W0258884

Informatik – Fachberichte

Band 7: GMR–GI–GfK. Fachtagung Prozessrechner 1977. Herausgegeben von G. Schmidt. XIII, 524 Seiten. 1977.

Band 8: Digitale Bildverarbeitung/Digital Image Processing. GI/NTG Fachtagung, München, März 1977. Herausgegeben von H.-H. Nagel. XI, 328 Seiten. 1977.

Band 9: Modelle für Rechensysteme. Workshop 1977. Herausgegeben von P. P. Spies. VI, 297 Seiten. 1977.

Band 10: GI – 7. Jahrestagung. Proceedings 1977. Herausgegeben von H. J. Schneider. IX, 214 Seiten. 1977.

Band 11: Methoden der Informatik für Rechnerunterstütztes Entwerfen und Konstruieren, GI-Fachtagung, München, 1977. Herausgegeben von R. Gnatz und K. Samelson. VIII, 327 Seiten. 1977.

Band 12: Programmiersprachen. 5. Fachtagung der GI, Braunschweig, 1978. Herausgegeben von Klaus Alber. VI, 179 Seiten. 1977.

Band 13: W. Steinmüller, L. Ermer, W. Schimmel: Datenschutz bei riskanten Systemen. X, 244 Seiten. 1978.

Band 14: Datenbanken in Rechnernetzen mit Kleinrechnern. Fachtagung der GI, Karlsruhe, 1978. Herausgegeben von W. Stucky und E. Holler. X, 198 Seiten. 1978.

Band 15: Organisation von Rechenzentren. Workshop der Gesellschaft für Informatik, Göttingen, 1977. Herausgegeben von D. Wall. X, 310 Seiten. 1978.

Band 16: GI – 8. Jahrestagung, Proceedings 1978. Herausgegeben von S. Schindler und W. K. Giloi. VI, 394 Seiten. 1978.

Band 17: Bildverarbeitung und Mustererkennung. DAGM Symposium, Oberpfaffenhofen, 1978. Herausgegeben von E. Triendl. XIII, 385 Seiten. 1978.

Band 18: Virtuelle Maschinen. Nachbildung und Vervielfachung maschinenorientierter Schnittstellen. GI-Arbeitsseminar. München 1979. Herausgegeben von H. J. Siegert. X, 231 Seiten. 1979.

Band 19: GI – 9. Jahrestagung. Herausgegeben von K. H. Böhling und P. P. Spies. XIII, 690 Seiten. 1979.

Band 20: Angewandte Szenenanalyse. DAGM Symposium, Karlsruhe 1979. Herausgegeben von J. Foith. XIII, 362 Seiten. 1979.

Band 21: Formale Modelle für Informationssysteme. Fachtagung der GI, Tutzing 1979. Herausgegeben von H. C. Mayr und B. E. Meyer. VI, 265 Seiten. 1979.

Band 22: Kommunikation in verteilten Systemen. Workshop der Gesellschaft für Informatik e.V.. Herausgegeben von S. Schindler und J. Schröder. VIII, 338 Seiten. 1979.

Band 23: K.-H. Hauer, Portable Methodenmonitoren. XI, 209 Seiten. 1980.

Band 24: N. Ryska, S. Herda: Technischer Datenschutz. Kryptographische Verfahren in der Datenverarbeitung. V, 401 Seiten. 1980.

Band 25: Programmiersprachen und Programmierentwicklung. 6. Fachtagung, Darmstadt, 1980. Herausgegeben von H.-J. Hoffmann. IV, 236 Seiten. 1980.

Band 26: F. Gaffal, Datenverarbeitung im Hochschulbereich der USA. Stand und Entwicklungstendenzen. IX, 199 Seiten. 1980.

Band 27: GI-NTG Fachtagung, Struktur und Betrieb von Rechensystemen. Kiel, März 1980. Herausgegeben von G. Zimmermann. IX, 286 Seiten. 1980.

Band 28: Online-Systeme im Finanz- und Rechnungswesen. Anwendergespräch, Berlin, April 1980. Herausgegeben von P. Stahlknecht. X, 547 Seiten, 1980.

Band 29: Erzeugung und Analyse von Bildern und Strukturen. DGaO – DAGM Tagung, Essen, Mai 1980. Herausgegeben von S. J. Pöppl und H. Platzer. VII, 215 Seiten. 1980.

Band 30: Textverarbeitung und Informatik. Fachtagung der GI, Bayreuth, Mai 1980. Herausgegeben von P. R. Wossidlo. VIII, 362 Seiten. 1980.

Band 31: Firmware Engineering. Seminar veranstaltet von der gemeinsamen Fachgruppe „Mikroprogrammierung" des GI Fachausschusses 3/4 und des NTG-Fachausschusses 6 vom 12. – 14. März 1980 in Berlin. Herausgegeben von W. K. Giloi. VII, 295 Seiten. 1980.

Band 32: M. Kühn, CAD Arbeitssituation. VII, 215 Seiten. 1980.

Band 33: GI – 10. Jahrestagung. Herausgegeben von R. Wilhelm. XV, 563 Seiten. 1980.

Band 34: CAD-Fachgespräch. GI - 10. Jahrestagung. Herausgegeben von R. Wilhelm. VI, 184 Seiten. 1980.

Band 35: B. Buchberger, F. Lichtenberger: Mathematik für Mathematiker I. Die Methode der Mathematik. XI, 315 Seiten. 1980.

Band 36: The Use of Formal Specification of Software. Berlin, Juni 1979. Edited by H. K. Berg and W. K. Giloi. V, 388 pages. 1980.

Band 37: Entwicklungstendenzen wissenschaftlicher Rechenzentren. Kolloquium Göttingen, Juni 1980. Herausgegeben von D. Wall. VII, 163 Seiten. 1980.

Band 38: Datenverarbeitung im Marketing. Herausgegeben von R. Thome. VIII, 377 pages. 1981.

Band 40: Kommunikation in verteilten Systemen. Herausgegeben von S. Schindler und J.C.W. Schröder. IX, 459 Seiten. 1981.

Band 41: Messung, Modellierung und Bewertung von Rechensystemen. GI-NTG Fachtagung. Jülich, Februar 1981. Herausgegeben von B. Mertens. VIII, 368 Seiten. 1981.

Band 42: W. Kilian, Personalinformationssysteme in deutschen Großunternehmen. XV, 352 Seiten. 1981.

Band 43: G. Goos, Werkzeuge der Programmiertechnik. VI, 262 Seiten. 1981.

Band 44: Organisation informationstechnik-gestützter öffentlicher Verwaltungen. Fachtagung, Speyer, Oktober 1980. Herausgegeben von Heinrich Reinermann, Herbert Fiedler, Klaus Grimmer und Klaus Lenk. 1981.

Band 45: R. Marty, PISA – A Programming System for Interactive Production of Application Software. VII. 297 Seiten. 1981.

Band 46: F. Wolf, Organisation und Betrieb von Rechenzentren. VII, 244 Seiten. 1981.

Band 47: GWAI – 81 German Workshop on Artificial Intelligence. Bad Honnef, January 1981. Herausgegeben von J. H. Siekmann. VII, 317 Seiten. 1981.

Band 48: W. Wahlster, Natürlichsprachliche Argumentation in Dialogsystemen. XI, 194 Seiten. 1981.

Band 49: Modelle und Strukturen. Herausgegeben von B. Radig. XII, 404 Seiten. 1981.

Band 50: GI – 11. Jahrestagung. Herausgegeben von W. Brauer. XIV, 617 Seiten. 1981.

Informatik-Fachberichte

Herausgegeben von W. Brauer
im Auftrag der Gesellschaft für Informatik (GI)

50

GI – 11. Jahrestagung

in Verbindung mit

Third Conference of the European
Co-operation in Informatics (ECI)
München, 20. – 23. Oktober 1981
Proceedings

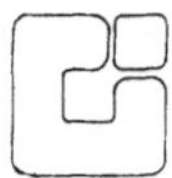

Herausgegeben von W. Brauer

Springer-Verlag Berlin Heidelberg GmbH

Herausgeber

Wilfried Brauer
Fachbereich Informatik, Universität Hamburg
Rothenbaumchaussee 67/69, 2000 Hamburg 13

AMS Subject Classifications (1979): 68A05, 68BXX, 68CXX, 68GXX, 68H05, 68K05

ISBN 978-3-540-10884-9 ISBN 978-3-662-01089-1 (eBook)
DOI 10.1007/978-3-662-01089-1

CIP-Kurztitelaufnahme der Deutschen Bibliothek

Gesellschaft für Informatik:
GI-Jahrestagung. – Berlin; Heidelberg; New York: Springer
ISSN 0343-3110
Bis 5.1975 u. d. T.: Gesellschaft für Informatik: Jahrestagung / GI, Gesellschaft für Informatik e. V.
11.1981. In Verbindung mit Third Conference of the European Co-operation in Informatics (ECI), München, 20. – 23. Oktober 1981: proceedings. – 1981.
(Informatik-Fachberichte; 50)

NE: GT

Ursprünglich erschienen bei Springer-Verlag Berlin Heidelberg New York 1981.

2145/3140 – 5 4 3 2 1 0

VORWORT

Die GI-Fachgespräche haben sich mehr und mehr zum tragenden Bestandteil der GI-Jahrestagungen entwickelt. In diesem Jahr, in dem der zentrale Teil der GI-Jahrestagung mit der ECI-Konferenz zusammenfällt, kommt den Fachgesprächen eine besondere Mittlerrolle zu.

Ich danke Herrn Kollegen Brauer, Hamburg, für seine Mühe bei der Planung und Organisation der Fachgespräche, sowie den Fachausschüssen der GI und ihren Leitern für ihre unermüdlichen Aktivitäten.

München, im August 1980

F.L. Bauer

P R O G R A M M K O M I T E E S
D E R G I - F A C H G E S P R Ä C H E

SEMANTIK VON PROGRAMMIERSPRACHEN

GI-Fachgespräch, veranstaltet von Fachausschuß 1
"Automatentheorie und formale Sprachen"

Programmkomitee:
K. Indermark, Aachen (Vorsitz) - J. Eickel, München
J. Loeckx, Saarbrücken - R. Wilhelm, Saarbrücken

QUANTITATIVE ASPEKTE DES SOFTWARE-ENGINEERING

GI-Fachgespräch, veranstaltet vom Fachausschuß 2
"Programmiersprachen und Programmiertechnik"

Programmkomitee:
J. Nehmer, Kaiserslautern (Vorsitz) - C. Haenel, München
W. Hesse, München - H.-J. Schneider, Erlangen

ENTWURFS- UND ENTWICKLUNGSWERKZEUGE FÜR RECHNERGESTÜTZTE INFORMATIONSSYSTEME

GI-Fachgespräch, veranstaltet von der Fachgruppe "Methoden und Modelle zur Entwicklung von Informationssystemen" des Fachausschusses 5/7 "Rechnergestützte Informationssysteme"

Programmkomitee:
H.C. Mayr, Karlsruhe (Vorsitz) - A. Blaser, Heidelberg
H.-J. Ehling, Berlin - H.J. Kreowski, Berlin
K. Lautenbach, Bonn - B.E. Meyer, Heilbronn
H. Noltemeier, Aachen - H.W. Schramm, Darmstadt

SICHERE SYSTEME

GI-Fachgespräch, gemeinsam veranstaltet vom Fachausschuß 8
"Methoden der Informatik für spezielle Anwendungen"
und der
"Gesellschaft für Datenschutz und Datensicherung"

Programmkomitee:
R. Dierstein, Wessling (Vorsitz) - R. Bayer, München
H. vor der Brück, Ottobrunn - F. Heymann, München
G. Merbeth, München

INFORMATIK IN DER SCHULE

GI-Fachgespräch, veranstaltet vom Fachausschuß 9/10
"Ausbildung" und seiner Fachgruppe
"Informatik in der Schule"

Programmkomitee:
R. Gunzenhäuser, Stuttgart (Vorsitz)
W. Hosseus, Mainz - R. Loos, Karlsruhe

SYSTEMATISCHER ENTWURF VON PDV-SYSTEMEN

GI-Fachgespräch, gemeinsam veranstaltet vom Fachausschuß 11
"Automatisierung technischer Prozesse"
und der
VDI/VDE-Gesellschaft für Meß- und Regelungstechnik

Programmkomitee:
G. Hommel, Würzburg (Vorsitz) - H.J. Ehling, Berlin
F. Hofmann, Erlangen - H. Keutgen, Aachen
B. Kühnel, Erlangen - H.-J. Schneider, Erlangen

AKTUELLE ENTWICKKUNGEN AUF DEM GEBIET
COMPUTERGESTÜTZTER PERSONAL-INFORMATIONSSYSTEME

GI-Fachgespräch, veranstaltet vom Fachausschuß 12
"Betriebliche Anwendungen der Informatik"
und seinem Unterausschuß
"Anwendungen im Personalwesen"

Programmkomitee:
D. Seibt, Essen - H.R. Hansen, Wien

ÄRZTLICHES URTEIL UND METHODEN DER INFORMATIK

GI-Fachgespräch, veranstaltet vom Fachausschuß 14
"Anwendung der DV in der Medizin"

Programmkomitee:
P. Reichertz, Hannover (Vorsitz) - S. Braun, München
G. Goos, Karlsruhe - P. Koeppe, Berlin
J. Möhr, Heidelberg - G. Stiege, Braunschweig
F. Wingert, Münster

BEAUFTRAGTER DES PRÄSIDIUMS
FÜR DIE JAHRESTAGUNG 1981
UND KOORDINATOR DER GI-FACHGESPRÄCHE

W. Brauer, Hamburg

TAGUNGSLEITER DER ECI/GI-TAGUNG

F.L. Bauer, München

ORGANISATIONSKOMITEE DER ECI/GI-TAGUNG

M. Paul, TU München (Vorsitz)

G. Bretschneider, Siemens, München (stellv. Vorsitz)

R. Gerold, F. Kröger, D. Hanisch,
H. Kuss, A. Gerold, Th. Ströhlein,
K.P. Wimmer, L. Zagler, H. Lommel (Sekretariat)

alle Institut für Informatik, Technische Universität München

Hinweis:

Der Tagungsband der ECI-Tagung (eingeladene und eingereichte Vorträge) erscheint als Band 123 der Lecture Notes in Computer Science des Springer-Verlages.

INHALTSVERZEICHNIS Seite

SEMANTIK VON PROGRAMMIERSPRACHEN

Seite

ENTWURFS- UND ENTWICKLUNGSWERKZEUGE FÜR RECHNERGESTÜTZTE INFORMATIONSSYSTEME

Seite

SICHERE SYSTEME

Seite

INFORMATIK IN DER SCHULE

Seite

SYSTEMATISCHER ENTWURF VON PDV-SYSTEMEN

Seite

AKTUELLE ENTWICKLUNGEN AUF DEM GEBIET
COMPUTERGESTÜTZTER PERSONAL-INFORMATIONSSYSTEME

Seite

ÄRZTLICHES URTEIL UND METHODEN DER INFORMATIK

INVARIANCE OF APPROXIMATIVE SEMANTICS WITH RESPECT TO PROGRAM TRANSFORMATIONS

Robert Giegerich *
Institut für Informatik
Technische Universität
Arcisstr. 21
8000 München 2

Ulrich Möncke **
Reinhard Wilhelm
FB 10 - Informatik
Universität des Saarlandes
6600 Saarbrücken

1. INTRODUCTION

Program transformations, as used for optimization and sometimes for program development, utilize information about the program which is derived by the method of abstract interpretation within various data flow analysis frameworks. Each transformation, as it changes the program, may render the flow information derived for the original program suboptimal or even invalid with respect to the new program. Although the outdated flow information may serve well as a starting point for rederivation, it appears profitable to look for conditions where passes of many transformations may be performed without recalculating flow information each time a transformation rule is applied.

We define the notion of invariance of an approximative semantics with respect to a given set of transformation rules. In the case of invariance, the original flow information remains valid and even optimal across transformations. We demonstrate for several traditional frameworks that they do not have this property, and show how they can be revised to yield invariant frameworks.

These revised, invariant approximate semantics are sometimes more expensive to calculate. Therefore, we also show that when an approximate semantics S is invariant with respect to a set T of transformation rules, T may also be used with an approximate semantics S' without intervening rederivation, if S' is itself an approximation of S. S' need not be invariant with respect to T, and T may safely use the original information derived with S', even if it becomes invalid in the traditional sense during transformations.

* Supported by SFB 49 - Programmiertechnik -, TU München
** Supported by DFG-Projekt "Manipulation attributierter Bäume"

2. DFA FRAMEWORKS AND TRANSFORMATIONS: DEFINITIONS

For reasons of space, we will have to be very terse with our definitions.

2.1 PROGRAMS

Syntactic objects:

V: set of values

X: set of program variables

EXP: set of (syntactic) expressions over X and V, written $e(x_1,\ldots,x_n)$ and not specified further

COM: set of commands, disjoined union of

ASS: set of assignment statements $x_0 := e(x_1,\ldots,x_n)$, $x_i \in X$

TESTS: set of tests $p(x_1,\ldots,x_n) \in$ EXP, and

{skip} the empty command

A program graph is a directed graph $G = (N,E,n_{in},n_{out})$,

N: set of nodes

$E \subseteq N \times N$ set of directed edges, written $e : n \to n'$

$n_{in}, n_{out} \in N$ "entry"- and "exit"-node

A program P is a pair (G,prog), where G is a program graph and prog : E → COM assigns a command (assignment, test or skip) to each edge in the intuitively obvious way.

2.2 PROGRAM SEMANTICS

Semantics are defined by giving some semantic domain S and an interpretation Int which associates a mapping $S \to S$ with each program. Correctness of program transformations will have to be defined relative to the semantics of programs. We will need two different semantics, "static semantics" and "traces semantics" for the optimizations dealt with in this paper. Common to both are the following definitions:

S $\cup$-lattice of semantic objects,

Int : COM → (S→S) is the (concrete) semantic interpretation of commands.

Example: s t a t i c s e m a n t i c s (CoC 77)

Let $S := (X \to V)$ set of states, $Z := 2^S$ powerset of states, also called "assertions"

Int_e : EXP → $(V^n \to V)$ associates a function f_e or f_p with each e or p ∈EXP

Int_{SS} : COM → (Z→Z) defines commands as state (set) transformers according to

$Int_{SS}(x_0 := e(x_1,\ldots,x_n)) :=$

$$\lambda z.\{s \in z \mid \exists v : s[x_0 \leftarrow v] \in z \wedge sx_0 = f_e(\ldots,(s[x_0 \leftarrow v])x_i,\ldots)\}$$

$Int_{SS}(p(x_1,\ldots,x_n)) := \lambda z.\{s \mid s \in z \wedge f_p(\ldots,sx_i,\ldots)\}$

$Int_{SS}(\underline{skip}) := \lambda z.z$

prog is extended to directed paths in G, yielding sequences of commands. Int_{SS} is extended to sequences of commands by composition.
The static semantics of (G,prog) is then given by ss : N→Z according to $ss(n) := \bigcup_p Int_{SS} \circ prog(p)\ (s_{in})$, where p is a path from n_{in} to n, and s_{in} is the set of possible entry states.

2.3 DATA FLOW ANALYSIS FRAMEWORKS AS APPROXIMATE SEMANTICS

When discussing various DFAs, the duality between ∪-lattices, with "≤" and ∩-lattices with "≥" gives rise to confusion. Note that in this paper, our concrete semantics are defined via ∪-lattices, while approximate semantics use ∩-lattices, which leads to simpler intuitive arguments in each case. However, monotonicity of a mapping $m : J \to I$ from a ∪-lattice J to a ∩-lattice I must be interpreted as $\forall\ i,j \in J:\quad i \le_J j \Longrightarrow m(j) \le_I m(i)$.

A data flow analysis framework (DFA) is a pair (M,L), where L is a complete ∩-lattice, $M \subseteq (L \to L)$ is a monoid of monotone functions.

A DFA is called an <u>approximate semantics</u>, if there are monotone mappings α, γ with the following properties:

1) $\alpha : S \to L$ is the <u>abstraction function</u>,
   $\gamma : L \to S$ is the <u>concretization function</u>,
   with $\gamma \circ \alpha$ <u>extensive</u> : $\forall s \in S: \quad s \le \gamma \circ \alpha(s)$;

2) There is another mapping, also denoted by α:
   $\alpha: (S \to S) \to M$, such that
   $\forall c \in COM : \forall s \in S : Int(c)\ (s) \le \gamma(\alpha(Int\ c)\ (\alpha s))$

Using (M,L) instead of (Int,S) therefore may mean some loss of information, but never derive incorrect information.

A <u>data flow problem</u> DFP is a tuple (P,Int,S,(M,L),α,γ), as defined above; we will write (P,Int,α) for short, assuming S to be implied by Int, and M,L,γ to be implied by α.

An <u>assignment</u> for a DFP (P,Int,α) is a mapping $\ell_N: N \to L$. Sometimes we will omit the index.

A DFP defines a set of <u>data flow equations</u> according to

$$\ell(n) = \bigcap_{e:n' \to n} \alpha \circ Int \circ prog(e)(\ell(n'))$$

This system corresponds to a so-called "forward"-DFP. For a "backward"-DFP, just think of all the edges inverted.

An assignment ℓ_N is a <u>fixpoint</u>, if it is a solution to the above system of equations (there is always a unique maximal fixpoint $\hat{\ell}_N$).

An assignment ℓ_N is conservative, if $\forall n$: $\ell_N(n) \leq \hat{\ell}_N(n)$.

<u>Example:</u> c o n s t a n t p r o p a g a t i o n

The DFP constant propagation CONST is defined by choosing:

$Int = Int_{SS}$

$S = X \to V$, $Z = 2^S$ static semantics

$L = 2^{X \times V}$

α: $Z \to L$ $\quad \alpha(z) = \{(x,v) | \forall s \in z \quad sx = v\}$

γ: $L \to S$ $\quad \gamma(\ell) = \{s \in [X \to V] | (x,v) \in \ell \to sx = v\}$

$\alpha(Int\ x_0 := e(x_1,\ldots,x_k)) = \lambda\ \ell.\ell \setminus KILL(x_0 := e(x_1,\ldots,x_k))\ell$

$\cup$ <u>if</u> $(x_1,v_1) \ldots (x_k,v_k) \in \ell$

<u>then</u> $\{(x_0,(Int_e e)(v_1,\ldots,v_k))\}$ <u>else</u> $\emptyset$

<u>fi</u>

$KILL(x_0 := e(x_1,\ldots,x_k)) = \lambda\ \ell.\{(x_0,y) \in \ell\}$

$\alpha(Int\ p(x_1,\ldots,x_k)) = \lambda\ell.\ell$

$\alpha(Int$ <u>skip</u>$) = \lambda\ell.\ell$

2.4 PROGRAM TRANSFORMATIONS

A (program) transformation rule r based on an approximate semantics $(Int,S,(M,L),\alpha,\gamma)$ is a triplet $(c,c',B) \subseteq COM \times COM \times (L \to BOOL)$, where B is the "applicability condition" and satisfies

$$B(\ell) \to \forall s \in \gamma(\ell) : Int(c)(s) \doteq Int(c')s,$$

for some appropriately defined relation $\doteq$ of semantic equivalence. Thus, $B(\ell)$ implies preservation of program correctness when a program $P = (G,prog)$ is transformed by r , which is defined as follows:

Let ℓ_N be a conservative assignment, $e : n \to n'$ for forward, $e : n' \to n$ for backward problems, $prog(e) = c$ and $B(\ell(n)) =$ <u>true</u>.

The transformed program $P' = (G,prog')$ is defined by $prog' := prog[e \leftarrow c']$.

Of course, the modified program P' gives rise to a modified DFP with a set of equations differing from the original one with respect to $\alpha \circ \text{Int} \circ \text{prog}(e)$. As an example, the rule (actually a rule schema) for constant folding is

$$r_c : (x := e(x_1,\ldots,x_k),\ x := v,\ \lambda\ell.(x_1,v_1) \in \ell \wedge \ldots \wedge (x_k,v_k) \in \ell \wedge$$
$$(\text{Int } e)(v_1,\ldots,v_k) = v).$$

3. SAFENESS AND INVARIANCE OF FRAMEWORKS WITH RESPECT TO TRANSFORMATIONS

3.1 Enabling and affected frameworks

As transformations modify programs and therefore the associated data flow equations, they may outdate the flow information calculated for the original program. In general, there are two frameworks to be considered:
The "enabling" framework, which the transformation is based on, and the "affected" framework - the one one is interested in for the next transformation step, whose flow information has also been calculated already. When we ask if a transformation modifies its "own" flow information, enabling and affected framework are the same. In this case, or in the case where both frameworks use the same lattice L of abstract information, we will be able to make stronger assertions about possible effects than in the case of totally unrelated frameworks.

For the rest of this section, let

$A = (P,\text{Int}_A,S_A,(M_A,L_A),\alpha_A,\gamma_A)$ be the enabling,

$O = (P,\text{Int}_O,S_O,(M_O,L_O),\alpha_O,\gamma_O)$ be the affected DFP, and let

$r = (c,c',B)$ be a transformation rule based on A, i.e. $B \in L_A \to \text{BOOL}$.

The transformed DFPs are referred to as A' and O'.

3.2 Safeness

The least we can ask for is that the information calculated for the affected framework remains valid (but not necessarily optimal). This means, a conservative assignment for O must also be one for O'.

Definition 1 Let $r = (c,c',B{:}L_A \to \text{BOOL})$ as before,
and B monotone, i.e. $\ell \leq \ell' \to (B(\ell) \to B(\ell'))$
O is safe with respect to r, if

a) for $L_A = L_0$, $\gamma_A = \gamma_0$

$\forall \ell \in L_A : B(\ell) \rightarrow ((\alpha_0 \circ Int_0)(c)(\ell) \leq (\alpha_0 \circ Int_0)(c')(\ell))$

b) for $L_A \neq L_0$ or $\gamma_A \neq \gamma_0$:

$\forall \ell \in L_A : B(\ell) \rightarrow ((\alpha_0 \circ Int_0)(c) \leq (\alpha_0 \circ Int_0)(c'))$

Theorem 1

If ℓ_A is a conservative assignment to A , and if ℓ_N is a conservative assignment to 0 , and 0 is safe with respect to r , then ℓ'_N is a conservative assignment for 0'.

Proof: Obviously, the system of equations for 0' differs from the one for 0 only with respect to the edge e: m→n, where r was applied.

Let $\hat{\ell}_N$ be the maximal fixpoint of 0, $\hat{\ell}'_N$ that of 0'.
We have to show that $\ell_N \leq \hat{\ell}_N \leq \hat{\ell}'_N$ is implied by $B(\ell_A(m))$.
In case b), $\alpha_0 \circ Int_0(c) \leq \alpha_0 \circ Int_0(c')$ implies $\hat{\ell}_N \leq \hat{\ell}'_N$.
In case a), the monotonicity of B implies that
$\alpha_0 \circ Int_0(c)(\ell) \leq \alpha_0 \circ Int_0(c')(\ell)$ for all $\ell \geq \hat{\ell}_N(m)$, ℓ in the Kleene sequence calculating $\hat{\ell}'_N$. Therefore we also have $\hat{\ell}_N \leq \hat{\ell}'_N$ in this case, q.e.d.

Examples: Let DEADVARS be the framework that determines at each node of a program graph the set of variables whose current value will not be used later on, either since no use is made of the variable until the end of the program, or since any use of the variable is preceded by a modification of the variable. Let COPIES be the framework that determines at each node the following relation copy between variables:

x copy y iff x and y hold the same value, every time execution of the program reaches this node, cf. (Hec 77), (AhU 77). Both frameworks can be used to eliminate "useless" assignments. Let r_e be the elimination of useless assignments, r_i the introduction of an assignment to a dead variable.

(1) DEADVARS is not safe with respect to r_e and COPIES,
(2) COPIES is not safe with respect to r_e and DEADVARS.

```
transformed using COPIES        original program          transformed using DEADVARS
COPIES     DEADVARS             COPIES     DEADVARS                COPIES     DEADVARS
      Ø  o {x}                        Ø  o {x}                          Ø  o {x}
         ↓ x := y                        ↓ x := y         r_e              ↓ skip
{(x,y)}  o {x}(*)      r_e      {(x,y)}  o {x}            ⟹       {(x,y)}  o {x}
         ↓ skip        ⟸                 ↓ x := y     x∈DEADVARS     (*)   ↓ x := y
         o Ø       (x,y)∈COPIES          o Ø                               o Ø
```

(3) DEADVARS is safe with respect to r_e and DEADVARS.
Clear, since $(\alpha \circ \mathrm{Int})(\underline{\mathrm{skip}})$ eliminates no dead variables, and $(\alpha \circ \mathrm{Int})(x_0 := e(x_1,\ldots,x_n))$ introduces no new dead variables when x_0 is dead.

(4) DEADVARS is not safe with respect to r_i and DEADVARS.

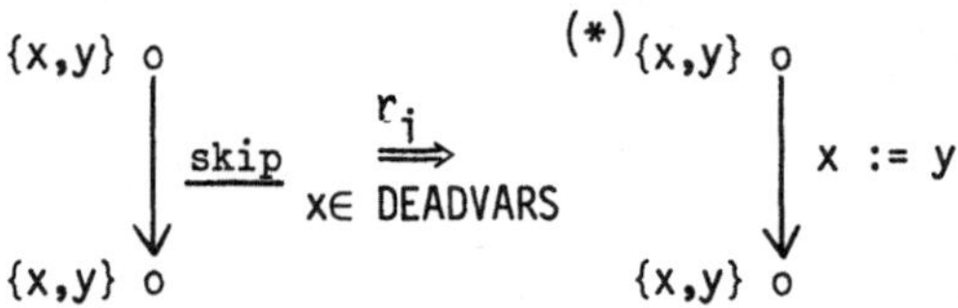

(*) invalid information!

3.3 Invariance

If we require that maximality of fixpoints be retained, or if we require safeness for a symmetric (with respect to c and c') set of transformation rules, we arrive at the notion of invariance:

Definition 2 Let $r = (c,c',B)$ as before, B monotone.
O is invariant with respect to r, if

a) for $L_A = L_0$, $\gamma_A = \gamma_0$:
$\forall \ell \in L_A : B(\ell) \rightarrow (\alpha \circ \mathrm{Int})(c)(\ell) = (\alpha \circ \mathrm{Int})(c')(\ell)$

b) for $L_A \neq L_0$ or $\gamma_A \neq \gamma_0$:
$\forall \ell \in L_A : B(\ell) \rightarrow (\alpha \circ \mathrm{Int})(c) = (\alpha \circ \mathrm{Int})(c')$.

Theorem 2 If O is invariant with respect to r and A, and $\hat{\ell}_N$ is the maximal fixpoint of O, then $\hat{\ell}_N$ is the maximal fixpoint of O'.

Proof: In case b), the system of equations of O and O' and hence their maximal fixpoints are identical. In case a), the monotonicity of B implies that the Kleene sequences calculating the maximal fixpoints, and hence the fixpoints themselves are identical, q.e.d.

Examples: DEADVARS, as used before, is apparently not invariant with respect to r_e and itself. CONST(Hec 77) is invariant with respect to constant folding (r_c) and itself. DEADVARS (CONST) is not invariant with respect to r_c and CONST (r_e and DEADVARS). DEADVARS is safe with respect to r_e and CONST is not safe with respect to r_e and DEADVARS.

From these examples, it becomes clear how the properties of invariance and safeness help the compiler designer with the structuring of optimization phases:

Invariance allows a phase of many transformations, all based on optimal information. Safeness allows to proceed with transformations before rederiving flow information, at the price of missing some chances this time. Otherwise, invalidated information must be corrected before optimization can go on, cf. (Wil 79).

Apparently, it is highly desirable that a DFA be invariant with respect to itself and the transformations it is used for. In the next section we show how to turn DEADVARS into such a framework.

4. DEAD VARIABLES, FAINT VARIABLES

4.1 Classical dead variables

It was shown in section 3 that the DEADVARS-framework is not invariant under the elimination (and insertion) of assignments to dead variables. Now, we construct a framework that is stronger than DEADVARS and invariant under the elimination (and insertion) of useless assignments. (Insertion is an important rule on the machine code level of optimization (Gie 81)). Let us first give an exact description of DEADVARS.

DEADVARS is an abstraction of a traces semantics (CoC 79). We will only give the $\alpha o \mathrm{Int}$ definition of the functions of the framework.

$$(\alpha o \mathrm{Int})(c)(a) = (a \cup \mathrm{KILL}(c)) \setminus \mathrm{USE}(c) \quad ,$$

where KILL(c) is the set of variables, whose value may be changed by the execution of command c,
USE(c) is the set of variables, whose value may be used when command c is executed.

DEADVARS is a backwards, meet framework. The system of equations for a given program P is usually written

$$\mathrm{DEADVARS}(m) = \bigcap_{e:m\rightarrow n} ((\mathrm{DEADVARS}(n) \cup \mathrm{KILL}(prog(e)) \setminus \mathrm{USE}(prog(e)).$$

4.2 Construction of an invariant framework for dead variables

Let the framework we look for be (M_a, L_a). The regarded transformation is

$$(c, c', B: L_a \rightarrow \mathrm{BOOL})$$

where

$$c \equiv x_0 := e(x_1, \ldots, x_n)$$

$$c' \equiv \underline{skip}$$

$$B \equiv x_0 \in \ell$$

The condition for invariance according to Def. 2 (a) is:

$\forall \ell \in L_a : B(\ell) \rightarrow ((\alpha_a \circ Int_a)(c)(\ell) = ((\alpha_a \circ Int_a)(c')(\ell))$.

Here, this reads:

$\forall \ell \in L_a : x_0 \in \ell \rightarrow ((\ell \cup \{x_0\}) \setminus \{x_1,\ldots,x_n\} = \ell)$.

The new framework, let us call it FAINTVARS, anticipates the elimination of assignments fo faint variables by the following definition of the abstract semantics of an assignment statement:

$$\alpha \circ Int(x_0 := e(x_1,\ldots,x_n))(\ell) =$$

$$\underline{\text{if}}\ x_0 \in \ell\ \underline{\text{then}}\ \ell\ \underline{\text{else}}\ (\ell \cup \{x\}) \setminus \{x_1,\ldots,x_n\}$$

The system of equations can then be written as

$$\text{FAINTVARS}(m) = \bigcap_{e:m \rightarrow n} \underline{\text{if}}\ \text{KILL}(\text{prog}(e)) \subseteq \text{FAINTVARS}(n)$$
$$\underline{\text{then}}\ \text{FAINTVARS}(n)$$
$$\underline{\text{else}}\ (\text{FAINTVARS}(n) \cup \text{KILL}(\text{prog}(e)) \setminus \text{USE}(\text{prog}(e)))$$

FAINTVARS has the following nice properties:

- it is invariant under elimination and insertion of assignments to faint variables (can be seen from the construction),
- it is stronger than DEADVARS, that is, any dead variable is also faint (can be seen by comparing the two systems of equations),
- it is exhaustive in the sense that, if a maximal fixpoint for FAINTVARS is computed, and all assignments to variables found to be faint are eliminated, then a new computation of a fixpoint of FAINTVARS would reveal no faint variables having assignments (follows from the invariance),
- it may be more expensive to compute than DEADVARS baut is still cheap (for every assignment we have an additional membership test),
- it ensures the preservation of semantic equivalence by the transformation regarded, since it is an implementation of an axiom of the traces semantics: When an assignment $x_0 := e(x_1,\ldots,x_n)$ is redundant, then the values of $x_1,\ldots,x_n$ are irrelevant at this point; therefore, the redundant assignment need not be considered as using the values of $x_1,\ldots,x_n$.

5. WORKING WITH APPROXIMATIONS OF INVARIANT FRAMEWORKS

In this section, we show by an example, which is very easily generalized, that one can benefit from the mere existence of invariant frameworks, while actually using "cheaper" approximations.

DEADVARS is itself an approximation of FAINTVARS. Assume DEADVARS is the one actually used for optimization. By application of r_e and r_i, DEADVARS-information may become invalid. But it must still be valid with respect to FAINTVARS, which we know to be invariant and hence safe wrt both r_e and r_i, and itself. Thus, in the "higher" sense, the outdated DEADVARS-Information is still valid and may safely be used for further transformations. Note that this would not be the case if it had been outdated by a rule with respect to which FAINTVARS is not safe, say r_e based on CONST.

6. CONCLUSION

An optimizing compiler performs a number of code improving program transformations. Most of these transformations are based on global data flow information. In this paper the properties of safeness and invariance of data flow analysis frameworks under transformations are defined. Several traditional DFA-frameworks are shown to be unsafe, or not invariant under some transformations: For the well known framework DEADVARS a stronger and invariant framework has been constructed. It is argued that the notions of safeness and invariance are valuable aids in devising the optimization phase of a compiler.

REFERENCES:

(AhU 77) Aho, A.V., Ullman, J.D.: Principles of Compiler Design, Addison Wesley, 1977

(CoC 77) Cousot, P., Cousot, R.: Abstract interpretation: a unified lattice model for static analysis of programs by construction or approximation of fixpoints, 4th ACM Symp. on Principles of Progr. Lang., 1977

(CoC 79) Cousot, P., Cousot, R.: Systematic design of program analysis frameworks, 6th ACM Symp. on Principles of Progr. Lang., 1979

(Gie 81) Giegerich, R.: Automatische Erzeugung von Maschinencode-Optimierern, Doct. Dissertation, TU München, 1981

(Hec 77) Hecht, M.S.: Flow analysis of computer programs, North Holland, 1977

(Wil 79) Wilhelm, R.: Computation and use of data flow information in optimizing compilers, Acta Informatica 12, 1979

DESCRIPTION OF PARAMETERIZED COMPILER MODULES

Harald Ganzinger

Institut für Informatik
Technische Universität München
Postfach 202420
D-8000 München 2
Fed. Rep. of Germany

1. INTRODUCTION

Attribute grammars are the basis of most compiler generating systems. An extension of context-free grammars, they allow to employ well-known parsing techniques for syntactic analysis. Compiler descriptions in form of attribute grammars are, like denotational semantics definitions in the sense of Scott and Strachey, monolithic and do not encourage modularization. Compiler descriptions, like any other specification of complex program systems, are nontrivial to write and reliability and modifiability can be achieved only through adequate structuring mechanisms.

There are approaches in the literature where language definitions are given as combinations of language concepts [Mos80], [GoP80]. The latter employs the methodology of parameterized abstract data types as suggested in [Zil75] and formally investigated in [ADJ80]. This paper is to give a parameterization mechanism for compiler descriptions based on attribute grammars.

Our approach is based upon the following observation: Attribute grammars constitute a meta-language that employs (attribute) types, functions, attributes, and cf-grammars as primitive concepts. Any of these primitives could be a parameter in a parameterized description of a compilation concept. Thus, for compiler modules to be described by attribute grammars, we will have to specify their specific requirements about input attributes and underlying cf-grammar (in addition to the requirements about attribute types and functions). In section 2 we shall exploit this fact. Section 3 introduces a mechanism, called grammar morphism, to pass grammars as actual parameters to formal parameters of a compiler module. In section 4 we give a nontrivial example. We shall define a compiler module for the identification problem in block-oriented languages. Finally, in section 5, we shall briefly list the results we have obtained so far.

2. GRAMMAR ABSTRACTIONS AS THE BASIS OF PARAMETERIZED COMPILER MODULES

At least since McCarthy's and Painter's pioneering work on compiler correctness [CaP67], it is agreed that a grammar that is suitable for parsing is usually too detailed for defining the semantics of a language. Also, different parsing methods require different grammar types. To be independent of parsing, the semantics of a language should be defined with respect to an abstract syntax of the language. We extend this view by claiming that the abstract syntax itself is too detailed for defining the specific <u>concepts</u> that are employed in a language or a compiler. To be independent of irrelevant details of a specific language, the definition of language or compilation concepts should be based upon further abstractions of the abstract syntax of the language.

To illustrate this argument, we introduce a simple compilation problem which we want to solve by combining standard concepts of compilation.

Abstract syntax of the source language (we use ¦ and $(...)^*$ to denote union and Kleene-star in regular expressions):

```
start      ->  program
program    ->  begin block end
block      ->  ( stmt )*
stmt       ->  assignment ¦ labelDef ¦ goto ¦ if ¦ begin block end
labelDef   ->  labelId :
goto       ->  goto labelId
if         ->  if bexp then block else block fi
assignment ->  var := exp
 ...
```

Our problem concerns the treatment of labels. We want to number the statements and to assign to an attribute labDef at any goto the number of that statement which is the corresponding label definition. As usual, labels may be redefined in inner blocks. Gotos that lead into parallel or into inner blocks are forbidden.

To solve the problem we want to give an attribute grammar that defines the attribute labDef in the way described above. The following modularization into simple subtasks, called phases, seems to be appropriate:

Phase 1: Numbering the statements
  Result: sn[labelDef] -- an attribute that represents the statement number of the label definition

Phase 2: Recognizing the block structure
  Result: bn[block] -- unique number of the block
  bn[labelDef], bn[goto] -- for any label definition and goto: number of the directly enclosing block

Phase 3: Identification of labels
  Input: sn[labelDef], bn[block], bn[labelDef], bn[goto], -- cf. above
  lexinf[labelId] -- lexical identification of the identifier as obtained during syntactic analysis
  Result: labDef[goto] -- number of the label definition to which the goto refers to

We conclude that phases can be described by separate attribute grammars together with a specification of input and result attributes. (We want the input-result dependencies between phases to be acyclic such that the attribute dependencies are acyclic, iff all phases are cycle-free attribute grammars.)

The pass-oriented methods to attribute evaluation always dealt with the structuring of attribute grammars into partial grammars. Thereby, the underlying cf-grammars are identical (and, thus, identical with the given grammar for the concrete or abstract syntax of the source language). Our experience shows that such a restricted type of modularization, although being helpful for efficiently implementing attribute grammars, cannot considered to be helpful for the compiler describer. It remains the problem to isolate the semantic issues of a compiler phase from the syntactic details. (The latter is required if a given description of a compiler phase is to be adapted to a similar compilation task or to a similar language construct.) Also, even small changes in the syntax of the language require to change the attribute rules correspondingly.

Therefore, we would rather be able to define phase-specific abstractions of the concrete syntax to hide those details that are irrelevant to the compilation phase in question.

In our example, phases 1 and 2 are closely related. In both cases nested compound constructs (stmts and blocks, resp.) that may contain elementary constructs (labelDefs and labelDefs or gotos, resp.) are involved. For any of the elementary constructs, a unique identification of the directly enclosing compound has to be determined. We could describe this process using a grammar that defines abstract compound constructs, their nesting and elementary components only:

```
start -> compound
    nmb[compound] = 1   -- we use attributes  nmb (inherited) and  nmb' (synthesized)
                           to maintain a counter
compound0 -> (elem | compound1)*
    -- A compound consists of a sequence  S  of components that are either elemen-
       tary or again compounds. (The syntactic ambiguity that is introduced with this
       rule causes no problems since we can obtain the actual nesting of compounds,
       e.g., blocks or stmts, from the concrete parse tree.)
    nmb[compound1] = (nmb'[pre] or nmb[compound0]) +1
    -- For any compound in  S, the counter is incremented. Its old value is repre-
       sented by  nmb'  at the predecessor in  S. If no predecessor exists (or-case),
       nmb  at the enclosing compound represents this old value.
    nmb[elem] = nmb'[pre] or nmb[compound0]
    -- For elementary constructs the counter is not increased.
    nmb'[compound0] = nmb'[last] or nmb[compound0]
    -- "last" refers to the last element in the list  S  of components. The or-case
       applies if the latter is empty.
    nec[elem] = nmb[compound0]  -- delivers into  nec  the number of the directly
                                   enclosing compound
elem -> empty  -- The structure of elementary constructs is irrelevant.
    nmb'[elem] = nmb[elem]
```

Using specific <u>abstract</u> grammars rather than the full grammar as the basis for the description of compiler phases has several advantages. First, trivial attribute rules for transferring relevant semantic information across irrelevant regions of the syntax tree can be avoided. These regions are left unspecified by the abstract grammar. Note, that abstract grammars in our sense are not merely defined by a subset of rules of the concrete grammar. Rather they represent logical units of their own. This is formally mirrored by the fact that they are reduced cf-grammars. (The use of abstract grammars seems to be the only way to achieve an elimination of redundancy in attribute grammars without introducing nonstandard concepts of attribute rules as defined for many definition languages, e.g. [WaM77], [Räi78], [Kas79], [Gan81].)

More importantly, the abstract grammar can be viewed as (part of) the <u>parameter</u> of the description of the phase. Different <u>instantiations</u> (e.g. phases 1 and 2) are obtained by establishing specific "correspondences" between concrete and abstract syntax and by passing the other parameters (e.g. attributes nec -> sn and nec, nmb -> bn, resp.) to and from the phase definition.

The next section is to discuss possible notions of correspondence between concrete and abstract syntax. The central role in establishing correspondences between abstract and concrete trees will be played by symbol maps s sending any symbol of the concrete syntax to either a symbol of the abstract grammar or to the empty string e. For phase 1 we could define

s1(start)=start, s1(program)=s1(stmt)=compound, s1(labelDef)=elem, and s1(X)= e, otherwise,

and for phase 2,

s2(start)=start, s2(block)=compound, s2(labelDef)=s2(goto)=elem, and s2(X)= e, otherwise,

Sending a concrete-syntax symbol X to e means that it has no counterpart in the abstract syntax. A symbol map s defines a correspondence, called parse tree morphism, between concrete and abstract parse trees, if renaming the labels X in concrete parse trees by s(X) and, then, erasing the e-nodes does always yield a parse tree of the abstract syntax. (Erasing an inner e-node should, however, not delete the complete subtree. Rather, all sons of a node u to be deleted are assumed to be inserted (preserving their order) into the sequence of sons of the father of u (at u's position).) Only symbol maps that define a parse tree morphism can be admitted. The following figure depicts the effect on a small sample program of the parse tree morphisms as defined by the maps s1 and s2:

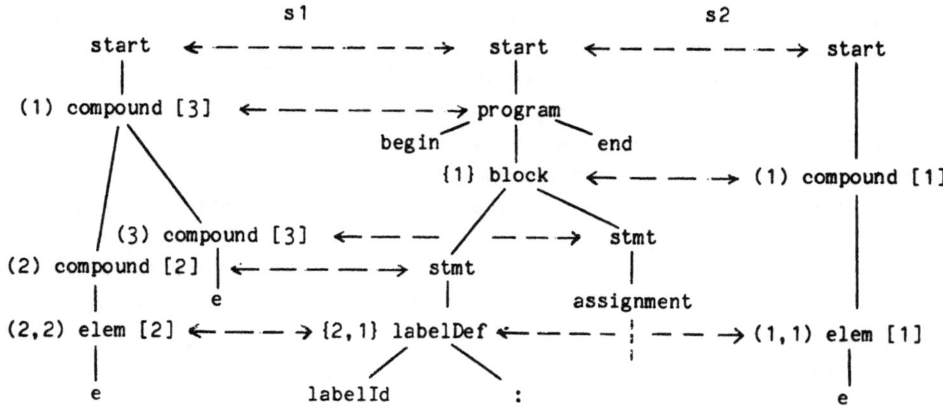

The arrows represent bijections between the X- and s(X)-nodes in the concrete and abstract tree, resp.. Such bijections come with any parse tree morphism. They allow to transfer the attributes that are defined for the nodes in the abstract tree to the corresponding nodes on the concrete tree. To illustrate the transfer of attributes according to these correspondences, we have attached their values with the nodes. The different brackets distinguish the attributes (nmb), (nmb,nec), [nmb'], and {sn,bn}.

Our example demonstrates clearly that cf-grammars without regular right parts are not sufficient for our purposes. Erasing internal nodes, e.g. s1 erases blocks and ifs, can make other grammar symbols, e.g. stmt, capable to directly generate an unbounded sequence of symbols, e.g. labelDefs. Therefore, the abstract parse tree must either involve auxiliary symbols that have no counterpart in the concrete tree or some of its rules, e.g. compound, must have regular right parts. The latter is more natural since auxiliary symbols in abstract grammars could only define semantically irrelevant structure.

3. MORPHISMS FROM CONCRETE TO ABSTRACT PARSE TREES

To study correspondences between derivations of structurally related grammars, a concept, called grammar covers, is known for quite a long time [ReH70]. (This topic has gained new interest recently, cf. [Nij80]. In [Boc79] it is extended to attribute grammars to allow for transformation of grammar and attribute rules during parser generation.) For our purposes a generalization to right part regular grammars is necessary.

Assume we are given an attribute grammar AG over an abstract syntax, represented by the cf-grammar Ga = (Na,Ta,Ra,Sa) (N: nonterminals, T: terminals, R: rules, S: start symbol. Rules have the form X->R, where R is a regular expression over $N \cup T$. It will be required that the regular languages L(R) and L(R') are disjoint for different rules X->R and X->R' for any X.) Let furthermore Gc = (Nc,Tc,Rc,Sc) define the concrete syntax of the language. By P(G) we denote the set of parse trees defined (for the programs of the language) by G.

g : Gc -> Ga is called a (grammar) morphism, if g = (s,r), where:
a) s is a function s : $Nc \cup Tc$ -> $Na \cup Ta \cup \{e\}$, such that s(Sc)=Sa, s(Nc)$\subset Na \cup \{e\}$, and s(Tc)$\subset Ta \cup \{e\}$,
b) r is a mapping r : P(Gc) -> P(Ga), such that for any $X \in Nc \cup Tc$ for which s(X)$\neq$e and for any $t \in P(Gc)$ there exists a bijection

r[t,X] : X[t] -> s(X)[r(t)]

of X[t], the set of X-nodes of t, onto the set of s(X)-nodes of r(t).

(b) is the weakest condition that allows to decorate, according to g, concrete syntax trees t with attributes defined in AG: The bijections r[t,X] serve to, first, transfer predefined X-attributes from t to r(t), and, then, to transfer the resulting s(X)-attributes specified by AG from r(t) back to t. We will immediately impose a stronger restriction on morphisms. We call g a strong morphism, if additionally,

c) each r[t,X] preserves hierarchy and orientation, i.e.,
(i) for X-nodes u,v of t it is u a descendant of v in t, iff r[t,X](u) is a descendant of r[t,X](v) in r(t),
(ii) it occurs u left of v in t, iff r[t,X](u) occurs left of r[t,X](v) in r(t), and
(iii) any node u' in r(t) occurs as r[t,X](u), for some u and X.
In this case we call r the parse tree morphism as given by g.

As motivation for (c) we remark that many properties of attributes can conveniently be specified in terms of the relations of hierarchy and orientation. We want to be able to directly infer properties of the attributes in the concrete parse tree from those of the corresponding attributes in the abstract tree. We note the following facts.

Facts: Let s be a mapping with the properties specified above.
(F1) There exists at most one parse tree morphism r such that (s,r) is a strong grammar morphism.
(F2) For any strong morphism g=(s,r), the bijections r[t,X] are uniquely determined.
(F3) The composition (obtained by composing the functions s, r, r[t,X]) of a (strong) morphism is again a (strong) morphism, as is the morphism given by the identities on symbols and parse trees.

From (F1) and (F2) it follows that in order to define a strong morphism it suffices to specify s. The decidability of the problem whether or not to a given s the parse tree morphism r exists is an open question. This question is, cf. section 5, equivalent to a well-known open problem in formal language theory.

The symbol maps s1 and s2 as defined in section 2 specify two strong grammar morphisms. The arrows in the figure in section 2 represent the bijections r[t,X].

In contrast to grammar covers, we do not require the two languages generated by Gc and Ga to be equal. Rather, the concrete parse tree for a given source program serves as master tree from which the different abstract trees are constructed. (This explains why abstract grammars may be arbitrarily ambiguous.) Furthermore, we deal with regular right part grammars. However, a simple consideration shows that our notion of parse tree morphism for strong grammar morphisms is a special case of parse homomorphisms in the sense of [Nij80], provided the latter is extended to grammars with regular right parts.

Parse tree morphisms are purely syntactic maps. It seems to be useful, c.f. motivation for EAGs in [WaM77], to allow the symbol map s to depend on the value of attributes. (E.g., one might want to map variables to boolean variables or to arithmetic variables depending on their type.) Such an extension would not cause any serious problem.

4. DEFINITION AND INSTANTIATION OF PHASES

We illustrate how a compiler description language that employs our modularization concept could look like. In order to explicitly distinguish the definition of parameterized phases from their instantiations, we shall call the former <u>modules</u>.

In section 2 we have already given the body of a module to be used for numbering compound constructs and we have specified the morphisms that make phases 1 and 2 to become instances of this module. To demonstrate some of the power of the modularization concept, we shall define a module that can handle the general identification problem in ALGOL-like languages. Declarations and applications of objects may be in arbitrary order.

```
module identification
  parameter  -- It begins the specification of all parameters of the module.
    syntax   -- The abstract syntax that underlies the module is one of its parameters.
                In this case it defines the nesting of declarations, applications, and
                blocks.
      program -> block
      block -> (decl | appl | block)*
      decl -> (appl | block)* -- This is much more than would be required for our
                                 label definitions.
      appl -> empty
            -- other parameters, e.g. types, constants, functions, attributes:
    type  declInf, id
        -- The structure  declInf  of declaration information and of the information id
           that serves to identify objects is irrelevant. Thus, the corresponding types
           are parameters of the module, too.
    const maxBlocks : int    -- implementation bound
```

```
   function  eq(id,id) : bool
       -- a predicate that decides whether or not two identifiers are
          equal with respect to identification
   attribute  i[decl, appl] : id  -- identifier that is declared and applied, resp.
              d[decl] : declInf   -- information about the object that the declara-
                                     tion defines
              bn[appl, decl, block] : 0 .. maxBlocks -- block numbers
 exports
         -- it begins the specification of those objects that are to be
            defined in the module body and made available for external use:
   attribute  a[appl] : declInf    -- properties of the applied object
                                      as specified in its declaration

is     -- ----------- it begins the body of the module -------------
       -- It follows the declaration of three (local) symbol table attributes iTab,
          sTab, tab.  The first two serve to collect all declarations. tab will be
          used to hold the final state of the symbol table.
   type symtab = << list of entries for declarations and blocks >>;
   attribute  iTab, tab : symtab inherited;
              sTab : symtab synthesized;
   function initTab : symtab ;  << initialization of the symbol table >> ;
            enterBlock(st:symtab,b:0..maxBlocks):symtab ;
            << enters into st a new entry for the block b and establishes its rela-
               tions with the enclosing blocks >> ;
            exitBlock(st:symtab,b:0..maxBlocks):symtab ;
            << reactivates the enclosing block b >> ;
            enterDecl(st:symtab,i:id,d:declInf,b:0..maxBlocks,eq(id,id):bool):symtab;
            << enters the declaration d for i in block b into st. The predicate eq
               is used for redeclaration checks. >> ;
            lookup(st:symtab,b:0..maxBlocks,i:id,eq(id,id):bool):declInf;
            << searches st for the declaration for i that is visible in block b.
               eq serves for testing the equality of identifiers. >> ;
   rules
   program -> block
       iTab[block] = initTab(bn[block]);
       tab[block] = sTab[block];    -- assigning the final state sTab[block] of the
                                       symbol table to tab
   block0 -> (decl | appl | block1)*
       iTab[(decl|appl)] = sTab[pre] or iTab[block0];
       iTab[block1] = enterBlock(sTab[pre] or iTab[block0], bn[block1]);
       tab[(decl|appl|block1)] = tab[block0];
       sTab[Block0] = exitblock(sTab[last] or iTab[block0], bn[block0]);
   decl -> (appl | block)*
       iTab[appl] = sTab[pre] or iTab[decl];
       iTab[block] = enterBlock[sTab[pre] or iTab[decl], bn[decl]);
       tab[(appl|block)] = tab[decl];
       sTab[decl] = enterDecl(sTab[last] or iTab[decl],i[decl],d[decl],bn[decl],eq);
   appl -> empty
       sTab[appl] = iTab[appl]
       a[appl] = lookup(tab[appl], bn[appl], i[appl], eq)
```

```
end module

     We obtain phase 3 as instantiation of "identification":
phase 3 = identification
  (  -- parameter passing; it begins with defining the strong morphism from concrete
        to abstract syntax which is, according to (F1), (F2) uniquely determined by
        the symbol map s. We use the notation Y<=s^-1(Y), for all Y ∈ Na ∪ Ta such that
        s^-1(Y)≠∅ :
     program <= start,
     block <= block,
     decl <= labelDef,
     appl <= goto;
   type declInf <= 0 .. maxNmbOfStmts,
        id <= 0 .. maxNmbOfIds;
   function eq <= function eq(x:id,y:id):bool is eq:= x=y end;
   attribute
     i[decl,appl] <= lexinf[labelDef,goto],
            -- lexinf is assumed to be some lexical coding of the labelId
               involved
     d[decl] <= sn[labelDef], -- obtained from phase 1
     bn[decl,appl,block] <= bn[goto,labelDef,block]; -- from phase 2
   out   -- renaming the exported attribute:
     attribute
       a[appl] => labDef[goto]  -- the final result );
```

5. RESULTS AND CONCLUDING REMARKS

We have demonstrated that the effect of any compilation phase is independent of many of the peculiarites of the syntax of a given source language. If one eliminates this irrelevant structure, then one obtains a specific abstraction of the concrete syntax. We have argued that the description of the phase should employ this specific abstraction rather than the concrete (or abstract) syntax of the language.

We briefly list the main results we have obtained so far.

1. The number of auxiliary attributes and of trivial attribute rules is drastically reduced.
2. Compiler modules can be parameterized and, thus, be viewed as implementation of a specific compilation concept.
3. It seems not to be difficult to implement the modularization concept on top of most given implementations of attribute grammars. The reason is that any attribute grammar AGa with underlying abstract grammar Ga can be transformed into an equivalent AGc over the concrete grammar Gc, when given a strong morphism g. In particular, AGc is cycle-free, iff Ga is cycle-free. (A proof of this fact depends on some technical details about attribute rules for syntactic rules with regular expressions and has to be omitted here.) This means in particular that a generated compiler will not have to transform the given parse tree into its individual abstractions. Also, if we restrict ourselves to pass-oriented attribute evaluation strategies, the structuring of the attribute definition phases helps to optimize storage allocation for attributes. Rather than introducing trivial transport rules for attributes, we can generate evaluation rules that store attributes into global variables where they remain during the traversal of irrelevant regions of

the tree.

4. According to (F3) we may construct hierarchies of parameterized modules. To put it differently, instantiations of modules may be employed for defining a new module. Thereby, the abstract grammar of the module to be defined becomes the concrete grammar that is passed to obtain the instantiations. Note, that one could view the first step in this hierarchy of grammar abstractions to represent the map from concrete to abstract syntax in the usual sense. This information could then be used by the compiler generator to automatically design the appropriate intermediate form for the source programs.

5. We finally turn once more to the problem of deciding whether or not a given symbol map s specifies a parse tree morphism r and, thus, a strong grammar morphism. It is an open problem of formal language theory as to whether the inclusion problem $L(G) \subset L(R)$, for context-free grammars G and regular expressions R, is decidable. Our problem is equivalent with this inclusion problem. Even if it turned out to be undecidable, it would not really affect the use of this modularization concept. The usual situation for parameter passing mechanisms is that many requirements about actual parameters (in our case concrete grammars) cannot be tested effectively, even not at runtime. Our situation is better. We can, at compile time, test whether the given concrete parse tree can actually be transformed into its individual abstractions.

REFERENCES

[ADJ80] Ehrig,H.,Kreowski,H.-J.,Thatcher,J.W.,Wagner,E.G.,Wright,J.B.: Parameter passing in algebraic specification languages. IBM Research, Yorktown Heights, 1980.

[Boc79] Bochmann,G.V.: Semantic equivalence of covering attribute grammars. Int'l. J. of Comp. and Inf. Science, 8,6 (1979) pp. 523-539.

[CaP67] McCarthy,J.,Painter,J.: Correctness of a compiler for arithmetic expressions. Mathematical Aspects of Comp. Sci., Proc. Symp. in Appl. Math., 19 (1967), pp.33-41.

[Gan81] Ganzinger,H.: ADELE - an attribute definition language. To appear.

[GoP80] Goguen,J.A.,Parsaye-Ghomi,K.: Algebraic denotational semantics using parameterized abstract modules. Manuscript, SRI-International, Menlo Park, Ca, Dec. 1980.

[Kas79] Kastens,U.: ALADIN - Eine Definitionssprache für attributierte Grammatiken. Univ. Karlsruhe, Fak. für Informatik, Bericht 7/79, 1979.

[Mos80] Mosses,P.: A constructive approach to compiler correctness. LNCS 94, 1980,

[Nij80] Nijholt,A.: Context-free grammars: covers, normal forms, and parsing. LNCS 93,

[Räi78] Räihä,K.-J.,Saarinen,M.,Soisalon-Soininen,E.,Tienari,M.: The compiler writing system HLP (Helsinki Language Processor). Dep't. of Comp. Sci., Univ. of Helsinki, Finland, Report A-1978-2, 1978.

[ReH70] Reynolds,J.C.,Haskell,R.: Grammatical coverings. Unpublished Manuscript, 1970.

[WaM77] Watt,D.A.,Madsen,O.L.: Extended attribute grammars. Univ. of Glasgow, Rep. 10, July 1977. (Revised version: Comp. Sci Dep't., Aarhus Univ., DAIMI PB-105, 1979)

[Zil75] Zilles,S.N.: An introduction to data algebras. Working draft paper. IBM Research, San Jose, 1975.

Static-Scope-LISP: ZERLEGUNG EINES INTERPRETIERERS IN ÜBERSETZER UND LAUFZEITSYSTEM

Henner Kröger
Institut für Informatik und Praktische Mathematik
Universität Kiel, D23oo Kiel, Olshausenstr. 4o-6o

Für den praktischen Bereich der Programmierung nimmt die Entwicklung korrekter Übersetzer einen lebenswichtigen Platz ein. Die bei der Übersetzerkonstruktion auftretenden Schwierigkeiten haben verschiedene prinzipielle Untersuchungen ausgelöst, so daß der Übersetzerbau zunehmend auch die Aufmerksamkeit der mehr theoretisch durchdrungenen Nachbargebiete auf sich zieht. Man ist seit langem bemüht, die traditionelle per-Hand-Konstruktion von Übersetzern durch (halb-) automatische Methoden zu ersetzen. Dabei sind auf *attributierte* Grammatiken abgestützte Verfahren (vgl. R. Wilhelm [10]; K.-J. Räihä [9]) unter anderem sehr gebräuchlich. P.D. Mosses [8] benutzt stattdessen eine *denotationelle* Semantikbeschreibung als Ausgangspunkt für die Compiler-Erzeugung. Eine andere Methode geht von einer *interpretativen* Sprachbeschreibung aus und verdient in jüngerer Zeit mehr und mehr Interesse (vgl. u.a.: L.A. Lombardi + B. Raphael [6]; L. Beckman + A. Haraldson + Ö. Oskarsson + E. Sandewall [1]; A.P. Ershov [2,3]; H. Kröger [4,5]).

In dieser Arbeit wird ein modifizierter LISP-Interpretierer vorgestellt, der einen vernünftigen Übersetzer samt Laufzeitsystem enthält. Dieser Interpretierer wurde gemäß dem *Prinzip der partiellen Auswertung* aus einer Variante jenes im LISP-Manual (McCarthy et al. [7]) S.13/7o angegebenen Interpretierers hergeleitet. Die Unterschiede zwischen dem modifizierten Interpretierer (inklusive Übersetzer und Laufzeitsystem) einerseits und der hier auch angegebenen ursprünglichen Interpretierervariante andererseits sind so "geringfügig", daß sich bei der Gegenüberstellung die Vermutung aufdrängt, der allgemeine Übergang vom Interpretierer zu einem Übersetzer samt Laufzeitsystem müsse kalkülmäßig in den Griff zu bekommen sein - zumindest für gewisse durchaus anspruchsvolle Sprachklassen und Interpretierertypen.

Die Zielsprache Z, die zugleich als Beschreibungssprache der Interpretierer/Übersetzer dient, sei in M-Ausdrücken geschriebenes LISP und zwar in der gebräuchlichen Kurzform und in dem Umfang etwa, wie vom Interpretierer von McCarthy et al. [7] her bekannt. Wegen der überwiegenden Buchstabengröße der Identifikatoren in dieser LISP-Version spreche man auch von *Klein-LISP*. Die Verwendung der Dynamic-Scope-Komponente der üblichen Semantik von (Klein-) LISP wird nur bezüglich der dynamischen Bindung der Identifikatoren ξ und α wesentlich und zwar besonders innerhalb der Funktion 'substitute' des modifizierten Interpretierers.

Die Quellsprache Q sei in S-Ausdrücken geschriebenes LISP, zur besseren Unterscheidung auch *Groß-LISP* genannt. Es empfiehlt sich bei der Lektüre der Gegenüberstellung des modifizierten Interpretierers und der ursprünglichen Interpretierervariante, den Sprachumfang von Groß-LISP schrittweise zu erweitern: ausgehend von den Standardfunktionen CAR bis EQ durch Hinzunahme von LAMBDA-Funktionen, Konditionalen (COND), FUNCTION-Argumenten und schließlich LABEL-Funktionen. Funktionale sowie das DEFINE- und PROGRAM-Konzept seien bezüglich der Quellsprache (Groß-LISP) späteren Untersuchungen vorbehalten. Im Gegensatz zum sonst üblichen LISP-Gebrauch wird für Groß-LISP eine *Static-Scope*-Semantik festgesetzt (die Interpretation von Funktionen erfolgt nicht in der Umgebung der Aufrufstelle sondern in der Umgebung der Deklarationsstelle, vgl. im Programm-Teil die Zeilen 55/56, 76, 60/62, 79/80): Damit soll dokumentiert werden, daß die hier benutzte Methode der Übersetzerentwicklung auch diese etwas aufwendigere Semantik-Philosophie meistert; die übliche Semantik von LISP oder gar eine konsequente Dynamic-Scope-Semantik wären in ähnlicher, etwas einfacherer Weise zu handhaben.

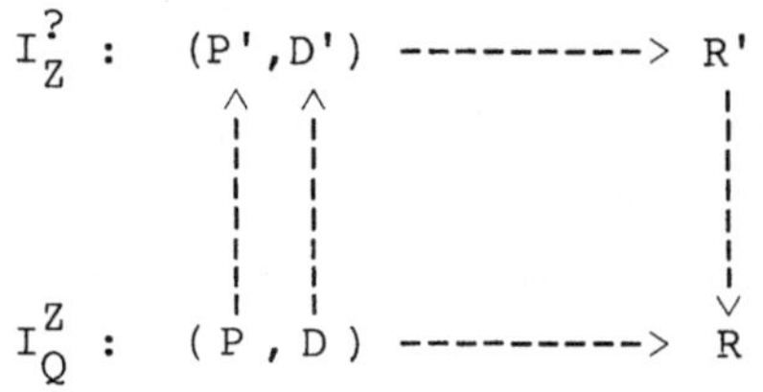

$$\begin{array}{lcr} I_Z^{?} : (P',D') & \longrightarrow & R' \\ \quad\;\; \uparrow \;\; \uparrow & & \downarrow \\ I_Q^{Z} : (P,D) & \longrightarrow & R \end{array}$$

Da außer den zugehörigen Daten D auch jedes Groß-LISP-Programm P und gewisse Bestandteile von P zugleich Konstanten in Klein-LISP sind, liegt folgender Versuch nahe: Man setzt den Groß-LISP-Interpretierer I_Q^Z auf (P,D) an, sperrt aber jeden Zugriff auf D und führt in einer ersten Rechenphase höchstens jene Handlungen von I_Q^Z durch, welche die Kenntnis der Programmdaten D nicht benötigen; über die Daten D soll als Information nur zur Verfügung stehen, daß sie im "Ernstfall" über die zweite Argumentstelle von I_Q^Z erreichbar sind. Um diese partielle Abarbeitung des Interpretierers zu steuern, wird Klein-LISP um ein Sondersymbol $\emptyset$, den Formalisierungsoperator, erweitert. Mit $\emptyset$ markierte Interpretiererhandlungen gelten als "eingefroren", "suspendiert" oder "blockiert". Mit solchen markierten Handlungen wird nur noch "formal" weitergerechnet; erst in einer zweiten Rechenphase, der Laufzeitphase, werden sie voll ausgewertet. Übrigens kann man sich die partielle Auswertung an einem hinreichend einfachen (arithmetischen) Ausdruck anschaulich in stark vereinfachter Weise als ein *Zerschneiden* des zugehörigen (verallgemeinerten) "Berechnungsbaumes" vorstellen.

In der ersten Rechenphase, der Code-Erzeugungsphase, wird man also in der Regel nicht das Endergebnis erreichen sondern den Auswertungsvorgang bei Beachtung gewisser Regeln aufgrund der Ø-Markierungen vorzeitig unterbrechen. Dabei bleibt als vorläufiges Zwischenergebnis ein Code C stehen, der sich aus Teilen von I_Q^Z (mit Ø-Markierungen), aus Teilen von P, Konstanten und dem Hinweis, wie D erreichbar ist, zusammensetzt. Dieser Code C kann als Übersetzung von P in die Zielsprache verstanden werden. Die im Code C verbliebenen Teile von I_Q^Z geben erste Hinweise über den Umfang des zur Code-Auswertung erforderlichen Laufzeitsystems. Wenn man die Ø-Markierungen aus dem Code C in geeigneter Weise "entfernt", kann man die restlichen, frei werdenden Auswertungen durchführen und erhält (hoffentlich!) das gesuchte Endergebnis - das setzt selbstverständlich voraus, daß die Auswertungen der Code-Erzeugungsphase und der anschließenden Laufzeitphase unter anderem in ihrer Reihenfolge und Wirkung von der bei normaler Gesamtauswertung nicht "wesentlich" verschieden sind.

Den Interpretierer in dieser Weise durch partielle Auswertung als Übersetzer zu "mißbrauchen", ist sicher dann sinnvoll, wenn die Ø-Markierungen so gesetzt werden können, daß in der Code-Erzeugungsphase die "komplizierten" Interpretiererhandlungen abgearbeitet werden, dagegen in der Laufzeitphase nur noch "einfache" Interpretiererhandlungen anfallen, die insbesondere nicht mehr den gesamten Interpretationsmechanismus erneut auslösen. Um dies auch bei der Behandlung von Rekursionen (LABEL) und Funktionen auf Argumentposition (FUNCTION) ohne Terminierungsprobleme zu erreichen, wird eine geringfügige Änderung der Reihenfolge einiger Handlungen erforderlich, die aber unter dem Stichwort *vorübersetzte* Funktionen ganz natürlich erscheint.

Das Herzstück dieser Arbeit ist der nachfolgende Programm-Teil. Dort wird der modifizierte Interpretierer (inklusive Übersetzer und Laufzeitsystem) angegeben. Es wird vom ernsthaften Leser erwartet, daß er diesen Interpretierer aktiv durcharbeitet; eine gewisse Hilfestellung soll ihm dabei der nachfolgende Kommentar sein, der eigene Arbeit aber nicht ersetzen kann. Die als Ausgangspunkt für die Modifikation dienende ursprüngliche Variante des LISP-Interpretierers kann man sich mit den angegebenen Hilfen in der rechten Spalte leicht rekonstruieren; man wird so die Ähnlichkeit sofort erkennen. Für genauere Details, theoretische Grundlagen und insbesondere eine Rechtfertigung des richtigen Zusammenspiels zwischen Ø-Markierung und Ø-Elimination wird auf die Arbeit [5] und nachfolgende Untersuchungen verwiesen.

KOMMENTAR zum modifizierten Interpretierer
(inklusive Übersetzer und Laufzeitsystem)

Bei Funktionsaufrufen in Klein-LISP greift man in der Regel nach dem call-by-value-Prinzip auf die Argumente zu. In Analogie zum Konditional sollen aber auch Funktionen mit call-by-need-Mechanismus in sparsamem Umfang erlaubt sein, ihre Identifikatoren mögen mit einem ! enden. Die in (Zeile) 2/3 deklarierte Startfunktion des modifizierten Interpretierers erlaubt also, den Zugriff über xx auf die tatsächlichen Programmdaten D möglichst lange hinauszuzögern. In 3 wird der Zugriff auf den Wert von xx durch ein Ø blockiert. Bei dem translate-Aufruf in 3 hat das zweite Argument die Zeichenreihe Øxx als Wert; dagegen wird über fn ein S-Ausdruck als Darstellung des Programmes P angeliefert. Die Funktion 'translate' löst den Übersetzungsvorgang aus und stellt schließlich zu P den oben erwähnten Code C zur Verfügung. Der Aufruf von 'run?' (man könnte dort einen Booleschen Schalter einbauen) sorgt über 'elim' für die Elimination der Ø-Markierungen in C, bewirkt also den Übergang in die Laufzeitphase. Mit einem "externen Trick" sind die Daten D also bis zu dem Augenblick "auswechselbar", wo in einem Teilstück Øxx des Codes C die Markierung Ø aufgehoben wird.

Einem markierten Funktionsaufruf Øf[a1;...;an] werde als Wert die *Zeichenreihe* Øf[$\overline{\text{a1}}$;...;$\overline{\text{an}}$] zugeordnet, wobei $\overline{\text{ai}}$ der Wert von ai sei. Diese Regelung soll auch gelten, wenn der Funktionsidentifikator mit einem ! endet. Derartige mit einem Ø beginnende Zeichenreihen heißen Ø-Werte; man zähle auch Øxx von 2 sowie Øξ und Øα von 56 und 61 dazu. Es ist sinnvoll, zur Menge der ursprünglichen LISP-Atome noch die Ø-Werte hinzuzunehmen und somit die Menge der ursprünglichen S-Ausdrücke unter Beibehaltung des Konstruktionsprinzips zur Menge der SØ-Ausdrücke zu erweitern. Jene SØ-Ausdrücke, die weder S-Ausdrücke noch Ø-Werte sind, sollen gemischte Werte heißen.

Offenbar müssen Aufrufe der Standardfunktionen 'car' und 'cdr' mit einem Ø markiert und blockiert werden, falls das Argument ein Ø-Wert ist (oder sein kann). Eine entsprechende Regelung ist für die Standardfunktionen 'atom' und 'eq' zwar nicht zwingend (Ø-Werte wurden zu Atomen erklärt), aber im Sinne einer Übersetzungs- und einer Laufzeitphase aus semantischen Gründen zweckmäßig; es sei denn, man beabsichtigt einen besonderen Trick. Bei Aufrufen der Standardfunktion 'cons' kann man dagegen ohne jede Auflage eine Ø-Markierung durchführen oder darauf verzichten, ganz wie es von Fall zu Fall opportun ist.

Das Setzen der Ø-Markierungen muß mit ihrer Elimination (durch die Funktion 'elim') abgestimmt sein. Dabei spielen Fragen der Lebensdauer- und Gültigkeitsbereiche von Variablen- und Funktionsidentifikatoren

PROGRAMM-TEIL

Eliminations-Algorithmus 'elim' :

Sei $\bar{z}$ der Wert der Variablen z. Der Wert des Aufrufes elim[z] berechnet sich wie folgt in einer *Hauptrechnung der Stufe o*, die sich in verschiedene Hauptrechnungen ebenfalls der Stufe o gemäß 2 aufspalten kann, mit untergeordneten *Nebenrechnungen* der Stufe $i \in \mathbb{N}$.

1. Sei $\bar{z}$ ein S-Ausdruck, so ist elim[$\bar{z}$] = $\bar{z}$.

2. Sei $\bar{z}$ ein gemischter Wert (a.b) . Dann ermittle man aus zwei neuen, elim[a] und elim[b] zugeordneten Hauptrechnungen der Stufe o die zugehörigen Teilergebnisse und setze

   elim[(a.b)] = (elim[a] . elim[b]) .

3. Sei $\bar{z}$ ein Ø-Wert:

a) entferne in $\bar{z}$ alle jene Ø, die nicht innerhalb eines gemischten Wertes stehen;

b) beginne, die entstandene Form auszurechnen; sobald während dieser Rechnung der Stufe $i \geq o$ aus einem gemischten Wert ein Ø-Wert herausgeholt wird, unterbreche man diese Rechnung der Stufe i und wende in einer Nebenrechnung der Stufe i+1 *außerhalb* des gemischten Wertes auf den Ø-Wert gemäß 3. 'elim' an;

c) wenn eine Nebenrechnung der Stufe $i+1 \geq 1$ endet (mit einem S-Ausdruck oder mit einem gemischten Wert), so setze man mit diesem Resultat die übergeordnete Rechnung der Stufe $i \geq o$ fort;

d) wenn eine Hauptrechnung der Stufe o mit einem gemischten Wert endet, so wende man auf diesen erneut 'elim' gemäß 2. an.

Modifizierter Interpretierer (inklusive Übersetzer und Laufzeitsystem):

```
begin
start![fn;xx] =
 run?[translate[fn;Øxx]]
translate[fn;x] =
 apply[fn;x;Nil]
```

Ursprüngliche Variante des LISP-Interpretierers:

```
begin
start[fn;xx] =
 evalquote[fn;xx]
evalquote[fn;x] =
 apply[fn;x;Nil]
```

```
apply[fn;x;a] =
 [atom[fn]->
  [eq[fn;CAR]->
        Øcar[Øcar[x]];
   eq[fn;CDR]->
        Øcdr[Øcar[x]];
   eq[fn;CONS]->
        Øcons[Øcar[x];Øcadr[x]];
   eq[fn;ATOM]->
        Øatom[Øcar[x]];
   eq[fn;EQ]->
        Øeq  [Øcar[x];Øcadr[x]];
   T->Øjumpid[fn;x;a] ];
  atom[car[fn]]->
   [eq[car[fn];LAMBDA]->
            callLAMBDA[fn;x;a];
    eq[car[fn];LABEL]->
            declLABEL[fn;x;a];
}
}  verlagert nach
}             'plycase'
}
    T->Øerror[28] ];
  T->Øerror[29] ]

callLAMBDA[fn;x;a] =
 eval[caddr[fn];
      Øpairlis[cadr[fn];x;a]]

eval[e;a] =
 [atom[e]->Øcont[e;a];
  atom[car[e]]->
   [eq[car[e];QUOTE]->Øcadr[e];
    eq[car[e];COND]->
             evcon[cdr[e];a];
    eq[car[e];FUNCTION]->
            evalFUN[e;a];
    T->functioncall[e;a] ];
  T->functioncall[e;a] ]

functioncall[e;a] =
 apply[car[e];evlis[cdr[e];a];a]
```

```
apply[fn;x;a] =
}
}
}
}
}
}  wie links, aber ohne Ø
}
}
}
}
}
   T->callid[fn;x;a] ];
}
}
}  identisch wie links
}
}
     eq[car[fn];ABEL]->
            callABEL[fn;x;a];
     eq[car[fn];FUNARG]->
            callFUNARG[fn;x];
}  wie links,
}      aber ohne Ø

callLAMBDA[fn;x;a] =
}  wie links,
}      aber ohne Ø

eval[e;a] =
}
}
}  wie links,
}      aber ohne Ø
}
}
}
}
}

functioncall[e;a] =
}  identisch wie links
```

```
evcon[c;a] =
 [null[c]->Øruntime-error[46];
  T->Øif![eval[caar[c];a];
          eval[cadar[c];a];
          evcon[cdr[c];a]] ]

evlis[m;a] =
 [null[m]->Nil;
  T->cons[eval[car[m];a];
          evlis[cdr[m];a]] ]

evalFUN[e;a] =
 Ølist3[FUNARGCODE;list1[
        apply[cadr[e];Øξ;Øα]];a]

declLABEL[fn;x;a] =
 apply[cadr[fn];x;
  Øcons[Øcons[cadr[fn];
   Ølist3[ABELCODE;list1[
          apply[caddr[fn];Øξ;Øα]];
          a]  ]; a ] ]

jumpid[fid;x;a] =
 plycase[cont[fid;a];x;fid]

plycase[fn;x;fid] =
 [atom[fn]->store-error[66];
  atom[car[fn]]->
   [eq[car[fn];ABELCODE]->
          substABEL[fn;x;fid];
    eq[car[fn];FUNARGCODE]->
          substFUNARG[fn;x];
    T->store-error[72] ];
  T->store-error[73] ]

substFUNARG[fn;x] =
 substitute[cadr[fn];x;
            caddr[fn] ]

substABEL[fn;x;fid] =
 substitute[cadr[fn];x;
  cons[cons[fid;fn];
       caddr[fn] ]]

substitute[codelist;x;a] =
 prog[[ξ;α]; ξ:=x; α:=a;
      return[car[codelist]] ]
```

```
evcon[c;a] =
}
}   wie links,
}       aber ohne Ø
}

evlis[m;a] =
}
}   identisch wie links
}

evalFUN[e;a] =
 list3[FUNARG;list1[
            cadr[e]];a]

declLABEL[fn;x;a] =
 apply[cadr[fn];x;
  cons[cons[cadr[fn];
   list3[ABEL;list1[
          caddr[fn]];
       a] ]; a] ]

callid[fid;x;a] =
 apply[cont[fid;a];x;fid]

}
}
}
}   entfällt  -
}   fand schon in 'apply'
}   statt
}
}
}

callFUNARG[fn;x] =
 apply[caadr[fn];x;
      caddr[fn] ]

callABEL[fn;x;fid] =
 apply[caadr[fn];x;
  cons[cons[fid;fn];
      caddr[fn] ]]

}
}   entfällt
}
```

Hilfsfunktionen	*Hilfsfunktionen*
end	end

Hilfsfunktionen für beide Interpretierer:

error[x] = SYNTAX-FEHLER Nr. ...
runtime-error[x] = LAUFZEIT-FEHLER Nr. ...
null[x] = }
pairlis[x;y;a] = } vgl. LISP-Manual
assoc[x;a] = }
cont[id;a] = cdr[assoc[id;a]]
if![p;q;s] = [p-> q; T-> s] (call-by-need!)
listo[] = Nil
listi[x_i;...;x_1] = cons[x_i;listi-1[x_{i-1};...;x_1]] ($1 \leq i \leq 3$)

Zusätzliche (Hilfs-) Funktionen für den modifizierten Interpretierer (inklusive Übersetzer und Laufzeitsystem):

run?[z] = elim[z]
elim[z] = *<Entfernung der Ø-Markierungen "nach Bedarf der Rechnung"; vgl. den vorangegangenen Eliminationsalgorithmus>*
store-error[x] = SPEICHER-FEHLER Nr. ...

Neben den Sprachelementen von Klein-LISP werden folgende Funktionen benötigt:

a) im Übersetzer:	b) im Laufzeitsystem:
start!	elim
run?	jumpid
translate	plycase
apply	substABEL
callLAMBDA	substFUNARG
declLABEL	substitute
eval	pairlis, null
evcon	cont, assoc, (equal)
evlis	error
evalFUN	runtime-error
functioncall	store-error
null	if!
list1, listo	list3, list2, list1, listo

FORTSETZUNG des Kommentarteiles auf der nächsten Seite!

eine zentrale Rolle. Wesentlich schwieriger sind jene Probleme zu handhaben, welche durch Mißachtung einer speziellen Reihenfolge in der Abarbeitung von Funktionsaufrufen (z.B. call-by-need) ausgelöst werden; das ist im Zusammenhang mit Seiteneffekten besonders gefährlich.

Der Parameter x in 'translate', 'apply', 'callLAMBDA', 'declLABEL' kann wegen 3, 56, 61 einen Ø-Wert bringen. Demzufolge sind die Aufrufe von 'car', 'cadr' und 'cdr' in 9, 11, 13, 15, 17 markiert. In 15, 17 werden die Aufrufe von 'atom' und 'eq' markiert, um die Simulation der "großen" Standardfunktionen durch die "kleinen" korrekt durchzuführen. Die Markierung des cons-Aufrufes in 13 erfolgt, um die Simulation aller Standardfunktionen einheitlich zu gestalten.

Da x in 32 einen Ø-Wert bringen kann, wird, um eine Markierung im pairlis-Rumpf zu vermeiden, der pairlis-Aufruf selbst markiert. Demzufolge kann der Parameter a in 'eval', 'evcon', 'evalFUN', 'functioncall', 'evlis', 'apply', 'callLAMBDA','declLABEL' einen Ø-Wert bringen. Folglich muß der cont-Aufruf in 34 markiert sein.

Die Markierung des cadr-Aufrufes in 36 geschieht nicht so sehr aus Analogiegründen zur Variablenbehandlung in 34, sondern mehr in der Absicht, während der Übersetzungsphase nur die "unbedingt nötige" Organisationsarbeit zu leisten, dagegen den "eigentlichen" Rechenablauf des ursprünglichen Interpretierers soweit irgendmöglich in der Laufzeitphase zu simulieren. Dem entsprechend werden in der Übersetzungsphase Syntaxfehler in 28, 29 zwar erkannt, aber die Meldung darüber wird durch Markierung in die Laufzeitphase verlegt und erfolgt nur, wenn der Syntaxfehler dann noch relevant ist, das heißt, wenn auch der ursprüngliche Interpretierer in Abhängigkeit von den Programmdaten D darüber gestolpert wäre. Die Fehlerbehandlung in 46 dagegen betrifft nur während der Laufzeitphase auftretende Komplikationen, darf also auf keinen Fall in der Übersetzungsphase aktiv werden und ist deshalb markiert. Über die Markierung des if!-Aufrufes in 47 sprechen wir später.

Der apply-Aufruf in 56, 61 sorgt jeweils für die *Vorübersetzung* von FUNCTION-Argumenten und LABEL-Deklarationen. Da in diesem Augenblick die aktuellen Argumente und auch die aktuelle Umgebung nicht bekannt sind (man denke etwa an LABEL-Deklarationen oder Aufrufe mit FUNCTION-Argumenten im Rumpf einer anderen LABEL-Funktion), wird in 56, 61 der Zugriff auf die Variablen ξ und α durch Ø-Markierungen gesperrt; die *Formen* Øξ und Øα sollen die *Zeichenreihen* Øξ beziehungsweise Øα als Wert haben. Hierzu sind einige Eigenarten sehr wesentlich: Wie in 3 wird auf den tatsächlichen Wert der Variablen ξ oder α erst in der Laufzeitphase nach Entfernen der Ø-Markierung zugegriffen. Bis dahin ist für diese Variablen/Identifikatoren weder eine Bindung noch eine Belegung mit Werten erforderlich. Diese Bindung und Versorgung mit Werten erfolgt erst im dynamischen Ablauf der Laufzeitphase innerhalb der Funktion 'substitute' in 82, 83 und wird durch die Dynamic-Scope-Komponente der Semantik von Klein-LISP sanktioniert. Aufgrund der in 'start!' an fn übergebenen Programmdarstellung P wird in der Übersetzungsphase der Code C aufgebaut. In C können an vielen verschiedenen Stellen ξ- und α-Identifikatoren, stets mit einer Markierung, auftreten. Während der Laufzeitphase werden gewisse Codestücke von C, die auch Øξ und Øα enthalten können, nach Bedarf dupliziert. Der in 56, 61 erzeugte Code wird während der Übersetzungsphase in einem gemischten Wert verpackt, damit die Markierung in Øξ und Øα möglichst lange in Kraft bleibt. Dieser gemischte Wert tritt in der Laufzeitphase in einer geeigneten Inkarnation von 'substitute' als Argument eines car-Aufrufes 83 wieder auf: erst im Anschluß an diesen car-Eingriff in den gemischten Wert wird die Markierung in dem zugehörigen Øξ und Øα gelöscht, und zwar nur in der Inkarnation *außerhalb* des gemischten Wertes. Damit wird die Bindung für ξ und α erforderlich und hergestellt. Die Markierung des äußeren cons-Aufrufes in 59 ist in Analogie zu der Markierung des pairlis-Aufrufes in 32 zu sehen. Der innere cons-Aufruf in 59 wird aus den gleichen Gründen markiert wie bei dem list3-Aufruf in 55, 6o: Der Wert des in 56, 62 auftretenden a kann Øα sein; dann muß diese Markierung aber beim Vollzug der Funktionsdeklaration beseitigt sein (dafür wird während der Laufzeitphase in einem umfassenderen substitute-Aufruf gesorgt), damit während der Laufzeitphase die korrekte Umgebung der jeweiligen Deklarationsstelle in das CODE-Tripel und dieses dann in der a-Liste eingetragen wird.

Da der Parameter a in 'apply' einen Ø-Wert bringen kann, muß der jumpid-Aufruf in 18 markiert sein. Dadurch wird die Entscheidung, ob das zum Identifikator gehörige Tripel ein ABEL- oder ein FUNARG-CODE-Tripel ist, in die Laufzeitphase verlegt, also von 'apply' nach 'plycase'. Der apply-Aufruf in 75, 78 des ursprünglichen Interpretierers erfolgt jetzt in der Übersetzungsphase offenbar schon vorzeitig (und nur noch einmalig vor der Speicherung) in 56, 49.

Das Groß-LISP-Programm

```
        ( LABEL, G, ( LAMBDA, ( X, Y ),  < Form >  ) )
```

erhält als Übersetzung

```
        Øjumpid[G;Øxx;Øcons[Øcons[G;Ølist3[ABELCODE;(
          < Übersetzung der  < Form >  in der
            Umgebung  Øpairlis[(X,Y);Øξ;Øα]    >
          ); Nil]]; Nil]]
```

Die Markierung des if!-Aufrufes in 47 ist erforderlich, da die Fallunterscheidung des zu übersetzenden Groß-LISP-Konditionals in der Regel erst zur Laufzeit getroffen werden kann. Nun wird aber die call-by-need-Eigenschaft von 'if!' bei der Ermittlung des *markierten* if!-Aufrufes während der Übersetzungsphase nicht beachtet; sie wirkt erst wieder, wenn die Markierung in der Laufzeitphase entfernt wird. Andererseits muß in der Übersetzungsphase der Code für die gesamte Fallkaskade vorbereitet werden, so daß eine Ø-Markierung der drei Argumente des markierten if!-Aufrufes in 47 wenig sinnvoll ist - in der Laufzeitphase würden sonst wieder Übersetzungsaufgaben anfallen. Man kann sich (durch Induktion über den Aufbau von Formen) klar machen, daß hier dieser Balance-Akt zwischen *Tun und Nicht-Tun* im speziellen Fall unseres modifizierten Interpretierers glückt: Während der Übersetzungsphase eines Groß-LISP-Programmes P wird keine Groß-LISP-Form von P ausgerechnet, sie wird nur in einen Ø-Wert umcodiert, und dies allein aufgrund ihrer syntaktischen Struktur (unter Kenntnisnahme der Standardsymbole) - selbst die korrekte Bindung von Variablen- und Funktionsidentifikatoren sowie die korrekte Parameteranzahl etc. bei Funktionsaufrufen wird erst in der Laufzeitphase geprüft; die Übersetzungsphase baut lediglich den Mechanismus für diese Prüfungen auf.

Der vorliegende modifizierte Interpretierer (inklusive Übersetzer und Laufzeitsystem) verarbeitet in der Übersetzungsphase jedes Groß-LISP-Programm (des angegebenen Sprachumfanges), wenn es nur *syntaktisch korrekt* ist, und überläßt dabei, wenn nur irgendmöglich, jede rechen- oder datenmäßige Interpretation der Laufzeitphase. In der Laufzeitphase schmiegt sich die nur organisatorisch vorbereitete Rechnung dann an die der ursprünglichen Interpretierer-variante *hautnah* an.

LITERATUR.

[1] L. Beckman, A. Haraldson, Ö. Oskarsson and E. Sandewall, *A partial evaluator, and its use as a programming tool*, Artificial Intelligence 7 (1976), 319-357.

[2] A.P. Ershov, *On the partial computation principle*, Information Processing Letters 6 (1977), 38-41.

[3] A.P. Ershov, *On the essence of compilation*, IFIP Working Conf. on Formal Description of Programming Concepts, 31 July to 5 August 1977, Saint Andrews, New Brunswick; Volume One, 1.1-1.28.

[4] H. Kröger, *A compiler-interpreter-problem*, Proceedings of the International Workshop on Semantics of Programming Languages, Bad Honnef, März 1977; Bericht 41, Abteilung Informatik, Universität Dortmund; Seite 6o-64.

[5] H. Kröger, *Ein Code erzeugender Formalisierungsoperator und seine*

Anwendung auf LISP-Interpretierer, Habilitationsschrift, Mathematisch-Naturwissenschaftliche Fakultät, Universität Kiel,1981.

[6] L.A. Lombardi, B. Raphael, *LISP as the language for an incremental computer*, in 'The Programming Language LISP: Its Operation and Applications', ed.: E.C. Berkeley, D.G. Bobrow; The MIT Press, Cambridge, Mass., 1964; fourth printing 1974, 2o4-219.

[7] J. McCarthy, P.W. Abrahams, D.J. Edwards, T.P. Hart, M.I. Levin, *LISP 1.5 Programmer's Manual*, The MIT Press, Cambridge, Mass., 1962; second edition, eight printing 1973.

[8] P.D. Mosses, *Compiler generation using denotational semantics*, MFCS 1976 Gdansk (ed.: A. Mazurkiewicz), Lecture Notes in Computer Science 45, Springer-Verlag 1976, 436-441.

[9] K.-J. Räihä, *On attribute grammars and their use in a compiler writing system*, Report A-1977-4, Department of Computer Science, University of Helsinki, 1977.

[1o] R. Wilhelm, *Attributierte Grammatiken*, Informatik Spektrum 2 (1979), 123-13o.

PROGRAMS AS TRANSFORMATIONS OF ALGEBRAIC THEORIES
(Extended Abstract)

Harald Ganzinger

Institut für Informatik
Technische Universität München
Postfach 202420
D-8000 München 2
Fed. Rep. of Germany

1. INTRODUCTION

Abstract specifications of data types have proved to be a powerful tool in the process of software development. Consequently, semantic theories for programs computing on abstractly specified data types have been studied. At least two different types of theories have emerged. Approaches of the first type view programming language constructs, such as assignment or if-then-else, as operators of algebras that contain as a sub-algebra the data types on which the programs compute. The approaches of [ADJ77], [CoN78], [Wan79a], and [BrW80], among others, belong to this class. This enrichment of the base type by the while-program control constructs is, because of aspects of nontermination, not sufficiently complete in the sense of e.g. [Gut75], [ADJ78a], [Wan79b]. Thus the theory of abstract data types has been extended by various concepts, among them partial algebras and homomorphisms or continuous algebras. The second class of approaches is concerned with programs as implementations of abstractly specified data types. Programs are viewed as data type specifications that extend the base type by the objects (variables, functions, types) it computes [ADJ78a], [Ehr79], [EKP80], [Hup80], [Gan81], among others. Then, the semantics of a terminating program is a "persistent" free functor from the base type theory to these objects.

This paper gives an algebraic semantics for while-programs that justifies the latter view. Programs will be associated with products of free and forgetful functors from "inputs" to "results" such that termination is indicated by certain persistency properties. The results we have obtained so far are the following. The semantics is a model of the Hoare-logic for while programs over abstract data types. It is compatible with certain notions of abstract implementation for data type specifications. Moreover, it is independent of a specific notion of semantics such as intial or terminal algebra semantics for the specification of the underlying data types. The latter is important for the development of concepts for abstract implementation based on observability concepts [Gan81].

2. NOTATION

We assume the reader to be familiar with the basic notions in the theory of parameterized algebraic specifications as developed in [ADJ80] or [BG80]. We repeat the notions that are introduced in these papers.

A signature consists of a pair (S,Σ), where S is the set of sorts and Σ is the

S^*xS-indexed family of sets of operators Σ_{us}, $u \in S^*$, $s \in S$. An operator $f \in \Sigma_{s1...sns0}$ will be written as f: s1...sn -> s0.

With $T_\Sigma(X)$ we denote the free Σ-algebra over X, if X is a S-indexed family of sets. It is the system of all terms that can be written with the constants from X and the operators from Σ. A (conditional) Σ-<u>equation</u> is a pair (X,e1& ... &en -> e0) where X is a S-indexed family of sets of <u>variables</u> and the ej are equations, i.e. pairs t1=t2 of terms $t1,t2 \in T_\Sigma(X)$. We omit X if it is the set of variables appearing in one of the ei. We call the equation unconditional, if n=0.

A <u>specification</u> SPEC is a triple (S,Σ,E), where (S,Σ) is a signature and E is a set of conditional Σ-equations. Alg[SPEC] is the category of all Σ-algebras A that satify E (the latter will be written A |= E). By E^{**} we denote the closure of E, i.e. the set of all Σ-equations that are satified by any $A \in$ Alg[SPEC].

The renaming of sorts and operators in specifications and the establishing of structural similarities between specifications is modelled by signature morphisms. A <u>signature morphism</u> $h:(S,\Sigma)->(S',\Sigma')$ is a pair (h_S,h_Σ) consisting of a mapping h_S:S->S' and a S^*xS-indexed family of mappings $h_\Sigma(us):\Sigma_{us}-> \Sigma'_{h_S(us)}$. Replacing the operators and variables in a term t or an equation e by their images under h yields translated terms h(t) or equations h(e). (Thereby, the variables of sort s are assumed to be injectively mapped to variables of sort $h_S(s)$.) A <u>specification morphism</u> h:SPEC->SPEC' between specifications is a signature morphism $h:(S,\Sigma) -> (S',\Sigma')$ for which $h(E) \subset E'$. For any signature or specification morphism h, the map Uh that sends any Σ'-algebra A' to the Σ-algebra A for which $(A)_s = (A')_{h(s)}$, $s \in S$, $o_A = h(o)_{A'}$, $o \in \Sigma$, is a functor. It is called the <u>forgetful functor</u> that comes with h.

A <u>parameterized specification</u> is a pair SPEC1(SPEC) of specifications SPEC1 and SPEC such that $S \subset S1$, $\Sigma_{us} \subset \Sigma 1_{us}$, for any $us \in S^*S$, and $E \subset E1$. Parameterized specifications are constructors for extending parameter algebras $A \in$ Alg[SPEC] to algebras $A \in$ Alg[SPEC1]. The map T that sends any such A to $T_{\Sigma 1}(A)/=$, where = is the congruence generated by E1 and the equations that are satified in A, is a free construction that is left-adjoint to the forgetful functor Ui that comes with the inclusion morphism i : SPEC->SPEC1. T is called the <u>free construction</u> T : Alg[SPEC]->Alg[SPEC1]. An algebra $A \in$ Alg[SPEC] is said to <u>persist</u> in the result of T, if Ui(T(A)) is isomorphic to A (written Ui(T(A))=A). T is called <u>persistent</u>, if any such A persists under T.

Let SPEC1(SPEC) be a parameterized specification, $SPEC=(S,\Sigma,E)$, $SPEC1=SPEC+(S1,\Sigma1,E1)$, let $SPEC2=(S2,\Sigma2,E2)$ be a specification and let h : SPEC->SPEC2 be a signature morphism. Then, $SPEC1*_hSPEC2 = (S3,\Sigma3,E3)$ is the result of passing the actual parameter SPEC2 to the (formal) parameter SPEC according to h. Thereby, SPEC is replaced by SPEC2 according to the correspondences specified by h. Formally,

$$S3 = S1+S2,\quad \Sigma3 = h'(\Sigma1)+\Sigma2,\quad E3 = h'(E1)+E2,$$

where h' is a signature morphism on $(S+S1,\Sigma+\Sigma1)$ defined by

$h'_S(s)$ = <u>if</u> $s \in S$ <u>then</u> $h_S(s)$ <u>else</u> s

$h'_\Sigma(o)$ = <u>if</u> $o:w->s \in \Sigma$ <u>then</u> $h_\Sigma(o)$ <u>else</u> $o: h'_S(w)->h'_S(s)$.

3. CONDITIONAL CONSTRUCTIONS

Our goal was to employ persistent functors for the definition of the semantics of programs.

As we shall see, the semantics of an assignment can easily be seen as such a construction. Then, the extension lemma of [ADJ80] can be applied to construct compositions, modelling the semantics of sequences of assignments. Any path in the flow graph of a program is a sequence of assignments and tests. Thus, we can represent the semantics of the program by a system of pairs consisting of persistent functors and finite sets of equations. The former model the effect of executing the assignments on a specific path, whereas the latter represent the boolean conditions on that path. Subsequently we will call such systems conditional functors and we will list their basic properties.

Let SPEC = (S, Σ, E), SPECi = SPEC+$(\emptyset, \emptyset, Ei)$, SPEC1i = SPECi+$(S1, \Sigma1, E1i)$, $i \in I$, be a finite or countably infinite family of specifications such that

a) at least for one $s \in S$ it is $(T_{\Sigma+\Sigma1})_s - (T_\Sigma)_s \neq \emptyset$,

b) SPEC1i(SPECi) is persistent for any $i \in I$,

c) if Ti is the free construction Alg[SPEC] -> Alg[SPEC1], then, for any pair $i,j \in I$, both functors Ti and Tj yield identical results on algebras $A \in$ Alg[SPEC+$(\emptyset, \emptyset, Ei+Ej)$],

d) the Ei are finite sets of unconditional Σ-equations in constant terms $t \in T_\Sigma$.

The family of persistent free constructors Ti can, under the above assumptions, be composed to yield again a free constructor T which is almost persistent and for which the extension lemma of [ADJ80] can be applied to construct compositions of such constructors. The domain of this composite functor will be SPEC. Its range will be SPEC1 = SPEC+$(S1, \Sigma1, E1)$, where, if $Ei = \{ei_1, \ldots ei_{ki}\}$,

$$E1 = \{ei_1 \& \ldots \& ei_{ki} \& f1 \& \ldots \& fk \rightarrow f \mid i \in I,\ f1 \& \ldots \& fk \rightarrow f \in E1i\}$$

Thus, E1 is the set of conditional equations that results from taking the equations from any of the E1i and add to their premisses the equations of Ei. Then we define

T : Alg[SPEC] -> Alg[SPEC1] by

T(A) = if A |= Ei, for some $i \in I$, then Ti(A) else undef(A), $A \in$ Alg[SPEC],

T(h) = if A |= Ei then Ti(h) else undef(h), for any Σ-homomorphism h:A->B.

Remains to be specified what "undef" is supposed to mean. Intuitively, T(A) is a conditional that tests upon the conditions Ei and selects then the corresponding Ti. The above specified assumptions guarantee that Ti and Tj yield the same result if A |= Ei+Ej. If we think of the Ei as being the guards of a guarded command, then a program does not terminate, if none of the guards are satisfied. Our handling of this situation will be to pollute the input algebra A by new terms that do not have equivalent terms in A. Therefore, we take undef to be the free construction

undef : Alg[SPEC] -> Alg[SPEC+$(S1, \Sigma1, \emptyset)$].

It follows from condition a) that no $A \in$ Alg[SPEC] persists under undef.

Theorem 1. T is the free construction Alg[SPEC] -> Alg[SPEC1] (up to isomorphy). For any $A \in$ Alg[SPEC] it is A |= Ei, for some $i \in I$, iff A persists under T. In this case it is T(A) = Ti(A).

We use the notation T = $[i \in I]$(SPECi -> SPEC1i) (or T=(SPEC1->SPEC11,...,SPECk->SPEC1k), if I={1,...,k}) and call T a (free) conditional construction (or, simply, a conditional).

3.1. Adding a condition to a conditional

Let T = $[i \in I]$(SPECi -> SPEC1i) and a finite set E of unconditional $\Sigma+\Sigma1$-equations be given such that the following is true: For any t1=t2 $\in$ E it is t1,t2 $\in (T_{\Sigma+\Sigma1})_s$, for some $s \in S$, i.e. the $t1,t2$ are constant terms, yielding a result of an S-sort.

Then from the persistency of the SPEC1i(SPECi) it follows for any $t1=t2 \in E$ the existence of terms $t1',t2' \in T_{\Sigma}$ such that $t1=t1'$ and $t2=t2'$ are equations in $(E+Ei+E1i)^{**}$. Let $E'=\{ t1'=t2' \mid t1=t2 \in E \}$ and assume that SPECi'=SPECi+$(\emptyset,\emptyset,E')$ and SPEC1i'= SPEC1i+$(\emptyset,\emptyset,E')$. (Note that then $E \subset (Ei+E1i+E')^{**}$, for any $i \in I$.)

Theorem 2. T' = [i ∈ I](SPECi' -> SPEC1i') is again a free conditional construction, denoted E & [i ∈ I](SPECi -> SPEC1i) subsequently. It is for any A ∈ Alg[SPEC] such that A |= E+Ei for some i ∈ I, T(A) = T'(A).

3.2. Composition of conditionals

Let T=[i ∈ I](SPECi -> SPEC1i) and T'=[j ∈ J](SPECj' -> SPEC1i') be two conditional constructions. Let, furthermore, $a:(S,\Sigma) \to (S'+S1', \Sigma'+\Sigma 1')$ be a signature morphism such that $a(E) \subset (E'+Ej'+E1j')^{**}$, for any j, and $a(S) \subset S'$. Then Ti = Ei & [j ∈ J](SPECj' -> SPEC1j') is defined. According to the above, any of the Ti is itself a conditional of form [j ∈ J](SPECij'->SPEC1ij').

Theorem 3. T'' = [(i,j) ∈ IxJ](SPECij' -> SPEC1i$*_a$SPEC1ij') is again a free conditional construction, denoted T'' = T$\cdot_a$T'. For any A ∈ Alg[SPEC'], A persists under T'', iff there exists a pair (i,j) ∈ IxJ such that A |= Ej' and T'(A) |= Ei. In this case, T''(A) = T$*_a$T'(A).

3.3. Forgetting sorts and operators in conditionals

Let (S', Σ') be a signature such that $S \subset S' \subset S+S1$, $\Sigma \subset \Sigma' \subset \Sigma + \Sigma 1$, and let g denote the inclusion morphism $g : (S', \Sigma') \to (S+S1, \Sigma + \Sigma 1)$. If [i ∈ I](SPECi -> SPEC1i) is a conditional construction then we define SPEC1i' = $(S', \Sigma', g^{-1}((E+Ei+E1i)^{**}))$.

Theorem 4. [i ∈ I](SPECi -> SPEC1i') is again a free conditional construction denoted g^{-1}\{[i ∈ I](SPECi -> SPEC1i)\}. Furthermore, if Ug is the forgetful functor that forgets the sorts (S+S1)-S' and operators $(\Sigma+\Sigma 1)-\Sigma'$ and if A ∈ Alg[SPEC] satisfies Ei, then it is Ug([i ∈ I](SPECi->SPEC1i)(A)) = g^{-1}\{[i ∈ I](SPECi->SPEC1i)\}(A).

3.4. Sum of conditionals

Let Tj = [i ∈ Ij](SPECij->SPEC1ij), j ∈ J, be a finite or countably infinite family of conditionals. Assume that SPECij = SPEC+$(\emptyset,\emptyset,$Eij) and that for any A ∈ Alg[SPEC] and any i,i' ∈ I, j,j' ∈ J it is A |= Eij+Ei'j', only if Tj(A) = Tj'(A).

Theorem 5. T = [(i,j) ∈ IxJ](SPECij->SPEC1ij) is again a conditional, denoted T = +[j ∈ J] Tj (or T=T1+...+Tk, if J=\{1,...,k\}).

4. PROGRAMS AS COMPOSITIONS OF FREE AND FORGETFUL FUNCTORS

We assume that SPECT = (S,Σ,E) is a specification of the data types on which the while programs may compute. Therefore we assume that SPECT contains a specification of the standard type BOOLEAN. In particular, BOOL ∈ S and true, false $\in \Sigma$.

Since we do not admit inequations in specifications nor do we employ concepts such as data constraints [BG80] or canons [Rei80], we have to explicitly exclude the trivial algebras in which true=false holds. From now on we will assume that for any specification SPEC, Alg[SPEC] is the full subcategory of SPEC-algebras in which true=false holds. The results and constructions of section 2 are not affected by this additional constraint. (The reason for this is that we required the components SPEC1i(SPECi) of the conditionals to be persistent, so that the sub-algebra A_{BOOL} of any SPECi-algebra A is not modified by the free construction Alg[SPECi] -> Alg[SPEC1i]. Also in the default case in which A satisfies none of the Ei, A is enriched consistently under the conditional constructs so that true=false remains true.)

The semantics definition which we now want to give is based upon the following ideas. Given a program p we assume that V is the set of variables occurring in p. V is a system of constants x->s, s ∈ S, over the set S of type names. x is the name of the program variable and s denotes its type. Then the execution of the program starts from a state that satisfies the specification

SPECV = SPECT + (∅,V,∅).

An assignment x:=t can now be viewed as consisting of an x->s ∈ V and a constant term t ∈ $(T_{\Sigma+V})_s$. Its elaboration consists of two steps:

a) The value of t is computed depending on the input state.

b) This value is assigned to x.

In our algebraic framework, program states will be modelled by algebras A ∈ Alg[SPEC]. In particular the mapping from program variables y to their values in this state is reflected by the A-values y_A of the operators y ∈ V. Thus, step a) can be seen as enriching A by a new constant x' and giving it the value of t in A. This is exactly what the free constructor

Alg[SPECV] -> Alg[SPECV+(∅,V',{x'=t}∪ {y'=y ¦ y ∈ V, y ≠ x})]

does, if V' denotes a set of new copies y' for the variables y ∈ V. Step b) is then the renaming of all the y' back into y, thereby forgetting the old values of the variables. (Actually, only the old value of x gets destroyed since the values of the other variables are not changed.) This can be modelled by the forgetful functor Uf that comes with the signature morphism

f : (S, Σ+V) -> (S, Σ+V+V')

sending s ∈ S to s, o ∈ Σ to o, and x ∈ V to x' ∈ V'. Note that the free constructor of step a) is persistent. Persistency will be the formal equivalent of termination.

This structuring of the state transformation into the product of a free functor Tp with the forgetful functor Uf is possible for any program p as will be demonstrated now. Since Uf is independent of p, it is sufficient to define Tp by structural induction over p. Tp will always be a conditional in the above sense. Any of its conditions will correspond to the properties of the input algebra that have to be satisfied so that one specific sequence of assignments constitutes the execution of p.

4.1. Assignments

p = x:=t, x->s ∈ V, t ∈ $(T_{\Sigma+V})_s$.

Tp is the free construction defined above.

Example 1. Let in the following be S = {INT, BOOL}, (Σ,E) be the usual specification of integers and boolean values, and V = {x->INT,y->INT}.

For p = x:=x+1 it is then
Tp = (SPECV -> SPECV+(∅,{x',y'}, {x'=x+1, y'=y}))

4.2. Conditional statements

p = if b then q else r, b ∈ $(T_{\Sigma+V})_{BOOL}$
Then, if ET = { b = true } and EF = { b = false },
Tp = (ET & Tq) + (EF & Tr).

Example 2. p = if x > 0 then x:=x+1 else y:=y+1 yields
Tq = (SPECV -> SPECV+(∅,{x',y'},{x'=x+1,y'=y}))
Tr = (SPECV -> SPECV+(∅,{x',y'},{x'=x,y'=y+1})), and, thus,
Tp = (SPECV+(∅,∅,{x>0=true}) -> SPECV+(∅,{x',y'},{x>0=true,x'=x+1,y'=y}),
SPECV+(∅,∅,{x>0=false})-> SPECV+(∅,{x',y'},{x>0=false,x'=x,y'=y+1}))

This demonstrates the principal application of free conditional constructs. The condition of a test and its negation are the guards for the "then"- and "else"-functor, respectively. The sum + is defined since for no algebra A ∈ Alg[SPEC] A |= b=true, b=false at the same time.

4.3. Sequencing

p = q ; r
We may assume that Tq and Tr are the free constructions
Tq : Alg[SPECV] -> Alg[SPEC1q], for some SPEC1q = SPECV+(∅,V'',Eq), and
Tr : Alg[SPECV] -> Alg[SPEC1r], for some SPEC1r = SPECV+(∅,V',Er).
(In order to distinguish the final values of the variables after the execution of r from those after the execution of q, we assume that we have used new copies x'' ∈ V'' of the variables x ∈ V in the definition of Tq.) Now three steps are to be taken:
a) The initial values x of the program variables at r are associated with the final values x'' of the variables after execution of q. This is modelled by the specification morphism io : SPECV -> SPEC1q, sending s ∈ S to s, o ∈ Σ to o, and x ∈ V to x'' ∈ V''.
b) The two functors Tr and Tq are composed according to io. Let T = Tr $\cdot_{io}$ Tq. Then, T is the free construction Alg[SPEC] -> Alg[SPEC1], for some SPEC1= SPEC+(∅,V''+V',E1).
c) The intermediate values x'' ∈ V'' of the program variables are hidden. This is established by the inclusion morphism
i : SPEC+(∅,V',∅) -> SPEC1,
sending s ∈ S to s, o ∈ Σ∪V∪V' to o. Altogether:
Tp = i^{-1}{ Tr $\cdot_{io}$ Tq }.

Example 3.
x:=x+1; if x > 0 then x:=x+1 else y:=y+1
Tq is given in example 1, Tr is given in example 2. Then:
T= (SPECV+(∅,∅,{x+1>0=true}) ->
SPECV+(∅,{x'',y'',x',y'},{x+1>0=true,x''=x+1,y''=y,x'=x''+1,y'=y''}),
SPECV+(∅,∅,{x+1>0=false}) ->
SPECV+(∅,{x'',y'',x',y'},{x+1>0=false,x''=x+1,y''=y,x'=x'',y'=y''+1}))
Tp = (SPECV+(∅,∅,{x+1>0=true} -> SPECV+(∅,{x',y'},{x+1>0=true,x'=(x+1)+1,y'=y}),
SPECV+(∅,∅,{x+1>0=false} -> SPECV+(∅,{x',y'},{x+1>0=false,x'=x+1,y'=y+1})).

4.4. While-loops

p = while b do q , $b \in (T_{\Sigma+V})_{BOOL}$.

Let Tq : Alg[SPECV] -> Alg[SPECV+(∅,V'',Eq)], where we again assume that the final values of the program variables after the execution of one iteration step are denoted by new copies $x'' \in V''$ of the $x \in V$. Then we can define conditionals Tj, j>=0, by

$T0 = (SPECV+(\emptyset,\emptyset,\{b=false\}) \rightarrow SPECV+(\emptyset,V',\{b=false\} \cup \{x'=x \mid x \in V\}))$.

(T0 represents the case where the loop condition evaluates to false. Then, the program variables remain unchanged.) For j>0 we define

$Tj = i^{-1} \{ T[j-1] \cdot_{io} (\{b = true\} \,\&\, Tq) \}$,

where io and i are the signature morphisms as defined for statement sequences, cf. 4.3. io makes the final values of the variables after execution of the first iteration step {b=true}&Tq to become the initial values of the variables for the rest T[j-1] of the execution of the while loop. i forgets the intermediate values of the variables. Then we define

$Tp = +[j>=0]\ Tj$.

It is not difficult to see that this sum is well-defined since the conditions of the conditionals Tj do not overlap. The conditions of Tj represent all possible executions of the loop with exactly j iterations of the loop body q.

Example 4. Let V={r->INT,q->INT,d->INT}, p = while r >= q do r:=r-q; d:=d+1 .
Then, Tq = (SPECV -> SPECV+(∅,{r'',q'',d''},{r''=r-q,q''=q,d''=d+1})),
T0=(SPECV+(∅,∅,{r>=q = false})->SPECV+(∅,V',{r>=q = false,r'=r,q'=q,d'=d})).
This makes
Tj=(SPECV+(∅,∅,{r-iq>=q = true|0<=i<j}∪{r-jq>=q = false}) ->
SPECV+(∅,{r',q',d'},
{r-iq>=q = true|0<=i<j}∪{r-jq>=q = false,r'=r-jq,q'=q,d'=d+j})).

5. SOME PROPERTIES OF THE ALGEBRAIC SEMANTICS

Definition. A program p is said to terminate on $A \in$ Alg[SPECV], if A persists under Tp. The functor $Sp = Uf \cdot Tp$ is called the semantics of p.

5.1. Correspondence to axiomatic semantics

It is necessary to justify that the above notion of semantics corresponds to the intuition about while-programs.

Theorem 6. The above semantics is a model of the Hoare-logic for while programs, i.e. if {E} p {E'} is provable for two sets E and E' of Σ+V-equations, then for any A $\in$ Alg[SPECV] the following is true: If A |= E and if p terminates on A, then Sp(A) |= E'.

By Hoare-logic we mean the usual system of proof rules with sets of Σ+V-equations as pre- and post-conditions, together with any sound oracle for implications E -> E' in the rule of consequence. (See [BeT80] for such a logic for a slightly nonstandard language of while-programs.) Also, our definition of termination is like what one would expect.

Theorem 7. a) Assignments terminate on any A $\in$ Alg[SPECV].
b) if b then q else r terminates on A, iff either A |= b=true and q terminates on A, or A |= b=false and r terminates on A.
c) q ; r terminates on A, iff q terminates on A and r terminates on Sq(A).
d) p = while b do q terminates on A, iff either A |= b=false or if A |= b=true and p terminates on Sq(A).

The proof follows immediately from the properties of conditionals in section 2.

We see that nontermination can be caused by three situations. First, a program can loop. Secondly, the specification SPECT of the underlying data types can be incomplete in the sense that there exist A $\in$ Alg[SPECV] and terms b $\in$ $(T_\Sigma)_{BOOL}$ for which neither A |= b=true nor A |= b=false. Finally, the initial value of one of the program variables x can be undefined in A in the sense that there exists no t $\in$ T_Σ such that A |= x=t. The second situation is independent of the specific program p. It demonstrates formally that one only should consider specifications SPECT that are consistent and sufficiently complete (and thus persistent) in the sense of e.g. [Gut75], [ADJ78b], [Wan79].

5.2. Implementations of the underlying data types

A notion of semantics for programs over abstract data types should be compatible with notions of abstract implementation for abstract data types. In the initial algebra approach to data types [ADJ78a], implementations are represented by certain monomorphisms between algebras. The semantics Sp of a program p is a functor that sends monomorphisms h : A->B to monomorphisms Sp(h) : Sp(A)->Sp(B). Additionally, if p terminates on A then it terminates on B, too. Altogether, the result of executing p on an implementation B of A is an implementation of the result of executing p on A.

5.3. Semantics of the underlying data types

The above notion of semantics for while-programs does not rely upon a specific notion of semantics for the specification SPECT of the underlying data types. The functors Sp are defined on all algebras A C Alg[SPECV]. We have argued that SPECT should be persistent w.r.t. its sub-specification of boolean values. Let us now assume that this is the case. Then consider the category C of all SPECT-algebras D for which D_{BOOL} is the "usual" algebra of boolean values. Any of these D can considered to be the semantics of SPECT. (E.g., Initial and final algebra semantics of SPECT are given by the initial and final algebra, resp., of C.) The question is whether or not the program behaviour depends on a specific choice of D. The answer in no in the following sense. Let A,B $\in$ Alg[SPECV] such that their restrictions to SPECT are, perhaps different, algebras D $\in$ C. Furthermore, assume that for any t,t' $\in$ $(T_{\Sigma+V})_{BOOL}$ it is A |= t=t', iff B |= t=t'. The latter means that the values of the program variables in A and B have identical properties w.r.t the result of any predicate that can be defined over them.

Theorem 8. Let p be a program. Then, p terminates on A, iff it terminates on B. Moreover, let t,t' $\in$ $(T_{\Sigma+V})_{BOOL}$ be two "predicates" as above. Then it is Sp(A) |= t=t', iff Sp(B) |= t=t'.

This theorem says that termination and all predicates over the behaviour of p are independent of a specific choice of a semantics for SPECT. It also says that if we replace the equations E in SPECT by an E' such that the observable properties (i.e. the predicates in the above sense) remain unchanged, then the behaviour of the programs is not affected. A notion of optimizing implementation for parameterized specification (based on observability concepts) has to make use of this fact to allow for the stepwise composition of implementations [Gan81].

REFERENCES

[ADJ77] Goguen,J.A.,Thatcher,J.W.,Wagner,E.G., and Wright,J.B.: Initial algebra semantics and continuous algebras. JACM, 24 (1977), pp. 68-95.

[ADJ78a] Goguen,J.A.,Thatcher,J.W.,and Wagner,E.G.: An initial algebra approach to the specification, correctness, and implementation of abstract types. Current trends in Programming Methodology, IV: Data Structuring (R.T. Yeh, ed.), Prentice Hall, 1978, pp. 80-149.

[ADJ78b] Thatcher,J.W.,Wagner,E.G., and Wright,J.B.: Data type specification: parameterization and the power of specification techniques. Proc. SIGACT 10th Annual Symp. on Theory of Comp., May 1978, pp. 119-132.

[ADJ80] Ehrig,H.,Kreowski,H.-J.,Thatcher,J.W.,Wagner,E.G.,and Wright,J.B.: Parameter passing in algebraic specification languages. IBM Yorktown Heights, Draft, 1980.

[BG80] Burstall,R.M., and Goguen,J.A.: The semantics of CLEAR, a specification language. Version of Feb. 80. Proc. 1979 Copenhagen Winter School in Abstract Software Specifications.

[BeT80] Bergstra,J.A., and Tucker,J.V.: Algebraically specified programming systems and Hoare's logic. Mathematisch Centrum Amsterdam, Rep. IW 143/80, 1980.

[BrW80] Broy,M.,and Wirsing,M.: Algebraic definition of a functional programming language and its semantic models. Techn. Univ. München, Rep. TUM-I8008, 1980.

[CoN78] Courcelle,B., and Nivat,M.: The algebraic semantics of recursive program schemes. 7th MFCS, Zakopane, LNCS 64 (1978), pp. 16-30.

[Ehr79] Ehrich, H.-D.: On the theory of specification, implementation, and parameterization of abstract data types. Report 82, Abt. Informatik, Univ. Dortmund, 1979.

[EKP80] Ehrig,H.,Kreowski,H.-J.,and Padawitz,P.: Algebraic implementations of abstract data types: concept, syntax, semantics, and correctness. LNCS 85, 1980, pp.142-156.

[Gan81] Ganzinger,H.: Parameterized specifications : parameter passing and implementation. Techn. Univ. München, Rep. TUM-I8110, 1981.

[Gut75] Guttag,J.: The specification and application to programming of abstract data types. CSRG Tech. Rep. 59, Univ. of Toronto, 1975.

[Hup80] Hupbach,U.L.: Abstract implementation of abstract data types. 9th MFCS, LNCS 88 (1980), pp. 291-304.

[Rei80] Reichel, H.: Initially restricting algebraic theories. 9th MFCS, LNCS 88, (1980), pp. 504-514.

[Wan79a] Wand,M.: First-order identities as a defining language. Techn. Rep. 29, Comp. Sci. Dept., Indiana Univ., Bloomington, Indiana, 1979.

[Wan79b] Wand,M.: Final algebra semantics and data type extensions. JCSS 19 (1979), pp. 27-44.

RELATING UNIFORM AND NONUNIFORM MODELS OF COMPUTATION

Bernd Mahr, Dirk Siefkes

Technische Universität Berlin, Fachbereich Informatik

Otto-Suhr-Allee 18/20, 1000 Berlin 10, Germany (West)

ABSTRACT

We relate uniform and nonuniform models of computation on a semantical level. As a uniform model we use a universal language based on recursive definitions over arbitrary data structures. Nonuniform models are represented by "term definitions" which describe functions by families of terms. We find the term definition inside a program, called calculation function, and show that exactly the recursive functions have recursive term definitions which can be realized as calculation functions. We give the examples of matrix multiplication and binary search to prove our concepts appropriate.

1. INTRODUCTION

Complexity analysis of computational problems employs many different kinds of computation models. Following /Karp and Lipton 1980/ we call a model uniform, if it works for arbitrary inputs, like Turing machines, register machines, or programs, and nonuniform, if it applies to inputs of a fixed "size" only, like straight line programs, circuits or computation trees. Concerning computational power and complexity the relations between different uniform models are well studied, but uniform and nonuniform models are related only on a rather intuitive ground.

The following examples show that the intuition might need some precision:

(i) Usually one defines the "school method" for matrix multiplication by a schema of terms for arbitrary but fixed matrix dimensions. While it is obvious how to build a program from this definition, the cost of the program might depend on the version choosen. The problem becomes subtler if one uses the recursive algorithm of /Strassen 1969/. (ii) The thesis /Mahr 1979/ shows how to compute optimally the shortest paths in an arbitrary but fixed cycle-free graph. It shows also that any program which realizes this method for all cycle-free graphs, is highly inefficient most certainly. (iii) For any (possibly non computable) function $f:\{0,1\}^* \longrightarrow \{0,1\}$ circuits for $f \upharpoonright \{0,1\}^n$ are bounded in size by 2^n.

All three examples have in common that one defines or analyzes only "segments" of functions (problems) and that one uses devices which are terms, tuples of terms, or objects definable from those. It is this observation which motivates our approach to relating uniform and nonuniform models of computation.

We introduce two concepts for the definition of functions $f:A_V \longrightarrow A_W$ over structures

A (partial heterogeneous algebras). One is called "term definition" and consists in a mapping $g:A_v \longrightarrow (T_{Sig}(X^{(v)}))_w$ which assigns to each b a tuple of terms over the signature of A such that their evaluation with respect to b yields f(b). We can visualize this situation by the following commutative diagram:

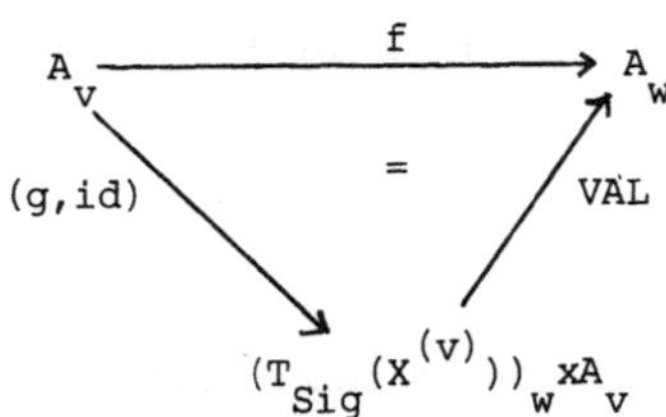

The other concept, called REC, is a uniform computation model; it uses systems of recursive equations over arbitrary data structures as programs to describe recursive functions. Our main result (Theorems 4.5 + 6) relates these two concepts as follows:
1. each REC-program specifies a recursive term definition in a natural way; thus each recursive function has a recursive term definition;
2. each REC-program for a term definition g of f can be changed into a program for f which specifies g as term definition.
Finally we give examples (matrix multiplication, binary search) which show that the theoretical concepts and relations cover the applications in mind.
Term definitions (first introduced in /Mahr 1979/) seem to be a unifying approach to study nonuniform models. REC-programs, in contrast to other models like Turing machines or register machines, seem to be the most natural and adequate formalism for relating uniform and nonuniform models on a semantical level. The language REC is introduced and studied in /Siefkes 1979/1980/. See also /Lynch 1980/ in comparison to our approach. /Karp and Lipton 1980/ study uniform and nonuniform complexity classes. J.R. Büchi has very much influenced the foundations of the work presented here during two extended visits of the second author at Purdue University, which were financed through a travel grant of the Stiftung Volkswagenwerk. This work will be published in the forth-coming paper /Büchi, Mahr, Siefkes 1981/. The present paper does not apply the treated concepts to cost analysis; for information see /Siefkes 1980/, Ch. 4 and 5.
To save parentheses we often write fx instead of f(x).

2. DATA STRUCTURES AND TERM DEFINITIONS

2.1 A <u>signature</u> is a pair Sig=(S,F) consisting of a set S of <u>sorts</u> and a family F of sets $F_{v,s}$ with $v\in S^*$ and $s\in S$. An element $f\in F_{v,s}$, also written $f:v\longrightarrow s$, is called an <u>operation symbol</u> with <u>I-type</u> v and <u>O-type</u> s. We assume that <u>bool</u>$\in S$ and true, false $\in F_{e,bool}$, where e denotes the empty word in S^*.

2.2 A <u>(data) structure</u> A <u>of signature</u> Sig=(S,F), for short <u>Sig-structure</u>, consists of
(1) for each $s\in S$ a set A_s of elements of sort s;
(2) for each $f\in F_{v,s}$ a partial mapping $f_A:A_v \longrightarrow A_s$ where $A_v:=A_{s1}x\ldots xA_{sr}$ for

$v=s_1 \dots s_r$, and $A_e := (\ )$.

(3) $A_{\underline{bool}} \cong \{true, false\}$

2.3 From a given signature Sig=(S,F) we derive the <u>term structure T_{Sig} of signature</u> Sig in the usual way: $(T_{Sig})_s$ for $s \in S$ contains all terms of sort s, and for $f: v \longrightarrow s$ there is a total function $f_T: (T_{Sig})_v \longrightarrow (T_{Sig})_s$ defined by $f_T(b) := f(b)$ for all term tuples $b \in (T_{Sig})_v$.

2.4 Let Sig=(S,F) be a signature and $Z=(Z_s)_{s \in S}$ be a family of sets of <u>data variables.</u> The <u>term-structure</u> $T_{Sig}(Z)$ <u>of signature</u> Sig <u>with variables</u> Z is defined to be the restriction of $T_{Sig'}$ to the signature Sig, where $T_{Sig'}$ is the term structure of signature Sig'=(S,F') with $F' := (F'_{v,s})_{v \in S^*, s \in S}$ so that $F'_{v,s} = F_{v,s}$ if $v \neq e$ and $F'_{e,s} := F_{e,s} \dot{\cup} Z_s$. Thus $T_{Sig}(Z)$ is a Sig-structure.

2.5 We assume that data variables are linearly ordered, and so have for any given set $X \subseteq \bigcup_{s \in S} Z_s$ of data variables a natural ordering $\varphi: X \longrightarrow \mathbb{N}_o$. With each set of data variables X we associate a <u>type</u> $w \in S^*$, also written w=type(X), such that card(X)=length(w) and for $x \in X \cap Z_s$ w has an s at position $\varphi(x)$.
For any given set $X \subseteq \bigcup_{s \in S} Z_s$ of data variables and structure A of signature Sig=(S,F) we call a mapping $d: X \longrightarrow A$ a <u>data assignment</u>, or short <u>data</u>, if for $x \in X \cap Z_s$ $d(x) \in A_s$. For $a=(a_1,\dots,a_r) \in A_v$ d_a denotes the <u>induced data assignment</u> given by $d_a(x) = a_{\varphi(x)}$ for $x \in X$.

2.6 Let Sig=(S,F) be a signature, let $Z=(Z_s)_{s \in S}$ be data variables, let A be Sig-structure. Any data assignment $d: X \longrightarrow A$ induces a <u>partial term evaluation</u>

$$VAL(-,d): T_{Sig}(X) \longrightarrow A$$

defined by

(1) $VAL(x,d) := d(x)$ for variables x

(2) $VAL(f(t_1,\dots,t_r),d) := f_A(VAL(t_1,d),\dots,VAL(t_r,d))$ if for $i=1,\dots,r$ $VAL(t_i,d)$ is defined, and f_A is defined on $(VAL(t_1,d),\dots,VAL(t_r,d))$.

2.7 For each term $t \in (T_{Sig}(X))_s$ we denote by VAR(t) the <u>set of variables in t.</u> For a Sig-structure A each tuple of terms $t=(t_1,\dots,t_r) \in (T_{Sig}(X))_w$ defines a <u>partial</u> function $VAL(t): A_v \longrightarrow A_w$ by v=type(X) and $VAL(t)(a) := (VAL(t_1,d_a),\dots,VAL(t_r,d_a))$. VAL(t) is called a <u>derived operation</u> of A. A more general method to define functions $f: A_v \longrightarrow A_w$ by terms is to specify a partial function $g: A_v \longrightarrow (T_{Sig}(X^{(v)}))_w$ such that

(1) g defined iff f defined

(2) $X^{(v)}$ is a set of data variables with $type(X^{(v)}) = v$

(3) $VAL(g(a))(a) = f(a)$ for $a \in A_v$.

Such g we call a <u>term definition of f.</u>

Each derived function has a term definition. Moreover if A is generated by its operations, then each function $f: A_v \longrightarrow A_w$ has a term definition, which simply assigns to $a \in A_v$ a tuple of generating terms for f(a). In Section 4 we show that each recursive function has a recursive term definition.

2.8 OBSERVATION: Let $f:A_v \longrightarrow A_w$ be a function with term definition g, then g defines a partition of A_v into "segments" $A_v^{(t)} := g^{-1}(t)$ and a "segmentation of f" into derived operations

$$(f^{(t)}:A_v^{(t)} \longrightarrow A_w)_{t \in range(g)}$$

such that $f^{(t)}(a)=f(a)$ for all $a \in A^{(t)}$ and all t. The set $\{g(a)/a \in A_v\}$ specifies a nonuniform model for the computation of the segments $f^{(t)}$, $t \in range(g)$.

3. REC-PROGRAMS

As a uniform computation model we now introduce the formalism REC. In REC we define computable functions by recursive definitions.

3.1 Let Sig be a signature and Z be data variables. Let H be a finite family of finite sets $H_{v,w}$ with $v,w \in S^*$ (function variables of I/O-type v/w). Using the two operators pairing (,) and test (if-then-else) we define inductively the set $RT := RT_{Sig}(Z,H)$ and simultaneously the function VAR on RT. $RT_{v,w}$ are the REC-terms over Sig(Z,H) of I/O-type v/w; VARt is the set of data variables of t. RT is the smallest family $(RT_{v,w})_{v,w \in S^*}$ which satisfies:

(0) the empty term $t_e \in RT_{e,e}$ (introduced for convenience) ,$VARt_e = \emptyset$;

(1) if $x \in Z_s$, then $x \in RT_{s,s}$, $VARx := \{x\}$;

(2) if $p_i \in RT_{vi,wi}$, then $(p_1,p_2) \in RT_{v,w}$ where $v = type(VAR(p_1,p_2))$, $w = w_1w_2$, $VAR(p_1,p_2) := VARp_1 \cup VARp_2$;

(3) if $r \in RT_{u,\underline{bool}}$, $p \in RT_{v1,w}$, $q \in RT_{v2,w}$, then (if r then p else q) $\in RT_{v,w}$ where v=type (VARr∪VARp∪VARq),VAR(if r then p else q)=VARr∪VARp∪VARq;

(4) if $p \in RT_{u,v}$, $f \in F_{v,w} \cup H_{v,w}$, then $fp \in RT_{u,w}$ and VAR(fp)=VAR(p).

We identify REC-terms without if-then-else and function variables with tuples from $T_{Sig}(Z)$.

3.2 A REC-program over Sig(Z,H) is a family $P=(P_{v,w})$, $P_{v,w}: H_{v,w} \longrightarrow RT(P) := RT_{Sig}(Z,H)_{v,w}$. We visualize a program as a family $(hx := P(h))_{h \in H}$ of recursive definitions. A program P together with data d from a structure A induces an evaluation function $VAL_{P,A}(-,d): RT(P) \longrightarrow A$ which on $T_{Sig}(Z)$ equals VAL(-,d) from 2.6. We define $VAL_{P,A}(-,d)$ inductively by a production system in the sense of Thue-Post; see /Post 1936/. The production system is parameterized by P,A and d; we omit the letters P and A:

(0) $VAL(t_e,d) \longrightarrow (\ )$;

(1) $VAL(x,d) \longrightarrow dx$ for variables x

(2) $VAL((p,q),d) \longrightarrow (VAL(p,d),VAL(q,d))$;

(3a) VAL((if r then p else q),d) ⟶ VAL((if VAL(r,d) then p else q),d);

(3b) VAL((if true then p else q),d) ⟶ VAL(p,d);

(3c) VAL((if false then p else q),d) ⟶ VAL(q,d);

(4) $VAL(fp,d) \longrightarrow f_A(VAL(p,d))$ if $f \in F$;

(5) $VAL(hp,d) \longrightarrow VAL(P(h),d')$ if $h \in H$, where $d' := d(VAL(p,d)/VAR(P(h)))$ results from d by assigning VAL(p,d) to VAR(P(h)).

3.3 The system has the following strong Church-Rosser property: If $t \longrightarrow p$ and $t \longrightarrow q$, then there is an r s.t. $p \longrightarrow r$ and $q \longrightarrow r$. Therefore it defines a partial function VAL as wanted. In /Siefkes 1980/ VAL is defined by recursion and the Church-Rosser property is proved to show that VAL does not depend on an "evaluation strategy" (see 6.1-4 there). For any P and A a REC-term $t \in RT_{v,w}$ <u>defines</u> the function $VAL(t): A_v \longrightarrow A_w$ as in 2.7. Normally some $g \in H$ (sometimes a set $\subseteq H$) is specified as <u>name(s) of</u> P; we then say that P <u>computes</u> or <u>defines</u> g, and has the <u>I/O-type</u> of g, and we write $VAL_{P,A}$ for $VAL_{P,A}(gx)$.

3.4 <u>REMARK</u>: Let A be a structure whose elements are (coded into) words. A Turing machine M has the <u>oracle</u> A if for each operation f_A it has a state "compute f" which makes M change the content p of a special "oracle tape" into $f_A(p)$. (See e.g. /Sasso 1975/). Then exactly the (partial) functions over A which are Turing-computable with oracle A are REC-computable over A. The proof extends easily from /Siefkes 1980, Thms. 3.7+9/.

4. RECURSIVE FUNCTIONS AND TERM DEFINITIONS

4.1 We show that each recursive function f on an algebra A has a recursive term definition by deriving from any program P for f a term definition $CT_{P,A}$ of f. The <u>Calculation Term</u> $CT_{P,A}(t,d)$ combines the operations evaluated during the computation of $VAL_{P,A}(t,d)$, and thus describes a "calculation" (Berechnung) in the sense of /Strassen 1972/73/. As the main results of this paper we show that exactly the recursive term definitions can be represented through calculation terms (Theorem 4.5+6).

4.2 Let A be structure of signature Sig=(S,F), let P be program over Sig(Z,H). As with VAL in 3.3 we define the function $CT:=CT_{P,A}(-,d):RT(P) \longrightarrow T_{Sig}(Z)$ (<u>Calculation</u> <u>(Term)</u> <u>function</u>) through a production system which extends the one for VAL:

(0) $CT(t_e,d) \longrightarrow t_e$;

(1) $CT(x,d) \longrightarrow x$ for variables x

(2) $CT((p,q),d) \longrightarrow (CT(p,d),CT(q,d))$;

(3a) CT((<u>if</u> r <u>then</u> p <u>else</u> q),d) ⟶ CT((<u>if</u> VAL(r,d) <u>then</u> p <u>else</u> q),d);

(3b) CT((<u>if</u> true <u>then</u> p <u>else</u> q),d) ⟶ CT(p,d);

(3c) CT((<u>if</u> false <u>then</u> p <u>else</u> q),d) ⟶ CT(q,d);

(4) $CT(fp,d) \longrightarrow f(CT(p,d))$ if $f \in F$;

(5) $CT(hp,d) \longrightarrow CT(P(h),d')[CT(p,d)]$ if $h \in H$, where $d':=d(VAL(p,d)/VAR(P(h)))$.

In rule (5) t[r] is the <u>substitution of</u> the term r <u>into</u> (the variables of) the term t, which is well-defined if I-type(t)=O-type(r).

4.3 <u>FACT</u> (/Siefkes 1980/ Thm. 5.4): For each program P and algebra A the calculation function $CT_{P,A}$ of P is a term definition for the function which P computes on A.

4.4 Our aim is to turn the definitions of VAL and CT into REC-programs. Let Sig be a signature, P a program over Sig(Z,H). We extend Sig to Sig(P) by adding sorts <u>term</u> and <u>data</u> together with the predicate and operation symbols on <u>term</u> necessary to describe compose, and decompose terms, and with operation symbols dat_s with $s\in S$. We extend a Sig-algebra A to the computation algebra AP:=A$\dot\cup$RT(P)$\dot\cup$Data(A) of signature Sig(P) with $dat_{AP}(d,z):=d(z)$. Note that the term operations on RT(P) are partial functions.

4.5 THEOREM: Let P be a program over Sig(Z,H) of I/O-type v/w. Then there is a program CP over Sig(P) of I/O-type v/term with range in $T_{Sig}(Z)_w$ which computes the calculation function of P, i.e. $VAL_{CP,AP}=CT_{P,A}$.

4.6 THEOREM: Let Q be a program over Sig(P) of I/O-type v/term with range in $T_{Sig}(Z)_w$. Then there is a program VQ over Sig(P) of I/O-type v/w such that Q computes the calculation function of VQ, i.e. $CT_{VQ,AP}=VAL_{Q,AP}$.

4.7 SKETCH OF PROOF: Define substitution by a REC-program over Sig(P); then translate the production systems for VAL and CT into REC-programs. The main steps are contained in the following equations which are proved by induction on the number of evaluation steps for the terms in question:

$$VAL(t[s],d)=VAL(t,d(VAL(s,d)/VARt))$$

$$CT(t[s],d)= CT(t,d(VAL(s,d)/VARt))\,[CT(s,d)]$$

$$VAL_{CP,CA}(Ct,d)= CT_{P,A}(t,d)$$

$$CT_{VP,CA}(Vt,d)=VAL_{Q,CA}(t,d)$$

4.8 COROLLARY: Exactly the recursive functions have recursive term definitions, which can be realized as calculation functions.

5. EXAMPLES

5.1 MATRIX MULTIPLICATION: We use the sorts bool, nat, data, matrix, and the operations:

create: nat nat ⟶ matrix ("initial" nxm-matrix),

rowdim, coldim: matrix ⟶ nat (dimensions of a matrix)

assign: matrix nat nat data ⟶ matrix (read data into a matrix)

entry: matrix nat nat ⟶ data (elements of a matrix)

error:⟶ matrix, zero:⟶ data, error:⟶ data, addition and multiplication on data, the necessary operations on bool and nat.

It is easy to specify the data type matrix over this signature with the help of equations. Define a function mult: matrix matrix ⟶ matrix by the program

```
mult(X,Y):=if coldim X ≠ rowdim Y then error else MULT(X,Y,rowdimX,coldimY)
MULT(X,Y,x,z):=if z=0 then if x=1 then create (rowdimX,coldimY)
    else MULT(X,Y,x-1,coldimY)
    else assign(MULT(X,Y,x,z-1),x,z,res(X,Y,x,coldimX,z))
res(X,Y,x,y,z):=if y=0 then zero else res(X,Y,x,y-1,z)+entry(X,x,y)·entry(Y,y,z)
```

For incorrect data the calculation term of mult is error. For data d with correct dimensions we get

$$CT(mult,d)=assign\{\ldots\{assign\{create(x_1,z_n),x_i,z_k,zero+\sum_{j=1}^{m} X_{i,j}\cdot Y_{i,k}\}\ldots\}_{k=1,\ldots,n}^{i=1,\ldots,l}$$

where $l:=rowdim_A(dX), m:=coldim_A(dX), n:=coldim_A(dY), x_i:=rowdim(X)-l+i$, $y_j:=coldim(X)-m+j, z_k:=coldim(Y)-n+k, X_{i,j}:=entry(X,x_i,y_j), Y_{j,k}:=entry(Y,y_j,z_k)$. Thus the term function of mult yields the term representation of the "school method" for matrix multiplication, in the concise notation of the data structure. If instead one represents matrices by sequences, then a similar program yields as calculation term the sequence

$$(zero+\sum_{j=1}^{m} x_{i,j}\cdot y_{j,k})_{k=1,\ldots,n.}^{i=1,\ldots,l}$$

In both cases the multiplication function is segmented by the dimensions of the matrices. - We urge the reader to write a program for Strassen's matrix multiplication, using an extended signature.

5.2 BINARY SEARCH: The program

search(list,x,y,z):=if y=z then z else if x = list($\overline{y/z}$)

then search(list,x,$\overline{y/z}$,z) else search(list,x,y,$\overline{y/z}$)

defines a function search: list data nat nat ⟶ nat which yields the position of an element x in an ordered list between positions y and z. We specify lists by specializing example 5.1; thus list(y) is short for entry(list,y). The program uses further = on nat, ≥ on data, and $\overline{y/z}$:= (y+z)/2, $\underline{y/z}$:= $\overline{y/z}$-1 on nat. One shows by induction that for a list of length n search calls itself $\lceil \log n \rceil$ times. Therefore for any n and k, $1\leq k\leq n$, there is a term $t_{n,k}$ where

(i) $t_{n,k}$ is built up with $\perp$ and $\top$ from variables y and z,

(ii) $t_{n,k}$ contains exactly $\lceil \log n \rceil$ operation symbols,

(iii) $VAL(t_{n,k},d)=k$ if $/dy-dz/=n-1$.

$t_{n,k}$ is unique up to exchanging y and z. One then shows that for data d where $dx=d(list)(k)$, $/dy-dz/=n-1$

$$CT(search(list,x,y,z),d)=t_{n,k}.$$

Thus the calculation term describes the search path, which depends on n and k. - If on the other hand we replace the second if-then-else in the program by an operation test: bool nat nat ⟶ nat in the signature, then the calculation term depends only on n. It describes the full search tree built up using test, $\perp$, and $\top$.

REFERENCES

Büchi, J.R., Mahr, B., Siefkes, D., 1981: Forthcoming paper to appear

Karp, R.M., Lipton, R.J., 1980: Some Connections between Nonuniform and Uniform Complexity Classes. Proc. 12th ACM Symp. Theory of Computing, 302-309

Lynch, N., 1978: Straightline Program Length as a Parameter for Complexity Measures. Proc. 10th ACM Symp. Theory of Computing, 150-161

Mahr, B., 1979: Algorithmische Komplexität des allgemeinen Wegeproblems in Graphen. Bericht Nr. 79-14, Informatik, Technische Univ. Berlin, 133 pp.

Post, E.L., 1936: Finite Combinatory Processes. J.Symb.Logic 1, 103-105

REFERENCES (cont'd)

Sasso, L.P., 1975: A survey of partial degrees. J.Symb. Logic 40, 130-140

Strassen, V., 1969: Gaussian elimination is not optimal. Numer. Math. 13, 354-356.

Strassen, V., 1972/73: Berechnung und Programm 1/2. Acta Informatica 1/2.

Siefkes, D., 1979: Recursive Equations as a Programming System. In: "Begriffs-schrift" Jenaer Fregekonferenz, Jena, 433-448

Siefkes, D., 1980: Programming with Recursion. Tech. Report CSD-TR 331, Purdue University, 72 pp.

Semantikdefinition im Rahmen eines Programmiersystemgenerators

Rolf Bahlke* , Manfred Daniel* , Thomas Letschert

Institut für Praktische Informatik
Technische Hochschule Darmstadt
Steubenplatz 12
D-6100 Darmstadt

Zusammenfassung

In diesem Bericht wird eine formale Semantikbeschreibungssprache sowie eine Methode zur Ausführung von Programmfragmenten vorgestellt. Die Überlegungen hierzu resultieren aus der Arbeit am PSG-Projekt ("Programmiersystemgenerator") und stellen Teilaspekte einer formalen Sprachdefinition und der aus ihr erzeugten Programmierumgebung dar. Die Semantikbeschreibung ist denotational unter Berücksichtigung von Strukturierungshilfsmitteln. Fragmente werden durch einen Lambda-Interpretierer ausgeführt, der zur Interpretation unvollständiger Terme erweitert wurde.

1. Einleitung

In letzter Zeit ist verstärkt ein Trend zu beobachten, das traditionelle Compiler-Konzept der Sprachübersetzung durch das Konzept einer sprachbezogenen, integrierten Programmierumgebung (siehe etwa [4], [5], [14]) abzulösen. Die bisher bekannten Systeme sind jedoch nur für eine Sprache (z.B. Pascal, PL/CS) ausgelegt. An der TH Darmstadt werden im Rahmen des PSG-Projekts ([1], [2]) die Möglichkeiten und Schwierigkeiten untersucht, die sich durch die Weiterentwicklung des Compiler-Compiler-Konzepts zu einem Generator für Programmierumgebungen ergeben. Ziel des Projekts ist es, aus einer formalen Sprachdefinition ein interaktives Programmiersystem zu erzeugen. Die generierten Programmiersysteme bestehen aus einem sprachbezogenen, struktur-orientierten Ediersystem zur Erstellung syntaktisch korrekter Programmfragmente und einem Interpretiersystem zur Ausführung von Programmfragmenten.

Gegenstand dieser Arbeit ist das Interpretiersystem und dessen Generierung. In Teil 2 werden die für das Interpretiersystem relevanten Konzepte von PSG vorgestellt. Teil 3 beschäftigt sich mit der Semantikbeschreibung, die Ausgangspunkt des Generierungsprozesses ist und ihren Niederschlag in der Sprachdefinitionssprache SDS findet. Die Semantikdefinition enthält (noch) keine Komponenten, die sich aus den besonderen Anforderungen einer Programmierumgebung ergeben. Spezifisch für Programmierumgebungen ist jedoch die Art, in der Programmfragmente ausgeführt werden. In Teil 4 wird ein interaktiver Interpretierer vorgestellt, der diese Aufgaben erfüllt.

*Diese Arbeit entstand im Rahmen des Projekts "Programmiersystemgenerator", das von der Deutschen Forschungsgemeinschaft unter Az. He 1170/1 gefördert wird.

2. System-Übersicht

Abstrakte Syntaxbäume dienen als gemeinsame interne Repräsentation der Programme im gesamten Programmiersystem. Ein Programmfragment ist ein Abstrakter Syntaxbaum, dessen Struktur durch eine Abstrakte Syntax der Programmiersprache beschrieben ist. Ein Fragment ist unvollständig, wenn ein Knoten des Abstrakten Baums durch eine Verfeinerungsstelle ersetzt ist. Einem Fragment kann ein Name zugeordnet werden, der das Abspeichern und Wiederauffinden des Fragments in einer Fragmentbibliothek ermöglicht. Ebenso kann einer Verfeinerungsstelle ein Name zugeordnet werden. Verfeinerungsstellen können durch Fragmente mit gleichem syntaktischen Typ ersetzt werden, benannte Verfeinerungsstellen nur durch benannte Fragmente mit identischem Namen.

Aufgabe des Ediersystems ist die Erstellung eines Fragments durch schrittweises Ersetzen von Verfeinerungsstellen durch Fragmente. Die Fragmentkonstruktion ist abgeschlossen, wenn das Fragment entweder keine oder nur noch benannte Verfeinerungsstellen besitzt. Das Ediersystem garantiert die syntaktische Korrektheit der erstellten Programmfragmente, eine Überprüfung der Kontextbedingungen ist in Vorbereitung.

Die Ausführung eines Fragments erfolgt in drei Schritten: In einer Bindephase werden alle vorhandenen Verfeinerungsstellen durch Fragmente aus der Fragmentbibliothek ersetzt. Es folgt die Übersetzung und Interpretation. Der Term, in den der Abstrakte Baum übersetzt wird, ist ein Ausdruck einer λ-Kalkül ähnlichen Sprache. Die Übersetzung beruht auf einer Semantikdefinition der jeweiligen Sprache, die damit einen wesentlichen Teil der gesamten Sprachbeschreibung ausmacht. Der von uns gewählte Stil ist denotational, jedem syntaktischen Konstrukt wird eine Bedeutung in einem semantischen Bereich zugeordnet. Diese beschreiben wir ausgehend von vorgegebenen Grunddatentypen konstruktiv durch reflexive Domaingleichungen als Retrakte eines universellen Bereichs [13]. In der Sprachdefinition wird zu jeder Klasse der Abstrakten Syntax ein semantischer Bereich angegeben und zu jedem Knoten der Abstrakten Syntax seine Bedeutung als Funktion seiner Unterkomponenten definiert. In algebraischer Terminologie [6] heißt das, daß wir die Definition der Abstrakten Syntax als Signatur einer Syntax-Algebra ansehen und in der Semantikdefinition durch die Angabe von semantischen Funktionen und semantischen Bereichen eine Semantik-Algebra mit gleicher Signatur definieren. Die Abbildung Syntax nach Semantik ist der eindeutig existierende Homomorphismus von der Syntax- in die Semantik-Algebra. Die Notation bringt diese Beziehung deutlich zum Ausdruck und macht die explizite Angabe einer Abbildung Syntax nach Semantik überflüssig.

Im Vergleich mit dem SIS-System von P. Mosses [11] ist die Übereinstimmung in den Grundideen festzustellen. Der Stil unserer Sprachdefinition ist jedoch von der algebraischen Sichtweise geprägt: Pro Klasse ein semantischer Bereich, pro Knoten eine semantische Funktion. In SIS kommt den Hilfsfunktionen und semantischen Funktionen, die dort auf die Klassen der Abstrakten Syntax bezogen sind, notationell der gleiche Rang zu, was die Übersichtlichkeit der Definition mindert. Wir fassen Hilfsfunktionen in Abstrakten Datentypen zusammen und kommen so zu einer stärkeren Modularisierung der Semantikdefinition. Die erzeugten Systeme sind als Programmierumgebungen stärker auf Interaktion mit dem Benutzer hin konzipiert, was vor allem in der Interpretation durch Benutzerrückfragen (s. Teil 4) zum Ausdruck kommt.

3. Semantikdefinitionssprache SDS

Nachdem im letzten Kapitel die Grundideen unserer Semantikdefinitionsmethode dargelegt worden sind, sollen nun anhand der ausschnittsweise wiedergegebenen Definition der Sprache Asple [10] die Elemente der Semantikdefinitionssprache SDS in ihrer notationellen Ausprägung vorgestellt werden. Die Abstrakte Syntax bestimmt die Menge der semantischen Funktionen und deren Funktionalität nach den o.a. Prinzipien.

```
abstract syntax
    terminal classes   id, intg;     // Menge von nullstelligen Knoten
    program   :: decllist statement; // Knotenregel:  Knotenname und Unterkomponenten
    ...
    statement =  assign | conditional | loop   ... ;  // Klassenregel
    assign    :: id expr;
    ...
abstract syntax end
```

Bei dem Konstruktionsprozeß hin zu den semantischen Bereichen werden auch Domains benannt, die nicht als semantische Bereiche fungieren: die sogenannten help domains. Die Basis der Domainkonstruktion bilden die elementaren Grunddatentypen Integer, Boolean und Identifier.

```
help domains
   State   :: s-in: Vallist,      // Baum mit  Knotenname :: Selektorname : Komponente
              s-out: Vallist,
              s-env: Environment,
              s-heap: Heap;
   Val     =  Integer | Boolean;       // disjunkte Vereinigung
   Store   =  Loc → Val;               // Abbildung
   Loc     =  Integer;                 // Domainumbenennung
   Vallist =  Val*;                    // Liste
help domains end
```

Bei der Definition der semantischen Funktionen werden Hilfsfunktionen verwendet, die mit der Manipulation zentraler semantischer Objekte (hier Environment und Heap) befaßt sind. Wir fassen sie geeignet zu Abstrakten Datentypen zusammen, die wir im Stile von [9] definieren: Es gilt das Prinzip, daß auf den Objekten eines solchen Typs nur die ihm zugeordneten Abstrakten Operationen angewendet werden dürfen.

```
abstract type  Heap;                   // Name des Abstrakten Typs
   intern representation
     Heap :: s-counter: Integer,       // Heap wird intern als Baum mit zwei Unterkom-
             s-store:   Store;         // ponenten repräsentiert
```

```
sorts      Integer, Val, Loc;           // Nebensorten des Typs
operations                              // "Abstrakte" Operationen des Typs
   'assign' : Heap × Loc × Val → Heap;
              λheap, loc, val. let c = s-counter (heap),
                                   s = s-store   (heap)
                               in  mk-Heap (c, s + [loc → val]);
   'newloc' : Heap → Loc × Heap;
              ...
   ...
abstract type end
```

Für jede Klasse der Abstrakten Syntax wird der semantische Bereich in der class-Kopfzeile definiert. Es folgen für jeden Knoten dieser Klasse die Angabe des Definitionsbereichs seiner semantischen Funktion (in der node-Kopfzeile) und die Beschreibung der Funktion als SDS-Term. Diese sind als Kontrollstrukturen und Operationsanwendungen aufgebaut. Mögliche Kontrollstrukturen sind Abstraktion, Applikation, if-then-else, McCarthy-Conditional, let-Klausel und Definition rekursiver Funktionen (vergleiche Meta IV-Notation [3]).

```
class  STATEMENT = State → State;  // Semantischer Bereich von statement
node   assign:  ID × EXPR;         // Definitionsbereich der semantischen Funktion
          λstate. let env = s-env (state),
                      heap = s-heap (state),
                      l-type = 'gettype' (env, ID),
                      l-reflevel = 'getrevlevel' (env, ID),
                      res = EXPR (env, heap),  // EXPR: Bedeutung der Unterkomponente
                                               //   expr von assign
                      newheap = (res ε Boolean → if (l-type = bool) ∧ (l-reflevel = 0)
                                                 then 'assign' (heap,
                                                          'getloc' (env, ID), res)
                                                 else context-error2,
                                 res ε Integer → ... ,
                                 is-Ref (res)  → ... )
                  in mk-State (s-in (state), s-out (state), env, newheap)
node   conditional:  EXPR × STATEMENT × STATEMENT
....
class end
```

Ein Element aus der syntaktischen Klasse statement bezeichnet ein Objekt aus dem semantischen Bereich STATEMENT, der alle stetigen Funktionen von State nach State umfasst. Das assign-Statement besteht aus einem Bezeichner (Element der syntaktischen Klasse id, deren Bedeutungen Elemente des Bereichs ID sind) und einem Ausdruck (expr). Die Bedeutung eines assign-Statements ist wegen der Homomorphie-Eigenschaft abhängig von der Bedeutung der Unterkomponenten, auf die in der Funktion mit ID und EXPR Bezug genommen wird.

4. Interpretation von Fragmenten

Wie bereits erwähnt werden Programmfragmente durch Übersetzung in eine, alle Programmierumgebungen gleiche, interpretierbare Sprache und anschließende Reduktion ausgeführt. Die Zielsprache des Übersetzungsprozesses, die sogenannten Meta-Expressions, ist eine Teilsprache der Semantikdefinitionssprache. Der Interpretierer für die Metaexpressions soll in diesem Kapitel kurz beschrieben werden, wobei die Betonung auf den Eigenschaften liegt, die eine Ausführung von Programmfragmenten erlauben. Eine gewisse Vertrautheit mit dem λ-Kalkül, seiner operationalen Semantik sowie der Continuation-Technik wird vorausgesetzt (siehe etwa [12]).

Handelt es sich bei dem auszuführenden Fragment nicht um ein vollständiges Programm sondern nur um ein Programmfragment, so ist es nicht im üblichen Sinne ausführbar. Seine Bedeutung ist ein Objekt höherer Ordnung, d.h. eine Funktion ohne Argumente: Die Übersetzung läßt sich nicht interpretieren. Für den Benutzer der Programmierumgebung, der nicht unbedingt etwas von der internen Darstellung seiner Fragmente wissen muß, stellt sich der Mangel an Argumenten als Fehlen von Deklarationen, Initialisierungen u.ä. dar: Es fehlen Informationen aus dem nicht vorhandenen Kontext des Fragments. In unserem System können auch solche Programmfragmente ausgeführt werden, indem der Interpretierer während der Interpretation fehlende Information (Verbesserung) nachfordert. Dabei soll folgende "Church-Rosser-Eigenschaft" erfüllt sein: Die Fragmentausführung mit nachgefragter Information und die Ausführung in einem Kontext, der die entsprechende Information enthält, liefern die gleichen Ergebnisse.

Um die Diskussion zu vereinfachen, führen wir eine reduzierte Version der Meta-Expressions als Terme ein und behandeln nur die Verbesserung elementarer Konstanten. Eine ausführliche und vollständige Beschreibung des Algorithmus' ist in [8] zu finden.

Definition (Terme)

Sei V eine abzählbar unendliche Menge von Variablen, Σ eine Menge von Konstanten. Die Menge T der Terme ist induktiv definiert:

(i)	$V \subseteq T,\ \Sigma \subseteq T$	(Variable, Konstante)
(ii)	$x \in V,\ M \in T \Rightarrow \lambda x.M \in T$	(Abstraktion)
(iii)	$M,N \in T \Rightarrow (MN) \in T$	(Applikation)

$\Omega \in \Sigma$ ist eine besondere Konstante, die einen noch nicht spezifizierten Teilterm symbolisiert. Den Termen kann man eine operationale Semantik zuordnen, die wiederum einen Interpretierer definiert. Eine besondere Behandlung erfährt die Ω-Konstante: Sie wird während der Interpretation durch einen anderen (besseren) Term ersetzt (der auch wieder Ω enthalten kann): die "Verbesserung des Benutzers".

Um die Verhältnisse vor und nach einer Verbesserung beschreiben zu können, wird der Interpretierer in Continuationform angegeben. Ein "sharing-Mechanismus" bewirkt, daß Veränderungen eines Teilterms sich auf andere Teilterme auswirken, falls diese vom veränderten Term abhingen. Die Grundidee des Verfahrens ist das der lazy-evaluation [7]: Ein Term wird dann, und nur dann, ausgewertet, wenn er benötigt wird, und diese Auswertung bleibt in Zukunft bestehen. Ω kann als unausgewerteter Term angesehen werden. Die Unterscheidung ist hier jedoch nicht zwischen ausgewertet und unausgewertet, sondern zwischen 'Graden der Auswertung'. Jede Benutzerrückfrage liefert mehr Informationen. Wir behandeln jedoch nur den Fall bei dem Ω einen Term von Grundtyp (mit diskreter Ordnung) vertritt und infolge dessen nur eine einzige Verbesserung (Rückfrage) möglich ist. Wir beschreiben beispielhaft die einfache Version des rückfragenden Interpretierers: evalask.

Im folgenden sei x eine Variable über V; M,N über T und c über Σ.

$cl \in Closure = T \times Loc$

$l \in Loc$ unspezifizierte Menge (von Locations)

$r \in Env = (Loc \times V \times (\underline{n} \mid \underline{r}) \times Closure \times Loc)^*$

$k \in Cont = Closure \times Env \rightarrow T$

Ein Environment besteht aus einer Liste von Environmenteinträgen, von denen jeder eine Adresse sowie die Adresse eines Folgeeintrags hat, sowie den Namen einer Variablen mit ihrer Bindung an eine Closure. Die Markierungen $\underline{r}$ bzw. $\underline{n}$ weisen auf ausgewertete und unausgewertete Closures hin. Der Interpretationsalgorithmus kann damit auf einem einzigen 'globalen' Environment operieren. Die Location in einer Closure stehtfür das Environment, dessen Einträge bei dieser Location beginnen.

<u>Definition</u> (evalask)

$evalask_N\ (<c,l>,r,k) = k(<c,l>,r)$

$evalask_N\ (<\lambda x.M,l>,r,k) = k(<\lambda x.M,l>,r)$

$evalask_N\ (<x,l>,r,k) = get_N\ (getenv(x,l),r,k)$

$evalask_N\ (<MN,l>,r,k) = evalask_N(<M,l>,r,\lambda cl,r.apply_N(cl,<N,l>,r,k))$

$get_N\ (<l_1,x,\underline{r},<N,l>,l_2>,r,k) = k(<N,l>,r)$

$get_N\ (<l_1,x,\underline{n},<N,l>,l_2>,r,k) =$
$\quad evalask_N\ (<N,l>\ ,r,\lambda cl,r.k(cl,ext(r,<l_1,x,\underline{r},cl,l_2>)))$

$get_N\ (<l_1,x,\underline{n},<\Omega,l>,l_2>,r,k) =$
$\quad evalask_N\ (<N,\underline{nil}>,r,\lambda cl,r.k(cl,ext(r,<l_1,x,\underline{r},cl,l_2>)))$

$apply_N\ (<c,l_1>,<N,l_2>,r,k) =$
$\quad evalask_N\ (<N,l_2>,r,\lambda cl,r.k(\ ca(<c,l_1>,cl),r))$

$apply_N\ (<\lambda x.M,l_1>,<N,l_2>,r,k) =$
$\quad evalask_N\ (<M,l_3>,ext\ (r,<l_3,x,\underline{n},<N,l_2>,l_1>),k)$

$ca\ (<c_a,l_1>,<c_b,l_2>) = <c_{a(b)},\underline{nil}>$

<u>ext</u> und <u>getenv</u> sind Funktionen, die einen neuen Eintrag im Environment vornehmen bzw. nach der Bindung einer Variablen (ab einer bestimmten Position) suchen.

<u>Satz</u> Sei M ein Term mit einer freien Variablen x und N ein geschlossener Term; dann gilt:

$$evalask_N\ (\lambda x.M(\Omega)) = eval\ (\lambda x.M(N))$$

wobei eval ein Standard-Interpretationsmechanismus ist.

Man sieht, daß in diesem Formalismus der Benutzer als Teil des Interpretierers erscheint. Größere Probleme treten auf, wenn mehr als nur eine Rückfrage nach einer Ω-Konstante möglich ist, da zwischen zwei Rückfragen u.U. das verbesserte, aber noch unvollständige Objekt zur Erzeugung anderer Objekte (mittels der Funktion ca) benutzt wurde. In [8] wird beschrieben, wie man in diesem Fall ohne aufwendiges Backtracking auskommen kann.

Abschließende Bemerkungen

Die Implementierung einer vorläufigen Version des Edier- und Interpretationssystems ist abgeschlossen und wird derzeit erprobt. Schwerpunkte der gegenwärtigen Arbeit sind auf dem Gebiet der Semantikdefinition die Implementierung der Semantikdefinitionssprache SDS und ihre Weiterentwicklung, insbesondere die Spezifikation von Dialogen bei Fehlsituationen. Nicht erwähnt wurden in dieser Arbeit Fragen der statischen Semantik, die auf Grund des Fragmentkonzepts eine Weiterentwicklung Attributierter Grammatiken notwendig machten.

Wir danken den Herren B. Austermühl und W. Henhapl sowie den Referenten für ihre wertvollen und kritischen Anmerkungen.

Literatur

[1] Austermühl,B., Bahlke,R., Daniel,M., Henhapl,W., Letschert,T.
Programmiersystemgenerator.
Projektbericht PU1R6/81, TH Darmstadt, 1981

[2] Bahlke,R., Henhapl,W.
Development of a Programming Environment Generator.
Bericht PU1R9/81, TH Darmstadt, 1981

[3] Bjørner,D., Jones,C.B. (Eds.)
The Vienna Development Method: The Meta-Language.
Lecture Notes in Computer Science 61, Springer 1978

[4] Celentano,A., Della Vigna,P., Ghezzi,C., Mandrioli,D.
Simple: A Program Development System.
Computer Languages 5, 1980, 103-114

[5] Feiler,P.H., Medina-Mora,R.
An Incremental Programming Environment.
Proc. 5th International Conference on Software Engineering, March 1981, 44-53

[6] Goguen,J.A., Thatcher,J.W., Wagner,E.G., Wright,J.B.
Initial Algebra Semantics and Continuous Algebras.
Journal ACM 24, 1, Jan. 1977, 68-95

[7] Henderson,P., Morris,J.H.
A Lazy Evaluator.
Proc. 3rd ACM Symp. on Principles of Progr. Lang., Jan. 1976, 95-103

[8] Letschert,T.
Evalask: Yet another Lambda Interpreter.
Bericht PU1R7/81, TH Darmstadt, 1981

[9] Liskov,B., Snyder,A., Atkins,R., Schaffert,C.
Abstraction Mechanisms in CLU.
Communications ACM 20, 8, Aug. 1977, 564-576

[10] Marcotty,M., Ledgard,H.F., Bochmann,G.V.
A Sampler of Formal Definitions.
ACM Computing Surveys 8, 2, June 1976, 191-276

[11] Mosses,P.
SIS - Semantics Implementation System. Reference Manual and User Guide.
Report DAIMI MD-30, Aarhus University, Aug. 1979

[12] Plotkin,G.D.
Call-by-Name, Call-by-Value and the λ-Calculus.
Theoretical Computer Science 1, 1975, 125-159

[13] Scott,D.S.
Data Types as Lattices.
SIAM Journal of Computing 5, 3, 1976, 522-587

[14] Teitelbaum,T., Reps,T., Horwitz,S.
The Why and Wherefore of the Cornell Program Synthesizer.
Proc. Sigplan-Sigoa Symp. on Text Manip., Sigplan Not. 16, 6, June 1981, 8-16

Die formale Entwicklung der maschinenunabhängigen Zwischensprache CAT

Uwe Schmidt Reinhard Völler

Institut für Informatik und Praktische Mathematik
Christian-Albrechts-Universität Kiel

Zusammenfassung:

Aus denotationellen Beschreibungen der dynamischen Semantik der Programmiersprachen BASIC, COBOL, FORTRAN und PASCAL, die in der Spezifikationssprache META IV vorliegen, wird eine gemeinsame, maschinenunabhängige Zwischensprache für die Übersetzung dieser Sprachen hergeleitet. In dieser Sprache werden die Programme als abstrakte Syntaxbäume dargestellt. Aus den Semantikbeschreibungen ergibt sich auch eine formale Spezifikation für die Übersetzung der Quellsprachen in die Zwischensprache.

1. Überblick über das Gesamtprojekt

In Zusammenarbeit mit der Firma H. Dietz, Computersysteme, Mülheim, wird eine gemeinsame Zwischensprache für die Programmiersprachen BASIC, COBOL, FORTRAN und PASCAL entwickelt.
Ziel dieses Projekts ist ein Übersetzersystem aus vier Compileroberteilen, die die Übersetzung in die Zwischensprache durchführen, und einem Codegenerator, der Code für verschiedene Zielmaschinen erzeugt. Im Gegensatz zum allgemeinen UNCOL-Problem sind die zu beachtenden Quellsprachen und die in Frage kommenden Zielmaschinen (im wesentlichen) bekannt.

In diesem Beitrag soll das Vorgehen bei der formalen Herleitung der Zwischensprache und der Übersetzeroberteile an zwei Beispielsprachen vorgestellt werden, in denen charakteristische Eigenschaften der Quellsprachen enthalten sind.

Als gutes Entwicklungswerkzeug erwies sich die Vienna Development Method (VDM) mit der Spezifikationssprache META IV [1]. Aus den vorliegenden Normen und Sprachdefinitionen der Quellsprachen [2,3,4,5] wird zunächst eine formale, denotationelle Beschreibung der dynamischen Semantik der Quellsprachen erstellt. Aus diesen Beschreibungen lassen sich die formale Spezifikation der gemeinsamen maschinenunabhängigen Zwischensprache CAT (Common Abstract Tree Language) und die zugehörigen Übersetzer systematisch herleiten. Die Verwendung von VDM erleichtert den Nachweis der Vollständigkeit der Zwischensprache und der Korrektheit der Übersetzer [6].

2. Sprachdefinitionen in META IV

Die denotationelle Spezifikation einer Programmiersprache läßt sich in die folgenden vier Komponenten gliedern:

(i) Abstrakte Syntax (Syntaktische Bereiche)

(ii) Statische Semantik

(iii) Semantische Bereiche

(iv) Dynamische Semantik

Die abstrakte Syntax abstrahiert die durch die konkrete Syntax einer Sprache gegebenen Zeichenketten zu mathematisch handhabbaren Objekten wie Bäumen, Tupeln, Mengen und Abbildungen. Hierdurch sind Gemeinsamkeiten oder auch Unterschiede verschiedener Sprachen, die sonst durch die konkrete Darstellung verdeckt werden, leichter zu erkennen.

Die statische Semantik formuliert zusätzliche, kontextabhängige Bedingungen an die syntaktischen Objekte, die erfüllt sein müssen, um eine Bedeutung für diese Objekte angeben zu können.

Die semantischen Bereiche enthalten im wesentlichen ein Speichermodell, das sich aus den Abbildungen

Environment = *Name* --> *Denotation*

Storage = *Location* --> *Value*

zusammensetzt [7].

Die dynamische Semantik besteht aus einer Menge von Funktionen, die syntaktischen Objekten Objekte aus den semantischen Bereichen zuordnen [8].

3. Vorgehen

Die Spezifikation einer gemeinsamen Zwischensprache soll nun aus den formalen Spezifikationen der Quellsprachen hergeleitet werden. Dazu ordnen wir jedem syntaktischen Objekt die Menge der Interpretationsfunktionen (I-Funktionen) zu, die diesem Objekt eine Bedeutung zuweisen. In der Regel enthält diese Menge genau eine Funktion. Wird aber ein Objekt nicht in allen Kontexten gleich interpretiert, so gibt es für dieses Objekt mehrere I-Funktionen. Ein Beispiel hierfür ist das syntaktische Objekt <variable> in PASCAL, das auf der rechten Seite einer Zuweisung für einen Wert, auf der linken Seite für einen Speicherplatz steht.

Eine triviale "Zwischensprache" erhält man durch die Vereinigung der syntaktischen und semantischen Bereiche sowie der I-Funktionen der Quellsprachen. Unser Ziel ist aber eine möglichst kleine Zwischensprache, die genügend syntaktische Objekte enthält, um den vollen Sprachumfang der Quellsprachen implementieren zu können. Gleichzeitig darf die Übersetzung in diese Sprache nicht zu aufwendig sein.

Ausgehend von der Sprache, die durch die Vereinigung der syntaktischen und semantischen Bereiche definiert wird, erfolgt die Herleitung der Zwischensprache in drei Schritten:

1. Vereinheitlichung der semantischen Bereiche
2. Verringerung der Anzahl der I-Funktionen
3. Verringerung der Anzahl der syntaktischen Objekte

Die Vereinheitlichung der semantischen Bereiche ist notwendig, um I-Funktionen verschiedener Sprachelemente vergleichen zu können; sie kann u.a. durch Zusammenlegen gleicher Bereiche oder durch Ersetzen spezieller Bereiche durch allgemeinere geschehen. Die Vereinheitlichung der semantischen Objekte bedingt, daß die I-Funktionen, die diese Objekte manipulieren, umgeschrieben werden müssen.

Im zweiten Schritt lassen sich die I-Funktionen vergleichen. Um ihre Anzahl zu verringern, simuliert man eine I-Funktion durch eine andere. Dazu muß man die syntaktischen Objekte, die von der zu simulierenden Funktion interpretiert werden, transformieren.

Gegeben seien die Funktionen *i-s1(s1,...)* und *i-s1'(s1',...)*. Wenn *i-s1* durch *i-s1'* simuliert werden soll, muß eine Transformationsfunktion gefunden werden, die das syntaktische Objekt *s1* in *s1'* so transformiert, daß gilt:

i-s1(s1,...) = i-s1'(t-s1-s1'(s1,...),...)

Die Entscheidung *i-s1* durch *i-s1'* zu simulieren, hängt von den folgenden Parametern ab:

- Komplexität der Transformationsfunktion *t-s1-s1'*
- Komplexität der I-Funktion *i-s1'*
- Reduktion des Umfangs der Zwischensprache

Diese Kriterien sind nicht immer gleichzeitig voll erfüllbar: es ist möglich, ein Sprachkonstrukt der Zwischensprache einfach zu beschreiben, während sich die Übersetzung in dieses Objekt sehr aufwendig gestalten kann. Wenn alle Objekte der Quellsprache direkt in die Zwischensprache übernommen werden, ist die Übersetzung trivial, der Umfang der Zwischensprache vergrößert sich aber zu sehr.

Es lassen sich verschiedene Klassen von Transformationen unterscheiden. Im einfachsten Fall wird nur die Wurzel des Baums, der das zu transformierende Objekt repräsentiert, umbenannt. Ein weiterer einfacher Fall ist die Verallgemeinerung von syntaktischen Objekten, z.B. die Darstellung von Feldern mit impliziten unteren Grenzen durch Felder mit expliziten Grenzen. Komplexe Operatoren lassen sich in eine Folge einfacherer Operatoren zerlegen, oder durch Prozeduren implementieren, um den Übersetzungsaufwand gering zu halten. Mehrere syntaktische Objekte können auf ein neues Objekt abgebildet werden, das noch in keiner der Quellsprachen enthalten ist, aber ein allgemeineres Konzept als die einzelnen Objekte implementiert.

Zum Schluß reduziert man die Anzahl der syntaktischen Objekte. Ein syntaktisches

Objekt kann vollständig eliminiert werden, wenn alle zugehörigen I-Funktionen durch andere simuliert werden, d.h. wenn das Objekt in allen Kontexten in ein anderes übersetzt wird. Die verbleibenden syntaktischen Objekte bilden zusammen mit den semantischen Bereichen und I-Funktionen die Spezifikation der Zwischensprache. Die Transformationsfunktionen geben die Übersetzung der Quellsprachobjekte in diese Sprache an.

4. Die Herleitung einer gemeinsamen Zwischensprache

Das Vorgehen bei der Entwicklung einer gemeinsamen Zwischensprache soll in diesem Abschnitt an zwei Beispielsprachen L1 und L2 dargestellt werden, die einige charakteristische Elemente der Quellsprachen enthalten.

In beiden Sprachen besteht ein Programm aus einer Deklarations- und einer Anweisungsliste. In L1 sind Deklarationen von einfachen Variablen sowie von beliebig dimensionierbaren Feldern mit beliebigen Grenzen möglich (PASCAL). Einfache Variablen können auch implizit deklariert werden (FORTRAN, BASIC). Es gibt keine Blockschachtelung, daher ist eine statische Speicherverwaltung möglich (BASIC, COBOL, FORTRAN).

L2 erlaubt Blockschachtelungen und die Deklaration von lokalen Variablen. Die Blockstruktur ist eine Vereinfachung der Prozedurschachtelung in PASCAL. Alle Variablen müssen vor ihrer Verwendung deklariert werden. Es gibt nur einfache Variablen und eindimensionale Felder mit fester unterer Grenze 1 (BASIC).

4.1 Die abstrakte Syntax von L1 und L2

```
            L1                              L2
Prog1   ::  Dcl1  Stl1          Prog2  =  Block2
                                Block2 :: Dcl2 Stl2
Dcl1    =   Dc1*                Dcl2   =  Dc2*
Dc1     ::  Id Bl1              Dc2    :: Id Ix2
Bl1     =   (INTG INTG)*        Ix2    =  [N1]
Stl1    =   Stm1*               Stl2   =  Stm2*
Stm1    =   ...                 Stm2   =  Block2 | ...
```

4.2 Die semantischen Bereiche

```
            L1                          L2
Stg1   =  Id  -->  Val1         Env2 = Id  -->  Loc
                                Stg2 = Loc -->  Val2
Val1   =  INTG | Aval1          Val2 = INTG | INTG +
Aval1 ::  INTG Val1*
```

Die Abbildung *Stg1* ordnet Identifikatoren Werte zu und modelliert so die statische Speicherverwaltung von L1. Für die dynamische Speicherverwaltung von L2 werden die

Abbildungen *Env2* und *Stg2* verwendet. *Env2* bildet Identifikatoren auf Speicherplätze (*Loc*ations) ab. Diese Abbildung ändert sich zur Laufzeit beim Betreten eines Blocks mit lokalen Variablen. *Stg2* bildet diese Speicherplätze auf Werte ab.

Die Werte in L1 und L2 sind entweder ganze Zahlen oder Felder. Felder in L1 bestehen aus unterer Grenze und Elementliste, in L2 nur aus einer Liste von ganzen Zahlen.

Diese Bereiche lassen sich zu

```
Stg    =  Loc --> Val1
Env2   =  Id  --> Loc
Val1   =  INTG | Aval1
Aval1 ::  INTG  Val1*
```

vereinheitlichen.

4.2 Die dynamische Semantik (Interpretationsfunktionen)

In L2 besteht die Interpretation eines Programms aus der Interpretation eines Blocks in einer leeren Umgebung. In beiden Sprachen werden zuerst die Deklarationen verarbeitet und die Speicher sowie das Adreßbuch initialisiert. In L2 werden vor der Interpretation der Anweisungen noch die impliziten Variablendeklarationen verarbeitet.

```
               L1                                      L2
                                        i-prog2(p,s) = i-block2(p,[ ], s)
                                        type: Prog2 Stg --> Stg

i-prog1(mk-prog1(dl,sl), s) =           i-block2(mk-block2(dl,sl),e,s) =
   let (e1,s1) = i-dcl1(dl,s) in         let (e1,s1) = i-dcl2(dl,s) in
   let (e2,s2) =
       i-impl-dcl1(sl,e1,s1) in
   let s3 = i-stl1(sl,e2,s2) in            let s2 = i-stl2(sl,e + e1,s1) in
       s3 | dom s                              s2 | dom s
type: Prog1 Stg --> Stg                 type: Block2 Env2 Stg --> Stg
```

Die Funktionen *i-dcl1* und *i-dcl2* bauen den Speicher und das Adreßbuch auf. *i-impl-dcl1* berechnet die implizit deklarierten einfachen Variablen.

```
i-dcl1(dl,s) =                          i-dcl2(dl,s) =
   if dl = <> then ([],s)                  if dl = <> then ([ ],s)
   else                                    else
   let (e1,s1) = i-dc1(hd dl,s) in         let (e1,s1) = i-dc2(hd dl,s) in
   let (e2,s2) = i-dcl1(tl dl,s1) in       let (e2,s2) = i-dcl2(tl dl,s) in
       (e1 ∪ e2, s2)                           (e1 ∪ e2, s2)
type: Dcl1 Stg --> (Env2 Stg)           type: Dcl2 Stg --> (Env2 Stg)
```

```
i-impl-dcl1(sl,e,s) =
   let svs = coll-idf(sl) \ dom e in
   let dcl-sv(ids,s1) =
   if  ids = { } then ([ ], s1)
   else let id ∈ ids in
        let (e2, s2) = i-dc1(mk-dc1(id,<>),s1) in
        let (e3,s3)  = dcl-sv(ids \ {id},s2) in
            (e2 ∪ e3, s3)
  in let (e4,s4) = dcl-sv(svs,s) in
        (e ∪ e4, s4)
type: Stl1 Env2 Stg --> (Env2 Stg)

coll-idf(sl) = {id | ''id ist enthalten in sl''}
type: Stl1 --> Id-set
```

Die Funktionen *i-dc1* und *i-dc2* ordnen einem Identifikator einen Speicherplatz zu, erweitern die Abbildung *Env2* und initialisieren den Speicher.

```
i-dc1(mk-dc1(id,bl),s) =
   let nloc ∈ Loc be s.t.
       nloc ~∈ dom s
   in ([id |-> nloc],
       s ∪ [nloc |-> e-bl1(bl)])
type: Dc1 Stg --> (Env2 Stg)

i-dc2(mk-dc2(id,ix),s) =
   let nloc ∈ Loc be s.t.
       nloc ~∈ dom s
   in ([id |-> nloc],
       s ∪ [nloc |-> e-ix2(ix)])
type: Dc2 Stg --> (Env2 Stg)

e-bl1(bl) =
   if bl = <> then 0
   else let (l,u) = hd bl in
        mk-aval1(l,<e-bl(tl bl)
                    | l  ≤ i  ≤ u>)
type: Bl1 --> Val1

e-ix2(ix) =
   if ix = nil then 0
   else
    mk-aval1(1,<0 | 1 ≤ i ≤ ix>)
type: Ix2 --> Val1
```

4.3 Reduktion der Anzahl der Interpretationsfunktionen

Die Funktion *e-ix2* läßt sich nach Anwendung der Transformationsfunktion *trans-ix2-bl1* auf ihr Argument *ix* durch die Funktion *e-bl1* simulieren. Ersetzt man den Aufruf von *e-ix2(ix)* durch *e-bl1(trans-ix2-bl1(ix))*, so kann man *i-dc2* durch *i-dc1* und in einem weiteren Schritt *i-dcl2* durch *i-dcl1* ersetzen:

```
trans-ix2-bl1(ix) = if ix = nil then <> else <(1,ix)>
type: Ix2 --> Bl1

trans-dc2-dc1(mk-dc2(id,ix)) = mk-dc1(id,trans-ix2-bl1(ix))
type: Dc2 --> Dc1

trans-dcl2-dcl1(dl) =  <trans-dc2-dc1(dl(i)) | i ∈ ind dl>
type: Dcl2 --> Dcl1
```

Diese Ersetzungen bringen eine Vereinheitlichung der Deklarations-I-Funktionen. Es sind aber noch implizite Deklarationen in der Sprache enthalten, die durch *i-dcl1(trans-impl-dcl1(sl,dom e'),s')* implementiert werden können.

Wegen der Blockstruktur in L2 gelingt die Vereinheitlichung von *i-prog1* und *i-block2* nicht mehr durch die Simulation der einen Funktion durch die andere Funktion. Nehmen wir an, daß eine Übersetzung *trans-stl1-stl2* existiert, so ist durch die Einführung eines neuen syntaktischen Objekts

```
Block :: Dcl1 Stl2
```

und der zugehörigen I-Funktion

```
i-block(mk-block(dl,sl),e,s) =
   let (e1,s1) = i-dcl1(dl,s) in
   let s2 = i-stl2(sl,e  +  e1,s1) in s2 | dom s
type: Block Env2 Stg -->  Stg
```

die Simulation von i-prog1 und i-block2 mit den folgenden Übersetzungen möglich:

```
trans-impl-dcl1(sl,ids) =
   let svs = coll-idf-(sl) \ ids in
   let cre-dcl(is) =
         if is = { } then <>
         else let id ∈ is in
              <mk-dc1(id,<>)> concat cre-dcl(is \ {id})
   in cre-dcl(svs)
type: Stl1 Id-set --> Dcl1
trans-prog1-block(mk-prog1(dl,sl)) =
   mk-block(dl concat trans-impl-dcl1(sl,{id | mk-dc1(id,) ∈ elems dl}),
            trans-stl1-stl2(sl))
type: Prog1 --> Block

trans-block2-block(mk-block2(dl,sl)) = mk-block(trans-dcl2-dcl1(dl),sl)
type: Block2 --> Block
```

4.4 Reduktion der Anzahl der syntaktischen Objekte

Nach der Vereinheitlichung der I-Funktionen können die syntaktischen Objekte *Prog1*, *Stl1*, *Stm1* aus L1 und *Prog2*, *Block2*, *Dcl2*, *Dc2* und *Ix2* aus L2 entfernt werden. Es ergibt sich

Block	::	*Dcl1 Stl2*	*Bl1*	=	*(INTG INTG)**
Dcl1	=	*Dc1**	*Stl2*	=	*Stm2**
Dc1	::	*Id Bl1*	*Stm2*	=	*Block* : ...

5. Stand der Arbeiten und Erfahrungen

Die Definition von CAT als gemeinsame Zwischensprache für BASIC, COBOL, FORTRAN und PASCAL liegt in META IV vor, ebenso die Transformationsfunktionen für die Objekte aus den Quellsprachen, die die Compileroberteile spezifizieren. Eine erste Pilotimplementierung für PASCAL hat gezeigt, daß die erzeugten CAT-Programme etwa die Länge der Quellprogramme haben.

Die Anwendung von VDM zwingt zu präzisen Entwürfen und Formulierungen, obwohl die Methode ohne Rechnerunterstützung arbeitet. Design-Fehler werden weitgehend vermieden. Man erhält Spezifikationen für einheitlich strukturierte Übersetzeroberteile, die in Programme einer höheren Programmiersprache umgesetzt werden können. Zusätzlich erleichtern die formal angegebenen Transformationen den Nachweis der Korrektheit der Compileroberteile.

6. Literatur

[1] Bjørner, D., Jones, C.B., The Vienna Development Method: The Meta Language, Berlin, Springer LNCS 61, 1978

[2] Jensen, K., Wirth, N., PASCAL User Manual and Report Berlin, Springer, LNCS 18, 1974

[3] ANSI X3.9, American National Standard Programming Language FORTRAN, New York, American National Standards Institute, 1978

[4] ANSI X3.23, American National Standard Programming Language COBOL, New York, American National Standards Institute, 1974

[5] Dietz 600, C-BASIC Benutzeranleitung, Mülheim, Dietz Computer Systeme, 1977

[6] Bjørner, D., The Systematic Development of a Compiling Algorithm, Techn. Rept. ID681, Dept. of Comp. Sci., Techn. University of Denmark, Kopenhagen, 1977

[7] Bjørner, D., Programming Languages: Linguistics and Semantics, in Morlet, E., Ribbens, D., International Computing Symposium 1977, Proceedings, Amsterdam, North-Holland Publ. Comp., 1977, S. 511

[8] Jones, C.B., The Meta-Language: A Reference Manual in [1], S. 218 (1978)

HOARE-STYLE PROOF SYSTEMS AND FORMAL COMPUTATIONS

Ernst-Rüdiger Olderog
Institut für Informatik und Praktische Mathematik
Christian-Albrechts-Universität Kiel
Olshausenstr. 40-60, D-2300 Kiel 1

1. Introduction

Hoare-style proof systems have been proposed for various language constructs [1]. Nevertheless, it is sometimes questioned as to what extent such systems can help to construct correct programs. One possible answer is provided by observing that efforts to find sound and complete Hoare-style proof systems can be considered as efforts to understand the formal computations of the considered programs. Stated in general terms this observation may seem quite obvious, but it is quite another matter to see what "understanding the formal computations" means for particular classes of programs.

The aim of the present paper is now to exemplify this observation for the class of $\mathcal{C}_{60}$-bounded ALGOL-like programs. Due to [12] this class is rich enough to display the essential ideas of presently known Hoare-style proof systems for ALGOL-like programs. To reach our aim, we outline a Hoare-style proof system $\mathcal{H}$ for partial correctness and show that formal correctness proofs in $\mathcal{H}$ have the same structure as certain upper subtrees of formal computation trees which are already important when decidability questions dealing with run time behaviour are studied. Intuitively speaking, these upper subtrees form the key to understand the formal computations of $\mathcal{C}_{60}$-bounded programs. Thus it is not surprising that rather different issues such as run time behaviour and partial correctness can be treated on a uniform basis.

2. ALGOL-like Programs and Units

By L_{Algol} we denote the set of all *ALGOL-like* programs π , i.e. of well-formed blocks

B = begin var ... proc ... S end

with declarations of variables and procedures followed by a statement S. "Well-formed" implies that all procedure identifiers g in B have a corresponding declaration

proc $g(\bar{x}_f:\bar{h}_f)$; B_1;

where $\bar{x}_f$ and $\bar{h}_f$ are lists of formal variables resp. formal procedure identifiers, all treated as if specified as name-parameters. The result type of procedures is here void in the sense of ALGOL 68. Since procedure bodies are again blocks, procedure nestings are allowed. By *environments* E we mean finite sets of declarations of distinct procedure identifiers, represented as sequences

$E ::= \emptyset \mid$ proc g(...);...; $\mid E_1E_2$.

Statements allow the usual language constructs:

$S ::= x{:=}e \mid S_1;S_2 \mid$ if b then S_1 else S_2 fi $\mid \ldots \mid B \mid g(\bar{x}_a:\bar{h}_a)$.

Since correctness proofs in Hoare-style proof systems proceed by structural induction, we need an appropriate notion of program segment. To this end, we introduce the notion of unit. A *unit* is a pair

$E \mid S$ such that begin E S end is in L_{Algol}.

Throughout this paper we identify programs π and the corresponding units $\emptyset|\pi$.

3. Formal Computations and Semantics

To investigate the computational behaviour of programs and units independently of actual operations on data, we consider *formal computation paths*

$$p : E \mid S \rightarrow E_1 \mid S_1 \rightarrow \dots \rightarrow E_n \mid S_n ,$$

i.e. sequences of units generated by a relation $\rightarrow$ between units defined as follows:

(1) $S = S_1;S_2$ or $S =$ if b then S_1 else S_2 fi.

Then $E \mid S \rightarrow E \mid S_1$ and $E \mid S \rightarrow E \mid S_2$.

(2) $S =$ begin var x; E_1 S_1 end.

Then $E \mid S \rightarrow E \cup E_1 \mid S_1$.

(3) $S = g(\bar{x}_a:\bar{h}_a)$, correct w.r.t. the declaration proc $g(x_f:h_f)$; B; in E.

Then $E \mid S \rightarrow E \mid B(\mathcal{C}_{60})$. $B(\mathcal{C}_{60})$ is the ALGOL 60 or static scope modification of B, obtained from B by (i) inserting actual for formal parameters and by (ii) renaming all local identifiers. Thus begin E g(...) end $\vdash$ begin E $B(\mathcal{C}_{60})$ end holds where $\vdash$ is the application of the ALGOL 60 copy rule $\mathcal{C}_{60}$ [8]. We note that $B(\mathcal{C}_{60})$ is not uniquely determined because the renaming (ii) is not deterministic. If uniqueness is needed we consider so-called deterministic specimens $\underline{\mathcal{C}}_{60}$ of $\mathcal{C}_{60}$ [13].

The set of all formal computation paths p, the so-called *formal computation* of $E \mid S$, is represented as a tree, namely the *formal computation tree* $C_{E|S}$. Strictly speaking $C_{E|S}$ depends on the considered specimen $\underline{\mathcal{C}}_{60}$ of $\mathcal{C}_{60}$: $C_{E|S} = C_{E|S}(\underline{\mathcal{C}}_{60})$. Compared with the formal execution tree T_{π} of a program π [8], the formal computation tree $C_{\pi} = C_{\emptyset|\pi}$ describes the computational behaviour of π more detailed, just detailed enough to serve as a "skeleton" for formal correctness proofs of Hoare assertions $\{P\}\ \pi\ \{Q\}$ (see Section 7).

The semantics Σ of L_{Algol} assigns a partially defined mapping $\Sigma(E \mid S)$ from states to states to every units $E \mid S$. A definition of Σ specifies first an approximating semantics $\Sigma^j(E \mid S)$, $j \geq 0$, which is the meaning of $E \mid S$ if we restrict ourselves to a copy depth of at most j in $C_{E|S}$. Then the full semantics Σ is given by $\Sigma(E \mid S) = \bigcup_{j \geq 0} \Sigma^j(E \mid S)$. Of course, Σ varies with the underlying interpretation $\mathcal{J}$ of expressions e and Boolean expressions b: $\Sigma = \Sigma^{\mathcal{J}}$.

4. Substitutional Equivalence

To compare units which differ only by a certain renaming of identifiers, we introduce

Definition 1. Two units $E \mid S$ and $E' \mid S'$ are *substitutional equivalent* if there exists a substitution σ : *Idf* $\longrightarrow$ *Idf* with $\sigma(\min(E \mid S)) = \min(E' \mid S')$ which is injective on *Idf*$(\min(E \mid S))$. As a shorthand we write $E \mid S \cong E' \mid S'$ or more precisely $E \mid S \ {}_{\sigma}\!\!\cong E' \mid S'$.

The minimal unit $\min(E \mid S)$ denotes that unit $E_o \mid S$ where $E_o = \min_{\subseteq} \{E' \mid \text{where } E' \subseteq E \text{ and begin } E' \text{ S end}^o \in L_{Algol}\}$. Intuitively, E_o contains only those procedures which are needed to understand S.

Example 1.

$$\sigma\cong\left(\begin{array}{ll} E \mid S = & \underline{\text{proc}}\ f(x:);\underline{\text{begin}}\ x:=y+1\ \underline{\text{end}}; \\ & \underline{\text{proc}}\ g;\underline{\text{begin}}\ u:=v\ \underline{\text{end}}; \\ E' \mid S' = & \underline{\text{proc}}\ h(u:);\underline{\text{begin}}\ u:=v+1\ \underline{\text{end}}; \end{array}\right. \begin{array}{|l} f(z:) \\ \\ h(w:) \end{array}$$

with $\sigma = [u,v,w,h/x,y,z,f]$. Note that the procedure g does not occur in min(E | S). The applicability of the concept of substitutional equivalence is guaranteed by the following

Substitution Lemma. [13] If $E \mid S\ {}_{\sigma}\!\cong E' \mid S'$ then there exists a deterministic specimen $\underline{\mathcal{C}}_{60}$ of $\mathcal{C}_{60}$ such that $C_{E \mid S}(\underline{\mathcal{C}}_{60})\ {}_{\sigma}\!\cong C_{E' \mid S'}(\underline{\mathcal{C}}_{60})$ holds, i.e. both formal computation trees have the same structure and corresponding nodes are marked by units which are also in relation ${}_{\sigma}\!\cong$.

Roughly speaking, the lemma states that ${}_{\sigma}\!\cong$ is invariant w.r.t. "applications" of $\longrightarrow\!\!\!\triangleright$, i.e. a congruence relation.

5. $\mathcal{C}_{60}$-bounded Programs

The notion of substitutional equivalence leads to the following

Definition 2. A program $\pi \in L_{Algol}$ is $\mathcal{C}_{60}$*-bounded* if the substitutional equivalence induces only finitely many equivalence classes, i.e. has a finite index, in the set of all units in C_{π}. (This definition is independent of the chosen specimen $\underline{\mathcal{C}}_{60}$ of $\mathcal{C}_{60}$.)

Next we give natural examples for this class of programs.

Remark 1. Every program $\pi \in L_{Algol}$ *without global formal procedure identifiers* [8] is $\mathcal{C}_{60}$-bounded. Examples of such programs are all programs without procedure nestings or without procedures as parameters.

Remark 2. Programs $\pi \in L_{Algol}$ with the *formal "most recent" property* [6] are in general not $\mathcal{C}_{60}$-bounded, but $\mathcal{C}_{mr}$-bounded. $\mathcal{C}_{mr}$ is the so-called "most recent" copy rule, it induces a semantics Σ_{mr} which coincides with the static scope semantics Σ for all programs with the formal "most recent" property [13].

In the following we study $\mathcal{C}_{60}$-bounded programs and in Section 6 we outline a Hoare-style proof system $\mathcal{H}$ for these programs. First we explain a method which can be applied to solve various decidability questions on $\mathcal{C}_{60}$-bounded programs. We focus here on the formal reachability of procedures (which is undecidable for the full language L_{Algol} [8,9]).

Theorem 1. For $\mathcal{C}_{60}$-bounded programs $\pi \in L_{Algol}$ it is decidable whether a given procedure f in π is *formally reachable,* i.e. whether there is a node E | f'(...) in C_{π} with f' being a copy of f.

The proof idea is as follows: Construct a certain *upper subtree*, i.e. an initial segment, of C_{π}, namely the smallest upper subtree U_{π} of C_{π} such that every maximal node E' | S' is either maximal in C_{π} too or of the form E' | S' = E' | g'(...) and has a substitutional equivalent predecessor node E | S = E | g(...):

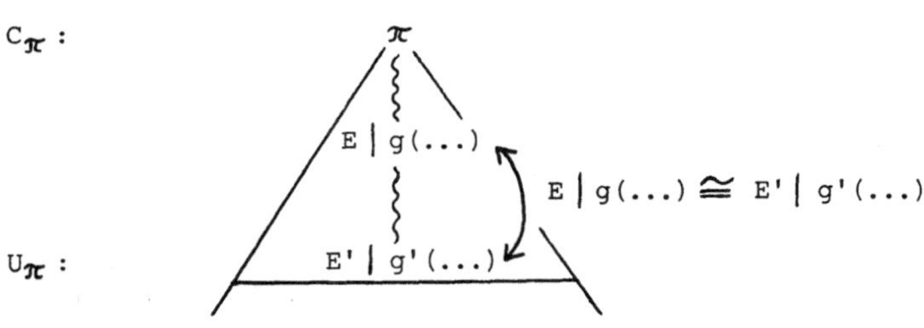

Since π is $\mathcal{C}_{60}$-bounded, U_π is finite and effectively constructable. Now the required decidability result follows immediately from

Lemma 1. If f is formally reachable in C_π then already in U_π.

The proof relies on the Substitution Lemma. Intuitively speaking, Lemma 1 states that all information about C_π is already concentrated in the finite upper subtree U_π.

Analogously also other questions such as the formal recursiveness of procedures or whether C_π is finite can be proved decidable for $\mathcal{C}_{60}$-bounded programs. The principal idea of this upper subtree method has already been used in [6] to show that the formal "most recent" property is decidable. We note that all these questions are closely related to the question whether run time systems can apply simplified working techniques when confronted with such programs.

Most interesting is now that exactly the same upper subtrees U_π which were used here to solve decidability questions form the skeleton for formal correctness proofs in Section 7.

6. The Hoare-style Proof System $\mathcal{H}$

Partial correctness of programs and units is described by assertions $\{P\}\ E \mid S\{Q\}$ where P and Q are logical formulas. Analogously to the validity $\models_{\mathfrak{I}}$ P of logical formulas P we write $\models_{\mathfrak{I}} \{P\}\ E \mid S\{Q\}$ if $\{P\}\ E \mid S\{Q\}$ is *valid* in $\mathfrak{I}$, i.e. if $\Sigma^{\mathfrak{I}}(E \mid S)(\widetilde{P}^{\mathfrak{I}}) \subseteq \widetilde{Q}^{\mathfrak{I}}$ holds where $\widetilde{P}^{\mathfrak{I}}$, $\widetilde{Q}^{\mathfrak{I}}$ are the sets of states expressed by P, Q in $\mathfrak{I}$.

We now outline a Hoare-style proof system $\mathcal{H}$ for assertions $\{P\}\ E \mid S\{Q\}$. $\mathcal{H}$ is presented as a *deduction system* [14] where formal proofs are deduction trees which can be easily compared with the already known formal computation trees. A *deduction tree* Δ is a finite tree with assertions occurring at the nodes. Associated with Δ is a set $\mathcal{A}$ of assertions occurring at the leaves of Δ, called *assumptions*. We write $\mathcal{A} \vdash_{\mathcal{H}} \{P\}\ E \mid S\{Q\}$ if there exists a deduction tree Δ with root assertion $\{P\}\ E \mid S\{Q\}$ and assumption set $\mathcal{A}$. If $\mathcal{A} = \emptyset$ holds Δ is called a *formal proof.*

Deduction trees Δ and the associated assumption sets $\mathcal{A}$ are constructed inductively with help of proof rules. To give the idea of this construction we display the central proof rules of $\mathcal{H}$. First we have the standard rules dealing with language constructs such as assignment, composition, conditional or block. The crucial proof rules for the completeness of $\mathcal{H}$ are (R) and (S).

(S) Substitution. If Δ_1 is a deduction tree with assumptions $\mathcal{A}_1$ then Δ is a deduction tree with assumptions $\mathcal{A} = \mathcal{A}_1$:

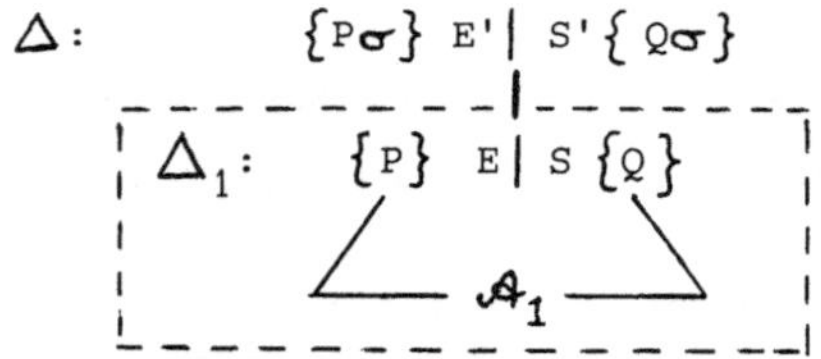

where the substitution σ is injective on *FreeVar*(P,Q) $\cup$ *Idf*(min(E | S)) and $E \mid S_\sigma \cong E' \mid S'$ holds.

Here Δ simply inherits all assumptions of Δ_1. (The same is true for the standard rules just mentioned. Of course, some have more than one premise.) This type of proof rule is called *inference rule.*

(R) Recursion. If Δ_1 is a deduction tree with assumptions $\mathcal{A}_1$ then Δ is a deduction tree with assumptions $\mathcal{A} = \mathcal{A}_1 \setminus \{P\}\ E \mid g(\bar{x}_a:\bar{h}_a)\ \{Q\}$:

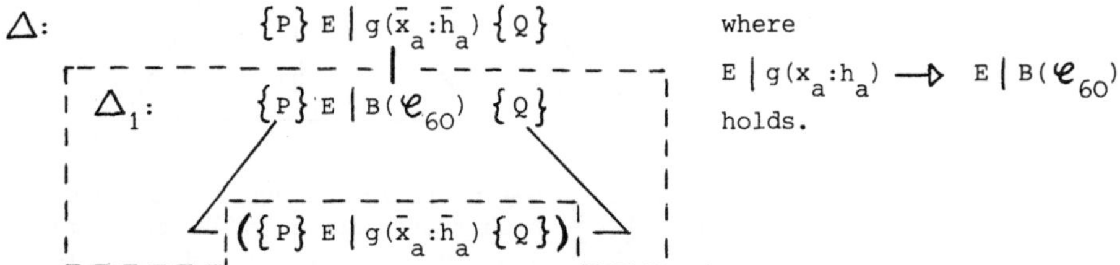

where $E \mid g(x_a:h_a) \rightarrow E \mid B(\mathcal{C}_{60})$ holds.

Here we are allowed to discharge an assumption. This type of proof rule is called *deduction rule* as opposed to simple inference rules. (R) is the only deduction rule in $\mathcal{H}$.

Also other standard rules such as the invariance rule or the rule of consequence are included in $\mathcal{H}$. To apply the latter one, $\mathcal{H}$ must be augmented with an oracle $\mathcal{O}$ for logical formulas, for example with the theory $Th(\mathcal{J}) = \{P \mid \models_{\mathcal{J}} P\}$ of $\mathcal{J}$. The augmented system will be denoted by $\mathcal{H}, \mathcal{O}$.

As explained in [12,13] the soundness of $\mathcal{H}$ can be conviently proved with help of the approximating semantics Σ^j. In particular, soundness of proof rule (R) is shown by induction on the index $j \geq 0$ of Σ^j and soundness of proof rule (S) relies on the Substitution Lemma.

Theorem 2. $\mathcal{H}$ is *sound* for L_{Algol}, i.e. for every $\mathcal{J}, \pi \in L_{Algol}$, P and Q

$$\vdash_{\mathcal{H},Th(\mathcal{J})} \{P\}\ \pi\ \{Q\} \text{ implies } \models_{\mathcal{J}} \{P\}\ \pi\ \{Q\} .$$

7. Relative Completeness

We now explain how to prove

Theorem 3. Let $L \subseteq L_{Algol}$ such that every $\pi \in L$ is $\mathcal{C}_{60}$*-bounded.*
Then $\mathcal{H}$ is *relatively complete* for L, i.e. for every $\mathcal{J}$ for which the logical formulas are *expressive*, $\pi \in L$, P and Q

$$\models_{\mathcal{J}} \{P\}\ \pi\ \{Q\} \quad \text{implies} \vdash_{\mathcal{H},Th(\mathcal{J})} \{P\}\ \pi\ \{Q\} .$$

The concepts of expressibility and relative completeness [3] are well-known. (Remember also that no proof system $\mathcal{H}$ can be sound and relatively complete for the full language L_{Algol} [2] .)

The proof outline is now as follows: Let an interpretation $\mathcal{J}$ satisfying the expressibility condition and a $\mathcal{C}_{60}$-bounded program $\pi \in L$ be given and assume that $\models_{\mathcal{J}} \{P\}\ \pi\ \{Q\}$ holds. Then we show the existence of a formal proof Δ of $\{P\}\ \pi\ \{Q\}$ in $\mathcal{H}$ such that Δ is a "decorated" or "pumped" version of exactly that finite upper subtree U_{π} of C_{π} which formed the basis for the decidability proof in Section 5:

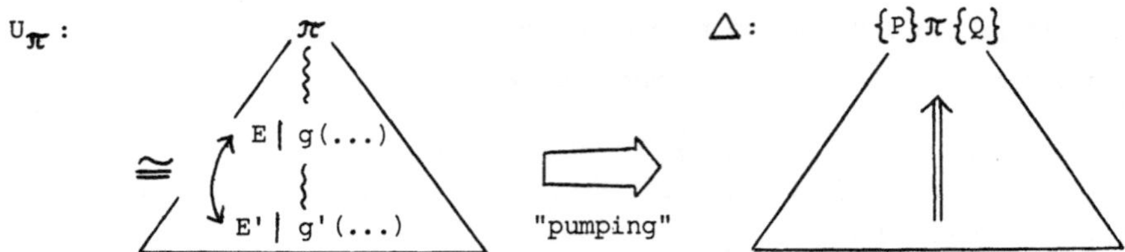

Pumped version means that Δ is obtained from U_π by replacing every node E | S of U_π by a branch $\beta_{E|S}$ of nodes {P'} E | S {Q'} which represents a couple of formal proof steps in $\mathcal{H}$ dealing with E | S. Only at leaves of Δ we additionally allow applications of rule (S), i.e. also nodes {P'} E' | S' {Q'} with E | S $\cong$ E' | S' in $\beta_{E|S}$. Informally speaking the strategy how to construct Δ is completely determined by U_π.

This construction proceeds bottom-up using the appropriate proof rules of $\mathcal{H}$. The non-trivial steps are those dealing with procedure calls in U_π. If such a procedure call E' | g'(...) occurs at a leaf there exists a substitutional equivalent predecessor node E | g(...) by definition of U_π. Then we apply rule (S) to produce a deduction tree of form Δ_1 with a most general formula [5] {G} E | g(...) {G'} as assumption. If later on in this construction process we hit the corresponding predecessor node E | g(...) we apply rule (R) to deduce {G} E | g(...) {G'} and at the same moment discharge the assumption made earlier in Δ_1:

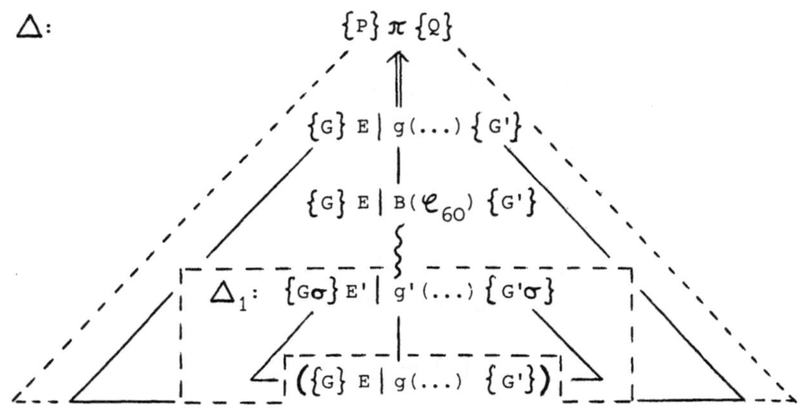

Thus the proof rules (R) and (S) reflect the structure of U_π.

8. Conclusion

In this paper we showed that the structure of the formal computations of $\mathcal{C}_{60}$-bounded programs is completely determined by certain finite upper subtrees of the formal computation trees. These upper subtrees are characterized by repetitions of units which are equivalent up to substitution. This basic principle is reflected both in decidability proofs dealing with questions related to the run time behaviour of the considered programs and in formal correctness proofs in the system $\mathcal{H}$ with (R) and (S) as essential proof rules.

Current dissertation work implies that these observations can be extended to all ALGOL-like programs with so-called regular formal call trees. To understand the formal computations of these programs an additional basic principle has to be identified, namely the so-called depth k property. Again this principle is reflected in both decidability proofs and formal correctness proofs for this extended class of programs. So we may say that for $\mathcal{C}_{60}$-bounded programs or more general for programs with regular formal call trees the structure of formal computations is fully understood.

This is not longer true for programs with non-regular formal call trees as the class of ALGOL-like programs with finite procedure modes in the sense of ALGOL 68 shows. Here presently known methods to solve certain termination problems [4,7,10,11] are (at the moment) not sufficient for designing a Hoare-style proof system [12], but we expect that also here it will be possible to identify the additional basic principles quite clearly. So this example indicates that whether there exists a sound and complete Hoare-style proof system for some programming language provides a good test to judge whether we fully understand the formal computations. We consider such a knowledge as a worthwhile basis for designing correct and efficient programs.

References

[1] Apt, K.R., Ten years of Hoare's logic, a survey, part I, Fac. Econom., Univ. of Rotterdam (1979); to appear in TOPLAS.

[2] Clarke, E.M., Programming language constructs for which it is impossible to obtain good Hoare axiom systems, J. ACM 26, pp. 129-147 (1979).

[3] Cook, S.A., Soundness and completeness of an axiomatic system for program verification, SIAM J. Comp. 7, pp. 70-90 (1978).

[4] Damm, W., Fehr, E., A schematological approach to the analysis of the procedure concept in ALGOL-languages, Proc. 5ième Coll. sur les Arbes en Algèbre et en Programmation, Lille, pp. 130-134 (1980).

[5] Gorelick, G.A., A complete axiomatic system for proving assertions about recursive and non-recursive programs, Tech. Rep. 75, Dept. Comp. Sc., Univ. of Toronto (1975).

[6] Kandzia, P., On the "most recent" property of ALGOL-like programs, in: Proc. ICALP 74, Lecture Notes in Computer Science 14, Springer Verlag, pp. 97-111 (1974).

[7] Klein, H.-J., Zur Charakterisierung von Programmen mit endlichen Arten, Diss., Univ. of Kiel, 180 pp. (1980).

[8] Langmaack, H., On correct procedure parameter transmission in higher programming languages, Acta Inform. 2, pp. 110-143 (1973).

[9] Langmaack, H., On procedures as open subroutines I, II, Acta Inform. 2, pp. 311-333 (1973) and Acta Inform. 3, pp. 227-241 (1974).

[10] Langmaack, H., On termination problems for finitely interpreted ALGOL-like programs, Bericht Nr. 7904, Inst. Inform. Prakt. Math., Univ. of Kiel (1979).

[11] Langmaack, H., Lippe, W.M., Wagner, F., The formal termination problem for programs with finite ALGOL 68-modes, Inform. Proc. Letters 9, pp. 155-159 (1979).

[12] Langmaack, H., Olderog, E.-R., Present-day Hoare-like systems for programming languages with procedures: power, limits and most likely extensions, in: Proc. ICALP 80, Lecture Notes in Computer Science 85, Springer Verlag, pp. 363-373 (1980).

[13] Olderog, E.-R., Sound and complete Hoare-like calculi based on copy rules, Bericht Nr. 7905, Inst. Inform. Prakt. Math., Univ. of Kiel, 57 pp. (1979); to appear in Acta Informatica.

[14] Prawitz, D., Natural deduction - a proof-theoretic study, Almquist & Wiksell, Stockholm, 113 pp. (1965).

A CHARACTERIZATION OF PROGRAM EQUIVALENCE IN TERMS OF HOARE'S LOGIC

J.A. Bergstra
Institute of Applied Mathematics
and Computer Science
University of Leiden
Leiden, The Netherlands

J. Terlouw
Mathematical Institute
University of Utrecht,
Utrecht, The Netherlands

Abstract

We discuss the equivalence of simple while-programs S_1 and S_2 in all datatypes that implement a specification (Σ,E). A sufficient condition is that S_1 and S_2 are indistinguishable in all program logics $HL(\Sigma',E)$ for $\Sigma' \supseteq \Sigma$. A necessary condition is that for each refinement (Σ',E') of (Σ,E) another refinement (Σ^*,E^*) of (Σ',E') exists such that S_1 and S_2 cannot be distinguished in $HL(\Sigma^*,E^*)$.

TECHNICAL INTRODUCTION

1.1. Program equivalence derives its interest both from a fundamental theoretical point of view (MH[7]) and from its role in a theory of program transformation. Especially in the case of transformations that replace a complicated, high-level program, S, by a simpler, lower-level but equivalent one, the correctness proof of such a transformation T must establish some kind of equivalence between S and T(S). In the present paper we concentrate on one possible form of equivalence: behaving equivalent w.r.t. Hoare's logic.

1.2. At this stage it is necessary to be precise about the main parameters that govern this situation. These are, in order of importance:

a) The program language. We will use while-programs over various finite signatures Σ. $WP(\Sigma)$ is the smallest class of programs, working on registers (variables) $x_0,x_1,x_2,\ldots$ that contains assignments $x_i := \tau$ with τ an expression (term) in $L(\Sigma)$, and which is closed under composition, the if b then else fi and the while b do od constructs. Here b denotes a boolean expression (quantifier free formula) of $L(\Sigma)$, the first oder logic of signature Σ.

b) The data structures on which to run our programs. Here each Σ'-algebra with $\Sigma' \supseteq \Sigma$, is a conceivable datastructure on which $S \in WP(\Sigma)$ can run.
In general, however, we work relative to a specification E, a theory in $L(\Sigma)$. Semantic program equivalence is then expressed as follows: for $S_1,S_2 \in WP(\Sigma)$, E a Σ-specification we write $S_1 \equiv_{ALG(\Sigma,E)} S_2$ if S_1 and S_2 compute the same partial function $\mathfrak{A}^n \to \mathfrak{A}^n$ on each $\mathfrak{A} \in ALG(\Sigma,E)$, i.e. on the collection of structures that satisfies the requirements of specification (Σ,E). The partial function: $\mathfrak{A}^n \to \mathfrak{A}^n$ that S defines on $\mathfrak{A}$ is defined using a standard operational semantics. In this

case we must choose n as the number of variables occurring in S_1 or in S_2.
For technical reasons we must assume in proposition 2 and in theorem 1 that (Σ,E) has no finite models.

c) The precise version of Hoare's logic that is used. For each specification (Σ,E), a logic $HL(\Sigma,E)$ is introduced. This is exactly standard Hoare's logic for proving correctness assertions of the form $\{p\}\ S\ \{q\}$ with $p,q \in L(\Sigma)$ $S \in WP(\Sigma)$ where in applications of the rule of consequence only those implications $r \rightarrow s$ can be used that are derivable from E.
A detailed account of $HL(\Sigma,E)$ can be found in Apt [1], de Bakker [3] or B & T [5]. In [5] a deduction theorem for HL is proved, using a quite straightforward induction on proof length, which we will need. It reads as follows:
for each closed assertion t, for all p,q,S:

$$HL(\Sigma,E \cup \{t\}) \vdash \{p\}\ S\ \{q\} \Leftrightarrow$$
$$HL(\Sigma,E) \vdash \{p \wedge t\}\ S\ \{q\}$$

d) Important notational conventions are the following: let (Σ,E) be a specification, a refinement of (Σ,E) is a specification (Σ',E') with $\Sigma' \supseteq \Sigma$ and $E' \vdash E$. We will usually assume that E' is consistent whenever E is. A refinement (Σ',E') of (Σ,E) is conservative if for all $p \in L(\Sigma)$: $E' \vdash p$ implies $E \vdash p$. Here is our main technical definition:

$$S_1 \equiv_{HL(\Sigma,E)} S_2 \text{ if for all } p,q$$
$$HL(\Sigma,E) \vdash \{p\}\ S_1\ \{q\} \Leftrightarrow HL(\Sigma,E) \vdash \{p\}\ S_2\ \{q\}.$$

SURVEY OF OUR RESULTS

The following results will be established, all having to do with the relationship between $\equiv_{HL(\Sigma,E)}$ and $\equiv_{ALG(\Sigma,E)}$.

PROPOSITION 1. There are a signature and programs $S_1,S_2 \in WP(\Sigma)$ such that $S_1 \equiv_{ALG(\Sigma,\phi)} S_2$ but $S_1 \not\equiv_{HL(\Sigma,\phi)} S_2$.
This solves a problem posed by J. Tiuryn [8].

PROPOSITION 2. If $S_1 \equiv_{ALG(\Sigma,E)} S_2$ then there is a conservative refinement (Σ',E') of (Σ,E) such that $S_1 \equiv_{HL(\Sigma',E')} S_2$.

THEOREM 1. CHARACTERIZATION OF PROGRAM EQUIVALENCE.

For each specification (Σ,E) and all pairs of programs $S_1,S_2 \in WP(\Sigma)$ the following are equivalent:

i) $S_1 \equiv_{ALG(\Sigma,E)} S_2$

ii) for each refinement (Σ',E') of (Σ,E) there is a refinement (Σ^*,E^*) of (Σ',E') such that
$S_1 \equiv_{HL(\Sigma^*,E^*)} S_2$.

THEOREM 2. A sufficient condition for $S_1 \equiv_{ALG(\Sigma,E)} S_2$ is that for all Σ' extending Σ:

$$S_1 \equiv_{HL(\Sigma',E)} S_2$$

We have the impression that this criterion could well be the basis for a formal proof system for program equivalence. This will be a subject of further work by the first author and J.W. Klop (Mathematical Center, Amsterdam).

RELATIONS TO PREVIOUS LITERATURE

Let us introduce the notation $S_1 \equiv_{PC(\Sigma,E)} S_2$ to express that for all $p,q \in L(\Sigma)$: $ALG(\Sigma,E) \models \{p\}\ S_1\ \{q\} \Leftrightarrow ALG(\Sigma,E) \models \{p\}\ S_2\ \{q\}$.
MH [7] and BTT [4] study the relationship between $\equiv_{ALG(\Sigma,E)}$ and $\equiv_{PC(\Sigma,E)}$.
Obviously $\equiv_{ALG(\Sigma,E)} \subseteq \equiv_{PC(\Sigma,E)}$ and, depending on (Σ,E) the inverse inclusion may or may not hold. If $HL(\Sigma,E)$ is complete, i.e. for all p,q,S $HL(\Sigma,E) \vdash \{p\}\ S\ \{q\} \Leftrightarrow ALG(\Sigma,E) \models \{p\}\ S\ \{q\}$ the relations $\equiv_{HL(\Sigma,E)}$ and $\equiv_{PC(\Sigma,E)}$ coincide.
In general, however, the relations are not so clear, because, according to Wand [9] $HL(\Sigma,E)$ may be incomplete. Semantic work on program equivalence occurs for instance in De Bakker [2].

SKETCHES OF PROOFS

5.1. Let Σ be the signature {0,S,P}. Then we can construct the following programs S_0,S',S'',S_1,S_2 :
S_0 = y := 0; <u>while</u> y ≠ x <u>do</u> <u>if</u> y = PS(y) <u>then</u> y := S(y) <u>else</u> DIV <u>fi</u> <u>od</u>.

S' = y := 0; <u>while</u> x ≠ 0 <u>do</u> y := S(y); x := P(x) <u>od</u>

S" = y := x; x := 0

$S_1 = S_0$; S' $S_2 = S_0$; S".

Here DIV = <u>while</u> x = x <u>do</u> x := x <u>od</u>.

First observe that $S_1 \equiv_{ALG(\Sigma,\phi)} S_2$. To see this note that $S_0(x,y)\downarrow$ if for some n $x = S^n(0)$ and for all $m < n$ $PS^{m+1}(0) = S^m(0)$. Then, however, S_1 just like S_2 results giving y the value of x and putting x := 0. Then we consider $HL(\Sigma,\phi)$. It is obvious that

$$HL(\Sigma,\phi) \vdash \{x=z\}\ S_2\ \{x=0 \wedge y=z\}$$

On the other hand $HL(\Sigma,\phi) \nvdash \{x=z\}\ S_1\ \{x=0 \wedge y=z\}$.
To prove this consider the structure $A = (\mathbb{Z},S,P,0)$. If
$HL(\Sigma,\phi) \vdash \{x=z\}\ S_1\ \{x=0 \wedge y=z\}$ then also $HL(\Sigma,Th(A))$ proves this fact.
Suppose that $r(x,y,z)$ is the invariant of the <u>while</u> loop in S' (in this second proof), then one can show that, in A,r defines the predicate $x+y = z$.
This, however, cannot be done by a first order formula of $L(\Sigma)$.

This proves proposition 1. In this situation we can already observe a version of the phenomenon indicated in proposition 2. Let $\Sigma' = \Sigma \cup \{+\}$ and
$E' = \{x+0 = x,\ 0+x = x,\ x \neq 0 \quad P(x) + S(y) = x+y\}$ plus all induction axioms. Then with some work one can show $S_1 \equiv_{HL(\Sigma',E')} S_2$.

5.2. For further proofs we need a lemma that is immediate from B & T [6].
Assume that (Σ,E) is a specification without finite models.
Let Γ_ω be the signature of $\mathbb{N} = (\omega,+,\cdot,0,1)$. With Σ_ω we denote a disjoint union of Σ and Γ_ω . We denote with E_ω the theory E plus Peano arithmetic, over Γ_ω, plus all induction axioms of $L(\Sigma_\times)$. First of all we observe that (Σ_ω,E_ω) is conservative over (Σ,E)
To prove this assume that $\phi \in L(\Sigma)$, ϕ closed, and $E \nvdash \phi$; acoording to the completeness theorem there is a countable model A of $E \cup \{\neg\phi\}$. Expanding A to a Σ_ω-structure A' such that $A'|\Gamma_\omega$ is a standard model of arithmetic, A' satisfies E_ω and $\neg\phi$, thus $E_\omega \nvdash \phi$.

5.3. LEMMA. For all p,S there is a formula SP(p,S) in $L(\Sigma_\omega)$ such that the following properties hold:

i) $HL(\Sigma_\omega,E_\omega) \vdash \{p\}\ S\ \{SP(p,S)\}$

ii) for all q: $HL(\Sigma_\omega,E_\omega) \vdash \{p\}\ S\ \{q\}$ if and only if $E_\omega \vdash SP(P,S) \rightarrow q$.

iii) if $A \in ALG(\Sigma_\omega,E_\omega)$ and $A|\Gamma_\omega \cong \mathbb{N}$ then SP(p,S) defines in A the strongest postconditon w.r.t. p of S.

iv) $E_\omega \vdash \forall(p \leftrightarrow q) \rightarrow (SP(p,S) \leftrightarrow SP(q,S))$. Here $\forall(p \leftrightarrow q)$ is the universal closure of $p \leftrightarrow q$.

v) if $x \notin VAR(S)$ then $E_\omega \vdash SP(\exists xp,S) \leftrightarrow \exists xSP(p,S)$

vi) if $FV(q) \cap VAR(S) = \emptyset$ then

$$E_\omega \vdash SP(p \wedge q,S) \leftrightarrow q \wedge SP(p,S) .$$

5.4. Suppose $S_1 \equiv_{ALG(\Sigma,E)} S_2$. With θ we denote the universal closure of the formula $SP(X = Z,S_1) \leftrightarrow SP(X = Z,S_2)$, where X is a list containing $VAR(S_1) \cup VAR(S_2)$ and Z is a list of variables disjoint from X. Now $E_\omega \cup \{\theta\}$ is conservative over E as well because the model A' constructed in 5.2 satisfies θ in view of property iii) of the

SP construct and the operational equivalence of S_1 and S_2 in A.

At this stage proposition 2 is proved by taking $\Sigma' = \Sigma_\omega$ and $E' = E_\omega \cup \{\theta\}$. We find that for all p,q:

$$HL(\Sigma',E') \vdash \{p\}\ S_1\ \{q\} \Leftrightarrow \text{(by the deduction lemma)}$$

$$HL(\Sigma_\omega,E_\omega) \vdash \{\theta \wedge p\}\ S_1\ \{q\} \Leftrightarrow \text{(by property II))}$$

$$E_\omega \vdash SP(\theta \wedge p,S_1) \rightarrow q \Leftrightarrow \text{(by vi))}$$

$$E_\omega \vdash \theta \wedge SP(p,S_1) \Leftrightarrow \text{(by iv))}$$

$$E_\omega \vdash \theta \wedge SP(\exists Z(X=Z \wedge p[X/Z]),S_1) \Leftrightarrow \text{(by v))}$$

$$E_\omega \vdash \theta \wedge \exists Z\ SP(X=Z \wedge p[X/Z]),S_1) \Leftrightarrow \text{(by vi))}$$

$$E_\omega \vdash \theta \wedge \exists Z(p[X/Z] \wedge SP(X=Z,S_1)) \Leftrightarrow \text{(by assumption)}$$

$$E_\omega \vdash \theta \wedge \exists Z(p[X/Z] \wedge SP(X=Z,S_2)) \Leftrightarrow$$

$HL(\Sigma',E') \vdash \{p\}\ S_2\ \{q\}$ by arguing backwards in a symmetrical way.

5.5. The i) $\Rightarrow$ ii) part of 1 now follows by observing that $S_1 \equiv_{ALG(\Sigma,E)} S_2$ implies $S_1 \equiv_{ALG(\Sigma',E')} S_2$ and then taking $\Sigma^* = \Sigma'_\omega$ and $E^* = E'_\omega \cup \{\theta\}$, repeating the above argument for (Σ^*,E^*).

5.6. At last we arrive at proving the negative parts, i.e. those working from the assumption $S_1 \not\equiv_{ALG(\Sigma,E)} S_2$. For theorem 2 we have to find an extension signature Σ' such that $S_1 \not\equiv_{HL(\Sigma',E)} S_2$; and for the ii) $\Rightarrow$ i) part of theorem 1 we must find a refinement (Σ',E') such that for each refinement (Σ^*,E^*) of (Σ',E'), $S_1 \not\equiv_{HL(\Sigma^*,E^*)} S_2$.

Let us assume that for some $A \in ALG(\Sigma,E)$ and some vectors a and b of elements of A, $A \models S_1[a] = b$ and $A \not\models S_2\ [a] = b$. (The symmetric other case is dealt with similarly.) Extend Σ to Σ^0 by adding constant names for the a's and b's, $\Sigma = \Sigma^0 \cup \{\underline{a},\underline{b}\}$. A^0 is the corresponding Σ^0-structure. Then $A^0 \models S_1\ [\underline{a}] = \underline{b}$ but $A^0 \not\models S_2[\underline{a}] = \underline{b}$. Now choose a closed assertion t of $L(\Sigma^0)$, true in A^0 such that $t \models S_1[\underline{a}] = \underline{b}$ (the construction of such t is quite straightforward, see BTT[4] for instance). Observe that $A \models \{X = \underline{a}\}S_2\{\neg(X = \underline{b})\}$, with X a vector of variables.

Take $\Sigma' = \Sigma^0$ and

$$E' = E_\omega \cup \{t\} \cup SP(X = \underline{a},\ S_2) \rightarrow \neg(X = \underline{b}).$$

Then (Σ',E') is a (consistent) refinement of (Σ,E).
Suppose now that (Σ^*,E^*) refines (Σ',E'), then clearly $HL(\Sigma^*,E^*) \vdash \{X = \underline{A}\}\ S_2\{\ (X = \underline{b})\}$. But because $E^* \vdash t$, $ALG(\Sigma^*,E^*) \not\models \{X = \underline{a}\}\ S_1\ \{\neg(X = \underline{b})\}$. This proves $S_1 \not\equiv_{HL(\Sigma^*,E^*)} S_2$ and theorem 1.

5.7. To obtain theorem 2 choose a closed assertion r such that $E' \vdash r$ and

$HL(\Sigma',E \cup \{r\}) \vdash \{X = \underline{a}\}\ S_2\ \{\neg(X = \underline{b})\}$. This r exists due to the (obvious) finiteness lemma from BT [5]. By the deduction lemma mentioned in the introduction this gives $HL(\Sigma',E) \vdash \{X = \underline{a} \wedge r\}\ S_2\ \{\neg(X = \underline{b})\}$; but if $HL(\Sigma',E) \vdash \{X = \underline{a} \wedge r\} S_1\ \{\neg(X = \underline{b})\}$ then arguing the other way around $HL(\Sigma',E') \vdash \{X = \underline{a}\}\ S_1\ \{\neg(X = \underline{b})\}$ which is not true, because of soundness.

This ends our proofs. It will not be so easy to extend these results to more complicated languages, including recursion and concurrency, because Lemma 1 depends heavily on the 'algebraic' structure of HL(Σ,E) for WP(Σ). But it is in fact quite likely that similar results can be obtained for each sound and relatively complete HL proof system.

REFERENCES

[1] K.R. Apt, Ten years of Hoare's Logic, a survey, F.V. Jensen, B.H. Mayoh & K.K. Møller (eds.). Proceedings from 5th Scandinavian Logic Symposium, Aalborg University Press, Aalborg 1979.

[2] J.W. de Bakker, Recursive procedures, Mathematical Centre Tracts 24, Math. Centre Amsterdam 1973.

[3] J.W. de Bakker, Mathematical Theorey of Program Correctness, Prentice Hall International, London 1980.

[4] J.A. Bergstra, J. Tiuryn & J.V. Tucker, Floyd's principle, correctnes theories and program equivalence, Math. Centre report IW 145/80, to appear in T.C.S.

[5] J.A. Bergstra & J.V. Tucker, On the refinement of specifications and Hoare's logic, Math. Centre report IW 155, Amsterdam 1980.

[6] J.A. Bergstra & J.V. Tucker, Peano's arithmetic and Hoare's logic, Math. Centre report IW 160, Amsterdam 1981.

[7] A.R. Meyer & J.Y. Halpern, Axiomatic definitions of programming languages, a theoretical assesment. Proceedings 6th POPL 1979.

[8] J. Tiuryn, private communication, november 1980.

[9] M. Wand, A new incompleteness result for Hoare's system, J.A.C.M. 25 (1) 1978.

SEMANTICS OF DISTRIBUTED PROCESSES DERIVED BY TRANSLATION

by

Egidio ASTESIANO and Elena ZUCCA

Istituto di Matematica-Via L.B.Alberti 4-16132 Genova-Italy

INTRODUCTION.

The aim of this paper is to show a technique for getting an operational semantics for the language of Distributed Processes(DP) introduced in /BH/,by means of a translation into the language of behaviour expressions in CCS,the Calculus of Communicating Systems developed in /M/.

The essential idea is as follows.Guided by an intuitive understanding of the semantics of DP,as exposed in /BH/,we can translate DP terms into CCS terms(Section 1);then,if P is a DP term and $[\![P]\!]$ denotes its translation,to P is associated a semantics,which is the semantics of $[\![P]\!]$ in CCS,obtained from a system of derivations $\mathcal{M}$.This semantics is not very manageable,since it is expressed in a kind of low level language.But from $\mathcal{M}$ we can deduce a simpler system of derivations $\mathcal{P}$ acting on CCS terms which are the translation of DP terms;thus,forgetting the CCS structure,and using a simplified notation,we get a system of derivations on DP terms.(Section 2).This system provides a way of defining an operational semantics which agrees completely with a semantics in CCS, to be made precise in the paper(Section 3).

One important point is that this technique relies on a quite general principle;and indeed it has been already applied to the case of CSP(see /AZ/;for a related paper see /HLP/).

From another viewpoint,if we accept as good the obtained operational semantics of Section 2,the results of Section 3 show that the translation in Section 1 is correct. Moreover the translation seems to give good hints and directions for a correct implementation.

Throughout the paper we assume the reader familiar with the basic concepts and notations about CCS as in /M/ and DP as in /BH/.

1.TRANSLATION OF DP PROCESSES.

1.1 Assumptions.

We recall here in outline the basic ideas of DP:

- a program consists of a fixed number of concurrent processes that start simultaneously and exist forever.
- each process can access its own variables only (there are no common variables).
- processes communicate only via common procedures.
- a process defines some procedures and an initial statement.
- the execution of a process begins with the execution of the initial statement;the execution continues until the statement either terminates or arrives at a "guarded

----

This work has been partially supported by a grant of "Progetto Finalizzato Informatica-P1-CNET" of CNR (Consiglio Nazionale delle Ricerche)-Italy.

region"(when or cycle statement) where all the boolean guards are false;then another operation starts(as the result of an external request) and an interleaving begins of the initial statement and external requests.

There is a common agreement on the following two assumptions:recursive procedures are not allowed and a process cannot call its own procedures (see /BH/ and,e.g.,/RDKR/). In this paper we shall also assume that a procedure can be accessed by only one process at a time,so that,in the case of several "contemporary" calls,one process is served, while the others have to wait.This is a restriction with respect to the DP originally proposed.The motivation is purely technical (see /M/ pg.134):in the version of CCS which we refer to no easy way can be found for allowing simultaneous activation of an unbounded number of copies of a procedure (it would be easy instead to allow for a fixed maximum number.).The easiest way for circumventing this difficulty,i.e. using a "return link",requires passing labels of channels as values,which is not allowed in CCS (see /M/ Ch.9).But it should be said that some work is in progress for an improved version of CCS without this limitation.

Finally our translation assumes that a process is an agent which exists forever,as in /BH/;i.e. we do not make any assumption about termination of programs (contrary to the way taken in /RDKR/).We could have taken the other approach,but in that case the translation should be different;that is the way taken in CSP and the reader is referred to /AZ/ for a translation dealing with this situation(Obviously,if processes exist forever,the results of a program are to be obtained through procedure calls from an external agent,say a printer).

Now let us recall some basic clauses of the DP syntax (lower level clauses will be be given when defining the translation).

<program> ::= <process> {‖<process>}
<process> ::= <process name> < declaration> { <procedure>} <initial statement>
<procedure> ::= <proc name> ({ <input param> } # { <output param> }) <declaration> <statement>
<statement> ::= <assignment> | <procedure call> | <if statement> | <do statement>
| <when statement> | <cycle statement> | <statement> ; <statement>
| <empty statement>

We denote by V the set of values of the expressions.In what follows S will range over statements;P,Q over process names;R,T over procedure names;E over expressions;B over boolean expressions;D over declarations;X,Y over variables;x,y,u,v,w over values.

1.2 Preliminary comments. Important remark:in what follows strong equivalence between behaviour expressions will be denoted by = instead of $\sim$ as in /M/ pg.77.

In what follows,we give the translation of the DP language into CCS;we recall that CCS is a model for concurrent computation where the only actions are communications between elementary agents;hence the effect of this translation is to represent every step in the execution of a DP program by communications of low-level components.To get just the flavour of the translation,let us consider the case of the assignment. A variable X can be represented by a register of sort $\{\alpha_X,\bar{\gamma}_X\}$,defined as follows:

$$REG(x) \Leftarrow\!\!= \ \underline{if}\ x{=}\emptyset\ \underline{then}\ \alpha y.REG(y)\ \underline{else}\ \alpha y.REG(y)+\gamma x.REG(x)$$ (see /M/ pg.127)

We will abbreviate $REG(x)[{}^{\alpha}X\ {}^{\gamma}X \backslash \alpha\ \gamma]$ by $REG_X(x)$.

Here a register of content x is an agent which can both receive a new value y on the line α and answer an external request sending its content x.These communication capabilities are expressed formally by means of derivation rules:

$REG(x) \xrightarrow{\alpha v} REG(v)$ for every v in the value set of y.

$REG(x) \xrightarrow{\overline{\gamma}x} REG(x)$.

If now we want to model an assignment in CCS, we can write, denoting translation by $[\![\ \ ]\!]$: $[\![X:=E]\!] = ([\![E]\!] \mid \rho u.\overline{\alpha}_X u.\overline{\varepsilon}.NIL)\backslash\rho$.

The behaviour expression $\rho u.\overline{\alpha}_X u.\overline{\varepsilon}.NIL$ can receive the result of the evaluation of E on the line ρ and then send this value to the register X on the line α_X.

The overall effect of the assignment can be represented, using parallel composition, by $B = [\![X:=E]\!] \mid REG_X(x)$.

B is an example of a behaviour expression which can evolve by means of an internal communication (denoted by τ), the one which takes place between the complementary ports α and $\overline{\alpha}$. For more details see /M/ Ch.5.

An expression E with variables $X_1,\dots,X_k$ will be represented by a behaviour program of sort $\{\gamma_{X_1},\dots,\gamma_{X_k}, \overline{\rho}\}$. We assume that the evaluation of an expression always terminates. An expression delivers its result at ρ and then dies; this means that, if $[\![E]\!]$ is the translation of E it has the property:

$[\![E]\!] \dots \xrightarrow{\overline{\rho}v} N$ implies N=NIL.

A procedure identified by R and declared in a process P will be denoted by P:R.

A statement S with variables $X_1,\dots,X_k$ and with calls of the procedures $Q_i:R_j$ for i, j $\in$ I will be represented by a behaviour program of sort $\{\overline{\alpha}_{X_1}, \gamma_{X_1}, \dots, \overline{\alpha}_{X_k}, \gamma_{X_k}, \varepsilon, go, \overline{go}, \overline{fail}, \overline{in\ Q_i:R_j}, out\ Q_i:R_j \mid i,j \in I\}$. $\overline{\alpha}_{X_i}$ and γ_{X_i} are the registers labels above; fail is the label of the channel for sending failure messages (to the external world); go and $\overline{go}$ are "synchronizing labels" for controlling the interleaving of the initial statement and the procedure calls: only one of these components can be active at each moment and the others wait until the active one either terminates or waits for a condition to become true.

A statement signals its termination through $\overline{\varepsilon}$ and then dies; this means that, for every statement S, it has the property:

$[\![S]\!] \dots \xrightarrow{\overline{\varepsilon}} N$ implies N=NIL.

A procedure R with local variables $X_1,\dots,X_k$ and body S_R will be represented by a behaviour program of sort $L([\![R]\!])$, with $L([\![R]\!]) = L(\overline{[\![S_R]\!]})\backslash\{\overline{\alpha}_X, \gamma_X \mid X=X_i \text{ for some } i\} \cup \{in\ R, \overline{out\ R}\}$; in R, $\overline{out\ R}$ will be relabelled P:R, $\overline{out\ P:R}$ via the relabelling function S_P, when inserting a procedure in a process P.

A process P with own procedures $R_1,\dots,R_n$ and calls of the external procedures $\overline{Q_i:T_j}$ for i,j $\in$ I, will be represented by a behaviour program of sort $\{in\ P:R_i, \overline{out\ P:R_i} \mid i=1,\dots,n\} \cup \{\overline{in\ Q_i:T_j}, out\ Q_i:T_j \mid i,j \in I\} \cup \{\overline{fail}\}$.

1.3 Translation.

- $[\![process]\!] = [\![P\ D\ S]\!] = ([\![S]\!] \mid \varepsilon.NIL)\backslash\varepsilon \mid [\![D]\!])\backslash L_D[S_P]$
- $[\![process]\!] = [\![P\ D\ R_1 \dots R_n\ S]\!] = ((([\![S]\!] \mid \varepsilon.\overline{go}.NIL)\backslash\varepsilon) \mid [\![D]\!] \mid [\![R_1]\!] \mid \dots \mid [\![R_n]\!])\backslash go\backslash L_D[S_P]$

where, if $D = X_1:type_1;\dots;X_k:type_k$, $L_D = \{\alpha_{X_1}, \gamma_{X_1}, \dots, \alpha_{X_k}, \gamma_{X_k}\}$ (we will denote by $B\backslash L$, $L = \{\alpha_1,\dots,\alpha_n\}$ the behaviour expression $B\backslash\alpha_1\backslash\dots\backslash\alpha_n$).

S_P is the following relabelling: $S(R) = P{:}R$ for every R procedure name in $L([\![S]\!])$.

Notice that the translation of a process without procedure declaration is slightly different from the translation of a process with procedure declaration; indeed the second one, when its initial statement S terminates (i.e. when $[\![S]\!]$ sends an $\bar{\varepsilon}$ signal) must send to the procedures a start signal $\overline{go}$, which is useless in the first case.

$[\![D]\!] = [\![X_1{:}type_1;\ldots;X_k{:}type_k]\!] = [\![X_1{:}type_1]\!]|\ldots|[\![X_k{:}type_k]\!]$

$[\![X{:}type]\!] = REG_X(\emptyset)$

$[\![\underline{procedure}\ call]\!] = [\![call\ Q{:}R(E_1\ldots E_n,\underline{Y}_1\ldots Y_m)]\!] = ([\![E_1]\!][^{\rho_1}/\rho]|\ldots|[\![E_n]\!][^{\rho_n}/\rho]|\rho_1 u_1.\ \ldots$
$\rho_n u_n.in\ Q{:}R(u_1,\ldots,u_n).out\ Q{:}R\ v_1,\ldots,v_m.\bar{\alpha}_{Y_1}v_1.\ \ldots\ .\bar{\alpha}_{Y_m}v_m.\bar{\varepsilon}.NIL)\backslash\rho_1\backslash\ldots\backslash\rho_n$

$[\![if\ statement]\!] = [\![\underline{if}\ B_1{:}S_1|\ldots|B_n{:}S_n\ \underline{end}]\!] = ([\![B_1]\!][^{\rho_1}/\rho]|\ldots|[\![B_n]\!][^{\rho_n}/\rho]|COND([\![S_1]\!],\ldots$
$\ldots,[\![S_n]\!],\overline{fail}.NIL)\backslash\rho_1\ldots\backslash\rho_n$

$COND(B_1,\ldots,B_{n+1}) = (\beta_1.B_1|\ldots|\beta_{n+1}.B_{n+1}|\rho_1 v_1.\ \ldots\ .\rho_n v_n.\underline{if}$ there exists i s.t. $v_i = tt$
$\underline{then}\ \sum_{i\ s.t.v_i=tt}\bar{\beta}_i.NIL\ \underline{else}\ \bar{\beta}_{n+1}.NIL)\backslash\beta_1\ \ldots\backslash\beta_n$

$[\![do\ statement]\!] = [\![\underline{do}\ B_1{:}S_1|\ldots|B_n{:}S_n\ \underline{end}]\!] = \omega$, a new behaviour identifier where
$\omega \Leftarrow ([\![B_1]\!][^{\rho_1}/\rho]|\ldots|[\![B_n]\!][^{\rho_n}/\rho]|COND([\![S_1]\!]\ before\ \omega,\ldots,[\![S_n]\!]\ before\ \omega,[\![skip]\!])\backslash\rho_1\ ..\backslash\rho_n$
$B\ before\ B' = (B[^{\beta}/\varepsilon]|\beta.B')\backslash\beta \qquad \beta\ new$

$[\![when\ statement]\!] = [\![\underline{when}\ B_1{:}S_1|\ldots|B_n{:}S_n\ \underline{end}]\!] = \psi$, a new behaviour identifier where
$\psi \Leftarrow ([\![B_1]\!][^{\rho_1}/\rho]|\ldots|[\![B_n]\!][^{\rho_n}/\rho],COND([\![S_1]\!],\ldots,[\![S_n]\!],\overline{go}.go.\psi)\backslash\rho_1\backslash\ldots\backslash\rho_n$

$[\![cycle\ statement]\!] = [\![\underline{cycle}\ B_1{:}S_1|\ldots|B_n{:}S_n\ \underline{end}]\!] = \phi$, a new identifier where
$\phi \Leftarrow ([\![B_1]\!][^{\rho_1}/\rho]|\ldots|[\![B_n]\!][^{\rho_n}/\rho]|COND([\![S_1]\!]\ before\ \phi,\ldots,[\![S_n]\!]\ before\ \phi,\overline{go}.go.\phi)\backslash\rho_1..\backslash\rho_n$

$[\![S_1;S_2]\!] = [\![S_1]\!]\ before\ [\![S_2]\!]$

$[\![empty\ statement]\!] = [\![skip]\!] = \bar{\varepsilon}.NIL$

$[\![procedure]\!] = [\![proc\ R(IP_1\ldots IP_n \# OP_1\ldots OP_m)\ D_R\ S_R]\!] = (\omega_R|sync)\backslash end$ where
$\omega_R \Leftarrow (REG_{IP_1}(\emptyset)|\ldots|REG_{IP_m}(\emptyset)|REG_{OP_1}(\emptyset)|\ldots|REG_{OP_m}(\emptyset)|in\ R(v_1,\ldots,v_n).\bar{\alpha}_{IP_1}v_1.\ \ldots$
$\ldots\ .\bar{\alpha}_{IP_n}v_n.go.([\![D_R]\!]|([\![S_R]\!]|\varepsilon.R\text{-}return)\backslash\varepsilon)\backslash L_{D_R})\backslash\alpha_{IP_1}\backslash\gamma_{IP_1}\backslash\ldots\backslash\alpha_{OP_m}\backslash\gamma_{OP_m}$

$R\text{-}return \Leftarrow \gamma_{OP_1}u_1.\ \ldots\ .\gamma_{OP_m}u_m.\overline{out}\ R(u_1,\ldots,u_m).\overline{end}.\omega_R$

$sync \Leftarrow end.go.sync$

sync is an auxiliary behaviour program needed in order to allow a procedure to be ready to answer a new call immediately after an execution.

2.INDUCED DERIVATIONS ON DP TERMS.

Following the hints of the previous Section and, formally, the derivation rules of CCS (/M/ Ch.5), to each translated term is associated a derivation tree. These derivations (together with some equivalence relations, to be discussed later) provide an operational semantics. Dealing with this semantics is not so convenient, since the relationship of CCS to DP is of the kind low-level to high-level language (say P-code to PASCAL). We are thus forced to keep track of many detailed intermediate informations (corresponding to CCS terms which have no significant counterpart at DP level) and transformations (corresponding to some internal communications).

Our aim is to show a method for deriving a higher level operational semantics, dealing only with DP terms and transformations between them.

We will first consider an example, and then outline our approach (omitting proofs, because of lack of space).

Set $B=[\![\text{call } Q:R(E,Y)]\!]$ (recall that we use "=" to denote strong equivalence.)

$[\![\text{call } Q:R(E,Y)]\!] = ([\![E]\!] \mid \rho u.\text{in } Q:R\ u.\text{out } Q:R\ v.\bar{\alpha}_Y v.\bar{\varepsilon}.NIL)\backslash\rho$

Every derivation sequence for $[\![E]\!]$ is of the form:

$[\![E]\!] \xrightarrow{\mu_1 v_1} \dots \xrightarrow{\mu_j v_j} \xrightarrow{\bar{\rho} w} N$ for some $w \in V, \mu_i v_i = \tau$ or $\gamma_X v_i$ for some variable $X (1 \leq i \leq j)$, $N=NIL$.

Then from the inference rules Com-Res (/M/ pg.70-71) every derivation sequence for B is of the form:

$B \xrightarrow{\mu_1 v_1} \dots \xrightarrow{\mu_j v_j} \xrightarrow{\tau} \xrightarrow{\overline{\text{in } Q:R\ w}} \xrightarrow{\text{out } Q:R\ v} \xrightarrow{\bar{\alpha}_Y v} N'$ s.t. $N'=\varepsilon.NIL = [\![\text{skip}]\!]$

Now let C be the behaviour expression $(REG_{Y_1}(y_1) \mid \dots \mid REG_{Y_k}(y_k) \mid (B \mid \varepsilon.W)\backslash\varepsilon)\backslash\alpha_{Y_1}\backslash\gamma_{Y_1}\backslash \dots \gamma_{Y_k}$ ($k \geq 1$) where W is any behaviour expression.

From Com-Res every derivation sequence for C is of the form:

a) if there exists i ($1 \leq i \leq k$) s.t. $Y=Y_i$ then:

$C \xrightarrow{\mu'_1 v'_1} \dots \xrightarrow{\mu'_j v'_j} \xrightarrow{\tau} \xrightarrow{\overline{\text{in } Q:R\ w}} \xrightarrow{\text{out } Q:R\ v} \xrightarrow{\tau} C'$

where C' is

$(REG_{Y_1}(y_1) \mid \dots \mid REG_{Y_i}(v) \mid \dots \mid REG_{Y_k}(y_k) \mid (N' \mid W)\backslash\varepsilon)\backslash\alpha_{Y_1}\backslash\gamma_{Y_1}\backslash \dots \backslash\alpha_{Y_k}\backslash\gamma_{Y_k}$

b) otherwise:

$C \xrightarrow{\mu'_1 v'_1} \dots \xrightarrow{\mu'_j v'_j} \xrightarrow{\tau} \xrightarrow{\overline{\text{in } Q:R\ w}} \xrightarrow{\text{out } Q:R\ v} \xrightarrow{\bar{\alpha}_Y v} C''$

where C'' is

$(REG_{Y_1}(y_1) \mid \dots \mid REG_{Y_k}(y_k) \mid (N' \mid W)\backslash\varepsilon)\backslash\alpha_{Y_1}\backslash\gamma_{Y_1}\backslash \dots \backslash\alpha_{Y_k}\backslash\gamma_{Y_k}$

where for every $i=1,\dots,j$ $\mu'_i v'_i = \mu_i v_i$ if $\mu_i \neq \gamma_{Y_j}$ for every $j (1 \leq j \leq k)$, τ otherwise.

Finally, let D be the behaviour expression

$(C \mid REG_{X_1}(x_1) \mid \dots \mid REG_{X_L}(x_L))\backslash\alpha_{X_1}\backslash\gamma_{X_1}\backslash \dots \backslash\alpha_{X_L}\backslash\gamma_{X_L}$ ($L \geq 1$)

where we suppose that $\{X_1,\dots,X_L\}$ contains all variable names which occur in C and do not in $\{Y_1,\dots,Y_k\}$. We consider two different levels of registers because a DP statement can be part of a procedure body, and in this case it can refer either to local or to global variables. Every derivation sequence for D is of the form:

a) if there exists i ($1 \leq i \leq k$) s.t. $Y=Y_i$ then:

$D\{\xrightarrow{\tau}\}^{*} \xrightarrow{\overline{\text{in } Q:R\ w}} D' \xrightarrow{\text{out } Q:R\ v} \xrightarrow{\tau} (C' \mid REG_{X_1}(x_1) \mid \dots \mid REG_{X_L}(x_L))\backslash\alpha_{X_1}\backslash\gamma_{X_1}\backslash \dots \backslash\alpha_{X_L}\backslash\gamma_{X_L} = D_1$

*) Here and in what follows $\{\xrightarrow{\tau}\}$ will indicate 0 to n consecutive arrows $\xrightarrow{\tau}$.

b) otherwise (and in this case there exists X_i s.t. $Y=X_i$) then:

$D\{\xrightarrow{\tau}\} \xrightarrow{\overline{\text{in } Q:R\ w}} D' \xrightarrow{\text{out } Q:R\ v} \xrightarrow{\tau} (C'' \mid REG_{X_1}(x_1) \mid \dots \mid REG_{X_i}(v) \mid \dots \mid REG_{X_L}(x_L))\backslash\alpha_{X_1}\backslash \dots \backslash\gamma_{X_L} = D_2$

It is clear that, with the following notations:

$B \xrightarrow{\mu_1 v_1 \dots \mu_k v_k} B'$ iff $B \xrightarrow{\mu_1 v_1} B_1 \dots \xrightarrow{\mu_k v_k} B'$ ($k \geq 1$)

$B \xrightarrow{\mu v} B'$ iff $B \xrightarrow{\tau^m \mu v \tau^n} B'$ $(m,n \geq 0)$

we can shortly write

$D \xrightarrow{\overline{\text{in}}\ Q:R\ w} D' \xrightarrow{\text{out}\ Q:R\ v} D_1$ in the case a)

$D \xrightarrow{\overline{\text{in}}\ Q:R\ w} D' \xrightarrow{\text{out}\ Q:R\ v} D_2$ in the case b).

We can apply this analysis to every behaviour expression of the form of D,provided that B=⟦S⟧ for some DP statement S,getting an analogous situation:i.e.,we will find that, after a finite number of derivations D will transform itself in an other behaviour expression of the same form.

At this stage we have found a shorter description of the original CCS derivations using more compact arrows.Now we will introduce shorter notations also for behaviour expressions like D and for some auxiliary elements,like D' above,needed to describe the evolution.

STAT will denote the set of behaviour expressions B s.t. one of the following clauses holds:

i) $B=(\llbracket S \rrbracket|\varepsilon.W)\backslash\varepsilon$ denoted by S

ii) $B=(go.\llbracket S \rrbracket|\varepsilon.W)\backslash\varepsilon$ denoted by start:$\bar{S}$

iii) $B=(out\ Q:R(y_1,\dots,y_m).\bar{\alpha}_{Y_1} y_1. \dots .\bar{\alpha}_{Y_m} y_m.\bar{\varepsilon}.NIL\ [\text{before}\ \llbracket S \rrbracket]\ |\varepsilon.W)\backslash\varepsilon$

denoted by return $Q:R(Y_1,\dots,Y_m)[\ ;S]$

iv) B=NIL denoted by nil.

A generic element of STAT will be denoted by t.

MEM will be the set of the behaviour expressions(generic element s) of the form:

$REG_{Y_1}(y_1)|\dots|REG_{Y_k}(y_k), k\geq 0$

We will denote by L_S the set $\{\alpha_{Y_1},\gamma_{Y_1},\dots,\alpha_{Y_k},\gamma_{Y_k}\}$ and by <t,s> the behaviour expression

$(t|s)\backslash\alpha_{Y_1}\backslash\gamma_{Y_1}\backslash\dots\backslash\alpha_{Y_k}\backslash\gamma_{Y_k}$ where $t \in$ STAT, $s \in$ MEM.

Clearly to each s in MEM we can associate an element ,also denoted by s,of the state-space $SS = VAR \longrightarrow (V \cup \{\bot,\emptyset\})$,defined by:

$s=\lambda X.\text{if } (\exists\ i \text{ s.t. } X=Y_i) \text{ then } y_i \text{ else } \bot$.

Finally we will denote by Bs the behaviour expression $(B|s)\backslash L_s$, $s\in$MEM,with the assumption that the sort of Bs does not contain α_X nor γ_X,for any variable X.

With these shortened notations the above example will become:

$\langle call\ Q:R(E,Y),s\rangle\ s' \xrightarrow{\overline{\text{in}\ Q:R}\ \llbracket E \rrbracket\ s\ s'} \langle return\ Q:R(Y),s\rangle\ s'$

$\langle return\ Q:R(Y),s\rangle\ s' \xrightarrow{\text{out}\ Q:R\ v} \langle skip,s[\frac{v}{Y}]\ s'[\frac{v}{Y}]$

where:

- ⟦E⟧ ss' denotes the value of E w.r. to the local state s and the global state s', names bound in that order;
- $s \in SS$, $s[\frac{v}{X}]=\lambda Y.\text{if } s(X)\neq\bot \text{ and } Y=X \text{ then } v \text{ else } s(Y)$.

We shall now prove that we can apply the technique shown in the example above in order to get an operational semantics on DP terms.More precisely,we will deduce from CCS derivations:

- a relation $\mathcal{S}$ on triples <t,s>s' corresponding to a statement t with local state s and global state s'
- a relation $\mathcal{R}$ on triples <R:r,s> s' corresponding to a procedure R with local state

s and global state s'.

- a relation $\mathcal{P}$ on couples <P:p,s> corresponding to a process P with state s.

The relations $\mathcal{S}$ and $\mathcal{R}$ are needed in order to define in a simpler way the relation $\mathcal{P}$.

Lemma 2.1 The following relations hold:

s1) $<X:=E,s>\ s' \xrightarrow{\tau} <skip, s[\frac{[\![E]\!]ss'}{X}]>\ s'[\frac{[\![E]\!]ss'}{X}]$

s2) $<call\ Q{:}R(E_1 \ldots E_n, Y_1 \ldots Y_m), s>\ s' \xrightarrow{\overline{in\ Q{:}R}([\![E_1]\!]ss', \ldots, [\![E_n]\!]ss')} <return\ Q{:}R(Y_1, \ldots, Y_m), s>\ s'$

s3) $<return\ Q{:}R(Y_1, \ldots, Y_m), s>\ s' \xrightarrow{out\ Q{:}R(v_1, \ldots, v_m)} <skip, s[\frac{v_1}{Y_1}, \ldots, \frac{v_m}{Y_m}]>\ s'[\frac{v_1}{Y_1}, \ldots, \frac{v_m}{Y_m}]$

s4) $<\underline{if}\ B_1{:}S_1|\ldots|B_n{:}S_n\ \underline{end}, s>\ s' \xrightarrow{\tau} <S_i, s>\ s'$ (if $[\![B_i]\!]$ ss'=tt)

$\xrightarrow{\overline{fail}} <nil, s>\ s'$ (if $[\![B_i]\!]$ ss'=ff for every i=1,...,n)

s5) $<\underline{do}\ B_1{:}S_1|\ldots|B_n{:}S_n\ \underline{end}, s>\ s' \xrightarrow{\tau} <skip, s>\ s'$ (if $[\![B_i]\!]$ ss'=ff for every i=1,...,n)

$\xrightarrow{\tau} <S_i; \underline{do} \ldots \underline{end}, s>\ s'$ (if $[\![B_i]\!]$ ss'=tt)

s6) $<\underline{when}\ B_1{:}S_1|\ldots|B_n{:}S_n\ \underline{end}, s>\ s' \xrightarrow{\tau} <S_i, s>\ s'$ (if $[\![B_i]\!]$ ss'=tt)

$\xrightarrow{\overline{go}} <start{:}\underline{when} \ldots \underline{end}, s>\ s'$ (if $[\![B_i]\!]$ ss'=ff for every i=1,...,n.)

s7) $<\underline{cycle}\ B_1{:}S_1|\ldots|B_n{:}S_n\ \underline{end}, s>\ s' \xrightarrow{\tau} <S_i; \underline{cycle} \ldots \underline{end}, s>\ s'$ (if $[\![B_i]\!]$ ss'=tt)

$\xrightarrow{\tau} <start{:}\underline{cycle} \ldots \underline{end}, s>\ s'$ (if $[\![B_i]\!]$ ss'=ff for every i=1,...,n.)

s8) $<start{:}S, s>\ s' \xrightarrow{\overline{go}} <S, s>\ s'$

s9) a) $<t_1, s_1> s'_1 \xrightarrow{c} <t'_1, s_2> s'_2 \Longrightarrow <t_1; t_2, s_1>\ s'_1 \xrightarrow{c} <t'_1; t_2, s_2>\ s'_2$

b) $<skip; S, s>\ s' \xrightarrow{\tau} <S, s>\ s'$

c) $<t_1, s_1> s'_1 \xrightarrow{\overline{fail}} <nil, s_2>\ s'_2 \Longrightarrow <t_1; t_2, s>\ s' \xrightarrow{\overline{fail}} <nil, s_2>\ s'_2$

s10) $<skip, s>\ s' \xrightarrow{\tau} <nil, s>\ s'$ if $W=\varepsilon.NIL$ in skip

$\xrightarrow{\overline{go}} <nil, s>\ s'$ if $W=\varepsilon.\overline{go}.NIL$ in skip. //

Definition 2.1 $\mathcal{S}$ denotes the labelled relation on triples <t,s> s'(t∈STAT,s,s'∈MEM) defined by s1-s10.(We will denote this relation by $\xrightarrow[\mathcal{S}]{c}$). //

Consider now a procedure $R(IP_1 \ldots IP_n \# OP_1 \ldots OP_m)\ D_R\ S_R$ where $D_R = VL_1{:}type_1; \ldots; VL_k{:}type_k$.

PRCD will denote the set of behaviour expressions B s.t. one of the following clauses holds:

i) $B=(\omega_R|sync)\backslash end$

ii) $B=(((REG_{IP_1}(v_1)|\ldots|REG_{IP_n}(v_n)|REG_{OP_1}(\emptyset)|\ldots|REG_{OP_m}(\emptyset)|go.<S_R,s>)\backslash\alpha_{IP_1}\backslash\gamma_{IP_1}\backslash\ldots\backslash\alpha_{OP_1}\backslash\gamma_{OP_m})|sync)\backslash end$

where in $<S_R,s>$ W is R-return, s∈MEM, $s=\lambda X.$if there exists i s.t. $X=VL_i$ then $\emptyset$ else $\perp$.

iii) $B=(((REG_{IP_1}(v_1)|\ldots|REG_{IP_n}(v_n)|REG_{OP_1}(u_1)|\ldots|REG_{OP_m}(u_m)|<t,s>)\backslash\alpha_{IP_1}\backslash\gamma_{IP_1}\backslash\ldots$
$\backslash\alpha_{OP_m}\backslash\gamma_{OP_m})|sync)\backslash end$

where $t\in STAT$, W in $<t,s>$ is R-return, $s\in MEM$, $s(VL_i)\neq\perp$ for every $i=1,\ldots,k$.

iv) $B=(\omega_R|\overline{go}.sync)\backslash end$

We will denote an element of PRCD:

- by $<R:call:start:S_R,\emptyset>$ in the case i) (where $\emptyset\in SS$, $\emptyset=\lambda X.$if there exists i s.t. $X=OP_i$ or $X=IP_i$ or $X=VL_i$ then $\emptyset$ else $\perp$);
- by $<R:start:S_R,\bar{s}>$ in the case ii) (where $\bar{s}=\lambda X.$if there exists i s.t. $X=IP_i$ then v_i else if there exists i s.t. $X=OP_i$ or $X=VL_i$ then $\emptyset$ else $\perp$);
- by $<R:t,\hat{s}>$ in the case iii) (where $\hat{s}=\lambda X.$if there exists i s.t. $X=IP_i$ then v_i else if there exists i s.t. $X=OP_i$ then u_i else $s(X)$);
- by $<R:end,\emptyset>$ in the case iv).

We will denote by $<R:r,s>$ a generic element of PRCD.

<u>Lemma 2.2</u> The following relations hold:

R1) $<t,s_1>s_1' \xrightarrow[\mathcal{S}]{c} <t',s_2>s_2' \Longrightarrow <R:t,s_1>s_1' \xrightarrow{c} <R:t',s_2>s_2'$

R2) $<R:call:start:S_R,\emptyset>s' \xrightarrow{in\ R(v_1,\ldots,v_n)} <R:start:S_R,\emptyset[\frac{v_1}{IP_1}\ldots\frac{v_n}{IP_n}]\ s'$

R3) $<R:skip,s>s' \xrightarrow{\overline{out}\ R(s(OP_1),\ldots,s(OP_m))} <R:end,\emptyset>s'$

R4) $<R:end,\emptyset>s' \xrightarrow{in\ R(v_1,\ldots,v_n)} <R:S_R,\emptyset[\frac{v_1}{IP_1}\ldots\frac{v_n}{IP_n}]\ s'$

$\xrightarrow{\overline{go}} <R:call:start:S_R,\emptyset>s'$ //

<u>Definition 2.2</u> $\mathcal{R}$ denotes the labelled relation on couples $<R:r,s>s'$ ($<R:r,s>\in PRCD$, $s'\in MEM$) defined by R1-R4. (We will denote this relation by $\xrightarrow[\mathcal{R}]{c}$).//

PROC will denote the set of behaviour expressions B s.t. one of the following clauses holds:

i) $B=<t,s>[S_P]$

ii) $B=(t|s_o|<R_1:r_1,s_1>|\ldots|<R_n:r_n,s_n>)\backslash go\backslash L_S[S_P]$ $n\geq 1$, for some $t\in STAT$ s.t. W in t is now $\overline{go}$.NIL, $s,s_o\in MEM$, $<R_i:r_i,s_i>\in PRCD(1\leq i\leq n)$, P process name.

We will denote an element of PROC:

- by $<P:t,s>$ in the case i);
- by $<P:t;R_1:r_1;\ldots,R_n:r_n,\hat{s}>$ in the case ii) (where $\hat{s}=s_o,\ldots,s_n$). In this case we denote also $t;R_1:r_1;\ldots;R_n:r_n$ by $c_o;\ldots;c_n$; we set $s_o'=\perp$, $s_i'=s_o$ $(1\leq i\leq n)$.

We will denote by $<P:p,s>$ a generic element of PROC.

<u>Lemma 2.3</u> The following relations hold:

P1) $<t,s_1> \xrightarrow[\mathcal{S}]{c} <t',s_2> \Longrightarrow <P:t,s_1> \xrightarrow{S_P(c)} <P:t',s_2>$

P2) $<c_i,s_i>s_i' \xrightarrow[\mathcal{L}]{c} <c_i',\bar{s}_i>\bar{s}_i'$

$$\Longrightarrow \langle P:c_o;\ldots;c_n,\hat{s}\rangle \xrightarrow{S_P(c)} \langle P:c_o;\ldots;c_i';\ldots;c_n,\hat{s}[\tfrac{\bar{s}_i'}{s_o}][\tfrac{s_i'}{s_i}]\rangle \quad c\neq go,\overline{go}$$

$\mathcal{L}$ ranges in $\{\mathcal{G},\mathcal{R}\}$

P3) $\langle c_i,s_i\rangle\, s_i' \xrightarrow[\mathcal{L}]{\overline{go}} \langle c_i',\bar{s}_i\rangle\, \bar{s}_i'$ and $\langle c_j,s_j\rangle\, s_j' \xrightarrow[\mathcal{L}]{go} \langle c_j',\bar{s}_j\rangle\, \bar{s}_j'$

$$\Longrightarrow \langle P:c_o;\ldots;c_n,\hat{s}\rangle \xrightarrow{\tau} \langle P:c_o;\ldots;c_i';\ldots;c_j';\ldots;c_n,\hat{s}\rangle \qquad //$$

Definition 2.3 $\mathcal{P}$ denotes the labelled relation on PROC defined by P1-P3.(We will denote this relation by $\xrightarrow[\mathcal{P}]{c}$). //

The relation $\mathcal{P}$ can be assumed as the basic relation giving an operational semantics on DP processes;indeed in the following section we shall see that from $\mathcal{P}$ we can derive the semantics we get when dealing in CCS with the terms obtained by translation.

3.SEMANTICS.

In CCS,semantics is assigned via equivalence relations.Different equivalences have been proposed,reflecting different points of view on what is meant intuitively by "equivalence of concurrent processes"(see /M/ Ch.5 and 7,and /HP/).Presently the best one seems to be a version of "observational equivalence"(/M/ pg.98) which takes into account the possibility of divergent computations(see,e.g. /HP/;technically we have $\tau^\omega \neq$ NIL).

Here we show in outline that the relation $\mathcal{P}$ on DP processes and the relation $\mathcal{M}$ on the CCS behaviour expressions obtained by translation from DP processes define the same equivalence classes,hence giving the same semantics.Proofs are omitted for lack of space(they are not trivial).

Let $\mathcal{R}$ be a labelled relation on (E,Σ) where we assume $\tau \in \Sigma$.

Definition 3.1 If $x,x',y,y' \in E, c \in \Sigma$

i) $x \overset{\tau}{\underset{\mathcal{R}}{\Longrightarrow}} x$

ii) if $x \overset{\tau}{\underset{\mathcal{R}}{\Longrightarrow}} x'$ and $x' \xrightarrow[\mathcal{R}]{c} y'$ and $y' \overset{\tau}{\underset{\mathcal{R}}{\Longrightarrow}} y$ then $x \overset{c}{\underset{\mathcal{R}}{\Longrightarrow}} y$.

iii) $x\Downarrow\mathcal{R}$ iff $[x \xrightarrow[\mathcal{R}]{\tau} x'$ implies $x'\Downarrow\mathcal{R}$,for every $x' \in E]$.//

Definition 3.2 Let $\mathcal{R}$,$\mathcal{R}'$ be two labelled relations on respectively (E,Σ) and (D,Σ); define inductively:

$-\langle x,\mathcal{R}\rangle \approx_o \langle y,\mathcal{R}'\rangle$ for $x \in E, y \in D$

$-\langle x,\mathcal{R}\rangle \approx_{k+1} \langle y,\mathcal{R}'\rangle$ iff i) and ii) hold:

i) $x \overset{c}{\underset{\mathcal{R}}{\Longrightarrow}} x'$ implies $y \overset{c}{\underset{\mathcal{R}'}{\Longrightarrow}} y'$and $\langle x',\mathcal{R}\rangle \approx_k \langle y,\mathcal{R}'\rangle$ and conversely;

ii) $x\Downarrow\mathcal{R}$ iff $y\Downarrow\mathcal{R}'$.

Then set $\langle x,\mathcal{R}\rangle \approx \langle y,\mathcal{R}'\rangle$ iff $\langle x,\mathcal{R}\rangle \approx_k \langle y,\mathcal{R}'\rangle$ for every k.//

We write $x \approx_{\mathcal{R}} y$ iff $\langle x,\mathcal{R}\rangle \approx \langle y,\mathcal{R}\rangle$.

In what follows $\mathcal{M}$ will denote the labelled relation defined in /M/,i.e. the relation generated by the derivations in CCS.

The main result is the following:

Theorem 3.1 $\langle P,\mathcal{M}\rangle \approx \langle P,\mathcal{P}\rangle$ for every $P \in$ PROC.//

Corollary 3.2 If $P,Q \in$ PROC,then:

$$\langle P,\mathcal{M}\rangle \approx \langle Q,\mathcal{M}\rangle \quad \text{iff} \quad \langle P,\mathcal{P}\rangle \approx \langle Q,\mathcal{P}\rangle\ .//$$

The interpretation of this result is straightforward,recalling that $\mathcal{P}$ can be seen as a relation on DP terms (with some extra terms),forgetting their CCS structure from which they have been derived.The necessary presence of some extra terms in the relation

$\mathcal{P}$ seems to be a contribution we have gained, without much effort, from the translation into CCS. Indeed it is interesting to note that terms of this kind look necessary for a definition of inference rules on DP terms; similar terms can be found, for example, in /RDKR/, where an Hoare-like system is considered.

Let us discuss briefly the case of programs. Recall that <program> ::= $\langle process_1 \rangle \| \ldots \| \langle process_n \rangle$, where $\|$ denotes parallel composition on DP processes. Since no special assumption is made about termination, we could simply set $[\![program]\!] = [\![process_1]\!] | \ldots | [\![process_n]\!]$ (notice that this is not true for CSP programs, see /AZ/). Then a new relation $\mathcal{O}$ on DP programs can be derived from $\mathcal{P}$, simply adding the inference clauses Com(/M/pg. 70) on parallel composition. That $\mathcal{O}$ defines the same equivalence classes on programs as $\mathcal{M}$, follows from the fact that $\approx_{\mathcal{M}}$ and $\approx_{\mathcal{P}}$ are congruences w.r. to the | operation. Moreover since a process is also a program, it follows that $\overset{c}{\approx}_{\mathcal{M}}$ and $\overset{c}{\approx}_{\mathcal{P}}$ coincide respectively with $\approx_{\mathcal{M}}$ and $\approx_{\mathcal{P}}$. (Recall from /M/ that $B \overset{c}{\approx} B'$ iff for every program context $\mathcal{C}[\ ]$, $\mathcal{C}[B] \approx \mathcal{C}[B']$). Hence the agreement between $\mathcal{O}$-operational semantics on DP programs and $\mathcal{M}$-operational semantics on the corresponding CCS programs could be considered satisfactory.

But now two problems arise, which we can only mention here.

First, the above translation is in principle incorrect, since parallel composition in CCS is explained via interleaving, while $\|$ does permit simultaneous independent actions. Though this difference should not affect in this case the resulting semantics, another formal treatment has to be adopted (see /M1/ for a theory of synchronous CCS).

Moreover the notion of program should be discussed. Indeed, here we have not a terminal global state, which could be considered the result of a computation, as in the case of CSP (see /AZ/); thus results can only be obtained by means of procedure calls. Hence obviously we cannot say that a program is closed w.r.to procedure names (as a CSP program is closed w.r.to process names) : some procedure names should be reserved for external communication, say for output to a line printer. Then two programs should be considered equivalent whenever they have the same set of (external) results, irrespective of their internal structure, which is instead taken into account in the equivalence $\approx$.

Some work is in progress on these topics. We hope to come out with a full answer to the two mentioned questions, together with a translation which does not make any restriction on contemporary calls of a procedure.

References.

/AZ/ E.Astesiano, E.Zucca, Semantics of CSP via translation into CCS, Quaderni CNET 22 ETS Pisa (March 1981), also to appear in Proc. MFCS'81, LNCS, Springer Verlag.

/BH/ P.Brinch Hansen, Distributed Processes, a concurrent programming concept, Comm. ACM 21,11,1978.

/HLP/ M.Hennessy, W.Li, G.Plotkin A first attempt at translating CSP into CCS, Proc. of the 2nd International Conference on Distributed Computing Systems, IEEE Comp.Soc.Press, Maryland, 1981.

/HP/ M.Hennessy, G.Plotkin, A term model for CCS, Proc.MFCS'80, LNCS 92, Springer Verlag 1980.

/M/ R.Milner, A calculus of Communicating System, LNCS 92, Springer Verlag 1980.

/M1/ R.Milner, On relating Synchrony and Asynchrony, preprint, Univ. Edinburgh, 1980.

/RDKR/ H.Roncken, N.van Diepen, M.Kramer, W.P.de Roever, A proof system for Brinch Hansen's Distributed Processes ,in this volume.

A PROOF SYSTEM FOR BRINCH HANSEN's DISTRIBUTED PROCESSES

M. Roncken
R. Gerth
W.P. de Roever
University of Utrecht, Holland

CONTENTS

We present a sketch of a proof system for proving partial correctness of Brinch Hansen's Distributed Processes as described in 'Distributed Processes: A Concurrent Programming Concept, CACM 21-11, p. 934-941, 1978. The organisation of this extended abstract is as follows:

1. THE LANGUAGE CONCEPT DP

1.1. Program execution

A DP program consists of a fixed number of concurrent and persistent processes, that are started simultaneously. We assume the processes as being numbered, hence the program is denoted as $(P_1 \| \dots \| P_n)$, $n \geq 2$. A process does not contain parallel statements, nor shared variables. The syntax of a process is as follows:

process *<name>*
<private variables>
<common procedures>
<initial statement>

A process P is executed by starting execution of its *initial statement*, which may then be interleaved with the execution of calls of other processes, named *external requests*, to *common procedures* of P. Executing new procedure-incarnations, activated by external requests, is the only form of communication between processes. Syntax of a procedure:

<u>proc</u> *<name>(<input parameter list> #<output parameter list>)*

<statements>

(The separator '#' is omitted when only input parameters occur)

The parameter transfer mechanism (dubbed *call-by-io*) works as follows: before executing the procedure body, the expression-values are assigned to the input parameters and afterwards the values of the output parameters are assigned to the output-variables of the call. Within a procedure body, we do not allow assignments to input-parameters. An external request is considered a *critical section* within the calling process: the caller is suspended until the callee has finished execution of the corresponding procedure-incarnation. Hence, in particular, recursive procedures and requests of a process to procedures declared within itself are illegal.

1.2. Synchronization and nondeterminism

Synchronization is established, primarily, by means of so called *guarded regions*. These are two of a kind:

when-statement: <u>when</u> $b_1 : S_1 \mid \ldots \mid b_n : S_n$ <u>end</u>
with meaning: *wait* until at least one of the (boolean) guards b_i is true, then select arbitrarily for execution one of the corresponging S_i.

cycle-statement: <u>cycle</u> $b_1 : S_1 \mid \ldots \mid b_n : S_n$ <u>end</u>
meaning: endless repetition of the corresponding <u>when</u>-statement.

Synchronization can occur in a process
(1) when waiting at a guarded region, because all guards were false on arrival,
(2) when waiting after execution of its initial statement,
(3) upon completion of an external request to one of its common procedures.

The points waiting at in 1-3 are called *waiting points*.
By synchronization we mean either
(1) the act of honouting an, arbitrarily selected, external request, or
(2) the act of resuming execution of a guarded region (having been a waiting point earlier on and still to be resumed) as result of a guard being true (this resembles a *coroutine-mode of execution* within the process). Notice that synchronization introduces an *implicit* form of nondeterminism.

2. THE PROOF SYSTEM

2.1. Introduction of general invariant, auxiliary variables, bracketed sections and process invariant

The main characteristic of DP, on which the proof system is built, is the *synchronization-at-waiting-points*, in particular the interplay between external requests and the coroutine-mode of operation (cf. 1.2). A clear picture of this is essential for understanding the proof system. Figure 1 shows the execution of 3 processes, P_1, P_2 and P_3. The horizontal lines represent the time-axes for each of the respective processes, on which execution proceeds. During execution of P_1 an external request is made, the action of which is atomic w.r.t. P_1, as indicated by the brackets '<' and '>'. Execution of P_2 proceeds until a waiting point is encountered, denoted by the (leftmost) vertical wriggles, at which synchronization takes place. P_2 continues by honouring P_1's request and starting execution of a new incarnation of pr_2. During this execution, other waiting points are encountered and external requests are made. Finally execution arrives at the end of the procedure-body, after which P_1 and P_2 proceed independently. At parameter-passing, external information from the caller (P_1) will be injected into the callee (P_2) by the input-parameters at the beginning of the procedure execution and vice versa at the end.

The proof system captures these process-interactions by introduction of the *general invariant, GI,* which will keep track of the changes in the process-states created by these external requests. To be able to express properties about each of the process-states, a new class, *AV,* of *auxiliary variables* is introduced, the need of which is a well-known phenomena for parallel programs (2) . Because the validity of GI is required only when parameter-passing takes place, updating the variables of GI may be restricted to these points. For each call, there are at most two places where parameter-passing occurs (on account of the call-by-io mechanism): at the beginning and at the end of procedure execution. We refine the notion of *bracketed section* (cf. figure 1, the execution axis of P_1) by associating with the opening bracket in P_1 the leftmost closing bracket in P_2, and with the closing-bracket in P_1 the rightmost opening bracket in P_2. Now, validity of GI is checked by examining whether GI is left valid by execution of each bracketed section.

While GI describes synchronization activities *globally,* a *process invariant, PI* (one for each process), describes the coroutine mechanism *within the process,* i.e., PI expresses a condition on the process-state at the moment that new requests can be accepted.

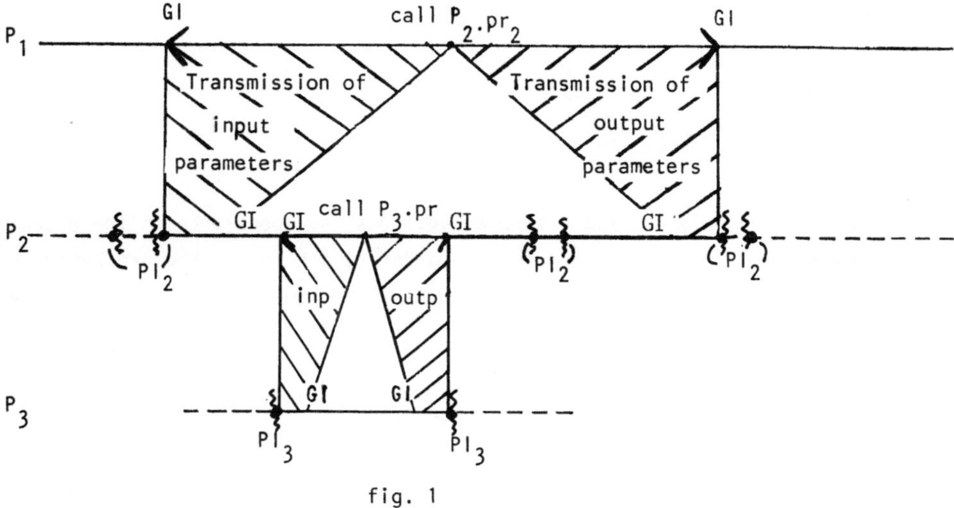

fig. 1

2.2. The proof-rules

We only discuss the rules that are characteristic for DP. A complete list of rules and axioms can be found in (4).

2.2.1. Rule for guarded regions: the when-rule

$$\frac{\{p\wedge b_1\}\ S_1\ \{q\},\ \ldots,\ \{p\wedge b_n\}\ S_n\ \{q\},\quad p\wedge\neg\bigvee_{j=1}^{n} b_j \rightarrow PI\wedge at(S),\quad \{b_1\wedge PI\wedge at(S)\}\ S_1\ \{q\},\ \ldots,\ \{b_n\wedge PI\wedge at(S)\}\ S_n\ \{q\}}{\{p\}\ \underline{\text{when}}\ b_1 : S_1\ |\ \ldots\ |\ b_n : S_n\ \underline{\text{end}}\ \{q\}}$$

This rule is of interest, because the when-statement may serve as a waiting point, and hence enable the process to synchronize. In the preceding section, we demanded that at this moment PI holds, which is expressed by the second premiss. Whenever the statement is resumed again, p need not hold. However, in this case process-control had arrived at "another" waiting point, which has made PI valid again. Thus, we have arrived at a situation equivalent to the guarded conditional with pre-assertion $PI\wedge at(S)$, whence the third premiss. Here $PI\wedge at(S)$ specializes to that part of PI applicable to S. The first premiss covers the case that the when-statement does not act as a waiting point. Observe that the specialization in PI to locations introduces the notion of *interference freedom test* (3), which will not be discussed in this abstract.

2.2.2. Rules for external requests: bracketed-section-rule and call-rule

bracketed section-rule

$$\frac{\{p \wedge GI\}\ S\ \{q \wedge GI\}}{\{p\}\ \langle S\rangle\ \{q\}}$$

GI's validity is assured only outside bracketed sections, so appearance of the bracketed section rule should not come as a surprise. In order to get inside the bracketed section surrounding the call, application of the call-rule is always preceded by an appeal to the bracketed-section-rule.

call-rule

$$\frac{\{p \wedge PI_j\}\ T\ (.)\ \{p_1(.) \wedge p_2 \wedge GI\},\quad \{p_1\}\ T\ \{q_1\},\quad \{p_2 \wedge q_1(.)\}\ T_2(.)\ \{q \wedge PI_j\}}{\{p\}\ \underline{\text{call}}\ P_j.pr(\bar{x},\bar{y})\ \{q\}}$$

where:

(1) P_i contains the call-statement ($i \neq j$)

(2) P_j contains the declaration proc $pr(\bar{u}\#\ \bar{v})\ T_1;\rangle\ T\ \langle;T_2$

(3) $(.) = (x/u, y/v)$

(4) $free(p) \cup free(q) \subseteq free(P_i) \cup free(GI)$

(5) $free(p_2) \subseteq free(P_i) \setminus (free(\bar{x}) \cup \bar{y})$

(6) $free(p_1) \cup free(q_1) \subseteq free(P_j)$

The form of the call-rule may be somewhat difficult to appreciate. To explain the particular form of the premisses, notice that the first premiss captures the assignment to the input parameters; likewise the third premiss expresses the transfer of the output parameter values. The second premiss is to be copied directly from the proof of the procedure body: hence the procedure body is proved correct only once. As for the appearance of GI, remember that the call-rule is always combined with the bracketed section rule which, moreover, implies that the assertions p and q may contain auxiliary variables free in GI but not necessarily owned by P_i. The intermediate assertion p_2 is needed because q may contain only free variables belonging to process P_i, which are not allowed to occur free in p_1 and q_1, as we want to keep the proofs of each of the processes as isolated from each other as possible. Finally, the appearance of the process invariant PI of process P_j should be clear from the fact that the call can be honoured only if P_j arrives at a waiting point and from the fact that its completion leaves control at a waiting point.

Note: It may inspire the reader's confidence to know that the call-rule, together with Apt's *variable-substitution-rule*, can be based completely on the call-rules in (1, ch. 6.1.1).

2.2.3. Rule for parallel composition

$$\frac{\{p_i\}\ \mathrm{Init}_i\ \{q\},\ \text{and}\ \mathrm{PI}_i\ \text{is interference free},\ i = 1..n}{\{\bigwedge_{i=1}^{n} p_i \wedge GI\}(P_1 \parallel \dots \parallel P_n)\{\bigwedge_{i=1}^{n} q_i \wedge GI\}}$$

where,

(1) PI_i denotes the process invariant of process P_i,
(2) Init_i is the initial statement of process P_i,
(3) $PI_i \wedge after(Init_i) \rightarrow q_i$.

This rule should be clear, except for the interference freedom test, introduced by the specialization in PI (cf. 2.2.1.).

2.2.4. Miscellaneous rules

Besides the above rules, we have the usual *composition, consequence, conjunction, disjunction, substitution, quarded selection, guarded loop, assignment* and *skip-rules* and *axioms*, completed with the *auxiliary variable (AV) rule* (3):

$$\frac{\{p\}\ S'\ \{q\}}{\{p\}\ S\ \{q\}}$$

, provided free(q) $\cap$ AV = $\emptyset$ and S is obtained from S' by deleting all assignments of the form x := t, for x $\in$ AV

used to remove auxiliary variables, introduced to execute the proof.

Literature references in this section:

(1) Apt, K.R., Ten years of Hoare logic, to appear.
(2) Clint, M., 1973, Program proving: Coroutines, Acta Inf. 2, p. 50-63.
(3) Owicki, S., D. Gries, 1976, An Axiomatic Proof Technique for Parallel Programs I, Acta Inf. 6, p. 319-340.
(4) Roncken, M., N. van Diepen, M. Kramer, W.P. de Roever, 1981, A Proof System for Brinch Hansen's Distributed Processes, Technical Report.

Further ideas of the proof system may be found in:

(5) Apt, K.R., N. Francez, W.P. de Roever, 1980, A Proof System for Communicating Sequential Processes, TOPLAS 2-3, p. 359-385.

3. EXAMPLE

Two monkeys are obliged to write the word 'HUMBUG' in order to get a banana. They can do this by requesting process writer to type one of the syllables 'HUM' or 'BUG', which in cooperation and depending on the typing order may lead to the desired result. The two monkeys are represented by a so called *process-array* monkey (2), which is a shorthand notation for having 2 identical processes in the DP-program. This example exhibits synchronization by means of a when-statement. The single guard "x=2" of the when-statement in process writer is initially made false, which implies that the when-statement will act as a waiting point. As a consequence, the outstanding requests for procedure type will be honoured. Because each execution of procedure type increases the value of x by 1, both requests must be honoured before execution of the when-statement can be resumed. Now, let the processes be numbered as follows: $P_1 \equiv$ monkey (1), $P_2 \equiv$ monkey (2), $P_3 \equiv$ writer. To prove:

$$\{\underline{true}\}\ (P_1 \| P_2 \| P_3)\{word = \langle HUMBUG\rangle \vee message = \langle NO\_BANANAS\_TODAY\rangle\}.$$

For this purpose, we choose the following invariants and proof outlines:

$PI_i \equiv h_i=1$ for $i=1,2$ and $PI_3 \equiv PI_3' \wedge len(word)=h_3 \wedge h_3=x$, where

$PI_3' \equiv (x=0 \rightarrow (\neg b \vee word = \langle\rangle) \wedge (x=1 \rightarrow ((b \wedge BUG \in word) \vee (\neg b \wedge HUM \in word)) \wedge$
$(x=2 \rightarrow (\neg b \vee word = \langle HUMBUG\rangle)) \wedge (after(Init_3) \rightarrow POST)$, and

$POST \equiv$ (HUM , BUG $\in$ word (in this order) $\vee$ message = $\langle NO\_BANANAS\_TODAY\rangle$),

$GI \equiv h_1 + h_2 = h_3$.

Here, the auxiliary variables h_1 and h_2 keep count of the number of calls to procedure type in P_1, respectively P_2, while h_3 keeps count of the number of honoured calls to procedure type and as such of the syllablelength of word (denoted len(word)). The original text, i.e., without additions of auxiliary variables, is lined out in normal lettertype.

<u>process</u> monkey (j)'
h_j : *int*
<u>proc</u> eat(x) $\{PI_j\}$ <u>begin</u> >"eat x"< <u>end</u> $\{PI_j\}$
$\{h_j=0\}$ <u>begin</u> $\{h_j=0\}$< <u>call</u> writer'.type; $h_j := 1$ > $\{PI_j\}$ <u>end</u> $\{PI_j \wedge after(Init_j)\}$

<u>process</u> writer'
b : boolean; x : int; word : <u>seq</u>(2) syllable; message : <u>seq</u> (16) <u>char</u>; h_3 : *int*
<u>proc</u> type $\{PI_3\}$ <u>begin</u> >
  $\{PI_3\}$ <u>if</u> <u>true</u> : $\{PI_3\}$ word := word^< HUM > ;b := <u>false</u>
    $\{PI_3' \wedge h_3=x \wedge len(word)=h_3+1 \wedge \neg b \wedge HUM \in word\}$
  | <u>true</u> : $\{PI_3\}$ word := word^< BUG>; b := ¬b;
    $\{len(word)=h_3+1 \wedge x=h_3 \wedge (x=0 \rightarrow b \wedge BUG \in word) \wedge (x=1 \rightarrow ((\neg b \wedge word=\langle BUGBUG\rangle)$
    $\vee (b \wedge word=\langle HUMBUG\rangle)) \wedge (after(Init_3) \rightarrow POST))\}$

```
      end;
      x := x+1; { PI_3'∧ x=h_3+1 ∧ len(word)=h_3+1 }
   <h_3:=h_3+1 end{ PI_3 }
   { h_3=0 } begin b := false; x := 0; message := word := <> ;
   { PI_3∧ x ≠ 2 } when x=2 : { PI_3∧ x=2 ∧ b} { word= <HUMBUG> }
                        if b : { word= <HUMBUG> }< call monkey (1 ).eat(banana)>;
                               < call monkey (2 ).eat(banana)>{ word= <HUMBUG> }
                        | ¬b : {PI_3} message :=  <NO_BANANAS_TODAY>
                               {message = <NO_BANANAS_TODAY>}
                        end {POST }
                    end {POST }
          end {PI_3 ∧ after(Init_3 ) }
```

We only prove the call to procedure type and the when-statement in writer. The rest is trivial or follows directly from the proof outline (using the assignment and skip-axioms and composition, consequence and conjunction-rules).

Consider the call in P_1'. We have to prove $\{h_1=0\}$ call writer.type; $h_1 := 1$ $\{PI_1\}$

By the bracketed-section-rule (and the assignment axiom) this reduces to proving:

$\{h_1=0 \wedge PI_3 \wedge GI\}$ skip $\{h_1=0 \wedge PI_3 \wedge GI\}$

$\{PI_3\}$ "body of type" $\{PI_3' \wedge x=h_3+1 \wedge len(word)=h_3+1\}$

$\{PI_3' \wedge x=h_3+1 \wedge len(word)=h_3+1 \wedge h_1=0 \wedge GI\}$ $h_3 := h_3+1$ $\{h_2=h_3-1 \wedge h_2 \leq 1 \wedge h_1=0 \wedge PI_3\}$.

All this follows readily from the definitions, the proof outline of P_3' and the assignment and skip-axioms.

We next consider the when-statement. As $(PI_3 \wedge x \neq 2 \wedge x=2) \leftrightarrow$ false and $PI_3 \wedge x \neq 2 \rightarrow PI_3$, we obtain by the usual rules the validity of the first two premisses of the when-rule. As to the third premiss, this is shown in the proof-outline, whence application of the when-rule is allowed.

Thus, we proved $\{h_j=0\}$ $Init_j$ $\{PI_j \wedge after(Init_j)\}$ for j=1,2,3.

Application of the parallel-composition-rule, consequence and conjunction-rules gives $\{h_1=h_2=h_3=0 \wedge GI\}$ $(P_1' \| P_2' \| P_3')$ $\{(\bigwedge_{j=1}^{3} (PI_j \wedge after(Init_j)) \wedge GI\}$.

Finally, using the AV-rule and substituting 0 for h_1, h_2, and h_3 delivers the desired formula {true}$(P_1 \| P_2 \| P_3)$ {word = <HUMBUG> ∨ message = <NO_BANANAS_TODAY>}.

There remains the interference freedom test, which is informally satisfied by noticing the invariance of POST w.r.t. the body of procedure type.

Implementations of abstract data types and their verification

Jacques Loeckx

Fachbereich 10
Universität des Saarlandes
D-6600 Saarbrücken

1. Introduction

Algorithmic specifications of abstract data types have been introduced in [Lo 81a]. While being strongly related to the algebraic specification method used by e. g. [GH 78a, GHM 78b, Mu 80] the algorithmic specification method avoids several of its problems; it provides for instance an elegant way for handling undefined and error values; moreover it is felt to be easier to use for the specification of non-trivial data types.

The purpose of the present paper is to introduce the notion of implementation of a data type in the framework of the algorithmic specification method and to present *implementation conditions* which guarantee the correctness of an implementation. The paper is a sketch rather than a full treatment of the subject; it contains no formal developments, no proofs and only a trivial example; for more details the reader is referred to [Lo 80b, Lo 81b].

Section 2 presents an overview of the algorithmic specification method. Section 3 introduces the notion of an implementation. Section 4 presents the implementation conditions. Section 5 contains an example.

2. The algorithmic specification method

2.1. Algorithmic specifications

According to [Lo 81a] an algorithmic specification of an abstract data type, say τ, consists of:

(i) a list of *constructors* of type τ, such as (for τ = *Stack*):

emptystack: $\rightarrow$ *Stack*

push : *Stack* x *Integer* $\rightarrow$ *Stack* ;

these constructors define a *term language* similar to the carrier set of the word algebra of [ADJ 78]; as a difference a constructor is a purely syntactical object which is <u>not</u> to be interpreted as a function;

(ii) a predicate noted Is.τ which defines a subset of the term language; this predicate may be viewed as an "invariant" of the type;

(iii) a predicate noted Eq.τ which defines an equivalence relation in the term language; this predicate may be viewed as defining the equality for the type;

(iv) some *external* (or: *user*) functions on term languages such as Push or Pop;

(v) possibly some *auxiliary* (or: *hidden*) functions.

Examples are in Figure 1, 3 and 4.

In the function definitions the following "basic" functions (defined over the term languages) may be used:

- for each constructor, say *cons*, a 1-ary predicate *Is.cons*, the value of which is <u>true</u> iff it starts with the constructor *cons*;
- a "projector function" which extracts an "argument" of a constructor; the value of this function is denoted by the array notation; for instance, if t is a term of the form $cons(u, v)$ then $t[1] = u$ and $t[2] = v$.

The formalism used for the function definitions is (pure) LCF [Mi 72], i. e. a function is defined as an LCF-term. Such a term is built up from constants, variables and functions by composition, λ-abstraction and minimal fixpoint abstraction. The latter is expressed with the help of the operator α : if t is an LCF-term and M a function variable, $[\alpha M.t]$ denotes the minimal fixpoint of $[\lambda M.t]$. In order to be able to apply the LCF-formalism each term language is transformed into a flat lattice by the addition of the *undefined value* ω as the bottom element and the *error value* Ω as the top element.

For more precision and details the reader is referred to [Lo 81a].

2.2 Hierarchical sets of specifications

Consider a finite set $\underline{H}$ of algorithmic specifications.

Let $\leq$ denote the reflexive transitive closure of the relation between specifications " makes use of external functions of".

(i) Constructors

emptystack : → *Stack*

push: *Stack* x *Integer* → *Stack*

(ii) Acceptor function

Is.Stack is the (doubly strict extension of the) function with the constant value true

(iii) Equivalence relation

Eq.Stack is the (doubly strict extension of the) syntactical equality (in the term language of type *Stack*)

(iv) External functions

Emptystack = emptystack

Push = [λs∈Stack, i∈Integer. push(s, i)]

Pop = [λs∈Stack.
    if Is.push(s) then s[1] else Ω]

Top = [λs∈Stack.
    if Is.push(s) then s[2] else Ω]

Isnew = [λs∈Stack.
    if Is.push(s) then false else true]

Figure 1: The specification of the data type *Stack*. Note that Emptystack is a 0-ary external function (i. e. a constant) and emptystack a 0-ary constructor (i.e. a term). It is implicitly assumed that Eq.Integer is the syntactical equality in the term language of type *Integer*.

The set $\underline{H}$ is called *hierarchical* if the relation ≤ is a partial ordering.

2.3. The algebra defined by a hierarchical set of specifications

A hierarchical set of specifications defines a heterogeneous algebra; this algebra consists of a carrier set for each data type and of an operation for each external function.

The carrier set of a type τ is the set constituted by the equivalence classes induced by Eq.τ on the subset of the term language defined by Is.τ and by the elements ERROR and UNDEFINED.

To each external function F of a specification is associated an operation F_{op} in the following way. Suppose F maps terms of type $\tau_1,\dots,\tau_n$ into terms of type τ_{n+1}, $n \geq 0$; let $\varphi(t)$ denote

- the equivalence class of t, if t is a term
- ERROR, if t = Ω
- UNDEFINED, if $t = \omega$;

then the corresponding operation F_{op} maps the carrier sets of $\tau_1,\dots,\tau_n$ into the carrier set of τ_{n+1} and its value is defined by:

$$F_{op}(\varphi(t_1),\dots,\varphi(t_n)) = \varphi(F(t_1,\dots,t_n)).$$

Note that this definition of F_{op} is consistent only if the external function F satisfies certain *verification conditions*, expressing e. g. that equivalent arguments lead to equivalent values. More details and a study of these conditions may be found in [Lo 81a].

In the sequel we assume that each element of each carrier set may be obtained as the value of an expression built with operations (cf [Lo 80b]).

3. Implementations

The main idea consists in defining the implementation of a data type as a "new" data type; this new data type has a particular structure in that it essentially consists of an n-tuple of "old" data types. The implementation is called correct if the replacement of the specification of the implemented data type by that of the implementing data type leads to an isomorphic algebra. In order to formalize these ideas a few definitions are needed.

3.1. Preliminary definitions and notations

Let T be a specification of a data type τ containing a single constructor; if this constructor is of the form

$$\dots : \tau_1 \times \dots \times \tau_n \rightarrow \tau$$

$n \geq 1$, $\tau_i \neq \tau$ for all i $(1 \leq i \leq n)$, then τ is called a *package of the data types* $\tau_1, \dots, \tau_n$.

Two specifications S and T are called *similar* if there exists a one-to-one correspondence between their external functions such that to each external function

$$F_S : \underline{\rho}_1 \times \dots \times \underline{\rho}_n \rightarrow \underline{\rho}_{n+1} \qquad , n \geq 0$$

of S corresponds an external function

$$F_T : \underline{\rho}'_1 \times \dots \times \underline{\rho}'_m \rightarrow \underline{\rho}'_{m+1} \qquad , m \geq 0$$

of T with m = n and, for all i, $1 \leq i \leq n + 1$:

$$\rho_i' = \begin{cases} \tau & \text{if } \rho_i = \sigma \\ \rho_i & \text{otherwise} \end{cases}$$

A specification T is *new* in a set $\underline{H}$ of specifications if the type defined by T is not used in the specifications of $\underline{H}$.

Let S and T be similar specifications defining the data types σ and τ respectively. If $\underline{H}$ is a hierarchical set of specifications containing S and if T is new in $\underline{H}$ then

$$\underline{H}_S^T$$

denotes the set of specifications obtained from $\underline{H}$ by replacing S by T and by replacing in each specification of $\underline{H}$ - $\{S\}$:

- each occurrence of σ by τ;
- each occurrence of an external function of S by the corresponding external function of T;
- each occurrence of Is.σ and Eq.σ by Is.τ and Eq.τ respectively.

3.2. Definition of an implementation

Let $\underline{H}$ be a hierarchical set of specifications containing the specification S. A specification T is called an *implementation of S (in $\underline{H}$)* if the following conditions are satisfied:

(i) T is a specification of a package which is new in $\underline{H}$;

(ii) S and T are similar;

(iii) $\underline{H}_S^T$ is hierarchical;

(iv) the algebras defined by $\underline{H}$ and $\underline{H}_S^T$ are isomorphic.

Note that by replacing successively in a hierarchical set of specifications each specification of a "non-elementary" data type by an implementation it is possible to reduce all data types to packages of "elementary" ones, for instance those available in a programming language; an example may be found in [Lo 81b].

3.3. Proving the correctness of an implementation

The correctness proof of an implementation consists in a proof of the conditions (i) through (iv) above. Checking the conditions (i), (ii) and (iii) is trivial. The condition (iv) is replaced by so-called *implementation conditions*; these conditions may be expressed either by using a *representation function* (cf. [SWL 77], [GHM 78b], [WSHF 81])

$$RP : \underline{\tau} \rightarrow \underline{\sigma}$$

or an *implementation function* (cf. [ADJ 78], [Ga 79], [Su 79])

$$IM : \underline{\sigma} \to \underline{\tau}$$

where σ and τ are the data types defined by the specifications S and T respectively. The study of these conditions is the subject of the next section.

4. The implementation conditions

4.1. The case of a representation function

The implementation conditions are:

(i) the representation function is doubly strict, i. e.

$$RP(\omega) = \omega$$

and $$RP(\Omega) = \Omega$$

(ii) for all terms d of type τ:

$$Is.\tau(d) = \underline{true} \quad \text{iff} \quad Is.\sigma(RP(d)) = \underline{true}$$

(iii) for all terms d_1, d_2 of type τ:

$$\text{if } Is.\tau(d_1) = Is.\tau(d_2) = \underline{true}$$

$$\text{then } Eq.\tau(d_1, d_2) = Eq.\sigma(RP(d_1), RP(d_2))$$

(iv) for each external function of S, say

$$F_S : \underline{\rho_1} \times \dots \times \underline{\rho_n} \to \underline{\rho_{n+1}} \quad , n \geq o,$$

and its corresponding function

$$F_T : \underline{\rho'_1} \times \dots \times \underline{\rho'_n} \to \underline{\rho'_{n+1}}$$

of T the following condition holds:

for each d'_i of type ρ'_i , $1 \leq i \leq n$:

$$\left[\begin{array}{l} \text{if } (Is.\rho'_i(d'_i) = \underline{true}) \textbf{ or} (d'_i = \omega) \text{ or } (d'_i = \Omega) \\ \qquad \text{for all } i, 1 \leq i \leq n \\ \text{then:} \end{array}\right.$$

$$\left[\begin{array}{ll} Eq.\sigma(F_S(d_1,\dots,d_n), RP(F_T(d'_1,\dots,d'_n))) = \underline{true} & \text{(a1)} \\ \quad \text{or } F_S(d_1,\dots,d_n) = RP(F_T(d'_1,\dots,d'_n)) & \text{(a2)} \\ \qquad \text{if } \rho_{n+1} = \sigma & \\ Eq.\rho_{n+1}(F_S(d_1,\dots,d_n), F_T(d'_1,\dots,d'_n)) = \underline{true} & \\ \quad \text{or } F_S(d_1,\dots,d_n) = F_T(d'_1,\dots,d'_n) & \\ \qquad \text{if } \rho_{n+1} \neq \sigma & \end{array}\right.$$

where for each i, $1 \le i \le n$:

$$d_i = \begin{cases} RP(d_i') & \text{if} \quad \rho_i = \sigma \\ d_i' & \text{if} \quad \rho_i \neq \sigma \end{cases}$$

Intuitively, (ii) expresses that RP maps "allowed" terms into "allowed" terms; (iii) expresses that two terms of τ are equivalent iff the corresponding terms of σ are equivalent or, more loosely, that RP corresponds to an injective mapping of the equivalence classes of τ into those of σ. In order to interpret (iv) consider the special case $n = 1$, $\rho_1 = \rho_2 = \sigma$ and none of the values $F_S(RP(d'))$ and $RP(F_T(d'))$ is ω or Ω; in that case the condition (a1) of (iv) becomes

$$Eq.\sigma(F_S(RP(d')), RP(F_T(d'))) = \underline{true} \qquad \text{(b)}$$

and is illustrated by Figure 2 (A); now as F_S is supposed to satisfy the verification conditions, equivalent arguments lead to equivalent values (see Section 2.3), i. e.

$$\text{if } Eq.\sigma(c, RP(d')) = \underline{true}$$
$$\text{then } Eq.\sigma(F_S(c), F_S(RP(d'))) = \underline{true} \;;$$

hence (b) is equivalent with

$$\text{if } Eq.\sigma(c, RP(d')) = \underline{true}$$
$$\text{then } Eq.\sigma(F_S(c), RP(F_T(d'))) = \underline{true} \;;$$

this condition is illustrated by Figure 2 (B) and expresses that the external functions F_T of T "simulate" the corresponding functions F_S of S up to equivalence. - The condition (a2) accounts for the case in which $F_S(d_1,\dots,d_n)$ and $RP(F_T(d_1',\dots,d_n'))$ are both ω or Ω.

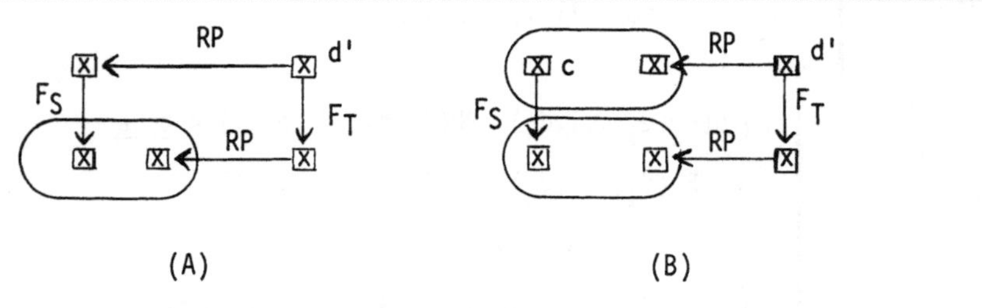

FIGURE 2: Illustration of the implementation condition (iv); points in the same enclosure are equivalent.

4.2. Theorem: Let $\underline{H}$ be a hierarchical set of specifications containing the specification S. Let moreover T be a specification satisfying the conditions (i), (ii) and (iii) of Section 3.2. The implementation conditions of Section 4.1 then imply that the algebras defined by $\underline{H}$ and $\underline{H}_S^T$ are isomorphic.

The proof of this theorem is in [Lo 80b].

4.3. The case of an implementation function

The use of an implementation function IM : $\underline{\sigma} \rightarrow \underline{\tau}$ instead of a representation function RP : $\underline{\tau} \rightarrow \underline{\sigma}$ puts no problem: due to the symmetry of the definitions it is sufficient to permute σ and τ and to replace RP by IM in the conditions of Section 4.1.

5. An example

5.1. The data types

The implementation to be proved correct is that of a stack by a vector and a pointer. More precisely, the specification to be implemented is that of Figure 1; the specification which constitutes the implementation is that of Figure 4.

It is assumed that for all specifications the verification conditions mentioned in Section 2.3 have been checked.

5.2. The implementation conditions

Consider the representation function (*)

```
RP = [αM.[λm∈Imstack.
        if m[2] = 0
        then Emptystack
        else Push ( M(pair(m[1], m[2]-1)),
                    Read(m[1], m[2]))     ]]
```

(*) As in the figures use is made here of the decimal notation and the infix notation for usual (external) functions of the type *Integer*; moreover Eq.Integer is replaced by the infix notation "=".

Intuitively the value of RP is the empty stack when the pointer is zero; otherwise the value is the stack consisting of the elements v[1],...,v[k] where v is the vector and k the value of the pointer.

Let us examine the implementation conditions of Section 4.1 with σ = *Stack* and τ = *Imstack*.

The conditions (i) and (ii) trivially hold.

The condition (iii) is:

if Is.Imstack(m_1) = Is.Imstack(m_2) = <u>true</u>

then Eq.Imstack(m_1,m_2) = Eq.Stack(RP(m_1), RP(m_2))

The condition (iv) consists of:

(a) Eq.Stack (Emptystack, RP(Imemptystack)) = <u>true</u>

(b) if (Is.Imstack(m) = <u>true</u>) or (m = ω) or (m = Ω)
and if (Is.Integer (i) = <u>true</u>) or (i = ω) or (i = Ω)
then
Eq.Stack (Push(RP(m), i), RP (Impush(m, i))) = <u>true</u> (b1)
or Push (RP(m), i) = RP (Impush(m, i)) (b2)

(c) similar to (b) with Pop instead of Push

(d) if (Is.Imstack (m) = <u>true</u>) or (m = ω) or (m = Ω)
then
Eq.Integer(Top(RP(m)), RP(Imtop(m))) = <u>true</u> (d1)
or Top(RP(m)) = RP(Imtop(m)) (d2)

(e) similar to (d) with Isnew instead of Top.

Note that (b1) may be dropped because (b1) implies (b2) due to the definition of Eq.Stack. A similar remark holds for (d1).

These conditions have been proved mechanically with the help of the AFFIRM-system [Mu 80]; the proofs are in [Lo 80a]. Essentially a proof consists in replacing functions such as Is.Imstack, Impush or Push by their definition and, if necessary, to apply structural induction on the term language.

5.3. The case of an implementation function

The condition (iv) of Section 3.2 can also be proved with the help of an implementation function such as

```
(i)    Constructors
              emptyvector : → Vector
              write: Vector x Integer x Integer → Vector
(ii)   Acceptor function
              Is.Vector is the (doubly strict extension of the) function
              with the constant value true
(iii)  Equivalence relation
              Eq.Vector = [λv1,v2∈Vector.
                 if Subvector (v1,v2)
                 then Subvector (v2,v1) else false ]
(iv)   External functions
                 Emptyvector = emptyvector
                 Write = [λv∈Vector, i, j∈Integer. write (v, i, j) ]
                 Read = [αM.[λv∈Vector, i∈Integer.
                     if Is.emptyvector (v)
                     then Ω else if i = v[2]
                                 then v[3] else M(v[1], i) ]]
                 Defined = [αM.[λv∈Vector, i∈Integer.
                     if Is.emptyvector (v)
                     then false else if i = v[2]
                                     then true else M(v[1], i)  ]]
(v)    Auxiliary functions
              Subvector = [αM.[λv1,v2∈Vector.
                     if Is.emptyvector (v1)
                     then true else if Defined (v2,v1[2])
                                    then if Read (v2,v1[2]) = v1[3]
                                         then M(Clear(v1[1],v1[2]), v2)
                                         else false
                                    else false      ]]
              Clear = [αM.[λv∈Vector, i ∈ Integer.
                        if Is.emptyvector (v) then emptyvector
                        else if v[2] = i then M(v[1], i)
                                         else write (M(v[1], i),v[2],v[3])]]
```

FIGURE 3: The data type *Vector*. Intuitively speaking "overwritten" values are not erased.

(i) Constructor

$\quad$ pair : *Vector* x *Integer* → *Imstack*

(ii) Acceptor function

```
        Is.Imstack = [λm∈Imstack.
           if m[2] ≥ 0 then true else false]
```

(iii) Equivalence relation

```
        Eq.Imstack = [αM.[λm1,m2∈Imstack.
           if m1[2] = m2[2]
           then if m1[2] = 0
                then true
                else if Read (m1[1], m1[2]) = Read (m2[1], m2[2])
                     then M(pair (m1[1], m1[2]-1),
                            pair (m2[1], m2[2]-1))
                     else false
           else false  ]]
```

(iv) External functions

```
        Imemptystack = pair(emptyvector, 0)
        Impush = [λm∈Imstack, i∈Integer.
                    pair (Write (m[1], m[2]+1, i), m[2]+1)]
        Impop = [λm∈Imstack.
                    if m[2] = 0 then Ω else pair (m[1], m[2]-1)]
        Imtop = [λm∈Imstack.
                    if m[2] = 0 then Ω else Read (m[1], m[2])]
        Imisnew = [λm∈Imstack. if m[2] = 0 then true else false]
```

FIGURE 4: The data type *Imstack* which is intended to be an implementation of the data type *Stack*. Intuitively the data type consists of a vector and a "pointer". According to (iii), pair (v_1,i_1) and pair (v_2,i_2) are equivalent if either $(i_1 = i_2 = 0)$ or $((i_1 = i_2)$ and $(i_1,i_2$ "point" to the same value in v_1, $v_2)$ and (pair (v_1,i_1-1) and pair (v_2,i_2-2) are equivalent)).

IM = [λs∈Stack. pair (*Construct*(s), *Depth*(s))]

where *Construct* and *Depth* are (auxiliary) functions:

```
Depth = [αM.[λs∈Stack. if Is.emptystack(s)
                        then 0
                        else M(s[1]) + 1 ]]
Construct = [αM.[λs∈Stack. if Is.emptystack(s)
                            then Emptyvector
                            else Write (M(s[1]), Depth(s), s[2])]]
```

Informally, *Depth* determines the number of elements of the stack and *Construct* constructs a vector for a given stack.

It is then sufficient to prove the implementation conditions (i) to (iv) of Section 4.1 with σ = *Imstack*, τ ≠ *Stack* and IM instead of RP.

6. A property

Let *S* be a specification for which the verification conditions hold. If *T* is an implementation of *S* or, more precisely, if the conditions (i) through (iii) of Section 3.2 and the implementation conditions of Section 4.1 or 4.3 hold, the verification conditions hold for *T*. The proof of this property is in [Lo 80b].

As a practical consequence it is not necessary to prove the verification conditions of the specification of an implementing data type.

7. Concluding remarks

Algorithmic specifications have been shown to lead to a simple and natural notion of implementation. The implementation conditions include the case of undefined and error values and may be verified mechanically.

Apart from these differences resulting from the use of algorithmic rather than algebraic specifications the present approach is characterized by its considering an implementation as a new data type. This approach which is already described in informal terms in [GHM 78b] naturally leads to the notion of isomorphic algebras; the symmetry of this notion in its turn leads to implementation conditions which may be expressed indifferently by using a representation function (as in [SWL 77], [GHM 78b], [EKP 80]) or an implementation function (as in [ADJ 78], [Su 79], [Ga 79]).

References

[ADJ 78] J. A. Goguen, J. W. Thatcher, E. G. Wagner, "An initial algebra approach to the specification, correctness and implementation of abstract data types" in "Current Trends in Programming Methodology IV" (R.Yeh, ed.), pp. 80-149, Prentice Hall, 1978

[EKP 80] H. Ehrig, H. J. Kreowski, P. Padawitz, "Algebraic Implementation of Abstract Data Types: Concept, Syntax, Semantics and Correctness", Lecture Notes in Computer Science 85, Springer-Verlag, 1980, pp. 142 - 156

[Ga 79] M. C. Gaudel, "Algebraic specification of abstract data types", Internal Report 360, IRIA, Le Chesney (August 1979)

[GH 78a] J. V. Guttag, J. J. Horning, "The algebraic specification of abstract data types", Acta Informatica 10, 1, pp. 27 - 52 (1978)

[GHM 78b] J. V. Guttag, E. Horowitz, D. R. Musser, "Abstract data types and software validation", Comm. ACM 21, 12, pp. 1048 - 1064 (1978)

[Ho 72] C. A. R. Hoare,"Proof of correctness of data representations", Acta Informatica 1, 4, pp. 271 - 281 (1972)

[Lo 80a] J. Loeckx, "Proving properties of algorithmic specifications of abstract data types in AFFIRM", AFFIRM-Memo-29-JL, USC-ISI, Marina del Rey, 1980

[Lo 80b] J. Loeckx, "Some properties of implementations of abstract data types", Internal Report A 80/14, Fachbereich 10, Universität des Saarlandes, Saarbrücken, 1980

[Lo 81a] J. Loeckx, "Algorithmic specifications of abstract data types", Proc. ICALP 81 (Haifa), to be published as Springer Lect. Notes (1981)

[Lo 81b] J. Loeckx, "The description of programming languages and the verification of their compilers by abstract data types", Internal Report, Fachbereich 10, Universität des Saarlandes, Saarbrücken (in preparation)

[Mi 72] R. Milner, "Implementation and applications of Scott's logic for computable functions", Proc. ACM Conf. on Proving Assertions about Programs, SIGPLAN Notices 7, 1, pp. 1 - 6 (1972)

[Mu 80] D. R. Musser, "Abstract data type specification in the AFFIRM-system", IEEE Trans. on Softw. Eng., SE-6, 1, pp. 24 - 32 (1980)

[Su 79] P. A. Subrahmanyam, "On proving the correctness of data type implementations", Internal report, Dept. Comp. Sc., University of Utah, Sept. 1979

[SWL 77] M. Shaw, W. A. Wulf, R. L. London, "Abstraction and verification in ALPHARD: Defining and specifying iteration and generators", CACM 20, 8, pp.553-564 (1977)

[WSHF 81] W. A. Wulf, M. Shaw, P. N. Hilfinger, L. Flon, "Fundamental structures of Computer Science", Addison-Wesley Publ. Co., 1981 (Chapter 11)

GOTOs -
A Study in the Algebraic Specification of Programming Languages*)
(Extended Abstract)

M. Broy, W. Dosch, B. Möller, M. Wirsing

Technische Universität München
Institut für Informatik
Postfach 20 24 20
D-8000 München 2

1. Introduction

During recent years the concept of algebraic specification (cf. e.g. /Guttag 75/, /Burstall, Goguen 77/, /Goguen et al. 78/, /Wirsing et al. 80/) has proved to be a powerful and flexible tool for the formal definition of data structures. Algebraic concepts have also been employed for the specification of programming language semantics, e.g. first-order identities (/Wand 77/) or continuous algebras (/Courcelle, Nivat 78/, /Goguen et al. 77/). In contrast to these "explicit" constructions of semantics, /Broy, Wirsing 80a/ have introduced a technique for characterizing the semantic models of a language by the axioms of an algebraic type without resorting to (the isomorphism class of) a fixed model. This approach is characterized by the following peculiarities (cf. /Wirsing et al. 80/, /Broy, Wirsing 80c/):

(1) As semantic models, finitely generated (cf. /Bauer, Wössner 81/) heterogeneous algebras with partial operations are considered.

(2) Their properties are specified in algebraic types using positive conditional equations and a definedness predicate D on the terms of the type.

(3) Within the equations, the metasymbol = is interpreted as strong equality, and D is total, so that the underlying logic remains two-valued.

(4) In general, the types are hierarchical, i.e. a type may be based on a subtype which is considered as the specification of primitive objects and operations. Models of hierarchical types are required to preserve the properties of the primitive type.

*) This research was carried out within the Sonderforschungsbereich 49, Programmiertechnik, Munich.

(5) *All* models of a type are considered. In order to compare them, especially with respect to the definedness of operations, partial and strong homomorphisms are used.

In the sequel we illustrate this approach with the specifications of two layers of a programming language. The first layer comprises simple statements based on integer arithmetic; its programs always terminate. Whereas this language layer can also be treated in the conventional framework of total algebras, the second layer containing general jumps introduces the possibility of non-termination and thus needs the generalized setting of partial algebras.

For each of the layers we analyse the class of semantic models, especially with respect to extremal (initial and terminal) algebras. Each semantic model is characterized by a special equivalence between the terms denoting programs; these equivalences range from textual identity over different operational equivalences to functional (mathematical) equivalence. Models corresponding to this latter equivalence (fully abstract models in the sense of /Milner 77/) can be constructed using the techniques of denotational semantics (cf. /Scott, Strachey 71/).

Due to lack of space we present only a short analysis of each specification and omit proofs. For an extended treatment we refer to /Broy et al. 81/.

2. Basic Definitions

In the sequel we give the most important definitions; for a detailed treatment compare e.g. /Wirsing et al. 80/, /Broy, Wirsing 80a, c/.

2.1. Partial Algebras

For a *signature* $\Sigma = (S, F)$ a *partial heterogeneous* Σ - *algebra* A is defined analogously to a total one; however, the operation symbols in F may also be interpreted by partial functions. The *term algebra* is denoted by W_Σ and the *interpretation* of a term or an operation symbol t in A is denoted by t^A. A Σ-algebra is called *finitely generated* if all elements of its carrier sets can be obtained as interpretations of terms in W_Σ. Given two Σ-algebras A, B, a family $\varphi = (\varphi_s : s^A \to s^B)_{s \in S}$ of partial functions is called a *partial* Σ*-homomorphism* if for all operation symbols $f : s_1 \times \ldots \times s_n \to s$ in F and all arguments $a_i \in s_i^A$ $(i = 1, \ldots, n)$

$$f^A(a_1,\ldots,a_n) \text{ defined} \Rightarrow [f^B(\varphi_{s_1}(a_1), \ldots, \varphi_{s_n}(a_n)) \text{ defined and}$$
$$\varphi_s(f^A(a_1,\ldots,a_n)) = f^B(\varphi_{s_1}(a_1),\ldots, \varphi_{s_n}(a_n))]$$

A partial homomorphism φ is called *strong*, if in addition, for all $f \in F$ and all arguments $(a_1,\dots,a_k)$: $f^B(\varphi(a_1), \dots, \varphi(a_n))$ defined $\Rightarrow$ $f^A(a_1,\dots, a_n)$ defined. Homomorphisms preserve the definedness of term interpretations.

For a class C of partial Σ-algebras, an algebra $I \in C$ is called *initial* (resp. *strongly initial*) in C if for every algebra $A \in C$ there is a unique partial (resp. strong) Σ-homomorphism $\varphi : I \to A$. An algebra $Z \in C$ is called *strongly terminal* in C if for every algebra $A \in C$ there is at least one strong Σ-homomorphism $\varphi : A \to Z$. Finitely generated initial and terminal algebras are determined up to isomorphism if they exist.

2.2. Algebraic Types and their Models

Consider two Σ-terms t_1 and t_2 containing free variables. We say that a Σ-algebra A *satisfies the equation* $t_1 = t_2$ (and write $A \models t_1 = t_2$) if for all instantiations of the free variables by elements of the carrier sets of A t_1^A and t_2^A are both undefined or both defined and equal.

Besides this strong equality we need as a basic predicate the *definedness predicate* $D(t)$ for a term t : $A \models D(t)$ iff t^A is defined for all instantiations of the free variables by objects of A.

A *positive conditional formula* has the form

$$\bigwedge_{i=1}^{k} D(p_i) \wedge \bigwedge_{j=1}^{m} [D(q_j) \wedge D(r_j) \wedge q_j = r_j] \Rightarrow C \quad (k, m \geq 0) ,$$

where C is either $D(s)$ or $s = t$ and p_i, q_j, r_j, s, t are Σ-terms (with free variables). In the following we omit $D(q_j)$ and $D(r_j)$. An *algebraic type* $T = < \Sigma, E >$ consists of a signature Σ and a (countable) set E of positive conditional formulas called *axioms*.
The class $PGEN(T)$ of *models* of T consists of all finitely generated partial Σ-algebras A with $A \models E$, where the sentential connectives have the usual (two-valued) interpretation. Every algebraic type T has an initial model, i.e. $PGEN(T)$ contains an initial algebra.

Since partial homomorphisms preserve definedness, the initial models I are *minimally defined* in $PGEN(T)$: for all terms $t \in W_\Sigma$ we have

$$I \models D(t) \Leftrightarrow \bigwedge_{A \in PGEN(T)} A \models D(t)$$

For an arbitrary class C of partial Σ-algebras we denote by

$$MDEF(C) = \{A \in C : \forall\, t \in W_\Sigma : A \models D(t) \Leftrightarrow \bigwedge_{B \in C} B \models D(t)\} ,$$

the class of minimally defined models.

Since the definedness of terms is fixed in MDEF(C) , all homomorphisms between models in this class are strong. Therefore I is strongly initial in MDEF(PGEN(T)). If there is also a strongly terminal model Z in MDEF(C) then Z is called *weakly terminal* in C .

2.3. Hierarchical Algebraic Types

In a *hierarchical algebraic type* $T = < \Sigma, E, T' >$ a *primitive (sub)type* $T' = < \Sigma', E' >$ with $\Sigma' \subseteq \Sigma$ and $E' \subseteq E$ is designated. In order to rule out trivial models of the primitive type we consider for hierarchical types the class

$$HGEN(T) = \{A \in PGEN(T) : A|\Sigma' \text{ is initial in } PGEN(T')\} ,$$

where $A|\Sigma'$ is the Σ-algebra comprising only those carrier sets and operations of A which are also mentioned in Σ'.

T is called *hierarchy-preserving* if HGEN(T) is nonempty. A necessary condition for this property is *hierarchy-consistency :* every equation $p_1 = p_2$ between primitive terms $p_1, p_2 \in W_{\Sigma'}$ which is provable in T must already be provable in T' .

We can identify the primitive algebras of all models in HGEN(T) since they are fixed up to isomorphism. This gives the possibility of characterizing the non-primitive objects by their "visible behaviour", i.e. by their behaviour under "output operations" leading into the primitives. Let $A, B \in HGEN(T)$. We call A and B *extensionally equivalent* if for all terms $t \in W_\Sigma$ of a primitive sort we have $t^A = t^B$. This holds if there is a strong homomorphism from B to A . All models in MDEF(HGEN(T)) are extensionally equivalent. Let us finally call a model A *fully abstract* if its nonprimitive objects are completely characterized by their visible behaviour, i.e. if for all terms s and t of a nonprimitive sort we have $s^A = t^A$ iff for all contexts c[.] of a primitive sort $c[s]^A = c[t]^A$ (cf. /Milner 77/).

Because of the importance of the visible behaviour one is interested in types that specify it sufficiently precisely : a hierarchical type T is said to be *partially sufficiently complete* iff for all terms $t \in W_\Sigma$ of a primitive sort for which $T \vdash D(t)$ holds there is a primitive term $p \in W_{\Sigma'}$ with $T \vdash t = p$.

3. The First Language: Simple Statements

In this section we define a type describing a simple statement language over the integers which comprises assignment, incrementation, and finite iteration.

3.1. Specification of the Type STAT

The type to be introduced contains a sort stat for the statements. The terms of this sort provide the *abstract syntax* (cf./Goguen et al. 77/, /Laut 81/) of statements ; each kind of statement is represented by a corresponding constructor operation. A homomorphism to strings can be used for defining a concrete syntax.

In order to leave freedom for the semantic models we do not give essential equations between statements; rather we characterize statements by an output operation value associating with each variable identifier its value after the execution of a statement.

STAT is hierarchically based on the primitive types BOOL , INT and ID for boolean values, integers and variable identifiers. We do not specify these types in detail, we only assume that INT provides the usual arithmetic and comparison operators and that ID specifies an operation eqid testing equality of identifiers.

In order to avoid lengthy context conditions we treat the statements as if all variable identifiers were declared and initialized with 0 .

```
type STAT ≡ stat, nop, semi, assign, incr, copy, cond, iterate, value :
      based on BOOL, INT, ID ,
      sort stat ,
      funct stat nop ,
      funct (stat, stat) stat semi ,
      funct (id, int) stat assign ,
      funct (id, int) stat incr ,
      funct (id, id) stat copy ,
      funct (id, stat, stat) stat cond ,
      funct (id, stat) stat iterate ,
      funct (int, stat) stat it ,
      funct (stat, id) int value ,

      semi(nop,s) = semi(s,nop) = s ,
      semi(r,semi(s,t)) = semi(semi(r,s), t) ,
      value(nop,z) = 0 ,
      value(semi(r, assign(x,n)),z) =
         if eqid(x,z) then n else value(r,z) fi ,
      value(semi(r,copy(x,y)),z) =
         if eqid(x,z) then value(r,y) else value(r,z) fi ,
      value(semi(r,incr(x,n)),z) =
         if eqid(x,z) then value(r,x) + n else value(r,z) fi ,
```

```
value(semi(r,cond(x,s,t)),z) =
   if value(r,x) ≥ 0 then value(semi(r,s),z) else value(semi(r,t),z) fi ,
value(semi(s,iterate(x,t)),z) = value(semi(s,it(value(s,x),t)),z) ,
it(n, t) = if n ≤ 0 then nop else semi(t,it(n-1,t)) fi
```

end of type

Before we analyse STAT , to aid the intuition let us give a homomorphism h specifying an ALGOL-like concrete syntax:

```
h(nop)            = skip
h(semi(s,t))      = h(s) ; h(t)
h(assign(x,i))    = x := i
h(incr(x,i))      = x := x+i
h(copy(x,z))      = x := z
h(cond(x,s,t))    = if x ≥ 0 then h(s) else h(t) fi
h(iterate(x,s))   = to x do h(s) od
```

One may also interpret value(s,x) as begin s ; x end as in ALGOL 68.

3.2. Analysis of Type STAT

First of all we note that the sequencing of statements is associative and has a neutral element nop . Therefore each term $t \in W_{STAT}$ of sort stat can be reduced to the *normal form* (NF) $STAT \vdash t = nop \vee t = semi(s,a)$ where a is an atomic statement (assign, incr, copy) or a is a compound statement (cond, iterate) the constituents of sort stat of which are in the same normal form, and s is again in normal form.

This implies also that the hidden operation it is not a constructor function since in each term of sort stat it can be eliminated by "unwinding" the finite iteration. STAT is partially sufficiently complete and hierarchy-consistent. The interpretation of every term is defined in all models, thus MDEF(HGEN(STAT)) = HGEN(STAT) and all homomorphisms are strong. In particular, all models in HGEN(STAT) are extensionally equivalent. There is an initial model I , and a terminal model Z which is both fully abstract and strongly terminal in HGEN(STAT). The fact that all terms of STAT are defined implies that all models are total algebras; thus this type can also be treated in the conventional framework.

In a (strongly) initial model I terms are interpreted as differently as possible: For all $s,t \in W_{STAT}$ of sort stat : $s^I = t^I \leftrightarrow STAT \vdash s = t$.

Thus the equality in I coincides with the syntactic equality of statements in normal form (NF) ; i.e. statements in normal form provide a (strongly) initial model.

Dually to (strongly) initial models, the equality in a strongly terminal model Z is characterized as follows: For all $s, t \in W_{STAT}$ of sort <u>stat</u> :

$$s^Z = t^Z \Leftrightarrow \forall\ \underline{stat}\ r,\ \underline{id}\ x : STAT \vdash value(semi(r,s),x) = value(semi(r,t),x)\ .$$

This implies that Z is fully abstract and that the equality in Z is the mathematical (functional) equality of statements. Therefore it can be constructed as a denotational model using the techniques of /Scott, Strachey 71/.

4. The Second Language: Jumps

4.1. Specifications of the Type LSTAT

Based on the type STAT , we shall now present a type LSTAT which specifies a sort <u>lst</u> containing sequences of labelled simple statements and conditional jumps. A sequence of labelled statements and conditional jumps is *context-correct* (i.e. syntactically correct) if every label is declared at most once. It can be evaluated (to a defined value) only if all used labels are declared. A sequence of labelled statements and jumps in which not all used labels are declared may be concatenated with another sequence of labelled statements and jumps, such that then all used labels are declared. A sequence of labelled statements with multiple declarations of a label, however, can never be completed in a correct way. Therefore we interpret such sequences as undefined. It is remarkable that the specification of the context conditions is as difficult as that of the semantics proper.

In addition to STAT, LSTAT is based on a type LABEL specifying a sort <u>label</u> and an equality test eql on labels; again, the exact definition of this type is omitted.

As a shorthand notation we use *parameter restrictions* in two of the operations of LSTAT : An occurrence of

$$\underline{funct}(\underline{s}_1 x_1,\ldots,\underline{s}_n x_n : p(x_1,\ldots,x_n))\ \underline{s}\ f$$

where p is a predicate of functionality $\underline{funct}(\underline{s}_1,\ldots,\underline{s}_n)\ \underline{bool}$ is equivalent to

$$\underline{funct}(\underline{s}_1,\ldots,\underline{s}_n)\ \underline{s}\ f$$

and the law

$$D(f(x_1,\ldots,x_n)) \Rightarrow p(x_1,\ldots,x_n) = true\ .$$

Also we abbreviate axioms $p = true \Rightarrow t_1 = t_2$ to $p \Rightarrow t_1 = t_2$.

```
type LSTAT ≡ lst, lnop, set, goto, conc, val :
   based on  LABEL, STAT ,

   sort lst ,

   funct lst lnop ,
   funct (label, stat) lst set ,
   funct (id, label) lst goto ,
   funct (lst c1, lst c2 : disjoint(c1, c2)) lst conc ,

   funct (lst, lst) bool disjoint ,
   funct (lst, lst) bool closed ,
   funct (label, lst) bool defined ,

   funct (lst c, id : closed(c, c)) int val ,
   funct (stat, lst c1, lst c2, id : closed(c1, c2)) int eval ,
   funct (label m, lst c : defined(m, c)) lst conti ,

   conc(c1, lnop) = c1 = conc(lnop, c1) ,
   conc(c1, conc(c2, c3)) = conc(conc(c1, c2), c3) ,

   defined(m, lnop) = false ,
   defined(m1, set(m2, s)) = eql(m1, m2) ,
   defined (m1, goto(x, m2)) = false ,
   disjoint(c1, c2)  ⇒  defined(m1, conc(c1, c2)) = (defined(m1, c1) or
                                                          defined(m1, c2)) ,
   closed(lnop, c) = true ,
   closed(set(m, s), c) = true ,
   closed(goto(x, m), c) = defined(m, c) ,
   disjoint(c1, c2)  ⇒  closed(conc(c1, c2), c) = (closed(c1, c) and closed(c2,c)),

   disjoint(lnop, c) = true ,
   disjoint(set(m, c), c) = not defined(m, c) ,
   disjoint(goto(x, m), c) = true ,
   disjoint(c1, c2)  ⇒  disjoint(conc(c1, c2), c) = (disjoint(c1, c) and
                                                          disjoint(c2, c)) ,
   val(c, x) = eval(nop, c, c, x) ,
   eval(s, lnop, c, x) = value(s, x) ,
   closed(conc(set(m, s1), c1), c)  ⇒
       eval(s, conc(set(m, s1), c1), c, x) = eval(semi(s, s1), c1, c, x) ,
   closed(conc(goto(y, m), c1), c)  ⇒
       eval(s, conc(goto(y, m), c1), c, x) =
            if value(s, y) ≥ 0 then eval(s, conti(m, c), c, x)
                               else eval(s, c1, c, x)                  fi ,
```

```
defined(m, conc(set(m1, s), c)) ⇒
                  conti(m, conc(set(m1, s), c)) =
                            if eql(m, m1) then conc(set(m1,s), c)
                                           else conti(m, c)        fi ,
defined(m, conc(goto(y, m1), c)) ⇒
     conti(m, conc(goto(y, m1), c)) = conti(m, c)

end of type
```

Again we give a concrete syntax for the language:

```
h(lnop)              =  skip
h(set(m, c))         =  m : h(c)
h(goto(x, m))        =  if x ≥ 0 then goto m  fi
h(conc(c1, c2))      =  h(c1) ; h(c2)
```

Let us also associate some intuitive meaning with the other operations of LSTAT :

eval(s, c1, c2, x) = << value of x after execution of "s; c1" , where the "continuations" for the labels are extracted from the "program" c2 >>

conti(m, c) = << "rest of program" following m in c >>

The context conditions are formulated with the help of the predicates

defined(m, c) = << the label m is declared in c >> ,
closed(c1, c2) = << all labels used in c1 are declared in c2 >> ,
disjoint(c1, c2) = << no label is declared both in c1 and in c2 >> .

Note that these predicates are specified sufficiently completely without referring to the semantic functions. So they can be checked "statically". Therefore the terms of sort lst can be divided into a class of terms which are defined and a class of terms which are undefined independently of particular models (cf. /Wirsing et al. 80/).

4.2. Analysis of LSTAT

With the jumps introduced we can write non-terminating programs. This is reflected in the fact that we can no longer prove the definedness of all terms val(p, x) even for context-correct p . The only way to do this would be to reduce such a term to a primitive term, i.e. a term value(s, x) of STAT. Consider, however, the following derivation in LSTAT (in concrete syntax) :

$$\begin{aligned}
& \mathrm{val}(m : \underline{skip} ; \underline{if}\ y \geq 0\ \underline{then}\ \underline{goto}\ m\ \underline{fi}\ , x) \\
= {} & \mathrm{eval}(\underline{skip}, m : \underline{skip}; \underline{if}\ y \geq 0\ \underline{then}\ \underline{goto}\ \underline{m}\ \underline{fi}, P, x) \\
= {} & \mathrm{eval}(\underline{skip}; \underline{skip}, \underline{if}\ y \geq 0\ \underline{then}\ \underline{goto}\ m\ \underline{fi}, P, x) \\
= {} & \mathrm{eval}(\underline{skip}, \underline{if}\ y \geq 0\ \underline{then}\ \underline{goto}\ m\ \underline{fi}, P, x) \\
= {} & \underline{if}\ \mathrm{value}(\underline{skip}, y) \geq 0\ \underline{then}\ \mathrm{eval}(\underline{skip}, \mathrm{conti}(m, P), P, x) \\
& \qquad\qquad \underline{else}\ \mathrm{eval}(\underline{skip}, \underline{skip}, P, x) \qquad \underline{fi} \\
= {} & \mathrm{eval}(\underline{skip}, \mathrm{conti}\ (m, P), P, x) \\
= {} & \mathrm{eval}(\underline{skip}, m : \underline{skip}; \underline{if}\ y \geq 0\ \underline{then}\ \underline{goto}\ m\ \underline{fi}, P, x) \\
= {} & - - -
\end{aligned}$$

where P denotes the sequence $m : \underline{skip}\ ; \underline{if}\ y \geq 0\ \underline{then}\ \underline{goto}\ m\ \underline{fi}$. The derivation is cyclic and does not lead to a primitive term. Thus the interpretation of val(P, x) is not fixed by the axioms and a natural interpretation besides arbitrary integers is "undefined". This necessitates the generalized setting of partial algebras.

Let us summarize the properties of LSTAT : LSTAT is partially sufficiently complete and hierarchy-consistent and moreover has an initial and a strongly terminal model in MDEF(HGEN(LSTAT)). In contrast to STAT , not all models are minimally defined and extensionally equivalent. Especially, the initial models are not strongly initial.

Similarly to section 3.2 we may define a normal form for terms of sort $\underline{\mathrm{lst}}$. In the partially initial model two terms of sort $\underline{\mathrm{lst}}$ are interpreted equally iff they both are interpreted as undefined or they both are interpreted as defined and have equal normal forms. Since LSTAT is partially sufficiently complete and initial models I are minimally defined, for each term c of sort $\underline{\mathrm{lst}}$ we have

$$I \models \mathrm{val}(c, x) = i \quad \text{iff} \quad \mathrm{LSTAT} \vdash \mathrm{val}(c, x) = i \ ,$$

i.e. "computability" coincides with "first order deducibility". Therefore the initial models define a kind of "operational semantics".

Call a term c of sort $\underline{\mathrm{lst}}$ *terminating* , if there exists an identifier x and an integer i with $\mathrm{LSTAT} \vdash \mathrm{val}(c, x) = i$. Note that for terminating c there is for every y a j such that $\mathrm{LSTAT} \vdash \mathrm{val}(c, y) = j$.

The equality of terminating "programs" c1, c2 in a weakly terminal model Z is characterized by the following formula:

$$\begin{aligned}
c1^Z = c2^Z \;\Leftrightarrow\; & \forall\ \underline{\mathrm{id}}\ x, \underline{\mathrm{lst}}\ c, c' : \mathrm{val}(\mathrm{conc}(c, \mathrm{conc}(c1, c')), x)^Z = \\
& \qquad \mathrm{val}(\mathrm{conc}(c, \mathrm{conc}(c2, c')), x)^Z \\
\Leftrightarrow\; & \forall\ \underline{\mathrm{id}}\ x, \underline{\mathrm{lst}}\ c, c', \underline{\mathrm{int}}\ i : \mathrm{LSTAT} \vdash \mathrm{val}(\mathrm{conc}(c, \mathrm{conc}(c1, c')), x) = i \Leftrightarrow \\
& \qquad \mathrm{LSTAT} \vdash \mathrm{val}(\mathrm{conc}(c, \mathrm{conc}(c2, c')), x) = i
\end{aligned}$$

Again a particular strongly terminal model in MDEF(HGEN(LSTAT)) can be given explicitly by the techniques of denotational semantics using continuations (cf. /Broy et al. 81/ where such a model is outlined).

Once more there is a host of other models for LSTAT. Most interestingly, there are models which are totally defined, i.e. models M in which $val(p, x)^M$ is defined even for non-terminating p. To rule out such models would mean fixing the definedness predicate D completely by the axioms which would solve the halting problem. Thus there can be no type both characterizing our language and avoiding such models (cf. /Broy, Wirsing 80b/).

For the construction of a denotational model one essentially uses an environment associating continuations with label identifiers. Because of the interdependence of these continuations, this environment must be defined recursively, i.e. as a fixpoint of a functional. If the *least* fixpoint is taken the resulting model lies in MDEF(HGEN(LSTAT)). Other fixpoints (maximal or optimal ones) lead to models which are no longer minimally defined. Still each denotational model is fully abstract and thus strongly terminal in its class of extensional equivalence. The relations between the various models of LSTAT are illustrated by the following picture:

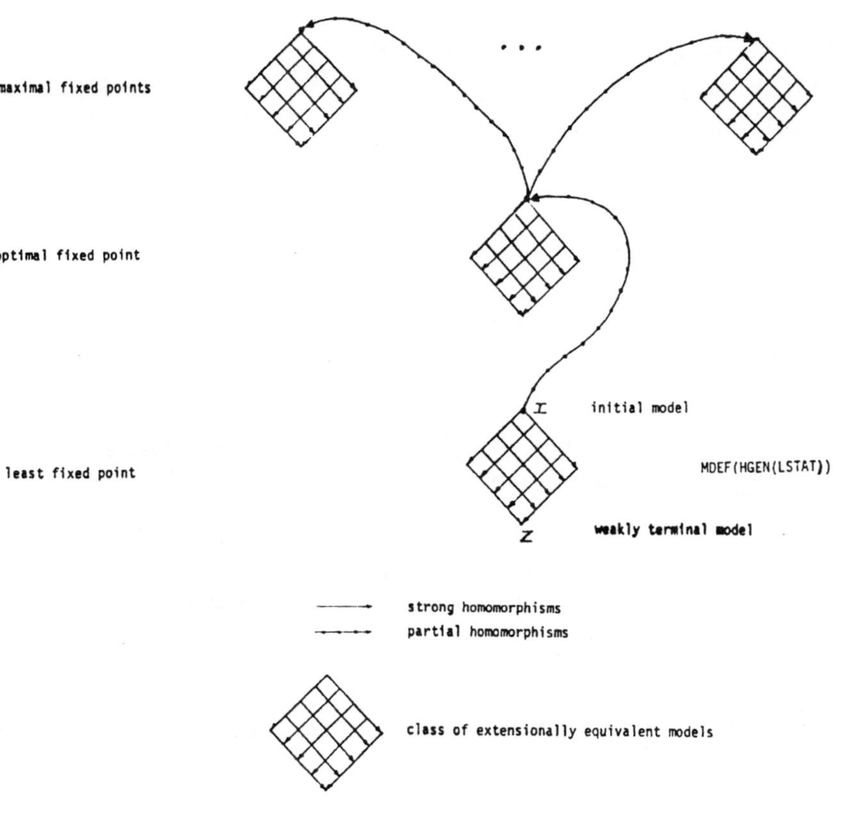

5. Concluding Remarks

Algebraic types characterize programming languages using the following transcriptions: The context-free syntax corresponds to the type's signature: Each production becomes a function symbol, the syntactic entities correspond to sorts. In this way every program is represented by a term of the term algebra. The context-conditions can e.g. be specified by incorporating into the type appropriate predicates on the abstract syntax. The semantics of the programming language is defined relative to the semantics of the primitive types using positive conditional formulas.

An algebraic specification of a programming language seems especially promising for the comparison of semantic descriptions when different description methods are used, for discussing the dependence and compatibility of various semantic requirements, for deriving complementary language specifications and constructing concrete models, and for establishing an "algebra of programs" which allows the development of programs by transformations and/or their verification.

Finally the algebraic method also seems to be a tool for treating data structures and control structures in a uniform way.

Acknowledgement:

We gratefully acknowledge valuable discussions with Prof. F.L. Bauer and our colleagues from the project CIP. Thanks go to A. Laut for reading a draft version and to D. Sannella for having a look at our English.

References

/Bauer, Wössner 81/
F.L. Bauer, H. Wössner: Algorithmische Sprache und Programmentwicklung. Berlin-Heidelberg-New York: Springer 1981

/Broy et al. 81/
M. Broy, W. Dosch, B. Möller, M. Wirsing: GOTOs - A study in the algebraic specification of programming languages. University of Edinburgh, Dept. of Computer Science, Rep. CSR-89-81

/Broy, Wirsing 80a/
M. Broy, M. Wirsing: Programming languages as abstract data types. In: M. Dauchet (ed.): Proc. 5th Colloquium on "Arbres en Algèbre et en Programmation", Lille (1980), 160-177

/Broy, Wirsing 80b/
M. Broy, M. Wirsing: Partial-recursive functions and abstract data types. Bulletin of the EATCS 11, 34-41 (1980)

/Broy, Wirsing 80c/
M. Broy, M. Wirsing: Initial versus terminal algebra semantics for partially defined abstract data types. TU München, TUM-I8018 (1980)

/Burstall, Goguen 77/
R.M. Burstall, J.A. Goguen: Putting theories together to make specifications. Proc. of the Fifth Int. Joint Conf. on Artificial Intelligence, MIT, Cambridge, Mass., 1045-1048 (1977)

/Courcelle, Nivat 78/
B. Courcelle, M. Nivat: The algebraic semantics of program schemes. 7th MFCS, LNCS 64, 16-30, (1978)

/Goguen et al. 77/
J.A. Goguen, J.W. Thatcher, E.G. Wagner: Initial algebra semantics and continuous algebras. JACM 24, 68-95 (1977)

/Goguen et al. 78/
J.A. Goguen, J.W. Thatcher, E.G. Wagner: An initial algebra approach to the specification, correctness and implementation of abstract data types. In: R.T. Yeh (ed.): Current trends in programming methodology. Vol. 4, Data structuring. Englewood Cliffs, N.J. : Prentice Hall (1978), 80-149

/Guttag 75/
J.V. Guttag: The specification and application to programming of abstract data types. Ph. D. Thesis, Univ. of Toronto, Dept. of Comp. Science, Rep. CSRG-59 (1975)

/Laut 81/
A. Laut: Von abstrakter Syntax zu verketteten Bäumen - Entwicklung einer Datenstruktur für die Programm-Manipulation. Dissertation, Technische Universität München, Fakultät für Mathematik (1981)

/Milner 77/
R. Milner: Fully abstract models of typed λ-calculi. TCS 4, 1-22 (1977)

/Scott, Strachey 71/
D. Scott, C. Strachey: Toward a mathematical semantics for computer languages. Oxford University Computing Laboratory, Technical Monograph PRG-6 (1971)

/Wand 77/
M. Wand: First-order identities as a defining language. Indiana University, Comp. Science Department, Technical Report No. 29 (1977)

/Wirsing et al. 80/
M. Wirsing, P. Pepper, H. Partsch, W. Dosch, M. Broy: On hierarchies of abstract data types. Technische Universität München, Institut für Informatik, TUM-I8007 (1980)

AN ORDER SEMANTICS FOR NON-DETERMINISTIC RECURSIVE PROGRAM SCHEMES

Axel Poigné

Informatik II
Universität Dortmund
Postfach 50 05 00
D-4600 Dortmund 50

0. INTRODUCTION

Non-deterministic recursive program schemes are investigated by Arnold and Nivat in several papers [5],[6],[7]. They prove the coincidence of operational and denotational semantics using greatest fixpoints and metric interpretations. The objective of this paper is to demonstrate that this result may be achieved using the standard least fix-point approach.

Non-deterministic recursive program schemes are systems of equations $\phi_i(x_{io},\ldots,x_{in_i}) = \tau_i$, $i \in \underline{n}$, where each term τ_i is built up from some basic function symbols, the function variables ϕ_i, the variables x_{ij} and a binary function symbol $\underline{or}$ which is a choice construct saying that a term $t_o \,\underline{or}\, t_1$ may either be evaluated to t_o or to t_1.

If we restrict our attention to formal computations [7] deterministic recursive program schemes naturally compute infinite trees being defined as least upper bounds of their finite approximations. Because of the choice construct in the non-deterministic case a set of finite and infinite trees may be the result of the computation. Thus to extend the least fixpoint approach we may ask what are finite approximations of (infinite) sets of finite and infinite trees. The natural choice is: finite sets of finite trees. This will be the basic idea of our approach. Our view is somewhat opposed to that of Arnold and Nivat [7] who understand 'the computed infinite tree as the result of an infinite computation rather then the lub of the results of a collection of finite computations'.

This paper extends the results of [16] where systems of non-deterministic equations are considered. It should be noted that many of our ideas are inspired by [7],[10],[15]. Due to the limitation of space we are only able to state the theorems. Proofs will be published elsewhere. For category theory we refer to [11],[13].

1. OPERATIONAL SEMANTICS

Dealing with recursive program schemes we believe that the appropriate level of discourse is that of algebraic theories.

1.1 *Definition:* An *(algebraic) theory* is a $\mathbb{N}\times\mathbb{N}$-sorted algebra with operators $\circ_{m,n,p}: T(m,n)\times T(n,p) \to T(m,p)$ for composition, $1_m: \underline{1} \to T(m,m)$ for identity $u_i: \underline{1} \to T(1,m)$ for inclusion and $()_m: T(1,n)^m \to T(m,n)$ for tupling, $m,n,p \in \mathbb{N}$ and $i \in \underline{m}:=\{0,\ldots,m-1\}$, satisfying the "category axioms" (indices omitted)

$$1 \circ f = f = f \circ 1 \qquad f\circ(g\circ h) = (f\circ g)\circ h$$

and the "coproduct axioms"

$(u_o \circ f,\dots, u_{m-1}\circ f) = f \qquad u_i \circ (f_o,\dots,f_{m-1}) = f_i$.

With the standard notion of homomorphism this defines a category Th (cf. [1]).

1.2 *Proposition*: Let Op be the category of operator domains (i.e. ranked sets $\Omega = (\Omega,\ a:\Omega \to \mathbb{N})$ with morphisms preserving the rank). Then the forgetful functor $V\colon \underline{Th} \to \underline{Op}$, $T \to (\{(n,t)\mid t\in T(1,n)\},a)$ with $a(n,t):= n$ has a left adjoint.[1]

A free theory T_Ω over an operator domain Ω is obtained by the Kleisli construction [13], explicitly: carriers are $T_\Omega(m,n) = T_\Omega(\underline{n})^{\underline{m}}$ (with $T_\Omega(X)$ being the canonical free term algebra over X [1]), composition is given by $f\circ g:= g^{\#}\cdot f$ where $g^{\#}:T_\Omega(\underline{n}) \to T_\Omega(\underline{p})$ is the unique homomorphic extension of $g\colon \underline{n} \to T_\Omega(\underline{p})$. Units are mappings $m\eta\colon \underline{m} \to T_\Omega(\underline{m})$ $i \to \{i\}$. The coproduct structure is given by $u_i\colon \underline{1} \to T_\Omega(1,n)$, $0 \to \{i\}$ and $()_m\colon T_\Omega(1,n)^m \to T_\Omega(m,n)$, $(f_o,\dots,f_{m-1}) \to [f_o,\dots,f_{m-1}]$, where $[f_o,\dots,f_{m-1}](i):= f_i(0)$ is uniquely defined by coproduct properties (in set).

Let $\Omega+$ be an operator domain Ω plus an additional binary operator or, moreover let Φ be an operator domain of *function variables*. Then *non-deterministic recursive program schemes* S (for short ndps) may be understood as morphisms of operator domains $S\colon \Phi \to T_{\Phi+\Omega+}V$, where $\Phi+\Omega+$ is the coproduct of the operator domains Φ and $\Omega+$ (explicitly the disjoint union of Φ and $\Omega+$ with appropriate arity function).

An *elementary step* in a *formal computation* with a ndps S then has one of the following forms
- replacing a function variable by the right hand side of the scheme
- making a non-deterministic choice.

Formally, on $T_{\Phi+\Omega+}(\underline{n})$ a relation $\to$ is defined by: $t \to t'$ iff

(i) $t = \phi(t_o,\dots,t_{a(\phi)-1})$ with $\phi\in\Phi$ and $t' = h^{\#}(S(\phi))$ where $h^{\#}\colon T_{\Phi+\Omega+}(\underline{a(\phi)}) \to T_{\Phi+\Omega+}(\underline{n})$ is the unique homomorphic extension of $h\colon \underline{a(\phi)} \to T_{\Phi+\Omega+}(\underline{n})$, $i \to t_i$, or

(ii) $t = t_o$ or t_1 and ($t' = t_o$ or $t' = t_1$),or

(iii) $t = \sigma(t_o,\dots,t_{a(\sigma)-1})$ with $\sigma\in\Phi+\Omega+$ and there exists a t_i' such that $t_i \to t_i'$ for $i\in\underline{a(\sigma)}$ and $t' = \sigma(t_o,\dots,t_i',\dots,t_{a(\sigma)-1})$.

Let $\to^r$ be the reflexive and $\to^*$ be the reflexive and transitive closure of $\to$.

Given a ndps $S\colon \Phi \to T_{\Phi+\Omega+}V$, a *computation sequence* is a sequence $(t_i|i\in\mathbb{N})$ with $t_i\in T_{\Phi+\Omega+}(\underline{n})$ such that $t_i \to^r t_{i+1}$ for all $i\in\mathbb{N}$ and that $t_i = t_{i+k}$ for all $k\in\mathbb{N}$ if $t_i = t_{i+1}$. In the latter case the computation sequence is called *finite* otherwise *infinite*.

According to [7] a computation sequence is considered to be successful if the resulting (possibly infinite) term only consists of basic operator symbols. As in [7] we use orders to give a formal definition:

Let pos and cpo be the categories of posets and ω-complete posets (cf. [2]). If the posets have a least element $\bot$ and if morphisms are strict we use $\underline{pos}_\bot$ and $\underline{cpo}_\bot$ as notation.

1.3 *Definition*: Let $B = \underline{pos}$ or $B = \underline{cpo}$. As in [3] $B_\bot$-*enriched theories* are theories such that for all $m,n,p \in \mathbb{N}$ $T(m,n) \in B_\bot$, $\circ_{m,n,p}: T(m,n)\times T(n,p) \to T(m,p) \in B$ and $\bot \circ f = \bot$, and $(\;)_m: T(1,n)^m \to T(m,n) \in B$. With homomorphisms such that $F(m,n): T(m,n) \to T'(m,n) \in B_\bot$ these data define categories $\underline{Th\text{-}B}_\bot$.

1.4 *Proposition*:[3] The forgetful functors $\underline{Th\text{-}pos}_\bot \to \underline{Op}$, $\underline{Th\text{-}cpo}_\bot \to \underline{Op}$ have left adjoints.

Again free theories are obtained by the Kleisli construction. Instead of free algebras free ordered algebras resp. free ω-complete algebras are to be used [2]. The resulting free ordered resp. ω-complete theory will be denoted FT_Ω resp. CT_Ω.

Now let $\Gamma: T_{\Phi+\Omega+} \to CT_\Omega$ be the theory morphism uniquely induced by $\gamma: \Phi+\Omega+ \to CT_\Omega V$, $\gamma(\sigma) := \bot$ for $\sigma \in \Phi+$ and $\gamma(\sigma) := \sigma(0,\dots,a(\sigma)-1)$ for $\sigma \in \Omega$. Intuitively Γ maps $\Phi+\Omega+$-terms to $\Omega_\bot$-terms ($\Omega_\bot := \Omega + \{\bot\}$) where the operators $\phi \in \Phi$ and the or-operator are replaced by $\bot$.

1.5 *Lemma*: For all $t,t' \in T_{\Phi+\Omega+}(\underline{n})$, $n \in \mathbb{N}$, $t \to t'$ implies $\Gamma(t) \le \Gamma(t')$.

1.6 *Definition*: (i) Let P be a poset. An element $x \in P$ is called *maximal* iff for all $y \in P$ $x \le y$ implies $x = y$.

(ii) A computation sequence $(t_n | n\; \mathbb{N})$ is called *successful* iff $\bigsqcup_n \Gamma(t_n)$ is maximal (in $CT_\Omega(1,m)$ if $t_n \in T_{\Phi+\Omega+}(\underline{m})$).

$\bigsqcup_n \Gamma(t_n)$ is called the *result* of the computation sequence $(t_n | n \in \mathbb{N})$. By $Res_S(t)$ we denote the set of results of all successful computation sequences starting in $t \in T_{\Phi+\Omega+}(\underline{n})$.

2. NON-DETERMINISM VERSUS ALGEBRAIC STRUCTURE VERSUS ORDER

Several authors [9],[10],[12] pointed out that semilattices (or commutative idempotent semigroups) are the appropriate structure to model bounded non-determinism. This is due to the observation that the finite power set functor $P_f: \underline{set} \to \underline{sl}$, $X \to (\{S \subseteq X | S \text{ finite, non empty}\}, \cup)$ is the left adjoint or "free structure" functor to the forgetful functor $\underline{sl} \to \underline{set}$. Here $\underline{sl}$ denotes the category of semilattices. (Bounded) non-deterministic functions are understood as one-many functions which may be characterized as functions $f: X \to P_f(Y)$. These are exactly the morphisms of the Kleisli category to the above adjunction.

In [16]we introduced Ω-algebras with respect to the tensorproduct in $\underline{sl}$ as non-deterministic Ω-algebras. This is due to the operational point of view which implies that the equation

$$\sigma(x_0,\dots,x_i \;\underline{or}\; x_i',\dots,x_{a(\sigma)-1}) = \sigma(x_0,\dots,x_i,\dots,x_{a(\sigma)-1}) \;\underline{or}\; \sigma(x_0,\dots,x_i',\dots,x_{a(\sigma)-1})$$

should hold for all operators σ and all $i \in \underline{a(\sigma)}$, i.e. the algebra operations are linear in each component.

2.1 *Definition*: A (non-deterministic) *OI-Ω-algebra* consists of a semilattice (A,+) and a Ω-indexed family of operations $\delta_\sigma : A^{a(\sigma)} \to A$ which are linear in each component. With Ω-homomorphisms being linear mappings this defines a category $\underline{\text{OI-}\Omega\text{-alg}}$.

2.2 *Proposition*: The forgetful functor $\underline{\text{OI-}\Omega\text{-alg}} \to \underline{\text{set}}$ has a left adjoint. Free structures are given by: carrier $PT_\Omega(X) := \{S \subseteq T_\Omega(X) \mid S \text{ finite, non empty}\}$, $S + S' := S \cup S'$, and $\delta_\sigma(S_o,\dots,S_{a(\sigma)-1}) := \{\sigma(t_o,\dots,t_{a(\sigma)-1}) \mid t_i \in S_i\}$.

2.3 *Remark*: (i) Let $\underline{\Omega\text{-alg}_\otimes\text{-sl}}$ be the category of Ω-algebras with respect to the tensor product in $\underline{\text{sl}}$ [16]. Then $\underline{\text{OI-}\Omega\text{-alg}} = \underline{\Omega\text{-alg}_\otimes\text{-sl}}$

(ii) It should be noted that the composition in the Kleisli category to the above adjunction is called OI-substitution in [8].

2.4 *Definition*: A theory is called *OI-theory* iff it is enriched in the following sense: For $m,n \in \mathbb{N}$ $T(m,n)$ is a semilattice, the mappings $\circ: T(m,n) \times T(n,p) \to T(m,p)$ are bilinear, the mappings $()_m : T(1,n)^m \to T(m,n)$ are linear (w.r.t.products in $\underline{\text{sl}}$). With linear homomorphisms this defines a category $\underline{\text{OI-Th}}$.

This definition is somewhat brute force as parts of the algebraic structure are defined with respect to products and other parts w.r.t. tensor products. But the bilinearity is necessary to model the non-deterministic composition. The background idea is that any equationally defined category of OI-algebras should correspond to an OI-theory and vice versa. This correspondance will be discussed elsewhere. Here we are interested in the following

2.5 *Proposition*: The forgetful functor $\underline{\text{OI-Th}} \to \underline{\text{Op}}$ has a left adjoint. Again given an operator domain Ω the free OI-theory PT_Ω over Ω is obtained by the Kleisli construction w.r.t. the adjunction in 2.2.

As a next step we introduce order. Hennessy and Plotkin pointed out that there are several possibilities to enrich semilattices with order[10]. We choose the following one: Semilattices may be understood as join-semilattices with order structure $x \le y$ iff $x + y = y$. A free join-semilattice over a poset $(P,\le)$ then is given by: carrier $\{[S]_{\eqsim} \mid S \subseteq X \text{ finite and non empty}\}$, operation $[S]_{\eqsim}+[S']_{\eqsim} := [S \cup S']_{\eqsim}$ with order induced by $S \sqsubseteq S'$ iff $\forall s \in S\, \exists s' \in S': s \le s'$ and $\eqsim$ being the congruence defined by $S \eqsim S'$ iff $S \sqsubseteq S'$ and $S' \sqsubseteq S$.

The same definition may be given for ω-complete posets, but the definition of the left adjoint is more elaborate (compare [10]).

We now combine non-determinism, algebraic structure and ω-completeness in an appropriate way:

2.6 *Definition*: Let $A = ((A,+),(\delta_\sigma|\sigma\in\Omega))$ be an OI-Ω-algebra. If $((A,\leq),(\delta_\sigma|\sigma\in\Omega))$ with the order induced from $(A,+)$ is as well a $\underline{\text{cpo}}_\perp$-enriched Ω-algebra, then A is called a *ω-complete OI-Ω-algebra.* With morphisms as well being algebra homomorphisms as linear and strict ω-continuous mappings this defines a category $\underline{\text{OI-}\Omega\text{-alg-cpo}}_\perp$.

2.7 *Proposition*: The forgetful functor $\underline{\text{OI-}\Omega\text{-alg-cpo}}_\perp \to \underline{\text{cpo}}$ has a left adjoint.

For discretely ordered sets we have a representation theorem which is essential to our approach (we assume X to be a set discretely ordered):

2.8 *Definition*: (i) Let P be a poset, $T\subseteq P$. An element $t\in T$ is called *maximal relative* T iff for all $t'\in T$ $t\leq t'$ implies $t = t'$. Let $MAX(T):=\{t\in T|t \text{ maximal rel. } T\}$.

(ii) For $T\subseteq CT_\Omega(X)$ let $\hat{T}:= \{t\in FT_\Omega(X)|\exists t'\in T: t\leq t'\}$ be the *ideal of finite subtrees generated by* T and $C(T):=\{\bigsqcup k|k \ \omega\text{-chain in } \hat{T}\}$ be the *chain-closure* of T. ($FT_\Omega(X)$ $(CT_\Omega(X))$ being the free (ω-complete) ordered Ω-algebra over X [2]).

(iii) A subset $T\subseteq CT_\Omega(X)$ is called *finitely generated* iff there exists a chain $(T_n|n\in\mathbb{N})$ of finite, non empty subsets of $FT_\Omega(X)$ with $T_n \sqsubseteq T_{n+1}$ for all $n\in\mathbb{N}$ such that $T = C_m(\bigcup_n T_n):= MAX(C(\bigcup_n T_n))$.

2.9 *Theorem*: A free $\underline{\text{OI-}\Omega\text{-alg-cpo}}_\perp$-object over a discretely ordered set X is given by the following data:

(i) $CPT_\Omega(X) := \{T\subseteq CT_\Omega(X)|\ T \text{ finitely generated}\}$

(ii) $T\leq T'$ iff $T\sqsubseteq T'$

(iii) $\bigsqcup_n T_n := C_m(\bigcup_n T_n)$ for ω-chains $(T_n|n\in\mathbb{N})$

(iv) $T + T' := C_m(\ T\cup T'\ )$

(v) $\delta_\sigma(T_o,\ldots,T_{a(\sigma)-1}) := C_m(\{\sigma(t_o,\ldots,t_{a(\sigma)-1})|\ t_i\in T_i\})$

Let us look what happens on the level of theories:

2.10 *Definition*: Let T be an OI-theory. If T with the order induced from $(T(m,n),+)$, $m,n\in\mathbb{N}$, is a $\underline{\text{cpo}}_\perp$-enriched theory, then T is called a *ω-complete OI-theory.* With OI-theory morphisms being as well morphisms of $\underline{\text{cpo}}_\perp$-enriched theories we have a category $\underline{\text{OI-Th-cpo}}_\perp$.

2.11 *Proposition*: The forgetful functor $\underline{\text{OI-Th-cpo}}_\perp \to \underline{\text{Op}}$ has a left adjoint. A free ω-complete OI-theory is again obtained by the Kleisli construction with respect to the adjunction in 2.7 resp. 2.9 . Hom-sets are $CPT_\Omega(m,n):= CPT_\Omega(\underline{n})^{\underline{m}}$ ($\underline{m}$ discretely ordered).

3. COINCIDENCE OF OPERATIONAL AND DENOTATIONAL SEMANTICS

With the definitions given so far we are able to follow the arguments of [16.3], but everything is lifted to the level of theories.

3.1 *Definition:* Let an Op-morphism $e: \Omega+ \to CPT_{\Phi+\Omega}V$ (CPT_Ω being the free ω-complete OI-theory given in 2.11) defined by $e(\sigma) := \sigma(0,\dots,a(\sigma)-1)$ and $e(\underline{or}) := \{0,1\}$ ($\{0,1\} \varepsilon CPT_{\Phi+\Omega}(1,2)$ is the 'elementary non-deterministic operator' in $CPT_{\Phi+\Omega}$). Then given an Op-morphism $f: \Phi \to CPT_{\Phi+\Omega}V$ coproduct properties induce an **arrow** $[f,e]: \Phi+\Omega+ \to CPT_{\Phi+\Omega}V$ and freeness of $T_{\Phi+\Omega+}$ a theory morphism $[f,e]^{\#}: T_{\Phi+\Omega+} \to CPT_{\Phi+\Omega}$. As the hom sets $\underline{Op}(\Phi, CPT_{\Phi+\Omega}V)$ are isomorphic to the product $\prod_{\phi\varepsilon\Phi} CPT_{\Phi+\Omega}(1,a(\phi))$ (in $\underline{set}$) we define (without explicitly stating the isomorphisms):

$$\hat{S}: \prod_{\phi\varepsilon\Phi} CPT_{\Phi+\Omega}(1,a(\phi)) \to \prod_{\phi\varepsilon\Phi} CPT_{\Phi+\Omega}(1,a(\phi)), \quad \hat{S}(f) := [f,e]^{\#}V \cdot S$$

where $S: \Phi \to T_{\Phi+\Omega+}V$ is the given ndps.

3.2 *Lemma:* $\hat{S}$ is ω-continuous with respect to the $\underline{cpo}_\perp$-structure induced from CPT_Ω. The least fixpoint $FIX(\hat{S})$ of $\hat{S}$ is $\bigsqcup_n \hat{S}^n(\perp)$ with $\perp: \Phi \to CPT_{\Phi+\Omega}V$, $\phi \to \perp$.

3.3 *Definition:* The *denotational semantics* Val_S of a ndps $S: \Phi \to T_{\Phi+\Omega+}V$ is defined by

$$Val_S := FIX(\hat{S}).$$

To obtain the result that operational semantics equals the denotational semantics the schemes are to be Greibach [5].

3.4 *Definition:* Let X be a set. A term $t \varepsilon T_{\Phi+\Omega+}(X)$ is said to *satisfy the Greibach condition* iff (i) $t = x$ with $x \varepsilon X$, or (ii) $t = \sigma(t_0,\dots,t_{a(\sigma)-1})$ with $\sigma \varepsilon \Omega$, or $t = t_0 \ \underline{or} \ t_1$ and t_0 and t_1 satisfy the Greibach condition.
A ndps $S: \Phi \to T_{\Phi+\Omega+}V$ is called *Greibach* iff for all $\phi \varepsilon \Phi$ $S(\phi)$ satisfies the Greibach condition.

3.5 *(Main) Theorem:* Let $S: \Phi \to T_{\Phi+\Omega+}V$ be a Greibach scheme. Then the operational and denotational semantics coincide, i.e.

$$Res_S(\ \phi(0,\dots,a(\phi)-1)\ ) = Val_S(\phi) \quad \text{for all } \phi \varepsilon \Phi \quad \text{(as sets)}.$$

The proof is a lifting of the proof given in [16] to the level of algebraic theories. A first lemma makes use of the fact that $CPT_{\Phi+\Omega}$ is a free ω-complete OI-theory. Intuitively it states that terms t_ϕ generated by S from terms $\phi(0,\dots,a(\phi)-1)$ either may be substituted for the ϕ's in the right hand sides $S(\phi)$ of the scheme S or that the $S(\phi)$'s may be substituted for the ϕ's in the terms t_ϕ and the result is the same.

3.6 *Lemma:* Let $\tilde{S}: CPT_{\Phi+\Omega} \to CPT_{\Phi+\Omega}$ be the OI-Th-cpo$_{\perp}$-morphism induced by $\hat{S}(\phi\eta): \Phi \to CPT_{\Phi+\Omega}V$ and $e: \Omega+ \to CPT_{\Phi+\Omega}V$ with $\phi\eta: \Phi \to CPT_{\Phi+\Omega}V$, $\phi \to \phi(0,\dots,a(\phi)-1)$ (compare 3.1). Then for all $n \in \mathbb{N}$ $\hat{S}^n(\phi\eta) = \tilde{S}^n \cdot \phi\eta$ and $\hat{S}^n(\perp) = [\perp,\bar{e}]^{\#} \cdot \tilde{S}^n \cdot \phi\eta$ with $[\perp,\bar{e}]^{\#}: CPT_{\Phi+\Omega} \to CPT_{\Phi+\Omega}$ induced by $[\perp,\bar{e}]: \Phi+\Omega \to CPT_{\Phi+\Omega}V$ with $\bar{e}(\sigma) := \sigma(0,\dots,a(\sigma)-1)$ for $\sigma\in\Omega$.

The next lemma establishes several connections between computation by substitution, i.e. applying S, and operational computation steps.

3.7 *Lemma:* (i) Let $t \in T_{\Phi+\Omega+}(1,n)$, $n \in \mathbb{N}$. Then there exists a $t' \in \Pi(t)$ s.t. $t \to^* t'$

($\Pi = [\phi\eta,\bar{e}]^{\#}: CPT_{\Phi+\Omega} \to CPT_{\Phi+\Omega}$)

(ii) Let $T \in CPT_{\Phi+\Omega}(1,n)$. Then for all $t \in T$ there exists a $t' \in \tilde{S}(T)$ s.t. $t \to^* t'$ and for all $t' \in \tilde{S}(T)$ there exists a $t \in T$ s.t. $t \to^* t'$.

(iii) Let $(t_n | n \in \mathbb{N})$ be a computation sequence. Then for all $n \in \mathbb{N}$ there exists a $t'_n \in \tilde{S}^n(\Pi(t_n))$ s.t. $t_n \to^* t'_n$.

The proofs are done by induction on length of terms. In (iii) we use that given $t,t' \in T_{\Phi+\Omega+}(1,n)$ s.t. $t \to t'$ for all $s' \in \tilde{S}^n(\Pi(t'))$ there exists a $s \in \tilde{S}^{n+1}(\Pi(t))$ s.t. $s' \to^* s$. In (i) all non-deterministic choices are to be executed. (ii) says that computation by substitution may be simulated by elementary computation steps. (iii) implies that computation by substitution involves at least one elementary computation step. The simulation results are needed to prove

3.8 *Lemma:* For any $t \in T_{\Phi+\Omega+}(\underline{m})$ $Res_S(t) \sqsubseteq C_m(\bigcup_n [\perp,\bar{e}]^{\#}(\tilde{S}^n(\Pi(t))))$.

Let $(t_n | n \in \mathbb{N})$ be a successful computation sequence. By 3.7(iii) there exists a $t'_n \in \tilde{S}^n(\Pi(t_n))$ s.t. $t_n \to^* t'_n$. Thus $\Gamma(t_n) \le \Gamma(t'_n)$. But $\Gamma(t'_n) = [\perp,\bar{e}]^{\#}(t'_n)$ as t'_n contains no choice operator. Maximality of $\bigsqcup_n \Gamma(t_n)$ implies the result.

To ensure the reverse direction we need that the scheme is Greibach. The argument uses the fact that for Greibach schemes after n substitutions all function variables in a term are at a distance at least n from the root.
Given a ω-chain $(x_n | n \in \mathbb{N})$ in $\overline{\bigcup_n [\perp,\bar{e}]^{\#}(\tilde{S}^n(\Pi(t)))}$ we use the above argument to show that there exists a term $t_n \in \tilde{S}^{|x_n|}(\Pi(t))$ ($|x_n|$ being the depth of x_n) such that $x_n \le t_n$. Again the same argument ensures for any such t_n the existence of a t_{n-1} with $x_{n-1} \le t_{n-1}$ and $t_{n-1} \to^* t_n$, $n < 0$. Then by König's lemma the existence of a possibly infinite computation sequence of such t_n's follows. Again using the distance argument it is easy to see that the computation sequence is successful. This yields (for details compare [16])

3.9 *Lemma:* For any $t \in T_{\Phi+\Omega+}(\underline{m})$ $C_m(\bigcup_n [\perp,\bar{e}]^{\#}(\tilde{S}^n(\Pi(t))) \sqsubseteq Res_S(t)$.

3.6, 3.8 and 3.9 imply 3.5 by an easy computation.

4. CONCLUSIONS

We have extended the methods introduced in [16] for systems of non-deterministic equations to the level of non-deterministic recursive program schemes. A canonical next step is to consider non-deterministic schemes of higher types. As the category of join-semilattices is monoidal closed we should be able to construct theories of higher types (for instance in the sense of [4]). We believe that then the same proof techniques should work.

5. REFERENCES

[1] ADJ-group: A junction between computer science and category theory. IBM research report RC-4526, 1973

[2] ADJ-group: Some fundamentals of order algebraic semantics. MFCS '76, LNCS 45, 1976

[3] ADJ-group: Rational algebraic theories and fixed-point solutions. 17th IEEE Symp. on Found. of Comp., Houston 1976

[4] ADJ-group: Programming languages as mathematical objects. MFCS '78, LNCS 64 1978

[5] Arnold,A.,Nivat,M.: Non deterministic recursive program schemes. FCT '77, LNCS 56, Poznan 1977

[6] Arnold,A.,Nivat,M.: Metric interpretations of infinite trees and semantics of non deterministic programs. Techn. Rep., Lille 1978

[7] Arnold,A.,Nivat,M.: Formal computations of non deterministic recursive program schemes. Math. Syst. Th. 13, 1980

[8] Engelfriet,J.,Schmidt,E.M.: IO and OI, JCCS 15, 1977

[9] Hennessy, M.C.B.,Ashcroft,E.A.: The semantics of non-determinism. 3rd ICALP, Edinburgh 1976

[10] Hennessy,M.C.B.,Plotkin,G.: Full abstraction of a simple programming language. MFCS '79, LNCS 74, 1979

[11] MacLane,S.: Kategorien.Berlin-Heidelberg-New-York, 1972

[12] Maibaum,T.S.E.: The semantics of non-determinism. Res. rep. CS-77-30, Waterloo 1977

[13] Manes,E.G.: Algebraic theories. Berlin-Heidelberg-New-York 1976

[14] Meseguer,J.:On order-complete universal algebra and enriched functorial semantics. FCT '77, LNCS 56, Poznan 1977

[15] Meseguer,J.: Ideal monads and Z-posets. to be published

[16] Poigné,A.: Using least fixed points to characterize formal computations of non-deterministic equations. Proc. Conf. Formal. of Progr. Conc.,LNCS 107, Peniscola 1981

[17] Smyth,M.B.: Power domains. JCSS 16, 1978

Quantifizierung der Qualität von Software

Udo Voges
Kernforschungszentrum Karlsruhe
Institut für Datenverarbeitung in der Technik
Postfach 3640, D-7500 Karlsruhe 1

Gliederung

1. Einleitung
2. Allgemeine Qualitätskriterien
3. Software Physik
4. Komplexitätsmaße
5. Zuverlässigkeitsmodelle
6. Testmaße
7. Ausblick
8. Literatur

Zusammenfassung

Die Quantifizierung der Qualität von Software ist noch nicht in allen Bereichen möglich und noch weniger üblich. Für die Mehrzahl der Qualitätskriterien lassen sich keine quantitativen, sondern höchstens relative Aussagen machen. Es wird auf verschiedene Komplexitätsmaße eingegangen, die eine Quantifizierung zulassen. Ebenso gibt es Zuverlässigkeitsmodelle, die Aussagen über die Fehleranzahl bzw. die Fehlerauftrittswahrscheinlichkeit machen. Darüber hinaus werden einige Testmaße aufgeführt, die den Grad der Testüberdeckung angeben. Weitere Arbeiten zur Quantifizierung sind aber erforderlich, insbesondere um einen integrierten Ansatz zu einer Gesamtaussage zu erhalten.

1. Einleitung

Im Software-Bereich ist immer stärker der Wunsch festzustellen, Zahlen über Software zu bekommen, die über die Informationen zu Größe, Preis und Leistung hinausgehen und die die Qualität betreffen. Bislang werden einige Qualitätsmerkmale nur recht vage beschrieben, d. h. teilweise nur als grobe Klassifizierung (schlechtere/bessere Qualität) angegeben. Es besteht aber der Wunsch, diese vagen Aussagen in numerische Aussagen zu erweitern.

In einigen Anwendungsgebieten ist dieser Wunsch besonders stark ausgeprägt. So ist im Bereich der sicherheitsrelevanten Anwendungen der Bedarf vorhanden, quantitative Aussagen über die Zuverlässigkeit und Sicherheit der Software zu bekommen, wie es für dort eingesetzte Hardware und Bauteile bereits seit langem üblich ist. In anderen Anwendungsbereichen möchte man quantitative Aussagen z. B. für Kosten- und Zeitaufwandabschätzungen, für Laufzeitabschätzung, für Portabilität und Änderbarkeit erhalten.

Es können unterschiedliche quantitative Aussagen gemacht werden. Hier soll unterschieden werden zwischen allgemeinen Qualitätskriterien und speziellen Aussagen zum Programm und zum Testen. Auf den Bereich der Abschätzung des Projektaufwandes soll nicht näher eingegangen werden.

2. Allgemeine Qualitätskriterien

Um über die Güte von Software eine Aussage zu machen, kann man verschiedene Qualitätskriterien heranziehen (vgl. Tab. 1). Teilweise wirken diese Kriterien in entgegengesetzter Richtung - größere Allgemeingültigkeit hat i.a. geringere Effizienz zur Folge - , teilweise zielen sie in dieselbe Richtung - Effizienz als Teil der Wirtschaftlichkeit, Dokumentation und Klarheit zur Verständlichkeit.

Diese Kriterien lassen sich aber nur schwerlich objektiv quantifizieren. Leichter ist es möglich, grobe subjektive Erfüllungszahlen anzugeben, eventuell als einfach Erfüllung oder Nichterfüllung (0/1-Bewertung), diese ggf. zu gewichten nach der Bedeutung der Kriterien für die jeweilige Anwendung bzw. nur die bedeutungsvollen Kriterien zu berücksichtigen. Die Summe der Erfüllungszahlen gibt dann die Güte und Qualität der Software an. Diese Zahl kann aber nicht als absolutes Maß genommen werden, sondern ist nur eine relative Bewertung im Vergleich zu Beurteilungen, die mit denselben Maßstäben gemacht wurden. Um zu objektiveren Bewertungen zu kommen, muß man auf Größen aufbauen, die sich

Allgemeingültigkeit	Portabilität
Änderbarkeit	Richtigkeit
Benutzerfreundlichkeit	Sicherheit
Dokumentation	Testbarkeit
Effizienz	Verständlichkeit
Flexibilität	Wartbarkeit
Gültigkeit	Wiederverwendbarkeit
Klarheit	Wirtschaftlichkeit
Modularität	Zuverlässigkeit

Tab. 1: Qualitätskriterien (nach /DACS79a/)

eindeutig bestimmen lassen (siehe Tab. 2). Mit Hilfe dieser Werte kann nun versucht werden, quantitative Aussagen über die Software zu gewinnen, die auch etwas über die Qualität aussagen. So läßt sich etwa die Modularität durch die Zahl der Statements je Modul und die Zahl der Moduln im System angeben, die Dokumentation durch das Verhältnis von Kommentarstatements zu Statements.

Zahl der Moduln
Zahl der Zeilen
Zahl der Statements
Zahl der ausführbaren Statements
Zahl der Statements eines Typs
Zahl der Operatoren (+,-,*,...)
Zahl der Operanden (Variablen)

Tab. 2: Meßbare Größen

3. Software Physik

Halstead /HALS77/ hat die Begriffe Software Physik und Software Science für seine Theorie über einige meßbare Größen und deren Zusammenhänge geprägt. Auf die wesentlichen Punkte soll hier eingegangen werden.

Halstead führt zunächst eine Reihe von Größen ein, die aus dem Programm direkt berechnet werden können:

n_1: Anzahl der unterschiedlichen Operatoren

n_2: Anzahl der unterschiedlichen Operanden

N_1: Gesamtzahl der Operatorverwendungen

N_2: Gesamtzahl der Operandenverwendungen.

Daraus läßt sich dann eine Reihe von weiteren Größen berechnen, die Aussagen über das Programm liefern. So kann man die Größe des Vokabulars

$$n = n_1 + n_2$$

und die beobachtete Programmlänge

$$N = N_1 + N_2$$

direkt ableiten.

Zwischen dem Vokabular und der Programmlänge besteht ein Zusammenhang, der zur Abschätzung der Programmlänge benutzt werden kann:

$$N_s = n_1 * \mathrm{lb}\, n_1 + n_2 * \mathrm{lb}\, n_2.$$

Untersuchungen haben gezeigt, daß zwischen der beobachteten Programmlänge N und der geschätzten Programmlänge N_s eine gute Übereinstimmung existiert /ELSH76/.

Ausgehend von der Programmlänge und dem Vokabular läßt sich der Umfang V (volume) eines Algorithmus bestimmen als

$$V = N * \mathrm{lb}\, n.$$

Der Umfang V wird dabei als Zahl der zur Implementierung erforderlichen Bits angegeben.

Neben dem Umfang V führt Halstead noch den potentiellen Umfang V^* ein. Dieser kann z. B. erreicht werden, wenn in einer Sprache die gewünschte Funktion bereits als aufrufbare Prozedur vorliegt. So ergibt sich z. B. für die Benutzung der Wurzelfunktion

X = SQR (Y)

mit zwei Operanden (X, Y) und zwei Operatoren (=, SQR()) der potentielle Umfang zu

$$V^* = 4 * \mathrm{lb}\, 4 = 8.$$

Das Ausprogrammieren der Wurzelfunktion z. B.in einer Assembler-Sprache, die keinen entsprechenden Prozeduraufruf enthählt, würde dagegen mehr Operanden, Operatoren und deren Verwendung verlangen und damit einen größeren Umfang V ergeben.

Über den Umfang läßt sich das Niveau L (level) eines Programms einführen:

$$L = V^{*} / V.$$

In einer idealen Programmiersprache kann man somit ein Niveau von 1 erreichen (indem $V = V^{*}$), während normalerweise L kleiner als 1 ist. L läßt sich abschätzen aus

$$L_s = (2 / n_1) * (n_2 / N_2).$$

Der Aufwand E (effort) zur Erstellung eines Programms wird definiert als

$$E = V / L.$$

Aufgrund der Definition von V und durch Ersetzen von L durch die Abschätzung L_s kann der Aufwand E damit bei Kenntnis des Vokabulars und der Programmlänge abgeschätzt werden gemäß

$$E_s = (N * lb\ n) / (2 / n_1) * (n_2 / N_2).$$

Der Aufwand E kann, insbesondere bei Vergleich von Implementierungen in Sprachen mit unterschiedlichem Niveau, nicht nur für die Erstellung, sondern auch zum Verständnis von Implementierungen herangezogen werden. Damit kann man E auch als Maß für die Programmkomplexität bezeichnen.

Versuche haben gezeigt, daß zwischen der Programmkomplexität E und der Anzahl der Fehler in einem Programm ein enger Zusammenhang besteht /FUHA75/ : je größer die Programmkomplexität, desto größer die Zahl der Fehler.

Als weitere Größen führt Halstead noch die geschätzte Zahl von Fehlern B, das Sprachniveau λ und unter Benutzung der Stroud-Zahl S die Programmierzeit T ein. Weitere Erläuterungen zu diesen Größen sowie Hinweise auf verschiedene Untersuchungen zur Unterstützung von Halsteads Theorie sind u. a. in /FILO78/ und /KNIJ78/ zu finden.

4. Komplexitätsmaß

Für die Bestimmung der Komplexität eines Programms bzw. eines Systems gibt es einige Verfahren, die mit unterschiedlichem Erfolg angewendet werden. Exemplarisch soll hier auf einige Hauptvertreter näher eingegangen werden.

Gilb /GILB76/ unterscheidet zwischen logischer und struktureller Komplexität. Die relative logische Komplexität berechnet sich aus dem Verhältnis der Verzweigungen und der Zahl der Befehle. Die relative strukturelle Komplexität ist das Verhältnis von Modulverbindungen (Zahl der Parameter und verwendeten globalen Größen) zur Zahl der Moduln. Diese beiden Maße lassen sich recht einfach berechnen, da die zugrundeliegenden Parameter leicht mit automatischen Hilfsmitteln bestimmt werden können. Die logische Komplexität läßt sich sowohl für Moduln als auch für Systeme angeben, während die strukturelle Komplexität nur für Systeme von Interesse ist.

Das Komplexitätsmaß von McCabe /MCCA76/ basiert auf Informationen, die aus dem Programmgraphen bzw. der Programmstruktur gewonnen werden können. Die Komplexität v berechnet sich als

$$v = e - n + 2 * p$$

wobei e die Anzahl der Kanten, n die Anzahl der Knoten und p die Anzahl der verbundenen Komponenten ist (i. a. ist p = 1). Das Komplexitätsmaß v gibt gleichzeitig die minimale Zahl der zu testenden Pfade an.

Untersuchungen zur Korrelation zwischen McCabes Komplexitätsmaß v und der Zahl der entdeckten Fehler in einem Modul haben eine Bestätigung des Zusammenhangs zwischen diesen Größen erbracht /BOWE78/.

In /TANI81/ werden vier Modelle zur einfachen Abschätzung vom Komplexitätsmaß v angegeben, die keine Programmgraph-Untersuchung voraussetzen, sondern auf einfacheren Programmanalysen basieren. So ist z. B. die Zahl der Sprungbefehle und der Kommentare, oder die Zahl der Prozeduraufrufe und der Parameter zu messen.

Verfeinerungen des McCabeschen Komplexitätsmaßes sind z. B. von Hansen /HANS78/ und von Myers /MYER77/ vorgeschlagen worden.

Harrison und Magel /HAMA81/ führen ein Scope Komplexitätsmaß ein, das eine aufwendigere Analyse des Programmgraphen verlangt, dafür aber auch Unterschiede zwischen Programmen aufzeigt, wo das McCabesche Komplexitätsmaß eine identische Bewertung vornimmt.

Die genannten Komplexitätsmaße können zur Qualitätsbestimmung herangezogen werden. So lassen sich daraus z.B. Aussagen über die Klarheit, Modularität, Testbarkeit und Verständlichkeit ableiten.

Ebenso können sie dazu benutzt werden, um zwischen verschiedenen Lösungen die bessere (weniger komplexe) herauszufinden.

Der festgestellte Zusammenhang zwischen Komplexität und Fehlerzahl hat auch Rückwirkungen auf die Vorgabe von Programmierrichtlinien. So gibt es Regeln, die die Modulgröße auf 50 Zeilen oder eine Seite einschränken (z. B. /IBM 74/), oder die das McCabesche Komplexitätsmaß v auf 10 beschränken /MCCA76/.

Die hier aufgezeigte Fülle von möglichen Komplexitätsmaßen zeigt allerdings, daß selbst in diesem kleinen Bereich die Meinungen und Interpretationen auseinandergehen. Je nach Auffassung und Einstellung legt man z. B. Wert auf die Unterscheidung zwischen Vor- und Rücksprüngen oder nicht. Für den Anwender bedeutet dies, daß er sich zunächst darüber im Klaren sein muß, was er bei der Berechnung der Komplexität berücksichtigt haben will, und daß er sich dann ein entsprechendes Komplexitätsmaß aussuchen muß.

5. Zuverlässigkeitsmodelle

Ein weiteres Gebiet im Bereich Software Engineering, in dem bereits seit einiger Zeit verschiedene Quantifizierungsansätze gemacht werden, ist die Zuverlässigkeits- und Fehleranalyse. Die bekanntesten Modelle sind die von Schick und Wolverton /SCWO78/, von Jelinski und Moranda /JEMO72/, von Shooman /SHOO75/ und von Littlewood und Verrall /LIVE73/.

Ziel dieser Modelle ist es, Aussagen über die Zahl der im Programm verbliebenen Fehler und die Zeit bis zum nächsten Auftreten eines Fehlers (MTBF) zu machen.

Im wesentlichen unterscheiden sich diese Modelle durch die zugrundegelegten Hypothesen über Fehlerverteilung, Fehlerbeseitigung etc. In verschiedenen Experimenten ist mit unterschiedlichem Ergebnis versucht worden, den Erfolg oder die Güte dieser Modelle nachzuweisen oder zu widerlegen. Befriedigend kann die Situation auf diesem Gebiet aber noch nicht genannt werden.

Eine Aufstellung weiterer Zuverlässigkeitsmodelle sowie auch weiterer Metriken kann in /DACS79b/ gefunden werden.

6. Testmaße

Auch auf dem Gebiet des Testens gibt es eine Reihe von Kriterien, die angeben, wie gut ein Programm ausgetestet ist /GMVO80/. Die meisten bauen auf der Programmstrukturinformation auf. Hierbei gibt es einfachere und komplexere Kriterien. Eine Aufzählung ist in Tab. 3 angegeben. Der Grad der Erfüllung der jeweiligen Testkriterien ergibt dann das zugehörige Testmaß.

Das einfachste Kriterium geht von den Befehlen aus. Das Verhältnis

TK1	Jedes Statement im Programm mindestens einmal ausgeführt
TK2	Jede Bedingungsalternative mindestens einmal ausgeführt
$TK3_n$	Jede Schleife mindestens n mal iteriert
TK4	Ausführung aller datenabhängigen Verzweigungskombinationen
TK5	Ausführung aller Pfade
TK6	Statistischer Test mit identisch verteilten Testdaten
TK7	Statistischer Test mit unterschiedlich verteilten Testdaten getrennt nach Teilbereichen

Tab. 3: Testkriterien

der ausgeführten Befehle zu den vorhandenen Befehlen gibt ein Überdeckungsmaß an (TK1, c_0). Dieses Maß ist recht einfach mit Trace-Programmen oder Instrumentierern zu messen.

Etwas mehr analytischen Aufwand erfordert das Messen der Ausführungshäufigkeit von Bedingungsalternativen (TK2, c_1). Bei diesem Testmaß muß z. B. auch ein leerer ELSE-Zweig gezählt werden, der beim ersten Testmaß nicht mitrechnet. Somit erhalten wir hier i.a. mehr Testfälle als vorher und damit bei 100%iger Erfüllung des Testmaßes auch einen höheren Grad des Ausgetestetseins. Die Erfüllung von TK2 wird häufig als die Minimalforderung beim Testen angesehen, da es einerseits i. a. ohne allzu großen Aufwand möglich ist, einen hohen Erfüllungsgrad (ca. 90%) zu erreichen, andererseits auch eine automatische Berechnung des Erfüllungsgrades über Instrumentierer gegeben ist. Diese Instrumentierer basieren auf Programmstrukturuntersuchungen (Programmgraph). Versuche haben gezeigt, daß bei Anwendung dieses Testmaßes mindestens 2/3 der Fehler entdeckt werden konnten /MILL77/.

Bei Schleifen interessiert nicht nur, ob sie - gemäß TK2 - mindestens einmal oder keinmal ausgeführt wurden, sondern es kann auch eine Mindesthäufigkeit der Durchläufe von Bedeutung sein ($TK3_n$). Weitere Testmaße, die aber sowohl schwerer zu erreichen als auch zu überprüfen sind, betrachten datenabhängige Verzweigungen, Einzelprädikate von Bedingungen, Teilstreckenkombinationen und alle Pfade.

In Ergänzung zu den o. g. strukturabhängigen Testmaßen sind weitere möglich, die sich auf statistische Testdatenauswahl und -überdeckung beziehen. Bei den strukturellen Testkriterien spielt die mehrfache

Ausführung eines Programmteils - mit Ausnahme von Schleifen - keine Rolle. Beim statistischen Test hingegen erhöht jeder zusätzliche Testlauf das Testmaß, unabhängig vom jeweiligen Programmpfad. Die Auswahl der Testdaten muß aber auch einer Gesetzmäßigkeit genügen, um z. B. auszuschließen, daß Testläufe mit identischen Daten eine gute Testüberdeckung vortäuschen. So sind von praktischer Bedeutung:

- identisch verteilte Auswahl über das gesamte System
- unterschiedlich verteilte Auswahl über Teilgebiete.

Mit Hilfe dieser statistischen Tests kann eine Wahrscheinlichkeitsaussage über die Korrektheit der Programme und die Restfehlerzahl gewonnen werden.

7. Ausblick

Die Themen Qualität, Qualitätsmessung und Qualitätssicherung rücken in vielen Publikationen in den Vordergrund. So gibt es kaum eine Software Engineering Tagung, auf der nicht einige Vorträge zu diesen Themen enthalten sind. Hierzu gehören insbesondere die IEEE COMPSAC und die Internationale Conferences on Software Engineering. Als Spezialtagung sei hier der Software Quality and Assurance Workshop /PROC78/ erwähnt.

Als Veröffentlichung soll auch auf /BBKL78/ und auf die letzte Tagung zu diesem Thema /PROC81/ verwiesen werden. Die hier angegebenen Beispiele zeigen, daß schon in einigen Bereichen der Übergang 'vom Glauben zum Messen' begonnen wurde. Teilweise sind die Ansätze noch recht zaghaft, teilweise gibt es schon ein breites Spektrum von Metriken unterschiedlicher Qualifikation. Die Anwendung dieser Verfahren ist aber noch nicht sehr verbreitet. Eine Unterstützung durch automatische Verfahren, wie sie bei Testmaßen teilweise schon üblich ist, ist erforderlich, um weiteren Benutzern diese Methoden nahezubringen. Dabei könnten dann auch die unterschiedlichen Ansätze auf einer breiten Basis miteinander verglichen und so die besten ausgewählt werden. Um für viele Sprachen anwendbar zu sein, ist eine Sprachunabhängigkeit bei den automatisch unterstützten Metriken erforderlich.

Ein weiteres Gebiet, in dem das Messen noch nicht Fuß gefaßt hat, ist die Spezifikation. Hier müssen, in Abstimmung mit den jeweiligen Spezifikationsverfahren, neue Ansätze gefunden werden, um Aussagen über die Güte und Qualität der Spezifikation zu bekommen.

Ebenso sind in den frühen Entwicklungsschritten - wie z. B.

Spezifikation und Entwurf - Aussagen über die Komplexität wünschenswert.

Ein weiteres Ziel ist es, die Ansätze in den verschiedenen Bereichen miteinander zu verbinden. So ist eine Verknüpfung von Komplexitätsmaß und Testmaß sinnvoll: je komplexer ein Programm ist, desto stärker muß es getestet werden. Dabei sollten sich möglichst auch die strukturellen und die statistischen Tests ergänzen.

Der Zusammenhang, der zwischen den Zuverlässigkeitsmodellen und den Komplexitätsmaßen von der Aussagezielrichtung her besteht - beide sollen u. a. Aussagen über die Fehler liefern - , ist noch genauer zu untersuchen. Die Untersuchung des Zusammenspiels dieser beiden Richtungen ist ein mögliches Forschungsthema.

Ein Gesamtansatz, der zu den verschiedenen Qualitätsfaktoren zugehörige Metriken liefert, die konsistent sind und eine integrierte Theorie darstellen, muß noch erarbeitet werden.

8. Literaturverzeichnis

/BBKL78/ Boehm, B.W.; Brown, J.R.; Kaspar, H.; Lipow, M.; Macleod, G.L.; Merritt, M.J.: Characteristics of Software Quality. Amsterdam, North-Holland Publ. Company 1978

/BOWE78/ Bowen, J.B.: Are Current Approaches Sufficient for Measuring Software Quality? in /PROC78/ S.148-155

/DACS79a/ DACS: The DACS Glossary A Bibliography of Software Engineering Terms. RADC, GAFB 1979

/DACS79b/ DACS: Quantitative Software Models. RADC, GAFB 1979

/ELSH76/ Elshoff, J.L.: Measuring Commercial PL/I Programs Using Halstead's Criteria. ACM Sigplan Notices, 11 (May 1976) S. 38-46

/FILO78/ Fitzsimmons, A.; Love, T.: A Review and Evaluation of Software Science. ACM Comp. Surv., 10 (March 1978) S. 3-18

/FUHA75/ Funami, Y.; Halstead, M.H.: A Software Physics Analysis of Akiyama's Debugging Data. CSD-TR144, Purdue Univ., Lafayette 1975

/GILB76/ Gilb, T.: Software Metrics. Lund, Studentlitteratur 1976

/GMVO80/ Gmeiner, L.; Voges, U.: Methods, Criteria and Automatic Tools for Software Testing. in: Ebert, R.; Luegger, J. (Hrsg.): Practice in Software Adaption and Maintenance. Amsterdam, North-Holland Publ. Company 1980, S. 183-192

/HALS77/ Halstead, M.H.: Elements of Software Science. New York, Elsevier North Holland 1977

/HAMA81/ Harrison, W.; Magel, K.:
A Topological Analysis of the Complexity of Computer Programs with Less than Three Branches.
ACM Sigplan Notices, 16 (April 1981) S. 51-63

/HANS78/ Hansen, W.:
Measurement of Program Complexity by the Pair (Cyclomatic Number, Operator Count).
ACM Sigplan Notices, 13 (March 1978) S. 29-33

/IBM 74/ IBM:
Structured Programming Guide.
IBM FSC 1974

/JEMO72/ Jelinski, Z.; Moranda, P.B.:
Software Reliability Research.
in: Freiberger, W. (Ed.):
Statistical Computer Performance Evaluation.
New York, Academic Press 1972, S. 465-484

/KNIJ78/ van der Knijff, D.J.J.:
Software Physics and Program Analysis.
The Australian Computer Journal, 10 (August 1978) S. 82-86

/LIVE73/ Littlewood, B.; Verrall, J.L.:
A Bayesian Reliability Growth Model for Computer Software.
J. R. Statist. Soc., C 22 (1973) S. 332

/MCCA76/ McCabe, T.J.:
A Complexity Measure.
IEEE Trans. Softw. Eng., SE-2 (Dec. 1976) S. 308-320

/MILL77/ Miller, E.F.:
Program Testing: Art Meets Theory.
IEEE Computer, 10 (July 1977) S. 42-51

/MYER77/ Myers, G.:
An Extension to the Cyclomatic Measure of Program Complexity.
ACM Sigplan Notices, 12 (Oct. 1977) S. 61-64

/PROC78/ Proceedings of the Software Quality and Assurance Workshop.
San Diego, November 15-17, 1978
ACM Softw. Eng. Notes, 3 (Nov. 1978)

/PROC81/ Proceedings of the 1981 ACM Workshop/Symposium on Measurement and Evaluation of Software Quality.
ACM Performance Evaluation Review, 10 (Spring 1981)

/SCWO78/ Schick, G.J.; Wolverton, R.W.:
An Analysis of Competing Software Reliability Models.
IEEE Trans. Softw. Eng., SE-4 (March 1978) S. 104-120

/SHOO75/ Shooman, M.L.:
Software Reliability: Measurement and Models.
Proceedings 1975 Annual Reliability and Maintainability Symposium,
Jan. 1975, S. 485-491

/TANI81/ Tanik, M.M.:
Prediction Models for Cyclomatic Complexity.
ACM Sigplan Notices, 16 (April 1981) S. 89-97

Ermittlung und Verwendung quantitativer Angaben zur Bewertung der Qualität von Software-Produkten

Rudolf van Megen; Heinz Bons

Zusammenfassung

Die Qualität von Software-Produkten drückt sich nicht nur in Eigenschaften des Endprodukts aus, sondern umfaßt ebenso Charakteristika der Vorgehensweise im Entwicklungs- und Wartungsprozess. Insofern ist die Bewertung der Qualität von Software-Produkten einerseits eine Aufgabe, die in den Software-Entwicklungsprozeß integriert ist und sowohl die einzelnen Zwischen/Endprodukte als auch den Erstellungsprozeß betrifft. Darüber hinaus ist die Bewertung der Qualität von Software im Einsatz bzw. in der Wartung von Bedeutung.

Neben einer Analyse der Zeitpunkte und Zwecke zur Ermittlung quantitativer Angaben für die Bewertung der Qualität wird auf die für unterschiedliche Zwecke und Zeitpunkte relevanten Informationen, die Eingangsgrößen möglicher Qualitätsmaße sind, eingegangen. Zudem werden die Möglichkeiten der Anwendung von Qualitätsmaßen sowie deren Grenzen aufgezeigt.

1 Problematik der Bewertung der Qualität von Software-Produkten

Qualität ist die "Gesamtheit von Eigenschaften und Merkmalen eines Produkts oder einer Tätigkeit, die sich auf die Eignung zur Erfüllung gegebener Erfordernisse beziehen" [5]. Im Kontext der Software-Entwicklung können sämtliche Zwischen-/ Endprodukte und Tätigkeiten des Entwicklungsprozesses, des Einsatz sowie der Wartung Gegenstand der Qualitätsbewertung sein. Die Qualitätsbewertung umfaßt die Analyse der unterschiedlichen Einheiten in Bezug auf ein oder mehrere vorgegebene Qualitätsmerkmale entweder zur Feststellung des Erreichens von Qualitätszielen oder zur objektiven Bestimmung von Qualitätsmaßen.

Qualitätsmerkmale für Software-Produkte sollen in vier Klassen differenziert werden, wobei im folgenden jeweils einige Beispiele für jede der Klassen genannt werden sollen, ohne jedoch den Anspruch auf Vollständigkeit zu erheben [15] (zu anderen Einteilungen von Qualitätsmerkmalen vgl. u.a. [2] , [10]):

- Qualität - die Entwicklung betreffend (Testbarkeit, Verständlichkeit, Übersichtlichkeit)
- Qualität - die Anwendung betreffend (Funktionsabdeckung, Handhabbarkeit, Richtigkeit, Robustheit, Sicherheit, Effizienz)
- Qualität - die Wartung betreffend (Verständlichkeit, Testbarkeit, Änderbarkeit)
- Qualität - die Übertragung betreffend (Portabilität, Allgemeingültigkeit)

Hinsichtlich der Definitionen der einzelnen Begriffe wird auf die angegebene Literatur verwiesen.

Die unterschiedlichen Qualitätsmerkmale sind in der vorliegenden Form nicht operational, sondern müssen in Submerkmale differenziert werden. So kann z.B. das Merkmal Richtigkeit in folgende, voneinander weitgehend unabhängige Submerkmale, die insgesamt die Richtigkeit ausdrücken, unterschieden werden:

- Genauigkeit,
- Abdeckung der Anforderungsspezifikation,
- sachlich richtige Verarbeitung.

Auch bei der hier vorgenommenen Differenzierung ist noch keine direkte Bewertung der Qualität möglich; es sind vielmehr für die entsprechenden Qualitätsmerkmale bzw. Submerkmale geeignete Maße zu definieren, die eine hohe Korrelation zu den Submerkmalen haben und anhand derer die Bewertung der Qualität ermöglicht wird.

Die Problematik der Bewertung von Software-Produkten hinsichtlich der Qualität ist u.a. durch folgende Faktoren bedingt:

- Die Qualität eines Software-Produkts - insbesondere auch die Anforderungen an die Qualität - sind in der Regel nicht hinreichend formuliert bzw. formulierbar.
- Die Begriffe für Qualitätsmerkmale sind im allgemeinen nicht operational und bedürfen einer Konkretisierung durch Submerkmale und entsprechende Maße.
- Die Verwendung von Maßen für unterschiedliche Qualitätsmerkmale ist nicht eindeutig festgelegt.
- Die vorhandenen Maße sind nicht vollständig bzw. nicht ausreichend qualifiziert, so daß nicht sämtliche Qualitätsmerkmale adäquat beschrieben werden können.
- Die Zeitpunkte zur Anwendung von Qualitätsmaßen und damit deren Ermittlung sowie Auswertung bzw. Kumulierung sind nicht eindeutig festgelegt.
- Zu unterschiedlichen Zeitpunkten und in Abhängigkeit vom Zweck sind u.U. verschiedene Maße erforderlich.
- Die im Software-Entwicklungsprozeß bzw. im Einsatz und in der Wartung verfügbaren Informationen werden nicht umfassend zur Ermittlung von Kenngrößen als Eingangsgrößen von Maßen genutzt.

2 Zeitpunkte, Objekte und Zwecke der Bewertung der Qualität von Software-Produkten

Software-Produkte sind alle Zwischen- bzw. Endprodukte, die im Software-Lebenszyklus, d.h.

- im Software-Entwicklungsprozeß und
- im Einsatz bzw. in der Wartung erstellt, angewendet oder modifiziert werden.

Qualitätsbewertungen werden - u.a. in Abhängigkeit vom Zeitpunkt ihrer Durchführung - für unterschiedliche Zwecke durchgeführt.

2.1 Zeitpunkte und Objekte von Qualitätsbewertungen

Während die Bewertung der Qualität von Software-Produkten im allgemeinen nur als Aufgabe des Software-Entwicklungsprozesses gesehen wird (vgl. z.B. [2], [4]), erscheint es notwendig, darüber hinaus auch den Einsatz bzw. die Wartung einzubeziehen, um so auch die hieraus resultierenden Auswirkungen auf die Qualität zu berücksichtigen. Es ist zwar zutreffend, daß Software nicht altert; durch die Anzahl der Änderungen bzw. Erweiterungen in einem Programmsystem sind jedoch vielfältige Auswirkungen auf die Qualität gegeben, die eine Überprüfung oder erneute Bewertung der Qualität erforderlich machen können. Die hier zugrundegelegte Differenzierung der Zeitpunkte ist aus Abb. 1 ersichtlich.

Im Entwicklungsprozeß können Qualitätsbewertungen zu folgenden Zeitpunkten durchgeführt werden:

- nach der Fertigstellung der Anforderungsspezifikation,
- nach der Fertigstellung der Entwurfsspezifikation,
- nach der Fertigstellung des Programmsystems durch den Entwickler und
- nach der Abnahme des Programmsystems durch den Anwender.

Sofern die Abnahme nicht direkt durch den späteren Anwender erfolgt - dies ist insbesondere bei mehrfach verwendbarer Software gegeben -, ist nach der Abnahme, die in diesen Fällen z.B. durch eine spezielle Abteilung der entwickelnden Institution oder einen Pilotanwender vorgenommen wird, der Zeitpunkt der "Übernahme" durch den unmittelbaren Anwender des Software-Systems in die Qualitätsbewertung einzubeziehen. Hierbei kann es sich sowohl um eine Qualitätsbewertung vor der Beschaffungsentscheidung (Bewertung hinsichtlich des möglichen Einsatzes) als auch um eine Bewertung nach der Beschaffungsentscheidung (Abnahme des Produkts) handeln.

Im Einsatz bzw. in der Wartung sind weitere Qualitätsbewertungen möglich. So kann einerseits in zeitlichen Abständen eine erneute Qualitätsbewertung des Produkts erfolgen; andererseits können bei Änderungen bzw. Anpassungen im Rahmen der Wartung Qualitätsbewertungen notwendig werden.

Hinsichtlich der Wartung ist davon auszugehen, daß wegen des engen zeitlichen Zusammenhangs der durchzuführenden Aktivitäten nur zu jeweils einem Zeitpunkt - nach der Durchführung der Änderungen etc. - eine Bewertung der Qualität des gesamten Software-Produkts bzw. der von der Änderung betroffenen Teile vorgenommen wird.

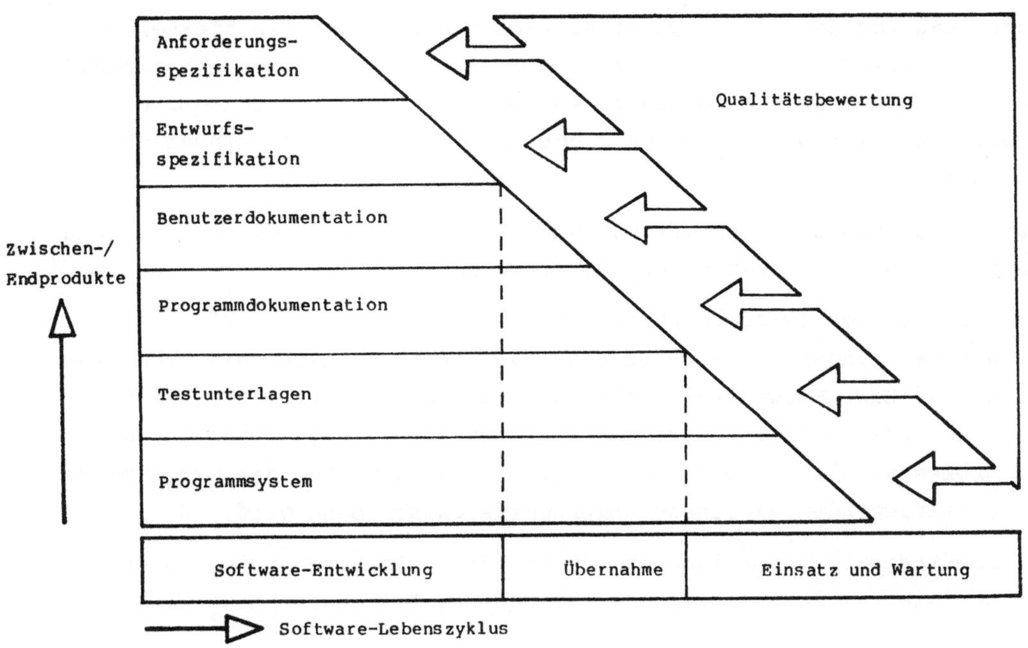

Abb. 1: Zeitpunkte und Objekte der Qualitätsbewertung im Software-Lebenszyklus

Gegenstand der zu unterschiedlichen Zeitpunkten durchzuführenden Qualitätsbewertungen können sowohl die Gesamtheit der bis dahin fertiggestellten Zwischen-/Endprodukte als auch das(die) ausschließlich in der zuletzt abgeschlossenen Phase erstellte(n) Produkt(e). Generell sind folgenden Objekte zu differenzieren:

- Anforderungsspezifikation,
- Entwurfsspezifikation,
- Programmsystem,

- Programmdokumentation,
- Benutzerdokumentation,
- Testunterlagen.

Art und Anzahl der einzubeziehenden Objekte ist u.a. abhängig vom Zweck der Qualitätsbewertung.

2.2 Zweck der Bewertung der Qualität von Software-Produkten

Qualitätsbewertungen können für unterschiedliche Zwecke durchgeführt werden; neben der Kontrolle der Vollständigkeit bestimmter Tätigkeiten im Software-Entwicklungs- und Wartungsprozeß (z.B. Testkontrolle zur Kontrolle der Vollständigkeit des Testens [16], [17]) ist die Bewertung eines oder mehrerer Zwischen-/Endprodukte nach deren Fertigstellung von Bedeutung (Qualitätskontrolle), wobei die hierbei zu verwendenden Maße teilweise für beide Zwecke, teilweise nur singulär nutzbar sind. In den folgenden Ausführungen soll ausschließlich auf Qualitätsbewertungen zum Zweck der Qualitätskontrolle eingegangen werden.

Die Bewertung der Qualität von Software-Zwischen-/Endprodukten kann aus folgenden Gründen durchgeführt werden:

- Freigabe von Zwischen-/Endprodukten
  Hierbei handelt es sich um eine von einem Projektbeteiligten (Anwender bzw. Entwickler etc.) durchzuführende Aktivität, bei der einer oder mehrere Werte für Qualitätsmaße mit entsprechenden Zielgrößen verglichen werden und aufgrund dessen über die Freigabe der entsprechenden Zwischen-/Endprodukte entschieden wird.

  Die Freigabe von Zwischenprodukten des Software-Entwicklungsprozesses dient i.a. als Freigabe für den nachfolgenden Entwicklungsschritt.

  Eine Qualitätsbewertung zum Zweck der Freigabe des Endprodukts, die ggf. in mehreren Stufen ablaufen kann, soll einerseits sicherstellen, daß seitens der Entwickler alle notwendigen Schritte durchgeführt wurden (Beendigung des Entwicklungsprozesses aus der Sicht der ADV-Abteilung) und die Abnahme durch den Anwender beginnen kann (vgl. hierzu [3]); andererseits erfolgt aus der Sicht der Anwenders die Freigabe für den Einsatz des Software-Produkts.

- Abnahme von Zwischen-/Endprodukten
  Dieser Zweck der Bewertung von Qualität kann sowohl beim Übergang der Verantwortung für ein Zwischen-/Endprodukt von einem Träger des Entwicklungs- bzw. Wartungsprozesses auf den nächsten (z.B. Abnahme

der Anforderungsspezifikation bei Fremdentwicklung von Software) erforderlich sein als auch bei der Abnahme eines Software-Systems durch einen Anwender. Hierbei werden Qualitätsmaße verwendet, für die seitens der Beteiligten Soll-Werte vorgegeben werden, die mit den in dem entsprechenden Produkt realisierten Ist-Werten verglichen werden.

- Bewertung von Zwischen-/Endprodukten
  Hierbei kann es sich einerseits um eine an individuellen Bedürfnissen ausgerichtete Bewertung z.B. eines Anwenders handeln. Diese Qualitätsbewertung erfordert die Bewertung hinsichtlich spezieller, die Einsatzmöglichkeiten eines Software-Produkts betreffender Qualitätsmerkmale; hierbei werden Qualitätsmaße, die aus der Sicht des Anwenders von Bedeutung sind, ermittelt und ggf. mit alternativen Software-Produkten bzw. mit Zielgrößen für die Maße verglichen.

  Darüber hinaus kann eine allgemeine Bewertung eines Software-Zwischen-/Endprodukts durchgeführt werden. Im Gegensatz zu den bisher genannten Zwecken werden bei der allgemeinen Bewertung eines Software-Produkts ausschließlich Ist-Werte für die Qualitätsmaße festgestellt; hierbei handelt es sich um eine objektive Feststellung der Eigenschaften eines Software-Produkts. Ziel ist die Bestimmung eines Güte-Merkmals.

Die Darstellung der unterschiedlichen Zwecke für die Qualitätsbewertung hat deutlich gemacht, unter welchen Aspekten Software-Zwischen-/ Endprodukte bewertet werden können. Hierbei wurde ausschließlich auf die Zwecke der Qualitätsbewertung im Rahmen der Qualitätskontrolle eingegangen, bei der die zu analysierenden Produkte fertiggestellt sind.

In Abhängigkeit von den möglichen Zeitpunkten zur Durchführung von Qualitätsbewertungen können hierfür unterschiedliche Zwecke relevant sein, wobei verschiedene Objekte Gegenstand der Bewertung sind (s. Abb. 2). So ist z.B. bei der Freigabe für den nachfolgenden Entwicklungsschritt nach der Fertigstellung des Programmsystems eine Bewertung der Qualität des Programmsystems, der Programmdokumenation und der Testunterlagen erforderlich. Die Qualitätsbewertung zwecks Freigabe der Software durch den Entwickler in der Wartung nach erfolgter Anpassung bezieht sich auf das Programmsystem, die Programm-/Benutzerdokumentation sowie die Testunterlage . Die Qualitätsbewertung zwecks Charakterisierung von Zwischen-/Endprodukten ist in nahezu allen Zeitpunkten möglich.

Zwecke / Zeitpunkte	Freigabe von		Abnahme von		Bewertung i.B. auf	
	Zwischen-produkten	End-produkten	Zwischen-produkten	End-produkten	individuelle Anforderungen	allgemeine Anforderungen
- Fertigstellung Anforderungen	AS, TU		AS, TU			AS
- Fertigstellung Entwurf	ES, TU		ES, TU			ES
- Fertigstellung Programmsystem	PS, DP, TU	PS, DP, TU	PS, DP, TU	PS, DP, TU		PS, DP
- Fertigstellung Softwaresystem		PS, DB, TU		PS, DP, DB TU		PS, DB
- Übernahme				PS, DB		
- Einsatz/Wartung		PS, TU		PS, TU		PS

Legende: AS: Anforderungsspezifikation ES: Entwurfsspezifikation PS: Programmsystem
DP: Programmdokumentation DB: Benutzerdokumentation TU: Testunterlagen

Abb. 2: Objekte der Qualitätsbewertung in Abhängigkeit vom Zeitpunkt und Zweck

Unter Berücksichtigung der Zeitpunkte und Zwecke der Qualitätsbewertung sind die hierfür erforderlichen Informationen sowie die entsprechenden Maße zu bestimmen.

3 Informationsarten als Eingangsgrößen der Qualitätsbewertung

Sofern Zeitpunkt und Zweck einer Maßnahme zur Qualitätsbewertung bekannt sind, ergibt sich die nächste wesentliche Frage nach den Daten bzw. Informationsarten, die bei der Qualitätsbewertung berücksichtigt und ausgewertet bzw. für die Ermittlung von Qualitätsmaßen zur Verfügung stehen oder bereitgestellt werden sollten. Zu einem bestimmten Zeitpunkt sind nicht unbedingt alle bisher verfügbaren Daten in eine Bewertung einzubeziehen. Der Zweck der Qualitätsbewertung sollte hierbei ein Auswahlkriterium bieten, um den Umfang der notwendigen Maßnahmen zur Vorbereitung und Durchführung zu begrenzen.

3.1 Informationsarten zur Ableitung von Qualitätsmaßen

Die Qualität ist nicht direkt und absolut meßbar. Daher sind Hilfsgrößen mit hoher Korrelation zu einzelnen Qualitätsmerkmalen zu ihrer Messung heranzuziehen. Hierbei werden in der Literatur eine Vielzahl von unterschiedlichen Informationsarten aus dem Umfeld der Software-Zwischen-/Endprodukte zur Ermittlung von relevanten Qualitätsmaßen verwendet (siehe [3], [6], [7],[13],[14]). Sie können gleichzeitig zu einer groben Klassifikation möglicher Qualitätsmaße dienen.

Einflußgrößen der Qualität und damit einzubeziehende Informationsarten können sein:

- Charakteristika des Software-Entwicklungsprozesses
  Hierzu zählen Tätigkeiten der Konstruktion sowie des Prüfens; das sind die einzelnen durchgeführten Konstruktions- oder Analyseschritte sowie der Umfang der jeweiligen Entwicklungsschritte. Ferner sind die genutzten Ressourcen wie Methoden, Verfahren sowie Werkzeuge, Kapazitäten (z.B. Personen in der Entwicklung) und Daten der Entwicklungsstatistik wie Anzahl Änderungen, Erweiterungen und Fehleraufkommen mögliche Elemente zur Definition von Qualitätsmaßen. Die Charakteristika des Entwicklungsprozesses können entsprechend untergliedert werden in
  o Charakteristika der Konstruktion und
  o Charakteristika der Analyse.

- Charakteristika der Zwischen-/Endprodukte
  Hierzu zählen der Umfang der Produkte sowie Kenngrößen der Produktstruktur. Diese Charakteristika sind zu differenzieren für die unterschiedlichen Produkte des Software-Entwicklungsprozesses.

- Charakteristika des Software-Einsatzes
  Hierzu zählen im wesentlichen Einsatzstatistiken wie Anzahl der Änderungen bedingt durch Fehler sowie Anzahl der Erweiterungen sowie Daten zur Einsatzintensität des Software-Produkts.

3.2 Informationsarten für unterschiedliche Zeitpunkte und Zwecke der Qualitätsbewertung

Die Berücksichtigung von Informationsarten bei der Bewertung der Qualität ist einerseits abhängig vom Zeitpunkt. So werden während der Software-Entwicklung im wesentlichen Charakteristika des Software-Entwicklungsprozesses mit direktem Bezug zu dem zu untersuchenden Objekt betrachtet. Nach Abschluß der Software-Entwicklung werden einerseits statisch ableitbare Charakteristika der Endprodukte sowie z.B.

Daten zum bisherigen Ablaufverhalten besondere Bedeutung finden. Daten des Software-Entwicklungsprozesses finden in diesem Fall nicht mehr umfassend, sondern lediglich als verdichtete Kenngrößen (z.B. als Bestandteil der Testdokumentation oder eines 'Gütepasses') Eingang in die Bewertung.

Neben dem Zeitpunkt ist der Zweck der Qualitätsbewertung eine wesentliche Bestimmungsgröße für die Auswahl der Informationsarten. So wird die Bewertung struktureller Qualitätsmerkmale (z.B. Änderbarkeit, Testbarkeit) in erster Linie von den statisch ableitbaren Charakteristika der Zwischen- und Endprodukte des Entwicklungsprozesses ausgehen[1)], die Bewertung verhaltensorientierter Merkmale (z.B. Richtigkeit, Effizienz) dagegen wird den Charakteristika des Software-Einsatzes besondere Beachtung schenken.

Dementsprechend führen unterschiedliche Informationsarten für verschiedene Zeitpunkte und Zwecke der Qualitätsbewertung zur Formulierung und Anwendung unterschiedlicher Qualitätsmaße im Software-Lebenszyklus, wobei diese gegebenenfalls auch bei gleichem zu bewertenden Qualitätsmerkmal differieren können.

4 Qualitätsmaße in der praktischen Anwendung

Ein Qualitätsmaß ist eine objektive, meßbare Größe; sie ist sensitiv in Bezug auf unterschiedliche Ausprägungen eines oder mehrerer Qualitätsmerkmale [3].

Ein Qualitätsmaß dient der qualitativen Bewertung eines Software-Zwischen- oder Endprodukts in Hinblick auf eine ergänzende Beschreibung des Software- Produkts sowie einen Vergleich mit einem vorgegebenen Soll oder mit anderen Software-Produkten. Vom Qualitätsmaß ist das Testmaß abzugrenzen. Das Testmaß mißt oder bewertet den Umfang der Testaktivitäten - zunächst unabhängig von einem angestrebten Qualitätsmerkmal. Ein Testmaß wird in der Regel auch als Qualitätsmaß verwendet.

Einem Maß ist in der Anwendung ein konkretes Ziel zugeordnet. Qualitätsziele definieren den angestrebten Wert eines Qualitätsmaßes. Bei Erreichen der Qualitätsziele wird die Qualität des Software-Produkts für die geplanten Einsatzziele als hinreichend betrachtet.

---

1) Zu einem späteren Zeitpunkt während des Software-Einsatzes wäre es wiederum denkbar, primär Charakteristika des Software-Einsatzes (z.B. Anzahl Änderungen, durchschnittlicher Aufwand der Änderungen, durchschnittliche Anzahl betroffener Moduln pro Änderung) einzubeziehen.

4.1 Qualitätsmaße

Eine Klassifizierung der unterschiedlichen Qualitätsmaße ergibt sich einerseits aufgrund der unterschiedlichen, relevanten Qualitätsmerkmale sowie andererseits aufgrund der (oben differenzierten) Informationsarten aus dem Umfeld der Software-Produkte.

Beispielhaft werden im folgenden für die Qualitätsmerkmale Richtigkeit und Robustheit mögliche Qualitätsmaße aufgeführt (vgl.[16],[18]).

Bei Betrachtung der "Charakteristika der Analyse" werden zur Bewertung der Richtigkeit und Robustheit im wesentlichen Testabdeckungskriterien und Testergebniskriterien unterschieden.

Testabdeckungskriterien sind tätigkeitsbezogene Maße, die den Umfang der Analyseschritte messen und diesen als Maß für die erreichte Qualität betrachten. Sie dienen vielfach auch als Testmaße. Der Umfang der Analysetätigkeit wird gemessen anhand vordefinierter Einzelprüfungen oder Prüfelemente sowie deren Berücksichtigung im Test [16], [18]. 'Prüfelemente' können z.B. Prüfpunkte einer Checkliste mit potentiellen Fehlerarten, Elemente der Produkte z.B. Dokumentationsseiten, Moduln des Programmsystems, Anweisungen oder Datenelemente sein. 'Berücksichtigung' beinhaltet das Ansprechen, das Ausführen oder das Durchlaufen der Prüfelemente.

Testergebniskriterien sind Maße, welche die Ergebnisse der Analyseschritte - Fehleraufkommen, Änderungen usw. - als Maß für die erreichte Qualität betrachten.

Bei Betrachtung der "Charakteristika der Zwischen- und Endprodukte" werden zur Bewertung der Richtigkeit und Robustheit im wesentlichen Komplexitätsmaße [23] aufgeführt. Sie ergeben sich aus der Ermittlung statischer Produkteigenschaften (vgl. [7], [8], [12], [24]).

Neben den hier aufgeführten Informationsarten können weitere Informationsarten für eine Bewertung der Richtigkeit und Robustheit herangezogen werden. Ihre Auswahl erfolgt u.a. unter Berücksichtigung der Zeitpunkte und des Zwecks der Qualitätsbewertung.

4.2 Die Anwendung von Qualitätsmaßen in der Praxis

Um zur Anwendung von Qualitätsmaßen in der Praxis einen ersten Eindruck zu gewinnen, sei auf die Ergebnisse einer Befragung bei 32 ADV-Mitarbeitern aus unterschiedlichen Bereichen der Bundesverwaltung im Rahmen einer Informationsveranstaltung [20] sowie auf die Ergebnisse eines Forschungsprojektes zum Thema 'Testen' an der Universität zu Köln [15] verwiesen, bei dem unter anderem eine Befragung von 256 Unternehmungen in der Bundesrublik Deutschland in Form einer Fragebogenaktion [19] durchgeführt wurde.

4.2.1 Die Stellung von Qualitätsmaßen und ihre Akzeptanz

Auswertungen zur Vorgehensweise in der Praxis zeigen, daß Qualitätsmaße im Sinne objektiv meßbarer Größen nicht, oder zumindest nur in wenigen Fällen, definiert und angewendet werden.

Bezogen auf die Vorgabe von Testzielen (dies setzt das Vorhandensein von Testmaßen voraus) ergab die oben angesprochene Informationsveranstaltung [20] , daß lediglich globale Qualitätsmerkmale sowie nicht objektiv meßbare Kriterien wie 'Testen aller praktisch relevanten Pfade, Aufgaben und Funktionen' (Angabe von jeweils 76% der Befragten) formuliert werden. Entsprechend hielten nur etwa 10% der Befragten die augenblickliche Situation für hinreichend; dagegen sprachen sich 83% dafür aus, im praktischen Test quantifizierbare Testziele vorzugeben und somit objektiv meßbare Testmaße zu verwenden.

Dieses Ergebnis überraschte insbesondere, als der Erreichungsgrad des Qualitätsmerkmals Richtigkeit in Bezug auf die geforderte Qualität von 78% der Befragten als sehr gut bezeichnet wurde, obwohl keine ausreichenden quantitativen Maße vorhanden sind. Diese Daten weisen darauf hin, daß eine hohe Unsicherheit vorherrscht und eine größere Objektivierung und Vergleichbarkeit der Qualitätsbewertung allgemein für wünschenswert und notwendig erachtet wird.

Die Aussagen gelten analog für alle Qualitätsmerkmale, insbesondere auch für die Merkmale Robustheit, Effizienz, Testbarkeit, Änderbarkeit und Portabilität, da hier der Erreichunggrad weniger positiv bewertet wurde. Lediglich 40 - 44% bzw. 25% der Befragten bewerteten diesen mit 'sehr gut'. Dies liegt zu einem wesentlichen Teil jedoch bereits in der mangelhaften Definition des Qualitätsbegriffs sowie seiner mangelnden Operationalisierung begründet.

Die geringe Anwendbarkeit von Qualitätsmaßen in der Praxis ist im wesentlichen auf folgende Gründe zurückzuführen:

- Nicht-Vorhandensein von objektiv meßbaren Kriterien
  Wenn auch zu einigen Qualitätsmerkmalen für bestimmte Zeitpunkte und Zwecke unterschiedliche Maße in der Literatur beschrieben und auf theoretischer und praktischer Ebene diskutiert werden, so fehlt es doch fast ausnahmslos selbst in der Theorie an allgemeingültigen, insbesondere allgemein anerkannten, empirisch fundierten Aus-

sagen über den Nutzen (Korrelation zur Qualität) zur Qualitätsbewertung.

- Mangelnde verfahrensmäßige Unterstützung, insbesondere durch Werkzeuge
  Da allgemeingültige Kriterien fehlen, ist das Angebot an automatischen Verfahren zur Bestimmung von Qualitätsmaßen entsprechend niedrig (siehe hierzu Punkt 4.2.2)

- Mangelnde Kenntnisse über die Verfügbarkeit und die Einsatzfähigkeit verfügbarer Qualitätsmaße in der Praxis

  Dies drückt sich einerseits in der mangelhaften Einschätzung der Zielerreichung aus. So gaben z.B. ca. 47 - 50% der Befragten auf der Informationsveranstaltung an, sie deckten im Testen auch bei nicht vorhandenen systematischen Verfahren zur Testfallermittlung und Hilfsmitteln der automatischen Erfassung der Testabdeckung ca. 75 - 99% der vorhandenen Programmverweigungen sowie der Programmpfade ab. Empirische Erhebungen zeigten, daß lediglich eine Abdeckung der Verzweigungen in der Größenordnung von ca. 50% erreicht wird [11], [22].

  Andererseits wird der Aufwand zur Realisierung von unterschiedlichen Testabdeckungskriterien gänzlich unterschätzt und entsprechend mangels Erfahrung ihr sinnvoller Einsatz in unterschiedlichen Testphasen falsch eingeschätzt. Dies zeigte sich besonders krass bei der Auswertung einer Frage zur Anwendung von Testzielen beim Modul- und Integrationstest bei 256 Befragten [19]. Das Ergebnis zeigte, daß das theoretisch sinnvolle und praktisch machbare in der Meinung des Praktikers oft völlig falsch gesehen wird (siehe Abb. 3).

Zusammenfassend kann man feststellen, daß die Notwendigkeit, Qualitätsmaße zu formulieren, gesehen wird und in der Praxis ihre Definition in der Zukunft zunehmend gefordert wird.

4.2.2 Verfahren zur Bestimmung von Qualitätsmaßen

Wie oben bereits angeführt wurde, ist ein Grund für die geringe Anwendung von Qualitätsmaßen in der Praxis die mangelnde Verfügbarkeit von Werkzeugen. Werkzeuge aber sind notwendig, da zum einen eine in der Regel sehr komplexe Analysetätigkeit zur Gewinnung von Qualitätsmaßen (z.B. statische Analyse von Programmen) notwendig ist, die wirtschaftlich vertretbar nur automatisiert durchgeführt werden kann. Zum anderen ist die Qualitätsbewertung zeitpunktbezogen, die Sammlung und Auswertung von Daten als Grundlage für Qualitätsmaße aber erstreckt sich teils über einen längeren Zeitraum und wird zudem von unterschiedlichen Personen initiiert und durchgeführt (z.B. Ermittlung von Ablaufstatistiken). Auch hier sind Werkzeuge notwendig.

Das Angebot an Werkzeugen am Markt sowie der Stand der Anwendbarkeit für eine Qualitätsbewertung ist für unterschiedliche Werkzeugklassen getrennt zu betrachten.

- Werkzeuge zur statischen Analyse von Programmen und Ermittlung von Qualitätsmaßen

  Aufgrund der oben angeführten Untersuchungen sind nahezu keine Werkzeuge im praktischen Einsatz bekannt. Werkzeuge, die schwerpunktmäßig Qualitätsmaße oder diese als zusätzliche Ergebnisse ihrer Analyse ermitteln, sind lediglich in der Literatur, also experimentell, verfügbar. Es sind jedoch Systeme in der Entwicklung, die auch am Markt angeboten werden könnten.

  Eine wesentliche Gruppe von Werkzeugen, die in dieser Klasse einzuordnen ist, stellen die Werkzeuge zur Analyse von Sprachkonventionen, insbesondere individuellen Sprachkonventionen, dar. Sie liefern in der Regel auch Maße zur Beschreibung von Programmeigenschaften. Hier sind zwar praktisch anwendbare Systeme bereits am Markt, ihr Einsatz aber ist nur minimal.

Testziele	Anwendung in Testphasen		theoretisch und praktisch sinnvoll in Testphasen	
	Modultest	Systemtest	Modultest	Systemtest
- Ausführung des Programms mit allen theoretisch möglichen Datenkonstellationen	50,0	60,5		
- Ausführung des Programms mit allen praktisch relevanten Datenkonstellationen	41,3	48,1		
- alle theoretisch denkbaren Programmpfade sind einmal durchlaufen worden	27,2	30,4	(X)	
- alle problemrelevanten Programmpfade sind einmal durchlaufen worden	26,3	16,1	XX	
- jede Programmfunktion ist mehrmals ausgeführt worden	23,2	21,8	X	(X)
- jede Programmfunktion ist einmal ausgeführt worden	21,0	17,9	XX	XX
- jede Programmanweisung ist einmal ausgeführt worden	16,1	10,8	XXX	X

Abb. 3: Antworten zur Frage nach der "Anwendung von Testzielen in der Praxis (%-Angaben der Befragten (inges. 256 Teilnehmer); Mehrfachnennungen zugelassen) [19]

- Werkzeuge zur Ablaufstatistik und Teststatistik

  Diese Klasse von Werkzeugen ist sowohl im Marktangebot als auch im praktischen Einsatz zahlenmäßig stark vertreten. Hier sind insbesondere Werkzeuge zur Ermittlung von Ablaufstatistiken bezogen auf die Strukturelemente Anweisungen, Verzweigungen und Moduln zu nennen. Diese waren zunächst nur für die Anwendungssprache FORTRAN, sind seit einigen Jahren jedoch auch für COBOL, PL/I usw. verfügbar.

  Schwächen im Funktionsumfang der Werkzeuge sind im allgemeinen bei der Teststatistik gegeben, bei der die Aufgabe u.a. darin besteht, die Ablaufdaten unterschiedlicher Testläufe zu kumulieren und eine Gesamtabdeckung als Test- und Qualitätsmaß zu ermitteln; die Probleme bei der Teststatistik sind insbesondere bei der Kumulierung durch die unterschiedlichen Bezugsgrößen nach Änderungen des Programms während einer Testphase gegeben.

- Werkzeuge zur Ermittlung von Testergebniskriterien
  Diese Werkzeugklasse kommt in der Regel immer in Verbindung mit Systemen zur Sammlung von Fehlermeldungen, deren Speicherung sowie der Verwaltung ihrer Bearbeitung (Fehlerbehebung) vor. Sie sind bisher lediglich bei ADVA-Herstellern vorhanden.

5 Ausblick

Die Anzahl der in der Literatur aufgeführen Qualitätmaße ist recht umfangreich. Erfahrungswerte zu einer konkreten Bestimmung der Abhängigkeit zwischen dem Wert eines Qualitätsmaßes und der damit sichergestellten Ausprägung eines Qualitätsmerkmals aber sind nur in unzureichendem Maße vorhanden.

Demgegenüber werden teilweise operationale Qualitätsziele als Erfahrungswerte angeführt. Als Qualitätsmaß für die Anforderungs-und Entwurfsspezifikation wird z.B. die "specification page densitiy" herangezogen [[21](zitiert nach [3])]. Angestrebt werden 18 bis 25 Seiten pro 1000 Anweisungen. Als Qualitätsmaß für die Richtigkeit von Programmen wird u.a. die "error rate" herangezogen (Anzahl Fehler pro CPU-Stunden Testzeit). Bowen nennt einen Wert von 0,5 [3]. Diese Qualitätsziele sind aber mangels einer gesicherten allgemeinen Erfahrungsbasis sowie der jeweils spezifischen Anwendungsumgebung nicht übertragbar und damit nicht allgemein anwendbar.

Zusammenfassend kann man sagen, daß bisher zu wenige Kenntnisse zu Qualitätsmaßen, besonders auch empirisch fundierte Erfahrungswerte vorhanden sind. Dies ist zum Teil bereits darin begründet, daß selbst der Qualitätsbegriff nicht eindeutig und allgemeingültig (standardisiert) definiert ist. Zu einer breiten abgesicherten Anwendbarkeit von Qualitätsmaßen sind in der Zukunft umfangreiche Untersuchungen in der Praxis notwendig.

Literaturverzeichnis

[1] Boehm, B. W.; Brown, J. R., Lipow. M.: Quantitative Evaluation of Software Quality. In: Proc. 2nd Int. Conf. on Software Engineering, 592-605 (1976)

[2] Boehm, B. W.; Brown, J. R.; Kaspar, H.; Lipow, M.; MacLeod, G. J.; Merrit, M. J.: Characteristics of Software Quality. Amster- dam-New York-Oxford, North-Holland, 1978

[3] Bowen, J. B.: A Survey of Standards and Proposed Metrics for Software Quality Testing. In: IEEE Computer Magazine, 37-42 (1979)

[4] Cho, C.-K.: An Introduction to Software Quality Control. New York-Chichester-Brisbane-Toronto, Wiley, 1980

[5] Deutscher Normenausschuss e.V.: Begriffe der Qualitätssicherung und Statistik. Begriffe der Qualitätssicherung. Grundbegriffe. Vornorm DIN 55 350, Teil 11, Teil 12. Berlin, Beuth, 1980

[6] Fitzsimmons, A.; Love, T.: A Review and Evaluation of Software Science. In: Computing Surveys 2, Vol. 10, 3-18 (1978)

[7] Gilb, T.: Software Metrics. Cambridge, Mass., Winthrop, 1977

[8] Halstead, M. H.: Elements of Software Science. New York-Oxford-Amsterdam, North-Holland, 1977

[9] Heidrich, W.: Maßnahmen zur Sicherung der Zuverlässigkeit von Softwareprodukten. In: Goerke, W. (Hrsg): Zuverlässigkeit von Rechnersystemen. Vorträge einer NTG/GI-Diskussionssitzung am 28. und 29. September in Karlsruhe. München-Wien, 257-265 (1979)

[10] Hemm, R.: Zur systematischen Entwicklung langlebiger Programme. Diss. RWTH Aachen, 1977

[11] Kishida, K.: Techniques of C1 Coverage Analysis. In: Testing Technique Newsletters 3, Vol. 3, 4-5 (1980)

[12] McCabe, T. J.: A Complexity Measure. In: IEEE Transactions on Software Engineering 4, Vol. SE-2, 308-320 (1976)

[13] McCall, J. A.; Richards, P. K.; Walters, G. F.: Factors in Software Quality. Vol. I. Concepts and Definitions of Software Quality. General Electric (Hrsg.), Sunnyvale, California, 1977

[14] Mohanty, S. N.: Models und Measurements for Quality Assessment of Software. In: Computing Surveys 3, Vol. 11, 251-275 (1979)

[15] Schmitz, P.; Bons, H.; van Megen, R.: Abschlußbericht zum Forschungsprojekt "Softwaretechnologische Methoden für das Programmtesten und für die Aufwandschätzung". Projektgruppe Softwaretechnologie, Rechenzentrum der Universität zu Köln (Hrsg.), Köln, 1980

[16] Schmitz, P.; Bons, H.; van Megen, R.: Methods and Techniques of Dynamic Program Testing. In: Practice in Software Adaption and Maintenance. Proceedings of the SAM Workshop, Berlin, 5.-6. April 1979. Edited by Ebert, R., Lügger, J. and Goecke, L., Amsterdam-New York-Oxford, North-Holland, 193 - 208 (1980)

[17] Schmitz, P.; van Megen, R.; Bons, H.: Methods of Systematic Test Case Determination and Test Data Preparation. In: Practice in Software Adaption and Maintenance. Proceedings of the SAM Workshop, Berlin, 5.-6. April 1979. Edited by Ebert, R., Lügger, J. and Goecke, L., Amsterdam-New York-Oxford, North-Holland, 209 - 221 (1980)

[18] Schmitz, P.; Bons, H.; van Megen, R.: Workshop "Ausgewählte Methoden und Verfahren für das Testen und für die Aufwandschätzung", Köln, 5.-6. Oktober 1980. Projektgruppe Softwaretechnologie, Rechenzentrum der Universität zu Köln (Hrsg.), Köln, 1980

[19] Schmitz, P.; Bons, H.; van Megen, R.: Situation des Testens und der Aufwandschätzung in der Praxis - Auswertung der Fragebogenaktion. Projektgruppe Softwaretechnologie, Rechenzentrum der Universität zu Köln (Hrsg.), Köln, 1978

[20] Schmitz, P.; Bons, H.; van Megen, R.: Methoden und Richtlinien für das Testen in Software-Entwicklungsprojekten für die öffentlichen Verwaltung (TMR-Studie). Köln, 1981

[21] Searle, L. V.: An Air Force Guide to the Computer Program Development Specification. ESD-TR-78-139, 1977

[22] Stucki, L. G.: Automatic Generation of Self-Metric Software. In: IEEE Symposium on Computer Software Reliability, 94 - 100 (1973)

[23] Thayer, T. A; Lipow, M.; Nelson, E. C.: Software Reliability. Amsterdam-New York-Oxford, North-Holland, 1978

[24] Woodward, M. R.; Hennell, M. A.; Hedley, D.: A Measure of Control Flow Complexity in Program Text. In: IEEE Transactions on Software Engineering 1, Vol. SE-5, 45-50 (1979)

Der Einfluß von Strukturierungsmethoden der Anwendungsprogrammierung auf die Durchlaufzeit von Programmen

A. Schulz
Institut für Informatik, Johannes Kepler Universität Linz

1. Einleitung:

Praktiker behaupten in Diskussionen über die strukturierte Programmierung und den strukturierten Programmentwurf häufig, daß herkömmlich erstellte Programme, die beispielsweise viele GOTO-Anweisungen aufweisen und nicht modularisiert wurden, in der Programmausführung schneller sind als Programme, die den Regeln der strukturierten Programmierung gehorchen. Dies soll auch der Grund dafür sein, daß sich strukturierte Entwurfsmethoden bisher in der Anwendungsprogrammierung nicht durchsetzen konnten. Auf die Frage, ob denn diese Behauptung quantitativ verifiziert wurde, erhält man im allgemeinen eine nichtssagende Antwort, etwa den Hinweis, daß bekanntlich auch Programme, die in einer problemorientierten Sprache abgefaßt wurden, langsamer sind als maschinenorientierte.

Dieses Beispiel ist symptomatisch für die gegenwärtige Situation in der Anwendungsprogrammierung, wo wenig experimentiert und gemessen wird, sondern häufig Halbwahrheiten weitergegeben werden; man denke nur an die Fachdiskussion über den dogmatischen Charakter der Jackson-Methode [1]. So behauptet auch Zemanek, daß die Computerkunst zu sehr zu einer mathematischen Kunst gemacht worden ist und daß Experimente in der Informatik selten zu finden und Beobachtungseinrichtungen als Voraussetzung für Experimente mehr als unterentwickelt sind [2].

In dieser Arbeit wird über ein Experiment aus dem Gebiet der Anwendungsprogrammierung berichtet. Es soll untersucht werden, wie sich verschiedene Strukturierungsmethoden aus dem Gebiet von Software-Engineering, wie das Abstraktionsstufenkonzept oder die Verwendung von Datenkapseln, auf die Durchlaufzeit von Programmen auswirken. Von theoretischer Seite aus wird dazu bisher nichts gesagt. Um noch einmal Zemanek zu zitieren: "Ein vernünftiges Maß an Mißtrauen gegen die Fähigkeit des Alles-voraus-Wissens, wie es vom algorithmischen Denken hochgezüchtet wird, wäre für den Entwerfer mehr als nützlich" [2]. Weiterhin soll gezeigt werden, in welcher Weise Experimente den Software-Designer in seiner Arbeit unterstützen können, wofür eine

Meßmethodik Voraussetzung ist, die in dieser Arbeit beschrieben wird.

2. Durchführung der Untersuchung:

Für unsere Versuche soll ein exemplarisches Beispiel aus dem Gebiet der betrieblichen Datenverarbeitung und nicht irgend ein Algorithmus herangezogen werden. Die Verarbeitung sequentiell organisierter Dateien nimmt dort nach wie vor einen breiten Raum ein. Viele Batch-Programme basieren auf dieser Ablauforganisation. Wegen ihrer großen praktischen Bedeutung wurde versucht, diesen Ablauf zu normen (normierte Programmierung) [3]. Auch die Software-Entwurfsmethode, die Jackson in seinem Buch "Principles of Program Design" seit 1975 propagiert, beruht auf derselben Modellvorstellung [4].

Im konkreten nehmen wir an, daß eine Stammdatei, die auf Magnetbändern steht und Kontenbestände enthält, durch Bewegungsdaten, die mit Lochkarten in eine Datenverarbeitungsanlage eingegeben werden, periodisch auf den neuesten Stand zu bringen ist. Das Ordnungsmerkmal beider Dateien stellt eine Kontonummer dar. Sowohl die Stammdatei als auch die Bewegungsdatei liegen in aufsteigender Folge sortiert vor. Es ist eine Liste zu drucken, die den alten Saldo, die Bewegungen und den neuen Saldo enthält.

In jeder Dateiverarbeitung gibt es grundsätzlich drei Teilfunktionen [5]:

1. die Verarbeitung von Stammsätzen, für die Bewegungsdaten in der Bewegungsdatei vorliegen, von den Praktikern häufig kurz "bewegte Stammsätze" genannt;

2. die Verarbeitung von Bewegungssätzen, für die, aus welchen Gründen auch immer, in der Stammdatei kein Stammsatz existiert und für die deshalb ein solcher neu angelegt werden muß, "Bewegungen ohne Stammsätze" genannt;

3. die Verarbeitung nichtbewegter Stammsätze, für die in der Bewegungsdatei kein Satz vorliegt und die beispielsweise, wie in unserem Fall mit ihrem alten Saldo ausgegeben werden.

Diese drei Teilfunktionen sind im Grunde genommen unabhängig von der verwendeten Dateiorganisation. Liegen die Dateien aber in aufsteigender Folge des Ordnungsmerkmals sortiert vor und ist B der Wert des Ordnungsmerkmals in der Bewegungsdatei und S der analoge Wert in der Stammdatei, dann werden nach einem Gruppenwechsel diese drei Teilfunktionen aus einem Vergleich von B mit S erhalten, nämlich:

B = S : bewegte Stammsätze

B > S : Bewegungen ohne Stammsätze

B < S : nichtbewegte Stammsätze.

In unseren Untersuchungen wurde darauf geachtet, daß alle drei Teilfunktionen in etwa gleich häufig von der Programmsteuerung angesprochen werden. Damit der Zeitaufwand für die Verwaltungsarbeiten eines Programms (Vereinbarungen) vernachlässigbar klein ist gegenüber dem Anweisungsteil, muß ein entsprechend großes Datenvolumen verarbeitet werden. In unserem Fall bestand es aus 1680 Datensätzen, die sich wie folgt verteilten:

Teilfunktion "bewegte Stammsätze": 330 Stammsätze
780 Bewegungssätze

Teilfunktion "Bewegungen ohne Stammsätze":
300 Bewegungssätze

Teilfunktion "nichtbewegte Stammsätze":
270 Stammsätze.

Das Ziel unserer Untersuchungen ist quantitative Aussagen derart zu bekommen, um wieviel Prozent eine bestimmte Strukturierungsstrategie die Durchlaufzeit eines Programms im Vergleich zu einem nichtmodularisierten Programm vergrößert. Mit Hilfe dieser Zeitanalyse soll es auch möglich sein, zeitkritische Wege eines Programms zu finden, um diese durch "tuning" zu verbessern. Deshalb muß das Software-Werkzeug, das für diese Analyse eingesetzt wird, in der Lage sein, alle in einem Programm während seiner Ausführung durchlaufenen Zweige aufzuzeichnen und die dafür verbrauchte Durchlaufzeit auszuweisen. Für diese Aufgabe verwendeten wir das Programm PRT7 des Softwarehauses HIS Consultants, Wettswil bei Zürich. Es basiert auf der Eigenschaft des PL/1-Optimizing Compilers, mit Hilfe der FLOW- und COUNT-Option alle durchlaufenen Programmzweige eines Objektprogramms verfolgen zu können und dabei die Anzahl der Durchläufe zu zählen und die "execution time" zu messen. Dieses Software-Werkzeug berechnet die Ausführungszeit zwischen zwei Verzweigungen und zwar einmal inklusive aller Unterbrechungszeiten und zum zweiten die reine Durchlaufzeit, ohne daß der Zeitaufwand für Unterbrechungen (z.B. Paging, EA-Unterbrechungen) berücksichtigt wird ("minimum flow path time"). Dabei stellt das Software-Werkzeug mit Hilfe der System Control Blocks zu Beginn und am Ende eines Programmzweigs fest, ob diese Control Blocks durch Programmunterbrechungen verändert wurden. Diese Technik ist auf allen IBM/370-Systemen anwendbar. Zwei verschiedene Fälle werden bei der Zusammenstellung der Zeitstatistik für die Minimum Flow Paths betrachtet:

- Jeder Durchlauf eines Programmzweigs wird unterbrochen
- mindestens ein Durchlauf ist unterbrechungsfrei.

Um die Durchlaufzeiten in diesen beiden Fällen zu erhalten, werden zwei verschiedene Techniken angewandt. Führt jeder Durchlauf zu einer Unterbrechung, wird eine Statistik für die beobachtete Minimum-Zeit aufgestellt. Sobald ein unterbrechungsfreier Zweig beobachtet wird, hält das Software-Werkzeug die aufaddierte Zeit aller unterbrechungsfreien Durchläufe fest. Die minimale Zeitangabe ist in dieser Weise entweder die kleinste beobachtete Zeit oder der Durchschnitt von allen unterbrechungsfreien Durchgängen Dieser zweite Wert entspricht der CPU-Zeit.

Alle Untersuchungen wurden auf dem Informatik-Rechner unseres Instituts (IBM/370-115) mit dem Betriebssystem OS/VS1 durchgeführt. Während der Untersuchungen war die Maschine "leer", so daß sich außer dem Betriebssystem kein anderes Programm auf der Maschine befand.

3. Untersuchungsergebnisse:

Als Bezugspunkt dient ein typisches nichtmodularisiertes Programm, das ohne methodischen Ansatz programmiert wurde (s.[6] S. 16 ff.). Es trägt die charakteristischen Merkmale der "Vor-Dijkstraschen-Zeit". Elshoff hat 1977 im General-Motors-Konzern 120 PL/1-Programme, die konventionell erstellt und 34 PL/1-Programme, die strukturiert programmiert worden sind, auf die Häufigkeitsverteilung der wichtigsten Anweisungsklassen wie Zuordnungsanweisungen, IF-, GOTO- und CALL-Anweisungen analysiert [7]. Aus diesen Untersuchungen hat er ein Anweisungsspektrum abgeleitet, aus dem sich gewisse qualitative Schlüsse über die Güte und die Art einer Strukturierung ziehen lassen. So sind in unserer konventionellen Lösung die GOTO-Anweisungen mit 11 % (bei Elshoff 11,7 %), die IF-Anweisung mit 16,5 % (bei Elshoff 17,8 %) und die CALL-Anweisung mit 0 % (bei Elshoff 2,0 %) vertreten.

Als erster Typ eines strukturierten Programms wurde ein mit dem Abstraktionsstufenkonzept entworfenes Programm untersucht. Seine Struktur, dargestellt in der Constantine-Methode [8], zeigt Bild 1. Allerdings wurden aus Übersichtlichkeitsgründen die Daten- und Steuerflußpfeile zunächst weggelassen. Die Top-down-Strukturierung unterhalb der Ebene der Teilfunktionen konnte aus Platzgründen nur für die Funktion "bewegte Stammsätze" in diese Darstellung mit aufgenommen werden. Die anderen beiden Teilfunktionen sind analog aufgebaut (Strukturierungstyp 1).

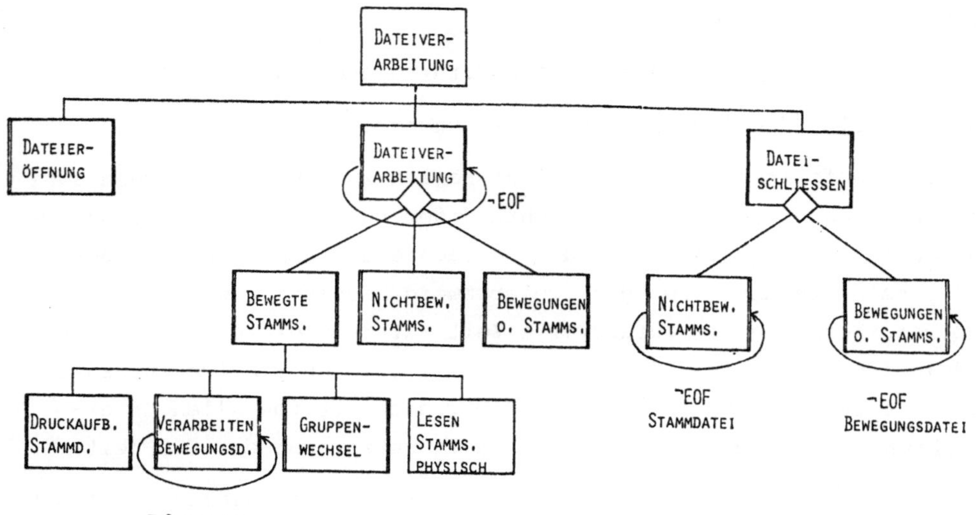

Bild 1: Entwurf der Fallstudie mit dem Abstraktionsstufenkonzept

Bild 2 zeigt den Versuch, die Durchlaufzeit der Prozedur "Dateiverarbeitung" des Bildes 1 dadurch zu verbessern, daß jede Teilfunktion so lange iterativ durchlaufen wird, bis ein Wechsel in der Teilfunktion auftritt. Dadurch vermeidet man, daß die Programmausführung nach jedem Gruppenwechsel in die übergeordnete Abstraktionsstufe zurückkehrt, um dort festzustellen, welche Teilfunktion als nächste zu durchlaufen ist. Diese Strukturänderung bedeutet, daß die Programmausführung in der Funktion Dateiverarbeitung nicht so viele CALL-Anweisungen wie im Strukturierungstyp 1 zu durchlaufen hat (Strukturierungstyp 1-V). Im konkreten Beispiel geht die Anzahl der ausgeführten CALL-Anweisungen um 61 % zurück, was sich natürlich auch auf die Durchlaufzeit der Funktion "Dateiverarbeitung" auswirkt (Rückgang von 2,023 µs auf 0,658 µs).

VERBESSERUNG DURCHLAUFZEIT PROZEDUR "DATEIVERARBEITUNG"

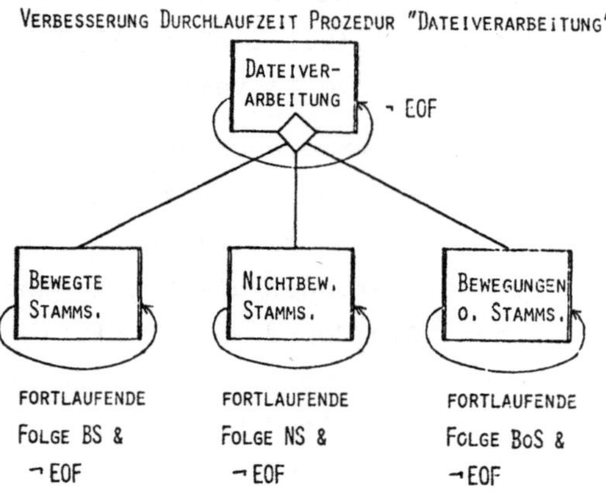

Bild 2: Verbesserung des Strukturierungstyps 1 durch Aufnahme zusätzlicher Iterationen (Strukturierungstyp 1-V)

In der Informatik wird heute gelehrt, beim Entwurf eines Programms vom Geheimnisprinzip auszugehen [9] und mit Datenkapseln ein Softwaresystem zu modularisieren. Bild 3 zeigt den Versuch, den gesamten Eingabeverkehr in eine Datenkapsel "Dateiverwaltung" zu legen. Nur sie kennt die physische Struktur der Bewegungs- und Stammdatei. Der "operationale" Programmteil, die Dateiverarbeitung, kommuniziert mit der Dateiverwaltung über funktionelle Datensätze, die Zeichenketten darstellen (Strukturierungstyp 2). Auch in diesem Fall wird analog zum Bild 2 untersucht, wie sich eine größere Verwendung von Iterationen in der Funktion Dateiverarbeitung auf die Durchlaufzeit auswirkt (Strukturierungstyp 2-V).

DATEIVERARBEITUNG: ANWENDUNG GEHEIMNISPRINZIP, DATENHALTUNG EINGABEVERKEHR IN EINER DATENKAPSEL

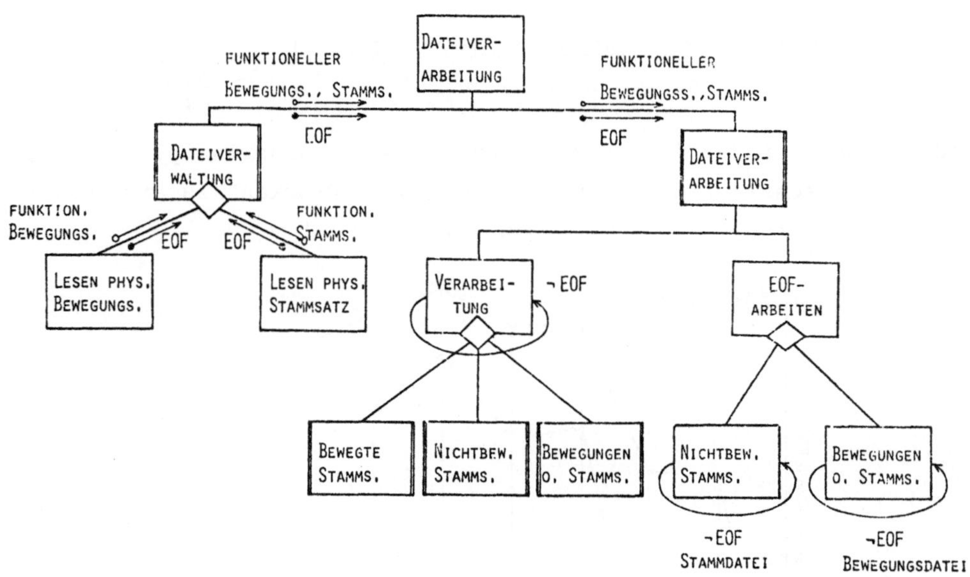

Bild 3: Entwurf der Fallstudie nach dem Geheimnisprinzip, der Eingabeverkehr liegt in der Datenkapsel "Dateiverwaltung" (Strukturierungstyp 2).

In Bild 4 wurde das Geheimnisprinzip in der Weise verstärkt angewendet, daß jetzt auch die Druckprozesse, die in Bild 3 noch im operationalen Teil liegen und damit im Grunde genommen diesem Prinzip widersprechen, zu einer eigenen Datenkapsel "Drucken" zusammengefaßt werden. Diese Datenkapsel verfügt über 3 Eingänge, die nach den verschiedenen Druckbildern differenzieren, nämlich Drucken der Stammdaten, Drucken eines Bewegungssatzes und Drucken einer Summenzeile (Strukturierungstyp 3). Auch hier wird die Variation untersucht, wie sich zusätzliche Iterationen über die Teilfunktionen bewegte Stammsätze, nichtbewegte Stammsätze und Bewegungen ohne Stammsätze auf die Durchlaufzeit auswirken (Strukturierungstyp 3-V).

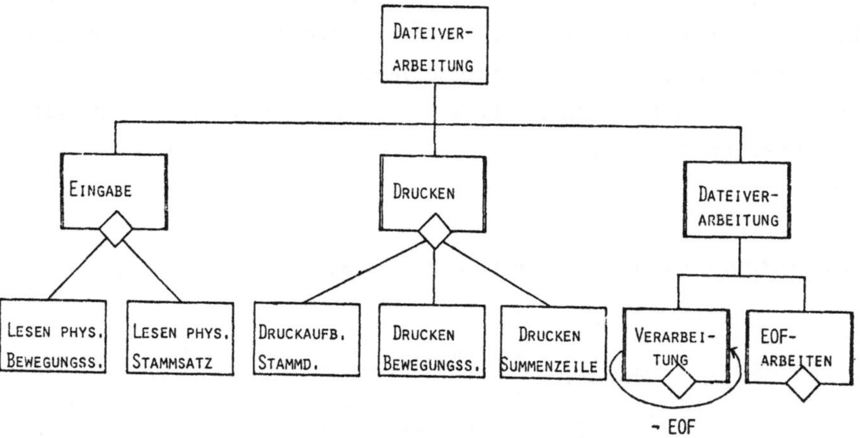

Bild 4: Entwurf der Fallstudie nach dem Geheimnisprinzip, alle Druckprozesse sind in einer Datenkapsel "Drucken" zusammengefaßt (Strukturierungstyp 3 und 3-V).

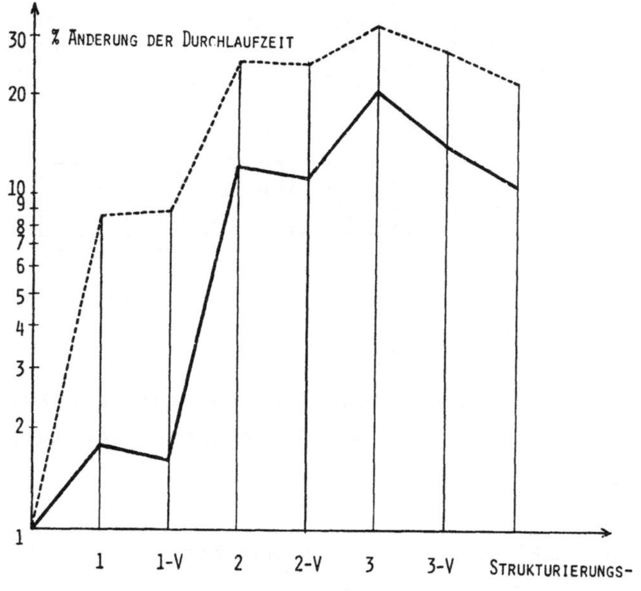

Bild 5: Durchlaufzeiten in Abhängigkeit von Strukturierungsstrategien.

Bild 5 zeigt nun die Ergebnisse unserer Messungen und zwar jeweils den Mittelwert aus sechs Meßreihen. Auf der Abzissenachse wurden die drei Strukturierungsstrategien mit ihren zwei Varianten aufgetragen. Die untere Kurve repräsentiert den prozentualen Anstieg der Durchlaufzeit im Vergleich zum nichtstrukturierten Programm inklusive aller Unterbrechungszeiten. Interessant ist, daß sich der Strukturierungstyp 1 nur gering (2 %) auf die Durchlaufzeit auswirkt. Erst wenn man ein Programm nach dem Geheimnisprinzip strukturiert, hat diese Maßnahme Einfluß auf die Durchlaufzeit. Für die untersuchte Programmstruktur steigt in den Meßreihen die Durchlaufzeit um maximal 21 % an und zwar für den Strukturierungstyp 3, bei dem der E/A-Verkehr über zwei Datenkapseln abgewickelt wird. Dieses Ergebnis läßt sich verbessern, indem der Software-Konstrukteur in die Datenkapsel "Dateiverarbeitung" zusätzliche Iterationen einbaut (Strukturierungstyp 3-V). Dann sinkt die maximale Durchlaufzeit um 4 % ab.

Die obere Kurve in Bild 5 stellt die Veränderungen der Durchlaufzeit ohne den Zeitaufwand für Unterbrechungen dar (minimum flow path time). In diesem Fall wirken sich die verschiedenen Strukturierungsstrategien stärker aus als in der unteren Kurve. So liegt jetzt die maximale Durchlaufzeit um 34 % über der nichtstrukturierten Lösung (Strukturierungstyp 3). Im Grunde genommen ist aber auch dieser Wert klein, wenn man bedenkt, daß die Verweilzeit eines Programms, verursacht durch die verschiedenen Belastungen des Betriebssystems, viel stärker schwankt und, wie wir beobachtet haben, bis +100 % variieren kann.

Die obere Kurve, die für den Anwender bedeutungslos ist, weil er von seiner Seite aus nur die gesamte Druchlaufzeit sieht, ist aber der Schlüssel, um die Ergebnisse unseres Versuchs interpretieren zu können. Wir unterstellen, daß der größte Teil der Untersuchungen durch E/A-Prozesse und nicht durch Seitenfehler im virtuellen System ausgelöst wird. Dann zeigt die obere Kurve in Bild 5, daß sich die Strukturierungsstrategien deshalb so wenig auf die Durchlaufzeit auswirken, weil diese primär von den E/A-Anweisungen, auf die Strukturierungsstrategien aber keinen Einfluß haben, bestimmt wird. Dieses Ergebnis läßt sich auch dadurch verifizieren, daß das Meßwerkzeug PRT7 den prozentualen Anteil der beiden Datenkapseln "Eingabe" und "Drucken" an der Gesamtdurchlaufzeit ausweist. Er beträgt 68 %.

Schließlich weist die von uns verwendete Meßmethode auch auf weitere Tuningmöglichkeiten hin. So wurde bisher in der Datenkapsel "Dateiverarbeitung" ein funktioneller Datensatz, an die nur dort bekannte interne Datenstruktur mit Hilfe der String-Funktion übergeben. Wenn man sie durch überlagerndes Definieren ersetzt, sinkt der maximale Anstieg der Durchlaufzeit in der oberen Kurve des Bildes 5 von 34 % auf 22 % ab (letzter auf der Abzissenachse nicht gekennzeichneter Meßwert der beiden Kurven in Bild 5).

4. Zusammenfassung:

Unsere Untersuchungen haben gezeigt, daß sich die Behauptung, strukturierte Programme sind in der Ausführung langsamer als nichtstrukturierte, quantitativ nachweisen läßt. Für den Bereich der betrieblichen Datenverarbeitung haben wir maximale Abweichungen gegenüber konventionellen Programmen, die nach außen in Erscheinung treten (untere Kurve in Bild 5) von 21 % beobachtet. Sie lassen sich durch den Einsatz von Tuningmaßnahmen auf 10 % begrenzen, ein Wert, den der Anwender in der realen Umgebung eines belasteten Betriebssystems kaum spüren wird. Aus diesen Meßergebnissen kann man schließen, daß die Vorteile, die ein wohlstrukturiertes Programm bietet, wie Wartungsfreundlichkeit, gute Lesbarkeit und hohe Zuverlässigkeit, die Nachteile durch eine geringfügige Vergrößerung der Durchlaufzeit ausgleichen. Deshalb kann man jedem Anwendungsprogrammierer bedenkenlos empfehlen, ein Programm mit Hilfe des Geheimnisprinzips gut zu strukturieren.

Literatur

[1] Schulz, A.: Software-Entwurfsmethoden: Ein Vergleich des LITOS-Verfahrens mit der Jackson-Methode; Stellungnahme zu einer Leserzuschrift. In: Angewandte Informatik 11 (1980), S.96 ff.

[2] Zemanek, H.: Entwurf und Verantwortung. In: NTG-Fachberichte. Band 62. Berlin 1978: Struktur und Betrieb von Rechensystemen. Vorträge NTG/GI-Fachtagung 15.-17.3. 1978

[3] DNA, Deutscher Normenausschuß, Fachnormenausschuß Informationsverarbeitung (FNI): DIN 66220, Informationsverarbeitung, Programmablauf für die Verarbeitung von Dateien nach Satzgruppen, Berlin 1977.

[4] Jackson, M.A.: Principles of Program-Design. London, New York, San Francisco 1975

[5] Schulz, A.: Einführen in das Programmieren in PL/1. Berlin, New York 1975, S. 180

[6] Schulz, A.: Methoden des Softwareentwurfs und Strukturierte Programmierung. Berlin, New York 1978, S. 16 ff.

[7] Elshoff, J.L.: The Influence of Structured Programming on PL/1 Program Profiles. In: IEEE Transactions on Software Engineering Vol. SE-3, No. 5 (1977), S. 364 ff.

[8] Yourdon, E., L.L. Constantine: Structured Design. 2. Auflage, New York 1976.

[9] Parnas, D.L.: On the Criteria To Be Used in Decomposing Systems into Modules. In: Communications of the ACM 15 (1972) S. 1053 ff.

Quantitative Ansätze zur Bestimmung der Komplexität von Software-Systemen

Helmut Balzert

Abteilung Software Engineering
TRIUMPH-ADLER AG Nürnberg

Zusammenfassung

Die Komplexität eines Software-Systems kann durch "geeignete" Strukturierung reduziert werden. Das Problem liegt in der Quantifizierung des Begriffes "geeignet" sowie in der Festlegung, was unter Strukturierung verstanden werden soll. Außerdem spielen psychologische Aspekte eine Rolle.

Die Strukturierung wird bestimmt durch Hierarchien, Modulkonzepte, Schnittstellenspezifikationen und Zugriffsrechte.

Um verschiedene Aspekte berücksichtigen und unterschiedlich gewichten zu können, wurden mehrere Komplexitätsmaße entwickelt, die es ermöglichen, eine Software-Struktur zu "vermessen".

Anhand mehrerer Systeme, die nach den gleichen Konstruktionsprinzipien entworfen wurden, werden mehrere berechnete Komplexitätsmaße angegeben und ihre Aussagekraft diskutiert.

1. Einleitung

Eine Forderung an ein Software-Produkt stellt "Einfachheit" dar. Einfachheit ist ein gegensätzlicher Begriff zu Komplexität, d.h. Einfachheit kann als "Mangel an Komplexität" gedeutet werden. Mit diesen Begriffen eng verbunden ist der Begriff Struktur. Eine gute Struktur bildet eine wesentliche Voraussetzung für Einfachheit.Daneben sind Transparenz, Klarheit und Verständlichkeit erforderlich, um Einfachheit, aber auch Korrektheit und Stabilität zu erreichen. Die Strukturierung eines Software-Produkts wird wesentlich durch Hierarchisierung und Modularisierung verbunden mit der Datenabstraktion erreicht.

2. Komplexität und Struktur

Nach Untersuchungen von /Stevens et al. 74/ wird die Komplexität in einem allgemeinen System sowohl durch die Wechselwirkungen zwischen Systemkomponenten (intersystem-Wechselwirkungen) als auch durch die Wechselwirkungen innerhalb der einzelnen Systemkomponenten selbst (intrasystem-Wechselwirkungen) bestimmt (siehe Abb. 1).
Zur Ausprägung einer Struktur läßt sich folgende These aufstellen:

These 1:

> Die Struktur eines Systems ist umso ausgeprägter, je stärker die intrasystem-Wechselwirkungen im Vergleich zu den intersystem-Wechselwirkungen sind.

Je stärker die Ausprägung einer Struktur ist, desto geringer ist auch die Komplexität dieser Struktur. Um von diesen qualitativen Aussagen zu quantitativen Aussagen zu gelangen, muß man von einem allgemeinen System zu einem spezialisierten, exakt definierten System übergehen.

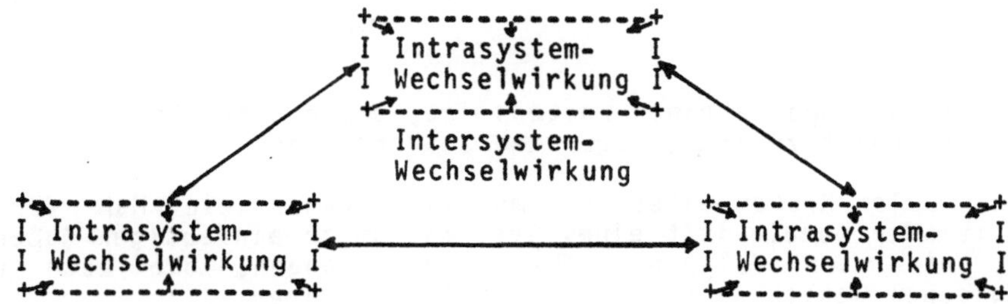

Abb. 1: Wechselwirkungsarten, die die Komplexität bestimmen

3. Intersystem-Wechselwirkungen

/Simon 62/ stellte fest, daß viele in der Natur vorkommenden komplexen Systeme über eine hierarchische Struktur verfügen. Eine solche Struktur bietet sich offenbar auch als geeignetes Mittel für den Aufbau von künstlichen Systemen an.

3.1 Komplexitätsmaße für statische Baumhierarchien

Wählt man als Systemstruktur eine Hierarchie, dann erhält man eine Spezialisierung gegenüber einem allgemeinen System. Eine im Bereich der Software-Systeme bereits durch klassische Programmiersprachen favorisierte Hierarchieart stellt die Baumhierarchie dar.

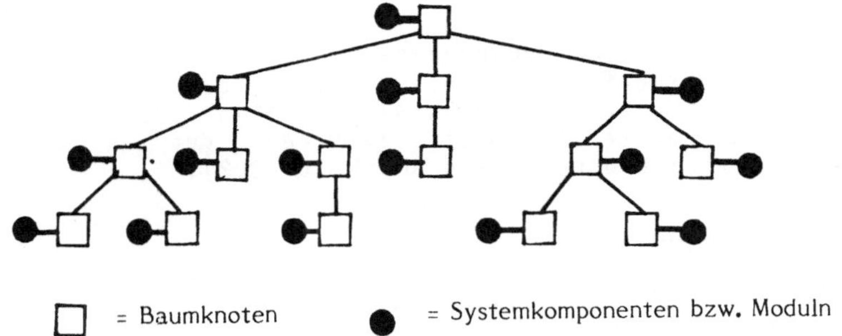

Abb. 2: Beispiel für eine Baumhierarchie mit "eingehängten" Systemkomponenten bzw. Moduln

Um zu einer klaren Entkoppelung zwischen Intersystem- und Intrasystem-Wechselwirkungen zu gelangen, muß man sich die Systemkomponenten bzw. Moduln in den Baum "eingehängt" denken. Die Hierarchisierung wird ausschliesslich im Systembaum und nicht in den Systemkomponenten vorgenommen.

Um nun zu Aussagen über die Komplexität einer Baumhierarchie zu gelangen, werden einige Definitionen und Thesen aufgestellt:

Definition 1

Unter der Spanne eines Knotens bei einer Baumhierarchie wird die Anzahl der direkten Untersysteme (Kinder) verstanden.

These 2

Je kleiner die Spanne eines Knotens ist, desto einfacher ist dieser Systemausschnitt zu analysieren und zu verstehen.

Die Spannen aller Knoten eines Systems bilden daher ein Maß für die Einfachheit oder Komplexität eines Systems. Um zu eindeutigen Maßen zu gelangen, wird von folgenden Thesen ausgegangen, die auch unter psychologischen Gesichtspunkten plausibel erscheinen:

These 3

Ein System mit n Knoten hat eine niedrigere Komplexität als ein System mit n+1-Knoten.

Unter Knoten werden alle Knoten, Blätter sowie die Wurzel verstanden. Diese These bedeutet nicht, daß ein System im Optimalfall nur aus einem Knoten besteht, da für die Intrasystem-Wechselwirkungen Strukturen anzustreben sind, die These 3 entgegenwirken (siehe Abschnitt 4).

Definition 2

$$\text{Spannenmaß} = SM = \sum \text{Spannen}^2$$

These 4

Bei gleicher Knotenzahl gilt: Ein System mit einem niedrigeren Spannenmaß hat eine niedrigere Komplexität; Systeme mit gleichem Spannenmaß sind gleich komplex.

Bei dieser These wird davon ausgegangen, daß ein System in Abstraktionsebenen entworfen wird. Zum Verständnis einer Abstraktionsebene reicht es aus, jeweils einen Knoten und alle seine Kinderknoten zu betrachten, wobei zwischen den Kinderknoten Wechselwirkungen bestehen können (siehe Abschnitt 3.2).

Beispiel

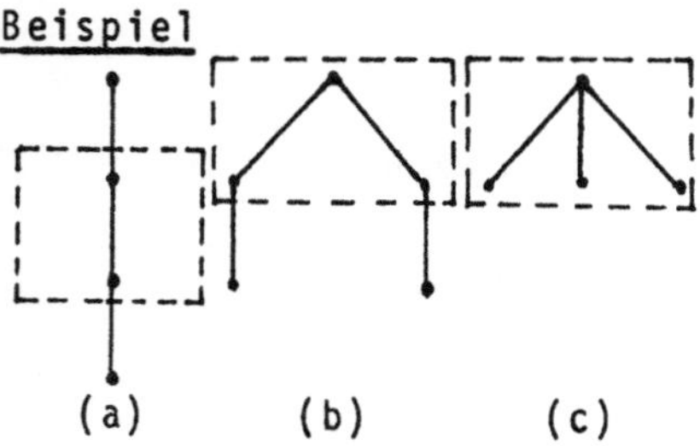

Zum Verstehen einer Abstraktionsebene muß maximal folgende Knotenanzahl betrachtet werden:
(a) 2 Knoten
(b) 3 Knoten
(c) 4 Knoten

Definition 3

Systeme mit gleichem Spannenmaß besitzen bei gleicher Knotenzahl keine unterschiedliche Struktur.

Unter Berücksichtigung dieser Thesen erhält man folgende Rangordnung:

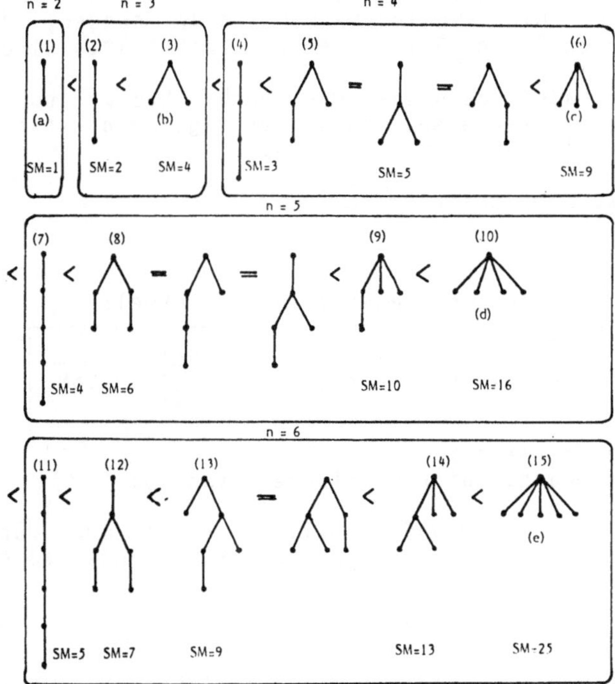

Abb. 3: Rangfolge für die Komplexität von Baumhierarchien

Zur Bestimmung der Komplexität benötigt man sowohl ein absolutes als auch ein relatives Komplexitätsmaß.

Ein <u>absolutes Komplexitätsmaß</u> soll folgenden Anforderungen genügen:

1. Je komplexer das System ist, desto größer sollte der errechnete Komplexitätswert sein.

2. Unterschiedliche Strukturen müssen sich im Komplexitätsmaß signifikant unterscheiden.

3. Mit dem Komplexitätsmaß müssen Baumhierarchien berechnet werden können, die in unterschiedlichen Zweigen verschieden tief sein können, d.h. verschieden viele Ebenen haben können.

4. Das Komplexitätsmaß sollte normierbar sein, d.h. sich zwischen festen Endwerten bewegen.

Ein absolutes Komplexitätsmaß sagt also immer etwas über den Umfang der Struktur aus. Mathematisch gesehen, muß die Formel zur Berechnung des absoluten Komplexitätsmaßes eine bijektive Abbildung der gegebenen Rangfolge auf ein monoton wachsendes Maß darstellen.

Ein <u>relatives Komplexitätsmaß</u> wird benötigt, um Komplexitätsvergleiche zwischen unterschiedlich umfangreichen Systemen vornehmen zu können. Die Anforderungen 1 und 3 für absolute Komplexitätsmaße gelten für relative daher nicht.

Wie man an den Beispielen sieht, reicht das Spannenmaß aus, um innerhalb einer Gruppe mit gleicher Knotenzahl eine eindeutige Rangfolge herzustellen.

Es muß nun eine Formel gefunden werden, die es ermöglicht, die Hierarchiestruktur mit unterschiedlicher Knotenanzahl auf ein Maßintervall abzubilden. Die Abbildung muß dafür sorgen, daß die relative Rangfolge innerhalb der Gruppe dennoch beibehalten wird.

Neben diesen beiden Maßen benötigt man noch Maße, um extrem asymetrische Strukturen zu erkennen. Dazu benötigt man statistische Maße wie Durchschnittsbildungen und Varianzen.

Vorschläge für absolute Komplexitätsmaße

Vorschlag 1

Eine mögliche Lösung des Problems bietet folgende Formel:

KM1 (BH) = Komplexitätsmaß 1 (Baumhierarchie) = $\sum_{i=1}^{n-2} i + \sqrt{SM}$

n = Knotenanzahl, SM = Spannenmaß
Tabelle 1 zeigt KM1 angewandt auf die Beispiele von Abb.1.

Eine Normierung auf das Intervall (0,1) erreicht man durch die Umwandlung: KM(BH) = 1 - 1 / KM1(BH). Ein aussagekräftiges Maß entsteht dadurch jedoch nicht.

Vorschlag 2

Bei diesem Vorschlag handelt es sich um ein algorithmisches Verfahren. Jeder Baum wird in elementare Grundbausteine zerlegt. Jedem Grundbaustein ist ein Zahlenwert zugeordnet. Diese Zahlenwerte werden addiert und ergeben das Komplexitätsmaß.

Folgenden Grundbausteinen wird folgender Maßwert zugeordnet:

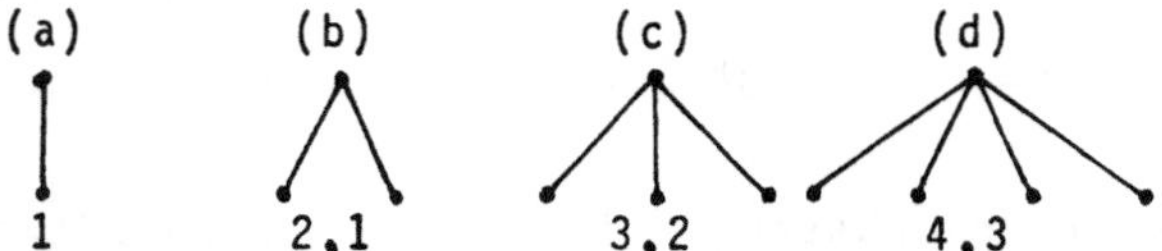

Zu diesen Maßwerten gelangt man durch die Ableitung von Ungleichungen anhand der vorgegebenen Rangfolge.

KM2 (BH) = $\sum$ Maßwerte über alle Grundbausteine

Diese Maßwerte gelten für einen Grundbaustein bis n = 10. Die Ungleichungen gelten jedoch auch bei folgenden Werten: 1, 2,01; 3,02; 4,03; usw.
Damit kann man Grundbausteine bis n = 100 messen.

	n = 2	n = 3		n = 4			n = 5				n = 6				
Maße / Beispiele	(1)	(2)	(3)	(4)	(5)	(6)	(7)	(8)	(9)	(10)	(11)	(12)	(13)	(14)	(15)
absolute Maße KM1 (BH)	1	2,41	3	4,73	5,23	6	8	8,44	9,16	10	12,23	12,64	13	13,6	15
KM2 (BH)	1	2	2,1	3	3,1	3,2	4	4,1	4,2	4,3	5	5,1	5,2	5,3	5.4
relative Maße KM3 (BH)	1	0,5	1	0,33	0,55	1	0,25	0,37	0,62	1	0,2	0,28	0,36	0,52	1
KM4 (BH)	1	0,80	1	0,78	0,87	1	0,8	0,84	0,91	1	0,81	0,84	0,86	0,9	1
KM6 (BH)	0,5	0,52	0,66	0,58	0,65	0,75	0,64	0,67	0,72	0,8	0,67	0,69	0,71	0,74	0,83
KM5 (BH)	0,5	0,66	0,7	0,75	0,77	0,8	0,8	0,82	0,84	0,86	0,83	0,85	0,86	0,88	0,9
KM7 (BH)	0,25	0,44	0,46	0,56	0,58	0,6	0,64	0,65	0,67	0,68	0,69	0,7	0,72	0,73	0,74

Tabelle 1: Maße für Baumhierarchien angewandt auf Beispiele

Zur Begründung der in Abb.3 angegebenen Rangfolgen sowie zur Wahl der Maße seien noch folgende Bemerkungen gemacht:
Es wird davon ausgegangen, daß sowohl beim Konstruieren als auch beim Analysieren eines Systems jeweils 1 Knoten mit seinen Kinderknoten betrachtet wird. Es spielt daher keinerlei Rolle, auf welcher Ebene innerhalb der Hierarchie sich der jeweis betrachtete Knoten befindet. Daher wird weder die Ebenenanzahl noch die Stellung eines Knotens innerhalb der Hierarchie berücksichtigt. Ein Sonderfall liegt jedoch bei den Blättern vor. Betrachtet man nur ein Blatt, dann besitzt es keine Nachfolgerknoten. Blätter sind daher besonders einfach zu verstehen. Es könnte daher noch ein Komplexitätskorrekturfaktor in die Maße eingebaut werden, der die Anzahl der Blätter berücksichtigt. Da ein solcher Korrekturfaktor jedoch keine Änderung der Komplexitätsreihenfolge bewirkt, wird auf ihn verzichtet.

Vorschläge für relative Komplexitätsmaße

Vorschlag 1

$$KM3\ (BH) = \frac{SM}{(n-1)^2}$$

Dieser Vorschlag beruht auf der Erkenntnis, daß das Spannenmaß pro Knotenklasse eine eindeutige Rangfolge herstellt. Die Division durch (n-1) sorgt dafür, daß die jeweils komplizierteste Hierarchie pro Klasse auf 1 abgebildet wird.

Vorschlag 2

Bei diesem Vorschlag wird das relative Mass aus dem absolutem abgeleitet.

$$KM4\ (BH) = \frac{KM1_i}{\max (KM1_i)}$$

i = Anzahl der Knoten
$KM1_i$ = absolutes Maß für den Baum in der Klasse i
$\max(KM1_i)$ = das maximale absolute Maß der Klasse i

Vorschlag 3

$$KM5\ (BH) = \frac{KM2_i}{\min (KM2_{i+1})}$$

i = Anzahl der Knoten
$KM2_i$ = absolutes Maß für den Baum in der Klasse i
$\min(KM2_{i+1})$ = das minimale absolute Maß der Klasse i+1, d.h. als Normierungsgröße wird das kleinste absolute Maß der Klasse mit der nächsthöheren Knotenzahl verwendet.

Vorschlag 4

Um im relativen Komplexitätsmaß auszudrücken, daß Hierarchien mit kleinen Knotenzahlen einfacher sind, können die relativen Komplexitaetsmaße mit (n-1)/n multipliziert werden:
KM6(BH) = KM4(BH) * (n-1)/n
KM7(BH) = KM5(BH) * (n-1)/n

Vorschläge für statistische Komplexitätsmaße

Ein Komplexitätsmaß reicht natürlich nicht aus, um die Komplexität der statischen Hierarchie ausreichend zu beschreiben.
Folgende Angaben geben noch weitere wichtige Informationen:

1. Angaben zu den Systemebenen

a. KM (ME) = maximale Anzahl der Systemebenen
b. KM (DE) = durchschnittliche Anzahl der Systemebenen

$$= \frac{\text{Kantenlängen} + 1}{\text{Kantenanzahl}}$$

c. KM (VE) = Varianz der Anzahl der Systemebenen

$$= \sqrt{\frac{1}{\text{Kantenanzahl}} \sum_{i=1}^{\text{Kantenanzahl}} (\text{Kantenlänge}_i - \text{KM (DE)})^2}$$

2. Angaben zu den Spannen

a. KM (MAXS) = maximale Spanne eines Knotens
b. KM (MINS) = minimale Spanne eines Knotens
c. KM (DS) = durchschnittliche Spanne eines Knotens

$$= \frac{\sum \text{Spanne}}{\text{Spannenanzahl}} = \frac{n - 1}{\text{n-Anzahl Blätter}}$$

d. KM (VS) = Varianz der Spannen =

$$= \sqrt{\frac{1}{\text{Spannenanzahl}} \sum_{i=1}^{\text{Spannenanzahl}} (\text{Spanne}_i - \text{KM (DS)})^2}$$

3. Angaben zum Umfang des Systems

a. KM (K) = Anzahl der Knoten
b. KM (B) = Anzahl der Blätter

Die von /Gilb 76, S. 181f./ vorgeschlagenen Metriken für Hierarchien umfassen nur die Maße 3a, 1a, 2c. Sie sind nicht ausreichend, um eine Hierarchie zu vermessen.

Der Entwurfssprache PLASMA/D /Balzert 79/, /Balzert, Weber 80/ liegt eine Baumhierarchie als Systemhierarchie zugrunde. Da mit PLASMA/D bereits eine Reihe von Software-Produkten entwickelt wurden, sollen diese als Beispiele genommen werden, um die Komplexitätsmaße anzuwenden.

Beispiel (1)

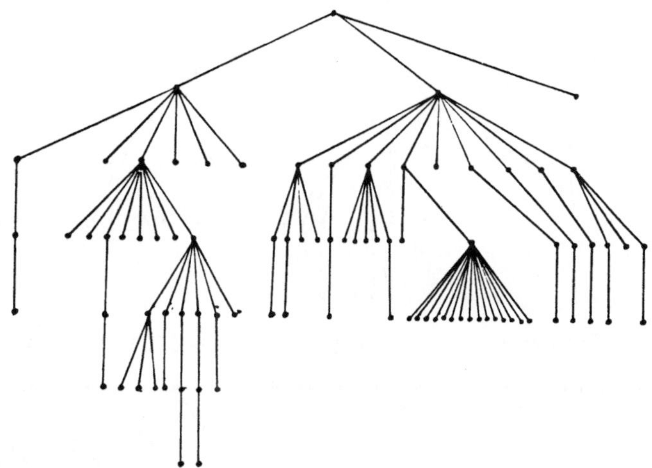

Systemhierarchie der PLASMA-Implementierung /Balzert 79,S.199ff/

Beispiel (2)

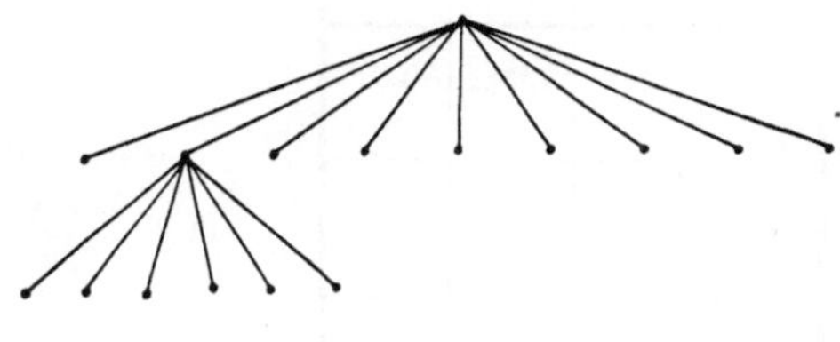

Systemhierarchie des Modul-Testrahmen-Generators für PLASMA /Prem 80/

Beispiel (3)

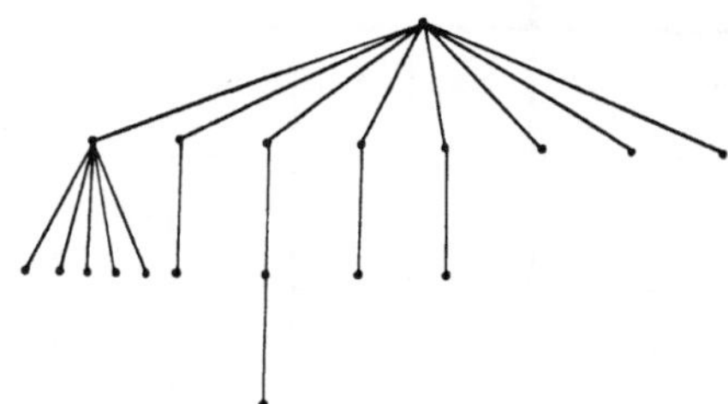

Systemhierarchie eines PLASMA-Änderungsanalysesystems /Sander 81/

Beispiel (4)

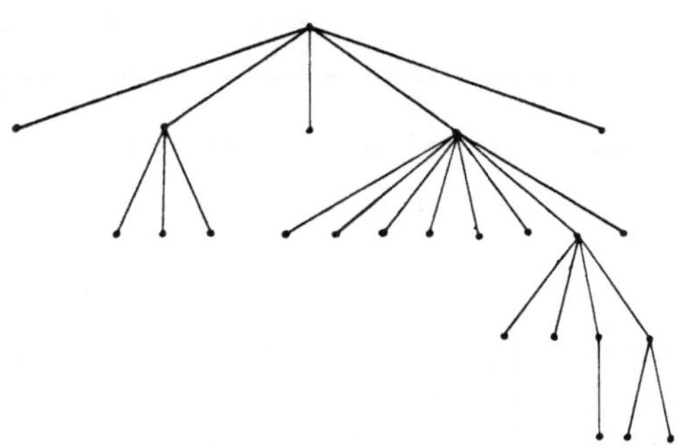

Systemhierarchie eines Struktogramm-Generators /Lonsdorfer 81/

Beispiel (5)

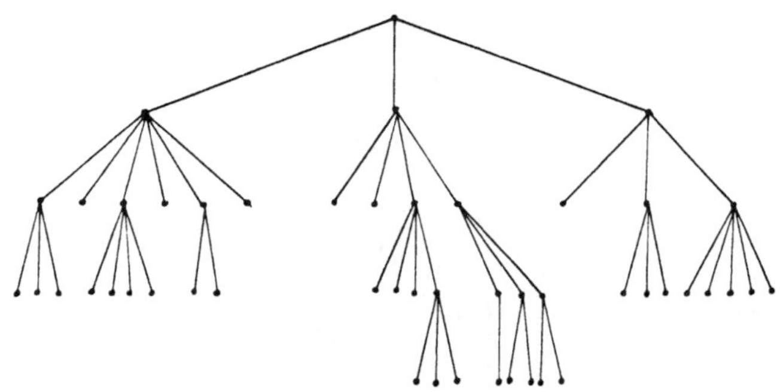

Systemhierarchie des Textverarbeitungssystems TA-AUTOTEXT /TA 81/

Maße / Beispiel	$KM1 = \sum_{i=1}^{n-2} i + \sqrt{SM}$	$KM2 = \sum$ Maßwerte über alle Grundbausteine Maßwerte: 1; 2,01; 3,02; usw.	$KM3 = \frac{SM}{(n-1)\,2}$	$KM4 = \frac{KM1_i}{\max(KM1_i)}$	$KM6 = \frac{KM4\,(n-1)}{n}$	$KM5 = \frac{KM2_i}{\min(KM2_{i+1})}$	$KM7 = KM5\,\frac{(n-1)}{n}$	$\sum \frac{\text{Kantenlänge} + 1}{\text{Kantenanzahl}}$	Varianz der Anzahl der Systemebenen	durchschnittliche Spanne $= \frac{n-1}{n - \text{Anzahl Blätter}}$	Varianz der Spannen
	KM1 (BH)	KM2 (BH)	KM3 (BH)	KM4 (BH)	KM6 (BH)	KM5 (BH)	KM7 (BH)	KM (DE)	KM (VE)	KM (DS)	KM (VS)
(1) PLASMA-Implem.	3763	87,53	0,070	0,983	0,9718	0,9962	0,9849	3,81	1,75	2,485	3,27
(2) PLASMA-Testrahmengenerator	114	15,13	0,596	0,964	0,9037	0,9993	0,9368	1,57	0,99	7,5	1,5
(3) PLASMA-Änderungsanalyse	161	18,11	0,325	0,951	0,9009	0,9966	0,9442	1,92	1,07	2,57	2,61
(4) Struktogrammgenerator	262	23,17	0,245	0,956	0,9161	0,9978	0,9562	2,33	1,33	3,83	2,71
(5) AUTO-TEXT	1140	48,33	0,076	0,970	0,9502	0,9971	0,9767	3,09	1,16	3,2	1,51
	absolute Maße		relative Maße					statistische Maße			

Tabelle 2: Komplexitätsmaße für Beispielhierarchien

Diskussion der Maße

Die Tabellen 1 und 2 zeigen einen zusammenfassenden Überblick ueber die Komplexitätsmaße fuer Baumhierarchien angewandt auf Beispiele. Die absoluten Maße KM1 und KM2 erfühlen die oben geforderten Krite- rien fuer absolute Komplexitätsmaße. Der Wunsch an ein absolutes Maß besteht auch darin, daß ein doppelt so hoher Wert auch eine doppelt so hohe Komplexität anzeigt. Da das subjektive Empfinden von Komplexität jedoch psychologisch bedingt ist, wird man kein objektives Maß finden. Ein Vergleich beider Maße zeigt Abb. 4. Beide Maße zeigen innerhalb der gleichen Knotenklasse ein fast lineares Anwachsen. Zwischen den Klassen entsteht jeweils ein Sprung. Beide Maße haben unter psychologischen Gesichtspunkten wahrscheinlich ihre Berechtigung. Nach Tabelle 1 ist Beispiel (15) nach KM1 ca. 3 mal so komplex wie Beispiel (5), nach KM2 jedoch nur ca. 2 mal.

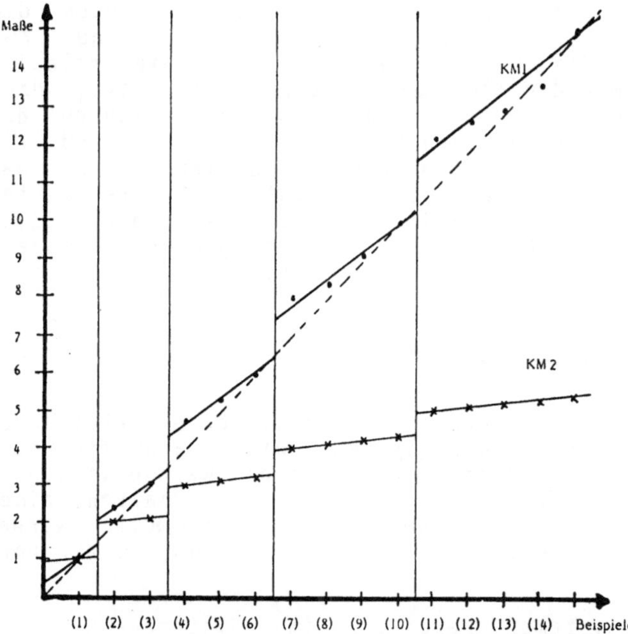

Abb. 4: Vergleich der Komplexitätsmaße KM1 und KM2

Bezogen auf die Beispiele der Tabelle 2 ergeben sich folgende Relationen:

Beispiele	(1)		(2)		(3)		(4)		(5)
KM1	1	:	1,41	:	2,29	:	10	:	33
							1	:	3,3
KM2	1	:	1,19	:	1,53	:	3,19	:	5,78
							1	:	1,8

Die Relation zwischen den Beispielen (4) und (5) scheint bei beiden Maßen vernünftig, während die Relation 1 : 33 zwischen (1) und (5) bei KM1 vielleicht zu hoch ist.

Die <u>relativen</u> <u>Maße</u> sollen einen Vergleich unterschiedlich umfangreicher Strukturen ermöglichen. Bezogen auf Tabelle 1 liefern die relativen Maße der Beispiele 1 bis 15 folgende Rangfolgen:

KM3: 11< 7<12< 4<13< 8< 2<14< 5< 9< 1= 3= 6=10=15
KM4: 4< 7= 2<11<12= 8<13< 5<14< 9< 1= 3= 6=10=15
KM6: 1< 2< 4< 7< 5< 3< 8=11<12<13< 9<14< 6<10<15
KM5: 1< 2< 3< 4< 5< 6= 7< 8<11< 9<12<10=13<14<15
KM7: 1< 2< 3< 4< 5< 6< 7< 8< 9<10<11<12<13<14<15

Bezogen auf die Tabelle 2 liefern die relativen Maße der Beispiele 1 bis 5 folgende Rangfolgen:

KM3: 1< 5< 4< 3< 2 Reihenfolge umgekehrt proportional Umfang
KM4: 3< 4< 2< 5< 1
KM6: 3< 2< 4< 5< 1
KM5: 1< 3< 5< 4< 2
KM7: 2< 3< 4< 5< 1 Reihenfolge proportional Umfang

Bei den relativen Maßen spielt noch stärker als bei den absoluten die psychologische Komponente eine Rolle. Die Maße KM5 und KM7 berücksichtigen sehr stark die Knotenanzahl, so daß die relative Reihenfolge fast identisch mit der Knotenanzahl der Systeme ist. Nach der persönlichen einschätzung des Autors sind die Systemstrukturen der Beispiele (2) und (3) relativ am komplexesten, die von (1) und (5) relativ am einfachsten. Dieser subjektiven Einordnung wird nur das Maß KM3 gerecht. Km3 hat außerdem über das Intervall gut gestreute Werte, während KM4 weniger als 1/4 des Intervalls ausnutzt (siehe Tabelle 1). Die statistischen Maße geben besonders für die großen Beispiele wichtige Informationen über die vermessene Struktur.

3.2 Komplexitätsmaße für Zugriffsstrukturen

Die bisher ermittelten Maße beschreiben die Komplexität der statischen Systemhierarchie. Die Komplexität eines Systems wird natürlich ganz wesentlich auch durch seine möglichen dynamischen Wechselwirkungen bestimmt. Da statistische Daten über das dynamische Verhalten eines Software-Systems nur während des Systembetriebs gesammelt werden können, stehen solche Daten während der Systementwicklung i.a. noch nicht zur Verfügung.

Um die Komplexität von Systemen bereits beim Systementwurf zu reduzieren, werden mögliche dynamische Wechselwirkungen durch Vergabe von Zugriffsrechten von vornherein eingeschränkt (siehe z.B./De Remer, Kron 76/, /Balzert, Weber 80/). Diese Zugriffsrechte werden bereits beim Systementwurf vergeben und geben ein Maß ab für den Grad der späteren dynamischen Wechselwirkungen.
Geht man beim Systementwurf nach der Methode der Abstraktionsebenen bzw. der virtuellen Maschinen vor, dann erscheinen folgende Zugriffsregelungen sinnvoll:

1. Ein Vatersystem kann implizit auf alle Ressourcen seiner Kinder zugreifen; die Nachkommen der Kinder sind für das Vatersystem jedoch unsichtbar.
2. Zwischen Geschwistern können explizit Zugriffsrechte vergeben werden.
3. Ein Vatersystem kann eigene Zugriffsrechte explizit an seine Kinder vererben. Dadurch ist es möglich, daß in der Hierarchie tief liegende Systeme auf weit oben im Systembaum stehende Ressourcen zugreifen können. Ein Vatersystem kann jedoch seine Zugriffsrechte auf seine Kinder nicht weitervererben; d.h. ein System kann nie auf seine Vorfahren in gerader Linie zugreifen.
4. Die explizit vergebenen Zugriffsrechte können auf Teilmengen von Ressourcen beschränkt werden.

Legt man alle Zugriffsbereiche, die sich aus den einzelnen Zugriffsrechten ergeben, übereinander, dann erhält man den kompletten Zugriffsbereich jeden Knotens.

Für die Konstruktion oder Analyse eines Knotens mit seinen direkten Nachfolgerknoten wird die Komplexität durch die implizit und explizit vergebenen Zugriffsrechte bestimmt. Die Komplexität des Gesamtsystems wird dann durch die Summe über alle Knoten charakterisiert.

Es wird daher zunächst die Komplexität aus der Sicht eines Knotens untersucht.

zu 1. Implizites Zugriffsrecht auf alle Kinder.

Da diese Zugriffsrechte implizit sind, hängt die Komplexität direkt von der Spanne des jeweiligen Knotens ab. Da zum Verstehen eines Knotens und seiner Kinderknoten alle Ressourcen der Kinderknoten betrachtet werden müssen, erscheint es sinnvoll, das Quadrat der Spanne als Komplexitätsmaß zu verwenden.

$$KM1(ZS) = \text{Komplexitätsmaß 1 (Zugriffsstrukturen)} = SM$$

zu 2. Explizites Zugriffsrecht zwischen Geschwistern.

Ein Kind kennt nur die Geschwister, auf die es explizit zugreifen darf. Die Zugriffsrechte sind nicht transitiv. Die Komplexität pro Vaterknoten wird also durch die Anzahl der Geschwisterzugriffsrechte bestimmt.

Da bei zunehmender Anzahl der Zugriffsrechte die konstruktive und analytische Komplexität mehr als linear steigt, sollte auch hier das Quadrat der Anzahl der Geschwisterzugriffsrechte genommen werden.

$$KM2(ZS) = \sum^{n\text{-Anzahl Blätter}} (\text{Anzahl Geschwisterzugriffe pro Vaterknoten})^2$$

zu 3. Explizites Vererben von Zugriffsrechten (siehe Abb. 5):

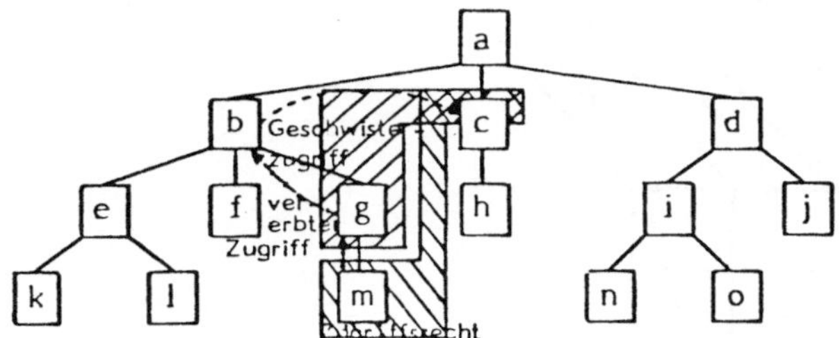

In der Abb. vererbt b seinen Geschwisterzugriff auf c an g. Dadurch kann g auch auf c zugreifen. g wiederum vererbt seinen geerbten Zugriff an m. Dadurch kann m ebenfalls auf c zugreifen.

Abb.5: Beispiel für mögliche dynamische Wechselwirkungen durch explizit vererbte Zugriffsrechte an Kinder

Aus der Sicht eines Knotens verhält sich ein vererbtes Zugriffsrecht wie ein Geschwisterzugriff. Eine Möglichkeit besteht darin, die Komplexität vererbter Zugriffe wie die Komplexität von Geschwisterzugriffen zu berechnen:

$$KM3(ZS) = \sum^{n\text{-Anzahl Blätter}} (\text{Anzahl vererbter Zugriffe an Kinder pro Vaterknoten})^2$$

Da Zugriffsrechte über mehrere Ebenen hinweg vererbt werden können, wird die Gesamtsystemkomplexität umso größer, je länger die jeweiligen Vererbungswege sind. Die Kantenlängen der Vererbungswege bilden daher ein zusätzliches Maß. Ein entsprechendes Maß wird aus Vereinfachungsgründen zunächst nicht angegeben.

Ein sinnvolles Gesamtmaß für die möglichen dynamischen Wechselwirkungen ergibt sich durch die Addition der Teilmaße:

$$KM4(ZS) = KM1(ZS) + KM2(ZS) + KM3(ZS)$$

Aus der Sicht eines Vaterknotens wird die Komplexität natürlich durch die Summe dieser Maße pro Vaterknoten bestimmt, während aus Gesamtsystemsicht die einzelnen Zugriffsrechte auch gleichmäßig über das Gesamtsystem verteilt sein können. D.h. wenn sich Zugriffsrechte bei verschiedenen Knoten konzentrieren, dann wird die Komplexität gegenüber einer weitgehenden Gleichverteilung erhöht. Solche Konzentrationen könnten daher mit einem "Komplexitätszuschlag" sozusagen "bestraft" werden.

Darauf wird jedoch zunächst verzichtet, ebenso wie auf eine unterschiedliche Bewertung, wenn nur auf Teilmengen von Ressourcen zugegriffen wird.

Um zu einem vergleichbaren relativen Maß zu gelangen, scheint es sinnvoll, KM4(ZS) in Relation zu den Maximalwerten für Kinder-, Geschwister- und vererbten Zugriff der jeweils vorliegenden Struktur zu setzen:

$$KM5(ZS) = \frac{KM4(ZS)}{\max(KM1(ZS)) + \max(KM2(ZS)) + \max(KM3(ZS))}$$

Maße / Beispiel	KM1 (ZS) (max KM1)	KM2 (ZS) (max KM2)	KM3 (ZS) (max KM3)	KM4 (ZS) (max KM4)	KM5 (ZS)
	$KM1(ZS) = SM$	$KM2(ZS) = \Sigma(\text{Anzahl Geschwisterzugriffe})^2$	$KM3(ZS) = \Sigma(\text{Anzahl vererbte Zugriffe})^2$	$KM4 = KM1 + KM2 + KM3$	$KM5(ZS) = \frac{KM4(ZS)}{\max(KM4(ZS))}$
(1) PLASMA-implem.	537 (537)	90 (54876)	134 (50812)	761 (111065)	0,0068
(2) Modul-Testrahmen-generator	117 (117)	125 (5784)	144 (2304)	386 (8205)	0,047
(3) PLASMA-Änderungsanalyse	94 (94)	241 (3536)	14 (1470)	349 (5100)	0,068
(4) Struktogramm generator	119 (119)	276 (3720)	54 (3636)	449 (7475)	0,060
	absolute Maße				relatives Maß

Tabelle 3: Komplexitätsmaße für Zugriffsstrukturen angewandt auf Beispiele

Durch statistische Maße können wieder Durchschnitts- und Varianzwerte ermittelt werden.

Diskussion der Maße

Um sich ein optisches Bild von den Geschwisterzugriffen und den vererbten Zugriffen machen zu können, sind die Beispiele (2) bis (4) im Anhang nochmals dargestellt. Die Zahlenwerte befinden sich in Tabelle 3.

Wie KM4 in Tabelle 3 zeigt, ist Beispiel (1) im Verhältnis zu den Beispielen (2) bis (4) relativ einfach. Das relative Maß KM5 zeigt dies noch deutlicher. Durch die Quadratbildung wird jedes zusätzliche Zugriffsrecht "bestraft" bzw. jeder Verzicht "belohnt". Werden alle möglichen Zugriffsrechte ausgenutzt, dann erhält KM5 den Wert 1. Die für die Beispiele (1) bis (4) ermittelten Werte zeigen, wie wenig Zugriffsrechte vergeben werden.

4. Intrasystem-Wechselwirkungen

Für Software-Systeme ergeben sich erst dann sinnvolle Komplexitätsmaße, wenn neben einer Spezialisierung und Präzisierung der Intersystem-Wechselwirkungen auch die Intrasystem-Wechselwirkungen konkretisiert werden. Die folgenden Ausführungen berücksichtigen Beiträge von /Parnas 71/, /Kopetz 76/, /Myers 73 und 78/ und /Stevens et al. 74/.

Die Verbindungen innerhalb einer Systemkomponente oder eines Moduls lassen sich durch sechs unterschiedliche Bindungsarten charakterisieren:

1. zufällige Bindung am schwächsten
2. logische Bindung
3. zeitliche Bindung
4. kommunikative Bindung
5. sequentielle Bindung
6. funktionelle Bindung am stärksten

Die Bindungsart stellt ein Maß für die Kompaktheit einer Systemkomponente dar.

Definition 4:

Eine funktionelle Bindung liegt vor, wenn alle Elemente an der Verwirklichung einer einzigen, abgeschlossenen Funktion beteiligt sind.

Definition 5:

Die Funktion einer Systemkomponente oder eines Moduls ist die Beschreibung der Transformationen oder Abbildungen der Eingabegrößen in abhängige Ausgabegrößen, die bei der Ausführung der Systemkomponente oder des Moduls durchgeführt werden.

These 5:

Die Intrasystem-Verbindung wird maximiert, wenn alle Elemente einer Systemkomponente oder eines Moduls funktionell gebunden sind.

Kriterien zum Prüfen, ob eine Systemkomponente funktionell gebunden ist, werden in /Stevens et al. 74, S. 124/ angegeben. Die Einhaltung dieser semantischen Kriterien kann nicht automatisch, sondern nur im Rahmen eines `code review` überprüft werden.

Bezogen auf die Datenabstraktion bedeutet dies, daß jede Zugriffsoperation oder Zugriffsfunktion für sich funktionell gebunden ist.

These 6:

Eine Gruppe von ungefähr 30 Anweisungen ist die oberste Grenze, was beim ersten Lesen eines Listings einer Systemkomponente, eines Moduls oder einer Ressource bewältigt werden kann.

Definition 6:

Eine kontextunabhängige Systemkomponente kommuniziert nur über explizite Import- Export- Schnittstellen mit ihrer Umwelt.

These 7:

Um den Grad der Verknüpfung eines Systems zu reduzieren, müssen alle Systemkomponenten kontextunabhängig sein.

Die Schnittstellenkomplexität wird durch folgende Komponenten bestimmt:

a. Anzahl der Schnittstellen zwischen Systemkomponenten

These 8:

Je weniger Schnittstellen vorliegen, desto geringer ist die Komplexität.

b. Anzahl der Parameter pro Schnittstelle

c. Art der Kommunikation

Es können folgende Kommunikationsarten unterschieden werden:
(1) reine Datenkommunikation
(2) Kontrollinformation in Form von Daten.

Die reine Datenkommunikation ist für das Funktionieren eines Systems notwendig. Die Übergabe von Kontrollinformation, d.h. von Information, die angibt, was die Systemkomponente tun soll (z.B. in Form von Schaltern) ist jedoch nicht erforderlich. Durch eine solche Kommunikationsart wird die Wechselwirkung zwischen Systemkomponenten erhöht, da die rufende Systemkomponente einige Kenntnisse über das "Innere" der gerufenen Systemkomponente besitzt.
Allgemein läßt sich durch Wahl einer geeigneten Entscheidungsstruktur die Übergabe von Kontrollinformation verringern.
Die Kommunikationsart kann nur durch ein code review festgestellt werden.
Anhand der Definitionen und Thesen lassen sich folgende quantitativen Maße ableiten:

KM1 (SK) = Komplexitätsmaß 1 (Systemkomponente) =

$$= \sum^{m} \text{Anzahl der Anweisungen ohne Vereinbarun. u. Kommentare}$$

m = Anzahl der Systemkomponenten bzw. Moduln

Geht man davon aus, daß eine Systemkomponente mehrere Schnittstellen besitzen kann und daß jede Schnittstelle genau eine Ressource bzw. Zugriffsoperation realisiert, dann sollten nach These 6 zu jeder Schnittstelle nicht mehr als 30 Anweisungen gehören.

$$\text{KM2 (SK)} = \frac{\text{KM1 (SK)}}{l}$$

durchschnittliche Anzahl der Anweisungen pro Schnittstelle
l=Anzahl der Schnittstellen bzw. Ressourcen

KM3 (SK) = minimale Anweisungsanzahl pro Schnittstelle

KM4 (SK) = maximale Anweisungsanzahl pro Schnittstelle

KM5 (SK) = l

Bezogen auf die Gesamtkomplexität des Systems führt eine größere Anzahl von Anweisungen zu einer Erhöhung der Komplexität. Da das Überschreiten der Anweisungsanzahl von 30 den Verständnisgrad überproportional erschwert, sollten die Differenzwerte quadriert werden.

$$KM6\ (SK) = \sum^{k} \triangle^{2}$$

$\triangle$ = Anzahl der Anweisungen - 30
k = Anzahl der Schnittstellen mit mehr als 30 Anweisungen

Ein relatives Maß erhält man durch:

$$KM8\ (SK) = \frac{KM6\ (SK)}{\sum^{l} (\text{Anzahl der Anweisungen pro Schnittstelle})^{2}}$$

Eine "Belohnung" für weniger als 30 Anweisungen pro Ressource erscheint nicht sinnvoll , da dadurch dann auf der anderen Seite Ressourcen mit mehr als 30 Anweisungen kompensiert werden können. Das Unterschreiten der Anzahl von 30 Anweisungen wirkt sich aber indirekt durch die Summenbildung

$KM7(SK) = \sum^{l} (\text{Anzahl der Anweisungen pro Schnittstelle})$

positiv aus.

Bezogen auf die Schnittstellen sind folgende Angaben informativ:

KM9 (PA) = durchschnittliche Länge einer Parameterliste
KM10(PA) = maximale Länge einer Parameterliste
Die minimale Länge einer Parameterliste dürfte i.a. Null sein.

Neben der Anzahl der Parameter pro Schnittstelle spielt natürlich auch eine Rolle, welche Datenstrukturen über die Parameter übertragen werden. Die Bewertung dieser Informationen ist i.a. nur durch ein `code review` möglich.

Wählt man trotz eingeschränkter Aussagekraft die Längen von Parameterlisten als zusätzliches Maß für die Komplexität von Systemkomponenten, dann kann man analog wie bei KM8 (SK) ein Maß definieren, wobei willkürlich angenommen wird, daß alle Parameterlisten mit mehr als 10 Parametern "bestraft" werden.

$$KM11\ (PA) = \frac{\sum^{k} \triangle^{2}}{\sum^{l} (\text{Anzahl der Parameter pro Parameterliste})}$$

$\triangle$ = Anzahl der Parameter - 10
k = Anzahl der Parameterlisten mit mehr als 10 Parametern
l = Anzahl der Parameterlisten

Maße / Beispiel	KM1(SK)	KM2(SK)	KM3(SK)	KM4(SK)	KM6(SK)	KM7(SK)	KM8(SK)	KM9(SK)	KM10(PA)	KM11(PA)
	$KM1(SK) = \sum^{m}$ Anzahl der Anweisungen	KM2(SK) = KM1(SK)	KM3(SK)=minimale Anweisungsanzahl pro Schnittstelle	KM4(SK)=maximale Anweisungsanzahl pro Schnittstelle	$KM6(SK)=\sum^{k} \Delta^2$	$KM7(SK)=\sum^{k}$(Anzahl Anw. pro Schnittstelle)	$KM8(SK)= \frac{KM6(SK)}{KM7(SK)}$	KM9(PA)=durchschn.Länge einer Parameterliste	KM10(PA)=max.Länge einer Parameterliste	$KM11(PA)=\frac{\sum^{k} \Delta^2}{\sum^{e}(\text{Anzahl Parameter})^2}$
(1) PLASMA-Implement.	6900	46	4	200	281.030	582.302	0,482	4	12	≈ 0,02
(2) Modul-Testrahmen-generator	4000	45	3	390	386.600	562.412	0,687	1,8	6	0
(3) PLASMA-Änderungs-analyse	2750	50	5	234	168.784	293.153	0,575	2	7	0
(4) Struktogramm generator	2350	35	4	330	128.972	224.628	0,574	3,5	9	0
	absolutes Maß	statist. Maß	absolute Maße				relatives Maß	statist. Maß	absolutes Maß	relatives Maß

Tabelle 4: Komplexitätsmaße für Systemkomponenten angewandt auf Beispiele

Diskussion der Maße

Wie das Maß KM8 zeigt, schneidet das Beispiel (1) am besten ab. Die drei anderen Beispiele sind ungefähr gleich gut. Bei den Parameterlisten geht nur Beispiel (1) über den Grenzwert von 10 in seiner Maximallänge hinaus.

5. Maße für die Gesamtkomplexität

Um zu einem Maß für die Gesamtkomplexität zu gelangen, müssen die Maße für die Intersystem-Wechselwirkungen mit den Maßen für die Intrasystem-Wechselwirkungen so kombiniert werden, daß ein ausgewogener Entwurf "belohnt" und extreme Entwürfe "bestraft" werden (siehe Abb. 6).

Intrasystem-Wechselwirkungen repräsentiert durch die Maße	Intersystem-Wechselwirkungen repräsentiert durch die Maße
KM5(BH)	KM8(SK)
KM5(ZS)	KM11(PA)

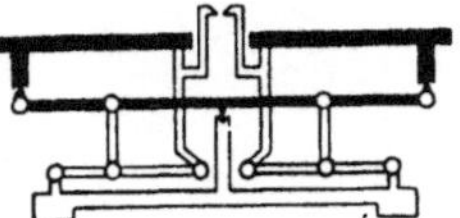

Abb. 6: Ausbalancierung der Maße zu einem Gesamtmaß

These 8:

Die Forderung nach Einfachheit wird erfüllt, wenn die

Intersystem-Wechselwirkungen minimiert <u>und</u> die Intrasystem-Wechselwirkungen maximiert werden.

Ein geeignetes Gesamtmaß ergibt sich damit durch:

KM(Gesamt) = KM3(BA) + KM5(ZS) + KM8(SK) + KM11(PA)

Dieses Maß liegt im Intervall (0,4). Je näher das Gesamtmaß sich der Null nähert, desto besser ist die Systemstruktur, je mehr das Maß sich der Vier nähert, desto schlechter ist die Systemstruktur.

<u>Beispiel</u>

(a) ausgewogene Intrasystem- und Intersystem-Struktur

(b) extrem schlechte Intrasystem-Struktur

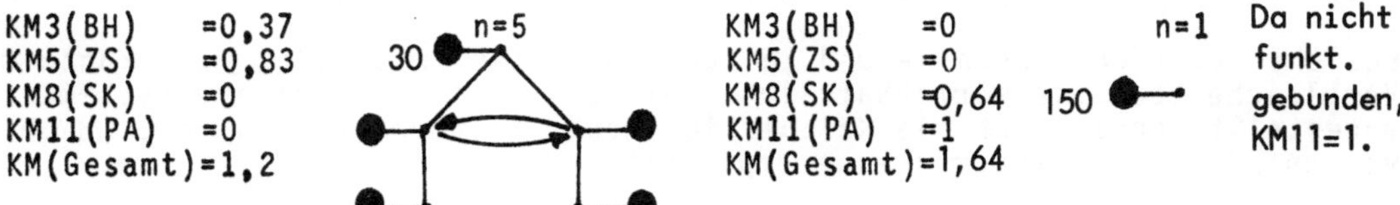

(c) extrem schlechte Intersystem-Struktur

KM3(SH) =1
KM5(ZS) =1
KM8(SK) =0
KM11(PA) =0
KM(Gesamt)=2

n=15

10

Annahme: Alle Geschwister dürfen auf alle anderen zugreifen

Maße / Beispiel	KM3(BH)	KM5(DS)	KM3+KM5	KM8(SK)	KM11(PA)	KM8+KM11	KM (Gesamt)
(1) PLASMA-Implement.	0,07	0,007	0,077	0,482	0,02	0,502	0,579
(2) Modul-Testrahmen-generator	0,596	0,047	0,643	0,687	0	0,687	1,33
(3) PLASMA-Änderungs-analyse	0,325	0,068	0,393	0,575	0	0,575	0,968
(4) Strukto-gramm-generator	0,245	0,060	0,305	0,574	0	0,574	0,879
möglicher Maximal-wert	1	1	2	≈ 1	≈ 1	≈ 2	≈ 4
	Intersystem-Maße			Intrasystem-Maße			

Tabelle 5: Gesamtkomplexitätsmaß angewandt auf Beispiele

6. Resümee und Ausblick

Die Komplexität eines Software-Systems wird durch eine ganze Reihe von Faktoren bestimmt. Nur ein Teil von Faktoren läßt sich zur Zeit quantitativ erfassen. Wesentlich erscheint, daß erst die geeignete Kombination von Intersystem- und Intrasystem-Maßen sowie die Einhaltung einer ganzen Reihe von Voraussetzungen zu Ansätzen für aussagekräftige Komplexitätsmaße führen.

Um zu einer ausgewogenen Gewichtung und Kombination der einzelnen Maße zu gelangen, sind noch weitere Erfahrungen nötig. Die hier dargestellten Ansätze zeigen jedoch bereits den Wert solcher Maße:

- objektivere Beurteilung von Systemstrukturen
- Unterstützung für den `design`- und `code review`
- Ermöglichung des Vergleichs unterschiedlicher Systeme.

Bezieht man noch Personal- und Zeitaufwandsdaten mit ein, so können Vergleiche über die wirtschaftliche Entwicklung von Software-Systemen angestellt werden. Für die Kalkulation neuer Systeme bieten die Maße von entwickelten Systemen eine empirische Grundlage.

Für Vorschläge, Anregungen und wertvolle Diskussionen danke ich Frau H. Willmer sowie den Herren K. König, R. Rüb und K. Schweizer.

Literatur

/Balzert 79/ Balzert H., Die Programmiersprache PLASMA 78, Dissertation, Fachbereich Informatik, Universität Kaiserslautern 1979

/Balzert,Weber 81/ Balzert H., Weber D., PLASMA/D - Eine Sprache für den Systementwurf, in: German Chapter of the ACM, Berichte 5, Stuttgart 1981, S. 175-201

/De Remer,Kron 76/ De Remer F., Kron H., Programmierung-in-the-large versus Programming-in-the-small in Informatik-Fachbericht Nr.1, Berlin 1976

/Gilb 80/ Gilb T., Software Metrics, Lund 1980

/Kopetz 76/ Kopetz H., Softwarezuverlässigkeit, München - Wien 1976

/Lonsdorfer 81/ Lonsdorfer C., Konzeption und Implementierung eines Struktogramm-Generators für PLASMA- und PASCAL-Programme, Projektarbeit, Fachbereich Informatik, Universität Kaiserslautern 1981

/Myers 73/ Myers G.J., Characteristics of Composite Design, Datamation, Sept. 1973, S. 100-102

/Myers 78/ Myers G.J., Composite/structured design, Van Nostrawd, Reinhold 1978

/Parnas 71/ Parnas D.L., Information Distribution

Aspects of Design Methodology, in: Information Processing 71, North-Holland 1972, S. 339-344

/Prem 80/ Prem R., Konzeption und Implementierung eines Modul-Testrahmen-Generators für PLASMA, Projektarbeit, Fachbereich Informatik, Universität Kaiserslautern 1980

/Sander 81/ Sander M., Automatische Analyse der Auswirkungen von Änderungen in PLASMA-Systemen, Projektarbeit, Fachbereich Informatik, Universität Kaiserslautern 1981

/Simon 62/ Simon H.A., The Architecture of Complexity, Proceedings of the American Philosophical Society, Philadelphia, Vol. 106, 1962,S. 467-482

/Stevens et al.74/ Stevens W.P., Myers G.J.,Constantine L.L., Structured design, IBM System Journal, No. 2, 1974, S. 115-139

/TA 81/ Triumph-Adler AG, Systemdokumentation TA-AUTOTEXT, Nürnberg 1981

Anschrift des Autors:

Dr. Helmut Balzert
c/o TRIUMPH-ADLER AG
Abteilung SBAM
Kunigundenstr. 75
85 Nürnberg 70

Anhang

Beispiel (2): Zugriffsrechte beim Modul-Testrahmen-Generator

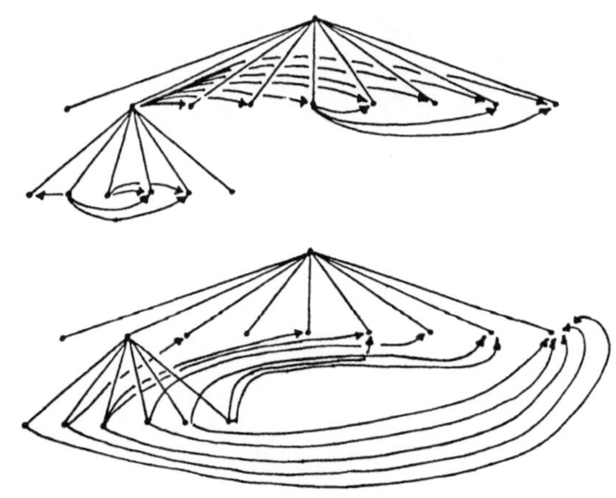

Beispiel (3): Zugriffsrechte beim Änderungsanalysesystem

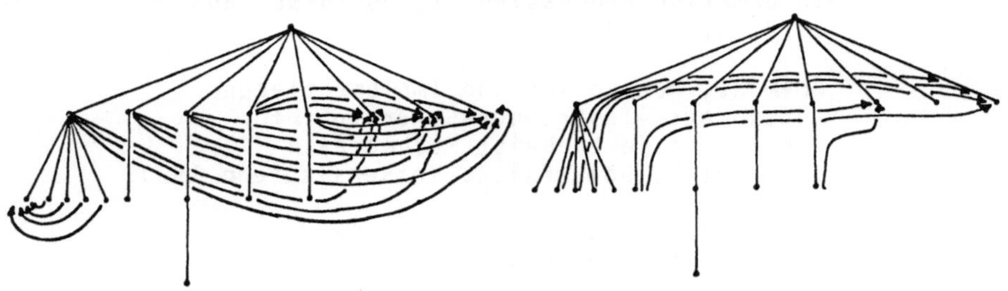

Beispiel (4): Zugriffsrechte beim Struktogramm-Generator

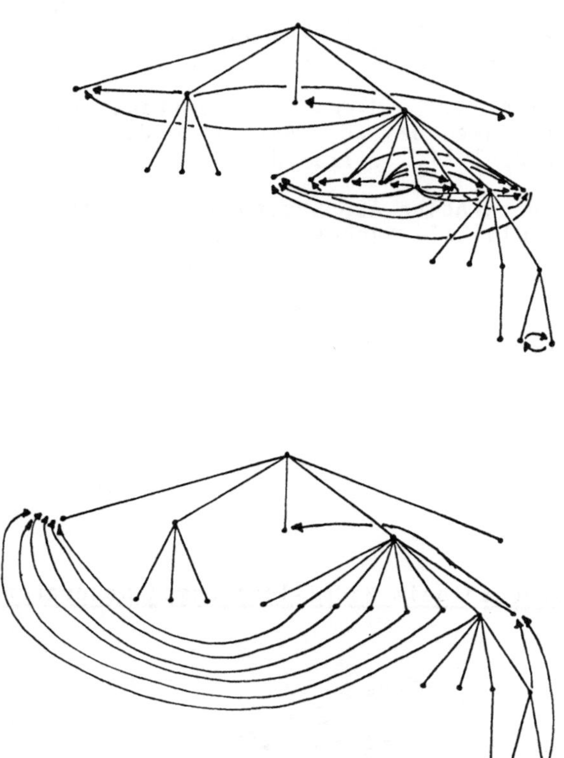

Eine Metrik zur Bewertung der Modularisierung

Hans Keutgen
GEI - Gesellschaft für Elektronische Informationsverarbeitung, Aachen

Zusammenfassung:

Die Metrik zur Bewertung der Modularisierung beruht auf Kriterien, die sich auf die intermodularen und die intramodularen Strukturen beziehen. Die intermodularen Strukturen werden aufgrund von Kenngrößen eines Schichtenmodells und ihres Export-/Importverhaltens bewertet. Die intramodulare Architektur wird mit einer Baumstruktur verglichen. Abschließend werden beide Teile an einem Beispiel verdeutlicht.

1. Einleitung

'What is needed is quantifiable measures of design goodness - a number, zero to one - which rates the design according to established guidelines' /Wi79/. Dieses Zitat zeigt das Ziel vieler Bemühungen, die alle noch nicht zu einem befriedigenden Ergebnis geführt haben. Grundlegend soll hier zunächst der Modulbegriff geklärt werden.

In diesem Beitrag wird unter einem Modul eine Einheit verstanden, die alle Funktionen (Programme) enthält, die zusammen entworfen und implementiert werden. Wenn Änderungen durchgeführt werden, dann ist das Objekt dieser Änderungen das Modul, nicht die einzelne Funktion. Das Kriterium, weshalb Funktionen zusammengefaßt werden, ist das des 'Information-Hiding'. Jedes Modul verbirgt eine oder mehrere Entwurfsentscheidungen nach außen; es versteckt die Implementierungsdetails. Die Kommunikation zwischen Moduln findet über Schnittstellen statt, die über die verborgenen Informationen nichts aussagen und damit unabhängig von der Implementierung sind.

Ein Modul stellt so eine abstrakte Maschine (oder einen Teil davon) dar, die 'Software'-Instruktionen zur Verfügung stellt, die auf einer bestimmten Datenstruktur arbeiten. Die Realisierung bleibt verborgen; das Modul ist leicht gegen ein anderes austauschbar, das die gleichen Instruktionen zur Verfügung stellt, diese aber anders realisiert.

Für die Schichten in einem Systementwurf ergibt sich folgender pragmatischer Ansatz: Moduln der untersten Schicht definieren die Datenstrukturen, auf denen das System arbeitet, und die einfachen Zugriffsoperationen auf einzelne Elemente einer Datenstruktur (eines Datentyps). Die darüberliegende Schicht enthält Moduln, deren Funktionen mehrere Elemente einer Struktur (eines Typs) manipulieren. Diese Moduln werden 'Verwaltungsmoduln' genannt.

Die Moduln der darüberliegenden Schicht enthalten Funktionen, die Elemente verschiedener Strukturen (Typen) miteinander kombinieren. Die Moduln dieser Schicht verbergen nicht mehr so stark die Implementierung von Datenstrukturen; eher verstecken sie die Implementierung der problemorientierten Funktionen, die das Benutzerproblem lösen.

Die Moduln der obersten Schicht enthalten Steuerfunktionen, die die Software-Instruktionen der darunter liegenden abstrakten Maschinen kombinieren.

Schicht	Bedeutung
1	Steuerungsmoduln
2	problemorientierte Moduln
3	Verwaltungsmoduln für abstrakte Datentypen
4	Realisierungsmoduln für abstrakte Datentypen

Ein Modul wird bestimmt durch seinen Namen und durch seine Schnittstelle. Die Schnittstelle enthält Angaben über die exportierten und importierten Funktionen.

2. Darstellung der Systemstruktur

Die intermodularen Beziehungen werden durch ein Modulstrukturdiagramm (siehe Abbildung 4.2) dargestellt. Es entsteht aus der Einordnung eines Moduls in die zugeordnete Schicht einerseits und durch die Hierarchisierung innerhalb einer Schicht andererseits. Jede Schicht kann aus mehreren Ebenen bestehen. Bei dem hier zugrunde gelegten Konzept der Modularisierung werden nur hierarchische Strukturen unterstützt (d.h. Zyklen dürfen im entsprechenden Graphen nicht auftreten). Das Modulstrukturdiagramm zeigt die hierarchische Gliederung des Gesamtsystems. Durch diese Form der Modularisierung ist gewährleistet, daß nur Funktionen aus tiefer gelegenen Ebenen und Schichten verwendet werden können.

Die intramodulare Struktur eines Moduls mit seinen importierten, exportierten und internen Funktionen wird im Strukturdiagramm (siehe Abbildung 4.1) dargestellt. In Strukturdiagrammen können auch Rekursionen auftreten.

Bei kleineren Systemen kann man beide Strukturen gut übersehen und die Struktur durch 'Anschauen' begutachten. Intuitiv läuft dabei ein Prozeß ab, der versucht, die Komplexität des Modulstrukturdiagramms zu bewerten. Dieser Prozeß versagt aber schon bei Softwarehierarchien mittlerer Größenordnung, da der entstehende Graph nicht mehr übersichtlich ist. Es ist deshalb erforderlich, aus beiden Strukturen Kenngrößen abzuleiten, die ohne Aufzeichnen der Struktur Aussagen darüber erlauben.

3. Bewertungsansätze

3.1 Intermodulare Bewertung

Praktische Erfahrungen mit dem obengenannten Schichtenmodell haben gezeigt, daß dabei Systeme entstehen, die ein charakteristisches Verhalten aufweisen. Die Anzahl der Module der oberen Ebenen wächst, während die der unteren Ebenen konstant bzw. abnehmend ist. E. Yourdon vergleicht die so entstehende Struktur mit einer Moschee /Yo78/, oft wird auch von einer Zwiebelform gesprochen.

Folgende Größen werden bestimmt:

i	Hierarchiestufe	
N(i)	Anzahl der Moduln auf der Hierarchiestufe i	
FO(i)	Anzahl der aufgerufenen Moduln aus Hierarchiestufe i	(fan-out)
EF(i)	Anzahl der exportierten Funktionen auf Hierarchiestufe i	(exported functions)
IF(i)	Anzahl der importierten Funktionen auf Hierarchiestufe i	(imported functions)

Zur Auswertung werden neben diesen Größen folgende Funktionen herangezogen:

R(i)	=	FO(i) / N(i)	(reference)
D(i)	=	EF(i) / N(i)	(define)
U	=	$\sum EF(i) / \sum IF(i)$	(usage)

Die charakteristische Zwiebelform kann man direkt an der Funktion N(i) ablesen. Die Funktion FO(i) macht eine Aussage über die Aufrufgesamtzahl und R(i) relativiert diese auf die Anzahl der Moduln der Hierarchiestufe.

Die durchschnittliche Anzahl von exportierten Funktionen wird durch D(i) festgestellt. Die Konstante U gibt die durchschnittliche Verwendung von exportierten Funktionen im Gesamtsystem an.

Durch die Konstruktion des Systems ist gesichert, daß nur hierarchische Strukturen mit einer Wurzel und ohne Rekursionen entstehen können.

Die angegebenen Größen und Abhängigkeiten sollten als Trendangabe gewertet werden. Die Veränderungen der Werte von Hierarchiestufe zu Hierarchiestufe sind meist wichtiger als die absoluten Werte.

- Der Wert N(i) wächst typischerweise zunächst, nimmt danach ab und läuft ziemlich konstant aus. Zeigt N(i) dieses Verhalten nicht, ist dies ein Anzeichen, daß die Ebenen der Modularisierung ungleichen Abstraktionsgrad aufweisen. Eine gründliche Untersuchung der gesamten Modulstruktur bezüglich des Abstraktionsgrads ist als Maßnahme vorzunehmen.

- Sowohl der Wert FO(i) als auch R(i) zeigen ein zu N(i) ähnliches Verhalten. Allerdings nehmen beide nach dem Maximum kontinuierlich ab. Ein anderer Funktionsverlauf ist oft mit einem Fehlverhalten von N(i) verbunden. Hier wird empfohlen, insbesondere die Modulstruktur für die Schichten 3 und 4 zu überprüfen.

- Die Werte D(i) hängen direkt von der Modularisierung ab. Dabei ist es als sicher anzusehen, daß sie für die Schichten 3 und 4 von vorne herein Werte in mittlerer Größenordnung annehmen. In den oberen Schichten - vor allem in Schicht 1 - besteht öfters die Tendenz, je Modul nur eine Funktion zu realisieren. Damit wird jedoch ein Sonderfall der Modularisierung erreicht. Es ist bei niedrigen D(i)-Werten zu überlegen, ob man durch andersgeartete Modularisierung höhere Werte erhält.

- Das Skalar U gibt eine grobe Vorstellung von der Güte der Systemzerlegung. Niedrige Werte von U zeigen an, daß exportierte Funktionen sehr wenig verwendet werden, woraus geschlossen werden kann, daß eine zu starke Modularisierung betrieben wurde. Sehr hohe Werte zeigen an, daß viele Funktionen in mehreren Moduln verwendet werden. In diesem Falle sollte die Einfügung einer weiteren Ebene überprüft werden, um die Komplexität der Schnittstellen zu senken.

Als Faustregel für die Interpretation sollte angestrebt werden, zunächst die Werte U, N(i) und R(i) zu betrachten und in Abhängigkeit von D(i) die Struktur nochmals zu analysieren.

3.2 Intramodulare Bewertung

Um dem Designer eine Beurteilungsgrundlage für die geschaffene Struktur zu geben, wird die vorliegende Struktur anhand einer Baumstruktur gemessen und bewertet.

Reine Baumstrukturen haben den Vorteil, daß sie

- einfach zu verstehen sind
  (um eine Funktion zu betrachten, braucht man nur deren Unterbaum zu untersuchen und hat keine Verbindungen mehr zu anderen Zweigen des Baumes),
- zuverlässig sind
  (die Abhängigkeit der Funktionen untereinander ist auf ein Mindestmaß reduziert),
- einfach wartbar und erweiterbar sind
  (Änderungen wirken immer nur auf einen Unterbaum des Baumes).

Die Bewertung gibt den Grad der Abweichung der geschaffenen Struktur von einer Baumstruktur durch folgende Größen /Yi78/ an:

i	Hierarchiestufe	
n(i)	Anzahl der Funktionen bis zur Hierarchiestufe i	
a(i)	Anzahl der Netzverbindungen bis zur Hierarchiestufe i	(arches)
t(i) = n(i) - 1	Anzahl der Netzverbindungen eines Baumes bis zur Hierarchiestufe i	(tree)

Durch

$$c(i) = a(i) - t(i) \qquad \text{(complexity)}$$

wird eine monoton steigende Funktion definiert, die die Komplexität des Netzes in bezug auf eine Baumstruktur angibt. Für Baumstrukturen gilt c(i) = 0.

Weiterhin seien die Funktionen

$$r(i) = c(i) \;/\; a(i) \qquad \text{(relative impurity)}$$

$$d(i) = (\; c(i) - c(i\text{-}1) \;) \;/\; (a(i) - a\,(i\text{-}1)\;) \qquad \text{(differential impurity)}$$

$$\text{mit } c(0) = 0,\; a(0) = 0$$

gegeben.

r(i) und d(i) können Werte zwischen 0 und 1 annehmen. Beide Größen sind gleich 0, falls eine reine Baumstruktur vorliegt. Die Werte steigen, falls sich die Struktur von einer Baumstruktur "entfernt".

Die Funktion r(i) gibt die relative Abweichung von der Baumstruktur auf der Verfeinerungsstufe i an. Die Funktion d(i) gibt den Zuwachs der Abweichung von der Baumstruktur auf der Verfeinerungsstufe i an.

Folgende formale Konstruktionsregeln für das Strukturdiagramm müssen beachtet werden:

- Für Strukturdiagramme mit mehreren Wurzeln wird formal eine gemeinsame Wurzel eingeführt. Da dadurch lediglich eine Baumstruktur erzeugt wird, hat diese Hilfskonstruktion keine Folge auf die Aussage der Metrik.

- Eine Funktion wird immer auf tiefstmögliche Hierarchiestufe heruntergezogen, um hierarchische Strukturen zu ermöglichen (siehe Abbildung 3.1).

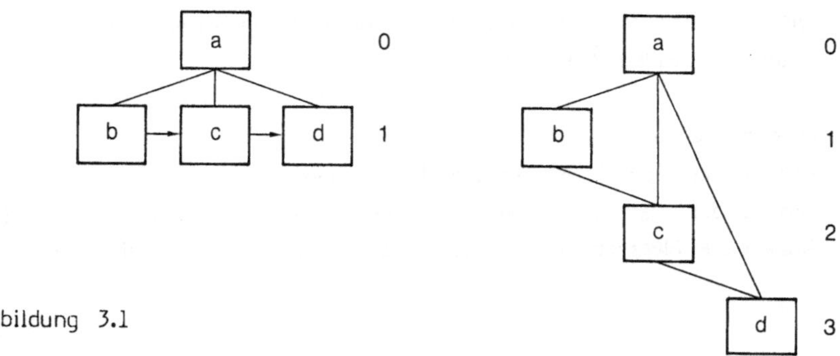

Abbildung 3.1

- Eine Rekursion erzeugt Funktionen auf einer Hierarchiestufe.

Die angegebenen Werte für die Komplexität der Struktur und der Abweichung von der Baumstruktur sollten als Trendangaben gewertet werden. Mehr als die absolute Angabe des Wertes sind die Veränderungen der Werte von Hierarchiestufe zu Hierarchiestufe wichtig.

- Der Wert von c(i) sollte so klein wie möglich gehalten werden. Da c(i) mit zunehmenden Hierarchiestufen meist wächst, können kaum obere Grenzen für c(i) angegeben werden. Wichtig für die Betrachtungsweise ist, daß größere Sprünge in den Werten von d(i) vermieden werden, denn solche Stellen deuten auf eine plötzliche Steigerung der Vermaschung hin.

- Der Wert von d(i) ist unabhängig von der Anzahl der Hierarchiestufen. Da d(i) jeweils die Änderung von einer Stufe zur nächstfolgenden Stufe angibt, sollte die Folge dieser Werte keine großen Schwankungen enthalten. Große Schwankungen können andeuten, daß keine konsequente und einheitliche Vorgehensweise im Modulentwurf vorliegt. Tritt eine starke Steigerung von d(i) in Verbindung mit einem großen Wertzuwachs von c(i) auf, so sollte die Hierarchiestufe i einer genauen Analyse unterzogen werden, um herauszufinden, welche Funktionen für diese Steigerung der Komplexität verantwortlich sind. Die so ermittelten Funktionen haben meist zentrale Bedeutung für die ordnungsgemäße Arbeit des Moduls.

- Die Berechnung und Angabe der Werte c(i) und d(i) sollen dem Designer vor Augen führen, wie komplex die von ihm geschaffene Struktur ist. Er sollte ggfs. die Struktur so ändern, daß die Komplexität über mehrere Hierarchiestufen hinweg gemindert wird.

Als Faustregel für die Interpretation der Werte von c(i) und d(i) kann gelten: je höher diese Werte sind, desto höher ist die Fehlerrate im System.

Neben den hier aufgeführten Überlegungen kommt den Parametern, die den Funktionen übergeben werden, besondere Bedeutung zu. Eine Metrik, die Auskunft über die Zusammenhänge zwischen Kopplung sowie Bindung einerseits und Güte des Strukturdiagramms andererseits gibt, wurde in /My75/ veröffentlicht.

4. Beispiele

Zur Bewertung einer intermodularen Struktur wird ein Beispiel aus der Praxis herangezogen. Es handelt sich um den Entwurf eines Systems, das die Verwaltung einer Bibliothek realisiert.

Der Übersichtlichkeit halber sind im Modulstrukturdiagramm (siehe Abbildung 4.2) die Moduln numeriert und nur die Verbindungen bis Modul 18 eingezeichnet.

Die Analyse des Beispiels (siehe Abbildungen 4.2 - 4.4) zeigt, daß die Zwiebelform zwar im wesentlichen erreicht ist, aber die Werte von D(i) für die Hierarchiestufen 2 i 5 und das Skalar U sind sehr niedrig. Es ist also zu analysieren, ob hier eine andere Modularisierung bessere Werte erzielen kann. Der Wert N(3), der sehr hoch ist, läßt ebenfalls darauf schließen.

Das zweite Beispiel (siehe Abbildung 4.1) ist eine theoretische intramodulare Struktur, bei der alle drei Konstruktionsregeln angewandt werden.

Obwohl die Struktur auf den ersten Blick vor allem durch die Rekursion recht komplex aussieht, werden die Werte r(i) und d(i) nicht sehr hoch. Der Anstieg von r(i) ist recht flach. Insgesamt ist die Struktur gemäß der Metrik positiv zu bewerten.

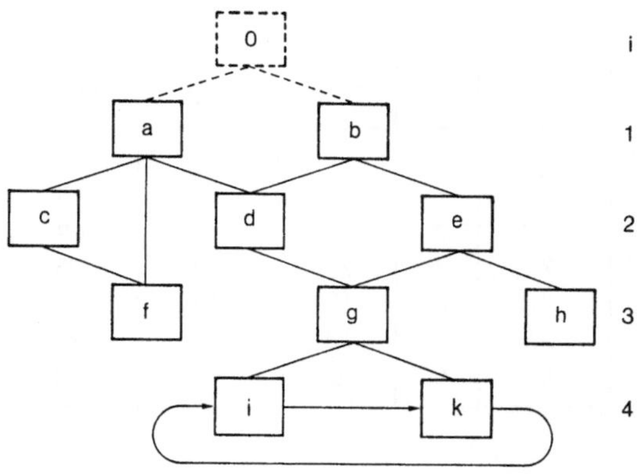

Abbildung 4.1

Auswertungstabelle

i	n(i)	a(i)	t(i)	c(i)	r(i)	d(i)
1	3	2	2	0	0.00	0.00
2	6	6	5	1	0.17	0.25
3	9	11	8	3	0.27	0.40
4	11	15	10	5	0.33	0.50

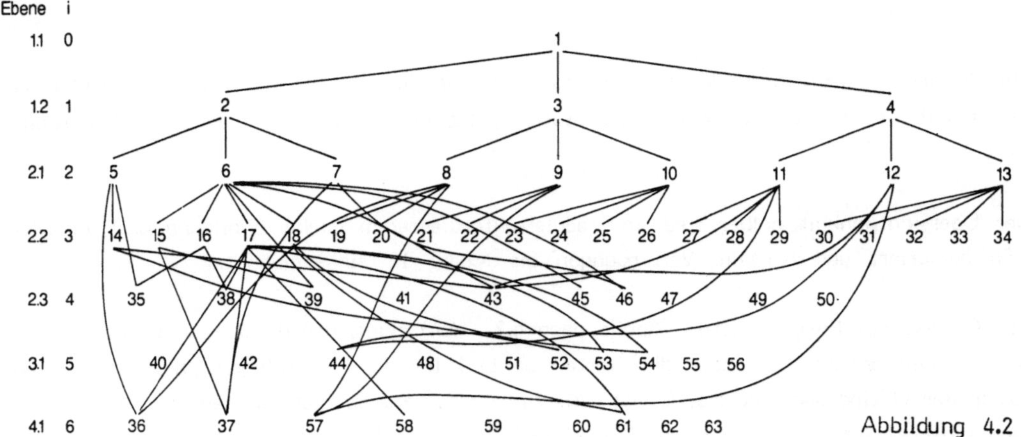

Abbildung 4.2

Auswertungstabelle

Ebene	i	N(i)	FO(i)	EF(i)	IF(i)	R(i)	D(i)
1.1	0	1	3	0	3	3.00	0.00
1.2	1	3	9	3	9	3.00	1.00
2.1	2	9	37	9	50	4.11	1.00
2.2	3	21	60	25	83	2.86	1.19
2.3	4	10	19	15	27	1.90	1.50
3.1	5	10	13	21	42	1.30	2.10
4.1	6	9	0	58	0	0.00	6.44
			Σ	131	214	U	1.63

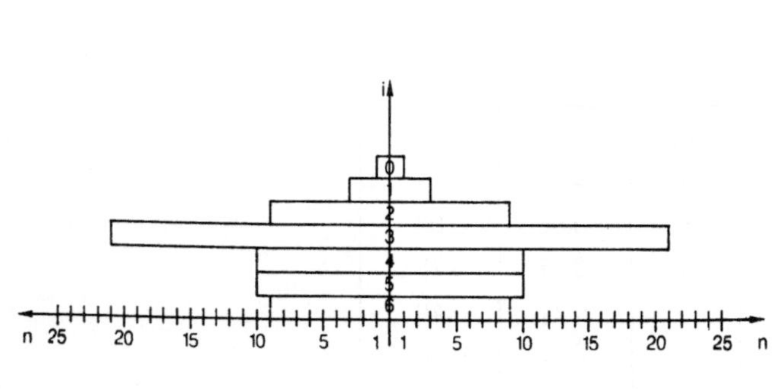

Abbildung 4.3

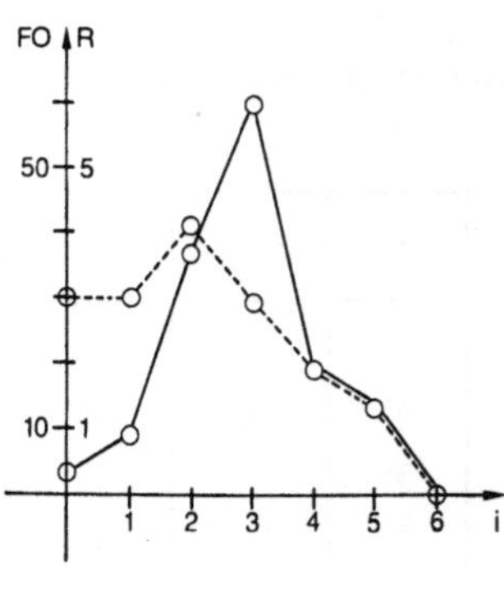

Abbildung 4.4

5. Schlußbemerkungen

Beide Ansätze werden zur Zeit weiter im praktischen Gebrauch erprobt. Die ersten Ergebnisse sind positiv zu bewerten und ermutigen zu weiteren Analysen. Die Überlegungen werden im Rahmen eines F&E-Vorhabens - gefördert vom BMFT unter der Projektträgerschaft der GMD - in ein Werkzeug zur Unterstützung des Systementwurfes integriert.

6. Literatur

/My75/ G.J. Myers
Reliable Software through Composite Design
von Nostrand Reinhold, 1975

/Wi79/ R.R. Willis, E.P. Jensen
Computer Aided Design of Software Systems
4. ICSE, München 1979

/Yi78/ B.A. Yin, J.W. Winchester
The Establishment and Use of Measures to Evaluate the Quality of Software Design
Hughes Aircraft, internal paper

/Yo78/ E. Yourdon, L.L. Constantine
Structured Design
Yourdon Press 1978

ISAC - eine Analyse- und Entwurfsmethode für komplexe Softwaresysteme

F. Jochum, D. Winter

ACTIS GmbH, Zweigniederlassung Berlin

Kurzfassung

Im vorliegenden Beitrag wird die Weiterentwicklung der Analyse- und Entwurfsmethode ISAC vorgestellt. Es werden die wichtigsten Konzepte des Ansatzes, wie Verfeinerungsregeln, Notationsregeln und die Darstellungssymbolik beschrieben und über Erfahrungen im praktischen Einsatz berichtet. Abschließend werden offene Probleme und geplante Erweiterungen andiskutiert.

1. Einleitung

Bei der Entwicklung computergestützter Problemlösungen gewinnen Methoden der Systemanalyse, des Systementwurfs und der Systemrealisierung in Wirtschaft und Verwaltung zunehmend an Bedeutung. In allen Phasen derartiger Projekte treten spezifische Probleme auf, wie z. B. gegenseitige Sprach- bzw. Verstehensprobleme in der Analysephase zwischen Fachabteilung und EDV-Abteilung bzw. Softwarehaus und Auftraggeber. Die Eignung einer Methode zeigt sich darin, in welchem Maße sie in der Lage ist, die Systementwicklung effektiv und effizient zu unterstützen. Das bedeutet, daß sie einerseits für alle Beteiligten verständlich und überschaubar und andererseits aber auch hinreichend exakt sein muß, um eine adäquate Beschreibung eines Problembereichs zu ermöglichen. Darüber hinaus sollte die Methode die modernen Prinzipien des Software Engineering unterstützen und selbst automatisierbar sein. Die in den letzten Jahren vorgestellten Ansätze wie z. B. SADT, HIPO, JACKSON, WARNIER, LITOS (s. z. B. /SCH 78/) weisen für bestimmte Projektphasen jeweils Vor- und Nachteile auf (vgl. /SNE 79/). Mit der Entwicklung der in diesem Beitrag fortgeschriebenen ISAC-Methode (Informationsfluß-Symbolik für Angewandte Computertechnik) wurde versucht, die oben genannten Maximen zu integrieren und ein geeignetes Werkzeug zur Verfügung zu stellen, daß für alle Projektphasen gleichermaßen geeignet ist.

Gegenüber /STU 79/ handelt es sich um eine in der Notation und Darstellungsart modifizierte Version. Bezüglich eines Vergleichs mit anderen Methoden sei auf /ACT 79/ verwiesen.

2. Allgemeine Eigenschaften von ISAC

ISAC ist eine Beschreibungstechnik zur Unterstützung von Problemlösungen und eignet sich insbesondere für die Analyse und den Entwurf komplexer Software-Systeme. Sie ermöglicht dem Analytiker die Beschreibung betrieblicher Abläufe und Organisationsstrukturen und dem Designer die funktions-, daten- oder betriebsmittelabhängige Darstellung des Softwaresystems sowie dessen Einbettung in den gesamtorganisatorischen Rahmen. Durch verschiedene Abstraktionsniveaus lassen sich unterschiedliche Sichten und somit je nach Fragestellung nur die dafür relevanten Sachverhalte darstellen. Damit reichen die Aggregationsstufen, die sowohl Daten als auch Funktionen umfassen, von einer groben Gesamtübersicht bis zum einzelnen Detail.

Die Methode basiert auf der Konzeption von Lundeberg et al. /LUN 79/ von der Universität Stockholm. Sie wurde von ACTIS - Angewandte Computertechnik für Informationssysteme GmbH - methodologisch vereinfacht, indem die Darstellungselemente auf zwei Sorten reduziert und die Notation vereinheitlicht wurde. Daraus resultiert eine einfache und übersichtliche Anwendung sowie die Möglichkeit einer Fundierung durch die Netztheorie (s. /PET 73/) und einer DIN-Normung über Instanzen und Kanäle.

3. Beschreibung der Methode

3.1 Darstellungselemente

Die Elemente von ISAC sind zweisortig (s. Tab. 1): Schwarz ausgezeichnete Quadrate symbolisieren Aktivitaeten (Tätigkeiten, Handlungen, Programme, ...), Ovale symbolisieren Informations-/Materialeinheiten (Kommunikationsmedien, Zustandsstrukturen, Daten, Bedingungen, ...).
Elemente aus verschiedenen Sorten sind durch Kanten miteinander verbunden, die einen Informations- oder Materialfluß (Strömungslinien) symbolisieren. Dabei handelt es sich um gerichtete Beziehungen, die aber nur dann durch einen Pfeil gekennzeichnet sind, wenn die Richtung nicht (eindeutig) in der Darstellung von "oben" nach "unten" verläuft. Ein Informationsfluß nach beiden Richtungen (z. B. lesender und schreibender Zugriff) kann abkürzend durch einen Doppelpfeil dargestellt werden. Es liegt immer eine alternierdende Reihenfolge vor, so daß eine Aktivität als Input eine oder mehrere Informationseinheiten hat und als Output ebenfalls eine oder mehrere Informations-

einheiten, die wiederum für eine andere Aktivität als Input dienen können.

Symbol	Interpretation
■	Aktivität (Ai)
⬭	Informationseinheit (Ii)
↑ ↕	Informationsfluß kennzeichnet die Beziehungen zwischen den Aktivitäten und den Informationseinheiten bzw. Materialeinheiten. Ein Fluß in beide Richtungen kann durch einen Doppelpfeil abgekürzt werden.
⬚	kennzeichnet auf der n-ten ($n > 1$) Ebene eine Aktivität der ($n - 1$)-ten Ebene
(- - -)	kennzeichnet auf der n-ten ($n > 1$) Ebene eine Informationseinheit der ($n - 1$)-ten Ebene

Tab. 1: ISAC-Symbolik

3.2 Verfeinerungsregeln und Notation

Ein wesentlichen Charakteristikum von ISAC ist die Möglichkeit, Aktivitäten und Informationseinheiten je nach Bedarf sukzessive zu verfeinern bzw. zu vergröbern. Auf diese Weise kann der Problembereich auf unterschiedlichen Abstraktionsebenen beschrieben werden (s. Abb. 1).
Verfeinerte Aktivitäten und verfeinerte Informationseinheiten können jeweils wiederum sowohl Aktivitäten als auch Informationseinheiten enthalten (Dualitätsprinzip).

Wurde eine Aktivität bzw. Informationseinheit verfeinert, so wird dies auf der feineren Ebene durch eine gestrichelte Umrandung angedeutet. Dabei ist eine Aktivität rechteckig und eine Informationseinheit rund umrandet (s. Tab. 1), um das Alternieren verschiedensortiger Elemente auf allen Ebenen zu gewährleisten. Außerdem dürfen Aktivitäten und Informationseinheiten nur innerhalb dieser gestrichelten Umrandungen neu entstehen. Diese Restriktion ist eine notwendige Voraussetzung dafür, das Netzmorphismen (s. /FER 76/) zwischen verschiedenen Ebenen definiert werden können.

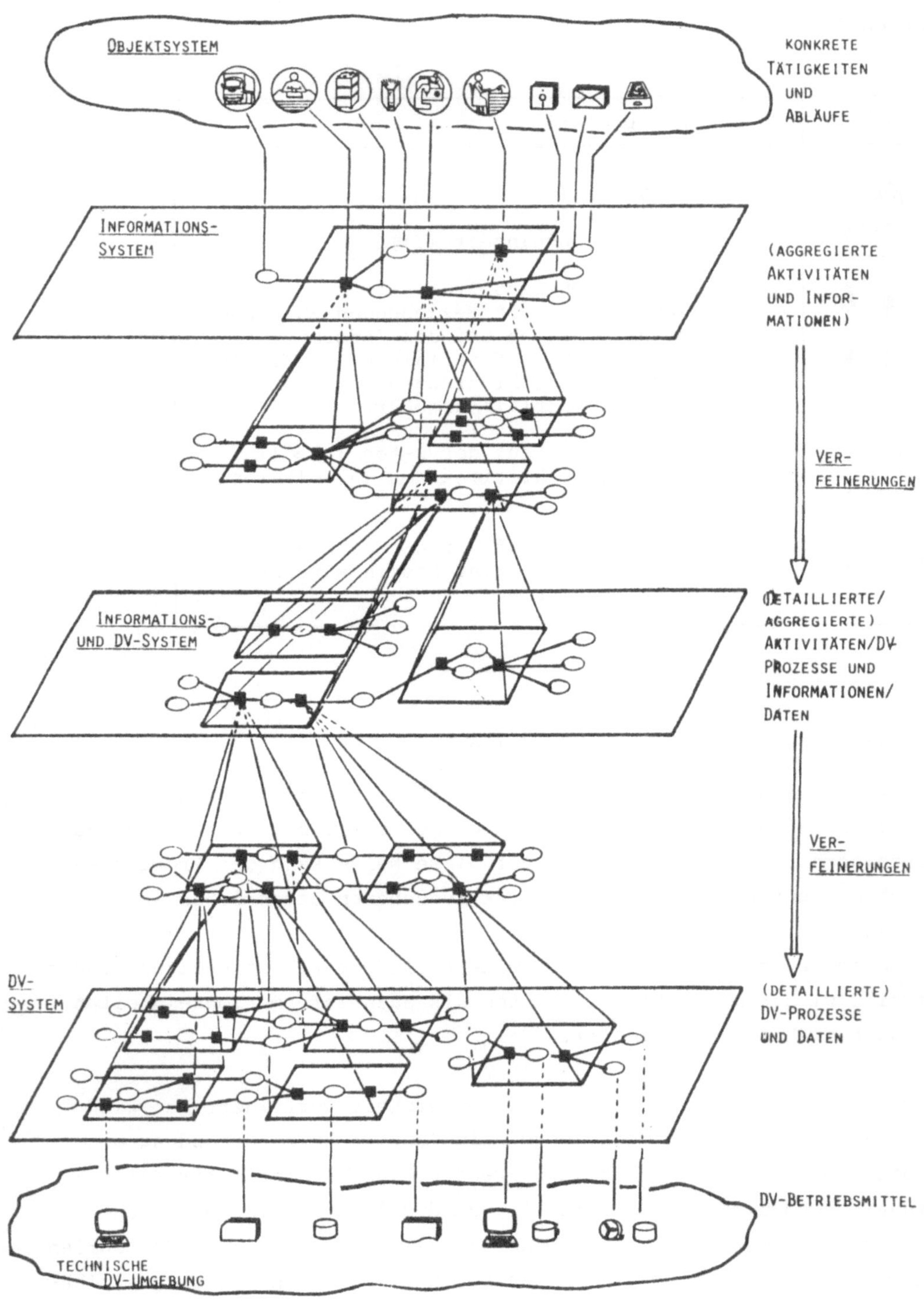

Abb. 1: Verfeinerungs-Hierarchie (vgl. /ACT 79/)

Die Beziehungen zu gröberen Ebenen werden, neben den gestrichelten Umrandungen, zusätzlich durch die Notation der Elemente angegeben: Elemente, die bei einer Verfeinerung neu entstehen, werden fortlaufend durchnumeriert und erhalten als Präfix die Bezeichnung des Elements der gröberen Ebene in Dot-Notation (Zugriffspfad). So bezeichnet beispielsweise A1.A3 in Abb. 2 den Zugriffspfad der Aktivität A3 aus Ebene 2, die aus der Verfeinerung der Aktivität A1 der Ebene 1 hervorgeht. Entsprechend bezeichnet I1.I2 den Zugriffspfad der Informationseinheit I2 in Ebene 2, die aus der Informationseinheit I1 der Ebene 1 durch die Verfeinerung entstand und A1.I2 den Zugriffspfad der Informationseinheit I2 innerhalb der verfeinerten Aktivität A1 von Ebene 1.

Eine solche Bezeichnungsweise ermöglicht den eindeutigen Zugriff auf alle Elemente der verschiedenen Abstraktionsebenen. Zur Kennzeichnung, ob eine Verfeinerung vorliegt, wird im Diagramm die Dot-Notation des betreffenden Elements auf der gröberen Ebene unterstrichen (s. Abb. 2).

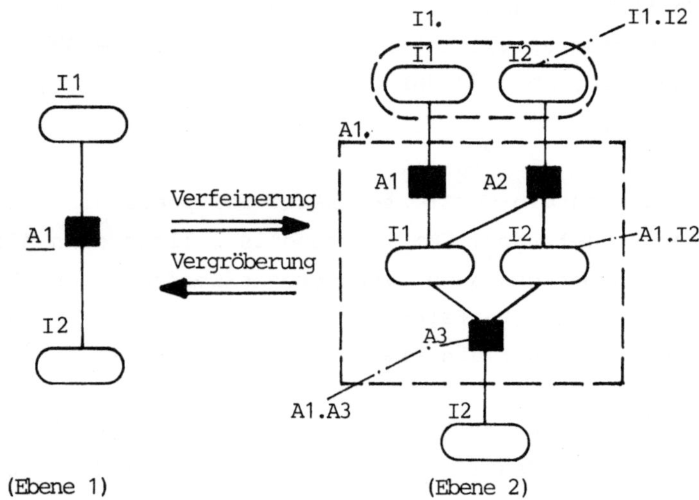

Abb. 2: Beispiel für eine Verfeinerung bzw. Vergröberung

Neben der Verwendung des Zugriffspfads zur eindeutigen Identifizierung, sind die Elemente eines ISAC-Diagramms zwecks vollständiger Beschreibung durch weitere Merkmale gekennzeichnet:

- NAME DES ZUGRIFFSPFADS (mnemotechnische Abkürzung) zur umgangssprachlichen Verwendung
- KURZTEXT (kurze natürlichsprachliche Beschreibung). Dieser kann im Diagramm unmittelbar neben (bei Aktivitäten) oder in (bei Informationseinheiten) die Elemente geschrieben werden (s. Pkt. 4.1)
- LANGTEXT als detaillierte verbale oder formale Beschreibung auf einem

separaten Blatt (z.B. Funktionsbeschreibung eines Moduls mit Input- und Outputparametern).

Darüber hinaus lassen sich alle Abstraktionsebenen durch Aktivitäts- und Informationsbäume (s. Pkt. 4.1) übersichtlich zusammenfassen, da die Verfeinerungen streng hierarchisch erfolgen. Dabei werden durch die Notationsweise Informationseinheiten und Aktivitäten außerhalb einer Komponente (eines Moduls) (z.B. I1, I2 in Abb. 2) von denen unterschieden, die innerhalb liegen (z.B. A1.I1 in Abb. 2).

4. Anwendung

4.1 Beispiel

Das folgende (fiktive) Beispiel veranschaulicht den Einsatz von ISAC für den Anwendungsfall 'Untersuchung der Verwaltungstätigkeit "Bearbeitung eines Weiterbildungsantrages" im Hinblick auf die Möglichkeiten einer Computerunterstützung'. Die Bilder Abb. 3 - Abb. 6 stellen die Istanalyse, Abb. 7a das Sollkonzept und Abb. 7b, Abb. 8 den Systementwurf dar.

Aus Platzgründen wurden die Kurztexte dieses Beispiels nicht in allen Abbildungen eingetragen. Zum Verständnis sollten dann die Aktivitäts- und Informationsbäume herangezogen werden. Ebenfalls aus Platzgründen wurde nur ein Verfeinerungspfad dargestellt, so daß von jeder Verfeinerungsebene nur ein Diagramm aufgeführt ist.

Beim Sollkonzept für den ausgewählten Teil der Istanalyse ist nur zufällig die äußere Form des ISAC-Diagramms gleich dem der Istanalyse. Die Aktivitäts- und Informationsinhalte sind unterschiedlich.

Da nur ein Verfeinerungspfad dargestellt ist, sind die Aktivitäts- und Informationsbäume entsprechend unvollständig und nur für die vorgestellten Diagramme aufgeführt, wobei Sollkonzept und Systementwurf durch Trennstriche untereinander und von der Istanalyse abgesetzt sind.

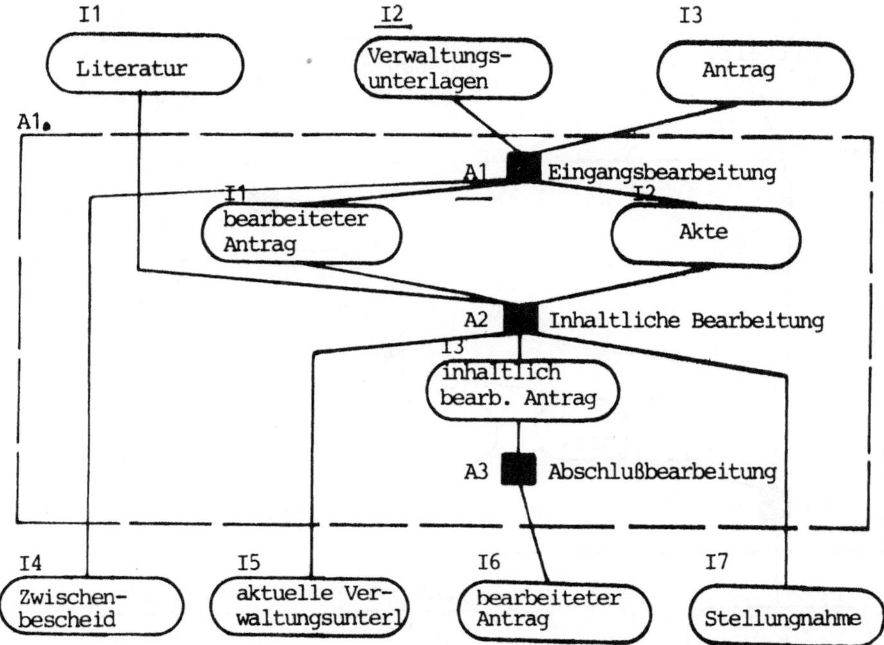

Abb. 3: Istanalyse "Bearbeitung eines Weiterbildungsantrages

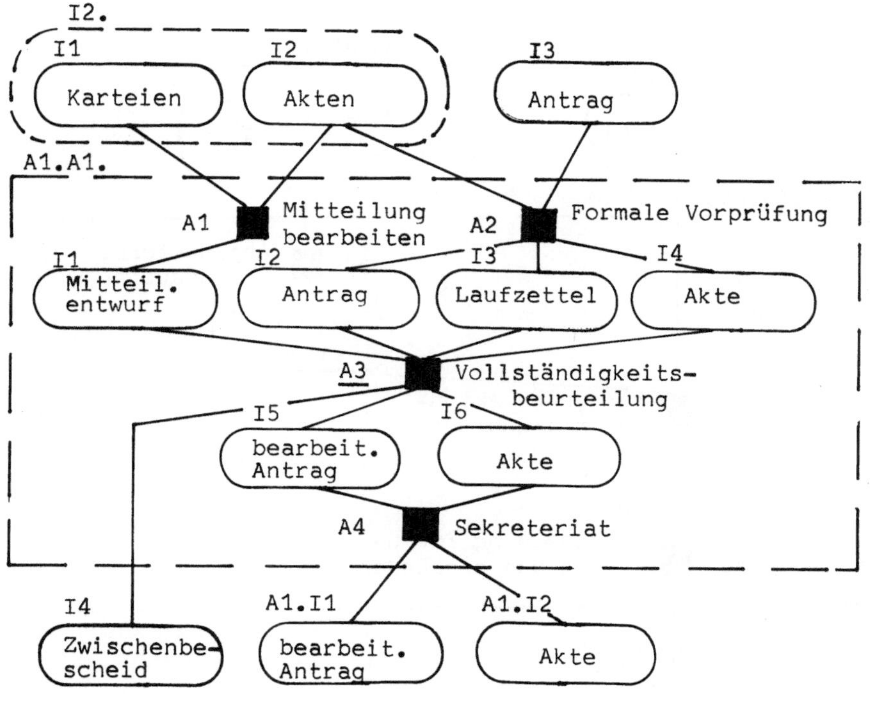

Abb. 4: Istanalyse (Verfeinerund "Eingangsbearbeitung")

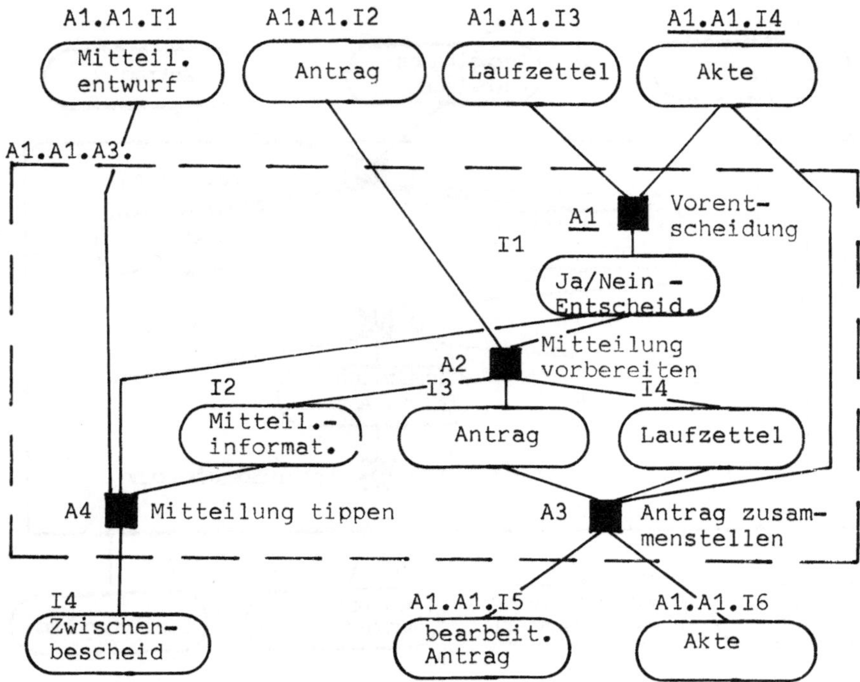

Abb. 5: Istanalyse (Verfeinerung "Vollständikeitsbeurteilung")

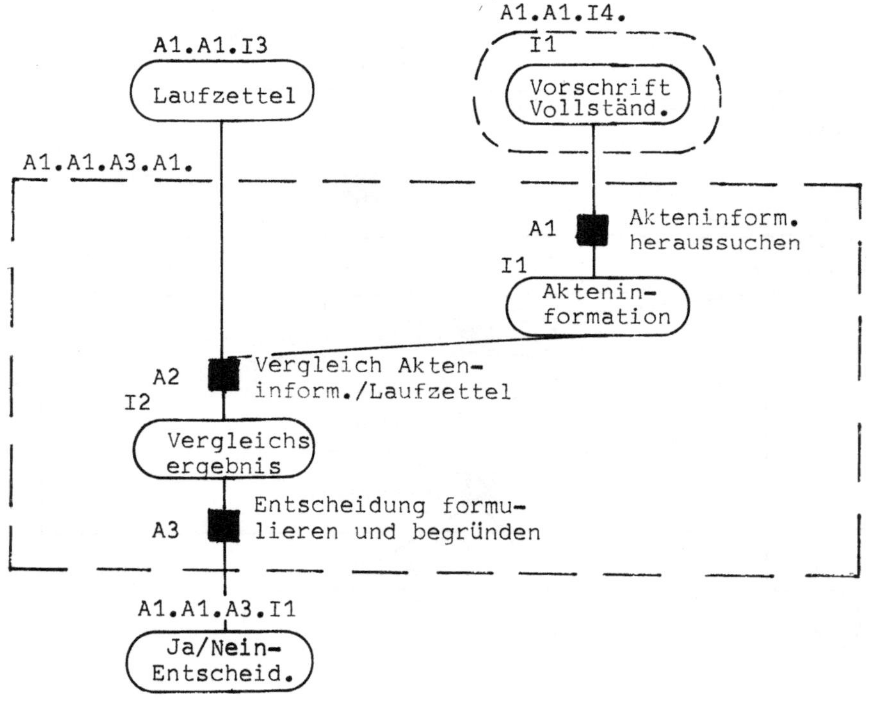

Abb. 6: Istanalyse (Verfeinerung "Vorentscheidung")

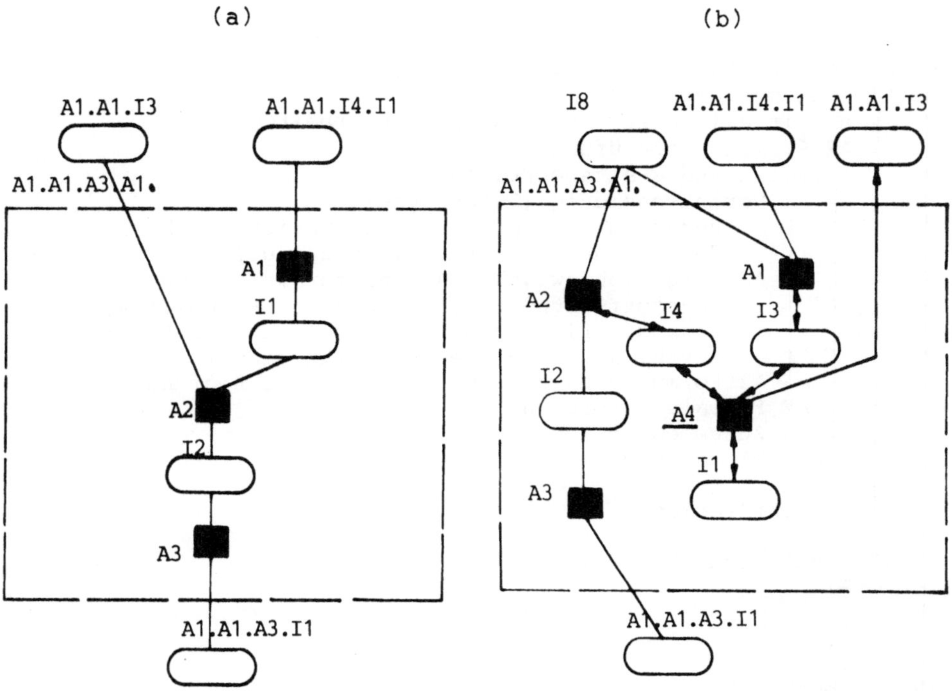

(a)

A1.A1.I3 A1.A1.I4.I1

A1.A1.A3.A1.

A1 I1 A2 I2 A3

A1.A1.A3.I1

(b)

I8 A1.A1.I4.I1 A1.A1.I3

A1.A1.A3.A1.

A1 A2 I4 I3 I2 A4 I1 A3

A1.A1.A3.I1

Abb. 7: Sollkonzept (a) und Systementwurf (b)

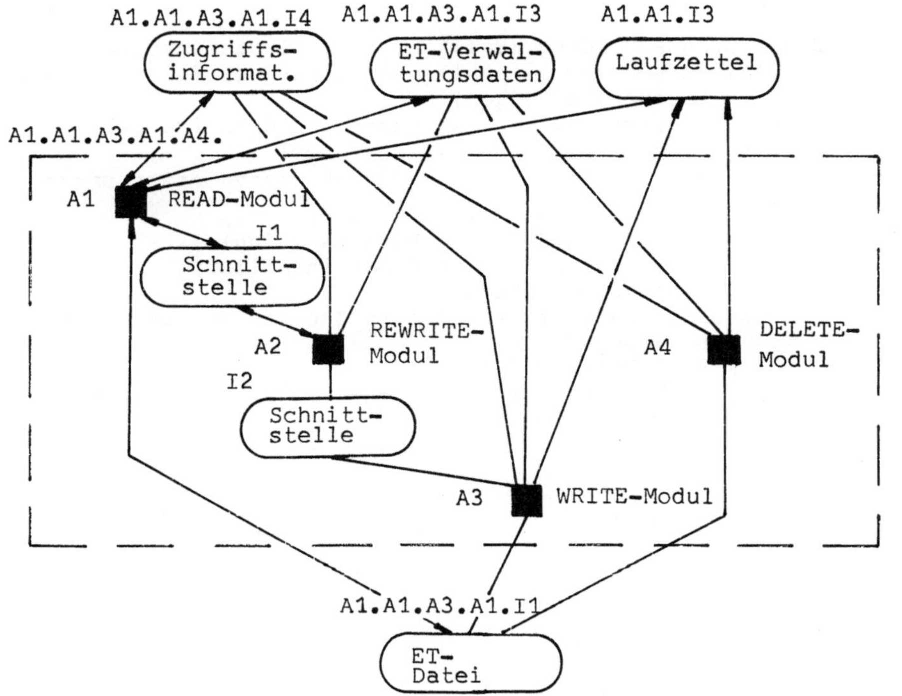

Abb. 8: Systementwurf (Verfeinerung "Dateihandler")

Aktivitätsbäume

```
A1.Weiterbildungsantragbearbeitung
├─ A1.Eingangsbearbeitung
│   ├─ A1 Mitteilung für Antragsteller bearbeiten
│   ├─ A2 Formale Vorprüfung
│   ├─ A3.Vollständigkeitsbeurteilung
│   │   ├─ A1.Vorentscheidung (Istanalyse)
│   │   │   ├─ A1 Heraussuchen der Akteninformation, nach
│   │   │   │     der ein Antrag als vollständig gilt
│   │   │   ├─ A2 Vergleich zwischen Akteninformation und
│   │   │   │     Laufzettel und Entscheidung (z. B. positiv,
│   │   │   │     wenn die richtigen Unterlagen auf dem Lauf-
│   │   │   │     zettel als vorhanden vermerkt sind.)
│   │   │   └─ A3 Formulieren der Entscheidung mit Begründung
│   │   ├─ A2 Formale Vorprüfung
│   │   ├─ A3 Zusammenstellen des Antrags
│   │   └─ A4 Mitteilung tippen
│   │
│   └─ A4 Sekretariat
│
├─ A2.Inhaltliche Bearbeitung
│   └─ A1
│       .
│       .
│       .
└─ A3.Abschlußbearbeitung
    └─ A1
        .
        .
        .
-----------------------------------------------------------------

A1.A1.A3.A1.Vorentscheidung (Sollkonzept f. Systemunterstützung)
            ├─ A1 Entscheidungstabellenverwaltung (Erfassen, Ändern,
            │     Löschen, Anzeigen)
            ├─ A2 Auswertfunktion zwischen ET und Laufzettel
            └─ A3 Druckaufbereitung (Textsystem)
-----------------------------------------------------------------

A1.A1.A3.A1.Vorentscheidung (Systementwurf)
            ├─ A1 Et-Verwaltung (ohne Dateihandling)
            ├─ A2 Auswertfunktion (ohne Dateihandling)
            ├─ A3 Druckaufbereitung
            └─ A4.Dateihandler (realisiert Zugriff auf Dateien)
                ├─ A1 READ-Modul
                ├─ A2 REWRITE-Modul
                ├─ A3 WRITE-Modul
                └─ A4 DELETE-Modul
```

Informationsbäume

```
I1 Literatur
I2.Verwaltungsunterlagen
 ├ I1 Karteien
 └ I2 Akten

I3 Antrag
I4 Zwischenbescheid
I5 aktualisierte Verwaltungsunterlagen
I6 bearbeiteter Antrag
I7 Stellungnahme

A1.I1 bearbeiteter Antrag
 ├ I2 Akte
 └ I3 inhaltlich bearbeiteter Antrag

A1.A1.I1 Mitteilungsentwurf
      ├ I2 Antrag
      ├ I3 Laufzettel
      └ I4.Akte
          └ I1 Vorschrift über Vollständigkeit
A1.A1.I5 bearbeiteter sortierter Antrag
      └ I6 Akte

A1.A1.A3.I1 Ja/Nein-Entscheidung mit Begründung
         ├ I2 Mitteilungsinformation
         ├ I3 Antrag
         └ I4 Laufzettel

A1.A1.A3.A1.I1 Akteninformation (Vorschrift) nach der ein
            │    Antrag als vollständig gilt
            └ I2 Ergebnis des Vergleichs, Entscheidung und
                 Begründung
------------------------------------------------------------------

A1.A1.I3 Datei - Laufzettel
A1.A1.I4.I1 Vorschrift über Vollständigkeit (siehe Istanalyse)
A1.A1.A3.A1.I1 Entscheidungstabelle
            └ I2 Schnittstelle zwischen Auswertfunktion
                 und Druckaufbereitung (Textsystem)
A1.A1.A3.I1 automatisch erzeugte J/N-Entscheidung mit
            Begründung
------------------------------------------------------------------

I8 Benutzerbildschirm (Daten-E/A, Steuerung)
A1.A1.A3.A1.I1 Datei-Entscheidungstabelle
            ├ I2 Schnittstelle zwischen Auswertfunktion und
            │    Druckaufbereitung (Textsystem)
            ├ I3 ET-Verwaltungsdaten für die (von der) ET-Datei
            └ I4 Informationen für Zugriff auf ET-Datei und
                 Laufzetteldatei
A1.A1.A3.A1.A4.I1 Schnittstelle zwischen REWRITE- und READ-Modul
               └ I2 Schnittstelle zwischen REWRITE- und WRITE-Modul
```

4.2 Praktische Erfahrungen

ISAC wird seit drei Jahren von ACTIS in Projekten mit unterschiedlicher Zielsetzung (Problemanalyse, Sollkonzeption, Systementwurf, Systemimplementierung) in Handel, Industrie, Behörden und Forschungsinstituten eingesetzt. Die dabei gewonnenen Erfahrungen umfassen hauptsächlich Anwendungen aus dem Bereich Computergestützte Informationssysteme (Groß- und Kleinrechner) und der kommerziellen Datenverarbeitung.

Dabei zeigen sich im wesentlichen die folgenden Vorteile der Methode:

1. Wegen der Einfachheit der graphischen Symbole und der Schichtung nach Abstraktionsebenen sind die ISAC-Diagramme ein leicht verständliches Hilfsmittel zur Kommunikation zwischen Fachabteilung und Datenverarbeitung (Auftraggeber und Softwarehaus). Die Erfahrung hat gezeigt, daß Entwurfsfehler und Terminverzögerungen durch Mißverständnisse wegen zu spätem Einschalten der Fachabteilungen vermieden werden können (partizipierende Vorgehensweise).

2. Die Verwendung der gleichen Darstellungsart bei Analyse und Entwurf ermöglicht:
   - einen konsistenten und nachvollziehbaren Übergang zwischen den Entwicklungsphasen
   - die einheitliche Dokumentation aller Projektphasen von der Problemanalyse über die Sollkonzeption bis zur Programmierung (Bildschirm- und Listen-Entwurf, Dateibeschreibung, Modul- und Komponenten-Spezifikation)
   - eine Überprüfung, inwieweit die analysierten Anforderungen beim Entwurf berücksichtigt wurden
   - eine bessere Fortschreibung und Schulung der Organisationskonzeption sowie der Festlegung des detaillierten Stufenplans zur Realisierung des Gesamtsystems.

3. Aufgrund des Alternierens von Aktivitäten und Informationseinheiten sind Schnittstellen zwischen verschiedenen Entscheidungsebenen und Funktionsbereichen klar darstellbar und erkennbar.

4. Die Verfeinerungs-/Vergröberungstechnik läßt sowohl ein Top-down- als auch ein Bottom-up-Vorgehen zu.

5. Die Einbeziehung der Verfeinerungsschritte in die Notation der dargestellten Objekte führt bei einem Top-down-Vorgehen zu einer einheitlichen Terminologie, was besonders in dezentral organisierten Unternehmen wichtig ist.

6. Durch das Dualitätsprinzip (Informationseinheiten können Aktivitäten, Aktivitäten können Informationseinheiten enthalten) und die konsequente Anwendung der Verfeinerungs-/Vergröberungstechnik werden wichtige Prinzipien des Software Engineering (s. /DEN 79/, /ROS 75/), wie Modularisierung, Verbergen modul-interner Informationen (information hiding), hierarchische Zerlegung des Systems und Daten-Abstraktion unterstützt.

7. Die eindeutige Identifikation aller Elemente durch den Zugriffspfad erleichtert ihre maschinelle Verwaltung und die automatische Generierung der Aktivitäts- und Informationsbäume.

Ein Nachteil, der sich besonders in der Anfangsphase eines Projektes bemerkbar macht, ist der relativ hohe Änderungsaufwand an den Diagrammen, bedingt durch die strengen Verfeinerungsregeln und dem anfänglich geringen Wissenstand über den zu modellierende Gegenstandsbereich. Dieser Nachteil kann durch eine maschinelle Unterstützung behoben werden.

Ein weiterer Nachteil könnte u. U. die fehlende Unterscheidung von Datenfluß und Kontrollfluß sein. Durch entsprechende Benennung der Elemente bzw. durch die Wahl der Kurztexte ist dies jedoch zu umgehen.

5. Schlußbemerkungen

Die mehrjährigen Erfahrungen mit ISAC haben die Praktibilität der Methode bestätigt. Der durchgängige Einsatz während der gesamten Projektdauer gewährleistet den konsistenten Übergang zwischen den einzelnen Entwicklungsphasen. Dies gilt insbesondere für die Schnittstelle zwischen Systemanalyse und Systementwurf und ist dadurch eine wesentliche Voraussetzung dafür, daß die Systemrealisierung an den Benutzeranforderungen orientiert ist und sich die späteren, tatsächlichen Systemleistungen mit den ursprünglichen Zielen decken. Durch die Einfachheit und Flexibilität der Methode sind die Ergebnisse für alle am Entwicklungsprozess beteiligten Personen (Sachbearbeiter und Abteilungsleiter der Fachabteilungen, Systemanalytiker, Programmierer) in gleicher Weise leicht verständlich, wodurch die Steuerung und Kontrolle bei allen Entwurfsentscheidungen durch die Betroffenen gewährleistet ist. Dies erhöht die Akzeptanz des zu entwickelnden Systems.

Einige noch offene Punkte, die z. T. in Angriff genommen wurden, sind:

- Automatisierung der Methode, d. h. die maschinelle Unterstützung der graphischen Seite durch Graphik-Terminal und Plotter sowie die Erweiterung durch zusätzliche Komponenten wie Bausteine für Konsistenzprüfungen und Bildschirmspezifikation, Data Dictionary, Information Dictionary (s. /MEY 79/) und Programmgeneratoren (s. /POR 79/).
- Formalisierung durch die Netztheorie zur Durchführung von Korrektheits- und Vollständigkeitsbeweisen und zur Simulation des dynamischen Systemverhaltens.

Allen Mitarbeiten, die durch ihre Diskussionsbeiträge während der Projektarbeit den Inhalt des vorliegenden Artikels mit beeinflußt haben, sei an dieser Stelle gedankt. Ebenso danken wir Prof. Dr. H.-J. Schneider (TU Berlin) für seine wertvollen Hinweise.

6. Literatur

/ACT 79/ ACTIS GmbH: Angewandte Softwaretechnik, ACTIS-Seminar, Stuttgart 1979 .

/DEN 79/ Denert, E.: Software-Modularisierung, in: Informatik-Spektrum 2, S. 204 - 218 (1979).

/FER 76/ Ferduandez, C. C.: Net Topology, Internal Reports 79-09 and 76-2, Gesellschaft für Mathematik und Datenverarbeitung, St. Augustin, W. Germany, (1979).

/LUN 79/ Lundeberg, M.; Goldkuhl, G.; Nilsson, A.: A systematic Approach to Information Systems Development - I. Introduktion, in: Information Systems, 4, pp. 1-12, (1979).

/MEY 79/ Meyer, B. E.; Schneider, H.-J.: The Concepts of a Problem Solution Support System, Interner CIS-Bericht Nr. 10/79, Institut für Angewandte Informatik, TU Berlin, 1979 .

/PET 73/ Petri, C. A.: Concept of Net Theorie, in: Proceedings of Symposium on Mathematical Foudation of Computer Sciene, pp. 146 - 157, Mathem. Institute of the Slovak Acedemy of Sciene, Bratislava, Sept. 1973 .

/POR 79/ Portner, N.; Stübel, G.: Computergestütztes Programmieren durch Spezifizieren am Bildschirm, in: Angewandte Informatik 10, (1979).

/ROS 75/ Ross, D. T.; Goodenough, J. B.; Irvine, C. A.: Software Engineering: Process, Principles and Goals, in: Computer, pp. 17-29, May (1975).

/SCH 78/ Schulz, A.: Methoden des Softwareentwurfs und strukturierte Programmierung, Berlin 1978 .

/SNE 79/ Sneed, H.: Programmentwurfsmethoden im Vergleich, Online, Sept. (1979).

/STU 79/ Stübel, G.: ISAC - eine formale Methode zur rechnergestützten Beschreibung von Betriebsabläufen, in: Mayr, H. C.; Meyer, B. E. (Hrsg.): Formale Modelle für Informationssysteme, GI-Fachberichte Nr. 21, Berlin, Heidelberg, New York, Springer Verlag 1979 .

DESIGNING THE CONCEPTUAL DATABASE SCHEMA - A FRAMEWORK FOR AN INTERACTIVE APPROACH

J. Karszt, R. Krieger, G. Lausen, W. Stucky
Institut für Angewandte Informatik
und Formale Beschreibungsverfahren
Universität Karlsruhe (TH)
Postfach 6380, D-7500 Karlsruhe 1

Abstract

A framework for interactive conceptual database design methods is proposed, which captures top-down and bottom-up approaches, as well. Several constraints are defined, which are to be fulfilled by the final conceptual schema. Some of them can be completely or partially tested by an automatic design tool. Further we show, how inconsistencies as homonyms, redundancies and synonyms can be automatically tested. Finally we sketch by examples, how bottom-up and top-down approaches can be used within our framework.

1. Introduction

Modern data design is a stepwise process of modelling the data base at different levels of abstraction. According to many authors ([1], [2], [3]) we distinguish between the conceptual (or enterprise), the logical and the physical schema of a database. The topic of our paper is the design of the conceptual schema, which describes the real world independently of implementation aspects.

Designing the conceptual schema is the first and very important task in the database design process. Since a poor database design can produce excessive processing and restructuring costs, the design cannot base only on designers experience and intuition. Methods must be used which include well defined rules and which guide the designer in developing the conceptual schema. Although this necessity is known, database design in practice is still less systematic. One reason for this fact might be, that the methods discussed in the academic environment (especially normalization theory [4], [5], aggregation and generalization [6], entity-relationship model [7]), are less known in practice. But it seams also, that these methods loose their attractiveness during the design process of large systems (e.g. this observation is made in [8] with respect to aggregation and generalization).

We feel that the latter problem can be solved by using an computer aided design method. Computer aided design methods have following advantages:

- They relieve the designer of routine, tedious and lengthy tasks (e.g. normalization, consistency checks) and enable him to concentrate on those design decisions, which are out of algorithmic control.
- The design process is less expensive, since it could be done faster.
- If needed, iterations can be easily performed. In reality it is not a realistic assumption, that all requirements are known in the moment of the beginning of the design process. Usually it is necessary to communicate with the users during the design process and to change the design decisions.
- Using computer aided design methods the design steps can be documented automatically. This makes manual documentation unnecessary, which usually is a tedious and disliked task.

In the literature there exist several approaches for the computer aided design of the conceptual schema (e.g. [9], [10], [11], [12], [13]). We propose interactive tools, with the following properties. Consistency checks and normalization are performed by a computer process, while corrections and further semantics can be introduced interactively by the designer. The following chapter gives a principal discussion of computer aided design approaches. A framework for interactive approaches is sketched and more formally described in chapter 3. Several constraints are defined, which are to be fulfilled by the final conceptual schema. Some of them can be completely or partially tested by an automatic design tool. In chapter 4 we show how the constraints can be fulfilled and in chapter 5 we discuss the problem of inconsistencies. Finally in chapter 6 we sketch how bottom-up and top-down approaches can be used within the framework.

2. Computer Aided Design Approaches

The "New Orleans workshop report" [3] divides the design process into the following steps:

1. Requirement Analysis,
2. Information Analysis and Definition,
3. Implementation Design,
4. Physical Design.

In the following, we refer to step 2. Information analysis and definition deal with view modelling and the design of the conceptual schema. The designer has to analyse the user views, to resolve conflicts and differences and to integrate the views into a single enterprise view of the database. This tasks should be supported by an automatic tool.

The suitability and the degree of automation of a computer aided design tool heavily depends on the properties of the underlying data model and the design method. In general we can say, that there exists a conflict between the possibility of including semantics during the design process and the degree of automation. Algorithms for automatic design are well-known for the relational model. For survey see [5]. But such approaches are not sufficient since the relational model hides many of the semantics of the real world. It is restricted to functional and multivalued dependencies.

Models based on aggregation and generalization [6] or the entity-relationship approach [7] are suited to capture more semantics of the real world. They consist of clear and simple constructs. Further they allow a dialogue between the user and the designer during the design process. That means, the conceptual schema can be developed step by step in cooperation with the users. Unfortunately, these approaches cannot be fully automated. They still need a final normalization step to achieve syntactical correctness.

The above discussion shows, that using a computer aided design approach, the designer still must be able to control the design -process and to enter additional information. On the other side, the analysis of his decisions should be supported by an automatic tool, which should perform the normalization, too.

We think, that the development of interactive design tools is a promising way to achieve these goals. Using an interactive design tool the designer can build the conceptual schema step by step including additional semantic information whenever needed. This interactive process can be characterized as shown in figure 1.

① realworld observation of the designer and dialogue with the users,

② input of relevant information, corrections,

③ analysis results, conceptual schema (intermediate or final)

Figure 1

An interactive design method can be found in [11]. This method is based on a binary data model. The conceptual schema is defined by sentences about the real world, which can be interpreted and analyzed by algorithms. We propose a framework for an interactive approach, which heavily depends on a construct which we call associationtype. Formally, an associationtype can be considered as a n-ary relation, describing a relationship between objects of the real world.

We can classify associationtypes into elementary associationtypes and compound associationtypes. Elementary associationtypes represent functional and nunfunctional dependencies between attributes which cannot be divided into smaller constructs without loss of information. Most of them will refer to attribute pairs or key pairs. Compound associationtypes represent high level objects of the real world. They can be used by the designer to specify objects with more or less semantic meaning: compound associationtypes can be considered either as aggregates in the sense of Smith and Smith [6] or entity-relationship-types in the sense of Chen [7] or relations without specific semantic meaning. Using associationtypes as a general concept in this sense has several advantages:

- The designer is free from semantic input-restrictions. He can enter all informations, which are expressable by n-ary relations.
- The designer is not restricted to a fixed design method. He can choose e.g. a synthesis (bottom-up) or a decomposition (top-down) approach, whatever seems to him most appropriate for the construction of the conceptual schema in a specific situation.

To clarify the concept of associationtypes let us consider for example the following user view resulting from document analysis:

EMPOLYEE(EMPNO,ADDR,HIRE-DATE,DEPARTURE-DATE,HOURS-WORKED,DEPARTMENT)

This user view can be interpreted as a compound associationtype EMPLOYEE. The designer can also perceive elementary associationytpes, which are included by the compound associationtype EMPLOYEE, e.g. EMPNO → ADDR,EMPNO → DEPT.

In the following we describe a framework for a family of design methods, which all have the principal structure shown in figure 2.

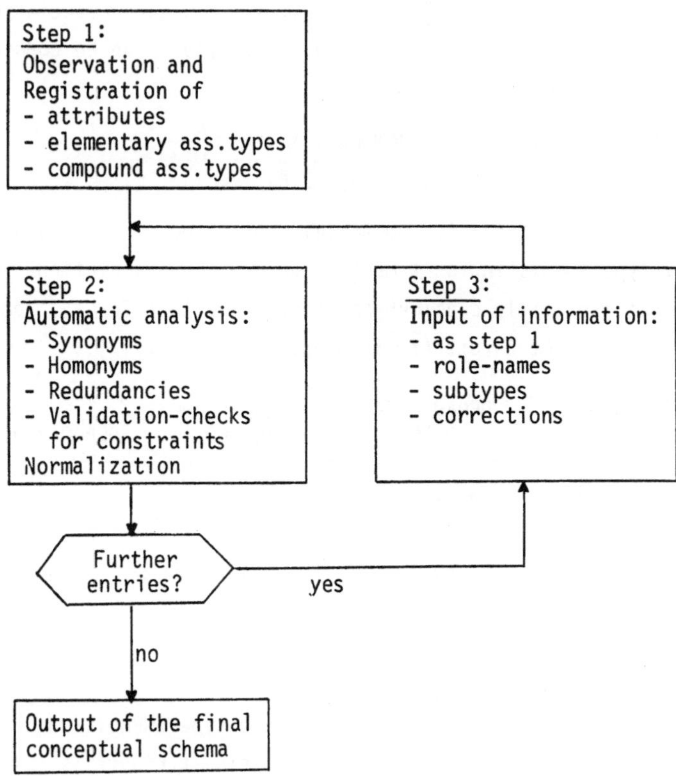

Figure 2: The interactive design process

Let us assume, that the information requirements of applications (user views) exist in the form of file descriptions, documents, forms and answers to questionnaires. The first step of the designer is to use this information to perceive an initial set of attributes and elementary and compound associationtypes. During the design process he has to transform this set of attributes and associationtypes via several intermediate steps to a semantically equivalent set of associationtypes, which has to fulfill a number of constraints (formally defined in the next chapter). This final set represents the conceptual schema. During each iteration step the automatic design tool analysis the current set of associationstypes, whether or not the constraints are fulfilled. Furthermore potential homonyms, synonyms and redundancies are indicated. The designer has to react on these results of the analyzation process by changing and/or extending the set of associationtypes to correct the violated constraints. The resulting set of associationtypes becomes the current set of the next iteration step.

3. Formal Framework

Consider a set of <u>attributes</u> $\overline{A} = \{a_1,\ldots,a_n\}$. We associate with each attribute $a \in \overline{A}$ a value set dom(a), called the domain of a. Each domain includes a special nullvalue "ω". Consider a set of associationtypes $\overline{F} = \{f_1,\ldots,f_m\}$. With each associationtype f is associated a set of attributes attr(f). An associationtype f can be considered as a class of timevarying relations

$$f_t \subseteq dom(b_1) \times \ldots \times dom(b_k), \text{ where}$$
$$attr(f) = \{b_1, \ldots, b_k\} \subseteq \overline{A}.$$

The order of the attributes $b \in attr(f)$ is immaterial, but fixed. f_t represents the concrete associations of type f existing at time t (e.g. see the associations shown in figure 3). If we do not explicitly consider the time we write f for f_t, too. The projection of f (f_t) to a subset $C \subseteq attr(f)$ is denoted by $f|_C$ ($f_t|_C$).

EMP-NO	ADDR	HIRE-DATE	DEPARTURE-DATE	HOURS WORKED	DEPARTMENT
1020	London	1.4.78	31.1.80	ω	A
1030	Bonn	1.6.75	ω	40	B
1050	Paris	1.4.78	ω	46	A
1060	London	1.7.79	ω	40	B

Figure 3

The above figure shows the associations of an associationtype EMPLOYEE at a given time. With "ω" we denote a nullvalue, which indicates, that this attribute is for the respective association semantically not defined ("property inapplicable", [14]). Hence nullvalues have a distinct semantic meaning. In the above table HOURS = ω indicates, that for the employee with NO = 1020 the attribute HOURS is not defined. This is due to the fact, that the employee has a departure date D-DATE = 31.1.80 and therefore is not an active employee. In contrast, the remaining employees are still active and therefore D-DATE is not defined for them.

Consider an associationtype f and sets of attributes A, $B \subseteq attr(f)$.

(a) f includes a functional associationtype (fa) from A to B ($A \xrightarrow{f} B$), iff for each t:
- $f_{t|A}$ contains no nullvalues,
- f_t represents a mapping from $f_{t|A}$ to $f_{t|B}$,

(b) f includes a strong functional associationtype (sfa) from A to B ($A \overset{f}{\rightarrowtail} B$), iff $A \xrightarrow{f} B$ and for each t:
- $f_{t|B}$ contains no nullvalues,

(c) f includes a weak functional associationtype (wfa) from A to B ($A \overset{f}{\circ\!\!\rightarrow} B$), iff $A \xrightarrow{f} B$ and not $A \overset{f}{\rightarrowtail} B$,

(d) f includes a nonfunctional associationtype (nfa) between A and B ($A \overset{f}{—} B$), iff neither $A \xrightarrow{f} B$ nor $B \xrightarrow{f} A$.

The associationtype shown in figure 3 includes at the given time:

$$NO \rightarrowtail \{ADDR, H\text{-}Date, DEPT\}; \quad NO \circ\!\!\rightarrow HOURS;$$
$$\{NO, ADDR\} \circ\!\!\rightarrow D\text{-}DATE; \quad ADDR — DEPT.$$

A key of an associationtype f is a minimal subset $key(f) \subseteq attr(f)$, such that $key(f) \rightarrow attr(f)$. We consider for each associationtype only one key - the primary key. An attribute $a \in \bar{A}$ is called keyattribute, iff $a \in key(f)$ for some $f \in F$. Otherwise it is called nonkeyattribute. The set of nonkeyattributes of an associationtype f is denoted by $nka(f) \subseteq attr(f)$. The keypart of an associationtype f is defined as $kpart(f) := attr(f) \setminus nka(f)$. The set of all functional associationtypes, which are included by an associationtype f, is called the dependency set dep(f). Let f_i, f_j be two different associationtypes. We say f_i is a subtype of f_j, iff $key(f_i) = key(f_j)$ and $f_{i,t|key(f_i)} \subseteq f_{j,t|key(f_j)}$ for each time t.

Now remember that designing the conceptual schema is an iterativ process. At each step the current set of associationtypes is checked, whether it fulfills some constraints. These constraints are defined below. To have a distinction between associationtypes which fulfill the constraints and those, which do not, we introduce the notion of an "aggregate".

Consider a set of associationtypes $\bar{G} \subseteq \bar{F}$. $\bar{G}$ is called "set of aggregates" (each $g \in \bar{G}$ is called aggregate), iff the following constraints are fulfilled:

(C0) each information resulting from requirement analysis and entered into the design process is derivable from $\bar{G}$,

(C1) each $g \in \bar{G}$ is semantically meaningfull [6],

(C2) for each $g \in \overline{G}$ exists a primary key,

(C3) for each $g \in \overline{G}$, dep(g) does not contain a wfa,

(C4) each $g \in \overline{G}$ fulfills 3NF with respect to dep(g),

(C5) for each $g_i, g_j \in \overline{G}$, $g_i \neq g_j$ holds: $nka(g_i) \cap nka(g_j) = \emptyset$,

(C6) each $g \in \overline{G}$ either is an entitytype in $\overline{G}$ or a relationshiptype in $\overline{G}$, where

(ET) g is an <u>entitytype</u> in $\overline{G}$, iff

- key(g) = kpart(g),
- for each $g' \in \overline{G}$:
  if $key(g) \cap kpart(g') \neq \emptyset$ then $key(g) \subseteq kpart(g')$),

(RT) g is a <u>relationshiptype</u> in $\overline{G}$, iff there exist entitytypes $g_1, \ldots, g_k \in \overline{G}$, $k \geqslant 2$ such that holds: $kpart(g) = key(g_1) \uplus \ldots \uplus key(g_k)$,
($\uplus$ = disjunct union [1])

(C7) for each entitytypes $g_i, g_j \in \overline{G}$, $g_i \neq g_j$ holds:
$key(g_i) = key(g_j) \Rightarrow$ either g_i is a subtype of g_j or g_j is a subtype of g_i.

<u>4. Discussion of the Constraints</u>

In this chapter we further discuss the transformation process of a set of associationtypes into a set of aggregates. Our constraints contain syntactic and semantic aspects. We have chosen this approach to obtain constraints, which can be checked automatically as much as possible, while on the other hand obviously the designer still must be able to direct the design process.

The constraint (C0) is a general requirement, which of course must be fulfilled. The definition of associationtypes and dependency sets can only be controlled by the designer. But derivability can be guaranteed to some extent via normalization (see also below). Further we can check automatically whether each attribute has been associated with an aggregate and whether each associationtype has become an aggregate or is included by an aggregate. Of course in the latter case, the designer has to decide whether this inclusion is semantically correct.

This leads us to (C1). Before an associationtype becomes an aggregate, the designer has to agree. If he cannot agree, he has to redefine or to erase the respective associationtype.

(C2) needs no further justification. It guarantees, that for each aggregate g there exists at least one fa, namely $key(g) \rightarrow attr(g)$. The definition of a key is a cooperative task between the designer and the automatic tool. The designer must decide, whether the key is semantically meaningful and whether the implied fa's really hold. The tool can check the consistency of the designers decision with other existing fa's (e.g. minimality, see (C4)).

---

[1] $A \uplus B$ means: for each element x in $A \cap B$, rename x at least once to obtain two distinct elements (cf. "role name") and perform $A \cup B$.

(C2) and (C3) together exclude nullvalues of aggregates. With respect to the attribute set attr(g)∖key(g) nullvalues can be avoided by removing wfa's. For example the wfa EMP-NO ○→ HOURS in figure 3 can be circumvented by defining a subtype ACTIVE-EMP of EMPLOYEE; HOURS and the wfa EMP-NO ○→ HOURS are removed from attr(EMPLOYEE), respectively, dep(EMPLOYEE). Then HOURS and a sfa EMP-NO ↦ HOURS are inserted into attr(ACTIVE-EMP), respectively dep(ACTIVE-EMP). Hence wfa's, which may result from requirement analysis, can be considered as "delayed triggers" for the definition of subtypes.

To achieve (C4) there exist synthesis and decomposition algorithms (for a detailed discussion see [5]). The input of a synthesis algorithm is a set of attributes and a set of sfa's. This approach is appropriated, if no information about compound associationtypes is available. The restriction to the synthesis approach limits the features of our framework. Hence the designer must be able to use a decomposition algorithm, as well. The input of a decomposition algorithm is a compound associationtype with its respective dependency set. The semantic information, concerning the interrelation of the attributes of a compound associationtype is preserved by a decomposition algorithm. But anyway, the results produced by a normalization algorithm still need a final check by the designer to guarantee (C0) and (C1). For example a decomposition approach may produce an associationtype X(PUPIL, CLASS, MOUNTAIN), which obviously describes no semantically meaningful interrelation and which should be replaced by two associationtypes ENROLLMENT (PUPIL, CLASS), CLIMB(PUPIL, MOUNTAIN) (the example is taken from [15] and is further explained there).

(C5) states, that nonkeyattributes must be uniquely associated with one aggregate. In other words, if an attribute is referenced by more than one aggregate, this attribute must be a keyattribute. The motivation behind is to avoid identification problems (see [10], [16]).

(C6) includes the definition of entitytypes and relationshiptypes. Entitytypes can be considered as atomic aggregates. On the other side, relationshiptypes can be used to represent associationtypes between entitytypes, or between entitytypes and relationshiptypes, or between relationshiptypes and relationshiptypes. To clarify this constraint let us consider the following set of associationtypes:

COURSE(COURSE-NO, DESCRIPTION),
CLASS(COURSE-NO, SEMESTER-NO, INSTRUCTOR).

Obviously, COURSE is an entitytype, but CLASS neither is an entitytype nor is a relationshiptype. This situation can be solved by introducing an additional entitytype SEMESTER(SEMESTER-NO). Now CLASS represents a relationshiptype between COURSE and SEMESTER, what describes the real world semantically more precisely. Note, that this additional entitytype is not needed in the model of [15]. Now let us assume, that due to requirement analysis we have an associationtype COURSE-ORD(COURSE-NO, COURSE-NO), which models the fact, that some courses have to be visited in a fixed order. COURSE-ORD is not an aggregate, since the keypart cannot result from a disjunct union. It becomes an aggregate, if we introduce rolenames as follows: COURSE-ORD(FIRST.COURSE-NO,

SEC.COURSE-NO). Hence fulfilling the constraint enforces a role-concept similar to [8]. Both situations, which have been discussed, are examples for the cooperative design between designer and automatic tool. The tool detects violations of the constraint and the designer solves the situation.

Finally (C7) together with (C5) require, that entitytypes must be disjunct or subtypes.

5. Inconsistencies

In certain situations inconsistencies can be detected automatically. Those situations have the common feature, that one attribute appears in more than one associationtype. In such a situation, the designer has to decide, whether there exist inconsistencies or not. We discuss this problem in the following examples.

Let us assume, that the designer has entered the following associationtypes resulting from requirement analysis:

DOCUMENT-A(NUMBER, PRICE, DATE),
DOCUMENT-B(NUMBER, PRICE, COLOUR)

The automatic tool detects this unclear situation and the designer has to reflect on the following interpretations:

(a) the associationtypes are different views of the same object,
(b) one associationtype is a subtype of the other,
(c) the associationtypes describe different semantic objects.

In the first case he will integrate the views to one associationtype. In the second case he has to define a subtype relationship and to assign the attributes according to (C3) and (C5). In the last case there exist homonyms (one name refers to different semantic objects) and the designer has to change the attribute names.

Another situation is as follows:

A(EMP-NO, COMPANY),
B(COMPANY, STATE),
C(EMP-NO, STATE).

The designer has to describe, whether STATE is a homonym or whether C reflects only a transitivity. In the first case he has to precise the associationtypes by entering the roles LIVING and WORKING of STATE. If we assume, that there exists an associationtype D(STATE, ...), too, the situation becomes different. Now B and C are potential relationshiptypes. The designer has to decide whether C is transitive or not. In the first case he can erase C.

Finally let us assume, that there exist associationtypes defining a 1 : 1-relationship:

A(CUSTOMERS-ORDER, PRODUCTION-ORDER),
B(PRODUCTION-ORDER, CUSTOMERS ORDER).

This may be a hint, that CUSTOMERS-ORDER and PRODUCTION-ORDER are synonyms (different names refer to the same semantic object) and the designer can erase one of them. On the other hand A and B can describe a real 1 : 1-relationship between different objects.

6. Conclusion

Within our framework the designer is not restricted to one specific design method. He can build the conceptual schema with a bottom-up or with a top-down design approach.

As an example for a top-down approach let us consider, how the aggregation method of Smith and Smith [15] fits into our framework:

The initial input consists on the one side of associationtypes, which correspond to the most abstract objects resulting from requirement analysis, and on the other side, of associationtypes, which describe the relationships of interest, in which these objects participate. What follows is a top-down design-process, in which the associationtypes of one level are decomposed into associationtypes of the next lower level. They correspond to lower-level objects. This process is continued until the abstract structure is completed. During each step the designer is supported by inconsistency checks, which are performed by the automatic tool (as described in the above chapter). These checks will help the designer to clarify his decisions. Finally the designer has to enter the respective dependency sets of the associationtypes. Now the complete structure is tested for 3NF. A rearranging step may result to transform the structure into 3NF. Further the keyattributes have to be declared. After this, all constraints (C0) - (C7) can be tested and the structure can be transformed into a entitytype-relationshiptype based schema.

As an example for a bottom-up approach we consider the method MICODD described in [13].

The initial input in this method are a set of attributes and a set of elementary functional associationtypes, which result from requirement analysis. Inconsistency checks are performed automatically and when all inconsistencies are removed,the designer can define entitytypes, relationshiptypes and subtypes. The attributes are assigned automatically to the entitytypes and relationshiptypes, such that the resulting conceptual schema is in 3NF and the constraints (C2) - (C7) are fulfilled. Finally, the designer has to test the constraints (C0) and (C1) and to rearrange the conceptual schema if necessary.

In general, top-down and bottom-up approaches can be combined during the design process. We think, that an implementation, which enables both approaches will be a flexible and valuable tool for conceptual database design. This integration is the topic of current research.

References

[1] Chen, P.: The entity-relationship model - A basis for the enterprice view of data Proc. AFIPS Conf., 1977

[2] Sakai, H.: Entity-relationship approach to the conceptual schema design Proc. SIGMOD 1980

[3] Lum, V.Y. et al.: 1978 New Orleans Data Base Design Workshop Report Proc. VLDB 1979

[4] Codd, E.F.: A relational model of data for large shared data banks Comm. ACM, vol. 13, 1970, no. 6

[5] Beeri, C., Bernstein, Ph.A. and Goodman, N.: A sophisticate's introduction to database normalization theory Proc. VLDB 1979

[6] Smith, J.M. and Smith, D.C.P.: Database abstractions: aggregation generalization ACM TODS, vol. 2, 1977, no. 2

[7] Chen, P.P.: The entity-relationship model: toward a unified view of data ACM TODS, vol. 1, 1976, no. 1

[8] Weldon, J.L.: Using data base abstraction for logical database design The Computer Journal, vol. 23, 1979, no. 1

[9] Raver, N. and Hubbard, G.: Automated logical data base design: concepts and applications IBM Systems Journal, vol. 16, 1977, no. 3

[10] Flory, A. and Kouloumdjian, J.: A model and a method for logical data base design Proc. VLDB 1978

[11] Baldissera, C., Ceri, S., Pelagatti, G. and Bracchi, G.: Interactive Specification and formal verification of user's views in data base design Proc. VLDB 1979

[12] Tardieu, H., Pascot, D., Nanci, D. and Heckenroth, H.: A method, a formalism and tools for database design (Three years of experimental practice) Proc. Entity-Relationship 1979, ed. P.P.Chen, 1980

[13] Günther, H., Krieger, R., Lausen, G.: A method for interactive conceptual database design ICS 81, Proc. of the 6. ACM European regional conference, 1981

[14] Codd, E.F.: Extending the data base relational model to capture more meaning ACM TODS, vol. 4, 1979, no. 4

[15] Smith, J.M. and Smith, D.C.P.: Database Abstractions: Aggregation Comm. ACM, vol. 20, 1977, no. 6

[16] Mijares, I. and Peebles, R.: A methodology for the design of logical database structures Modelling in DBMS, ed. Nijssen, North Holl. 1977

Entwurfs- und Entwicklungswerkzeuge für rechnergestützte Informationssysteme

RECHNERGESTÜTZTE SATZHERSTELLUNG

Carl-Otto Mertin

1. ALLGEMEINES

Satzsysteme müssen für die Satzherstellung, Speicherung, Umfangsermittlung, Zusammenbindung, Verteilung usw. alle erforderlichen Funktionen ausführen können. Daher müssen Ordnungsbegriffe den aufgabenspezifischen Anforderungen entsprechen und an den Ursprungsstellen bzw. bei der Auswahl für die Veröffentlichung bekannt sein.

Dies gilt für alle Satzarbeiten, also
- für Texte und Anzeigen in Zeitungen, Illustrierten und Zeitschriften;
- für Berichte und Bekanntmachungen von Parlamenten, Gremien usw.;
- für Buchtexte (Werksatz) der verschiedensten Arten und Formen;
- für allgemeine Satz- und Druckaufträge (Akzidenzen)

einschließlich spezieller Satzarbeiten, wie Formelsatz, Notensatz, Fremdschriftensatz usw.

Für die Verarbeitung der Satzarten im Satzsystem sind die Eigenarten der Satzaufgaben entsprechend zu berücksichtigen. So werden Satzarbeiten im Satzsystem als durchlaufende Arbeiten geführt, wenn sie an Veröffentlichungstermine bzw. Herstellungstermine gebunden sind und danach verfallen. Hierbei kann es sich um aktuelle Texte für den nächsten Veröffentlichungstermin, um vorbereitete Satzarten für bestimmte Veröffentlichungstermine oder auch um nicht terminisierte Texte für zu erwartende Veröffentlichungen handeln. In allen Fällen muß die Steuerung für die termingerechte Ausgabe vom Satzsystem übernommen werden können. Ebenso müssen Texte beliebig aufbewahrt werden können, um sie gegebenenfalls in irgendeiner Form wiederverwenden zu wollen. Besondere Anforderungen werden an Satzsysteme für die Verarbeitung von organisatorischen Texten gestellt, die aus einer Texterfassung mehrere Formen und Inhalte automatisch herstellen und in entsprechenden Satzformatierungen ausgeben müssen.

Um hier nicht auf alle Eigenarten, Zielbildungen und Fähigkeiten der unterschiedlichsten Satzsystem eingehen zu müssen, wird hier ein leistungsfähiges Satzsystem, nämlich MOPAS von deltaconsult in Frankfurt, mit seinen Komponenten dargestellt [*].

2. SYSTEMKOMPONENTEN MOPAS-Satzsystem

Die Satzherstellung und die flexible Organisationsmöglichkeit aller erdenklichen Satzausgaben erfordern ein Höchstmaß an Zeichen. Es sind daher über Bildschirme nicht nur die reinen Schriftzeichen und Ziffern, sondern auch möglichst viele Sonderzeichen für symbolische Darstellungen, für Kennzeichnung festzulegender Funktionen besonders für organisatorische Satzarbeiten, Formelzeichen, Musiknoten und auch Fremdschriften zu erzeugen und darzustellen. Dabei muß auf die Erzeugung dieser Zeichen mit möglichst wenig Tastenanschlägen großer Wert gelegt werden können.

Auch die Setzmaschinen müssen dieser Zeichendarstellung folgen können, womit bereits Typen von CRT-(Cathod-Ray-Tube-)Setzmaschinen festgelegt sind. Diese Setzmaschinen bilden in einem Bildspeicher das bit-Muster der Zeichen, Texte, Abbildungen usw. aus einzelnen bits auf und entleeren diesen Bildspeicher bei der Belichtung bit für bit als Punkt für Punkt. Damit können alle Zeichen, Abbildungen usw. aus einem Bildspeicher mit digitalen Aufzeichnungen auf Fotopapier oder Film sowie auf Mikrofilm und Mikrofiche belichtet werden. Die Belichtungsstärke der einzelnen Punkte kann in 64 verschiedenen Grautönen gehalten werden, so daß auch fotografische Abbildungen schwarz-weiß von solchen Setzmaschinen aus einem Bildspeicher zu belichten sind. Die Abbildungen müssen dann jedoch vorher über einen Scanner in das notwendige digitale Bit-Muster umgesetzt werden.

Die Verarbeitung im Satzsystem erfolgt für viele Funktionen über gespeicherte Tabellen, die teils vom Anwender und teils vom Lieferanten aufgebaut und festgelegt werden müssen. Gerade das Satzsystem MOPAS bietet hier ein Höchstmaß an Komfort, weil es als neutrales Satzsystem den Anschluß aller Ein- und Ausgabegeräte und solcher Typen gewährleistet. Damit sind Voraussetzungen zu schaffen, die von der Übersetzung von systemfremden Codes bis zur Verwaltung der Rüstmöglichkeiten und -zustände reichen.

Die Satzbefahlssprache muß alle erdenklichen Funktionen bewältigen, wozu auch Rechenoperationen für horizontale und vertikale Abmessungen, Vergleiche und Modifikationen gehören. MOPAS ist dafür hervorragend geeignet. Die schwierigen Aufgaben können mit der Befehlssprache MEDIA gelöst werden, die von MUMPS im medizinischen Bereich abgeleitet wurde.

Die Konfiguration des Satzsystems MOPAS ist richtungweisend für alle Informationssysteme, weil größter Wert auf die absolute Verarbeitungssicherheit gelegt wurde.

Die Bildschirme sind mit Doppelanschlüssen versehen, die den Anschluß jedes Bildschirmes an zwei Rechner mit Umschaltung am Bildschirm ermöglichen. Damit können Bildschirme für gemischte Verarbeitung - z.B. für die Anzeigenproduktion über Satzsystem - sowohl an das Satzsystem als auch an das kommerzielle EDV-System angeschlossen werden.

Als Rechner werden Typen von DATA-GENERAL eingesetzt, wie früher NOVA 830 und heute NOVA 4X und alle Eclipse-Typen. Die Festlegung auf diese Rechnertypen hat den Vorteil, daß bei Stromausfall bzw. Stromschwankungen automatisch, und zwar sofort, eine Batterieversorgung bis zu 90 Minuten für den Rechner dessen Verarbeitung für entsprechende Notabschlüsse usw. gewährleistet. Die Umstände für aufwendiges Neuaufsetzen des Systems und der Verarbeitungszustände sind damit vermieden. Die Hauptspeichererweiterung kann entsprechend der Bildschirmzahlen mit den unterschiedlichen Rechnertypen angepaßt werden; an NOVA 4X mit 256 KB werden maximal bis zu 24 in Dauerbelastung arbeitende Bildschirme angeschlossen. Abbildung 1

Die externen Speicher sind aufgrund der speziellen Anforderungen als mixed Hardware konfiguriert. Die Plattensteuereinheit ist mit Dual-port versehen und erlaubt damit den ständigen Anschluß an zwei Rechner. Damit ist auch die Systemkonfiguration als Rechnerpaare begründet, wobei zwei Rechner mit der Rechnerkopplung IPB verbunden sind. An eine Plattensteuereinheit können bis zu 8 80-MB-Platten bzw. 4 300-MB-Platten von CDC angeschlossen werden. Jede Wechselplatteneinheit ist mit Doppelanschluß versehen und fest an zwei Steuereinheiten angeschlossen. Aus Sicherheitsgründen werden nur Wechselplatteneinheiten eingesetzt.

Um den Datenzugriff von allen Bildschirmen und Rechnern auf jede Platteneinheit zu ermöglichen, sind alle Rechner mit dem Spezialkanal MCA verbunden. Das Betriebssystem RDOS von Data-General wurde entsprechend modifiziert, wobei die MCA-Funktionen programmautomatisch ausgeführt werden. Peripheriegeräte sind auf die einzelnen Rechner verteilt, wobei die notwendigen Übertragungen ebenfalls über MCA erfolgen.

Jedem Rechner ist eine Wechselplatte als Zwischenspeicher zugeordnet. Hier sind alle Tabellen und Programme aufgezeichnet, die für das Satzsystem benötigt werden. Ebenso sind alle Dateiverzeichnisse korrespondierend mit allen anderen Rechnern auf dieser Magnetplatte mit dem je-

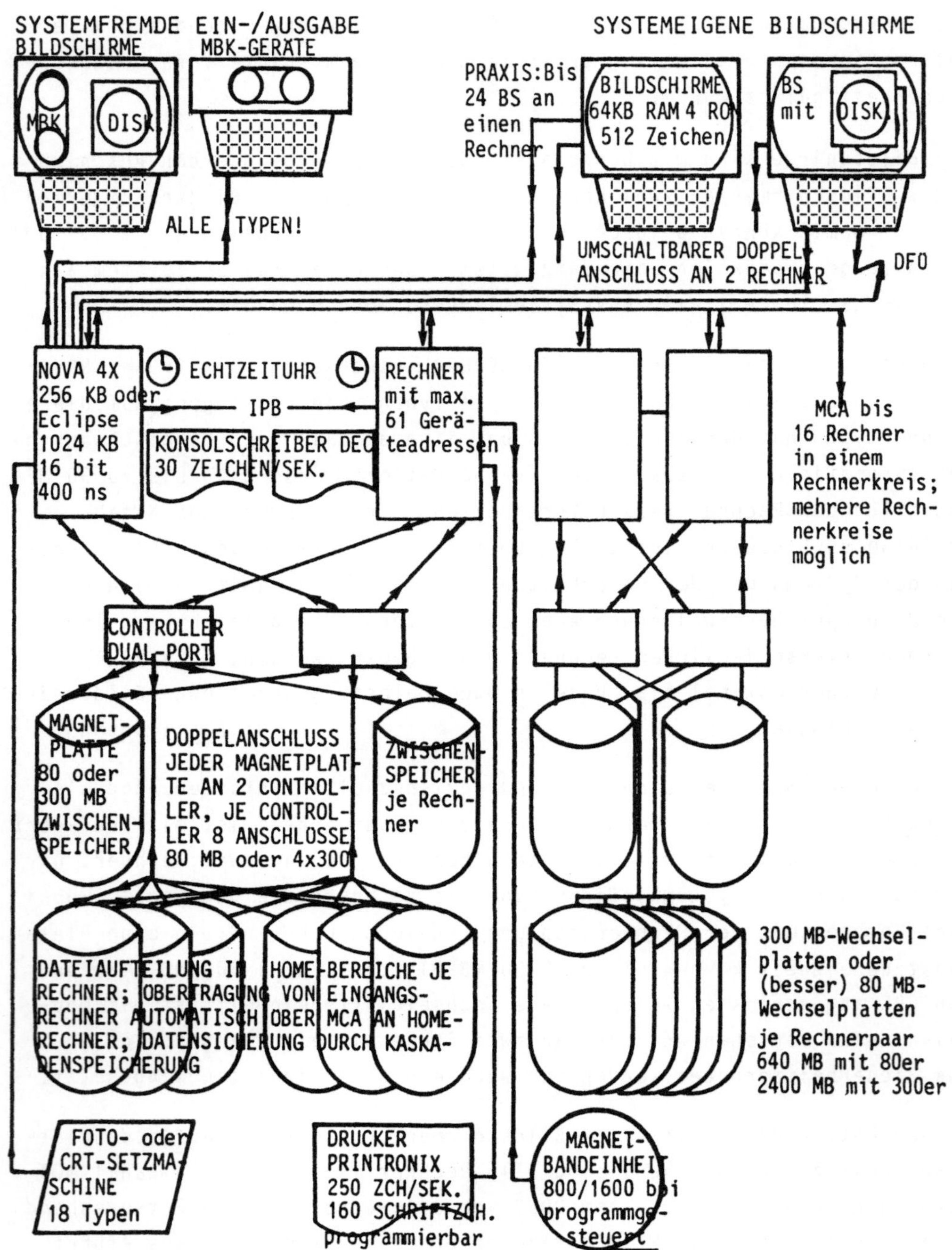

Abbildung 1: Konfiguration Satzsystem

weiligen neuesten Stand vorhanden, die ständig aktualisiert werden. Die über Bildschirm an einen Rechner abgegebenen Texte werden mit der Ersteingabe im Zwischenspeicher aufgezeichnet, von Satzprogrammen verarbeitet (ausgeschlossen einschließlich silbengerechter Worttrennung usw.) und in dieser Form der Satzverarbeitung ebenfalls aufgezeichnet. Dann erst werden beide Formen, 1. Ersteingabe und 2. Satzverarbeitung laut Dateiverzeichnis an den Rechner übertragen, der diese Datei mit seinen Wechselplatteneinheiten führt (Home-Rechner). Abbildung 2

Wird eine Korrektur des Textes durch Fehlerfeststellungen usw. der verschiedenen Korrekturvorgänge erforderlich, so wird diese Korrektureingabe mit irgendeinem Bildschirm durchzuführen sein. Die vorliegende Korrekturfahne enthält das Manuskriptkennzeichen; dieses wird über den Bildschirm eingegeben und stellt über die im Zwischenspeicher geführten Dateiverzeichnisse die Verbindung zum Home-Rechner her. Aus dessen Aufzeichnung wird der zu korrigierende Text über MCA an den aufrufenden Rechner in dessen Zwischenspeicher übertragen und dem Bildschirm direkt zugeordnet. Die Korrektureingabe kann über Zeilennummern - die in der Korrekturfahne belichtet bzw. ausgedruckt sind - an den vermerkten Korrekturstellen am Bildschirm erfolgen. Nach Bearbeitung des Textes am Bildschirm wird dieser korrigierte Text abgeschlossen. Der Rechner überprüft den korrigierten Text mit seiner vorhergehenden Aufzeichnung und stellt die Textabsätze mit Korrekturstellen fest. Nur diese werden über Programme neu bearbeitet und dabei die Korrekturteile indisziert den unveränderten Textteilen zugeordnet. Auch hierbei entstehen zwei Aufzeichnungen; aus der übertragenen Form 2. Satzverarbeitung des vorhergehenden Textes wird mit der Korrektureingabe eine neue Version mit Form 1. Erstform bzw. unausgeschlossene Textform gebildet. Mit der Satzverarbeitung entsteht für diese neue Version die Form 2.; beide Formen der neuen Version werden über MCA an den Home-Rechner übertragen und stehen dort für alle weiteren Bearbeitungen zur Verfügung. Belichtungen usw. als Verarbeitungsvorschriften vom bearbeitenden Bildschirm werden vom Home-Rechner gesteuert und veranlaßt. Für jeden Aufruf von Satzarbeiten wird immer auf die Form 2. Satzverarbeitung der letzten und damit neuesten Version zugegriffen. Abbildung 2

Die vollständige Datensicherung ist dadurch gewährleistet, daß für jede neue Version die Aufzeichnungszustände 1. unausgeschlossen und 2. satzverarbeitet auf verschiedenen Plattenspeichern aufgezeichnet sind. Der Form 1. unausgeschlossen sind die indizierten Korrekturteile zugeordnet. Bei Plattenfehlern kann daher auf die neueste Version mit

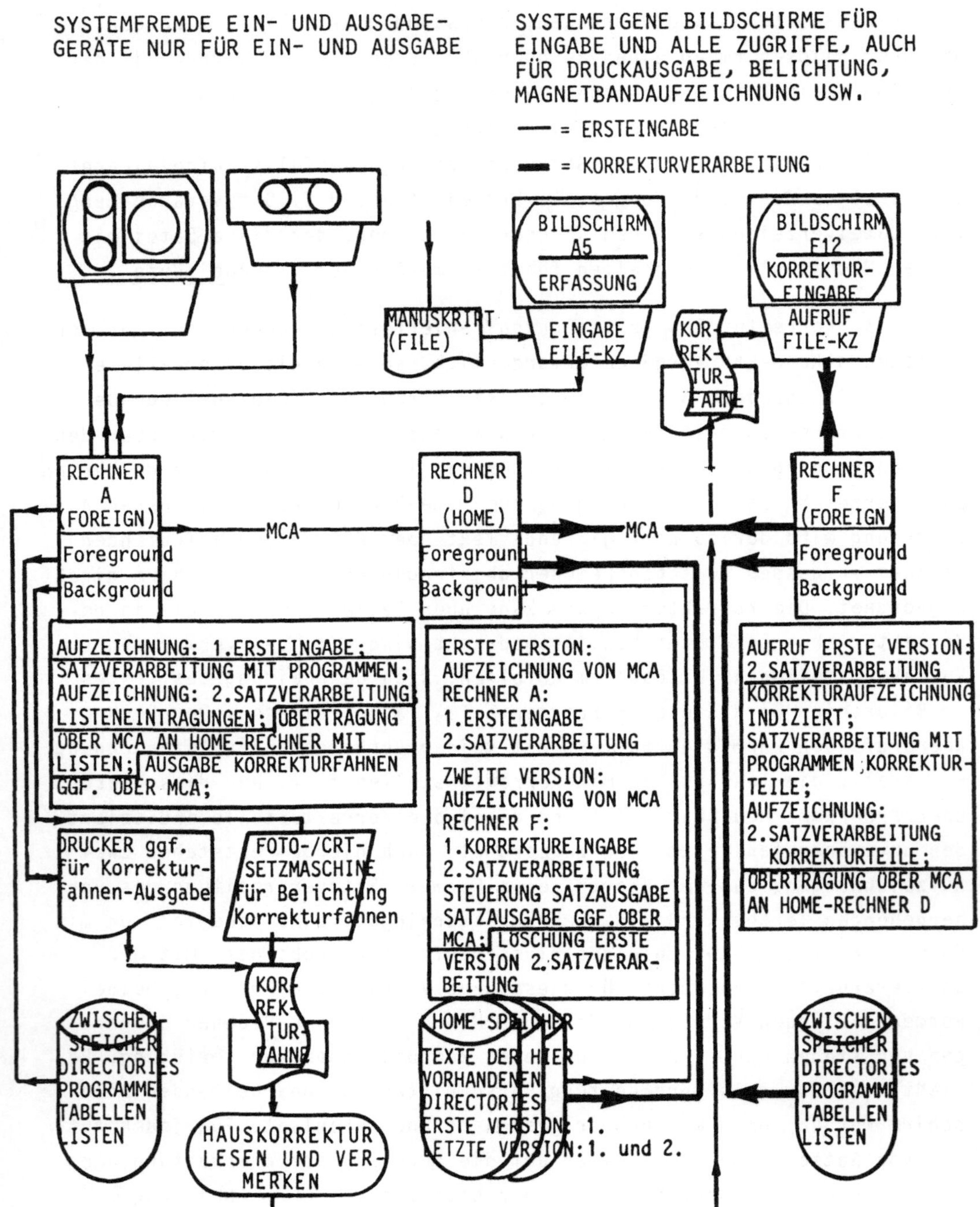

Abbildung 2: Ablaufsteuerung Satzsystem

Form 1. unausgeschlossen zugegriffen und der Zustand der Form 2. satzverarbeitet über die Bildschirmanweisung Satzverarbeitung von den entsprechenden Programmen hergestellt werden.

Damit ist ein Höchstmaß an Sicherheit und Beweglichkeit im Satzsystem sichergestellt. Allerdings ist zwangsläufig eine große Anzahl von Zugriffen auf die Wechselplatteneinheiten erforderlich. Dies kann als Engpaß in der Arbeitsdurchführung angesehen werden und ist die Begründung für die dargestellte Systemkonfiguration. Nur die Verteilung von großen Datenmengen auf möglichst viele Magnetplatteneinheiten und mehrere Rechner bietet die Möglichkeit, die Zahl der Zugriffe auf die benötigten Dateien wesentlich zu erhöhen. Innerhalb einer Zugriffszeit von durchschnittlich 35 Millisekunden bei normaler Plattenfüllung kann ein Rechner etwa 10.000 Befehlsoperationen ausführen, was für die Satzverarbeitung eine ausreichende Programmverarbeitung ermöglicht. Die Zugriffe auf nachzuschiebende Textteile, Listen und programmbedingte Speicheraufzeichnungen erfordern daher viel eher eine Verteilung der Aufzeichnungen auf 80-MB-Wechselplatten als auf größere, etwa 300-MB-Platten. Bei gleichem Datenbestand kann auf 4 Wechselplatteneinheiten je 80 MB (4xnetto 66,5 MB = 266 MB) viermal so oft zugegriffen werden, wie auf eine 300-MB-Wechselplatte (netto 256 MB).

Weil auch die Funktionsleistungen für Programmverarbeitungen auf mehrere Rechner verteilt sind, kann eine sehr viel höhere Durchsatzleistung erreicht werden, als vergleichbare Satzsysteme mit Universalrechnern. Letztere müssen allein für die Abarbeitung umfangreicher Betriebssysteme einen erheblichen Zeitaufwand leisten, bis die anwenderspezifischen Aufgabenprogramme ausgeführt werden können.

Gemessene Vergleichswerte bei gleicher Zykluszeit von 400 ns haben gezeigt, daß größere Universalrechner mit gleichen Anforderungen an die Satzherstellung pro Rechner etwa 260 Zeichen pro Sekunde und innerhalb der maximal möglichen Doppelkonfiguration 520 Zeichen pro Sekunde leisten können. Rechnersysteme, wie die hier genannten, erbringen pro Rechner 300 Zeichen und damit in einem Satzsystem mit beispielsweise 6 Rechnern 1.800 Zeichen pro Sekunde, also über das Dreifache der maximalen Universalrechnerleistungen. Zu bemerken ist noch, daß die Kosten der Prozeßrechner-Satzsysteme wesentlich geringer sind und sich diese Systeme noch viel weiter ausbauen lassen, als es hier beschrieben ist.

3. ORDNUNGSBEGRIFFE

Für die Satzherstellung der verschiedensten Satzarbeiten und Satzarten sind Ordnungsbegriffe festzulegen.

So ist für die Zuordnung von Dateien und Subdateien allgemein das Manuskript-Kennzeichen zu bestimmen. Für die Satzarten können dafür verschiedene Begriffe gebildet werden, die naturgemäß mit den Satzarbeiten zusammenhängen. Für Texte und Anzeigen in Zeitungen, Illustrierten und Zeitschriften bietet sich die Aufteilung der Satzprodukte als Ordnungsbegriffe an, wie auf jeden Fall Produkt, Ressort oder Rubrik oder Fachbereich, gegebenenfalls Unterteilungen davon, usw. Abbildung 3

Für Bücher (Werksatz) und Aufträge (Akzidenzen) gelten andere Unterteilungen, die mehr auf die Verarbeitungsorganisation zielen können. Hier sind auch Manuskriptaufteilungen in verarbeitungsfähige Satzmengen (als Schübe) bzw. nach Satzarten stärker zu berücksichtigen.

Manuskriptkennzeichen sind Identifikationsmerkmale jeder Satzarbeit für das einzelne Manuskript; vielfach wird dieses Kennzeichen auch als Jobnummer (Job = gleich Manuskript) bezeichnet. Hier ist es dem Kennzeichen für ein File (kleinste Dateieinheit) gleichzusetzen.

Je nach Satzarbeit sind unterschiedliche Ordnungsbegriffe auch hinsichtlich der Anzahl von Begriffen erforderlich. Diese Begriffe werden formulärartig in Bildschirmmasken aufgebaut; sie sind vom Anwender für die einzelnen Anforderungen genau festzulegen.

Im Satzsystem MOPAS können die Bildschirmmasken frei gewählt und aufgebaut werden; die maximale Bildschirmmaske kann einen Bildschirminhalt ausmachen, die Anzahl der Bildschirmmasken innerhalb eines Satzsystems ist beliebig.

Damit können die organisatorischen Voraussetzungen für alle zu setzenden bzw. über Satzsysteme herzustellenden Satzausgaben erfüllt werden. Für organisatorische Satzarbeiten stehen zusätzlich mit besonders zu belegenden Bildschirmtasten Möglichkeiten zur Verfügung, bestimmte Begriffe, Worte, Wortgruppen, Titel in freier Gliederung usw. mit Anschlag einer solchen Taste zu kennzeichnen. Diese Kennzeichnung kann in Satzprogrammen für die Steuerung zusätzlicher Funktionen entsprechend der gestellten Satzaufgaben verwendet werden, die sowohl an die Dateigruppe als auch an die einzelne Satzarbeit gebunden werden kann.

Z.B. 12 STELLEN JE BILDSCHIRMMASKE — XX XX XX XX XXXX

BELIEBIG BELEGBAR

DATEIKENNZEICHEN

SUBDATEI, WENN NOTWENDIG

TEXT ZEITUNGEN — PP RR UU TT ZZZZ

VOM REDAKTEUR VERGEBEN

P = PRODUKT

R = RESSORT

U = UNTERTEILUNG RESSORT

T = TAG DER ERSTELLUNG

Z = UHRZEIT DER ERSTELLUNG
(TAG UND UHRZEIT ALS REIHENFOLGE!)

ANZEIGEN ZEITUNGEN — PP RR UU NN NNNN

AUS ANZEIGENAUFTRAG

P = PRODUKT

R = RUBRIK

U = UNTERRUBRIK

N = FORTLAUFENDE ANZEIGENNUMMER
VOM SATZSYSTEM VERGEBEN

BÜCHER (WERKSATZ) — TT TT TT KK SSSS

VON ARBEITSVORBEREITUNG VERGEBEN

T = BUCHTITEL-KURZKENNZEICHEN

K = KAPITEL-KENNZEICHEN

S = SCHUB-KENNZEICHEN
(MANUSKRIPTAUFTEILUNG)

AUFTRÄGE (AKZIDENZEN) — AA AA AA UU SSSS

VON ARBEITSVORBEREITUNG VERGEBEN

A = AUFTRAGS-KURZKENNZEICHEN

U = UNTERTEILUNG (MANUSKRIPT-SCHUB)

S = SATZART-KENNZEICHEN
(TEXT, TABELLEN, FORMELN USW.)

Abbildung 3: Manuskript-Kennzeichen

Die in einer Bildschirmmaske enthaltenen Begriffe bzw. Ordnungsbegriffe können mit unterschiedlichen Wirksamkeiten festgelegt werden. Bei der Maskengenerierung wird die Verknüpfung zu den entsprechenden Programmfunktionen vorgenommen.

Ein Beispiel einer umfangreicheren Bildschirmmaske ist dargestellt in Form der Bildschirmmaske ANZEIGEN. Hier sind alle für die Anzeigenproduktion über Satzsystem erforderlichen Begriffsfelder aufgenommen. Es ist damit auch sichergestellt, daß dieses Anzeigenmanuskript für alle Bearbeitungen in der Satzherstellung, Abrechnung und Verwaltung nur einmal erfaßt werden muß und dann in der Ablage verschwinden kann; es muß nach der Anzeigenproduktion nicht mehr in die Hand genommen werden.

Diese Bildschirmmaske zeigt aber auch, welche gründliche Vorbereitung für spezifische Satzaufgaben und deren vollständige Erfüllung über Satzsysteme erforderlich ist. Jedoch ist damit die Gewähr gegeben, daß mit Aufbau einer Bildschirmmaske alle Funktionen erfüllt werden können.

Die in Manuskriptkennzeichen (in gekürzter Form) und in Bildschirmmasken enthaltenen Begriffe können für bestimmte Funktionsveranlassungen verwendet werden. Eine besondere Form sind als zwangsläufige Folge der in Systemen durchgeführten anonymen Speicherung die Listen für unterschiedliche Zwecke.

So gibt es Listen für die Umfangserfassung, für die Placierung von Anzeigen, für die Vorlagen- und Abbildungsverarbeitung usw., die alle mit der Satzproduktion entsprechender Satzarten usw. zusammenhängen.

Ebenso muß es aber auch Listen geben, die als zusammenfassende Textaufstellungen oder auch als direkte Suchlisten verwendet werden können. Diese Listen werden bei Ersterfassung einer Satzarbeit mit den zu bestimmenden Begriffen aus der Bildschirmmaske (für diese Satzarbeit) oder des Manuskriptkennzeichens angelegt und ständig geführt. Das Satzsystem übernimmt die vollständige Verwaltung dieser Listen, nimmt neue Satzarbeiten auf, löscht verfallene bzw. diese erst nach besonderer Veranlassung. Damit ist sichergestellt, daß ohne Kenntnis von genauen Manuskriptkennzeichen oder Ordnungsbegriffen alle Satzarbeiten im Satzsystem gefunden werden können.

So sind aus den Manuskriptkennzeichen Listen aufzurufen, die nur Teile des Manuskriptkennzeichens enthalten können.

Ebenso können Listen gebildet und später aufgerufen werden unter Aufruf bestimmter Ordnungsbegriffe aus der Bildschirmmaske über Bildschirm bzw. über Anweisung als Druckausgabe. Abbildung 4

Für die Listenformen sind im Satzsystem MOPAS bezüglich des Informationswunsches vorgesehen:

- Gesamtverzeichnis aller Manuskripte einer Datei;
- Verzeichnis mit ausgewählten Begriffen aus der Bildschirmmaske einer Datei, wobei die Begriffe festgelegt sind. Die entsprechende Gruppe dieser Datei ist mit den entsprechenden Begriffen aufzurufen;
- Verzeichnis der vollständigen Bildschirmmasken einer aufzurufenden Dateigruppe mit zugehörigen Begriffen.

Der jeweilige Suchvorgang wird durch die Führung des Positionsanzeigers am Bildschirm (Kursor) unterstützt. Wird in dem Gesamtverzeichnis ein Manuskript gefunden, so kann der Kursor an diese Stelle prositioniert und eine besondere Taste betätigt werden. Es erscheint dann auf dem Bildschirm dieser damit aufgerufene Inhalt des Manuskriptes.

Ebenso können aus diesem Gesamtverzeichnis Gruppen erkannt und als andere Verzeichnisse - wie oben aufgeführt - aufgerufen werden, um letztlich genau die Satzarbeit auf den Bildschirm zu holen, die man wünscht. Hat man dieses erreicht, ist die Druckausgabe dieser Satzarbeit über Druckbefehl am Bildschirm möglich; der Ausdruck kann in kürzester Zeit dem Drucker entnommen werden.

Mit solchen Listenführungen ist nicht nur die Vollständigkeit aller im Satzsystem gespeicherten Satzarbeiten gegeben; es kann auch der Verarbeitungszustand und damit der Fortschritt für umfangreichere Produkte geprüft werden.

BEISPIELE: **SUCHBEGRIFFE AUS BILDSCHIRMMASKE:**

BEGRIFFE:

PRODUKT	ZEITUNG
ERSCHEINUNGSTAG	AB 4.11.
LOKALAUSGABE	
EREIGNIS	ERDBEBEN ITALIEN
REDAKTEUR	
SEITE	
SEITENABSCHLUSSZEIT	
USW.	

AUFRUF: EREIGNIS ERDBEBEN ITALIEN
ERSCHEINUNGSTAG 4.11.- (AB 4.11.)

LISTENFOLGE:

ERDBEBEN ITALIEN 4.11.
ERDBEBEN ITALIEN 5.11.
ERDBEBEN ITALIEN 6.11.
: : :
ERDBEBEN ITALIEN 26.11.

BEGRIFFE:

PRODUKT	PARLAMENTSBERICHTE
VERHANDLUNGSTAG	
THEMA	SPARMASSNAHMEN
UNTERTHEMA	VERTEIDIGUNGSKOSTEN
SPRECHER	
DISKUSSIONSPARTNER	
USW.	

AUFRUF: PRODUKT PARLAMENTSBERICHTE
THEMA SPARMASSNAHMEN

LISTENFOLGE:

PARL.BER.	SPARMASSN.	VERT.KO.	VERH.TAG	SPRECHER	DISK.PARTNER
:	:	:	:	:	:

Abbildung 4: Suchlisten

4. VERARBEITUNGSSTEUERUNG

Die Verarbeitungssteuerung der unterschiedlichen Satzarbeiten wird mit Kennzeichen im System durchgeführt, die dem Manuskriptkennzeichen angehängt werden.

So stellt das Satzsystem fest, wann durch Veränderung der vorhergehenden Speicheraufzeichnung eine neue Version der Satzarbeit entsteht. Im Satzsystem MOPAS wird die erste Form grundsätzlich mit Version 99 gekennzeichnet; jede weitere Version verringert diese Zahl um 1.

Diese Versionsnummer wird vom Satzsystem dem Manuskriptkennzeichen nach einem Punkt angehängt, ist also mit der Ersteingabe dann mit .99 vorhanden.

Zusätzlich zu der Versionsnummer wird vom System automatisch der Aufzeichnungszustand vermerkt. Das Satzsystem unterscheidet je Version die Zustände unausgeschlossen (auch für den Aufruf von vorher satzverarbeiteten und dann geänderten Satzarbeiten), ausgeschlossen, satzverarbeitet und belichtet. Aufbewahrt wird von der ersten Version die Urform unausgeschlossen. Mit jeder neuen Version und der Aufzeichnung im satzverarbeiteten Zustand werden die Vorversionen gelöscht; es kann in bestimmten Dateigruppen, und damit in solchen spezifischen Arbeitsanweisungen bestimmt werden, daß alle Versionen in der satzverarbeiteten Form aufgezeichnet bleiben sollen.

In dem Verarbeitungsetikett - welches vom Betriebssystem RDOS automatisch jedem Manuskript als Verarbeitungssatz bei jeder Systemverarbeitung hinzugefügt wird - können unter anderen festliegenden Begriffen auch Kennzeichen für Verarbeitungszustände eingegeben werden. Damit ist die Produktionsfolge und der Fortschritt besonders für Satzarbeiten größeren Umfangs erkennbar.

Dieses Verarbeitungsetikett wird im Satzsystem MOPAS für verschiedene Zwecke benutzt; so z.B. für die Vorauswahl von Schriftarten und Schriftgrößen und den damit zusammenhängenden Rüstzuständen von Setzmaschinen. Mit der Eingabe des Kennzeichens Verarbeitungszustand und dem Namenskurzzeichen des am Bildschirm Bearbeitenden führt das System eine genaue Zeitstatistik für die Dauer der Bildschirmbenutzung sowie der vom Satzsystem durchgeführten Funktionen. In einem besonderen Programm können diese Angaben zu einer Leistungsstatistik für die einzelnen Satzarbeiten verdichtet und damit für Abrechnungszwecke verwendet werden.

In der Praxis werden damit die Häufigkeiten und benötigten Zeiten mit Zahl der Korrekturzeichen und Korrekturen für Autorkorrekturen und Kundenkorrekturen den Auftraggebern nachgewiesen und in Rechnung gestellt.

Für die unterschiedlichen Systemfunktionen werden in den einzelnen Programmen je Rechner Warteschlangen gebildet, die reihenfolgemäßig aufgebaut und abgearbeitet werden. Im Satzsystem MOPAS sind solche Warteschlangen je Funktion nach Prioritäten festgelegt; d.h. je Priorität werden die Warteschlangen geführt.

Es wird nach drei verschiedenen Prioritäten unterschieden, A, B und C in der Dringlichkeitsfolge. Je nach Fertigstellungstermin und Dringlichkeit der Satzarbeit wird von der Arbeitsvorbereitung für die Ersterfassung die Priorität festgelegt und mit der Ersterfassung am Bildschirm eingegeben.

Allgemein wird mit der Eingabe der Hauskorrektur diese Priorität der Satzarbeit nicht verändert. Nach betriebsindividuellen Vorschriften kann bei Eingabe der Autor- und Kundenkorrekturen vom Eingebenden die Prioritätsstufe um eine Stufe höher gesetzt werden; in das Verarbeitungsetikett wird dann die neue Priorität eingetragen. Damit wird die Verarbeitungsfolge entsprechend umrangiert. Für späte und Revisions-Korrekturen gilt allgemein die Priorität A, die mit einer solchen Korrektureingabe eingegeben wird.

Das Satzsystem prüft bei jeder Funktion das Vorhandensein von Warteschlangen mit Priorität A und B, die der Verarbeitung von C-Warteschlangen vorgezogen werden. Damit ist eine Anpassung an den fortschreitenden Produktionsablauf der unterschiedlichen Satzarbeiten möglich.

Es werden Entwicklungen betrieben, unter anderem für Satzprodukte mit engen Terminen die vorzugebenden Abschlußzeiten für Seiten, Ressorts und Fachbereiche sowie auch für Anzeigenrubriken pro Kalendertag (unterschiedliche Produktionsfolge, Vordruck der Teile für Wochenendausgaben usw.) für die Prioritätensteuerung zu verwenden. Damit ist dann die jeweils früheste Abschlußzeit die höchste Priorität.

Die Protokollschreiber jedes Rechners weisen alle Funktionen mit den einzelnen Satzarbeiten aus. Auch die Übertragungen von einem Rechner an einen anderen über MCA werden entsprechend protokolliert. Im Zusammenhang mit den Zeitangaben im Verarbeitungsetikett ist damit die Verfolgung von Fehlerfällen jederzeit und genau möglich.

5. ZUSAMMENFASSUNG

Mit diesem Vortrag wird versucht, die Verwirklichung eines EDV-Einsatzes in der Textverarbeitung mit gehobenen Ansprüchen darzustellen. Die Ansätze der Verarbeitung organisatorischer Satzarbeiten mit ihrer unbegrenzten Vielfältigkeit hier genauer auszuführen, würde den Rahmen dieser Veranstaltung sprengen.

Um einige Beispiele von Satzarbeiten über Satzsystem zu zeigen, sind Original-Belichtungen ausgehängt. Diese zeigen u.a. auch die mit einigen CRT-Setzmaschinen möglichen Bilddrehungen, mit welchen die Spalten im rechten Winkel zur Materialbahn belichtet werden können. Erkennbar sind auch der Zeichenumfang solcher Satzsysteme, der vom Bildschirm bis zur Setzmaschine reichen muß.

Veröffentlichungen über Satzsysteme gibt es kaum; die Hersteller haben entsprechende Handbücher hergestellt, die teils genaue und teils ungenaue Auskünfte über Möglichkeiten geben. Darin sind Systembeschreibungen enthalten, die nichts über Leistungsfähigkeiten aussagen.

---

[*] MOPAS-Dokumentation. delta consult H. Th. Hermann GmbH, Frankfurt (1979)

Das Data Dictionary :

Ein universelles Werkzeug beim Aufbau und Einsatz von Informationssystemen

Peter J. A. Reusch

Ausgerichtet auf die Vermittlung einer Übersicht über die Grundkonzeption und die Verwendungsmöglichkeiten von Data Dictionaries werden im folgenden

- Grundaufgaben und Grundaufbau eines Data Dictionary
- die Stellung eines Data Dictionary beim Aufbau und Einsatz betrieblicher Informationssysteme
- die Anforderungen der Praxis an ein Data Dictionary
- der Aufbau eines übergreifenden Data Dictionary für alle Informationssysteme eines Unternehmens
- die Anforderungen an die zukünftige Entwicklung von Data Dictionary Systemen

beschrieben. Dabei wird deutlich, wie ein Data Dictionary zu einem universellen Werkzeug für den Aufbau und den Einsatz betrieblicher Informationssysteme werden kann.

1. Einleitung

Die Entwicklung betrieblicher Informations- und Abrechnungssysteme in den vergangenen Jahren ist geprägt durch eine fortgesetzte Integration einer Vielzahl parallel geführter Anwendungssysteme. Im Zuge dieser Integration entstehen komplexe Systeme, die unternehmensübergreifend vielfältige Informations- und Abrechnungsaufgaben wahrnehmen. Die Entwicklung und die Führung dieser integrierten Systeme kann erhebliche Schwierigkeiten bereiten. Sie müssen so gestaltet werden, daß man nicht nur ihre statische Komplexität beherrschen kann, sondern daß man auch die bei ihrem Einsatz auftretenden Wünsche nach Ausweitungen und Modifikationen mit systemimmanenten Mitteln erfüllen kann.

Hier bieten sich Data Dictionaries als Werkzeuge an sowohl für den Aufbau als auch für den Einsatz von Informationssystemen. Diese Werkzeuge sind dabei insoweit universell als sie unabhängig vom Anwendungsbereich und der Komplexität von Informationssystemen stets mit Gewinn eingesetzt werden können.

Ein Data Dictionary (-System) ist ein Informationssystem, in dem der Struktur- und Verwendungsnachweis für die Daten von Informationssystemen geführt wird, und ist damit ein Metainformationssystem, bezogen auf die zugrundeliegenden anwendungsorientierten Informationssysteme.

Wie in Abbildung 1 angedeutet, basiert ein solches Metainformationssystem auf zwei Grundpfeilern : Einer Metadatenbank mit den Spezifikationsdaten der Anwendungssysteme und einer Programm- und Methodenbank mit Routinen zur Spezifikation und Dokumentation von Anwendungssystemen.

Eine Metadatenbank ist hier eine auf die Systemspezifikation von Anwendungssystemen ausgerichtete Systemdatenbank mit Angaben über die zugrundeliegenden Anwendungsdatenbanken , und zwar Angaben über die Struktur und die Verwendung der Anwendungsdaten.

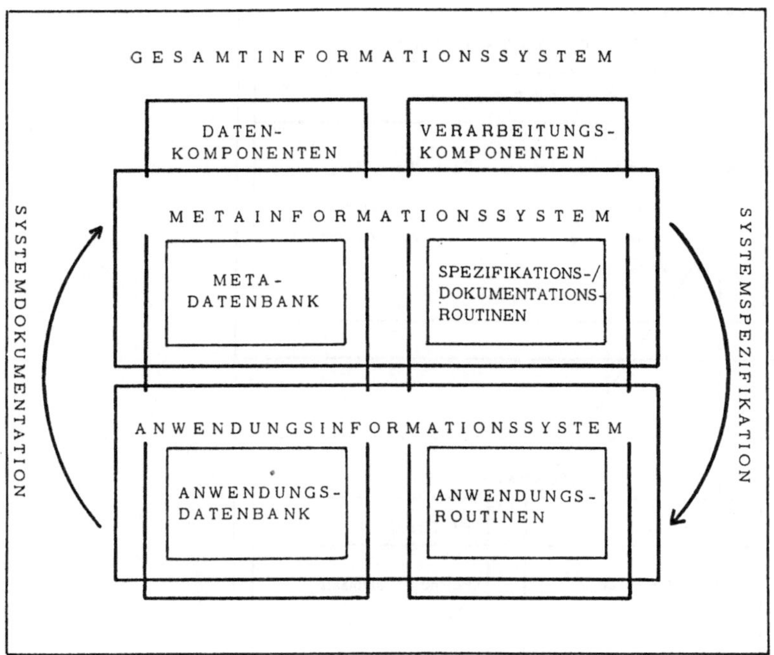

Abbildung 1 : Metainformationssystem und Anwendungssystem als Komponenten eines Informationssystems

Die Beziehung zwischen einer Anwendungsdatenbank und der zugehörigen Metadatenbank wird in Abbildung 2 noch weiter verdeutlicht. Die Metadatenbank zeigt hier Satzdefinitionen für die Anwendungsdaten. In den Anwendungsdateien werden nur noch die Schlüssel der Satzdefinition geführt (Satz 01, Feld 01,...) und die Satzinhalte. Die Bedeutung und die Verwendung der Satzinhalte ist alleine aufgrund der Satzdefinition festgelegt und kann durch Änderung der Satzdefinition umgesteuert werden. Die Metadatenbank wird damit zu einem mächtigen Werkzeug für den Aufbau und Einsatz von Anwendungssystemen, wenn der Endbenutzer - geführt vom Data Dictionary System - hier seine Spezifikationen so einbringen kann, daß sie unmittelbar wirksam werden.

Wie Abbildung 1 zeigt, ist ein Data Dictionary System ein Metainformationssystem, das Aufgaben der Systemspezifikation und der Systemdokumentation übernimmt. Gerade durch die Übernahme dieser Doppelaufgabe kann ein Data Dictionary zu einem leistungsfähigen Werkzeug werden. Dabei ist die Aufgabe der Systemdokumentation von einem Data Dictionary System noch relativ leicht zu lösen. Hier reichen oft schon einfache Auswertungsverfahren für Datenbankdatendefinitionen, für Programmspezifikationen, ... aus. Dagegen verlangt eine leitungsfähige Systemspezifikation mächtigere Hilfsmittel, wie z. B. Metadatenbanken.

Es gibt Data Dictionary Systeme, die die Systemspezifikation lediglich insoweit unterstützen als sie ausgereifte Datendefinitionen aufnehmen wie ein herkömmlicher DDL-Prozessor (Data Definition Language ...). Diese Datendefinitionen sind aber dann schon ein Endprodukt eines langen Spezifikationsprozesses.

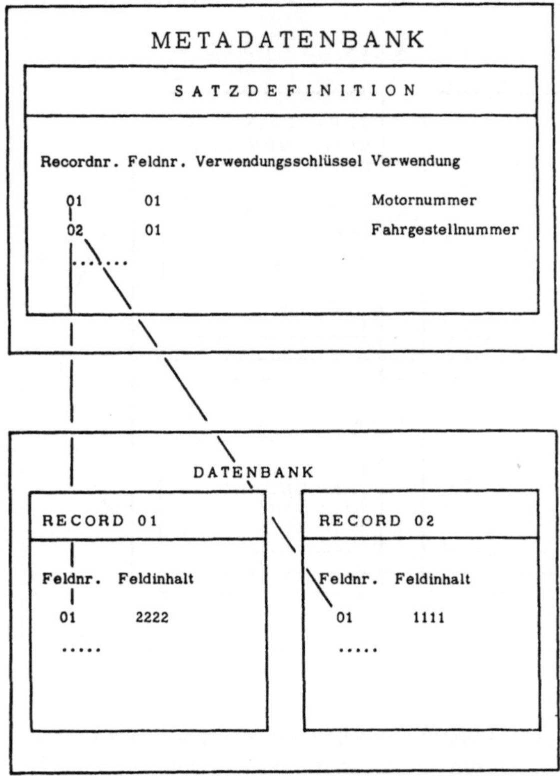

Abbildung 2 : Datendefinition durch eine Metadatenbank

Vor der Aufnahme einer Spezifikation in eine Datenbankdatendefinition liegen noch die aufwendigen Entwicklungsphasen der Informationsanalyse und der Datenanalyse. Bei der Informationsanalyse gilt es, reale Objekte, Beziehungen und Informationsverarbeitungsprozesse zu erkennen und insoweit zu spezifizieren, wie sie von einem geplanten Informationssystem repräsentiert werden sollen (vgl. Abbildung 3: 1). Daneben müssen die Einbettungen dieser realen Objekte, Beziehungen und Informationsverarbeitungsprozesse in bereits vorhandene Informationssysteme analysiert werden, um die notwendigen Verflechtungen zwischen dem geplanten und den vorhandenen Informationssystemen zu erkennen und zu spezifizieren (vgl. Abbildung 3: 2,3).

In der anschließenden Entwicklungsphase der Datenanalyse müssen für die realen Objekte und Beziehungen geeignete Repräsentanten aufgebaut werden, die alle erforderlichen Attribute der Objekte repräsentieren können und alle erforderlichen Beziehungen zwischen realen Objekten wiedergeben können. Dabei muß diese Wiedergabe vielfältigen Grundsätzen und Anforderungen genügen : minimale Datenredundanz, maximale Zugriffssicherung, ...

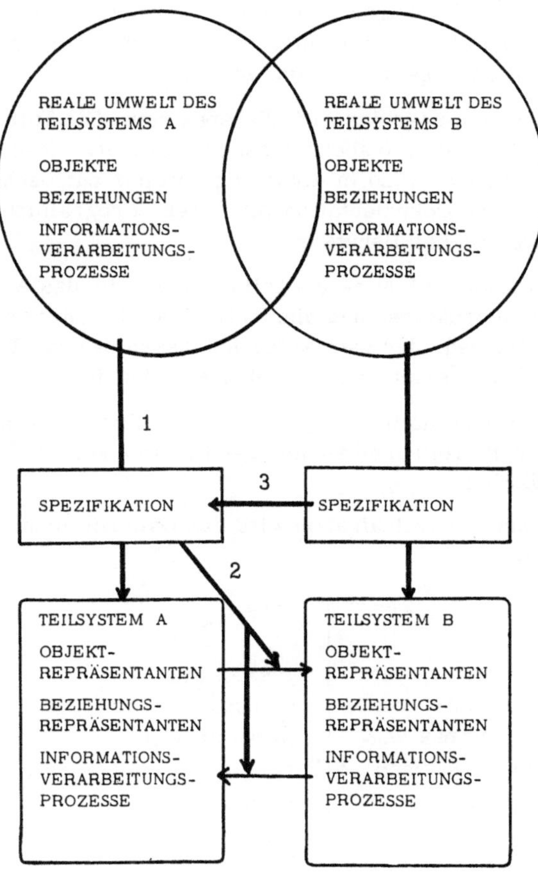

Abbildung 3 : Der Aufbau eines Informationssystems

Der Aufbau eines Informationssystems ist ein komplexer Prozess, der viele Analyse- und Spezifikationsschritte umfaßt. Dieser Prozess ist nicht isoliert - es ist vielmehr ein offener und iterativer Prozess. Beim erstmaligen Aufbau eines Informationssystems müssen Spezifikationen eingebracht und immer wieder überprüft, ergänzt und modifiziert werden. Auch nach Inbetriebnahme des Informationssystems bleiben die Einwirkungen der realen Umwelt und der angrenzenden Informationssysteme bestehen.

Dieser offene Prozess des Aufbaus und Einsatzes von Informationssystemen kann nur mit geeigneten Werkzeugen wirtschaftlich abgewickelt werden. Dabei nimmt das Data Dictionary eine herausragende Stellung ein.

2. Die Grundaufgaben eines Data Dictionary

Ein Data Dictionary deckt ein weites Spektrum von Aufgaben ab. Dieses Spektrum soll hier mit Hilfe von zwei Abbildungen erschlossen werden. Dabei werden die zentralen Teilaufgaben eines Data Dictionary aufgezeigt mit ihren Wechselbeziehungen untereinander und zum Anwendungssystem, das sie umschließen.

Abbildung 4 gibt eine Übersicht über das Aufgabenspektrum. Die Teilaufgaben eines Data Dictionary werden hier vier Aufgabenklassen zugeordnet. Diese Teilaufgaben mit ihren Beziehungen zueinander sind in Abbildung 5 weiter aufgeschlossen. Sie umfassen die Spezifikation und Dokumentation von Daten, Programmen, Konsistenzbedingungen und Arbeitsgängen der Benutzer.

Jede der vier Aufgabenklassen umfaßt aktive Teilaufgaben, die das Anwendungssystem steuern und in seinen Datenstrukturen und hinsichtlich der Datenverwendung verändern können. Ebenso umfaßt jede der vier Aufgabenklassen passive Teilaufgaben, nämlich die Führung von Nachweisen und die Dokumentation des Anwendungssystems.

Durch diese Aufgabenaufteilung bleibt die Spezifikation selbst bei komplexen Informationssystemen überschaubar. Teilaufgaben der Spezifikation können damit weiter zum Endbenutzer verlagert werden.

Durch die Erfüllung der aktiven Teilaufgaben wird das Data Dictionary zu einem mächtigen Spezifikationswerkzeug.

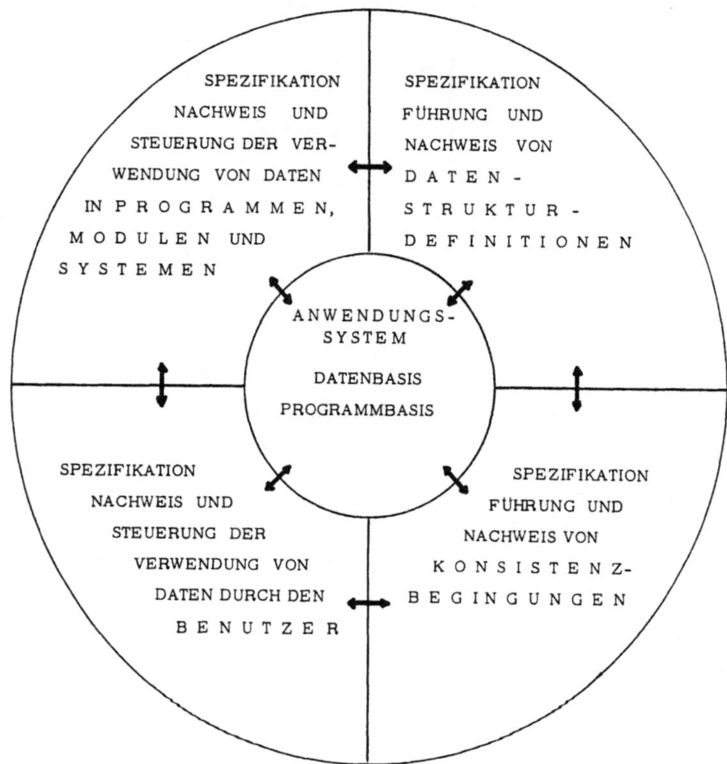

Abbildung 4 : Das Aufgabenspektrum eines Data Dictionary

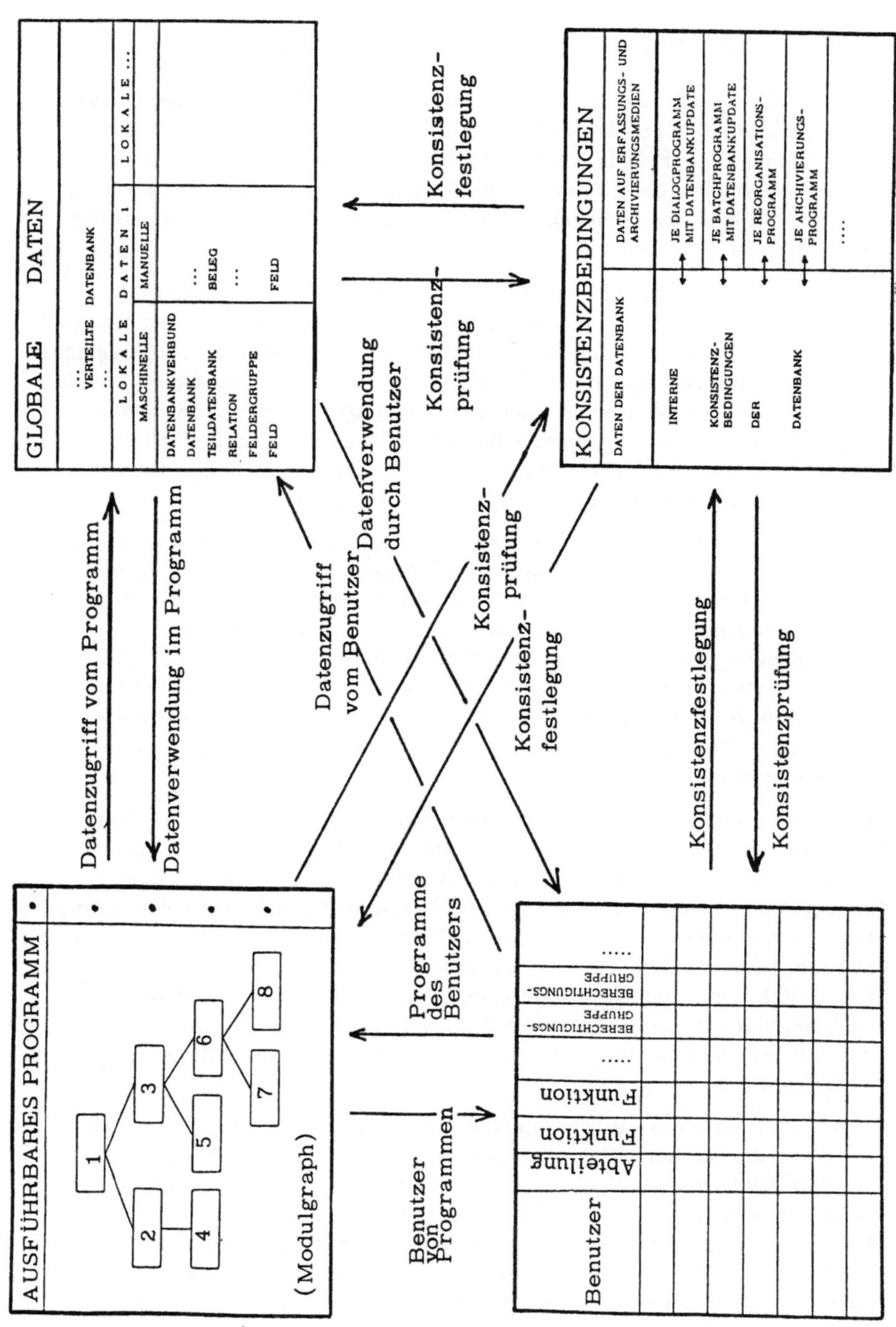

Abbildung 5 : Das Aufgabenspektrum eines Data Dictionary (Teil 2)

3. Die Anforderungen der Praxis an ein Data Dictionary

Ein Data Dictionary für die zuvor skizzierten Spezifikations- und Dokumentationsaufgaben bei der Führung einzelner moderner Anwendungssysteme kann noch relativ leicht aufgebaut werden. Dringender und zugleich problematischer wird aber die Aufgabe, ein übergreifendes Data Dictionary für alle Anwendungssysteme eines Unternehmens oder einer Verwaltung zu schaffen.

In einem gewachsenen Unternehmen findet man Anwendungssysteme unterschiedlichster Art (vgl. Abb. 6/7). Hier stehen neuere datenbankunterstützte und dialogorientierte Systeme neben klassischen Anwendungssystemen mit ihren Assembler- und COBOL-Programmen, die z. T. seit 10 - 20 Jahren von DV-Anlage zu DV-Anlage übernommen werden. Ferner findet man heute immer häufiger endbenutzerorientierte interaktive Planungs- und Berichtssysteme, die eigenständig neben den anderen Systemen geführt werden (vgl. R. KRAUSE (2)).

Diese unterschiedlichen Systeme sind miteinander verflochten. Insbesondere ist hier oft ein umfangreicher Datenaustausch zwischen den zentralen datenbankunterstützten Systemen und den klassischen Batchsystemen realisiert (Pfeil b, Abb. 6). Die eigenständigen Berichts- und Planungssysteme bauen z. T. auf den Daten auf, die originär in den anderen Systemen geführt werden (Pfeile a,c, Abb.6). Schließlich müssen alle Anwendungssysteme an die jeweilige lokale Rechnersteuerung (Operating, Arbeitsplanung,...) und an das jeweilige lokale Datenarchiv angebunden werden.

In dieser betrieblichen Systemumgebung wird ein übergreifendes Data Dictionary benötigt, das alle Einzelsysteme gleichartig und mit ihren Verflechtungen dokumentiert und so weit wie möglich auch die Anwendungssysteme steuert. Darin liegt insofern eine besondere Problematik, als die Einzelsysteme nach unterschiedlichen Prinzipien aufgebaut sind und nicht immer ausreichend aufeinander abgestimmt sind. So kann es hinsichtlich der Datenspezifikation durchaus möglich sein, daß ein Datum des Anwenders in unterschiedlichen Anwendungssystemen mit unterschiedlichem Namen, unterschiedlicher Länge, unterschiedlichem Code, ... geführt wird.

Diese Spezifikationskonflikte müssen von einem Data Dictionary aufgefangen werden können, ohne die Anwendungssysteme zu überarbeiten. Das Data Dictionary muß also u. a. Werkzeuge enthalten, die es erlauben, unterschiedliche Spezifikationen eines Datums zusammenzuführen und gleichartige Spezifikationen unterschiedlicher Daten zu trennen. Werkzeuge hierfür sind im Bereich der Linguistik und Dokumentationswissenschaften geschaffen worden und können auf Data Dictionaries übertragen werden (vgl. P. REUSCH (5)).

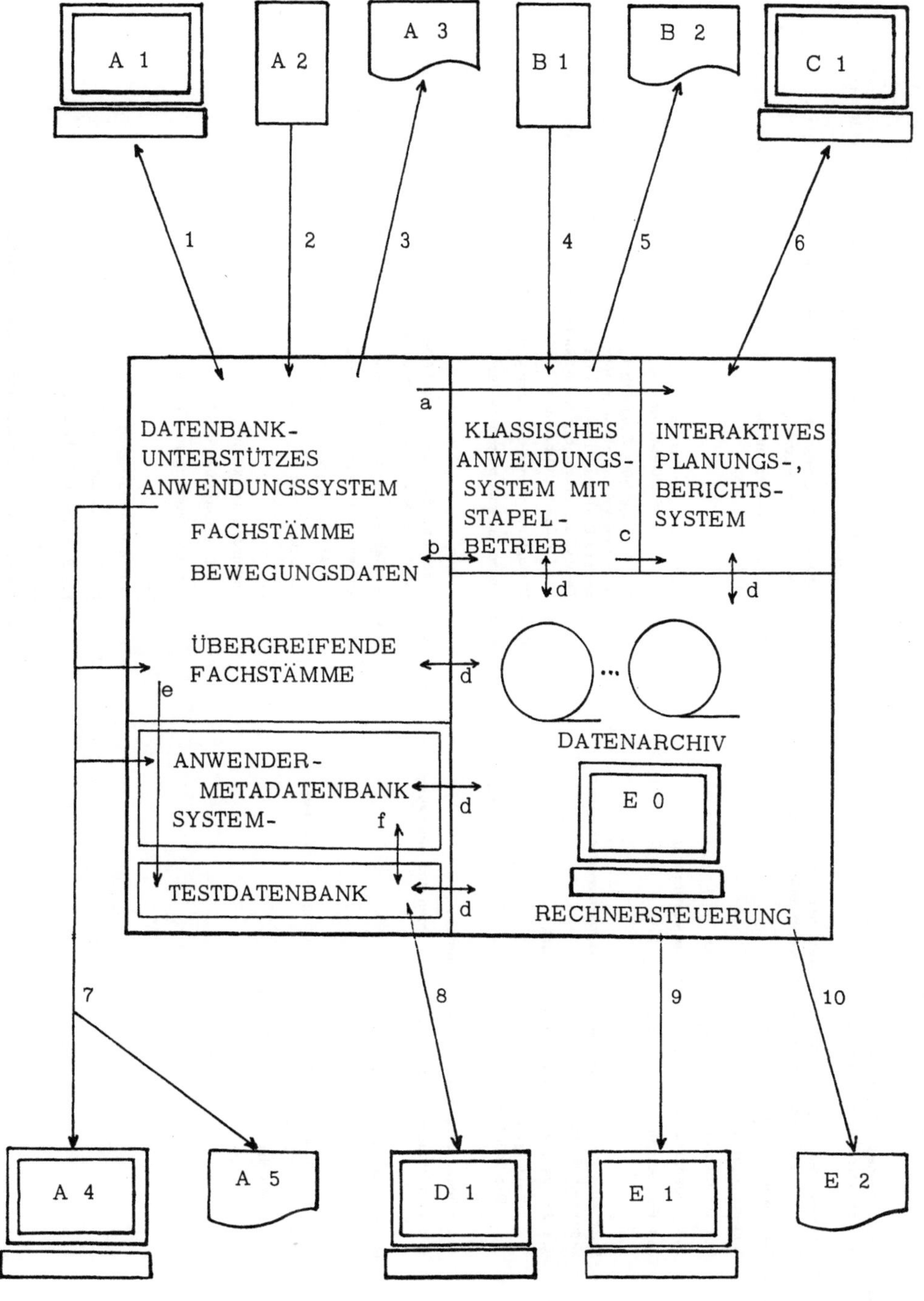

Abbildung 6 : Typische betriebliche Anwendungssysteme und ihre Beziehungen zueinander (vgl. Abbildung 7)

Komponenten eines lokalen betrieblichen Informationssystems

A Umfassendes datenbankunterstützes betriebliches Anwendungssystem mit Dialogkomponenten

A 1 Erfassungsdialoge und sachbearbeiterorientierte Dialoge mit Zugriff auf die Fachstämme und Bewegungsdaten des Systems

A 2 Belege für die Stapelverarbeitung

A 3 Listenauswertungen

- 3.1 Protokolle zu den Vorgängen nach A 1 und A 2
- 3.2 Umfangreiche oder übergreifende Auswertungen
- 3.3 Periodische Auswertungen
- ...

A 4 Fachliche Steuerung des Anwendungssystems durch eine Zentralstelle im Fachbereich

- 4.1 Pflege der Anwendermetadatenbank
  - Felddefinitionen
  - Dialogdefinitionen
  - ...
- 4.2 Pflege übergreifender Fachstämme
- 4.3 Spezialauswertungen bei Fachstämmen und Bewegungsdaten

A 5 Listen zu den Funktionen nach A 4

B Klassisches begrenztes stapelverarbeitungsorientiertes Anwendungssystem

B 1 Belege für die Stapelverarbeitung

B 2 Listen

C Endbenutzerorientiertes interaktives Planungs- und Berichtssystem

C 1 Offene dialogorientierte interaktive Methoden zur Berichtsspezifikation, Planungsrechnung, ...

C 2 Listenauswertungen nach C 1 (sind oft von untergeordneter Bedeutung)

D Testsystem für das umfassende datenbankunterstützte betriebliche Anwendungssystem

Wegen der großen Einsatzbreite der Anwendungssysteme nach A und wegen der oft sehr hohen Verfügbarkeitsanforderungen an ihre Dialogkomponenten ist die Führung eines integrierten Testsystems notwendig zur Absicherung des Systemeinsatzes und für den Systemausbau.

D 1 Dialogkomponente des Testsystems

D 2 Auswertungskomponente des Testsystems

E System für die Führung und Überwachung der Anwendungssysteme durch das betriebliche Rechenzentrum

E 0 Betriebssteuerung des Rechners über Systemkonsole (Operating)

E 1 Aufgabenbezogene Rechnersteuerung durch die Arbeitsplanung (i.w.S)

- 1.1 Abwicklung von Arbeiten nach Terminplan
- 1.2 Abwicklung laufender Benutzeranforderungen
- ...

Datenadministration

- 1.3 Bereitstellung von Daten
- 1.4 Archivierung von Daten
- ...

Systemadministration

- 1.5 Durchsatzüberwachung
- 1.6 Sicherheitsprüfungen
- ...

E 2 Auswertungen über Systemzustände, Systemdurchsatz, usw.

Abbildung 7 : Typische betriebliche Anwendungssysteme und ihre Beziehungen zueinander (Erläuterungen zu Abbildung 6)

4. Der Aufbau eines übergreifenden Data Dictionary

Ein übergreifendes Data Dictionary kann sinnvoll nur maschinell geführt werden. Zur Führung und Auswertung der Spezifikations- und Dokumentationsdaten von Anwendungssystemen gibt es auch eine Reihe von Softwareprodukten (vgl. LEFKOVITS (3)). Beim Einsatz derartiger Systeme wird aber i. d. R. vom Benutzer erwartet, daß er die erforderlichen Daten selbst - z. T. manuell - in das Data Dictionary einbringt. Dies würde aber in der oben skizzierten Umgebung bei einem übergreifenden Data Dictionary für alle Anwendungssysteme eines Unternehmens nicht mehr mit vertretbarem Aufwand möglich sein.

Wer ein übergreifendes Data Dictionary aufbauen will, der benötigt zunächst Softwarewerkzeuge zur automatisierten Analyse der Anwendungssysteme (Analyse der vorliegenden Datendefinitionen anhand der symbolischen Codes,...) und zur Extraktion der Spezifikationsdaten. Danach müssen die extrahierten Spezifikationsdaten harmonisiert und für die Aufnahme in ein Data Dictionary aufbereitet werden. Für diese Aufgaben gibt es i. d. R. keine fertigen Werkzeuge, dafür hängt die Analyse und die Harmonisierung meist zu sehr von der speziellen betrieblichen Umgebung ab.

Da z. B. Datenspezifikationen, die von Einzelsystemen extrahiert werden, für das übergreifende Data Dictionary in vieler Hinsicht unvollständig sind, da sie mit ihren Basisdaten wie Feldname, Code,... auch nicht eindeutig in Beziehung zu den übrigen Anwendungssystemen gebracht werden können, ist es erforderlich, die extrahierten Spezifikationsdaten möglichst vielfältig zu klassifizieren. So empfiehlt es sich , jedem Datum Herkunfts- und Verwendungsinformationen zuzuordnen. Dies kann z. B. durch eine Analyse von Programm- bzw. Systemabläufen DV-unterstützt durchgeführt werden.

Solche syntaktischen Analysen von Datendefinitionen, Ablaufeinheiten, ... können bei Einsatz von hochwertiger Textverarbeitungssoftware, Compiler-Sprachen , o. ä. relativ leicht durchgeführt werden (z. B. mit MACRO 1100 (7)).

Von besonderer Bedeutung sind aber auch die semantischen Klassifikationen. So ist es für die Einordnung eines 9-stelligen numerischen Feldes wichtig, ob es sich bei seinen Werten um Schlüsselattribute (identifizierende Attribute) oder um beschreibende Attribute handelt. Ein Schlüsselattribut identifiziert meist ein Objekt im Unternehmen, auf das meist in vielfacher Hinsicht bezug genommen wird. Bei beschreibenden Attributen kann man weiter danach differenzieren, ob es sich bei dem Datum in dem 9-stelligen numerischen Feld um Längenangaben, Flächen-, Raum- , Gewichts-, Preisangaben,... handelt.

Diese semantischen Analysen sind wesentlich aufwendiger als die elementaren syntaktischen Analysen. Daher können semantische Analysen oft nur nach und nach aufgebaut werden. Für ein übergreifendes Data Dictionary sind diese semantischen Analysen aber letztlich unersetzlich, weil nur durch eine vielfältige Charakterisierung der Komponenten beim Einzelsystem Zusammenhänge zu Nachbarsystemen erkannt werden können (vgl. R. MRASEK (4), P. REUSCH (6)).

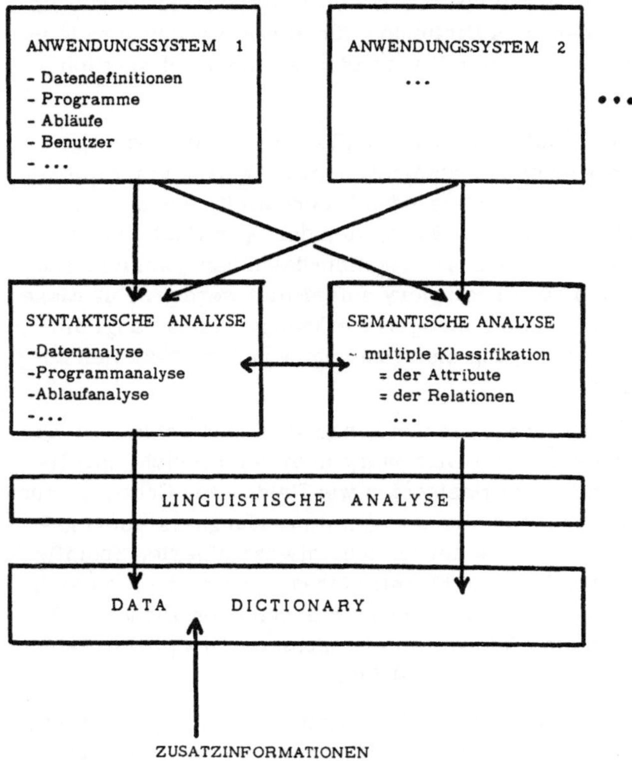

Abbildung 8 : Syntaktische, semantische und linguistische Analysen von Anwendungssystemen zum Aufbau des Data Dictionary

Bei der syntaktischen Analyse werden u. a. Felddefinitionen aus den Anwendungssystemen extrahiert und aufbereitet. Bei der semantischen Analyse werden dann den jeweiligen Attributen Bedeutungen zugeordnet. Dabei kann eine vielfältige semantische Klassifikation solche Felder, die unterschiedliche Attribute mit gleichem Namen bezeichnen, differenzieren, bzw. solche Felder, die in den Anwendungssystemen unterschiedliche

Namen tragen, aber stets diegleiche Attributart aufnehmen, zusammenführen. Diese Aufgabe der Homographendifferenzierung und Synonymenzusammenführung kann auch durch linguistische Verfahren unterstützt werden, die in den Aufbau eines Data Dictionary mit einbezogen werden können - siehe Abbildung 7 , vgl. R. MRASEK (4) , P. REUSCH (6) .

Mit der kombinierten syntaktischen, semantischen und linguistischen Analyse kann bei jedem Attribut seine Rolle in den Anwendungssystemen eines Unternehmens DV-unterstützt ermittelt werden. Auf der Basis dieser Rollenanalyse kann dann ein übergreifender Verwendungsnachweis geführt werden. Ferner können Konsistenzbedingungen übergreifend dokumentiert und spezifiziert werden.

Insgesamt kann mit dem Aufbau eines übergreifenden Data Dictionary die Dokumentation der Anwendungssysteme entscheidend verbessert werden und der Einsatz und Ausbau von Anwendungssystemen wesentlich erleichtert werden.

5. Anforderungen an die zukünftige Entwicklung von Data Dictionary Systemen

Data Dictionary Systeme werden am Softwaremarkt meist zusammen mit Datenbanksystemen angeboten. Dies liegt im wesentlichen daran, daß ein Data Dictionary oft als notwendige Ergänzung für ein Datenbanksystem angesehen wird. Daneben gibt es auch Data Dictionary Systeme, die losgelöst von speziellen Datenbanksystemen entwickelt wurden. Unabhängig von der Herkunft und Einbettung leiden alle Data Dictionary Systeme daran, daß es keine gültigen Normen für den Aufbau und Einsatz von Data Dictionary Systemen gibt. Dies ist um so gravierender als man heute eine rasche Ausbreitung von Data Dictionary Systemen verfolgen kann, ähnlich wie bei Datenbanksystemen vor einem Jahrzehnt. Während aber die Entwicklung vieler Datenbanksysteme sich an weithin anerkannten Normungsansätzen anlehnen konnte (CODAYSL-Report u. ä.), fehlt eine ähnliche Orientierung für die weitere Entwicklung von Data Dictionary Systemen völlig.

Vom NATIONAL BUREAU OF STANDARDS (USA) wurde kürzlich das Interesse am Aufbau von Normen für Data Dictionary Systeme bekundet. Mit der Festlegung von Normen wird in diesem Kreis aber erst in einigen Jahren gerechnet (vgl. DATABASE NEWSLETTER März/April 1981).

Das Zögern in den Normungsbemühungen steht im krassen Gegensatz zu den Erwartungen der Anwender von Data Dictionary Systemen in der Praxis. Nach einer Umfrage der COMPUTERWOCHE (2.11.1979) wurde von einem repräsentativen Kreis von Anwendern eines Data Dictionary Systems die Erwartung ausgesprochen, daß innerhalb der nächsten Jahre Data Dictionaries

- zur zentralen Quelle aller Datendefinitionen und aller EDV-Dokumentation werden
- Datenbanken steuern und kontrollieren
- Datenanalysen und Programmspezifikationen ermöglichen
- eine Hilfe bieten für die Analyse von Systemabbrüchen und das Wiederaufsetzen von Abläufen

usw.

Die weitere Verbreitung von Data Dictionary Systemen und die Ausweitung ihrer Aufgaben machen eine Normung immer notwendiger, aber zugleich auch immer problematischer. Die Arbeit, die hier geleistet werden muß, ist auch nur bedingt mit den bisherigen Normungen im Bereich der Informatik zu vergleichen. Ein Data Dictionary ist letztlich eine Dokumentationssprache im Sinne der Dokumentationswissenschaften und bietet auch ähnliche Probleme bei einer Normung wie die übrigen Dokumentationssprachen (vgl. P. REUSCH (5)). Auf der anderen Seite können aber auch die Normungserfahrungen der Dokumentationswissenschaften mit eingebracht werden.

Ein Verzicht auf die Erstellung von Normen für Data Dictionary Systeme etwa im Hinblick auf die weitere und noch offene Entwicklung im Bereich der Datenbanksysteme ist wenig sinnvoll. Eine rechtzeitige und pragmatische Norm für Data Dictionary Systeme kann mindestens soviel leisten wie der CODASYL-Report von 1971, der die Entwicklung von Datenbanksystemen für ein Jahrzehnt geprägt hat.

6. Anmerkung

Diese Ausführungen sind Auszüge aus P. REUSCH (6) und werden im dortigen Rahmen weiter verfolgt.

7. Literatur

(1) CONRAD, G. : Data Dictionary, Integrationsbasis für Datenbankstrukturen und Programmgeneratoren , in : J. NIEDEREICHHOLZ : Datenbanktechnologie , Stuttgart 1979.

(2) KRAUSE, R. : Der Einsatz einer anwenderorientierten Dialogsprache, zfbf, Kontaktstudium 31 , 1979 .

(3) LEFKOVITS, H. C. : Data Dictionary Systeme , Wellesley 1977 .

(4) MRASEK, R. : Data Dictionaries - Grundzüge, betriebliche Anwendungen und Einsatzmöglichkeiten, Diplomarbeit , Bonn 1981 .

(5) REUSCH, P. J. A. : Informationssysteme, Dokumentationssprachen, Data Dictionaries , Mannheim 1980 .

(6) REUSCH, P. J. A. : Aufbau und Einsatz betrieblicher Informationssysteme, Skriptum zur Vorlesung , Bonn 1981 , 1981/82 .

(7) UNIVAC : MACRO 1100 , Systemunterlagen .

(8) SOKOLOVSKY : Bemerkungen zu Data Dictionary Systemen , in : Angewandte Informatik 3 , 1981 .

Peter J. A. Reusch
Ringstr. 18
5030 Hürth

Juli 1981

METHODOLOGY FOR THE SPECIFICATION OF SOFTWARE SYSTEMS: FROM FORMAL REQUIREMENTS TO ALGEBRAIC DESIGN SPECIFICATIONS

Hartmut Ehrig

Werner Fey

Technische Universität Berlin, FB Informatik

Institut für Software und Theorëtische Informatik

D-1000 Berlin 10, Otto-Suhr-Allee 18/20

July, 1981

ABSTRACT

Algebraic specifications of abstract data types and software systems have been studied mainly with respect to the design phase and stepwise refinement towards implementation up to now. This paper shows how to extend the algebraic specification techniques to obtain also a methodology for systematic software development from the requirements to the design phase. This methodology is based on parameter passing techniques for parameterized specifications with requirements where the notion of requirements is general enough to cover general predicate formulas and different kinds of integrity and consistency constraints.

As an example for this new methodology we consider a parts system and give the main steps from requirements specification, via a parameterized refinement towards a design specification.

INTRODUCTION

Although the phase oriented approach to software system development has been modified by a number of authors recently (see /Flo 81/, /Leh 81/) there is still common agreement that there are some phases which should be considered within the-possibly cyclic-development process. We consider the following phases

1. Informal specification of the user problem
2. Requirements (or functional) specification
3. Design specification
4. Implementation
5. Modification (or maintenance)

where requirements as well as design specification are intended to be formal specifications (i.e. with formal syntax and formal semantics). The main difference is that in the requirements specification we allow a logical formalism to express our require-

ments which have a well-defined class of models.
However, the class may be empty in the case that the requirements are contradicting each other. In the design specification we only allow the algebraic formalism (with equational or conditional axioms) which has (up to isomorphism) one unique model, the initial (or quotient term) algebra. Since there are already a number of interpreters for algebraic specifications available a design specification (in our sense) is in principle already a running system.
In /Kre 80/ and /EFK 80/ we have shown how to use the algebraic implementation technique to support stepwise refinement from the design specification towards implementation, and how to apply these techniques to a parts system. In general the algebraic technique is suitable for the specification of all kinds of software systems. Up to now, however, it cannot be used to specify the concurrency aspects.

In this paper we give a formal framework for requirements specifications which can be used immediately after the informal specification of the user problem. This notion of requirements specifications was sketched already in /Ehr 81/ where requirements are introduced and mainly used with respect to parameterized specifications. We will use the concept of parameter passing to build up a methodology how to proceed in a correct way from requirements specifications to design specifications. Moreover this methodology supports the stability of the system in the sense of /Tur 81/ because it allows to modify the specification in a systematic and correct way. In order to give first an intuitive idea of our methodology we start with a specific application in the field of information systems in Section 1 while the general methodology for stepwise refinement from requirements to algebraic design specifications is given in Section 2. The presentation in this paper is based on the algebraic specification techniques developed in /ADJ 76-78/, /Kre 80/ and /Ehr 81/. The application we are going to study is the specification of a parts system from requirements to design specification in contrast to stepwise refinement towards implementation which was studied in /EFK 80/. In this paper we only give some typical features of the corresponding specifications. But the full case study including correctness proofs will be given in /Fey 81/. The verification of two typical requirements is given in the APPENDIX.

1. STEPWISE REFINEMENT OF A PARTS SYSTEM

Before we consider specific features of our parts system let us give an overview of the different steps within our methodology we are going to study.
We start with an INFORMAL SPECIFICATION (in natural language) of our parts system. The first formal step is the REQUIREMENTS SPECIFICATION where we fix the signature of the operations of the system but not yet their full semantics. The main idea in this step is to give a precise formulation of main parts of the INFORMAL SPECIFICATION in terms of logical formulas. We cannot expect to be able to show correctness of the REQUIREMENTS SPECIFICATION with respect to the INFORMAL SPECIFICATION because natural language does not allow such proofs but only informal reasoning and agreement.

Within our general methodology the REQUIREMENTS SPECIFICATION ⟨parts-system0,RPS⟩ can be considered as a specification parts-system0 which consists of several formal parameter parts (attr+key+comp+system-signature) together with corresponding requirements RPS but no actual parameter part. Replacing part of these formal parameter parts by actual parameters is exactly a process of parameter passing. This means that part of the logical formulas are replaced by algebraic equations for the corresponding operations while the remaining part of the logical requirements remains unchanged. This process is a special case of PARAMETERIZED PARAMETER PASSING because the result in this step is a PARAMETERIZED SPECIFICATION ⟨key+attr,parts-system,RKEY⟩. In this parameterized specification the remaining part of the formal parameters is in the parameter declaration key+attr, the algebraic equations are in the target specification parts-system, and RKEY is the remaining part of the requirements.
In the last step the formal parameters key+attr together with the requirements RKEY are replaced by actual parameters nat1+A-string including algebraic equations for the operations such that the requirements RKEY are satisfied. This process is called STANDARD PARAMETER PASSING because the actual parameter is not parameterized. The result of this step is the DESIGN SPECIFICATION parts-system(nat1+A-string) where all formal parts and requirements have been replaced by actual (non parameterized) specifications.

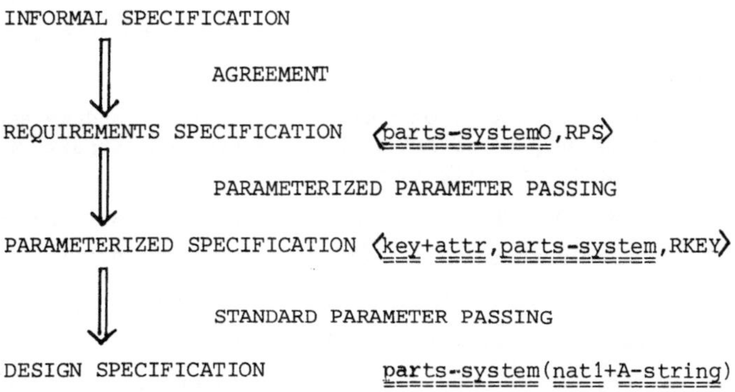

In the following we give the different steps in more detail:

1.1 INFORMAL SPECIFICATION

Bills of material keep information about products and their parts for manufacturing of all kinds of technical systems. Therefore a parts system has to provide descriptions of parts, the relationship between these parts - which are the subparts of a part and which quantity of each one is necessary to produce this part - and some operations to build and manipulate such bills of material. A special role play parts which have no subparts. They are called atomic parts and must be in stock before the production starts, while all the other parts are intermediate products or products of a specific production budget.

INFORMAL REQUIREMENTS FOR A PARTSSYSTEM

Each bill of material includes all descriptions of parts and their relationship for a product.

A part description consists of a key to uniquely identify a part and a list of characteristic attributes like color, material, weight, etc. Related to each part are all its direct subparts and also a number for the quantity of each one of these subparts. Again subparts may also have subparts such that the part-subpart-relationship reaches over several levels. But not allowed are cycles, because no part can be its own subpart.

Because of different application areas keys and also the attribute lists may change significantly.

To generate and manipulate such bills of material and to get some information out of them the parts system must have some specific operations:

- create an empty bill of material [CREATE];
- add a part with key KEY and attribute list ATTR to a bill of material BILL, if BILL has no part with KEY already [ADD-PART(KEY,ATTR,BILL)] ;
- is there a part with key KEY in the bill of material BILL? [PART?(KEY,BILL)] ;
- delete the part with key KEY in the bill of material BILL, if this part has no subparts and is not subpart of any other part in BILL [DELETE-PART(KEY,BILL)] ;
- add to the bill of material BILL a direct part-subpart-relation between two different parts of BILL with keys KEY, KEY' and quantity N, if the reverse relation does not exist in BILL [ADD-SUBPART(KEY,KEY',N,BILL)] ;

Remark: If KEY is part of KEY' already - not necessarily direct - and we add without condition "KEY' is subpart of KEY", then KEY becomes subpart of itself. Hence we get an inconsistent parts system.

- are the two parts with keys KEY and KEY' in a (not necessaryly direct) part-subpart-relation of the bill of material BILL? [SUBPART?(KEY,KEY',BILL)] ;
- delete all direct part-subpart-relations between the two parts with keys KEY, KEY' in the bill of material BILL [DELETE-SUBPART(KEY,KEY',BILL)] ;
- wich atomic parts and how many of each one are necessary to produce N pieces of the part with key KEY and bill of material BILL? [ATOMIC-PARTS(KEY,N,BILL)] .

To illustrate the INFORMAL SPECIFICATION we give a short slice of a parts system for bicycles. The table for attributes below together with the graph, where the nodes are the keys, the edges are the direct part-subpart-relation and edge labels are the (quantity) numbers of direct subparts, keep the information of the bill of material BILL in which for example:

direct subparts of the part with key 3 are the parts with keys 5,6 and 10;
subparts of the part with key 3 are the parts with the keys 5,6,10,8 and 9;
atomic parts of BILL are the parts with the keys 8,9 and 10.

To produce 10 bikes for men we need 20 tires, 700 spokes and 20 pedals, that is

ATOMIC-PARTS(1,10,BILL)= $\{(8,20),\ (9,700),\ (10,20)\}$.

KEY	ATTRIBUTE LIST
1	bike for men with 10 gears
2	bike for ladies with 6 gears
3	frame for men
4	frame for ladies
5	front-wheel
6	back-wheel for 10 gears
7	back-wheel for 6 gears
8	tyre
9	spoke
10	pedal

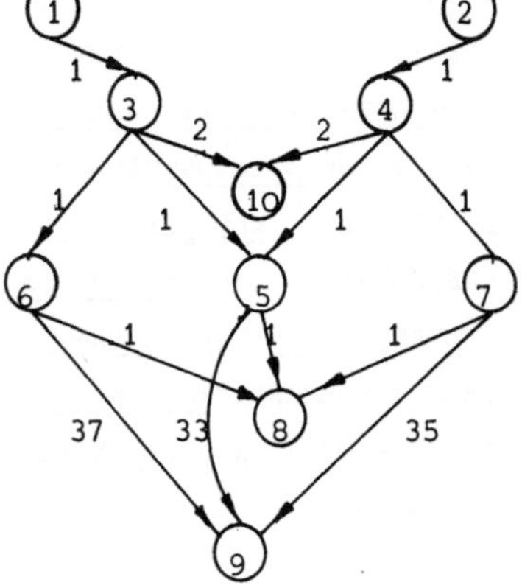

1.2 REQUIREMENTS SPECIFICATION ⟨parts-system0, RPS⟩

The main idea in this step is to fix the signature of the operations given in the INFORMAL SPECIFICATION and to replace the informal requirements by corresponding logical formulas RPS. In order to define the signature of the operations (system-signature) we need some other formal parameters attr+key+comp. The specification attr for attributes consists of a single sort attr without operations, equations and requirements. The requirements specification ⟨key,RKEY⟩ for keys is defined as follows:

key:=bool +

sorts: key

opns: EQ: key key ⟶ bool

RKEY: initial(bool)

EQ(KEY,KEY')=TRUE ⟷ KEY = KEY'

This means that key contains as fixed parameter a specification bool for boolean values with the usual operations TRUE,FALSE,AND,OR and NON. The requirement initial (bool) makes sure that no other than the well-known 2-valued initial bool-algebra TRUE,FALSE can be used as bool-parameter such that EQ: key key ⟶ bool together with the remaining requirement becomes an equality predicate on the set A_{key} for all models A of ⟨key,RKEY⟩.

For the range of the operation ATOMIC-PARTS we need a sort comp for the corresponding set of key-number pairs. This sort comp belongs to a parameter comp which includes also a specification nat1 for natural numbers with sort nat.

Now we are able to formulate the REQUIREMENTS SPECIFICATION ⟨parts-system0,RPS⟩ with sort parts-system for the set of bills of material. However, only requirements for the operations ADD-PART, DELETE-PART, ADD-SUBPART and DELETE-SUBPART are given in this paper.

The REQUIREMENTS SPECIFICATION ⟨parts-system0,RPS⟩ is given by

parts-system0=attr+key+comp+

sorts: parts-system

opns: CREATE: ⟶ parts-system

ADD-PART: key attr parts-system ⟶ parts-system

PART?: key parts-system ⟶ bool

DELETE-PART: key parts-system ⟶ parts-system

ADD-SUBPART: key key nat parts-system ⟶ parts-system

SUBPART?: key key parts-system ⟶ bool

DELETE-SUBPART: key key parts-system ⟶ parts-system

ATOMIC-PARTS: key nat parts-system ⟶ comp

RPS= RKEY∪{initial(nat1), r1,r2,r3,r4}

with

r1:ADD-PART(KEY,ATTR,BILL)=BILL ⟷ PART?(KEY,BILL)=TRUE

r2:PART?(KEY,DELETE-PART(KEY,BILL))=FALSE ⟷

∀KEY' [SUBPART?(KEY,KEY',BILL)=FALSE ∧ SUBPART?(KEY',KEY,BILL)=FALSE]

r3:SUBPART?(KEY,KEY',ADD-SUBPART(KEY,KEY',N,BILL))=TRUE

⟷ EQ(KEY,KEY')=FALSE ∧ PART?(KEY,BILL)=TRUE ∧

PART?(KEY',BILL)=TRUE ∧ SUBPART?(KEY',KEY,BILL)=FALSE

r4:SUBPART?(KEY,KEY',DELETE-SUBPART(KEY,KEY',BILL))=FALSE

⟷ ∀KEY" [SUBPART?(KEY,KEY",BILL)=FALSE ∨

SUBPART?(KEY",KEY',BILL)=FALSE

∨ EQ(KEY",KEY')=TRUE ∨ EQ(KEY",KEY)=TRUE]

The requirements r1-r4 are formalizing the informal conditions given for the operations ADD-PART,DELETE-PART,ADD-SUBPART resp. DELETE-SUBPART given in the INFORMAL SPECIFICATION.

Note, that we could add more requirements for these operations, like the obvious requirement r1':PART?(KEY,ADD-PART(KEY,ATTR,BILL))=TRUE.

But for this paper we have decided to give only one requirement for each of the manipulating operations. Requirements for the other operations, especially ATOMIC-PARTS, including also integrity constraints are given in /Fey 81/.

The semantics of the REQUIREMENTS SPECIFICATION ⟨parts-system0,RPS⟩ is the class of models which have for each sort in parts-system0 a set A_s and for each operation symbol σ:s1...sn⟶ s an operation $\sigma_A : A_{s_1} \times \ldots \times A_{s_n} \longrightarrow A_s$ such that the equations in comp and all requirements in RPS are satisfied. Especially the requirement initial (nat1) makes sure that A_{nat} is isomorphic to the natural numbers $\mathbb{N}$ (without zero) which is the initial algebra in the category of all nat1-algebras.

1.3 PARAMETERIZED SPECIFICATION ⟨key+attr,parts-system,RKEY⟩

In the first formal refinement step we replace the formal requirements r1,...,r4 for the operations by algebraic equations, and the formal parameter comp in parts-system0 is considered now as actual parameter in parts-system such that we can ommit the requirement initial(nat1). But the formal parameters attr+key together with the requirements RKEY remain unchanged. Hence we obtain the following PARAMETERIZED SPECIFICATION ⟨key+attr,parts-system,RKEY⟩ given by

```
PARAMETER DECLARATION: key+attr
REQUIREMENTS:          RKEY(see 1.2)
TARGET SPECIFICATION:  parts-system =
    parts-system0 +
    eqns: e1,...,e20 with
    e1: ADD-PART(KEY,ATTR,ADD-PART(KEY',ATTR',BILL))=
         if PART?(KEY,ADD-PART(KEY',ATTR',BILL))
            then ADD-PART(KEY',ATTR',BILL)
            else ADD-PART(KEY',ATTR',ADD-PART(KEY,ATTR,BILL))

    e2: ADD-PART(KEY,ATTR,ADD-SUBPART(KEY',KEY",N,BILL)) =
         if PART?(KEY,BILL)
            then ADD-SUBPART(KEY',KEY",N,BILL)
            else if EQ(KEY,KEY') OR EQ(KEY,KEY")
                    then ADD-PART(KEY,ATTR,ADD-SUBPART(KEY',KEY",N,BILL))
                    else ADD-SUBPART(KEY',KEY",N,ADD-PART(KEY,ATTR,BILL))

    e3: PART?(KEY,CREATE)=FALSE
    e4: PART?(KEY,ADD-PART(KEY',ATTR,BILL)) =
             EQ(KEY,KEY') OR PART?(KEY,BILL)

    e5: PART?(KEY,ADD-SUBPART(KEY',KEY",N,BILL)) = PART?(KEY,BILL)
```

The remaining equations e6-e20 (see /Fey 81/) are those for the operation DELETE-PART, ADD-SUBPART, SUBPART?, DELETE-SUBPART and ATOMIC-PARTS. Because of space limitation we only give one of the equations for ADD-SUBPART which reflects the requirement r3 of the REQUIREMENTS SPECIFICATION

```
e10: ADD-SUBPART(KEY,KEY',N',ADD-SUBPART(KEY1,KEY2,N,BILL)) =
      if EQ(KEY,KEY') OR NON PART?(KEY,BILL) OR NON PART?(KEY',BILL)
         OR SUBPART?(KEY',KEY,ADD-SUBPART(KEY1,KEY2,N,BILL))
      then ADD-SUBPART(KEY1,KEY2,N,BILL)
      else ADD-SUBPART(KEY1,KEY2,N,ADD-SUBPART(KEY,KEY',N',BILL))
```

The specification parts-system has three generating operations for the sort parts-system: CREATE, ADD-PART and ADD-SUBPART. Due to requirement r1 in RPS an entry of (KEY,ATTR) into the BILL does not take place if KEY is already part of BILL. This requirement is reflected in the then-part of equation e1. The else-part of e1 makes sure that adding is commutative. In equation e2 we specify the effect of ADD-PART with respect to the other generating operation ADD-SUBPART. There is no effect if KEY is already part of BILL. Due to the else-else-part ADD-PART and ADD-SUBPART commute with each other provided that the corresponding keys are different. But if we have KEY=KEY' and KEY' is not in BILL then the else-then-part of e2 is equal to ADD-PART(KEY,ATTR,BILL) which in general is different from the else-else-part. Note, that the else-then-part of e2 is equal to the left hand side of e2 which means that this term cannot be reduced in the case KEY=KEY' or KEY=KEY" if also no other equation can be used therefore.

The equations e3-e5 for PART? are enrichment equations with respect to the generating operations CREATE, ADD-PART and ADD-SUBPART respectively. In a similar way we have three equations for each of the remaining operations DELETE-PART, ADD-SUBPART, SUBPART?, DELETE-SUBPART and ATOMIC-PARTS.

In the semantic of ⟨key+attr, parts-system, RKEY⟩ we have for each model of the parameter key+attr satisfying the requirements RKEY exactly one parts-system-model defined by the equations e1-e20. Correctness of this first formal refinement step means that all these models are also models of the REQUIREMENTS SPECIFICATION ⟨parts-system0, RPS⟩.

This means we have to show that all these parts-system-models are satisfying the requirements r1,...,r4 of RPS. There is no general procedure to give such proofs because of well-known undecidability results. But the proof for requirement r1 in the APPENDIX is typical for such verification.

In terms of our general methodology the step from ⟨parts-system0, RPS⟩ to ⟨key+attr, parts-system, RKEY⟩ is given by a parameter passing morphism h': parts-system0 ⟶ parts-system which is an inclusion of sorts, operations and equations (that of bool and nat in key and comp) in our special case.

1.4 DESIGN SPECIFICATION parts-system(nat1+A-string)

In the second formal refinement step we replace the remaining formal parameter key+attr by the actual parameter nat1+A-string given by

```
nat1:=bool +                                  A-string:=
sorts:nat                                     sorts:string,char
opns: 1:⟶ nat                                 opns: A_1,...,A_n :⟶ char
      SUCC: nat⟶ nat                                ε :⟶ string
        ≡: nat nat ⟶bool                            RADD:string char ⟶ string
eqns :                                        eqns: — no equation —
E 1  : (1≡1)=TRUE
E2,E3: (1≡SUCC(M))=(SUCC(N)≡1)=FALSE
E 4  : (SUCC(N)≡SUCC(M))=(N≡M)
```

The corresponding parameter passing morphism h: key+attr⟶ nat1+A-string is defined by: bool is bool; key is nat; EQ is ≡; attr is string.

Hence the DESIGN SPECIFICATION parts-system(nat1+A-string) is the value specification in the following parameter passing diagram

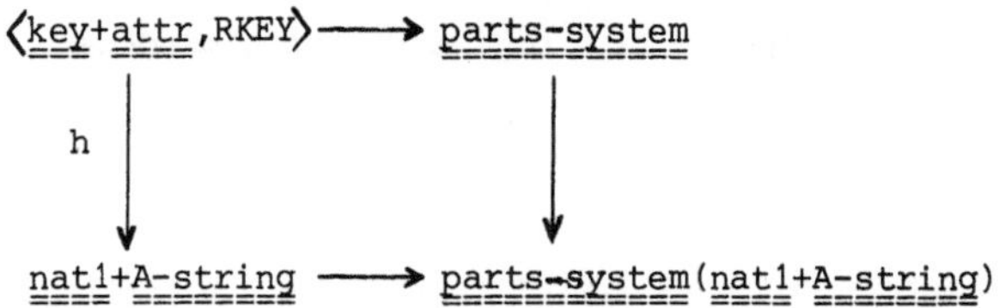

Explicitly we have

parts-system(nat1+A-string) =

nat1+A-string + comp +

sorts: parts-system

opns: CREATE: → parts-system

ADD-PART: nat string parts-system → parts-system

PART?: nat parts-system → bool

DELETE-PART: nat parts-system → parts-system

ADD-SUBPART?: nat nat nat parts-system → parts-system

SUBPART?: nat nat parts-system → bool

DELETE-SUBPART: nat nat parts-system → parts-system

ATOMIC-PARTS: nat nat parts-system → comp

eqns: e1-e20 as in 1.3 but with EQ replaced by ≡ and variables KEY and ATTR replaced by variables NAT and STR of sort nat and string respectively.

For correctness in this step it sufficies to show that the parameter passing morphism h is passing consistent, i.e. the initial model of nat1 considered as key-model has to satisfy the requirements RKEY. Since the initial model of nat1 is isomorphic to the well-known natural numbers $\mathbb{N}$ (without zero) in sort nat and boolean values in bool it remains to show that ≡ in nat1 is exactly the equality (see APPENDIX).

The semantics of the design specification parts-system(nat1+A-string) consists exactly of the initial model which can be constructed as quotient term algebra. It turns out that the parts-system domain of the initial model can be considered as specific colored graphs where the nodes correspond to parts (key-attribute pairs) and the edges to direct part-subpart relationships. Passing consistency of h implies within the general methodology that this initial parts-system(nat1+A-string)-model belongs to the semantics of the PARAMETERIZED SPECIFICATION ⟨key+attr,parts-system,RKEY⟩ (see 1.3).

Together with the correctness result in 1.3 we obtain the following

THEOREM (Correctness of the Refinement Process)

The DESIGN SPECIFICATION parts-system(nat1+A-string) is correct with respect to the

REQUIREMENTS SPECIFICATION $\langle$parts-system0,RPS$\rangle$, i.e. the initial parts-system (nat1+A-string)-model satisfies (regarded as a parts-system0-model) the requirements RPS.

This theorem is a direct application of the corresponding general correctness theorem in the next section, provided that passing consistensy of both steps is verified (see APPENDIX).

Note, that we have given only one specific example of a parts system design. Using other actual parameters for keys and attributes we can adapt this design to several different applications. Moreover this methodology supports the stability of the system in the sense of /Tur 81/ if we modify the design in such a way that first same old actual parameters are replaced by the corresponding formal ones and then the formal ones are replaced by new actual parameters satisfying the requirements of the formal part.

2. THE GENERAL METHODOLOGY

In this section we give the general framework for our refinement methodology. Algebraic specifications are used in the sense of /ADJ 76-78/ and /Kre 80/. This means that a specification SPEC=$\langle S,\Sigma,E\rangle$ consists of three sets S,Σ, and E called set of sorts, operations(symbols) and equations (or conditional axioms) respectively. Each specification SPEC has a well-defined semantics T_{SPEC}, the initial algebra within the category of all SPEC-algebras. Hence such a specification corresponds to a design specification in terms of software engineering. Due to /Ehr 81/ a requirements specification RSPEC=$\langle$SPEC,R$\rangle$, short R-specification, consists of a specification SPEC=$\langle S,\Sigma,E\rangle$ as above - however, with empty set E in most examples - and a set R, called set of requirements. As requirements we can take predicate formulas based on a declaration $\langle S,\Sigma\rangle$ (also called signature). Another example of requirements are initial restrictions like initial(bool) where in our example the bool-part is required to be initial (see also /BG 80/). In general we assume that for each $r\in R$ there is a well-defined subclass VALID(r) of all SPEC-algebras. The class VALID(R) is defined to be the intersection of all VALID(r) for $r\in R$ and the corresponding algebras are called RSPEC-algebras. In other words an RSPEC-algebra is a SPEC-algebra satisfying all requirements in R. The semantics of a requirements specification RSPEC is the class of all RSPEC-algebras. Hence the semantics of a requirements specification is significantly different from that of a design specification, which consists exactly of the initial algebra. Note, that the class of all RSPEC-algebras might be quite big but also possible empty in the case that the requirements are contradicting each other. The problem is now to find a methodology how to develop a correct design specification from a given requirements specification. If all requirements R in RSPEC are already equations the corresponding design specification is easy to obtain, namely SPEC'=$\langle S,\Sigma,E+R\rangle$. Another trivial case is that T_{SPEC} satisfies already the requirements R in RSPEC=$\langle$SPEC,R$\rangle$ such that we can take SPEC as design specification. In general, however, we have to replace the logical requirements by corresponding algebraic equations, where also parts of the signature $\langle S,\Sigma\rangle$ may be renamed and/or extended.

We propose to use the technique of parameter passing for parameterized specifications with requirements as developed in /Ehr 81/. A parameterized specification with requirements PRSPEC=$\langle$SPEC,SPEC1,R$\rangle$ consists of a parameterized specification PSPEC=$\langle$SPEC,SPEC1$\rangle$ (with parameter declaration (also called formal parameter part) SPEC included in the target specification SPEC1) and a set of requirements R on SPEC. Roughly spoken the semantics of PRSPEC is the class of all SPEC1-algebras F(A) which are freely generated by some parameter A. As parameters we allow SPEC-algebras satisfying the requirements R, i.e. RSPEC-algebras, which are assumed to be persistent in F(A). In the special case SPEC=SPEC1 a parameterized specification with requirements is (with respect to syntax and semantics) nothing else but a requirements specification RSPEC. On the other hand R=∅ and SPEC=∅ implies that the semantics consists only of the initial SPEC1-algebra T_{SPEC1} such that we obtain a design specification. Given a parameterized specification with requirements PRSPEC, like $\langle$data,set(data),R$\rangle$, the technique of (parameterized) parameter passing (see /Ehr 81/) allows to replace the formal parameter part data by another parameterized specification with requirements like $\langle$item,stack(item),R'$\rangle$. The result is the composite parameterized specification $\langle$item,set*stack(item),R'$\rangle$. If in a second step we use the technique of standard parameter passing and replace the formal parameter item by an actual parameter like int we obtain the (nonparameterized) specification set*stack(int) which can be considered as design specification. Let us note that we have set*stack(int)=set(stack(int)) as corollary of Theorem 4.7 in /Ehr 81/. In general we have the following situation: Given two parameterized specifications PRSPEC=$\langle$SPEC,SPEC1,R$\rangle$ and PRSPEC'=$\langle$SPEC',SPEC0',R'$\rangle$ we first have to define a parameter passing morphism h:SPEC⟶ SPEC0'. This is a pair of functions $h=(h_S,h_\Sigma)$ where h_S is a mapping from sorts of SPEC to sorts of SPEC0' and h_Σ a mapping between the operations such that for each σ:s1...sn⟶s in SPEC we have $h_\Sigma(\sigma):h_S(s1)\dots h_S(sn)\longrightarrow h_S(s)$ for the corresponding operation in SPEC0'. Moreover we assume that the translation h(E) of the equations E in SPEC are equations in SPEC0'. In other words h is a specification morphism in the sense of Def. 2.5 in /Ehr 81/.

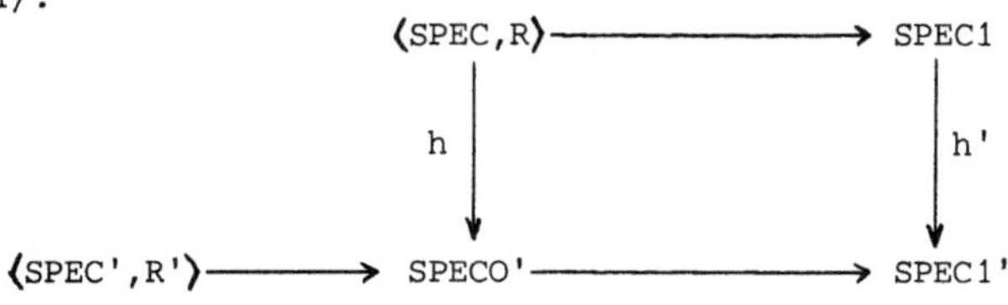

The result of parameterized parameter passing is the parameterized specification PRSPEC"=$\langle$SPEC',SPEC1',R'$\rangle$. Let SPEC1=SPEC+$\langle$S1,Σ1,E1$\rangle$ then SPEC1' is given by

$$SPEC1'=SPEC0'+\langle S1,h'(\Sigma 1),h'(E1)\rangle$$

where h':SPEC1⟶ SPEC1' is a specification morphism defined by

$$h'_S(x)=\text{if } x\in S1 \text{ then } x \text{ else } h_S(x)$$
$$h'_\Sigma(y)=\text{if } y\in\Sigma 1 \text{ then } y \text{ else } h_\Sigma(y)$$

Correctness of parameter passing should imply that for each SPEC1'-algebra in the semantics of PRSPEC" the corresponding SPEC1-part (with respect to h') belongs to the semantics of PRSPEC. In /Ehr 81/ it is proved that it sufficies to show that the parameter passing morphism h:SPEC⟶ SPEC0' is passing consistent. That means for each SPEC'-algebra A' which satisfies R' the SPEC-part (with respect to h) of the corresponding free SPEC0'-algebra F'(A') satisfies the requirements R of PRSPEC. In most practical cases this means to show that the operations in SPEC0' defined by the equations in SPEC0' are satisfying the translated logical requirments h(R) in SPEC0'. But it is not necessary to show this for all operations in SPEC1'. In the special case of standard parameter passing we have R'=∅ and SPEC'=∅ such that the semantics of PRSPEC" consists only of the initial SPEC1'-algebra $T_{SPEC1'}$. Passing consistency of h implies that the SPEC1-part (with respect to h') of $T_{SPEC1'}$ belongs to the semantics of PRSPEC. But in order to verify passing consistency we only have to show that the SPEC-part (with respect to h) of $T_{SPEC0'}$ satisfies the requirements R. For precise definition concerning syntax, semantics and correctness of parameter passing and main results how to obtain correctness we again have to refer to /Ehr 81/.

Our general methodology for stepwise refinement from requirements to design specification is given in the following picture where correctness of all parameter passing steps implies correctness of the design with respect to the requirements specification.

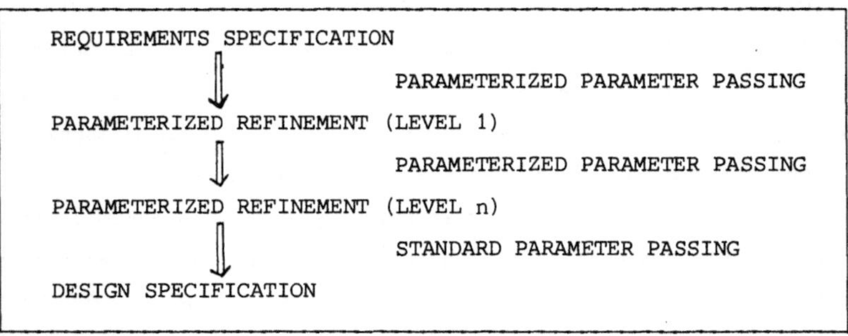

As mentioned above the requirements specification as well as all parameterized refinements are parameterized specifications with requirements. From level 1 to level n, however, more and more design details are added by replacing corresponding formal parameter parts by actual parts or other parameterized specification parts. In the case study above, we have considered only one refinement level.

Now we give a precise formulation of the refinement methodology. Let RSPEC=⟨SPEC,R⟩ be the given requirements specification and h0,h1,...,hn parameter passing morphisms with respect to parameterized refinements ⟨SPEC',SPEC0',R'⟩, ⟨SPEC",SPEC0",R"⟩,.... and the actual parameter $\overline{SPEC}$. Then the resulting design specification $\overline{SPECn}$ is constructed stepwise in the following diagram (for n=2).

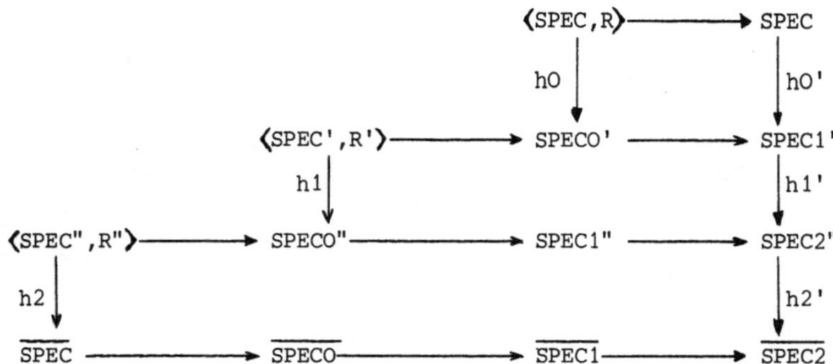

Moreover we have an induced specification morphism $\bar{h}:SPEC \to \overline{SPECn}$ defined by $\bar{h}=hn' \circ \ldots \circ h0'$. This allows to give a precise formulation of the correctness result which is a corollary of the R-EXTENSION-LEMMA in /Ehr 81/:

THEOREM (Correctness of the General Methodology)

The SPEC-part (with respect to $\bar{h}$) of the semantics $T_{\overline{SPECn}}$ of the design specification $\overline{SPECn}$ satisfies the requirements R of the requirements specification RSPEC provided that all the parameter passing morphisms h0,h1,...,hn are passing consistent. In other words passing consistency for all refinement steps implies the correctness of the design specification with respect to the requirements specification.

ACKNOWLEDGEMENTS

This paper is part of the DFG-project ACT at TU Berlin. We are most grateful to the members of this project and to the referees for several valuable discussions resp. comments concerning the material of this paper. Thanks also to H. Barnewitz for excellent typing.

REFERENCES

/ADJ 76-78/ Goguen, J.A., Thatcher, J.W., Wagner, E.G.: An initial algebra approach to the specification, correctness, and implementation of abstract data types, IBM Research Report RC-6487, Oct 1976. Current Trends in Programming Methodology, IV: Data Structuring (R.T.Yeh,Ed.) Prentice Hall, New Jersey (1978), pp. 80-149

/BG 80/ Burstall, R.M, Goguen, J.A.: The Semantics of CLEAR, a Specification Language, Proc. 1979 Copenhagen Winter School on Abstract Software Specifications (1980)

/Ehr 81/ Ehrig, H.: Algebraic Theory of Parameterized Specifications with Requirements, Proc. 6th CAAP, Genove 81, Italy, LNCS 112(1981),pp.1-24

/EFK 80/ Ehrig, H., Fey, W., Kreowski, H.-J.: Algebraische Spezifikation eines Stücklistensystems - Eine Fallstudie; Software Engineering - Entwurf und Spezifikation, Teubner Berichte des German Chapter of the ACM, Band 5, Stuttgart (1981), pp. 75-90

/Kre 80/ Kreowski, H.-J.: Algebraische Spezifikation von Softwaresystemen; Software Engineering-Entwurf und Spezifikation, Teubner Berichte des German Chapter of the ACM, Band 5, Stuttgart(1981), pp. 46-74

/Fey 81/ Fey, W.: Specification of a Parts System: From Requirements to Design; to appear

/Flo 81/ Floyd, Ch.: A process-oriented approach to software development, Proc. 6th ACM European Regional Conf. on Systems Architecture, London 1981, pp. 285-294

/Leh 81/ Lehmann, M.M.: The environment of program development and maintenance, Proc. 6th ACM European Regional Conf. on System Architecture, London 1981, pp. 273-284

/Tur 81/ Turski, W.M.: Software Stability, Proc. 6th ACM European Regional Conf. on Systems Architecture, London 1981, pp. 107-116

APPENDIX (VERIFICATION OF REQUIREMENTS)

For correctness of the design specification of our parts system (see the Theorem in Sect. 1.4) we have to show correctness of the two refinement steps in Section 1. Due to our theorem i.e. in Section 2 we have to show passing consistency of both parameter passing morphisms h' and h. This means that the translated requirements h'(RPS) and h(RKEY) have to be satisfied by parts-system and nat1+A-string respectively.

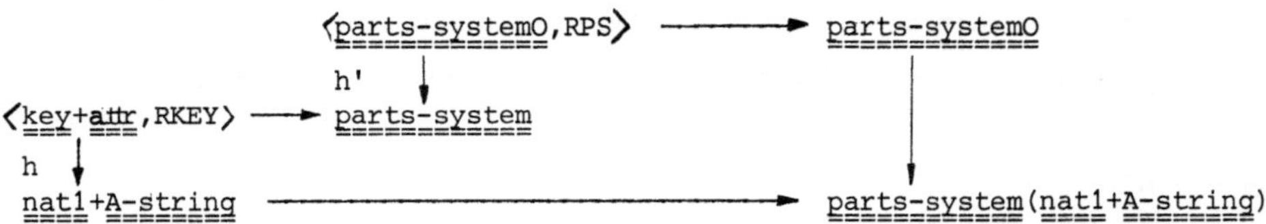

To give an impression of such correctness proofs we verify one of the requirements in each step:

Lemma 1:

For r1∈RPS is the translated requriement h'(r1)=r1=[ADD-PART(KEY,ATTR,BILL)=BILL ⟷ PART?(KEY,BILL)=TRUE] satisfied by parts-system.

Lemma 2:

For r:=[EQ(KEY,KEY')=TRUE ⟷ KEY=KEY'] ∈RKEY is the translated requrirement h(r)= [(N≡M)=TRUE ⟷ N=M] statisfied by nat1, i.e. ≡ in nat1 is the equality on natural numbers.

Proof of Lemma 1:

First we show ADD-PART(KEY,ATTR,BILL)=BILL → PART?(KEY,BILL)=TRUE. Using equation e4 and the requirements RKEY we have

PART?(KEY,BILL)=PART?(KEY,ADD-PART(KEY,ATTR,BILL))
=EQ(KEY,KEY)OR PART?(KEY,BILL)=TRUE

Vice versa we show PART?(KEY,BILL)=TRUE ⟶ ADD-PART(KEY,ATTR,BILL)=BILL.
We consider three cases for BILL, since all bills of material are generated by the operations CREATE, ADD-PART and ADD-SUBPART:

Due to equation e3 we have PART?(KEY,CREATE)=FALSE s.t. BILL $\neq$ CREATE.
For BILL=ADD-PART(KEY',ATTR',BILL') we have by e1

ADD-PART(KEY,ATTR,BILL)
= <u>if</u> PART?(KEY,BILL) <u>then</u> BILL <u>else</u> ...
= BILL
because PART?(KEY,BILL)=TRUE by assumption.

For BILL=ADD-SUBPART(KEY',KEY'',N,BILL') we have by e2, e5 and assumption:

ADD-PART(KEY,ATTR,BILL)
= <u>if</u> PART?(KEY,BILL') <u>then</u> BILL <u>else</u> ...
= <u>if</u> PART?(KEY,BILL) <u>then</u> BILL <u>else</u> ...
= BILL □

<u>Proof of Lemma 2:</u>

First let us start with N=M and N:=$SUCC^n(1)$ für some $n \in \mathbb{N}$ to show N=M ⟶ (N≡M)=TRUE.
Using E4 inductively and E1 we have:

$$(N \equiv M) = (N \equiv N) = (SUCC^{n-1}(1) \equiv SUCC^{n-1}(1)) = (1 \equiv 1) = TRUE$$

To show (N≡M)=TRUE ⟶ N=M let (N≡M)=TRUE, N=$SUCC^n(1)$, M=$SUCC^m(1)$ for some $n,m \in \mathbb{N}$ and assume w.l.o.g. $n \geq m$. Inductive use of E4 shows

$$TRUE = (N \equiv M) = (SUCC^n(1) \equiv SUCC^m(1)) = (SUCC^{n-m}(1) \equiv 1)$$

Now ist follows from E1-E3 that n=m and hence N=M. □

DURCH PRÄDIKATION ZU OBJEKTTYPEN

E. Ortner
Universität Erlangen-Nürnberg
IMMD VI, Martensstraße 3

Zusammenfassung: Ein Ansatz für das Konstruieren von Datenbank-Anwendungen wird vorgeschlagen. Dabei wird in Begriffen konstruiert, die zu Objekttypen führen. Diese werden schrittweise und kontrolliert eingeführt, d.h.:

- durch (exemplarische)Prädikation und Aufstellen der Prädikatorenregeln,
- durch Reflexion und kritische Prüfung des Regelsystems auf Konsistenz und Ableitbarkeit,
- durch Konstruktion der Objekttypen unter Angabe der Integritätsbedingungen.

Auf logischer Ebene erfolgt zuletzt die Darstellung der (re-)konstruierten Objekttypen entweder relational, als Coset oder hierarchisch.

1. Einleitung

Eine der wesentlichen Schwierigkeiten beim Entwurf von Datenbank-Anwendungen ist die Umsetzung von Fachbegriffen in Objekttypen. Objekttypen sind rekonstruierte Begriffe, die explizit jene Fachtermini repräsentieren, die implizit das Geschehen in den Anwendungsbereichen bestimmen. Sie bilden die Grundlage für den Aufbau der Dateien eines Datenbank-Systems sowie für die Verarbeitung der Daten in Programmen. Es gibt viele Versuche, diese Aufgabe wenigstens in gewissem Umfange durchgehend, d.h. von der Aufgabenstellung bis zur Lösung, systematisch zu bewältigen. Schwierigkeiten treten insbesondere auf, je näher man den Aufgabenstellungen in den Anwendungsbereichen kommt. Die Diskussion, wie von hier aus die ersten Hürden kontrolliert genommen werden können, ist in vollem Gange (1).

In dem vorliegenden Beitrag geht es um den "ersten" Konstruktionsschritt - aus einer Mangelsituation in der Informationsversorgung über die Spezifikation zu einer Objekttypenkonstruktion. Sonst spricht man in diesem Zusammenhang von "semantischer Modellierung" und meint den Entwurf eines Datenmodells auf noch nicht formaler Ebene. D.h. also noch vor der Entscheidung, ob diesen Entwurf eine Konstruktion basierend auf dem hierarchischen Modellansatz (12), auf Netzwerk-Modellen (11) oder auf dem Relationenmodell (3) repräsentiert.

Das war das Motiv der Suche nach "höher liegenden" Modellansätzen in den letzten zehn Jahren. Dabei sollten die Fundamente intensional tiefer gelegt werden, bzw. es geht um ein "extending ... to capture more meaning" nach Codd (5).

Die verschiedenen Ansätze in Richtung semantische Modellierung, z.B. die von Schmid/Swenson (9), Chen (4) oder Smith/Smith (10), werden bekannt sein. Die eleganteste Lösung hat zuletzt McLeod (8) geliefert. Form und Extension aber ist im Hinblick auf Begriffsbildung noch nicht alles.

Es wird ein Ansatz vorgeschlagen, der im wesentlichen in Anlehnung an Frege (6) entstand und der von den Begriffsinhalten ausgeht. Methodologisch folgen wir der Vorgehensweise der Konstruktivisten (7) mit dem Ziel, den Gebrauch fachsprachlicher Termini (re-)konstruktiv einzuführen. Diskutiert werden in diesem Zusammenhang:

1. Die Frage nach den Fachbegriffen und ihre Repräsentation durch Objekttypen.
2. Die Prädikation als elementare Konstruktionshandlung im Hinblick auf die Einführung von Attributen.
3. Die Rolle der Integritätsbedingungen, die im Zuge der Konstruktion von Objekttypen aus Prädikatorenregeln abgeleitet werden.

Der begriffliche Ansatz, der dabei zugrundegelegt wird, besagt, daß die Begriffe, mit denen wir es zu tun haben, eine Kombination von Teilbegriffen sind.

2. Begriffsbildung

Der Aufbau von Dateien zum Zweck der automatisierten Verarbeitung der Daten in Programmen macht es notwendig, die in den Anwendungsbereichen benutzten Begriffe zu präzisieren, damit zuverlässige Kriterien bereitstehen zur Unterscheidung und Strukturierung der Daten im Hinblick auf ihre Verarbeitung in Programmen. Dies ist nur möglich über die Erforschung jenes logischen Verfahrens, das unter der Bezeichnung "Begriffsbildung" bekannt ist.

Traditionsgemäß unterscheidet man bei einem Begriff seinen Inhalt oder seine Intension und seinen Umfang oder seine Extension. Die Intension eines Begriffs besteht aus anderen Begriffen bzw. Merkmalen. Die Extension eines Begriffs ist die Klasse derjenigen Gegenstände, denen der Begriff zukommt. Der Inhalt des Begriffs "Kunde" z.B. wird durch ein Verzeichnis der Merkmale bestimmt, die einem Gegenstand zukommen müssen, damit er als Kunde anerkannt wird. Der Umfang des Begriffs "Kunde" ist die Klasse aller Kunden.

Die Art, wie die Logiker heute das Wort "Begriff" gebrauchen, ist weitgehend von Frege beeinflußt worden. Frege nennt den Begriff eine Funktion, deren Wert immer ein Wahrheitswert ist (6). Demgemäß ist ein Begriff "unvollständig", "ergänzungsbedürftig", "ungesättigt", aber auch "prädikativ", d.h. die Bedeutung eines grammatischen Prädikats. Die Bezeichnung eines Begriffs ist ein Funktionsausdruck, aus dem ein Vollausdruck, ein Satz mit einem bestimmten Wahrheitswert dadurch entsteht, daß für die Argumentvariable Namen von Argumenten eingesetzt werden. Die Bedeutung dieses Satzes ist sein Wahrheitswert, entweder das Wahre oder das Falsche. Der Wahrheitswert ist zugleich der Wert der betreffenden Funktion für das Argument, dessen Namen in die Funktion eingesetzt wird.

Wir legen uns folgende Arbeitsdefinition zu: Ein Begriff ist prädikativ, er hat eine Intension und eine Extension.

Prädikation ist stets Bezugnahme (Referenz) und Beschreibung (Deskription). Wir befassen uns hier mit Prädikationen vom Typ:

Lutz ε (ist) Kunde (Prädikation)
Lutz $\vee$ (hat) KUNDEN-NR (Attribution)
4711 $\bar{\varepsilon}$ (ist) KUNDEN-NR (Metaprädikation)
usw.

Sie dienen dem Aufbau von Objekttypen und der Feststellung des Gebrauchs von Zeichen für die Bezugnahme auf Gegenstände und die Beschreibung ihrer Eigenschaften. Prädikationen vergegenwärtigen Sachverhalte, die wahr oder falsch sind. Die Feststellung der Wahrheit oder Falschheit eines Sachverhaltes findet durch Beurteilung des Sachverhaltes statt. Urteilen (u) ist eine Funktion, z.B.:

$$u : x \; \varepsilon \; \text{Kunde} \longrightarrow \omega \; ,$$

die jedem Sachverhalt genau einen Wahrheitswert zuordnet. Dabei werden für x der Reihe nach Argumente eingesetzt, während ω für die Wahrheitswerte "wahr" oder "falsch" steht.

Die Intension eines Begriffs ist die Eigenschaft, die ein Gegenstand haben muß, damit er unter den Begriff fällt (2). Man kann sie spezifizieren, indem Teilbegriffe bzw. Attribute, die die Intension eines Begriffs repräsentieren, zu einem Objekttyp zusammengefaßt werden.

z.B.:

$$\begin{aligned} x \;\varepsilon\; \text{Kunde} \Longrightarrow\;& x \;\text{v}\; \text{KUNDEN-NR} \\ \wedge\;& x \;\text{v}\; \text{BERUF} \\ \wedge\;& x \;\text{v}\; \text{ADRESSE} \\ & \text{usw.} \end{aligned}$$

Vereinfacht kann man jetzt sagen, daß die Attribute KUNDEN-NR, BERUF, ADRESSE usw. die Intension des Begriffs "Kunde" sind. Tatsächlich aber stellen sie seine Intension nur dar, indem sie die Eigenschaften von Gegenständen, die "Kunde sind", näher bestimmen.

Die Klasse derjenigen Gegenstände, die unter einen Begriff, einen Objekttyp oder ein Attribut fallen, bildet schließlich die Extension eines Begriffs.

Welche Konsequenzen ergeben sich daraus für das logische Verfahren der Begriffsbildung?

Das Ergebnis der Begriffsbildung sind Aussagen in einer bestimmten Sprache, in der das beschrieben wird, was durch das betreffende Verfahren erreicht wurde. Unser Sprachmittel sind Prädikatorenregeln. Man kann sie auch Transformationsregeln nennen, die von wahren Aussagen zu wahren Aussagen führen. Wahr in dem Sinne, daß die Sachverhalte, die die Aussagen vergegenwärtigen, entweder gegeben sind oder man nimmt an bzw. man weiß es, daß zur Lösung der Aufgabe eben diese Sachverhalte herbeigeführt werden müssen.

Um sicherzustellen, daß ein Begriff in der Weise rekonstruiert wird, daß er zur Lösung einer Aufgabe etwas beiträgt, führen wir im Übergang von Begriffen zu Objekttypen den Terminus "Adäquatheit" ein. Im Hinblick auf den Zweck, der mit der Lösung verfolgt wird, führt er uns weiter zu der Unterscheidung von Funktionalität, Performanz und Akzeptanz der Objekttypenkonstruktionen, die in einer Datenbankumgebung die rekonstruierten Begriffe vertreten. Die Beziehung zwischen den Begriffen und den Objekttypen wird Repräsentation ($=_{RP}$) genannt. Sie hat den Charakter einer Gleichung der Form:

$$\text{Begriff} =_{RP} \text{Objekttyp.}$$

Das was repräsentiert wird, was in der Repräsentation links steht, trägt die Bezeichnung "Repräsentat" - hier Begriff. Das wodurch der Begriff repräsentiert wird, was in der Repräsentation rechts steht, heißt "Repräsentant" bzw. in unserem Falle Objekttyp.

In diesem Sinne ist Begriffsbildung eine nach bestimmten Regeln geführte Rede (vgl. Abschnitt 5), die angibt:

a) Welche Eigenschaften müssen Gegenstände haben, damit sie unter einen Begriff fallen?
b) Welche Beziehungen bestehen zwischen den Begriffen?
c) In welcher Weise werden Wörter gebraucht, um einerseits die Begriffe zu repräsentieren und andererseits die Eigenschaften zu bezeichnen, die jene Gegenstände haben, die unter die Begriffe fallen?

D.h. es geht darum, verständlich zu machen, welche Begriffe in welcher Form gelten sollen.

3. Objekttypen

Betrachten wir als nächstes die Konstruktion eines Objekttyps (Bild 1), der rekonstruktiv eingeführt wurde. Ein Objekttyp ist die im Hinblick auf einen Begriff (z.B.: Kunde) erfolgte Zusammenfassung von Attributen (z.B.: KUNDEN-NR,BERUF,KREDITLINIE usw.), in denen die Objekte, die unter den Objekttyp fallen, zunächst bezeichnet (KUNDEN-NR) und dann beschrieben (BERUF,KREDITLINIE usw.) werden. Die Beziehung zwischen dem Begriff und dem Objekttyp wird , wie vereinbart , Repräsentation ($=_{RP}$) genannt. Sie ist eine dreistellige Relation der Form "x ist repräsentationsäquivalent y bezüglich z". Hier steht "x" für den Objekttyp, "y" für den repräsentierten Begriff und "z" für Adäquatheit, die, gemessen an dem Zweck, der verfolgt wird, weiter zu der Unterscheidung von Funktionalität, Performanz und Akzeptanz der Konstruktionen führt.

Repräsentiert wird der Begriff sowohl intensional ($=_{RI}$) durch die Attribute, die zum Objekttyp zusammengefaßt wurden, als auch extensional ($=_{RE}$) durch die Beschreibung der Objekte, die unter den Objekttyp fallen. Wir schreiben:

$$P(x) =_{RP} OTN(NA_1,NA_2,\ldots;PA_1,PA_2,\ldots)$$

und nennen "P(x)" bzw. "$x \in P$" die Aussageform, die den repräsentierten

Begriff darstellt. "OTN" ist der Name des Objekttyps. "NA" sind Nominatorattribute (z.B. KUNDEN-NR). Sie bestimmen den Gebrauch von Nominatoren (z.B. 4711). "PA" sind Prädikatorattribute (z.B. BERUF), die den Gebrauch der Apprädikatoren (z.B. Krämer) festlegen.

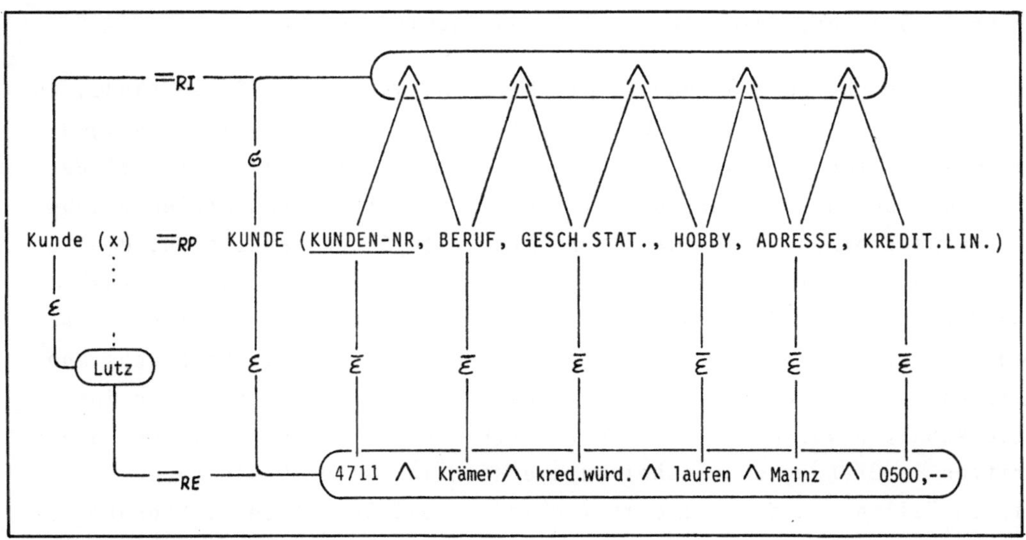

Bild 1: Objekttyp KUNDE

Ein Apprädikator ist ein Prädikator, der nicht in der Hauptsache das Objekt, über das geredet wird, bestimmt - das ist die Aufgabe des Eigenprädikators (EP) -, sondern der das Objekt in weiteren Eigenschaften beschreibt. Man abstrahiert in der Regel vom Eigenprädikator (z.B. Kunde) zum Objekttypnamen (KUNDE) und von den Apprädikatoren (z.B. Krämer) zu den Eigenschaften ("Krämer sein") der Objekte, die unter den Objekttyp fallen.

Streng unterscheiden muß man den Übergang von Gegenständen, die unter einen Begriff fallen, zu der Beschreibung dieser Gegenstände, die jetzt unter einen Objekttyp fallen:

$$\bigwedge_x (x \in EP \longleftrightarrow \overset{1}{\bigvee}_N \bigvee_{AP} (x \equiv N \wedge N \,\sigma_R\, AP))$$

D.h. z.B.: Von allen x gilt: wenn x ein Kunde (EP) ist, dann gibt es genau ein N (z.B. 4711) und wenigstens ein AP (z.B. Krämer), so daß x und N identisch sind und N in einer durch Prädikatorenregeln näher bestimmten Beziehung (hier: 4711 ε Krämer) zu AP steht.

von der Betrachtung der internen Struktur (Schlüsselattribute, Nichtschlüsselattribute) eines Objekttyps. Intern stellen Begriffe 2. Ordnung, die wir Attribute nennen, einen Begriff 1. Ordnung, genannt Objekttyp, dar. Das ganze Konstrukt aber repräsentiert wieder einen Begriff 1. Ordnung, in unserem Falle den Begriff "Kunde".

Diese Unterscheidung wurde getroffen, um Aussagen über Gegenstände, zu deren Zweck der Objekttyp konstruiert wird, abzugrenzen von Aussagen zur Feststellung des Gebrauchs von Zeichen für die Bezugnahme auf Gegenstände und die Beschreibung ihrer Eigenschaften. Demzufolge bedeuten Aussageformen, deren sämtliche Argumente Gegenstände sind, die unter den rekonstruierten Begriff fallen, Begriffe 1. Ordnung. Aussageformen, unter deren Argumenten Merkmale oder Eigenschaften dieser Gegenstände, vor allem aber Wörter zur Feststellung des Gebrauchs von Zeichen für die Bezugnahme auf Gegenstände und die Beschreibung ihrer Eigenschaften vorkommen, führen zu Begriffen 2. Ordnung. Von den Begriffen 1. Ordnung unterscheiden sie sich in erster Linie dadurch, daß in Fällen, in denen sie in Verbindung mit Begriffen 1. Ordnung zu Aussagen führen, z.B.:

$$\text{Lutz } \varepsilon \text{ Krämer} \wedge \text{Krämer } \bar{\varepsilon} \text{ BERUF} \not\Rightarrow \text{Lutz } \varepsilon \text{ BERUF},$$

der Sachzusammenhang, den sie vergegenwärtigen, nicht transitiv ist.

Prädikatoren bedeuten Begriffe 1. Ordnung. Sie werden Gegenständen zu- oder abgesprochen. Attributoren dagegen sind Wörter, sie werden auch Metaprädikatoren genannt, die von anderen Wörtern (Nominatoren oder Prädikatoren) ausgesagt, den Gebrauch dieser Wörter festlegen und ein Attribut bzw. einen Begriff 2. Ordnung darstellen.

Während bei der Prädikation (z.B. Lutz ε Krämer) die Kopula "ε" die Beziehung zwischen Subjekt und Prädikat angibt, schlagen wir für Metaprädikationen (z.B. 4711 $\bar{\varepsilon}$ KUNDEN-NR) vor, die Kopula "$\bar{\varepsilon}$" einzusetzen. Auf der intensionalen Ebene dagegen, von der aus Attribute zu einem Objekttyp zusammengefaßt werden, stellt die Präposition "σ", von **συντάττειν** - im Deutschen für das grammatische Zusammenstellen oder Konstruieren, die Beziehung her.

4. Prädikationenschemata

Prädikation ist stets Bezugnahme (Referenz) und Beschreibung (Deskription). Durch Bezugnahme (Namengebung oder Kennzeichnung) wird eine Rede gewissermaßen "eröffnet". Das Zeichen, das dabei ins Spiel kommt, bedeutet einen Individual- oder Allgemeinbegriff, lenkt die Rede auf einen bestimmten Gegenstand und führt ihn mit der einen oder anderen Eigenschaft in die Rede ein. Frege (6) sprach in diesem Zusammenhang von der Art und Weise des Gegebenseins eines Gegenstandes und nannte dieses "Gegebensein" den Sinn eines Nominators oder einer Kennzeichnung. Durch Deskription wird der in die Rede eingeführte Gegenstand in weiteren Eigenschaften beschrieben. Dabei resultiert aus der Analyse des Verbs "sein" die Feststellung, daß zwischen Bezugnahme und Beschreibung entweder die Kopula "sein" (ε), die Kopula "haben" (ν) oder die Kopula "tun" (π) die Beziehung zwischen einem Individualbegriff (Subjekt) und einem Allgemeinbegriff (Prädikat) herstellt.

z.B.:

a) Lutz ε Krämer
b) Lutz ν Kreditwürdigkeit
c) Lutz π laufen.

Bild 2 zeigt, daß wir im Schlüsselbereich eines Objekttyps entweder durch einfache Namengebung (Bezugnahme Form A) oder durch Verbindung von Nominatoren (Bezugnahme Form B) auf Gegenstände bezug nehmen. Die Beschreibung (Beschreibung Form A) erfolgt dann durch Substantiv-Prädikation (ε), durch Adjektiv-Prädikation (ν) oder durch Verb-Prädikation (π). Für die Beschreibung der Objekte, die unter einen Objekttyp fallen, ist das aber nur ein erster Ansatz, mit dem man am Ende ist, noch bevor die wichtigsten Fälle unter Dach und Fach sind.

z.B.:

d) Lutz ? Mainz
e) Lutz ? 500,--
f) Lutz ? Z

Durch Verallgemeinerung der spezifischen Bedeutung der Kopulae wird der Bogen zuletzt soweit gespannt (Beschreibung Form B), daß sämtliche Fälle berücksichtigt werden können. Die Fragezeichen in (d), (e) und (f) werden durch " σ_R" ersetzt. Hier steht " σ_R" für jede in Prädikatorenregeln vereinbarte Zusammengehörigkeit von Zeichen, wenn das eine Zeichen einen Gegenstand bezeichnet und das andere etwas von ihm aussagt.

Der Ansatz (Bild 2) ist damit abgeschlossen und vollständig. Er bildet die Grundlage für die systematische Einführung von Designatoren zur

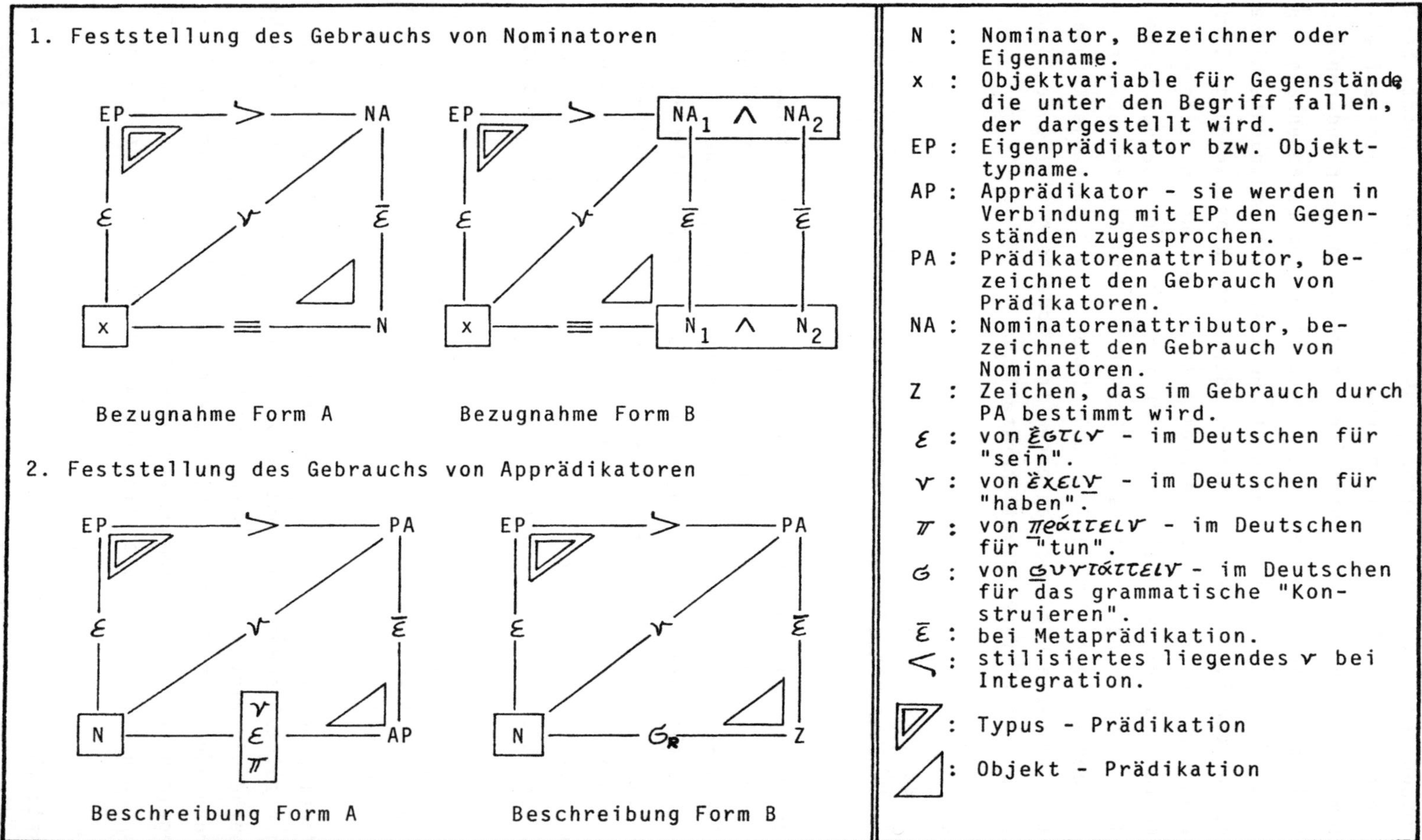

Bild 2: Prädikationenschemata

Bezeichnung und Beschreibung von Gegenständen und für die Konstruktion von Objekttypen aus Attributen. Denn wie wir bereits festgestellt haben ist ein Attributor ein Metaprädikator, der eine Aussagefunktion

$$u : (AP \; \bar{\varepsilon} \; AT) \prec EP \longrightarrow \omega$$

bedeutet, die im Hinblick auf einen Begriff 1. Ordnung (z.B. Kunde) einen Begriff 2. Ordnung (z.B. BERUF) darstellt. "AP" (bzw. "N") ist die Variable für Apprädikatoren (Nominatoren), "AT" ("NA" oder "PA") und "EP" sind Schemabuchstaben, die den Attributor und den Eigenprädikator repräsentieren und "ω" ist die Variable für die Wahrheitswerte "wahr" oder "falsch", während "$\bar{\varepsilon}$" für die (Meta-)Kopula "ist" und "$\prec$" für die Präposition "in" stehen. Gegenstände, die unter einen Begriff fallen, bilden die Extension eines Begriffs. Die Eigenschaft, die ein Gegenstand haben muß, damit er unter den Begriff fällt, nennt Carnap (2) die Intension des Begriffs. Durch Einsetzen von Namen für Gegenstände in eine Aussagefunktion werden Sachverhalte vergegenwärtigt, die wahr oder falsch sind. Die Feststellung der Wahrheit oder Falschheit erfolgt durch Beurteilung der Sachverhalte. Logisch ist ein Urteil (u) die Abbildung einer Menge von Sachverhalten in eine Menge von Wahrheitswerten, d.h. eine Funktion, die jedem Sachverhalt genau einen Wahrheitswert zuordnet. Auf diese Weise kommt man zu der Bestimmung der Extension von Begriffen oder wie in obigem Falle zu der Feststellung des Gebrauchs von Zeichen.

Beispielsweise sind KUNDEN-NR(N,KUNDE), gelesen: "N ist KUNDEN-NR in KUNDE" oder BERUF(AP,KUNDE), gelesen: "AP ist BERUF in KUNDE", Attributformen, die im Hinblick auf den Begriff KUNDE die Attribute KUNDEN-NR und BERUF darstellen. Dabei werden in dem einen Falle Nominatoren (4711, 4712 usw.) und in dem anderen Apprädikatoren (Krämer, Händler usw.) in ihrem Gebrauch festgelegt.

Die dargestellten Attribute sind atomare Semanteme, aus denen die Objekttypen konstruiert werden. Beim Zusammenfassen der Attribute zum Objekttyp - einer Art molekularem Semantem - handelt es sich dann im wesentlichen nur noch um ein Ausklammern, d.h. um ein Voranstellen des Objekttypnamens (OTN) einerseits und um ein Aufzählen der Attributnamen (NA u. PA), in Klammern dahinter, andererseits.

5. Integritätsbedingungen

Es muß noch geklärt werden, wie wir im Zuge der Konstruktion von Objekttypen zunächst zu Prädikatorenregeln und dann zu Integritätsbedingungen kommen.

Ausgehen kann man von fachsprachlichen Dialogen. Das sind unvollständige Argumentationen in einer besonderen Situation. Unvollständig deshalb, weil ein gewisses Vorverständnis (Fachwissen) immer vorausgesetzt wird. Hier helfen Regeln weiter, die explizit den Gebrauch von Fachbegriffen festlegen und Verbindungen zwischen ihnen vorschreiben. Diese Regeln heißen Prädikatorenregeln und sind Sätze über die Beibehaltung einer einmal vereinbarten Verwendung von Termini.

Wir unterscheiden Prädikatorenregeln

1. auf begrifflicher Ebene,
2. im Übergang von Begriffen zu Objekttypen,
3. auf Ebene der Objekttypen.

<u>zu 1</u>: Auf begrifflicher Ebene gibt es zwei Typen von Prädikatorenregeln:

1. Prädikatorenregeln, die einen Art/Gattungs-Zusammenhang liefern:

$x \varepsilon$ Kunde $\Longrightarrow x \varepsilon$ Geschäftspartner
$x \varepsilon$ Kunde $\Longrightarrow x \varepsilon'$ Lieferant
$x \varepsilon$ Gesch.Part. $\Longleftrightarrow x \varepsilon$ Kunde $\vee x \varepsilon$ Lieferant
usw.

2. Prädikatorenregeln, die einen Teil/Ganze-Zusammenhang einrichten:

$x \varepsilon$ Kunde $\Longrightarrow x \nu$ Adresse
$x \varepsilon$ Kante $\Longrightarrow x \nu$ Anzahl
$x \varepsilon$ Kante $\Longleftrightarrow x \nu$ Oberteil $\wedge x \nu$ Unterteil
usw.

Die Regelpfeile "$\Longrightarrow$" und "$\Longleftrightarrow$" stehen für: "Es ist erlaubt von ... überzugehen zu ... (und umgekehrt)". Statt der Kopulae "ist" bzw. "ist nicht" und "hat" werden die Abkürzungen ε, ε' und ν geschrieben.

<u>zu 2</u>: In Prädikatorenregeln, die von der begrifflichen Ebene auf die Objekttypen-Ebene führen, werden Gegenständen Attribute im Hinblick auf den einzurichtenden Objekttyp zugeteilt. Das erfolgt in zwei Teilschritten:

1. Einführung der Attribute im Hinblick auf den einzurichtenden Objekttyp:

$x \, \varepsilon$ Kunde $\Longleftrightarrow x \, \mathrm{v}$ KUNDEN-NR
$x \, \varepsilon$ Kunde $\Longrightarrow x \, \mathrm{v}$ BERUF
$x \, \varepsilon$ Kunde $\Longrightarrow x \, \mathrm{v}$ HOBBY
usw.

2. Apprädikation bzw. Identifikation mit Einbeziehung der Attribute in den Objekttyp:

$x \, \varepsilon$ Kunde $\wedge$ N,x ε KUNDEN-NR $\Longleftrightarrow$ N $\bar{\varepsilon}$ KUNDEN-NR,KUNDE $\wedge$ $x \equiv$ N
$x \, \varepsilon$ Kunde $\wedge$ Q,x ε BERUF $\Longleftrightarrow$ Q $\bar{\varepsilon}$ BERUF,KUNDE $\wedge$ $x \, \varepsilon$ Q
$x \, \varepsilon$ Kunde $\wedge$ S,x ε HOBBY $\Longleftrightarrow$ S $\bar{\varepsilon}$ HOBBY,KUNDE $\wedge$ $x \, \pi$ S
usw.

<u>zu 3</u>: Schließlich geht es in Prädikatorenregeln auf der dritten Ebene, auf Ebene der zu konstruierenden Objekttypen, um die Feststellung der internen Struktur eines Objekttyps. Es geht um die Frage, was sind Schlüsselattribute und was sind Nichtschlüsselattribute und welche Beziehungen bestehen zwischen den nominativen und den apprädikativen Eintragungen in das Schema.

<u>z.B.</u>:

Q $\bar{\varepsilon}$ BERUF,KUNDE $\Longrightarrow$ N $\bar{\varepsilon}$ KUNDEN-NR,KUNDE
$N_1 \bar{\varepsilon}$ OTNR,KANTE $\Longleftrightarrow$ $N_2 \bar{\varepsilon}$ UTNR,KANTE
T $\bar{\varepsilon}$ ANZAHL,KANTE $\Longrightarrow$ $N_1 \bar{\varepsilon}$ OTNR,KANTE $\wedge$ $N_2 \bar{\varepsilon}$ UTNR,KANTE
usw.

Integritätsbedingungen dagegen sind Allsätze über die Beibehaltung einer einmal vereinbarten Verwendung von Zeichen im Geltungsbereich eines Datenbanksystems. Zu den Integritätsbedingungen kommen wir durch schrittweises Distanzieren von besonderen Situationen. Prädikatorenregeln, als praktische Implikationen, bilden den Ausgangspunkt. Man kann aber auch eine andere Regelung treffen, wenn das zweckmäßig ist.

Es gibt Integritätsbedingungen, die die Bezugnahme auf Objekte regeln:

$$\bigvee_P \bigwedge_x (x \, \varepsilon \, P \longleftrightarrow \overset{1}{\bigvee}_N (N \, \bar{\varepsilon} \, NA,P \wedge x \equiv N))$$

und solche, die angeben, wie die Objekte zu beschreiben sind:

$$\bigvee_P \bigwedge_x (x \, \varepsilon \, P \longleftrightarrow \bigvee_Q (Q \, \bar{\varepsilon} \, PA,P \wedge x \, \sigma_R \, Q))$$

Links von "<->" findet die Eigenprädikation, rechts die Namengebung oder die Apprädikation statt. Für unser Beispiel, in dem KUNDE für P gesetzt wird, gelten z.B. folgende Integritätsbedingungen:

$$\bigwedge_x (x \in \text{KUNDE} \leftrightarrow \overset{1}{\bigvee}_N (N \bar{\in} \text{KUNDEN-NR,KUNDE} \wedge x \equiv N))$$
$$\bigwedge_x (x \in \text{KUNDE} \leftrightarrow \bigvee_Q (Q \bar{\in} \text{BERUF,KUNDE} \wedge x \in Q))$$
$$\bigwedge_x (x \in \text{KUNDE} \leftrightarrow \overset{\nabla}{\bigvee}_S (S \bar{\in} \text{HOBBY,KUNDE} \wedge x \pi S))$$

usw.

Dabei steht "$\overset{1}{\bigvee}$" für: "Es gibt genau ein ..., so daß gilt ...", "$\bigvee$" steht für: "Es gibt wenigstens ein ..., so daß gilt ..." und "$\overset{\nabla}{\bigvee}$" wird für: "Es gibt möglicherweise ein ..., so daß gilt ..." geschrieben.

Auf logischer Ebene erfolgt zuletzt die Darstellung der (re-)konstruierten Objekttypen entweder in Tabellenform, als Coset oder hierarchisch. Dabei müssen je nach Datenmodell oft Randbedingungen in Kauf genommen werden, die die rekonstruierte Struktur der aufgenommenen Begriffe wieder "entstellen". So wird im Relationenmodell z.B. der Objekttyp RECHNUNG, der eine komplexe, teils netzwerkartige, teils baumartige Struktur im Schlüsselbereich hat (Bild 3), tabellarisch dargestellt. Oder man geht im CODASYL-Ansatz dazu über, den Begriff "Auftrag" als Coset darzustellen usw.

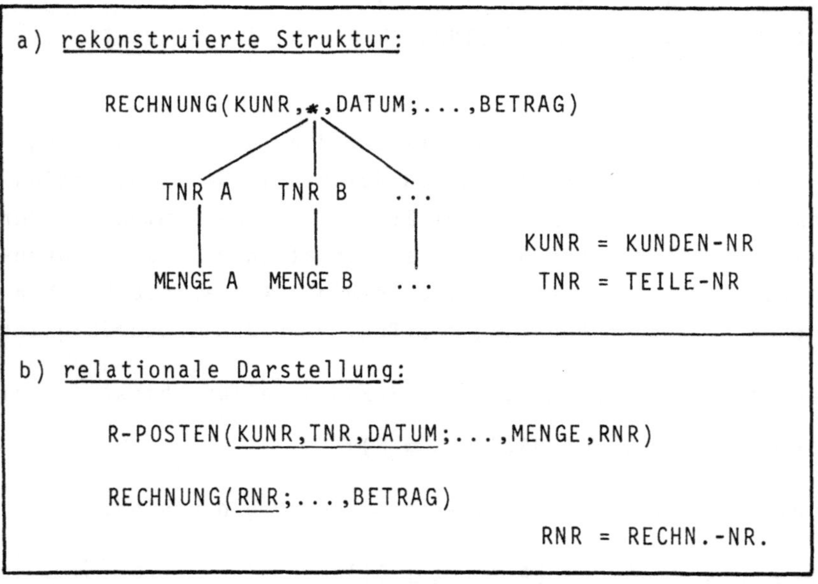

Bild 3: Objekttyp RECHNUNG

Objekttypen sind verschieden von Relationen in 3. Normalform. Sie repräsentieren explizit jene Begriffe, die implizit das Geschehen in den Fachabteilungen bestimmen. Dabei nützt es gar nichts, wenn man sich z.B. eine Rechnung tabellarisch oder einen Auftrag als Coset vorzustellen hat. Oder in anderem Zusammenhang: Den Begriff "Bilanz" als einfache Tabelle darzustellen ist ebenso eine Verfälschung der "semantischen Struktur" dieses Begriffs, wie wenn man den Begriff "Betriebsabrechnungsbogen" bloß hierarchisch darstellen wollte.

Zunächst jedenfalls ist es uninteressant sich den Kopf darüber zu zerbrechen, wie hierarchische Gegebenheiten als "flat relations" darzustellen sind oder wie "multivalued dependencies" im Relationenmodell behandelt werden sollen. Auf der semantischen Ebene sind deshalb Konstruktionshandlungen zugelassen und es stehen Ausdrucksmittel bereit, die im Hinblick auf die Struktur der rekonstruierten Begriffe zu keinen Einschränkungen führen. Dazu wurden verschiedene Möglichkeiten der Bindung von Prädikatenbuchstaben eingeführt und relativ weit gefaßte Rahmenbedingungen zur Bildung von Objekttypen aufgestellt. Da es dabei zu Existenzaussagen über Begriffe und die intensionalen Beziehungen zwischen den Begriffen kommt, beruht der Ansatz formal auf der Prädikatenlogik höherer Stufe.

6. Schlußbemerkung

Im vorliegenden Beitrag ging es uns

a) um die Begriffsbildung bzw. um die Rekonstruktion der in den Anwendungsbereichen gebrauchten Begriffe und
b) um die Repräsentation dieser Begriffe durch Objekttypen,

die schließlich in einem der bekannten Datenmodelle formal-logisch dargestellt werden.

Die Arbeit ist ein Beitrag zur Lösung eines Teilproblems im Rahmen eines größeren Projekts der konstruktiven Spezifikation von Anwendungssystemen, dem Entwurf von Programmen sowie dem Aufbau von Dateien, auf Basis des Datenbank-Konzepts.

Literatur:

(1) Brodie, M.L.; Zilles, S.N. (eds.): Proceedings of Workshop on Data Abstraction, Databases and Conceptual Modelling, Pingree Park, Colorado June 23-26, 1980.

(2) Carnap, R.: Bedeutung und Notwendigkeit - Eine Studie zur Semantik und modalen Logik, Library of Exact Philosophy Bd. 6, Springer-Verlag, Wien - New York 1972.

(3) Chamberlin, D.D.: Relational Database Management Systems, in: Computing Surveys, 8(1976)1, S. 43-66.

(4) Chen, P.P.S.: The Entity-Relationship Model - Toward a Unified View of Data, in: ACM Transactions on Database Systems, 1(1976)1, S. 9-36.

(5) Codd, E.F.: Extending the Data Base Relational Model to Capture More Meaning, IBM Research Report RJ2599, San Jose, California 1979.

(6) Frege, G.: Funktion, Begriff, Bedeutung - Fünf logische Studien, Patzig, G. (Hrsg.), Kleine Vandenhoeck-Reihe 1144, Göttingen 1975.

(7) Lorenzen, P.; Schwemmer, O.: Konstruktive Logik, Ethik und Wissenschaftstheorie, B.I. 700, Mannheim 1975.

(8) McLeod, D.: A Semantic Data Base Model and its Associated Structures user Interface, Diss. MIT/LCS/Tr-214, Cambridge, Mass. 1978.

(9) Schmid, H.A.; Swenson, J.R.: On the Semantics of the Relational Data Model, Proceedings of ACM SIGMOD International Conference on the Management of Data, San Jose, California 14-15 May 1975.

(10) Smith, J.M.; Smith, D.C.P.: Database Abstractions: Aggregation and Generalization, in: ACM Transactions on Database Systems, 2(1977)2, S. 105-133.

(11) Taylor, R.W.; Frank, R.L.: CODASYL Database Management Systems, in: Computing Surveys, 8(1976)1, S. 67-103.

(12) Tsichiritzis, D.C.; Lochovsky, F.H.: Hierarchical Database Management: A Survey, in: Computing Surveys, 8(19767)1, S. 105-123.

SELF-DIAGNOSIS FOR PARALLEL COMPUTERS

M. Dal Cin
Institut für Informationsverarbeitung
Universität Tübingen

Abstract

The growing importance of fault-tolerance for computing systems has made self-diagnosis a topic of considerable interest, since efficient self-diagnosis is a prerequisite for any fault-tolerant system behavior. In this paper, self-diagnosis of systems with multiple processing elements is considered where each element may enter into the diagnosis of other elements. We shall develop a formal model for self-diagnosis based on comparison testing. In particular, we consider tree machines suitable for VLSI-implementation.

1. Introduction

Technology has made possible the development of powerful computing systems as networks of many VLSI-components with the complexity of sophisticated processors [1]. It has been estimated that networks (parallel computers) comprising as many as 10^5 interconnected modules will soon be technically feasible. Since reliability decreases with increasing system complexity it will then be necessary to provide for redundancy and to incorporate into the network modules the ability to test one another and to diagnose malfunctions. We shall assume that testing among modules is done by comparison. That is, two modules test one another by executing the same specific test program; a third module compares their outputs and signalizes an error if and only if these outputs disagree. We have, however, to make sure that from the begin of a test round up until the end of diagnosis no additional failures occur. Hence, tests and diagnosis must not be time consuming.

A (binary) tree structured network computer, the tree machine, efficiently implementable in VLSI-technology is described by Bentley and Kung [2]. The structure of the tree machine is illustrated by Figs. 1 and 2. It contains three types of modules: processing elements (PE, squares) which store and compute data, input elements (circles) which broadcast data (from the root to the PEs), and output elements (OE, triangles) which combine their inputs. The tree machine is controlled by a control unit CU. Bentley and Kung identified a large set of problems which can be solved efficiently by the tree machine. The tree machine can be simulated by a set of conventional processors operating on a shared memory. It also provides a convenient model for understanding and analysing parallel algorithms. In the following we shall show how self-diagnosis can be efficiently implemented into parallel computers such as the tree machine.

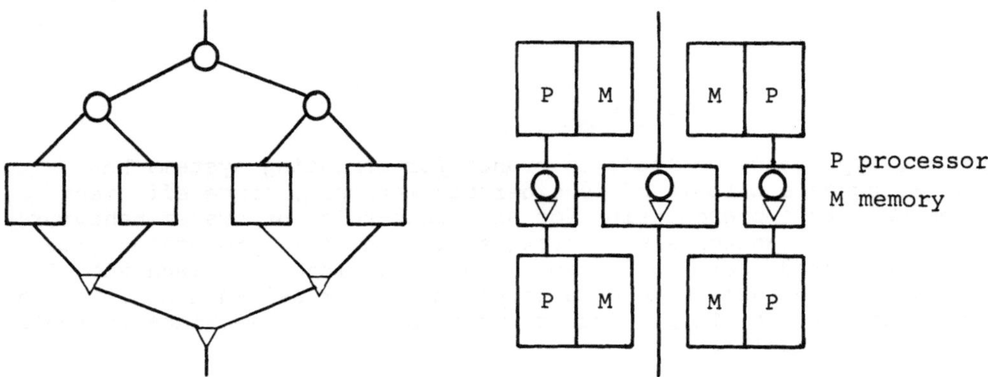

Fig. 1 Structure of the tree machine

Fig. 2. A layout of the tree machine

2. Diagnostic model

Consider a system S (a parallel computer) consisting of set N of n modules u1,u2,...,un, and a test assignment E={(ui,uj)| ui and uj test one another by comparison}. Thus, the test arrangement is given by the finite, undirected testing graph G=(N,E). Without loss of generality we can assume that G is connected. When units ui and uj test one another the test outcome tij is 1 if both units are fault-free and 0 otherwise. Thus, tij=0 indicates a malfunction of ui or uj or both. A complete set of test outcomes is called a syndrome. Given a syndrome SYN, the system S has to identify its faulty modules from the knowledge of SYN (diagnosis). That is, S has to partition N into fault-set F and its complement H where F is the set of all faulty modules. Each partition (H,F) of N determines a syndrome uniquely. A syndrome, however, can be generated by several partitions. In order to accomplish reliable self-diagnosis we have to limit the number of faulty modules in S. In practice, only a small fraction t/n of all modules will be faulty. Further, in order to prevent congestion of the system by tests, it is reasonable to avoid unnecessary tests. Therefore, we define:

Definition: A self-diagnosing system S and its testing graph G are t-diagnosable (t-db) if for all syndromes of S all faulty modules in S can be identified, provided the number of faulty modules present does not exceed t. Testing graph G is t-optimal if G is t-db and has the smallest number of test links with respect to all t-db testing graphs with n nodes. G is optimal if it is n-2-optimal (cf. Lemma 1 below).

Examples of testing graphs:

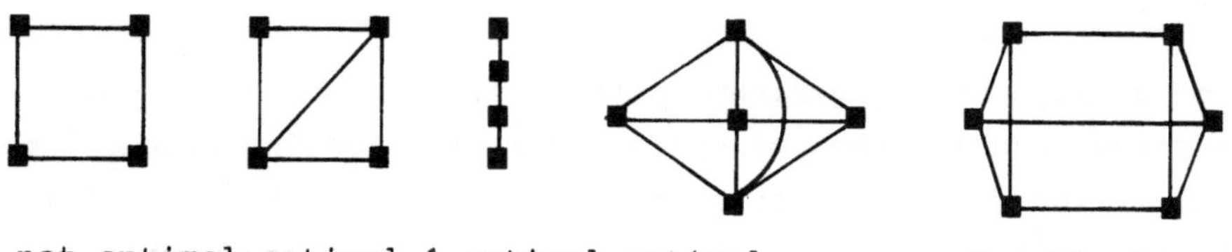

not optimal, optimal, 1-optimal, optimal, 3-optimal

Fig. 3 Testing graphs

Let G=(N,E) and $N_G(u)=\{uj\,|\,(u,uj)\in E\}$. Then $n_G(u)=|N_G(u)|$ is the <u>degree</u> of node u. By dG we denote the minimal node degree of G. (We omit subscript G whenever confusion cannot arise). A syndrome with all test outcomes equal to 0 is called a <u>0-syndrome</u>.

<u>Lemma 1</u>: G t-diagnosable implies dG≥t and t≤n-2. Hence, G is t-optimal if $|E|=\lceil nt/2\rceil$.

<u>Proof</u>: Suppose, n(u)<t for some u∈N. Then the fault-sets N(u) and N(u)∪{u} of cardinality ≤t produce the same syndrome. Hence, G is not t-db. Suppose, G is n-1-db. Then dG≥t implies that G is complete and, hence, all partitions (u,N-{u}) of N, u∈N, produce the 0-syndrome. Thus, G is not n-1-db. From dG≥t follows that $|E|\geq\lceil nt/2\rceil$.

<u>Lemma 2</u>: If dG≥t+1, then G is t-diagnosable.

<u>Proof</u>: In N(u)∪{u} there are at least two fault-free units. Hence, u is fault-free iff at least one testoutcome for u is 1, and u is faulty iff all testoutcomes of u are 0. Of course, this holds true only if not more than t units are faulty.

Fig. 3 shows that the conditions of Lemma 1 (Lemma 2) are not sufficient (necessary). The following theorem states necessary and sufficient conditions.

<u>Theorem</u>: G is t-diagnosable if and only if dG≥t and for each (ui,uj)∈E with n(ui)=n(uj)=t there exists at least one node u, either u∈N(ui)-N(uj) with N(u)≠N(uj) or u∈N(uj)-N(ui) with N(u)≠N(ui).

<u>Proof</u>: Similar to proof of Theorem 2 in [3].

<u>Remark</u>: Preparata et al. have proposed a similar model for self-diagno-

sis [4]. Their model, however, is based on directed testing graphs; it is well-known and theoretical results are available in the literature [5,6]. A model based on comparison testing similar to ours has been proposed by G. Malek [7].

3. Diagnosis of parallel computers

The task of a diagnostic algorithm is to identify all faulty modules, given a syndrome and information contained in the testing graph. A sequential algorithm for t-db testing graphs is given in [8]. Its time complexity is $O(n^2)$. For large parallel computers, however, this complexity may still be toohigh (cf. Sec. 1). It may then be reasonable to distribute among the network modules not only the test duties but also the diagnosing duty. In the next section we shall present for tree machines a parallel version of the diagnostic algorithm which exploits fully the intrinsic parallelism present in these machines.
The tree machine is ideally suited for implementing self-diagnosis as described by our model. Test duties are assigned to the PEs by CU according to a given testing graph. When ui and uj execute a test routine, the OE connecting both compares their outputs and sends the test outcome (via CU) back to the corresponding PEs. As soon as a test round is completed the diagnosing phase starts.

When dealing with the tree machine, we shall assume that the CU and i/o-elements never fail. This assumption is justified to some extent, since these elements are less complex than the PEs (see below). We have to assume, however, that also certain operations of the PEs belong to the hard-core, i.e., are immune from failure. Therefore, a problem we encounter in the design of parallel diagnostic routines is to keep the hard-core of a PE as small as possible.

It is unlikely that two or more processing elements fail in the same way. Comparison testing, therefore, provides a high fault-coverage. Above all it is a relatively simple test strategy. One may, therefore, use the tree machine also as a special purpose device for diagnosing large computer networks. In this case, the network is augmented by a tree machine which concurrently diagnoses the network's state (see Fig. 4). The PEs of the tree machine then represent the processing elements (modules) of the computer network and are loaded with test outcomes obtained by comparing pairs of modules. As soon as enough test information is gathered the tree machine starts diagnosing the computer state.

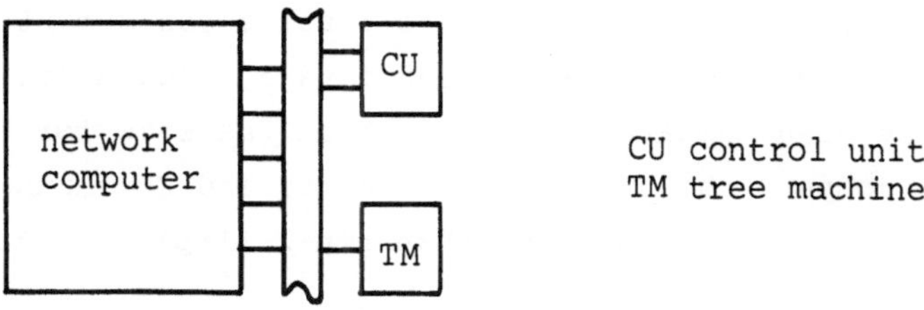

Fig. 4 The tree machine as diagnostic device

In order to learn about the feasability of this approach, a simulation study of the tree machine as diagnosing device is under way. To this end, we assume that the computer network can operate in a degraded mode. To simulate the fault-behavior of the network we have first to choose failure rates for each module and two parameters c and s, say, with $c<1$ and $s<n$ (number of modules). Then, the fault-behavior of the modules is simulated and the diagnosis is performed by the tree machine according to a given t-optimal testing graph with $t=\lfloor cn \rfloor$. The next simulation step is performed with $t=\lfloor c(n-n') \rfloor$ where n' is the number of identified faults. We continue with the simulation until either more than s modules have failed or until we encounter a diagnostic error. This may be the case when more than t modules failed between two test rounds. Our goal is to determine, for instance, the MTTF of the network computer and the percentage of breakdowns due to diagnostic errors.

4. Parallel algorithms for diagnosis

First we present a straightforward diagnostic algorithm for optimal testing graphs. Recall that PEs of the tree machine may also represent the modules of a computer network.

Parallel diagnosis for optimal testing graphs

Processing element PEi stores a list of identifiers of all PEs with which it has been compared, and a list $T[i,j]$ of the corresponding test outcomes. As soon as a test round is completed, all PEs with $T[i,j]=1$ for some j broadcast successively their T-values. That is, PEi broadcasts $T[i,1]$ if it has been compared with PE1, otherwise it remains inactive. One time step later, PEi broadcasts $T[i,2]$ and so on. The OEs compute the logical AND of their inputs. (If an OE receives only one input value it passes this value; if it receives no inputs it remains inactive). If CU receives 0 at the j-th step after the begin of the broadcasting phase, it turnes PEk with $k=j-\lceil \log_2 n \rceil$ (or the corresponding network module) off. It is assumed that broadcasting data from node to node and from node to CU takes one time step. The diagnosis is complete if the syndrome is not the O-syndrome (explicit state assignments). If the tests generated the O-syndrome, PEi broadcasts a 1 (parallel to the other PEs) iff it has been compared with PE1, then the same for PE2, and so on. Now, the OEs compute the sum of their inputs and CU turns PEk off if the corresponding sum D[k] is greater than t=n-2 (implicit state assignments).

In order to see that this algorithm works for optimal testing graphs if at least two PE are fault-free, we have to consider two cases.

1) Let SYN be different from the O-syndrome. Then, at least two fault-free PEs are identified. Since both test all other PEs, all PEs are identified by explicit state assignments.

2) Let SYN be the O-syndrome. Since at least two units, say u1 and u2, are fault-free, they do not test one another; however, they test all other PEs ($dG \geq n-2$). Hence, $n(u1)=n(u2)=n-2$. In $\bar{N}=N-\{u1,u2\}$ all PE test each other; (if not, the O-syndrome is not uniquely decodable). Hence, $n(u)=\bar{n}-1+2=n-1$ for all $u \in \bar{N}$. It follows that all PEs with $n(u)>n-2$ are faulty.

The complexity of the parallel diagnosis is proportional to $n-1+\log_2 n$, i.e., $\Theta(n)$. We have, however, to make sure that a faulty PE cannot broadcast its SYN-values. On the other hand, the CU-operations involved are very simple.

The algorithm we shall now present is not proposed to be the best possible diagnostic algorithm. Rather, it is put forward only as evidence that for any t-db testing graph an effective parallel diagnosis is possible, provided not more than t units are faulty. The diagnosis proceeds in four steps.

<u>Step 1</u>: Execute the explicit state assignments as explained above. When this step is completed, N can be partitioned into set N1 (NO) of all identified, fault-free (faulty) units and set V1 (VO) of all still unidentified, fault-free (faulty) units. Fig. 5 shows the possible test links between these sets. Now, (we denote the cardinality of set A by a) $n1 \geq n-t$ implies $VO \cup V1=\emptyset$ since $dG \geq t$, and $nO=t$ implies $VO=\emptyset$.

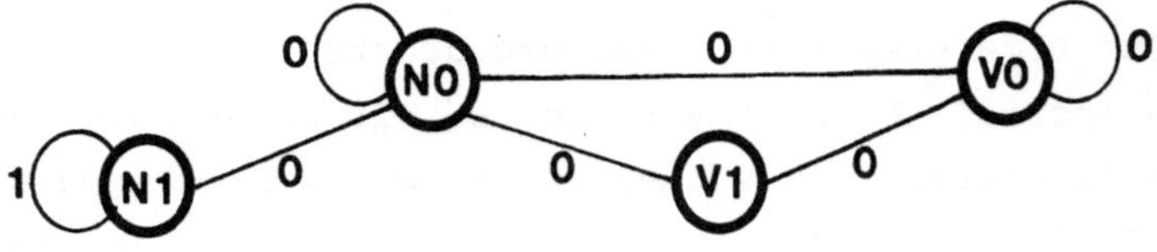

Fig. 5 Partition of N

Step 2: Each active PEi broadcasts E[i]=1 if its state has been identified and E[i]=-1 otherwise. The OEs compute $S1=\sum_{ui\ active} |E[i]|$ and $S3=\sum_{ui\ active} E[i]$. (Note that S1=n-n0 and S3=n1-v1-v0). Then CU executes the following program segment.

```
IF (S1+S3≥2(N-T)) OR (S1=N-T)
   THEN halt  (* all faulty PEs are identified *)
   ELSE S:=T+S1-N; continue with step 3;
```

Let G^+ be the subgraph of G with node set V^+=V0∪V1. The remaining task is to decode the 0-syndrome of G^+. V^+ contains exactly s=t+S1-n=t-n0>0 faulty units (see Lemma 3 below).

Step 3: 3.1 All PEs in N1 are (temporarily) turned off and CU broadcasts the numbers of all active PEs down the tree.

3.2 Parallel to all other active PEs, PEi first broadcasts A[i,k1]; A[i,k1]=1 if PEi has been compared with PEk1 where PEk1 is the first active PE and A[i,k1]=0 else. Then PEi broadcasts A[i,k2] where PEk2 is the next active PE, and so on. The OEs compute

$$C[j]=\sum_{E[i]=-1} 2^i A[i,kj]$$ and CU broadcasts C[j] to PEkj which stores C[j].

This step takes at most $n-1+2\log_2 n+const$ time steps.

3.3 With respect to G^+ the OEs compute $D^+[i]$ as explained in Sec. 3 (implicit state assignment) and CU marks PEi as "faulty" if $D^+[i]$<>S (see Lemma 3).

Step 4: If there are still unidentified PEs left CU broadcasts their C-values down the tree. Upon receiving C[j], PEi compares it with its own C-value and broadcasts a 1 iff both C-values are equal. The OEs add these bits. Let R[j] be the sum (i.e., R[j] active PEs have C-value C[j]). If R[j]<>$N-T-\frac{1}{2}(S1+S3)$ then CU marks PEj as "faulty" (s. Lemma 4). Finally, all marked PEs are turned off and all PE in N1 are turned on again. This completes the diagnosis. Step 4 takes at most O(n) time steps.

The complexity of the parallel diagnosis including the overhead due to broadcasting is O(n).

It remains to prove Lemmata 3 and 4.

Lemma 3: Let r=n-t-n1 and s=t-n0. Subgraph G^+ of G contains exactly r fault-free nodes and $n_{G^+}(u)=s$ if $u\in V^+$ is fault-free.

Proof: At most t units are faulty and V1≠∅ since n1<n-t. Let u∈V1. Then $N_G(u)\subsetneq V0\cup N0$. Hence, $n0+v0\le t\le n_G(u)$ implies $n0+v0=t=n_G(u)$. Hence, $n_{G^+}(u)=t-n0$ and v1=n-n0-v0-n1=n-t-n1.

Lemma 4: Let $u \in V^+$ and $N(u)=N_{G^+}(u)$. There is exactly one subset $\hat{V}$ of V^+ with cardinality r, $N(u)=N(u')$ for $u,u' \in \hat{V}$, and $N(u) \neq N(u')$ for $u \in \hat{V}$, and $u' \in V^+ - \hat{V}$, and all nodes of $\hat{V}$ have degree s. Furthermore, u is fault-free iff $u \in \hat{V}$.

Proof: No two nodes of $V1 \subseteq V^+$ are directly connected. All nodes of V1, however, are directly connected with all nodes of V0 (Lemma 3). Hence, $N(u)=N(u')$ for all $u,u' \in V1$ and $v1=r$ (Lemma 3). Let $u' \in V0$. Since u' is connected with all nodes of V1, $N(u') \neq N(u)$. All directly connected pairs of nodes have different N-sets. Suppose now that there are r not pair-wise connected nodes in V0 with degree s. Call the set of theses nodes $\bar{V}0$. Then, (V1,V0) and $(\bar{V}0,(V0-\bar{V}0) \cup V1)$ are two partitions of V^+ with s faulty nodes and consistent with the 0-syndrome of G^+. This contradicts the t-diagnosability of G.

5. Conclusion

We have presented parallel diagnostic algorithms for computer networks. These algorithms are designed to run on a tree machine. They may also be used by the tree machine for self-diagnosis. Then, however, it remains to develop a diagnostic procedure for i/o-trees which uses a minimum of PE-operations so that it can be executed before diagnosing the processing elements of the tree machine.

Acknowledgement: The author would like to thank E. Ammann for valuable discussions.

References

[1] Mead C.A., Conway L.A.; Introduction to VLSI Systems, Addison-Wesley, Reading (Massachusetts) (1980)

[2] Bentley J.L, Kung H.T.; A tree machine for searching problems, in "Proc., IEEE 7th Int. Conf. on Parallel Processing, Aug. 1979", 257 (1979)

[3] Barsi F. et al.; A theory of diagnosability of digital systems, IEEE Trans. Comp. Vol. C-25, 585 - 593 (1976)

[4] Preparata F.P. et al.; On the connection assignment problem of diagnosable systems, IEEE Trans. on Elec. Compt. Vol. EC-16, 843 (1967)

[5] Friedman A.D., Simoncini L.; System-level fault-diagnosis, Computer Vol. 13, 47 - 53 (1980)

[6] Dal Cin M.; Fehlertolerante Systeme, Teubner-Verlag Stuttgart,(1979)

[7] Malek M.; A comparison connection assignment for diagnosis of multiprocessor systems, Proc. 7th Symp. on Comp. Architecture, La Baule, 31 - 35 (1980)

[8] Ammann E., Dal Cin M.; Efficient algorithms for comparison-based self-diagnosis, Self-Diagnosis and Fault-Tolerance, Proc. Tübingen (1981)

VERFAHREN ZUR ERKENNUNG VON EINFACH- UND DOPPEL-AUSFÄLLEN IN EINEM ZWEIKANALIGEN SCHALTKREISSYSTEM

R. Konakovsky

Institut für Regelungstechnik
und Prozeßautomatisierung
Universität Stuttgart

Zusammenfassung:

Ein Verfahren, das die Erkennung von Einfach- und Doppelausfällen in einem zweikanaligen Schaltkreissystem ermöglicht, wird vorgestellt. Um auch Doppelausfälle zu erkennen, werden dynamische Signale zur Darstellung der logischen "Null" und "Eins" verwendet. Jede logische Grundfunktion wird redundant realisiert und überwacht. Das Verfahren ist auch für hoch integrierte Schaltkreise (LSI, VLSI) geeignet, da keine Anforderung an den Ausschluß von Doppelausfällen gestellt wird. Alle Ausfallarten sind daher erkennbar. Das Verfahren ist auch zur Erkennung der n-fachausfälle in einem n-kanaligen System anwendbar. Die Realisierung eines dreikanaligen Systems wird kurz beschrieben. Das neue Verfahren wurde an einem zweikanaligen System praktisch erprobt. Die Anwendung des Verfahrens bietet insbesondere bei der Realisierung von sicheren Systemen Vorteile.

1. Einleitung

Die Mikroelektronik ist in den letzten Jahren in immer mehr Anwendungsbereiche vorgedrungen. Dabei ist das Problem der Zuverlässigkeit und Sicherheit insbesondere durch die enorm gestiegene Komplexität der Mikrobausteine und -systeme auch immer mehr in den Vordergrund gerückt. Fehlertoleranz und Entwurf fehlertoleranter Systeme ist eine Möglichkeit dieses Problem zu lösen. Auf diesem Gebiet hat Avizienis mit dem Entwurf und der Realisierung des STAR-Rechners bereits vor mehr als 10 Jahren einen bemerkenswerten Beitrag geleistet [1]. Eine Übersicht hierzu hat er in [2,3] gegeben.
Die möglichen Zuverlässigkeits- und Sicherheitsmaßnahmen in der Prozeß-

automatisierung wurden in [9] übersichtlich dargestellt. Eine wichtige Hilfe für den Entwurf sicherer Systeme ist die Möglichkeit, die Sicherheit quantitativ zu erfassen. Die Grundlagen für eine systematische Methodik zur Berechnung der Sicherheitskennwerte von Automatisierungssystemen wurden in [6] gelegt. Solche Berechnungen sind insbesondere beim Einsatz komplexer Mikroelektronik in sicherheitsrelevanten Bereichen wertvoll.

Es gibt nur wenige Versuche ein sicheres Mikrorechnersystem vorzuschlagen oder aufzubauen [4,7,12] . Zu einem Durchbruch ist es dabei leider noch nicht gekommen.

Im vorliegenden Beitrag wird ein neues Verfahren vorgestellt, das eine vollständige Ausfallerkennung, also beispielsweise eine Einfach- und Doppelausfallerkennung in einem zweikanaligen Schaltkreissystem ermöglicht. Wird dieses Verfahren an einem Mikroprozessor oder Speichermodul angewandt, so lassen sich alle Signale in diesen Bausteinen in jedem Verarbeitungstakt überwachen. Ein beliebiger Ausfall kann somit sehr schnell, in der Regel innerhalb eines Takts, erkannt werden.

2. Allgemeines Prinzip der Erkennung von Fehlern und Ausfällen

Parallele Redundanz mit Vergleich der Signale ist die wohl bekannteste Methode für die Erkennung von Ausfällen. Ist eine der parallel arbeitenden Einheiten ausgefallen, so kann sie durch Vergleich der Signale erkannt werden. Das hier verwendete Prinzip der Ausfallerkennung kann verallgemeinert werden:

In einem beliebigen Verfahren zur Erkennung von Fehlern bzw. Ausfällen werden mindestens zwei Signale/Daten verglichen, die die gleiche Information darstellen, die jedoch auf verschiedener Weise gewonnen wurden.

Bild 1 zeigt das allgemeine Prinzip der Erkennung von Fehlern und Ausfällen [8] . Darin bedeuten E_1, E_2, ... die verschiedenen Wege der Signal-/Datenverarbeitung und x_1, x_2, ... die zum Vergleich zur Verfügung gestellten Signale/Daten.

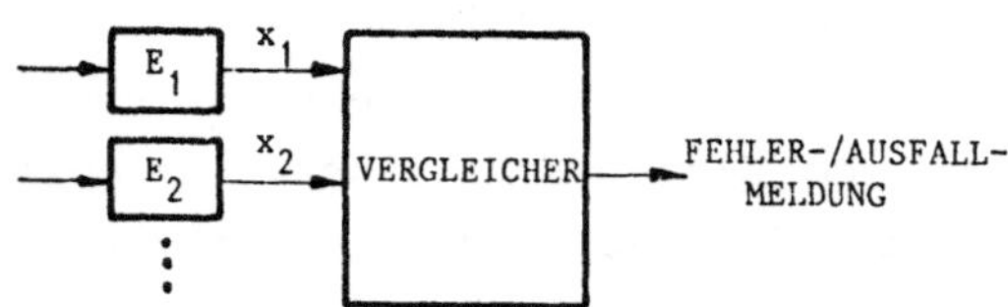

Bild 1 Allgemeines Prinzip der Fehlererkennung

Die Art der Verschiedenheit (Diversität) zwischen E_1, E_2, ... bestimmt die Art der erkennbaren Fehler und Ausfälle. Um diesen Zusammenhang zu verdeutlichen, werden Beispiele von Diversitätsarten und die dadurch erkennbaren Fehler-/Ausfallarten gebracht.

Diversität in Bedingungen

Die verschiedenen Wege E_1, E_2, ... stellen physikalisch die gleiche Einheit dar. Identische Eingangswerte werden unter verschiedenen Bedingungen verarbeitet. Die erhaltenen Ergebnisse x_1, x_2, ... werden verglichen. Die einfachste Form dieser Diversitätsart ist die "Zeitredundanz". Der unterschiedliche Zeitpunkt hat eigentlich unterschiedliche Bedingungen bei der Verwendung der gleichen Einheit zur Folge (interne und externe Bedingungen, wie Störfelder, physikalische/chemische Prozesse in der Einheit).
Erkennbare Fehler-/Ausfallarten: Sporadische Ausfälle.

Physikalische Diversität

Die verschiedenen Wege E_1, E_2, ... stellen physikalisch getrennte jedoch identische Einheiten dar, zum Beispiel identische Mikroprozessoren der gleichen Herstellungsserie.
Erkennbare Fehler-/Ausfallarten: Sporadische und statische Ausfälle.

Herstellungsdiversität

Die verschiedenen Wege E_1, E_2, ... stellen die gleiche Einheit dar, zum Beispiel identische Mikroprozessoren, die jedoch von verschiedenen Herstellern stammen.
Erkennbare Fehler-/Ausfallarten: Sporadische, statische Ausfälle sowie Herstellungsfehler.

Implementationsdiversität

Die verschiedenen Wege E_1, E_2, ... realisieren die gleiche Funktion, sie werden jedoch auf verschiedene Weise implementiert, zum Beispiel durch Verwendung der komplementären Logik.
Erkennbare Fehler-/Ausfallarten: Sporadische, statische Ausfälle, Herstellungsfehler, Implementationsfehler.

Diversität in der Funktion

Die verschiedenen Wege E_1, E_2, ... realisieren unterschiedliche Funktionen. Beispiel: Durch E_1 wird der Soll- und durch E_2 der Maximalwert (z.B. der Zuggeschwindigkeit) bestimmt. Der Vergleicher prüft ob $x_1 \leq x_2$. Vergleiche dieser Art sind als Plausibilitätsprüfungen bekannt.
Erkennbare Fehler-/Ausfallarten: Sporadische, statische Ausfälle, Herstellungsfehler, Implementationsfehler, Entwurfs-/Spezifikationsfehler.

In den drei ersten Beispielen, wenn E_1, E_2, ... identische Einheiten darstellen, wird der Begriff "Diversität" i.A. nicht verwendet, da die Diversität nicht unmittelbar ersichtlich ist und unterhalb der Herstellungs- bzw. Einsatztoleranzen liegt.

Während allen Phasen der Systementwicklung und -herstellung kann man jede beliebige Aktivität oder Systemkomponente diversitär ausführen oder realisieren. Zum Beispiel lassen sich verschiedene Entwurfsverfahren, Hilfsmittel, Programmiersprachen, Übersetzer, Betriebssysteme, Testsysteme, Hardware-Komponente, Kodes usw. anwenden.
Jede Diversitätsart trägt zu der Wirksamkeit der Fehler-/Ausfallerkennung im System bei. Die Gesamtwirksamkeit hängt noch von der Strategie ab, wie und wo eine Diversität angewandt ist. Eine gute Strategie kann wirkungsvoller sein als die "vollständige" Diversität.

In den folgenden Abschnitten wird gezeigt, wie man mit einer besonderen Strategie in zweikanaligen Systemen auch die Doppelausfälle bzw. im n-kanaligen auch die n-fachausfälle erkennen kann.

3. Zweikanalige Signalverarbeitung

Bei der Anwendung einer zweikanaligen Signalverarbeitung können verschiedene Signaldarstellungen verwendet werden (H/L bedeutet hoher/niedriger Signalpegel):

(a) Äquivalente statische Signale (Positive Logik)

Logisch Null	Kanal 1 :	L
	Kanal 2 :	L
Logisch Eins	Kanal 1 :	H
	Kanal 2 :	H

(b) Antivalente statische Signale (Positive Logik)

Logisch Null	Kanal 1 :	L
	Kanal 2 :	H
Logisch Eins	Kanal 1 :	H
	Kanal 2 :	L

(c) Äquivalente dynamische Signale (Positive und negative Logik)

Logisch Null	Kanal 1 :	L H L H ...
	Kanal 2 :	L H L H ...
Logisch Eins	Kanal 1 :	H L H L ...
	Kanal 2 :	H L H L ...

(d) Antivalente dynamsiche Signale (Positive und negative Logik)

Logisch Null	Kanal 1 :	L H L H ...
	Kanal 2 :	H L H L ...
Logisch Eins	Kanal 1 :	H L H L ...
	Kanal 2 :	L H L H ...

(e) Äquivalente und antivalente dynamische Signale (alle 4 Phasen)

Logisch Null { Kanal 1 : L L H H ...
Kanal 2 : L H H L ...

Logisch Eins { Kanal 1 : H H L L ...
Kanal 2 : H L L H ...

In jedem Verarbeitungsschritt wird entweder die Äquivalenz oder die Antivalenz der Signale ständig oder wechselweise geprüft. Bei der statischen Signaldarstellung (a) bzw. (b) ist die Ausfallerkennung datenflußabhängig, während bei der dynamischen Darstellung (c) bis (e) die Ausfallerkennung vom Datenfluß unabhängig ist.

Der Fall (a) tritt bei einer einfachen Parallelredundanz identischer Schaltkreise auf. Zum Beispiel wird diese Signaldarstellung beim Parallelbetrieb von zwei identischen Mikroprozessoren oder Mikrorechnern mit Vergleich der Ausgangs- bzw. Bussignale verwendet [12] . Im Fall (b) wird der zweite Kanal in komplementärer Technik implementiert. Die komplementäre Signaldarstellung kann auch bei hochintegrierten Schaltkreisen angewandt werden [11] .

Die kürzeste Ausfallerkennungszeit z.B. nur ein Verarbeitungsschritt, erhält man durch Anwendung der dynamischen Darstellung, falls nicht nur Ausgangssignale, sondern alle Signale der beiden Kanäle miteinander verglichen werden [1o,13] . Eine solche Eigenschaft bietet insbesondere bei der Realisierung sicherer Systeme große Vorteile.

Doppelausfälle, die entweder unabhängig oder wegen gemeinsamen Ursachen auftreten, können trotz der Verwendung der dynamischen Signaldarstellung (c) oder (d) unerkannt bleiben. Dagegen werden sie mit Hilfe der Signaldarstellung (e) erkannt. Eine genaue Beschreibung des Verfahrens der Doppelausfallerkennung ist im folgenden Abschnitt dargestellt.

4. Erkennung von Doppelausfällen in einem zweikanaligen Schaltkreissystem

Die verwendete Signaldarstellung (e) zeigt nochmals das Bild 2.

Zur Erprobung des Verfahrens kann für die Verknüpfung und Speicherung von Daten mit der gewählten Signaldarstellung auf die Bausteine des URTL-Schaltkreissystems U1 zurückgegriffen werden [12] . Im URTL-Schaltkreissystem U1 werden, da in den relativ niedrig integrierten Bausteinen Doppelausfälle sicherungstechnisch beherrscht werden, nur antivalente dynamische Signale verwendet (siehe oben (d)).

Der Verknüpfungsbaustein muß daher noch um eine Überwachungseinheit für äquivalente Signale erweiter werden. Für die Überwachung der äquivalenten Signale muß entweder ein neuer Überwachungsverstärker entworfen werden, oder es kann der im URTL-System vorhandene Antivalenz-Überwachungsverstärker verwendet werden. Im zweiten Fall wird die Äquivalenz - auf die Antivalenzüberwachung zurückgeführt.

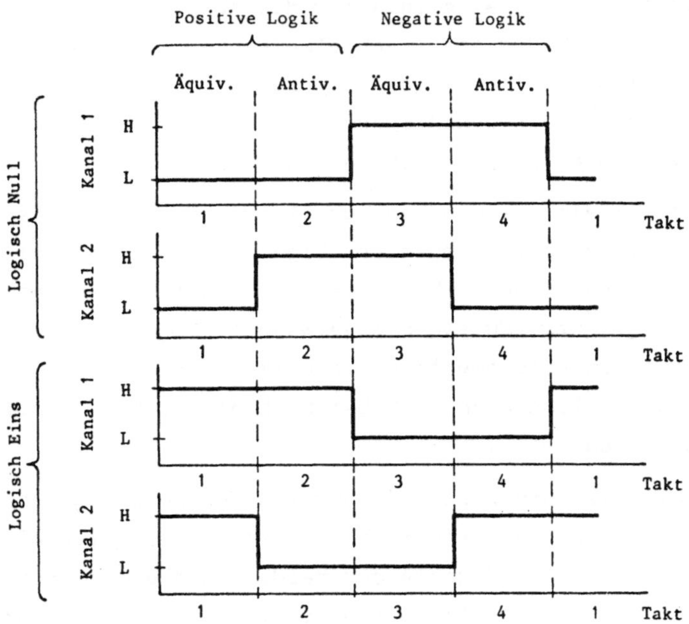

Bild 2 Signaldarstellung für logisch Null und Eins

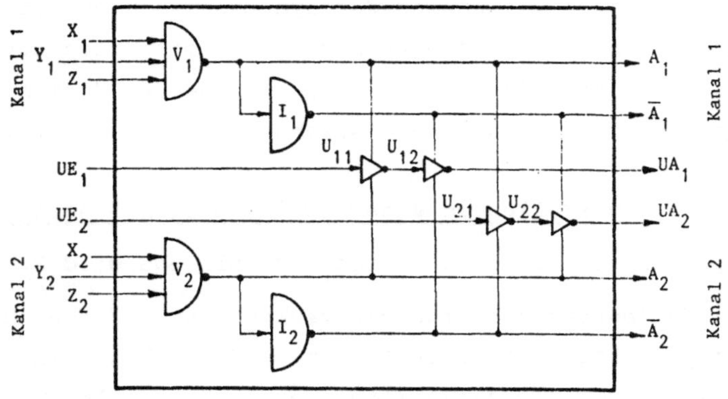

Bild 3 Verknüpfungsbaustein

In Bild 3 ist der Verknüpfungsbaustein mit vier Antivalenz-Überwachungsverstärkern dargestellt.

Mit den Invertierern I_1, I_2 werden die Ausgangssignale der Verknüpfungselemente V_1, V_2 invertiert. Die Überwachungsverstärker U_{11}, U_{12} sind bei antivalenten Signalen an V_1, V_2 bzw. I_1, I_2 durchlässig, d.h. ein am Eingang UE_1 angelegter Überwachungspuls erscheint am Ausgang UA_1. Die Verstärker U_{21}, U_{22} sind dagegen bei äquivalenten Signalen an V_1, V_2 bzw. I_1, I_2 d.h. bei antivalenten Signalen an V_1, I_2 bzw. V_2, I_1 an denen sie auch angeschlossen sind, durchlässig.

Die Verknüpfungselemente V_1, V_2 realisieren eine negierte 2 aus 3 Mehrheitslogik. Wird dem Eingangspaar Z_1, Z_2 die logisch Null (Eins) aufgeprägt, so läßt sich mit den übrigen zwei Eingangspaaren X und Y die NOR (NAND)-Verknüpfung realisieren.

Durch Verwendung der negierten Ausgänge ergibt sich daraus die OR (AND)-Verknüpfung. Das Vertauschen der Kanäle entspricht hier nicht der Inversion wie es bei dem URTL-System der Fall ist.

Mit dem Verknüpfungsbaustein läßt sich also eine der 7 Funktionen OR, NOR, AND, NAND, 2v3, $\overline{2v3}$ und NICHT realisieren. Die NICHT-Funktion ist meistens nicht erforderlich, da an jedem Baustein auch die negierten Signale zur Verfügung stehen.

Für die Speicherung von Daten wird ein Flip-flop-Baustein mit zwei getakten RS-Master-Slave-Flip-flops verwendet, der einer Modifizierung des Flip-flop-Bausteins im URTL-System entspricht [13] .

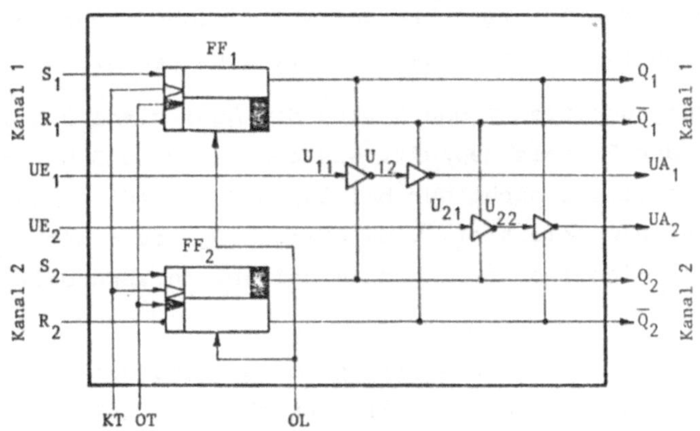

Bild 4 Flip-flop-Baustein

Beide Flip-folps FF_1, FF_2, werden durch beide Taktsignale OT und KT (Original-, Komplementärtakt) gesteuert. Sie übernehmen bei der negativen Flanke von OT das negierte und bei der positiven Flanke von KT das nichtinvertierte Eingangssignal und geben es am Ausgang wieder. Im Kanal 2 wird der invertierte Ausgang verwendet.

Bild 5 zeigt links vier Verarbeitungsschritte, wenn am Eingang des Flipflops der Wert logisch Null ansteht, danach weitere 4 Schritte wenn sich dieser Wert auf Eins ändert (Signalwechsel im dritten Schritt), und schließlich 4 Schritte wenn die Signale logisch Eins darstellen.

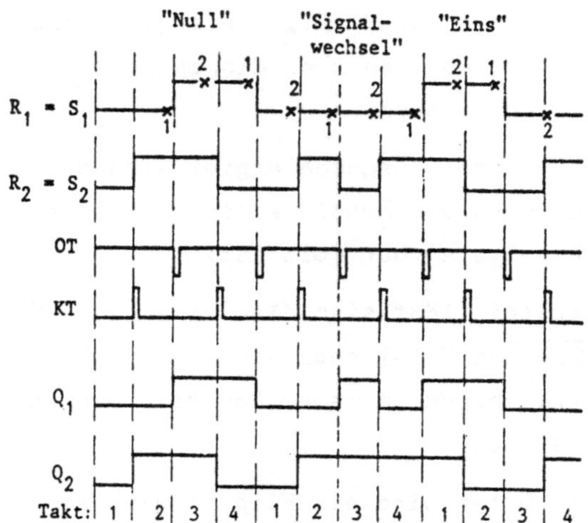

Bild 5 Zeitdiagramm der Signale am Flip-flop-Baustein beim Signalwechsel

Es werden die Werte Nr. 1 invertiert und Nr. 2 nicht invertiert am Ausgang des Flip-flops (Q_1) im nächsten Schritt ausgegeben.

In den Verarbeitungschritten 1 und 3 wird die Äquivalenz und in 2 und 4 die Antivalenz der Signale geprüft. Wie aus dem Bild 5 hervorgeht, ist die Äquivalenz/Antivalenz nicht nur bei logisch Null/Eins, sondern auch beim Signalwechsel gewährleistet. Eine Abweichung davon wird als Ausfall interpretiert. Der Signalwechsel kann im beliebigen Verarbeitungsschritt stattfinden.

Aufgrund der gewählten Signaldarstellung und an Hand der beschriebenen Verknüpfungs- und Speicherbausteine ist ersichtlich, daß ein beliebiger statischer Einfach- sowie Doppelausfall entweder durch die Äquivalenz- oder Antivalenzprüfung im gleichen oder nachfolgenden Verarbeitungsschritt erkannt wird.

Die Verwendung dieser besonderen dynamischen Signaldarstellung kann z.B. insofern vorteilhaft sein, als sie bei einer Entwicklung komplexerer URTL-Bausteine die bisher im lay out der URTL-ICs FUH 105 und FUJ 105 realisierten Maßnahmen zum Erkennen von Doppelausfällen ersetzen kann. Da es einen engen Zusammenhang zwischen Diversitätsarten und den erkennbaren Fehler-/Ausfallarten gibt (s. Abschnitt 2), hängt diese Verbesserung der Ausfallerkennbarkeit mit der Erweiterung der vorhandenen Diversitätsarten zusammen: Erweiterung der Diversität in Bedingungen hinsichtlich der wechselnden Betriebsarten zwischen positiver und negativer Logik jeweils mit äquivalenten und antivalenten Signalen.

In Bild 6 ist das Blockbild des zweikanaligen Schaltkreissystems dargestellt. Es entspricht dem Blockbild des URTL-Systems [1o] . Der Unterschied in der Signaldarstellung und in der Realisierung der Bausteine ist im Blockbild nur durch eine andere Überwachungseinheit erkennbar, die vier Überwachungsverstärker enthält.

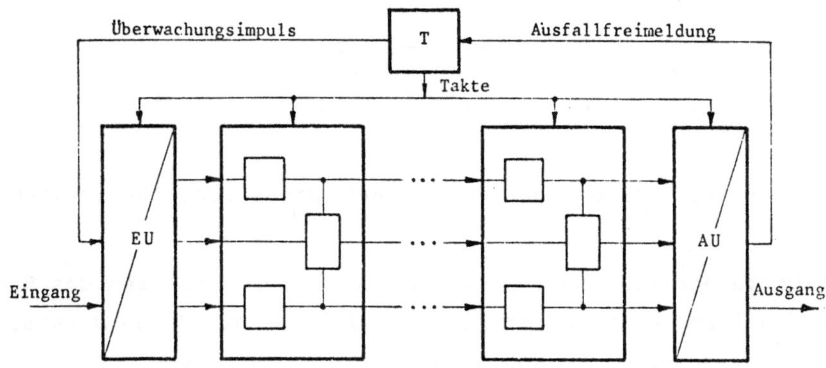

Bild 6 Blockbild des Schaltkreissystems

Die Ein/Ausgangssignalumsetzer sowie die Taktversorgung und Überwachung müssen der neuen Signaldarstellung angepaßt werden (EU, AU, T).

5. Erweiterung des Verfahrens auf Drei- und Mehrkanalige Systeme

Die in Abschnitt 3 beschriebenen Signaldarstellungen lassen sich zum Teil (b und d) oder vollständig (a, c und e) in mehrkanaligen Systemen verwenden. Zwischen den Kanälen kann zwar die Äquivalenz jedoch nicht die Antivalenz in allen Kanal-Kombinationen auftreten. Ist zwischen zwei Kanälen eine Antivalenz vorhanden, so kann der dritte Kanal nur noch mit einem Kanal antivalent sein.

Bild 7 zeigt die vollständige und eine gekürzte Signaldarstellung für logisch Null vom Typ (e). In der vollständigen Darstellung werden alle 8 Kombinationen und in der Gekürzten 6 Kombinationen der Signalpegel

(H/L) verwendet. Den Wert logisch Eins erhält man durch die Negation der drei Signale.

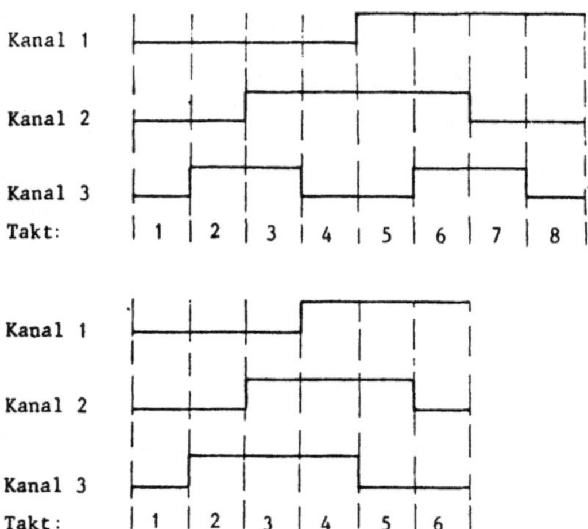

Bild 7 Vollständige und gekürzte Signaldarstellung für logisch Null

Die gekürzte Darstellung ergibt sich durch das Versetzen des Signals vom 1. Kanal um $\pm$ 1 Schritt im 2. und 3. Kanal. Beide Darstellungen sind auch allgemein in n-kanaligen Systemen verwendbar. In der gekürzten Darstellung ist die Periode 2 n Schritte groß und die Signale sind je um 1 Schritt versetzt.

Der Verknüpfungsbaustein von Bild 3 ist für ein dreikanaliges System in Bild 8 dargestellt.

Die Äquivalenz und Antivalenz zwischen den Kanälen wird durch die Überwacher entsprechend der Definition der Signaldarstellung getrennt in jedem Verarbeitungsschritt geprüft. Ein beliebiger am Ausgang eingetretener statischer Einfach-, Doppel- sowie Dreifachausfall kann dadurch im gleichen oder im nachfolgenden Schritt erkannt werden. Das dreikanalige System kann beim Ausfall eines Kanals als ein zweikanaliges System ohne Unterbrechung weiter betrieben werden.

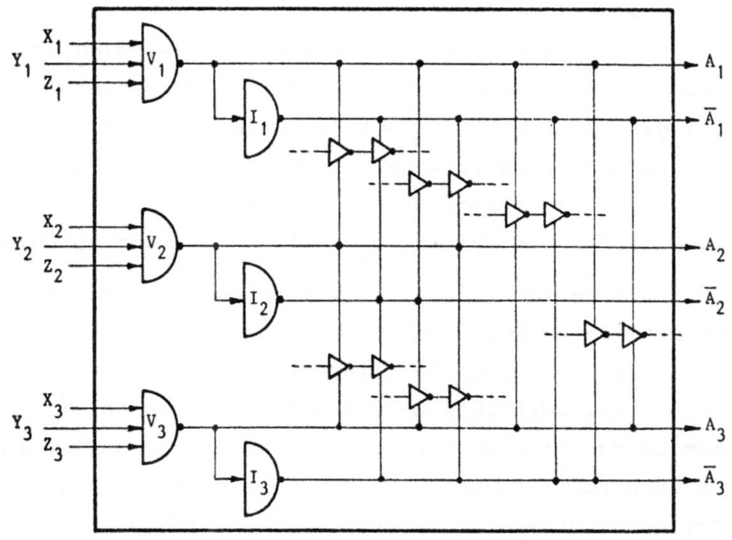

Bild 8 Verknüpfungsbaustein eines dreikanaligen Systems

6. Anwendung des Verfahrens für die Realisierung von sicheren Systemen

Bei der Realisierung von sicheren Systemen spielt das Problem einer vollständigen und schnellen Erkennung von Fehlern bzw. Ausfällen eine wichtige Rolle.

Das hier beschriebene Verfahren zur Erkennung von Einfach- und Doppelausfällen erfüllt beide Anforderungen. Ein beliebiger am Ausgang eines Bausteins eingetretener Einfach- oder Doppelausfall wird entweder sofort oder spätestens im nachfolgenden Verarbeitungsschritt erkannt. Da man im zweikanaligen System höchstens mit einem Doppelausfall zu rechnen hat, ist die Vollständigkeit der Ausfallerkennbarkeit erreicht. Mehrfachausfälle die in einem Kanal auftreten, werden als Einfachausfälle erkannt. Mehrfachausfälle die verteilt auf den beiden Kanälen auftreten werden als Doppelausfälle erkannt.

Ausfälle, die im Überwachungsverstärker oder in der Überwachungseinrichtung auftreten, müssen gesondert behandelt werden. Beim Überwachungsverstärker läßt sich, wie beim URTL-System, eine vorgegebene Ausfallrichtung erreichen, so daß die möglichen Ausfallarten sofort erkannt werden.

Die Überwachungseinrichtung ist so aufzubauen, daß sie nur bei der Ausfallfreimeldung die erforderlichen Signale (z.B. Takt) im nächsten Verarbeitungsschritt bereitstellt (Bild 6). Wenn ein Überwachungspuls (Ausfallfreimeldung) nicht ankommt, so wird die Taktversorgung unterbrochen und die gesamte Schaltung ruht (sicherer Zustand). Das tritt z.B. dann auf, wenn an einem Verknüpfungs- oder Speicherbaustein die geforderte Äquivalenz/Antivalenz nicht vorhanden ist. Der Überwachungsverstärker ist dann für den Überwachungspuls nicht mehr durchlässig.

Der Hauptvorteil des neuen Verfahrens, die Doppelausfallerkennung ohne die bisherigen besonderen Maßnahmen im lay out der integrierten Bausteine, kann dann eine große Rolle spielen, wenn eine Implementierung von Bausteinen mit LSI oder VLSI angestrebt wird. Die Anforderung, daß Ausfälle in den beiden Kanälen statistisch unabhängig auftreten, um Doppelausfälle unwahrscheinlich zu machen, muß nicht gestellt werden, da diese Ausfallarten erkennbar gemacht worden sind und wie Einfachausfälle behandelt werden.

Ein nach diesem Verfahren implementierter Mikroprozessor-Baustein, Speichermodul oder ein kompletter Mikrorechner hat hinsichtlich des Einsatzes in sicherheitsrelevanten Bereichen eine Reihe von Vorteilen:

(1) Jedes Signal (Bit) wird in jedem Verarbeitungsschritt überwacht, d.h. der Mikroprozessor oder andere LSI-, VLSI-Bausteine werden in jedem Takt vollständig überwacht.

(2) Ein beliebiger Ausfall wird sehr schnell, in der Regel innerhalb eines Takts, nachdem er sich am Ausgang eines Bausteins bemerkbar gemacht hat, erkannt.

(3) Nicht nur statische sondern auch sporadische Ausfallarten werden erkannt.

(4) Die meist sehr schwierig erkennbaren Ausfallarten, die von der augenblicklichen Bedingung, z.B. von der Verteilung der 0/1 Signale im Speichermodul oder von der Folge der 0/1 Signale im Mikroprozessor (von der Hardware-Software-Interaktion) abhängig sind, d.h. eine deterministische Ursache haben, jedoch einen sporadischen Charakter aufweisen, werden ebenfalls in der Regel innerhalb eines Takts erkannt.

Das hier beschriebene Verfahren erfüllt die für die Sicherheit wichtige Anforderung nach vollständiger Ausfallerkennung und kurzer Ausfalloffenbarungszeit wesentlich besser als alle bisher bekannten Verfahren.

Das neue Verfahren wurde praktisch erprobt. Ein Demonstrationsgerät wurde aufgebaut, mit dem man die Ausfallerkennbarkeit direkt am Verknüpfungs- und Speicherbaustein (Bild 3 und 4) zeigen kann [5] .

7. Schlußbemerkungen

Ein neues Verfahren zur Erkennung von Einfach- und Doppelausfällen in einem zweikanaligen Schaltkreissystem wird vorgestellt.

Zunächst wird ein allgemeines und einheitliches Prinzip der Erkennung von Fehlern und Ausfällen beschrieben. Darin wird der enge Zusammenhang zwischen Diversitätsarten und erkennbaren Fehler-/Ausfallarten herausgestellt und an Beispielen erläutert. Die Wirksamkeit der Fehler-/Ausfallerkennung im Gesamtsystem hängt von der Wahl der verwendeten Diversitäten ab. Diese Zusammenhänge werden auch in dem vorgestellten Verfahren deutlich. Durch volle Dynamisierung der Signaldarstellung, d.h. durch eine ständige Umschaltung der Signalpegel zwischen allen 4 Kombinationen wird eine vollständige Ausfallerkennung erreicht. Diese volle Dynamisierung der Signaldarstellung kann man als eine Vergrößerung der sog. Diversität der Bedingungen betrachten.

Das neue Verfahren kann auch auf drei- und mehrkanalige Systeme angewandt werden. Dadurch werden dann auch die Drei- bzw. n-fach-Ausfälle erkennbar. Beispielhaft wurde ein Verknüpfungsbaustein für ein dreikanaliges System angegeben.

Die noch mit keinem Verfahren erreichte so weitgehend von der Gestaltung des lay outs unabhängige vollständige Ausfallerkennung wie z.B. Einfach- und Doppelausfallerkennung in einem zweikanaligen Schaltkreissystem, ist mit dem hier beschriebenen Verfahren verwirklicht worden. Diese Eigenschaft ist für die Realisierung von sicheren Systemen mit LSI bzw. VLSI sehr vorteilhaft, da der sicherheitsrelevante Teil der lay out-Arbeiten wesentlich vereinfacht wird.

Literaturverzeichnis

[1] Avizienis, A. et. al (1971). The STAR (Self-Testing-And-Repairing) Computer: An investigation of the theory and practice of fault-tolerant computer design. IEEE Trans. Computers Vol. C-2o, No. 11, pp 1312-1321

[2] Avizienis, A. (1977). Fault-Tolerant Computing-Progress, Problems and Prospects. Proceedings of the IFIP Conference, pp 59-72

[3] Avizienis, A. (1978). Fault-Tolerance: The Survival Attribute of Digital Systems. Proceedings of the IEEE, Vol. 66, No. 1o, pp 11o9-1125

[4] Brauer, H. (1981). Das sichere Mikrorechnersystem LOGISAFE. Fachtagung Prozeßrechner, München 1981, pp 261-269

[5] Fleckenstein, J. (1977). Erkennung von Einfach- und Doppelfehlern in einem zweikanaligen Schaltkreissystem. Studienarbeit, Universität Stuttgart

[6] Konakovsky, R. (1977). Definition und Berechnung der Sicherheit von Automatisierungssystemen. Vieweg-Verlag Braunschweig

[7] Konakovsky, R. (1979). On Diversified Parallel Microcomputer System. Proceedings of the IFAC-Workshop on Safety of Computer Control Systems in Stuttgart, pp 81-88

[8] Konakovsky, R. (1979). On Safe Information Processing System. Proceedings of the IFAC-Congress, August 22-28, 1981, Kyoto/Japan

[9] Lauber, R. (1981). Zuverlässigkeit und Sicherheit in der Prozeßautomatisierung. Fachtagung Prozeßrechner, München 1981, pp 52-64

[10] Lohmann, H.L. (1974). URTL Schaltkreissystem U1 mit hoher Sicherheit und automatischer Fehlerdiagnose, Siemens-Zeitschrift 48, No. 7, pp 49o-494

[11] Sedmak, R.M. and Liebergot, H.L. (1978). Fault-Tolerance of a General Purpose Computer Implemented by Very Large Scale Integration. Proceedings of the FTCS-8, Toulouse, pp 137-143

[12] Strelow, H., Uebel, H. (1978). Das Sichere Mikrocomputersystem SIMIS. Signal + Draht 7o, No. 4, pp 82-86

[13] Wießell, R. (1974). Grundbausteine und Logikbaugruppe des URTL-Schaltkreissystems U1. Siemens-Zeitschrift 48 (1974), Heft 7, pp 495-499.

EIN BAUKASTENKONZEPT FÜR FEHLERTOLERANTE MULTI-MIKROPROZESSORSYSTEME

Erik Maehle
Shi-Cheng Hu

Universität Erlangen-Nürnberg
Institut für Mathematische Maschinen
und Datenverarbeitung (III)

Zusammenfassung:

Vorgestellt wird ein Baukastenkonzept für fehlertolerante Multi-Mikroprozessorkonfigurationen. Kernstück des Konzepts bilden Mikrocomputer-Module, die über Multiportspeicher baukastenartig zu redundanten Konfigurationen zusammengesetzt werden können. Der Beitrag geht ausführlicher auf die in einem experimentellen System implementierten Fehlertoleranztechniken (z.B. Transparente Selbsttestprogramme, Nachbarschaftsüberwachung, Fail-Soft-Verhalten) ein und gibt eine quantitative Abschätzung der erzielbaren Zuverlässigkeitskenngrößen anhand analytischer Zuverlässigkeitsmodelle.

0. Einleitung

Ein fehlertolerantes Computersystem ist nach Avizienis ein System, das die eingebaute Fähigkeit besitzt, die fortgesetzte korrekte Ausführung seiner Programme und Ein/Ausgabefunktionen (ohne äußere Hilfe) selbst bei der Anwesenheit einer bestimmten Menge physikalischer Fehler aufrecht zu erhalten [1]. Es sind bereits eine ganze Reihe Beispiele für fehlertolerante Rechner in der Literatur bekannt. Bei nahezu allen diesen Ansätzen handelt es sich allerdings um Spezialentwürfe z.B. aus dem Bereich der Raum- und Luftfahrt, der Vermittlungstechnik, der Prozeßrechentechnik, der Arbeitsplatzcomputer [2 - 5], die auf ihr relativ enges Einsatzgebiet zugeschnitten sind und sich nicht immer leicht verallgemeinern lassen.

Mit dem weiteren Vordringen der Mikrocomputertechnik in Anwendungsgebiete mit oft recht unterschiedlichen Anforderungen an Verarbeitungsleistung, Zuverlässigkeit und Verfügbarkeit, liegt der Wunsch nahe, eine Art Baukastensystem zu besitzen, mit dem je nach den gestellten Anforderungen und tragbaren Kosten ein spezieller, zugeschnittener fehlertoleranter Rechner aus wenigen preiswerten vorgefertigten Komponenten leicht konfiguriert werden kann. Als Bausteine eines solchen Systems bieten sich möglichst universelle Mikrocomputerkomponenten an, aus denen sich ein weites Spektrum fehlertoleranter Multi-Mikroprozessorsysteme zusammensetzen läßt. Der Einsatz mehrerer kooperierender Prozessoren erlaubt sowohl die Fehlertoleranz (Nutzung von Redundanz) als auch die Verarbeitungsleistung (Nutzung von Parallelarbeit) in weiten Grenzen zu variieren.

Ein solcher Ansatz wird derzeit im Rahmen des Projekts DIRMU (Distributed Reconfigurable Multiprocessor Kit)* an der Universität Erlangen-Nürnberg verfolgt [6]. Im folgenden wird zunächst ein kurzer Überblick über das Grundkonzept des DIRMU-Multi-Mikroprozessor-Baukastens gegeben. Etwas ausführlicher wird anschließend auf einen experimentellen Baustein eingegangen und schließlich das Fail-Soft-Verhalten einer ringförmigen Beispielkonfiguration beschrieben.

1. Das DIRMU-Baukastenkonzept

Die verschiedenen Aspekte des DIRMU-Konzepts sind bereits in [6] ausführlich beschrieben. Einige grundsätzliche Untersuchungen über fehlertolerante DIRMU-Konfigurationen sind in [7] enthalten. Hier sollen daher nur die wichtigsten Grundlagen vorgestellt werden, soweit sie für das fehlertolerante Experimentiersystem von Bedeutung sind.

Grundelement des DIRMU-Baukastens ist ein universeller Baustein (Abb. 1), bestehend aus einem Prozessor (P-Modul) und einem Multiportspeicher (M-Modul). Über die sog. P-Ports kann der Prozessor sowohl auf 'seinen' M-Modul als auch auf die M-Moduln anderer benachbarter Bausteine zugreifen. Die Verbindungen zwischen P-Ports und M-Ports sind steckbar ausgeführt, so daß der Systementwickler leicht eine Vielzahl verschiedener Multiprozessorstrukturen aus mehreren gleichartigen DIRMU-Bausteinen konfigurieren kann.

Die Kommunikation zwischen den einzelnen Bausteinen wird softwareseitig durch ein lokales Betriebssystem in jedem P-Modul unterstützt.

Soll ein spezielles Multimikroprozessorsystem für ein bestimmtes Anwendungsgebiet aufgebaut werden, kann z.B. folgendermaßen vorgegangen werden:

(1) Zerlegen des Anwenderproblems in klar strukturierte Teilaufgaben
(2) Zuordnung der Teilaufgaben zu einzelnen Bausteinen
(3) Verbindung der Bausteine
    (a) je nach Problemstruktur (datenflußorientiert)
    (b) je nach Fehlertoleranzanforderungen (redundanzorientiert)
(4) Programmierung der Bausteine unter Ausnutzung des lokalen Betriebssystems.

* gefördert von der DFG unter Gz 322 647

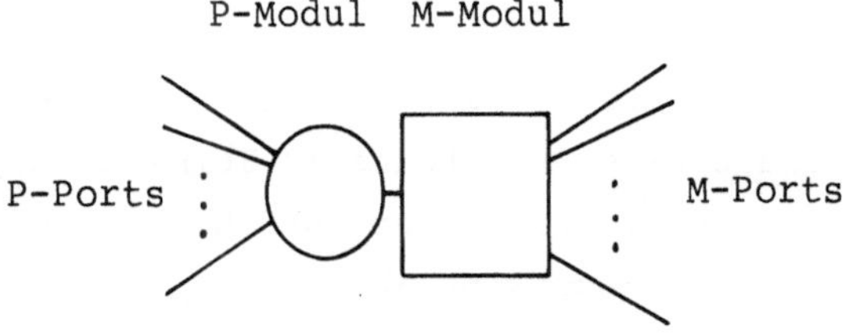

Abb. 1: Prinzipieller Aufbau eines DIRMU-Bausteins

2. Ein experimenteller Baustein für fehlertolerante DIRMU-Konfigurationen

2.1 Hardwarestruktur

Den prinzipiellen Aufbau des experimentellen Bausteins zeigt Abbildung 2. Der P-Modul enthält außer dem Mikroprozessor (SC/MP II) privaten RAM-Speicher (4KB), privaten ROM-Speicher (18KB) und E/A-Schnittstellen. Die Portlogik [8],[9] ist auf Platinen am P-Modul Ausgang und M-Modul Eingang verteilt und besteht im wesentlichen aus Logik zur Adreßumsetzung, Leitungstreibern und Einrichtungen zum Hardware-Speicherschutz. Die Verbindung zwischen den verschiedenen Moduln ist steckbar ausgelegt (64 pol. Flachbandkabel von max 1-2m Länge). Zur Auflösung von Speicherzugriffskonflikten auf den M-Modul (4KB RAM) dient die Kontrolleinheit CTR, die außerdem noch Spezialhardware zur Unterstützung der Nachbarschaftsüberwachung enthält. Jeder Baustein bestehend aus P- und M-Modul hat ein eigenes Netzgerät.

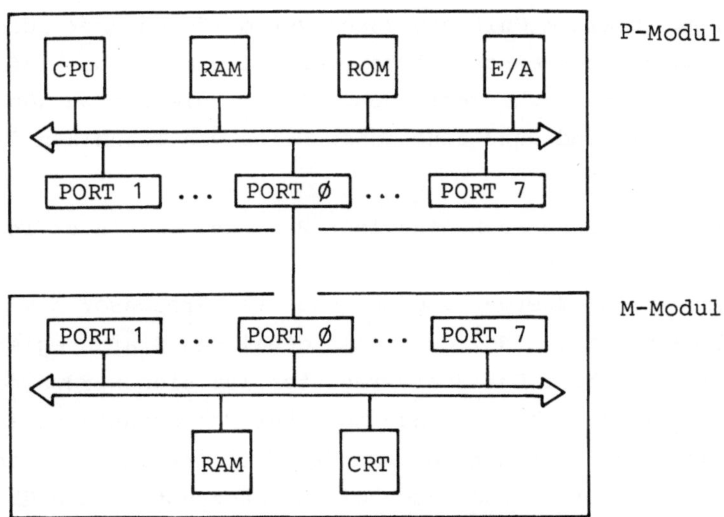

Abb. 2: Hardwarestruktur eines experimentellen Bausteins

2.2 Transparente Selbsttestprogramme

Da preiswerte Standardhardware eingesetzt werden sollte, wurde die Fehlererkennung innerhalb eines Bausteins in Form von Selbsttestprogrammen [10],[11] realisiert. Sie laufen zunächst als ganzes unmittelbar nach dem Rücksetzen des Bausteins ab um sicherzustellen, daß die Hardware intakt ist. Um auch Fehler während des laufenden Betriebs aufdecken zu können, werden sie außerdem entweder in festen Zeitabständen oder anstelle von Leerschleifen zyklisch in kurzen Abschnitten eingeblendet und laufen damit sozusagen transparent für die übrige Software ab. Dabei ist es wesentlich, daß der Test möglichst schnell unterbrochen werden kann. Testalgorithmen für Mikrocomputerkomponenten, die diese Eigenschaft besitzen, wurden bereits in [11] vorgestellt und konnten ohne Schwierigkeiten auf dem experimentellen Baustein implementiert werden [12]. Der Programmumfang beträgt für CPU-, ROM- und RAM-Test zusammen ca. 4KB, die maximale Unterbrechungsantwortzeit 433 μsec (Befehlszyklus des Mikroprozessors 5-22 μsec). Ein vollständiger Testzyklus dauert je nach verwendeten Speichertests bis zu einigen Sekunden. Das gesamte Testprogramm ist im ROM-Bereich des P-Moduls abgelegt.

Erkennt das Selbsttestprogramm einen Fehler, wird die defekte Karte durch eine Anzeige auf der Frontplatte identifiziert und der Mikroprozessor in den HALT-Zustand versetzt.

2.3 Nachbarschaftsüberwachung

Transparente Selbsttestprogramme können nur Fehler innerhalb eines Bausteins erkennen. In einem Multiprozessorsystem müssen aber auch die übrigen Prozessoren über einen solchen Vorfall unmittelbar informiert werden, um eine automatische Fehlerbehandlung einleiten zu können. Im Experimentiersystem sind dazu eine ganze Reihe von Techniken implementiert worden (Abb. 3).

Die Kommunikation zwischen den einzelnen Prozessoren findet in DIRMU-Konfigurationen lediglich über den Multiportspeicher statt, der folglich auch zur gegenseitigen Überwachung benachbarter Prozessoren verwendet werden muß. Eine besondere Rolle spielen dabei das Statusregister und die Testergebnis-Mailbox. Das Statusregister ist eine Hardwareeinrichtung, mit deren Hilfe sich ein Prozessor über Fehlerzustände in seinen Nachbarprozessoren durch einen lesenden Zugriff informieren kann. Einige Bits des Statusregisters können auch einen Interrupt in den überwachenden Prozessoren auslösen. Realisiert sind derzeit u.a. Statusbits für den HALT-Zustand (Fehlermeldung Selbsttestprogramme!), Stromversorgungsausfall und die Verletzung des Speicherschutzes.

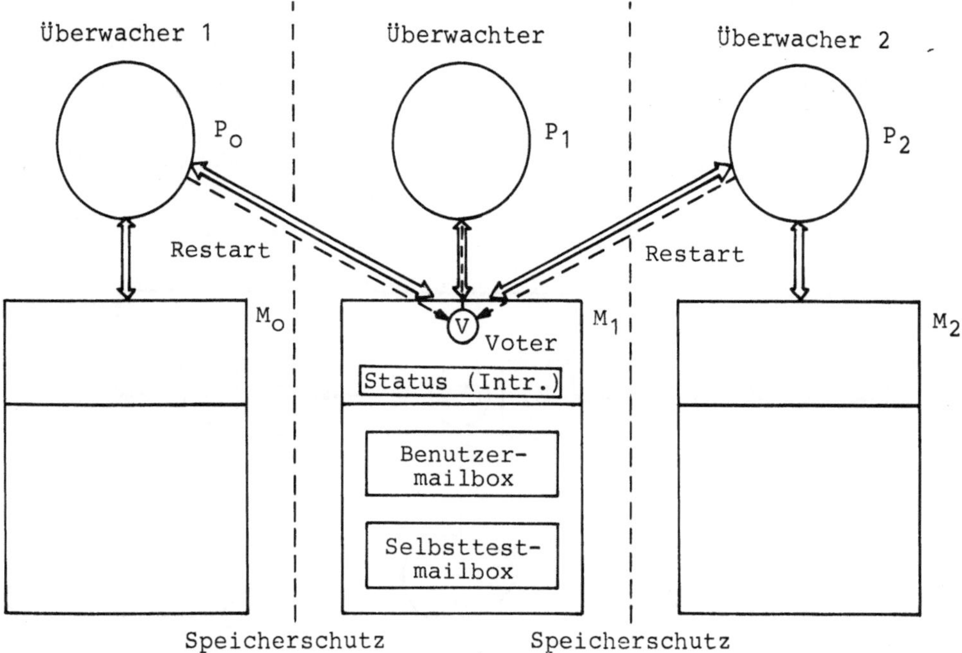

Abb. 3: Nachbarschaftsüberwachung

In einer späteren Ausbaustufe können auch die Ausgänge von Prüfschaltkreisen bei der Verwendung fehlererkennender Codes angeschlossen werden.

Nach jedem Durchlauf einer Testroutine wird das Testergebnis in der Testergebnis-Mailbox abgelegt und ein Zähler erhöht. Anhand des Zählerstandes können die überwachenden Prozessoren feststellen, ob überhaupt noch Testprogramme ausgeführt werden, anhand des Inhalts der Testergebnis-Mailbox können genauere Informationen über den aufgetretenen Fehler ausgelesen werden. Zum Schutz des überwachten Prozessors vor unerlaubten Zugriffen seiner Überwacher (die ja ebenfalls defekt werden können), ist ein Hardware-Schreibschutz in den Ports vorgesehen.

Haben die überwachenden Prozessoren einen Fehler in einem gemeinsamen Nachbarn erkannt, müssen sie ihn im Rahmen der Fehlerbehandlung wieder neu starten können. Dazu können sie über die Ports ein Restart-Signal absetzen. Um einen Mißbrauch durch einen defekten Prozessor zu verhindern, kann das Restart-Signal hardwaremäßig von einer Mehrheitsentscheidung sämtlicher Nachbarn abhängig gemacht werden (Hardware Voter).

3. Beispielkonfiguration

3.1 Systemstruktur und Zeitverhalten

Als Beispiel eines fehlertoleranten Multi-Mikroprozessorsystems aus den beschriebenen Bausteinen wurde die in Abb. 4 gezeigte Konfiguration aufgebaut. Baustein B_i ist dabei ringförmig mit Baustein $B_{i+1 \bmod 3}$ verbunden und kann ihn nach den oben beschriebenen Verfahren überwachen. Solange nur maximal ein Baustein defekt ist, kann diese Situation automatisch erkannt werden und das System bis zur Reparatur der defekten Komponente mit Hilfe der verbleibenden zwei Bausteine mit verminderter Leistung weiterarbeiten.

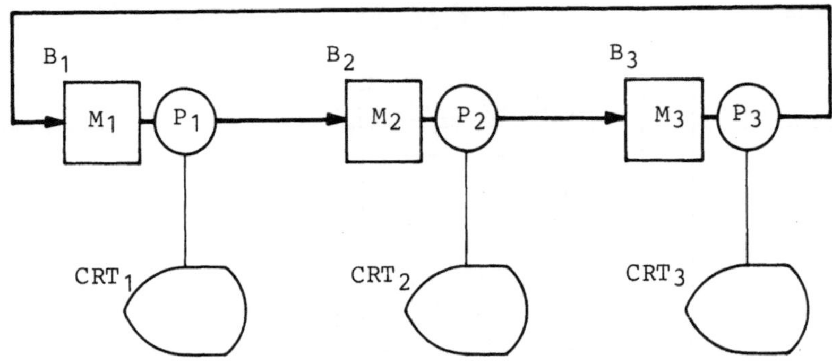

Abb. 4: Ringförmige Beispielkonfiguration aus experimentellen DIRMU-Bausteinen

Die dabei ablaufenden Vorgänge sind in Abb. 5 etwas genauer dargestellt. Das obere Diagramm zeigt den Fehlerzustand des Systems abgetragen über der Zeit. Dabei wird für jeden Baustein B_i eine Zustandsvariable X_i vorgesehen mit X_i=1, falls B_i intakt, X_i=0 sonst. Da das System einfachfehlertolerant ist, ist jeder Fehlerzustand bis zur gestrichelten Linie tolerierbar. Im fehlerfreien Fall soll jeder Baustein B_i nur eine Task T_i ausführen (transparent dazu natürlich die Selbsttestprogramme und Überprüfung des Nachbarn). Die Fehlerbehandlung bei einem Fehler im Nachbarprozessor wird durch eine Task T_R vorgenommen. Wird ein permanenter Fehler im Nachbarn entdeckt, kann außerdem dessen Task mit übernommen werden.

Dargestellt ist in Abbildung 5 zunächst ein permanenter Fehler in Baustein B_1, der zum 'Absturz' von Task T_1 führt. B_3 bemerkt als Überwacher diese Situation und beginnt mit der Ausführung von T_R. T_R setzt an B_1 ein Restart-Signal ab und startet damit das Selbsttestprogramm. Wird dieses nicht fehlerfrei beendet, liegt tatsächlich ein permanenter Fehler vor und B_3 führt alternierend T_1 und T_3 aus. B_1 kann nun zur Reparatur entfernt werden, während der Rest des Systems mit verminderter Leistung weiterarbeitet (Fail Soft, Graceful Degradation). Nach der Reparatur von B_1 registriert B_3 im Rahmen der Nachbarschaftsüberwachung, daß B_1 wieder eingeschaltet ist, startet über T_R die Selbsttestprogramme und überspielt bei fehlerfreier Ausführung T_1 zurück an B_1.

Transiente Fehler werden dadurch identifiziert, daß sie zwar die Nachbarschaftsüberwachung ansprechen lassen, der anschließende Selbsttest jedoch fehlerfrei abläuft. In diesem Fall setzt der Überwacher die unterbrochene Task unmittelbar wieder auf.

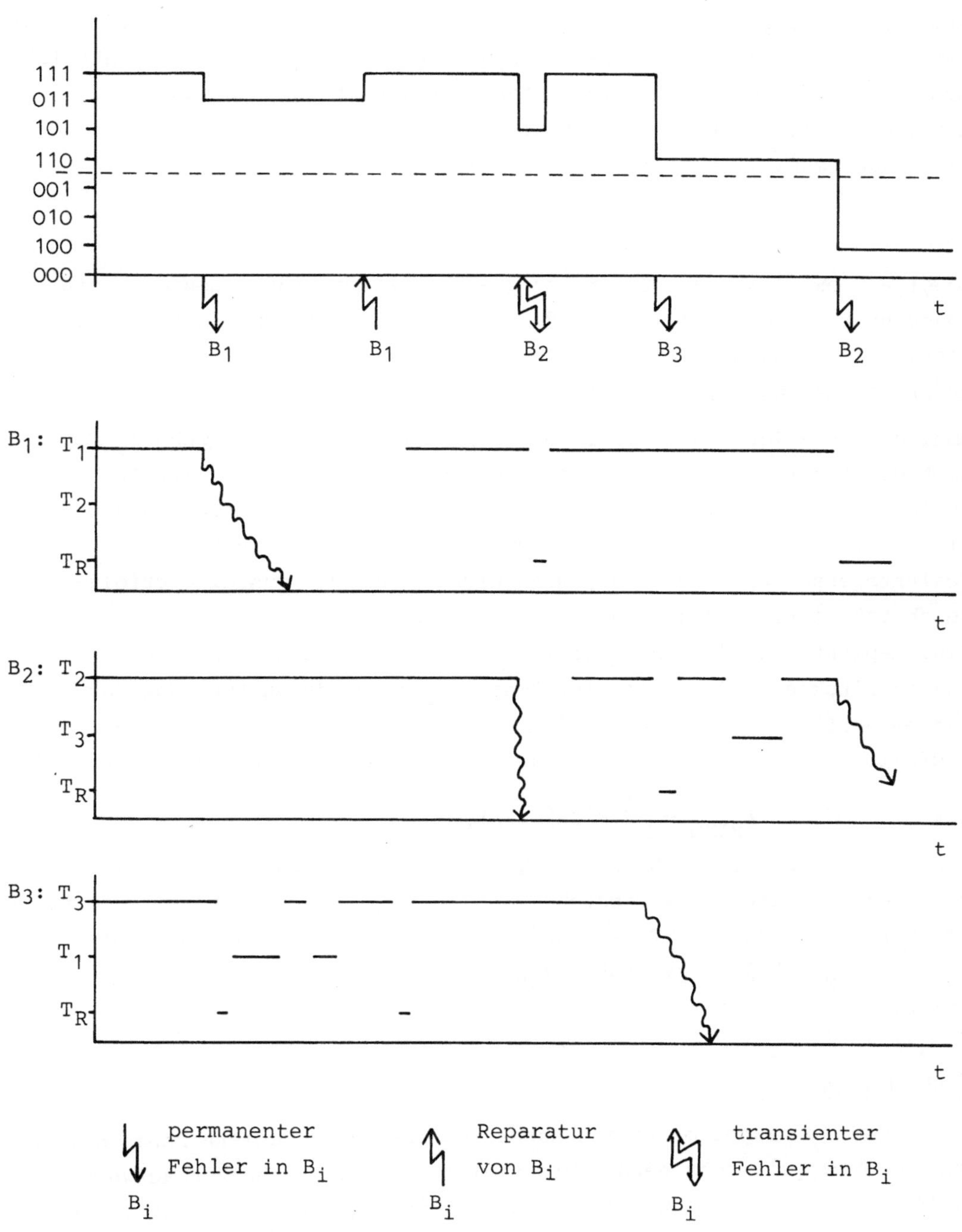

Abb. 5: Zeitverhalten des Ring-Systems

3.2 Zuverlässigkeitsberechnung

Es stellt sich natürlich die Frage, welcher Gewinn an Zuverlässigkeit und Verfügbarkeit sich mit einem derartigen System erzielen läßt. Eine erste quantitative Abschätzung hierzu läßt sich anhand analytischer Zuverlässigkeitsmodelle [13] gewinnen.

Zunächst sei angenommen, daß das System zum Zeitpunkt t=O fehlerfrei sei und nicht repariert werde. Da das System offenbar genau dann intakt ist, wenn mindestens zwei Bausteine intakt sind, gilt bei stochastischer Unabhängigkeit der Ausfälle für die Zuverlässigkeitsfunktion (Überlebenswahrscheinlichkeit) des Ring-Systems

$$R_{RING} = R^3 + 3cR^2(1-R),$$

wobei $R = \exp(-\lambda t)$ die Zuverlässigkeitsfunktion eines Bausteins mit konstanter Ausfallrate λ ist und c der sog. Überdeckungsfaktor (die Wahrscheinlichkeit dafür, daß ein Ausfall erfolgreich toleriert wird unter der Bedingung, daß er auftritt).

Abbildung 6 zeigt den Verlauf von R_{RING} über der Zeit t, wobei λ nach der Literatur (z.B. [14]) angegebenen Ausfallraten ermittelt wurde (ohne Terminals). Man sieht, daß sich auch dann noch ein deutlicher Zuverlässigkeitsgewinn gegenüber dem gleichen System ohne Fehlertoleranz erzielen läßt, wenn nicht sämtliche Ausfälle erfolgreich toleriert werden können.
Sind Reparaturen möglich, läßt sich die Verfügbarkeit als Zuverlässigkeitskenngröße ermitteln. Geht man wieder davon aus, daß das System verfügbar ist, wenn mindestens zwei Bausteine intakt sind und Ausfälle sowie Reparaturen stochastisch unabhängig sind, gilt für c=1:

$$A_{RING} = A^3 + 3A^2(1-A),$$

wobei A = MTBF/(MTBF + MTTR) die Verfügbarkeit eines Bausteins ist. Bei gleichem mittleren Fehlerabstand (MTBF = $1/\lambda$) wie oben und einer mittleren Reparaturdauer MTTR = 24h ergibt sich z.B. für das Fail-Soft System A_{RING}=99,999% gegenüber A_{NFT} = 99,482% für den nichtfehlertoleranten Ring.

4. Schlußbemerkung

Die bisherigen Experimente mit künstlich erzeugten Fehlern haben gezeigt, daß das Ringsystem das gewünschte fehlertolerante Verhalten aufweist. Weitere Untersuchungen werden darin bestehen, das Zuverlässigkeitsverhalten des Systems bei Dauerbetrieb mittels Fehlerstatistiken zu ermitteln. Außerdem ist eine Weiterentwicklung der beschriebenen Techniken (z.B. zusätzlicher Anwendung fehlererkennender Codes) und ihr Einsatz in leistungsfähigeren DIRMU-Bausteinen und größeren Konfigurationen auf Basis des Mikroprozessors 8086 in Arbeit.

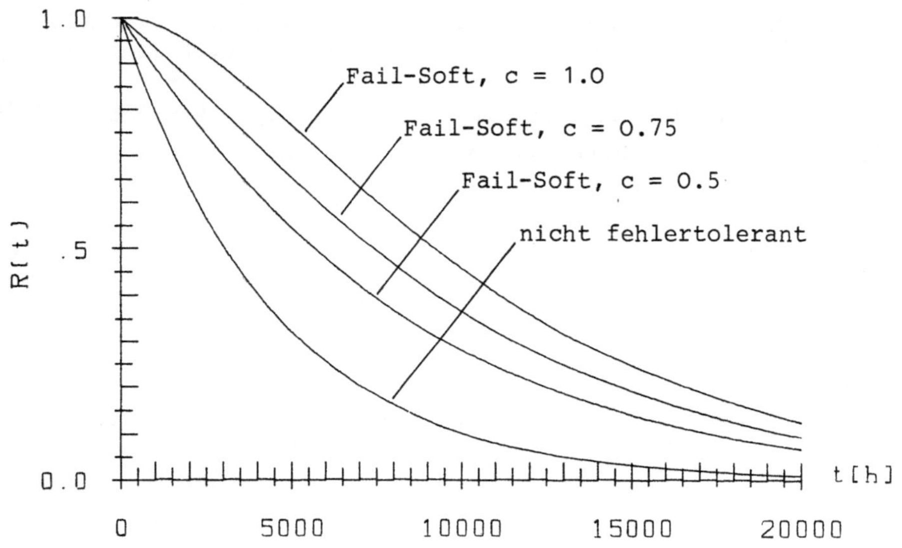

Abb. 6: Zuverlässigkeit des Ringsystems

Literatur

[1] Avizienis, A.: Fault-Tolerance in Computer Systems. Infotech State of the Art Report: System Reliability and Integrity 2, 39-67 (1978)

[2] Rennels, D.A.: Distributed Fault-Tolerant Computer Systems. Computer 13, No. 3, 55-65 (1980)

[3] Katsuki, D. et al.: Pluribus - An Operational Fault-Tolerant Multiprocessor. Proc. IEEE 66, No. 10, 1146-1159 (1978)

[4] Heger, D.; Peschke, P.; Syrbe, M.: Fehlertolerantes, verteiltes Prozeßrechensystem mit Lichtleiterbus. Elektronik 29, No. 16, 27-34 (1980)

[5] Bernhardt, D.; Schmitter, E.: Design and Implementation of a Fault-Tolerant Multimicrocomputer System. Proc. ICS 81, 256-261, London (1981)

[6] Händler, W.; Rohrer, H.: Gedanken zu einem Rechner-Baukasten-System. Elektr. Rechenanlagen 22, H. 1, 3-13 (1980)

[7] Maehle, E.: Modulare fehlertolerante Multi-Mikroprozessorsysteme nach dem Baukastenprinzip. VDI/DGQ/NTG/DKIN-Tagung "Technische Zuverlässigkeit", Nürnberg (1981) (erscheint demnächst)

[8] Sollmann, W.: Entwurf und Implementierung einer Prozessor-Speicher-Schnittstelleneinheit für einen fehlertoleranten Multi-Mikrorechner. Studienarbeit, Univ. Erlangen-Nürnberg (1980)

[9] Künecke, P.: Entwurf und Implementierung eines Mehrtorspeichers für einen fehlertoleranten Multi-Mikrorechner. Studienarbeit, Univ. Erlangen-Nürnberg (1980)

[10] Giodano, A.; Nilssen, S.A.: Vollständiger Selbsttest eines Mikrorechnertestkerns. ACM Workshop "Microcomputing", 217-230, München (1979)

[11] Maehle, E.: Entwurf von Selbsttestprogrammen für Mikrocomputer. ACM Workshop "Microcomputing", 204-216, München (1979)

[12] Joseph, H.: Entwurf und Implementierung eines Mikrocomputermoduls mit transparenter Selbstdiagnose. Studienarbeit, Univ. Erlangen-Nürnberg (1980)

[13] Dal Cin, M.: Fehlertolerante Systeme. Teubner Verlag, Stuttgart (1979)

[14] Reliability Reports, Firmenschriften der Firma Intel

Entwurf eines hochzuverlässigen redundanten Mikrorechnernetzes

F. Fetsch, L. Gmeiner, U. Voges
Kernforschungszentrum Karlsruhe GmbH
Institut für Datenverarbeitung in der Technik
Postfach 3640, D-7500 Karlsruhe

Zusammenfassung :

Ein integrierter Ansatz zur Erstellung eines hochzuverlässigen redundanten und rechnergestützten Reaktorschutzsystems wird dargestellt. Insbesondere werden die Maßnahmen zur Strukturierung, Konstruktion sowie Qualitätssicherung sowohl der Hardware wie der Software erläutert.

Das Gesamtsystem wird funktional aufgeteilt in Einzelmoduln, die redundant ausgelegt werden. Die Software wird ausgehend von einer formalen Spezifikation diversitär und unter Beachtung von Programmierrichtlinien erstellt. Das Gesamtsystem wird mittels Review-Techniken und automatischen sowie manuellen Testverfahren getestet. Alle Entwicklungs- und Testschritte werden von unabhängigen Gutachtern überprüft.

Schlüsselwörter :

Reaktorschutzsystem, Mikrorechner, Redundanz, Zuverlässigkeit, Sicherheit, diversitäre Software, Qualitätssicherung, Testverfahren

Gliederung :

1. Einleitung

In immer stärker werdendem Maße werden Rechner in Bereichen eingesetzt, in denen hohe Anforderungen an die Zuverlässigkeit und Sicherheit der Systeme gestellt werden. Zu diesen Bereichen zählen insbesondere die Verkehrssteuerung (Bahn, Luft, Raumfahrt), Medizin und Kerntechnik sowie einige Bereiche der Industrie. Diese Anwendungsbereiche erfordern einen hohen Einsatz bei der Planung und Realisierung der Rechnersysteme, um Fehlerquellen weitgehend auszuschließen bzw. Fehlererkennung und -toleranz einzubauen.

In diesem Papier soll an einem Beispiel aus der Kerntechnik gezeigt werden, welche Überlegungen hier angestellt werden, um den Anforderungen gerecht zu werden und ein hochzuverlässiges und sicheres System zu erhalten. Zunächst wird auf die Anforderungen an das System eingegangen. Anschließend werden die Hardware- und die Softwarestruktur vorgestellt. Die Besonderheiten bei der Qualitätssicherung werden erläutert. Zum Schluß wird der Stand des Projektes geschildert.

2. Anforderungen

Das hier behandelte System ist ein Reaktorschutzsystem, das den natriumgekühlten schnellen Brüter KNK II in Karlsruhe auf Temperaturüberschreitung des Kühlmittels überwachen soll. Liegt eine Grenzwertüberschreitung vor, so soll eine Schnellabschaltung des Reaktors durchgeführt werden.

Die Temperatur des Kühlmittels Natrium soll beim Eintritt in den Reaktorkern und am Ausgang der 35 Brennelemente gemessen werden. Jeder Messwert ist dreifach redundant vorhanden. Der Verlauf der Temperaturen wird nach fünf verschiedenen Kriterien überprüft. Eine Reaktorschnellabschaltung soll spätestens drei Sekunden nach Auftreten einer Störung (Nichterfüllung eines Kriteriums) erfolgen.

Die Systemzuverlässigkeit soll so dimensioniert sein, daß im Durchschnitt nicht mehr als eine unnötige Abschaltung pro Jahr von diesem System ausgelöst wird.

Die Konzeption des Systems soll eine Erweiterung der Zahl der zu überwachenden Brennelemente sowie Modifikationen der Abschaltkriterien zulassen.

Da das System Sicherheitsfunktionen in einem Reaktor zu erfüllen hat, muß es einem Genehmigungsverfahren unterzogen werden. Das bedeutet, daß alle Entwurfs- und Prüfschritte der Genehmigungsbehörde bzw. den entsprechenden Gutachtern vorgelegt werden müssen.

3. Hardware-Struktur

Um die korrekte Funktion von Rechnersystemen insbesondere bei sicherheitsrelevanten Einsatzbereichen nachweisen zu können, ist die Komplexität des Gesamtsystems auf überschaubare Einzelmoduln zu reduzieren. Ein solcher Ansatz führt weg von bisher üblichen Realisierungen von Sicherheitssystemen mit Prozeßrechnern zu einer Lösung mittels eines verteilten Systems auf der Basis von Mikrorechnern. Der Aufteilung des Systems liegt die funktionale Trennung in Einzelaufgaben zugrunde, verbunden mit der Zuordnung der Einzelaufgaben zu separaten Rechnern. Ausfälle, Fehlverhalten und deren Auswirkungen sollen sich auf einzelne Rechner beschränken und das Restsystem unbeeinflußt lassen.

Am Beispiel des Schutzrechnersystems kann eine funktionale Aufteilung folgendermaßen vorgenommen werden:

Verarbeitungseinheit 1: Entgegennahme der Meßdaten,
Umwandlung analog/digital,
Plausibilitätsprüfung,
Mittelwertbildung,

Verarbeitungseinheit 2: Berechnung der Kriterien mittels aktueller Meßdaten,

Verarbeitungseinheit 3: Berechnung der Kriterien mittels gefilterter Meßdaten eines größeren Zeitintervalls,

Verarbeitungseinheit 4: Auswertung der Ergebnisse der verschiedenen Kriterien, ggf. Abschaltung des Reaktors.

Damit ergibt sich eine relativ einfache Struktur des Gesamtsystems mit einfach gerichteter Datenflußrichtung und der Möglichkeit zur Parallelarbeit zwischen den Verarbeitungseinheiten 2 und 3.

Um die Ausfallsicherheit und Verfügbarkeit des Systems zu erhöhen, muß das System redundant ausgelegt werden, üblicherweise mit einer dreifachen Redundanz mit 2-von-3 Mehrheitsbewertung /JÜNG76/. Zu diesem Zweck wird jede Verarbeitungseinheit aus drei Rechnern gebildet. Diese kommunizieren untereinander, um einerseits Daten auszutauschen, andererseits um sich gegenseitig zu überwachen. Das Gesamtsystem besteht damit aus zwölf Rechnermoduln, die verschiedene

Möglichkeiten der Kopplung und Vermaschung zulassen. Eine Fehlerbaumanalyse ergab, daß eine mittlere Vermaschung (s. Abb. 1) den günstigsten Kompromiß zwischen Aufwand, Fehleranfälligkeit und Gewinn an Sicherheit ergab.

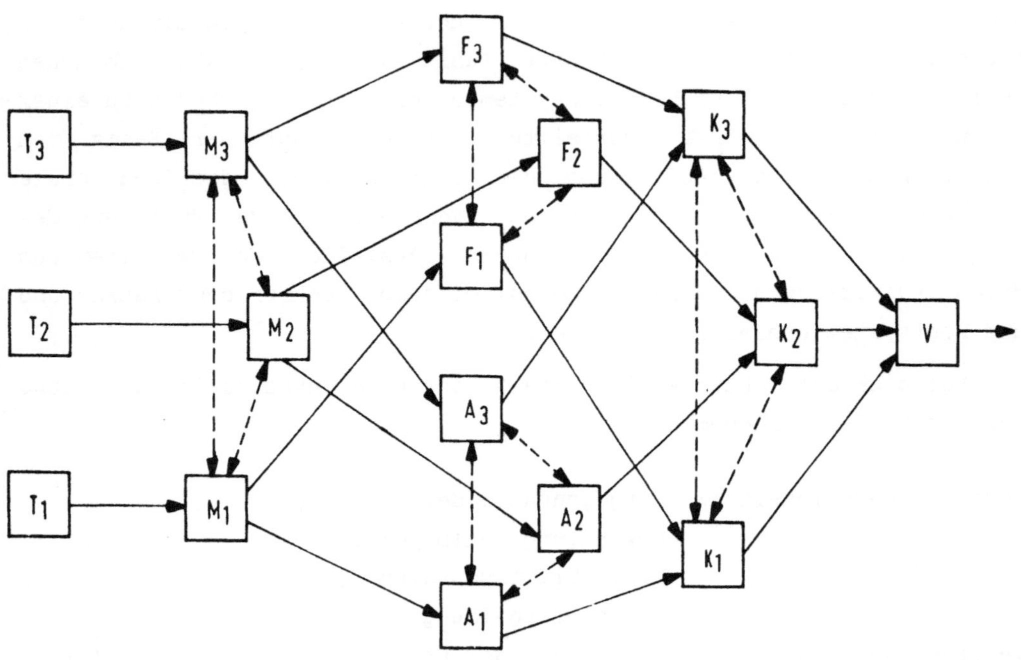

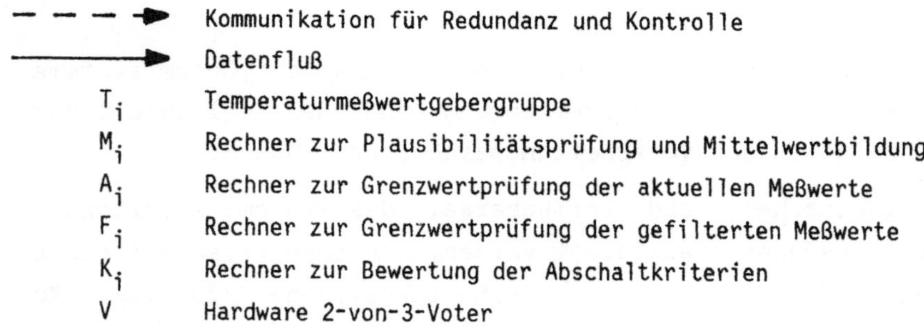

T_i Temperaturmeßwertgebergruppe
M_i Rechner zur Plausibilitätsprüfung und Mittelwertbildung
A_i Rechner zur Grenzwertprüfung der aktuellen Meßwerte
F_i Rechner zur Grenzwertprüfung der gefilterten Meßwerte
K_i Rechner zur Bewertung der Abschaltkriterien
V Hardware 2-von-3-Voter

Abb. 1: Struktur des Schutzrechnersystems.

Da ein Buskonzept wegen der Gefahr von Common-Mode-Fehlern nicht in Frage kommt, müssen die einzelnen Rechner über getrennte Datenübertragungsleitungen miteinander kommunizieren. Diese müssen, bedingt durch die Zeitanforderungen, einen "schnellen" Datentransfer zwischen den Rechnern ermöglichen. Aus Sicherheitsgründen müssen die Rechner verschiedener Redundanzgruppen jedoch räumlich getrennt untergebracht werden, so daß u.U. auch größere Entfernungen überbrückt werden müssen. Eine Mischung aus parallelen und seriellen Datenleitungen bietet sich an.

Die Hardware eines Einzelrechners setzt sich folgendermaßen zusammen:

- Chassis, Stromversorgung,
- CPU (Mikroprozessor),
- Hauptspeicher (Kombination von ROM, RAM, insgesamt 64 kB),
- I/O-Einrichtungen (8 Schnittstellen parallel/seriell)

Die einzelnen Rechner erhalten keine Peripherie. Um jedoch auch den Verlauf der Verarbeitung verfolgen und nach Ausfällen den Systemzustand rekonstruieren zu können, ist ein Protokollrechner mit entsprechender Peripherie vorgesehen, der jedoch nur zur Entgegennahme von Daten an alle Einzelrechner angeschlossen ist.

Die Ergebnisse der letzten Rechnergruppe gelangen als digitale Signale (Reaktor abschalten bzw. weiterarbeiten) an einen hochzuverlässigen 2-aus-3 Hardware-Voter, der das Endergebnis liefert.

4. Softwarestruktur

Aus der Aufgabenstellung ergab sich für die Software eine Grobgliederung in folgende vier Komponenten:

- Ablaufsteuerung/Betriebssystem
- Kommunikationssoftware
- Anwendungssoftware
- Prüfsoftware

Da die Hardware keine besonderen Anforderungen an ein Betriebssystem stellt (keine Peripherie) und auch von der Anwendungssoftware nur wenige Betriebsfunktionen benötigt werden, genügt in diesem Fall eine einfache Ablaufsteuerung, die die Anwendungs-, Kommunikations- und Prüfsoftware aktiviert und den zeitlichen Ablauf kontrolliert.

Die Kommunikationssoftware ist für den E/A-Verkehr, die Überwachung der Datenleitungen und die Datenübertragungsprotokolle zuständig. Durch die feste Zuordnung der Datenleitungen und der damit verbundenen einfachen Identifizierung der Daten kann das Übertragungsprotokoll sehr einfach gehalten werden, lediglich eine Fehlererkennungsmöglichkeit muß vorhanden sein.

In der Anwendungssoftware ist die eigentliche Problemlösung realisiert.

Die Prüfsoftware dient zum rechtzeitigen Entdecken von Hardwarefehlern. Sie soll einerseits die korrekte Funktion des Rechners selbst überprüfen (on-line Wartungsprogramme), andererseits aber auch die Nachbarrechner und die Kommunikationswege kontrollieren. Werden Unstimmigkeiten entdeckt, die auf Fehler hindeuten, so wird eine entsprechende Nachricht an den Protokollrechner und an die Nachfolgerechner gegeben.

Da auf jeder Ebene drei Rechner vorhanden sind, kann - unter der Voraussetzung, daß innerhalb eines Zeitintervalls nur ein Einzelfehler auftritt - in der Regel ein Fehler auch einer Einheit zugeordnet werden. Das Gesamtsystem bleibt somit in einem sicheren Zustand.

Die o.g. Punkte betreffen die Struktur des Systems. Auch in weiteren Punkten ist dafür Sorge getragen, daß ein korrektes und sicheres System aufgebaut wird. Hierfür sind konstruktive Maßnahmen zu ergreifen, die beispielsweise durch Programmierrichtlinien und die Verwendung von formalen Spezifikationssprachen und von höheren Programmiersprachen zum Ausdruck kommen.

So wird das Gesamtsystem weitgehend mit Hilfe einer formalen Spezifikationssprache /LUDE81/ definiert. Dadurch sollen Fehler während der Spezifikation sowie Mehrdeutigkeiten vermieden werden. Für die Implementierung ist ein diversitärer Ansatz vorgesehen: Ein Teil der Software (Anwendungssoftware) soll von drei verschiedenen Teams in drei verschiedenen Sprachen implementiert werden (IFTRAN, PASCAL, PL/M). Frühere Experimente haben den Vorteil dieser Methode gezeigt /GMVO79/. Bei dieser Implementierung sind Programmierrichtlinien einzuhalten (vgl. /VOEH75, EWIC81/), die z. B. die Regeln der strukturierten Programmierung beinhalten. Zusätzlich ist das System so zu initialisieren, daß im Fehlerfall immer sicherheitsgerichtete Werte geliefert werden (Fail-Safe-Initialisierung).

5. Qualitätssicherung

Da es sich bei dem hier behandelten Schutzsystem, wie bereits in der Einleitung erwähnt, um eine hohe Zuverlässigkeit und Sicherheit erfordernde Anwendung handelt, ist es nötig, insbesondere der Qualitätssicherung bei der Systemerstellung eine hohe Priorität einzuräumen. Während sich im Hardwarebereich bereits allgemein anerkannte Verfahren der Qualitätssicherung herausgebildet haben /INTE79/, existieren auf dem Gebiet der Software bisher nur rudimentäre Ansätze.

Im folgenden wird für die Software ein Ansatz beschrieben, der sowohl auf konstruktiven als auch auf analytischen Maßnahmen basiert. Während im Kapitel 4 bereits die konstruktiven Maßnahmen beschrieben wurden, werden wir uns im folgenden auf analytische Verfahren zur Qualitätssicherung konzentrieren.

Die beiden Hauptkomponenten der analytischen Vorgehensweise sind Reviews und Testverfahren.

Die Review- oder auch Walk-Through-Technik /FAGA76/ setzt voraus, daß der Systementwicklungsprozeß durch Meilensteine unterteilt ist, an denen genau definierte Entwicklungsdokumente (Anforderungsspezifikation, Entwurfsbeschreibung, usw.) vorliegen.

Die Reviews laufen zweistufig ab. Zunächst wird nach der Erstellung eines Dokuments innerhalb des Entwicklungsteams ein Review durchgeführt. Wenn das Dokument innerhalb des Entwicklungsteams anerkannt wurde, kann als nächste Stufe der Gutachter eingeschaltet werden. Dieser führt als externer und unabhängiger Prüfer einen Review durch, bei dem er sich als Vergleichsbasis auf die Richtlinien und Dokumente der davor liegenden Systementwicklungsphasen bezieht. Durch diese Art der entwicklungsbegleitenden Prüfungen und Inspektionen wird der Entwicklungsprozeß transparent.

Im Gegensatz zu der Review-Technik setzen die Testverfahren die Existenz von ausführbarem Programmcode voraus. Wir unterscheiden verschiedene Stufen, auf denen Tests durchgeführt werden:

- den Erstellertest,
- den Softwaretest,
- den Systemtest.

Im Erstellertest wird das Programm vom Entwickler einem Test unterzogen, dessen Umfang nur vom Ermessen des Programmierers abhängt.

Der Softwaretest wird von unabhängigen Personen nach folgenden Kriterien durchgeführt:

- Testdaten werden aus der Programmstruktur und der Entwurfsbeschreibung abgeleitet, und die erwarteten Testresultate werden aus der Programm- bzw. der Anforderungsspezifikation manuell gewonnen.
- Das Programm wird einer statischen und dynamischen Analyse unterzogen. Hierzu werden automatische Werkzeuge, wie z.B. RXVP /RXVP80, GEGM80/, eingesetzt.

Die statische Analyse bereitet die im Programm enthaltene Information in Form von Tabellen und Listen auf, so daß eine leichtere Überwachung der Richtlinien möglich ist. In der dynamischen Analyse wird das Verhalten des Programms während der Ausführung ermittelt. Um festzustellen, welche Teile des Programms ausgeführt werden und welche Werte die Variablen annehmen, werden die Programmbausteine vom Testsystem automatisch instrumentiert, d. h. es werden an bestimmten Stellen im Programm Anweisungen zur Zählung der Ausführungshäufigkeit und zur Protokollierung der Variablenwerte eingefügt. Während der Ausführung werden die Meßergebnisse der Instrumentierung von einem Überwachungsprogramm festgehalten und anschließend für einzelne Tests und Testreihen automatisch ausgewertet. Damit lassen sich Informationen über Datenfluß, Variablenwerte und Ausführungsprofil gewinnen. Das Ausführungsprofil beschreibt die Testüberdeckung und ermöglicht die Testüberwachung gemäß bestimmter Kriterien (z. B. Ausführung aller Programmverzweigungen).

Zusammenfassend läßt sich sagen, daß im Softwaretest die einzelnen Programme "off-line", d. h. getrennt vom Prozeß, einem intensiven Modul- und Integrationstest unterzogen werden.

Im Systemtest wird das komplett aufgebaute System im Echtzeitablauf getestet. Die hierfür nötigen Testdaten werden im Gegensatz zum Softwaretest weniger aus der Programmstruktur gewonnen. Vielmehr werden die Testdaten spezifikationsorientiert und applikationsorientiert ausgewählt. Im spezifikationsorientierten Systemtest werden die einzelnen Funktionen aus der Programmspezifikation abgeleitet mit dem Ziel, alle darin enthaltenen Fälle systematisch zu erfassen. Als Hilfsmittel für die Beschreibung dieser Testfälle dient eine Kombinationstabelle. Diese entscheidungstabellenähnliche Darstellungsform erlaubt eine systematische und vollständige Beschreibung der Testfälle. Im applikationsorientierten Systemtest bildet das gesamte Rechnersystem das Testobjekt. Ziel dieses Tests ist es, aus der Sicht des tatsächlichen Einsatzes (Applikation) die korrekte Systemfunktion nachzuweisen. Dies geschieht durch Simulation von charakteristischen Normal- und Störfällen. Die Anzahl der Tests für die einzelnen Fälle richtet sich dabei nach ihrer angenommenen Eintrittswahrscheinlichkeit.

Die letzte Phase des Systemtests läuft dann so, daß die originalen Prozeßdaten auf das Rechnersystem geschaltet werden. Während dieses Probebetriebs läuft das Schutzrechnersystem ohne Abschaltberechtigung im Prozeß mit.

6. Schlußbemerkung

Das hier vorgestellte Projekt zeigt einen integrierten Ansatz von Hardware und Software zur Lösung des Problems, ein hochzuverlässiges und sicheres System zu entwickeln. Konstruktive wie auch analytische Verfahren werden gemeinsam eingesetzt, um das Ziel zu erreichen.

Der augenblickliche Stand (1.8.81) des Projektes sieht eine Systemstruktur gemäß Abb. 1 vor. Als Rechner kommen Mikrocomputer vom Typ Siemens SME-E8 auf der Basis Intel 8088 zum Einsatz. Bei der Hardware-Auswahl wurde insbesondere auf Großserien-Platinensysteme zurückgegriffen.

Die Implementierung der Software soll in diesem Jahr in Angriff genommen werden. Der Test ist für 1982 vorgesehen. Das System soll 1983 mit Original-Reaktordaten versorgt werden, um Betriebserfahrung zu gewinnen.

7. Literatur

/EWIC81/ EWICS TC7
Development of Safety Related Software
EWICS TC7 WP 235, April 1981

/FAGA76/ M.E. Fagan
Design and Code Inspections to Reduce Errors in Program Development
IBM Systems Journal 1976

/GEGM80/ W. Geiger, L. Gmeiner
Automatische Test- und Dokumentationshilfsmittel für FORTRAN-Programme
KfK-Nachrichten, 12(1980) No. 1-2, S. 23 - 28

/GMVO79/ L. Gmeiner, U. Voges
Software Diversity in Reactor Protection Systems: An Experiment
in: R. Lauber (Hrsg.) Safety of Computer Control Systems. Proc. of the IFAC Workshop, Stuttgart, May 16-18, 1979, Pergamon Press, Oxford, S. 75-81

/INTE79/ Intel Corporation
Intel iSBC 86/12A Single Board Computer
Reliabitity Report RR-23, 1979

/JÜNG76/ U. Jüngst
Design Features of the Fuel Element Computerized Protection System BESSY
IAEA/NPPCI Specialists' Meeting on Use of Computers for Protection Systems and Automatic Control
Neuherberg, May 1976

/LUDE81/ J. Ludewig
PCSL und ESPRESO - zwei Ansätze zur Formalisierung der Prozeßrechner-Softwarespezifikation
Fachtagung Prozeßrechner, München, 10.-11.3.1981

/RXVP80/ RXVP80 Users Manual
General Research Corporation, Santa Barbara 1980

/VOEH75/ U. Voges, W. Ehrenberger
Vorschläge zu Programmierrichtlinien für ein Reaktorschutzrechnersystem
KFK-Ext. 13/75-02

SICHERUNG STATISTISCHER DATENBANKEN: OUTPUT VON INTERVALLEN [1)]

Jan Schlörer
Klinische Dokumentation, Universität Ulm
Prittwitzstr. 6, 7900 Ulm

Eine statistische Datenbank soll statistische Angaben - etwa Häufigkeiten, Prozentzahlen, Mittelwerte - über Personengruppen oder Gruppen von Organisationen zugänglich machen, ohne dabei Information über erkennbare Einzelpersonen oder Organisationen preiszugeben. Dieses doppelte Ziel ist nicht leicht zu erreichen. In den letzten Jahren tauchten immer neue Techniken auf, die erlauben, aus prima vista unschuldig wirkenden statistischen Angaben den Inhalt einzelner Datensätze, teils sogar der ganzen Datenbank zu rekonstruieren [Dal.77, DeS 79, DeS 80, DeJ 81, Mic 80, Rei 78, Sch 75, Sch 80, SDD 79]. Parallel dazu liefen theoretische Untersuchungen der Möglichkeit, eine statistische Datenbank zu attackieren, bei der die Schnittmengen zwischen den Datensatzteilmengen, die aufeinanderfolgende Anfragen verwenden dürfen, auf wenige Datensätze beschränkt bleiben [DJL 79]. Aber selbst diese extreme, für die Praxis nicht akzeptable Einschränkung half wenig; auch ein solches System kann mit recht geringem Aufwand unterlaufen werden.

Es genügt nicht, den Inhalt von Datensätzen zu kennen. Man muß diese - hier als anonym angenommenen - Datensätze dann auch identifizieren, also den richtigen Personen zuordnen können. Dies erfordert Zusatzwissen über die interessierenden Personen, das aber nicht immer umfangreich sein muß. Intuitiv leuchtet ein, daß unter ungünstigen Umständen die Kenntnis weniger Merkmale ausreichen kann, um einen Datensatz eindeutig zu identifizieren. Dies ist auch praktisch nachgewiesen worden [BlO 76, Sch 75]. Kernprobleme für die Sicherheit statistischer Datenbanken sind demnach :

(1) Das Identifikations-Problem: Ist ein gegebener Bestand anonymer Datensätze identifikationsgefährdet ?

[1)] Diese Arbeit wurde von der Stiftung Volkswagenwerk unterstützt.

(2) Das Output-Problem: Erlaubt eine gegebene Menge an Output, also eine Menge statistischer Angaben, Rückschlüsse auf den Inhalt einzelner Datensätze in der Datenbank ?

Entsprechend kann man die wichtigsten bis heute diskutierten Gegenmaßnahmen - mit Randunschärfen - in zwei Hauptgruppen einteilen. Zur ersten Gruppe zählen Verfahren, die beim Identifikationsproblem ansetzen und versuchen, die Daten selbst so zu verändern, daß Identifikationen schwierig oder unmöglich werden. Gelingt dies, dann braucht man in der Regel den Output nicht mehr zu überwachen, weil es nun gleichgültig ist, ob der genaue Inhalt der Datensätze bekannt wird. Beispiele sind: Verwendung von Stichproben anstelle von Grundgesamtheiten, Streichen oder Vergröbern der Klasseneinteilung "gefährlicher" (als Zusatzwissen geeigneter) Merkmale. Komplexere Verfahren wie kontrolliertes Einbringen von Zufallsfehlern (z.B. [Ree 73]) oder Transformation der Datenbank [DaR 78, Sch 77, Sch 81a] sind vorläufig von eher theoretischem Interesse; sie eignen sich auch nicht für Mehrzweckdatenbanken, weil sie die Daten im allgemeinen irreversibel verändern.

Die zweite Gruppe bilden Techniken der Output-Kontrolle, die den Output so beschränken oder verändern sollen, daß Details einzelner Datensätze nicht oder nur schwer erkennbar bleiben. Dabei geht natürlich Information verloren. Kein bisher bekanntes Verfahren vereinigt in sich die Idealkombination von minimalem Informationsverlust und geringem Aufwand bei maximaler Sicherheit [WeS 81]; ein solches Verfahren ist auch kaum zu erhoffen. Bei Techniken, die den Output beschränken, also bestimmte Antworten verweigern, werden die von der einzelnen Anfrage verwendeten Merkmalsausprägungen (etwa [Cox 80, FrH 80, Den 81]) oder auch nur die verwendeten Merkmale [Sch 76] überprüft; dann wird entschieden, ob eine Antwort erfolgt oder nicht. Eine Variante sind Verfahren zur Partitionierung der Datenbank [Ala 81, ChO 79, ChO 81, YuC 77], die ebenfalls Angaben über zu kleine - und damit kritische - Datensatzteilmengen unzugänglich machen sollen. Auf der anderen Seite stehen Techniken der Output-Modifikation. Verfahren, die kontrollierte Zufallsfehler in den Output einbringen [Bec 80, Den 80] bilden einen recht wirksamen Schutz, sind auch nicht allzu aufwendig, haben allerdings den Nachteil, daß der Benutzer nicht exakt weiß, wie weit ein ausgegebener Wert vom wahren Wert entfernt ist. Systematisches Runden [AcC 79, Sch 77] oder, gleichwertig, Ausgabe eines Intervalles [x,y], das den wahren Wert t ($x \leq t \leq y$) enthält, vermeidet diesen Nachteil und ist sehr einfach zu implementieren. Der Schutzeffekt dieser Technik ist aber nicht leicht zu beurteilen und auch erst in Ansätzen bekannt. In der Folge werden einige beim Output von Intervallen auftretende Probleme beschrieben. Zuvor wird das verwendete Modell skizziert.

Verwendetes Modell

Die meisten einschlägigen Arbeiten und auch wir gehen von einer <u>statistischen Datenbank</u> aus, die weitgehend einer Relation mit m Spalten (Merkmalen, attributes) und n Zeilen (logischen Datensätzen, m-Tupeln) gleicht. Zwischen den Zeilen oder Datensätzen einerseits und den Personen oder Merkmalsträgern andererseits besteht eine 1:1-Beziehung; in der Statistik spricht man dann auch von Individual- oder Mikrodaten. Das Datenelement x_{ij} in Zeile i und Spalte j ist eine Ausprägung v_{jk} des Merkmals V_j für die Person bzw. den Datensatz i (Beispiel: Wenn V_j = GESCHLECHT, dann v_{j1} = männlich, v_{j2} = weiblich). Anders als bei einer Relation kann in einer statistischen Datenbank, die anonyme Datensätze enthält, der gleiche Tupel auch mehrfach auftreten. Man kann dieses Problem umgehen, indem man die Datensätze fortlaufend durchnumeriert; das Merkmal LAUFENDE NUMMER bleibt für die statistische Auswertung irrelevant. Es sei betont, daß unser Modell nichts über die physische Speicherung der Daten aussagt; die konkreten Datenstrukturen können völlig anders aussehen.

Wir beschränken uns meist auf die für die Sicherheit statistischer Datenbanken gefährlichste Form des Output. Das sind absolute Häufigkeiten, also <u>Kardinalitäten</u> $|T|$ von Teilmengen $T \subset D$ der gespeicherten Datensätze; D ist die Datenbank, also die Menge aller Datensätze, $|D| = n$, $0 \leq |T| \leq n$. Eine Teilmenge T wird durch eine logische Bedingung Q(T) definiert, in der als Operanden die Ausprägungen der vorkommenden Merkmale, als Operatoren logisches UND ($\wedge$), ODER ($\vee$), NICHT ($\neg$) auftreten können. Q(T) könnte zum Beispiel lauten "GESCHLECHT = weiblich $\wedge$ BERUF = Informatiker" oder kurz "weiblich $\wedge$ Informatiker". T ist dann die Menge aller in der Datenbank gespeicherter Datensätze weiblicher Informatiker, $|T|$ ist die Anzahl oder absolute Häufigkeit, $|T| / n$ die relative Häufigkeit dieser Datensätze, und so fort. Eine ein- oder mehrdimensionale <u>Tabelle</u> im landläufigen Sinn (Figur 1a und 1d) ist eine Zusammenstellung von Kardinalitäten von Datensatzteilmengen.

Output von Intervallen

Grundgedanke des Verfahrens ist, anstelle der wahren Kardinalität $t = |T|$ ein Intervall [x,y] auszugeben, das den wahren Wert enthält; $x \leq t \leq y$, $y-x = b-1$, wobei $b \geq 2$ die Rundungsbasis oder kurz <u>Basis</u> ist. Das herkömmliche systematische oder determinierte Runden [AcC 79, Sch 77] hat Alagar [Ala 80] um eine kleine, aber wichtige Verbesserung bereichert: er hat die Intervalle halber Länge im Bereich $0 \leq t \leq \lfloor b/2 \rfloor$

m	w	Σ
4	5	9

(a)

m	w	Σ
[3,5]	[3,5]	[9,11]

(b)

m	w	Σ
[4,5]	[4,5]	[9,10]

(c)

	m	w	Σ
Ar	4	5	9
An	1	8	9
B	6	2	8
S	3	3	6
Σ	14	18	32

(d)

	m	w	Σ
Ar	[3, 5]	[3, 5]	[9,11]
An	[0, 2]	[6, 8]	[9,11]
B	[6, 8]	[0, 2]	[6, 8]
S	[3, 5]	[3, 5]	[6, 8]
Σ	[12,14]	[18,20]	[30,32]

(e)

	m	w	Σ
Ar	4	5	9
An	1	8	9
B	6	[0,2]	[6,8]
S	3	[3,5]	[6,8]
Σ	14	18	32

(f)

Figur 1: Eindimensionale (a-c) und zweidimensionale (d-f) Tabellen mit Randsummen (Σ). a und d: wahre Werte; b und e: Intervalle zur Basis b = 3; c und f: Intervalle soweit reduziert, wie ohne zusätzliche, nicht in den Tabellen enthaltene Information möglich. Merkmalsausprägungen: m = männlich, w = weiblich, Ar = Arbeiter, An = Angestellter, B = Beamter, S = selbständig .

beseitigt. Nimmt man die Basis b = 5 als Beispiel, dann liefert herkömmliches systematisches Runden für die wahren Werte 0,1,2 den gerundeten Wert 0, für die wahren Werte 3 - 7 den gerundeten Wert 5; die gerundete 0 entspricht also dem Intervall [0,2], 5 bedeutet [3,7] und so fort. Das Intervall [0,2] ist nur halb so lang wie die restlichen Intervalle und entsprechend stärker exponiert. Alagar schlägt vor, Intervalle der Form [kb, (k+1)b - 1] auszugeben ($k \geq 0$). Die wahren Werte zwischen 0 und 4 liefern für b = 5 jetzt das Intervall [0,4] ; es ist genau so lang wie alle übrigen Intervalle. Wendet man das Verfahren mit der Basis b = 3 auf die Tabellen in Figur 1a und 1d an, dann bekommt man Figur 1b und 1e.

Die Schutzwirkung nimmt mit b zu. Wir sind aber noch ein gutes Stück davon entfernt, einen genauen Zusammenhang zwischen b und dem erreichten Schutz angeben zu können. Gegenwärtig werden Teilprobleme untersucht; erst nachdem sie geklärt sind, kann man ein Gesamturteil wagen. Die folgenden Abschnitte sind den wichtigsten dieser Probleme gewidmet.

Verteilung der Reste der Kardinalitäten

Die meisten der folgenden Probleme werden sehr kompliziert, wenn man nicht unterstellt, daß die Reste modulo b der Kardinalitäten aller mit logischen Bedingungen definierbaren Datensatzteilmengen annähernd gleichverteilt sind. Bei b = 3 hieße das zum Beispiel, daß die Reste 0, 1, und 2 etwa gleich häufig auftreten, wenn man die Kardinalitäten sämtlicher definierbarer Teilmengen betrachtet. Wir gingen dieser Frage nach und stellten fest, daß diese Annahme in der Regel durchaus berechtigt ist [Sch 81b]. Ausnahmen können vorkommen, wenn praktisch alle Elementarmengen - das sind mit logischen Bedingungen nicht weiter zerlegbare Datensatzteilmengen [Sch 80] - Kardinalitäten von 0 oder 1 haben, und wenn gleichzeitig die Basis b größer als etwa $\sqrt{n}$ ist ; n ist die Gesamtzahl der Datensätze. Eine derart hohe Basis wird aber der Normalbenutzer kaum akzeptieren. Wir gehen hier von einer Gleichverteilung der Reste modulo b aus.

Reduktion von Intervallen

Der Benutzer kann manchmal ein ausgegebenes Intervall reduzieren (verkleinern) und damit einem oder mehreren der wahren Werte näher kommen.

(a) Eindimensionale Tabellen : Figur 1b liefert die Intervallgleichung [3,5] + [3,5] = [9,11]. Da 3 + 5 = 8 (< 9) und 5 + 5 = 10 (< 11), läßt sich diese Gleichung auf [4,5] + [4,5] = [9,10] reduzieren (Figur 1c). Für das herkömmliche systematische Runden haben Achugbue und Chin [AcC 79] Teile dieses Problemes studiert. Alagar hat für die Ausgabe von Intervallen eine eingehende Untersuchung angefangen [Ala 80]; darin noch enthaltene Lücken scheinen überwindlich, so daß eine vollständige Klärung des Problemes in Aussicht steht. Ob eine Reduktion vorkommen kann und wie groß sie ist, hängt von der Zahl der Ausprägungen (Zahl der möglichen Werte) c des betreffenden Merkmales und von der Basis b ab. Für $c \equiv z$ modulo b kann eine Reduktion der Intervall-Länge um (z-1) modulo b auftreten. Bei Annahme gleichverteilter Reste modulo b der Kardinalitäten läßt sich die Wahrscheinlichkeit dafür angeben, daß eine Reduktion tatsächlich auftritt. Überraschenderweise scheint sie mit abnehmendem wahrem Wert $t = |T|$ kleiner zu werden; sie hängt außerdem von b und c ab.

(b) Mehrdimensionale Tabellen (nur logisches UND verwendet): Figur 1e und 1f illustrieren das Problem für zwei Dimensionen. In Figur 1e kann man zunächst nur die beiden oberen Zeilen auf [4,5] + [4,5] = [9,10] bzw. [1,2] + [7,8] = [9,10] reduzieren. Danach wird aber eine vollständige Reduktion der linken Spalte möglich, deren Summe nun mindestens und höchstens, also genau 14 ist; und so fort. Fellegi und Phillips [FeP 74] wiesen schon auf dieses Problem hin; bisher wurde es nicht näher untersucht, weil vorher das Problem (a) geklärt sein mußte. Was man inzwischen weiß, läßt vermuten, daß auch Simulationen eine geeignete Lösungsmethode sein können.

(c) Reduktion mit logischem ODER bzw. NICHT : Dieses Problem ist in der mir bekannten Literatur nirgends erwähnt und ebenfalls noch nicht näher untersucht. Ein Beispiel mit b = 4 :

FAM.STAND	ledig		verh.		verw.		gesch.		sonst.		Summe
Wahre Werte	11	+	15	+	7	+	3	+	3	=	39
Intervalle	[8,11]	+	[12,15]	+	[4,7]	+	[0,3]	+	[0,3]	=	[36,39]

Diese Intervallgleichung läßt sich nicht reduzieren. Aber :

$$\begin{aligned} |\neg \text{ledig}| &= |\text{verh.} \vee \text{verw.} \vee \text{gesch.} \vee \text{sonst.}| = [28,31] = \\ &= |\text{verh.}| + |\text{verw.}| + |\text{gesch.}| + |\text{sonst.}| = \\ &= [12,15] + [4,7] + [0,3] + [0,3] \end{aligned}$$

läßt sich vollständig auf 28 = 15 + 7 + 3 + 3 reduzieren. Der fehlende Wert |ledig| = 11 läßt sich zum Beispiel mit Hilfe von $|\neg$sonst.$|$ ergänzen. Die Quelle des Übels ist, daß das Zusammenlegen (Falten) von Klassen mittels ODER die effektive Ausprägungszahl des Merkmals verringert. Für c > b ist das Problem besonders ernst zu nehmen, weil die dann mögliche Verringerung auf $c' = b$ zu einer vollständigen Reduktion führen kann, wenn auch nicht muß.

Intervalle und Individualtracker

Der Individualtracker ist ein Werkzeug zum Identifizieren und Retrieval von Datensätzen auf dem Umweg über Kardinalitäten [Sch 75, Sch 80]. M_{jk} sei die Menge der Datensätze, die eine bestimmte Merkmalsausprägung v_{jk} enthält. Die einfachste Form eines Individualtrackers für Datensatz X ist ein Paar {T1,T2} von Datensatzteilmengen (Figur 2) mit der Eigenschaft :

$$|(T1 \cup M_{jk}) \cap T2| = \begin{cases} |T2| & \longleftrightarrow \quad \text{Datensatz X enthält Merkmalsausprägung } v_{jk} \\ |T2| - 1 & \quad \text{sonst} \end{cases}$$

Wenn Intervalle ausgegeben werden, kann es geschehen, daß |T2| in einem höheren Intervall liegt als |T2| - 1. Die Funktion eines solchen Trackers wird durch die Ausgabe von Intervallen nicht behindert [Sch 77]. Nur muß der Benutzer vorher nachweisen, daß {T1,T2} tatsächlich einen echten und nicht nur einen Pseudotracker bilden. Sonst ist kein Verlaß auf die gewonnene Information. Für einen Pseudotracker gilt (s. Figur 2) :

$$|(T1 \cup M_{jk}) \cap T2| = |T2| - k \quad (0 \leq k \leq u) \quad \longleftrightarrow$$

u-k der u Datensätze in $X \cup Y$ enthalten Merkmalsausprägung v_{jk} ($u \geq 2$).

Ein Pseudotracker ist praktisch nutzlos, wenn Intervalle ausgegeben

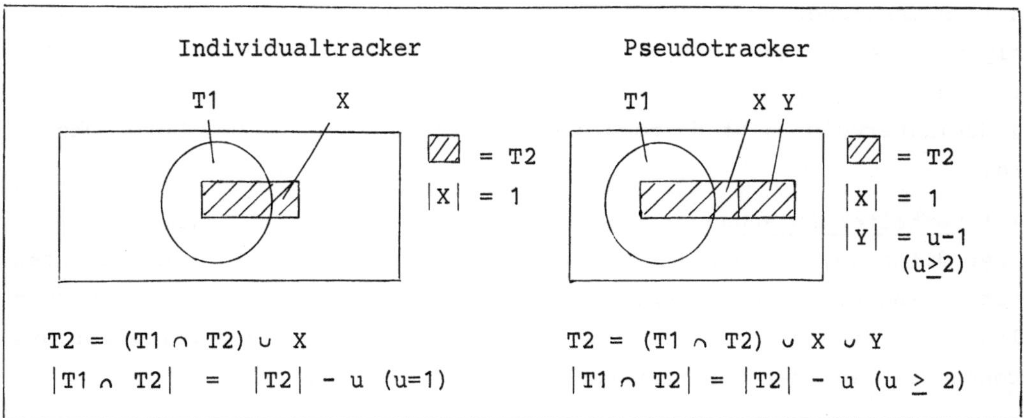

Figur 2: Individual- und Pseudotracker

werden. Die "Differentialdiagnose" zwischen Pseudo- und echtem Individualtracker ist auf zwei Wegen möglich :

(1) Trefferhäufigkeit : Trifft das vorhandene Zusatzwissen eines Benutzers auf u Datensätze zu, dann entsteht für u = 1 ein echter, für u $\geq$ 2 ein Pseudotracker. Bei gegebenem Zusatzwissen lassen sich sehr viele funktionsgleiche Paare {T1,T2} bilden; stets gilt $|T1 \cap T2| = |T2| - u$, aber $|T2|$ kann beliebige Werte zwischen u und n annehmen; für die hier vorgestellte Form der Tracker sind Werte um n/3 am häufigsten [Sch 80]. Die Wahrscheinlichkeit, daß ein zufällig gebildetes Paar {T1,T2} ein Treffer ist, daß also $|T1 \cap T2|$ im Intervall $[(k-1)b, kb-1]$, $|T2|$ dagegen im nächsthöheren Intervall $[kb, (k+1)b - 1]$ liegt, beträgt bei gleichverteilten Resten modulo b der Kardinalitäten u/b. Daraus folgt einmal, daß bis zum ersten Treffer im Mittel etwa b/u (für u=1 also etwa b) Versuche - mit je zwei Anfragen - nötig sind. Zweitens kann man über die Binomialverteilung B(z,p) = B(Zahl der Versuche, u/b) berechnen, wieviele Versuche erforderlich sind, um anhand der erzielten Trefferzahl einen Pseudotracker (u $\geq$ 2) als solchen erkennen zu können. Die folgenden Zahlen gelten für $\alpha = 0.01$ und $\beta = 0.5$; tabelliert ist also die kleinste Zahl von Versuchen, nach der ein Benutzer in 50 % aller Versuchsreihen eine Trefferzahl erzielt hat, die ausreicht, um einen Pseudotracker - falls er vorliegt - mit 1 % Irrtumswahrscheinlichkeit zu erkennen :

b	u = 2	u = 3	u = 4	u = 5
10	64	19	9	5
20	137	45	24	15
30	205	67	35	22
50	342	111	59	37

Eine ausführlichere Tabelle wird in [Sch 81b] erscheinen. Schon diese wenigen Zahlen zeigen, daß sich auf diesem Weg ein Pseudotracker mit hohem u rasch, einer mit niedrigem u dagegen nur mühsam erkennen läßt. Unglücklicherweise gibt es noch eine zweite Möglichkeit der Unterscheidung.

(2) Verhaltensforschung : Ein Pseudotracker gibt sich früher oder später durch sein Verhalten zu erkennen. $M_1, \ldots, M_c$ seien die c Datensatzteilmengen, die die Ausprägungen $v_1, \ldots, v_c$ eines Merkmales V enthalten. Die Mengen sind paarweise disjunkt und bilden eine Partition der Datenbank. Fragt der Benutzer nach den c Kardinalitäten

$$|(T1 \cup M_i) \cap T2| \qquad (i = 1 \ldots c) \qquad (\&1)$$

dann liefert ein echter Individualtracker in genau einem der c Fälle das höhere, in allen anderen Fällen das niedrigere der zwei Intervalle: der Datensatz X muß genau eine der c Ausprägungen des Merkmales V enthalten. Ein Pseudotracker kann sich verschieden verhalten :

(a) wie ein echter Individualtracker,

(b) das höhere Intervall kommt bei keiner der c Anfragen vor,

(c) das höhere Intervall kommt zweimal oder öfter vor.

Man kann den Pseudotracker rascher erkennen, wenn man statt der Anfrageserie (&1) eine Binärsuche ähnlich wie in [Sch 80] durchführt und - falls dabei genau eine einzige Menge, sagen wir M_k, das höhere Intervall liefert - noch die Fangfrage nach der Kardinalität

$$|(T1 \cup \bigcup_{i \neq k} M_i) \cap T2| \qquad (\&2)$$

nachschiebt. Schon die Binärsuche wird oft den Pseudotracker aufdecken, wo eine Fragenserie der Form (&1) versagt hätte. In manchen weiteren Fällen wird die Frage (&2) das höhere Intervall liefern und damit den Pseudotracker erkennen. Nimmt man vereinfachend an, daß alle vom Benutzer bei einem solchen Test verwendeten Merkmale gleichverteilt sind und die gleiche Zahl c ($c \geq 3$) von Ausprägungen haben, dann braucht dieses Verfahren rund $r(1 + \log_2 c)$ Anfragen, um einen Individualtracker von einem Pseudotracker abzugrenzen. Die Größe r hängt von c und der angestrebten Irrtumswahrscheinlichkeit α ab, sie sinkt mit wachsendem c [Sch 81b]. Für $\alpha = 0.01$ und $c = 4$ liegt r bei 10, für $c = 8$ bei 5, so daß sich im ersten Fall etwa 30, im zweiten Fall rund 20 Anfragen ergeben. Daß r anwächst, wenn das verwendete Merkmal V nicht gleichverteilt ist, ist erfreulich; weniger erfreulich ist, daß r nicht von b abhängt, also auch nicht steigt, wenn man die Intervalle verlängert. Interessant, wenn auch vermutlich selten von praktischem Nutzen, ist das Nebenergebnis, daß man einen Individualtracker äußerst schwer erkennen kann, wenn alle in der Datenbank vorkommenden Merkmale nur c = 2 Ausprägungen aufweisen.

Schlußbemerkung

Einige weitere Probleme seien gestreift. Auch für arithmetische Mittel wird man sicher Intervalle ausgeben müssen; spätestens seit der Arbeit von de Jonge [DeJ 81] verbietet sich der Output der exakten Werte. Die Gefährlichkeit des "general tracker" [DeS 79] und verwandter Techniken bei der Ausgabe von Intervallen bleibt zu klären; auf den ersten Blick scheint es, als ob diese Verfahren durch Intervalle weitgehend unschädlich gemacht würden.

Der Output von Intervallen ist eine so einfache Technik, daß sich einiger Aufwand lohnt, um seine Brauchbarkeit - oder das Gegenteil - zu zeigen. Derzeit läßt sich die Schutzwirkung des Verfahrens noch nicht schlüssig beurteilen. Man kann vermuten, daß es sich am ehesten zur Kombination mit einem einfachen Verfahren der Output-Beschränkung eignet. Ein möglicher Kandidat für eine solche Kombination ist die Beschränkung der Anzahl der Merkmale, die eine Anfrage verwenden darf.

Danksagung

Linda Zick schrieb einen großen Teil der benötigten Programme und half auch bei den immer wieder vorkommenden Rechnungen "zu Fuß". Ich danke ihr herzlich.

Literatur

[AcC 79] Achugbue, J.O., Chin, F.Y.: The effectiveness of output modification by rounding for protection of statistical data bases. INFOR 17 (1979), 209-218.

[Ala 80] Alagar, V.S.: Complexity of compromising statistical databases. Dept. Comp. Sci., Concordia Univ., Montreal, Nov. 1980.

[Ala 81] Alagar, V.S., Blanchard, B., Glaser, G.: Effective inference control mechanisms for securing statistical databases. Proc. AFIPS NCC 50 (to appear 1981).

[Bec 80] Beck, L.L.: A security mechanism for statistical databases. ACM Trans. Database Syst. 5 (1980), 316-338.

[BlO 76] Block, H., Olsson, L.: Bakvägsidentifiering. Stat. Tidskrift 14 (1976), 135-144.

[ChO 79] Chin, F.Y., Oszoyoglu, G.: Security in partitioned dynamic statistical databases. Proc. IEEE COMPSAC Conf. (1979), 594-601.

[ChO 81] Chin, F.Y., Oszoyoglu, G.: Statistical database design. ACM Trans. Database Syst. 6(1981), 113-139.

[Cox 80] Cox, L.H.: Suppression methodology and statistical disclosure control. J.Am.Stat.Ass. 75 (1980), 377-385.

[Dal 77] Dalenius, T.: Towards a methodology for statistical disclosure control. Stat. Tidskrift 15 (1977), 429-444.

[DaR 78] Dalenius, T., Reiss, S.P.: Data swapping - a technique for disclosure control. Confid.in Surveys, Rep.31, Dept.Stat., Univ.Stockholm, May 1978.

[DeJ 81] De Jonge, W.: Compromising statistical databases responding to queries about means. Vakgroep Informatica, Vrije Univ.,Amsterdam, Jan. 1981.

[Den 80] Denning, D.E.: Secure statistical databases with random sample queries. ACM Trans. Database Syst. 5 (1980), 291-315.

[Den 81] Denning, D.E.: Restricting queries that might lead to compromise. Dept.Comp.Sci., Purdue Univ., W.Lafayette, Jan.1981.

[DeS 79] Denning, D.E., Denning, P.J., Schwartz, M.D.: The tracker: a threat to statistical database security. ACM Trans.Database Syst. 4 (1979), 76-96.

[DeS 80] Denning, D.E., Schlörer, J.: A fast procedure for finding a tracker in a statistical database. ACM Trans.Database Syst. 5(1980), 88-102.

[DJL 79] Dobkin, D., Jones, A.K., Lipton, R.: Secure databases: protection against user influence. ACM Trans.Database Syst. 4(1979), 97-106.

[FeP 74] Fellegi, I.P., Phillips, J.L.: Statistical confidentiality: some theory and applications to data dissemination. Ann.Econ.Soc.Measurement 3 (1974), 399-409.

[FrH 80] Friedman, A.D., Hoffman, L.J.: Towards a fail-safe approach to secure databases. GWU-EECS-80-01, Dept.Electr.Eng.Comp.Sci., George Washington Univ., Washington, D.C., Jan. 80.

[Mic 80] Michalewicz, Z.: Compromisability of a statistical database. ICS PAS Rep.420, Inst.Comp.Sci., Polish Acad.Sci., Warschau, Juli 1980.

[Ree 73] Reed, I.S.: Information theory and privacy in data banks. Proc. AFIPS NCC 42 (1973), 581-587.

[Rei 78] Reiss, S.P.: Medians and database security. In DeMillo, R.A., Dobkin, D., Jones, A.K., Lipton, R.J. (eds.): Foundations of Secure Computation. New York, Acad.Press, 1978, pp. 57-91.

[Sch 75] Schlörer, J.: Identification and retrieval of personal records from a statistical data bank. Meth.Inform.Med.14(1975), 7-13.

[Sch 76] Schlörer, J.: Confidentiality of statistical records: a threat-monitoring scheme for on line dialogue. Meth.Inform.Med.15(1976), 36-42.

[Sch 77] Schlörer, J.: Confidentiality and security in statistical data banks. In Gaus,W.,Henzler,R.(eds.): Data documentation: some principles and applications in science and industry. München, Verlag Dokum., 1977, S.101-123.

[Sch 80] Schlörer,J.: Disclosure from statistical databases: quantitative aspects of trackers. ACM Trans.Database Syst.5(1980),467-492.

[Sch 81a] Schlörer,J.: Security of statistical databases: multidimensional transformation. ACM Trans.Database Syst. 6(1981), 95-112.

[Sch 81b] Schlörer,J.: Security of statistical databases: ranges and trackers (1981, in Vorbereitung).

[SDD 79] Schwartz,M.D., Denning, D.E., Denning, P.: Linear queries in statistical databases. ACM Trans.Database Syst.4(1979), 156-167.

[WeS 81] Wehrle, E., Schlörer, J.: Sicherung statistischer Datenbanken durch Output-Kontrolle. Vortrag, 26.Jahrestagung der GMDS, Giessen, Sept. 1981.

[YuC 77] Yu, C.T., Chin, F.Y.: A study on the protection of statistical databases. Proc. ACM SIGMOD Int.Conf.Management of Data, Toronto, 1977, pp. 169-181.

Schutz, Sicherung und Sicherheit

Versuch einer Begriffsklärung aus der Sicht der Informatik

Klaus Dittrich
Institut für Informatik II
Universität Karlsruhe
Postfach 6380
7500 Karlsruhe 1

Zusammenfassung

Schutz, Sicherung und Sicherheit gehören zu den Begriffen, die im Zusammenhang mit Datenverarbeitungssystemen häufig verwendet werden, ohne daß ein allgemein anerkanntes Verständnis über ihre genaue Bedeutung vorliegt. Der Beitrag möchte aus der Sicht des Informatikers einen Diskussionsanstoß zur Begriffsklärung geben. Er geht aus vom allgemeinen Sprachgebrauch und entwickelt die vielfältigen Begriffsanwendungen an einem einfachen Beschreibungsmodell. Eine Reihe von Schutzmaßnahmen und Anwendungsfällen werden dabei beispielhaft aufgezählt, verwandte Begriffe werden erläutert und voneinander abgegrenzt.

Schutz, Sicherung und Sicherheit sind Schlagworte, die gerade auch im Zusammenhang mit der automatisierten Datenverarbeitung ausgesprochen uneinheitlich und oft sogar widersprüchlich verwendet werden (mit "protection", "security" usw. im englischen Sprachbereich ist es nicht besser). Kommen verschiedene Fachgebiete zusammen, etwa Jurisprudenz und Informatik, so entsteht schnell vollkommene Begriffsverwirrung. Dieser Beitrag will aus der Sicht eines Informatikers versuchen, die genannten Begriffe wenigstens informell zu klären und gegeneinander abzugrenzen. Eine formale Definition wäre nur bei überaus starker Einschränkung des Gegenstandsbereichs möglich und somit für unsere Zwecke wenig hilfreich.

1 Schutz, Sicherung und Sicherheit im allgemeinen Sprachgebrauch

Da die Informatik keine grundlegende Erklärung der zu untersuchenden Begriffe kennt, versuchen wir, ihre Bedeutung aus dem allgemeinen Sprachgebrauch heraus zu erfassen und sie anschließend für den hier interessierenden Bereich zu konkretisieren.

Schutz und Sicherung tragen in ihrer täglichen Verwendung mehrere Bedeutungen und werden häufig auch gleichwertig gebraucht. Wir benutzen folgende Auffassung, die an Gedanken aus [BD 79] anknüpft:

Wo eine Gefahr und eine Schwachstelle zusammentreffen, entsteht ein Risiko. Tritt das als Gefahr betrachtete Ereignis tatsächlich ein, so führt das Risiko zu einer Beeinträchtigung (einem Schaden), d.h. zu einem schlecht oder nachteilig empfundenen, also unerwünschten Zustand oder Zustandsübergang ("der Schadensfall tritt ein"). Gefahr, Schwachstelle, Beeinträchtigung usw. sind dabei durchaus weitläufig und meist subjektiv zu verstehen.

Unter <u>Schutz</u> verstehen wir die Verhinderung oder Begrenzung von Beeinträchtigungen; <u>Sicherung</u> hingegen ist die Vermeidung, Beseitigung oder Verminderung zugrunde liegender Risiken. Beide Begriffe stehen recht nahe beieinander, wiewohl Schutz eine umfassendere, abstraktere Bedeutung zukommt (die Vermeidung von Risiken dient stets der Verhinderung von Beeinträchtigungen). Da jedoch zwischen Risiken einerseits und daraus erwachsenden Beeinträchtigungen andererseits häufig nicht unterschieden wird und auch nicht unterschieden werden muß, kann eine gleichartige Verwendung beider Begriffe vielfach akzeptiert werden.

So spricht man vom Umweltschutz (Verhinderung nachteiliger Eingriffe in die Natur), von der Einkommenssicherung (Verminderung/Beseitigung der Risiken, Einkommenseinbußen zu erleiden), aber sowohl von Brandschutz (...Beeinträchtigungen durch Feuer) als auch von Brandsicherung (...Risiko eines Brandausbruches; gemeint ist die Beseitigung entsprechender Schwachstellen; trotzdem werden beide Begriffe meist gleichartig verwendet).

Wir werden in dieser Arbeit vorwiegend Schutz und damit den umfassenderen beider Begriffe verwenden (für Sicherung gelten die meisten noch zu treffenden Aussagen analog); erst später wird für den Bereich der Informatik noch einmal unterschieden.

Schutz ist unserer Erklärung zufolge als Aktivität zu betrachten (vgl. die Existenz des Verbs "schützen", aus dem sich das Substantiv herleitet). Vorkehrungen aller Art zur Durchführung von Schutz heißen Schutzmaßnahmen, sind sie technischer Natur auch Schutzmechanismen. Sie lassen sich grob klassifizieren in solche, die

(a) Beeinträchtigungen verhindern,
(b) Beeinträchtigungen erkennen,
(c) entstandenen Schaden beheben.

Gerätschaften, die im Zuge von Schutzmaßnahmen eingesetzt werden, nennt man Schutzeinrichtungen.

Unter Sicherheit verstehen wir den Zustand des Nichtvorhandenseins von Risiken und/oder Beeinträchtigungen. Ein solcher Zustand besteht, wenn Sicherung und/oder Schutz gewährleistet ist oder Risiken a priori nicht vorliegen. [Eine andere Interpretation sieht Sicherheit als (subjektive) Gewißheit über die Wirksamkeit von Schutzmaßnahmen ("sich in Sicherheit wiegen").]

Sicherheit kann somit als das Ziel oder Ergebnis der Aktivitäten Schutz und Sicherung aufgefaßt werden. Alle bisher eingeführten Begriffe sind jedoch in den seltensten Fällen universell gemeint (alle Arten von Beeinträchtigungen, Schäden, Risiken). Vielmehr liegen meist spezielle Gegebenheiten vor, gegen die geschützt werden soll. Diese müssen bei genauer Sprechweise stets näher spezifiziert werden (z.B. "Brandschutz").

Für die folgenden Betrachtungen legen wir ein einfaches Modell zugrunde, das einige wichtige Zusammenhänge der besprochenen Begriffe veranschaulicht (Abb. 1). Es spiegelt folgende Auffassung wider: Schutz, d.h. die Verhinderung spezifischer Beeinträchtigungen, führt gegenüber eben diesen zu Sicherheit. Die abstrakte Aktivität Schutz wird dabei durch den Einsatz von Schutzmaßnahmen konkret realisiert. Als ein Zwischenschritt ist es erforderlich, die ebenfalls zunächst als abstrakte Vorstellungen bestehenden Beeinträchtigungen in Form einer Menge von Regelungen (explizit oder in manchen Lebensbereichen auch implizit) zu konkretisieren. Diese Regelungen legen auf genaue (und für die Schutzmaßnahmen "verständliche") Weise fest, welche Zustände/Zustandsübergänge im vorliegenden Fall eine Beeinträchtigung darstellen (also nicht eintreten/stattfinden sollen) und/oder für welche dies nicht zutrifft (solche Zustände/Zustandsübergänge sollen ausschließlich eintreten/stattfinden). Die Durchsetzung der Regelungen durch die Schutzmaßnahmen führt zu ihrer Einhaltung, d.h. zum regelgerechten Verhalten des betrachteten Systems. Dies wiederum stellt die konkrete Bedeutung des abstrakten Begriffs Sicherheit dar.

Aus dem vorgestellten Modell lassen sich bereits in dieser allgemeinen Form eine Reihe von Fragen erkennen, die für Einsatz oder Entwicklung von Schutzmaßnahmen zu beantworten sind:

- Welche Sicherheit kann man bei welcher Anwendungsweise einer Reihe vorliegender Schutzmaßnahmen erzielen?
- Welche Schutzmaßnahmen muß man wie einsetzen, um eine bestimmte Sicherheit zu erreichen?

Beide Fragestellungen haben ihre Berechtigung, da man in vielen Fällen mit gegebenem Mitteleinsatz Maximalziele erreichen möchte, in anderen Fällen aber fest vorgegebene Ziele unter minimalem Mitteleinsatz realisiert werden sollen.

- Spiegeln die spezifizierten Regelungen die Intentionen wider (d.h. führt ihre Einhaltung zur gewünschten Sicherheit)?
- Setzen die Schutzmaßnahmen die spezifizierten Regelungen durch?

Schließlich verwendet man für die in unserem Modell als Rechtecke dargestellten Bestandteile (samt ihrer Verbindungen) häufig den Begriff Schutzsystem als Teil eines umfassenden Systems, in dem Sicherheit gewünscht wird.

2 Grobstrukturierung von Schutzsystemen

Das erläuterte Grundmodell eines Schutzsystems vermittelt einen nur groben Eindruck. Tatsächlich sind Schutzsysteme meist selbst wieder aus Teilsystemen aufgebaut. Für je zwei Teilsysteme kann eine horizontale (parallele) oder eine vertikale (hierarchische) Strukturierung erfolgen; mehrere Teilsysteme können durch sukzessive Anwendung der beiden Techniken (auch in Kombinationen) zusammengesetzt werden.

- horizontale (parallele) Strukturierung (Abb. 2)

Die spezifizierten Regelungen werden hierbei gemeinsam durch beide Schutzmaßnahmen durchgesetzt, wobei jede einen Teil der Regelungen übernimmt (R1 bzw. R2). R1 und R2 können sich überschneiden oder auch identisch sein (redundante Schutzmaßnahmen). Bezüglich der Einbettung eines horizontal strukturierten Schutzsystems in seine Umgebung gilt, daß an der Schnittstelle (repräsentiert letztlich durch die zu spezifizierenden Regelungen) die Kenntnis der Existenz beider Schutzmaßnahmen erforderlich ist.

- Vertikale (hierarchische) Strukturierung (Abb. 3)

Hier liegt die Durchsetzung der spezifizierten Regelungen (R1) zunächst voll bei der Schutzmaßnahme 1. Diese kann der Aufgabe jedoch durch vollständige oder teilweise Delegation an das zweite Teilsystem gerecht werden. Dazu müssen (durch die Schutzmaßnahme 1) Regelungen R2 für Schutzmaßnahme 2 spezifiziert werden. Die Einbettung in die Umgebung sieht hier so aus, daß an der Schnittstelle lediglich Kenntnisse der Schutzmaßnahme 1 vorhanden zu sein brauchen.

Darüber hinaus stellen die als R2 spezifizierten Regelungen nach dem Grundmodell wieder die Repräsentation irgendwelcher (abstrakter) Beeinträchtigungen dar, die durch Schutzmaßnahme 2 verhindert werden. Damit kann R2 zusätzlich eine Schnittstelle zur Umgebung darstellen (zu einem anderen Ausschnitt als R1), andererseits kann man die gestrichelt dargestellten Beeinträchtigungen auch als (durch die Hierarchiebildung der Teilsysteme) künstlich entstanden betrachten, ohne daß sie explizit in der Systemumgebung auftreten.

3 Schutz, Sicherung und Sicherheit im Zusammenhang mit automatisierter Datenverarbeitung

Mit dieser allgemeinen Begriffs- und Modellbildung im Hintergrund wollen wir nun erläutern, welche Bedeutung Schutz, Sicherung und Sicherheit im Zusammenhang mit dem Einsatz automatisierter DV-Systeme haben. Dazu gehen wir der Frage nach,

- wer oder was im Zusammenhang mit DV-Systemen beeinträchtigt werden kann.

Darüber hinaus versuchen wir beispielhaft zu erfassen,

- welcher Art hierbei Risiken und Beeinträchtigungen sind,
- wie diesen Risiken und Beeintrachtigungen begegnet wird.

3.1 Schutzobjekte

Wir überlegen zunächst, wer oder was im Zusammenhang mit DV-Systemen beeinträchtigt werden kann, also potentiell geschützt werden muß, und verwenden als Sammelbegriff dafür die Bezeichnung (Schutz-)Objekte.

Je nach ihrer Stellung zum DV-System teilen wir die Schutzobjekte in drei Klassen ein, die man naheliegenderweise als übereinandergeschichtete Ebenen betrachtet:

E_1: Objekte, die durch Einsatz von DV-Systemen indirekt beeinträchtigt werden können, d.h. selbst nicht unmittelbar mit dem DV-System in Berührung stehen,

E_2: Objekte, die unmittelbar mit DV-Systemen umgehen und damit direkt durch sie beeinträchtigt werden können,

E_3: Objekte, die Bestandteile des DV-Systems selbst sind und in dieser Eigenschaft beeinträchtigt werden können.

Innerhalb und zwischen den Ebenen geht es meist nicht um Einzelobjekte selbst, sondern um die Rollen, die sie einnehmen. Mehrere Objekte können gemeinsam eine Rolle übernehmen, andererseits kann ein Objekt in verschiedenen Rollen auftreten. Insbesondere kann das gleiche Objekt in einer Rolle auf E_1 und in einer anderen auf E_2 erscheinen.

Objekte der Ebene E_1 sind Personen, Personengruppen oder Institutionen (also natürliche und juristische Personen), über oder für die Informationen mit DV-Systemen gesammelt und verarbeitet werden. Beeinträchtigt werden können die Rechte und Interessen dieser Personen. Beispiele sind der Bürger als Versicherungsnehmer (nachteilige Folgen für sein Arbeitsverhältnis, wenn Arbeitgeber im Zuge eines Datenverbundes Liste seiner Krankheiten einsehen kann, also seine Rollen als Arbeit- und Versicherungsnehmer nicht mehr scharf voneinander getrennt sind), Unternehmen (Wettbewerbsnachteile, wenn Konkurrenz Ergebnisse der eigenen Marktforschung einsehen kann), oder der Mensch als Verkehrsteilnehmer (Unfallschaden durch falsch gesteuerte Verkehrsampel). Wir sprechen hier von den Schutzobjekten als den <u>Betroffenen</u> der Anwendung von DV-Systemen.

E_2-Objekte treten in Rollen wie Systemverwalter, Operateur, Programmierer und Endbenutzer (evtl. weiter unterschieden nach Datenbankbenutzer, Anwender Platzbuchungssystem X usw.) auf. Auch andere technische Systeme können direkt mit dem gegebenen DV-System kommunizieren und daher ebenfalls als E_2-Objekte auftreten. Wir sprechen auf dieser Ebene zusammenfassend von <u>(externen) Benutzern</u> des DV-Systems.

Die Einführung einer Ebene E_3 trägt der Tatsache Rechnung, daß auch innerhalb des DV-Systems selbst einzelne Komponenten in verschiedener Weise beeinträchtigt werden können: Hardwareeinheiten, Programme, Daten. Wir sprechen hier von <u>Systemobjekten</u>.

3.2 Risiken und Beeinträchtigungen

In diesem Abschnitt soll anhand von Beispielen ein Eindruck davon vermittelt werden, welcher Art die Risiken und Beeinträchtigungen für Objekte der einzelnen Ebenen sein können.

E_1:
- persönliche Nachteile materieller und/oder immaterieller Art,
- Nachteile für Institutionen (finanzielle Verluste, Wettbewerbsnachteile, Unzufriedenheit unter Belegschaft)

<u>durch</u>
a) Verlust, Beschädigung, Preisgabe, Veränderung von im DV-System abgelegter Information an/durch Unberechtigte
b) nicht rechtzeitige Verfügbarkeit oder Ausfall von Leistungen, auf deren Erbringung durch das DV-System sich die Betroffenen verlassen (z.B. Ausfall von Ampelanlagen, Verzögerung der Gehaltsabrechnung)
c) fehlerhafte Leistungen des DV-Systems, auf deren Korrektheit sich die Betroffenen verlassen (z.B. falsche Meldung von Raketenangriffen)
d) Belästigung durch DV-Systeme (z.B. "unlesbare" Stromrechnungen)

E_2:
a) falsche Durchführung verlangter Leistungen (wegen Fehler in Hardware, Programmen, Daten)
b) Nichtverfügbarkeit erwarteter Leistungen (wegen Monopolisierung des DV-Systems durch andere Benutzer, Eigenverbrauch des Systems, usw.)
c) unerlaubte (d.h gegen die Intentionen des Benutzers erfolgende) Manipulation oder Kenntnisnahme von Hardware, Progammen, und Daten durch andere Benutzer
d) Beeinträchtigung durch organisatorische Maßnahmen bzgl. der Verwendung des DV-Systems

E_3:
a) von einer Komponente benutzte Hardware, Programme, Daten fehlerhaft
b) Beeinträchtigung einer Komponente durch Aktivitäten anderer Komponenten (z.B. falsche Synchronisation, Monopolisierung von Betriebsmitteln, fehlende gegenseitige Abschirmung)

3.3 Schutzmaßnahmen

Die Schichteneinteilung der Schutzobjekte erfordert konsequenterweise auf jeder Ebene ein Schutzsystem. Wie die aufgezählten Beeinträchtigungsmöglichkeiten nahelegen, kann man aber E_1-, E_2- und E_3-Schutzsystem als Teile eines Gesamtschutzsystem betrachten, das gemäß Abschnitt 2 strukturiert ist. Wegen der Hierarchie der Ebenen handelt es sich um eine vertikale Strukturierung mit horizontaler Aufteilung innerhalb der Ebenen. Wir sehen folgende Zusammenhänge (Abb. 4):

Schutzmaßnahmen auf E_1 und E_2 lassen sich horizontal jeweils zerlegen in solche, die vollständig auf der einzelnen Ebene durchgeführt werden können (E_1^A, E_2^A) und solche, die die Schutzmaßnahmen der nächsttieferen Ebene mit einbeziehen (E_1^B, E_2^B). Als tiefste Ebene muß E_3 dort anfallende Schutzaufgaben vollständig selbst realisieren. Alle angeführten Beispiele setzen sich in der Regel selbst wieder aus mehreren Einzelmaßnahmen zusammen:

E_1: Beeinträchtigungen auf dieser Ebene versuchen die Gesetzgeber durch entsprechende Gesetze und sonstige Regelungen sowie die betroffenen Institutionen durch analoge Vorschriften und organisatorische Maßnahmen zu verhindern. Hierbei handelt es sich häufig um Maßnahmen im Vorfeld von DV-Systemen (z.B. Vorkehrungen, auch ohne DV-System den Betrieb aufrecht erhalten zu können), teilweise kann jedoch eine Delegation der zu treffenden Schutzmaßnahmen an Benutzer des Rechensystems erfolgen (z.B. Vorschriften für die Operateure bzgl. Umgang mit Datenträgern).

Zur Durchsetzung der Maßnahmen gehört die Einrichtung von Überwachungsinstanzen (z.B. Datenschutzbeauftragter) sowie Strafandrohung für Fälle der Zuwiderhandlung. Auch Betroffene selbst können einen Teil der Risiken vermeiden, indem sie etwa besonders sorgsam mit schutzwürdigen Informationen umgehen (typische E_1^A-Maßnahme!). Die Verhinderung von E_1d) hingegen kann nur durch E_1^B-Maßnahmen angegangen werden, da sie auf jeden Fall (externe) Benutzer des Rechensystems erfordert (Systemanalytiker/Programmierer zur Verbesserung der Rechnungsgestaltung für unser Beispiel).

E_2: Ein beträchtlicher Teil der hier möglichen Maßnahmen liegt im Bereich organisatorischer Vorkehrungen (und ist damit E_2^A zuzuordnen), z.B. sachgerechte Autorisierung usw., aber auch die Verhinderung physikalischer Beeinträchtigungen durch bauliche und installatorische Maßnahmen (Schutz vor Beschädigung/Zerstörung des Rechensystems) sowie durch Rechnerwartung. Insbesondere ist hier auch für den angemessenen Einsatz auf E_3 vorhandener Mittel und für deren Entwicklung zu sorgen. Beiträge zu E_2-Maßnahmen sind von allen hier angesiedelten Benutzerrollen zu erbringen, insbesondere auch von Systemherstellern (und damit für ihr Teilgebiet auch von Programmierern), die für eine korrekte Erstellung von Hard- und Software zu sorgen haben.

E_3: Hierunter fallen alle soft- und hardwareseitig realisierbaren Schutzmaßnahmen. Neben ihrem Einsatz gegen Beeinträchtigungen auf E_3 stehen sie für die darüberliegenden Ebenen zur Verfügung.

3.4 Datenschutz und Datensicherung

Durch die Angabe von Schutzobjekten, Möglichkeiten der Beeinträchtigung und der Beeinträchtigungsverhinderung wurde die Verwendung des Begriffs Schutz im Zusammenhang mit DV-Systemen illustriert. Damit liegt auch der Begriff Sicherheit für den betreffenden Bereich fest.

Wir haben in diesem Abschnitt meist umfassend von Schutz gesprochen und Sicherung nicht gesondert erwähnt, was nach den Ausführungen in Abschnitt 1 gerechtfertigt ist. Hingegen ist sehr wohl zwischen den Begriffen Datenschutz und Datensicherung zu unterscheiden:

Datenschutz ("Schutz vor Daten") meint die Verhinderung von Beeinträchtigungen für die Betroffenen der Verwendung von DV-Systemen, ist also auf der Ebene E_1 anzusiedeln (oftmals dort sogar nur eingeschränkt auf den juristischen Aspekt). Bei Datensicherung ("Sicherung der Daten", gemeint ist aber das gesamte DV-System) hingegen ist, in Übereinstimmung mit unserer allgemeinen Erklärung von Sicherung, an die Beseitigung oder "Entschärfung" von Schwachstellen im DV-System und seiner Verwendung gedacht, also an die Verhinderung von Risiken. Schutz auf den Ebenen E_2 und E_3 ist also stets Datensicherung. Man beachte besonders, daß Datensicherung keineswegs auf E_2/E_3-Maßnahmen zur Gewährleistung von Datenschutz im gesetzlich geregelten Sinn beschränkt bleibt. Ebenso ist die Sicherung gespeicherter Daten vor Verlust oder Beschädigung (verursacht durch fehlerhafte Soft- oder Hardware) nur ein Teilaspekt der Datensicherung.

4 Schutz in und mit DV-Systemen

4.1 Motivation für Schutzmaßnahmen im DV-System

Schutz umfaßt im Zusammenhang mit DV-Systemen ein recht weites Feld. Insbesondere gehört dazu eine große Anzahl juristischer und organisatorischer Regelungen auf den Ebenen E_1 und E_2.

Die Durchsetzung solcher Regelungen ist oft nicht einfach. Dies legt es nahe, wo möglich und sinnvoll das DV-System selbst dazu einzusetzen. Ziel der Informatik ist es daher, Schutzmaßnahmen auf E_3 anzubieten, mit denen Regelungen auf E_2 (und indirekt auch auf E_1) durchgesetzt werden können. Unbeschadet davon müssen Schutzmaßnahmen gegen E_3-Beeinträchtigungen zwangsläufig ebenfalls auf E_3 angesiedelt sein.

Das Delegieren von Schutzaufgaben an tiefere Ebenen ist nicht nur bequemer, sondern wird auch unterstützt durch die folgende

Prämisse: Schutzmaßnahmen sind umso wirkungsvoller, je tiefer in einem hierarchischen System sie eingerichtet sind.

Selbstverständlich wird dabei vorausgesetzt, daß die Schutzmaßnahmen korrekt arbeiten und richtig verwendet werden (beides im intuitiven Sinne verstanden). Die Gültigkeit der Prämisse läßt sich dann vor allem durch zwei Feststellungen untermauern:

1. Schutzmaßnahmen auf höheren Hierarchieebenen sind meist leichter umgehbar (und damit unwirksam) als solche auf niederen. So ist es etwa für einen "Schutzverletzer" meist wesentlich einfacher, Einblick in eine herumliegende Gehaltsliste zu nehmen, als ein Paßwort zu ermitteln und die entsprechende Datei zu lesen.

2. Die Gefahr, Einsatz oder Einrichtung von Schutzmaßnahmen zu vergessen, ist auf tieferen Ebenen in der Regel geringer. So ist z.B. der Kreis der beteiligten Personen auf E_2 verglichen mit E_1 wesentlich kleiner und kann außerdem entsprechend geschult werden. Hinsichtlich E_2/E_3 gilt, daß Einrichtung und teilweise auch Einsatz von E_3-Maßnahmen einmalig bei Herstellung des DV-Systems zu bedenken sind und anschließend aufgrund der technischen Gegebenheiten automatisch "funktionieren". Auf E_2 besteht hingegen für jeden Fall von Neuem die Notwendigkeit, die Voraussetzungen korrekte Funktion und richtiger Einsatz zu erfüllen bzw. vorhandene Schutzmaßnahmen überhaupt zu verwenden.

Natürlich hat auch die hier vorliegende Prämisse Ausnahmen. So ist die E_1-Schutzmaßnahme "wo immer möglich, keine persönlichen Informationen preisgeben" außerordentlich wirksam, wiewohl auf oberster Ebene angesiedelt. Dies ändert jedoch nichts daran, daß die Prämisse eine angemessene Arbeitsgrundlage ist.

Schutzmaßnahmen in DV-Systemen werden also sowohl zur Verhinderung von Beeinträchtigungen auf E_3 selbst als auch zur Unterstützung der Schutzmaßnahmen auf E_2 und (indirekt) E_1 benötigt. Hierzu müssen Regelungen von E_2 auf "passende" E_3-Regelungen abgebildet werden, die dann durch das DV-System durchgesetzt werden können. Für E_1 tritt eine zusätzliche Abbildung auf E_2-Regelungen hinzu.

Zusammenfassend wollen wir festlegen: <u>Schutz aus der (technischen) Sicht des Informatikers</u> ist die Verhinderung von Beeinträchtigungen mithilfe von DV-Systemen. Beeinträchtigungen sind dabei sowohl solche, die

(a) das DV-Systems durch seine technische Beschaffenheit, Konstruktion etc. verursachen kann, als auch solche, die

(b) durch die Verwendung des DV-Systems entgegen
(i) implizit (durch die Konstruktion) oder
(ii) explizit (durch Systembenutzer)
festgelegten Regeln entstehen.

4.2 Schutzmaßnahmen in DV-Systemen

Betrachten wir die Ebene E_3 genauer, so können wir hier erneut eine interne Unterteilung in Schichten treffen. Folgende groben Ebenen bieten sich an:

E_3:
- RS_1 : Anwendungssoftware (z.B. Datenbanksysteme)
- RS_2 : Betriebssoftware (Betriebssysteme etc.)
- RS_3 : Hardware

Schutzmaßnahmen finden sich auf allen Ebenen, wobei Zusammensetzung und Zusammenwirken der Schutzsysteme in RS_1, RS_2 und RS_3 vollkommen analog wie für E_1, E_2 und E_3 besprochen aussehen. Insbesondere gilt auch hier obige Prämisse.

Bei der Betrachtung der einzelnen Bausteine (Moduln) von DV-Systemen unterscheidet man auf RS_1, RS_2 und RS_3 gleichermaßen zwischen Schnittstelle einerseits und deren Implementierung (Realisierung) andererseits. In ähnlicher Weise ist bei Schutzmaßnahmen in DV-Systemen zu unterscheiden (für Maßnahmen auf E_1 und E_2 gilt dies in leicht abgewandelter Form übrigens auch):

- Operationale Schutzmaßnahmen sind explizit an einer Schnittstelle angebotene Funktionen (Schutzfunktionen), mit denen

  (a) Regelungen spezifiziert werden können, deren Verletzung verhindert wird, oder
  (b) Regelungen spezifiziert werden können, deren Verletzung entdeckt wird, oder
  (c) Auswirkungen der Verletzung von Regelungen beseitigt werden können.

- Methodische Schutzmaßnahmen sind Verfahren und Methoden, die eine korrekte Realisierung ("sichere Realisierung") der Schnittstelle eines Systems gewährleisten oder unterstützen, so daß durch die Konstruktion des Systems keine Beeinträchtigungen entstehen.

Für den Bereich der Software sind methodische Schutzmaßnahmen somit gerade die Hilfsmittel der Programmkonstruktion, die zur korrekten Realisierung von Modulschnittstellen zur Verfügung stehen. Dazu gehören etwa die Verwendung höherer Programmiersprachen, der Einsatz von Verifikations- und Testwerkzeugen oder die Anwendung geeigneter Programmiermethoden (Modularisierung, defensives Programmieren, Programmtransformationen etc.). Auch der sachgerechte Einsatz vorhandener operationaler Schutzmaßnahmen (insbesondere die Formulierung der dort benötigten Regelungen) ist ein methodischer Gesichtspunkt. Derartige Schutzmaßnahmen verursachen Aufwand in erster Linie im Zuge der Systementwicklung, weniger aber während des Systembetriebs.

Operationale Schutzmaßnahmen - obwohl zusätzlichen Aufwand während des Systembetriebs verursachend - sind schon aus den folgenden Gründen unbedingt notwendig:

(i) Die zur Erzielung der gewünschten Sicherheit von einem System einzuhaltenden Regelungen können häufig nicht fest darin "eingebaut" werden, sondern müssen über eine Schnittstelle spezifizierbar sein. Dies gilt insbesondere dann, wenn die Regelungen sich während der Lebensdauer des Systems ändern können.

(ii) Mit methodischen Schutzmaßnahmen allein ist nach heutigem Kenntnisstand meist nur für stark eingeschränkte Schnittstellen das gewünschte Maß an Sicherheit zu erzielen (siehe etwa Verifikationstechniken). Dem läßt sich dadurch begegnen, daß man für die Realisierung der vorgegebenen Schnittstelle geeignete "Unterschnittstellen" - insbesondere in Form operationaler

Schutzmaßnahmen - sucht oder konstruiert. Damit können rein methodische Maßnahmen auf einen Umfang reduziert werden, der mit heutigen Mitteln zufriedenstellend bewältigt werden kann.

Somit ergeben sich folgende Zusammenhänge: Einerseits erfordert die sichere Realisierung operationaler Schutzmaßnahmen (wie die sichere Realisierung anderer Schnittstellen auch) den Einsatz methodischer Schutzmaßnahmen. Auf der anderen Seite ist es ein wichtiger Aspekt methodischer Schutzmaßnahmen, geeignete operationale Schutzmaßnahmen (und andere Schnittstellen) zur sicheren Realisierung einer vorgegebenen ("höheren") Schnittstelle aufzufinden und heranzuziehen. Dies führt zusammengenommen zu einer Maßnahmenhierarchie, bei der operationale und methodische Maßnahmen einander abwechseln.

4.3 Verwandte Begriffe

In der Fachterminologie der Informatik existieren eine Reihe von Begriffen, die im Zusammenhang mit Schutz häufig auftreten und sich in der Regel den von uns vorgeschlagenen Erklärungen als Spezialfälle unterordnen lassen. Hierzu gehört insbesondere die Zuverlässigkeit als Sammelbegriff für Korrektheit (funktionale Richtigkeit gegenüber einer Spezifikation des Systems), Ausfallsicherheit (Sicherheit vor der Beeinträchtigung "System fällt aus") und Robustheit (Sicherheit gegenüber Beeinträchtigungen durch fehlerhafte Benutzung des Systems). Ein zuverlässiges DV-System (Datenbank-, Betriebssystem, zuverlässige Hardware) bietet somit Sicherheit gegenüber Beeinträchtigungen nach (a) und (b)(i) aus Abschnitt 4.1. Maßnahmen zur Erzielung von Zuverlässigkeit sind somit spezielle Schutzmaßnahmen; ihr Einsatz ist auf allen Ebenen RS_1, RS_2 und RS_3 angezeigt.

Unter Datenkonsistenz versteht man die Sicherheit vor Beeinträchtigungen durch die Nichtübereinstimmung der im System vorhandenen Daten mit der durch sie darzustellen beabsichtigten Information. Konsistenz von Daten ist vergleichbar mit funktionaler Richtigkeit von Programmen. Bei den betreffenden Daten kann es sich um systeminterne Verwaltungsdaten (--> Zuverlässigkeit), oder um von Benutzern zur Speicherung angelieferte (--> Schutz für E_2) handeln. Sicherheit vor Beeinträchtigungen durch fehlende oder mangelhafte Koordination verschiedener Prozesse eines DV-Systems nennt man Prozeßintegrität.

Schließlich sei noch der Ausdruck "sicheres System" erwähnt, der in der einschlägigen Literatur häufig ohne nähere Erläuterung auftaucht. Meist wird darunter ein zuverlässiges System gemäß obiger Erläuterung verstanden. Unterstellt ist dabei oft, daß der Teilaspekt "Korrektheit gegenüber der Systemspezifikation oder einer dedizierten formalen Sicherheitsdefinition" mehr oder minder formal nachgewiesen wurde. Darin ist eingeschlossen, daß ein solches System nur so benutzt werden kann, wie es die vorgesehene Schnittstelle vorsieht. "Sicheres System" ist auf jeden Fall nur dann eine zulässige Redewendung, wenn die jeweiligen Beeinträchtigungen, gegen die das System Sicherheit bietet, eindeutig festgelegt sind.

5 Zusammenfassung

Die Verwendung von Begriffen in einem Fachgebiet sollte in einheitlicher Weise erfolgen, die Bedeutung von Fachbegriffen aus der Bedeutung im allgemeinen Sprachgebrauch ableitbar sein. Wir hoffen, daß unsere Ausführungen als Diskussionsgrundlage dienen, um in der Informatik für das weite Feld Schutz zu einem gemeinsamen Verständnis zu kommen.

Wenn es dabei um Hard- und Software geht, halten wir es nicht unbedingt für erforderlich, zwischen Schutz und Sicherung sprachlich streng zu unterscheiden (wiewohl die festgefügten Begriffe Datenschutz und Datensicherung wie besprochen differenziert zu verwenden sind). Viel wichtiger erscheint es uns, durch Angabe von Risiken/Beeinträchtigungen stets zu präzisieren, "welche" Sicherheit gemeint ist.

Literatur

Den Anstoß zu diesem Beitrag gab ein aus anderen Gründen durchgeführtes Literaturstudium. Eine Einzelaufzählung würde hier zu weit führen; stattdessen sei nur die hervoragende Bibliographie [HER 78] zitiert. Für Abschnitt 1 wurde eine größere Anzahl von Herkunfts- und Bedeutungswörterbüchern verwendet.

[BD 79] Bayer, R.; Dierstein, R.: Rahmenkonzept für die Systematik der Datensicherung. GDD-Dokumentation 19, 1979

[HER 78] Herda, S.: Datensicherung und Datenschutz - Glossar und annotierte Bibliographie. Bericht Nr. 38 des IST, Gesellschaft für Mathematik und Datenverarbeitung mbH Bonn, 1978

Herrn R. Dierstein, DFVLR Oberpfaffenhofen, und meinen Karlsruher Kollegen danke ich für ausgiebige Diskussionen über das behandelte Thema.

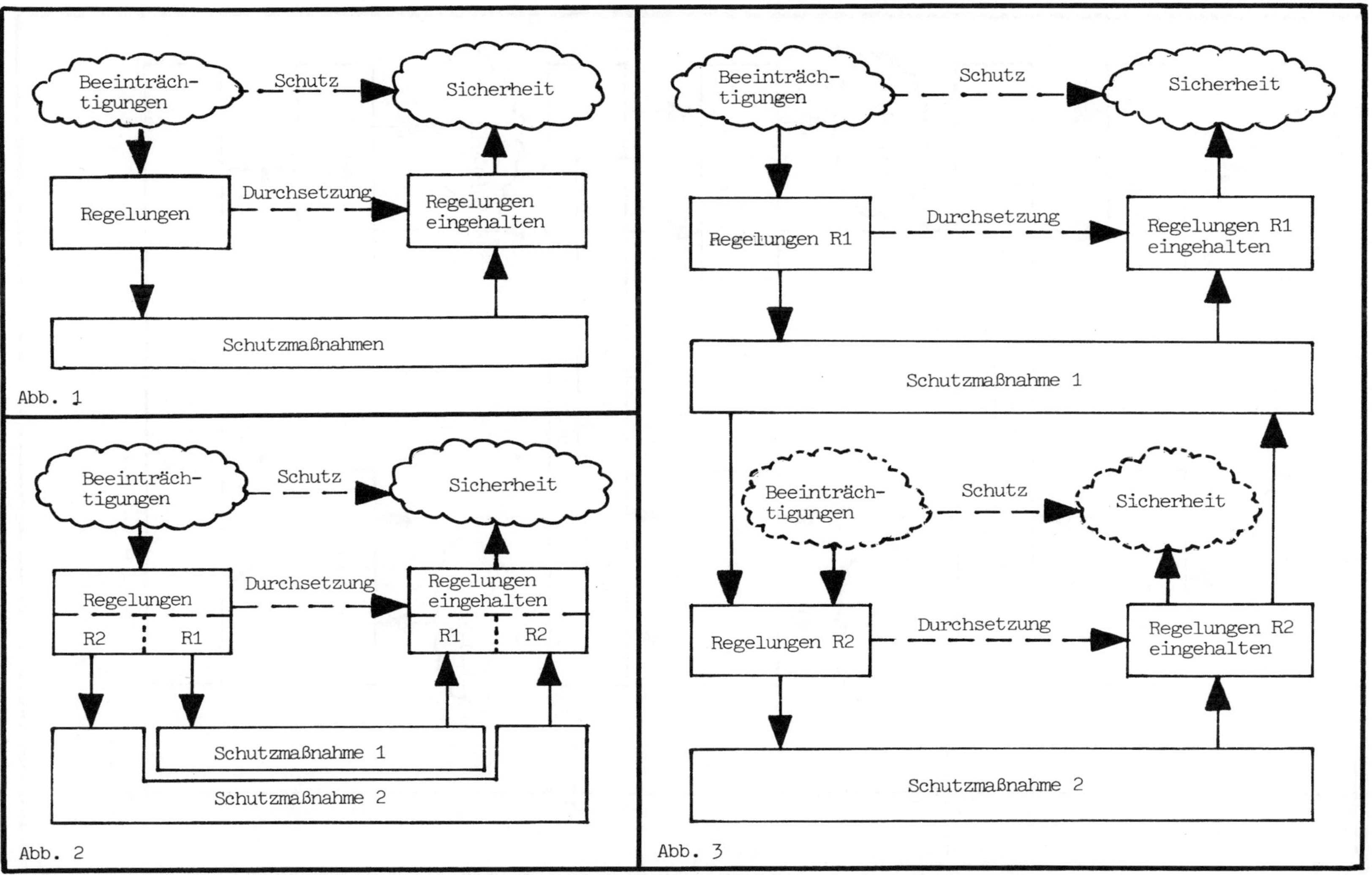

Abb. 1

Abb. 2

Abb. 3

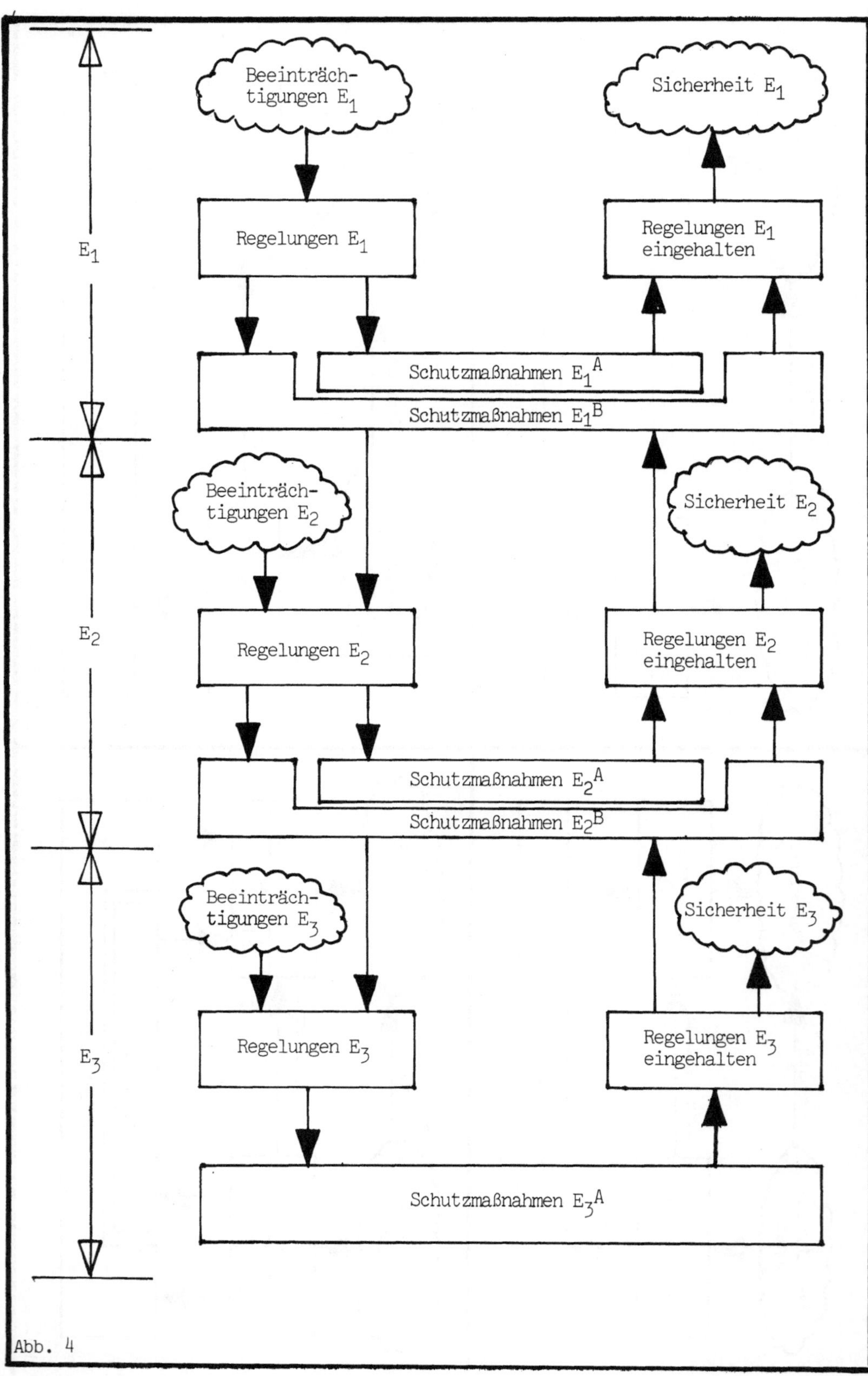
Beeinträchtigungen E1
Sicherheit E1
Regelungen E1
Regelungen E1 eingehalten
E1
Schutzmaßnahmen E1A
Schutzmaßnahmen E1B
Beeinträchtigungen E2
Sicherheit E2
E2
Regelungen E2
Regelungen E2 eingehalten
Schutzmaßnahmen E2A
Schutzmaßnahmen E2B
Beeinträchtigungen E3
Sicherheit E3
E3
Regelungen E3
Regelungen E3 eingehalten
Schutzmaßnahmen E3A

Abb. 4

COMPUTER AN DER SCHULE IM WANDEL

Karl-August Keil

Zentralstelle für Programmierten Unterricht
und Computer im Unterricht
Schertlinstr. 7, D 8900 Augsburg

Zusammenfassung

Nach Versuchen mit numerischen Tischrechnern und Forschungsprojekten mit größeren Rechenzentren wurden zunächst Einplatz- und Mehrplatzsysteme eingesetzt. Seit einigen Jahren halten die Microcomputer Einzug in die Schulen. Die Software bietet zunehmend bessere Möglichkeiten in bezug auf verfügbare Betriebssysteme, Sprachen, Graphik u. a. Informatiklehrpläne entstanden, die sich vor allem unter dem Einfluß der GI-Empfehlungen wandelten. Der Einsatzbereich der Computer an den Schulen verbreiterte sich: Informatik/DV-Fächer, anderer Fachunterricht und Schulverwaltung. Es beginnt nun der Schritt von einer kleinen Zahl von Schulen hin zu allen Schulen. Dabei muß Vorsorge getroffen werden, daß der Computereinsatz auch dann noch gelingt, wenn er nicht mehr nur von hochmotivierten Lehrern getragen wird. Auch der Übergang von Wahl- zu Pflichtunterricht ist nicht problemlos; die Beliebtheit der Informatik bei den Schülern könnte sich rasch wandeln.

1. Einleitung

Computer und Informatik sind noch jung, erst recht an der Schule. Trotzdem oder gerade deshalb ist der Computereinsatz in der Schule ständigen Veränderungen ausgesetzt. Die heutigen Zielvorstellungen haben sich erst im Laufe der Jahre herauskristallisiert und sind noch keineswegs festgeschrieben. Die Entwicklungen der Hardware, der Software und der Kommunikationstechnik sowie die Veränderungen in der Berufswelt haben Rückwirkungen auf die Schule.

Aus Gründen der Gleichbehandlung der Schüler müssen in absehbarer Zeit alle Schulen, in denen Schüler ab einer bestimmten Altersgruppe unterrichtet werden, den Computer benutzen. Angesichts der Bedeutung der Datenverarbeitung und der Kommunikationstechnik in Beruf und Alltag wird Informatik/EDV auch nicht auf den Wahlunterricht und damit auf einen Kreis von besonders interessierten Schülern beschränkt bleiben.

Diese Ausweitung auf alle Schulen und alle Schüler ist ein tiefgreifender Einschnitt; er bringt Probleme und Gefahren, die sorgfältig bedacht sein müssen.

2. Frühphase

Zunächst gab es ab Ende der 60er Jahre Pionierarbeiten einzelner Lehrer mit rein numerischen Rechnern und Projekte des Forschungsministeriums [1,2] die auf Terminalanschluß der Schulen an Großrechner als zentrale Lösungen ausgerichtet waren. Eine Veränderung in mehrfacher Hinsicht zeigte sich um die Mitte der 70er Jahre. Es kamen verhältnismäßig preiswerte Rechner als Mehrbenutzersysteme auf den Markt und außerdem Tischcomputer, die gegenüber ihren Vorgängern, bei etwa gleichem Preis, statt der Maschinensprache über BASIC verfügten, Stringverarbeitung zuließen und externe magnetische Speicher, nämlich Kassetten und bald auch Disketten verwendeten. Zu diesem Zeitpunkt konnte man absehen, daß dezentrale Lösungen allgemein finanzierbar werden würden. Ein Sachverständigenkreis des Bundesministeriums für Forschung und Technologie veröffentlichte 1974 eine entsprechende Empfehlung für Rechnerausstattung und koordinierte Maßnahmen[3]. Die dort genannten Hardwarekosten stellten sich später noch als zu hoch angesetzt heraus.

Die Lehrpläne zeigten, nicht zuletzt unter dem Einfluß der Empfehlungen der Gesellschaft für Informatik von 1976 [4], ein Zurücktreten von Inhalten wie Hardware, Maschinensprache, Schaltalgebra, und eine Betonung der Schwerpunkte Computer als Werkzeug, algorithmische Lösungen von Problemen, Top-down-Programmierung, Auswirkungen der Datenverarbeitung. Die bisherigen Aktivitäten wurden abgelöst durch Modellversuche in den Bundesländern, die Informatik-Curricula, höhere Programmiersprachen für den Unterrichtsgebrauch oder multifunktionalen Einsatz des Computers für Informatik, andere Fachrichtungen und Schulverwaltung erprobten.

3. Hardware

Den Zeittakt des Wandels bestimmten in den folgenden Jahren hauptsächlich die Entwicklungen auf der Hardwareseite. Etwa ab 1978 wurden Microcomputer verfügbar. Zunehmende Leistungsfähigkeit, umfangreicher werdende Peripherie und abnehmender Preis ließen sie für die Schule interessant werden. Vielfach stehen heute interne Speicher bis zu 64 KB zur Verfügung, was 10 Jahre vorher einem kleineren Rechenzentrum entsprach. Externe Speicher mit Diskettendoppellaufwerken von über ein MB oder sogar mit Festplatten können angeschlossen werden.

Der multifunktionale Einsatz wurde etwa ab 1979 auch mit diesen Geräten realisierbar wie ein Modellversuch des Bayerischen Kultusministeriums mit 17 Schulen zeigt. Möglichkeiten der Graphik auf dem Bildschirm eröffneten sich, die vorher für Schulen utopisch erschienen. Beschränkte Tonausgabe ist erhältlich, die vorläufig allerdings meist nur spielerisch benutzt wird.

Auch wenn ein Mehrbenutzersystem nicht finanzierbar ist, entfällt nun die Notwendigkeit, sich auf einen einzigen Arbeitsplatz zu beschränken. Bei einfachster Peripherie kosten 6 bis 10 autonome Rechner heute soviel wie Mitte der 70er Jahre ein Einplatzsystem. Neuerdings werden sogar gemeinsame Zugriffe auf Disketten und Drucker angeboten, z.B. für 4 Microcomputer zum Preise unter DM 2.000,--. Die Diskussion um geeignete Rechner bleibt im Gange. Der Arbeitskreis Schulrechner des BMFT veröffentlichte 1980 Empfehlungen[5], in Berlin fand im Juni 1981 ein Kolloquium statt, bei dem die Rechnerausstattung ein wichtiger Punkt war, in Bayern werden seit einiger Zeit jährliche Ausschreibungen durchgeführt. Angesichts der finanziellen Engpässe wird man sich auch in den kommenden Jahren mit verhältnismäßig bescheidener Ausstattung zufriedengeben müssen, wenn man nicht auf viele Jahre bei einer kleinen Minderheit von Schulen stehenbleiben will. Zentraler Einkauf kann die Kosten senken.

Sehr wichtig ist für die Schulen auch eine preiswerte Instandhaltung der Geräte. Dies ist immer noch ein schwieriger Punkt für den Schuletat, obwohl heute im Vergleich zu früher erstaunlich billige Lösungen gefunden wurden. Wartungsverträge können in der Regel nicht abgeschlossen werden. Hardwareanschaffung und -instandhaltung sind für die Schulen die entscheidenden Kostenpunkte. Die Situation ist anders als in der Wirtschaft, denn die Anwendersoftware fällt auf Grund ihrer Art bzw. der großen Zahl von Schulen kostenmäßig nicht ins Gewicht. Spezielle Personalkosten wurden jedenfalls zur Zeit noch nicht berücksichtigt.

4. Software

Die Software der Microcomputer hatte Mühe mit der raschen Hardwareentwicklung Schritt zu halten. Die Betriebssysteme der ersten Hobby-Computer waren noch sehr primitiv und verdienten kaum diese Bezeichnung. Inzwischen werden schon recht komfortable Versionen benutzt, wenn man ihnen auch meist noch anmerkt, daß sie aus einfachen Vorgängern entstanden sind. Die Sprache BASIC bieten nahezu alle an und dadurch fand diese Sprache eine enorme Verbreitung im Schulbereich. PASCAL oder ELAN [6] können inzwischen außerdem eingesetzt werden, allerdings erst bei größerem Arbeitsspeicher, Diskettenlaufwerk und zusätzlichen Kosten. Die Folge ist, daß zur Zeit BASIC sehr stark dominiert. Obwohl moderne BASIC-Dialekte reichhaltigere Sprachelemente enthalten als früher, führt es zu einem gewissen Konflikt mit den Prinzipien modernen Programmierens: Top-down-Methode, Strukturiertes Programmieren, Selbstdokumentierende Programme usw., wie es den GI-Empfehlungen entspricht. Eine brauchbare Kompromißlösung ist es, wenn man die Algorithmen zunächst unabhängig von der verwendeten Computersprache formulieren läßt und dann zeigt, wie man die Umsetzung in BASIC durchführen kann, sogar nach festen Regeln. Bei der Lehrerfortbildung gehen wir in Bayern in dieser Weise vor [7]. Da String- und Dateiverarbeitung möglich sind und ein freier Anwenderspeicher von 32 KB durchaus üblich ist, können größere Projekte realisiert werden. Wenn ein interpretierendes System, z.B. bei Simulationen, Laufzeitprobleme bringt, werden Routinen in Maschinensprache eingefügt. Bei manchen Microcomputern steht allerdings neben dem Interpretierer schon ein Compiler zur Verfügung.

Durch die Ausbreitung der Micros im privaten Sektor zeigt sich die neuartige Situation, daß Programmieren nicht mehr nur eine Sache der Fachleute ist, sondern zum Hobby wird. In Clubs und Zeitschriften, die in großer Zahl gegründet wurden, wird vielfältig Anwendersoftware angeboten. Die Qualität ist allerdings sehr unterschiedlich. Lehrer und Schüler benutzen sie und beteiligen sich auch.

5. Multifunktionaler Einsatz

Der Multifunktionale Einsatz der Rechner wird inzwischen aus den Modellversuchen vielfach in die Praxis anderer Schulen übernommen.

Die Erfahrung zeigt, daß die Entwicklung eines Softwarepakets für die Schulverwaltung kein Freizeitjob ist, der nebenbei erledigt werden kann. Das muß man feststellen, obwohl einzelne Lehrer ganz Erstaunliches entwickelt haben. Sie ernten aber in der Regel wenig Dank: Wenn Pannen auftreten, werden nicht die Leistung und der Zeitaufwand gesehen, sondern der Programmierer ist der Sündenbock. Außerdem richtet sich der Ärger auf den Computer, was seine Aufnahme in die Schule nicht gerade erleichtert. Meist konnten die Programme nicht so benutzerfreundlich, bedienungssicher und dokumentiert ausgebaut werden, daß die Schulsekretärin problemlos damit zurecht kommt. Es führte dann zu der grotesken Situation, daß für Dateneingabe, Änderungsdienst, Abruf von Statistik- oder Listendruckprogrammen z. B. ein Mathematiklehrer mit A14-Einstufung eingesetzt wurde. Außerdem ist es wenig rationell, daß an jeder Schule das gleiche Programmpaket neu entwickelt wird. Man kann also nur davor warnen! Zu berücksichtigen ist auch, daß man einen Computer nicht einfach in eine vorhandene Verwaltungsstruktur einfügen kann. Es ist eine Überprüfung und Anpassung notwendig. Besonders wenn das gleiche Programmpaket an einer großen Zahl von Schulen verwendet werden soll, sind einheitliche Festlegungen, z.B. des Schülerdatensatzes, erforderlich. Dies gilt auch dann, wenn wie heute vorherrschend ein schuleigener Rechner zur Verfügung steht, über den frei verfügt werden kann.

Im Rahmen der Modellversuche wurden in Bayern [8] in Zusammenarbeit von Hersteller- oder Vertriebsfirmen und Versuchsschulen nach detaillierten Vorgaben Verwaltungsprogramme bereits für mehrere Fabrikate entwickelt. Die Freigabe erfolgt erst nach gründlicher Erprobung der Programme und des Arbeitsablaufs in den Versuchsschulen, um das Akzeptanzproblem bei Schulleitern und Lehrerkollegium zu entschärfen.

Besondere Fragen wirft der Einsatz im Unterricht der verschiedenen Fächer auf. Welche Rolle kann der Computer hier jeweils übernehmen? Der Lehrer hat kein Vorbild aus der eigenen Schulzeit oder aus der Ausbildung. Vorschläge in der Literatur sind noch rar und nicht ohne weiteres zugänglich. Die Vorbereitung auf solchen Unterricht kann für den Lehrer sehr zeitaufwendig werden; es sind Überlegungen und Planungen erforderlich, die aus dem üblichen Rahmen fallen. Der Computereinsatz kostet Unterrichtszeit. Der Lehrer fragt sich, ob er dies verantworten kann, sei es im Blick auf den Gewinn für das betreffende Fach, oder auf die mitbehandelten Informatikaspekte, oder einfach im Blick auf die Motivationswirkung. Schließlich sind die Lehrpläne etwa in Mathematik, Physik, Wirtschaftskunde nicht darauf abgestimmt, daß ein Computer verfügbar ist. Sie bieten noch wenig Ansatzpunkte für den Computereinsatz. Lehrpläne ändern sich nicht so rasch. Auch ist der Erfahrungshintergrund für solche Maßnahmen noch zu schmal und nicht alle Schulen haben schon einen Computer. Die Nutzung der Graphikfähigkeiten z. B. beginnt gerade erst.

Mit Computerprogrammen zu den einzelnen Fächern allein ist dem Lehrer noch nicht sehr viel gedient. Wichtiger sind Unterrichtsbeispiele. In Bayern hat die Zentralstelle in Augsburg einen Austausch von Programmen und Unterrichtsmodellen unter den Schulen organisiert, der bereits gut eingespielt ist. Die ca. 500 Programme sind allerdings von sehr unterschiedlicher Qualität und gerade die zugehörige Funktion im Unterricht ist oft noch wenig befriedigend dargestellt. Ausführliche Beschreibungen von Unterrichtsbeispielen werden den Schulen zusätzlich in der internen Fortbildungszeitschrift BUS zur Verfügung gestellt.

Dagegen sind die Schwierigkeiten in dem Haupteinsatzbereich, den Informatik/EDV-Fächern weniger gravierend. Die bereits vorhandenen Lehrpläne geben dem Lehrer meist eine verläßliche Richtschnur für sein Vorgehen und in der Literatur findet er Hilfen und Anregungen für Problemstellungen und Programme. Voraussetzung ist allerdings, daß er selbst bereits ein ausreichendes Kenntnisniveau erreicht hat, nicht nur in der Bedienung des Rechners und im Codieren. Er muß die Prinzipien und Ziele der Informatik an der Schule verstanden haben.

Derjenige Lehrer, der die Beschaffung eines Rechners durchgesetzt hat, übernimmt verständlicherweise auch die Betreuung des Computersystems und die Organisation des Rechnerbetriebs an der Schule. Dies ist zunächst, wenn erst wenige Lehrer der Schule damit arbeiten, noch nicht sehr aufwendig; wird die Zahl aber größer, läuft die Schulverwaltung auf dem Rechner, wollen immer mehr Schüler außerhalb ihrer Unterrichtszeit an das Gerät, sollen Facharbeiten damit angefertigt werden usw., so ist es keine zu unterschätzende Aufgabe, die ständige Betriebsbereitschaft, eine reibungslose Organisation sowie Beratung und Hilfestellung für Kollegen, Verwaltungspersonal und Schüler zu gewährleisten. Oft kommen noch Programmieraufgaben hinzu. Es ist dringend erforderlich, daß diese Aufgaben und Belastungen präzisiert und in den Planungen mit entsprechenden Entlastungen berücksichtigt werden.

6. Ausdehnung auf alle Schulen

Es bedeutet keineswegs eine stetige Weiterentwicklung sondern vielmehr einen ganz neuen Schritt, wenn alle Schulen der in Frage kommenden Schularten mit Computern ausgestattet werden, nicht nur Versuchsschulen und Schulen, an denen Lehrer sich für die Anschaffung eingesetzt haben.

Der Übergang von Versuchsschulen zu der Gesamtheit der Schulen bringt stets eine veränderte Situation. Manches Problem, mancher Seiteneffekt wird erst dann erkannt. Beispiele aus Lehrplan-Neugestaltungen oder der Oberstufenreform belegen dies. Der Einsatz muß jetzt von einer sehr großen Zahl von Lehrern getragen werden, auch solchen, die nicht besonders daran interessiert sind. Die Motivationslage ist ganz anders. Wesentliche zusätzliche Belastungen werden nicht mehr stillschweigend akzeptiert wie vorher von den Enthusiasten. Nicht alles läuft so gut, wenn der Lehrer nicht mit seinem vollen Engagement und mit großem Idealismus dahintersteht. Manches wird nüchterner, kritischer gesehen. Zumindest die Schulleitung und die Fachkollegen der betroffenen Fächer können die Existenz des Schulrechners nicht mehr ignorieren. Der Wechsel eines Lehrers, der mit dem Computer nichts zu tun haben will, zu einer Schule ohne Computer ist nicht mehr möglich.

Ein weiterer tiefgreifender Wandel ist es, wenn Informatik nicht nur Wahlunterricht ist, sondern als eigenes Fach oder als Bestandteil anderer Fächer in den Pflichtunterricht eingeht, wie es heute zum Teil schon geschieht. Der Unterricht sieht anders aus, wenn nicht nur interessierte Schüler freiwillig teilnehmen und wenn die üblichen Leistungsnachweise verlangt werden. Im Pflichtunterricht muß man sich, im Gegensatz zu Wahlkursen, mehr um die Motivation kümmern. Man muß berücksichtigen, daß mancher Schüler ganz andere Interessenschwerpunkte hat oder, daß er schon vom Elternhaus mit einer negativen Einstellung kommt. Es besagt noch nicht viel, daß es in jeder Klasse immer einige geben wird, die begeistert darauf eingehen und sich jede freie Minute an den Computer setzen wollen. Auch die Mathematik fasziniert eine ganze Reihe von Schülern, ist andererseits bei vielen sehr wenig beliebt. Ist die Situation in der Informatik so vollständig anders? Jedenfalls kommt hier das Gerät und Medium Computer dazu. Der Vergleich mit Medien wie Dias, Film und Fernseher, an die die Schüler längst gewöhnt sind, fällt für den Computer günstig aus. Zum einen ist der Computer noch neu, der Heimcomputer zu Hause doch noch recht selten. Wichtiger ist, daß die Möglichkeit des eigenen aktiven Arbeitens mit der Maschine hinzukommt, die man den Schülern auch unbedingt eröffnen muß. Das Interesse erlahmt sehr rasch, wenn der Computer nur ein Instrument in der Hand des Lehrers oder einiger weniger Schüler ist, auch wenn die ganze Klasse das Bildschirmgeschehen auf Fernsehern mitverfolgen kann. Durch die Tatsache, daß sich stets ein Teil der Schüler außerhalb der Unterrichtszeit intensiv mit dem Computer befaßt, wird das Leistungsgefälle in einer Klasse größer als in jedem anderen Fach. Mancher Schüler findet in der Arbeit am Computer ein Feld, wo er sich hervortun kann. Er fühlt sich bald als Experte gegenüber seinen Klassenkameraden. Besonders wichtig ist dies für solche Schüler, die im anderen Unterricht weniger erfolgreich sind. Hier ist allerdings Vorsicht geboten [9].

Um das Interesse der Schüler an der Informatik auch im Pflichtunterricht wachzuhalten bzw. erst zu wecken, ist es vor allem wichtig, alle Schüler bald und immer wieder zur aktiven Arbeit am Rechner zu bringen und sie dort Erfolge beim Lauf fremder und vor allem eigener Programme erleben zu lassen. Man muß die konstruktive Seite der Informatik nutzen, die bei keinem anderen Schulfach in diesem Maße vorhanden ist. Dies ist möglich, auch wenn die Durchführung größerer Projekte in Gruppenarbeit im Routinebetrieb nicht immer im vorgeschlagenen Umfang realisierbar ist. Die Beispiele, die Programmstellungen sollten interessant sein. Auch bei Spielen mit dem Computer kann man lernen. Weiter darf man sich nicht dazu verleiten lassen, den Schwerpunkt auf Wissensstoff zu legen, der in der Informatik dazu noch besonders rasch veraltet. Man muß den Schülern klarmachen, daß ihnen das, was sie in diesem Unterricht lernen, in der künftigen Berufswelt von Wert sein kann.

Wie in allen Fächern ist der Lehrer, sein Interesse, sein Engagement für das Fach, ein nicht zu unterschätzender Faktor. Solange es möglich ist, sollte man sich daher auf Lehrer beschränken, die freiwillig und gerne Informatik lehren. In der Regel müssen ja nicht alle Kollegen etwa der Mathematik in dieses Gebiet einsteigen. Da nicht alle Schulen in kurzer Zeit mit Computern ausgestattet werden können, sollten zuerst diejenigen zum Zuge kommen, die über die entsprechenden Lehrer verfügen. Man sollte es vermeiden, daß einer Schule ein Computer aufgedrängt wird. Eine Aufgabe der Fortbildung und längerfristig der Ausbildung ist es, Schwellen abzubauen und mit der Zeit überall ein entsprechendes Lehrerpotential zu schaffen. Insbesondere sind Lehrer für Informatik heranzubilden. Von der Gesellschaft für Informatik wurden 1979 Empfehlungen dazu herausgegeben [10]. Den Lehrern muß man Hilfen anbieten in Form von guten Beispielen und Unterrichtsmodellen. Um zu erreichen, daß auch weniger motivierte Lehrer auf die Dauer bereit sind, den Computer einzusetzen, muß dafür gesorgt werden, daß keine wesentliche zusätzliche Belastung damit verbunden ist und der Rechnerbetrieb an der Schule so organisiert ist, daß technische Pannen möglichst vermieden werden.

In Bayern erhielt unsere Zentralstelle in Augsburg die Aufgabe übertragen, die Fortbildung koordinierend und helfend zu unterstützen. Informatik/EDV wurde zu einem Schwerpunkt der gesamten Fortbildungsaktivitäten ab 1981 erklärt. Richtlinien für Einführungs-, Aufbau- und Spezialkurse wurden erarbeitet. Die Zentralstelle entwickelte einen Kursleitfaden in Form von Hilfen für die Referenten und Materialien für die Kursteilnehmer. Zur Erleichterung und Rationalisierung der Arbeit der Lehrer dienen Beschreibungen zur Handhabung der Geräte, zu den Computersprachen u. a. Daneben wird die Zeitschrift BUS als Fortbildungsmedium herausgebracht.

7. Ziele

Daß Informatik als eigenes Fach oder als Bestandteil anderer Fächer in die Schule aufgenommen wird, daß der Computer den Unterricht verschiedener Fächer unterstützt, ist nicht selbstverständlich [11]. Man sollte sich nicht auf den Standpunkt stellen: Der Computer ist da; was kann man in der Schule damit machen? Die Frage sollte lauten: Was sind die Aufgaben der Schule in unserer Zeit? Was kann der Computer zu ihrer Lösung beitragen?

Wenn man bedenkt, wie stark viele Berufszweige heute und in Zukunft durch die EDV geprägt werden, ja sogar schon von ihr abhängig sind, welchen Einfluß die Informationstechnik in der Gesellschaft bis hinein in die Privatsphäre des Einzelnen gewinnt, sieht man, daß es in der Schule kein zurück geben kann. Im Berufsbildenden Schulwesen muß auf die Berufe vorbereitet werden, wie sie sind und sein werden, nicht wie sie waren. Auch die allgemeinbildende Schule kann einen derart prägenden Faktor nicht außer Acht lassen. Hier kann es nicht darum gehen, einigen Schülern eine Basis für einen späteren DV-Beruf zu vermitteln. Möglichst alle Schüler müssen Methoden der Informatik und eine Einschätzung der Datenverarbeitung soweit kennenlernen, wie es für ihr Leben wichtig ist. Es sollte erreicht werden, daß die Diskussion um die Datentechnik in der Breite sachlich geführt werden kann und nicht so stark von Emotionen geprägt ist, wie heute die Kernenergiedebatte. Die Ziele müssen danach ausgerichtet werden, in Abhängigkeit von den Aufgaben der einzelnen Schulart und von dem jeweiligen Alter der Schüler. Man sollte die Chance nutzen, daß es sich um ein junges Gebiet handelt, das nicht von früheren Lehrzielen belastet ist. Man sollte flexibel bleiben und die Curricula nicht überfrachten. Leider zeigt sich hie und da auch in DV-Fächern schon unnötiger Ballast.

8. Zukünftiger Wandel

Wir stehen mitten im Wandel und sind uns im klaren, daß dieser nicht so schnell zu einem Abschluß kommt. Nur mit einigen kurzen Andeutungen kann darauf hingewiesen werden, was sich heute schon abzeichnet.

Zunächst inhaltlich: Die Mikroelektronik gewinnt zusehends größere Bedeutung in vielen Bereichen. Dies muß Auswirkungen in den Berufsschulen der betroffenen Berufsfelder haben. Zu fragen ist, inwieweit dem in den Informatikkursen allgemein Rechnung zu tragen ist.

Themen wie Meßwerterfassung, Steuerung, Analog-Digital-Wandlung und Texteditieren seien genannt.

Speziell in den mathematischen Anwendungen handelt es sich bisher fast immer um numerische Berechnungen, z.T. auch mit graphischer Ausgabe oder sogar Eingabe. Verfügbar sind heute aber schon, sogar für Microcomputer, Programmsysteme für mathematische Symbol-Manipulation, Termumformung, Gleichungslösen mit Parameter, Differenzieren und Integrieren von Funktionstermen. Es wäre zumindest interessant in Versuchen diese Möglichkeiten für die Schule auszuloten.

Auf der Hardwareseite zeichnen sich neue Angebote ab: Taschencomputer, also Geräte, die eher den Taschenrechnern gleichen, aber die Software- und Peripherieausstattung heutiger Micros haben; Nutzung des Bildschirmtextsystems in der Schule; Videoplatten als Digitalspeicher sehr hoher Kapazität, etwa mit Informationssystemen.

Schließlich könnte die Situation des Computers an den Schulen verändert werden durch eine zunehmend kritischer werdende Öffentlichkeit gegenüber Computern, Kommunikationstechnik und Automation. Auch dadurch werden die Fragen immer wieder aufgeworfen, was in der Schule in diesem Bereich getan werden soll, in welcher Weise, für welche Schüler.

Die Fachleute sind aufgerufen, Hilfen zu geben. Die Gesellschaft für Informatik hat durch ihre Empfehlungen einen wichtigen Beitrag geleistet. Sie hat die Verpflichtung, sich auch weiterhin um das Problemfeld 'Computer in der Schule' zu bemühen.

Literatur

1 Der Bundesminister für Forschung und Technologie: BMFT Förderungskatalog 1976; (1977)

2 Keil, K.-A., Red.(Hrsg): Das Projekt Computerunterstützer Unterricht Augsburg;(1976)

3 Sachverständigenkreis DV im Bildungswesen, Haefner, K.(Hrsg): Empfehlung an Bund, Länder und Kommunen - Der Computer als Werkzeug des Schülers in der SII; Paderborn (1974)

4 Fachausschuß Ausbildung der GI, Eickel, J. (Red.): Zielsetzungen und Inhalte des Informatikunterrichts; ZMD, 8, 35, (1976)

5 Arbeitskreis Schulrechner, Haefner, K. (Hrsg): Schulrechner 1985; Stuttgart, B.G. Teubner(1980)

6 Hosseus, W., u.a.: PASCAL in Beispielen; München, Oldenbourg (1980)
Jähnichen, S. u.a.: ELAN: Ziele und Konzepte bei der Entwicklung einer Sprache für die Ausbildung; LOG IN, 1,68, (1981)

7 Keidel, K.: Strukturiertes Programmieren in BASIC? BUS, 1-4, (1979-81)

8 Schmittlein, K.: Schuleigene Computer für den multifunktionalen Einsatz; in Schorb,A.O., VISODATA 78, München (1978)

9 Karl, U.: Hinweise für die Gewährung der freien Schülerarbeitszeiten; BUS, 4,55,(1980)

10 Fachausschuß Ausbildung der GI, Claus, V. (Red.): Empfehlungen zur Ausbildung, Fortbildung und Weiterbildung von Lehrkräften für das Lehramt Informatik für die Sekundarstufe I und II; Informatik Spektrum, 2, 53, (1979)

11 Goos, G.: Informatik an der Schule?; Informatik Spektrum, 2, 1, (1979)

PROJEKTBEZOGENES ARBEITEN IN EINEM GRUNDKURS INFORMATIK

Ernestina Dittrich

Helmholtz-Gymnasium
Kaiserallee 6
7500 Karlsruhe 1

Kurzfassung

Die Arbeit berichtet über Konzeption und Ergebnisse eines Versuches, im Rahmen eines Grundkurses Informatik ein Softwareprojekt zur Vertiefung, Erweiterung und praktischen Erprobung des Lehrstoffes durchzuführen. Die Aufgabe besteht in der Automatisierung der Schulbibliotheksorganisation. Positive und weniger positive Erfahrungen werden dargestellt, wobei die programmtechnischen Aspekte des entstandenen Produktes nicht weiter erläutert werden.

Mehr als in vielen anderen Fachgebieten besteht im Informatikunterricht die Notwendigkeit, den Lehrstoff in solchen Teilen darzubieten, die erst in ihrer Gesamtheit betrachtet für praktische Nutzanwendungen ausreichend und geeignet sind. Umso wichtiger ist es, den Unterricht nicht auf die Einübung der einzelnen Teile zu beschränken. Ein wesentlicher Bestandteil eines Informatik-Kurses sollte daher die Durchführung eines umfangreicheren, gleichwohl aber noch gut überschaubaren Softwareprojektes sein. Bei geeigneter Themenwahl hierzu wird nicht nur die vertiefende Wiederholung des vorhergehenden Stoffes erreicht, sondern auch dessen praktische Bedeutung und Einbettung in einen umfassenderen Rahmen demonstriert. Der Schüler kann seine bislang erworbenen Kenntnisse auf konkrete und nichttriviale Probleme anwenden, sich in Gruppenarbeit üben und Erfahrungen "aus dem Programmieralltag" sammeln. Nicht zuletzt wird er damit konfrontiert, daß aufgabenspezifische Spezialkenntnisse - zusätzlich zu bisherigem Wissen - bestimmt und selbständig beschafft werden müssen.

Vorliegende Arbeit berichtet über die Konzeption und die erzielten Ergebnisse projektbezogenen Arbeitens, wobei als konkretes Thema die Organisation des Schulbibliotheksbetriebs mit Hilfe einer Datenverarbeitungsanlage gewählt wurde.

1. Rahmenbedingungen

1.1 Zielgruppe

Das Projekt wurde von Schülern der Klassenstufe 12 des Helmholtz-Gymnasiums Karlsruhe durchgeführt. Aus zwei Grundkursen "Informatik" (2 Wochenstunden) mit zusammen 19 Schüler(inne)n wurden mehrere Teams von 2-3 Teilnehmern gebildet. Jede dieser Gruppen übernahm einen abgeschlossenen Teil der Gesamtaufgabe (neben den gemeinsam gelösten Arbeiten zur genaueren Problemspezifikation usw.). Alle Beteiligten waren überwiegend mathematisch-naturwissenschaftlich interessiert (meist gleichzeitig in Leistungskursen Mathematik und/oder Physik), gut motiviert und durchaus bereit, einen Teil ihrer Freizeit am Rechner zu verbringen. Insgesamt kann man diesbezüglich wohl von überdurchschnittlich günstigen Bedingungen sprechen.

1.2 Vorkenntnisse

Die Schüler wurden in der 12. Klassenstufe durchweg erstmals mit dem Themenbereich Informatik konfrontiert. Der erste Teil des Unterrichts wurde zur Erarbeitung des Algorithmenbegriffs, des Problemlösungsprozesses sowie der Realisierung von Algorithmen in einer algorithmischen Sprache verwendet. Als Programmiersprache habe ich PASCAL gewählt, da aus meiner Sicht hiermit eher als mit allen anderen denkbaren Sprachen (BASIC oder gar Maschinensprache) Lernziele des Informatikunterrichts (der ja mehr als ein Programmierkurs sein sollte) zu erreichen möglich wird. Im Hinblick auf die Projektarbeit konnte somit von Anfang an auf die Anwendung allgemein anerkannter Prinzipien wie Modularisierung, schrittweise Verfeinerung, strukturierte Programmierung usw. hingearbeitet werden, ohne beim Übergang auf den Rechner diese Grundsätze wieder über den Haufen werfen oder zumindest aufweichen zu müssen. Der vorhandene Rechner (siehe unten) erlaubte glücklicherweise ein solches Vorgehen, das bereits an dieser Stelle als wesentlich für den Erfolg des Projektes genannt werden sollte.

Der Umgang mit PASCAL wurde an zahlreichen kleineren Programmierbeispielen im Laufe des Schuljahres eingeübt. Die Schüler entwickelten mit der Zeit eine beachtliche Gewandtheit beim Testen und bei der Fehlersuche. Sie erfanden auch gerne eigene Beispiele, meist spielerischer Art oder zur Textverarbeitung (Drucken von Anzeigenrechnungen für die Schülerzeitung).

Als Lehrbuch stand /1/ zur Verfügung, erwies sich aber nur als bedingt geeignet. Als Sprachbeschreibung wurde /2/ und /3/ angeboten, womit die Schüler nach anfänglichen Schwierigkeiten gut zurecht kammen.

1.3 Rechner und Arbeitsbedingungen

Zur Durchführung von Unterricht und Projekt stand ein Tischrechner APPLE II zur Verfügung; Die Konfiguration umfaßte 48 KB Hauptspeiher, PASCAL - System (UCSD), 2 Floppy Disk-Laufwerke, Bildschirm und Drucker. Der Rechner wurde gleichzeitig von der Schulverwaltung benutzt. Alle Teams hatten wöchentlich 1-2 Stunden Rechenzeit zur Verfügung. Während der Programmierphase konnten die "Denkzeiten" bei der Fehlersuche eines Teams durch andere Gruppen genutzt werden, jedoch war diese Organisation von den Schülern selbst im Laufe der Arbeiten eingerichtet worden.

2. Projektthemenstellung

Hinsichtlich Auswahl und Durchführung des Projekts habe ich mich an den GI-Empfehlungen über "Zielsetzungen und Inhalte des Informatikunterrichts" /4/ orientiert. Die Schüler wählten aus mehreren Vorschlägen die Organisation des Schulbibliotheksbetriebs aus. Die Vorteile gerade dieses Themas liegen auf der Hand: es benötigt kaum Spezialkenntnisse zur Analyse der Problemstellung, jeder Teilnehmer kennt aus eigener Anschauung die bei manueller Organisation anfallenden Dokumente und Arbeitabläufe. Ganz nebenbei sorgt das Thema für einen gewissen Ehrgeiz, den Mitschülern anderer Kurse etwas "Vorzeigbares" zu entwickeln. Zudem ist die Aufgabe recht leicht gliederbar und in vieler Hinsicht ausbaufähig, so daß das gewünschte Produkt in kleinen Schritten entsteht und somit zwischendurch Teilerfolge sichtbar werden, die gerade bei Schülern eine sehr wichtige weitere Motivation darstellen.

2.1 Einfache Form des Projekts

Nach einer umfassenden "Generaldiskussion" der Aufgabe unter Beteiligung aller Teams, wobei insbesondere eine strukturierende, teilweise hinsichtlich des beabsichtigten Arbeitsumfangs bremsende Steuerung erforderlich war, wurden als Bestandteile der Grundstufe festgelegt:

- Erfassung des Bücherbestandes eines Fachgebietes der Schülerbibliothek: Festlegung der Beschreibungsmerkmale eines Buches (Verfasser, Titel usw.), Eingabe der erforderlichen Daten am Bildschirm, Speicherung auf Diskette.

- Ausgabe einer Liste der existierenden Bücher (geeignet formatiert), d.h. des Katalogs, in alphabetischer Reihenfolge der Verfasser (↗ Sortieren der Eingabedaten).

- Aufnahme von Neuerwerbungen ("Einsortieren").

Mit Abschluß dieser Ausbaustufe liegt bereits ein Produkt vor, das die regelmäßig fällige Inventur des Bücherbestandes erheblich erleichtert. Die Erweiterung auf mehrere Fachgebiete wurde bereits berücksichtigt und lediglich deshalb unterlassen, weil die Eingabe mehrerer hundert Buchdaten eine wenig lukrative Tätigkeit für die Schüler darstellt.

2.2 Ausbaustufe

Als Ausbaustufe bietet sich der "Kundenbetrieb" an, also die Buchausleihe und -rückgabe. Folgende im Dialog durchführbaren Funktionen wurden ausgewählt:

- Nachfrage, ob ein bestimmtes Buch vorrätig ist,

- Buchführung über Entleiher und Fälligkeitsdatum eines entliehenen Buches,

- Feststellen des Entleihers und des Fälligkeitsdatums eines gewünschten, nicht vorrätigen Buches.

2.3 Vertiefung

Zusätzlich zur Grund- und Ausbaustufe läßt sich der Komfort einer automatisierten Bibliotheksorganisation nahezu beliebig steigern, wobei die Schüler ihrer Phantasie freien Lauf lassen konnten. Folgende gut realisierbaren Vorschläge gingen ein:

- Erstellung von Mahnungen bei Überschreiten der Rückgabetermine
- Vormerkung von Entleihwünschen bei augenblicklich verliehenen Büchern
- Registrierung von Neuanschaffungswünschen.

Weitere Möglichkeiten führen hingegen schon zu eigenen Projekten. Sie dienen jedoch als Anknüpfungspunkte, im gemeinsamen Unterricht ergänzende Themen zumindest oberflächlich zu besprechen. Insbesondere fällt hierunter:

- Stichwortkataloge; Suchen von Büchern aufgrund von angegebenen Stichwörtern
- automatische Indexierung auf der Basis von Kurzfassungen (abstracts)

Auf diese Weise konnte vertiefend das Teilgebiet "Information Retrieval" als wichtige Anwendung elektronischer Rechenanlagen angesprochen werden. Dies verband sich harmonisch mit dem Besuch des Fachinformationszentrums (FIZ 4) in Leopoldshafen, wo die Schüler eine Großanwendung der besprochenen Verfahren begutachten konnten.

Selbstverständlich gehen die hier aufgezählten Funktionen i.a. über den Bedarf einer Schulbibliothek hinaus. Das konkrete Anwendungsbeispiel ist jedoch als Hintergrund außerordentlich wichtig.

3. Projektdurchführung

Neben den in der Einleitung genannten Lernzielen sollte den Schülern auch die systematische Durchführung von EDV-Projekten wenigstens in groben Zügen vermittelt werden. Als Projektphasen wurde daher von folgenden drei Punkten ausgegangen:

- Systemanalyse
- Programmierung
- Dokumentation

a) Systemanalyse

Der Istzustand ließ sich an der eigenen Schulbibliothek leicht ermitteln. Daran schlossen sich Erörterungen der Möglichkeiten einer Automatisierung des Betriebes an.

Nach der ersten Einkreisung des Problems wurden Datenflußpläne erstellt und davon ausgehend die benötigten Funktionen der Programme erarbeitet. Außerdem wurden die erforderlichen Dateien festgelegt und Abschätzungen über den Bedarf an Speicherplatz dafür angestellt.

Diese Phase wurde für Grund- und Aufbaustufe gemeinsam durchgeführt, wobei auch bereits die zur Realisierung vorgesehenen Teile der Vertiefungsstufe einbezogen wurden. Die Phase endete mit einer Spezifikation in Form (abstrakt) sprachlich formulierter Programmabläufe sowie einer Beschreibung der benötigten Datenformate. Damit lagen auch die Schnittstellen für die einzelnen Teams fest, auf die die Arbeiten nunmehr verteilt werden konnten. An dieser Stelle wurde auch ein Zeitplan für den weiteren Projektverlauf angefertigt.

b) Programmierung

Die Programmierphase begann mit der Erstellung von Struktogrammen durch die einzelnen Teams. Durch die Parallelarbeit kann besonders in dieser Phase der zeitliche Aufwand auf ein vertretbares Ausmaß reduziert werden.

Der logische Test der erstellten Programme wurde am noch bescheidenen Bücherbestand des Faches Informatik (ca. 40 Bände) in unserer Bibliothek durchgeführt. Dies war jedoch durchaus ausreichend, eine Vielzahl von kleineren und auch grundsätzlicheren Fehlern zu entdecken. Seitens der Lehrkraft muß hier einige Zeit investiert werden, bei der Klärung von Fehlerursachen zwischen verschiedenen Teams zu vermitteln.

c) Systemdokumentation

Zusätzlich zur Dokumentation der Programme zu Wartungszwecken, die bereits in der vorhergehenden Phase weitgehend stattzufinden hatte, sollte in dieser Phase in erster Linie die Benutzerdokumentation angefertigt werden. Mehr als jede Ermahnung, kein "Insiderwissen" vorauszusetzen, hilft es dabei, die erstellten Papiere unbeteiligten Mitschülern in die Hand zu drücken. Diese sollten, damit ausgerüstet, das fertige Produkt verwenden. Eine sehr lehrreiche Übung!

4. Erfahrungen und Konsequenzen

Bei der Durchführung eines solchen Projekts sammeln Schüler wie Lehrer gleichermaßen eine Fülle von Erfahrungen. An dieser Stelle sollen einige erreichte und nicht erreichte Lernziele, methodische und didaktische Gesichtspunkte sowie gezogene Konsequenzen aufgeführt werden.

4.1 Programmiersprache PASCAL

Als die Auswahl des Rechners und damit auch der im Unterricht zu lehrenden Programmiersprache zur Debatte stand, wurden sehr preisgünstige Geräte mit BASIC angeboten. Nach einem Jahr Erfahrung und Diskussion mit Kollegen, die kein PASCAL zur Verfügung hatten, erscheinen mir die etwas höheren Ausgaben dafür vollauf gerechtfertigt. Gerade bei "größeren" Projekten erweist sich die Strukturierungsfähigkeit der Sprache für didaktische Zwecke als optimal. Der Schüler, der am Unterrichtsbeginn eine "theoretische Durststrecke" überstanden hat, wird mit algorithmischer Denkfähigkeit belohnt, die ihm auch die Analyse von größeren und komplizierten Zusammenhängen gestattet. Ich warne deshalb davor, sich von dem schnellen Progammierkönnen der "BASIC-Anhänger" blenden zu lassen.

4.2 Apparative Ausstattung

Die apparative Ausstattung war nicht ideal. Ein Handicap war insbesondere die Teilung des Rechners zwischen Informatikunterricht und Schulverwaltung. Vor solchen Symbiosen bei Kleinrechnern möchte ich meine Kollegen nachdrücklich warnen, da sie zwangsläufig für Reibungsflächen sorgen. Bei 19 Teilnehmern ist ein einziger Rechner im Prinzip zu wenig; ist aus (verständlichen) finanziellen Gründen nicht mehr möglich, so sollte er wenigstens auch am späten Nachmittag noch zugänglich sein - ein schwieriges Aufsichtsproblem.

Mit dem Gerät APPLE II selbst sind die Erfahrungen recht gut. Ein Nachteil sind lediglich die Disketten, die nur eine begrenzte Lebensdauer haben und bei ungeschickter Handhabung von Dateien leicht zu einem "Diskjockey-Effekt" führen. In unserem Projekt war jede Gruppe mit eigenen Disketten für ihre Programme/Dateien ausgestattet.

4.3 Didaktische Erfahrungen

Da sich mit steigenden Programmierkenntnissen auch die Erfolgserlebnisse der Schüler häufen, sind die Kursteilnehmer an immer grösseren Aufgaben interessiert. Während manche Kollegen über mangelnde Leistungsbereitschaft der Grundkursbesucher klagen, scheinen mir Informatikteilnehmer gut motiviert zu sein. Insbesondere trifft dies für die 3-4 Monate am Schuljahrsende (!) zu, in denen durch die projektbezogene Arbeit ein gutes Lern- und Leistungsklima entsteht. Als Gründe dafür sind zu nennen:

- Die Phantasie und Eigeninitiative der Schüler wird angesprochen,
- Teamarbeit (leider im Schulalltag selten erlaubt, obwohl im Berufsleben meist unabdingbar),
- Der Nutzen der Projektarbeit bzw. des Erlernten wird direkt sichtbar.

Selbstverständlich gibt es auch einige weniger erfreuliche Gesichtspunkte aufzuzählen, die jedoch die positive Gesamtbeurteilung nicht entscheidend zu beeinflussen vermögen:

- Der Arbeitsaufwand für den Lehrer ist erheblich,
- Einige (glücklicherweise sehr wenige) Schüler, die mit Eifer begonnen haben, geben unterwegs auf (der Zeitaufwand ist natürlich auch für Schüler beachtlich),
- Die Aufteilung in Teams und deren Abhängigkeit untereinander erfordert eine gute Organisation, da sonst aufgrund weniger "Aussteiger" der gesamte Projekterfolg gefährdet ist und damit statt Erfolgserlebnissen das Gegenteil erzeugt wird.

5. Zusammenfassung

Natürlich sind die Ergebnisse unseres Projekts nicht in allen Punkten perfekt und in jedem Falle verbesserungsbedürftig. Es wurde beschlossen, den Bibliotheksdienst in freiwilliger Weiterarbeit zu vervollkommnen. Aufgrund meiner Erfahrung kann ich aber jedem Kollegen nur dringend empfehlen, projektbezogenes Arbeiten zum festen Bestandteil des Informatikunterrichts zu machen. Der Unterrichtserfolg rechtfertigt den eigenen Einsatz.

Literatur

/1/ Balzert,H.: Informatik 1, Hueber-Holzmann Verlag, 1980

/2/ Jensen,K./Wirth,N.: PASCAL user manual and report, Springer Verlag, 1978

/3/ APPLE PASCAL reference manual, Apple Computer Inc., 1979

/4/ Zielsetzungen und Inhalte des Informatikunterrichts, Zentralblatt für Didaktik der Mathematik, 1976/1, 34-43.

Informatik im zweiten Bildungsweg - Erfahrungen mit einem Informatikkurs am Abendgymnasium

Ulrike Wabel-Frenk

1. Zusammenfassung

Nach einigen Vorbemerkungen zur Schulart und ihrer Stellung zwischen Gymnasium und Erwachsenenbildungsinstitutionen wie z.B. Volkshochschulen werden kurz die Voraussetzungen für Informatikunterricht (Computer, Qualifikationsmöglichkeiten für Lehrer, Eingliederung in den Fächerkanon) skizziert. Eine Erläuterung des Kurskonzepts - entstanden aus den Kursvorschlägen und Materialien der Forschungsgruppe CUU/Projekt PROKOP unter Berücksichtigung der GI-Empfehlungen sowie methodischer Gesichtspunkte der Erwachsenenpädagogik - schließt sich an. Schließlich werden spezielle Erfahrungen und Probleme bei der Kursdurchführung angeschnitten, und es wird eine Charakterisierung der Kursteilnehmer versucht.

2. Vorbemerkung zur Schulart

Da es - verglichen mit anderen Schularten - nur wenige Abendgymnasien gibt, möchte ich einige Informationen über diese Schulen an den Anfang stellen.

Abendgymnasien sind Schulen des zweiten Bildungswegs, auf denen berufstätige Erwachsene in 7 bzw. 8 Semestern (je nachdem, ob Realschulabschluß vorhanden ist oder nicht) das Abitur nachholen können. Sie müssen dazu mindestens 19 Jahre alt sein und 3 Jahre eine regelmäßige Arbeit ausgeübt haben, außerdem ist Berufstätigkeit bis zu Beginn des drittletzten Semester verpflichtend.

Das Darmstädter Abendgymnasium ist mit ca. 400-500 Studierenden eines der großen hessischen Abendgymnasien, jedoch kleiner als die meisten Tagesgymnasien. Von den Studierenden sind etwa 60% Frauen, das Durchschnittsalter beträgt ungefähr 24 Jahre, die häufigsten Berufe liegen im kaufmännischen oder Verwaltungsbereich [9].

Ein wesentlich kürzerer Zeitabschnitt als an Tagesschulen steht für den Unterricht zur Verfügung: er findet in der Zeit zwischen 17.15 und 22 Uhr statt und muß fast alle Übungsphasen mitenthalten, da die wenigsten Studierenden wegen ihrer Mehrfachbelastung besonders in den Anfangssemestern zu Hause regelmäßg für die Schule arbeiten oder üben können. Es gibt nur 6 Kernfächer: Deutsch, Englisch, Mathematik, Physik, Gemeinschaftskunde, 2. Fremdsprache und eines der Wahlfächer Biologie, Chemie, Wirtschaftswissenschaften. In vielen anderen Fächern werden freiwillige zweistündige Arbeitsgemeinschaften angeboten. Mit der bundesweiten Einführung des Kurssystems für den zweiten Bildungsweg wird sich jedoch in diesem Jahr das Unterrichtsangebot verändern - allerdings wohl kaum vergrößern [12].

Insgesamt gesehen nehmen die Abendgymnasien eine Zwischenstellung ein: einerseits müssen sie Studierfähigkeit vermitteln, also einen Abschluß garantieren, der mit dem Tagesschulabitur vergleichbar ist; andererseits gehört die Schule wegen ihrer erwachsenen Schüler, deren Berufs- und Lebenserfahrung, Interessen und Verhaltensweisen oft einen ganz anderen Unterricht erfordern als an Tagesschulen üblich [14], eher in den Bereich der Erwachsenenbildung wie etwa Volksshochschulen.

3. Voraussetzungen für Informatikunterricht

3.1 Rechner

Anfang 1977 ergab sich für das Abendgymnasium Darmstadt die Gelegenheit, einen Computer zu kaufen. Es wurde eine Anlage von General Turtle mit Rechner LSI-11, Textschirm, Grafikschirm, Floppy-disk und einem einfachen Drucker ausgewählt, wobei die Beratung durch eine Darmstädter Forschungsgruppe (Computerunterstützter Unterricht, Projekt PROKOP) den Ausschlag gab für diese Entscheidung. Ab August 1979 konnte die Schule einen zweiten Computer mit gleicher Ausstattung bis auf den Drucker unbefristet vom HIBS (Hessisches Institut für Bildungsplanung und Schulentwicklung) leihen.

3.2 Lehrerfortbildung

Nach dem Rechnerkauf wurde für interessierte Lehrer unserer Schule ein Informatikeinführungskurs von einem Mitglied der Projektgruppe PROKOP durchgeführt. Dies geschah im Rahmen von Kaufberatung und Fortbildungskursen, die verschiedene Arbeitsgruppen des HIBS hessischen Schulen anbieten. Neben der Vermittlung von Grundkenntnissen der Programmiersprache unseres Rechners - LOGO, einer listenorientierten Programmiersprache, die speziell für pädagogische Zwecke entwickelt wurde [10,11] - wurde das didaktische Konzept der Projektgruppe vorgestellt [2,6,7], und allgemeine Fragen zum derzeitigen Stand von Computereinsatz und -anwendungsmöglichkeiten wurden andiskutiert. Nach einem halbjährigen Kurs mit zwei Wochenstunden und einem einwöchigen Intensivkurs, dessen Teilnehmer vom Unterricht freigestellt waren, war die weitere Vorbereitung eines Unterrichtsangebots den einzelnen Lehrern überlassen. Obwohl weiterhin Mitarbeiter der Forschungsgruppe für Fragen und Diskussionen zur Verfügung standen und der erste Kurs für Studierende von einen Forschungsgruppenmitglied drei Semester lang mit- bzw. zeitweise allein betreut wurde, blieb der Computereinsatz im Unterricht bis jetzt auf diesen einen Kurs beschränkt. Dies zeigt, wie wichtig es ist, ein breites Angebot institutionalisierter Fortbildungsmöglichkeiten für Lehrer im Fach Informatik bei angemessener Entlastung vom Unterricht zu fordern.

3.3 Stellung als Unterrichtsfach

Für das Abendgymnasium kommt ein Informatikkurs nur als Arbeitsgemeinschaft in Frage: Die Vergleichbarkeit mit dem Tagesschulabitur muß garantiert sein, und dort gibt es in Hessen im allgemeinen keinen Informatikunterricht im Pflichtbereich; außerdem erlaubt der ohnehin enge zeitliche Spielraum keine Integration in ein anderes Fach. Es besteht jedoch die Chance, daß diese Situation mit der bevorstehenden Einführung des Kurssystems geändert wird.

Durch den Status als Arbeitsgemeinschaft sind folgende Vorbedingungen festgelegt:

- Die Teilnahme an einer Arbeitsgemeinschaft ist immer freiwillig, und sie sollte Studierenden aller Semester möglich sein, also keine Vorkenntnisse aus anderen Fächern voraussetzen.
- Ein Kurs muß bei zwei Wochenstunden nach drei Semestern einen gewissen Abschluß erreichen, da die Studierenden für erfolgreiche Teilnahme an einer Arbeitsgemeinschaft eine 7. Abiturnote bekommen können - wobei auch die Möglichkeit einer mündlichen Prüfung besteht.

4. Ziele, Inhalte und Methoden des Kurses

Als Orientierung für ein methodisch-didaktisches Kurskonzept wurden die GI-Richtlinien [8] als von einer relativ großen Gruppe vorgeschlagener Curriculumentwurf zugrunde gelegt, sowie die von der Forschungsgruppe Projekt PROKOP entwickelten Kursvorschläge und Unterrichtsmaterialien [1,2,6,7], die durch die Zusammenarbeit mit der Forschungsgruppe besonderes Gewicht erhielten. Einige Einschränkungen und Akzentuierungen sind durch den engen zeitlichen Rahmen sowie durch die speziellen Anforderungen erwachsenengerechten Lernens vorgegeben.

4.1 Erste Kursphase

Die erste Kurshälfte - ca. eineinhalb Semester - wird benötigt, um Programmierkenntnisse zu vermitteln. Dabei wird Programmieren im Sinn von Punkt 1 und 2 der GI-Empfehlungen verstanden, nämlich als Weg vom Problem zum (LOGO-) Programm; d.h. systematische Untersuchung eines Problems mit heuristischen Verfahren steht am Anfang, die Lösung wird schrittweise formalisiert und verfeinert, bis als Ergebnis ein Programm entstanden ist. Beim Arbeiten mit der Programmiersprache LOGO steht von Kursbeginn an der Begriff der Prozedur im Mittelpunkt: die Möglichkeiten, damit umzugehen, werden dabei so entwickelt:

Auf eine kurze Phase des Kennenlernens des Computers und der Benutzung des Terminals - etwa durch bereits geschriebene Spiel- oder Dialogprogramme - folgt das Einüben grundlegender Befehle und Operationen im direkten Ausführungsmodus am Rechner (z.B. drucken und manipulieren der beiden grundlegenden Datenstrukturen Wort und Liste). Hierbei schaffen einerseits differenzierte Fehlermeldungen am Terminal, andererseits Hilfsmittel zur Analyse eines LOGO-Befehls wie etwa das Kästchenmodell [6] die Möglichkeit für die Studierenden, selbständig in kleinen Gruppen zu üben oder etwas auszuprobieren; diese Arbeitsform wird im weiteren Kursverlauf immer stärker vorherrschen, und sie trägt gerade bei Erwachsenen dem starken Bedürfnis Rechnung, nicht wie kleine Kinder gegängelt zu werden, sondern in eigener Verantwortung zu lernen [14].

Anschließend wird das Definieren von Prozeduren eingeführt, die als neue "Begriffe" die Programmiersprache erweitern. Besonders auf Verständlichkeit und Übersichtlichkeit der Programme wird hier Wert gelegt (etwa durch schrittweise Übertragung eines zunächst umgangssprachlich formulierten Algorithmus in die Programmiersprache, durch Verwendung semantischer Namen für Prozeduren und alle Variablen, durch kurze Zeilen usw.), während Gesichtspunkte wie Effizienz bei der Ausführung höchstens am Rande zu einem viel späteren Zeitpunkt interessant werden.

Nach der Einführung von Bedingungen besteht der nächste wichtige Schritt in der Behandlung rekursiver Prozeduren. Nach diesem Abschnitt können die Studierenden bereits Probleme bearbeiten, die durch mehrere Prozeduren auf verschiedene Arten gelöst werden können: z.B. Drucken verschiedener geometrischer Figuren aus beliebigen Zeichen, Auszählen der Häufigkeit bestimmter Buchstaben in Texten, Durchführen einfacher Mengenoperationen, usw.

Erst wenn die Studierenden ein solchen Problem lösen können, werden Sprachelemente wie z.B. der Zuweisungsbefehl "MAKE", der "RUN"-Befehl (entspricht dem LISP-"EVAL" oder dem APL "aktiviere") und kompliziertere Datenstrukturen (Eigenschaftslisten, Arrays, usw.) besprochen [6].

4.2 Zweite Kursphase

Der Inhalt der zweiten Kursphase wird noch stärker von den Interessen der Studierenden bestimmt: im Mittelpunkt stehen immer Projekte, deren Themen sich die einzelnen Kursteilnehmer oder zwei gemeinsam auswählen. Dabei kommen auch Beispiele in Betracht, wie sie in den GI-Empfehlungen zu Punkt 3A vorgeschlagen werden: Steuerabrechnung, Textverarbeitung, Spielprogramme, usw. [2]. Allerdings erzwingt hier der Zeitmangel eine Beschränkung auf diese eine Möglichkeit der Empfehlungen, die anderen darin genannten Alternativen (3B-3D sowie Punkt 4) müssen unter unseren Bedingungen weggelassen werden. Die Entscheidung fiel zugunsten der Projektkurse aus, weil hier erwachsenengerechtes Lernen besonders gut realisiert werden kann: gerade als Gegensatz zum herkömmlichen naturwissenschaftlichen Unterricht, der im allgemeinen bis in Einzelheiten vorstrukturiert ist, können hier die Studierenden nach ihren eigenen Bedürfnissen lernen und sogar das Thema selbstbestimmen. Der Lehrer hat hauptsächlich beratende Funktion als "Experte" im Hintergrund.

Ebenfalls typisch für eine Schule mit erwachsenen Lernenden erscheint mir die Tatsache, daß der von der GI als 5. Abschnitt empfohlene Themenkreis "Informatik in der Gesellschaft" nicht weggelassen werden kann, weil Studierende immer wieder darauf zurückkommen. Während jugendliche "Normalschüler" auf Erfahrungen vorbereitet werden, d.h. Methoden zu ihrer Bewältigung im vorhinein lernen, kommen die Erwachsenen in die Schule zurück, um bereits gewonnene Erfahrungen einordnen, strukturieren und werten zu lernen. Dies gilt mit Sicherheit auch für die elektronische Datenverarbeitung: allein im Beruf hatte schon jeder dritte aller Studierenden mit EDV zu tun. So verwundert es nicht, daß eigene Erfahrungen mit Computern im Beruf, die Problematik ihres Einsatzes in verschiedenen Bereichen, immer wieder von den Kursteilnehmern thematisiert werden, Referate zu Computerproblemen gewünscht und einzelne Zeitungs- oder Zeitschriftenartikel gelesen und gemeinsam diskutiert werden.

5. Charakterisierung der Kursteilnehmer

Um Hinweise zur Charakterisierung der Teilnehmer am Informatikunterricht zu bekommen, wurde eine Fragebogenaktion bei einer als repräsentativ anzusehenden Gruppe von ca. 160 Studierenden des Darmstädter Abendgymnasiums durchgeführt. Die Fragen beziehen sich auf Gründe für die Teilnahme oder Nicht-Teilnahme an der Informatik-Arbeitsgemeinschaft, auf bestimmte Vorurteile und Teilaspekte zu den Stichwörtern EDV und Computer, auf das Bedürfnis, Fragen zu Computereinsatz und -problematik in der Schule zu behandeln sowie auf das Interesse an einigen Schulfächern und außerschulischen Themenkreisen.

Ein Ergebnis erklärt die relativ niedrigen Teilnehmerzahlen der Informatik-AG: für den Anfängerkurs melden sich etwa 12 Studierende, von denen am Semesterende noch ca. 4-8 Interessenten für das zweite Semester übrig bleiben; länger als zwei Semester kommen noch einzelne (1-3) Studierende, so daß parallel zum dritten Semester ein jeweils neuer Anfängerkurs angeboten werden kann. Bei anderen Arbeitsgemeinschaften sehen die Teilnehmerzahlen ähnlich aus. Die Gründe dafür liegen außer an einer schulintern schlechten Information über das Unterrichtsangebot wesentlich beim Faktor Zeit: ca. 2/3 der Nicht-Teilnehmer gaben Terminüberschneidungen, zu große schulische oder außerschulische Beanspruchung an, während inhaltliche Gründe nur von etwa 20% dieser Gruppe genannt wurden. Demgegenüber steht der Wunsch von ca. 80% aller Befragten, Themen zu Computer oder EDV in der Schule zu behandeln.

Als Hauptgrund für die Teilnahme an der Informatik-AG wurde die Computerverbreitung angegeben, also eine richtige Einschätzung als gesamtgesellschaftlich relevantes Phänomen. Mit den Teilnehmern an anderen AGs gemeinsam haben die Besucher des Informatikkurses ein überdurchschnittliches Interesse an Schulfächern sowie außerschulischen Themenbereichen. Die Statements zum Thema Computer, EDV wurden von ihnen etwa so angekreuzt wie von allen Befragten, das bedeutet, daß auch bei dieser Gruppe negative Assoziationen eindeutig überwiegen. Im Zusammenhang mit den anderen Ergebnissen deute ich dies aber eher als Kritikfähigkeit, die sich positiv von einer blinden Fortschrittsgläubigkeit auf der einen Seite und einer irrationalen Ablehnung alles Technischen auf der anderen Seite abhebt. Erstaunlich scheint, daß im Informatikkurs diejenigen mit Berufen aus Naturwissenschaft und Technik häufiger, Studierende mit Verwaltungsberufen seltener vertreten sind als in der Gesamtgruppe, obwohl in diesem Bereich besonders viele Computer eingesetzt werden. Vielleicht hängt dieses Resultat mit dem auffälligsten Merkmal der AG-Gruppe zusammen: Der Männeranteil im Informatikkurs beträgt ca. 70%, obwohl die Frauen in der Gesamtzahl der Schüler eine deutliche Mehrheit besitzen. Dies kann man sicher nicht mit informatikspezifischen Gesichtspunkten sondern eher mit einer verbreiteten Einschätzung von Naturwissenschaft und Technik ganz allgemein als unweiblich erklären; diese Interpretation wird durch andere Fragebogenteile bestätigt [13].

Sieht man als wichtiges Ziel des Unterrichts in Informatik und Naturwissenschaften in der Schule, möglichst jedem die Fähigkeit zu einem rationalen und verantwortungsbewußten Umgang mit gesellschaftlich relevanten Technologien zu vermitteln [4,5], so muß auch im Informatikunterricht das irrationale Verständnis der männlichen und weiblichen Rolle in dieser Beziehung abgebaut werden. Ansätze, dem Ziel näherzukommen, könnten die Punkte bieten, in denen sich der Informatikkurs vom üblichen naturwissenschaftlichen Unterricht unterscheidet, z.B. Betonung von Zusammenarbeit statt Konkurrenz, Einbeziehung von Randbedingungen und konkreten Erfahrungen statt rein fachwissenschaftlicher Orientierung; bei freiwilligen Kursen liegt jedoch das Problem zunächst darin, Frauen überhaupt zur Teilnahme zu motivieren. Vielleicht zeigen neue Konzepte von Naturwissenschaft [3], die sowohl sozialwissenschaftliche Aspekte integrieren wie normative Fragen diskutieren, dazu langfristig gesehen bessere Möglichkeiten auf.

6. Erfahrungen und Probleme bei der Kurdurchführung

6.1 Schulspezifische Unterrichtsschwierigkeiten

Schultypische Unterrichtsprobleme resultieren meistens aus dem Erwachsenenstatus der Schüler des zweiten Bildungswegs: im Vordergrund stehen dabei neben dem Zeitproblem die Vielfalt und Unterschiedlichkeit der Vorerfahrungen der Studierenden, womit sowohl spezielle Vorkenntnisse aus dem Beruf wie auch Lernerfahrungen und Erfahrungen im Umgang mit anderen Menschen gemeint sind. In der Arbeitsgemeinschaft lassen sich diese Probleme oft besser als im Unterricht der Kernfächer lösen, da die Lerngruppe klein ist und die Inhalte weniger stark festgelegt sind.

Wenn im Informatikkurs Studierende überhaupt keine Übungszeit aufbringen können oder häufig fehlen, so können für diese Gruppe etwa nach einem Semster Wiederholungsstunden angeboten werden, während gleichzeitig die Fortgeschritteneren etwas Zusätzliches lernen - z.B. die Benutzung des Grafiksystems. Trotzdem geben die Studierenden, wenn sie Probleme haben, die freiwillige Teilnahme an einer Arbeitsgemeinschaft meistens zuerst auf, um zeitliche Entlastung zu spüren.

Die verschiedenen Vorerfahrungen und Interessen können besonders im zweiten Teil des Kurses zum Ausdruck kommen ohne sich gegenseitig zu behindern - so sind einige Finanzbeamte oder in der Verwaltung Tätige daran interessiert, Programme zur Steuerberechnung oder zur Einrichtung und Benutzung von Personalkarteien zu schreiben.

6.2 Inhaltlich bedingte Probleme

Durch die gewählte Kurskonzeption treten in einigen Situationen die folgenden Schwierigkeiten auf:

Vorerfahrungen mit programmierbaren Taschenrechnern oder BASIC-Programmen erschweren den Studierenden manchmal einen direkten Zugang zu einem Algorithmus ausgehend von einer genauen Beschreibung der menschlichen Tätigkeiten und Überlegungen während des Lösungsvorgangs.

Schwieriger für alle wird der Kurs meist bei der Einführung rekursiver Prozeduren - trotzdem machen passende Modellvorstellungen ("kleine Brüder" [7]), konkrete überschaubare Aufgaben (ein Wort rückwärts schreiben, ein bestimmtes Zeichen aus einem Wort streichen, usw.) in abgestufter Schwierigkeit, gute Fehlermeldungen und die Möglichkeit, ein Aufrufprotokoll drucken zu lassen, den Unterricht verständlicher, als er bei vergleichbaren Mathematikthemen - wie etwa vollständige Induktion - im allgemeinen ist.

In seiner Doppelfunktion als Kontrollstruktur und Befehl zur Datenübergabe bereitet am Anfang des Kurses der OUTPUT-Befehl Verständnisschwierigkeiten, die erst durch die häufige Verwendung des Befehls ausgeräumt werden. Zu einem späteren Zeitpunkt ist der RUN-Befehl wegen seiner Allgemeinheit schwer zu durchschauen; sein Gebrauch bleibt auf Spezialfälle beschränkt, die dann ausführlich behandelt werden.

Verständnisschwierigkeiten an anderen Stellen sind mir selten aufgefallen, problemlos erläutern läßt sich z.B. sowohl der Zuweisungsoperator, Befehle zur Dateneingabe, wie auch das Prinzip iterativer Programme (BASIC-Stil) nach Einübung der Rekursion.

6.3 Abschließende Bewertung

Fast immer macht der Unterricht allen Beteiligten Spaß, nicht zuletzt deshalb, weil immer wieder spontan von Erfahrungen mit Computern im Beruf berichtet wird oder aus anderen Gründen Diskussionen über EDV und Computer - Anwendung und Auswirkungen, Möglichkeiten und Gefahren auf dem Hintergrund des in der Arbeitsgemeinschaft Gelernten entstehen, so daß immer neue Aspekte ins Blickfeld rücken. Betrachtet man neben diesen insgesamt positiven Erfahrungen mit dem Informatikunterricht noch das große Interesse bei fast allen Studierenden an Fragen zu Computerproblemen und EDV-Einsatz, das sicher bei vielen durch die Berührung mit EDV im Beruf begründet ist, so ist die Forderung nach Informatikkursen im Kurssystem des zweiten Bildungswegs unausweichlich.

7. Literatur

[1] Böcker, H.-D.: LOGO-Manual, Darmstadt, HIBS (Projekt PROKOP), 1978

[2] Böcker, H.-D., Fischer, G.: Arbeitsmaterialien zum interaktiven Problemlösen mit Computerhilfe, Bd. 2 Teil 1-5: Mathematik, Linguistik, Informatik, Künstliche Intelligenz, Spiele. Darmstadt, HIBS (Projekt PROKOP), 1978

[3] Böhme, G.: Alternativen der Wissenschaft, Frankfurt, Suhrkamp, 1980

[4] Claus, V.: Informatik in der Schule: Begründung und allgemeinbildender Kern, Bielefeld, Schriftenreihe des IDM, Bd. 15, 1977

[5] Deller, H.: Informatik in der Sekundarstufe II: zur Grundlegung der Informatik als Unterrichtsfach, Frankfurt, Diesterweg, 1980

[6] Fischer, G.: Arbeitsmaterialien zum interaktiven Problemlösen mit Computerhilfe, Bd. 1: Einführung in das interaktive Programmieren, Darmstadt, HIBS (Projekt PROKOP), 1977

[7] Fischer, G.: Das Lösen komplexer Problemaufgaben durch naive Benutzer mit Hilfe des interaktiven Programmierens, Darmstadt, HIBS (Projekt PROKOP), 1977

[8] Gesellschaft für Informatik: Zielsetzungen und Inhalte des Informatikunterrichts, ZDM 1 S. 35 (1976)

[9] Huchthausen, R.: Herkunft, sozialer Status und Motivation von Studierenden am Abendgymnasium, Frankfurt (Diplomarbeit) 1978

[10] Papert, S.: The Uses of Technology to Enhance Education, Cambridge, MIT AI-Memo 298, 1973

[12] Rößler, H.: Die Neugestaltung des zweiten Bildungswegs - ein Lehrstück von der Macht bildungsbürgerlicher Tradition, HLZ 11, 1980

[13] Schildkamp-Kündiger, E.: Special Problems of Women in Mathematics, ZDM 1 S. 12, 1981

[14] Tietgens, H.: Lernen mit Erwachsenen, Braunschweig, Westermann, 1979

Zum Beginn des Rechnereinsatzes im Informatikunterricht

Mario Spengler
Staatliches Gymnasium
D 55o8 Hermeskeil

Zusammenfassung: In Lehrplänen und Empfehlungen zum Informatikunterricht finden sich kaum Hinweise über den Zeitpunkt des ersten Rechnereinsatzes im Unterricht. Im folgenden Beitrag sollen mehrere praktizierte Verfahren beschrieben und kommentiert werden. Abschließend stellt der Autor einen rechnerbegleiteten Anfangsunterricht vor, in dem der Rechner frühzeitig eingesetzt wird, jedoch nicht zum Programmieren.

1 Vorgaben

Ausganspunkt für den heutigen Informatikunterricht waren die "Zielsetzungen und Inhalte des Informatikunterrichts" [1] , die im Auftrag des Fachausschusses "Ausbildung" der "Gesellschaft für Informatik" von einem Unterausschuß erarbeitet wurden. Es folgen die Wichtigsten Ziele und Inhalte zum gegebenen Thema:

1.1 Zielsetzungen des Informatikunterrichts (GI)
1.1.1 Systematisches Finden algorithmischer Lösungen von Problemen
1.1.2 Formulierung algorithmischer Problemlösungen in einem Programm
1.1.3 Vertiefung durch Anwendung auf praxisorientierte Probleme
1.1.4 Erkennung der Auswirkung der Datenverarbeitung auf die Gesellschaft
1.1.5 Vertiefung durch Erarbeitung von theoretischen oder technischen Grundlagen der Informatik

1.2 Inhalte des Informatikunterrichts (GI)

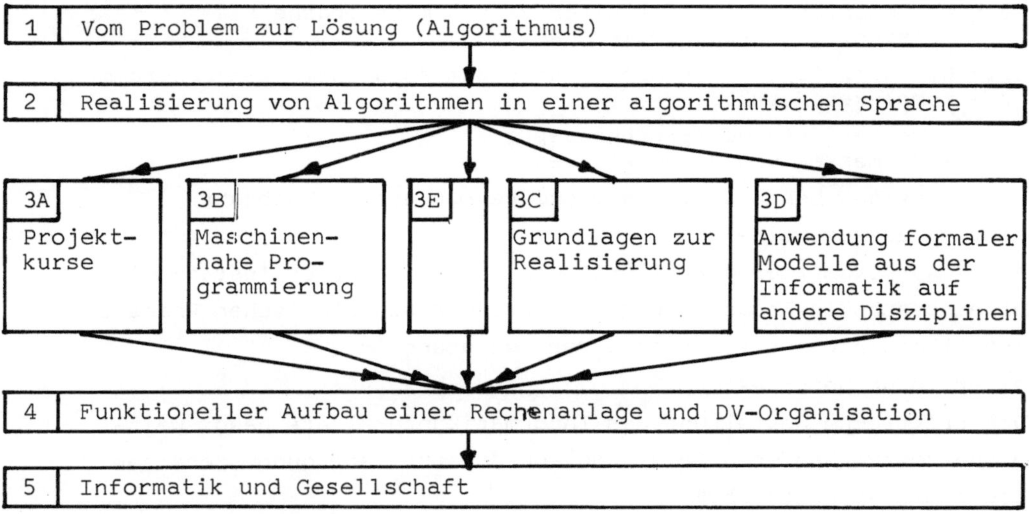

1.Abbildung : Inhalte des Informatikunterrichts aus [1]

Es folgt nun eine Verfeinerung der Ziele für die ersten beiden Blöcke 1.1.2 und 1.2.2 :

1.2.1 Vom Problem zur Lösung

- Alltagsalgorithmen
- Bekannte Algorithmen aus dem Schulunterricht
- Der intuitive Begriff des Algorithmus
- Elementare Objekte
- Elementare Anweisungen
- Kontrollstrukturen
- Datenstrukturen
- Strukturierung von Algorithmen

1.2.2 Realisierung von Algorithmen in einer algorithmischen Sprache

- Elementare Objekte (Konstante,Variable,Vereinbarungen)
- Elementare Anweisungen(Zuweisungen,Ausdrücke,Ein-/Ausgabe)
- Kontrollstrukturen (Zusammenfassung,Auswahl,Wiederh.,Abbruch)
- Weiterführende Sprachelemente (Ind.Var.,Prozeduren,Datenstr.)

Diese Zielsetzungen und Inhalte der GI finden sich nun in den Lehrplänen der Bundesländer wieder. Es folgen die entsprechenden Inhalte des Lehrplans Informatik von Rheinland-Pfalz [2] , der dem Autor am besten bekannt ist:

1.3 Inhalte des Informatikunterrichts (Lehrplan)

1.3.1 <u>Halbjahr 11/1</u> : Vom Problem zum Algorithmus

- Problemspezifikation
- Begriff des Algorithmus
- Methode der schrittweisen Verfeinerung
- Korrektheit und Aufwand von Algorithmen
- Formalisierte Darstellung von Algorithmen in der Umgangssprache

1.3.2 <u>Halbjahr 11/2</u> : Vom Algorithmus zum getesteten Programm einfacher Struktur

- Elementare Bausteine einer Programmiersprache
- Technik des Programmierens

1.3.3 <u>Halbjahr 12/1</u> : Vom Algorithmus zum dokumentierten Programm komplexer Struktur

- Weiterführende Sprachkonzepte
- Vermessen und Dokumentieren

Im Vorwort des Lehrplans, insbesondere zum ersten Halbjahr, heißt es auszugsweise:

"Als Ausdrucksmittel der Algorithmen kommt in erster Instanz die Muttersprache in Frage, die gerade bei der schöpferischen Phase des Algorithmenentwurfs von besonderer Bedeutung ist."

Weiter vorne heißt es:

"Die praktische Gestaltung des Informatikunterrichts hängt weitgehend vom vorhandenen Gerät und von den zur Verfügung stehenden Programmiersprachen ab."

Und als letztes Zitat und zum Abschluß der Bestandsaufnahme:

"Andererseits sollte trotz der verständlichen Faszination durch die

Maschine niemals die gründliche Vorarbeit, wie sie besonders im Halbjahr 11/1 in der Erarbeitung des Algorithmus erstrebt wird, übersprungen werden."

2 Problematik

Weder im GI-Papier noch in dem zitierten Lehrplan ist ein genauer Zeitpunkt angegeben, zu dem der Rechner zum ersten Mal in das Unterrichtsgeschehen einbezogen wird.

Innerhalb zweier Schulversuche wurden unter anderem die Erfahrungsberichte vieler Kollegen über ihren Anfangsunterricht in Informatik gesammelt und ausgewertet. Es zeigte sich, daß ein Teil den Rechner im ersten Halbjahr gar nicht einsetzte, ein zweiter Teil jedoch gleich zu Beginn, und ein dritter Teil unterrichtete 2-3 Monate wie die erste Gruppe der Kollegen, anschließend genau wie die zweite Gruppe. Bei der ersten Methode wird genau nach GI-Vorschlag und lehrplankonform der Schritt "Vom Problem zum Algorithmus" sorgfältig ein ganzes Halbjahr lang erarbeitet und in allen Einzelheiten erörtert, erst im nächsten Halbjahr erfolgt der Übergang vom "Algorithmus zum Programm". Also ist bei dieser Methode der Rechnereinsatz erst nach dem 1.Halbjahr erforderlich. Da bei diesem Verfahren die stark motivierende Wirkung des Rechners nicht ausgenutzt wird, haben die Verfechter der 2.Methode die verfügbare Unterrichtszeit in Unterrichtseinheiten eingeteilt. Innerhalb einer jeden Einheit wird an einem Beispiel das Problem analysiert, strukturiert und ein Algorithmus in der Umgangssprache formuliert und graphisch veranschaulicht. Anschließend wird in derselben Einheit der Algorithmus in ein Programm umgesetzt und an der Maschine ausgetestet. Zwangsläufig wird der Rechner bei diesem Verfahren schon in den ersten Unterrichtsstunden intensiv eingesetzt.

Bei der folgenden 2.Abbildung finden sich die beiden Verfahren in einer Gegenüberstellung, ergänzt durch einen dritten Vorschlag, der sich sowohl an die GI-Richtlinien und den bestehenden Lehrplan hält, als auch die motivierende Kraft des Computers im Anfangsunterricht ausnutzt. Dieser 3.Vorschlag soll im weiteren Verlauf dieses Beitrags näher ausgearbeitet werden. Für die vergleichende Übersicht gelten folgende Bezeichnungen:

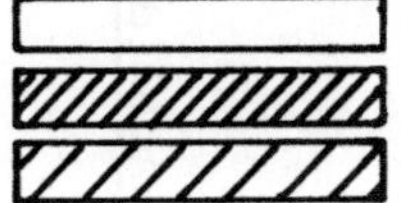

Unterricht ohne Rechnerbenutzung
Unterricht mit intensiver Rechnerbenutzung
Unterricht, teilweise mit Rechnerbenutzung

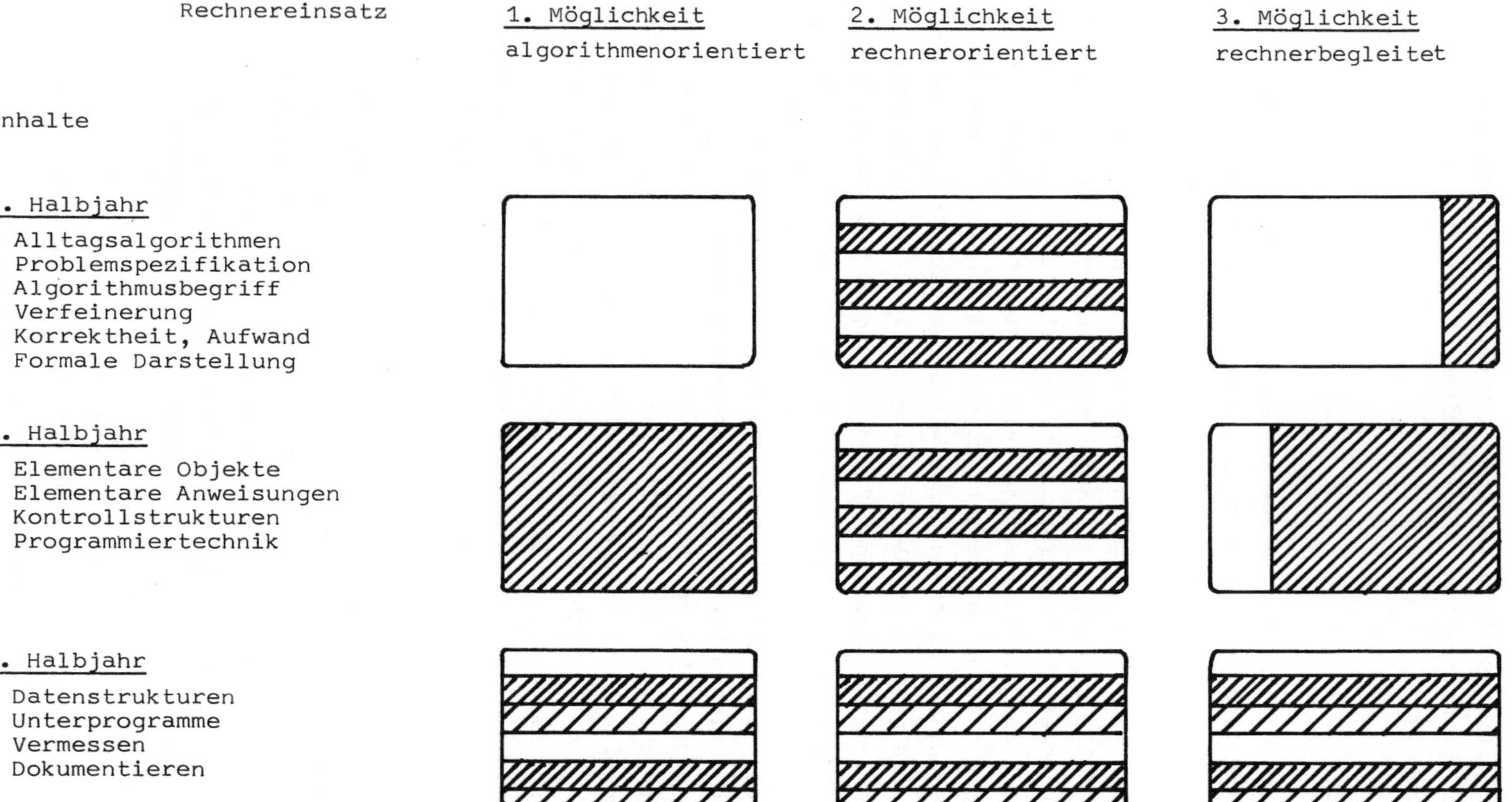

2. Abbildung : Möglichkeiten des Rechnereinsatzes in den ersten drei Halbjahren

3 Wertung

Bei der algorithmenorientierten Vorgehensweise ist der erste Einsatz des Rechners zu Beginn des zweiten Halbjahres vorgesehen. Hier erfolgt die Einführung in eine höhere Programmiersprache wie PASCAL. In jeder Unterrichtseinheit werden neue Sprachelemente vorgestellt und anschließend am Rechner in kleinen übersichtlichen Programmen ausgetestet. Problematisch ist hier meist nur die geringe Zahl der verfügbaren Arbeitsplätze, die dennoch bei geeigneter Unterrichtsorganisation jedem Schüler gestattet, praktische Erfahrungen im Umgang mit der Rechenanlage zu sammeln.

Die rechnerorientierte Vorgehensweise setzt die im Unterricht an Algorithmen abgeleiteten Sprachstrukturen sofort in die Programmiersprache um und realisiert die Programmierung des Rechners noch in derselben Unterrichtseinheit. Je nach Beispiel werden auch hier Korrektheitsnachweise besprochen und Aufwandsbetrachtungen angestellt, so daß sich dieses Verfahren über zwei Halbjahre hinzieht.

Das rechnerbegleitete Verfahren stimmt inhaltlich mit dem algorithmenorientierten Verfahren überein, wie es auch in "Zielsetzungen und Inhalte des Informatikunterrichts" der "Gesellschaft für Informatik" vorgeschlagen wurde. Der Computer wird ab und zu mit fertigen Programmen, jedoch nicht in jeder Unterrichtsstunde, zur Demonstration und als Hilfsmittel eingesetzt. Damit wird zum einen die starke Motivation des Faches Informatik aufrecht gehalten, zum anderen werden die wichtigen Ziele des ersten Halbjahres intensiv erarbeitet. Nebenbei wird das Handling der Anlage erlernt, so daß die Sprachelemente des Betriebssystems zum Zeitpunkt des Erlernens der Programmiersprache bereits bekannt sind. Es ist notwendig, die Einführung in die Programmiersprache und die Hinführung zum Bedienen der Anlage zeitlich zu trennen. Gründe hierfür werden später angeführt.

Im 3. Halbjahr werden übereinstimmend bei allen Vorgehensweisen komplexe Probleme zunächst umgangssprachlich aufbereitet. Problemspezifikation, Groblösung, Verfeinerungen und Struktogramm erfordern noch keinen Rechnereinsatz. Sehr intensiv wird der Rechner in der Programmierphase eingesetzt. In der Optimierungs- und Dokumentationsphase wird schließlich die Maschine nur sporadisch benutzt. Die Dokumentation sollte natürlich bereits parallel zur Programmentwicklung erfolgen.

4 Rechnereinsatz ohne Programmierung

Das Gespräch mit Schülern, die das Fach Informatik im Rahmen der reformierten gymnasialen Oberstufe im 1. oder im 2. Halbjahr abwählten, zeigte unter Vernachlässigung taktischer Gründe wie Noten, Lehrerpersönlichkeit und Überbelastung folgende Ursachen für die Abwahl:

	Abwahl im 1.Halbjahr	Abwahl im 2.Halbjahr
1.Verfahren	"Ich habe mir unter Informatik etwas anderes vorgestellt."	"Ich traue mich doch nicht an die Anlage, wenn so viele andere da sind."
2.Verfahren	"Es geht mir zu schnell, ich verstehe das ganze nicht."	"Die anderen sind schon so gut, ich komme da nicht mehr mit."

3. Abbildung : Gründe für die vorzeitige Abwahl von Informatik

Die exemplarischen Schülerantworten als Begründung für eine vorzeitige Abwahl decken sich mit einer Beobachtung, welche alle Kollegen machen, die Informatik unterrichten: Ein paar Wochen nach den ersten Programmierübungen eilt ein Teil des Kurses ein halbes Jahr voraus, während der andere Teil des Kurses weder die Handhabung des Rechners beherrscht, noch in der Lage ist, einfachste Programme zu schreiben.

Um diesen Begleiterscheinungen Rechnung zu tragen, wurde das rechnerbegleitete Verfahren konzipiert. Im ersten Halbjahr wird an fertigen Programmen demonstriert, was machbar ist. Dadurch bleibt weiterhin die Motivation erhalten, bereits gelöste Probleme zu einem späteren Zeitpunkt in eine Programmiersprache zu übersetzen. Durch spielerischen Umgang mit dem Rechner ist der Befehlsvorrat von Editor und Betriebssystem allen Kursteilnehmern bekannt, so daß das erste Halbjahr seinen eigentlichen Sinn, nämlich die Anpassung der unterschiedlichen Vorkenntnisse, voll erfüllt. Der Editor kann zur Auflockerung theoretischer Unterrichtsphasen eingesetzt werden, ohne daß Programmtexte erstellt und korrigiert werden. Für Schüler allgemeinbildender Schulen ist es äußerst lehrreich, einen Programmablaufplan oder ein Struktogramm im Terminalbetrieb zu editieren. Die folgende Übersicht zeigt exemplarisch einige Möglichkeiten des Rechnereinsatzes, ohne daß Schüler programmieren müssen.

Einsatz / Inhalte	Demonstration	Spiel und Handling	Austesten	Editorübungen
Alltagsalgorithmen, bekannte Algorithmen	Gaußscher Algor.	Nimm - Spiel		
Problemspezifikation	Häufigkeit von Zeichen im Text			Texteingabe
Algorithmusbegriff		Nachfolger suchen	Vorgänger suchen	
Schrittweise Verfeinerung			Sonderfälle bei automatischer Geldrückgabe	Textkorrektur
Objekte, Anweisungen und Kontrollstrukt.		Plattenzugriff üben		
Korrektheit und Aufwand	verschiedene Sortierverfahren		Laufzeiten ausmessen	
Formale Darstellung von Algorithmen				Editieren von Baumdiagrammen, Struktogrammen

4. Abbildung : Möglichkeiten des Rechnereinsatzes ohne Programmierung durch die Schüler

5 Empfehlungen

Unter Berücksichtigung der genannten Aspekte komme ich zu folgenden Empfehlungen über den Rechnereinsatz im Anfangsunterricht des Schulfaches Informatik:

5.1 Um eine solide Grundausbildung zu gewährleisten, sollte im ersten Halbjahr nicht programmiert werden.

5.2 Um die Motivation aufrecht zu halten, sollte der Rechner im ersten Halbjahr wohl dosiert zur Demonstration und zum Austesten fertiger Programme eingesetzt werden.

5.3 Um die Programmiersprache von den Betriebssystembefehlen abzuheben, sollten die Kommandos der Betriebssystemebene vor der Programmierphase spielend am Rechner erarbeitet werden.

5.4 Um allen Schülern die gleichen Chancen am Rechner zu geben, sollten die Editor-Befehle an neutralen Texten vor dem Erlernen der Programmiersprache mit dem Rechner geübt werden.

6 Literatur

[1] Brauer,W.; Claus,V.; Deussen,P.; Eickel,W.; Haacke,W.; Hosseus,W.; Koster,C.H.A.; Ollesky,D.; Weinhart,K.
Zielsetzungen und Inhalte des Informatikunterrichts
Sonderdruck aus Zentralblatt für Didaktik der Mathematik ZDM 76/1
Stuttgart, Klett, 1976

[2] Laubenheimer,N.; Rissberger,A.; Schmitt,R.; Stimm,H.; Wache,R.; Welzel,M.; Werner,W.

Entwurf der Revision des Lehrplans Informatik Grundfach Gymnasium
Mainz, Kultusministerium, 1981

Erste Erfahrungen mit Informatik als Abiturprüfungsfach in Niedersachsen

Dierk Buse, Gymnasium Soltau

Zusammenfassung:

Zur Zeit legen in Niedersachsen etwa 1% der Schüler eines Jahrgangs das Abitur im Fach Informatik ab. Die fachlichen Qualifikationen, die der Schüler in der Prüfung nachweisen soll, werden nachfolgend kurz beschrieben und an einem Beispiel aus der mündlichen Prüfung erläutert. Aus den ersten Erfahrungen mit der Abiturprüfung werden Folgerungen für die Zukunft der Informatik am Gymnasium gezogen.

1. Organisatorische Voraussetzungen

Informatik ist in Niedersachsen ein eigenständiges Fach in der Sek.II und gehört zum mathematisch-naturwissenschaftlich-technischen Aufgabenfeld. Einzelne Informatikgrundkurse können ohne besondere Genehmigung im Wahl- und Pflichtbereich angeboten werden.
Gymnasien, die Informatik als Abiturprüfungsfach einführen wollen, müssen dies beim Kultusministerium beantragen. Sie müssen drei qualifizierte Lehrer und eine unterrichtsgeeignete Rechnerausstattung nachweisen. Die Genehmigung wird dem gegenwärtigen Entwicklungsstand des neuen Faches entsprechend zur Zeit nur für Informatik als drittes oder viertes Prüfungsfach erteilt. Unterricht und Prüfung sind nach den Rahmenrichtlinien bzw. den einheitlichen Prüfungsanforderungen in der Abiturprüfung für dieses Fach durchzuführen. Im dritten Prüfungsfach findet eine schriftliche und falls das Ergebnis von den bisherigen Leistungen abweicht, auch eine mündliche Prüfung statt; im vierten Prüfungsfach wird der Schüler ausschließlich mündlich geprüft. Ein Schüler, der Informatik als drittes oder viertes Prüfungsfach wählt, muß mindestens fünf Grundkurse in diesem Fach belegen (das sind etwa 225 Unterrichtsstunden). Durch diese Wahl kann er seine Pflichtauflagen in Mathematik und den Naturwissenschaften nicht erfüllen. Somit muß dieser Schüler in der Regel mehr leisten, als jene, die statt Informatik Mathematik oder eine Naturwissenschaft als Prüfungsfach wählen.

2. Abiturprüfungsanforderungen

Grundlage der niedersächsischen Abiturprüfungsanforderungen sind die "Einheitlichen Prüfungsanforderungen in der Abiturprüfung Informatik"

(EPA), die von der Kultusministerkonferenz am 23.2.81 verabschiedet worden sind.
Sie enthalten

- eine Beschreibung in diesem Fach nachweisbarer Qualifikationen
- Kriterien, mit deren Hilfe überprüft werden kann, ob eine Prüfungsaufgabe das anzustrebende Anspruchsniveau hat
- Angaben über Aufgabenarten
- Hinweise zum Bewerten von Prüfungsleistungen
- Aufgabenbeispiele mit Bewertungsvorschlägen, die der Erläuterung dienen aber nicht als Festlegungen mißverstanden werden dürfen.

Als Hilfsmittel bei der Auswahl der Prüfungsinhalte und der Entwicklung von Prüfungsaufgaben werden drei Anforderungsbereiche fachspezifisch beschrieben. Sie charakterisieren vor allem den Grad der Selbständigkeit bei der geistigen Arbeit und stellen damit auch eine Abstufung nach der Schwierigkeit der Aufgabe dar. Die Schwerpunkte der Aufgaben liegen im Anforderungsbereich II, der mit selbständigem Auswählen, Verarbeiten und Darstellen bekannter Sachverhalte sowie Übertragen des Gelernten auf vergleichbare neue Situationen beschrieben werden kann. Bei der Aufgabenstellung wird jede im Rahmen eines Arbeitsauftrags erwartete Leistung auf die drei Anforderungsbereiche bezogen. Dieser Bezug ist ganz wesentlich vom vorangegangenen Unterricht abhängig.
Die Inhalte und Lernziele des zu erteilenden Unterrichts sind in den niedersächsischen Rahmenrichtlinien festgelegt und lassen sich folgendermaßen zusammenfassen:
Der Schüler soll

- numerische und nichtnumerische Probleme beschreiben, analysieren und für sie geeignete Modelle entwickeln,
- Problemlösungsmethoden beschreiben und anwenden,
- systematisch algorithmische Lösungen von Problemen entwickeln,
- Beschreibungselemente und Darstellungsformen von Algorithmen anwenden,
- Datenstrukturen und Datenorganisationen in ihrer Bedeutung für den Lösungsalgorithmus verstehen und bewerten,
- die algorithmische Problemlösung in einer Programmiersprache formulieren,
- Programme testen und aus den Ergebnissen Rückschlüsse ziehen,
- Organisationsformen von DV-Anlagen kennen und problemorientiert auswählen,

- Aufbau und Funktionsweise informationsverarbeitender Systeme verstehen,
- Wechselbeziehungen zwischen theoretischen Ansätzen und praktischen Realisierungen beschreiben und analysieren,
- Auswirkungen auf die Gesellschaft durch Gebrauch und Mißbrauch der Datenverarbeitung erkennen und beurteilen.

Die Aufgaben der Abiturprüfung sollen diese fachlichen Qualifikationen und Inhalte in möglichst großer Breite überprüfen.

2.1 Schriftliche Prüfung

Der Fachlehrer muß zwei etwa gleichschwere Prüfungsvorschläge bei der unteren Schulbehörde zur Auswahl einreichen. Jeder Prüfungsvorschlag besteht aus drei von einander unabhängigen Aufgaben aus mindestens zwei Sachgebieten. Jedem Vorschlag sind folgende Erläuterungen beizufügen:

- Eine kurze Beschreibung des Bezugs der Teilaufgaben zum vorangegangenen Unterricht sowie die Angabe der Kursthemen
- eine stichwortartige Darstellung der Ergebnisse und Lösungswege
- eine Zuordnung der Teilaufgaben zu den Anforderungsbereichen sowie die geplante Gewichtung im Rahmen der Gesamtaufgabe.

Der Schüler muß die drei von der Schulbehörde ausgewählten Aufgaben innerhalb von 210 Minuten bearbeiten. Soll der Schüler dabei die vorhandene Rechenanlage benutzen, kann die Bearbeitungszeit um 60 Minuten verlängert werden.

Von den Aufgabenbeispielen aus den EPA können hier nur die Themen genannt werden.

(1) Analyse eines numerischen Algorithmus

Übersetzung eines als Programmablaufplan vorgelegten Algorithmus in die Programmiersprache PASCAL mit Korrektheitsnachweis.

(2) Sortierverfahren

Vergleich und Untersuchung von in Struktogrammen vorgelegten Sortieralgorithmen.

(3) Verschmelzung zweier Listen

Analyse eines Programms

(4) Mandatsverteilung

Erstellen eines Programms für das in einem Beispiel vorgelegten d'Hondt-Verfahren und Probeläufe auf dem Rechner

(5) Zeilendehnung und Worttrennung

Erstellen von Programmen zur Textverarbeitung mit Probeläufen auf dem Rechner

(6) Dateiverarbeitung

Datenorganisation, Speichermedien, Datensicherung anhand eines vorgelegten Beispiels aus dem Großhandel

(7) Serienaddierer

Analyse und Variation eines als Schaltplan vorgelegten Schaltwerkes

(8) Steuerung und Überwachung einer Maschinenstraße

Erstellen der Schaltfunktion und der Schaltung zu einer vorgelegten Beschreibung

(9) Algorithmisierung eines Problems mit Hilfe eines endlichen Automaten

Interpretation einer vorgelegten Umfüllaufgabe als endlicher Automat

(10) Endliche Automaten

Analyse eines als Transitionsgraph vorgelegten endlichen Automaten

(11) Kundendatei

Planung einer Datei und Erstellen eines Abfrageprogramms zu einem vorgelegten Datenschema. Fragen zum Datenschutz.

2.2 Mündliche Prüfung

Damit in der zur Verfügung stehenden Zeit von zwanzig Minuten die in den EPA beschriebenen Qualifikationen überprüft werden können, muß sich die Aufgabenstellung für die mündliche Prüfung grundsätzlich von der für die schriftliche Prüfung unterscheiden.
Als Ausgangspunkt für die mündliche Prüfung dient eine begrenzte, gegliederte Aufgabe. Die Darstellung und Begründung von Sachverhalten und Verfahren soll im Vordergrund stehen. Falls in der Aufgabe ein Programm erstellt werden soll, kann dies nur als Einstieg dienen. Daher ist der Programmieraufwand gering zu halten.
Die Prüfungsaufgabe muß einen einfachen Einstieg erlauben, aber so angelegt sein, daß in der Prüfung grundsätzlich jede Note erreichbar ist. Bei der Aufgabenstellung muß berücksichtigt werden, daß sich der Prüfling bis etwa zur Hälfte der Prüfungszeit im zusammenhängenden Vortrag zu dieser Prüfungsaufgabe äußern kann. In dem anschließenden Prüfungsgespräch soll festgestellt werden, ob der Prüfling fähig ist, sein Wissen in einem Fachgespräch darzustellen.

Das folgende Beispiel für die mündliche Prüfung soll verdeutlichen, wie die Qualifikationen überprüft werden können.
Dem Schüler wird ein PASCAL-Programm vorgelegt, das eine vorgegebene Datei von Schülerstammdaten mit Hilfe zweier Sortierverfahren (bubble-sort und quick_sort) nach Schülernummern oder Schülernamen

sortiert. Im Programm werden die drei Prozedurarten (call by value, call by reference, call by name) verwendet.

Die Aufgabenstellung lautet:

Das anliegende Programm ist unter dem Namen SORT abgespeichert. Führen Sie Testläufe unter Verwendung der Datei STAMM durch.

(1) Stoppen Sie die Zeit bei der Sortierung mit SORT1 und SORT2.

(2) Erläutern Sie die beiden Sortierverfahren.

(3) Erläutern Sie das unterschiedliche Laufzeitverhalten.

(4) Erläutern Sie die unterschiedlichen Prozedurarten, die im Programm verwendet werden.

(5) Was würden Sie am Programm ändern, wenn die Datei nicht in den Arbeitsspeicher paßt?

Der Schüler hat eine Vorbereitungszeit von zwanzig Minuten. Während dieser Zeit soll er u.a. zeigen, daß er mit der Rechenanlage vertraut ist. Die beiden Sortierverfahren und die Prozedurarten wurden in anderem Zusammenhang im Unterricht behandelt. Aufwandsberechnungen wurden an anderen Beispielen geübt. Die Erklärung der Rekursion im Algorithmus quick-sort bietet dem Schüler Gelegenheit auch anspruchsvollere Prüfungsleistungen zu erbringen.

3. Bestandsaufnahme und Zukunftsaspekte

Rund 10% der niedersächsischen Gymnasien (25 von 230) dürfen Informatik als Prüfungsfach anbieten. In diesen Schulen nehmen etwa 40 - 50 % der Schüler eines Jahrgangs an wenigstens einen Grundkurs teil, während nur 5 - 10 % Informatik als Prüfungsfach wählen. In der Regel wird hierbei Informatik als viertes Prüfungsfach in der Kombination mit Mathematik als Leistungsfach (1. Prüfungsfach) bevorzugt.

In Niedersachsen haben in diesem Jahr schätzungsweise 100 Schüler von den 20 000 des Abiturjahrgangs die Prüfung in Informatik abgelegt. Damit spielt das Abiturfach Informatik zur Zeit eine untergeordnete Rolle. Dies wäre meiner Ansicht nach nicht weiter gravierend, wenn möglichst alle anderen Schüler wenigstens einmal in ihrer Schulzeit mit Informatikinhalten vertraut gemacht würden.

Dies kann auf zweierlei Weisen geschehen:

(1) Informatik wird als Pflichtfach in der Sek.I und Sek.II eingeführt

(2) Informatikinhalte werden in allen dafür in Frage kommenden Fächern der Sek.I und Sek.II gelehrt.

Der zweiten Lösung gebe ich eine größere Chance, da die erste wegen der derzeitigen schulpolitischen Lage nicht durchsetzbar ist.

BERUFSQUALIFIZIERENDER DATENVERARBEITUNGSUNTERRICHT

ANFORDERUNGEN AN DEN DATENVERARBEITUNGSUNTERRICHT KAUFMÄNNISCHER BERUFSBILDENDER SCHULEN AUS DER SICHT DER EDV-ANWENDER UND VORAUSSETZUNGEN IHRER UMSETZUNG

B. KRETSCHMER, WOLFSBURG

ZUSAMMENFASSUNG

Ausweitung des EDV-Einsatzes und Veränderung der Rechnernutzung in Wirtschaft und Verwaltung verändern tiefgreifend die Tätigkeiten kaufmännischer Sachbearbeiter. Diese benötigen für den aktiven Umgang mit DV-Systemen neue Qualifikationen, während auf frühere Arbeitsabläufe bezogene Kenntnisse und Fertigkeiten entwertet werden. Anknüpfend an eine empirische Untersuchung [3] über Veränderungen in kaufmännischen Berufsfeldern und Forderungen der Wirtschaft soll hier ein Anforderungsprofil für einen berufsqualifizierenden Datenverarbeitungsunterricht abgeleitet werden. Dessen Umsetzung setzt nicht nur die Beschaffung geigneter Rechnersysteme für die Schulen voraus. Spätestens nach der Rechnerbeschaffung werden die Fehlsteuerung durch fehlqualifizierende starre Curricula und Prüfungssysteme und die Engpässe in der Aus- und Fortbildung der Lehrer und in der abgestimmten Gestaltung von hard-,soft- und teachware und lehrer-und schülergeeigneten Hand- und Lehrbüchern sichtbar.

GLIEDERUNG

1. VERÄNDERUNGEN IM BERUFSFELD KAUFMÄNNISCHER SACHBEARBEITER

1.1 MENGENMÄSSIGE AUSWEITUNG DES EDV-EINSATZES

Bis 1985 werden über 90 % der kaufmännischen Sachbearbeiter über Datensichtgeräte Zugang zu Datenverarbeitungssystemen haben und und diese so selbstverständlich zur Kommunikation nutzen wie das Fernsprechnetz. Immer mehr Teilaufgaben werden statt manuell im Zusammenwirken von EDV-System und Sachbearbeiter bearbeitet oder voll automatisiert.

1.2 VERÄNDERUNGEN DER RECHNERSYSTEME

Rechnerverbundsysteme lösen isolierte Einzelsysteme ab, automatische Prozesse und Dialogverarbeitung ersetzen weitgehend eine belegorientierte Stapelverarbeitung und das Arbeiten am Bildschirm mit Dateien bzw. Datenbanken verbannt DV-Listen und Belegberge.

1.3 VERSCHIEBUNG DER TÄTIGKEITEN AN BILDSCHIRMARBEITSPLÄTZEN

Bis Mitte des Jahrzehnts werden im Zuge weiterer Automatisierung Routinearbeiten an Bildschirmarbeitsplätzen von derzeit 80% auf 20% abnehmen und die verantwortlichen Arbeiten mit Datenbanken bzw. Dateisystemen als Grundlage von Entscheidungen auf 80% zunehmen.

1.4 AUFGABENVERLAGERUNG VON DEN DV-ABTEILUNGEN AUF DIE FACHABTEILUNGEN

Von den EDV-Abteilungen werden die folgenden Aufgaben vermehrt auf die Fachabteilungen übertragen:

- Problemformulierung, Aufgabenstellung und Entwicklung von Detailkonzepten
- Entwurf, Weiterentwicklung und Pflege von (nur in der jeweiligen Fachabteilung genutzten) Programmsystemen
- Datenerfassung
- Datei- bzw. Datenbankauswertungen
- Dezentrales, fallweises Ausdrucken von Daten (z.T. in selbst gestalteten Formaten).

Kaum berührt wird hingegen die fachübergreifende Systemkonzeption und -verantwortung durch die EDV-Abteilung.

1.5 MITBESTIMMUNG BEI ORGANISATORISCHEN MASSNAHMEN

Konkretes Ausfüllen betrieblicher und überbetrieblicher Mitbestimmungsregelungen bei organisatorischen Änderungen bzw. Rationalisierungsmaßnahmen erfordert sachkundige Interessenvertretung und ihre Unterstützung durch ebenso sachkundige Mitarbeiter.

2. NOTWENDIGE QUALIFIKATIONEN KAUFMÄNNISCHER SACHBEARBEITER

Besonders für die Phase der Umstellung auf integrierte, weitgehend automatisierte Organisationsformen wird noch eine größere Zahl umfassend qualifizierter Sachbearbeiter benötigt. Von kaufmännischen Sachbearbeitern wird daher erwartet, daß sie sich über eine breite, problemlösungs- und entscheidungsorientierte kaufmännische Grundbildung hinaus dazu qualifizieren, DV-Anlagen aktiv zum Problemlösen nutzen zu können.

Dazu müssen sie u.a.

- systematisch Benutzeranforderungen formulieren und begründen können

und dabei gebräuchliche

- Problemlösungs- und darstellungsmethoden anwenden können.

Sie müssen ferner Dialoge mit Datenbank-/Dateiverwaltungssystemen führen können, d.h.

- im Dialog Datenbanken bzw. Dateien für ihre Entscheidungen auswerten können

und

- Daten strukturieren und ordnungsgemäß in Datenbanken bzw. Dateisysteme eingeben können.

Vermehrt werden sie

- Programme anpassen, verändern und z.T. selbst konzipieren, verfassen, eingeben und testen können müssen.

Hierbei werden sie allerdings bei der Detailprogrammierung durch immer anwendungsnähere und benutzerfreundlichere Programmiersysteme und Hilfsprogramme (z.B. zum Gestalten von Bildschirmmasken und Druckbildern) durch DV-Systeme unterstützt bzw. entlastet.

Ohne Ausnahme wir von Sachbearbeitern erwartet, daß sie mit Datenbeständen sehr sorgfältig umgehen und die

- Normen, Erfordernisse und Verfahren des Datenschutzes und der Datensicherung sicher beherrschen.

3. ANFORDERUNGEN AN DEN DATENVERARBEITUNGS - UNTERRICHT

Ich setze voraus, daß der EDV-Unterricht sowohl

- im Interesse des Beschäftigungssystems

als auch

- im Interesse der Beschäftigten

auf zukünftige Berufe vorbereiten soll.

Damit muß der Datenverarbeitungs-Unterricht auf

- Vertrautheit, Selbstverständlichkeit, Handlungsfähigkeit und Flexibilität im Umgang mit Datenverarbeitungssystemen

aber auch auf eine

- begründete kritische Haltung gegenüber unnötigem, unwirtschaftlichem oder ihren Interessen zuwider laufendem EDV-Einsatz

abzielen.

Nicht zuletzt muß der Datenverarbeitungs-Unterricht dem Schüler für seine Berufswahl klare Vorstellungen darüber vermitteln, auf welchen Gebieten DV-Systeme menschlicher Informationsverarbeitung überlegen sind oder bald sein werden und welchen Einfluß dies auf die Arbeitsplätze haben kann.

Im einzelnen sollte der Datenverarbeitungs-Unterricht an kaufmännischen berufsbildenden Schulen die folgenden Lernziele verfolgen:

- Ist-Analysen anfertigen und Organisationsstrukturen beschreiben und entwerfen können
- Ziele des DV-Einsatzes und Benutzeranforderungen formulieren können
- Betriebliche Organisation und Informationssystem abstimmen können
- Auswirkungen organisatorischer Lösungen mit verschiedenem Anteil an menschlicher und automatischer Informationsverarbeitung vergleichen und bewerten können
- Wirkungen von organisatorischen und von Rationalisierungs- und Kontrollmaßnahmen beurteilen können
- Datenstrukturen (einschließlich Dateistrukturen, Bildschirminhalten und Druckbildern) und Programmstrukturen entwerfen können
- Daten- und Programmstrukturen auf einen Rechner übertragen können
- aktiv mit Dateien und Datenbanken arbeiten können

und

- rationell und sicher mit Daten unter Beachtung gesetzlicher Normen arbeiten können.

4. VORAUSSETZUNGEN FÜR EINEN BERUFSQUALIFIZIERENDEN DV-UNTERRICHT

4.1 LEHRPLÄNE UND PRÜFUNGSORDNUNGEN

Das kaufmännische berufsbildende Schulwesen ist in den einzelnen Bundesländern teils uneinheitlich geregelt und stark gegliedert (Fachklassen der kaufmännischen Berufsschule, Berufsfachschulen, Wirtschaftsgymnasien usw.).

Für eine große Zahl der Schulformen sind in den einzelnen Ländern bereits Datenverarbeitungs-Lehrpläne erlassen.

Der überwiegenden Zahl dieser Lehrpläne ist gemeinsam, daß sie durch

- ihren geringen Zeitansatz für das Fach Datenverarbeitung (meist 30-40 Stunden),
- ihre Überfrachtung mit inhaltlich überholter Begriffskunde (Datenträger - und Rechnerkunde)

und

- ihren Mangel an wirklich bedarfsgerecht berufsqualifizierenden DV-Lerninhalten

einen längerfristig qualifizierenden praxisnahen Datenverarbeitungs-Unterricht verhindern.

Dies trifft besonders für die von den einzelnen Bundesländern erlassenen Lehrpläne für die Fachklassen der kaufmännischen Berufsschule zu, die in den letzten Jahren an die neuen Rahmenlehrpläne der Kultusministerkonferenz angepaßt wurden [4].

Verstärkt wird diese fehlqualifizierende Entwicklung durch die im multiple-choice-Verfahren durchgeführten überregionalen Abschlußprüfungen der Industrie- und Handelskammern, deren Stoffkatalogen in der Schulpraxis oft mehr Gewicht als den offiziellen Lehrplänen beigemessen wird und die zum Andrillen von Begriffsballast zwingen.

In den "Pionierzeiten" der EDV hervorgehobene Lerninhalte wie

- Axiome und Aussagen der Informationstheorie,
- mathematische Grundlagen der Informatik,
- verschiedene Codierungsarten und -systeme

und

- Übertragung von Problemlösungen in eine Maschinensprache

können ebenso problemlos aus den Lehrplänen gestrichen werden wie

- technische Details zur Zentraleinheit, zu Peripheriegeräten und zu Datenträgern.

Stattdessen sollte den oben unter 3. aufgeführten Lernzielen Vorrang gegeben werden!

Mehr Unterrichtszeit für DV-Unterricht kann leicht gewonnen werden, sobald die Curricula der anderen Fächer um Lernziele zu Tätigkeiten bereinigt werden, die von EDV-Systemen bereits heute oder in naher Zukunft wesentlich schneller, korrekter und billiger erledigt werden können. Bei der fälligen Überarbeitung der Lehrpläne für die "kaufmännischen Kernfächer" (Wirtschaftslehre, Rechnungswesen) gilt es, die Auswirkungen des Einsatzes von Informationstechnik zu integrieren.

Im Fachausschuß Ausbildung der Gesellschaft für Informatik arbeitet seit 2 Jahren eine Gruppe von Lehrern, Praktikern und Wissenschaftlern an einem Lehrplanentwurf für kaufmännische berufsbildende Schulen. Die Durchsetzung einer Lehrplanreform erfordert angesichts der verbürokratisierten Strukturen sehr große Anstrengungen.

4.2 LEHRERQUALIFIKATION

In den staatlichen berufsbildenden Schulen kommt bis heute dem Lehrer die zentrale Rolle bei der Qualifikationsvermittlung zu.
Wie steht es aber mit den hierbei vorauszusetzenden Qualifikationen der Lehrer?
Für einen systematischen praxisorientierten DV-Unterricht benötigt ein DV-Lehrer

- solide theoretische Grundlagen,
- aktuelle praktische Anwendungserfahrung und eine
- fachdidaktische Basis.

Derart "rundum" qualifizierte Berufsschullehrer kann man in der Bundesrepublik wohl an wenigen Händen zählen.
Zu den DV-Praktikern, die in den Schuldienst wechselten und den Autodidakten kommen nur langsam sehr wenige in Universität und Studienseminar ausgebildete Junglehrer hinzu.
Qualifikationslücken werden in einigen Bundesländern wenigstens durch meist 4-wöchige EDV- Grundlagen vermittelnde Lehrerfortbildungskurse und durch Betriebspraktika in ersten Ansätzen gefüllt. Diese erreichen aber bisher nur unverhältnismäßig wenige Lehrer: ich schätze, daß bisher ca. 1 °/oo der Lehrer an kaufmännischen berufsbildenden Schulen EDV-Grundlagenkurse besucht hat [1].
Doch eine einmalige Vermittlung von DV-Grundlagen an DV-Lehrer reicht nicht:

- Im DV-Unterricht und im Unterricht kaufmännischer Kernfächer müssen die Lehrer erst lernen, das Instrument DV-Anlage gezielt einzusetzen.
- Durch die rasche Entwicklung der Datenverarbeitung werden die Qualifikationen der DV-Lehrer etwa in 4-Jahres-Abschnitten zu einem großen Teil entwertet, wenn sie nicht einen großen Teil ihrer Arbeitskraft dazu verwenden, den Anschluß zu halten.
- Auch den Lehrern der kaufmännischen Kernfächer müssen laufend die Auswirkungen der einschneidenden Veränderungen im Beschäftigungssystem durch den Einsatz von Informationstechnik auf ihren Unterricht vermittelt werden.

Für die hierfür notwendigen echten Fortbildungskurse und notwendigen Stundenentlastungen werden die Bundesländer weitere Belastungen auf sich nehmen müssen, wenn sie dem Bildungsauftrag ernsthaft gerecht werden wollen.
Bei Beschaffung und Erweiterung von Schulrechnern müssen zudem für die Einweisung der Lehrkräfte in die Systemhandhabung wesentlich mehr Mittel als bisher bereitgestellt werden, um überhaupt eine sachkundige Gerätenutzung zu ermöglichen.

4.3 LEHRMITTELAUSSTATTUNG

4.3.1 RECHNERAUSSTATTUNG

Da die angestrebten Lernziele (Vgl. 3.) nicht in rein theoretischen Kursen vermittelt werden können, sind in den kaufmännischen Schulen Datenverarbeitungssysteme bereitzuhalten, die den Schülern ein praxisgerechtes Üben bei extrem einfach handhabbar gestalteter Benutzerschnittstelle ermöglichen.

Erforderlich ist eine ausreichende Zahl ergonomisch befriedigender Bildschirmarbeitsplätze (ein Gerät für je zwei Schüler einer Klasse, d.h. i.d.R. ein Dutzend Datensichtgeräte pro Klasse) mit einfach gehaltenem Dialogsystem.

Zur Software-Mindestausstattung gehören

- eine möglichst einfache, für Programmier-Anfänger geeignete Programmiersprache mit einfacher Systemeinbettung und integriertem, seitenorientiertem Editor,
- eine weitverbreitete kaufmännisch orientierte Programmiersprache (mit Programmgeneratoren)

und

- einfache Demonstrationsprogramme mit Übungsdateien für typische kaufmännische und Verwaltungsanwendungen.

Entsprechend der Entwicklung der Praxis, den Anwender bei der Detail-Programmierung zu unterstützen und zu entlasten, sind zusätzlich erforderlich:

- ein komfortables Dateiverwaltungs-/Datenbanksystem,
- einfach zu handhabende Datendefinitionssprachen, sowie Bildschirm- und Druckbildgestaltungssysteme (Masken- und Listgeneratoren)

und

- benutzerfreundliche Datei-/Datenbankabfragesprachen.

Obwohl die letzgenannten Softwarepakete bereits im Anfangsunterricht die Bearbeitung realer kaufmännischer Aufgabenstellungen ermöglichen würden, fehlen sie bisher an kaufmännischen Schulen.

Beim gegenwärtigen Stand der Technik sind für kaufmännische Schulen Mehrplatzsysteme mit echtem time-sharing und multiprogramming besonders geeignet. Zunehmende Bedeutung dürften in Zukunft Netze kommerzieller Microrechner bekommen.

Von den Gebietskörperschaften muß bei der Beschaffung von DV-Anlagen für Schulen in den nächsten Jahren trotz schwieriger Kassenlage ein wesentlich stärkeres Engagement als bisher erwartet werden.

Mindestens auf Landesebene müssen den Systemlieferanten klarere und detailliertere Kriterien für schulgeeignete Software an die Hand gegeben werden.

Hier sind als Ergebnis der länderübergreifenden Modellversuche im nächsten Jahr konkrete Aussagen zu erwarten.

4.3.2 SYSTEM - UND ANWENDUNGSBESCHREIBUNGEN

Zu den im letzten Abschnitt genannten Softwarebausteinen sind schülergerechte Beschreibungen erforderlich. Diese müssen vom Systemlieferanten in ausreichender Zahl mitbezogen werden.
Die bisherige Praxis, das Erstellen von schülergerechter Dokumentation den jeweiligen Lehrern zu überlassen, bedeutet unökonomische Doppelarbeit und überfordert die betroffenen Lehrer zumindest zeitlich.
Auch hier sind wenigstens auf Landesebene Mindestanforderungen für bei der Systembeschaffung mitzuliefernde Systembeschreibungen zu formulieren.

4.3.3 LEHRBÜCHER

Neben den systemspezifischen Schülertexten sind für Schüler verständliche Lehrbücher erforderlich, die auf die

- oben genannten Anforderungen an den DV- Unterricht (Vgl. 3.),
- und auf einfache Anfängersprachen mit ihrer Systemumgebung
- und und auf kaufmänniche Standard- Programmpakete
- und möglichst auch auf moderne Programmierhilfen (Maskengeneratoren, Abfragesprachen etc.)

abgestimmt sind.
Hierfür sind von den Kultusministerien zentrale Vorgaben zu entwickeln.
Diese sollten in gemeinsamen Projekten von Verlagen und Systemlieferanten oder durch Angebotserweiterung der Systemlieferanten rasch umgesetzt werden.

5. FEHLQUALIFIKATION ODER GEMEINSAME AKTION ?

Die Umsetzung berufsqualifizierender DV- Curricula in die Praxis berufsbildender Schulen fordert viel Engagement und gemeinsame Anstrengungen gegen heftige Widerstände und Finanzierungsengpässe.

Gelingt in diesem Bereich eine flexible stetige Anpassung an die in der Berufswelt vollzogenen tiefgreifenden Änderungen in der Qualifikationsnachfrage nicht, so wird durch die immer krasser zu Tage tretende Fehlqualifikation der Schüler schnell ein schmerzhafter Beitrag zur Krise im Ausbildungssystem der 80er Jahre erbracht [2].

Ein erstes Beispiel für zentral koodinierte, gemeinsame Aktionen von

- Bundes- und Landesministerien,
- DV- Herstellern,
- Softwarehäusern und
- Schulbuchverlagen

gibt z.B. Österreich mit landeseinheitlich realisierten Projekten zur Datenverarbeitung im Rechnungswesen und in der Textverarbeitung.

Dort werden landeseinheitlich hard- und software und Begleittexte konzipiert, produziert und beschafft und Lehrer geschult.

LITERATUR

[1] Buse, D. Lehrerfort- und -weiterbildung für den Bereich Informatik/Datenverarbeitung in Niedersachsen
in: log in H.1 1981 S. 7 f

[2] Haefner, K. Die neue Bildungskrise Manuskript Bremen 1981

[3] Kretschmer, B., Müller,H.D., Studie über die Entwicklung des Einsatzes des Computers in den Fächern Informatik und Datenverarbeitung in der kaufmännischen Schule bis 1985
in: Haefner, K. (Hrsg.) Arbeitskreis Schulrechner (ASR) Studien zu Schulrechner 1985, Paderborn 1980

[4] Kretschmer, B. Datenverarbeitungslehrpläne kaufmännischer Schulen Stand April 1980, Heft 1, HIBS, Wiesbaden 1980

Lernziele im Informatik-Datenverarbeitungs-Organisationslehre-Unterricht kaufmännischer Schulen

Std J. Loff, Osnabrück

1. Vorbemerkungen

Der Einsatz von Kommunikations- und Informationssystemen in unserer Gesellschaft beeinflußt in einem zunehmend stärker werdenden Umfang die berufliche und auch persönliche Lebenssituation jedes Einzelnen. Der technologische Fortschritt der Hard- und Softwareentwicklung sowie die ständig günstiger werdenden Kosten-Nutzen-Relationen im Bereich der Informationsverarbeitung führen zu einer nahezu "kopernikanischen Wende" in der gegenwärtigen Informations- und Kommunikationssystemumwelt.

Angesichts der sich hieraus ergebenden tiefgreifenden Strukturveränderungen in der Berufs- und Arbeitswelt kommt dem Bildungssystem eine Schlüsselrolle zu: Es gilt deshalb, geeignete Strategien zu entwickeln, mit denen man antizipatorisch auf die sich ändernde Umwelt reagieren kann.

Dabei bilden reale Informationssysteme in Unternehmungen und Verwaltungen einen zunehmend größer werdenden Anwendungsbereich betrieblicher "Informationsprozesse". Das kaufmännische Bildungswesen muß hierauf in geeigneter Form reagieren und Voraussetzungen schaffen, die künftig noch stärker erforderliche Mobilität und Flexibilität des kaufmännischen Mitarbeiters zu gewährleisten. Der vorliegende Beitrag soll helfen, die erkennbar größer werdende Kluft zwischen den Strukturveränderungen der Betriebspraxis und den derzeit überwiegenden Zielen des Informatik-(Datenverarbeitungs- und Organisationslehre-) Unterrichts in den kaufmännischen Schulen zu überwinden.

Wenn es weiterhin oberstes Bildungsziel kaufmännischer Schulen sein soll, eine praxisgerechte Ausbildung auf der Grundlage eines allgemeinen Verständnisses betrieblicher Funktionen und Abläufe zu bewirken, gilt es, die zunehmend rechnergestützten informationsverarbeitenden Prozesse und Systeme in den Unternehmungen und Verwaltungen zu verstehen. Hierbei führt ein grundlagenorientierter, auf die Vermittlung allgemeingültiger Organisations- und Informatikmethoden ausgerichteter Fachunterricht zu einer höheren und längerfristig gültigen Berufsqualifikation.

2. Zur gegenwärtigen Situation des Informatikunterrichts in kaufmännischen Schulen

Die vielfältigen Aufgaben und Ziele der kaufmännischen Grundbildung haben zu einer starken Differenzierung des kaufmännischen Schulwesens geführt. Äußere Kennzeichen dieser Entwicklung sind die vielfältigen Schulformen innerhalb des kaufmännischen Bildungswesens sowie die Vielzahl der Fachbezeichnungen und Unterrichtsfächer für den Informatikunterricht. Als Fachbezeichnungen findet man z.B. Datenverarbeitung, EDV, Organisation/Datenverarbeitung, Organisaton mit EDV, Bürowirtschaft, Rechnungswesen mit EDV. Wenn sich auch in einigen Bundesländern eine Integration von Informatik- und Organisationsinhalten zu einem eigenständgen Unterrichtsfach abzeichnet, so bleiben dennoch die angestrebten Unterrichtsziele und -inhalte hinter den in der Betriebspraxis und der Informatikwissenschaft gewonnenen Erkenntnissen zurück.

Die curriculare, organisatorische und institutionelle Situation des Informatikunterrichts an kaufmännischen Schulen ist heute allgemein gekennzeichnet durch

- eine überwiegend technologisch und hardwareorientierte Ausrichtung der Lerninhalte, Beispiele hierfür sind: Datenträger, Grundkenntnisse über DV-Maschinen und Peripheriegeräte, physische Daten- und Dateiorganisationsformen;

- eine mangelhafte Abstimmung der geforderten Lernziele mit den vorgegebenen Lerninhalten;

- die Vermittlung eines häufig überholten Faktenwissens, Beispiele hierfür sind die Prüfungsaufgaben der Industrie- und Handelskammern;

- ein allgemein geforderter, jedoch kaum realisierter Praxisbezug im Unterricht;

- eine unzureichende Berücksichtigung des Faches Informatik in den Stundentafeln;

- eine ungenügende Rechneraustattung der Schulen;

- eine ungenügende Lehreraus- und -weiterbildung.

Zusammenfassend kann festgestellt werden, daß trotz des Bemühens um Vereinheitlichung (vgl. die Empfehlungen der Kultusministerkonferenz) der Informatikunterricht in kaufmännischen Schulen weder in qualitativer noch in quantitativer Hinsicht den heute zu stellenden Anforderungen entspricht. Den wiederholt erhobenen Forderungen, z.B. der Gesellschaft für Informatik, nach Vermittlung von Problemlösungsstechniken oder allgemein anwendbaren Methoden der Informatik, DV und Organisation wird kaum entsprochen.

3. Der lernzielorientierte Curriculumsansatz im Informatikunterricht kaufmännischer Schulen

Angesichts der inneren und äußeren Heterogenität des kaufmännischen Bildungswesens im allgemeinen und der Situation des Informatikunterrichts im besonderen kann es nicht das Ziel des vorliegenden Beitrags sein, ein für alle kaufmännischen Schulen gültiges Gesamtcurriculum aufzuzeigen. Es kann auch nicht das Ziel darin gesehen werden, eine Vielzahl schulformbezogener Einzelcurricula zu entwickeln. Es gilt mit dem vorliegenden Beitrag vielmehr, diejenigen Qualifikationen aufzuzeigen, über die ein Schüler des kaufmännischen Schulwesens verfügen sollte, um seine mehr und mehr rechnergestützte betriebliche Umwelt zu verstehen. Stichworte hierfür sind Begriffe wie Problemanalyse, systematische Problemlösungsfindung, Algorithmisierng, Analyse- und Darstellungsformen informationsverarbeitender Prozesse, Systementwurfstechniken, Datenstrukturen, Text- und Dateiverarbeitung, Organisationsformen für Projekte sowie Planung und Einsatz betrieblicher Standardsoftware.

Die angegebenen Lernziele sind deshalb eher der Richt- bzw. Grobzielebene zuzuordnen. Unter Richtzielen sollen dabei die allgemeingültigen Unterrichtsziele verstanden werden, die teils fachbezogen teils fächerübergreifend definiert sind; Grobziele stellen demgegenüber eindeutige, aber nicht ins Detail gehende Lernziele dar, die innerhalb des Informatikunterrichts erreicht werden sollen. Die hierzu im einzelnen zu definierenden Lernziele, z.B. die Feinziele des kognitiven, affektiven und psychomotorischen Bereichs, sollten der einzelnen kaufmännischen Schulform sowie der Leistungsfähigkeit der Schüler angepaßt werden; im Rahmen dieses Beitrags wird deshalb auf eine weitergehende Verfeinerung, Hierarchisierng und Taxonomierung der Lernziele verzichtet.

Methodisch ist darauf zu achten, daß auf der Grundlage praxisgerechter konkreter betrieblicher Problemstellungen der gesamte Prozeß der systematischen Problemlösungsfindung mit den wesentlichen Schritten Problemanalyse, Teilproblemfindung und Teilproblemlösung unterrichtlich erarbeitet wird. In einer darauf aufbauenden Unterrichtsstufe gilt es dann, die Allgemeingültigkeit der erarbeiteten Methoden und Darstellungsformen herauszustellen.

Der zunehmende Einsatz der für die Betriebspraxis entwickelten Methoden, Verfahren und Darstellungsformen der Informatik <u>und</u> Organisation unterstützt diese unterrichtlichen Zielvorstellungen. Die didaktischen Grundlagen bilden größtenteils Modelle der entscheidungsorientierten Betriebswirtschaftslehre, die die rechnergestützten informationsverarbeitenden Prozesse im Unternehmen abbilden.

Unter Berücksichtigung der angestrebten Ziele und Annahmen können die Lernzielformulierungen den folgenden fünf Bereichen zugeordnet werden:

1. Informationsverarbeitende Prozesse in Unternehmen und Verwaltungen

2. Algorithmen und Programme

3. Daten und ihre Organisation

4. Abwicklung von rechnergestützten Problemlösungen

5. Informatik und Gesellschaft

3.1. Informationsverarbeitende Prozesse in Unternehmen und Verwaltungen

Die Schüler sollen die folgenden Qualifikationen erwerben:

3.1.1. Kaufmännische Tätigkeiten in Unternehmen und Verwaltungen als Informationsverarbeitung mit oder ohne Unterstützung von Computersystemen unterscheiden.

3.1.2. Innerhalb von informationsverarbeitenden Prozessen realisierte und mögliche DV-Aufgaben voneinander unterscheiden:
Kennzeichen dieser Prozesse sind:
Algorithmisierbarkeit
Wirtschaftlichkeit (Kostenstruktur, Mengengerüst)
Zeitstruktur
Wiederholbarkeit und Häufigkeit der Wiederholung
Arbeitsbedingungen und Arbeitsplatzgestaltung

3.1.3. In einem informationsverarbeitenden Prozess die entsprechenden Handlungsanweisungen und die zu verarbeitenden Daten einander zuordnen.

3.1.4. Mit Hilfe allgemeiner Verfahren, Darstellungsformen und Methoden der Organisation und Informatik betriebliche informationsverarbeitende Prozesse erfassen.

3.1.5. Die zur Erfassung der Informationsstruktur und des betrieblichen Tätigkeitsbereiches wesentlichen Methoden der schrittweisen Verfeinerung benutzen.
Beispiele:
Black-box-Verfahren, SADT-Entwurfstechnik,
Top-down-Vorgehensweise.

3.1.6. Algorithmische Problemlösungen betrieblicher Teilprobleme systematisch finden, verbal formulieren, mit geeigneten Darstellungsformen dokumentieren und auf einem Computer abbilden.

3.1.7. Vorgegebene algorithmische Problemlösungen (kommerzielle Software) sowie deren Planung, Entwicklungsphasen und Einsatz im betrieblichen Ablauf organisatorisch und wirtschaftlich beurteilen:

Beispiele:

Planung des Problems
Definition des Problems
Entwurf der Problemlösung
Implementierung der Problemlösung
Einführung, Betrieb und Wartung der Problemlösung

3.1.8. Verschiedene Dialoganwendungen selbsterstellter oder implementierter betrieblicher DV-Systeme einsetzen.

Beispiele:

Abfragesysteme
Dokumentationssysteme
Informations- und Auskunftssysteme
Entscheidungssysteme

3.2. Algorithmen und Programme

Die Schüler sollen die folgenden Qualifikationen erwerben:

3.2.1. Algorithmische von nicht-algorithmischen Problemlösungen unterscheiden.

3.2.2. Eigenschaften von Algorithmen erläutern.

Eigenschaften sind:

eindeutig
endlich
allgemein
ausführbar

3.2.3. Bei der Algorithmenkonstruktion die Elemente der Algorithmen anwenden.

Elemente sind:

Objekte
Vorschriften zur Manipulation von Objekten
Steuerung der Manipulation (Kontrollstruktur)

3.2.4. Die Standardstrukturen von Algorithmen unterscheiden und anwenden.
Beispiele:
Zuweisung
Sequenz
Auswahl
Wiederholung

3.2.5. Algorithmische Darstellungsformen bei der Problemlösungsfindung einsetzen.
Beispiele:
verbal (umgangssprachlich bezogen auf die algorithmischen Standardstrukturen)
graphisch (Struktogramm u.a)

3.2.6. Die gesuchte Problemlösung systematisch durch schrittweises Verfeinern entwickeln, darstellen, mit konkreten Daten testen und dokumentieren.

3.2.7. Die gefundene Problemlösung (Algorithmus) in einer problemorientierten Programmiersprache 1) formulieren und auf einem Computer überprüfen.

3.2.8. Zwischen Algorithmus, Programm und Prozeß unterscheiden.

3.3. Daten und ihre Organisaation

Die Schüler sollen die folgenden Qualifikationen erwerben:

---

1) Dabei sollte eine Programmiersprache verwendet werden, die folgenden Anforderungen genügt:
-direkte Umsetzung von Datenstrukturen und Kontrollstrukturen in die Programmiersprache (ohne logischen Bruch, sondern im Sinne einer Verfeinerung oder Konkretisierung)
-Erhaltung der Struktur der Problemlösung im Programm
-Möglichkeiten der sinnvollen Verbalisierung (lange Variablennamen müssen möglich sein)

3.3.1. Daten in Variable, Konstante, Skalare und zusammengesetzte Datentypen unterscheiden und anwenden.
Beispiele:
- skalare Datentypen:
  ganz, reell, logisch, Zeichen

- zusammengesetzte Datentypen:
  Bereich
  Verbund
  Datei (sequentiell, wahlfrei, index-sequentiell)

3.3.2. Bei Daten deren Bezeichnung, Wert, Format und Art voneinander unterscheiden.

3.3.3. Daten zu Datenstrukturen zusammenfassen und darstellen.

3.3.4. Die Zusammenfassung von Daten zu logischen Sätzen, von logischen Sätzen zu Dateien sowie Dateien zu Datenbanken erklären.

3.3.5. Organisationsformen von Dateien und Zugriffsformen zu Datensätzen von Dateien (direkt, indirekt) erklären.

3.3.6. Aufgaben der Datenverwaltung erklären.
Beispiele:
Organisation
Zugriff
Datenschutz
Datensicherung
Änderungsdienst

3.3.7. Aufgaben, Aufbau und Grundzusammenhänge der Datenverwaltung in inner- und außerbetrieblichen Datenverwaltungssystemen (Datenbanksystemen) erläutern.

3.4. Abwicklung von rechnergestützten Problemlösungen

Die Schüler sollen die folgenden Qualifikationen erwerben:

3.4.1. Die Komponenten eines Rechnersystems einschließlich deren Funktionen erläutern.
Komponenten sind:
Hardware
Software

Funktionen:
automatische Verarbeitung von Informationen
Speicherung von Programmen und Daten
Kommunikation mit der Systemumwelt

3.4.2. Aufgaben eines Betriebssystems erklären.
Beispiele:
Steuerung der Rechnerkomponenten
Ausführung von Benutzerprogrammen
Interpretation von Benutzerkommandos

3.4.3. Möglichkeiten der direkten und indirekten Datenerfassung anwenden sowie zugehörige Datenträger kennen.

3.4.4. Bei den Betriebsarten von Rechnersystemen die betrieblichen Anforderungen formulieren und die Einsatzmöglichkeiten beurteilen.
Betriebsarten:
Dialogverarbeitung
Stapelverarbeitung
Echtzeitverarbeitung
Datenfernübertragung

3.4.5. Die Zusammenhänge von Datenverarbeitung, Textverarbeitung und Nachrichtenübertragung erläutern.

3.5. Informatik und Gesellschaft

Die Schüler sollen die folgenden Qualifikationen erwerben:

3.5.1. Die betriebliche und gesamtwirtschaftliche Bedeutung des Hardware- und Software-Einsatzes abschätzen.

3.5.2. Die Notwendigkeit der Ausfall- und Datensicherung für den Betrieb und für den Mitarbeiter einschätzen.

3.5.3. Die durch den Computereinsatz hervorgerufenen Veränderungen und Anforderungen an die individuelle und berufliche Qualifikation abschätzen.

3.5.4. Die besondere Schutzbedürftigkeit personenbezogener Daten sowie die hierfür vorgeschriebenen gesetzlichen Maßnahmen kennen und bewerten.

Anmerkung:
Der vorliegende Beitrag stellt Ergebnisse der Beratungen des Unterausschusses "Informatik an berufsbildenden Schulen kaufmännischer Richtung" (Sprecher: Prof.Dr.Griese) der Gesellschaft für Informatik in vorläufiger Form dar.

Computer als konviviale Werkzeuge

Gerhard Fischer
Abteilung Dialogsysteme / Mensch-Maschine Kommunikation
Institut fuer Informatik, Universitaet Stuttgart

Abstract

Die Gestaltung von geeigneten Lernumgebungen erfordert ein vertieftes Verstaendnis von informationsverarbeitenden Prozessen beim Menschen und seinen modernen Werkzeugen und neue Formen der Mensch-Maschine Kommunikation. Um diesem Anspruch gerecht zu werden, muss der Computer ein **konviviales Werkzeug** fuer den Schueler sein. Der Informatikunterricht sollte deshalb darauf ausgerichtet sein, wichtige kognitive Prozesse (wie z.B. Problemloesen, Entwerfen symbolischer Artifakte, usw) zu foerdern.

1. Einleitung

Die bisherige Diskussion ueber den Informatikunterricht an den Schulen hat sich in ihrer Gesamtheit noch nicht ausreichend darum bemueht, die grundlegenden Ziele eines solchen Unterrichts zu definieren und diese Ziele durch umfassende theoretische und experimentelle Untersuchungen auf ihre Validitaet zu ueberpruefen. Eine wichtiges Ziel muss es sein, sich klar abzeichnende Probleme in solche prinzipieller und solche eher zufaelliger Art zu trennen; letztere entstehen z.B. durch die im Augenblick unzureichende Technologie. Wohlwollende aber letztlich unwissende Anwender (z.B. Lehrer, die zu wenig Zeit und Gelegenheit haben, sich staendig mit dem neuesten Stand der Technik auseinanderzusetzen) laufen in hohem Masse Gefahr, **lokale** Probleme ueberzubewerten. Bei einer sich so schnell fortentwickelnden Technologie wie der Informationsverarbeitung ist die Gefahr, technologisch und methodisch moeglicherweise bereits veraltete Ansaetze zur Basis von Zukunftsplanung und -bewertung zu machen, besonders gross. Wir sind der Ansicht, dass die Untersuchung aller mit der Entwicklung und Bewertung von Informatikunterricht zusammenhaengenden Fragestellungen kein isoliertes Problem der Informatik ist und nicht durch ausschliesslich technisch orientierte Forschungsansaetze abgedeckt werden kann. Andererseits kann aber weder die Bewertung von Entwicklungen, noch die Konzipierung alternativer Vorstellungen in diesem Bereich **ohne die Fachkompetenz** der Informatik durchgefuehrt werden.

Unsere Erfahrungen basieren einerseits auf langjaehriger Mitarbeit in dem Forschungsprojekt PROKOP (KLING et al, 1977; BOECKER und FISCHER, 1977 und 1979) und in mehreren vom BMFT gefoerderten Arbeitskreisen und anderseits auf Forschungsaufenthalten an amerikanischen Universitaeten (LOGO Gruppe am Massachusetts Institute of Technology (MIT), siehe PAPERT, 1980; Artificial Intelligence Group der Carnegie Mellon University (CMU), siehe SIMON, 1979) und Forschungszentren (Learning Research Group am Xerox Palo Alto Research Center, siehe KAY, 1977).

2. Konviviale Werkzeuge

Langfristig ist unsere Forschungsarbeit (zunaechst im Projekt PROKOP (FISCHER, 1977) und derzeitig im Projekt INFORM (BOECKER, FISCHER und GUNZENHAEUSER, 1980)) darauf ausgerichtet, Computersysteme so zu gestalten, dass sie sich als **konviviale Werkzeuge** (ILLICH, 1975 und 1978) benutzen lassen. Dies bedeutet, dass der Einzelne sie zur

Verwirklichung seiner **eigenen** Ziele benutzen kann, so oft oder so selten er will, und dass zu dieser Benutzung keine Spezialkenntnisse erforderlich sind. Konviviale Werkzeuge sollten sich moeglichst neutral gegenueber Arbeitsmethoden verhalten, damit das zu loesende Problem die Methode bestimmt und nicht das Werkzeug das zu loesende Problem oder die Methode.

Die von uns ins Auge gefassten Anwendungen unterscheiden sich grundlegend von den ersten Anwendungen von Computern in der Schule im Rahmen des traditionellen computerunterstuetzten Unterrichts, die darauf ausgerichtet waren, dass der Lernende durch den Computer "programmiert" und kontrolliert wurde. Einfache behavioristische Lerntheorien und ein unzureichender technologischer Entwicklungsstand (insbesondere im Bereich der Mensch-Maschine Kommunikation) fuehrte zu Entwicklungen und CUU-Systemen, die dem Schueler keine Moeglichkeit boten, eigenstaendig zu arbeiten.

Die "**Entzunftung**" der Informatik im Hinblick auf die Abschaffung einer entmuendigenden Expertenherrschaft stellt fuer den Informatikunterricht in der Schule ein wichtiges Ziel dar. Es muss verhindert werden, dass die von gewissen "Experten" vorgegebenen Sachzwaenge (aus dem Bereich der Datenverarbeitung und der Computerhersteller), die einerseits oft zu wenig Wissen und wenig Interesse an Schule und didaktischen Fragestellungen haben, andererseits aber anderen vorschreiben, was fuer diese richtig ist, zur staendigen Einrichtung wird.

Zu dieser Entzunftung kann der Computer selbst wesentliches beitragen. Im Mittelpunkt des Interesses stehen dabei nicht irgendwelche Computer mit irgendwelchen Programmiersprachen (BOECKER 1979; LAUBSCH, FISCHER und BOECKER 1979), sondern **integrierte Informationsmanipulationssysteme** (FISCHER 1980), mit deren Hilfe geeignete Lernumgebungen (FISCHER, 1981) und neue Formen der Mensch-Maschine Kommunikation (BOECKER, FISCHER und GUNZENHAEUSER, 1980) gestaltet werden koennen. Informationsmanipulationssysteme sind integrierte Systeme, die Programmieren, Textverarbeitung, Zugriff zu Datenbasen, Manipulation graphischer Objekte in einer einheitlichen begrifflichen Umgebung ermoeglichen und damit die kognitiven Belastung der Benutzer entscheidend reduzieren.

3. Konviviale Werkzeuge: Forschungsgegenstand der Mensch-Maschine Kommunikation

Ein wesentliches Ziel der technischen und paedagogischen Bemuehungen besteht in der Steigerung der **Benutzerunabhaengigkeit** und **-bestimmtheit**, die ein zukuenftiges Computersystem bieten kann.

Neben Teilgebieten technischer und paedagogischer Disziplinen liefert insbesondere die "**Cognitive Science**" (FISCHER und KLING, 1980) die begrifflichen Grundlagen unserer Untersuchung ueber die Konsequenzen moderner Kommunikationsmittel fuer die Mensch--Maschine-Kommunikation. Die innerhalb der Cognitive Science entwickelten Methoden erlauben es, Fragen der relativen Anteile von Mensch und Maschine an der beim Umgang mit informationsmanipulierenden Systemen beteiligten kognitiven Prozesse auf einer einheitlichen begrifflichen Basis zu untersuchen.

Die Abbildung 1 zeigt die verschiedenen bei Problemloese- und den meisten Informationsmanipulationsprozessen unterscheidbaren Phasen, die moeglichst **alle** von einem Informationsmanipulationssystem unterstuetzt werden sollten. (Herkoemmliche Computer unterstuetzen beim Programmieren z.B. im wesentlichen nur die Phase 4).

Abbildung 1: Phasen von Informationsmanipulationsprozessen

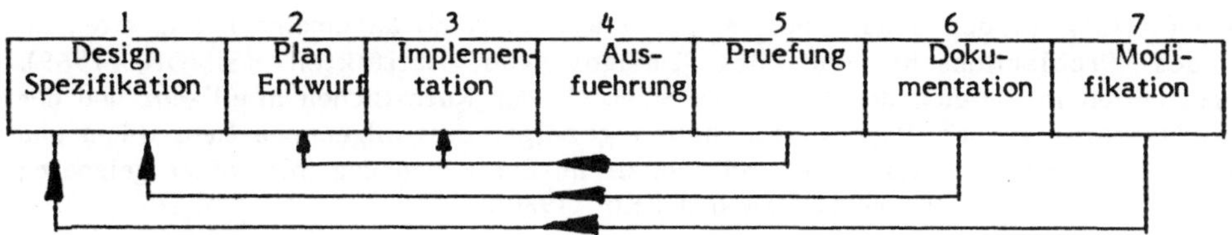

Als weiteres wichtiges Ziel, neben der Unterstuetzung des gesamten Designprozesses, soll die Entwicklung von komplexen Systemen und nicht nur von einzelnen Algorithmen unterstuetzt werden. Der **Algorithmus**-Begriff stand lange Zeit im Mittelpunkt des Interesses der Informatik. Versteht man die Informatik jedoch als eine konstruktive Wissenschaft, die sich mit der Synthese und Analyse von komplexen Artifakten beschaeftigt, dann kommt **Systemen** eine ungleich groessere Bedeutung zu. Einige der wichtigsten Unterschiede zwischen Algorithmen und Systemen sind in Abb. 2 zusammengefasst.

Abbildung 2 : Algorithmen versus Systeme

	Algorithmen	**Systeme**
Problem-loeseterminologie	wohldefiniertes Problem abstraktes Problem	schlecht-strukturiertes Problem semantisch reichhaltiges Problem
Spezifikationen	exakt, vollstaendig; veraendern sich nicht mit der Zeit	ungenau, unvollstaendig; veraendern sich mit der Zeit
lokale Transparenz	"vertrackte" Logik; stark optimiert; Richtigkeit beweisbar	lokal meist transparent; komplex durch Vielfalt der Komponenten
Verwendung	nuetzliche kleine Bausteine in groesseren Zusammenhaengen	Anwendungssysteme
Design Kriterien	Effizienz, Korrektheit	Transparenz, Zuverlaessigkeit, Uniformitaet, Modifizierbarkeit
Beispiele	Fakultaet, Fibonacci Zahlen	Textverarbeitungssysteme, Expertensysteme (MACSYMA)

Ein spezieller Forschungschwerpunkt unserer Arbeit ist es, ergaenzende Guetekriterien fuer Software zu erarbeiten. Es hat sich dabei als notwendig erwiesen, das Kriterium der maschinellen Effizienz eines Systems dem der **kognitiven Effizienz** unterzuordnen (FISCHER, 1977) und die nahezu ueberfluessig gewordenen Kriterien der **technologischen Machbarkeit** durch Kriterien der kognitiven Effizienz bzw. Wuenschbarkeit zu ersetzen. Solche Guetekriterien sollten unter anderem sein: Transparenz, Zuverlaessigkeit, Uniformitaet in Benutzung und Implementation und Aenderungsfaehigkeit eines Systems. Wir benoetigen Prinzipien, die ein Design nicht nur nach den Kriterien falsch und richtig, sondern vor allem nach den Kriterien gut und weniger gut bewerten (DeMILLO et al, 1979; SIMON 1969).

4. Problemloesen und Design Prozesse

Wissensvermittlung in der Schule muss ergaenzt werden durch allgemeine Fertigkeiten im Bereich des Problemloesens und des Designs von Artifakten (SIMON 1969). Forschungsarbeiten im Bereich der "Cognitive Science", der Kuenstlichen Intelligenz und der informationsverarbeitenden Psychologie haben gezeigt, dass allgemeine Heuristiken und Problemloesefaehigkeiten existieren und explizit im Zusammenhang mit dafuer geigneten Problemen gelehrt werden koennen (TUMA und REIF, 1980).

Zum Problemloesen haben wir eine Vielzahl von Fallstudien in verschiedenen inhaltlichen Bereichen (z.B. nicht-numerische Mathematik, Linguistik, Informatik, Kuenstliche Intelligenz und Spiele) mit Schuelern bearbeitet und ausfuehrlich dokumentiert (BOECKER und FISCHER, 1977 und 1979). In verschiedenen inhaltlichen Bereichen (Programmieren, Konstruktion von physikalischen Modellen mit Fischertechnikbaukaesten, Entwurf von Lernumgebungen) haben wir unser Verstaendnis fuer Design Prozesse vertieft (FISCHER und BOECKER, 1981). Diese Arbeiten haben gezeigt, das Design ein inkrementeller Prozess ist, bei dem ein partiell fertig gestelltes Produkt eine wichtige Funktion erfuellt, um zu einem vertieften Verstaendnis fuer eine Problem zu gelangen. Unsere Werkzeuge und Methoden muessen diesen Arbeitstil unterstuetzen (LOETHE 1978). Wir sollten uns vor allem im paedagogischen Bereich vor einer "geistigen Unredlichkeit" hueten, indem wir den Lernenden gegenueber unsere eigenen Loesungsversuche verheimlichen und ihnen nur Fertigprodukte vorstellen. Eine der wichtigsten Funktion, die ein Computer haben kann, ist es, ein Medium zur Konkretisierung und zum Austesten unserer "Gedankenexperimente" zu sein.

5. Prototypische Entwicklungen: LOGO und SMALLTALK

Richtungsweisende Impulse zum Thema "Informatik in der Schule" sind von den LOGO- (PAPERT 1980; KLING et al 1976) und SMALLTALK-Projekten (KAY 1977) ausgegangen. LOGO und SMALLTALK sollen hier nicht nur als die Namen von Programmierumgebungen verstanden werden, sondern sie veranschaulichen richtungsweisende Ansaetze einer Computernutzung fuer naive Benutzer im Hinblick auf Lehren und Lernen, die ueber die Alltagsproblematiken hinausgehen. Da unser Vorstellungsvermoegen, eine Vielzahl von moeglichen Zukuenften zu erahnen und vorherzuplanen, sehr beschraenkt ist, dienen diese Projekte als wichtige Orientierungspunkte.

Beide Entwicklungen hatten sich bereits Anfang der siebziger Jahre zum Ziel gesetzt (relativ unabhaengig vom damaligen technologischen Entwicklungsstand), grundlegende Aspekte der Computernutzung fuer Lehren und Lernen explorativ zu erforschen. Die Modifikation von Bestehendem spielte dabei eine untergeordnete Rolle.

Ein umfassendes LOGO Projekt (PROKOP) wurde auch in der Bundesrepublik durchgefuehrt (KLING et al, 1976). Umfangreiche Informationsmaterialien dazu sind vorhanden. Einer der Hauptkritikpunkte dieses Ansatzes ist in der Zwischenzeit ausgeraeumt: die dortigen Erfahrungen sind auch im Schulalltag nachvollziehbar, da seit kurzem ein LOGO System auf einem Kleinrechner (APPLE II) zur Verfuegung steht.

Das Leitziel der Arbeit der Learning Research Group am Xerox Palo Alto Research Center ist es seit langem, ein DYNABOOK zu schaffen. Darunter ist ein Computersystem in der Groesse einer Aktentasche zu verstehen, dass in seiner Leistung heutigen Grossrechnern vergleichbar ist. Dieses Ziel hat der Arbeit der Gruppe eine grosse Kohaerenz verliehen. Die wichtigsten Aspekte dieser Entwicklung sind die folgenden:

1) die Entwicklung eines **integrierten** Systems, dessen wichtigster Bestandteil ein breiter Kommunikationskanal zwischen Mensch und Maschine ist (Raster Grafik, Systeme mit multiplen Fenstern); dieses System ermoeglicht z.B. die direkte Manipulation von Informationsstrukturen auf dem Bildschirm (d.h. symbolische Anweisungen werden

ueberfluessig; diese Methodik hat z.B. der Textverarbeitung zum entscheidenden Durchbruch verholfen).

2) die Entwicklung der Programmiersprache **SMALLTALK**, die sich grundlegend von bestehenden Sprachen unterscheidet und die eine Reihe von neuen Programmiermethoden (z.B. Modifikation und Erweiterung von bestehenden Programmen durch weitergehende Spezialisierung) ermoeglicht (FISCHER und LAUBSCH 1979).

6. Empirische Arbeiten und Erfahrungen

Unsere Erfahrungen beruhen vor allem auf Unterrichtsversuchen, die im Rahmen des Projektes PROKOP an Darmstaedter Schulen durchgefuehrt worden sind. Dabei wurden verschiedene Innovationsstrategien exemplarisch erprobt (z.B. Integration in bestehenden Unterricht im Gegensatz zu Entwicklung von neuen Lerneinheiten, Kooperation mit Fachlehrern usw.). In vielen Zusammenhaengen haben wir dabei versucht, die traditionellen Schranken zwischen Curriculumeinheiten zu ueberwinden und mit den Schuelern zusammen an interessanten Projekten zu arbeiten (siehe hierzu auch den Beitrag von Wabel-Frenk in diesem Tagungsband).

Insbesondere wurde uns auch bewusst, dass **nicht-kognitive** Aspekte eine wichtige Rolle spielen. Davon sollen einige kurz erwaehnt werden:

1) viele Schueler konnten nach kurzer Zeit mehr als die Lehrer; dies befluegelte das Interesse der Schueler, fuehrte aber in unserer Kooperation mit Lehrern zu nicht unerheblichen Problemen

2) der Computer kann eine wesentliche Rolle uebernehmen, bestimmte Vorurteile und Abneigungen (z.B. vor der Mathematik; LAUBSCH, FISCHER und BOECKER 1979) abzubauen. Ein Schueler, der urspruenglich nicht an unserem Unterrichtsversuch teilnehmen wollte, weil er eine grosse Abneigung gegen Mathematik hatte, arbeitete ueber Monate hinweg an einem Programm zur Erzeugung von "Gedichten". Dabei loeste er eine Vielzahl von interessanten mathematischen Problemen, ohne sich dessen bewusst zu sein.

3) die (zum grossen Teil sehr fragwuerdigen) Vorstellungen, die Erwachsene (Lehrer, Eltern) von Computern haben, werden oft unbewusst von den Schuelern uebernommen. Dies fuehrt dazu, dass zusaetzliche Lernschranken aufgebaut werden, obwohl es erklaertes Ziel ist, gerade solche mit Hilfe des Computers abzubauen. Die spielerischen Ansaetze der LOGO Projekte (mit "Turtles", "Music-Box", usw) und die kuenstlerischen Aspekte des SMALLTALK Systems scheinen in der Lage zu sein, diese unbegruendeten Vorurteile abzubauen und damit einer grossen Anzahl von Schuelern einen erfolgreichen Einstieg zu ermoeglichen (FISCHER, 1981).

4) Piagetsches Lernen (PAPERT 1980; dh Lernen ohne explizit gelehrt zu werden, ohne extrinsische Belohnung) kann mit Hilfe konvivialer Werkzeuge gefoerdert werden. Die Vielzahl der interessanten und visuell ansprechenden Phaenomene, die mit einfachen Programmen erzeugt werden koennen, bieten dafuer einen wichtigen Ausgangspunkt.

7. Ein Blick in die Zukunft

Es ist schwierig vorherzusehen, wie sich die Informatik in der Schule im Spannungsfeld verschiedener Interessen und Sachzwaenge entwickeln wird. Wir wollen abschliessend eine Zukunft charakterisieren, wie sie unserer Meinung nach sein koennte. Die Definition eines Zielzustandes gestattet uns dann, darueber zu entscheiden, ob ein Entwicklung / Entscheidung als ein Schritt nach vorne oder nach hinten zu betrachten ist.

Folgende Aspekte erscheinen uns wesentlich:

1) Computersyteme muessen konvivale Werkzeuge sein; der Lernende muss das Gefuehl haben, dass er die Kontrolle hat und selbstbestimmtes Lernen und aktives Gestalten unterstuetzt wird

2) die Nutzung des Computers sollte eng mit anderen Taetigkeiten in Schule und Umwelt des Schuelers integriert werden

3) die Grenzen des Computers werden schon in naher Zukunft nicht mehr durch die Technologie, sondern durch unsere Vorstellungskraft, etwas Interessantes mit diesem Werkzeug anzufangen, gegeben sein; dabei duerfen wir nicht in eine Technologie-Falle fallen: naemlich nur das fuer wichtig zu erachten, was sich in einer computer-orientierten Umgebung realisieren laesst

4) wir sollten uns frei machen von der Einschraenkung, allein bestehendes Wissen und bewaehrte Methoden mit dem Medium Computer darzubieten; gleichzeitig ist zu erforschen, welche neuen Lehr- und Lernziele (z.B. im Hinblick auf Problemloesen und Design) erarbeitet werden koennen

5) Computer ermoeglichen eine neue Aufteilung kognitiver Leistungen zwischen Mensch und Maschine; wir muessen uns mit den menschlichen Beduerfnissen (ueber neue Moeglichkeiten, ueber Gefahren) in einer "Computer Zivilisation" auseinandersetzen

Zur weiteren Praezisierung unserer Zielvorstellungen geben wir ergaenzend an, in welche Richtungen sich die Informatik in der Schule **nicht** entwicklen sollte:

1) Informatik in der Schule ist kein reduziertes Hochschulstudium dieser wissenschaftlichen Disziplin; insbesondere ist Informatik keine deduktive, sondern primaer eine konstruktive Wissenschaft

2) auf die Erarbeitung expliziter Modellvorstellungen (ueber informationsverarbeitende Prozesse beim Menschen, ueber Wissensstrukturen in verschiedenen inhaltlichen Bereichen, ueber Vorkenntnisse verschiedener Benutzergruppen) kann nicht verzichtet werden; diese bieten einen Ausgangspunkt fuer Design Kriterien von Systemen, die ueber die reine informatische Machbarkeit hinauskommen wollen

3) die Relevanz von Programmiersprachen steht nicht im Vordergrund (siehe dazu Abbildung 1 und BOECKER 1979)

4) der Computer darf nicht nur als eine gigantische Rechenmaschine benutzt werden (z.B. zu enge Anlehnung an bestehenden Mathematikunterricht, Ueberbetonung von numerischen Beispielen)

5) wir sollten nicht dem Irrglauben zu verfallen, dass jeder Informatiker etwas ueber Psychologie und Paedagogik versteht und umgekehrt (dies erfordert die Foerderung von interdisziplinaeren Projekten)

Betrachtungen dieser Innovation, die sich ausschliesslich an den derzeitigen Hardwarekosten orientieren, koennen nur in die Irre fuehren. Informatik in der Schule beinhaltet:

1) kognitive Kosten -- zum Lernen von neuen Formalismen und Vorgehensweisen; falls falsche Wege eingeschlagen werden, wird der Aufwand zum "Umdenken" im Nachhinein umso schwerwiegender sein; nur langfristiges Planen und gezielte Experimente koennen vermeiden, dass unzureichende Entwicklungen festgefroren werden

2) soziale Kosten -- die Einfuehrung von Formen einer "geistigen Fliessbandarbeit" muss vermieden werden

3) emotionale Kosten -- der Einzelne darf sich nicht von Computern beherrscht fuehlen; dies wuerde zu einer erweiterten Technologiefeindlichkeit fuehren

Computer haben in der Schule nichts zu suchen (selbst wenn sie billig zur Verfuegungn stehen), wenn

1) sie nur Leistungen anbieten, die von anderen Werkzeugen besser angeboten werden

2) sie so umstaendlich zu benutzen sind, dass der Aufwand ungleich groesser ist als der Nutzen

3) sie nur dazu dienen, Wissen zu vermitteln, das in kurzer Zeit durch die fortschreitende technologische Entwicklung irrelevant wird

8. Schlussbemerkung

In diesem kurzen Beitrag ist es unmoeglich, ausfuehrlich auf theoretische Modellvorstellungen, empirische Erfahrungen und Beispiele einzugehen, die wir in den vergangenen Jahren erarbeitet haben. Nur mit deren Hilfe koennen die Behauptungen und Thesen dieses Beitrags auf ihre Richtigkeit ueberprueft werden. Aus diesem Grunde geben wir ein umfassendes Verzeichnis der Publikationen an, die die angefuehrten Themen ausfuehrlich behandeln.

Literatur

Boecker, H.-D. (1979): "Warum ist BASIC nur der Anfang und PASCAL schon am Ende", in LOGIN, Dezember, pp 8-14

Boecker, H.-D. und G. Fischer (1977, 1979): "Arbeitsmaterialien zum interaktiven Problemloesen", Band 2, Teil 1: "Mathematik"; Teil 2: "Linguistik"; Teil 3: "Informatik"; Teil 4: "Kuenstliche Intelligenz"; Teil 5: "Spiele"; Hessisches Institut fuer Bildungsplanung und Schulentwicklung, Wiesbaden

Boecker, H.-D., G. Fischer und R. Gunzenhaeuser (1980): "Die Funktion von integrierten Informationsmanipulationssystemen (IMS) in der Mensch-Mschine Kommunikation (Projekt INFORM)", Mensch-Maschine Kommunikation (MMK) Memo, Institut fuer Informatik, Universitaet Stuttgart, 1980

DeMillo, R. A., R.J. Lipton und A.J. Perlis (1979): "Social Processes and Proofs of Theorems and Programs", CACM, Vol 22, No 5, pp 271-280

Fischer, G. (1977): "Das Loesen komplexer Problemaufgaben durch naive Benutzer mit Hilfe des interaktiven Programmierens" Forschungsgruppe CUU, Projekt PROKOP, Darmstadt, Juli 1977

Fischer, G. (1979): "Powerful Ideas in Computational Linguistics - implications for problem solving and education", in Proceedings of the 17th Annual Meeting of the Association for Computational Linguistics, San Diego, pp 111-125

Fischer, G. (1980): "Cognitive Dimensions of Information Manipulation Systems", in Tagungsband der GI Fachtagung "Textverarbeitung und Informatik", Springer Verlag, Heidelberg, pp 17-31

Fischer, G. (1981): "Computational Models of Skill Acquisition Processes", 3rd World Conference on Computers and Education, Lausanne, Switzerland, July 1981

Fischer, G. und J. Laubsch (1979): "Object-oriented Programming", in Heft 2 der Notizen zum Interaktiven Programmieren, Fachausschuss 2 der Gesellschaft fuer Informatik, Stuttgart, Februar 1979, pp 121-140

Fischer, G. und U. Kling (1980): "Die Erforschung kognitiver Phaenomene - zum Stellenwert der Arbeiten von Herbert A. Simon fuer die Informatik", Angewandte Informatik, Heft 6, Juni 1980, Vieweg Verlag, Wiesbaden, pp 215-223

Fischer, G. und H.-D. Boecker (1981): "The nature of design processes and how computer systems can support them", Mensch-Maschine Kommunikation (MMK) Memo, Institut fuer Informatik, Universitaet Stuttgart

Illich, I. (1975): "Selbstbegrenzung: eine politische Kritik der Technik", Rowohlt

Illich, I. (1978): "Fortschrittsmythen", Rowohlt

Kling, U., et al (1976): "PROKOP - Projektbericht 1974-1976", Forschungsgruppe CUU, Projekt PROKOP, Darmstadt, Dezember 1976

Laubsch, J., Fischer, G. und H.-D. Boecker (1979): "LISP-based systems for educational applications", BYTE, Vol 4. No 8, August 1979, pp 18-25

Loethe, H. (1978): "Zum Arbeitsstil der Computernutzung in der Schule", Beitraege zur ACU-Tagung II/78, FEOLL, Paderborn, pp 208-213

Papert, S. (1980): "Mindstorms: Children, Computers and Powerful Ideas", Basic Books, New York

Simon, H. (1969): "The sciences of the artificial", MIT Press, Cambridge, Ma

Simon, H. (1980): "Problem solving and Education", in Tuma und Reif (1980), pp 81-96

Tuma, D.T. und F. Reif (eds, 1980): "Problem solving and Education", Lawrence Erlbaum Associates, Hillsdale

Der Bildschirmcomputer im Physikunterricht

K. Wagner, Klagenfurt

Der vorliegende Beitrag untersucht die Einsatzmöglichkeiten des Bildschirmcomputers im Physikunterricht. Zur Stützung des Unterrichts kann in mehrfacher Art die Bildschirmgraphik ausgenützt werden. Der Computer dient dabei nicht primär als Rechner, sondern als Demonstrationsgerät von Programmen, deren Ablauf vom Lehrer oder Schüler in weiten Grenzen beeinflußt und variiert werden kann. Rasches Zeichnen von Funktionsgraphen, Simulation einfacher und komplizierter physikalischer Versuche, sowie die Bearbeitung anwendungsorientierter Probleme sind mögliche Einsatzgebiete. Beispiele für jedes dieser Gebiete werden vorgeführt. Der Einsatz des Bildschirmcomputers im Physikunterricht erscheint durchführbar und wird in vielen Fällen einen nicht unwesentlichen Beitrag zum Erreichen und Festigen von Lernzielen erbringen können. Nicht zuletzt kann er zur Steigerung der Attraktivität des Unterrichts beitragen.

Das Angebot von Bildschirmcomputern wird immer reichhaltiger und das Preisniveau ist so gehalten, daß diese Geräte auch für den Einsatz in der Höheren Schule interessant geworden sind. Die Möglichkeit, jedes TV-Gerät als Bildschirm zu verwenden, bringt ein für die Klasse genügend großes Bild und einen relativ einfachen Vorgang der Vorführung. Beim Vorliegen von fertigen Programmen sind für den Lehrer nur minimale EDV-Kenntnisse notwendig. Was kann der Bildschirmcomputer neben anderen audiovisuellen Medien wie Folie, Dia oder Film leisten? In den folgenden vier Abschnitten soll versucht werden, diese Frage zu klären. Zum besseren Verständnis der verfolgten Absicht wird jeweils ein Beispiel genauer dargestellt.

1. Zeichnen von Funktionsgraphen

In der Physik besteht laufend die Notwendigkeit, den Ablauf eines Vorgangs in einem Graphen festzuhalten. Natürlich wird man Graphen auf die Tafel zeichnen, auf Overheadfolien bereit haben und auf Abbildungen in Büchern verweisen. Der Bildschirmcomputer bringt die Möglichkeit, die Kurve immer sehr schnell zur Hand zu haben, sie vor Augen der Schüler von Abszissenwert zu Abszissenwert wachsen zu lassen und vor allem die Parameter der Kurve frei zu verändern. Gerade die letzte Möglichkeit scheint mir ein besonderer Vorteil des Computers zu sein: Freie Wahl der Parameter. Ich glaube, daß damit den Schülern die Rolle eines Parameters in einem physikalischen Gesetz sehr anschaulich gemacht werden kann. Es wäre wünschenswert, ein Programm zu erstellen, das eine kleine Bibliothek der in der Physik relevanten Funktionen enthält. Der Computer zeichnet die Funktion erst mit vorgegebenen Parametern, anschließend können über die Tastatur beliebig andere Belegungen der Parameter vorgenommen werden. In dieser Sammlung könnten unter anderen die Gaußsche Glockenkurve, die Maxwellsche Geschwindigkeitsverteilung, verschiedene Schwingungsformen, Potentialkurven und auch kompliziertere Funktionen aus Relativitätstheorie und Atomphysik enthalten sein.

Als Beispiel betrachten wir das radioaktive Gleichgewicht zwischen einer Muttersubstanz und ihrem selbst wieder radioaktiven Zerfallsprodukt, der Tochtersubstanz.

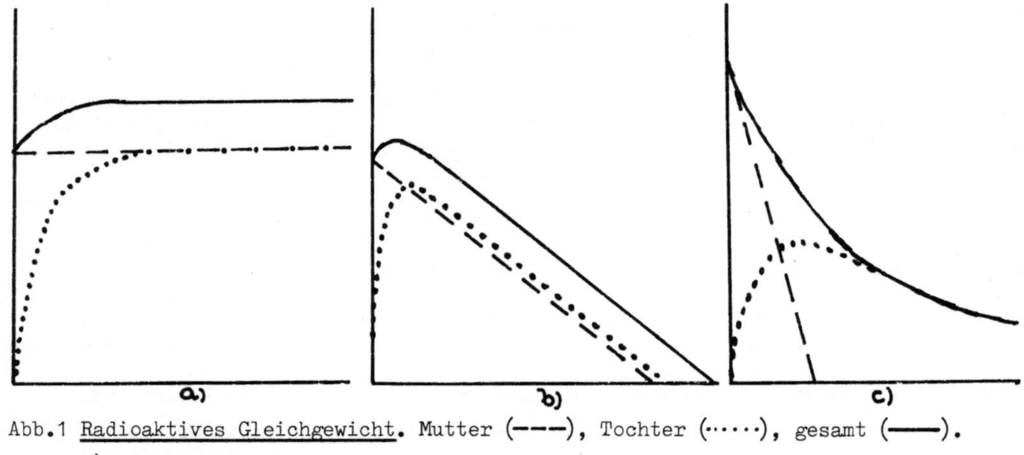

Abb.1 Radioaktives Gleichgewicht. Mutter (– – –), Tochter (·····), gesamt (——).

a) Dauerndes Gleichgewicht T_1= 6oo ooo d, T_2= 15 d
b) Laufendes Gleichgewicht T_1= 36 d, T_2= 3 d
c) Kein Gleichgewicht T_1= 1o d, T_2= 2o d

Die Aktivität eines radioaktiven Stoffes ist der Quotient aus der Anzahl der Zerfallsakte und der Zeit, in der diese Zerfallsakte erfolgen. Sie ist proportional der Anzahl der noch vorhandenen Atome: $A = \lambda . N$. λ ist die Zerfallskonstante, sie hängt mit der Halbwertszeit T durch die Beziehung $\lambda = \ln 2/T$ zusammen.
Für die Aktivität von Mutter (Index 1), Tochter (Index 2) und für die Gesamtaktivität gilt:

$$A_1 = A_o . e^{-\lambda_1 t}$$
$$A_2 = A_o . T_1/(T_1 - T_2) . (e^{-\lambda_1 t} - e^{-\lambda_2 t}) \qquad (1)$$
$$A = A_1 + A_2$$

A_o ist die Aktivität der Muttersubstanz zur Zeit t=0, während angenommen wird, daß bei Beginn der Zeitzählung noch keine Tochteratome vorhanden waren. Es ist nicht notwendig, die Gleichungen (1) für den Schüler herzuleiten. Interessant ist vielmehr das zeitliche Verhalten der drei Aktivitäten nach Vorgabe der beiden Halbwertszeiten. Der Computer zeichnet die drei Kurven Punkt für Punkt auf, ähnlich wie man sie mit dem Zeichenstift ausführen würde. Die Aktivitäten werden im logarithmischen Maßstab gegenüber der Zeit in Tagen (von 0 bis 139) aufgetragen. Wir können drei Klassen von Ereignissen unterscheiden:

Dauerndes Gleichgewicht $T_1 \gg T_2$, $T_1 \gg t$ (Abb.1a)
$A_1 = A_2$=konstant z.B. Radium 226 und Radon 222

Laufendes Gleichgewicht $T_1 > T_2$, jedoch in Größenordnung von t (Abb.1b)
A_2/A_1=konstant, $A \sim e^{-t}$ z.B. Barium 14o und Lanthan 14o

Kein Gleichgewicht $T_1 < T_2$ (Abb.1c)
A_2/A_1 wächst dauernd, A_2 hat ein Maximum, z.B. Jod 135 und Xenon 135 (Ursache der sogenannten Xenonvergiftung in Atomkernreaktoren).

Ergebnis: Ein und dasselbe Gleichungssystem (1) kann je nach Belegung der Parameter einen unterschiedlichen zeitlichen Verlauf nehmen. Nach Betrachtung des Computerprogramms besteht möglicherweise der Anreiz, die Ergebnisse auch rein arithmetisch aus den Gleichungen (1) herzuleiten. Für die Schüler ist dies eine gute Übung im Umgang mit e-Potenzen und im Abschätzen von Größenordnungen.

2. Simulation von Versuchen, deren reale Ausführung im Unterricht möglich ist

Es gibt Themenkreise in der Physik, bei deren Behandlung viele Experimente ausführbar sind. Der Lehrer kann und soll einige dieser Experimente in seinem Unterricht vorführen. Der Computer erscheint hier überflüssig, wenn nicht störend. Bei näherer Überlegung zeigt sich jedoch, daß auch hier der Computer sinnvoll eingesetzt werden kann. Versuche, die real durchgeführt werden, kann man in gleicher oder etwas veränderter Form am Bildschirm simulieren. Sie können zur Festigung und Vertiefung des Gesehenen und Gelernten beitragen. Da der Versuchsablauf beliebig langsam gestaltet werden kann, ist ein besserer Einblick in das physikalische Geschehen möglich. Oft wird man auch die Versuchsbedingungen auf dem Bildschirm viel komplexer gestalten können, als im real ablaufenden Versuch. In anderen Fällen wird gerade das Umgekehrte zielführend sein. Es kann auch reizvoll sein, den Versuchsablauf unter Bedingungen zu simulieren, die in der Natur gar nicht vorkommen. (Etwa Totalreflexion bei sehr hohen Brechungsindizes). Bei nicht wenigen Versuchen, die man durchführen kann, sieht man zwar das Ergebnis, jedoch nicht wie es zustande kommt. Bei einem optisch aktiven Stoff etwa beobachtet man im Experiment die Drehung der Polarisationsebene des linear polarisierten Lichtes. Am Bildschirm kann man die Addition ungleich orientierter, zirkularpolarisierter Schwingungen mit unterschiedlichen Phasengeschwindigkeiten durchführen lassen und so die Ursache der Drehung erkennen.

Als einfaches Beispiel sei die Mehrfachreflexion angeführt. Zur Anwendung und Vertiefung des Reflexionsgesetzes betrachten wir einen Billardtisch mit zwei Kugeln. Die Stoßkugel soll nach ein- oder mehrmaliger Reflexion an bestimmtem Banden unter Einhaltung des Reflexionsgesetzes die Zielkugel treffen. H,R,T bzw. L bedeuten Reflexion an der oberen (=hoch), an der rechten, an der unteren (=tief) bzw. an der linken Bande.

Die Eingabe	Koordinaten der Stoßkugel	5o,12o
	Koordinaten der Zielkugel	22o, 8o
	Reihenfolge der Reflexionen	HTR

erzeugt das Schirmbild der Abb.2.

Durch Änderung der Kugelkoordinaten und Variation der Reihenfolge der Reflexionen ergibt sich ein sehr nettes Experimentierfeld. Nicht jede eingegebene Reihenfolge ist durchführbar. Stößt der Computer auf eine nicht ausführbare Aufgabe, so erfolgt die Ausgabe: NICHT MÖGLICH!

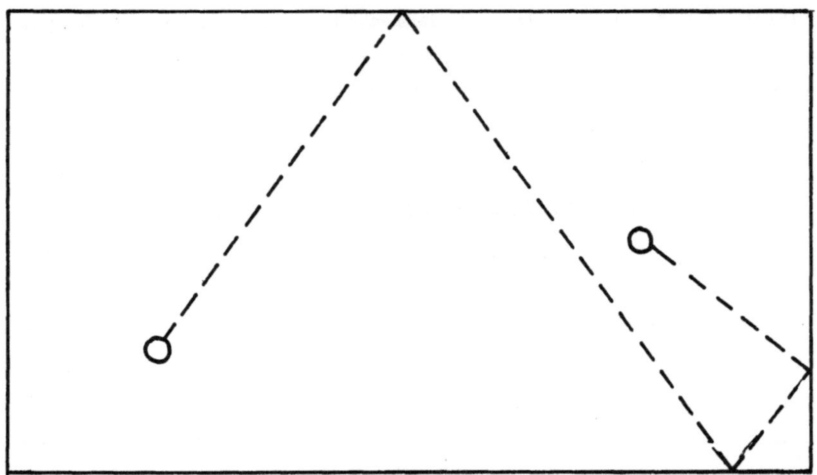

Abb.2 Mehrfachreflexion

Wir können mit dem Computer parallel arbeiten und die gestellte Aufgabe durch Zeichnung oder durch Rechnung lösen. Wir erkennen dabei, daß in jedem Fall die gleichen Schritte durchzuführen sind, wie bei der Erstellung des Computerprogramms, nämlich:

Eingabe
Spiegelung
Bestimmung der Auftreffpunkte an der Bande
Zeichnung.

3. Simulation von Versuchen, deren reale Ausführung im Unterricht nicht möglich ist

Es gibt Versuche, die zwar in vielen Physiklehrgängen genannt werden, jedoch im Unterricht wegen des zu hohen Zeit- oder Gerätebedarfes nicht durchgeführt werden können. Hier kann der Bildschirmcomputer neben dem Lehrfilm sinnvoll zum Einsatz kommen. Neben den Nachteilen, die jedes auf einer Fläche simulierte Experiment sicher hat, bieten sich wieder die Vorteile der freien Parameterwahl, des verlangsamten oder beschleunigten Ablaufs und der beliebigen Wiederholbarkeit an. Besondere Vorteile bringt die Verwendung des Zufallsgenerator, mit seiner Hilfe kann man Vorgänge aus der statistischen Physik simulieren. In Frage kommen Experimente aus der Wärmelehre, wie Brownsche Bewegung oder Entropieänderungen, alle Streu- und Absorptionsexperimente, wie etwa der Comptoneffekt, das Rutherfordsche Streuexperiment oder die Bestimmung der Anzahl der reflektierten, der absorbierten und der durchgelassenen Neutronen beim Auftreffen auf eine Metallschicht. Bei Beschäftigung mit solchen Programmen lernt man den mathematischen Begriff der Wahrscheinlichkeit und seine Auswirkung auf den Ablauf physikalischer Experimente erst so richtig kennen.

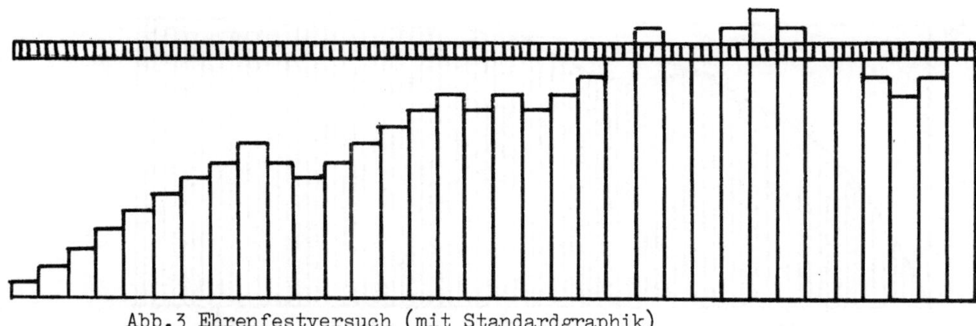

Abb.3 <u>Ehrenfestversuch</u> (mit Standardgraphik)

Als Beispiel für einen nach den Gesetzen der Statistik ablaufenden physikalischen Vorgang betrachten wir den <u>Ehrenfestversuch</u>. Dieses Gedankenexperiment wurde von P.Ehrenfest zur Erläuterung des Entropiebegriffes und zur Begegnung des Wiederkehreinwands vorgeschlagen. Eine Anzahl von n Kugeln, die die Zahlen von 1 bis n als Aufschrift tragen, befinden sich im Becher 1. Der Becher 2 ist zu Beginn des Versuches leer. Ein Zufallsgenerator erzeugt fortlaufend Zahlen zwischen 1 und n. Wird gerade die Zahl k geliefert, so wechselt die Kugel mit der Aufschrift k den Becher. Befindet sie sich also im Becher 1, so wird sie in den Becher 2 gelegt, ist sie bereits im 2.Becher, so kehrt sie bei abermaligen Aufruf in den Becher eins zurück und so fort. Beobachtet wird die Anzahl der Kugeln im zweiten Becher.

Dieser Versuch eignet sich sehr gut zur Simulation am Computer. Wir benützen zunächst die Standardgraphik und eine kleine Anzahl von Kugeln. Der Bildschirm zeigt für jeweils 4o Versuche die Anzahl der Kugeln im zweiten Becher. Der zu erwartende Mittelwert n/2 ist ebenfalls auf der Graphik sichtbar. Die Abb.3 zeigt den ersten Teil eines Versuches mit 3o Kugeln. Ihre Anzahl im zweiten Becher steigt zunächst linear an, wächst dann weniger stark und schwankt schließlich um den Wert 15.

Nach der Anlaufphase, wenn die Anzahl der Kugeln den Wert n/2 das erste Mal erreicht hat, beginnt der Computer mit der Zählung der Versuche und errechnet Erwartungswert und Streuung. Eine Serie von 1o ooo Versuchen mit 3o Kugeln ergab den Erwartungswert E=15,o26 und die relative Streuung σ/E=0,183.

Wir wollen dieses Ergebnis mit den theoretischen Werten vergleichen. Die Wahrscheinlichkeit $P_n(k)$ für den Aufenthalt von k Kugeln im zweiten Behälter berechnen wir

k/n (k+1)/n

k-1 k k+1

(n-k+1)/n (n-k)/n

aus der Gleichgewichtsbedingung Zufluß=Abfluß. Diese ergibt:

$$P_n(k) = P_n(k-1).\frac{n-k+1}{n} + P_n(k+1).\frac{k+1}{n} \qquad (2)$$

Die Rekursionsbedingung (2) wird von der binomischen Verteilung erfüllt, so daß wir erhalten

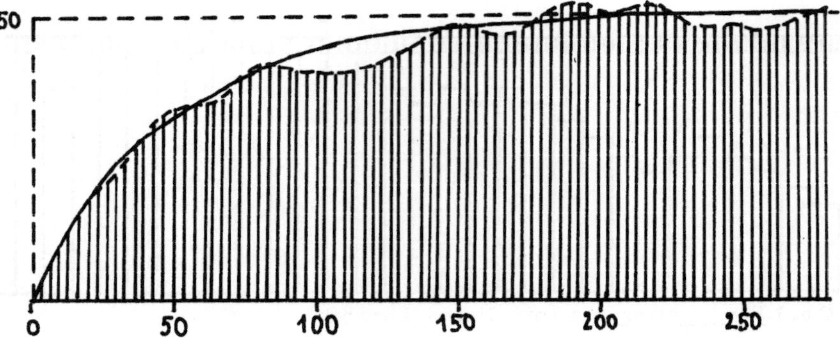

Abb.4 Ehrenfestversuch (mit hochauflösender Graphik)

Wahrscheinlichkeit des Zustands k	$P_n(k) = \binom{n}{k}.2^{-n}$	(3)
Erwartungswert	$E_n = n/2$	
Streuung absolut (relativ)	$\sigma = \sqrt{n}/2 \quad (\sigma/E = 1/\sqrt{n})$	

Die oben erwähnte Versuchsreihe bestätigt diese Werte recht gut.

Welche physikalische Aussage macht der Ehrenfestversuch? Die Anzahl der Kugeln im zweiten Becher kann als Maß für die Entropie angesehen werden. Zu Beginn der Versuchsreihe nimmt die Entropie dauernd zu. Dies entspricht dem Übergang des Systems in einen Zustand größerer Wahrscheinlichkeit. In der Nähe der Gleichgewichtseinstellung treten jedoch merkliche Schwankungen auf, die relativ zum Erwartungswert mit wachsender Zahl der Kugeln immer kleiner werden. Der Vorgang ist irreversibel. Denn nach (3) ist die Wahrscheinlichkeit, daß das System aus dem Gleichgewichtszustand von selbst in den Zustand 0 (Ausgangszustand) zurückkehrt sehr gering, schon für die kleine Zahl von 1o Kugeln ist sie kleiner als ein Promille. Eine "Wiederkehr" ist also praktisch ausgeschlossen. Diese Tatsache kann man am Bildschirm sehr schön beobachten. Nur bei sehr kleiner Kugelzahl läßt sich die Wiederkehr in den Zustand 0 in vernünftigen Zeitspannen erwarten.

Es ist interessant den Ehrenfestversuch auch während der Anlaufphase, also vor dem Erreichen des Gleichgewichtszustandes zu untersuchen. Der Erwartungswert nach Durchführung von x Versuchen kann ohne Kenntnis der Einzelwahrscheinlichkeiten angegeben werden.

$$E_n(x) = n/2.(1-(1-2/n)^x) = n/2.(1 - e^{-x\ln a}), \quad \text{mit } a=n/(n-2) \tag{4}$$

Für große x nähert sich $E_n(x)$ immer mehr dem Wert n/2. Wir können auch abschätzen, wie lange die Anlaufphase dauert, wenn wir annehmen, daß sie beendet ist, wenn sich $E_n(x)$ nur mehr um den Betrag der Streuung σ von $E_n(\infty)=n/2$ unterscheidet.

$$\frac{n}{2}(1-e^{-x\ln a}) = \frac{n}{2}\left(1-\frac{1}{\sqrt{n}}\right) \Rightarrow x\ln a = \frac{1}{2}\ln n \Rightarrow x \approx \frac{3}{2}n \text{ mit } \ln a \approx \frac{2}{n} \text{ u. } \ln n < 6$$

Für n<4oo ist die Anlaufphase nach etwa 1,5n Versuchen beendet.

Die Abb.4 zeigt den Ehrenfestversuch in hochauflösender Graphik mit 1oo Kugeln. Es sind 28o Versuche auf dem Bildschirm gleichzeitig zu sehen. Der Erwartungswert während der Anlaufphase wird nach (4) in das Schaubild eingezeichnet.

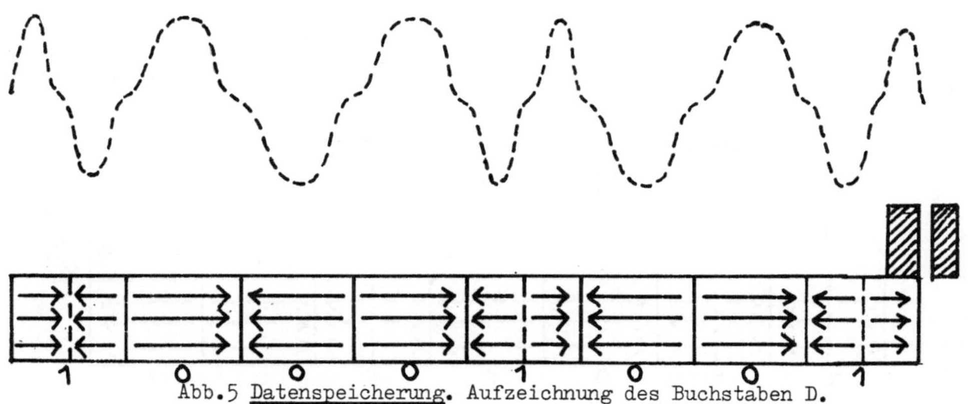

Abb.5 Datenspeicherung. Aufzeichnung des Buchstaben D.

4. Anwendungsorientierte Probleme

Häufig ist es im Unterricht nur schwer möglich, den Schülern Anwendungen des eben besprochenen Kapitels in Technik, Wirtschaft oder auch nur in anderen Bereichen der Physik genügend klar zu machen. Oft muß man sich mit einigen Sätzen begnügen. Der Bildschirmcomputer kann hier helfend einspringen. Es ist für den Lehrer leichter, an Hand der am Bildschirm entstehenden Graphik in kurzer Zeit komplexe Vorgänge zu erläutern, als durch bloße Schilderung oder Betrachten von Bildern. Im besonderen eignen sich alle Steuervorgänge zur Simulation auf dem Bildschirm. Ich lasse z.B. einen Lift zwischen fünf Stockwerken arbeiten, der von (rechteckigen) "Passagieren" gerufen und benützt wird. Es zeigte sich, daß die Aufstellung einer alle möglichen Fälle berücksichtigenden Logik für die Fahrten des Lifts und ihr Einbau in das Programm gar nicht so einfach ist, wie es zunächst scheint. Andere automatische Abläufe, die sich zur Simulation eignen, sind ampelgeregelte Kreuzungen, das Blocksystem zur Sicherung des Bahnverkehrs und ähnliches.

Als Beispiel eines anwendungsorientierten Problems betrachten wir die magnetische Datenspeicherung. Bei der Aufzeichnung von Daten gleitet ein Schreibkopf über die mit magnetisch aktivem Material beschichtete Platte. Er besteht aus einem ringförmigen Eisenkern und einer über diesen Kern gewickelten Spule, die vom Magnetisierungsstrom durchflossen wird. An einer Stelle ist der Kern aufgeschnitten, praktisch nur dort kann das Magnetfeld austreten und den darunterliegenden Abschnitt der Platte magnetisieren.

Alle zu speichernden Daten müssen als Dualzahlen vorliegen. Beim häufig verwendeten Frequenzverdoppelungsverfahren wird 1 durch eine Richtungsumkehr der Magnetisierung, 0 durch das Fehlen einer solchen Umkehrung dargestellt. Zusätzlich kehrt man nach jedem Bit die Magnetisierungsrichtung um. Die Verhältnisse werden am Bildschirm, wie in Abb.5 unten zu sehen, dargestellt. Man verwendet mehr Richtungsänderungen

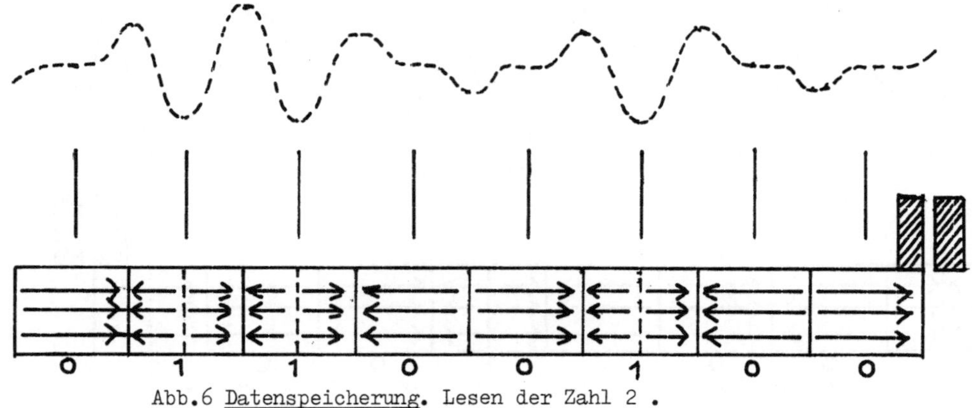

Abb.6 <u>Datenspeicherung</u>. Lesen der Zahl 2 .

als unbedingt nötig, gewinnt jedoch ein Signal zur Synchronisation des Datenflusses und eine geringere Fehleranfälligkeit. In Abb.5 oben ist der zeitliche Verlauf des Magnetisierungsstromes gezeichnet. Beim realen Vorgang bewegt sich die Platte sehr schnell unter dem Schreibkopf, bei der Simulation sind die Bewegungen vertauscht. Die "Platte" (gestrecktes Rechteck) ist in Ruhe und der "Schreibkopf" gleitet langsam von links nach rechts. Über ihm wird die Kurve des Magnetisierungsstromes punktweise gezeichnet und unter ihm entstehen Pfeile, die die fortschreitende Magnetisierung der Platte andeuten.

Die Verschlüsselung der Zeichen erfolgt nach dem ASCII - Code. Dabei wird jedes Zeichen durch eine siebenstellige Binärzahl dargestellt. Dem Buchstaben "D" z.B. ist die Zahl 1 0 0 0 1 0 0 zugeordnet. Ein achtes Bit, das Paritätsbit, wird so angefügt, daß jedes Zeichen insgesamt aus einer ungeraden Anzahl von Einsern besteht. Damit erkennt man jeden Fehler, der nur in der Änderung eines einzigen Bits besteht. Andere Fehler sind sehr viel seltener.

Der Schreibkopf ist gleichzeitig Lesekopf. Wenn sich die Platte unter ihm dreht, so induzieren ihre wechselnden magnetischen Felder in seiner Spule Spannungsstöße. Auch das Lesen wird in unserem Programm simuliert. In Abb.6 oben ist der zeitliche Verlauf der Induktionsspannung beim Lesen des Zeichens 2 gezeichnet. Die Striche darunter deuten die Stellen an, an denen die Information über die gespeicherte Binärzahl entnommen wird. Die übrigen Spannungsstöße dienen zur Synchronisation des Datenflusses.

OStR. Mag. Kurt Wagner
Bundesgymnasium A 9o2o Klagenfurt
Völkermarkter Ring 27

Auswertungen naturwissenschaftlicher Meßreihen und sozialwissenschaftlicher Erhebungen mit Computerunterstützung

Leo H. Klingen, Bonn

Zusammenfassung: Nachdem angesichts der Lehrerschwemme computerunterstützte Lernverfahren im Sinne von maschinengesteuertem programmiertem Lernen nur noch für Sonderfälle Anwendung finden, kommt dem computerorientierten Fachunterricht erhöhte Bedeutung zu. E i n Sektor möglichen Computereinsatzes ist die Auswertung empirischer Ergebnisse, die sich sowohl in den Natur- wie in den Sozialwissenschaften anbietet.

Die Aufarbeitung empirischer Ergebnisse ohne Computer wird behindert durch die auftretende numerische Belastung, aber auch durch den nicht immer präsenten algorithmischen Apparat und teilweise durch den Umfang vorhandener Daten. Andererseits wird die Möglichkeit des Computereinsatzes heute durch mehrere Faktoren gegeben, die in den frühen siebziger Jahren bei den Tischrechnern nicht vorgelegen haben:

a) Die mit dem Gedanken an Informatik-Unterricht, mitunter auch an Einsatz in der Schulverwaltung installierten Zentraleinheiten mit 128 - 256 k besitzen keine Einschränkungen mehr bezüglich des Umfangs aufzuarbeitenden empirischen Materials.

b) Neben der bekannten überall vorhandenen Vollauslastung des "Rechenzentrums" an der Schule am Nachmittag durch freie Arbeitsgemeinschaften ist die Vormittagsauslastung durch 9 Wochenstunden für 3 Grundkurse Informatik und 4 Wochenstunden Wahldifferenzierung in der Mittelstufe zu schmal. Erst 5 -10% "algorithmischer Strang" im mathematischen Unterricht und eben die hier angezogene Besetzung schaffen hinreichend breite Auslastung über den ganzen Tag.

c) Die formalsprachliche Darstellung von Auswertungsalgorithmen hat ein gutes Transparenzniveau erreicht. Es existieren Betriebssysteme, die hinreichend einfache Erstellung, Dokumentation, Archivierung und schnellen ad-hoc-Einsatz fertiger Moduln erlauben. Das ist gerade für eine nicht alltägliche Benutzung, die ein Behalten unlogischer Betriebssysteme nicht gestattet, eine wesentliche Voraussetzung. [1]

d) In den meisten Fällen wird das Endergebnis der Auswertung empirischer Ergebnisse nicht nur die Berechnung bestimmter Werte beinhalten, sondern wird auch eine graphische Ausgabe erwünscht sein. Kleine DIN A 4 - Digitalplotter aus der Mikroperipherie, die ggf. mehrfarbig direkt mit Permanentstiften auf Overheadfolie mit 1/10 mm Schrittweiten in allen Hauptrichtungen malen, stellen sehr kostengünstige Mittel dar, Demonstrationen für die ganze Klasse herzustellen, solange graphische Terminals mit parallelen Monitoren noch einen zu großen Aufwand bedeuten. Die Schüler können dann über die an Schulen üblichen Kopiergeräte Abzüge erhalten.

Für die zugrundeliegende Didaktik sollte ein einziger klarer Grundsatz ausreichen und vernünftige Grenzen ziehen:
Die Schüler müssen Einsicht über die Gültigkeit und die Reichweite der angewendeten Auswertungsverfahren erlangen.
In der Tat reicht dieses Prinzip für Ausgleichsrechnung und Statistik erheblich weiter, als es zunächst den Anschein hat. Zugleich wird damit das Lernziel, nicht nur die Erhebungen sorgfältig zu interpretieren, sondern auch die Methoden der Auswertung kritisch zu hinterfragen, entschieden angegangen. Erwähnt sei auch noch, daß häufig die Kosten der - oft nur begrenzt einsetzbaren- Experimentiereinrichtung und der Lerneffekt bei einer anschließenden bloß groben Versuchsauswertung in einem ungünstigen Verhältnis stehen.
Die weiteren Ausführungen dienen der Darstellung an konkreten Beispielen.

Zunächst wird das Protokoll der Meßreihe oder der Erhebung vor der Auswertung gefordert. Das bedeutet die Modularisierung einer einfachen Dateierstellung, ggf. auch der Sortierung der anfallenden Urwerte nach einem geeigneten Schlüssel. Ausgaberoutinen für diese Datei mit bündiger Tabellendarstellung, Kopfbeschriftung und Dimensionsangabe ergänzen den Modul. Vielleicht ist sogar für Zwecke der Schulverwaltung ein Datenbankkonzept geschaffen worden, das an dieser Stelle übernommen werden kann. Wenn die Mühe der Tastatureingabe der Eingangswerte für jede anschließende Auswertung neu aufgebracht werden muß, z.B. weil nur ein Feld mit manuellem Input vorgesehen worden ist, schwindet rasch und mit Recht das Vertrauen auf behauptete Ökonomie computerunterstützter Verfahren.
Das Protokoll in graphischer Form wird

a) durch Streudiagramme mit verschiedenartigen Punktsymbolen,
b) durch Polygonzüge für i.a. relative Häufigkeiten,
c) durch Balkendiagramme für absolute oder relative Häufigkeiten,
d) seltener durch prozentuale Kreissektor-Diagramme

wiedergegeben.

Dafür sollten geeignete Routinen vorliegen, wobei in den Fällen a - c ein Koordinatensystem mit Skalierung, Angabe der Einheiten und Titelbeschriftung, evt. auch wahlweise mit Bezeichnung aller Skalenteile, notwendig wird. Dagegen wird man auf automatische Skalierung, die aus Bereichsgrenzen ermittelt,in der Regel lieber verzichten, da sie zu sehr unüblichen Abbildungen (z.B. der Sinusfunktion) führen kann. Eine Ausschnittvergrößerung mit Maßstabveränderung sollte jederzeit leicht möglich sein.

Für weitere Berechnungsarbeit auf einer Datei werden hier nur wenige weitere Ausführungen gemacht. Erwähnt sei, daß für Integrationen die Simpson-Prozedur für die Schule nach ihrer theoretischen Grundlage (Parabelinterpolation zwiscken drei Stützpunkten) und ihrer einfachen Handhabung angemessen ist. (Beispiel: Auswertung eines thermodynamischen Kreisprozesses). Rein beschreibende Statistik mit Mittelwert $\overline{x}$, Standardabweichung s_x , absolutem Fehler des Mittelwertes $\Delta x = \pm \frac{s_x}{\sqrt{n}}$ und relativem Fehler $\frac{\Delta x}{x}$ auf der Eingangsseite und Fehlerfortpflanzungsrechnung mit $\Delta y \approx dy = f' \Delta x$ auf der berechneten Ausgangsseite können unmittelbar an das Protokoll automatisch angefügt werden.

Bisher wenig üblich war ein breiterer Einsatz der Ausgleichsrechnung an der Schule. Zunächst lassen sich Ausgleichsgeraden mit ausgezeichnetem Nullpunkt (Beispiel: Ohmsches Gesetz, Hookesches Gesetz) schon in der Sekundarstufe I durch Scheitelbestimmung der Parabel

$$\sum_i (y_i - m x_i)^2$$

und damit Minimalisierung der Fehlerquadratsumme bestimmen. Für allgemeinere Ausgleichsgeraden

$$y = m x + b \qquad m = \frac{\sum x_i y_i - (\sum x_i y_i)/n}{\sum x_i^2 - (\sum x_i)^2 /n}$$

wird man entweder den Zusammenhang

$$y - \overline{y} = m (x - \overline{x})$$

behandeln und kann dann m ohne Differentialrechnung ermitteln, oder man verwendet die anschaulich sofort einleuchtende notwendige Bedingung für eine waagerechte Tangentialebene an ein Paraboloid, daß in m-Richtung und in b-Richtung Nullanstiege vorhanden sein müssen in Analogie zum eindimensionalen Fall.

Die Ausgleichsgerade liefert nicht nur eine geeignete Interpretation linear zusammenhängender Meßergebnisse, sondern in manchen Fällen auch über ihren Anstieg oder ihren y-Achsenabschnitt wichtige Einzelresultate.(Beispiel: Berechnung des Wirkungsquantums h aus Messungen mit der Fotozelle und einem Energie-Frequenz-Diagramm [2]; Berechnung des Ausdehnungskoeffizienten eines Gases im Gay-Lussacschen Gesetz).
Zugleich bietet die naheliegende Übertragung desselben Ansatzes auf den multivariaten Fall eine Möglichkeit, Regressionspolynome n-ter Ordnung

$$y = a_n x^n + a_{n-1} x^{n-1} + \dots + a_1 x + a_0$$

einzuführen, deren Konstruktion nach demselben partiellen Differentiationsprinzip auf die Lösung eines linearen Gleichungssystems führt. Besonders für sozialwissenschaftliche Erhebungen (Schulbeispiel: Verlauf der Schüleranmeldungen an einem Gymnasium) läßt sich das wichtige Prinzip der angepaßten Informationsreduktion durch die Wahl der richtigen Ordnung der Ausgleichskurve treffend demonstrieren. Weiß man z.B., daß die Gründung eines Nachbargymnasiums und die seinerzeitigen Kurzschuljahre die einzigen wesentlichen Einbußen in den Anmeldungen brachten, wird eine Regressionskurve 4.Ordnung reichen, die 2 Minima wiedergeben kann.
Ausgleichsgeraden, die man früher auf - oft nicht gerade vorrätiges Funktionsnetzpapier gezeichnet hat, lassen sich jetzt z.B. als Ausgleichshyperbeln (Beispiel:Boylesches Gesetz, Adiabatenhyperbel; Linsenformel:optische Bildweite als Funktion der Gegenstandsweite) oder als Ausgleichs-e-Funktion(Beispiel:Entladung eines großen Kondensators über einen Widerstand, Zerfall von Thorium-Emanation) wiedergeben.
Wenn man so nicht nur lineare, sondern verschiedene Ausgleichszusammenhänge zur Verfügung hat, kann man über das berechnete

$$r^2 = \frac{s_{xy}^2}{s_x^2 \, s_y^2} \qquad \text{mit} \quad s_{xy} = \frac{\sum (x_i - \bar{x})(y_i - \bar{y})}{n - 1}$$

den aus der angesetzten Gesetzmäßigkeit vorhersagbaren Varianzanteil und den verbleibenden zufälligen Varianzanteil bestimmen und durch Minimierung von r sogar den wahrscheinlichsten Zusammenhang automatisch bestimmen.

Es verbleiben auch Meßreihen, wo man verlangt, daß gemessene Punkte vom Graphen der Meßfunktion angenommen werden.(Beispiele: p_H-Werte bei einer chemischen Titration einer gepufferten Lösung; Frank-Hertz-Versuch). Hier werden Lagrange-Interpolationen durch eine einzige ganzrationale Funktion, wie sie die Schüler meistens aus ihrem Erfahrungshorizont vorschlagen, wegen ihrer Welligkeit vor allem an den Intervallenden bei höherer Stützpunktzahl n rasch enttäuschen. Dagegen ist die Interpolation durch n-1 kubische Splines hervorragend geeignet und auf der Schule auch theoretisch herleitbar. Im Prinzip reichen die n Punktbedingungen und die Forderung nach glatter erster und zweiter Ableitung an den n-1 Zwischenstellen, um zusammen mit einer plausiblen Randbedingung ein Gleichungssystem mit $4\cdot(n-1)$ Variablen dem Computer zu übergeben, das wiederum durch den Modul "Gaußelimination" gelöst wird. Elegantere Verfahren findet man z.B. in [3].

Für Kurvenscharen(Beispiel: van der Waals Zustandsgleichung für reale Gase; Resonanz von Bandfiltern bei zunehmender Kopplung der Schwingungskreise) bieten sich räumliches Plotting oder auch Schablonendarstellung im räumlichen Modell an.

Für Häufigkeitsverteilungen(Beispiel: Zählraten für radioaktive Messungen mit Geiger-Müller-Zählrohren) gibt es noch anderweitige Vergleiche. Man kann in (0,1) gleichverteilte Zufallszahlen so an der Stammfunktion der Verteilung spiegeln, daß die empirisch ermittelte Verteilung simuliert wird; bezeichnet man die gleichverteilten Zufallszahlen mit g_i und die gespiegelten mit h_i, so gilt nach Definition der Gleichverteilung:

$$p(h_i < F(x)) = p (F^{-1}(g_i) < x) = p (g_i < F(x)) = F (x)$$

So haben z.B. die oben genannten Zählraten die Wahrscheinlichkeitsfunktion

$$\lambda e^{-\lambda x} \quad \text{mit der Stammfunktion} \quad 1 - e^{-\lambda x}$$

Die Spiegelung an der Stammfunktion führt auf $x = -\frac{1}{\lambda}.\ln(1-y)$ was man auch einfacher durch komplementäre Zufallszahlen

$$x = -\frac{1}{\lambda}.\ln y$$

in eine Simulationsprozedur "exponentialzufall" bringen kann. Jede empirische Wahrscheinlichkeitsdichte kann man durch Übergang zum Histogramm in eine Treppenfunktion verwandeln, die sich leicht integrieren läßt.

Der Biologe wird begrüßen, daß die Grundlagen der Chiquadrat-Verteilung auf der Schule durchaus zu erarbeiten sind (vgl. [4]) und der Rechenausdruck

$$\frac{\sum (x_i - n\, p_i)^2}{n\, p_i}$$

bei Zufallsgrößen mit r verschiedenen Ausfällen (z.B. Züchtungsergebnissen) und Erwartungswerten $n\, p_i$ vom Computer ermittelt wird.

Schließlich kann auch der Grundansatz einer Fourier-Analyse auf der Schule demonstriert werden. Für eine Klangkurve am Oszillographen mag auf diese Weise das Spektrum der Obertöne ermittelt werden; lehrreich ist dann dazu auch die geplottete Fourier-Synthese desselben Spektrums unter Vernachlässigung zu kleiner Amplituden der Obertonreihe.

Neben diese Verfahren mit fest vorgegener Methode werden natürlich im Einzelfall Darstellungen treten, die eine Auswertung in eine Simulation überführen. Als konkretes Beispiel aus den Sozialwissenschaften sei die graphische Darstellung einer Bevölkerungspyramide auf dem Bildschirm genannt. In 20 Zeilen lassen sich Fünfjahres-Statistiken für Männer und Frauen, evt. auch mit getrennten Symbolen für die erwerbstätige und die nicht erwerbstätige Bevölkerung unterbringen. Der Maßstab erlaubt es im allgemeinen, zwei solcher Pyramiden nebeneinander unterzubringen, z.B. die von Deutschland und Frankreich, oder die eines Industrielandes gegen eine Pyramide eines Entwicklungslandes. Obwohl man sich für feinere Details ein graphisches Terminal oder einen Plotter wünscht, verrät schon die Darstellung auf dem normalen Bildschirmraster manche historische Zäsur. Den Übergang zur Simulation gewinnt man nun durch jährliches Fortschreiben der Pyramide unter Berücksichtigung der Fruchtbarkeitsraten der Frauen zwischen 15 und 45 Jahren und der Sterblichkeitsraten der Männer und Frauen über alle Altersstufen mit besonderer Berücksichtigung der Säuglingssterblichkeit. Dabei wird besonders zu diskutieren sein, wieweit eine solche Fortschreibung, die Konstanz der Einstellungen voraussetzt, sinnvoll ist. Auf einem genügend schnellen Rechner - ggf. auch durch Vorwegberechnung und Ablagerung aller Daten über 100 Jahre in einem größeren Datenraum - kann man die graphische Ausgabe zu einem Trickfilm umfunktionieren, der eindrucksvolle Zukunftssituationen darstellt.

Im mehr numerischen Bereich kann man z.B. den Energieverbrauch eines Einfamilienhauses in Abhängigkeit vom täglichen Temperaturverlauf graphisch nach dem prozentualen Wärmeverlust durch Dach und Keller, durch Außenwände und Fenster und durch den Kamin darstellen; die dazu nötigen Erfahrungswerte können heute mit reichlich angebotener Literatur leicht beschafft werden. Schüler können sich bemühen, herauszufinden, wie sich zusätzliche Wärmedämmung, Isolierverglasung etc. auswirken und die Simulation bis zum Heizölverbrauch durchrechnen lassen.

Die beiden letztgenannten Beispiele setzen eine Lerngruppe mit einem Lehrer voraus, der im Rahmen eines kleinen Projekts selbständig mit Computerprogrammen umgehen kann. Für die breitere Nutzung des Geräts wäre es aber auch viel wert, wenn jeder Lehrer sich fertige Pakete zu eigen machen würde. Ein solches Paket müßte enthalten:

a) Plotting-Routinen für Punkte, Polygone,Histogramme,
b) Plotting-Routinen für Koordinatensysteme, Funktionen und Funktionenscharen,
c) Tabellenprotokolle ; Sortieren von Urlisten,
d) Berechnungen von $\bar{x}$, s_x , Δx, $\Delta x/ x$, Fehlerfortpflanzungen, Chiquadratberechnungen,
e) Ausgleichsgeraden, Ausgleichspolynome und andere Ausgleichskurven,
f) Splines für n Stützpunkte und ggf. Fourierzerlegungen,
g) numerische Lösungen gewöhnlicher expliziter Differentialgleichungen erster und zweiter Ordnung,
h) Transformationen von Zufallszahlen auf vorgegebene Verteilungen.

Alle angegeben Prozeduren passen in vorübersetzter Form auf eine einzige Diskette, die mehrfach kopiert werden kann. Damit kann einem größeren Fachlehrerkollegium ein Instrumentarium zur Verfügung gestellt werden, dessen theoretische Grundlagen auf der Schule dargestellt werden können und dessen Anwendung die Sorgfalt der experimentellen Arbeit durch eine gewissenhafte Auswertung mit Hilfe des Computers ergänzt.

Die Konstruktion der reformierten Oberstufe mit Leistungskursen von 6 Wochenstunden nach der Bonner Vereinbarung der Kultusminister ist seinerzeit davon ausgegangen, daß wissenschaftspropädeutisches Arbeiten in einem zweistündigen Übungsrahmen betrieben werden kann: die geschilderten Auswertungen von Meß- und Erhebungsreihen können dazu einen idealen Beitrag leisten. Andererseits bleiben solche Arbeiten liegen, wenn nicht leistungsfähiges Werkzeug für sie bereitsteht. Angesichts mancher Verwässerung guter Reformansätze in der neueren Praxis der Schule darf an diese Chance sinnvollen Computereinsatzes erinnert werden.

Literatur:

[1] Klingen, L. H. , Elementare Algorithmen, Prozeduren und Probleme, Freiburg, Herder, 1981

[2] Sprockhoff, G. ,Physikalische Schulversuche der Sekundarstufe I, Struktur der Stoffe, Köln, Aulis, 1980

[3] Carnahan,B. und Wilkes,J.O., Digital Computing and Numerical Methods, New York, Wiley, 1973

[4] Strick, H.K., Der Chiquadrat-Anpassungstest im Mathematik- und Biologieunterricht, MNU 34, S.139 (1981)

Ein Projektmodell und Werkzeuge zu dessen Unterstützung

Peter Hruschka
Gesellschaft für Elektronische
Informationsverarbeitung m.b.H.
Aachen

In den letzten Jahren hat die Botschaft der Software Engineers in verstärktem Maße Eingang in die Ohren der Software-Anwender gefunden. Nachdem es in der Zwischenzeit mindestens genauso viele Methoden zur Systemerstellung wie verschiedene Programmiersprachen gibt, ist es unserer Meinung nach an der Zeit, eine Pause bei der Erfindung neuer Methoden einzulegen und die Zeit dafür zu nutzen, bestehende Methoden in der Praxis verstärkt einzusetzen, ihre Stärken und Schwächen kennenzulernen und Werkzeuge zu schaffen, die dem Systemanalytiker mindestens soviel helfen, wie der Compiler dem Programmierer.

Nach umfangreichen Literaturstudien und zahlreichen praktischen Versuchen kamen wir zur folgenden Bewertung der Methoden, die in unsere engere Auswahl kamen. (Die Länge der Pfeile zeigt, in welchen Phasen die Methode Unterstützung gibt, die Dicke ist eine subjektive Einschätzung der Stärke der Methode.)

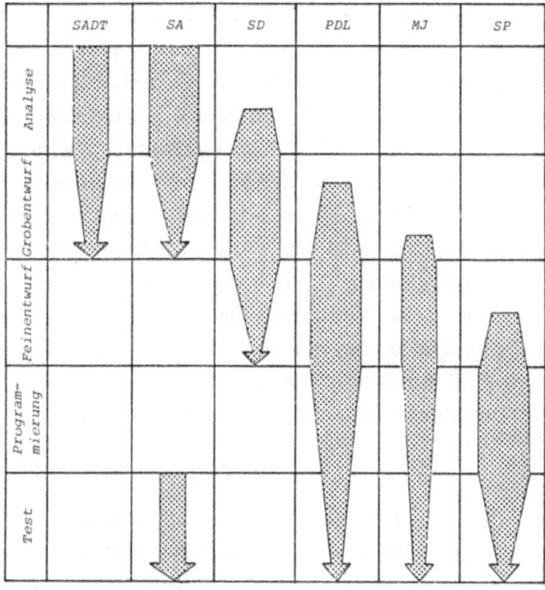

SADT = Structured Analysis and Design Technique

SA = Structured Analysis

SD = Structured Design

PDL = Program Design Language

MJ = Michael Jackson Design

SP = Structured Programming

Die Kriterien, die wir bei dieser Bewertung hauptsächlich verwendeten, waren folgende:

- Die ausgewählten Methoden sollen zusammen den ganzen Software Cycle abdecken.

- Sie sollen allgemein genug sein, um bei verschiedensten Problemstellungen angewandt werden zu können.

- Sie sollen spezifisch genug sein, um für bestimmte Anwendungsgebiete (z.B. PDV) effizient und hilfreich zu sein.

- Sie sollen ähnliche Grundphilosophien aufweisen (z.B. Top-down Strukturierung; informelle Notation, die der Kreativität noch Raum läßt).

- Sie sollen benutzerfreundlich und leicht erlernbar sein.

Die letzten beiden Punkte sollen die "Schwellenangst" bei den Personen verringern, die neuen Methoden grundsätzlich skeptisch gegenüberstehen. Aus der Bewertung ergibt sich für uns folgendes Projektmodell:

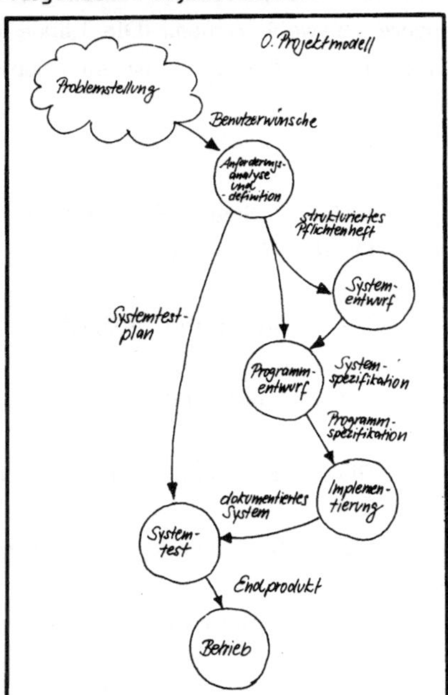

Für die Anforderungsanalyse und Definitionsphase erscheint uns die strukturierte Analyse /DEM79/ am geeignesten. Daraus läßt sich dann durch Transformationsanalysen /STE80/ ein erstes Systementwurfsmodell ableiten.
Zur weiteren Detailierung bietet sich strukturierter Entwurf an /MYE75/. Danach können unsere bewährten, auf Pseudocode basierenden Werkzeuge PDL und DARTS eingesetzt werden. Der Schritt zur strukturierten Programmierung /DDH72/ bildet die selbstverständliche Fortsetzung des Modells. Alle Methoden schließen schritthaltende Dokumentationen ein. Begleitet wird diese Vorgehensweise durch unsers Qualitätssicherungsprogramm, dem beispielsweise diverse Firmenstandards, ein Projektplanungs- und Berichtssystem, etc. zuzurechnen sind.

Die einzelnen Methoden, die den Phasen des Projektmodells zugeordnet sind, wurden ursprünglich (mit Ausnahme von DARTS) für den Bereich "kommerzielle DV" entwickelt. Durch einige Pilotprojekte im Bereich Industrieautomation und Systemprogrammierung wurden wir jedoch in unserer Überzeugung bestärkt, daß die Prinzipien der Methoden universell anwendbar sind.

Anforderungsanalyse und -definition (AAD)

Den Ausgangspunkt für unser Modell bilden die Wünsche eines Kunden, die informell in Form von vorhandenen Daten (z.B. Lieferscheine, Stückzahlen) und Funktionen (z.B. Walzstraße steuern, Wareneingang automatisieren) vorgebracht werden. Nach den Vorgehensregeln von strukturierter Analyse werden diese Angaben in drei Formen systematisiert:

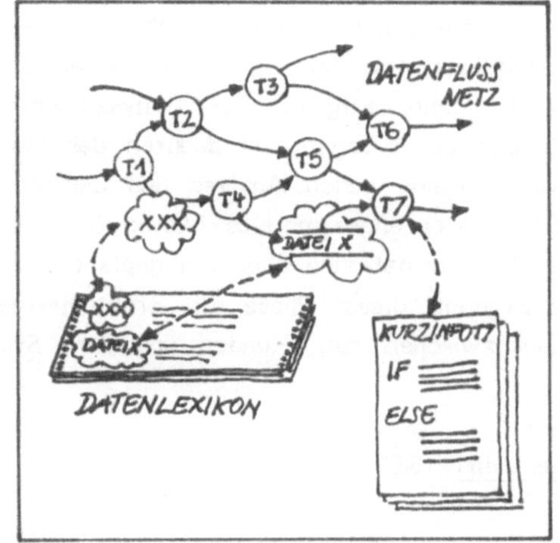

- die Daten, die durch ein System fließen und die Funktionen werden in Form eines Datenflußnetzes (DFN) graphisch dargestellt,
- die Aufgabe jeder einzelnen Funktion wird in Kurzinfos (KI) festgehalten,
- im Datenlexikon (DL) beschreibt man, wie die Datenflüsse und Dateien des Systems strukturell aufgebaut sind.

Dieser Vorgang ist durch das untenstehende Datenflußnetz dargestellt. Für jede der

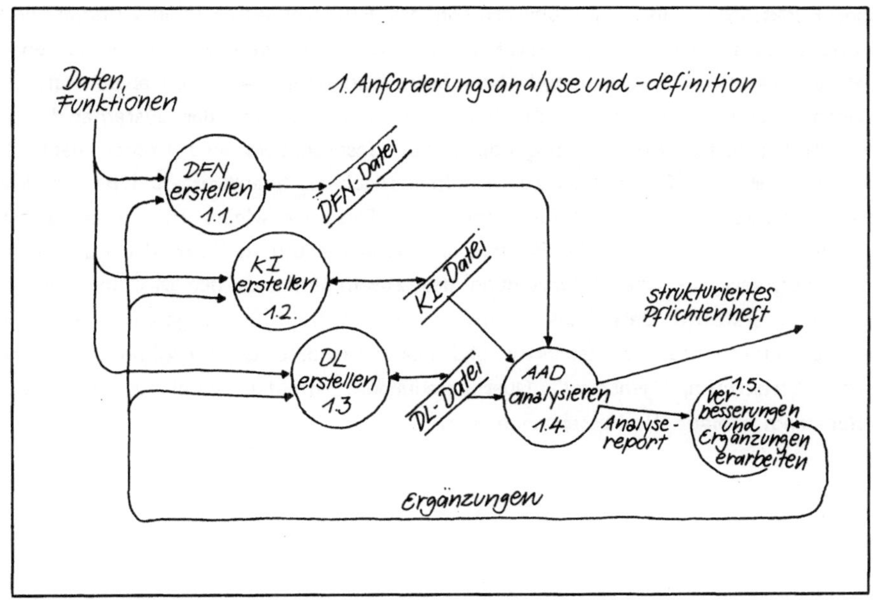

Erfassungstätigkeiten wird ein interaktives, rechnergestütztes Werkzeug zur Verfügung gestellt, das den Systemanalytiker bei der Erarbeitung eines funktionalen Modells des realen Systems unterstützt.

Sind alle drei Teile erfaßt, so kann ein Analyseprogramm die Zusammenhänge zwischen den Teilen feststellen, Inkonsistenzen suchen, Querverweise erzeugen, Prüfungen und Optimierungen durchführen und dem Systemanalytiker die Ergebnisse zur Verfügung stellen. Dessen Aufgabe ist dann, aufgrund der Analysen Verbesserungen zu erarbeiten, weitere Angaben vom Kunden zu erfragen und dadurch das Modell weiter zu vervollständigen. Bei diesem iterativen Vorgang gehen Analyse und Definition Hand in Hand. Zu jedem Zeitpunkt hat man das bereits angesammelte Wissen in geordneter und übersichtlicher Form verfügbar. Sobald alle Informationen über ein geplantes System eingearbeitet sind, stellt der Analysator als Ergebnis dieser Phase ein strukturiertes Pflichtenheft zur Verfügung, das als Vertragsbasis zwischen dem Kunden und dem Systemersteller dienen kann.

Systementwurf (SE)

Ziel der Systementwurfsphase ist es, aus den Funktionen, die im strukturierten Pflichtenheft aufgeführt sind, ein hierarchisches, modulares System abzuleiten. Dabei sollen die Moduln intern eine sehr starke Bindung aufweisen, untereinander aber nur lose gekoppelt sein. Solche Strukturen erreicht man durch Anwendung der Konzepte des strukturierten Entwurfs /MYE75, STE80/ und durch Verwendung eines Schichtenmodells. Das zugrundegelegte Modulkonzept basiert auf abstrakten Datentypen, Information Hiding und dem Zusammenfassen gleichartiger Funktionen. Eine erste Umformung des Pflichtenheftes kann automatisch durch Transformationsanalyse /DEM79/ gewonnen werden. Dabei werden aus den Schichten des in der AAD-Phase erstellten Systemmodells Schichten abstrakter Maschinen abgeleitet. Die dabei entstehende Modulstruktur kann natürlich nur so gut sein, wie der Systemanalytiker die Regeln der strukturierten Analyse eingehalten hat. Insbesonders sind Fragen nach Zusammenfassung von mehreren Funktionen zu Moduln kritisch zu beantworten. Die Struktur wird dann interaktiv weiterbearbeitet. Dafür stehen dem Designer wieder Hilfsmittel zur Verfügung. Ein Prozessor erlaubt ihm die Beschreibung von Moduln in Form der Funktionen, die dieses Modul definiert und die Beschreibung des Zusammenhangs der Moduln. Auch das in der ersten Phase erstellte Datenlexikon wird weiter gepflegt und ergänzt. Der Analysator untersucht die entstandene Modulstruktur und das erweiterte Datenlexikon (EDL), erkennt pathologische Strukturen, generiert Querbeziehungen, meldet nicht zusammenpassende Schnittstellen und schlägt Verbesserungen vor.

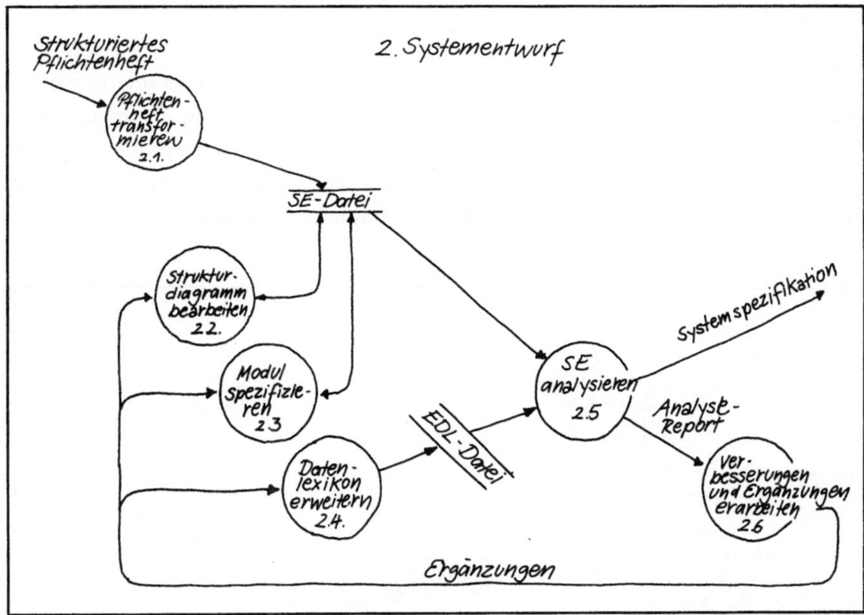

Danach liegt es wieder beim Designer, diese Ergebnisse zu verwerten, neue Ideen zu produzieren und in das System zu integrieren.

Die fertige Systemspezifikation enthält verschiedene Dokumente, wie z.B. die Modulstruktur des Gesamtsytems, alle einzelnen Module mit Parametrisierung der Funktionen und die bisher auftretenden Daten (,für die sowohl die Struktur als auch die Verwendungsstellen angegeben werden). Insbesonders werden auch Metriken erstellt, die eine Bewertung der entworfenen Struktur ermöglichen und dadurch wertvolle Hinweise für eine Verbesserung geben /KTG81/.

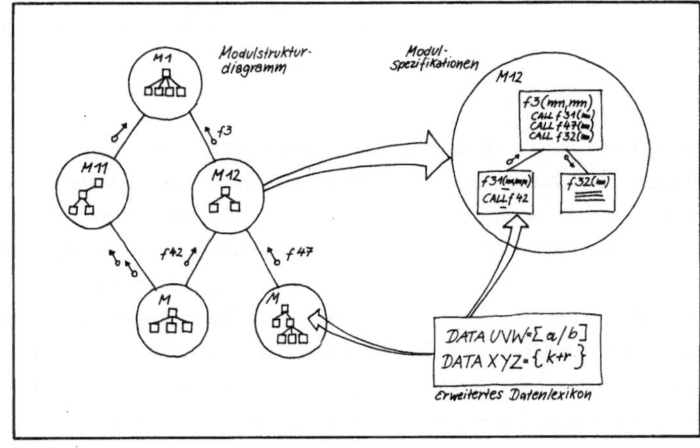

Die Metriken stützen sich auf Untersuchungen der Komplexität von Moduln, ihrer Zusammenhänge, der Art der Verbindungen (Benutztrelation, Zyklenfreiheit) und Abweichungen von der als ideal angesehenen Baumstruktur.

Programmentwurf (PE)

Was nach Abschluß der Systementwurfsphase noch zu endgültigen Programmiervorgabe fehlt, sind einerseits die detaillierte Beschreibung der Algorithmen und die Zuordnung der Datendefinitionen zu den Algorithmen. Zur exakten Formulierung von Algorithmen bewährten sich seit langem unsere auf Pseudocode basierenden Prozessoren PDL (Program Design Language) /CAI75/ und DARTS (Design Aid for Real-Time Systems) /KTG80/.

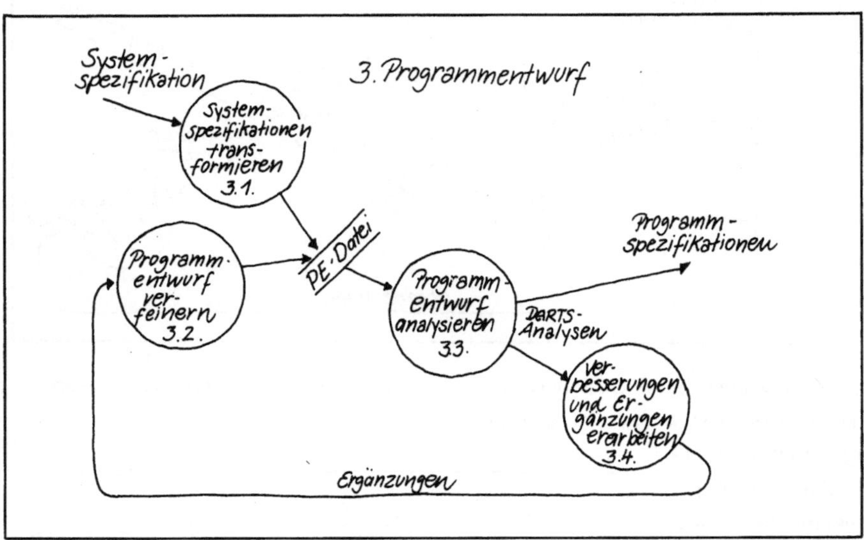

Im ersten Schritt wird die Systemspezifikation in einen Programmentwurf umgesetzt. Dabei werden die Daten aus dem Datenlexikon an den Stellen in die Funktionen integriert, an denen sie bei heute gängigen prozedur- und blockorientierten Sprachen geschrieben werden müssen. In einem ähnlichen, iterativen Prozeß wie bei den vorigen Phasen kann der Designer nun seine Algorithmen bis zu dem Level verfeinern, der zur Umsetzung in die verwendete Programmiersprache notwendig ist. Die notwendigen Konsistenzprüfung während dieser Phase werden vom DARTS-Prozessor durchgeführt. Nach Abschluß der Entwurfsphase steht dem Designer eine codierfertige Programmspezifikation zur Verfügung, die unter Verwendung der Single-Source-Philosophie (Code und Kommentar stehen auf einer Quelldatei) weiter bearbeitet werden kann.

Zusammenfassung

Durch die Auswahl von einigen bekannten Methoden, die bei der Projektabwicklung und bei der Softwareerstellung einheitliche Grundphilosophien aufweisen entstand ein einfaches, durchgängiges Modell zur Systemerstellung. Alle Phasen dieses Modells laufen rechnergestützt ab. Dadurch werden insbesonders die Probleme an den Schnittstellen zwischen den Phasen auf ein Minimum reduziert. Jedes einzelne Werkzeug dieses Methodenpakets ist für sich betrachtet sehr klein, leicht handhabbar und unabhängig von anderen einsetzbar. Dies ermöglicht eine stufenweise Einführung der Methoden in die Praxis und verringert den Ausbildungsaufwand für Systemanalytiker, Designer und Programmierer. Die verwendeten Methoden sind seit Jahren in der Industrie erprobt. Die GEI setzt seit 1979 PDL und seit 1980 verstärkt Structured Analysis, Structured Design und DARTS in verschiedenen Bereichen ein. Die Rechnerunterstützung, die bis Ende 1981 als Pilotversion fertiggestellt sein wird, läßt durch die Reduzierung des Verwaltungsaufwandes von Projekten aus eine noch höhere Akzeptanz und noch bessere Effizienz hoffen.

Literatur:

/DEM79/ T. DeMarco
Structured Analysis and System Specification
Yourdon Press, 1979

/STE80/ W.P. Stevens
Using Structured Design
Wiley, 1980

/MYE75/ G.J. Myers
Reliable Software through Composite Design
Van Nostrand Reinhold Company, 1975

/DDH72/ O.-J. Dahl, E.W. Dijkstra, C.A.R. Hoare
Structured Programming
Academic Press, 1972

/KTG81/ H. Keutgen
Eine Metrik zur Bewertung der Modularisierung
gleiche Publikation

/CAI75/ S.H. Caine, E.K. Gordon
PDL - A Tocl for Software Design
Proc. NCC 1975

/KTG80/ H. Keutgen, H.-H. Meyer
DARTS - Ein Softwareentwurfssystem für Echtzeitprogramme
in: Informatik Fachberichte, GI - 10. Jahrestagung
Springer Verlag, 1980

Erfahrungen beim softwareorientierten Entwurf eines portablen Betriebsleitsystems des öffentlichen Personennahverkehrs

von Dr.Walter Sonnenberg
Institut für Angewandte Informatik, Transport- und Verkehrssysteme
der Universität Karlsruhe

1. Einführung

Als Betriebsleitsystem wird im öffentlichen Personenverkehr ein Informationssystem bezeichnet, das dem Betreiber der Verkehrsmittel einen vollständigen und genauen Überblick über den Betriebszustand gibt und ihm damit erlaubt, kurzfristig dispositiv oder längerfristig planend sein Verkehrsangebot qualitativ zu verbessern und den Einsatz der Verkehrsmittel zu optimieren /Girnau/.

Ohne Datenfunk waren der zentralen Erfassung von Fahrzeugstandorten, Fahrplanlagen etc restriktive Grenzen gesetzt. Erst durch den Einsatz zentraler Rechenanlagen, die über Datenfunk mit den Fahrzeugen ständig kommunizieren, ist eine Echtzeitdisposition möglich. In den 70-er Jahren entstanden erste Prototypen rechnergesteuerter Betriebsleitsysteme (RBL). Mit der Entwicklung des BON-Systems (Betriebsleitsystem für den öffentlichen Nahverkehr) bei der USTRA, Hannoversche Verkehrsbetriebe AG, beginnt eine Phase der Normierung und STANDARDISIERUNG, die einer weiteren Verbreitung der Betriebsleitsysteme vorausgehen muß.

Unter dem Entwicklungsziel der Standardisierung sind vor allem die Unterziele der RECHNERUNABHÄNGIGKEIT = PORTABILITÄT sowie der ADAPTIERBARKEIT an veränderliche Randbedingungen und wachsende Aufgaben weitgehende Anforderungen an die BON-Software und an die Hilfsmittel von der Softwareerstellung bis zur -wartung. Trotzdem müssen mögliche Rechnerkonfigurationen und Rechnerlasten ausgelotet werden, um für die marktgängigen Rechner Software ausreichender Effizienz zu erhalten.

* diese Arbeit entstand im Rahmen des Forschungsvorhabens BON der *
* USTRA, Hannoversche Verkehrsbetriebe AG mit Förderung durch *
* das Bundesministerium für Forschung und Technologie (TV 79615) *

Wir berichten über unsere Erfahrungen beim Systementwurf in der Reihenfolge unserer Projektphasen bis zu der Programmcodierung. Die Testphasen laufen erst an.

2. Grobkonzept

Aufgrund der betrieblichen Vorgaben der Hannoverschen Verkehrsbetriebe (USTRA), die über die Gremien des Verbandes öffentlicher Verkehrsbetriebe (VÖV) abgesichert werden, wurde zuerst ein Software-Funktionskonzept standardisierter Betriebsleitsysteme entwickelt. Dies soll in verschiedenen Ausbaustufen und verschiedenen Varianten eingesetzt werden können, um unterschiedlichen Betreiberanforderungen und Betriebsgrößen gerecht zu werden. Über notwendige und mögliche Rechnerausrüstungen der Leitzentralen wurde erst sekundär gesprochen.

Im ersten Anlauf wurden aus den Begriffen der betrieblichen Aufgabenstellung solche herausgefiltert, für die Programmmoduln zu realisieren sind. Diese Moduln sind funktionale Instanzen, die jeweils einen abgeschlossenen Teilbereich der Aufgabenstellung vollständig bearbeiten sollen. Ihre interne Realisierung soll nach dem "Geheimnisprinzip" von /Parnas/ unabhängig von der aller anderen Moduln gewählt werden können.

Z.B. wurden hier Moduln für den Fahrplan Soll/Ist-Vergleich, eine Fahrzeugstatustabelle, eine Fahrplanvorlage und das Liniennetz definiert.

Insgesamt erhielten wir über 30 derartige Moduln. Einzelne Moduln waren noch zuwenig gegeneinander abgegrenzt. Deswegen wurden im zweiten Durchgang solche Moduln zusammengefaßt, die bei späteren Programmrevisionen voraussichtlich zusammen abzuändern wären, sei es daß während der Programmentwicklung Fehler zu korrigieren oder sei es daß Weiterentwicklungen zur Berücksichtigung neuer Randbedingungen oder zur Bearbeitung neuer Aufgabenstellungen notwendig wären. Dadurch entstanden die von uns sogenannten Modulpakete.

Die oben beispielsweise aufgezählten Moduln wurden im Paket SOLL/IST-VERGLEICH zusammengefaßt. Eine Übersicht über alle Modulpakete enthält Bild 1:

- *FAHRZEUGAUFRUF koordiniert den Datenverkehr zwischen der Zentrale und den Fahrzeugen.*
- *FUNKBEDIENUNG stellt Fahrzeugmeldungen dar, vermittelt Funkgespräche zwischen Disponent und Fahrer und leitet codierte Anweisungen an die Fahrzeuge weiter.*
- *STANDORTVERFOLGUNG rechnet von den Fahrzeugen übergebene Wegzählerstände in Streckennetzkoordinaten um und stößt ortsabhängige Steuermaßnahmen an (z.B. Beeinflußung von Lichtsignalanlagen).*
- *SOLL-VORGABEN enthält Editoren zur Eingabe und Änderung der Fahrzeugbestandslisten, Verkehrsnetzbeschreibungen, Fahrpläne und Bilddarstellungen der Betriebsinformation.*

- *SOLL/IST-VERGLEICH ermittelt Fahrplanabweichungen und erkennt elementare Störungssituationen.*
- *BETRIEBSINFORMATION stellt dem Disponenten grafische und tabellarische Darstellungen des Betriebszustandes und Formulare für Störungsmeldungen zur Verfügung.*
- *STATISTIK sammelt Kenndaten und wertet sie statistisch aus.*
- *DISPOSITION BEI STÖRFÄLLEN analysiert Störungen, schlägt dispositive Reaktionen vor und unterstützt bei deren Durchführung.*
- *EXTERNE KOPPLUNGEN stellen Verbindungen zu anderen Leitzentralen zwecks Fahrzeugübergabe, zu Verkehrsrechnern zwecks LSA-Beeinflußung, zu Stellwerken zur Vorgabe von Prioritäten, zu Fahrgastinformationsrechnern und zu Einrichtungen zur Erfassung von Fahrtwünschen bei bedarfsgesteuerter Verkehrsbedienung her.*
- *TECHNISCHE DIAGNOSE erfaßt Störungen an Fahrzeuggeräten, Funkgeräten und Ortssendern und unterstützt die Fehlersuche an diesen Geräten.*
- *BEDARFSSTEUERUNG optimiert in Echtzeit Fahrplanvorgaben für bedarfsgesteuerte Verkehrsbedienung.*

Der Begriff "Funktionale Modularisierung" wird von uns zur Charakterisierung dieses Entwurfsprozesses benutzt, in dem jeder Modul und jedes Modulpaket eine Instanz mit funktional definierter Aufgabe wird.

3. Hardwarekonzept

Die Fahrzeuge werden mit Mikroprozessorgeräten ausgestattet, die mit den zentralen Rechenanlagen über Datenfunk kommunizieren. *Dazu wird das Sprechfunkgerät des Fahrzeugs mit einem Datenmodem versehen und auf einen Datenfunkkanal umgeschaltet. Der Sprechfunkkanal wird im Regelbetrieb nur auf besondere Anforderung benutzt. Beim Ausfall des Fahrzeugrechners oder des Datenfunkträgersignals wird das Sprechfunksystem als Rückfallebene genutzt.*

Für je einen Datenfunkduplexkanal wird ein mit dem Fahrzeugrechner weitgehend baugleiches Mikroprozessorgerät als Funkinterface in der Zentrale eingesetzt.

Die zentrale Rechenanlage wird vorerst aus drei Rechnern zusammengesetzt,

einem Basisrechner,
einem Dispositionsrechner und
einem stand-by-Rechner

Der BASISRECHNER *übernimmt die Basisaufgaben FAHRZEUGAUFRUF, FUNKBEDIENUNG und STANDORTVERFOLGUNG, sowie die damit eng verbundenen Funktionen der TECHNISCHEN DIAGNOSE und die EXTERNEN KOPPLUNGEN zu anderen Leitrechnern, zu Stellwerken und zur LSA-Beeinflußung. Diese Funktionen erbringen eine* fast gleichmäßige Rechnerauslastung ohne wesentliche externe Eingriffmöglichkeiten. Fehlerträchtige Hardware wird nicht benötigt. Dieser Rechner bietet dem Betrieb ein Informationssystem mit minimalem Komfort, *das die Fahrzeugstandorte nach verschiedenen Ordnungskriterien auflisten kann (Modul Basisbetriebsinformation im Paket FUNKBEDIENUNG),* das noch nach Ausfall zweier zentraler Rechner funktionsfähig bleibt.

Arbeiten mit ungleichmäßiger Rechnerauslastung und aufwendiger Hintergrundperipherie fallen dem DISPOSITIONSRECHNER zu. *Der SOLL-IST-VERGLEICH ist hier wegen aufwendiger Fahrplanunterlagen angesiedelt. Die Datenerfassung zur STATISTIK erfordert Massenspeicher. BETRIEBSINFORMATION und DISPOSITION werden auf Anforderung des Disponenten aktiv und können im Einzelfall erhebliche CPU- und Peripherielasten zur Folge haben.*

Der STAND-BY-RECHNER soll bei Bedarf *(z.B. bei Hardwareausfällen oder bei Wartungsarbeiten)* die Arbeiten des Basis- oder des Dispositionsrechners übernehmen. *Sonst wird er mit Hintergrundarbeiten beschäftigt, z.B. zur Eingabe der SOLL-VORGABEN oder für offline-STATISTIK-Auswertungen.*

Für die BEDARFSSTEUERUNG wird diese Zentrale voraussichtlich erweitert werden. Die dazu benötigte Software soll aus einem anderen Projekt übernommen werden.

Jeder DISPONENTENARBEITSPLATZ wird mit einem separaten Mikrorechner ausgerüstet. Dieser verwaltet drei semigrafische Farbmonitore und eine Tastatur. Er besitzt je eine serielle Schnittstelle zum Basisrechner *(FUNKBEDIENUNG)* und zum Dispositionsrechner *(BETRIEBSINFORMATION)*. Darüberhinaus können weitere nicht direkt zum RBL-System gehörende Geräte *z.B. Fernsehmonitore für die Haltestellenüberwachung* gesteuert werden, um die Anzahl verschiedener Tastaturen und Monitore am Leittisch zu minimieren.

4. Schnittstellenstrukturierung

Zwischen den Moduln und Modulpaketen aus der ersten Phase existieren Schnittstellen, deren Verfeinerung für den weiteren Projektablauf der Programmerstellung als kritisch angesehen wurde. Daher haben wir uns erstens von vornherein auf besonders robuste, sogenannte Funktions-Schnittstellen beschränkt und zweitens diese weitgehend formalisiert unter den Projektpartnern abgestimmt.

FUNKTIONS-SCHNITTSTELLEN sind gegenüber Daten-Schnittstellen bei Programmänderungen WENIGER FEHLERTRÄCHTIG. Bei der Änderung des Layouts von Datenbereichen, der Datencodierung und ähnlich häufiger Eingriffe bewirken Daten-Schnittstellen, daß auch alle auf die Daten zugreifenden Moduln abzuändern sind. Bei Funktions-Schnittstellen werden Änderungen dieser Art durch die im selben Modul realisierten Schnittstellenfunktionen abgefangen, außerhalb des Moduls werden keine funktionellen Folgewirkungen spürbar. Durch konsequente Anwendung von Funktionsschnittstellen bei der modularen Datenorganisation entsteht der sogenannte Datentypmodul, dessen Daten nur mittelbar über Zugriffsfunktionen zugänglich sind (Bei *Goos&Kastens* Moduln der Klasse 4).

SYNCHRONISIERUNGSMAẞNAHMEN zum Schutz der Konsistenz modulinterner Daten beschränken sich auf die Funktionen des Moduls, sie TRETEN NICHT NACH AUẞEN IN ERSCHEINUNG. Der Modul ist daher ein verallgemeinerter Monitor */Hoare/*. Ein Aufrufer kann durch eine Synchronisierung verzögert werden, erhält jedoch keine Kenntnis über die interne Technik der Synchronisierung. Echtzeitrandbedingungen treten folglich nur als Laufzeitbeschränkungen oder Reihenfolgebedingungen auf.

Um umfangreiche Reihenfolgebedingungen zu vermeiden, erhielten einige Schnittstellenfunktionen STRUKTURIERTE RESULTATE. Damit ist der gesamte Ablauf zwischen Beginn und Ende einer Synchronisierungsmaßnahme im selben Modul ausprogrammiert. Dagegen können zwischen den Aufrufen von Schnittstellenfunktionen mit Reihenfolgebedingungen außerhalb des Moduls unkontrollierbare Zeitprobleme induziert werden.

5. Feinstrukturierung

Die ersten Produktionsphasen können unabhängig von Rechnertypen und Programmiersprachen durchgeführt werden. Bei der Feinstrukturierung werden die Modulpakete strukturell verfeinert, die Modulebene überarbeitet, Moduln in Submoduln und Einzelkomponenten untergliedert. Auf der tiefsten Ebene dieser Modularisierungshierarchie werden die Schnittstellenfunktionen eingeordnet. Die Abschlußberichte der Produktionsphasen sind nach dem gleichen Hierarchieschema aufgebaut. Auf der unteren Berichtsgliederungsebene werden in jeder Produktionsphase phasenspezifische Standardkapitel ergänzt. AM ENDE ERGEBEN DIE GESAMMELTEN PHASENBERICHTE DIE PROGRAMMDOKUMENTATION.

Mit der Verfeinerung der Komponentenhierarchie war auch die Ausarbeitung der Daten- und Kontrollstrukturen verbunden. Dabei mußten die ARBEITSMETHODEN NACH DER AUFGABENSTELLUNG DIFFERENZIERT werden:

- die meisten Pakete wurden datenstrukturorientiert bearbeitet. *Bei FAHRZEUGAUFRUF, FUNKBEDIENUNG, STATISTIK und TECHNISCHE DIAGNOSE sind die Datenstrukturen auf die Fahrzeuge ausgerichtet, bei STANDORTVERFOLGUNG, SOLL/IST-VERLEICH und SOLL-VORGABEN geben die Beschreibungen des Betriebsnetzes, der Linien, ihrer Fahrwege, der Fahr- und Dienstpläne die Struktur vor, bei der BETRIEBSINFORMATION wird die Struktur durch Bildinhalte bestimmt.*
- Echtzeitbedingungen *waren für FAHRZEUGAUFRUF, STANDORTVERFOLGUNG und SOLL/IST-VERGLEICH* erst in zweiter Linie betrachtet worden. Dabei gab es jedoch erhebliche Rückwirkungen auf die Schnittstellen *zu FUNKBEDIENUNG und BETRIEBSINFORMATION* (vgl. Kap. 4 letzter Absatz).
- Bei der Rechnerauswahl wurden Probleme mit Adreßraumbeschränkungen auf allen Rechnern offenbar, für die derzeit PEARL implementiert war (sämtlich 16 bit-Strukturen). *Daher haben wir Datenstrukturen auf diese Rechnerstrukturen hin unterteilt und mögliche Programmcodeüberlagerungen*

diskutiert und vorbereitet. Durch Erweiterung der Firmware der bestellten Rechner wurde diese Situation inzwischen entschärft. Bei der Ubertragung der Software auf andere Rechner wird an dieser Stelle sicherlich noch Arbeit anfallen.

- *FUNKBEDIENUNG, BETRIEBSINFORMATION, DISPOSITION und SOLL-VORGABEN realisieren ein* Mensch-Maschine-Interface. *Hierzu waren Entwürfe zu Bedienstrategien und Analysen zur Einbindung in die Betriebsorganisation zu erarbeiten. Während für FUNKBEDIENUNG und BETRIEBS-INFORMATION anhand vorhandener RBL-Systeme detaillierte Vorgaben existierten, verursachten DISPOSI-TION und SOLL-VORGABEN hier erheblichen Aufwand.* Die Bedienstrategien induzieren in allen vier Modulpaketen wesentliche Ablaufstrukturen.

6. Programmiervorgaben

Unter idealen Bedingungen hätten wir während der Entwurfsarbeiten über Rechnertypen und Programmiersprachen nicht zu sprechen brauchen. Dennoch haben wir eine Programmiersprache für die spätere Realisierung relativ früh ausgewählt. PEARL verspricht als einzige Programmiersprache bei moderner Programmstrukturierung eine Portabilität auch in Bereichen der Kontrolle paralleler Tasks und der Ein/Ausgabe.

Durch die Abstraktion mit Funktionen und Datentypen zur Parameterdefinition lag eine "natürliche" Umsetzung in PROCEDURE- und TYPE-Programmstrukturen nahe. Wir setzen daher über Basis PEARL hinaus entsprechende Sprachelemente von Full PEARL ein.

PROCEDUREs werden in den PEARL-Implementierungen nach der Technik der geschlossenen Unterprogramme in Objektcode umgesetzt. Durch unsere funktionalen Abstraktionen sind die Funktionen oft in der Realisierung wenig aufwendig, so daß der Verwaltungsaufwand für Prozeduraufrufe und Parameteranschlußmechanismen zu erheblichen Ineffizienzen führt. Die Codeumsetzung nach der Technik offener Unterprogramme (auch als Makros bekannt) wäre hier effizienter. Wir haben dies durch einen einfachen Präprozessor zur Programmtextmanipulation in PEARL realisiert.

PEARL enthält, wie die meisten anderen Programmiersprachen auch, keine sprachlichen Hilfsmittel, mit denen verschiedene Programmvarianten im Quelltext nebeneinander realisiert und vor der Umsetzung in Objektcode die gewünschten Varianten ausgewählt werden können. Ein solches Hilfsmittel ist bei unserer Aufgabenstellung aber unbedingt notwendig, wenn ein wartbares Produkt entstehen soll. Da das Programmprodukt außerdem portabel sein soll, muß auch ein solches Hilfsprogramm portabel sein *(s. auch /Winkler/)*. Dies leistet unser Präprozessor, der im PEARL-Quellprogramm vor der Ubersetzung die ungewünschten Varianten eliminiert und betreiberspezifische Parameter einsetzt.

7. Schlußbetrachtungen

Beim Entwurf des BON-Systems hat sich die HARDWARE UND SOFTWARE INTEGRIERENDE, teilweise formalisierte VORGEHENSWEISE FUNKTIONALER MODULARISIERUNG BEWÄHRT. Es entstand eine Systemstruktur, die sowohl verschiedene Betriebsgrößen als auch unterschiedliche Betreiberwünsche bezüglich Funktionsumfang und Leitstellenausrüstung in der Betriebsleittechnik abdeckt.

Die Ziele der Adaptierbarkeit und Portabilität können mit Einschränkungen erreicht werden. Die ADAPTIERBARKEIT WURDE IN ANSÄTZEN BEREITS NACHGEWIESEN, indem Ubergangslösungen zum Anschluß von Teilsystemen aus einem älteren Prototyp-Leitsystem und nachträgliche Änderungen der betrieblichen Aufgabenstellung problemlos eingefügt werden konnten. Der Nachweis der Portabilität wird erst in ca. 1 1/2 Jahren möglich sein.

ADAPTIERBARKEIT UND PORTABILITÄT werden nicht aufgrund passender Hilfsmittel wie Programmiersprachen o.ä. erzielt, sondern ERGEBEN SICH AUS EINER WEITGEHEND VON DER IMPLEMENTIERUNG UNABHÄNGIGEN BEARBEITUNG DES PROGRAMMENTWURFS UND EINER PROGRAMMCODIERUNG MIT GEGENÜBER IMPLEMENTIERUNGEN INVARIANTEN KONSTRUKTIONEN. Hierzu bieten höhere Programmiersprachen geeignete Formulierungshilfen, PEARL insbesondere auch für die bei dieser Anwendung wichtigen Tasksteuerung und Ein/Ausgabe. Zur effizienten Programmcodierung und für die Manipulation von Programmvarianten mußte ein sprachfremder Präprozessor zu Hilfe genommen werden.

Literatur

*Girnau,G: Betriebsleitsysteme aus der Sicht des VÖV
in VDI Fortschrittsberichte Reihe 12, No 38, VDI-Verlag, Düsseldorf 1979*

Forschungsvorhaben BON: Betriebliche Anforderungen zur Entwicklung und Erprobung eines standardisierten Betriebsleitsystems für den ÖPNV Hannoversche Verkehrsbetriebe (USTRA) 1979

*Goos, G & Kastens, U: Programming languages and the design of modular programs
in Hibbard, P. G. & Schuman, S. A: constructing quality software, IFIP North - Holland (78) 153-186*

*Gruhl,A & Sonnenberg,W: Software-Dokumentation (Handbuch)
Forschungsvorhaben BON, USTRA Hannover 1980*

*Parnas, D.L: On the criteria to be used in decomposing systems into modules
CACM 15(12-72)1053-1058*

*Hoare, C.A.R: Monitors: an operating system structuring concept
CACM 17(10-74)549-557 + Corrigendum CACM 18(2-75)95*

Schweizer,G. & Sonnenberg,W. & Fritsche,D: Erfahrungen mit funktionaler Modularisierung beim Entwurf der Realzeitsoftware eines portablen Betriebsleitsystems des öffentlichen Nahverkehrs
GI-GMR Prozeßrechner '81 Springer Verlag IFB 39 p356-365

Winkler, J. & Stoffel, G:
Methoden zur Betriebssystemgenerierung und Modularisierung für Prozeßrechnensysteme

DIN 66253 Informationsverarbeitung: Programmiersprache PEARL
Teil 1 Basic PEARL, Beuth Verlag, 1978
Teil 2 Full PEARL, Beuth Verlag, 1979

Bild 1
BON und Software Hardware

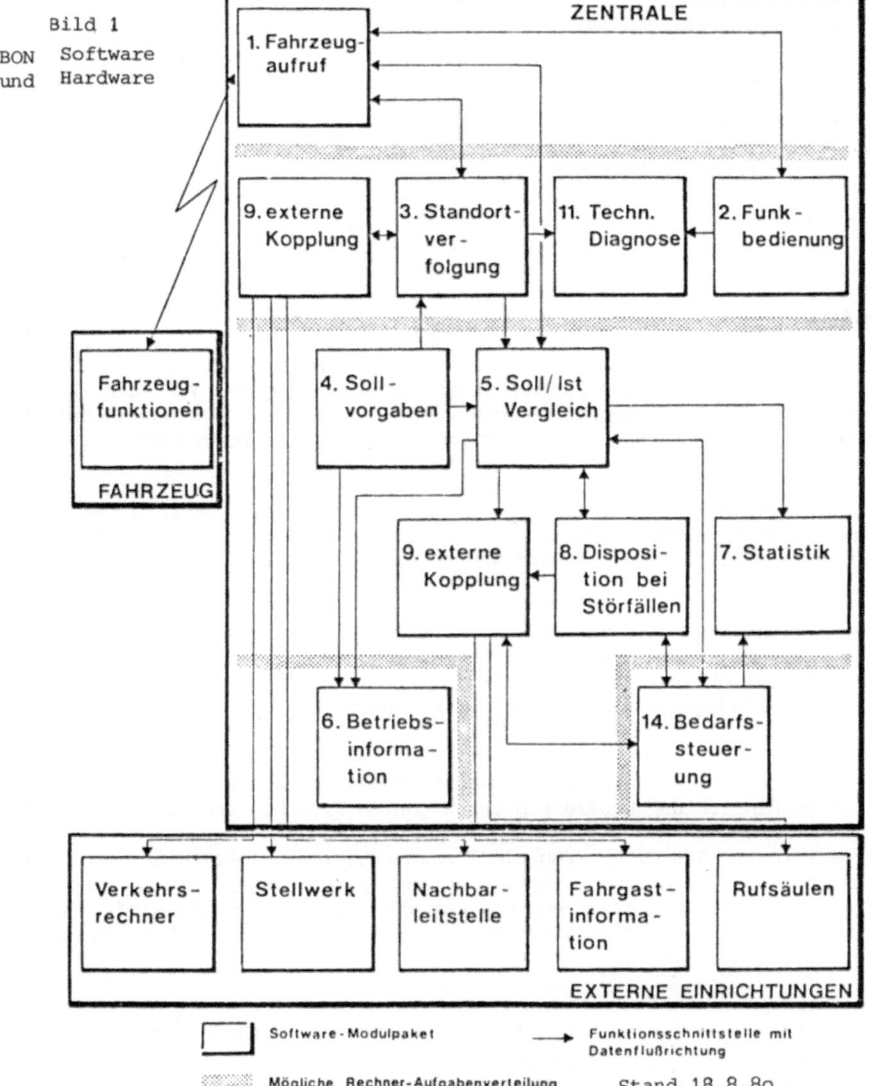

Stand 18.8.80

EINIGE BEMERKUNGEN ZUM VERSTÄNDNIS NEBENLÄUFIGER PROZESSE UND SYSTEME

Reinhard Budde

Institut für Software-Technologie
Gesellschaft für Mathematik und Datenverarbeitung mbH
Postfach 1240, D-5205 St.Augustin 1

<u>Inhalt</u>

1 Einleitung

Dieser Beitrag beschreibt ein System- und Prozeßverständnis für den Entwurf dezentraler Systeme. Viele Überlegungen sind der RELATIVITÄTSTHEORIE entlehnt und auf die DISKRETEN PROZESSE UND SYSTEME der Informationsverarbeitung angewandt worden.

Ein relativistischer Effekt tritt in der Physik dann auf, wenn die Zeit zwischen dem Abschicken eines Signals an ein anderes System und der Antwort des anderen Systems nicht vernachlässigt werden darf (wie das die klassische Physik tut).

Bei informationsverarbeitenden Systemen treten relativistische Efekte gut meßbar in Erscheinung, wenn die Verarbeitungsgeschwindigkeit von Signalen in den einzelnen Komponenten eines DV-Systems in der gleichen Größenordnung liegt wie die Signalgeschwindigkeit zwischen diesen Komponenten. Das ist beispielsweise der Fall

- beim Schaltwerksentwurf, wenn die Verarbeitungsgeschwindigkeit einzelner Gatter im Bereich der Laufzeiten von Signalen zwischen den Gattern liegt, oder
- bei dezentralen Systemen, wenn die Transportgeschwindigkeit für Nachrichten durch die Geschwindigkeit der Übertragungsleitungen, durch Hard- und Software-Systeme in Knoten- und Endrechnern soweit abgesenkt wird, daß sie im Bereich der Verarbeitungsgeschwindigkeit für die Nachrichten in der Anwendungssoftware liegt.

Ziel dieses Beitrages ist es, ein Prozeß- und Systemverständnis zu skizzieren, von dem ich hoffe, daß es GRUNDLAGE für die Ausarbeitung sicherer Kommunikationsstrukturen dezentraler Systeme sein kann. Wesentliche Arbeiten stammen von C.A. Petri ([1, 2, 3] in [4]) und A. Holt [5, 6]. Auf mathematische Formulierungen ist soweit wie möglich verzichtet worden, siehe dazu [7, 8].

2 Kausalität und Zeit

Viele Modelle enthalten implizit oder explizit die Annahme, daß alle Erscheinungen in der Zeit TOTAL GEORDNET sind. Das bedeutet, daß von zwei Erscheinungen eine entweder vor, nach oder aber zugleich mit der zweiten stattfindet. Das wird häufig "Existenz einer globalen Zeit" genannt. Diese Annahme ist der klassischen Physik entlehnt. Dort wird die Totalordnung von Ereignissen aber abgeleitet, und nicht wie ein Axiom vorausgesetzt.

So sagt KANT bei der philosophischen Begründung der klassischen Physik: Die Bestimmung von Erscheinungen in der Zeit "kann nun nicht von dem Verhältnis der Erscheinungen gegen die absolute Zeit entlehnt werden, (denn die ist kein Gegenstand der Wahrnehmung) sondern umgekehrt, die Erscheinungen müssen einander ihre Stellen in der Zeit selbst bestimmen" [9].

Das, was Erscheinungen ihre Stelle in der Zeit zuordnet, ist das KAUSALVERHÄLTNIS:

Wenn eine Erscheinung A Ursache einer Erscheinung B ist, (A —> B oder A verursacht B), dann ist deren zeitliche Reihenfolge festgelegt (A vor B). GLEICHZEITIGKEIT von Erscheinungen liegt bei WECHSELSEITIGER kausaler Beeinflussung vor (C —> D und D —> C).

Unausgesprochen liegt der klassischen Anschauung die Annahme einer UNENDLICH GROSSEN SIGNALGESCHWINDIGKEIT zugrunde: Gleichzeitige Erscheinungen (an verschiedenen Orten) müssen einander ohne Verzögerung beeinflussen können.

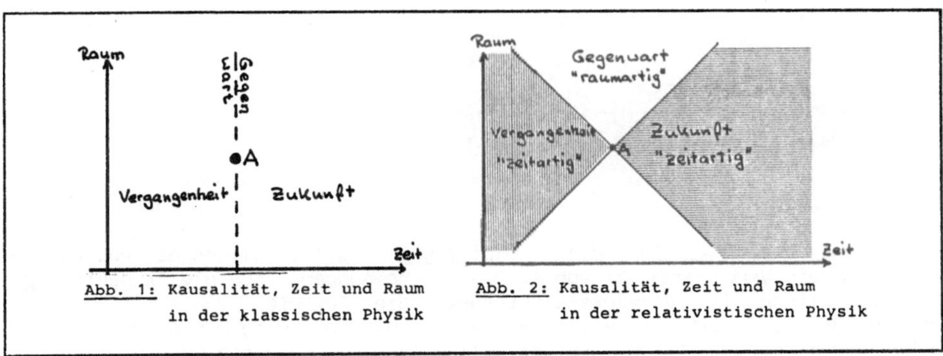

Abb. 1: Kausalität, Zeit und Raum in der klassischen Physik

Abb. 2: Kausalität, Zeit und Raum in der relativistischen Physik

Weil in der Realität die maximale Ausbreitungsgeschwindigkeit von Signalen die LICHTGESCHWINDIGKEIT ist, wird in der Relativitätstheorie das Raum-Zeit-Diagramm der Abb. 1 modifiziert (Abb. 2):

Eine von der Erscheinung A verursachte Erscheinung B muß im VORWÄRTS-LICHTKEGEL von A liegen, da A nur in diesem Bereich Einfluß ausüben kann. Solche Ereignisse heißen ZEITARTIG verbunden, da wegen der kausalen Abhängigkeit B's von A die Zeitordnung A vor B OBJEKTIV ist. Objektiv soll bedeuten: es gibt keinen Beobachter, der ein gegenteiliges Ergebnis "B vor A" feststellen kann.

Anders ist das bei raumartig zueinander liegenden Erscheinungen wie A und C. Sie können einander nicht kausal beeinflussen. Deshalb sind sie nicht durch die Kausalität natürlich geordnet. Verschiedene Beobachter können durchaus für sich A vor C, C vor A oder A gleichzeitig mit C beobachten. Diese Ordnung ist aber vom Beobachter abhängig und in diesem Sinne SUBJEKTIV und nicht objektiv. Für RAUMARTIGE, d.h. kausal unabhängige Erscheinungen ist nur ihre UNORDNUNG objektiv. Objektiv gleichzeitige Erscheinungen sind demnach nur am selben Ort möglich.

Feststellung 1: Schon die Annahme IRGENDEINER objektiven Totalordnung von Erscheinungen schließt eine REALITÄTSGETREUE Modellierung räumlich verteilter Systeme von vornherein aus.

3 Kausalgefüge

"A verursacht B" heißt, daß die Erscheinung A Ursache für die Erscheinung B ist.

"A beeinflußt F" bedeutet, daß eine Menge E1, ..., En existiert mit
A verursacht E1 verursacht E2 ... En verursacht F.
Wenn A beeinflußt F gilt, ist die Zeitordnung A vor F objektiv, ebenso auch F nach A.

Eine durch die Relation beeinflußt zusammenhängende Menge von Erscheinungen ohne Zyklen nenne ich KAUSALGEFÜGE (Abb. 3).

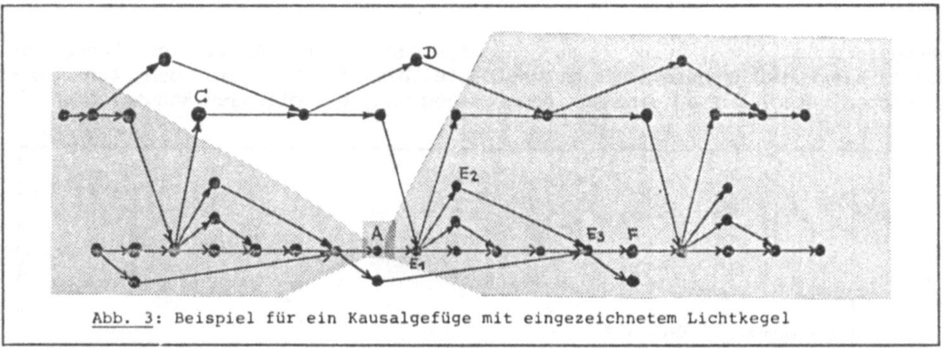

Abb. 3: Beispiel für ein Kausalgefüge mit eingezeichnetem Lichtkegel

Alle Erscheinungen X, für die "X beeinflußt A" gilt, bilden den Rückwärts-Lichtkegel (die Vergangenheit) von A. Die Erscheinungen, für die "A beeinflußt X" gilt, bilden den Vorwärts-Lichtkegel (die Zukunft) von A. Alle diese Erscheinungen sind zeitartig mit A verbunden. Die raumartig mit A verbundenen Erscheinungen, dazu will ich A selbst auch rechnen, bilden die Gegenwart von A. Zu A raumartige Erscheinungen X bezeichne ich als NEBENLÄUFIG (CONCURRENT) zu A und schreibe "X co A".

Für verschiedene Erscheinungen A und B gilt:
genau dann, wenn A beeinflußt B oder B beeinflußt A gilt, gilt NICHT A co B.
Weil beeinflußt eine partielle ORDNUNG ist, kann man deshalb co mit gutem Recht eine UNORDNUNG nennen.

Die Relation co hat folgende Eigenschaften (siehe z.B. Abb. 3):

Es gilt: A co A

Es gilt: Aus A co D folgt D co A

Aber: Aus A co D, D co B folgt NICHT A co B

co ist also nicht transitiv, anders als etwa die Gleichzeitigkeit der klassischen Physik.

Liegen einem Modell transitive Relationen wie die Gleichzeitigkeit zugrunde, so suggeriert der Modellierer, er wüßte genau darüber Bescheid, wie die Dinge wirklich SIND: Bei der Konstruktion solcher Modelle wird davon abgesehen, daß man Dinge erst BEOBACHTEN muß, bevor man Aussagen über sie machen kann. Diese Situation ist PRINZIPIELL weniger klar. Selbst wenn man von den Einflüssen des Beobachters auf das Beobachtete absieht (man denke an Tests in Realzeitsystemen), kann man zwar über zwei Dinge sagen: "Ich kann sie NICHT UNTERSCHEIDEN", aber niemals "Sie sind gleich". Die Ununterscheidbarkeit beim Beobachten ist aber nicht transitiv, wie folgendes Gedankenexperiment zeigt. Deshalb kann man das nichttransitive co auch UNUNTERSCHEIDBARKEITSRELATION oder ÄHNLICHKEITSRELATION nennen.

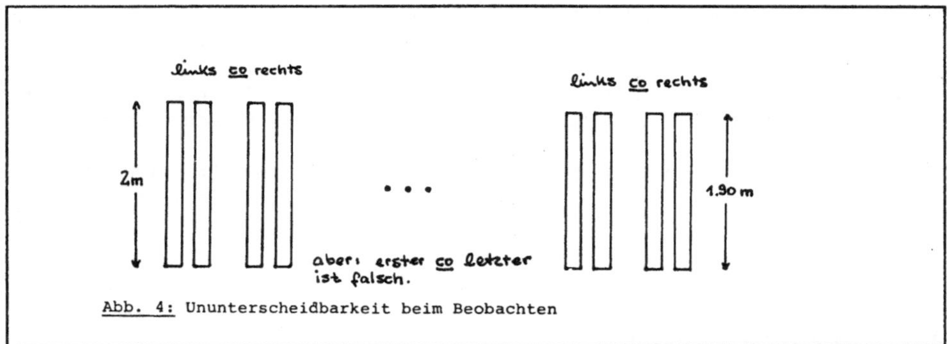

Abb. 4: Ununterscheidbarkeit beim Beobachten

Aus 5 m Entfernung werden zwei Stäbe beobachtet, von denen der linke 2 m lang ist. Der rechte ist

entweder gleich (+- 0.001 mm) dem linken
oder 1 mm (+- 0.001 mm) kürzer.

Der Beobachter kann nicht unterscheiden, ob der erste oder zweite Fall vorliegt. Nun wird ein neuer Stab rechts neben den verbliebenen gestellt, der auch entweder gleich seinem linken Nachbar ist oder 1 mm kürzer. Dieser ganze Vorgang wird so oft wiederholt, bis 100 mal ein kürzerer rechter Stab verwendet wurde. Obwohl bei den Vergleichen die Längen von je zwei Stäben für den Beobachter ununterscheidbar sind, kann er trotzdem leicht den ersten (2 m langen) Stab vom letzten (1.90 m langen) unterscheiden: Die Ununterscheidbarkeitsrelation ist nicht transitiv.

Feststellung 2: Weil man nicht modellieren kann, wie die Dinge "an sich" sind, sondern nur wie man sie beobachtet, sollte eine nicht transitive, aber reflexive Relation wie co (und dazugehörige Teilordnungen wie vor und nach) Grundlage der Modellbildung sein. Transitive Relationen wie gleich (und dazugehörige Totalordnungen) verzerren das Bild, da sie Beobachtungsmöglichkeiten unterstellen, die objektiv nicht vorhanden sind.

Unter einer WELTLINIE li (A) verstehe ich eine maximale Menge von Erscheinungen, die paarweise in der Relation beeinflußt stehen.
Ein SCHNITT cut (A) bezeichnet eine maximale Menge von Erscheinungen, die paarweise in der Relation co stehen.

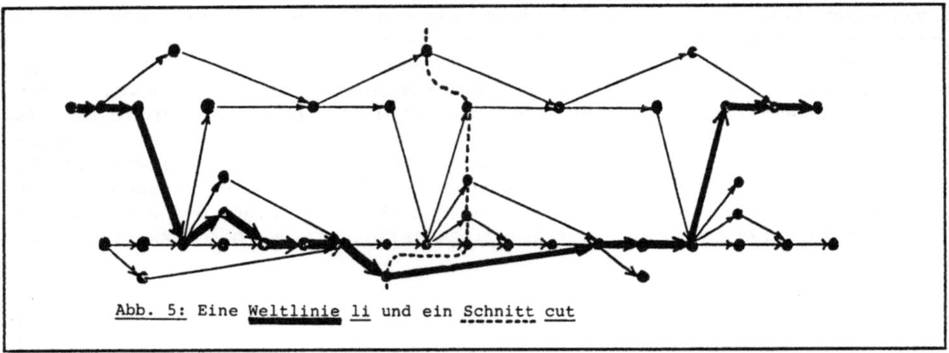

Abb. 5: Eine Weltlinie li und ein Schnitt cut

Die Vereinigung aller li (A) ergibt den Lichtkegel von A, die Vereinigung aller cut (A) die Gegenwart von A. A selbst ist in beiden Vereinigungen enthalten.

Jeder Beobachtung des Kausalgefüges, die A enthält (ein sog. "SCHNAPPSCHUSS"), entspricht genau ein cut (A) .

4 Bedingungen und Ereignisse

Bislang habe ich den Kausalzusammenhang untersucht, ohne weiter auf die Erscheinungen im Kausalgefüge einzugehen. Das soll jetzt geschehen. Ereignisse (Lesen einer Variablen usw.) gehören sicherlich zu den Erscheinungen, die an Kausalgefügen beteiligt sind. Nun hängt der Begriff des Ereignisses mit dem der Veränderung insofern zusammen, als man ein Ereignis nur beobachten kann, wenn sich etwas ändert. Das, worauf Ereignisse wirken, das, was sich ändern kann, nenne ich BEDINGUNGEN. Eine Erscheinung soll nicht zugleich Bedingung und Ereignis sein, denn:

Ein Ereignis kann sich nicht ändern (es kann nur stattfinden), eine Bedingung kann sich nicht ereignen (sie gilt oder gilt nicht). Bedingungen und Ereignisse stehen in folgendem Zusammenhang:

- Eine Bedingung ist genau durch die Ereignisse charakterisiert, die verursachen, daß die Bedingung gilt oder nicht gilt.
- Ein Ereignis läßt sich genau charakterisieren durch die Bedingungen, die vor dem Ereignis gelten und nachher nicht mehr gelten, und durch diejenigen, die vor ihm nicht gelten und nachher gelten.

Die Festlegung eines Begriffs ausschließlich durch die mit ihm wechselwirkende Umgebung wird in der Wissenschaftstheorie EXTENSIONAL genannt. Das boolesche und ist extensional, denn der Wert von "A und B" ist durch den Wert von A und den Wert von B bestimmt, das weil ist dagegen INTENSIONAL, weil der Wert von "A weil B" nicht durch die Werte von A und B allein erklärt werden kann. Mittels extensionaler Begriffe kann man gut kommunizieren, allerdings nicht so kurz wie mit intensionalen.

Formale Sprachen (Kalküle), wie z.B. die Aussagenlogik, die Arithmetik, aber auch Programmiersprachen, sind extensional. DV-Anlagen sind Interpreter formaler, damit extensionaler Sprachen. Deshalb gilt für die Systementwicklung die

<u>Feststellung 3</u>: Die Spezifikation eines Systems besteht darin, intensionale Bedingungen und Ereignisse extensional festzulegen. Der Entwurf eines Systems besteht darin, extensionale Bedingungen und Ereignisse durch feinere zu realisieren.
Das Ergebnis einer Spezifikation soll extensional (formal) sein, das Gespräch zwischen System-Nutzer und -Entwickler über das System muß teilweise intensional (informell) geführt werden. Deshalb sollte eine Spezifikationssprache sowohl formale wie informelle Beschreibungen zulassen.

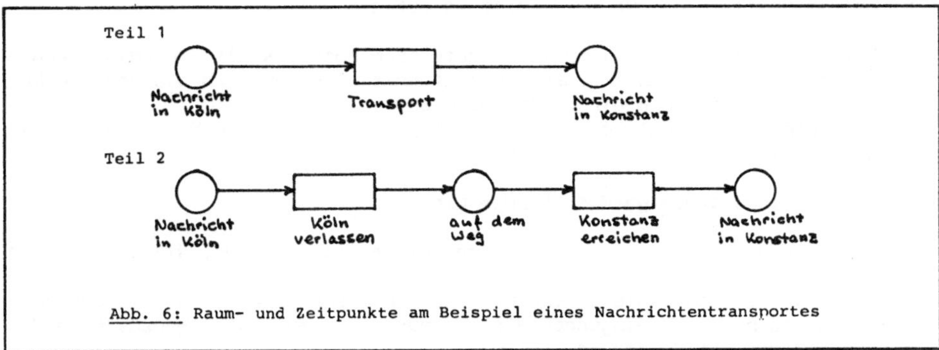

Abb. 6: Raum- und Zeitpunkte am Beispiel eines Nachrichtentransportes

Ereignisse drücken aus, wie Bedingungen miteinander zusammenwirken. Das bedeutet: Die Bedingungen müssen zu dem ZEITPUNKT, an dem das Ereignis geschieht, an BENACHBARTEN RAUMPUNKTEN vorliegen. Ein Beispiel:

Der Datentransport zwischen Köln und Konstanz kann auf einem Abstraktionsniveau wie in Abb. 6 Teil 1 modelliert werden. Durch die Grafik lege ich fest, daß ich den Abstand von 548 km zwischen den Orten auf BENACHBARTE Raumpunkte zusammenziehe. Denn: Das Transportereignis verlangt das Zutreffen der Vorbedingung und das Nichtzutreffen der Nachbedingung ZUGLEICH, und das bedeutet (wegen des relativistischen Kausalitätsbegriffes), daß keine Raumpunkte zwischen den Bedingungen liegen dürfen. Der Transport der Nachricht geschieht auch zu genau EINEM ZEITPUNKT.

Auf den Einwand, daß das ja gar nicht WIRKLICH so sei, denn jemand habe beobachtet, daß eine Nachricht zwar schon Köln verlassen habe (1. Ereignis), aber noch nicht in Konstanz angekommen sei (2. Ereignis), kann ich zweierlei antworten:

- Wenn ich diesen Aspekt mitmodellieren will, muß ich meine Ereignisse (und damit die möglichen Zeitpunkte) feiner modellieren, in der Folge aber auch die Bedingungen vermehren (die möglichen Raumpunkte), wie das in Abb. 6 Teil 2 geschehen ist.
- Wenn ich messen will, ob es einen solchen Zwischenzustand gibt oder nicht, muß ich ein Gerät zwischen den Orten aufbauen, daß feststellen kann,

  - daß eine Nachricht auf der Leitung ist,
  - daß eine Nachricht Köln verlassen hat und
  - daß die Nachricht in Konstanz noch nicht angekommen ist.

  Ich muß also sogar ein System BAUEN, von dem Abb. 6 Teil 2 einen Teil darstellt.

Auf den ersten Blick verwunderliche Aussagen wie "zwischen zwei (verschiedenen Raum-)Punkten liegt kein weiterer", werden erst durch ein diskretes Modell sinnvoll. Kontinuierliche Modelle, die meist (Raum- und Zeit-)Punkte auf der reellen Zahlengerade abbilden, provozieren "unendlich oft" die Frage "was aber, wenn zwischen diesen Punkten ...". Bei diskreter Modellierung stelle ich diese

Frage nur so lange, wie ich beobachten kann, daß Erscheinungen aus noch feineren Teilen zusammengesetzt sind.

Ich kann z.B. eine Bedingung zwischen zwei Ereignissen durch ein bedingungsberandetes Gefüge verfeinern, so daß nun zwischen den Ereignissen ein drittes liegt. Irgendwann ist diese "Ereignis-Intervallschachtelung" nicht mehr von Interesse. Dann befindet sich zwischen den feinsten zwei Ereignissen aber kein "Loch", sondern immer noch eine Bedingung.

Mit Hilfe der Begriffe des vorigen Kapitels definiere ich:

- Enthält ein Schnitt cut eines Kausalgefüges mindestens ein Ereignis, nenne ich ihn einen ZEITSCHNITT oder den Zeitpunkt, an dem sich die von den Ereignissen betroffenen Bedingungen änderten.
- Enthält ein Schnitt cut kein Ereignis, nenne ich ihn einen FALL, d.h. die Situation, in der alle seine Bedingungen zugleich gelten.

Weltlinien li eines Kausalgefüges können wir

- eine ZEITREIHE nennen, in der die Ereignisse die Änderung, die Bedingungen das Vorliegen einer Uhrzeit bedeuten, oder auch
- einen SEQUENTIELLEN PROZESS nennen. Dabei interpretiere ich die in den Prozeß hineinführenden Bedingungen als Voraussetzungen, die herausführenden als Ergebnisse des Prozesses.

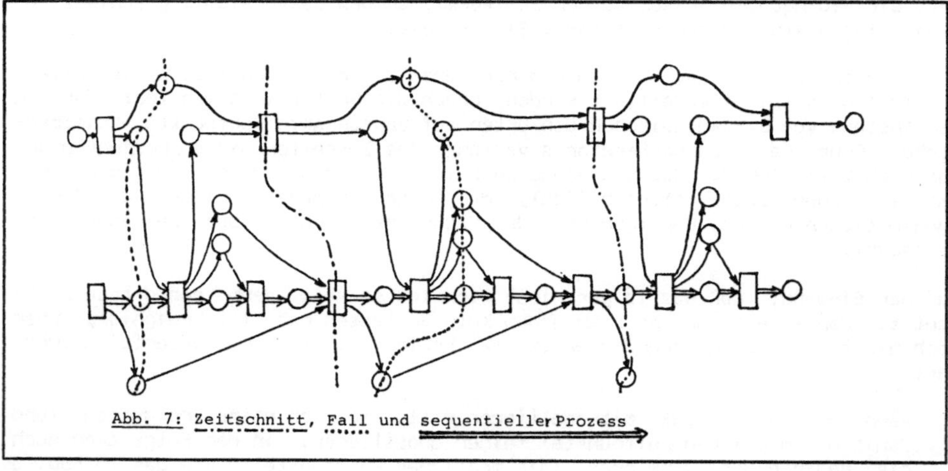

Abb. 7: Zeitschnitt, Fall und sequentieller Prozess

5 Prozeßnetze

Ein PROZESSNETZ ist ein Kausalgefüge aus miteinander verknüpften Bedingungen und Ereignissen. Jeder Bedingung ist genau ein Ereignis zugeordnet, das die Bedingung eintreten läßt, und ein Ereignis, das sie beendet.

Ereignisse müssen mit MINDESTENS zwei Vor- und zwei Nachbedingungen verknüpft sein, weil sie das ZUSAMMENWIRKEN zwischen Bedingungen an benachbarten Orten und deren Wirkung in den Raum hinein beschreiben sollen.

Das Zusammenwirken mehrerer Bedingungen in einem Ereignis kann man als WECHSELWIRKUNG zwischen Objekten interpretieren, wie in folgendem Beispiel:

Man wählt eine Weltlinie in einem Prozeßnetz aus und interpretiert sie als sequentiellen Prozeß in einem DV-System. Den Ereignissen auf der Weltlinie entsprechen die Operationen des Prozesses. Den Bedingungen auf der Weltlinie entsprechen die Werte der Variablen des Prozesses, die Schritt um Schritt transformiert werden. Die Vorbedingungen außerhalb der ausgewählten Weltlinie betrachtet man nun als VORAUSSETZUNG eines Ereignisses, die Nachbedingungen als ERGEBNIS. Dann hat ein Ereignis alle Voraussetzungen abzuwarten, die benötigt werden, damit sich die Werte der Variablen ändern können (eine neue Bedingung auf der Weltlinie gilt).

<u>Feststellung 4</u>: Grundbaustein einer Theorie von Prozessen ist die SYNCHRONISATION von Bedingungen durch Ereignisse. Synchronisation ist kein "high-level"-Konstrukt, sondern ein Grundkonzept eines Informationsverarbeitenden Systems.

Wenn ich in Netzen Ereignisse mit nur einer Vor- oder Nachbedingung konstruiere, was häufig passiert, sehe ich von Einwirkungen des Restmodells auf das Ereignis ebenso ab wie von Auswirkungen des Ereignisses auf den Rest. Eine Voraussage des Zeitverhaltens eines so definierten Programmes ist problematisch: Weil ich explizit von der Synchronisation des Programms mit seiner Umwelt abgesehen habe, verliere ich auch die Möglichkeit, über eine Verzögerung des Programmablaufs zu sprechen, den ich ja nur nur durch Synchronisations"verluste" bestimmen kann.

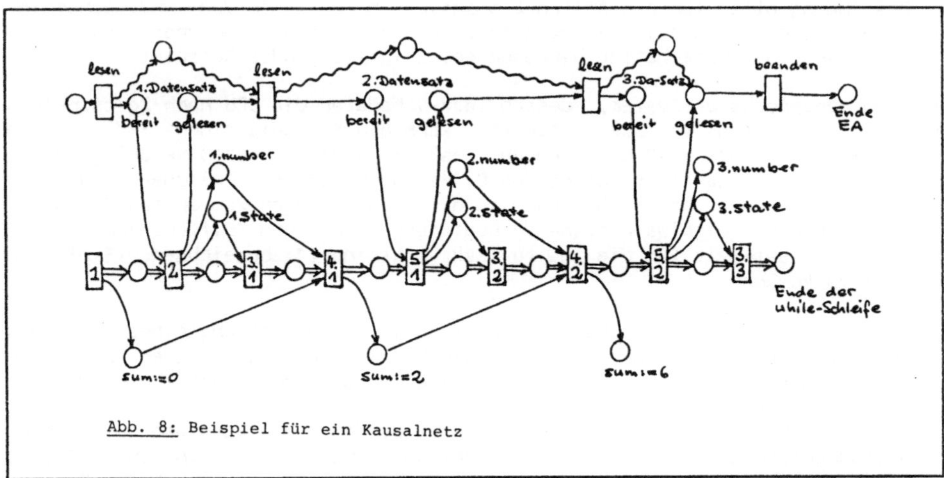

Abb. 8: Beispiel für ein Kausalnetz

Abb. 8 zeigt ein Beispiel für ein Prozeßnetz. Es ist eine ABWICKLUNG (Ausführung) des Pseudocodes von Abb. 9. Den Zusammenhang zwischen den beiden Teilen habe ich durch informelle Anschriften dargestellt.

```
Eingabedatensätze:
   ⟨ok,2⟩ , ⟨ok,4⟩ , ⟨eof,0⟩

Pseudocode:
   sum:=0 ;
   input (state,number) ;
   while state≠ eof do
     sum:=sum+number ;
     input (state,number) ;
   endwhile ;
```

Abb. 9

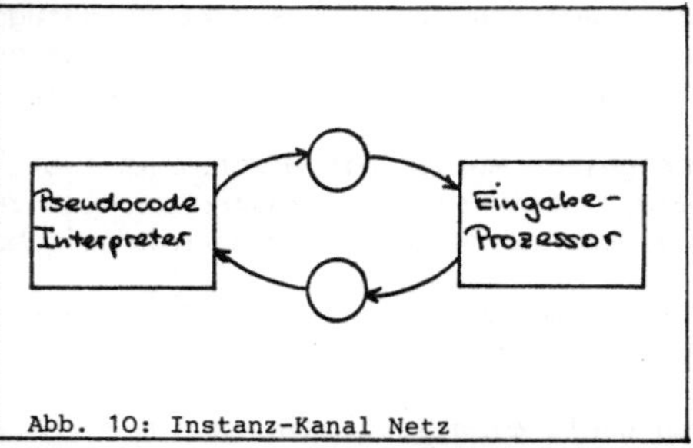

Abb. 10: Instanz-Kanal Netz

Durch Auszeichnung einer Weltlinie li kann ich andeuten, daß zwischen den so ausgezeichneten Erscheinungen ein organisatorischer Zusammenhang besteht, daß sie nämlich einer INSTANZ oder einem BAUTEIL zugehörig sind. In Abb. 8 sind durch den Doppelpfeil die Erscheinungen des Prozeßnetzes ausgezeichnet, die von der Instanz "Interpreter des Pseudocodes" herrühren. Die Erscheinungen einer zweiten Instanz, eines Eingabeprozessors, sind durch die geschlängelten Pfeile hervorgehoben.

Sind alle Instanzen identifiziert, läßt sich das Prozeßnetz zu einem INSTANZ-KANAL-NETZ vereinfachen (Abb. 10). Solche Netze sind "sehr" intensional und lassen nicht mehr den Grund der gegenseitigen Beeinflussung der Instanzen erkennen. Im Gegensatz dazu ist dem Prozeßnetz anzusehen, daß z.B. gilt:

Datensatz i bereit vor Datensatz i gelesen vor Datensatz i+1 bereit
sum:=0 co lesen Datensatz 2
sum:=0 co Datensatz 2 bereit
sum:=0 li Datensatz 2 gelesen

Dabei ist die letzte Abhängigkeit nur durch die sequentielle Interpretation des Pseudocodes bedingt ("Übersequentialisierung"). Von solchen und ähnlichen Überlegungen (Teilnetze, die keine Effekte auf ihre Umgebung ausüben, können entfallen usw.) gehen Optimierungsstrategien bei Übersetzern, Data-flow-languages u.ä. aus.

Die Bestimmung aller für ein Abstraktionsniveau bedeutsamen Vor- und Nachbedingungen eines Ereignisses ist kompliziert. Daß die Bedingungen über Lesen und Schreiben von Speicherinhalten hinausgehen, zeigt folgendes Beispiel:

In einem Monoprozessor-System, dessen Task-Scheduler die CPU nach Zeitscheiben an CPU- und EA-intensive Tasks verteilt, kann ein Ereignis einer Task "werde für 10 sec CPU-intensiv" dazu führen, daß ein anderer Prozeß verdrängt wird. Ein Ereignis in dieser Task "bilde den Differenzenquotient zwischen CPU-Zeit- und Real-Zeitverbrauch" steht dann in der Relation nach zum ersten Ereignis. Die zwischen den Ereignissen stehende Bedingung könnte man "Differenzenquotient CPU-Zeit zur Real-Zeit für die zweite Task verkleinert" bezeichnen. Einflüsse dieses Typs können

- Ursache komplizierter Fehler (RACES) sein. Eine Meldung eines Benutzers "dies Programm läuft immer, außer zwischen 13 und 15 Uhr" (der Zeit der Spitzenlast) ließ sich auf eine derartige Kausalkette zurückführen. Wirkungen dieses Typs können aber auch
- zur KOMMUNIKATION ZWISCHEN TASKS benutzt werden, die aufgrund von Sicherheitsüberlegungen nicht miteinander kommunizieren dürfen. In einer Studie über die Verletzlichkeit der Sicherheitskonstrukte des MULTICS-Systems schildert J. Saltzer [10] mehrere Möglichkeiten, wie Ereignisse einer Instanz (illegal) auf Ereignisse einer anderen einwirken.

6 Systemnetze

Die Prozeßnetze des vorigen Kapitels sind ungeeignet, das VERHALTEN eines Systemteils zu definieren. Das ist der Zweck der SYSTEMNETZE. Mit ihnen will ich folgende Verhaltensweisen modellieren:

1. WIEDERHOLUNGEN: "immer, wenn dieses Signal von H nach L wechselt, soll die Software ...".
2. ALTERNATIVEN: "Wenn der Eingabebefehl abgeschlossen ist, soll bei einem Fehler ..., sonst ...".

Um die Forderung 1 zu erfüllen, dürfen Systemnetze -anders als die hier behandelten Prozeßnetze- Zyklen enthalten. Der in Abb. 11 mit <u>cycl</u> bezeichnete Pfeil ist in einem Prozeßnetz nicht zugelassen. Als Folge davon kann eine Bedingung in einem Systemnetz mehrmals gelten (auf einer Weltline, also in mehreren Fällen). Um darzustellen, was gerade gilt, werden MARKEN verwendet. In Abb. 11 gilt die dem Ereignis 2 folgende Bedingung und trägt deshalb eine Marke. Die Menge aller markierten, d.h. geltenden Bedingungen heißt ein FALL in einem Systemnetz.

Um die Forderung 2 zu erfüllen, lasse ich in Systemnetzen zu, daß mehrere Ereignisse die Möglichkeit haben, eine Bedingung gültig oder ungültig zu machen. In Abb. 11 z.B. können die Ereignisse <u>3. eof</u> und <u>kein eof</u> die in der Figur markierte Bedingung ungültig machen. Die derart einer Bedingung zugeordneten Ereignisse nenne ich ALTERNATIVEN.

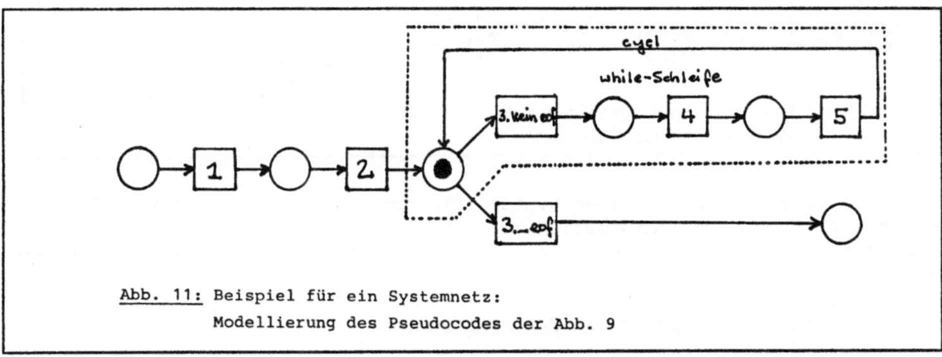

<u>Abb. 11:</u> Beispiel für ein Systemnetz: Modellierung des Pseudocodes der Abb. 9

Nachdem ich die Erweiterungen der Prozessnetze zu den Systemnetzen beschrieben habe, muß ich nun festlegen, wie die Änderung der Bedingungen in dem neuen Netztyp zustande kommt, wann also Ereignisse stattfinden können:

> Ein Ereignis heißt AUSFÜHRBAR, wenn alle seine Vorbedingungen markiert und alle seine Nachbedingungen nicht markiert sind. Ein ausführbereites Ereignis kann SCHALTEN. Schalten bedeutet: die Marken der Vorbedingungen werden entfernt, die Nachbedingungen werden markiert.

Haben zwei ausführbare Ereignisse gemeinsame Vorbedingungen, so liegt ein KONFLIKT vor, genauer ein Vorwärtskonflikt. Welches der beiden Ereignisse stattfindet, kann man im Rahmen des modellierten Systemteils nicht entscheiden. In Abb. 11 besteht ein Konflikt zwischen den alternativen Ereignissen <u>3. eof</u> und <u>3. kein eof</u> . Der Konflikt muß durch Rückgriff auf die Umgebung des Systems entschieden werden, nämlich dadurch, daß geprüft wird, ob ein eof-Satz vorliegt oder nicht.

<u>Feststellung 5</u>: Um Konflikte zu entscheiden, muß INFORMATION aus der Umgebung in das System eingespeist werden. Die Informationseinheit, die benötigt wird, um einen Konflikt zwischen zwei Ereignissen zu entscheiden, nenne ich ein BIT.

Ein Bit, wie das in Abb. 11 benötigte "eof oder nicht-eof" besteht zwangsläufig aus ZWEI Bedingungen, die so miteinander verkoppelt sind, daß höchstens eine von ihnen gilt. Abb 12 Teil 1 zeigt, wie der Konflikt der Abb. 11 durch ein Bit des Eingabe-Prozessors, der im umgebenden System des Netzes der Abb. 11 liegt, gelöst werden kann. In dem so veränderten Netz ist wieder ein Konflikt vorhanden, der in der Umgebung gelöst werden muß, z.B. durch einen Bediener eines Sichtgerätes, der sich ENTSCHIEDEN hat, eine eof-Bedingung einzugeben, oder durch ein Peripheriegerät, das VOREINGESTELLT war, zwei Meßwerte und dann eof zu liefern (Abb. 12 Teil 2).

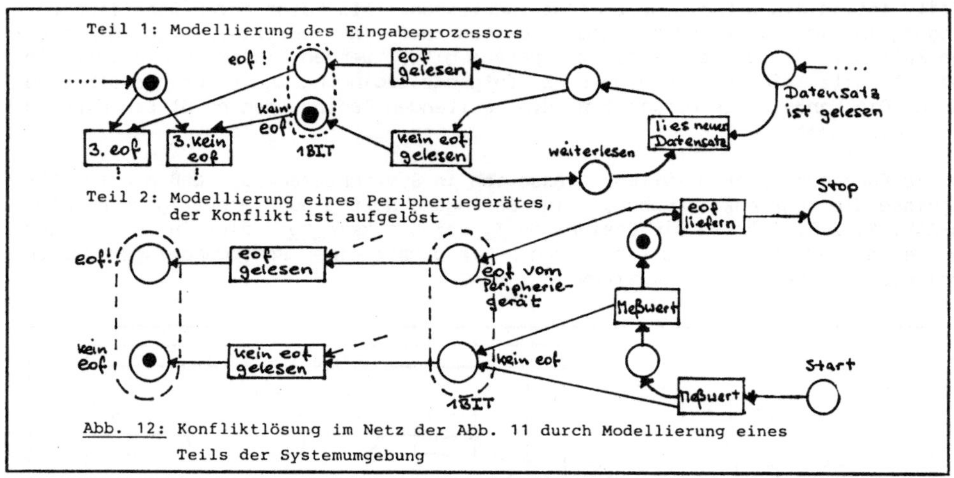

<u>Abb. 12:</u> Konfliktlösung im Netz der Abb. 11 durch Modellierung eines Teils der Systemumgebung

Neben den Punkten, an denen einem System Information zugeführt werden muß, lassen sich auch Punkte des Informationsabflusses definieren (RÜCKWÄRTSKONFLIKTE). Darauf kann ich nicht weiter eingehen, obwohl daraus interessante Überlegungen über eines INFORMATIONSERHALTUNGSSATZES folgen.

Prozeßnetze sind ABWICKLUNGEN von Systemnetzen:

- Einem Fall eines Systemnetzes (einer Menge markierter Bedingungen) entspricht ein Fall des Prozeßnetzes (ein Schnitt nur aus Bedingungen).
- Konflikte in Systemnetzen sind in zugehörigen Prozeßnetzen nicht mehr sichtbar, weil sie bei der Abwicklung (durch Informationszufuhr) GELÖST werden mußten.
- Wiederholungen von Bedingungen und Ereignissen in Systemnetzen lassen sich in Prozeßnetzen durch geeignete BESCHRIFTUNGEN wiederfinden. Davon würde in Abb. 10 (Ereignis 3.1, 3.2) schon Gebrauch gemacht.
- Ausführbare Ereignisse in Systemnetzen, die keine Vor- und Nachbedingungen gemeinsam haben, können NEBENLÄUFIG SCHALTEN. Das ist im Prozeßnetz dadurch sichtbar, daß die zugehörigen Prozeßnetz-Ereignisse in der <u>co</u> Relation zueinander stehen. <u>co</u> läßt sich also auch auf der Systemebene definieren.

7 Zusamenfassung

Ingenieurmäßige Konstruktion und Qualitätssicherung eines DV-Systems verlangen, daß nur beobachtbare Erscheinungen Grundlage von Modellbildungen sind. "Verborgene Parameter", also nicht nachprüfbare Effekte, sollen nicht in die Modellbildung eingehen. Nicht nachprüfbare Effekte sind solche, die auf Annahmen aufbauen wie beliebig genaue Uhren und beliebig genau übereinstimmende Uhren in räumlich verteilten Komponenten. Mit Hilfe solcher Effekte kann man zwar modellieren, nach diesen Modellen gebaute Systeme können aber nicht so funktionieren, wie sie sollen.

Von der elementaren Struktur der Kausalgefüge ausgehend habe ich versucht, ein Modell zu erläutern, daß solche Effekte NICHT voraussetzt.

Die Verwendbarkeit von darauf aufbauenden Entwurfsmethoden wird z.Zt. bei der Konstruktion eines dezentralen Systems überprüft.

Literaturverzeichnis

1. C.A. Petri: Introduction to General Net Theory, S.1 in [4].

2. C.A. Petri: Concurrency, S.251 in [4].

3. C.A. Petri: Non-Sequential Processes, ISF-Report 77.05, St. Augustin, GMD, 1975.

4. W. Brauer, Ed.: Net Theory and Applications, LNCS 84, Springer-Verlag, Berlin, ISBN 3-540-10001-6, 1980.

5. A. Holt, W. Commoner: Events and Conditions, Record of the Projekt MAC Conference on Concurrent Systems and Parallel Computation, ed. by J.B. Dennis, published by the A.C.M., New York, 1970.

6. A. Holt, et al.: Information System Theory Project, Final Report, RADC-TR-68-305, NTIS AD 676972, 1968.

7. H.J. Genrich, K. Lautenbach, P.S. Thiagarajan: Elements of General Net Theory, S.21 in [4].

8. H.J. Genrich, E. Stankiewecz-Wiechno: A Dictionary of some Basic Notions of Net Theory, S.519 in [4].

9. I. Kant: Kritik der reinen Vernunft, Aufl. B, S.33.

10. J.H. Saltzer: Protection and the Control of Information Sharing in Multics, MIT, MAC-TR-123, 1974.

DER ENTWURF NEBENLÄUFIGER SYSTEME MIT HANDLUNGS-ENTSCHEIDUNGS-NETZEN

Bernd Krämer und Heinz W. Schmidt

Institut für Software-Technologie
Gesellschaft für Mathematik und Datenverarbeitung mbH
Postfach 1240, D-5205 St. Augustin 1

Eine anschauliche grafische und zugleich formal begründete Methode zur Spezifikation und Analyse verteilter Systeme wird eingeführt. Wir verknüpfen Konzepte der Allgemeinen Netztheorie mit Prinzipien des modularen Entwurfs, der schrittweisen Verfeinerung und der schrittweisen Formalisierung von Softwaresystemen. Die Methode ermöglicht weitgehend formale und maschineninterpretierbare Spezifikationen von Systemfunktionen und zugleich anschauliche und damit verständliche Systemdarstellungen. Benutzerkenntnisse und -anforderungen zu Aufgaben und Einbettung des Softwaresystems können so besser berücksichtigt werden als bisher.

1 EINLEITUNG

Zahlreiche Probleme bei der Entwicklung und Anwendung von Softwaresystemen können zurückgeführt werden

- auf unzureichendes Problemverständnis der Entwickler,
- auf ungenügende Kommunikation zwischen Benutzer und Entwickler und
- auf einen Mangel an Hilfsmitteln zur präzisen Beschreibung, zur Analyse und Verwaltung von Auftragsdaten.

Mit großen Anstrengungen versucht man daher, formale Methoden so aufzubereiten, daß man sie bei der Anforderungsanalyse und bei der funktionalen Spezifikation von Anwendungssystemen einsetzen kann [1]. Algebraische Methoden werden z.Z. besonders intensiv untersucht [2].

Man verspricht sich davon, die Kommunikation zwischen Auftraggebern, Benutzern und Entwicklern auf eine präzisere Grundlage zurückzuführen und die Vollständigkeit, Widerspruchsfreiheit und Plausibilität einer Systemkonzeption wesentlich früher und möglichst rechnergestützt überprüfen zu können. Hierin sieht man den entscheidenden Ansatzpunkt, um Folgekosten von Fehlern und Unterlassungen und damit die gesamten Entwicklungskosten erheblich zu reduzieren.

Jedoch bleiben Auftraggebern und Systemnutzern formale Methoden der Informatik meist ganz unzugänglich. Im übrigen sind sie selbst gut ausgebildeten Software-Ingenieuren oft nur zum Teil vertraut. Hinzu kommt, daß Probleme nebenläufiger Systeme, wie sie z.B. beim Entwurf von Prozeßrechner-Software auftreten, nur nachrangig oder überhaupt nicht behandelt werden.

Andere Ansätze zu Entwurfssprachen wie SADT setzen auf die Anschaulichkeit und Aussagekraft grafischer Darstellungen. Sie wurden auch schon mit Erfolg in der Praxis eingesetzt. Sie bauen aber häufig nicht auf einem formalen Beschreibungsmodell auf, so daß ihre Implementierung erschwert ist und Korrektheits- oder Plausibilitätsüberprüfungen mehr oder weniger auf heuristischen Ansätzen beruhen. Ausdrucksmittel für Konzepte zur Spezifikation und Analyse nebenläufiger Systeme und Prozesse sind auch hier häufig nicht vorhanden oder haben keine formale Grundlage.

Daneben setzt sich immer mehr die Erkenntnis durch, daß nicht nur die Systementwicklung Probleme aufgibt. Bedingt durch technischen Fortschritt oder Veränderungen des organisatorischen oder technischen Umfelds sind immer neue Änderungen während der Lebenszeit eines Softwaresystems zu bewältigen. Häufig werden aber noch technische oder organisatorische Umgebungsbedingungen als unveränderlich vorausgesetzt, und viele Entwurfs- und Programmiersprachen bieten keine Begriffe an, um über die Umgebung des Softwaresystems zu reden. Daher gehen Umgebungsbedingungen nur implizit in

Anforderungsdefinition, Systementwurf und Implementation ein; Task- und Modulstruktur, Benennungen von Programmeinheiten und verbale Systemdokumentationen geben meist nur rudimentäre Hinweise auf äußere Einflußgrößen, die das betrachtete Softwaresystem mitstrukturierten.

Wir wollen im folgenden einen graphischen Ansatz zur Spezifikation nebenläufiger Systeme grob skizzieren, der das Verständnis von Systemen und die Kommunikation über Systeme verbessern will. Die Modellierungskonzepte zielen darauf ab, unabhängig von konkreten Realisierungen und Systemkonfigurationen Struktureinsichten über das nebenläufige Zusammenwirken zwischen den Komponenten eines Softwaresystems und mit dessen technischer und organisatorischer Umgebung zu vermitteln [3]. Es handelt sich um ein Systembeschreibungsmodell, das auf der Anschaulichkeit graphischer Netzdarstellungen und auf formalen Konzepten der Allgemeinen Netztheorie aufbaut.

Eine Einführung in einige Grundprinzipien und -begriffe der Netztheorie, auf die wir im folgenden aufbauen, findet sich in [4], einen umfassenden Überblick über Teiltheorien und Ergebnisse der Netztheorie vermittelt [5], in [6] werden Hinweise auf Anwendungen der Netztheorie gegeben, Anwendungsbeispiele sind in [7, 8] zu finden.

2 BEISPIEL

Abb. 1 zeigt ein Netz, das Ausschnitte aus einer Paketverteilanlage [8] grob modelliert. Für ein intuitives Verständnis wollen wir im Augenblick nur die Knoten unterscheiden in eckige, die Aktivitäten bezeichnen, und runde, die lokale Systemzustände oder Objekte bezeichnen. Die Kanten stehen für eine Kausalrelation zwischen den Knoten. Eine ausführliche Diskussion der Elemente unserer Darstellung folgt in Abschnitt 3.

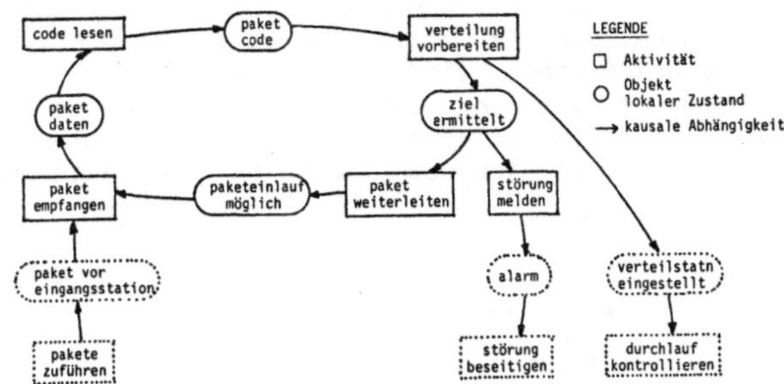

Abb. 1 Ausschnitt einer **Paketverteilanlage:**
Einige Funktionen einer Eingangsbehandlung

Das Netz modelliert ein kleines zyklisches System, das folgendermaßen interpretiert werden kann (fettgedruckte Begriffe verweisen auf die Abbildung):

Wir nehmen an, ein **paket** sei **vor** der **eingangsstation** der Verteilanlage und soll dort weiterbehandelt werden. Nachdem das **paket empfangen** wurde und damit bestimmte **paketdaten** vorliegen, wird die Paketbeschriftung gelesen **(code lesen)** und in einen internen **paketcode** umgewandelt. Dieser **paketcode** wird ausgewertet, um die **verteilung** des Pakets **vorzubereiten.** Sobald die **verteilstationen** der Anlage **eingestellt** sind und zugleich das **ziel ermittelt** ist, kann der weitere **durchlauf** des Pakets **kontrolliert** werden. Unabhängig von dieser Aktivität werden, ausgehend von **ziel ermittelt,** alternative Aktivitäten möglich: Entweder muß eine **störung** an irgendeine beaufsichtigende Instanz **gemeldet** werden, die diese **störung beseitigen** muß, oder das betrachtete **paket** kann jetzt zum Transport durch die Anlage **weitergeleitet** werden. (Eine detailliertere Beschreibung würde zeigen, daß man in der Vervollständigung und Verfeinerung von **durchlauf kontrollieren** und **paket weiterleiten** doch synchronisieren muß, um den Bezug zwischen dem in der Eingansstation behandelten und dem durch die Verteilstationen laufenden Paket zu modellieren; d.h. die beiden Aktivitätenstränge sind letztlich nicht völlig unabhängig.) Sobald das **paket** aus der Eingangsstation in die Verteilanlage **weitergeleitet** ist und ein neues **paket** von außen **zugeführt** wurde, kann ein neuer Systemzyklus beginnen. (Ein lokaler Zustand "paket in verteilanlage" und eine weitere korrespondierende Aktivität sind nicht dargestellt.)

Die gepunktet gezeichneten Netzknoten stehen für Aktivitäten (eckig), die in der Umgebung des zu entwickelnden Systems stattfinden und nicht als Funktion des betrachteten Systems realisiert werden, und für Situationen (rund), über die die Interaktion zwischen internen und externen Aktionen abgewickelt wird.

3 HANDLUNGS-ENTSCHEIDUNGS-NETZE

Netze sind mathematische Objekte, die in der Literatur auf unterschiedliche Weise eingeführt werden: als Tupel von Mengen, linear algebraisch oder als topologische Struktur. Wir wollen hier Netze in einer grafischen Darstellung einführen. Mit gewisser Vorsicht können wir Netze als gerichtete Grafen mit zwei geordneten disjunkten Knotenmengen verstehen. Zusätzlich gilt die Bedingung, daß Kanten immer nur zwischen einem Knoten der einen und einem Knoten der anderen Menge zugelassen sind. Weiterhin definieren unsere Diagramme über die grafische Struktur hinaus in Verbindung mit einer Markierung eine Interpretation dieser Struktur. Durch die Beschriftung eines Netzes gemäß einer Anwendungssystematik spiegelt sein Verhalten das Verhalten des modellierten Systems wider.

3.1 Beschreibungskonzepte im Kleinen

Handlungs-Entscheidungs-Netze sind durch eine endliche Menge von Situationen (s.u.) und eine endliche Menge von Handlungen und eine Einflußbeziehungen zwischen Handlungen und Situationen gegeben. Handlungen bezeichnen Veränderungen, Situationen stehen für die Zustände eines Systems. Im Unterschied zum Zustandsbegriff sequentieller Systeme bezeichnen Situationen keine globalen, sondern nur lokale Zustände (lokal einer Handlung). Man kann Handlungen auch als Prozeßelemente und Situationen als Datenelemente verstehen, die Begriffspaare sind nur Abstraktionen zur implementationsunabhängigen Beschreibung von Systemen. Diese Abstraktionen verfeinert und verfolständigt man schrittweise, bis man auf einer bekannten Ebene anlangt. Handlungen und Situationen bezeichnen wir als elementar, wenn es für sie im betrachteten Zusammenhang keine Zerlegung gibt.

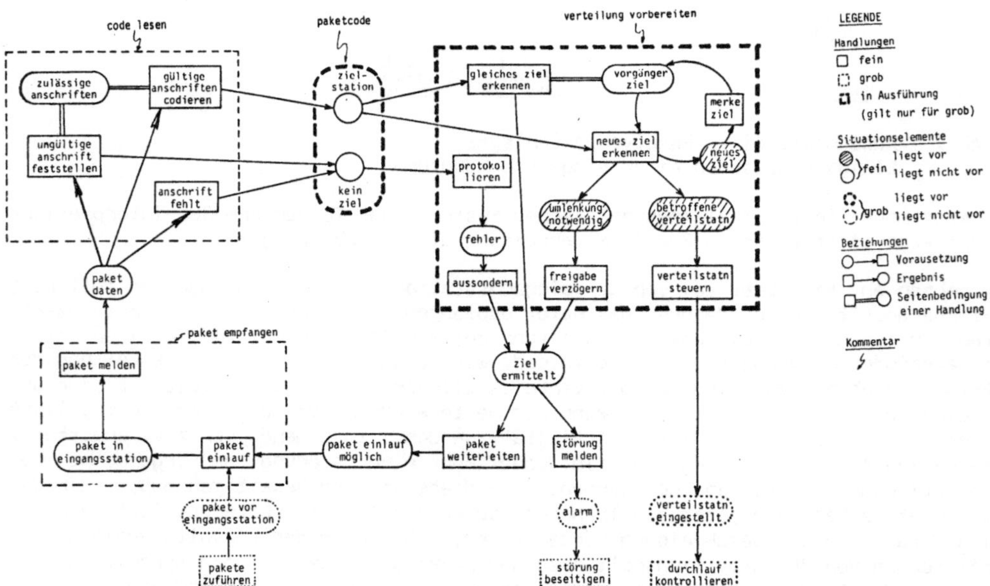

Abb. 2 Ausschnitte einer Paketverteilanlage: Grob und fein zugleich

In Abb. 2 haben wir das Netz aus Abb. 1 verfeinert. Die gestrichelt gezeichneten Netzelemente stellen den Zusammenhang zu der gröberen Darstellung in Abb. 1 her und fassen die sie verfeinernden Netzelemente zusammen.

Situation. Die aktuelle Situation des modellierten Systems besteht in dem (lokalen) Zusammentreffen mehrerer Situationselemente, für die man durch Beobachtung feststellen kann, ob sie gerade vorliegen oder nicht vorliegen. Situationselemente stellen wir durch abgerundete Umrisse dar; ihr Vorliegen heben wir gegenüber dem Nicht-Vorliegen hervor (durch Schraffur von Elementarsituationen oder durch fette gestrichelte Umrandung von vergröbernden Situationselementen). Die aktuelle Situation in Abb. 2 ist durch die Situationen **umlenkung notwendig, betroffene verteilstationen, neues ziel** und **paket code** gegeben. **paket code** besteht aus **zielstation** und **kein ziel.** Die Beziehung "besteht aus" ist durch eine gestrichelte Umrandung der Konstituenten dargestellt.

Situationen sind Voraussetzung und Ergebnis von Handlungen; Handlungen ändern Situationen. Wir unterscheiden reine Voraussetzungen und reine Ergebnisse von solchen Situationen, die gleichermaßer Voraussetzungen und Ergebnisse derselben Handlung umfassen. Solche Situationen nennen wir Seitenbedingungen bezüglich einer Handlung. Die beteiligten Handlungen werden nur bedingt ausgeführt und haben in der Regel einen noch nicht näher bezeichneten Seiteneffekt. Im Beispiel ist **vorgänger ziel** eine Seitenbedingung für **gleiches ziel erkennen,** nicht aber für **neues ziel erkennen.**

Handlung. Eine Handlung ist durchführbar, wenn alle ihre Voraussetzungen gegeben sind und keines ihrer Ergebnisse vorliegt. Sie ist erfüllt, wenn ihre Ergebnisse erreicht sind und ihre Voraussetzungen nicht mehr gegeben sind. Ist eine Hanlung erfüllt, hat sie die aktuelle Situation verändert. Die Durchführung nicht-elementarer Handlungen setzt sich zusammen aus der Durchführung sie verfeinernder Handlungen, wie bei der Aktivierung einer Prozedur die in ihrem Rumpf aufgerufenen Prozeduren aktiviert werden. Handlungen stellen wir durch Rechtecke dar. Die Ausführung einer nicht-elementaren Handlung repräsentieren wir durch ein Hervorheben des zugehörigen Rechtecks (im Unterschied zu üblichen Netzinterpretationen). Die Ausführung einer elementaren Handlung ist durch die von ihr verursachte Veränderung der lokalen Situationselemente beschrieben.

Kausalität. Die Beziehung zwischen Handlungen und ihren Voraussetzungen und Ergebnissen, oder umgekehrt zwischen Situationen und den in ihnen oder aus ihnen resultierenden Handlungen, stellen wir durch gerichtete Pfeile (von Voraussetzungen zu Handlungen, von Handlungen zu Ergebnissen) dar. Seitenbedingungen werden mit den zugehörigen Handlungen durch ungerichtete Doppelkanten verbunden. In Abb. 2 ist **paket code** Voraussetzung für **verteilung vorbereiten.** Die Ausführung dieser Handlung beginnt (fett markiert) in der gegebenen Situation. Ihre Ergebnisse **ziel ermittelt** und **verteilstationen eingestellt** liegen noch nicht vor.

Konflikt. Sind mehrere Handlungen mit gemeinsamen Voraussetzungen durchführbar, so kann genau eine von ihnen durchgeführt werden. Durch die Ausführung einer Handlung entfällt mindestens eine wesentliche Voraussetzung für die anderen Handlungen. Welche der widerstreitenden Handlungen jedoch ausgeführt wird, läßt sich in der gegebenen Situation nicht vorhersagen. Auch erledigte Handlungen können im Konflikt stehen, wenn sie gemeinsame Ergebnisse haben. Dann kann man im nachhinein nicht sagen, welche von ihnen hat zu dem Ergebnis geführt hat. Die Ausführung einer Handlung ist also mit einer spezifischen Entscheidung verbunden, die abhängt von Information, die von außen dem System zugeführt wird (Eingabedaten, Unterbrechungen). Mit Konflikten lassen sich Entscheidungspunkte in einem Systemmodell bezeichnen, ohne daß zugleich über eine Reihenfolge der Auswertung von Alternativen oder über Prioritäten geredet werden muß. Handlungen, die in Konflikt stehn können, bezeichnen wir als Entscheidungen. (Im Unterschied zur gängigen Bezeichnung von Netzinterpretationen nach den beiden Arten von Netzelementen haben wir nur die aktiven Netzelemente in die Bezeichnung unseres Modells eingehen lassen, da wir sie als die wesentlichen Konstruktionsbegriffe auffassen.)

In Abb. 2 stehen die Entscheidungen **paket weiterleiten** und **störung melden** in Konflikt, falls **ziel ermittelt** vorliegt (und die Ergebnisse der beiden Handlungen nicht vorliegen). Die Entscheidungen **aussondern**, **gleiches ziel erkennen** und **freigabe verzögern** stehen in Konflikt, falls alle ihre Voraussetzungen in einer Situation gegeben sind und **ziel ermittelt** nicht vorliegt.

Nebenläufigkeit. Durchführbare Handlungen, die nicht im Konflikt stehen, sind kausal unabhängig. Elementare Handlungen werden nebenläufig ausgeführt. Für sie ist dann eine Aussage über die Reihenfolge der Ausführung nicht objektiv; verschiedene Beobachter können zu unterschiedlchen Schlüssen kommen: Manche können die Handlungen nicht unterscheiden, einige nehmen eine bestimmte Handlung vor anderen wahr, während andere Beobachter eine andere Handlung für die zuerst durchgeführte halten. Dies alles sind Aspekte ein und desselben objektiven Sachverhaltes. **freigabe verzögern**, **merke ziel** und **verteilstatn steuern** in Abb. 2 sind in der gegebenen Situation nebenläufig ausführbar.

3.2 Pseudocode für Handlungs-Entscheidungs-Netze

Wir wollen an dieser Stelle aus zwei Gründen eine programmiersprachliche Transkription von Handlungs-Entscheidungs-Netzen einführen, die sich an [10, 11] anlehnt:

- Als Pseudocode soll sie das Verständnis der Konzepte und Beispiele für diejenigen erleichtern, die im Umgang mit grafischen oder gar netzartigen Beschreibungen weniger erfahren sind.
- Als ersten Ansatz zu einer nichtsequentiellen Programmiersprache mit netztheoretischer Fundierung soll sie Hinweise geben, (1) wie Handlungs-Entscheidungs-Netze in eine Programmiersprache übersetzt werden können, (2) wie wir zu einer Beschriftungsdisziplin kommen können oder (3) wie die elementarsten Handlungen eines solchen Modells mit Hilfe dieser Sprache implementiert werden können.

Handlungen wollen wir mit Prozeduren gleichsetzen. Wir spezifizieren Entscheidungen als decisions, andere Handlungen als actions. Die Situationen werden als Parameter von Prozeduren aufgefaßt und in einer Parameterliste angegeben. Voraussetzungen sind durch ein den Parameterbezeichner vorangestelltes ">" gekennzeichnet, Ergebnisse durch ein nachgestelltes ">" und Seitenbedingungen durch ">...>".

Die verwendeten Kontrollstrukturen either ... or, and then (nacheinander), and also (nebenläufig), where ... is ... do sprechen für sich. Die Priorität der Kontrollstrukturen stellen wir hier durch Einrückung dar. (Die Unterscheidung von and then und and also ist redundant, da wir das "and" bereits aufgrund der Kausal- oder der Datenflußbeziehung zwischen Handlungen über Ein-, und Ausgabeparameter unterscheiden können.) Das Prädikat benötigen wir, um die Zerlegung von Situationen zu beschreiben.

Die Umschreibung von **verteilung vorbereiten** aus Abb. 2 sieht wie folgt aus:

```
action
  verteilung vorbereiten (>paket code, ziel ermittelt>, verteilstatn eingestellt>):
    where paket code is zielstation do
     either gleiches ziel erkennen (>zielstation, >vorgänger ziel>, ziel ermittelt>)
     or neues Ziel erkennen (>zielstation, >vorgänger ziel, umlenkung notwendig>,
                                  betroffene verteilstatn>, neues Ziel>)
        and then freigabe verzögern (>umlenkung notwendig, ziel ermittelt>)
          and also verteilstatn steuern (>betroffene verteilstatn,
                                      verteilstatn eingestellt>)
          and also merke ziel (>neues Ziel, vorgänger ziel>)
    where paket code is kein ziel do
     protokollieren (>kein ziel, fehler>)
     and then aussondern (>fehler, ziel ermittelt>).
```

Bestimmte Wohldefiniertsheitsbedingungen zur Struktur solcher Prozeduren [11] sind die Grundlage für statische Plausibilitäts- und Korrektheitsüberprüfungen und für eine mechanische Transformation in eine Netzdarstellung und umgekehrt.

3.3 Struktur im Großen

Systemarchitektur. Alle Netze werden immer als Teil einer Systemmodellstruktur konstruiert und modifiziert. Das Systemmodell besteht aus Subsystemen, die miteinander über Schnittstellen in Beziehung stehen. Subsysteme bestehen aus Handlungen und Situationen, ihrer Zerlegung und kausalen Beziehung. Für jedes Netz einer Beschreibungsebene, geformt durch die Handlungen und Situationen, muß eine Ausgangssituation angegeben werden, sofern sie sich nicht eindeutig aus der Netzstruktur ableiten läßt.

Vertikale Zerlegung. Jedes Subsystem macht zusammengesetzte Handlungen und die sie verknüpfenden Situationen über Schnittstellen sichtbar, alle übrigen Systemelemente sind nur systemintern bekannt (information hiding, visibility [12]). Sichtbare Systemelemente dürfen nur genau einem Subsystem zugeordnet sein.

Das Netz aus zusammengesetzten Handlungen und Situationen bestimmt das äußere Verhalten des Subsystems: Die Kausalbeziehung macht Aussagen über die Reihenfolge sichtbarer Handlungen (erst a dann b), über Entscheidungsmöglichkeiten (entweder a oder b), über zyklische Abhängigkeiten zwischen Handlungen, über Seitenbedingungen von Handlungen und über die kausale Unabhängigkeit von Handlungen.

Sichtbare Handlungen können unter Berücksichtigung ihrer kausalen Abhängigkeiten in gröberen Systemen angewendet werden. Mittels Morphismen ist eine Überprüfung möglich, ob die im äußeren Verhalten eines feineren Systems angegebenen Abhängigkeiten zwischen Handlungen bei der Anwendung in gröberen Systemen eingehalten werden. Die elementaren Handlungen des gröberen Systems werden aufgrund ihrer Beschriftung mit den sichtbaren Handlungen und Situationen feinerer Systeme identifiziert.

Das angewandte Auftreten elementarer Handlungen erfüllt das äußere Verhalten des betrachteten Systems. Auf diese Weise wird ein System schließlich auf vordefinierte oder vorimplementierte Systeme zurückgeführt. Ähnlich dem "open end"-Ansatz in CDL2 [13] erhalten wir eine ablauffähige Implementation des Systems durch den Rückgriff auf eine vorgegebene Implementation der Netzstrukturen (Aktivierung von Handlungen, Verändern von Situationen) und die jeweilige Implementierung der primitiven Handlungen in einer geeigneten Programmiersprache.

In Abb. 3 ist das Netz aus Abb. 2 in drei Systeme (a, b, c) zerlegt dargestellt. Die sichtbaren Handlungen und Situationen sind in dieser Darstellung nicht durch besondere Umrandung hervorgehoben, da wir zur Vereinfachung nur jeweils eine Zerlegungsstufe angegeben haben, nämlich das äußere Verhalten des Subsystems (oben) und seine Verfeinerung (darunter) durch die Anwendung sichtbarer Handlungen feinerer Subsysteme. System a in Abb. 3 benutzt die sichtbaren Handlungen der Systeme b und c. (Die Erweiterungen unseres Pseudocodes um System- und Schnittstellenkonzepte system, supplies, applies etc spricht für sich selbst.)

In Abb. 4 sind die Systeme wieder zu einem größeren System zusammengefügt. Diese Abbildung zeigt auch, wie die Schnittstellen aufeinander aufbauender Systeme miteinander identifiziert werden können. Der Morphismus zwischen den Schnittstellen belegt, daß die in den Subsystemen spezifizierten Restriktionen (z.B. "erst **paket melden** dann **verteilung vorbereiten**" aus **eingangssteuerung**) in der Anwendung eingehalten werden.

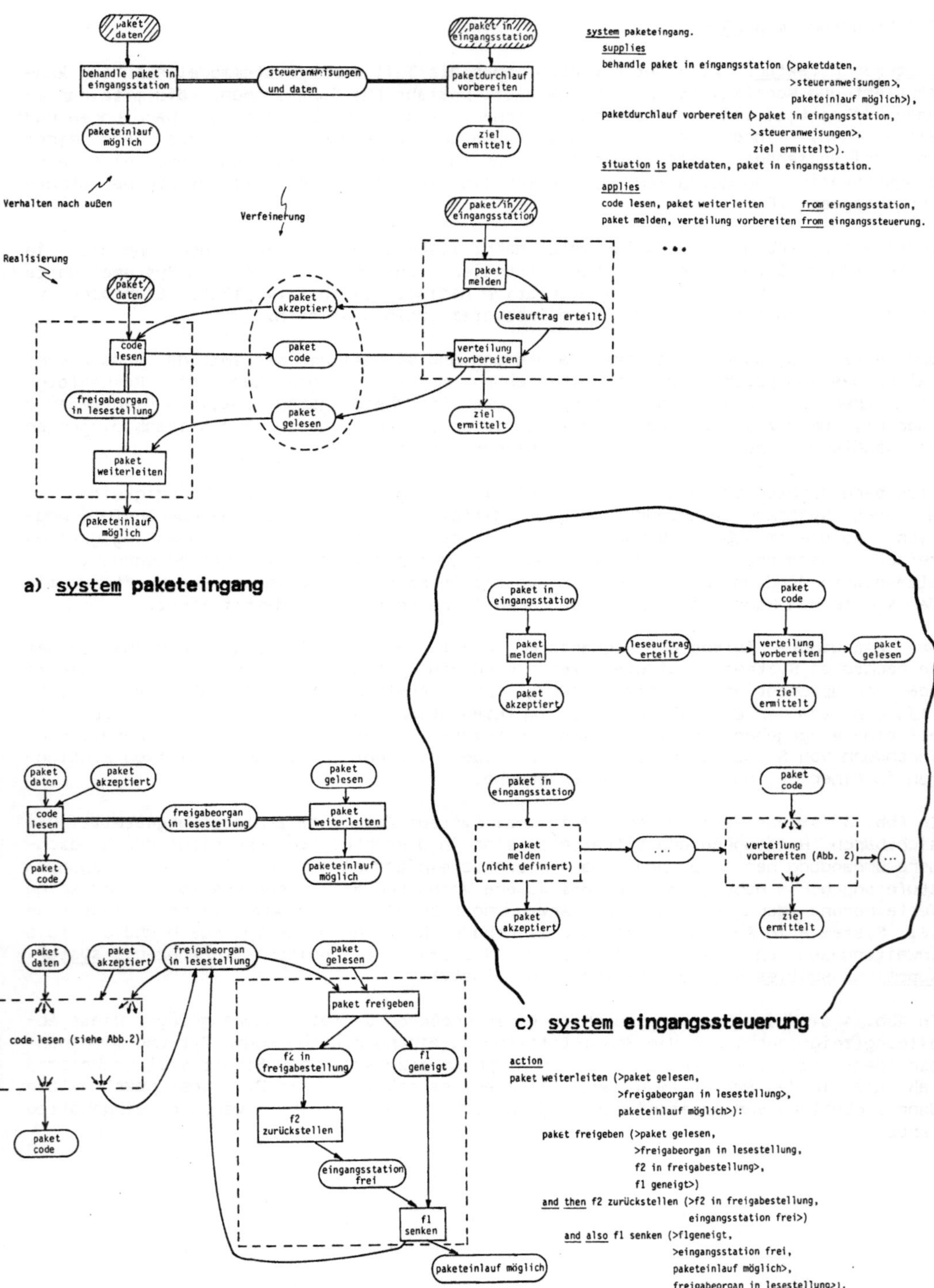

b) **system eingangsstation**

Abb. 3 Drei Subsysteme der **Paketverteilanlage**

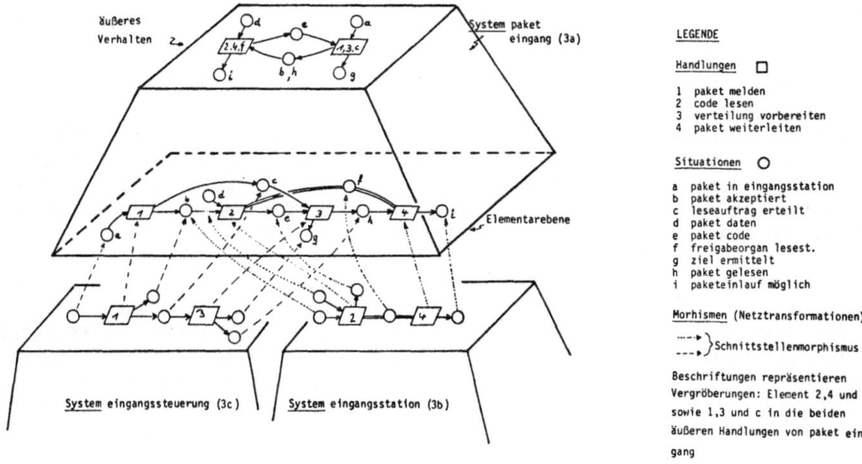

Abb. 4 Die Verknüpfung der Systeme aus Abb. 3

Horizontale Zerlegung. Wir gehen davon aus, daß jedes modellierte System nur einen begrenzten Ausschnitt eines größeren Systems, in das es eingebettet ist, angibt. Um den Zusammenhang mit der Umgebung (soweit er das betrachtete Systeme beeinflußt) beschreiben zu können, enthält das System auch immer ein Modell seiner Umgebung. Wir fassen das Zusammenwirken mit der Umgebung auf als eine aufgabenbezogene Kommunikation zwischen Systemen. Die Kommunikation wird dabei über bestimmte Situationen abgewickelt. Das Modell der Umgebung umfaßt in unserer Betrachtungsweise alle dem System und der Umgebung gemeinsamen Situationen. Diese Situationen sind Ergebnis sichtbarer Handlungen unseres Systems und zugleich Voraussetzung für Handlungen der Umgebung oder umgekehrt. Wir bezeichnen sie als Kommunikationssituationen. Das Modell der Umgebung umfaßt darüber hinaus die Handlungen der Umgebung, die für das System sichtbar sind und vom System angewandt werden. Das Modell umfaßt schließlich auch Situationen, die Abhängigkeiten zwischen Handlungen und Entscheidungen der Umgebung modellieren. Das betrachtete System hat jedoch auf diese äußeren Situationen, Handlungen und Entscheidungen nur über die Schnittstelle einen Einfluß.

In Abb. 2 sind die Handlungen der Umgebung **(pakete zuführen, störung beseitigen, durchlauf kontrollieren)** und die Kommunikationssituationen zeichentechnisch hervorgehoben. Die von der Kommunikation des Netzes mit der Umgebung betroffenen systeminternen Handlungen **(paket einlauf, störung melden, verteilstatn steuern)** wären über die Kommunikationsschnittstelle sichtbar.

4 ZUR SYSTEMKONSTRUKTION

Wir können den Prozeß der iterativen Verfeinerung der Systemelemente als schrittweise Formalisierung von Handlungs-Entscheidungs-Netzen begreifen: zunächst gibt es nur präformale Netze mit wenig Struktur und abstrakten Anschriften. Diese werden umgesetzt in Netze mit immer mehr Struktur und konkreteren Anschriften, bis schließlich eine Detaillierungsebene erreicht ist, die nur noch auf präzisierte, existierende Grundelemente Bezug nimmt. Die Netzstruktur kann jeweils formal behandelt werden, die Anschriften erklären das Netz, indem sie informell den Bezug der Netzstruktur zur Realität wiedergeben. Die Transformation der Netzstruktur und der Anschriften ist konstruktiv vom Entwickler anzugeben. Dabei sind bestimmte Regeln der Netztransformation einzuhalten, auf die wir hier nur exemplarisch eingehen können.

4.1 Verfeinerung, Vergröberung.

Transformationen von Netzen, wie sie bei der Konstruktion von Systemmodellen benutzt werden, sind netztheoretisch durch Morphismen gegeben. Morphismen respektieren die Netzstruktur insofern, als die Kausalbeziehung und die Nachbarschaftsbeziehung zwischen Netzelementen bei der Transformation erhalten oder auf Identität zurückgeführt werden [9]. Da wir darüber hinaus fordern, daß sich verfeinernde Netze auf verschiedenen Detaillierungsebenen gleich interpretierbar sein sollen, sind weitere Einschränkungen für zulässige Morphismen notwendig.

Abb. 2 bezeichnet einen Netzmorphismus, der das voll gezeichnete Netz in das gestrichelte Netz transformiert. (Die Kausalbeziehungen des Grobnetzes sind nicht eingezeichnet; sie ergeben sich aus der Bündelung der Kausalbeziehungen des feinen Netzes.) Dabei werden alternative Handlungen (alle Entscheidungen, die **code lesen** erklären) und dazu korrespondierende Situationen **(zielstation, kein ziel)** aufeinander gefaltet. Die durch den Morphismus angegebenen Zusammenfassungen von Netzelementen zu **code lesen** und **paket code** sind nicht unabhängig voneinander.

Einen Morphismus, der etwa die Entscheidungen von **code lesen,** nicht aber ihre Ergebnisse **(zielstation, kein ziel)** vergröbern würde, wollen wir nicht zulassen. In diesem Fall lägen nach der Durchführung von **code lesen** die Ergebnisse **zielstation** und **kein ziel** gemeinsam, in der Verfeinerung von **code lesen** nach der Durchführung einer ihrer inneren Entscheidungen dagegen alternativ vor. Die Tranformation nebenläufiger Handlungen in alternative Handlungen würde ebenfalls gegen die Forderung nach einer einheitlichen Interpretation verstoßen.

4.2 Sichten

Handlungs-Entscheidungs-Netze ermöglichen es, ein Objekt von einem bestimmten Blickpunkt aus zu modellieren. So entstehen verschiedene Sichten des Objekts, die verschiedene Aspekte beleuchten. Oft kann ein Gesamteindruck erst vermittelt oder erhalten werden aus der Betrachtung aus verschiedenen Blickwinkeln, kann der Kontext eines Modells, d.h. was enthalten ist und was in dem Modell ausgeschlossen ist, bestimmt werden.

Bei der Systementwicklung ist Information unter verschiedenen Gesichtspunkten anzugeben und zu analysieren. Datenfluß, Prozeßzerlegung, Kontrollfluß entsprechen solchen Sichten, aber auch die unterschiedlichen Perspektiven, unter denen in verschiedenen Entwicklungsphasen ein und dasselbe System gesehen wird (Spezifikation versus Test etc.) oder Perspektiven, unter denen verschiedenen Gruppen ein System sehen (Auftraggeber, Benutzer, Entwickler, Projektmanager).

Sichten werden bei der top-down Konstruktion zunächst als (i.S. der Netztopologie) unabhängige Netze und Netzhierarchien entwickelt. Ihre Beziehung wird schließlich in einer gemeinsamen Verfeinerung durch Überdeckung von Systemelementen hergestellt.

Aus einem gegebenen Netz können aber auch neue Sichten durch Vergröberung nach unterschiedlichen Aspekten gewonnen werden, um Plausibilitätsbetrachtungen zu unterstützen oder um das Modell für Experten unterschiedlicher Gebiete zu veranschaulichen.

Einen formalen Hintergrund zur Bestimmung dieses Konstruktionskonzepts liefert der Begriff des Netzmorphismus. Wir erhalten damit eine polyhierarchische Systemstruktur im Großen. Sie erweist sich im Unterschied zu klassischen hierarchischen Strukturen als Überdeckung mehrerer verschiedener Abstraktions-Hierarchien. Ein Element der polyhierarchischen Struktur kann somit mehr als ein Vaterelement oder eine Vergröberung besitzen.

In Abb. 5a und b sind die Verhalten zweier Teile des Freigabeorgans (Abb. 5c) der Eingangsstation getrennt modelliert.

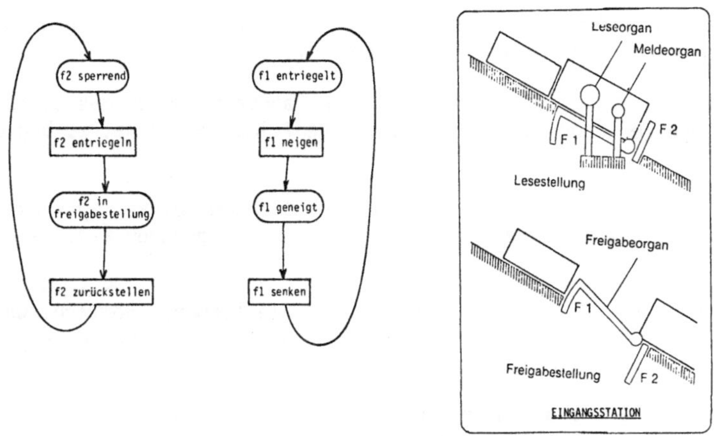

Abb. 5a,b,c Verhalten von Teil 1 und 2 des Freigabeorgans und die Eingangsstation aus [8]

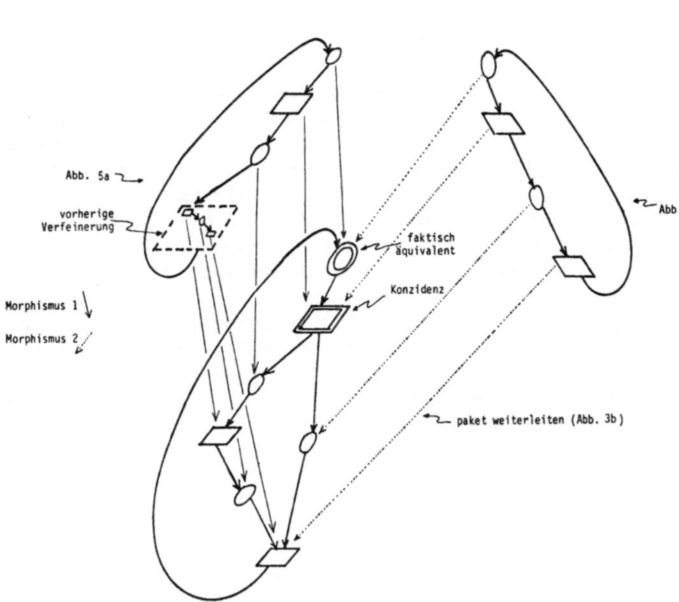

Abb. 6 Zwei Sichten des Freigabeorgans und ihre Überdeckung

Abb. 6 zeigt, wie die beiden unabhängigen Netze durch zwei **Netzmorphismen** zu einer gemeinsamen Darstellung des Verhaltens des Freigabeorgans überdeckt werden. Bei dieser Erweiterung des Betrachtungskontextes in der gemeinsamen Verfeinerung werden Situationen aus verschiedenen Sichten faktisch äquivalent; Handlungen aus verschiedenen Sichten werden zu koinzidenten Handlungen. Damit haben wir modelliert, daß im selben Schritt **f1** geneigt und **f2** entriegelt werden sollen (d.h. Paket kann weiterlaufen), **f1** aber erst gesenkt werden soll, nachdem **f2** zurückgestellt ist (um den Durchlauf neuer Pakete zu verhindern).

ZUSAMMENFASSUNG

Aufbauend auf der Anschaulichkeit grafischer Netzdarstellungen und formaler Konzepte der Netztheorie haben wir ein Systemmodell zur Beschreibung nebenläufiger Systeme eingeführt:

- **Das Modell bietet auf allen Ebenen** eine einheitliche Interpretation und die Möglichkeit, Strukturen unterschiedlichen Abstraktionsgrades "logisch" oder "funktionell" miteinander zu verknüpfen. Die Interpretation folgt dabei partiell der Interpretation von Bedingungs-Ereignis-Netzen [11]. Die Idee ist, die korrekte Umsetzung der Systemdaten von einer Beschreibungsebene zur anderen zu erleichtern und den Übergang zwischen unterschiedlichen Entwicklungsphasen (etwa Grobentwurf, Feinentwurf, Implementation) nachvollziehbar zu machen.

- Der Begriff des Netzmorphismus wird benutzt, um wohlbekannte Methoden des Software Engineering wie modulare Zerlegung und schrittweise Verfeinerung formal zu begründen.

- Der Morphismenbegriff ermöglicht es, unterschiedliche Sichten eines Systems zu modellieren, ineinander überzuführen oder aus einer einer gegebenen Beschreibung zu extrahieren.

- Morphismen können auch zur Gegenüberstellung unterschiedlicher, möglicherweise alternativer Entwürfe herangezogen werden. Entwurfsentscheidungen können leichter identifiziert und systematischer revidiert werden.

- Die Konzepte der Netztheorie und die hier benutzte Netzinterpretation ermöglichen es nicht nur, Programmstrukturen oder Prozesse zu beschreiben, sondern auch die technische und organisatorische Umgebung, in die das Softwaresystem eingebettet ist.

Dieser Artikel gibt den Stand einer noch im Gang befindlichen Diskussion wieder. Vieles konnte nur exemplarisch angedeutet werden, auf die Diskussion anderer Ergebnisse der Allgemeinen Netztheorie (etwa zur synchronischen Struktur von Systemen, auf die sich beispielsweise die Angabe von Prioritäten zwischen widerstreitenden Handlungen zurückführen ließe) mußte ganz verzichtet werden.

Dennoch sollte deutlich geworden sein, daß die Ergebnisse der Netztheorie verschiedene Fragestellungen formal zu beantworten erlauben. Wir können illegales oder unerwünschtes Systemverhalten durch Simulation des Netzmodells oder durch eine Analyse der Netzstruktur feststellen. Wir können nach den möglichen Verläufen von Handlungen fragen, nach kausalen Abhängigkeiten zwischen bestimmten Handlungen. Wir können bestimmen, ob ein System widerspruchsfrei oder vollständig ist (d.h. ob unbenutzte Handlungen oder Situationen vorkommen oder ob eine faktische Aussage aus dem gegebenen System ableitbar ist) oder ob das System lebendig und sicher ist [9].

Anders als bei der von der Fa. Siemens [14] entwickelten Petrinetz-Entwurfstechnologie können wir bisher kein rechnerunterstütztes System anbieten. Dieses Entwurfssystem stellt bisher aber nur Stellen-Transitions-Netze [9] zur Verfügung. Es sind nur Verfeinerungen von Transitionen möglich, so daß nur einfach-hierarchische Systemstrukturen entwickelt werden können. Ein formaler Umgang mit Beschriftungen ist - abgesehen von einer Gewichtung der Kanten - nicht vorgesehen. Systemmodelle können nur auf Lebendigkeit und Sicherheit überprüft werden. Uns ist nicht bekannt, inwieweit die Absicht realisiert ist, in einer Nachfolgeversion eine höhere Netzinterpretation und weitere Entwurfs- und Analysefunktionen bereitzustellen. Mit den Ansätzen zur Systemstruktur und zu Entwurfsprinzipien streben wir ein mächtigeres Systemmodell an. Die Polyhierarchie und die Möglichkeit zu vergröbern und Sichten zu extrahieren führen über einfach-hierarchische Systemstrukturen hinaus. Der in Abschnitt 3.2 eingeführte Pseudocode und an die Aussagen über zulässige Morphismen zeigen einen Weg, wie man zu einer formal abgesicherten Beschriftungsdisziplin kommt und zu Regeln der inkrementellen Entwicklung von Netzbeschreibungen. Solche Regeln bestimmen den Funktionsumfang rechnergestützten Entwicklungssystems.

LITERATUR

[1] Jones, C. B.: Towards More Formal Specifications. German Chapter of the ACM, Berichte Nr. 5, pp. 19-45, Stuttgart: B.G. Teubner (1981)

[2] Kreowski, H.-J.: Algebraische Spezifikation von Softwaresystemen. German Chapter of the ACM, Berichte Nr. 5, pp. 46-74, Stuttgart: B.G. Teubner (1981)

[3] Krämer, B. und Schmidt, H. W.: Interactive Software Development by Stepwise Formalisation. Proceedings of the sixth ACM European regional conference (pp.134-143), Guildford, England: IPC Press Ltd. (1981)

[4] Budde, R.: Einige Prinzipien zum Verständnis nebenläufiger Systeme und Prozesse. Beitrag dieser Tagung (1981)

[5] Brauer, W. (ed.): Net Theory and Applications. Lecture Notes in Computer Science, vol. 84. Berlin, Heidelberg, New York: Springer (1980)

[6] Petri, C.A.: Über einige Anwendungen der Netztheorie. GI - 9. Jahrestagung, Informatik-Fachberichte, vol. 19. Berlin, Heidelberg, New York: Springer (1979)

[7] Bretschneider, G.: Petri Heil. Computerwoche, Juni 1980.

[8] Hommel, G. (Hrsg.): Vergleich verschiedener Spezifikationsverfahren am Beispiel einer Paketverteilanlage. PDV-Berichte, Karlsruhe: KfK-PDV 186, Teile 1 und 2 (1980)

[9] Genrich, H.J., Lautenbach, K., und Thiagarajan, P.S.: Elements of General Net Theory. In [5], pp. 21-163 (1980)

[10] Genrich, H.J.: Ein systemtheoretischer Beitrag zur Handlungslogik. In: ed. H. Lenk, Handlungstheorien interdisziplinär I, München: Wilhelm Fink Verlag (1980)

[11] Dehottay, J.P., Feuerhahn, H., Koster, C.H.A. und Stahl, H.M.: Syntaktische Beschreibung von CDL2. Bericht des Informatik Forschungsprojekts CDL2, Berlin: Technische Universität (1976)

[12] Koster, C.H.A.: Visibility and Types. Conference on Data, Salt Lake City, SIGPLAN Notices Special Issue, pp. 179-190 (1976)

[13] Feuerhahn, H. und Koster, C.H.A.: Static Semantic Checks in an Openended Language. In: Constructing Quality Software. Amsterdam: North Holland Publishing Company (1978)

[14] Bretschneider, G.: Petrinetze - Ein leicht verständliches Vefahren zum Systementwurf. München: Siemens AG, Bereich Daten- und Informationssysteme (1980)

Anforderungen an die Software zur Gestaltung humaner Arbeitsplätze in computergesteuerten Fertigungsprozessen

T. Martin
Projektträgerschaft Fertigungstechnik,
Kernforschungszentrum Karlsruhe GmbH,
Postfach 3640, 7500 Karlsruhe

Zusammenfassung
Bei der humanen Gestaltung von Arbeitsplätzen in computergesteuerten Fertigungsprozessen fällt dem Entwurf der Software eine Schlüsselrolle zu, weil sie es ist, die den Computer lenkt. Der Aufsatz geht der Frage nach, wie humane Anforderungen an die Software definiert und spezifiziert werden können. Als wichtigstes Humankriterium beim Entwurf ist der von Arbeitspsychologen definierte Begriff der Persönlichkeitsförderlichkeit zu nennen. Hinsichtlich seiner Realisierung bestehen im methodischen wie im empirischen Bereich große Defizite, die nur durch interdisziplinäre Anstrengung behoben werden können. Als methodischer Ansatz für die Spezifikation humaner Anforderungen wird die Funktionen/Kriterien-Matrix vorgeschlagen und am Beispiel eines flexiblen Fertigungssystems vorgeführt. Am Schluß wird ein Beispiel von Arbeitsbereicherung geschildert.

Einleitung

Das öffentlich geförderte Programm "Fertigungstechnik", das die Fertigungsindustrie bei der Einführung neuer Technologien, insbesondere der Informationstechnologie, unterstützen soll, ist mit dem Anspruch angetreten, dabei darauf zu achten, daß möglichst humane Arbeitsplätze entstehen. Die im Programm "Humanisierung des Arbeitslebens" gewonnenen arbeitswissenschaftlichen Erkenntnisse sollen mitberücksichtigt und in die Praxis umgesetzt werden.

Nicht nur in der Produktion ist eine wachsende Anzahl von Arbeitsplätzen von Prozeßdatenverarbeitungssystemen geprägt. Computer dringen ebenso auch in die Büros, in Dienstleistungsbereiche und in private Bereiche vor. Die Art und Weise, wie sich der Computer auf den beteiligten Menschen auswirkt, wird einerseits durch die Arbeitsorganisation (Mensch-Maschine-Funktionsteilung), andererseits durch die Eigenschaften der Programme (Software) bestimmt; denn sie sind es, die den Computer, mit dem der Mensch in einer Produktionseinheit arbeitet, lenken. Der Software fällt daher heute bei der Gestaltung humaner Arbeitsplätze eine Schlüsselrolle zu.

Sind wir überhaupt schon in der Lage, Anforderungen dieser Art, nämlich humane Qualitätsmerkmale von computerbestimmten Arbeitsplätzen zu spezifizieren und dem Softwareingenieur als Aufgabenstellung an die Hand zu geben? Dieser Frage soll im folgenden - bezogen auf Arbeitsplätze in der Fertigung - nachgegangen werden (das Gesagte gilt jedoch sinngemäß auch für andere Computeranwendungsbereiche).

Vorab soll nach der Gestaltungsbedürftigkeit computerbestimmter Arbeitsplätze und nach den Zielen einer solchen Gestaltung gefragt werden.

Sind computerbestimmte Arbeitsplätze gestaltungsbedürftig?

Die Entwicklung der industriellen Produktion ist gekennzeichnet durch wachsende Mechanisierung, sich steigernde Automatisierung und zunehmend zerlegende und hierarchisierende Arbeitsorganisation. Bei der Arbeitszerlegung bzw. -teilung werden einerseits die einzelnen Arbeitsgänge durch Personen unterschiedlicher Qualifikation ausgeführt, andererseits werden auch einzelne Arbeitsaufgaben (z.B. das Planen und Vorbereiten der Arbeit) gegenüber der eigentlichen Arbeit am Werkstück vorverlagert, so daß diese inhaltlich verarmt. (Eine Definition des Begriffs 'Arbeitsinhalt' ist beispielsweise folgende (frei nach /1/, S. 23): Der Inhalt der Arbeit sind diejenigen Funktionen, die sich aus der Realisierung des Arbeitsauftrages und den Ausführungsbedingungen zur Erreichung des geforderten Arbeitsfortschrittes ergeben.)
Die heutige Industriearbeit ist mehrfach nach Gesichtspunkten der Arbeitsqualität untersucht worden. Einige Erkenntnisse aus diesen Untersuchungen seien im folgenden wiedergegeben.
Eine extreme Form der oben erwähnten Vorverlagerung ist die Hochautomatisierung, bei der dem 'Bediener' als anspruchsvollste Tätigkeitskomponente nur noch ein monotones Überwachen (Überforderung durch Unterforderung) verbleibt. Ein Beispiel dafür sind NC-gesteuerte Werkzeugmaschinen /2/, bei denen der Arbeitsinhalt auf das Überwachen und das Zuführen und Entnehmen der Werkstücke und Werkzeuge eingeengt ist. Ein weiteres Beispiel sind Resttätigkeiten, die beim Einsatz von Robotern übrigbleiben /3/. Bei hochautomatisierten Anlagen (zuerst in der Großchemie beobachtet) kann es zu einer Differenzierung der Industriearbeit in dem Sinne kommen, daß einerseits höherqualifizierte Arbeitsplätze verbunden mit Leistungsverdichtung (Anlagenfahrer) entstehen, andererseits unqualifizierte Hilfsarbeiten übrigbleiben (Polarisierung der Qualifikation) /4/. Ähnliches kann bei der Anwendung von CAD (Computer Aided Design) im Konstruktionsbüro geschehen, wenn einige Benutzer (Ingenieure) sich höher qualifizieren, die Qualifikation technischer Zeichner jedoch entwertet wird /5/.
An hochautomatisierten Anlagen ist aber auch gezeigt worden /6/, daß bei der Gestaltung der Arbeitsplätze weite Spielräume bestehen. Der steigende Automatisierungsgrad wirkt sich nicht zwangsläufig verändernd auf den Inhalt der Arbeit in der einen oder anderen Richtung aus, wohl aber die Verwendungsweise und die Gestaltung des Automatisierungsmittels im einzelnen. Jede technische Entscheidung ist daher immer auch eine soziale.
Die moderne Produktionsweise bringt vielfältige Belastungsarten für die Arbeitspersonen mit sich. Belastungsuntersuchungen ergaben, daß 15 bis 30% aller Arbeitsplätze als dringend gestaltungsbedürftig einzustufen sind. Besonders gesundheitsschädlich sind Belastungskombinationen, und zwar Kombinationen von physikalisch-chemischen Belastungen (z. B. Lärm) mit arbeitsorganisatorischen Belastungen (Schichtarbeit, Monotonie) /7/.

Somit läßt sich folgendes feststellen: Computerbestimmte Arbeitsplätze sind in der Tat gestaltungsbedürftig. Die technische und arbeitsorganisatorische Entwicklung verläuft nicht zwangsläufig, vielmehr bietet sie Gestaltungsspielräume. Der Gestaltungsspielraum des Computers liegt in seiner Freiprogrammierbarkeit. Sie gilt es - geleitet von Humankriterien - zu nutzen.

Was sind die Ziele und Bewertungsmerkmale bei der menschengerechten Gestaltung von Software?

Will man die Gestaltung menschlicher Arbeitsplätze bewerten, so sollte man die neueren Erkenntnisse der Arbeitswissenschaft, insbesondere der Arbeitspsychologie, zu Rate ziehen. Die dort gewonnenen Befunde besagen, daß die Arbeitstätigkeit entscheidenden Einfluß auf das Erleben, das Verhalten und die Entwicklung der Persönlichkeit hat, und zwar weit über den Bereich der Arbeit hinaus auch auf das ganze menschliche Leben. Die Entscheidung darüber, was menschengerecht ist, muß vom Verständnis des Menschen als denkendes und handelndes Wesen ausgehen. Die psychologische Handlungstheorie hat dafür die Grundlage gelegt. Sie versteht menschliches Handeln als bewußt, zielgerichtet, rückgemeldet und hierarchisch-sequentiell organisiert /8/. Von dieser (von der Kybernetik beeinflußten) Modellvorstellung soll hier nur der Aspekt der hierarchisch-sequentiellen Organisation kurz erläutert werden.

Die Ausführung einer Handlung wird je nach dem Grad der Komplexheit der Aufgabe und der Geübtheit des Handelnden auf verschiedenen Ebenen reguliert. Mindestens drei miteinander in Wechselwirkung stehende Regulationsebenen lassen sich unterscheiden. Die <u>intellektuelle</u> (höchste) <u>Regulationsebene</u> umfaßt Prozesse der Analyse und Synthese komplexer Situationen, die subjektiv neue Anforderungen stellen. Sie ermöglicht ein Probehandeln am gedanklichen Modell und die Entwicklung einer planenden Strategie. In der <u>perzeptiv-begrifflichen</u> (mittleren) <u>Regulationsebene</u> geschieht das Erkennen und Ausfiltern tätigkeitsrelevanter Signale. Sie werden mit flexiblen Handlungsmustern ("einfachen" Tätigkeiten) beantwortet. Auf der <u>sensumotorischen</u> (untersten) <u>Regulationsebene</u> werden Bewegungsmuster geschaffen bzw. aktiviert, die bei gleichförmigen Anforderungen zu automatisierten Bewegungsstereotypien werden /9/. Die höhere Ebene umfaßt Ziele und Aktionsprogramme der jeweils niedrigeren, wobei die unteren Ebenen einen möglichst großen Teil der Aufgabe übernehmen sollten, um so die intellektuelle Ebene für die Bewältigung komplexer Planungsvorgänge zu entlasten. Ausgehend von dieser Handlungstheorie läßt sich für die Bewertung menschengerechter Gestaltung von Arbeit folgende Zielrichtung ableiten.

Zunächst sollte die menschliche Handlungsorganisation in ihrer Ganzheit (alle Ebenen) beteiligt werden. Will man die planende Strategie als höchste menschliche Fähigkeit nutzen, und berücksichtigt man den Zusammenhang von Arbeitstätigkeit und Persönlichkeit, so folgt für unsere Fragestellung:
Software sollte so gestaltet werden, daß sie dazu beiträgt, an dem betroffenen Arbeitsplatz das Erwerben und Vertiefen planender Strategie zu ermöglichen. Und umgekehrt: Wenn automatisierte Prozesse den beteiligten Menschen daran hindern, mit dem Bewußtsein in der Technik zu bleiben /9/, so müssen seine Handlungskompetenz und seine Motivation verfallen. Tatsächlich "setzt eine zugleich zu hohen Leistungen motivierende Befriedigung nicht vorrangig an Arbeitsumgebungsbedingungen, sozialen Beziehungen und auch nicht am Lohn an, sondern mit großem Abstand dominiert der Inhalt der Arbeit selbst ....., insbesondere die Möglichkeit, in der Tätigkeit die geistigen Fähigkeiten anwenden zu können" (aus /11/, S. 376).

Es geht also nun darum, den Inhalt der Arbeit danach zu bewerten, wie er Beiträge für die Realisierung der Einheit von Persönlichkeitsförderlichkeit, Leistungsförderung und Beanspruchungsoptimierung als allgemeine Merkmale humaner Gestaltung der Arbeit liefert. Macher /1/ gibt dafür folgende fünf Bewertungsgrößen an:

- Niveau der geistigen Tätigkeitsanforderungen (Aspekt der planenden Strategie)
- Grad der Vielfalt
- Kombinationsgrad
- Grad der Verantwortung (für die Effektivität des Arbeitsprozesses und die Qualität des Produktes)
- Grad der Beanspruchung (Belastung, Monotonie, psychische Sättigung)

(In der DDR sind Versuche schon weit fortgeschritten, diese Merkmale in der Form von Kennzahlen quantifizierbar zu machen /1/.)

Zur Veranschaulichung der Ergebnisse solcher Bewertung von Inhalten der Arbeit diene das folgende Beispiel. Verglichen sei die Arbeit an Werkzeugmaschinen (Drehmaschinen) unterschiedlichen Technisierungsniveaus, nämlich

- konventionellen Maschinen
- verketteten konventionellen Maschinen
- teilautomatisierten Maschinen (NC-gesteuert) mit großer Tiefe der Arbeitsteilung.

Im zusammenfassenden Kennzahlenprofil (Bild 1) wird die unterschiedliche Ausprägung der einzelnen Aspekte anschaulich (nach Macher /1/).

In einem ergonomischen Bewertungsschema steht das Kriterium der Persönlichkeitsförderlichkeit an der Spitze einer Hierarchie von Bewertungsebenen. Sie bedeutet, daß jeweils vor dem Übergang zur nächsten Bewertungsebene die Mindestanforderungen der darunter liegenden erfüllt werden müssen, notfalls durch Umgestaltung des Arbeitsplatzes (Bild 2; nach Hacker /11/).

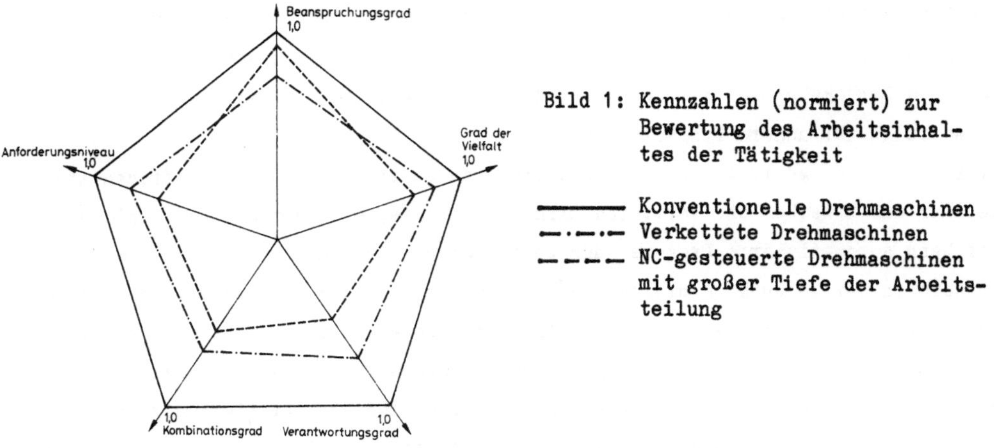

Bild 1: Kennzahlen (normiert) zur Bewertung des Arbeitsinhaltes der Tätigkeit

——— Konventionelle Drehmaschinen
—·—·— Verkettete Drehmaschinen
— — — NC-gesteuerte Drehmaschinen mit großer Tiefe der Arbeitsteilung

Bewertungsebenen	Unterebenen	Mögliche Kriterien (Beispiele)
Persönlichkeitsförderlichkeit ↑	o Höherqualifizierung o Erhaltung der Qualifikation o Dequalifizierung	o Handlungsspielraum o erforderliche Lernaktivität
Beeinträchtigungsfreiheit (Zumutbarkeit) ↑	o ohne Beeinträchtigung o verminderte Effektivität o funktionelle Störungen	Stufen psychischer und physischer Belastungswirkungen
Schädigungslosigkeit ↑	Gesundheitsschäden o ausgeschlossen o möglich o sehr wahrscheinlich	o MAK-Werte (gesundheitsschädlicher Arbeitsstoffe) o Unfallgefahr
Ausführbarkeit ↑	Normwerte o eingehalten o teilweise nicht eingehalten o überwiegend nicht eingehalten	o anthropotechnische o sinnesphysiologische o psychische Normwerte

Bild 2: Hierarchisches System zur ergonomischen Bewertung von Arbeitsgestaltungsmaßnahmen

Lösungsansätze zur menschengerechten Gestaltung von Computersoftware

Beim Festlegen von Technologien und der Arbeitsteilung im Fertigungsprozeß und bei der Entwicklung technischer Komponenten werden stets künftige Inhalte der Arbeit und damit Qualitäten des Arbeitsplatzes festgelegt. Häufig findet Arbeitsgestaltung erst im Nachhinein statt, nachdem Nachteile für die Betroffenen festgestellt worden sind (z.B. wird Monotonie durch Job Enrichment abgebaut). Die Nachteile solcher korrektiver Arbeitsgestaltung können vermieden werden, wenn man bereits im Stadium des Entwurfs von Produktionssystemen die arbeitswissenschaftlichen Erfordernisse berücksichtigt. Die Berücksichtigung des Kriteriums der Persönlichkeitsförderlichkeit verlangt darüber hinausgehend prospektive Arbeitsgestaltung /12/, das heißt, die gedankliche Vorwegnahme von Möglichkeiten der Persönlichkeitsentwicklung durch Schaffung objektiver Handlungsspielräume.

Im Prozeß solcher Arbeitsgestaltung gibt es im wesentlichen vier Ansatzstellen, an denen der Inhalt der Arbeit festgelegt wird. Sie sind einander mit zunehmender Einschränkung der Wahlmöglichkeiten nachgeordnet /13/.

a) Fertigungs-(speziell arbeitsprozeß-)bezogene Erzeugnisgestaltung.
Ein Produkt sollte so konstruiert werden, daß seine Fertigung (ohne Einschränkung seiner Gebrauchswerteigenschaften und ohne Erhöhung der Kosten) unter Einhaltung der Humankriterien möglich ist.

b) Funktionsverteilung zwischen Mensch und Maschine.
Darüber wird bei der Wahl der Technologie und des Mechanisierungs- und Automatisierungsgrades entschieden. Zu berücksichtigen sind (neben der Wirtschaftlichkeit) die Anforderungen an den Menschen (mit dem Einfluß auf die Systemzuverlässigkeit), daraus resultierende Belastungen und der Qualifikationsaspekt (mit dem Einfluß auf die Persönlichkeitsentwicklung, die Produktionseffektivität und die Produktqualität).

c) Aufgabenverteilung zwischen den Menschen.
Hier geht es vor allem darum, die (aus dem Taylorismus stammende) Teilung von geistiger (vorbereitender, planender, organisierender, kontrollierender) und manueller Arbeit zu vermeiden.

d) Festlegung von Aufgaben mit Freiheitsgraden.
Dadurch kann die individuelle Befähigung von Arbeitspersonen ausgenutzt werden. Sie kann durch neuere Methoden der Qualifizierung (z.B. sprachgestütztes mentales Training) gesteigert werden.

Es ist festzustellen, daß für das systematische Berücksichtigen solcher Aspekte bei der Gestaltung von Software sowohl im methodischen wie im empirischen Bereich große Defizite bestehen. Einiges geschieht gegenwärtig auf dem Gebiet der dialogorientierten Bildschirmarbeitsplätze /14/. Neben Handlungsanleitungen zur ergonomischen Gestaltung des Bildschirms im engeren Sinn /15/ gibt es Erkenntnisse der "kognitiven" Ergonomie, die berücksichtigt werden sollten, z.B. /16/

- sollte es Varianten für vorgedachte Benutzerkommandos geben (Dialogflexibilität);
- sollte die Programmstruktur ein optimierbares Antwortzeitverhalten berücksichtigen;
- sollten Ausgabeformate variabel gestaltbar sein;
- sollte es die Möglichkeit geben, vorgedachte Denkstrukturen zu verkürzen;
- sollte der Arbeitsumfang im Rahmen des Lernverhaltens ausgeweitet werden können.

Diese Hinweise sollten bei der Gestaltung von bildschirmgestützten Fertigungssteuerungssystemen in der Produktion und von CAD-Systemen (siehe dazu Hinweise in /9/) beachtet werden.

Systematisches Vorgehen bei der menschengerechten Gestaltung von Software

Bei der Gestaltung von Software ist die Spezifikation der funktionellen Anforderungen die erste und - wie man heute weiß - für den Erfolg in hohem Maße entscheidende Phase.

Die geforderten Funktionen müssen insgesamt die übergeordneten Kriterien (Qualitätsmerkmale) erfüllen. Solche Qualitätsmerkmale sind z.B. Zuverlässigkeit, Testbarkeit, Speichereffizienz. Dazu müssen nun noch die personenbezogenen Kriterien wie Persönlichkeitsförderlichkeit und Zumutbarkeit (bzw. davon abgeleitete Bewertungsgrößen) treten. Nach der Phase der Anforderungsspezifikation folgt die Phase des Entwurfs der Software. Hier hat der Softwareingenieur die Aufgabe, Maßnahmen zu ergreifen, die zur Erfüllung des Anforderungsfeldes geeignet sind. Das Anforderungsfeld läßt sich formal als Funktionen/Kriterien-Matrix beschreiben /17/.
Diese Matrix ist bisher nur für rein technische Anforderungen verwendet worden. Es wird vorgeschlagen, sie für die Berücksichtigung humaner Anforderungen an Software aufzugreifen. Das folgende Beispiel soll erläutern, wie dabei vorzugehen ist.
Gegeben sei die Aufgabe, ein flexibles Fertigungssystem (FFS) zu gestalten (das ist ein System von verketteten Werkzeugmaschinen, mit dem ein Spektrum von Werkstücken komplett bearbeitet werden kann). Man geht nun so vor, daß man allen funktionellen Anforderungen (Einzelfunktionen) sämtliche zu berücksichtigenden Humankriterien in einer Matrix gegenüberstellt. Bild 3 zeigt einen Ausschnitt möglicher Funktionen und Humankriterien (vgl. Bild 2) für ein hypothetisches FFS. In jedem Feld der Matrix steht (sofern erforderlich) ein Verweis auf die Maßnahme zur Erfüllung des Kriteriums. Maßnahme M7 beispielsweise soll dem Bediener ermöglichen, Störungen in der Hydraulik selbst zu beseitigen. Dafür muß er zusätzlich zur Zerspanungstechnik in Hydraulik ausgebildet sein, jedoch wird ein gesonderter Hydraulik-Fachmann nicht benötigt.

Diese Maßnahmen stehen zunächst (wie im Beispiel) auf einem hohen Abstraktionsniveau mit funktionellem Charakter. Sie sind "top-down" bis herunter zu programmiertechnischen Entscheidungen zu verfeinern. So entsteht in mehreren iterativen Durchgängen aus dem Maßnahmenkatalog die Entwurfsspezifikation der Software. Zu beachten ist, daß sich in der Regel zur Erfüllung eines Kriteriums mehrere technische Lösungsmöglichkeiten anbieten. Diese technischen Alternativen sind alle nach den obigen Gesichtspunkten (vier Ansatzstellen) zu durchdenken. Ausgeführt können letztendlich nur diejenigen werden, die sich in einem Prozeß des Aushandelns zwischen den Entscheidungsträgern (Betriebsverfassungsparteien) durchsetzen lassen. Dieser Prozeß verläuft umso einvernehmlicher, je besser humane und wirtschaftliche Gesichtspunkte bei der Softwaregestaltung konvergieren. Die Beispiele, bei denen nachgewiesen werden konnte, daß die humanere technische Alternative auch die wirtschaftlichere ist, sollten uns ermutigen. Ein solches Beispiel sei zum Schluß kurz geschildert.

HUMANE KRITERIEN / FUNKTIONELLE ANFORDERUNGEN	Schädigungslosigkeit			Beeinträchtigungsfreiheit			Persönlichkeitsförderlichkeit			
	Unfallgefahr	Umgebungs-bedingungen	...	Entkopplung von der Maschine	Kontrolle der Arbeitsperson	...	Qualifikations-vielfalt	Lernmöglichkeit	Dispositions-spielraum	...
Manueller Werkzeugwechsel an der Werkzeugmaschine	M1	S		M3	O		O	M8	S	
Automatische Werkzeug-brucherkennung	O	O		M4	O		O	O	O	
Überwachung der Hydraulik	S	M2		S	O		M7	M8	S	
⋮										
Fertigungssteuerung	O	O		M5	M6		S	M8	M5	

Mi Maßnahmenkatalog (Entwurfsspezifikation)

M1 Einrichtung zum Schutz gegen Greifen in den Arbeitsraum bei laufender Maschine.

M2 Lärmbegrenzung

M3 Automatisches Erfassen des Werkzeugverschleißes. Rechtzeitiges Ausgeben einer Meldung mit Angabe der voraussichtlichen Reststandzeit des Werkzeugs (auch auf Anforderung).

M4 Automatisches Abschalten der Maschine bei Werkzeugbruch verbunden mit Signalgabe.

M5 Fertigungsvorgaben und -daten auf Anforderung vom Bildschirm frühzeitig abrufbar.

M6 Trennung der Werkstückdaten von den personenbezogenen Daten bei der Betriebsdatenerfassung.

M7 Hydraulik-Funktionsanzeige und -Diagnosefunktion für den Bediener.

M8 Rückmeldung nach jedem Bedienungseingriff, die eine Ergebnisbeurteilung erlaubt.

⋮ ⋮

Bild 3: Funktionen/Kriterien-Matrix (Beispiel für die Berücksichtigung humaner Anforderungen an ein flexibles Fertigungssystem)

Mi ... Verweis von Matrixpunkten auf Maßnahmen
S ... noch zu spezifizieren
O ... keine Maßnahme erforderlich

Beispiel eines humanen Arbeitsplatzes an einer NC-gesteuerten Werkzeugmaschine

Oben wurde bereits dargestellt, wie die Teilautomatisierung der Werkzeugmaschine mittels NC-Steuerung zu einer Tätigkeit geführt hat, deren Arbeitsinhalt gegenüber der konventionellen Maschine erheblich reduziert ist (Bild 1). Dabei fand die Programmierung der NC-Steuerung personell und räumlich getrennt von der Produktion statt /2/.

Die Verfügbarkeit von Mikrocomputern gestattet nun, die benötigte Datenverarbeitungskapazität in die NC-Steuerung zu integrieren, und eine Rückverlagerung der NC-Programmerstellung an die Werkzeugmaschine zu ermöglichen (Werkstattprogrammierung) /18/. Dazu ist notwendig, für das Programmieren eines Teileprogramms eine Programmiersprache und ein Dialogbedienfeld zu entwickeln, die der technologischen Denkweise des Facharbeiters entsprechen /19/. Damit umfaßt sein Arbeitsplatz die Tätigkeiten Programmieren, Einrichten, Korrigieren und Produzieren, wodurch sein Entscheidungsspielraum und sein Tätigkeitsfeld wesentlich erweitert worden sind.

Diese Arbeitsbereicherung geht nicht mit der Integration der EDV automatisch einher, sondern muß arbeitsorganisatorisch abgesichert werden. Sie läßt sich durch Hinzunahme weiterer Tätigkeiten wie Wartung und Maschinenbelegung (dispositive Tätigkeit) noch wesentlich steigern /1/.

Resümee

Die Qualität der Arbeit von Personen, die in rechnergesteuerten Fertigungsprozessen tätig sind, ist nur gestaltbar, indem humane Anforderungen ebenso wie die technischen und wirtschaftlichen geplant werden. Die Computersoftware sollte so entworfen werden, daß der Fertigungsprozeß der Arbeitsperson Spielraum zum Handeln und die Möglichkeit dazuzulernen beläßt. Eine in diesem Sinne zeitgemäße Softwaretechnologie zur Lösung dieser Aufgabe gibt es zur Zeit nur in Ansätzen. Die hier vorgeschlagene Matrix und Vorgehensweise sollte in enger interdisziplinärer Zusammenarbeit von Ingenieuren, Informatikern und Arbeitswissenschaftlern - mit frühzeitiger Beteiligung der zukünftigen Benutzer - methodisch ausgestaltet und in einem Pilotprojekt erprobt werden.

Literatur

/1/ Macher, F.(Hrsg.): Wissenschaftlich-technischer Fortschritt und Inhalt der Arbeit.
Berlin, Verlag Die Wirtschaft, 1980.

/2/ Nobel, D.F.: Maschinen gegen Menschen - Die Entwicklung numerisch gesteuerter Werkzeugmaschinen.
Stuttgart, Alektor-Verlag, 1980.

/3/ Gizycki, R. von: Rationalisierung und Humanisierung durch Industrieroboter - Vorläufige Ergebnisse einer Fallstudie.
VDI-Zeitschrift 121, S. 1057-1066 (1979).

/4/ Kern, H.; Schumann, M.: Industriearbeit und Arbeitsbewußtsein.
Frankfurt, Edition Suhrkamp, 1977.

/5/ Bechmann, G.; Vahrenkamp, R.; Wingert, B.: Mechanisierung geistiger Arbeit.
Frankfurt/New York, Campus, 1979.

/6/ Mickler, O.: Arbeitsorganisatorische Gestaltungsmöglichkeiten bei automatisierter Produktion.
Zeitschr. Arb.wiss. 29, S. 158-162 (1975).

/7/ Volkholz, V.: Gestaltungsbedürftige Arbeitsplätze. In: Pöhler, W.(Hrsg.): ... damit die Arbeit menschlicher werde.
Bonn, Verlag Neue Gesellschaft, 1979.

/8/ Groskurth, P.; Volpert, W.: Lohnarbeitspsychologie.
Frankfurt, Fischer Taschenbuch Verlag, 1975.

/9/ Fischbach, D.; Nullmeier, E.; Reimann, F.: Planung und Gestaltung der Mensch-Maschine-Funktionsteilung.
Journal TU Berlin, November-Heft, S. 8-15 (1980).

/10/ Volpert, W.: Für eine neue Arbeitswissenschaft.
WSI-Mitt. 31, S. 113-118 (1978).

/11/ Hacker, W.: Allgemeine Arbeits- und Ingenieurspsychologie.
Berlin, Dt. Verlag d. Wiss. (2. Aufl.), 1978.

/12/ Ulich, E.: Psychologische Aspekte der Arbeit mit elektronischen Datenverarbeitungssystemen.
Schweiz. Techn. Zeitschr. 75, S. 66-68 (1980).

/13/ Hacker, W.(Hrsg.): Spezielle Arbeits- und Ingenieurpsychologie 1.
Berlin, Dt. Verlag d. Wiss., 1980.

/14/ Dzida, W.: Kognitive Ergonomie für Bildschirmarbeitsplätze.
Humane Produktion 10, S. 18-19 (1980).

/15/ Bundesanstalt für Arbeitsschutz und Unfallforschung (Hrsg.): Handlungsanleitung für Bildschirmarbeitsplätze.
Bremerhaven, Wirtschaftsverlag, 1979.

/16/ Fröhner, K.-D.: Personenbezogene Aspekte bei der Gestaltung von dialogorientierten EDV-Systemen.
In: Informatik-Fachberichte 28, Berlin/Heidelberg/New York, Springer, 1980.

/17/ Boehm, B.: Some steps towards formal and automated aids to software requirements analysis and design.
In: Information Processing 74, Amsterdam, North Holland, 1974.

/18/ Martin, W.; Klotz, V.; Dickmann, T.: Ansätze zur Arbeitsbereicherung an NC-Maschinen durch Mikrocomputer.
Rationalisierung 30, S. 39-42 (1979).

/19/ Hammer, H.: Technische, betriebliche und wirtschaftliche Aspekte der Werkstattprogrammierung.
VDI-Z 121, S. 999-1007 und 1095-1099 (1979).

Wie formal soll und darf die Beschreibung des Pflichtenheftes für ein Prozeßautomatisierungs-system sein?

von R. Lauber und S. Jovalekić

1. Einführung

"Die Antwort auf die Probleme der Software heißt: Software" [1]. Diese Erkenntnis hat dazu geführt, daß in den letzten Jahren eine Reihe von rechnergestützten Spezifikations- und Entwurfssystemen entwickelt wurden mit dem Ziel, die kreative Tätigkeit des Entwickelns von Rechner-Software und -Hardware zwar den beteiligten Menschen zu überlassen, ihnen dabei aber unterstützende Software-Werkzeuge verfügbar zu machen [2]. Die Unterstützung besteht - neben der automatischen Herstellung der Dokumentation - vor allem in der Bereitstellung von Hilfen und Prüfungen zur Erkennung möglicher Fehler im Sinne einer Vermeidung der oben angesprochenen "Probleme der Software". Diese Probleme entstehen nämlich durch (von einem gewissen Komplexitätsgrad an unvermeidliche) sog. "menschliche Fehlermechanismen", wie z.B. Denkfehler, Kommunikationsfehler, Interpretationsfehler, Flüchtigkeitsfehler usw. [3]. Die Auswirkungen dieser Fehlermechanismen (bezüglich der Kosten für ihre Beseitigung) sind umso schwerwiegender, je "früher"sie auftreten. Aus diesem Grunde kommt der Rechnerunterstützung gerade in den früheren Phasen eines Projekts (d.h. bei der Problemanalyse und der Pflichtenhefterstellung) große Bedeutung zu.

Da die Rechnerunterstützung zwangsläufig beinhaltet, daß Sachverhalte in einer von einem Rechner verstehbaren Form zu beschreiben sind, stellt sich die Frage nach der Art und dem möglichen Grad an Formalisierung einer solchen Beschreibung. Im Folgenden wird diese Frage vor allem in Bezug auf die Beschreibung der frühen Projektphase der Pflichtenheft-Erstellung behandelt.

2. Zum Begriff "Pflichtenheft"

Der Begriff "Pflichtenheft" ist in einem Norm-Entwurf DIN 69 901 vom Juni 1979 als "Zusammenstellung der technischen, wirtschaftlichen und sonstigen Spezifikationen für eine Leistung" erklärt. Eine Spezifikation wird dabei definiert als "ausführliche Beschreibung der Leistungen, die gefordert werden, damit Teilziele des Projekts erreicht werden". Da diese Definition wenig hilfreich erscheint, soll versucht werden, den Begriff "Pflichtenheft" an Hand von Bild 1 genauer festzulegen.

Als Grundlage für die Begriffdefinition wird in diesem Bild ein vereinfachtes Modell für den Ablauf eines Projekts angenommen: Die bekannte Unterteilung in Projektphasen wird insofern erweitert, als unterschieden wird zwischen Tätigkeiten eines Auftraggebers (Betreiber, Anwender) und eines Auftragnehmers (Hersteller, Lieferant). Die in der Praxis vorkommendenvielfältigen Möglichkeiten des Zusammenwirkens zwischen Auftraggeber und Auftragnehmer [4] werden dabei auf einen - allerdings häufig vorkommenden - Fall eingeschränkt: Es wird unterstellt, daß die Problemanalyse vom Auftraggeber durchgeführt wird und daß der Auftragnehmer auf Grund einer Ausschreibung mit der Entwicklung und Lieferung beauftragt wird. Unter dieser Annahme wird das Ausschreibungsdokument, in dem die Anforderungen an das zu entwickelnde System aus der Sicht des Auftraggebers zusammengestellt sind, als Lastenheft bezeichnet. Es wird (vor oder nach Auftragsvergabe) vom Auftragnehmer - im allgemeinen gemeinsam mit dem Auftraggeber - auf Grund einer Aufgabenstellungs- und Anforderungsanalyse überarbeitet. Das Ergebnis dieser Überarbeitung wird Pflichtenheft genannt. Dieses stellt somit die zwischen Auftraggeber und Auftragnehmer vereinbarte Vertragsgrundlage dar,in der die Aufgabenstellung und die zu erfüllenden Anforderungen möglichst detailliert, vollständig und widerspruchsfrei aufgeführt (spezifiziert) sind.

3. Widersprüchliche Forderungen an Beschreibungsmittel

An Beschreibungsmittel als Grundlage für eine Rechnerunterstützung bei der Entwicklung von Prozeßautomatisierungssystemen werden in allen Projektphasen, ganz besonders aber in der frühen Phase der Pflichtenheft-Erstellung, widersprüchliche Forderungen gestellt.

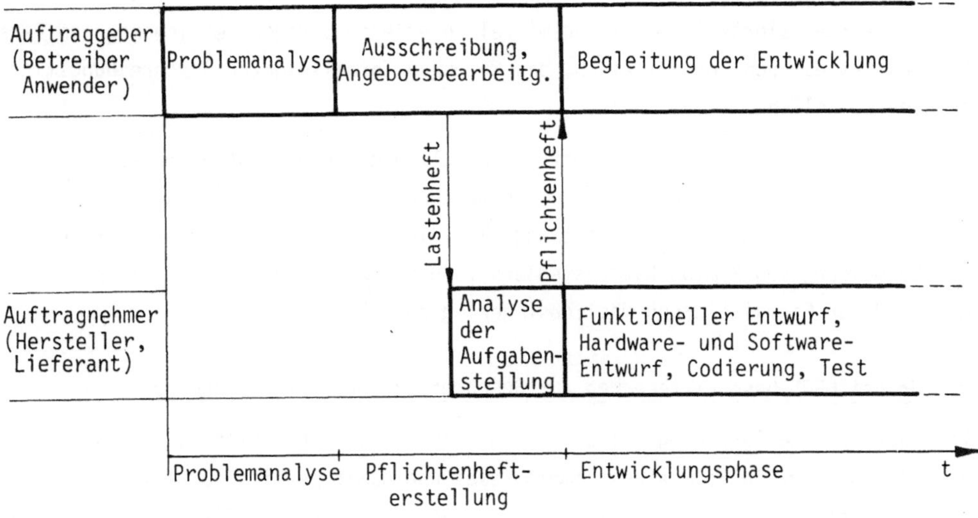

Bild 1: Phasenmodell für den Projektablauf mit Aufteilung der Tätigkeiten zwischen Auftraggeber und Auftragnehmer.

Auf der einen Seite sollen die zu beschreibenden Sachverhalte so genau und vollständig beschrieben werden, daß keine Interpretationsspielräume verbleiben, die zu Interpretationsfehlern führen könnten. Da mit natürlichen Sprachen als Beschreibungsmittel diese Bedingungen nur schwer zu erfüllen sind, wird die Forderung nach formalisierten Beschreibungsmitteln erhoben. Darunter werden speziell definierte Zeichen und Regeln verstanden, die eine eindeutige und vollständige Beschreibung erlauben. Solche Beschreibungsmittel weisen darüberhinaus den Vorteil auf, daß sie in einfacher Weise in die Datenbasis eines Rechners abbildbar sind. Die formalisierte Beschreibung wird bisher vielfach als Voraussetzung für den Einsatz eines Rechners zur Durchführung von Prüfungen angesehen. Bezüglich des Pflichtenheftes kann z.B. rechnergestützt geprüft werden, ob die Aufgabenstellungen und Anforderungen vollständig und untereinander verträglich sind und es kann der darauf aufbauende Entwurf dahingehend überprüft werden, ob er den Aufgabenstellungen entspricht und ob die gestellten Anforderungen vollständig erfüllt werden.

Auf der anderen Seite sollen die Beschreibungsmittel als Ausdrucks- und Kommunikationsmedium für Menschen dienen.
Viele Fehler entstehen bekanntlich - insbesondere in den frühen Projektphasen - dadurch, daß Verständigungsprobleme zwischen den beteiligten Menschen auftreten. Daraus folgt: Die zu verwendenden Beschreibungsmittel müssen von allen an einem Automatisierungsprojekt beteiligten Menschen verstanden werden. In der Phase der Pflichtenheft-Erstellung sind dies Projektleiter von Auftraggeber und Auftragnehmer, Prozeßfachleute, Systemanalytiker, Software- und Hardwareentwickler usw., d.h. Menschen mit sehr unterschiedlicher Vorbildung. Die allen gemeinsamen Beschreibungsmittel sind natürliche Sprache und zeichnerische Darstellungen. Dagegen sind formalisierte Beschreibungen für viele dieser Menschen unlesbar [9]. Darüberhinaus besteht wenig Bereitschaft, formalisierte Beschreibungsmittel zu erlernen. Wegen des inhomogenen Personenkreises ist es auch unrealistisch, das Erlernen formalisierter Beschreibungsmittel erzwingen zu wollen.

Die Forderungen an Beschreibungsmittel bezüglich des erwünschten Grades an Formalisierung widersprechen sich also: Zur Vermeidung von Interpretationsfehlern und zur Vereinfachung der Rechnerunterstützung wäre ein hoher Grad an Formalisierung erwünscht; zur Vermeidung von Kommunikationsfehlern (und auch im Interesse der Akzeptanz) muß der Grad der Formalisierung möglichst gering sein.

4. Der bei EPOS beschrittene Weg zur Beschreibung des Pflichtenheftes

Widersprüchliche Forderungen lassen sich - falls es nicht gelingt, den Widerspruch aufzulösen - nur in Form eines Kompromisses und damit jeweils nur teilweise erfüllen. Bei der Festlegung der Beschreibungsmittel von EPOS für die Pflichtenheft-Erstellung wurde ein Kompromiß gesucht zwischen der Versuchung, im Sinne der Rechnerunterstützung einen möglichst hohen Grad an Formalisierung vorzusehen, und dem Zwang, ein in der industriellen Praxis einsetzbares Entwicklungswerkzeug zu schaffen [5-8].

Dieser Kompromiß bedeutet:

- Formalisierte Beschreibungsmittel werden nur sehr sparsam und in einer solchen Weise angewandt, daß das Verständnis durch unterschiedliche Personen möglichst nicht beeinträchtigt wird.
- Es werden in großem Umfang die Beschreibungsmittel "Natürliche Sprache" und "Zeichnerische Darstellungen" zugelassen.
- Die Erstellung eines vollständigen und widerspruchsfreien Pflichtenheftes wird erleichtert,insbesondere durch einen einheitlichen Aufbau und ein Gliederungsschema.
- Die Anwendung und Änderung natürlich-sprachlicher Beschreibungen wird durch ein rechnergestütztes Begriffslexikon unterstützt.

4.1 Einheitlicher Aufbau und Gliederungsschema in EPOS-R

Die Beschreibung der Aufgabenstellung und der Anforderungen erfolgt mit Hilfe eines einheitlichen Gliederungsschemas, das natürlich gemäß den Erfordernissen des jeweiligen Projekts oder Anwenders ergänzt oder geändert werden kann. Das Gliederungsschema enthält u.a. folgende Abschnitte:

- Zielsetzung des Prozeßautomatisierungssystems
- Ist-Zustand des technischen Prozesses und eventuell des schon vorhandenen Automatisierungssystems
- Soll-Konzeption des neuen Automatisierungssystems und Rolle des Menschen
- Beschreibung der Schnittstellen (Signale, Daten usw.) zwischen
  - . Automatisierungssystem und technischem Prozeß
  - . Automatisierungssystem und übergeordnetem System
  - . Bedienpersonal und Automatisierungssystem
- Beschreibung der logischen und zeitlichen Zusammenhänge beim regulären und irregulären Betrieb des Prozeßautomatisierungssystems
- Beschreibung der Zuverlässigkeits- und Sicherheits-relevanten Aspekte
- Forderungen an die mechanische und elektrische Ausführung
- Forderungen an den Betrieb des Prozeßautomatisierungssystems (Umweltbedingungen, Wartung, Weiterentwicklung usw.)
- Forderungen bezüglich der Projektabwicklung (Methoden, Strategien, Richtlinien, Schulung, Management).

Inhaltsverzeichnisse mit allen Abschnittsnummern, Überschriften und Seitenzahlen, sowie Übersichten über den Dokumentationsstand einzelner Bearbeitungsabschnitte mit Abschnittsnummern und Datum der letzten Änderung können rechnergestützt erstellt werden.

4.2 Prüfung des Entwurfs auf Erfüllung der gestellten Anforderungen

Einzelne Elemente der Anforderungen im Pflichtenheft können in EPOS-R mit einem Schlüsselwort und einer Identifikations-Nummer gekennzeichnet werden. Da dabei die betreffende Anforderung mit natürlich-sprachlichen oder zeichnerischen Mitteln beschrieben wird, ist eine inhaltliche Erfüllung vom Rechner nicht prüfbar. Es ist jedoch eine Unterstützung des Menschen dadurch möglich, daß

- durch Software-Werkzeuge (EPOS-A) geprüft wird, ob alle Anforderungen mindestens einmal referenziert werden
- dem Anwender eine Cross-Referenz-Liste bereitgestellt wird, die ihn bei der inhaltlichen Prüfung auf Erfüllung der Anforderungen unterstützt.

4.3 Hilfsmittel zur Vermeidung von Verständigungsproblemen zwischen den Bearbeitern eines Projekts

Bei der Formulierung des Pflichtenheftes wird im allgemeinen die Fachsprache eines bestimmten Anwendungsgebiets (z.B. Hochregallager, Prüfstände usw.) verwendet werden. Zur Erleichterung der Verständigung zwischen den Bearbeitern wird in EPOS-R ein Lexikon mit definierten Begriffen des betreffenden Anwendungsgebiets erstellt, wobei den Begriffen Attribute und Kategorien, sowie Relationen zu anderen Begriffen, zugeordnet werden können. Dadurch wird einerseits die Begriffswelt verschiedener Bearbeiter angeglichen und vereinheitlicht, andererseits wird neuen Bearbeitern der Zugang erleichtert.

Die Rechnerunterstützung beinhaltet:

- Die Erstellung eines Gesamtlexikons aus verschiedenen Dokumenten
- Die Änderung (Wartung) des Lexikons bei Änderung in den Dokumenten
- Die Übernahme von Lexikon-Teilen aus schon durchgeführten Projekten.

4.4 Implementierung

Die Implementierung ist so aufgebaut, daß eine Änderung und Anpassung von Beschreibungsmitteln in einfacher Weise möglich ist. Dies wird dadurch erreicht, daß alle Aspekte der Beschreibungsmittel tabellengesteuert sind.

Das EPOS-R-Verarbeitungsprogramm besteht aus folgenden Komponenten (siehe Bild 2):

- Lexikalanalysierer
- Syntaxanalysierer
- Semantikanalysierer
- Protokollgenerator
- Datenbasis-Handler

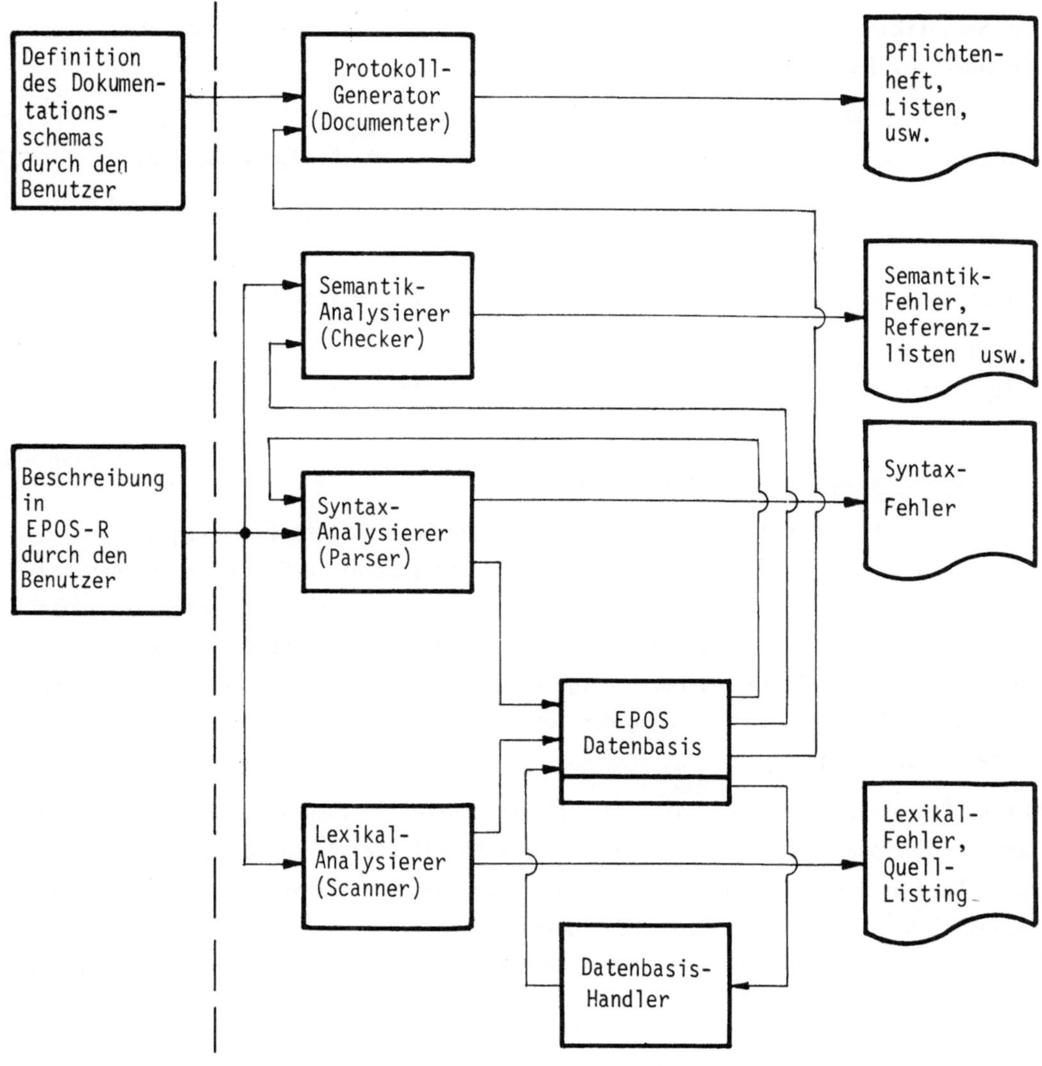

Bild 2: Aufbau des EPOS-R-Verarbeitungsprogrammsystems

Der Lexikalanalysierer wird mit Hilfe eines endlichen Zustandsgraphen ausgelegt. Die Definition der Lexikaleigenschaften erfolgt durch die Zeichenklassentabelle, die Zustandsübergangstabelle und eine Fehlermeldetabelle.

Die Syntaxeigenschaften werden durch eine formale Grammatik definiert. Mit dem Syntaxanalysierer werden Syntaxregeln überprüft und in Syntaxtabellen abgebildet. Die Analyse erfolgt durch einen Bottom-up Parser.

Der Semantikanalysierer besteht aus einer Bibliothek von Programmen, die verschiedene Aufgaben ausführen:

- Überprüfung des Pflichtenhefts auf formale Vollständigkeit
- Überprüfung einiger Teile des Pflichtenhefts (z.B. Entscheidungstabellen) auf Konsistenz
- Überprüfung der Konsistenz der verwendeten Begriffe.

Der Datenbasis-Handler hat die Aufgabe, die Datenbasis zu verwalten. Dazu gehört:

- Wartung der Symboltabelle
- Verwaltung des Textfiles (Lückenverwaltung) bei Änderungen.

5. Zusammenfassung und Schlußbemerkungen

Die Frage nach dem erforderlichen oder zulässigen Grad an Formalisierung bei der Beschreibung des Pflichtenhefts (d.h. der Verwendung speziell definierter Zeichen und Regeln, die keine Interpretationsspielräume mehr zulassen) führt zu gegensätzlichen Wünschen: Vom Standpunkt des Einsatzes leistungsfähiger Software-Werkzeuge wäre ein hoher Grad an Formalisierung zweckmäßig. Wegen der Inhomogenität der beteiligten Personen ist dagegen zur Ermöglichung der Kommunikation nur ein geringer Grad an Formalisierung zulässig.

Dieser Gegensatz ist in der Phase der Pflichtenhefterstellung am größten. In den späteren Projektphasen nimmt die Homogenität der beteiligten Personen zu, so daß ein höherer Grad an Formalisierung zulässig wird. Bei dem Spezifikations- und Entwurfssystem EPOS wurde daher versucht, das geschilderte Problem dadurch zu lösen, daß insgesamt drei verschiedene Beschreibungssprachen mit unterschiedlichen Formalisierungsgrad eingeführt wurden (Bild 3):

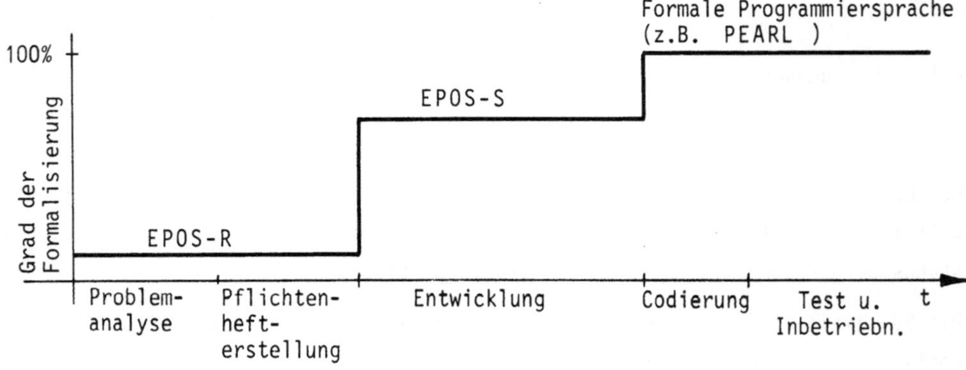

Bild 3: Formalisierungsgrad der Beschreibungsmittel bei der Anwendung von EPOS.

- Der Beschreibung des Pflichtenhefts und des konzeptionellen Entwurfs dient die "Sprache" EPOS-R, die nur wenige formale Elemente aufweist.
- Die Beschreibung des Grob- und Feinentwurfs erfolgt mit der Spezifikationssprache EPOS-S, die eine formale Syntax und eine definierte Semantik besitzt.
- Die Codierung efolgt schließlich in einer formalen Programmiersprache(z.B.PEARL).

Ein solcher Kompromiß ist erforderlich, solange formalisierte Beschreibungsmittel als Voraussetzung für den Rechner-Einsatz gelten. Falls es in der Zukunft gelingen sollte, auch den Inhalt natürlich-sprachlicher Texte mit Rechnern zu erfassen und zu analysieren (die Erfolge auf diesem Teilgebiet des "artificial intelligence" sind durchaus vielversprechend), wäre ein Kompromiß nicht mehr erforderlich. Denn damit ließe sich die menschen-gemäße, natürlich-sprachliche Beschreibung mit der Anwendung von Rechnern (Maschinen) als unterstützendes Werkzeug in Einklang bringen.

Literatur:

[1] Krüger, G.: Auswirkungen des Wandels der rechnergestützten Automatisierungstechnik auf die Aus- und Weiterbildung von Ingenieuren und Informatikern. Fachtagung Prozeßrechner '81, Informatik-Fachberichte Bd. 39, S.17-30 Springer-Verlag 1981

[2] Lauber,R.: Rechnergestützter Entwurf und Dokumentation von Prozeßautomatisierungssystemen. GI-Jahrestagung Bonn 1979. Springer-Verlag 1979

[3] Lauber, R.: Zuverlässigkeit informationsverarbeitender technischer Systeme unter den Bedingungen der Zukunft.Tagung Technische Zuverlässigkeit Nürnberg 1981. VDI-Bericht Nr. 395, VDI-Verlag Düsseldorf 1981

[4] Richtlinie VDI/VDE-GMR 3550: Einsatzvorbereitung für Prozeßrechnersysteme. Beuth-Verlag, Berlin 1976

[5] Biewald, J., Göhner,P., Lauber,R. und Schelling, H.: Das Software-Werkzeug EPOS zur Unterstützung der Ingenieurtätigkeiten beim Entwurf und bei der Wartung von Prozeßautomatisierungssystemen. Regelungstechnik 28 (1980) S.11-15

[6] Biewald, J.: Rechnergestützte Erzeugung der Dokumentation für den Funktions- und Softwareentwurf in EPOS. Fachtagung Prozeßrechner 1981 Informatik-Fachberichte 39, Springer-Verlag 1981, S.97-106

[7] Joho,E., Jovalekiĉ, S.: Rechnergestützte Umsetzung von EPOS-Spezifikationen in PEARL-Programme. Fachtagung Prozeßrechner 1981 Informatik-Fachberichte 39, Springer-Verlag 1981, S.119-128

[8] Göhner, P.: Spezifikation der Synchronisierung paralleler Rechenprozesse in EPOS. Fachtagung Prozeßrechner 1981, Informatik-Fachberichte 39, Springer-Verlag 1981, S.107-118

[9] Balzer, R.M.: GIST Specification Language, Final Report, Information Sciences Institute, University of Southern California, Los Angeles, Feb. 1981

KONTEXTVERLUSTE IN COMPUTERGESTÜTZTEN PERSONALINFORMATIONSSYSTEMEN

von Manfred Pils, Linz/ Österreich

Zusammenfassung: Bei der Planung von Personalinformationssystemen, die über Abrechnungssysteme hinausgehen, ist mit sogenannten Kontextverlusten zu rechnen. Es handelt sich dabei um bislang kaum identifizierte, auf methodische, psychische, soziale, rechtliche, wirtschaftliche und technologische Ursachen zurückzuführende Informationsverluste, die zu Verzerrungen des Bildes führen können, das sich der im Personalbereich tätige Benutzer insbesondere über Mitarbeiter und Arbeitsplätze macht. Die Gefahr besteht, daß weittragende Entscheidungen im Personalbereich aufgrund einer unzureichend fundierten Datenbasis bzw. ohne ausreichende Synthese der Daten zu größeren Zusammenhängen gefällt werden. Abwehrreaktionen der Betroffenen gegen den EDV-Einsatz im Personalbereich bzw. informationsfeindliche Rechtsnormen sind in solchen Fällen zu erwarten.

1. Grundsätzliches zur Planung von Personalinformationssystemen

Zur Unterstützung der Personalarbeit in Unternehmungen und öffentlichen Verwaltungen sind (auch über die Personalabrechnung hinausgehend) sinnvolle Anwendungen moderner Computertechnologie denkbar. Entsprechendes, auf diese Problematik bezogenes know-how und viel Fingerspitzengefühl werden für die Planung solcher Personalinformationssysteme vorausgesetzt. Anders als bei herkömmlichen Anwendungsgebieten (wie Fakturierung, Buchhaltung, Lager usw.) üblich, stellen beim EDV-Einsatz im Personalbereich nicht Kostensenkungen das primäre Planungsziel dar, sieht man von der Personalabrechnung einmal ab. Der Personalwirt soll vielmehr seine Aufgaben und Probleme leichter und effektiver lösen können. Positive Effekte durch die EDV sind vor allem durch qualitativ bessere Entscheidungen und durch ein gesteigertes Mitarbeiterservice zu erwarten. [1]

Beim Planen von Personalinformationssystemen bildet man drei Schwerpunkte [2]: Die personalwirtschaftlichen Aufgaben (z. B. das Ermitteln des Personalbedarfs für einen bestimmten Zeitraum), die dafür verwendeten Methoden (z. B. ein Rechenverfahren, das Personalbedarfe ermittelt) sowie die erforderlichen Daten (z. B. über das zukünftige Produktionsprogramm). Gleichzeitig mit der Planung des Aufgaben-, Methoden- und Datensystems wird auch über die zweckmäßigen Computer-Nutzungsformen und darauf aufbauend über Hardware und Software entschieden. Als Voraussetzungen für Personalinformationssysteme sollen hier insbesondere genannt werden: Dialogverarbeitung (und zwar freie Abfragemöglichkeit im benutzergesteuerten Dialog) sowie eine einfache und einprägsame Abfragesprache, die eine ad-hoc formulierbare, rasche Auswertung der Personaldatenbank ermöglicht [3]. Schließlich bedarf es der Lösung jener Probleme, die in diesem Beitrag mit dem Begriff "Kontextverluste" bezeichnet werden.

2. Überblick über potentielle Quellen für Kontextverluste

Personenbezogene Daten, Arbeitsplatzdaten und andere Daten des betrieblichen Personalbereiches sind - unabhängig von ihrer Schutzwürdigkeit - in besonders hohem Ausmaß nur in ihrem jeweiligen situativen, sozialen, räumlichen und zeitlichen Kontext zu verstehen und zu verwenden. Dies wird an einem Beispiel deutlich: Ergebnisse einer Mitarbeiterbeurteilung - etwa als "Beurteilungsdaten" bezeichnet - sind, wenn überhaupt, nur dann einigermaßen verläßlich zu interpretieren, falls etwa auch der Beurteiler, der Zweck oder Anlaß der Beurteilung, das Bewertungsschema, Beurteilungszeitpunkt und ähnlich wichtige Tatbestände bekannt sind.

"Kontext" bedeutet, daß eine Menge von Wissenselementen und Wissensfragmenten sinnvoll geordnet ist. "Ohne synthetisierenden Kontext bestünde das Wissen aus lauter singulären Aussagen, die ohne Zusammenhang wären. Erst die Existenz eines Kontextes ermöglicht es, einzelne Wissensfragmente einzuordnen und zueinander in Beziehung zu setzen." [4]

Bei der Planung von Personalinformationssystemen ist in zwei Bereichen mit potentiellen Informationsverlusten aufgrund mangelnden Kontextes (nachfolgend "Kontextverluste" genannt) zu rechnen: Erstens bei der datenmäßigen Abbildung von Mitarbeitern, Arbeitsplätzen und anderen Realitätsausschnitten in das Computersystem; zweitens bei der späteren Verwendung der gespeicherten Daten, also beim Zugreifen, Ausgeben, Auswerten bzw. Verknüpfen der Daten.

Kontextverluste lassen sich vor allem auf aufgabenseitige, theoretisch-methodische, objektspezifische, benutzerseitige, rechtliche, wirtschaftliche und technologische Ursachen zurückzuführen. In nachfolgender Tabelle sind lediglich Beispiele für solche Ursachen angegeben. An dieser Stelle muß wegen der großen Anzahl differenzierter Aussagen zu den einzelnen angesprochenen Bereichen auf eine detaillierte Darstellung der Ursachen für Kontextverluste verzichtet werden. [5]

Ursachenbereich	Beispiele für Ursachen für Kontextverluste
Methoden	Mangel an geeigneten psychologischen Testverfahren
Objekte	Abwehrreaktionen der betroffenen Mitarbeiter, mangelnde Abbildbarkeit von Menschen
Benutzer	kognitive Eigenschaften des Personalfachmannes
Rechtsnormen	Datenschutzbestimmungen
Wirtschaftlichkeit	Kosten kontextsichernder Maßnahmen
Technologie	mangelnde Unterstützung durch Software

Die Forderung nach einer Vergrößerung der Datenbasis und nach dem Einsatz moderner Informationstechnologien auch für den in zunehmenden Maße zum Engpaß werdenden betrieblichen Personalbereich hat nur dann Chance verwirklicht zu werden, wenn das noch größtenteils ungelöste Problem, wie Kontextverluste begrenzt oder vermieden werden können, analysiert und in weiterer Folge wenigstens einer für alle Betroffenen als befriedigend empfundenen Lösung zugeführt werden kann. Bei der Einführung von Personalinformationssystemen aufflammende Konflikte deuten ein Unbehagen der Betroffenen gegenüber potentiellen Verfälschungen und Verzerrungen von personenbezogenen Daten an.

So verbieten beispielsweise die bei Daimler Benz auf Druck der Arbeitnehmervertreter abgeschlossenen "Betriebsvereinbarungen zum Schutz personenbezogener Daten von ISA" (ISA = Informationssystem Arbeitseinsatz und Arbeitsplatzplanung für Arbeiter), daß die Eignung eines Mitarbeiters für einen Arbeitsplatz maschinell geprüft wird, weiter daß die Eignung mehrerer Mitarbeiter maschinell verglichen sowie daß zu versetzende und freizusetzende Mitarbeiter maschinell ermittelt werden [6]. Um ähnliche Einschränkungen zu verhindern, kann es zur Zeit zweckmäßig sein, mit der Computerunterstützung weiterer Bereiche der Personalarbeit behutsam und abwartend vorzugehen, um computerfeindliche Einstellungen unter den betroffenen Mitarbeitern und deren Vertretungen zu verhindern oder wenigstens nicht zu fördern.

3. Ansatzpunkte zur Kontextsicherung

Was sind nun die wesentlichsten Teilbereiche, denen beim Design eines Personalinformationssystems erhöhtes Augenmerk zuzuwenden ist? Welche Maßnahmen sind geeignet, potentielle Kontextverluste abzubauen? Systemgestalter sollten sich vorrangig mit der Harmonie zwischen personalwirtschaftlichen Aufgaben, Methoden und Daten befassen. Weiter ist das Verhalten des Benutzers, also des Personalfachmannes von zentralem Interesse. Schließlich müssen auch Besonderheiten der abzubildenden "Objekte" und deren Eigenschaften, diverse rechtliche Normen, der Ablauf des Systemplanungsprozssese sowie einsetzbare Hardware- und Softwaretechnologien in die Betrachtung einbezogen werden. Kontextverlusten kann durch Maßnahmen der Kontextsicherung sowohl im Bereich der Datenfindung, als auch bei der Datenverwendung begegnet werden.

Das Personalinformationssystem wird dem Personalfachmann bei der Erfüllung seiner Aufgaben (z. B. beim Ermitteln des Personalbedarfes, beim Beschaffen, beim Einsetzen oder beim Entwickeln der Mitarbeiter) nur dann eine echte Hilfe sein, wenn Aufgabe, Methoden und Daten eng aufeinander abgestimmt sind. Eine umfangreiche Personaldatenbank mit vielen Detailinformationen ist unsinnig, wenn z. B. entsprechende Methoden fehlen, die helfen, sinnvolle Zusammenhänge zwischen den Daten und zu anderen Informationen außerhalb des computergestützten Informationssystems herzustellen, und die somit effektive Auswertungen erst ermöglichen. Umgekehrt sind aufwendige Rechenmodelle kaum von Nutzen, wenn die erforderlichen Daten nicht erfaßt werden können. Da es gerade im Personalbereich an rechnerischen Methoden mangelt, lassen sich programmierbare, automatische Lösungen nur teilweise finden. Ein erster wesentlicher Schritt zur Kontextsicherung besteht darin, Aufgaben, Methoden und Daten harmonisch aufeinander abzustimmen und dabei einseitiges Automatisierungsstreben zu vermeiden.

Um Personalarbeit effektiv durch den Computer unterstützen zu können, bedarf es insbesondere einer kritischen Betrachtung der erfaßten oder noch zu erfassenden Daten; es ist genau zu überprüfen, ob diese richtig und aktuell sind. Aber auch an und für sich "richtige" Daten können zu falschen Schlüssen führen, wenn man z. B. den jeweiligen Zusammenhang, in dem sie erfaßt wurden, nicht bei der Auswertung der Daten berücksichtigt. So kann beispielsweise angenommen werden, daß ein Bewerber speziell jene persönlichen Eigenschaften hervorhebt, die von der freien Stelle gefordert werden. Wird dann - vielleicht Jahre später - durch den Computer auf Basis dieser Informationen eine Auswertung des Datenmaterials vorgenommen, so kann es leicht zu einem verfälschten Urteil über den Mitarbeiter kommen.

Die Mängel bestehender Konzeptionen und der zur Verfügung stehenden Methoden zur Gestaltung von Personalinformationssystemen, die in sich potentielle Quellen für Kontextverluste bergen, müssen vom Systemplaner erkannt und aufgezeigt werden. In der Kontextsicherung darf dabei nicht ein auf eine oder wenige Dimensionen reduziertes Problem gesehen werden, das durch simple technologische oder kostenwirtschaftliche Überlegungen in den Griff zu bekommen ist, so wie man dies in der Vergangenheit mit ähnlich strukturierten Problembereichen des öfteren getan hat. Will man kontextsichernde Methoden bzw. Informationssysteme entwickeln, so setzt dies voraus, daß man von möglichst realistischen Vorstellungen über den zu gestaltenden Bereich ausgeht, d. h. es müssen insbesondere auch wichtige Erkenntnisse der Verhaltenswissenschaften einbezogen werden.

Daß bei der Beurteilung von Informationssystemen und von Methoden zur Aufgaben- bzw. Entscheidungsunterstützung in starkem Maße von der Sicht des Benutzers auszugehen ist, gilt heute als anerkannt [7], desgleichen die Forderung nach Benutzerpartizipation bei der Systemgestaltung. Er ist es letzten Endes, der die Synthese von Daten zu einem möglichst viele wesentliche Tatbestände einbeziehenden Gesamtbild über einen Realitätsausschnitt zu vollziehen hat. Gemeint ist hierbei erstens der Personalfachmann (z. B. der das Einstellungsgespräch führende Vorgesetzte), der Realitätsausschnitte (z. B. den Bewerber) abbildet, indem er Daten im Computersystem dokumentiert. Einbezogen ist zweitens auch jener Benutzer, dem - womöglich in einer inadäquaten Weise - Daten vom Computersystem zur Durchführung seiner Aufgabe angeboten werden (z. B. dem Personalplaner). Dieser nimmt - durch die beschränkte Fähigkeit des Menschen, Informationen wahrzunehmen und zu "verarbeiten" bedingt, sowie unter der Wirkung anderer psychischer und sozialer Bedingungen - eine stets subjektive Einordnung der dargebotenen Daten in einen ebenfalls subjektiv gefärbten Zusammenhang vor.

Gerade bei den für die Personalarbeit typischen komplexeren Aufgabenstellungen kommt es nicht nur auf die Dateninhalte, sondern u. a. auch auf die Reihenfolge der Informationsdarbietung, auf Widersprüchlichkeiten, auf den Denkstil des Benutzers, auf dessen Aktivierungsgrad und schließlich auf äußere Einflüsse (z. B. auf Sanktionsmechanismen von Bezugspersonen) an, welcher Art der im Einzelfall hergestellte Kontext ist, und zu welchem Ergebnis somit der Personalfachmann bei der Durchführung einer Aufgabe kommt.

Man kann zwar Kontexte beispielsweise mittels der Dimensionen Reichhaltigkeit, Reichweite und Strukturierbarkeit quantifizieren; es fehlen allerdings weitgehend Meßmethoden, die eine Operationalisierung und somit auch eine detaillierte Planung erlauben.

Es wurde versucht, den Anforderungen, die sich von Seiten einer komplexen Realität an deren Abbildung in ein Datensystem ergeben, z. B. durch das Aufstellen überaus detaillierter Persönlichkeits- und Arbeitsplatzprofile, also durch eine große Anzahl elementarer Indikatoren, Rechnung zu tragen. Die Forderungen nach Objektivität und Operationalisierbarkeit der Datenfindung beschränken sich jedoch hauptsächlich auf die einzelnen Elemente der Abbildung. Die datenmäßig abbildbaren elementaren Indikatoren (etwa die punktartig wirkenden Daten eines Persönlichkeitsprofils) stellen jedoch manchmal triviale Äußerungen dar, die sich vom eigentlichen Abbildungsobjekt weit entfernt haben. Welche Werte als Daten erfaßt werden, kann in vielen Fällen nur subjektiv beantwortet werden. Zudem erweist sich die nachträgliche Vereinigung punktueller Datenelemente als äußerst problematisch, da es dazu sowohl an theoretisch fundierten als auch praktikablen Modellen und Verfahren mangelt. Ein Zusammenfügen der Daten zu einem einigermaßen geschlossenen Bild (z. B. über einen Arbeitsplatz) wird dann in vielen Fällen gänzlich unterbleiben, oder es kommt zu nichtssagenden oder verzerrten Abbildern der Realität. Als Schwachstelle kommt hierbei die Tatsache zum Tragen, daß die gegenseitigen Wechselwirkungen der erfaßten und der nicht erfaßten (weil nicht beobachtbaren) Elemente nicht beachtet werden.

In naher Zukunft ist von Seiten der Hardware- und der Softwaretechnologie mit keinen bahnbrechenden Neuentwicklungen zu rechnen, die - ohne eine entsprechend fundierte Ausbildung der Benutzer auf den betreffenden sozial- und wirtschaftswissenschaftlichen Disziplinen - in der Lage wären, Kontextverluste auf ein zu vernachlässigendes Minimum zu reduzieren.

Es hat sich gezeigt, daß Vermutungen von Praktikern, daß von Seiten der einschlägigen wissenschaftlichen Disziplinen (Psychologie, Soziologie, Informatik, Betriebsinformatik, Betriebswirtschaftslehre u. a.) ausreichend fundierte Theorien existieren, einer kritischen Prüfung nicht standzuhalten vermögen. Tatsächlich fehlen zur Zeit brauchbare Datenfindungsmethoden. Es mangelt auch an Verfahren, mittels derer aus einer größeren Anzahl (elementarer) Indikatoren, in der praktischen Personalarbeit verwertbare Aggregationen zusammengestellt werden können, ohne daß gleichzeitig wesentliche Details des Bildes außer acht gelassen werden. Einzelne hoffnungsvolle Ansätze, etwa in Form der Theorie der Mustererkennung [8], haben gegenwärtig noch mit erheblichen Schwierigkeiten zu kämpfen. Eine Realisierung dieser Ansätze würde nicht nur aus rechtlichen Gründen unzulässig sein, darüber hinaus zu sicherlich berechtigten, massiven Abwehrreaktionen der Betroffenen führen.

Des weiteren fehlen Aussagen zur Gestaltung der Mensch-Computer-Interaktion. Wie sollen die Informationen dem Benutzer des Personalinformationssystems aufbereitet werden, damit eine dem Personalfachmann sowie der Aufgabe angepaßte Wissenssynthese zwischen den Daten unter Einbeziehung seiner spezifischen Kenntnisse und Fähigkeiten möglich ist? Gerade hier zeichnet sich gegenwärtig noch ein erhebliches know-how-Defizit der Systemplaner ab.

Es soll hier darauf hingewiesen werden, daß durch die Entwicklung der Datenschutzbestimmungen dem Gedanken der Kontextsicherung nur teilweise Rechnung getragen wurde. Zum Teil wurde es nunmehr schwieriger, aus personenbezogenen Daten größere Zusammenhänge zu rekonstruieren. Enge Zusammenhänge und Auswirkungen auf die Kontextsicherung ergeben sich unter anderem mit dem im Rahmen der Datenschutzdiskussion aufgeworfenen Problematik der Privatsphäre und des informationellen Selbstbestimmungsrechtes des Menschen. Die hier in der Zukunft gefundenen gesellschaftspolitischen und rechtlichen Lösungen werden nicht unwesentlich die weitere Entwicklung computergestützter Personalinformationssysteme in Wirtschaft und Verwaltung prägen.

4. Konsequenzen

Die Sicherung des Kontextes, also eine sinnvolle Ordnung von Wissenselementen, die auch die Validität der einzelnen Datenelemente umfaßt, erweist sich als ein komplexes Problem, das es in der strategischen, in der administrativen und in der operativen Ebene der Gestaltung eines Personalinformationssystems zu berücksichtigen gilt. Gelingt es nicht, in absehbarer Zeit hier Fortschritte zu erzielen, so bestehen zwei Gefahren:

(1) Potentielle Anwender resignieren angesichts der aufgeworfenen Problemkreise. Somit könnten enorme potentielle Nutzeneffekte aufgrund einer breiten Datenbasis in der Personalarbeit verloren gehen.

(2) Werden Personalinformationssysteme ohne Berücksichtigung der Kontextproblematik implementiert, so droht die Gefahr von Abwehrreaktionen der betroffenen Arbeitnehmer und deren Vertreter, was Bestrebungen zugunsten informationshemmender rechtlicher Normen (z. B. Verschärfen von Datenschutzbestimmungen, Erfassungsverbote für personenbezogene Daten, Verarbeitungsverbote) verstärken könnte.

Beide Fälle führen letztlich dazu, daß trotz der Informationsintensität des modernen Wirtschaftslebens, zu dessen Bewältigung es zur Zeit keine sinnvolle Alternative zur elektronischen Datenverarbeitung gibt, auf die Computerunterstützung für weite Bereiche der Personalarbeit in Wirtschaft und Verwaltung verzichtet werden müßte. [9]

Bezüglich der Gestaltung von Personalinformationssystemen ergeben sich weitere Konsequenzen. Diese können dahingehend zusammengefaßt werden, daß die Kontextsicherung als zentrales Anliegen der Computerunterstützung in der Personalarbeit - analog etwa zum Datenschutz -zu betrachten ist. Kontextsicherung ist nicht in einem oder in wenigen Planungsanläufen zu bewältigen, Kontextsicherung kann nur durch eine Fülle von Einzelmaßnahmen betrieben werden.

Einzelmaßnahmen sind etwa die fundierte und intensive sozial- bzw. betriebswirtschaftliche Schulung der Benutzer, z. B. hinsichtlich der Problematik der Erfassung und Verarbeitung personenbezogener Daten und deren Verknüpfung. Ohne einen entsprechend fundierten theoretischen und praktischen Background ist ein adäquater Umgang mit diffizilen Informationen und das Einschätzen von potentiellen Informationsverzerrungen und -verfälschungen unmöglich und muß daher trotz oder - sollte man sagen - wegen vorliegender Computerunterstützung abgelehnt werden. Gehen Personalinformationssysteme über Abrechnungs- und einfachere Analysesysteme hinaus, so erfordert die Computerunterstützung eine wesentlich höhere Qualifikation des Benutzers, und zwar in betriebswirtschaftlicher, soziologischer und psychologischer Sicht, einschließlich dem Gebiet der Betriebsinformatik.

In Anbetracht der Gefahren, die aus Kontextverlusten drohen, liegt auch der Gedanke nahe, die computergestützte Verarbeitung personenbezogener Daten an bestimmte benutzerseitige Voraussetzungen zu knüpfen. Zum gegenwärtigen Stand der Forschung und Praxis ist es nicht möglich, Kontexte für eine größere Anzahl personalwirtschaftlicher Aufgaben allein durch organisatorische oder software- und hardwaretechnologische Maßnahmen auf einem wenigstens befriedigendem Niveau herzustellen.

Einen nicht unwesentlichen Aspekt bildet die Frage der Akzeptanz von Informationssystemen von Seiten des Benutzers [10]. Die Ergebnisse der Akzeptanzforschung sind mit großem Interesse zu verfolgen, zumal gerade das Erzeugen von Wissenssynthesen stark von aktivierenden Prozessen des Benutzers abhängig ist.

Trotz Intensivierung der Ausbildungs- und Schulungsmaßnahmen und der Bemühungen zur Verbesserung etwa der motivationalen Bedingungen für den Benutzer bedarf es zusätzlicher Maßnahmen betreffend die organisatorische und computertechnologische Ausgestaltung des Personalinformationssystems. Um den Grad der Wissenssynthese zu verbessern, sind verschiedene Formen der Computerunterstützung einzusetzen. Grundsätzlich lassen sich zwei Gestaltungsalternativen unterscheiden, die hier vereinfachend mit "freier Kontextsicherung" und "geplanter Kontextsicherung" charakterisiert werden sollen. Sowohl bei der freien als auch bei der geplanten Kontextsicherung ist eine Reihe sinnvoller Varianten denkbar.

Von <u>freier Kontextsicherung</u> soll dann gesprochen werden, wenn der Benutzer über das Erfassen kontextsichernder Daten und über den Einsatz kontextsichernder Aktivitäten weitgehend selbst entscheiden kann. Freie Kontextsicherung bedeutet jedoch nicht, daß nicht Teilbereiche vorausschauend und methodisch festgelegt werden; ausschlaggebend ist die Größe des dem Benutzer verbleibenden Gestaltungsspielraumes. Im Bereich der Datenfindung soll etwa das Finden, Erfassen bzw. Dokumentieren kontextsichernder Daten dank der Computerunterstützung ermöglicht bzw. erleichtert werden, analog dazu das Zugreifen, Auswählen, Auswerten bzw. Verarbeiten der gespeicherten Daten.

Bei den Formen einer aktiven, freien Kontextsicherung wird der Benutzer nicht vom Computersystem automatisch z. B. auf die Notwendigkeit der Erfassung kontextsichernder Daten aufmerksam gemacht. Im Gegensatz dazu geht bei den Formen der passiven, freien Kontextsicherung die Initiative zur Kontextsicherung vom Computersystem aus.

Im Falle der geplanten Kontextsicherung ist der Benutzer weitgehend an vorgegebene Regelungen (Kontextnormen) gebunden. Der verbleibende Gestaltungsspielraum ist relativ gering und unbedeutend. Im Bereich der Datenfindung soll der Benutzer gezwungen werden, z. B. kontextsichernde Daten zu erfassen, indem etwa eine Speicherung von "aus dem Zusammenhang gerissenen Daten" immer dann verhindert wird, wenn nicht bestimmte zusätzliche Daten gleichzeitig miterfaßt werden. Der Benutzer soll zudem gezwungen werden, Daten nur in einem definierten Kontext (z. B. nur für eine konkrete Aufgabe, nur in Verbindung mit bestimmten anderen Daten oder Auswertungsmethoden) zu sehen und zu verwenden. Dies könnte etwa in der Weise realisiert werden, daß das Anzeigen von Daten auf Bildschirm nur gemeinsam mit weiteren, für das Verständnis unbedingt erforderlichen Daten möglich ist, oder daß unerwünschte Formen der Datenverknüpfung vom System verhindert werden.

Zusätzlich besteht die Möglichkeit, sogenannte Anwendersoftware-Konventionen einzusetzen, bei denen der Benutzer selbst Ausmaß, Zeitpunkt und Art der Inanspruchnahme von Systemhilfen bestimmen kann. In Frage kommen Anwendersoftware-Konventionen z. B. bezüglich der Formate, Programmeldungen, Eingaben oder in Form von HELP-, Korrektur-, Duplizier- und Systemanmeldungsfunktionen [11].

In jedem Einzelfall sollte man unter Einbeziehung der Betroffenen prüfen, ob die diversen Typen der computergestützten Kontextsicherung in der jeweiligen Situation den Kontext der Daten bzw. Methoden wenigstens in einem befriedigenden Ausmaß sicherstellen. Dies kann nur aufgaben-, objekt- und benutzerspezifisch unter Berücksichtigung der wirtschaftlichen und technologischen Konsequenzen entschieden werden.

Es liegt auf der Hand, daß für eine akzeptable Kontextsicherung mit nicht unerheblichen Kostenbelastungen zu rechnen ist. Diese sind auf die anspruchsvollere Ausstattung mit Hardware und Systemsoftware zur Kontextsicherung zurückzuführen, etwa auf leistungsstarke Datenspeicher und Datenbank- bzw. Datenbankmanagementsysteme, weiter auf die umfangreichen Datenschutzmaßnahmen, auf die aufwendigere Anwendersoftware (durch den Einbau von kontextsichernden Routinen bedingt), auf akzeptable Antwortzeiten des Computersystems oder schließlich auf entsprechende, zur Zeit nicht vorhandene kontextorientierte Sprachen.

Kurz- und mittelfristiges Ziel von Wissenschaft und Praxis muß es sein, Negativeffekte durch krasse Kontextverluste solange zu verhindern, bis das zweifellos bestehende know-how-Defizit bei der Planung von Personalinformationssystemen allmählich ausgeglichen werden kann. Es gilt daher vorerst, Implementierungen von Systemen zu vermeiden, die das Kontextproblem negieren und daher berechtigte Abwehrreaktionen der Betroffenen herausfordern.

----

[1] Vgl. dazu Pils, M.: EDV im Personalbereich macht neue Planungsphilospophie erforderlich, in: Computerwoche 43, S. 6 (1978)

[2] Vgl. Heinrich, L. J./ Pils, M.: Betriebsinformatik im Personalbereich - Die Planung computergestützter Personalinformationssysteme, Würzburg/Wien, Physica-Verlag 1979, S. 75ff.

[3] Vgl. Schricker, R.: Anwendung einer Abfragesprache durch die Fachabteilung im Personalinformationssystem - Erfahrungsbericht. Unterlage zur Sitzung der Erfahrungsaustauschgruppe "EDV im Personalwesen/Personalinformationssysteme", Linz, 22. Okt. 1980, S. 2

[4] Kirsch, W./ Klein, H. K.: Management - Informationssysteme II. Auf dem Wege zu einem neuen Taylorismus? Stuttgart/ Berlin/ Köln/ Mainz, Verlag Kohlhammer, 1977, S. 113

[5] Vgl. Pils, M.: Kontextsicherung in computergestützten Personalinformationssystemen, Habilitationsschrift, Linz 1980 (im Druck)

[6] Vgl. Biermann, F.: Vortrag anläßlich der Sitzung der Erfahrungsaustauschgruppe "EDV im Personalwesen/Personalinformationssysteme", Linz, 22. Okt. 1980

[7] Vgl.Heinrich, L. J. (Hrsg.): Computerleistung am Arbeitsplatz - Benutzerorientiertes Distributed Processing (DDP), München/ Wien 1978, S. 7ff.

[8] Vgl. Scholz, C./ Rumpf, H.: Patterns of Capability - Ein informationstheoretischer Ansatz zur Personalplanung, Regensburg 1979

[9] Vgl. dazu Marr, R.: Datenschutz und betriebliche Personalplanung. Ein Appell an die personalwirtschaftliche Forschung, in: DBW 41 (1981), S. 29ff.

[10] Vgl. dazu z. B. Reichwald, R.: Zur Notwendigkeit der Akzeptanzforschung bei der Entwicklung neuer Systeme der Bürotechnik, München 1978

[11] Vgl. Heinrich, L. J. (Hrsg.): Computerleistung am Arbeitsplatz - Benutzerorientiertes Distributed Processing (DDP), München/ Wien 1978, S. 179ff.

ERFAHRUNGEN ÜBER DIE IMPLEMENTIERUNG EINES KONZEPTES FÜR EIN PERSONALINFORMATIONSSYSTEM (PERSIS) IM BEREICHE DES ÖSTERR. BUNDESHEERES

R. Reichel

Bundesministerium für
Landesverteidigung

Zusammenfassung: Nach einem geschichtlichen überblick werden die Probleme dargestellt, die sich während der Realisierung des Personalinformationssystemes ergaben. Bei PERSIS handelt es sich um ein IBM-Standardanwendungskonzept, welches im Bereich des österreichischen Bundesheeres sowohl den militärischen Bedürfnissen als auch den Erfordernissen des Dienst- und Besoldungsrechtes angepaßt werden mußte. Schließlich wird noch über praktische Erfahrungen bei der Datenerfassung, Fehlerkorrektur, Entwicklung und Test der Programme sowie Inbetriebnahme berichtet.

1. Geschichtlicher überblick

Die Absicht ein Personalinformationssystem im Bereich des österr. Bundesheeres zu erstellen, reicht bis in das Jahr 1968 zurück. Nach längeren theoretischen überlegungen und Untersuchungen wurde im Jahre 1970 konkret mit der IST-Aufnahme begonnen. Es folgte die Analyse des IST-Zustandes und die Festlegung des SOLL-Konzeptes. Ab 1971 wurde einerseits mit der EDV-Organisation, der Programmierung der Personalvorgänge und derer vorgesehenen periodischen Auswertungen, andererseits mit der Erstellung von Dienstrechtsbehelfen, Schlüssel- und Schulungsunterlagen, begonnen. Hierauf erfolgte im Oktober 1971 nach einer ersten Schulung die Datenerfassung durch die Standesführer.

Im Sommer 1972 folgte die zweite Schulung der Standesführer und die Korrektur der gespeicherten Daten. Schließlich wurde im Jänner 1973 die dritte Schulung und die Korrektur der Daten durchgeführt. Da Anfang 1973 schon mit dem Test begonnen werden konnte, stand dem Start des PERSIS mit 15. Mai 1973 nichts mehr im Wege. Das Projekt wurde in einer Arbeitsgemeinschaft zwischen dem Bundesministerium für Landesverteidigung und der Fa. IBM-Österreich entwickelt. Die Analyse und Organisation wurden von militärischer Seite durchgeführt, die Programmierung und EDV-Unterstützung von der Fa. IBM-Österreich geleistet. Insgesamt erforderte das Projekt einen Aufwand von mehr als 100 Mannjahren, wovon mehr als 50 % auf Datenerfassung und Korrektur der Daten entfielen.

2. Gegenüberstellung des angebotenen Konzeptes mit dem tatsächlichen Bedarf der Personalsektion

Nach Präsentation und Annahme des Grobkonzepts, ergaben sich bei einer Detailanalyse Auffassungsunterschiede über die Ziele und Zwecke des PERSIS zwischen den Ausarbeitern des Konzepts und den Mitarbeitern der Personalabteilung. Nachdem bereits die Grundentscheidung darüber gefallen war, daß ein ADV-gestütztes Besoldungssystem nur vom Bundesministerium für Finanzen zu errichten ist, verblieb für den Bereich des Bundesministerium für Landesverteidigung nur ein PERSIS ohne Besoldungsteil. Von der Personalabteilung wurde daher versucht, die Ideen und Vorstellungen der Fachseite zu diesem System zu verwirklichen. Im wesentlichen ging es dabei um folgendes: Das Grobkonzept sah rund 50 Datenfelder und etwa 30 Personal-Veränderungscodes vor, die diese Felder verändern sollten; eine klare Trennung von aktuellen und historischen Daten und ein "Strukturdatenbestand" waren nicht vorgesehen. Von der Fachabteilung wurde gefordert, daß alle für die Bearbeitung der dienst und besoldungsrechtlichen Maßnahmen relevanten, aktuellen und historischen Daten einer Person erfaßt und verändert werden sollten. Außerdem sollte nach Auffassung der Fachseite für die Personalplanung und Steuerung ein Datenbestand vorgesehen werden, der die Grunddaten der Personen, die Strukturdaten und die Organisationsplandaten enthält. Auf Grund dieser Problematik kam es zu Verzögerungen im geplanten Ablauf. Schließlich konnte das Grobkonzept noch in einigen wesentlichen Punkten im Sinner der Vorstellungen der Personalabteilung verändert werden.

3. Ziele des PERSIS

Das PERSIS ist ein ON-LINE-Abfragesystem, das gestützt auf einen täglichen

Veränderungsdienst (Personalanmeldungen) den abfrageberechtigten Stellen, Informationen über alle Angehörigen des BMLV in einer 24-Stunden-Aktualität zur Verfügung stellt. Mit dem PERSIS soll den planungs-und personalverantwortlichen Stellen ein Instrument zur Erleichterung der

-Personalverwaltung,
-Personalplanung,
-Personalführung und
-Steuerung der Kaderausbildung- und Fortbildung

zur Verfügung stehen.

Dies wird erreicht durch folgende Möglichkeiten:

a) tägliche Abfrage mittels Bildschirm,
b) periodische und sporadisch ablaufende Batsch-Auswertungen auf Listen.

4. IST-Aufnahme

Bei Aufnahmen des IST-Zustandes wurde festgestellt, daß zu diesem Zeitpunkt ca 40 verschiedene Personalkarteien und ca 75 unterschiedliche Antrags-, Melde- und sonstige Formulare in Verwendung standen. Die periodischen Meldungen wurden auf der nächsthöheren Ebene jeweils verdichtet und weiter vorgelegt. Da die gesammelten Daten auf oberster Ebene einen zu großen Umfang angenommen hatten, fand in der Praxis eine Auswertung aus zeitlichen Gründen nicht mehr statt.

5. Datenerfassung, Personalbogen, Korrektur, Fehlerprotokoll, Entwicklung der Programme

Nach dem Grobkonzept sollte die Datenerfassung bei großen Standeskörpern nach drei Monaten, bei kleinen Standeskörpern nach zwei Monaten abgeschlossen sein. Die Erfassung war auf einem Personalbogen vorgesehen, der durch die EDV abgelocht und über ein Aufnahmeprogramm bei Vornahme einer Reihe von logischen und formalen Datenprüfungen gebucht werden sollte. Als Nachricht über die Verarbeitung für den Standesführer wurde ein Fehlerprotokoll mit Fehlertexten erstellt, aus dem alle erforderlichen Korrekturmaßnahmen ableitbar waren. In der Folge stellte es sich heraus, daß der Zeitplan für die Datenerfassung und Programmierung nicht eingehalten werden konnte. Da die Datenerfassung von den Standesführern neben der Normalarbeit verlangt wurde, traten schon hier Verzögerungen ein. Auf der anderen Seite zeigt sich, daß die drei eingerichteten Lochereien nicht in der Lage waren, die gelieferten Personalbögen zeitgerecht abzulochen. Weiter wurde das Aufnahmeprogramm von der Personalabteilung so lange getestet, bis Fehler nicht mehr feststellbar waren. Die Verzögerung zum geplanten Ablauf betrug fast zwei Jahre.

6. Implementierung des Systemes, schließen der Lücken zwischen aktuellem Stand und gespeicherten Daten

Da der Aufnahmelauf erst rund zwei Jahre nach dem Beginn der Datenerfassung möglich war, entstand eine Lücke zwischen den gespeicherten Daten und dem aktuellen Stand. Erst ab diesem Zeitpunkt konnten die Personalveränderungsmeldungen über das heereseigene Fernschreibnetz an das EDV-System abgesetzt werden. Eine weitere Verzögerung in der Berichtigungsphase der Daten trat deshalb ein, weil die Fernschreibleitungen nicht zur Gänze für das PERSIS benützt werden durften und deshalb die Anzahl der täglich abzusetzenden Meldungen begrenzt werden mußten. Auf Grund der Meldedisziplin der Standesführer sowie der Referenten in den Personalabteilungen konnte drei Jahre nach Abschluß der Datenerfassung ein sehr hoher Wahrheitsgehalt der gespeicherten Daten erreicht werden.

7. Laufender Betrieb, Personalmeldung, Automatik

Mit Einführung des PERSIS war es möglich, alle Meldungen auf dem Personalsektor auf eine einzige Personalmeldung zu reduzieren. Diese Personalmeldung enthält einerseits das für das EDV-System erforderliche Format und anderseits den Klartext. Für jeden Personalvorgang wurde ein Personalvorgangscode (PVC) festgelegt. Die Verarbeitung der Personalmeldungen und die Veränderung der Datenbestände (=Buchung) erfolgt im Batch-Verfahren nach Abschalten der ON-LINE-Verbindungen für Abfragen, das ist täglich ab 1500 Uhr. Die Standeskörper erhalten unmittelbar nach der Buchung über FS-Journale Nachricht,ob die Personalmeldung gebucht wurde oder ob eine Korrektur erforderlich ist. Darüberhinaus werden auf Grund entsprechende PVC´s automatische Anträge mit Angaben der für den jeweiligen Antrag erforderlichen Daten der Bediensteten gedruckt und an die zuständige Stelle weitergeleitet (zB Anträge auf Gewährung von Dienstjubiläen, Beförderungsanträge an das Bundeskanzleramt, Überstellungsanträge usw.)

8. Abfrage (direkt und variabel)

Die PERSIS Abfrage ermöglicht die Auswertung der "Personaldatenbank". Es kann auf einen konkreten Datensatz mit seinen Feldinhalten zugegriffen werden oder es können alle Datensätze, auf die bestimmte Kriterien zutreffen, selektiert werden. Weiter ist jederzeit ein SOLL-IST Vergleich über die momentane Situation der Arbeitsplatzbesetzung möglich. Schwierigkeiten bei der Implementierung der Abfrage gab es keine. Probleme bei der Benützung gab es nur solange, bis durch gezielte Aufklärungsarbeit allen einsichtig gemacht werden konnte, daß die gefundenen Antworten nur in Relation zum Wahrheitsgehalt der gespeicherten Daten richtig und brauchbar waren. Mit der Steigerung der Richtigkeit der Daten verschwanden schließlich alle Schwierigkeiten.

9. Weiterer Ausbau

Das PERSIS ist ein "lebendes System", dh es unterliegt einem unbedingten Anpassungszwang an
a) gesetzliche Gegebenheiten (Änderung des Dienstrechts),
b) strukturelle Gegebenheiten (Heeresumgliederung)
und dem Wunsche nach Verbesserung und Erweiterung der Auswertungen. Seit Betriebsbeginn gab es Änderungen der Betriebssoftware und der Hardware. Auf Grund der gewonnenen Erkenntnisse wurde 1977 ein neues Buchungsprogramm und wesentliche Änderungen im Aufbau durch das neue Beamtendienstrechtsgesetzt, das mit 1.1.1978 wirksam wurde, notwendig.
Weiter wurde entwickelt:
-VARLI (=über eine variable Abfrage können weitere Daten selektiert ausgegeben werden),
-ETIKETT-(Ausgabe von Adreßetiketten),
-PERSIM-(Durchführung der Personalsimulation zu Steuerung des Bedarfs),
-ANONYM-(Anonymisierung von Personaldaten für statistische Zwecke),
-ALTER-(variable Statistik über Altersschichtungen, zahlenmäßig und graphisch).

10. Nutzen des PERSIS

Abschließend soll die Frage beantwortet werden, ob die Vorstellung der "Personalverwaltung mittels Computer" verwirklicht werden konnten. Dies muß auf Grund folgender Vorteile bejaht werden:
-verkürzter Meldeweg (von bisher durchschnittlich 6 Wochen auf 24 Stunden),
-Wegfall manueller Karteien-durch Bildschirmabfrage und periodischen Ausdruck von bestimmten Auswertungen,
-Personalführung mit aktuellen Daten,
-Querschnittsinformation - durch die variable Abfrage,
-rationelle Ausbildungsplanung,
-Entfall einer Vielzahl von Meldungen und Vereinheitlichung und Verringerung des Formularwesens,
-exakte Personalstatistik,
-einheitliche Information aller Führungssysteme.

ERFAHRUNGEN BEI KONZEPTION, ENTWICKLUNG UND EINFÜHRUNG DES PERSONALINFORMATIONS-SYSTEMS DER IBM DEUTSCHLAND GMBH

K. Ulmer
IBM Deutschland GmbH
Unternehmensbereich Datenverarbeitung
Informationssysteme Personalsysteme 1

Die Ausgangssituation

Die Gestaltung eines Personalinformations-System wird stark beeinflußt vom bereits erreichten Mechanisierungsgrad und der Art der Organisation (zentral oder dezentral) eines Unternehmens in diesem Bereich.

Es ist daher unumgänglich, die Situation präzise zu analysieren, den erwarteten Nutzen zu definieren, alternative Lösungswege zu suchen und dann im Rahmen des Wirtschaftlichen und Machbaren einen Konsens über die Aufgabenstellung herbeizuführen.

Die Ausgangssituation stellte sich in unserem Unternehmen wie folgt dar:

Das neu zu organisierende System würde das dritte sein, welches mit Recht als EDV-Informationssystem bezeichnet werden kann, also die dritte Generation. Die zweite Generation, an deren Entwicklung ich noch selbst mitgearbeitet hatte, war ein respektables Verfahren mit rund 80 Anschlußverfahren und verfügte über einen beachtlichen Komfort und eine äußerst klare Systemarchitektur. Entscheidendes Merkmal dieser Architektur war die Tatsache, daß, obgleich ein System der späten 60-er Jahre, ein Grundgedanke der Datenbank-Philosophie darin verwirklicht war, nämlich einen zentralen, führenden Datenbestand zu haben. Für den Änderungsdienst also nur ein Verfahren zuzulassen und alle angrenzenden Verarbeitungssysteme über ein generalisiertes Extraktionsverfahren mit einem maßgeschneiderten Informationsvolumen zu versorgen.

Dieser Umstand erleichterte die Beantwortung der Frage nach der Projektabgrenzung enorm. Wir waren somit in der Lage, den gesamten Datenbankteil zu ersetzen, ohne dadurch auch gezwungen zu sein, in den Anschlußverfahren gravierende Änderungen vorzunehmen.

Die Notwendigkeit für eine Neuorganisation hatte ihre wesentlichen Gründe im Fehlen historischer Daten, den aufwendigen Fehlerkorrekturen eines reinen Stapelsystems sowie den Anforderungen der deutschen Datenschutz-Gesetzgebung.

In die Alternativ-Untersuchung wurden eine Eigenentwicklung, eine Erweiterung des bestehenden Verfahrens und ein Programmprodukt unseres Hauses - nämlich INTERPERS - einbezogen.

Die Bewertung der Alternativen ergab schließlich eine Entscheidung für die Verwendung von INTERPERS.

Vorgehensweise bei der Entwicklung

Bei der Verwirklichung eines Großprojektes, und ein solches war PDS II, ist es unabdingbar, die einzelnen Projektentwicklungsphasen, Tätigkeiten und Ergebnisse zu beschreiben, um damit eine Basis für Schätzungen und Fortschrittskontrollen zu haben.

Die Identifikation aller unmittelbar Beteiligten mit der Projektaufgabenstellung und der Art der Realisierung wird von der gewählten Projektorganisation stark beeinflußt.

Ich möchte Ihre Aufmerksamkeit nicht allzu lange strapazieren mit der Aufzählung unterschiedlicher Phasenkonzepte für die Entwicklung von EDV-Systemen, da Ihnen diese hinlänglich bekannt sein dürften. Alle mir bekannten Konzepte haben in ihrer graphischen Darstellung ihre Aufwandsspitze im Zeitraum der programmtechnischen Realisierung. Die Überlappung einzelner Entwicklungsphasen unterscheidet sich auch nicht signifikant und ist in der Praxis ohnehin weitgehend in das Ermessen des Projektverantwortlichen gestellt und versetzt ihn in die Lage, Kapazitätsschwankungen auszugleichen.

Wenn ich dennoch von Entwicklungsphasen spreche, so deshalb, weil wir eine Entwicklungsphase in unser Konzept aufgenommen haben, welche noch nicht sehr häufig anzutreffen ist. Es handelt sich hierbei um eine sogenannte "Anwendungskonzeption".

Anwendungskonzeptionen werden jeweils für Funktionskreise eines Unternehmens erstellt. Als Beispiele hierfür mögen dienen der Funktionskreis Vertrieb, der Funktionskreis Finanzen oder eben der Funktionskreis Personal.

Ziel und Inhalt einer Anwendungskonzeption ist es, alle in einem Funktionskreis erforderlichen Daten, Anwendungen und Informationsbedürfnisse zu sichten, zu gruppieren und zu bewerten. Als Ergebnis entstehen neben der Beschreibung der Geschäftsabläufe der Funktion auch die Aufgabenstellungen für definierte Projekte.

Eine Anwendungskonzeption wird von der EDV-Abteilung gemeinsam mit der Benutzerfachabteilung erarbeitet und erfordert infolge ihrer hohen Abstrahierungsanforderungen echte Spitzenkräfte mit langjähriger Erfahrung. Es ist darauf zu achten, daß der Aufbau und die Formulierung so zu gestalten sind, daß das Dokument für jeden Hierarchie-Level verständliche, klare Aussagen macht. Unsere Erfahrungen sind bislang sehr positiv.

Ebenso wie bei der Erarbeitung der Anwendungskonzeption arbeiten EDV- und Fachabteilung auch bei der eigentlichen Projektentwicklung sehr eng zusammen. Die beim PDS II-Projekt verwendete Projektorganisation sehen Sie in Abb. 1 schematisch dargestellt. Diese Organisation wurde auch sachlich umgesetzt bis hin zur räumlichen Zusammenlegung der Mitarbeiter.

Reviews des Projektfortschritts wurden von unabhängigen Stellen in unregelmäßigen Abständen durchgeführt.

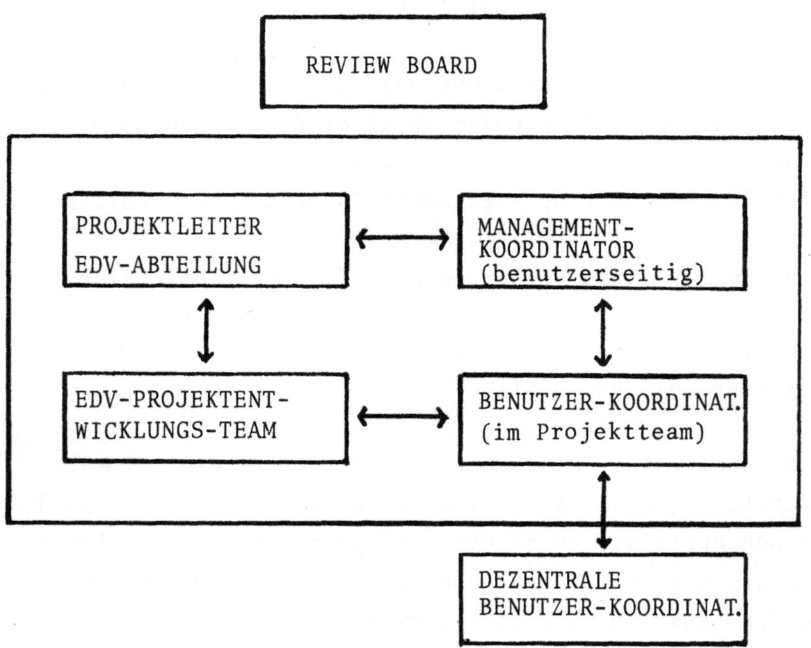

Abb. 1 PDS II-Projektorganisation (schematisch)

Implementierungs-Strategie

In den zurückliegenden Jahren konnte man bei EDV Anwendungssystemen einige signifikante Beobachtungen machen. Die Systeme werden zunehmend mächtiger und komfortabler, aber auch technisch komplexer und sie stellen höhere Ansprüche an die Benutzer. Deshalb ist bei gravierenden Eingriffen in die Geschäftsabläufe des Anwenders ein behutsamer stufenweiser Übergang ratsam.

In unserem Fall handelte es sich in der Tat um ein sehr breit gefächertes Spektrum von Veränderungen. Nicht nur, daß ca. 300 Benutzer mit dem für sie neuen Medium Bildschirm konfrontiert wurden, auch die Geschäftslogik wurde durch die Anpassung an die Direkteingabe stark modifiziert. Die ursprüngliche Absicht, das neue System in einem Zug zu entwickeln und einzuführen, wurde nach Vorliegen der Geschäftslogik-Konzeption revidiert. Wir entschlossen uns dazu, das System in vier Stufen zu entwickeln und einzuführen. Wir hatten hierbei das Glück, daß die Reihenfolge der Stufen einherging mit einer Zunahme an Umfang und Komplexität. Diese Vorgehensweise begünstigte den Aufbau von Erfahrung, erleichterte die Schulung der Anwender und verminderte das Einführungsrisiko ganz erheblich.

Allerdings mußte die Fachabteilung in Kauf nehmen, daß der Ausbau zu einem Personaldatensystem erst in der letzten Stufe vorgenommen wurde. Denkbar ist aber auch eine umgekehrte Implementierungsstrategie, nämlich zunächst die Minimalanforderungen zu realisieren und das System dann zu erweitern. Erfahrungsgemäß bleiben dabei aber viele der ursprünglichen Zielsetzungen auf der Strecke.

Zugegebenermaßen fällt es nicht leicht, ein solches System in logisch sinnvolle, überschaubare Blöcke aufzuteilen, was letztlich auch dazu führte, dass wir im Projektverlauf zwei Stufen inhaltlich umdefinieren mußten. Auch darf man sich der Tatsache nicht verschließen, daß sich der Gesamtaufwand durch Stufenbildung, bedingt durch Integrations- und Regressionsarbeiten erhöht. Dennoch kann ich Ihnen nur zur Stufenbildung raten.

Ein weiteres Implementierungsproblem ist in der Qualität der existierenden Datenbestände zu sehen. Hier wird es gegebenenfalls erforderlich sein, durch separate Prüfprogramme die normalerweise strengeren Plausibilitäten des Nachfolgesystems schon im bestehenden System quasi zu simulieren und die erforderlichen Korrekturen zu veranlassen. Je nach Dezentralisierungsgrad der Fachabteilungen ist hierfür angemessene Zeit zu planen.

System-Umfang

Wir leben in einer Zeit immer leistungsfähiger Computer, fortschreitender Technologien und eines explodierenden Informationsbedarfs. Man erliegt leicht der Gefahr, von einem neu zu entwickelndem Informationssystem die Lösung aller Probleme zu erwarten. Je weiter dieser Erwartungshorizont gespannt ist, desto schmerzlicher ist die Ernüchtungsphase. So darf man beispielsweise von einem Personaladministrations-System keine planerischen Qualitäten verlangen und ein Personalabfrage-System hat üblicherweise Schwächen auf Gebieten der Administration.

Wir haben uns dazu entschlossen, ein Personaladiminstrations-System zu erstellen, welches die Ausgangsdaten für Planungssysteme und mächtigere Informationssysteme darstellt.

Ich möchte Ihre Aufmerksamkeit nicht unnötig strapazieren durch die Aufzählung der Änderungsvorgänge und Anzeigeanwendungen, welche in unserem System realisiert sind, und anstatt dessen auf einige Besonderheiten eingehen.

Die erste Besonderheit bezieht sich auf die unterschiedlichen Zeitebenen, welche in ein und demselben System abgebildet sind. Es sind historische, aktuelle und zukunftswirksame Daten enthalten. Die größte Problematik liegt in den zukunftswirksamen Daten. Es handelt sich dabei nicht um Plandaten, sondern um solche Eingaben, welche zu einem zukünftigen Zeitpunkt tatsächlich wirksam werden, was wiederum bedingt, daß die Plausibilität der Eingabe auch bezogen auf diesen Zeitpunkt, sowie der dazwischenliegende Zeitraum im Moment der Eingabe sichergestellt werden muß, will man sich täglich wiederkehrende aufwendige Bestandsprüfungen mit anschließender Fehlerkorrektur ersparen. Ich weise nachdrücklich darauf hin, daß dieser Service ganz erheblichen Design- und Programmieraufwand sowie hochqualifizierte Spezialisten erfordert.

Eine weitere Besonderheit ist in einer systemgesteuerten Nachrichten-Datenbank zu sehen. Es handelt sich dabei um eine Art elektronischen Briefkasten. Sie kennen sicherlich die weitverbreiteten Formulare mit mehr oder minder langen Laufwegen auf der Randleiste. Genau dieses Zirkulieren von Papier, meist verbunden mit mehreren Kopiervorgängen, ist die Angriffsrichtung unserer Nachrichten-Datenbank.

Wird nämlich ein Vorgang durch einen Benutzer angestoßen, erhalten automatisch alle am Vorgang beteiligten Funktionen eine Nachricht. Über eine gesonderte Anzeige kann auch der aktuelle Stand des Vorgangs sichtbar gemacht werden. Wichtig ist auch, daß die Nachricht erst nach erfolgreich abgeschlossener Bearbeitung automatisch gelöscht wird. Wie ich glaube, haben wir damit eine wirkungsvolle Einsatzmöglichkeit des Computers als Kommunikationsmittel gefunden.

Datenbank-Konzept

Der Begriff der Datenbank ist aus modernen Informationssystemen nicht mehr wegzudenken. Auch die Verarbeitung von Datenbanken stellt qualifizierte Programmierer nur noch in wenigen Fällen vor ernsthafte Probleme. Die eigentliche Schwierigkeit liegt darin, den Aufbau der Datenbank so zu gestalten, daß sie der Summe der an sie gestellten Anforderungen optimal gerecht wird.

Üblicherweise, zumindest bei Firmen ab einer gewissen Größenordnung, übersteigen sogenannte Unternehmens-Datenbanken noch die Leistungsfähigkeit der Computer.

Die meisten Datenbanken decken daher nur Teilbereiche einer Unternehmung ab. Das langfristige Ziel eines Unternehmensinformations-Systems wird aber dennoch fast immer beibehalten. Soll ein Wildwuchs von Datenbanken, in etwa vergleichbar mit dem Wildwuchs von herkömmlichen Datenbeständen, vermieden werden, so bedarf dies einer sorgfältigen Analyse und Planung bis hin zum einzelnen Datenelement. In unserem Haus ist mit dieser Aufgabe für die internen Anwendungen ein 4-Mann-Team betraut, welches unter Anwendung entsprechender Methoden und technischer Hilfsmittel seit nunmehr drei Jahren recht erfolgreich arbeitet.

Doch zurück zum Personalinformations-System. Ich habe den Aspekt der Datenbankplanung angerissen, um Sie nun darauf aufmerksam zu machen, daß unser Haus unter dem Namen INTERPERS ein Programmprodukt anbietet, das vor allem "Einsteigern" diese Aufgabe abnimmt. Wir selbst verwendeten diese Anwendungssoftware. Neben einem Datenbankmodell liefert INTERPERS die 40 häufigsten Anwendungen des Personalbereichs mit, was einen Anwender in die Lage versetzt, mit minimalem Aufwand in sehr kurzer Zeit ein funktionsfähiges Online-Personalinformations-System zu installieren. Diese Anwendungen sind in einer eigenen Sprache codiert, die sich in ihrer Einfachheit an einem Endbenutzer orientiert und dadurch die Personalfachabteilung bezüglich zusätzlicher Anwendungen nicht mehr so stark von der EDV-Abteilung abhängig macht.

Die EDV-Abteilung profitiert in zweifacher Hinsicht. Zum Einen sind beachtliche Produktivitätserfolge bei der Anwendungsentwicklung erzielbar, und zum Anderen werden nicht so viele Mitarbeiter mit einem Spezialwissen benötigt, wie beim Einsatz herkömmlicher Programmiermethoden.

Unser Datenbankverbund ist in Abb. 2 schematisch dargestellt:

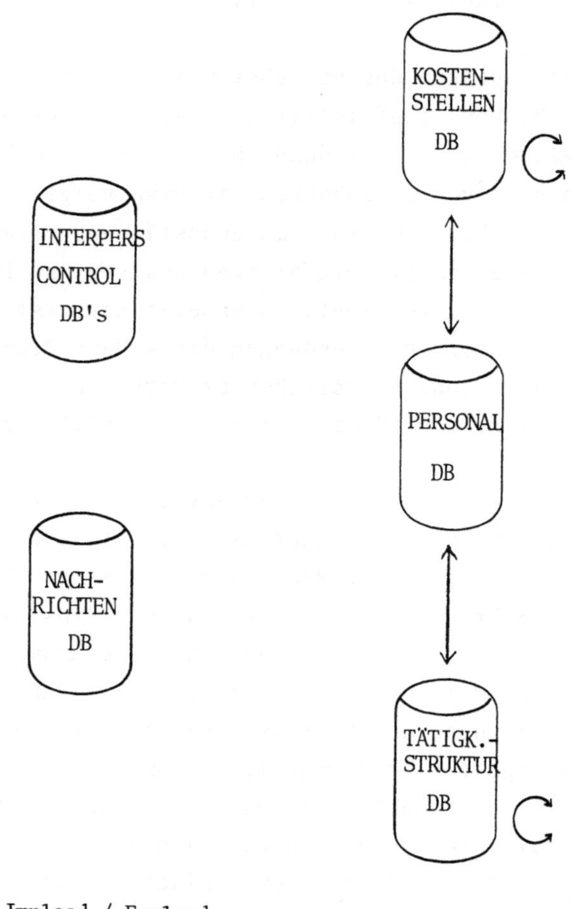

Abb. 2 PDS II - Datenbankverbund

Ausblick

Mit der Einführung des Systems wurde in diesem Jahr der wichtigste Schritt getan. Es wurde damit die Basis geschaffen, völlig neue Verfahren anzuschließen, bestehende Verfahren zu überarbeiten und von den neuen Möglichkeiten Gebrauch zu machen bis hin zur völligen Neuorganisation angrenzender Verfahren. Konzeptionelle Erweiterungen, wie zum Beispiel die Integration einer Stellen-Datenbank sind möglich, aber derzeit nicht geplant. Die unmittelbar anstehende Erweiterung hat vorwiegend die Behandlung historischer Daten zum Thema, wie etwa die Auslagerung solcher Informationen nach einer bestimmten Zeitdauer aus dem Online-Bestand.

INTEGRIERTES PERSONALINFORMATIONSSYSTEM
DER SIEMENS AG

M. Behr
B. Sperling
SIEMENS AG MUENCHEN

Zusammenfassung: Das Personalinformationssystem ist integrierter Bestandteil des bei der Siemens AG entwickelten Systems IVIP (Integriertes Verarbeitungs- und Informationssystem für Personaldaten). Das System wird zentral gepflegt und dezentral in den Betrieben zur Personalabrechnung, für Verwaltungsarbeiten und zu Informationszwecken im Personalbereich eingesetzt. Außerdem wird aus dem Abrechnungssystem eine zentrale Datenbank für die Berichterstattung und Auswertung versorgt; sie ist die Basis für das zentrale Informationssystem, dessen Aufgabe und Funktionsweise in diesem Beitrag hauptsächlich beschrieben wird.

Das dv-technische Konzept von IVIP berücksichtigt voll die Prinzipien des Software-Engineerings;

- es ist insbesonders flexibel zur Anpassung an neue fachliche Anforderungen
- sowie weitgehendst betriebssystemneutral
- gerüstet für zukünftige Hard- und Software-Entwicklung.

1. Ziele

Ein zentrales Personalinformationssystem ist notwendig, wenn sich der Personaldatenbestand wegen der Größe oder der Struktur des Unternehmens nicht mehr ohne weiteres überblicken läßt.

Es dient

- . als Lenkungsmittel der Unternehmensleitung (z.B. bessere Transparenz der Personalkosten)
- . zur Unterrichtung der Mitarbeiter, Betriebsräte und Aktionäre (z.B. über Entwicklung der Mitarbeiterzahlen und -strukturen, Auswirkung von Tarifabschlüssen)
- . zur Berichterstattung an öffentliche Stellen und Verbände (z.B. Unterstützung von Studien des Instituts für Arbeitsmarkt- und Berufsforschung)
- . als Datenbasis für Vergleiche mit externen Stellen (z.B. Personalstruktur- und Kostenvergleiche mit anderen Firmen)

2. Inhalt

Das Personalinformationssystem beinhaltet alle für Strukturauswertungen relevanten objektiven Daten der Mitarbeiter, nicht dagegen Daten wie z.B. Förderungsangaben, Beurteilungs-, Eignungsdaten, Testergebnisse, medizinische Daten, Vorstrafen.

Die Dateneingabe wird innerhalb des Abrechnungssystems aufgrund des "Anwenderhandbuchs" vorgenommen. Hier sind die einzelnen Daten, die für einen Mitarbeiter zu speichern sind, definiert und entsprechend den Erfordernissen der personalwirtschaftlichen Vorgänge gruppiert (z.B. Einstelldaten).

Für das Informationssystem ist es erforderlich, daß die Einzeldaten für Auswertungszwecke strukturiert gegliedert werden (z.B. Vorbildungsdaten) und Auswertungsbegriffe einheitlich für das Unternehmen geprägt werden. Hierzu dienen der Merkmalskatalog und der Begriffskatalog. Der Merkmalskatalog enthält eine Auswahl der für Abrechnungs- und Verwaltungszwecke erforderlichen Daten, ergänzt um einige reine Informationsdaten. Der Begriffskatalog ermöglicht die einheitliche Bestimmung und Interpretation von Standard- und Sonderauswertungen.

Art und Umfang der Auswertungen richten sich nach dem Informationsbedarf. Für den bekannten regelmäßigen Informationsbedarf werden die im Tabellenverzeichnis beschriebenen Standardauswertungen angeboten. Sie geben dem Anwender durch Zeilen- und Spalten-Varianten und variable organisatorische Tiefengliederung ein Höchstmaß an Flexibilität innerhalb der standardisierten Rahmenbedingungen. Für den unregelmäßigen Informationsbedarf steht eine Standardsoftware zur Verfügung, die dem Anwender unter Beachtung der Zugriffsberechtigung die freie Kombination der vorhandenen Merkmale zu Sonderauswertungen ermöglicht.

3. Aufbau der Datenbank

Abb. 1

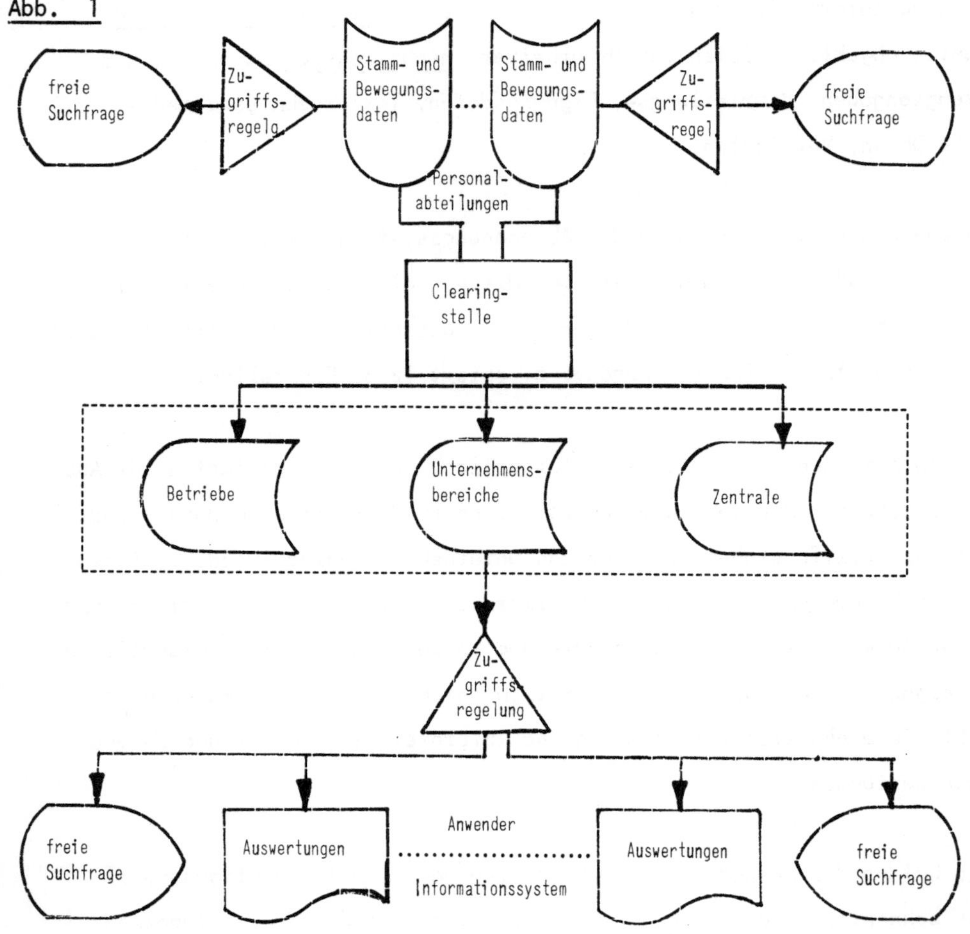

Die Informationsdatenbank wird durch Transformation der Daten der Personalabrechnung in einer zentralen Clearingstelle aufgebaut. Aus wirtschaftlichen Gründen ist es möglich, auf die Einrichtung von organisatorisch getrennten Teil-Datenbanken zu verzichten. Der Direktzugriff der einzelnen Bereiche der Siemens AG auf die Datenbank wird durch ein abgestuftes Zugriffssystem geregelt. Die Zugriffsberechtigung bezieht sich auf die organisatorische Einheit (z.B. Betrieb, Unternehmensbereich) und auf den Merkmalsumfang (z.B. "alle Merkmale außer Entgeltdaten"). Der Datenfluß ist in Abb. 1 dargestellt. Die Aktualisierung der Informationsdatenbank erfolgt monatlich zu einem einheitlichen Berichtsstand.

4. Praktische Anwendungsbeispiele für Auswertungen

Aus den Tätigkeiten des Personalwesens erfüllt IVIP die Funktionen

- Personalabrechnung
- Personalverwaltung
- und Information über Personaldaten.

Die Auswertungen des Personalinformationssystem geben dem Anwender die Möglichkeit

. zu informieren
. Entscheidungshilfen zu geben
. Alternativen aufzuzeigen
. Hypothesen zu bestätigen bzw. zu entkräften
. Tendenzen zu erkennen
. Prognosen anzufertigen
. die Datenerfassung zu beeinflussen.

Die Schaffung der dv-technischen und organisatorischen Voraussetzungen für ein Informationssystem ist als eine notwendige Basis anzusehen, wichtiger noch sind die Analyse- und Auswertemethoden, um ein derartiges Instrumentarium nutzbringend anzuwenden. Aus der Vielzahl der Anwenderbeispiele kann hier nur stichwortartig ein kleiner Ausschnitt aufgeführt werden:

. Lebens- und Dienstalterstruktur bestimmter Mitarbeitergruppen zur Ermittlung des künftigen Ersatzbedarfs

. Kombination von Einkommen, Vorbildung und Tätigkeit zur Darstellung der Entwicklungsmöglichkeiten qualifiziert ausgebildeter Mitarbeiter

. Untersuchung der Vorbildungsstruktur im Zeitvergleich als Grundlage der künftigen Aktivitäten bei der kaufmännischen Ausbildungspolitik

. Ermittlung von Ausmaß, Struktur und Ursachen der Fluktuation sowie der Fluktuationskosten

. Quantifizierung der Einflußfaktoren zur Bestimmung von Volumen-/Strukturänderungen und Verteuerungen bei der Analyse des Personalaufwands

. Berechnung von Rückstellungen/Verbindlichkeiten für den Jahresabschluß (z.B. Urlaubsrückstellungen)

. Regelmäßige Beobachtung der bereinigten Lohndrift, d.h. derjenigen durchschnittlichen Einkommensveränderung, die nicht durch die tarifliche Entwicklung bedingt ist

. Ermittlung der Kosten alternativer Regelungen bei geplanten sozialpolitischen Maßnahmen

. Berechnung der Auswirkungen tariflicher Vereinbarungen (im Vorfeld der Verhandlungen und nach Abschluß der Verträge)

. Kennzahlensystem "Personalwesen" zur Darstellung wichtiger Komponenten des Personalbestands und insbesondere des Personalaufwands.

Entscheidend für die Effektivität eines Personalinformationssystems ist nicht die wirtschaftliche technische Abwicklung, sondern in erster Linie die Fähigkeit des Anwenders, die Daten mit wohldurchdachten Systemen aufzubereiten, zu analysieren und zu entscheidungsrelevanten Informationen zu verarbeiten. Schwerpunkte sind hierbei die Bereitstellung von derartig aufbereiteten Daten und Informationen zu aktuellen personal-, sozial- und bildungspolitischen Themen sowie das rechtzeitige Erkennen und Bewerten von Maßnahmen auf dem Personalsektor, die der Gesetzgeber, die Tarifpartner und das Unternehmen planen.

5. Ziele und Gliederung des dv-technischen Konzeptes

Bei der Grundsatzüberlegung zum dv-technischen Konzept von IVIP sind Ziele festgelegt worden, die voll die Prinzipien des Software-Engineerings berücksichtigen.
Im Vergleich zu bisherigen Personalsystemen besitzt IVIP eine zukunftsichere Technologie.
Charakteristisch für das IVIP-Konzept ist

- die Kompatibilität zu unterschiedlichen Betriebssystemen
- die Flexibilität zur Anpassung an unterschiedliche Gegebenheiten in den Einsatzorten
- die Integrationsfähigkeit mit angrenzenden betriebswirtschaftlichen Aufgaben
- und Transparenz durch Strukturierung des gesamten Programmkomplexes.

Um gesetzliche, tarifliche und betriebliche Änderungen schnell realisieren zu können, wurde ein umfangreiches Tabellensystem implementiert, das die Anpassungsfähigkeit erhöht und die Wartung des Systems erleichtert.

Die Anwender-Software ist benutzerfreundlich, zuverlässig und portabel.

Zur rationellen Programmverwaltung wurde ein

- zentraler Programmdienst
- und zentrales Dokumentationsarchiv

eingerichtet.

Zu Beginn der Entwicklung des dv-technischen Konzeptes wurden aufgrund von Anforderungen die fachlichen Aufgaben von den dv-technischen Problemen getrennt und somit entstand das IVIP-Schalenmodell (Abb. 2).

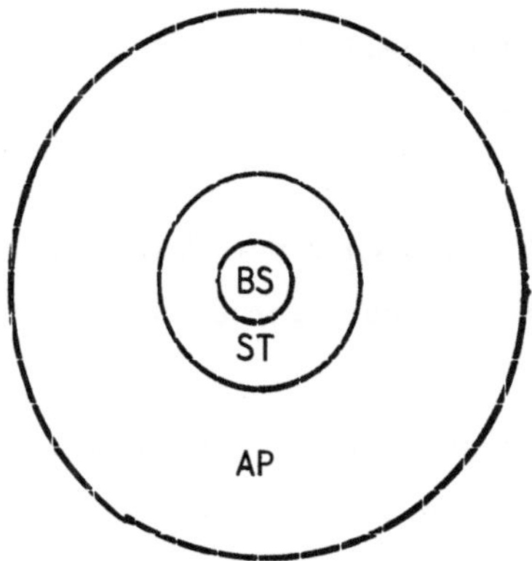

Im Innersten des Schalenmodells befindet sich das Betriebssystem (BS).
In der nächsten Schale verbindet der IVIP-Systemteil (ST) die Anwenderprogramme (AP) mit dem BS.

Der Systemteil führt eine Betriebssystemanpassung aus, setzt logische Ein-/ Ausgabeanforderungen in physikalische Anweisungen um und enthält mehrfach - verwendbare Bausteine, die von der Problemlösung her zu den Anwenderprogrammen (anwendernahe-Software) gehören.

Somit enthält der Systemteil betriebssystemnahe sowie anwendersystemnahe Komponenten.
Zu den wichtigsten BS-nahen Teilen gehören das

- Datenverwaltungssystem (DAVESY)
- und das umfangreiche Kriterienbanksystem (Tabellen).

6. Vorgehen und Technologie der Implementierung

Bei der Realisierung ist der Top-down-aproach mit dem bottum-up sinnvoll ergänzt worden. Zur Implementierung des Konzeptes wurde die Strukturierte - Programmierung angewendet. Hierfür wurde COLUMBUS eingesetzt, ein Siemens-Softwarewerkzeug zur Unterstützung der Strukturierten - Programmierung.
Die Anwenderprogramme sind zu 90 % in COBOL geschrieben, der Rest in ASSEMBLER realisiert.

Als Datenzugriffsmethode ist ISAM gewählt worden, ergänzt um eine sehr leistungsfähige Abfragesprache.

Das realisierte System ermöglicht auch andere Datenbanksysteme einzusetzen, ohne daß die Anwenderprogramme geändert werden müssen.

Zur Vereinheitlichung der Implementierung entstanden Projektkonventionen und eine Reihe von Werkzeugen, die die Implementierung rationalisieren und vereinfachen.

7. Datenfluß und Abwicklung

Abb. 3

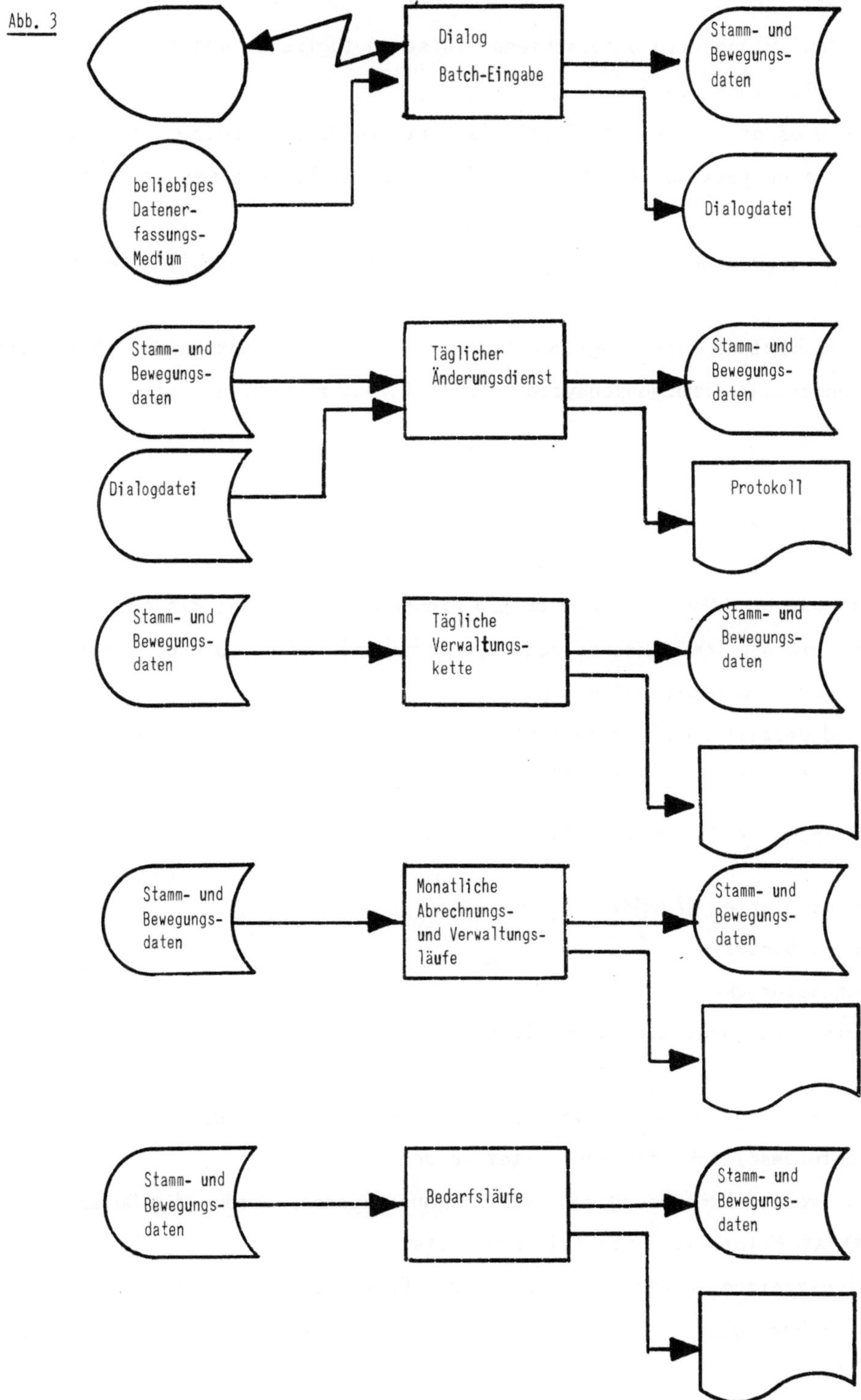

IVIP läuft auf allen Siemens-Anlagen des Systems 7.xxx unter dem BS2000.
Das Projekt wird dezentral bei den Anwendern abgewickelt.
Bei der Abwicklung wird unterschieden zwischen täglichen und monatlichen Läufen sowie Bedarfsläufen.
Die Bewegungsdaten können an Terminals über ein Dialogprogramm oder über ein anderes Datenerfassungsmedium mit Hilfe eines Batchprogrammes eingegeben werden.
In beiden Programmen sind die gleichen Bausteine der Plausibilitätenprüfung enthalten.
Für die Abwicklung sind Programme zu Ketten zusammengefaßt worden, die durch ein umfangreiches Prozedurensystem (JCL) einfach zu bedienen sind.

8. Mengengerüst

Derzeit besteht IVIP aus mehr als 220 Programmen, mit mehr als 630 Moduln, die mehr als 650 000 lines of code (geschrieben) und ca. 350 000 generierte Befehle und Kommentare enthalten.
IVIP wird derzeit in 22 Rechenzentren in der Bundesrepublik abgewickelt.
Die Mindestausstattung für IVIP:

Siemens-Anlage 7.738 oder ähnliche Leistung ASP 2 MB

1 Magnetplatte (72 MB)
2 Magnetbänder
1 Schnelldrucker
1 Datensichtgerät mit Ausweisleser

Im Juli 1981 sind Daten von mehr als 100 000 Mitarbeiter der Siemens AG und Töchtergesellschaften bearbeitet worden.
Nach der vollen Einführung von IVIP im Hause Siemens werden die Daten von ca. 200 000 Mitarbeiter von IVIP bearbeitet.
Die Antwortzeiten an den Terminals in den Personalabteilungen dauern ca. 3 - 4 Sekunden.

9. Speicherbedarf

Für die Verarbeitung werden für die Stamm-, Bewegungs- und Abrechnungsdaten sowie für Rückrechnungen und Auflaufwerte ca. 25 PAM-S/MA benötigt. (1 PAM-S = 2048 Bytes).

10. Datenschutz und Datensicherung

Die Speicherung und Verwendung von personenbezogenen Daten in einem Informationssystem unterliegt den Erlaubnistatbeständen und den Datensicherungsvorschriften des BDSG (Bundesdatenschutzgesetz).

Personenbezogene Daten, die auf keinen Fall zu Informationszwecken gespeichert werden dürfen, sind in einer internen Unternehmens-Richtlinie festgelegt.

Für die Gewährleistung der Datensicherung sind die 10 Kontrollen der Anlage zu Paragraph 6 des BDSG eingehalten. So ist insbesondere sichergestellt, daß Daten durch selbsttätige Einrichtungen (On-Line-Verkehr von Rechner zu Rechner ohne zwischengeschaltete menschliche Kontrolle) unbefugt an Dritte außerhalb der Siemens AG nicht übermittelt werden.

Durch eine geeignete Zugriffskontrolle wird erreicht, daß auf Informations-Dateien nur die befugten Personen und die Programme des Informationssystems zugreifen können. Das gilt sowohl für die Eingabe als auch die Ausgabe im Dialog- oder Batch-Betrieb. Zum Dialog-Betrieb ist dem Benutzer der Zugriff nur über Ausweisleser mit zulässiger Kennung möglich. Im Batch-Betrieb ist sichergestellt, daß das Personal des Rechenzentrums keinen Zugriff hat, ohne gleichzeitige Freigabe durch die verantwortliche personalfachliche Stelle (Vier-Augen-Prinzip). Ferner wird verhindert, daß die im Informationssystem eingebauten Zugriffssicherungen und insbesondere die Zugriffsberechtigungsregelung durch den Einsatz von unbefugten Programmen unterlaufen werden.

Die Zugriffskontrolle regelt den generellen Zugriff auf die Informations-Dateien. In der Zugriffsberechtigungsregelung ist der Zugriff auf die einzelnen Merkmale (Datenfelder) und die Art der Auswertungen (personenbezogene oder anonymisierte) festgelegt. Ferner ist der Datenumfang für den Berechtigten geregelt.

Um die Anforderungen des Datenschutzes zu erfüllen, wurden

1. Maßnahmen zur Datensicherheit des Betriebssystems genutzt

   - Abwicklung unter einer Benutzerkennung (Benutzerberechtigung)
   - getrennter Dateikatalog für jeden Benutzer
   - kein Zugriff falls nicht mehrfach benutzbar
   - Benutzung privater Platten
   - unregelmässige Schlüsselwortvergabe für Lese- und Schreibvorgänge auf IVIP-Dateien.

2. Projekteigene datenschutzunterstützende Lösungen implementiert

   - so führt z.B. das Datenverwaltungssystem eine von den Programmen getrennte Merkmalsbeschreibung (Formatdatei)
   - im Dialogprogramm ist eine mehrstufige Zugriffsberechtigung realisiert

     - Maskenart
       Änderungen, Abfragen
     - Sachgebiet
     - eigene Pers.-Nr.

   - es wird eine Terminalberechtigungsprüfung durchgeführt und
   - der Anstoß der Stapelprozesse wird über ein spezielles Programm kontrolliert, in dem eine dynamische Schlüsselwortvergabe und Terminalprüfung enthalten ist.

COMPUTERGESTÜTZTE MOTIVATIONS- UND ZUFRIEDENHEITSFORSCHUNG ALS INSTRUMENT DER BETRIEBLICHEN PERSONALPOLITIK

- ERGEBNISSE EINER PILOTSTUDIE IN EINEM MITTELSTÄNDISCHEN UNTERNEHMEN DER BAUMASCHINENINDUSTRIE -

von

Prof. Dr. Karl-Friedrich Ackermann
Universität Stuttgart

I. Zur personalpolitischen Anwendbarkeit verhaltenswissenschaftlicher Basistheorien in Unternehmen. Anspruch und Wirklichkeit

Betriebliche Personalpolitik setzt als selbstverständliche Tatsache voraus, daß das Verhalten der Organisationsmitglieder zumindest in gewissen Grenzen beeinflußbar ist und auch beeinflußt werden muß, um die Ziele des Unternehmens im angestrebten Ausmaß zu erreichen. Dies gilt sowohl für die Partizipationsentscheidungen, also für den Bereich der Eintritts- und Austrittsentscheidungen der Organisationsmitglieder, als auch für deren individuelle Beitragsentscheidungen, welche die tatsächlich erbrachten Arbeitsleistungen bestimmen (March u. Simon 1958). Nach herrschender Wissenschaftstheorie (Albert 1964) ist unstrittig, daß die Verhaltenswissenschaften einschließlich der sozialwissenschaftlich orientierten Betriebswirtschaftslehre (Reber 1977) zur Effizienzsteigerung der betrieblichen Personalpolitik beitragen können, indem sie empirisch gehaltvolle Theorien bzw. Hypothesen mit möglichst allgemeinen Aussagen des Typs "Wenn A - dann B" über das personale Verhalten in Betrieben bereitstellen. Bezeichnet die B-Komponente einen erwünschten Soll-Zustand oder eine erwünschte Änderung des bestehenden Ist-Zustandes, so gibt die A-Komponente der Hypothese an, was getan werden muß, um dieses Ziel zu erreichen.

In der wissenschaftlichen Fachdiskussion wird seit langem ein eklatantes Theoriedefizit der Personalpraxis konstatiert und auf den schnell wachsenden Bestand an - vermeintlich abrufbereiten - Erkenntnissen hingewiesen. Allerdings hat die letztlich entscheidende Frage nach den Bedingungen eines verbesserten "Theorie-Technologie-Praxis"-Transfers (Ackermann 1978, S. 54 ff) erst in jüngster Zeit die notwendige Beachtung gefunden. Zu diesen Bedingungen gehört neben der Innovationsfähigkeit und Innovationsbereitschaft vor allem auch die technologische Anwendbarkeit und Umsetzbarkeit verhaltenswissenschaftlicher Erkenntnisse im einzelnen Unternehmen für personalpolitisch relevante Entscheidungen. Wenig ist bislang seitens der wissenschaftlichen Forschung getan worden, um die Personalpraxis von der Brauchbarkeit und von dem Nutzen ihrer Erkenntnisse zu überzeugen. Dies gilt in besonderer Weise für den Bestand der motivationalen und kognitiven Basistheorien des personalen Verhaltens im Betrieb (Ackermann u. Reber 1981), deren hoher Bekanntheitsgrad und wissenschaftlicher Stellenwert in keinem vernünftigen Verhältnis zu ihrer geringen Akzeptanz als praktisch verwertbare Entscheidungshilfen stehen.

In der vorliegenden Untersuchung wird der Frage nachgegangen, ob und in welcher Weise bestimmte Basistheorien des personalen Verhaltens tatsächlich geeignet sind, den Belangen des einzelnen Unternehmens zu dienen und zur Effizienzsteigerung der betrieblichen Personalpolitik beizutragen. Zu diesem Zweck wurden zwei, auch in der Personalpraxis weithin bekannte Verhaltenstheorien ausgewählt und auf ihre praktische Anwendbarkeit in einem mittelständischen Unternehmen der Baumaschinen-Industrie geprüft.Ausgewählt wurden einmal die sog. "dynamische Motivationstheorie" Maslows (Maslow 1954; Wahba u. Bridwell 1976), zum anderen die sog. "Dual-Faktoren-Theorie" Herzbergs (Herzberg et al 1959; Herzberg 1971; Zink 1975). Im einzelnen stehen die folgenden anwendungsbezogenen Fragen zur Diskussion: (1) Welche Anforderungen stellen die beiden Theorien an die Gestaltung des betrieblichen Personalinformationssystems? (2) Was leisten diese Theorien für die personalwirtschaftliche Istzustandsanalyse eines Unternehmens; (3) Welche praktischen Konsequenzen lassen sich aus den gewonnenen Personalinformationen für die betriebliche Personalpolitik ableiten?

II. Gestaltung des BIS auf der Grundlage der verhaltenswissenschaftlichen Basistheorien Maslows und Herzbergs

Die Anwendung der verhaltenswissenschaftlichen Basistheorien Maslows and Herzbergs impliziert den Aufbau eines neuen Personalinformationssystems, das zur Unterscheidung gegenüber den traditionellen, vorwiegend zur Lohn- und Gehaltsabrechnung konzipierten Systemen als "Behavioral Information System" BIS bezeichnet werden soll (zur Grundkonzeption des BIS vergl. Starke u. Ferrat (1976) S. 26 ff).

Das BIS läßt sich wie andere betriebliche Informationssysteme in die Subsysteme "Aufgabensystem", "Methodensystem" und "Datensystem" gliedern (vgl. Heinrich u. Pils 1979, S. 38 ff). Die Basistheorien Maslows und Herzbergs geben bestimmte Rahmenbedingungen für die Gestaltung dieser Subsysteme vor.

1. Gestaltung des personalwirtschaftlichen Aufgabensystems

Maslow und Herzberg betonen die Notwendigkeiten und Bedeutung von systematischen Motivations- und Zufriedenheitsuntersuchungen als Aufgabe der Personalwirtschaft und damit des BIS. Die Durchführung solcher Untersuchungen dient letztlich dem Zweck, Daten für die Erfüllung der typischen Personalfunktionen im Betrieb bereitzustellen, so z. B. für das Beschaffen, Einsetzen, Erhalten und Entwickeln des Personals; sie wird daher gelegentlich als eine - den einzelnen Personalfunktionen oder Kernaufgaben vorgelagerte - Uraufgabe bzw. Datenfindungsgabe des Personalbereichs bezeichnet (Heinrich u. Pils 1979, S. 41).

Der Theorie Maslows zufolge hat das BIS die Grundbedürfnisse der Organisationsmitglieder nach dem subjektiv wahrgenommenen Befriedigungsgrad und nach ihrer wahrgenommenen Bedeutung bzw. Wichtigkeit zu erfassen. Es sind dies in der Reihenfolge der vermuteten Vorrangigkeit: physiologische Bedürfnisse, Sicherheitsbedürfnisse, soziale Bedürfnisse, Achtungs- und Anerkennungsbedürfnisse sowie die Selbstaktualisierungsbedürfnisse. Durch die Theorie Maslows wird die Aufmerksamkeit auf jene Bedürfniskategorien gelenkt, die relativ wenig befriedigt sind und eine hohe Bedeutung bzw. Wichtigkeit für die einzelnen Organisationsmitglieder besitzen. Diese Bedürfniskategorien bestimmen vor allen anderen die Verhaltensrichtung und die Verhaltensstärke der Individuen.

Nach Herzberg hat das BIS die Vorkommenshäufigkeit bestimmter, artmäßig vorgegebener Arbeitsfaktoren in der jeweiligen Arbeitssituation zu erfassen. Diese Faktoren sind als Ursachen besonderer Zufriedenheit und hoher Arbeitsmotivation (= Zufriedenmacher bzw. Motivatoren M) oder als Ursachen besonderer Unzufriedenheit und geringer Arbeitsmotivation (= Unzufriedenmacher bzw. Hygienefaktoren H) wirksam.

Zwischen den Maslowschen Grundbedürfnissen und den Arbeitsfaktoren Herzbergs bestehen noch nicht ganz geklärte Zusammenhänge. Die Vermutung liegt nahe, daß letztere auch als Bedürfnisbefriedigungsmittel interpretiert werden können (vgl. Kast u. Rosenzweig 1970, S. 231 ff). Mit der gleichzeitigen Berücksichtigung der genannten Basistheorien im BIS soll bewußt die Frage offen gehalten werden, welche davon für technologische Anwendungen im Betrieb besser geeignet erscheint. Vorläufig gehen wir von der Annahme aus, daß beide Konzepte personalpolitisch relevante, sich wechselseitig ergänzende oder auch bestätigende Personalinformationen zu liefern imstande sind.

2. Gestaltung des personalwirtschaftlichen Methodensystems

Die verhaltenstheoretisch geforderten Personalinformationen können durch verschiedene Methoden gewonnen werden. Ohne auf das schwierige Problem der Methodenwahl einzugehen, die einen nicht unerheblichen Einfluß auf die Erhebungsergebnisse haben dürfte, beschränken wir uns im folgenden auf die Kennzeichnung der Vorgehensweise, wie sie sich für den untersuchten Betrieb als praktikabel und zweckmäßig erwiesen hat.

Die Maslow-orientierten Personalinformationen wurden mit Hilfe eines anonymen Fragebogens, nämlich mit dem "Porter-Need Satisfaction-Questionnaire" (PNSQ) ermittelt (Porter 1961, S. 1 ff). Der PNSQ enthält 13 Einzelmerkmale (Items), die in bestimmter Weise mit den fünf Grundbedürfnissen verknüpft sind.[1] Hinzu treten zwei weitere Items; sie können keiner der genannten Bedürfnisschichten allein zugeordnet werden. Eines dieser Items betrifft das Bedürfnis nach angemessener Entlohnung ("Entlohnungsbedürfnis"), das andere jenes nach angemessener Information ("Informationsbedürfnis") über alle Vorgänge im Unternehmen, die für die betroffenen Organisationsmitglieder relevant sind. Für jedes der 15 Bedürfnis-Items wird der Befriedigungsgrad ermittelt, indem auf einer 7-Punkte-Skala

1) Abweichend von dem ursprünglichen 5-Schichten-Bedürfniskonzept Maslows vernachlässigt der PNSQ die physiologischen Bedürfnisse, die bereits als weitgehend befriedigt und daher für das aktuelle Verhalten als irrelevant gelten; dafür werden die Autonomie-Bedürfnisse als gesonderte Bedürfniskategorie berücksichtigt. Wie wir noch sehen werden, ist im vorliegenden Anwendungsbeispiel die Vernachlässigung der physiologischen Bedürfnisse nicht unproblematisch.

(1 = Min., 7 = Max.) zunächst die gewünschte Soll-Ausprägung ("Wieviel sollte davon vorhanden sein"), daran anschließend auf einer gesonderten 7-Punkte-Skala die tatsächliche Ausprägung ("Wieviel ist davon tatsächlich vorhanden") anzugeben ist. Der Befriedigungsgrad ergibt sich dann durch Berechnung der Differenz zwischen Soll und Ist. Je größer diese - meist positive - Differenz, d. h. das Befriedigungsdefizit ist, um so geringer ist der jeweilige Befriedigungsgrad. Demgegenüber wird die unterschiedliche Wichtigkeit der einzelnen Items durch Beantwortung der einfachen Frage: "Wie wichtig ist das für Sie?" auf der 7-Punkte-Skala erhoben.

Für die Ermittlung der Herzberg-orientierten Personalinformationen wurde ein gesonderter Fragebogen entwickelt. Abweichend von der ursprünglich vorgeschlagenen "Methode der kritischen Ereignisse", die auf Erlebnisschilderungen der Befragten und nachträglicher Codierung durch den Fragesteller aufgebaut ist, sind in neueren Untersuchungen verschiedene Erhebungs- und Auswertungsmethoden verwendet worden (vgl. King 1970). Die vorliegende Pilotstudie stützt sich auf einen vollstrukturierten Fragebogen, der für jeden der 16 Arbeitsfaktoren Herzbergs eine Antwort der Befragten verlangt, ob der Faktor im Rahmen der ausgeübten beruflichen Tätigkeit als Ursache für besondere Zufriedenheit und/oder als Ursache für besondere Unzufriedenheit im Betrieb wirksam gewesen ist.

3. Gestaltung des personalwirtschaftlichen Datensystems

Das Datensystem des BIS wurde in strikter Trennung vom bereits bestehenden Personalinformationssystem des untersuchten Unternehmens aufgebaut, um gegenüber den Befragten die geforderte Anonymität und Objektivität der Datenerhebung und Datenauswertung zu demonstrieren. Angesichts der Fälle der gewünschten Daten - von jeder befragten Vpn. mindestens 77 Einzeldaten - und der angestrebten differenzierten Auswertung für verschiedene Zwecke[1)] war die Computerunterstützung der Auswertung und der Einsatz des SPSS-Programms eine notwendige Voraussetzung.

---

1) Die technologische Anwendung der gewonnenen Personalinformationen für die betriebliche Personalpolitik, die in dem vorliegenden Beitrag allein interessiert, ist nur einer dieser Zwecke. Andere betreffen z. B. die empirische Prüfung und Weiterentwicklung der Theorie. Über die diesbezüglichen Befunde wird an anderer Stelle gesondert zu berichten sein.

III. Einführung und Anwendung des BIS in einem mittelständischen Unternehmen der Baumaschinen-Industrie

1. Einführungsprobleme des BIS

Systematische Mitarbeiterbefragungen werden z. Z. von einigen wenigen Großunternehmen - mit unterschiedlicher Zielsetzung - durchgeführt. Für mittlere und kleinere Unternehmen scheint die Auffassung vorherrschend zu sein, daß derartige Befragungen entweder nicht sinnvoll oder nicht realisierbar sind. Mit dem vorliegenden Anwendungsbeispiel des BIS wird zumindest die grundsätzlich bestehende Möglichkeit nachgewiesen, daß auch mittelständische Unternehmen sich dieses Instrumentariums bedienen können.

Die Einführung und Anwendung des BIS erfolgte nach längerer Vorbereitung in einem Unternehmen der Baumaschinen-Industrie mit rd. 160 beschäftigten Arbeitern und Angestellten. Die Vorbereitungsphase umschließt die Vorbesprechung und detaillierte Ablaufplanung der Fragebogenerhebung mit der Unternehmensleitung und dem Betriebsrat, Pretest der Einzelfragen auf Verständlichkeit, Erstellung schriftlicher Beantwortungshilfen einschließlich Übersetzungen des Fragebogens für bestimmte Ausländergruppen, Vorankündigung der Befragung durch Aushang am Belegschaftsbrett und zusätzliche individuelle Erläuterungen auf Wunsch der Befragten.
Unter Berücksichtigung des erheblichen Fragebogenumfangs und der mangelnden Erfahrung der Belegschaft mit dem verwendeten BIS ist der Rücklauf von N = 60 auswertbaren Fragebogen (Rücklaufquote rd. 37 % der Gesamtbelegschaft) als befriedigend zu bezeichnen. Hauptursache für die verweigerte Beteiligung Einzelner an der Befragung war nach unseren Beobachtungen weniger die anfallende Zeitbelastung durch das Ausfüllen des Fragebogens,[1] auch nicht die Überforderung durch ungewohnte Fragestellungen, sondern eindeutig die tiefsitzende Sorge, daß die Anonymität der Befragung im nachhinein durch geschickte Merkmalskombinationen gebrochen werden könnte.

1) Mit Ausnahme einer Gruppe türkischer Arbeitnehmer, die der sprachlichen Unterstützung durch einen Betriebsdolmetscher bedurften, waren die Fragebogen von den übrigen Belegschaftsmitgliedern außerhalb der Arbeitszeit - über das Wochenende - auszufüllen. Diese Regelung hat sich grundsätzlich bewährt, jedenfalls dann, wenn die Qualität und Vollständigkeit der Antworten als Beurteilungskriterien herangezogen werden.

Diese Befürchtung ist bei mittleren und kleineren Unternehmen wohl nicht ganz unangebracht und zwingt zu einer restriktiven Ausgestaltung des verwendeten Fragebogens insbesondere im Bereich der persönlichen Lebens-, Berufs- und Tätigkeitsdaten. Im vorliegenden Anwendungsbeispiel erwies sich die gewählte Gestaltung des Datensystems aus der Sicht der befragten Organisationsmitglieder als hilfreich im Sinne einer vertrauenswerbenden Maßnahme; die Daten wurden von einem betriebsexternen - neutralen - Team erhoben, ausgewertet und erst in hochaggregierter Form den betriebsinternen Benutzern (Unternehmensleitung, Betriebsrat) wieder verfügbar gemacht. Verschiedene Stellungnahmen aus dem Kreis der Belegschaft deuten an, daß bei einer Wiederholung der Befragung unter gleichen oder ähnlichen Bedingungen die beim ersten Probelauf erzielte Rücklaufquote von rd. 37 % noch erheblich übertroffen werden würde.

2. Ergebnisse des BIS: Maslow-orientierte Unternehmensanalyse im Personalbereich

Im folgenden werden lediglich die ermittelten Durchschnittswerte der Befriedigungsdefizite $\bar{D}$ und Bedürfniswichtigkeiten $\bar{W}$ für die einzelnen Bedürfniskategorien angegeben. Differenzierte Auswertungen liegen vor für einzelne Bedürfnis-Items und für bestimmte ausgewählte Merkmalsgruppen der befragten Organisationsmitglieder. Sie ermöglichen einen sehr detaillierten Einblick in die Stärken und Schwächen des untersuchten Unternehmens bezüglich seiner Fähigkeit, die Bedürfnisse der Mitarbeiter zu befriedigen. Dabei erweist es sich als fruchtbar, für jede Bedürfniskategorie - oder auch für jedes Item - einen Indikator zu bestimmen, der das Produkt aus "Defizit" und "Wichtigkeit" angibt (vgl. Tab. 1). Wir bezeichnen diesen Indikator als "Dringlichkeits-Indikator", und zwar in einem doppelten Sinne des Wortes. Einmal läßt der Indikator erkennen, wie dringlich die einzelnen Bedürfnisse für die Organisationsmitglieder sind und von ihnen zu befriedigen gewünscht werden.[1] Zum anderen zeigt der Indikator die Dringlichkeit personalpolitischer Maßnahmen an, die darauf gerichtet sind, die Bedürfnisbefriedigung der Organisationsmitglieder zu verbessern.

1) Die zugrundeliegende Annahme erscheint plausibel: Je höher das Befriedigungsdefizit in einer bestimmten Bedürfniskategorie und je wichtiger diese Kategorie für ein Individuum ist, um so stärker wird der subjektiv wahrgenommene Drang zu Befriedigung sein. Die Dringlichkeit tendiert nach dieser Annahme gegen ein Mindestniveau, wenn das betreffende Bedürfnis entweder bereits voll befriedigt ist ($D \rightarrow 0$) oder nicht als wichtig angesehen wird ($W \rightarrow 1$).

Bedürfnis-kategorien nach PNSQ	Befriedigungs-defizite $\bar{D}$ $(0 \leq \bar{D} \leq +6)$		Bedürfnis-wichtigkeiten $\bar{W}$ $(1 \leq \bar{W} \leq 7)$		Dringlichkeits-indikatoren $\bar{I} = \bar{D} \times \bar{W}$ $(0 \leq \bar{I} \leq 42)$	
	$\bar{D}$	Rang	$\bar{W}$	Rang	$\bar{I}$	Rang
Sicherheit	2,314	1	5,769	2	13,35	1
Soziale Bedürfnisse	1,000	5	5,765	3	5,77	5
Anerkennungs-bedürfnisse	0,609	7	5,383	6	3,28	7
Autonomiebedürfnisse	0,840	6	5,755	4	4,83	6
Selbstverwirklichung	1,229	4	5,625	5	6,91	4
Angemessenes Arbeitsentgelt	2,100	2	5,100	7	10,71	3
Informations-bedürfnis	1,820	3	6,000	1	10,92	2

Tab. 1: Durchschnittliche Befriedigungsdefizite $\bar{D}$, Bedürfniswichtigkeiten $\bar{W}$ und Dringlichkeitsindikatoren in einem mittelständischen Unternehmen der Baumaschinen-Industrie 1980 (PNSQ - Porter-Need Satisfaction-Questionnaire)

Die Hauptergebnisse lassen sich wie folgt zusammenfassen:

(1) Nach Tab. 1 sind drei Bedürfniskategorien erkennbar, die ein deutlich erhöhtes Befriedigungsdefizit und Dringlichkeitsniveau im Vergleich zu allen anderen Bedürfniskategorien aufweisen. Dazu gehören in der Reihenfolge der Dringlichkeits-Indikatoren: das Sicherheitsbedürfnis, das Informationsbedürfnis und das Bedürfnis nach einem angemessenen Arbeitsentgelt;

(2) die Durchschnittsbetrachtung in Tab. 1 zeichnet ein etwas zu günstiges Bild der gegenwärtigen Unternehmenssituation. So schließt das relativ niedrige Durchschnittsniveau der Befriedigungsdefizite keineswegs das Vorhandensein extrem unzufriedener Organisations-

mitglieder mit D≥ 5,0 aus. Eine gesonderte Analyse der Vorkommenshäufigkeiten D≥ 5,0 für die einzelnen Bedürfniskategorien ergibt ein wesentlich ungünstigeres Bild der Unternehmenssituation. Danach erfahren 20 % der Befragten beim Sicherheitsbedürfnis, mehr als 18 % beim Arbeitsentgelt und 10 % beim Informationsbedürfnis ein extrem hohes Befriedigungsdefizit. Dies bedeutet: Mindestens ein Fünftel der Belegschaft in dem untersuchten Betrieb hat wenigstens einen Grund, besonders unzufrieden zu sein; maximal sind nahezu die Hälfte besonders unzufrieden;

(3) die Unternehmenssituation erscheint dann besonders ungünstig, wenn das BIS - bei differenzierter Auswertung der gewonnenen Personalinformationen nach Personengruppen - als überdurchschnittlich vertretene Träger extrem hoher Befriedigungsdefizite jüngere qualifizierte Facharbeiter nachweist, die zur Stammbelegschaft gehören und nicht oder nur sehr schwer ersetzt werden können.

3. Ergebnis des BIS: Herzberg-orientierte Unternehmensanalyse im Personalbereich

Die empirischen Befunde sind in Abb. 1 in der von Herzberg bevorzugten Standardform dargestellt. Die Arbeitsfaktoren sind mit M (= Motivator) oder mit H (= Hygienefaktor) gekennzeichnet, je nachdem, ob der betreffende Faktor nach den vorangehenden Untersuchungen Herzbergs häufiger besondere Zufriedenheit oder häufiger besondere Unzufriedenheit hervorrufen sollte. Der Vergleich mit dem Balkendiagramm, das die relativen Vorkommenshäufigkeiten der einzelnen Faktoren als Zufriedenheits- und Unzufriedenheitsursachen im untersuchten Unternehmen unter besonderer Hervorhebung der jeweiligen Vorkommensdominanz durch das Symbol ■ ausweist, läßt erhebliche betriebsspezifische Abweichungen von der ursprünglichen M-H-Klassifikation erkennen (vgl. ähnlich auch Rühl u. Zink 1974; Zink 1975). Für die Unternehmensanalyse ist diese Frage freilich nur von sekundärem Interesse. Sie orientiert sich in erster Linie an den faktorbezogenen Unzufriedenheitsäußerungen; sind diese relativ zahlreich, so ist eine größere Dringlichkeit für personalpolitische Verbesserungsmaßnahmen zu vermuten als bei einer geringeren Vorkommenshäufigkeit. In dem Maße, wie es gelingt, eine Reduzierung der Unzufriedenheitsnennungen für einen bestimmten Arbeitsfaktor zu bewirken, ist auch eine tendenzielle Erhöhung der Zufriedenheitsnennungen zu erwarten.

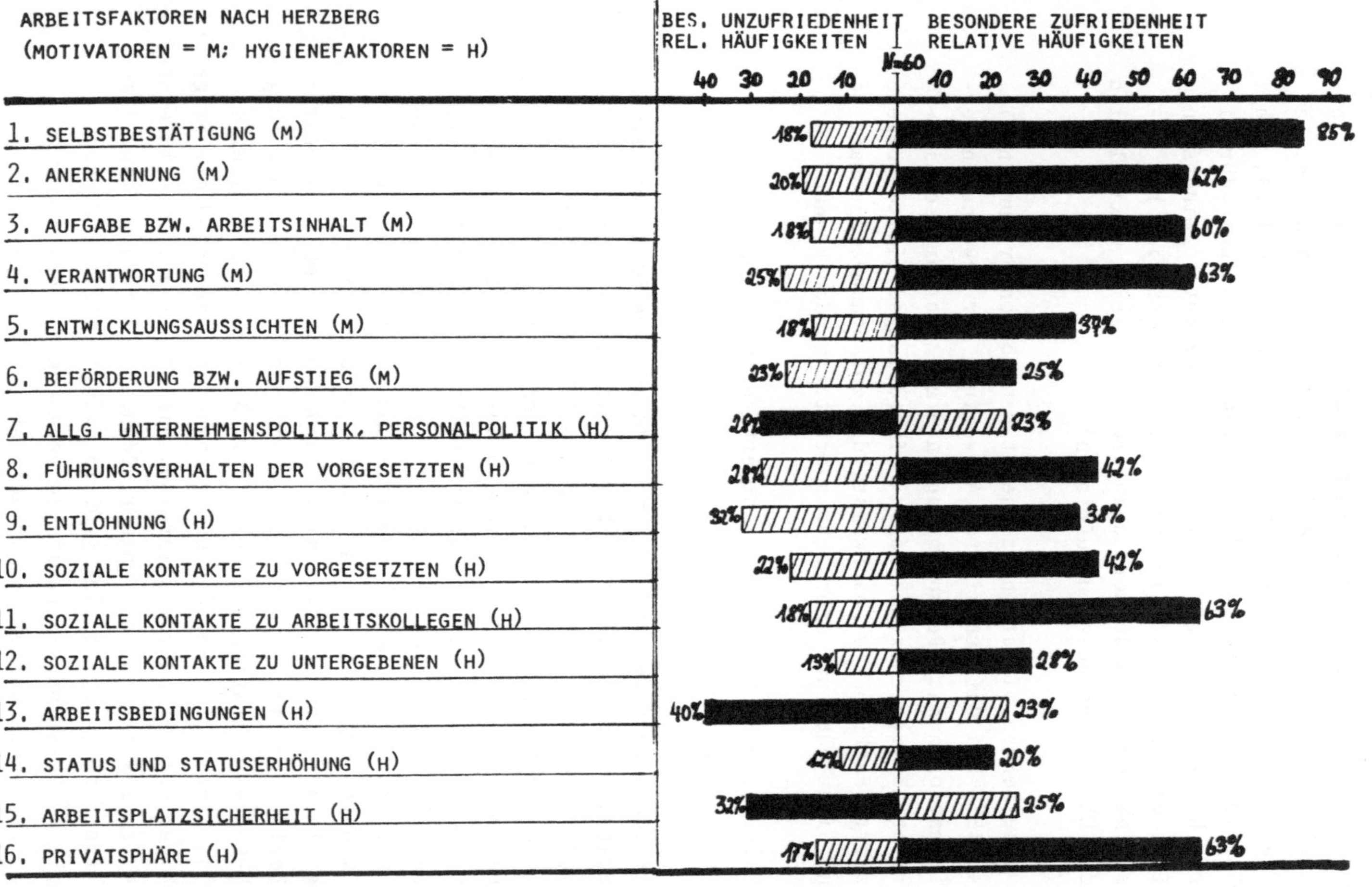

ABB. 1: DIE BEDEUTUNG DER ARBEITSFAKTOREN HERZBERGS ALS URSACHEN BESONDERER ZUFRIEDENHEIT UND UNZUFRIEDENHEIT IN EINEM UNTERNEHMEN DER METALLINDUSTRIE 1980 (N = 60 ARBEITER UND ANGESTELLTE)

Die Hauptergebnisse lassen sich wie folgt zusammenfassen:

(1) Die wesentlichen Befunde der Maslow-orientierten Unternehmensanalyse werden bestätigt. Die Arbeitsfaktoren "Arbeitsplatzsicherheit", "Entlohnung" und "Unternehmens- bzw. Personalpolitik" (als wichtigster Addressat für Informationswünsche) gehören zu den 4 am häufigsten genannten Anlässen für besondere Unzufriedenheit. Insoweit wurden keine neuen Erkenntnisse gewonnen, wohl aber - mit einer anderen Methode - die bereits vorliegenden Aussagen zur Unternehmenssituation im Personalbereich bekräftigt, ihre Glaubwürdigkeit erhöht. Dies gilt auch für eine Reihe anderer Arbeitsfaktoren, die unmittelbar auf bestimmte Grundbedürfnisse bzw. auf einzelne Bedürfnis-Items im PNSQ bezogen werden können;

(2) neu, weil im PNSQ durch Vernachlässigung der physiologischen Bedürfnisse nicht enthalten, ist insbesondere die Feststellung, daß die Arbeitsbedingungen im Sinne physiologischer Belastungen (Lärm, Temperaturschwankungen und Erkältungsgefahr etc.) die häufigste Ursache für besondere Unzufriedenheit darstellen. Zusätzliche Personalinformationen werden im übrigen überall dort gewonnen, wo ein unmittelbarer und eindeutiger Zusammenhang zwischen den Arbeitsfaktoren Herzbergs auf der einen und den Bedürfniskategorien und -items des PNSQ auf der anderen Seite nicht besteht. Dies ist aber nur bei einer Minderzahl der Arbeitsfaktoren wirklich der Fall.

IV. Bedeutung des BIS als personalpolitische Entscheidungshilfe - eine Zwischenbilanz

Die Pilotstudie in dem Unternehmen der Baumaschinen-Industrie ist noch nicht abgeschlossen, der wohl interessanteste Teil liegt wohl noch vor uns. Im wesentlichen handelt es sich um zwei eng zusammenhängende Problemkreise: (1) Soll und kann aufgrund der vorliegenden Unternehmensanalyse im Personalbereich überhaupt etwas getan werden? und (2) Was soll und kann konkret getan werden?

Die zuerst genannte Grundsatzfrage ist mittlerweile nach Absprache mit der Unternehmensleitung und dem Betriebsrat des Unternehmens positiv entschieden worden. Hervorzuheben ist, daß das BIS und seine Ergebnisse, gleichgültig, wie sie im einzelnen ausgefallen sind oder hätten ausfallen können, diese Entscheidung nicht zu präjudizieren vermag. Dazu bedarf es stets einer Bewertung des ermittelten Istzustandes durch Kriterien, die angeben, daß z. B. hohe Befriedigungsdefizite und Unzufriedenheit im Unternehmen unerwünscht, viele zufriedene Organisationsmitglieder dagegen erwünscht sind. Erst dann, also nach Vergleich mit einem mehr oder weniger präzise definierten Sollzustand, erhalten die Informationen des BIS den Charakter von aktuellen Aktionsstimuli. Im vorliegenden Anwendungsbeispiel wurden die bereitgestellten Personalinformationen durchaus als änderungsbedürftig, teilweise sogar als alarmierend bewertet. Die vorgebrachten Gründe für die Forderung nach personalpolitischen Aktionen lassen sich im wesentlichen auf zwei Positionen zurückführen:

(1) Bedürfnisbefriedigung und hohe Arbeitszufriedenheit der Organisationsmitglieder sind eigenständige soziale Ziele der Unternehmung, ebenso wie die ökonomischen Ziele ihren Eigenwert haben;

(2) Bedürfnisbefriedigung und hohe Arbeitszufriedenheit der Organisationsmitglieder sind instrumentelle Voraussetzungen für die Erreichung der ökonomischen Ziele. Die verhaltenswissenschaftliche Forschung hat Wirkungszusammenhänge zwischen Arbeitszufriedenheit auf der einen und Fluktuation, Absentismus und - mit Einschränkung - Arbeitsleistung auf der anderen Seite nachgewiesen.

Aus der Sicht beider Positionen, die sich in den Argumenten der personalpolitischen Entscheidungsträger wiederfinden, kann das BIS die Funktion eines Warn- und Kontrollsystems erfüllen, vor allem, wenn es regelmäßige und standardisierte Messungen in Verbindung mit Zeit- und Betriebsvergleichen vorsieht. Möglicherweise kann das BIS zu einem personalwirtschaftlichen Frühwarnsystem ausgebaut werden.

Für das zweite Teilproblem, die Frage: "Was soll bzw. was kann getan werden?" vermag das BIS zwei wesentliche Funktionen zu erfüllen. Es stellt Personalinformationen bereit, die bereits mögliche Problemlösungen angeben oder wenigstens den Suchraum begrenzen, in dem nach Handlungsalternativen mit Aussicht auf Erfolg gesucht werden kann. Betrachten wir z. B. die Ergebnisse der Maslow-orientierten Unternehmensanalyse. Sicherlich ist die Kritik zutreffend, daß die Kenntnis von vorhandenen Befriedigungsdefiziten bei einzelnen Grundbedürfnissen noch nichts darüber aussagt, wie man diese Defizite beseitigen könnte (v. Rosenstiel 1979, S. 51 ff). Grundsätzlich ist es jedoch möglich, durch Rückgriff auf die Bedürfnis-Items des PNSQ die Entstehungsursachen der Defizite und damit zugleich die Ansatzmöglichkeiten zur Verbesserung der Befriedigungslage aufzudecken. Nach unseren Erfahrungen im untersuchten Betrieb war es den Mitgliedern der Unternehmenleitung und des Betriebsrates stets und ohne weiteres möglich, verbleibende Lücken des BIS ad hoc zu schließen und generelle Personalinformationen zu spezifizieren.

Eine weitere wichtige Funktion des BIS besteht darin, daß sie Informationen zur personalpolitischen Prioritätensetzung bereitstellt.

Im vorliegenden Anwendungsfall bietet sich folgende Prioritätensetzung für die Durchführung von Aktionsprogrammen an:

(1) Verbesserung der Arbeitsbedingungen durch Abbau besonderer physiologischer Belastungen (Klimaschutz gegenüber Außenwelt, Lärmschutz) und Stellung bzw. Bezuschussung der Ausgaben für Arbeitskleidung in der Produktion;

(2) Verbesserung der Sicherheit am Arbeitsplatz durch zusätzliche Unfallschutzmaßnahmen, mehr und ausführlichere Informationen über die Lage und die Entwicklung des Unternehmens (siehe Punkt 3), gegebenenfalls Einführung eines Systems der betrieblichen Altersversorgung;

(3) Verbesserung des Informationsflusses zwischen Unternehmensleitung, Betriebsrat und Belegschaft durch Überprüfung und Änderung des bestehenden Kommunikationssystems;

(4) Verbesserung der Entlohnungsbedingungen durch Modifizierung der Entlohnungsgrundlagen (Arbeitsbewertung, leistungsbezogene Zulagen) und gegebenenfalls durch Einführung einer Erfolgsbeteiligung.

Die Ausarbeitung, Prüfung der Realisierbarkeit und Einführung dieser Aktionsprogramme einschließlich Erfolgskontrolle durch das BIS sind Gegenstand der zweiten Phase der Pilotstudie, in die wir jetzt eingetreten sind.

Für ein abschließendes Urteil über die personalpolitische Brauchbarkeit und Zweckmäßigkeit des vorgestellten BIS auf der Grundlage der verhaltenswissenschaftlichen Basistheorien Maslows und Herzberg ist es sicherlich noch zu früh. Mehr praktische Erfahrungen müssen gesammelt, Alternativuntersuchungen mit anderen Konzeptionen des BIS durchgeführt werden. Dennoch ist nicht zu übersehen, daß das eingesetzte Instumentarium im vorliegenden Anwendungsfall eine erste Bewährungsprobe recht erfolgreich bestanden hat.

LITERATURVERZEICHNIS

Ackermann, K.-F. (1978), Konzeptionen des Praxisbezugs im betriebswirtschaftlichen Studium, in: Hron, A. (Hrsg.), Praxisbezug im wirtschaftswissenschaftlichen Studium, Bd. 1, Hochschuldidaktische Materialien der Arbeitsgemeinschaft für Hochschuldidaktik, Hamburg 1978, S. 37 - 61;

Ackermann, K.-F. u. Reber, G. (Hrsg.), (1981), Personalwirtschaft. Motivationale und kognitive Grundlagen, Stuttgart 1981;

Albert, A. (Hrsg.), (1964), Theorie und Realität. Ausgewählte Aufsätze zur Wissenschaftslehre der Sozialwissenschaften, Tübingen 1964;

Heinrich, L. J. u. Pils, M. (1979), Betriebsinformatik im Personalbereich. Die Planung computergestützter Personalinformationssysteme, Würzburg - Wien 1979;

Herzberg, F. et al (1959), The Motivation to Work, New York 1959;

Herzberg, F. (1971), Work and the Nature of Man, 4. Aufl., Cleveland - New York 1971;

Kast, F. E. u. Rosenzweig, J. E. (1970), Organization and Management, New York 1970;

King, N. (1970), Clarification and Evaluation of the Two-Factor-Theory of Job Satisfaction, in: Psychological Bulletin, 74. Jg. (1970), S. 18 - 31;

March, J.G. u. Simon, H.A. (1958), Organizations, New York 1958;

Maslow, A. H. (1954), Motivation and Personality, New York 1954;

Porter, L. W. (1961), A study of perceived need satisfactions in bottom and middle management jobs, in: Journal of Applied Psychology, Vol. 45 (1961), S. 1-10;

Reber, G. (Hrsg.), (1977), Personal- und Sozialorientierung der Betriebswirtschaftslehre, Stuttgart 1977;

Rosenstiel L. v. (1979), Die Ermittlung personaler Eigenschaften motivationaler Art, in: Reber, G. (Hrsg.), Personalinformationssysteme, Stuttgart 1979, S. 51-73;

Rühl, G. u. Zink, K.J. (1974), Zur Kritik an der Herzbergschen Motivationstheorie, in: Fortschrittliche Betriebsführung, Vol. 23 (1974), H. 3, S. 173-185;

Starke, F.A. u. Ferrat, Ph.W. (1976), Behavioral Information Systems, in: Journal of Systems Management, Vol. 27 (1976), H. 3, S. 26 - 30;

Wahba, M.A. u. Bridwell, L.G. (1976), Maslow Reconsidered: A Review of Research on the Need Hierarchy Theory, in: Organizational Behavior and Human Performance, Vol. 15 (1976), S. 212 - 240;

Zink, K. J. (1975), Differenzierung der Theorie der Arbeitsmotivation von F. Herzberg zur Gestaltung sozio-technologischer Systeme, Frankfurt - Zürich 1975;

PERSONALINFORMATIONSSYSTEME UND GEWERKSCHAFTSPOLITIK

Paul Kolm
Gewerkschaft der
Privatangestellten
Wien

Zusammenfassung: Nach einer einleitenden Bemerkung zum Problem der Veränderung gesellschaftlicher Machtverhältnisse durch die interessensspezifische Anwendung von Informationstechnologien werden Aufbau und Wirkungsweise von Personalinformationssystemen aus gewerkschaftlicher Sicht behandelt. Schließlich beschäftigt sich der Beitrag mit Fragen der Beschränkung und Kontrolle dieser Systeme auf den verschiedenen Ebenen gewerkschaftlichen Handelns.

Vorbemerkung

Wenn von den sozialen Auswirkungen moderner Informationstechnologien im Betrieb gesprochen wird, kristallisiert sich das Denken zumeist um die Frage "Jobkiller oder Jobknüller ?". Abgesehen davon, daß nicht irgendeine Technologie Arbeitsplätze "killt", sondern die aus der ökonomischen Struktur entspringende Bewegungsform des Kapitals, wirkt zumindest in Österreich eine andere soziale und politische Bedrohung trotz Datenschutzdebatte noch weitgehend im Verborgenen: die Veränderung der gesellschaftlichen Machtverhältnisse durch die interessensspezifische Anwendung von Informationstechnologien.

Natürlich gibt es ein mehr oder weniger klares Wissen darüber, daß Information mit Macht und Herrschaft zu tun hat. Für den lohnabhängig beschäftigten Arbeiter oder Angestellten gehört es zur tagtäglichen Erfahrung, daß der Unternehmer seine Rolle durch das Sammeln und Verfügen von Information über Personal, Zeit,Leistung und Entgelt wahrnimmt. Allerdings hat der Kampf der Gewerkschaften dieser Verfügung bestimmte Grenzen gesetzt, die sich je nach den Kräfteverhältnissen und politischen Rahmenbedingungen verändern.

Ein Blick in die Geschichte zeigt, daß die Richtung dieser Veränderung nicht immer die gleiche ist. Es dürfte daher von Interesse sein, hier den vollständigen Wortlaut einer Stellungnahme der größten österreichischen Einzelgewerkschaft zum Thema computergestützter Personalinformationssysteme wiederzugeben.

Stellungnahme der Gewerkschaft der Privatangestellten Österreichs, März 1981

Tausende EDV-Anlagen sind in Österreich bereits in Verwendung. Da in zunehmendem Maß kostengünstige Systeme auf den Markt gelangen, die in Klein- und Mittelbetrieben vielfältig einsetzbar sind, wird ihre Zahl rasch weiterwachsen.

Die Anwendung moderner Informationstechnologien - dazu gehören Computer, Textverarbeitungssysteme, Bildschirmtext, Telefonsystme, maschinenlesbare Ausweise usw. - kann nicht nur als Ergebnis eines einmaligen Rationalisierungsschrittes mit oft einschneidenden sozialen Folgen gesehen werden. Diese Technologien wirken als universelle Steuerungs- und Kontrollinstrumente. Sie sind daher auch Mittel laufender Rationalisierungsprozesse im Betrieb.

Computergestützte Personalinformationssysteme zeichnen sich gerade dadurch aus, daß sie nicht nur zur rascheren, effektiveren Bewältigung administrativer Aufgaben dienen, sondern vor allem für plandende dispositive Funktionen im Personalbereich entwickelt sind. Diese Systeme bergen große Gefahren für die Arbeitnehmer. Schon im Planungsstadium ist eine wirksame Kontrolle notwendig. Nur so können negative Entwicklungen von Anfang an verhindert werden.

1. Aufbau und Wirkungsweise von Personalinformationssystemen

Es gibt heute schon Datensammlungen über Arbeitnehmer, sogenannte Personalinformationssysteme (PIS), in die bis zu mehrere tausend persönliche Daten pro Arbeitnehmer einfließen. Die Daten stammen aus verschiedenen Quellen und werden mit unterschiedlichen Instrumenten erfaßt (z.B. Dokumente, Fragebogen, Bedienungsstatistiken, maschinelle Direkterfassung), jedoch zentral gespeichert und ausgewertet. Der Arbeitnehmer soll möglichst in seiner ganzen Persönlichkeit abgebildet werden. Es besteht die Tendenz, den herkömmlichen, nun EDV-gespeicherten Personalakt, immer detaillierter zu gestalten. Die Skala reicht dann von den einfachen Identifikationsdaten wie Name, Alter, Geschlecht, Eintritt in den Betrieb usw. über Eignungsdaten wie Qualifikation, Auflistung der Fähigkeiten und Fertigkeiten, Belastbarkeit sowie detaillierte Gesundheitsdaten (Krankheiten, Fehlzeiten) bis zu Merkmalen des Charakters oder auch der gewerkschaftlichen Zugehörigkeit und politischen Einstellung. Darüber hinaus entsteht der "Datenschatten" des

Arbeitnehmers durch die bei der Arbeit an der Maschine - sei es eine Werkzeugmaschine oder ein Bildschirmterminal - gegebene Möglichkeit, ständig alle Leistungsdaten zu speichern. Es ist dann nicht mehr nötig, die Arbeitsleistung direkt zu beobachten oder zu messen. Zeiterfassungssysteme mit maschinenlesbaren Ausweisen sind ein weiterer Baustein des perfektionierten Instrumentariums.

Aus der Verknüpfung von Personaldaten und personenbezogener Betriebsdatenerfassung entstehen die für Rationalisierungszwecke wirkungsvollsten Personalinformationssysteme. Durch die systematische Gegenüberstellung von Eignungsdaten des Arbeitnehmers mit den Anforderungsmerkmalen der Arbeitsplätze und gestützt auf eine dauernde, umfassende Kontrolle jedes einzelnen Arbeitnehmers, ist der Unternehmer in der Lage, Personalabbau, Versetzungen, Aufstieg, die Entwicklung der Qualifikations- und Gehaltsstruktur zu steuern und vor allem die Leistung zu intensivieren. Die Auslese von einzelnen oder von Gruppen von Arbeitnehmern nach allen nur denkbaren Merkmalen ist möglich, zumal die Daten im Computer beliebig lange gespeichert werden können.

Die Entwicklung ist inzwischen so weit gediehen, daß in Österreich Systeme erprobt werden, wo etwa der maschinell lesbare Betriebsausweis neben der Funktion der Zeiterfassung auch als Schlüssel fungieren kann. Zum Beispiel wird mit ihm die Maschine am Arbeitsplatz in Betrieb genommen oder der Bereich abgegrenzt, in dem sich ein Arbeitnehmer aufhalten darf. Gleichzeitig können auch die Bewegungen und Kontakte des Arbeitnehmers im Betrieb aufgezeichnet werden. Die automatische Kantinenabrechnung mit diesen Ausweisen läßt die Ernährungsgewohnheiten der Kantinenbenützer erkennen, die der Unternehmer im Hinblick auf Krankenstände oder Leistungsschwächen verwerten könnte.

2. Beschränkung und Kontrolle von Personalinformationssystemen

2.1. Rechtliche Grundlagen zur Beschränkung und Kontrolle von Personalinformationssystemen sind im Arbeitsverfassungsgesetz und Datenschutzgesetz gegeben.

Das Arbeitsverfassungsgesetz enthält im § 1o9 eine Informationsverpflichtung des Unternehmers bei Rationalisierungs-

und Automatisierungsmaßnahmen von erheblicher Bedeutung, sowie bei Änderungen der Arbeits- und Betriebsorganisation.

Die Einführung von Personalfragebögen, sofern in diesen nicht bloß die allgemeinen Angaben zur Person und Angaben über die fachlichen Voraussetzungen für die beabsichtigte Verwendung des Arbeitnehmers enthalten sind, bedürfen der Zustimmung des Betriebsrates nach § 96 Arbeitsverfassungsgesetz. Das gleiche gilt für die Einführung von Kontrollmaßnahmen und technischen Systemen zur Kontrolle der Arbeitnehmer, sofern diese Maßnahmen (Systeme) die Menschenwürde berühren. Der Aufbau eines Personalinformationssystems ist daher eine zustimmungspflichtige Maßnahme. In Betrieben mit gewählten Belegschaftsvertretungen können Einzelvereinbarungen mit Arbeitnehmern nicht rechtskräftig geschlossen werden.

Das Datenschutzgesetz unterstützt die Position des Betriebsrates. In Anwendung des Grundrechtes auf Datenschutz ergibt sich, daß eigentlich alle die Persönlichkeit des Arbeitnehmers betreffenden Kontrollverfahren die Menschenwürde berühren. Die Ermittlung von Leistungsdaten ist daher auch unabhängig davon, ob sie zur Entgeltfindung dient, nach § 96 Abs. 1 Z. 3 Arbeitsverfassungsgesetz zustimmungspflichtig.

Diese Interpretation der Rechtslage sollte bei der bevorstehenden Novellierung des Arbeitsverfassungsgesetzes ausdrücklich verankert werden, d.h.:

o Aufnahme von personenbezogenen Daten im Sinne des Datenschutzgesetzes und deren Auswertung in den Katalog der zustimmungspflichtigen Maßnahmen;

o Kontrollmaßnahmen und technische Systeme zur Kontrolle der Arbeitnehmer sowie die Ermittlung von Leistungsdaten sollen in jedem Fall der Zustimmung des Betriebsrates bedürfen;

o die Informationsverpflichtung über Personalinformationssysteme an den Betriebsrat und die betroffenen Arbeitnehmer sollte im Gesetz fixiert werden. Die Verletzung dieser Bestimmung sollte mit wirksamen Sanktionen, z.B. Stillegung der Datenverarbeitungsanlage belegt werden.

Für Betriebe mit mehr als fünf Arbeitnehmer und Betrieben gemäß § 4o Arbeitsverfassungsgesetz sollte eine gesetzliche Grundlage geschaffen werden, die den jederzeitigen Widerruf ohne Nachwirkungen von Einzelvereinbarungen über Personalinformationssysteme vorsieht.

2.2. Rechtliche Bestimmungen können zur Durchsetzung der Interessen der Arbeitnehmer immer nur einen unterstützenden Rahmen bilden, die Entscheidungen fallen im Betrieb. Die Planung und Realisierung von Personalinformationssystemen, eingebettet in den Zusammenhang von Personal- und betrieblicher Gesamtplanung, ist ein jahrelanger Vorgang, in den sich der Betriebsrat rechtzeitig in Absprache mit der Gewerkschaft einschalten muß. Eine wirksame Kontrolle ist nur über eine Betriebsvereinbarung erreichbar, die folgende Punkte berücksichtigen sollte:

- o Verständliche Beschreibung des Personalinformationssystems und der verwendeten Programme mit Zweck;
- o genaue Festlegung, welche Technologien für den Aufbau eines Personalinformationssystems angewendet bzw. nicht angewendet werden dürfen (Textverarbeitungssystem ? maschinenlesbare Ausweise ? usw.);
- o Beschränkung auf ganz bestimmte Datensammlungen und Auswertungen, Verzeichnis dieser Daten unter Angabe ihres Verwendungszweckes;
- o Beschränkung und genaue Festlegung der Datenlieferanten (Fragebogen, Meßgeräte, Vorgesetzte usw.) und der Datenempfänger;
- o kostenlose Einsichtnahme des Arbeitnehmers in die ihn betreffenden Daten;

- o mindestens jährliche Benachrichtigung des Arbeitnehmers über die ihn betreffenden Daten und Auswertungen durch das Unternehmen;

- o Richtigstellung und Löschung von Daten analog zum Datenschutzgesetz und Vereinbarung von Fristen über die vollständige Löschung von Daten;

- o Zugangsrechte des Betriebsrates zum Informationssystem (d.h. zu Maschinen, Programmen und Daten);

- o wenn das Unternehmen seine Daten extern verarbeiten läßt, sind analoge Regelungen erforderlich;

- o Verpflichtung des Unternehmens, die notwendige Schulung der Betriebsräte oder vom Betriebsrat beauftragten Vertretern sicherzustellen.

Die GPA wird prüfen, ob nicht der Abschluß eines Generalkollektivvertrages auf dem Gebiet Personalinformationssysteme angestrebt werden soll.

Bei der Diskussion des Problems Personalinformationssysteme ist der Begriff des Datenschutzes etwas irreführend; denn es geht um den Schutz der Arbeitnehmer. Die Einschränkung der Verfügung des Unternehmers oder anders ausgedrückt, erweiterte Mitbestimmungsmöglichkeiten der Arbeitnehmer bei der Planung von Computersystemen, sind eine zwingende Notwendigkeit, wenn dieser Schutz gewährleistet werden soll.

------oOo------

Soweit also die Stellungnahme der Gewerkschaft der Privatangestellten. Sie ist Ausdruck der Erkenntnis, daß der Einsatz von Informationstechnologien im Betrieb nie einfach nur eine rentabilitätsorientierte Maßnahme darstellt, die am status quo nichts ändert, sondern einen tiefen Eingriff in das betriebliche Machtgefüge mit sich bringt. Planung, Steuerung, Kontrolle der Arbeitskraft und die Zentralisierung von Information, d.h. des Wissens um den Gesamtzusammenhang der Produktion in einer nur dem Kapitaleigner oder seinen Vertretern zugänglichen Maschinerie unterlaufen mühsam errungene Mitbestimmungsrechte. Sie können langfristig nur gesichert und ausgebaut werden, wenn sich die Diskussion nicht auf die Informationssysteme beschränkt, sondern die zugrunde liegende Organisationsform der Arbeit einbezogen wird.

WESEN UND PROBLEME DER URTEILSFINDUNG IN DER MEDIZIN

P.L. Reichertz
Institut für Medizinische Informatik,
Medizinische Hochschule Hannover

Zusammenfassung:

"Medizin" umfasst die medizinische Wissenschaft und die Tätigkeit des Arztes und seines Hilfspersonals in der Gesundheitsversorgung. Die Methoden der Urteilsfindung in der medizinischen Wissenschaft entsprechen denen der angewandten naturwissenschaftlichen, psychologischen und sozialwissenschaftlichen Forschung. Verfahren der Informatik vermögen gleiche Hilfeleistungen zu geben wie in den genannten Bereichen: zur Dokumentation von Literatur, Fakten, Versuchsverläufen, zur Datenverarbeitung und -haltung, als Teil der Auswertverfahren in Instrumenten und in Informationssystemen im weiteren Sinne.

Grundsätzlich ist eine gleiche Unterstützung auch bei der ärztlichen Urteilsfindung im Behandlungsprozeß möglich. Jedoch ist der Prozeßcharakter dieses Vorgangs entscheidend. Nicht die wissenschaftlich wichtige topologische Endklassifikation steht klinisch im Vordergrund, sondern die Unterstützung bei der Auswahl der meist unter Zeitzwängen zu treffenden Maßnahmen. Es resultiert eine hierarchisch gestufte Urteilsfindung mit unterschiedlicher Auflösung. Sie kann weitere diagnostische oder die Einleitung therapeutischer Maßnahmen implizieren, deren Resultate in den weiteren Entscheidungsprozeß eingehen.

Sinnvolle Modelle müssen diesen Prozeßcharakter und seine zeitlich-räumlichen Zwänge berücksichtigen, wobei in allen Stufen des Entscheidungsprozesses eine Verbesserung durch eine Optimierung der Informationslogistik möglich ist.

Ärztliche Entscheidungen sind keine Wahrscheinlichkeitsaussagen im Hinblick auf eine Grundgesamtheit. Sie sind bezogen auf einzelne Patienten. Entscheidungsmodelle haben daher spezielle Gegebenheiten und entsprechende Risiko- oder Nutzenüberlegungen im Hinblick auf den weiteren Verlauf zu berücksichtigen.

1. Die Entscheidungsfindung in der wissenschaftlichen Medizin

Die wissenschaftliche Medizin wendet überwiegend naturwissenschaftliche Verfahren zur Erkenntnisgewinnung und Problemlösung an. Das Methodenspektrum ist erweitert durch Verfahren der Psychologie und der Sozialwissenschaften im weiteren Sinne. Je nach Arbeitsrichtung überwiegen physikalische oder chemische resp. biochemische Verfahren.

Methoden der Informatik vermögen bei der Datenerfassung, -speicherung und -auswertung Hilfestellung zu geben wie in anderen wissenschaftlichen Bereichen. Die Bearbeitung großer Mengen von Beobachtungen, besonders im Rahmen klinischer Versuche oder von Feldstudien epidemiologischer Natur, ist durch die Anwendung von Informations- und Softwaresystemen zur Datenanalyse und -auswertung außerordentlich bereichert worden. Insbesondere interaktive Systeme gestatten das rasche Erfassen von Datenmengen, die orientierende Exploration und die Testung von Hypothesen.

2. Schaffung neuer Informationsqualitäten

Die Entwicklung chemischer und physikalischer Meßmethoden hat zu einer Vergrößerung des Methodenspektrums geführt, wobei zunehmend die vom Kranken oder dem untersuchten Substrat ausgehenden Signale direkt aufgearbeitet und ausgewertet werden. Demzufolge werden an vielen Stellen Mikroprozessoren Teile des medizinischen Instrumentariums. Bei der Computertomosynthese ist es gelungen, räumliche Absorptionswerte von Röntgenstrahlen rechnerisch aufzuarbeiten und zu Querschnittsdarstellungen zu synthetisieren. Dies hat ungeahnte Möglichkeiten zur Erkennung von pathologisch-anatomischen Veränderungen in sonst nicht zugänglichen Körperbereichen gebracht. Unmittelbar vor der Anwendungsreife stehen Verfahren, Elektronenspin-Resonanzphänomene in der Molekularstruktur auszunutzen, um ähnliche räumliche Bilder und möglicherweise Hinweise auf biochemische Prozesse zu erhalten. Es steht außer Frage, daß hierdurch die ärztliche Entscheidung hinsichtlich der somatischen Ausgangsbasis erneut verbessert werden wird.

3. Informationslogistik

Die zunehmende Fülle von Informationen in der wissenschaftlichen Medizin und über den einzelnen Kranken infolge Zunahme der Untersuchungsmethoden, einer besseren Chance zum Überstehen von ernsthaften Erkrankungen und somit größerer Wahrscheinlichkeit des Erlebens chronischer Leiden und größere Inanspruchnahme der Einrichtungen der Gesundheitsversorgung machen die Erstellung von Informationssystemen in allen Bereichen der Gesundheitsversorgung sinnvoll. In Krankenhausinformationssystemen werden von den verschiedensten Stellen kommende Daten zusammengetragen und am Ort der Entscheidungsfindung in einem geeigneten Format zur Verfügung gestellt. Zunehmend finden sich Anwendungen in der Praxis des niedergelassenen Arztes zur Bewältigung administrativer Aufgaben und zur Verbesserung des Wissensstands über den einzelnen Patienten, die getroffenen Maßnahmen und deren wirtschaftliche und medizinische Auswirkungen.

4. Informatik und ärztliches Urteil

Die beschriebenen Verfahren zur Anwendung im Vorfeld der ärztlichen Entscheidung vermögen deren Qualität wesentlich zu verbessern und sie reproduzierbarer zu machen. Im Behandlungsprozeß muß die Urteilsfindung im Rahmen der gegebenen räumlichen und zeitlichen Zwänge erfolgen. Eine Verbesserung der Voraussetzungen ist auf jeden Fall erstrebenswert. Die eigentliche Entscheidung steht sodann in einem untrennbaren Zusammenhang mit dem Patienten.

Es liegt nahe, Modelle zur Klassifizierung von Krankheitsbildern zu schaffen im Sinne einer topologischen Einordnung des Krankheitsbildes, ähnlich der Bestimmung einer Art oder Rasse in einem botanischen oder zoologischen System. Abbildung 1 stellt eine solche Einordnung schematisch dar als Resultat des Vergleichs der beobachteten resp. erhobenen Muster mit Krankheitsmustern aus der Literatur, dem ärztlichen Wissensstand und der eigenen Erfahrung. Die Abbildung deutet eine gewisse Dynamik insofern an, als z.B. Untersuchungsmethoden vom Erhebungsbefund her angeregt und Verbesserungen der diagnostischen Einstufung vom Therapieerfolg oder Mißerfolg her ausgelöst werden können.

Das in Abbildung 1 wiedergegebene Modell mit seinem quasi -linearen Charakter trifft aber nur sehr ungenau die tatsächliche Situation. In Wirklichkeit verläuft dieser Prozeß in vielen Stufen mit unterschiedlichen Rückkopplungen und unter äußeren Zwängen. Diagnostische und therapeutische Modelle werden vom ersten Moment des Kontakts her gebildet, gegenüber den Gegebenheiten geprüft, angewandt, verändert, verworfen oder bestätigt. Krankheit ist die nach außen in Erscheinung tretende Reaktion des kranken Menschen auf Störfaktoren unterschiedlicher Genese, welche sich kombinieren und überlagern können. Oft sind Aktionen zur Behebung von Sekundärauswirkungen vordringlicher als die Beseitigung der eigentlichen Ursache.

In diesem Sinne kann, im Hinblick auf die notwendige Aktion, eine Globaldiagnose "akuter Bauch" von ebenso großer Bedeutung sein wie die schließliche Einstufung des Krankheitsbildes als eine stielgedrehte Ovarialzyste;

wird doch die unmittelbar nachfolgende Handlung eindeutig determiniert. Eine differentialdiagnostische Überlegung im Hinblick auf eine Lebererkrankung legt Maßnahmen weiterer Diagnostik in eine bestimmte Richtung fest und wählt diese aus dem weiten Spektrum der gegebenen Möglichkeiten aus. Das Resultat gestattet es sodann, weitere Differenzierungen vorzunehmen bzw. Aktionen festzulegen.

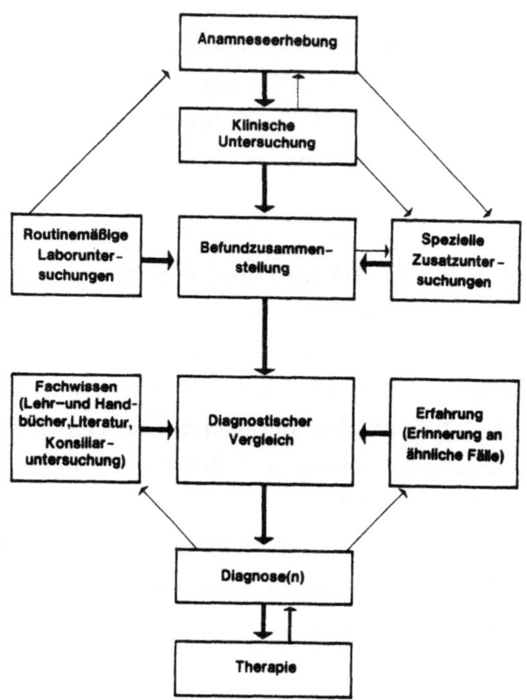

Abbildung 1: Darstellung der ärztlichen Urteilsfindung bei der Diagnosestellung als quasi-linearer Prozeß des Vergleichs erhobener mit bekannten Mustern /nach 4/.

So entsteht im Verlauf der ärztlichen Handlung eine mehr oder minder lange diagnostisch-therapeutische Kette /4/. Nach jeder diagnostischen oder therapeutischen Aktion stehen neue Informationen zur Verfügung, um die weiteren Maßnahmen gezielt ablaufen zu lassen. Dabei kann eine Parallelität diagnostischer oder therapeutischer Aktionen eintreten, (wie z.B. die Gabe von Antibiotika bei einem bedrohlichen Krankheitsbild bei gleichzeitig laufender Resistenzbestimmung).

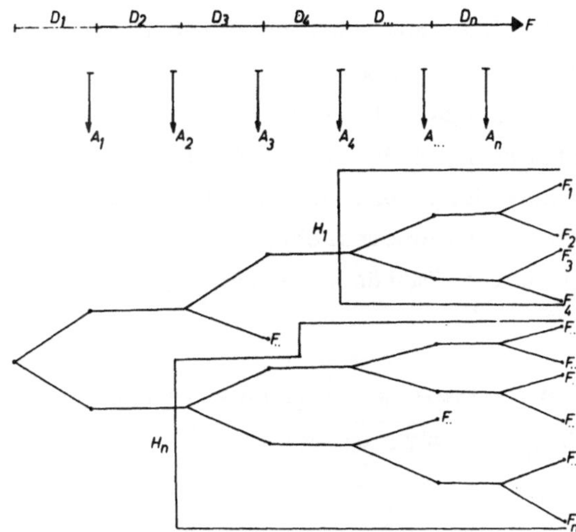

Abbildung 2: Darstellung der ärztlichen Handlung als diagnostisch-therapeutische Entscheidungskette. Vor der endgültigen klassifizierenden Diagnose (F_1-F_n) erfolgt die Aufteilung in Handlungs- resp. Krankheitshierarchien (H_1-H_n) /aus 4/.

In Abb. 2 ist eine solche Entscheidungskette im oberen Teil dargestellt. Vor der endgültigen Klassifizierung (F) erfolgen diagnostische (D_1-D_n) und Aktionsentscheidungen (A_1-A_n). Ergebnis solcher Aktions- und diagnostischer Ketten sind Entscheidungshierarchien (H_1-H_n), welche durchaus den Charakter: "Notwendigkeit der Krankenhauseinweisung", "Gynäkologisches Krankheitsbild", "Schock" (mit der Notwendigkeit der unmittelbaren Behandlung vor Abklärung, ob die Magenblutung durch ein Karzinom oder ein Ulcus bedingt gewesen ist) haben können.

5. Zeitlicher Ablauf

Auf die Nichtlinearität des Ablaufs des Entscheidungsprozesses wurde bereits hingewiesen, auch wenn er in Abb. 2 erneut linearisiert dargestellt worden ist. Tatsächlich erfolgt er iterativ, in Phasen und auf die jeweiligen zeitlich-räumlichen Gegebenheiten abgestimmt. So ist selbst bei einer optimalen Konzeption ein Verfahren nicht anwendbar, wenn es das Mehrfache der Zeit in Anspruch nimmt, welche in der klinischen Gegebenheit zur Verfügung steht.

Eine modellhafte Beschreibung dieses Ablaufs gibt das Struktogramm in Abbildung 3. In den in der Mitte dargestellten Verarbeitungsprozeß gehen die auf der linken Seite aufgeführten Informationen, teilweise als

Ergebnis der auf der rechten Seite dargestellten Handlungen und Maßnahmen, ein. Am Anfang des Kontakts wird eine diagnostische Vorstellung entwickelt, die, je nach den Zwängen zum unmittelbaren Handeln, durch Beobachtung, Befragung und Untersuchung modifiziert und durch zusätzliche Labor- oder andere Untersuchungen ergänzt wird. Das dann entwickelte therapeutische Modell führt, entsprechend den individuellen Gegebenheiten, zu einer therapeutischen Entscheidung, und das Ergebnis der therapeutischen Maßnahmen wird wiederum mit dem diagnostischen Modell rückgekoppelt, wobei der Entscheidungsprozeß unter Umständen erneut durchlaufen wird.

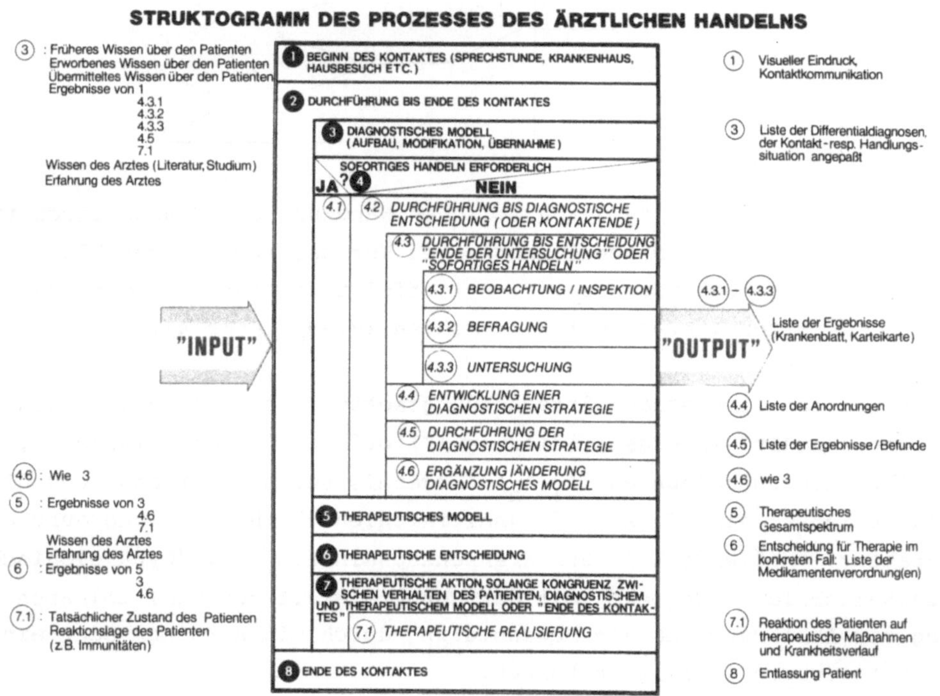

Abbildung 3: Struktogramm des Prozesses des ärztlichen Handelns. In den iterativen Verarbeitungsprozeß (Mitte) gehen Informationen (linke Seite) ein, welche teilweise als Ergebnis der veranlaßten Handlungen (rechte Seite) erhalten worden sind. Jederzeit kann der Zwang zu sofortigem Handeln entstehen /aus 4/.

6. Entscheidungsräume

Entsprechend der Abbildung 2 werden im Verlauf der ärztlichen Urteilsbildung verschiedene Krankheitshierarchien angesprochen, welche unterschiedliche Verifikationsmaßnahmen (Laboruntersuchungen etc.) erfordern. Vorliegende Daten können einen unterschiedlich diskriminierenden Wert in den einzelnen Entscheidungshierarchien haben. Deswegen wurde auch früh bereits schon von einer strategischen Kombination verschiedener Maßnahmen gesprochen, wie z.B. der Kombination von deterministischen Verfahren zur Abgrenzung von Hierarchien und der Anwendung probabilistischer Verfahren zur Einzeldiagnostik innerhalb dieser Bereiche /siehe 2/. Tatsächlich wird für den Entscheidungsprozeß eine jeweils andere Wissensbasis benötigt mit dem Hinweis auf andere Hierarchien, Folgebilder, Risiken, Therapiemöglichkeiten etc. /1/. Wegen des unterschiedlichen diskriminierenden Werts einzelner Daten kann durch eine globale Anwendung von Algorithmen ohne Differenzierung in die einzelnen Hierarchien eine Verwischung der Grenzen zwischen den einzelnen Krankheitsbildern auftreten; eine Beobachtung, die beim Ansatz von diagnostischen Verfahren immer dann gemacht wird, wenn die betrachteten Krankheitsbilder unterschiedlichen Klassen (z.B. hämodynamisch geprägte Krankheitsbilder bei Veränderungen oder Anomalien der Herzklappen gegenüber Gewebsveränderungen bei entzündlichen Herzmuskelprozessen) angehören. Auf der anderen Seite wird ein computerunterstütztes Diagnoseverfahren umso mehr Aussicht auf Erfolg haben, je mehr die betrachteten Krankheitsbilder einer einheitlichen Kategorie angehören (z.B. unterschiedliche Funktionszustände der Schilddrüse, Unterscheidung angeborener Herzfehler etc.).

7. Individueller Bezug

Diagnostische Aussagen sind ungleich wissenschaftlichen Aussagen solche, die sich auf einen einzelnen Menschen, also ein Element einer Grundgesamtheit beziehen und zum Teil zu Konsequenzen führen können, welche sich von dem Normalverhalten unterscheiden. In das einzelne ärztliche Urteil müssen also zusätzlich Risikoabwägungen, prognostische Überlegungen und individuelle Gegebenheiten eingehen, besonders dann, wenn diese Entscheidungen zu Handlungen (Operationen, medikamentösen Maßnahmen, etc.) führen. Auf der anderen Seite wird das individuelle Risiko bei der zunehmenden Möglichkeit unterschiedlicher Maßnahmen immer unüberschaubarer, z.B. bei der Auswahl eines Klappenersatzes, der Wahl einer differenten Maßnahme, wie dem Einführen einer Aortenballonpumpe oder der Unterscheidung zwischen einer erhaltenden oder verstümmelnden Operation. Hier kann von der medizinischen Informatik und der Erstellung entsprechender Programme entscheidende Hilfestellung erwartet werden. Einzelne Ansätze in der Literatur sind vielversprechend /siehe 3/.

Aber auch im Hinblick auf das Risiko diagnostischer Verfahren und ihre ökonomischen Auswirkungen für das Individuum wie für die Volkswirtschaft sind Risikoabwägungen resp. sinnvolle Stufungen möglich, welche im Sinne einer Teststrategie Entscheidungen mit weniger oder weniger belastenden Maßnahmen ermöglichen.

8. Möglichkeiten der Unterstützungen

Aus dieser Beschreibung des ärztlichen Entscheidungsprozesses ergeben sich Erwartungen für sinnvolle Anwendung entscheidungsunterstützender Verfahren. Diese haben zunehmend die zeitlichen und handlungsbezogenen Zwänge zu berücksichtigen ebenso wie den Prozeß der ärztlichen Handlung. Dies ist kein einmaliges Ereignis, sondern hat Prozeßcharakter mit wechselnden Zielrichtungen und Anforderungen. Entscheidungsunterstützende Maßnahmen haben ferner die zeitlichen und räumlichen Zwänge der klinischen Umgebung zu berücksichtigen. Im Hinblick auf das Individuum sind spezielle Risikoabwägungen erforderlich. Hieraus resultiert aber auch die Möglichkeit, handlungsorientierte Modelle zu schaffen, welche als Ziel diagnostische Hierarchien oder Handlungsdiagnosen haben mit unmittelbarem Nutzen für die klinische Entscheidung, die sich von endgültigen pathologisch-anatomischen Diagnosen unterscheiden können. In den einzelnen Krankheitshierarchien sind unterschiedliche Datenbanken und Entscheidungsalgorithmen erforderlich.

Weitere Arbeiten in der medizinischen Informatik werden sich an diesen Gegebenheiten orientieren müssen, um zu der Entwicklung von in der klinischen Routine sinnvollen Instrumenten beitragen zu können. Aufgrund dieser Anforderungen sind die gegebenen mathematisch-statistischen und Informatikverfahren zu untersuchen im Hinblick darauf, wie ihre speziellen Qualitäten für die jeweilige Aufgabenstellung genutzt werden können.

Literatur

/1/ Gory,G.: Knowledge-Based Systems for Clinical Problem Solving. In: de Dombal,F.T., Gremy,F. (Edit.): Decision Making and Medical Care: Can Information Science Help?, Amsterdam,North-Holland, 1976, 23-32

/2/ Lodwick,G.S., Reichertz,P.L.: Computerunterstützte Diagnostik von Tumoren und tumorähnlichen Veränderungen des Knochens. Das begrenzte Bayes-Konzept. Röntgenblätter 22, 162-168, (1977)

/3/ Gunselmann,W.: Prognosestellung beim Rektumkarzinom mit Hilfe des Cox-Modells. In: Horbach,L., Duhme,D. (Hrsg.): Nachsorge und Krankheitsverlaufsanalyse. 25.Jahrestagung der GMDS, Reihe: Med. Informatik und Statistik, Band 28, Berlin/Heidelberg,Springer-Verlag, 1981, 70-76

/4/ Reichertz,P.L.: Computerdiagnostik: Möglichkeiten und Grenzen. In: Schlegel,B.(Hrsg.): Verhandlungen der Deutschen Gesellschaft für Innere Medizin, 84. Band, München,J.F. Bergmann, 1978, 238-240

PROBLEME DES EINSATZES ENTSCHEIDUNGSTHEORETISCHER METHODEN IN DER MEDIZINISCHEN DIAGNOSTIK*

N. VICTOR
Abteilung Biomathematik, FB 18, Universität Gießen

1. Einleitung

Ich möchte in diesem Vortrag die Problematik der Anwendung entscheidungstheoretischer Verfahren in der medizinischen Diagnostik und die Grenzen ihrer Anwendbarkeit diskutieren. Ich werde nicht im einzelnen auf die zahlreichen verschiedenen und mit den unterschiedlichsten Namen belegten Methoden der sogenannten computerunterstützten Diagnostik eingehen, sondern die entscheidungstheoretischen Zuordnungsregeln als Gesamtheit behandeln. Diese pauschale Betrachtungsweise hat den Vorteil, grundsätzliche Probleme der Anwendbarkeit offenzulegen und nicht durch Detailprobleme der verschiedenen Verfahren zu überdecken.

2. Problemstellung

Aus dem Prozeß der ärztlichen Entscheidungsfindung, der Anamnese- und Symptomerhebung, Diagnosestellung sowie Entscheidungen zur Durchführung diagnostischer und therapeutischer Maßnahmen zu einem komplexen Netz gekoppelt umfaßt, greife ich - ohne das eigentliche Ziel ärztlichen Handelns aus dem Auge zu verlieren - das "einfache" Diagnostikproblem heraus, da dieses zur Demonstration der Problematik ausreicht. Dieses Problem kann folgendermaßen formuliert werden:
Eine Gesamtpopulation $\mathcal{P}$ (eine Menge von Patienten) läßt sich derart in m Gruppen $\mathcal{P}_i$ (i=1,...,m) einteilen, daß für alle Elemente einer Gruppe eine der m zur Auswahl stehenden Entscheidungen die günstigste ist, und zwar für jede Gruppe eine andere. Die Entscheidungen können wir dann der Zuordnung zu einer dieser Gruppen gleichsetzen. Jeder Patient aus $\mathcal{P}$ ist Träger einer Reihe von Merkmalen $X_1,...,X_s$, deren Ausprägungen einfach und gefahrlos für den Patienten festgestellt werden können. Dagegen ist die Gruppenzugehörigkeit der Patienten (die Diagnose) unbekannt bzw. schwer bestimmbar. D.h. definierende Merkmale sind nicht direkt beobachtbar und/oder zur Abklärung nötige Untersuchungen sind mit Risiken für den Patienten verbunden. Wir setzen zur Vereinfachung noch voraus, daß die Einteilung erschöpfend und disjunkt und keine der Gruppen leer ist:

---

* Nach einem Vortrag auf "6th Conference on Probability Theory", Brasov/Romania, 10. - 15.9.1979

(1) $\mathcal{P} = \mathcal{P}_1 \cup \mathcal{P}_2 \cup \ldots \cup \mathcal{P}_m$; $\mathcal{P}_i \cap \mathcal{P}_j = \emptyset$ $(i \neq j)$; $\mathcal{P}_i \neq \emptyset$.

Das Diagnostikproblem im Einzelfall besteht nun darin, aufgrund der an einem Patienten festgestellten Merkmalsausprägungen $x_1,\ldots,x_s$ diesen einer der m Gruppen zuzuordnen. Das allgemeine Diagnostikproblem besteht in der Angabe einer Diagnostikregel, die allen Patienten aus $\mathcal{P}$ eine Diagnose zuordnet und dabei mit möglichst großer Sicherheit richtig entscheidet.

Wir betrachten nur Probleme, für die nicht für alle Ausprägungen von $X_1,\ldots,X_s$ die richtige Entscheidung eindeutig festgelegt ist, d.h. zwei verschiedene Träger der gleichen Merkmalskombination können durchaus zu verschiedenen Gruppen gehören. Dies trägt der Tatsache Rechnung, daß die ärztliche Diagnose - abgesehen von Trivialfällen - probabilistischen Charakter hat und den Arzt oft zur Entscheidung bei Unsicherheit zwingt.

3. Das mathematische Modell zur Behandlung des Diagnostikproblems

Wir fassen die Merkmale als s-dimensionalen Zufallsvektor $X = (X_1,\ldots X_s)^T$ auf, der seine Werte in einem Merkmalsraum $\mathcal{X}$ annimmt. Diesen Zufallsvektor erweitern wir um eine "Indikatorvariable" I, die die Gruppenzugehörigkeit des Trägers angibt, und haben damit die Zufallsvariable $\tilde{X} = (X_1,\ldots,X_s,I)^T$. I kann nur die Werte $1,\ldots,m$ annehmen, und $I=i$ bedeutet: Der Träger gehört zur Gruppe $\mathcal{P}_i$. Eine Entscheidungsfunktion R, die $\mathcal{X}$ auf $\{1,\ldots,m\}$ abbildet, heißt Zuordnungsregel und entspricht der Diagnostikregel im Anwendungsfall. Jede Zuordnungsregel läßt sich durch eine disjunkte und erschöpfende Aufteilung von $\mathcal{X}$ angeben:

$R = \mathcal{R}_1,\ldots,\mathcal{R}_m$ mit $\bigcup_i \mathcal{R}_i = \mathcal{X}$ und $\mathcal{R}_i \cap \mathcal{R}_j = \emptyset$ $(i \neq j)$.

Um die Optimalität von Zuordnungsregeln betrachten zu können, führen wir Kosten für richtige und falsche Entscheidungen ein, und zwar K_{ij} zur Bewertung des Schadens, der durch die Zuordnung eines Elementes aus $\mathcal{P}_i$ zu $\mathcal{P}_j$ entsteht. An die Kostenmatrix $K = ((K_{ij}))$ stellen wir die sinnvolle Forderung $K_{ii} < K_{ij}$ $(i \neq j)$.

Die Verteilung von $\tilde{X}$ beschreiben wir aus praktischen Gründen durch die A-priori-Wahrscheinlichkeiten der Gruppen $q_i = Pr(I=i)$ und die bedingten Dichten $f_i(x) = f(x|I=i)$. Die Wahrscheinlichkeiten richtiger bzw. falscher Zuordnung für ein Element aus $\mathcal{P}_i$ bei Verwendung von R sind $p_{ij}(R) = \int_{\mathcal{R}_j} f_i(x)dx$. Die mit diesen Wahrscheinlichkeiten gewichteten Summen der Kosten $r_i(R) = \sum_j K_{ij}\ p_{ij}(R)$ heißen Risiken von R für $\mathcal{P}_i$ und $\bar{r}(R) = \sum_i q_i\ r_i(R)$ heißt verallgemeinertes oder Bayes-Risiko.

Die Regel R* mit $\bar{r}(R^*) = \min_R \bar{r}(R)$ heißt Bayes-Lösung und ist die optimale Zuordnungsregel in dem Sinne, daß sie bei häufiger Anwendung auf eine Zufallsstichprobe auf $\mathcal{P}$ die Gesamtkosten minimiert.

Führen wir durch

(2a) $w_i(x) = Pr(I=i|X=x) = q_i f_i(x) \,/\, (\sum_{j=1}^{m} q_j f_j(x))$

die sogenannten A-posteriori-Wahrscheinlichkeiten ein, so ist für konstante Kosten die Bayes-Lösung durch

(2b) $R^*\colon x \rightarrow \mathcal{P}_i$, falls $w_i(x) = \max_j w_j(x)$,

gegeben.

4. Algorithmische Probleme

Ist die Theorie der Zuordnungsverfahren auch so gut wie abgeschlossen, so treten bei praktischen Anwendungen doch zahlreiche algorithmische Probleme auf, die durch die Tatsache bedingt sind, daß man in der Praxis stets mit unvollständiger Information arbeiten muß. Ferner treten Probleme auf, die nicht direkt die Konstruktion von Zuordnungsregeln, sondern die Reduktion des für eine Zuordnung nötigen Aufwandes betreffen; auf letztere kann ich hier allerdings nicht eingehen.

Die zur optimalen Lösung eines Zuordnungsproblems nötige Information kann unvollständig sein bezüglich der Kosten und/oder der A-priori-Wahrscheinlichkeiten und/oder der bedingten Dichten.

(a) Unbekannte Kosten

Sind die Kosten (d.h. die Folgen der zu treffenden Entscheidung) vollkommen unbekannt, so ist es sinnlos, ein Zuordnungsproblem anzugehen. Hat man nur Näherungswerte, so kann man mit diesen arbeiten und den Einfluß von Kostenschwankungen auf die Lösung untersuchen. Ein häufig gewählter — zweifelhafter — Ausweg ist die Benutzung der Kostenmatrix $K_0 = \mathbb{1} - I$. Die Bedeutung der Benutzung problemadäquater Kosten darf keinesfalls unterschätzt werden, und wir werden im folgenden Abschnitt auf die spezielle Bedeutung dieses Problems für die medizinische Entscheidungsfindung zurückkommen.

(b) Unbekannte A-priori-Wahrscheinlichkeiten

Sind die A-priori-Wahrscheinlichkeiten q_i unbekannt, so gibt es folgende Auswege:

- Annahme des Bayesschen Postulates: $\bar{q}_i = \frac{1}{m}$,
- Schätzung der q_i aus einer Zufallsstichprobe durch $\hat{q}_i = n_i/\Sigma n_i$,
- Verwendung anderer Optimalitätskriterien.

Bei den beiden zuerst genannten Vorgehensweisen ersetzt man lediglich die q_i in der Bayes-Lösung nach (2) durch $\bar{q}_i$ bzw. $\hat{q}_i$. Die Annahme gleicher A-priori-Wahrscheinlichkeiten ist jedoch selten gerechtfertigt und meist sind nur Zufallsstichproben aus den Teilpopulationen möglich. Als alternative Optimalitätskriterien kommen MINIMAX-Lösungen, MINIMAX-Regret-Lösungen und Neyman-Pearson-Lösungen in Frage. MINIMAX-Lösungen sind Bayes-Lösungen für die ungünstigsten A-priori-Wahrscheinlichkeiten q_i^*, d.h. für q_i^* mit $r_i(q_1^*,\ldots,q_m^*) = c, \forall i$. Im allgemeinen sind die numerischen Probleme (hochdimensionale Integralgleichungen) zur Bestimmung dieser q_i^* unüberwindlich. Das Vorgehen bei MINIMAX-Regret-Lösungen ist analog; anstelle der r_i sind die "vermeidbaren" Risiken zu benutzen. Für Neyman-Pearson-Lösungen (Zweigruppenfall) ist eine Fehlzuordnungswahrscheinlichkeit fest vorgegeben und die andere muß minimiert werden. Sie können ebenso wie Zweigruppen-Bayes-Lösungen als Vergleich von $f_1(x)/f_2(x)$ mit einem Schwellenwert dargestellt werden. Die Bestimmung dieses Schwellenwertes (bei bekannten q_i ein simpler Quotient) erfordert wiederum die numerische Lösung einer Integralgleichung. Für Neyman-Pearson-Lösungen im Mehrgruppenfall wachsen die numerischen Probleme.

(c) Unbekannte Dichten

Die Information über f_i ist in der Praxis stets unvollständig und liegt in Form einer objektivierten Stichprobe vor. Unter einer objektivierten Stichprobe vom Umfang n verstehen wir eine Menge von n Realisationen der Zufallsvariablen $\tilde{X}$, d.h. bei n Elementen wurden sowohl die Ausprägungen der X_i als auch die Gruppenzugehörigkeit festgestellt.

Man unterscheidet die Fälle ohne (Verteilung vollkommen unbekannt) und mit zusätzlicher Information über die Form der Verteilung (unbekannt ist nur ein Parameter ϑ) und kommt zur klassischen Einteilung der Zuordnungsprobleme bezüglich der Information über f_i:

(i)	f_i bekannt	(vollständige Information),
(ii)	$f_i = f(x, \vartheta_i)$; ϑ_i unbekannt	(parametrisches Problem),
(iii)	f_i vollkommen unbekannt	(nichtparametrischen Problem).

Der Fall (i) ist durch die vorn angegebene Bayes-Lösung abgehandelt. Im Fall (ii) schätzt man die ϑ_i aus der objektivierten Stichprobe durch $\hat{\vartheta}$ und die Dichten durch $\hat{f}_i(x) = f(x, \hat{\vartheta}_i)$. Anschließend benutzt man die Regel, die sich aus (2) ergibt, wenn man dort $f_i(x)$ durch $\hat{f}_i(x)$ ersetzt. Solche Regeln heißen Parameter-Einsetz-Regeln (parameter-plug-in-rules). Die numerischen Probleme sind die der verwendeten Schätzmethoden (ML, LS etc.) und hängen von der gewählten Familie $\{f(x,\vartheta)\}_{\vartheta}$ ab. Problematischer ist die Entscheidung der Frage, welche Methode für endliches n besser ist und ab welchem n man asymptotischen Ergebnissen vertrauen kann. Es ist z.B. bekannt, daß für relativ kleine n_i plug-in-rules unter der falschen Annahme einer einfacheren Verteilungsfamilie (weniger Parameter) zu besseren Ergebnissen führen als die sich unter Annahme der richtigen Familie ergebenden Regeln. Die Plug-in-Regeln sind Zufallsvariable und ihre Güte hängt von der jeweiligen Stichprobe ab; unsere Aussagen gelten demnach für die Erwartungswerte der Fehlerraten.

Beispiele für parameter-plug-in-rules sind:

- die sogenannte lineare Diskriminanzanalyse für Normalverteilungen mit gleicher Kovarianzmatrix,
- die quadratische Diskriminanzanalyse für Normalverteilungen,
- die (mißverständlich) "Verfahren nach dem Satz von Bayes" genannte Regel für qualitative Daten mit insgesamt unabhängigen X_i,
- die Multinomial-Regel für beliebige qualitative Daten,
- die log-linearen Regeln für qualitative Variable ohne höhere Wechselwirkungen (im Sinne des log-linearen Modells).

Im nichtparametrischen Fall (iii) schätzt man die $f_i(x)$, ohne den Umweg über die ϑ_i direkt unter Verwendung eines nichtparametrischen Dichteschätzers. Die so erhaltenen $\hat{f}_i(x)$ setzt man wieder in (2) ein und erhält nichtparametrische-Einsetz-Regeln (nonparametric-plug-in-rules), die asymptotisch ebenfalls optimal sind und ohne parametrische Annahmen auskommen. Viele Dichteschätzer sind äußerst rechenaufwendig. Die Anwendung einer solchen Regel auf einen neuen Fall erfordert den Zugriff auf die gesamte objektivierte Stichprobe; die Entwicklung günstiger Algorithmen hierzu ist auch heute noch von Interesse. Ferner ist für manche Verfahren die Wahl eines Glättungsparameters und einer Funktionenfamilie als Basis nötig und oft problematisch.

Beispiele für nichtparametrische-plug-in-rules sind:
- Nearest-neighbour-rules (NN-Rules),
- Regeln mit Kernschätzern verschiedener Typen (u.a. Parzenschätzer),
- Regeln mit Dichteschätzern durch Orthogonalreihenentwicklung.

5. Diskrepanzen zwischen ärztlichem Entscheidungsprozeß und vorgestelltem Modell

Der einen Patienten betreffende ärztliche Entscheidungsprozeß ist so komplex, daß man ohne nährere Analyse das vorgestellte Modell als zu einfach zu dessen Beschreibung bezeichnen kann. Andererseits ist in allen biologisch-medizinischen Bereichen aus Gründen der Praktikabilität das Arbeiten mit vereinfachenden Modellen nötig. Die Frage lautet also: Ist das vorgestellte Modell zu stark vereinfacht, um für die Anwendung nützlich zu sein? Eine pauschale Antwort auf diese Frage ist nicht möglich; die Antwort hägt zu stark von der speziellen Anwendung ab. Wir beschränken uns deshalb auf das Herausarbeiten der wichtigsten Diskrepanzen zwischen Modell und Realität, um damit von Fall zu Fall differenziertere Aussagen zu ermöglichen.

Wir wollen zuerst auf drei Bedingungen eingehen, die nur aus Vereinfachungsgründen gemacht werden und denen durch geeignete Modifikation des Modells Abhilfe geschaffen werden kann (oft jedoch nur auf Kosten der Praktikabilität). Diese Bedingungen - im wesentlichen in (1) enthalten - sind: Abgeschlossenheit bezüglich der zugelassenen Diagnosen, Ausschluß von Mehrfachdiagnosen und Entsprechung zwischen Entscheidung und Diagnose.

Im Modell setzen wir eine fest vorgegebene Anzahl von Diagnosen voraus und schließen den Fall aus, daß bei Anwendung der Regel eine "andere" Diagnose auftritt. Aus Praktikabilitätsgründen muß außerdem die Zahl der zulässigen Diagnosen sehr klein gewählt werden: $m < 10$. Der Arzt sieht sich aber einem offenen Problem gegenüber: Jede Diagnose ist möglich, und Angaben zur Zahl der derzeit bekannten Diagnosen bewegen sich in der Größenordnung 10^4. Das Modell ist damit inadäquat für das generelle Diagnostikproblem und die Einsetzbarkeit beschränkt sich auf die Differentialdiagnostik und Probleme mit wenigen, oft diagnoseübergreifenden, evtl. auch vorläufigen Entscheidungsmöglichkeiten, wie die Einteilung in verdächtige und nichtverdächtige Personen beim Health Screening.

Auch in der Differentialdiagnostik muß der Arzt stets den Weg zu anderen Diagnosekategorien offenhalten. Das Modell kann, um dieser Forderung zu genügen, durch die Einführung einer Gruppe $\mathcal{P}_{m+1} = \{\text{Patienten mit "anderen" Diagnosen}\}$ den praktischen Gegebenheiten angepaßt werden (auch die "Diagnose" $\mathcal{P}_{m+2} = \{\text{Patienten ohne Krankheit}\}$ wird häufig eingeführt). Nicht vergessen darf man jedoch, daß Zuordnungsregeln stets ein Hilfsmittel für die diagnostizierenden Arzt bleiben und durch das Wissen des Arztes über die Grenzen des Modells Fehlschüsse bei dessen Benutzung vermeidbar sind.

Die Forderung $\mathcal{P}_i \wedge \mathcal{P}_j = \emptyset$ $(i \neq j)$ bedeutet im Klartext: Jeder Patient ist nur mit einer Krankheit behaftet. Selbstverständlich ist dies in der Realität nicht der Fall, und Mehrfacherkrankungen sind z.B. im Alter durchaus häufig. Durch Einführung von Mehrfacherkrankungen als eigene Diagnosegruppe kann das Modell geeignet modifiziert werden, jedoch ist die Einführung aller möglichen Krankheitskombinationen als Diagnosen nicht möglich. Diese Diskrepanz sollte jedoch nicht überbewertet werden. Meist ist der ärztliche Erkenntnisprozeß auf eine für die vorliegenden Beschwerden bzw. die anschließende Behandlung ausschlaggebende Diagnose gerichtet unter Kenntnis und/oder unter Vernachlässigung eventueller Nebendiagnosen. Zum gleichen Problemkreis gehört das Vorgehen bei seltenen Diagnosen. Da wir stets mit geschätzten Regeln arbeiten, ist ihrer Berücksichtigung unmöglich. Das Übergehen solcher Diagnosen in automatischen entscheidungsstützenden Systemen, ohne daß der Arzt ständig auf diese Lücke hingewiesen wird, ist äußerst gefährlich.

Unzutreffend ist auch die Annahme einer eindeutigen Entsprechung zwischen Entscheidung und Zuordnung zu einer Diagnose. Die Zahl der möglichen Entscheidungen des Arztes ist meist ungleich der Zahl der Diagnosen; diese kann sowohl größer als auch kleiner als jene sein. Oft sind nur zwei Entscheidungen möglich: Durchführung einer Therapie T oder Unterlassung von T. Die Berücksichtigung von $m > 2$ verschiedenen Diagnosen ist jedoch auch in diesem Fall nötig, da die Kosten (Risiken von T) für die verschiedenen Diagosen unterschiedlich sind. Andererseits besteht oft nicht der - im Modell vorausgesetzt - unmittelbare Zwang zur endgültigen Entscheidung; der Arzt kann einen Fall als nicht entscheidbar betrachten und weitere diagnostische Maßnahmen anordnen. Geeignete Modellanpassungen (rechteckige Kostenmatrizen, Unentschiedenheitsbereiche u.ä.) sind möglich, die Theorie dazu ist jedoch noch nicht abgeschlossen, und vielen bleibt heuristisch.

Abschließend wollen wir auf einige grundlegende Probleme der Anwendung entscheidungstheoretischer Methoden als Entscheidungshilfe für den Arzt eingehen, deren Lösung nicht durch einfache Modellmodifikation möglich ist. Diese Probleme sind teilweise nicht modellspezifisch, teilweise entstehen sie durch die isolierte Betrachtungsweise der Diagnostik innerhalb des gesamten, einen Patienten betreffenden ärztlichen Handelns und verlangen nach umfassenderen Modellansätzen.

Die Bedeutung der Einführung geeigneter "Kosten" wird häufig unterschätzt, und man arbeitet unkritisch mit der Kostenmatix K_0. Dieses Vorgehen bedeutet "keine Kenntnisse über mögliche Folgen" und führt auf das zu pauschale Gütekriterium "Zahl der Treffer" bzw. auf die Diagnostikregel "Diagnose = Krankheit mit der höchsten Wahrscheinlichkeit". SAVAGE hat auf der 2. Konferenz über Diagnostikprozesse dieses

Vorgehen als eine Degradierung und einen Mißbrauch der Wahrscheinlichkeit gebrandmarkt. Vollkommene Unkenntnis über Folgen von Fehlentscheidungen ist - im Gegensatz zu häufig anzutreffenden derartigen Behauptungen - bei diagnostischen Problemen nie gegeben. Der behandelnde Arzt muß auch ohne entscheidungstheoretische Unterstützung die Folgen seiner Entscheidungen für die verschiedenen möglichen Situationen abwägen. Die Quantifizierung dieser Folgen ist nicht ein durch die Benutzung von Zuordnungsverfahren geschaffenes Problem, sondern typisch für jede Entscheidungssituation. In diesem Punkt besteht das größte Problem der Einführung von Modellen darin, den Arzt dazu zu bringen, seine intuitive Risikoabwägung explizit zu quantifizieren.

Das Einsetzen von Kosten in diskriminanzanalytische Verfahren bleibt auch beim Vorliegen ärztlicher Risikoabschätzungen problematisch, und viele Fragen bleiben offen:

- Welche Kostenart ist zu verwenden?
  * Schaden- bzw. Nutzenziffern für die Gesundheit des Patienten?
  * Die monetären Folgen für den Patienten?
  * Die der Allgemeinheit entstehenden Kosten?
- Sind alle drei vorgenannten Aspekte zur berücksichtigen?
- Ist man überhaupt berechtigt, allgemeine Schaden- bzw. Nutzenwerte einzuführen? D.h., darf man mit Werten arbeiten, die die Beurteilung des Schadens für einen abstrakten Patienten aus der Sicht des Arztes darstellen?
- Muß man für jeden Fall individuelle Werte benutzen, die die Bewertung der Folgen durch den Patienten selbst ausdrücken?

Die letzten Fragen werden derzeit unter Ärzten heftig diskutiert; ihre Beantwortung ist für das Ergebnis der Zuordnungsregel von großer Relevanz, da die Bewertungen der Folgen einer Behandlung und der evtl. mit ihr verbundenen Einschränkungen der Lebensqualität sicherlich sehr stark von Patient zu Patient differieren.

Die Gefahr, durch automatische Diagnostikuntersützungssysteme das Verhältnis Arzt-Patient negativ zu beeinflussen, darf nicht verschwiegen werden: Man darf bei der Benutzung von Diagnostikmodellen nie aus dem Auge verlieren, daß das eigentliche Ziel ärztlichen Handelns nicht das Stellen der richtigen Diagnose, sondern die Besserung des Gesundheitszustandes des Patienten durch geeignete Therapie ist. Die richtige Diagnose ist oft nur von einem akademischen Interesse. So bedeutet die Diagnose einer unheilbaren, tödlichen Krankheit für die meisten Patienten eine große psychische Belastung, und ihre Abklärung durch schmerzhafte diagnostische Maßnahmen ist nicht vertretbar. Auch sind mit Risiko verbundene diagnostische Maßnahmen unsinnig, wenn eine risikolose Therapie zur Heilung führt, ohne daß die genaue differentialdiagnostische Frage geklärt ist. Die Sentenz: "Bevor man eine diagnostische Maßnahme einleitet, die den Kranken belästigt, muß man sicher sein, im Falle eines krankhaften Befundes die therapeutischen Konsequenzen in Kauf zu nehmen", ist eine bekannt Regel ärztlichen Handelns. Derartige Regeln sind wichtig und zahlreich und lassen sich nur schwer in Diagnostikmodelle einbinden.

Zwei weitere Probleme, die vor jedem praktischen Einsatz von Zuordnungsverfahren in der Diagnostik gelöst werden müssen, sind der Nachweis der Durchführbarkeit im klinischen Routinebetrieb und der Nachweis ausreichender Sicherheit. Zum ersten Problem sein darauf hingewiesen, daß in einer Klinik die Meßwerte $x_1 \ldots, x_s$ zu verschiedenen Zeitpunkten von verschiedenen Personen an räumlich getrennten Orten erhoben werden und ihre saubere Erfassung, Zusammenführung und Eingabe in den Rechner große Probleme aufwerfen. Ferner ist eine hinreichend genaue Prognose der Sicherheit bestimmter Regeln derzeit nicht möglich, da z.B. die theoretischen und numerischen Probleme einer unverzerrten Schätzung der Trefferrate für die meisten Verfahren nicht gelöst sind. Ein Kliniker wird sich zu Recht, auch falls solche Schätzungen vorliegen, nicht damit zufrieden geben, sondern solche automatischen Hilfen erst akzeptieren, wenn sie sich in einer langen Pilotstudie neben dem klinischen Routineverfahren bewährt haben. Erwähnt sei auch, daß eine theoretisch optimale Regel für praktische Belange unzureichend sein kann; die Optimalität bezieht sich nämlich auf $\mathcal{X}$ und kein noch so langer Meßwertvektor beschreibt den Träger vollständig.

Die gerade geschilderten Probleme machen die wichtigste, bereits einleitend erwähnte Diskrepanz zwischen Modell und Realität deutlich: Die Modellvorstellung

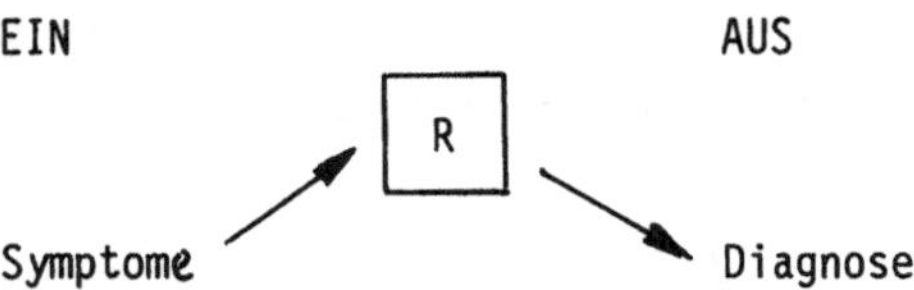

entspricht nicht der Realität. Analysiert man den ärztlichen Entscheidungsprozeß, so erkennt man, daß der Arzt in dessen Verlauf eine ganze Reihe von Entscheidungen fällt, die teilweise Diagnosen, teilweise zu erhebende Symptome bzw. durchzuführende Labortests, teilweise die Therapie betreffen. Während dieses Prozesses ändert sich seine Blickrichtung mehrmals: Teilweise schließt er induktiv von den Symptomen auf in Frage kommende Diagnosen, teilweise schließt er deduktiv von den noch möglichen Diagnosen auf die zu ihrer Differenzierung nötigen Symptome. Daneben hat er ständig die Möglichkeit der Einleitung einer notwendigen Therapie auch ohne endgültige Diagnose zu berücksichtigen. Die Analyse führt notwendigerweise zu mehrstufigen Modellen, innerhalb derer die Entscheidungen nicht nur die Diagnosen und Therapie, sondern auch die zu erhebenden Symptome betreffen. Der Merkmalsvektor X ist nicht mehr fest vorgegeben, sondern von Fall zu Fall verschieden. Modellierungsansätze in dieser Richtung wurden mehrfach begonnen, sind jedoch in den Anfängen stecken geblieben, da sich die Möglichkeit praktischer Anwendung nicht abzeichnete.

Noch komplexer werden die Modelle, falls man berücksichtigen will, daß es sich bei den meisten biologischen Größen nicht um für den Träger feste Werte, sondern um stochastische Prozesse handelt. Für eine Reihe medizinischer Meßwerte ist dieser Aspekt der relativ geringen intraindividuellen Schwankungen wegen vernachlässigbar, andere Größen gewinnen jedoch erst durch den zeitlichen Verlauf ihre diagnostische Bedeutung. Diskriminationsprobleme für stochastische Prozesse wurden auch in der theoretisch orientierten Literatur bisher kaum behandelt, und die Zahl der Ergebnisse ist gering.

6. Schlußfolgerungen

Entscheidungstheoretische Modelle vereinfachen den ärztlichen Entscheidungsprozeß sehr stark und sind nur für Teilbereiche dieses Prozesses adäquat. Es ist eine irrige, von seriösen Wissenschaftlern nie vertretene Ansicht, durch solche Methoden die ärztliche Diagnostik ersetzen zu können. Ernstzunehmende Ansätze hatten stets lediglich die Unterstützung des Arztes bei der Entscheidungsfindung zum Ziel (Schlagwort: computergestützte Diagnostik). In diesem Sinne von einem Arzt eingesetzt, der sich der Grenzen des Modells bewußt ist, können Zuordnungsverfahren durchaus hilfreich und nützlich sein. Den derzeitigen Hauptnutzen sehe ich in dem von der Benutzung dieser Verfahren für den Arzt ausgehenden Zwang, sich seiner Entscheidungssituation bewußt zu werden und die nötigen Risikoabwägungen nicht zu umgehen.

Im gesamten medizinisch-biologischen Bereich ist wegen der Ungenauigkeit der Parameterschätzungen nur der Einsatz von vereinfachenden Modellen praktikabel. Komplexe, der Realität angepaßte Modelle sind nur von theoretischem Interesse. Die Anwendung des Modells muß auf Teilbereiche des gesamten Problems beschränkt und dann als ein Baustein in den Gesamtprozeß eingebettet werden. So behalten auch die diskriminanzanalytischen Einschritt-Diagnostikmodelle im komplexen, mehrstufigen ärztlichen Entscheidungsprozeß ihre Bedeutung.

Den Hauptgrund für das Scheitern der meisten bisherigen Ansätze sehr ich im Fehlen einer gründlichen Analyse des ärztlichen Entscheidungsprozesses. Diese muß für jedes Teilproblem getrennt durchgeführt bzw. verfeinert werden. Weitere Gründe sind das blinde Vertrauen vieler Mediziner in den schwarzen Kasten (black box) "Diagnosealgorithmus" und der fehlende Kontakt vieler Methodiker zur klinischen Praxis. Diese beiden Gründe lassen sich auf den gemeinsamen Nenner mangelhaftes Teamwork bringen.

Ein Hauptmißverständnis vieler Diagnosemodellkonstrukteure gilt es auszuräumen. Hauptziel des ärztlichen Handelns ist nicht die Diagnose, sondern die Behebung von Beschwerden bzw. die Verbesserung des Gesundheitszustandes des einzelnen Patienten. Neben der Abwägung der Risiken von Fehldiagnosen muß der Arzt den Nutzen richtiger Diagnosen und mögliche Therapierisiken in seine Überlegungen einbeziehen sowie eine Risikominimierung der diagnostischen Maßnahme und eine Kostenminimierung für den Patienten anstreben. Auch Forderungen nach Verringerung des apparativen Aufwandes und Berücksichtigung betriebs- und volkswirtschaftlicher Randbedingungen können den Entscheidungsprozeß beeinflussen. Schließlich muß der Arzt bereit sein, nicht überall von seinen eigenen Bewertungen der Folgen seiner Handlung auszugehen, sondern auch von seinen Ansichten differierende Bewertungen der Folgen durch den Patienten (z.B. Beurteilung der Lebensqualität) zu akzeptieren. In praktikablen Modellen kann dies nicht alles berücksichtigt werden. Die unkritsche Anwendung von Diagnostikmodellen durch mit der Problematik unvertraute Ärzte ist daher äußerst gefährlich und muß unterbunden werden. Nützlich können Diagnostikmodelle nur eingesetzt werden, wenn die Ärzte sie als ergänzende Hilfsmittel zur Lösung ihres Entscheidungsproblems einzusetzen lernen.

Literaturhinweise:

GROSS, R.: Analyse des ärztlichen Diagnostikvorganges. In: Lange, H.-J. und Wagner, G.: Computerunterstützte ärztliche Diagnostik. Schattauer-Verlag, Stuttgart 1973, pp 31-38.

JACQUEZ, J.A.: Computer Diagnosis and Diagnostic Methods. Ch.C. Thomas Publ., Springfield 1972.

VICTOR, N. und LANGE, H.-J.: Influences de l'ordinateur sur le diagnostic médical. In: Marois, M.: Man and Computer. North-Holland Publ. Comp., Amsterdam 1974, pp 239 - 247.

KI-VERFAHREN ZUR UNTERSTÜTZUNG DER ÄRZTLICHEN URTEILSBILDUNG

Wolfgang Wahlster

Universität Hamburg[1]

ZUSAMMENFASSUNG. Expertensysteme sind wissensbasierte KI-Systeme, die Expertenwissen und die darauf beruhenden Fähigkeiten maschinell verfügbar machen. Der Aufsatz gibt einen einführenden Überblick über Expertensysteme, die zur Unterstützung der ärztlichen Urteilsbildung entwickelt wurden. Es wird der Forschungs- und Entwicklungsstand im Bereich der Inferenz-, Planungs-, Erklärungs-, Wissenserwerbs- und Dialogkomponenten medizinischer Expertensysteme dargestellt. Die in medizinischen Expertensystemen verwendeten Wissensquellen und ihre Codierung in Wissensrepräsentationssprachen wie Produktionensystemen, Semantischen Netzen, Frame-Systemen, Inferenznetzen, Actor-Systemen und PLANNER-artigen Programmiersprachen werden skizziert. Zum Schluß werden die Anwendungs- und Forschungsperspektiven des vorgestellten Teilgebietes der Medizinischen Informatik und Künstlichen Intelligenz diskutiert.

Medizinische Expertensysteme als wissensbasierte KI-Systeme

Während sich die Informatik ganz allgemein mit der systematischen Verarbeitung von Information mit Hilfe von Rechenanlagen beschäftigt, werden im Teilgebiet *Künstliche Intelligenz* (KI) speziell solche Informationsverarbeitungsprozesse untersucht, die in besonders starkem Maße Strategien menschlicher Intelligenz voraussetzen (vgl. [50],[4], [29]. Eines der Fachgebiete der KI, in dem erste Anwendungserfolge verzeichnet werden können, ist die Entwicklung von Expertensystemen (vgl. [26],[10],[34]).

Als *Expertensysteme* bezeichnet man KI-Systeme, die Expertenwissen und die darauf beruhenden Fähigkeiten maschinell verfügbar machen. Dabei wird unter *Wissen* in der KI eine Ansammlung von Kenntnissen, Erfahrungen und Problemlösungsmethoden verstanden, die den Hintergrund für komplexe Informationsverarbeitungsprozesse bildet. Das Wissen besteht aus Daten über Objekte, Relationen und Prozesse. Obwohl die Wahl einer problemgerechten Darstellung von Daten eine allgemeine Fragestellung innerhalb der Informatik ist, stellt sich das Problem der *Repräsentation von Wissen* (vgl. [23],[27],[42]) bei der Konstruktion von Expertensystemen verschärft, da solche Systeme auf einen umfangreichen Wissensfundus zurückgreifen müssen, der aus vielen heterogen strukturierten Einheiten bestehen kann.

In der KI wurden im Teilbereich 'Knowledge Engineering' verschiedene Hilfsmittel zur systematischen Repräsentation von Wissen entwickelt, die man als *Wissensrepräsentationssprachen* bezeichnet. Die durch eine Wissensrepräsentationssprache definierten Ausdrücke nennt man *Repräsentationskonstruktionen*. Die Gesamtheit an Wissen, die einem KI-System zur Verfügung steht, nennt man *Wissensbasis*. Die Wissensbasis gliedert sich in *Wissens-*

1) Der vorliegende Aufsatz entstand im Rahmen des Projektes HAM-ANS, das mit Mitteln des BMFT gefördert wird.

quellen, die wiederum aus einzelnen *Wisseneinheiten* bestehen. Wissen, das sich auf anderes Wissen innerhalb der Wissensbasis bezieht, nennt man *Metawissen*. Es sind im allgemeinen mehrere Metaebenen zu unterscheiden.
Expertensysteme sind *wissensbasierte Systeme*, deren wesentlichen Bestandteile eine Wissensbasis und eine *Inferenzkomponente* sind. Die Fähigkeit eines KI-Systems, eine Performanz auf Expertenniveau zu erreichen, hängt nur in geringem Maße von den in ihm implementierten allgemeinen Problemlösungsmethoden ab, sondern in erster Linie vom Umfang und semantischen Gehalt seiner Wissensbasis. Expertensysteme unterscheiden sich von traditionellen Informationssystemen u.a. dadurch, daß sie über einen Bestand an allgemeinem Hintergrundwissen verfügen und für komplexe, heterogene Wissensbereiche, aber weniger für homogene Massendaten entwickelt werden. Abstrakt betrachtet, stellen Expertenwissen ein Kommunikationsmedium zwischen dem Benutzer und den für den Aufbau der Wissensbasis verantwortlichen Experten dar.

Für viele Anwendungen aus Wissenschaft und Technik wurden in der KI Expertensysteme entwickelt, z.B. um Chemikern bei der Strukturanalyse chemischer Verbindungen zu helfen (DENDRAL, [5]), um Geologen bei der Suche nach Erzlagern zu unterstützten (PROSPECTOR, [18]), um Bauingenieure z.B. bei der Brückenplanung zu entlasten (SACON, [2]), um Informatikern bei der Konfigurierung von Rechensystemen zu helfen (R1 für die VAX, [24]), um Juristen im Körperschaftsrecht zu beraten (TAXMAN, [22]), um Elektrotechnikern bei der Analyse von Schaltkreisen zu helfen (EL, [38]) und schließlich auch um Ärzte bei ihrer diagnostischen und therapeutischen Tätigkeit zu unterstützen (vgl. [21], [12]).

Ziel des vorliegenden Aufsatzes ist es, Expertensysteme als *eine* Möglichkeit zur Unterstützung der ärztlichen Urteilsbildung einzuführen und einen Überblick zum Entwicklungsstand medizinischer Expertensysteme zu geben.

Bis auf wenige Ausnahmen (z.B. das Expertensystem PUFF, [30]) sind medizinische Expertensysteme als interaktive *Beratungssysteme* konzipiert.(vgl. Fig. 1, [37]). Für den Einsatz als Beratungssystem muß ein Expertensystem zusätzlich mit *Beratungskompetenz* (vgl. [34]) ausgestattet werden, d.h. es muß dazu in der Lage sein, Beratungswunsch und -ziel des Benutzers zu verstehen, sein Expertenwissen für den Benutzer verständlich zu machen und seine Lösungsvorschläge auf Anfrage zu erklären. Die Beratungskompetenz wird in Expertensystemen durch die Integration von *Dialog*- und *Erklärungskomponenten* aufgebaut.

Prinzipiell gibt es zwei wesentliche Motivationen zur KI-Forschung:

- eine technische Motivation: die Entwicklung von Systemen, die solche Aufgaben übernehmen können, von denen gegenwärtig gesagt wird, sie erforderten Intelligenz
- eine theoretische Motivation: die wissenschaftliche Beschreibung und Erklärung von kommunikativen und kognitiven Prozessen mit informatischen Mitteln.

Während die technische Motivation zur Entwicklung von *Leistungsmodellen* führt, in denen lediglich das Ein-/Ausgabeverhalten im Vordergrund steht, wird bei einer theoretischen Motivation der KI-Forschung eher die Simulation kommunikativer und kognitiver

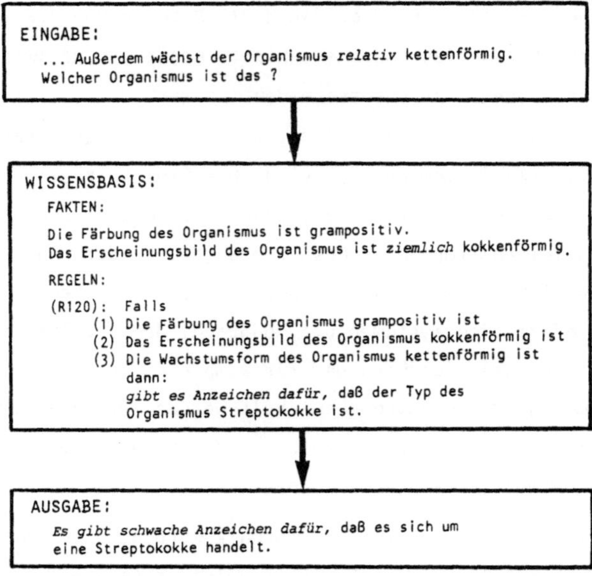

Fig. 1: Ein Beratungsdialog mit MYCIN

Prozesse durch *Funktionsmodelle* angestrebt, die Analogien zwischen der Arbeitsweise des Modells und des nachgebildeten Originals enthalten. Die hier betrachteten Expertensysteme sind als Ergebnisse anwendungsorientierter KI-Forschung primär als Leistungsmodelle konzipiert, bei denen einige Überlegungen aus dem Bereich der Simulation kognitiver Prozesse bei der ärztlichen Entscheidungsfindung einfließen. Keines der hier betrachteten KI-Systeme erhebt den Anspruch, ein vollständiges Funktionsmodell für den kognitiven Prozeß der ärztlichen Urteilsbildung darzustellen.

Die in der KI-Forschung entwickelten Expertensysteme sollen und können keineswegs das ärztliche Gespräch mit dem leidenden Patienten ersetzen. Vielmehr dienen Expertensysteme in der klinischen Situation dazu:

- das Qualitätsniveau der Diagnostik zu erhöhen
- den Diagnoseprozeß zu beschleunigen
- den Arzt von langwierigen Dosierungsberechnungen zu entlasten
- neuste medizinische Forschungsergebnisse im Not- und Behandlungsfall unmittelbar zur Verfügung zu stellen
- Fehldiagnosen zu vermeiden

Durch Expertensysteme kann auch die medizinische Lehre und Forschung unterstützt werden [7], da sie nicht nur das aus Lehrbüchern und der Fachliteratur hervorgehende Wissen, sondern erstmals auch eine explizite Repräsentation von Heuristiken, Strategien und Erfahrungswerten enthalten, die sich der Mediziner bisher nur durch eine langjährige praktische Tätigkeit aneignen konnte. Darüberhinaus hat die Repräsentation von Wissen in KI-Systemen gegenüber der Fachliteratur den Vorteil, daß sie kompakter, jederzeit verfügbar und für eine maschinelle Verarbeitung geeignet ist.

Die Architektur medizinischer Expertensysteme

Um die Pilotversion eines Expertensystems, das lediglich aus einer Wissensbasis und einer Inferenzkomponente besteht, in ein produktreifes Beratungssystem zu überführen, müssen die in Fig. 2 zusätzlich angegebenen Systemkomponenten ergänzt werden.

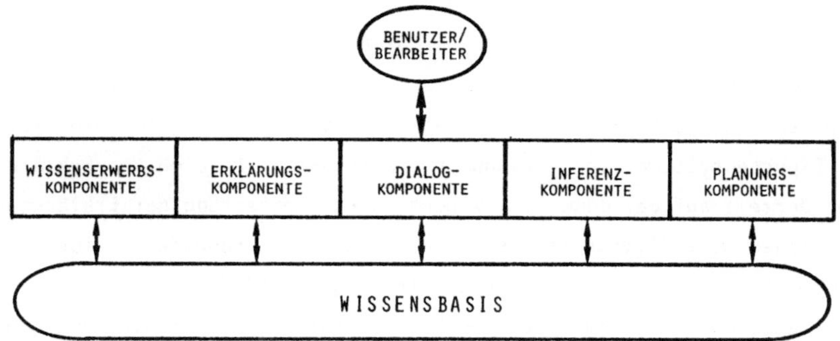

Fig. 2: Komponenten eines Expertensystems

Die Übersetzung der Benutzereingaben in die interne Wissensrepräsentationssprache und die Generierung kommunikativ adäquater Systemantworten wird von der *Dialogkomponente* eines Expertensystems übernommen. Auch die Formulierung von Anfragen des Expertensystems an den Benutzer gehört zu den Aufgaben der Dialogkomponente. Für medizinische Expertensysteme besonders geeignet ist der Einsatz von *natürlichsprachlichen KI-Systemen* (vgl. [43], die es dem Benutzer ermöglichen sollen, die medizinische Fachsprache zu benutzen. Da die Anwendung anspruchsvollerer KI-Verfahren zur Sprachverarbeitung mit hohen Betriebsmittelanforderungen verbunden ist, beschränkt man sich beim heutigen Stand der Technologie in der Dialogkomponente von Expertensystemen auf einfache Schlüsselwort- und Pattern-Matching-Verfahren sowie die Aufbereitung vorbereiteter Textpassagen.
Mithilfe der *Inferenzkomponente* können Aussagen, die nicht explizit als *Faktenwissen* gespeichert sind, unter Anwendung von *Inferenzregeln* aus dem Faktenwissen abgeleitet werden. Die Inferenzkomponente von Expertensystemen wird meist als *pattern-gesteuertes Inferenzsystem* (vgl. [45]) realisiert. Um die *kombinatorische Explosion* von Rechenzeit- und Speicherplatzanforderungen in der Inferenzkomponente zu vermeiden, muß die Anwendung der Inferenzregeln strategisch gesteuert werden. Dabei greift man auf *Metainferenzregeln* (vgl. [18]) zurück, in denen strategisches Wissen codiert ist. Bei der Konstruktion von Inferenzkomponenten für medizinische Expertensysteme sind auch *approximative* und *nicht-monotone Inferenzen* (vgl. [49]) zu berücksichtigen, da im Diagnoseprozeß häufig mit Unsicherheit behaftete bzw. rein hypothetische Schlußfolgerungen notwendig sind.
Für eine vorgegebene Zielbeschreibung erzeugt die *Planungskomponente* aufgrund von strategischem Wissen eine Folge von Handlungsschritten. Typisch für die in der KI entwickelten Planungssysteme (vgl. [36]) ist, daß das System die von ihm zunächst erzeugten Vorversionen eines Plans mehrfach einer Kritik und Revision unterwirft und den Plan bei veränderten Randbedingungen jederzeit abändern kann. Einsatzbereiche für Planungskompo-

nenten in medizinischen Expertensystemen sind z.B. die Planung des Diagnoseprozesses und die Erstellung des Behandlungsplanes für chronisch Kranke, wobei Randbedingungen wie die Minimierung der Therapiekosten oder des Risikos beim Patienten vorgegeben werden können.

Aufgabe der *Erklärungskomponente* ist es, auf Anfrage eine für den Benutzer verständliche und im jeweiligen Dialogzustand angemessene Erklärung für eine inferenz-basierte Systemantwort zu generieren (vgl. [44]). Da der Arzt bei der Verwertung und Weitergabe von Systemauskünften eine besonders große Verantwortung trägt, ist die durch eine Erklärungskomponente erzielte Systemtransparenz eine Voraussetzung für die Akzeptanz medizinischer Expertensysteme. Der Forschungsschwerpunkt im Bereich von Erklärungskomponenten liegt derzeit auf der Generierung kohärenter, mehrsträngiger Erklärungen auf einer angemessenen Detaillierungsebene, in denen das beim Benutzer vermutete Vorwissen und der Informativitätsgrad berücksichtigt wird (vgl. [44]).

Die *Wissenserwerbskomponente* hat die Aufgabe, den Aufbau, die Erweiterung und die Korrektur der Wissensbasis zu unterstützen. Die Integration einer Wissenserwerbskomponente soll es ermöglichen, Eintragungen in die Wissensbasis allein von einem Experten des jeweiligen Anwendungsgebietes vornehmen zu lassen, ohne daß dieser dabei auf die Hilfe eines Informatikers mit KI-Kenntnissen zurückgreifen muß (vgl. [8], [16]). In medizinischen Expertensystemen umfaßt die Wissenserwerbskomponente eine benutzerfreundliche Schnittstelle zur Eingabe von Faktenwissen, begrifflichem Fachwissen, Inferenzregeln und Inferenzstrategien sowie Möglichkeiten zur Konsistenzprüfung der Wissensbasis und zur experimentellen Validierung des eingegebenen Regelwissens anhand von Testfällen mit vorgegebenen Diagnoseergebnissen. Da letzlich die diagnostischen Fähigkeiten eines Spezialisten weitgehend auf persönlicher Erfahrung und Heuristiken beruhen, die er durch eine langjährige praktische Tätigkeit erworben hat, muß die Wissenserwerbskomponente als interaktives System konzipiert werden, das dem Benutzer Hilfestellungen bei der Explikation seines Spezialwissens anbietet.

Da jede der genannten Komponenten eine Entwicklungszeit von mehreren Mannjahren erfordert, existieren bisher noch keine medizinischen Expertensysteme, in denen alle genannten Komponenten vollständig ausgebaut sind, obwohl in der KI-Literatur für jede Komponente implementierte Beispiele dokumentiert sind. Vielmehr unterscheiden sich die in Fig. 4 zusammengestellten medizinischen Expertensysteme gerade dadurch, daß einzelne der angeführten Komponenten beim Entwurf unberücksichtigt blieben oder nur ansatzweise implementiert wurden.

Die Wissensbasis eines medizinischen Expertensystems besteht aus dem begrifflichen und referentiellen Wissen. Das *begriffliche Wissen* ist weitgehend anwendungsunabhängig und bezieht sich auf grundlegende medizinische Begriffe, Zusammenhänge und Verfahren, die eine Verständigung mit dem Arzt erst ermöglichen. Das *referentielle Wissen* kann wiederum in anwendungsspezifisches und patientenbezogenes Wissen gegliedert werden. Das *anwendungsspezifische Wissen* setzt sich aus dem Faktenwissen, Inferenzregeln und den Heuristiken eines medizinischen Fachgebietes zusammen. Das *patientenbezogene Wissen* kann aus der Krankenakte des Patienten, den erhobenen Befunden, den aktuellen Angaben des Patienten und/oder den Labordaten bestehen. Falls das Expertensystem als Dialogsystem eingesetzt wird, können als *dialogbezogene Wissensquellen*, in denen während des Dialogs temporär Information gespeichert wird, noch ein Partnermodell, ein Inferenzgedächtnis, der Fokus sowie syntaktische und semantische Dialoggedächtnisse hinzukommen.

Im *Partnermodell* ist Information über das beim Dialogpartner vermutete Vorwissen und seine voraussichtlichen Dialogziele gespeichert (vgl. [35]). Es enthält sowohl Wissen über prototypische Benutzerklassen (z.B. medizinischer Laie, Medizinstudent, Hausarzt, Facharzt, Wissenschaftler) als auch Information über das Dialogverhalten des Benutzers, die aus den bisherigen Dialogen extrahiert wurde. Durch die Integration eines Partnermodells wird ein Expertensystem wesentlich flexibler, da es sein Antwortverhalten auf das jeweilige Benutzerprofil einstellen kann.

Im *Inferenzgedächtnis* (vgl. [44] wird eine formale Beschreibung der vom Expertensystem durchgeführten Inferenzen gespeichert, um später mithilfe der Erklärungskomponente inferenz-basierte Systemantworten erklären zu können.

Die als *Fokus* bezeichnete Wissensquelle enthält Information über die jeweiligen thematischen Schwerpunkte eines Gesprächsabschnittes (vgl. [15]). Diese Wissensquelle dient u.a. zur Disambiguierung von Benutzereingaben und zur Erzeugung von Kohärenz durch die Dialogkomponente sowie zur Steuerung von Suchprozessen in der Inferenz- und der Planungskomponente.

Die *syntaktischen und semantischen Dialoggedächtnisse* (vgl. [17]) dienen zur Analyse und Generierung von Ellipsen und anaphorischen Ausdrücken. Genauso wie für die oben genannten Systemkomponenten gilt auch für die hier angeführten Wissensquellen, daß in jedem der in Fig. 4 zusammengestellten medizinischen Expertensysteme nur eine spezifische Auswahl der genannten Wissensbereiche realisiert ist.

Wissensrepräsentationssprachen für medizinische Expertensysteme

Zur Darstellung von Wissen in Expertensystemen werden die in der KI zu diesem Zweck entwickelten Wissensrepräsentationssprachen (vgl. [3], [11]) eingesetzt. Es gehört zu den Aufgaben des in der Medizinischen Informatik arbeitenden KI-Spezialisten, die jeweils adäquate Wissensrepräsentationssprache zur Codierung der unterschiedlichen Wissensquellen eines medizinischen Expertensystems zu wählen. Man spricht von einer *heterogenen Wissensbasis*, falls in einem KI-System verschiedene Wissensrepräsentationssprachen verwendet werden.

Für den Aufbau der in Fig. 4 zusammengestellten medizinischen Expertensysteme wurden folgende Wissensrepräsentationssprachen benutzt:

- Produktionensysteme
- Semantische Netze
- Frame-Systeme
- Inferenznetze
- Actor-Systeme
- PLANNER-artige Programmiersprachen

In dem hier behandelten Teilgebiet der KI sind Produktionensysteme die am häufigsten verwendete Wissensrepräsentationssprache. Ein *Produktionensystem* besteht aus drei Komponenten: einer geordneten Menge von *Produktionen*, einer *Datenbasis* und einem *Interpreter*. Jede Produktion hat die Form <Bedingung> → <Aktion>. Sowohl die linke als auch die rechte Seite einer Produktion kann Variablen enthalten. Die linke Seite ist ein bedingter Ausdruck, der sich auf den Inhalt der Datenbasis bezieht und, falls er vom Interpreter zu Wahr ausgewertet wird, die in der rechten Seite der Produktion codierten Aktionen auf der Datenbasis auslöst. Da das zu repräsentierende Wissen gerade im medizinischen Bereich meist aus approximativen Inferenzregeln besteht, sind in allen hier betrachteten Produktionensystemen Möglichkeiten zur Spezifikation der *Implikationsstärke* einer Produktion vorgesehen. Die verschiedenen in der KI entwickelten Interpreter für Produktionensysteme können danach unterschieden werden , ob die Produktionen von links nach rechts (Vorwärtverkettung) oder von rechts nach links (Rückwärtsverkettung) gelesen werden, wie *Regelkonflikte* gelöst werden, ob nur eine Ableitung oder *Mehrfachableitungen* mit *Evidenzverstärkungsoperationen* durchgeführt werden und wie neue Evidenzwerte bei der Anwendung des Modus ponens und der Substitutionsregel berechnet werden (vgl. [44]).

Ein *Semantisches Netz* ist ein bewerteter, gerichteter Graph, in dem semantische Einheiten, die als Knoten des Graphen repräsentiert werden, in verschiedenen semantischen Relationen zueinander stehen, die als bewertete, gerichtete Kanten dargestellt werden. Durch *Partitionierung* von Semantischen Netzwerken können Netzteile zu Einheiten zusammen gefaßt werden, zwischen denen dann wiederum semantische Relationen definiert werden (z.B. zur Darstellung von Zeitabläufen). Die Semantik der meist aus einer kleinen Zahl von Kantenprimitiven aufgebauten Graphen wird erst durch die für das Semantische Netzwerk definierten Such-, Traversierungs- und Inferenzalgorithmen spezifiziert. So gehen z.B. die Transitivität der Oberbegriffsrelation und die beschränkte Transitivität der Teil-von-Relation in die über Semantischen Netzen definierten Inferenzprozesse ein.

Frame-Systeme bestehen aus einer Hierarchie von zusammengesetzten Datenstrukturen, die speziell zur Repräsentation von *prototypischem Wissen* entworfen wurden. Solche Prototype-Frames, denen ein eindeutiger Bezeichner zugeordnet wird, sind aus einer Menge von innerhalb des Frames eindeutig bezeichneten Attributen aufgebaut, an die *Deskriptoren*, *Metadeskriptoren* und *objektbezogene Prozedurdefinitionen* gebunden sind. Deskriptoren geben Bedingungen an, die von den Werten der entsprechenden Attribute der Objektframes, die meist durch *partielle Instantiierung* eines Prototype-Frames entstehen, erfüllt sein müssen. Metadeskriptoren ermöglichen die deklarative Darstellung von Eigenschaften der Attribute und Deskriptoren eines Frames. Beispielsweise werden durch Metadeskriptoren diejenigen Deskriptoren gekennzeichnet, die als Voreinstellung (DEFAULT) oder als grundlegendes Merkmal des durch den Frame repräsentierten Konzeptes aufgefaßt werden (CRITERIAL). Die Instantiierung eines Frames und der Vergleich mit anderen Frames kann durch objektbezogene Prozedurdefinitionen gesteuert werden. Außerdem ergänzen diese die in Frame-Systemen enthaltenen *Vererbungsmechanismen* bei der Suche und der Weiterverbreitung von eingegebenen Attributbelegungen.

Inferenznetze sind bewertete, gerichtete Graphen ohne Schleifen und Kreise, deren Kanten als Implikationsrelationen und deren Knoten als Aussagen oder Hypothesen interpretiert werden. In einem Inferenznetz gibt es Knoten mit positiven und negativen Evidenzwerten, die der Datenbasis eines Produktionensystems entsprechen, sowie Knoten mit unbekanntem Evidenzwert. Zu jedem Inferenznetz gehört ein Traversierungsalgorithmus, dem die Funktion des Interpreters in Produktionensystemen zukommt. Unter Verwendung von verschiedenen im Rahmen der *Fuzzy Logiken* entwickelten Operatoren zur Verknüpfung von Evidenzwerten werden durch den Traversierungsalgorithmus vom Benutzer vorgegebene Evidenzwerte im gesamten Inferenznetz, das man als ein compiliertes Produktionensystem auffassen kann, weiterverbreitet.

Der *Actor-Formalismus* ist ein von C. Hewitt (vgl. [20]) entwickeltes Verfahren zur prozeduralen, heterarchisch verteilten Repräsentation von Wissen. Ein Actor-System besteht aus einem Netzwerk kooperierender, jeweils nebenläufiger und unabhängig voneinander sequentiell arbeitender Actors, die aufgrund definierter Kontrollbeziehungen untereinander Botschaften austauschen. Jeder Actor ist eine abstrakte Maschine, die bei Aktivierung durch Eingang einer Botschaft ein sequentielles Programm unter einem lokalen Zustand abarbeitet und danach den lokalen Zustand ändert und/oder Botschaften an Actors absendet (vgl. [33]). Ein Actor-System kann als eine Gesellschaft kooperierender Experten aufgefaßt werden, in der nebenläufig eine Informationsverarbeitungsaufgabe gelöst wird.

PLANNER-artige Programmiersprachen enthalten zusätzlich zum Sprachumfang von LISP (vgl. [51]) einen Pattern-Matcher, automatische Deduktionsmechanismen, eine Verwaltung für mehrere unabhängige assoziative Datenbasen sowie Möglichkeiten zum *pattern-gesteuerten Prozeduraufruf*, zur pattern-gesteuerten Suche und zum gesteuerten oder automatischen *Backtracking*. Insgesamt wurden diese Sprachen ausgehend von PLANNER als sehr hohe Pro-

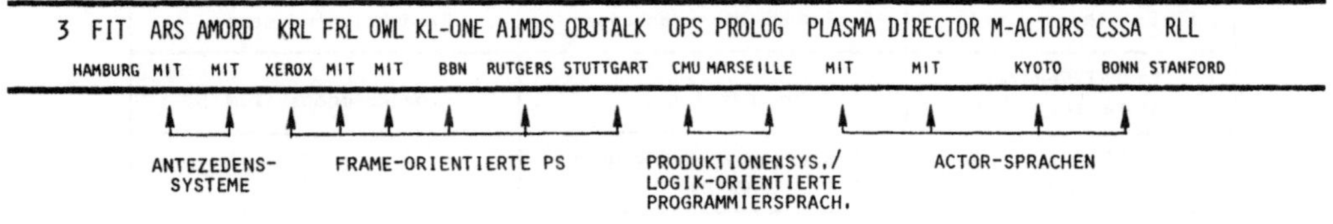

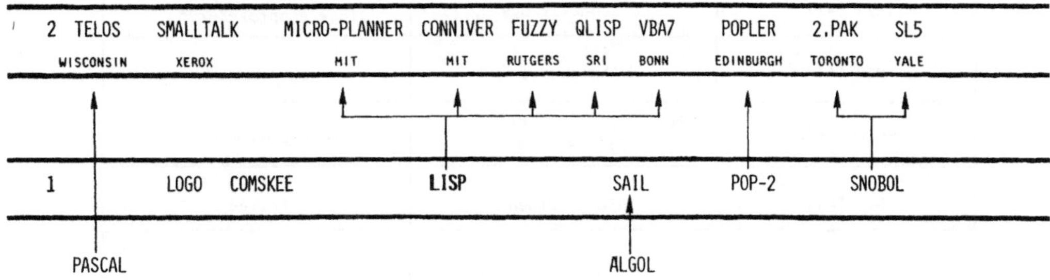

Fig. 3: Drei Generationen von KI-Sprachen

grammiersprachen konzipiert, deren Daten- und Kontrollstrukturen eine flexible Darstellung, eine modulare Organisation und eine effiziente Verarbeitung komplexer Wissensstrukturen fördern sollen.

Im strengen Sinne handelt es sich bei den genannten Wissensrepräsentationssprachen um Sprachfamilien, die ein breites Spektrum von verschiedenen Ausprägungen des Grundparadigmas der jeweiligen Repräsentationssprache enthalten. Einige der in der KI entwickelten Wissensrepräsentationssprachen sind in Fig. 3 zusammen mit dem Ort ihrer ersten Implementation verzeichnet.

Obwohl es bereits eine große Zahl von Wissensrepräsentationssprachen gibt, müssen in KI-Projekten wegen spezieller Randbedingungen der zu lösenden Repräsentationsprobleme häufig neue Varianten von KI-Sprachen entworfen werden. Es lag daher nahe mit dem System RLL (Representation Language Language, vgl. [14]) eine programmiersprachliche Umgebung zu schaffen, die den Benutzer bei der Spezifikation der Syntax und Semantik neuer Wissensrepräsentationssprachen unterstützt.

SYSTEMNAME/LITERATUR	MEDIZINISCHES FACHGEBIET	WISSENSREPRÄSENTATIONSSPRACHE
CASNET [47]	Glaucoma	Inferenznetz
CENTAUR [1]	Auswertung von Lungenfunktionsprüfungen	Frames & Produktionensysteme
DIGITALIS ADVISOR [39]	Digitalis-Dosierung	OWL-Prozeduren
EMYCIN/HEADMED [19]	Präskription von Psychopharmaka	Produktionensystem
EMYCIN/PUFF [30]	Auswertung von Lungenfunktionsprüfungen	Produktionensystem
EXPERT/PI [13]	Innere Medizin	Produktionensystem
EXPERT/Thyroid [13]	Schilddrüsenerkrankungen	Produktionensystem
EXPERT/General Rheumatology [13]	Rheumatologie	Produktionensystem
EXPERT/Connective Tissue Diseases [13]	Erkrankungen des Bindegewebes	Produktionensystem
INTERNIST I/II [32]	Innere Medizin	Produktionensystem
IRIS [41]	Augenheilkunde	Semantisches Netz & Inferenzprozeduren
MDX [6]	Cholestase	Actor-System
MYCIN [37]	Bakterielle Infektionen & Antibiotika-Therapie	Produktionensystem
PIP [40]	Nierenleiden	Frames
VM [9]	Datenauswertung in der Intensivstation	Produktionensysteme

Fig. 4: Medizinische Expertensysteme

Der Entwicklungsstand medizinischer Expertensysteme

Wie Fig. 4 zeigt, wurden für medizinische Fachgebiete sehr unterschiedlicher Größe Expertensysteme entwickelt. Das Spektrum reicht von großen Fachgebieten wie der Inneren Medizin (INTERNIST, EXPERT/PI) bis zu speziellen Erkrankungen wie der Cholestase (MDX). Entsprechend variiert auch die Größe der Wissensbasis. Die derzeit größte Wissensbasis eines medizinischen Expertensystems ist die von INTERNIST. Sie besteht aus 24 000 Inferenzregeln, die durch weitere 3000 Einheiten referentiellen Wissens und 400 Einheiten begrifflichen Wissens ergänzt werden. Am Ende des Spektrums liegt das System PUFF mit nur 250 Inferenzregeln. Eine Wissensbasis mittlerer Größe (z.B. MYCIN) enthält 500 bis 1000 Inferenzregeln.
Seit zwei Jahren zeichnet sich ein Trend zur Entwicklung von Rahmensystemen ab, die aus einer Verallgemeinerung bisheriger Expertensysteme bestehen und als Werkzeuge zum Aufbau wissensbasierter KI-Systeme dienen sollen. Beispiele für solche Rahmensysteme sind EMYCIN (vgl. [25]), EXPERT (vgl. [48]) und AGE (vgl. [28]).

Eine effiziente Implementation von Expertensystemen erfordert Speichermedien mit großer Kapazität und kurzer Zugriffszeit sowie Rechnerarchitekturen mit großen Adressräumen (≥ 24 Bits) und Befehlssätzen, die auf die Anforderungen der Symbolverarbeitung abgestimmt sind. Obwohl für die Entwicklung von Expertensystemen z.Z. fast ausschließlich Rechenanlagen vom Typ DECsystem 10 und DECsystem 20 verwendet werden, wird allgemein ein Wechsel zu den speziell in Hinblick auf die genannten Anforderungen entwickelten LISP-Maschinen erwartet (vgl. [46]). Da mithilfe der heute erhältlichen LISP-Maschinen schlüsselfertige Expertensysteme (Hardware und Software) zu einem Preis von rd. 250 TDM hergestellt werden können, ist der dezentrale Einsatz von Expertensystemen auch in mittleren und kleinen medizinischen Instituten und Krankenhäusern technologisch und ökonomisch möglich geworden.

Die wichtigsten drei Fragen, die in den nächsten Jahren im Bereich medizinischer Expertensysteme durch KI-Grundlagenforschung geklärt werden müssen, lauten:

- Wie kann der Zeit- und Personalaufwand für den Aufbau der Wissensbasis von Expertensystemen reduziert werden?
- Wie können verschiedene medizinische Expertensysteme gekoppelt werden, um durch eine auf breiterem Fachwissen beruhende Gesamtsicht die Diagnosequalität weiter zu erhöhen?
- Welche allgemeinen Hilfsmittel zur Validierung von Expertensystemen gibt es (vgl. [31])?

Ob die dargestellten KI-Techniken nach Klärung dieser Fragen auf breiterer Basis bis hin zu den niedergelassenen Ärzten eingesetzt werden, hängt im Gegensatz zu technisch-wissenschaftlichen Anwendungen von Expertensystemen weniger von der KI-Forschung, sondern vor allem von empirischen Ergebnissen der Akzeptanz- und Wirkungsforschung ab, durch die u.a. sichergestellt sein muß, daß der Einsatz von Expertensystemen keine negativen Auswirkungen auf die Vertrauenssphäre zwischen Arzt und Patient hat.

Literatur

[1] Atkins, J.: Prototype and production rules: An approach to knowledge representation for hypotheses formation. In: Proc. of the 6th Intern. Joint Conf. on Artificial Intelligence, S. 1-3, Tokio, 1979.

[2] Bennet, J., Creary, L., Engelmore, R.S., Melosh, R.: SACON: a knowledge-based consultant for structural analysis. Stanford Univ., Dept. of Computer Science, Memo HPP-78-28, 1978.

[3] Bobrow, D., Collins, D.A. (eds.): Representation and understanding: Studies in ve Cognitive Science. New York: Academic 1975.

[4] Boden, M.A.: Artificial Intelligence and natural man.Hassocks: Harvester 1977.

[5] Buchanan, B.G., Feigenbaum, E.A.: DENDRAL and META-DENDRAL: Their applications dimensions. In: Artificial Intelligence, 11, S. 5-24, 1978.

[6] Chandrasekaran, B., Gomez, F., Mittal, S., Smith, J.: An approach to medical diagnosis based on conceptual structures. In: Proc. of the 6th Intern. Joint Conf. on Artificial Intelligence, S. 134-142, Tokio, 1979.

[7] Clancey, W.J.: Tutoring rules for guiding a case method dialogue. In: Intern. Journal of Man-Machine Studies, 11, S. 25-49, 1979.

[8] Davis, R.: Applications of meta-level knowledge to the construction, maintenance and use of large knowledge bases. Stanford Univ., Ph.D. Thesis, 1976.

[9] Fagan, L.M., Kunz, J.C., Feigenbaum, E.A., Osborn, J.J.: Representation of dynamic clinical knowledge: measurement interpretation in the intensive care unit. In: Proc.of the 6th Intern. Joint Conf. on Artificial Intelligence, S. 260-262, Tokio, 1979.

[10] Feigenbaum, E.A.: Expert systems: looking back and looking ahead. In: Wilhelm, R. (ed.): GI-10. Jahrestagung 1980, Saarbrücken, Informatik-Fachberichte Nr. 33, Heidelberg: Springer, S. 1-14, 1980.

[11] Findler, N.V. (ed.): Associative networks. Representation and use of knowledge by computers. New York: Academic, 1979

[12] Freiherr, G.: The seeds of artificial intelligence: SUMEX-AIM. NIH Publication No. 80-2071, März 1980.

[13] Goldberg, R.N., Weiss, S.M.: An experimental translation of a large expert knowledge-base. Rutgers Univ., Dept. of Computer Science, Technical Report CBM-TR-110, Mai 1980.

[14] Greiner, R., Lenat, D.B.: A representation language language. In: Proc. of the 1st annual national Conf. on Artificial Intelligence, Stanford, S. 165-169, 1980.

[15] Grosz, B.J.: The representation and use of focus in a system for understanding dialogs. In: Proc. of the 5th Intern. Joint Conf. on Artificial Intelligence, Cambridge, S. 67-76, 1977.

[16] Haas, N., Hendrix, G.G.: An approach to aquiring and applying knowledge. In: Proc. of the 1st annual national Conf. on Artificial Intelligence, Stanford, S. 235-239, 1980.

[17] v. Hahn, W., Hoeppner, W., Jameson, A., Wahlster, W.: The anatomy of the natural language dialogue system HAM-RPM. In: Bolc, L. (ed.): Natural Language Based Computer Systems. München/London: Hanser/Macmillan, S. 119-235, 1980.

[18] Hart, P., Duda, R.: PROSPECTOR - computer-based consultation system for mineral exploration. SRI International, Menlo Park, AI Center, Tech. Note 155, 1977.

[19] Heiser, J.F., Brooks, R.E.: A computerized psychopharmacology advisor. In: Proc. of the 4th annual Artificial Intelligence in Medicine Workshop, Rutgers Univ., S. 68-69, Juni 1978.

[20] Hewitt, C.: Viewing control structures as patterns of passing messages. In: Artificial Intelligence, 8, S. 323-364, 1977.

[21] Kulikowski, C.A.: Artificial intelligence methods and systems for medical consultation. In: IEEE Transact. on Pattern Analysis and Machine Intelligence, VOL-PAMI-2, 5, S. 464-476, 1980.

[22] McCarty, L.T., Sridharan, N.S., Sangster, B.C.: The implementation of TAXMAN II: An experiment in AI and legal reasoning. Rutgers Univ., Dept. of Computer Sc., Report LRP-TR-2, 1979.

[23] McDermott, D.: The last survey of representation of knowledge. In: Proc. of AISB/GI Conf. on Artificial Intelligence, Hamburg, S. 206-221, 1978.

[24] McDermott, J.: R1: an expert in the computer systems domain. In: Proc. of the 1st annual national Conf. on Artificial Intelligence, Stanford, S. 269-271, 1980.

[25] van Melle, W.: A domain-independent production-rule system for consultation programs. In: Proc. of the 6th Intern. Joint Conference on Artificial Intelligence, S. 923-925, Tokio, 1979.

[26] Michie, D. (ed.): Expert systems in the micro-electronic age. Edinburgh: Univ. Press 1979.

[27] Mylopoulos, J.: An overview of knowledge representation. In: SIGART Newsletter, No. 74, S. 5-12, 1981.

[28] Nii, H.P., Aiello, N.: AGE (Attempt to generalize): A knowledge-based program for building knowledge-based programs. In: Proc. of the 6th Intern. Joint Conf. on Artificial Intelligence, S. 645-655, Tokio, 1979.

[29] Nilsson, N.: Principles of artificial intelligence. Palo Alto: Tioga 1980.

[30] Osborn, J., Fagan, L., Fallat, R., McClung, D., Mitchell, R.: Managing data from respiratory measurement. In: Medical Instrumentation, 13, 6, 1979.

[31] Politakis, P., Weiss, S.M.: A system for empirical experimentation with expert knowledge. Rutgers Univ., Dept. of Computer Sc., Submitted to IJCAI-81.

[32] Pople, H.: The formation of composite hypotheses in diagnostic problem solving. In: Proc. of the 5th Inten. Joint Conf. on Artificial Intelligence, Cambridge, S. 1030-1037, 1977.

[33] Raulefs, P.: Actors und Agenten. In: Rundbrief der Fachgruppe Künstliche Intelligenz der GI, Nr. 20, S. 16-18, 1980.

[34] Raulefs, P.: Expert systems: state of the art and future prospects. In: Siekmann, J. (ed.): Proc. of the 5th German Workshop on Artificial Intelligence, Bad Honnef, Informatik-Fachberichte, Heidelberg: Springer 1981

[35] Rich, E.: Building and exploiting user models. Carnegie-Mellon-Univ., Dept. of Computer Science, Report CMU-CS-79-119, 1979.

[36] Sacerdoti, E.D.: A structure for plans and behavior. New York: Elsevier 1977.

[37] Shortliffe, E.H.: Computer-based medical consultations: MYCIN. N.Y.: Elsevier 1976.

[38] Stallman, R.M., Sussman, G.J.: Forward reasoning and dependency-directed backtracking in a system for computer-aided circuit analysis. In: Artificial Intelligence, 9, S. 135-196, 1977.

[39] Swartout, W.R.: A digitalis therapy advisor with explanations. MIT Lab. for Comp. Sc., Report TR-176, 1977.

[40] Szolovits, P., Pauker, S.G.: Categorical and probabilistic reasoning in medical diagnosis. In: Artificial Intelligence, 11, S. 115-144, 1978.

[41] Trigoboff, M., Kulikowski, C.A.: IRIS: A system for the propagation of inferences in a semantic net. In: Proc. of the 5th Intern. Joint Conf. on Artificial Intelligence, S. 274-280, Cambridge, 1977.

[42] Wahlster, W.: Die Repräsentation von vagem Wissen in natürlichsprachlichen Systemen der Künstlichen Intelligenz. FB Informatik der Univ. Hamburg, Bericht IfI-HH-B-38/77, 1977.

[43] Wahlster, W.: Natürlichsprachliche KI-Systeme: Entwicklungsstand und Forschungsperspektive. In: Siekmann, J. (ed.): Proc. of the 5th German Workshop on Artificial Intelligence, Bad Honnef, Informatik-Fachberichte, Heidelberg: Springer 1981.

[44] Wahlster, W.: Natürlichsprachliche Argumentation in Dialogsystemen. KI-Verfahren zur Rekonstruktion und Erklärung approximativer Inferenzprozesse. Informatik-Fachberichte, Heidelberg: Springer 1981.

[45] Waterman, D., Hayes-Roth, F. (eds.): Pattern-directed inference systems. New York: Academic 1978.

[46] Weinreb, D., Moon, D.: The Lisp Machine Manual. 4th Edition, Symbolic Inc., Woodland Hills, Order No. LMM-4, Juni 1981.

[47] Weiss, S., Kulikowski, C., Amarel, S., Safir, A.: A model-based method for computer-aided medical decision-making. In: Artif. Intelligence, 11, S. 145-172, 1978.

[48] Weiss, S., Kulikowski, C.: EXPERT: A system for developing consultation models. In: Proc. of the 6th Intern. J. Conf. on Artif. Intelligence, S. 942-947, 1979.

[49] Winograd, T.: Extended inference modes in reasoning by computer systems. In: Artificial intelligence, 13, S. 5-26, 1980.

[50] Winston, P.H.: Artificial intelligence. Reading: Addison-Wesley 1977.

[51] Winston, P.H., Horn, B.K.P.: LISP. Reading: Addison-Wesley 1981.

PROBLEME DER STANDARDISIERUNG MEDIZINISCHER DATEN AM BEISPIEL DER ERSTELLUNG EINER STANDARDISIERTEN SYMPTOMANAMNESE

J.R. Möhr, H.-J. Seelos, W. Raufmann und M. Rothemund

Universität Heidelberg, Arbeitsgemeinschaft für Gemeinschaftsaufgaben der Krankenversicherungen Essen, Medizinische Hochschule Hannover, Fachhochschule Heilbronn

Zusammenfassung

Über die Bedeutung der Anamnese im ärztlichen Entscheidungsprozess gibt es keinen Zweifel. Verschiedene Ansätze sind gemacht worden, die Anamnese zu automatisieren.
Im Rahmen des Projektes DVDIS wurde ein Konzept für eine Screeninganamnese zur Unterstützung der begutachtenden Ärzte realisiert und an fast 6000 Patienten getestet.
Konstruktionsverfahren und Ergebnisse der Untersuchung werden dargestellt und mit den Ergebnissen vorheriger Studien verglichen.

1. Einleitung

Klassifikations- und Entscheidungsalgorithmen haben sich in der automatischen Zellerkennung in der Hämatologie und bei der automatischen Interpretation von EKG-Signalen durchgesetzt. Sie stehen damit für Routineanwendungen in eng begrenzten Bereichen der spezialisierten Medizin zur Verfügung. Die breite Alltagsmedizin profitiert davon recht wenig, obwohl auch hier eine Unterstützung zu einer Verbesserung von Effizienz und EffEktivität sinnvoll wäre. Im folgenden soll durch eine Übersicht über Untersuchungen, welche die automatisierte Anamnese betreffen, aufgezeigt werden, welche Probleme in diesem Bereich existieren und damit eine Anregung zu ihrer Lösung gegeben werden.

2. Gegenstand und Bedeutung der Anamnese

Die Effektivität der ärztlichen Behandlung wird in vielen wichtigen Situationen entscheidend von der Anamnese bestimmt:

- von der Erhebung der Vorgeschichte des Patienten und seiner Erkrankung,
- von der Kenntnis dieser Vorgeschichte und
- von der Qualität der Dokumente, in denen diese Vorgeschichte festgehalten wird.

Die wichtigste, die diagnostische Funktion, soll in der folgenden Darstellung im Vordergrund stehen. Auf sie wurde früher mehrfach hingewiesen (5,6,7,11).

Wie Untersuchungen zeigten, wird sowohl bei den Allgemeinmedizinern und praktischen Ärzten als auch bei den Klinikern aus der Anamnese der grösste Teil der zur Diagnostik notwendigen medizinischen Information gewonnen (4,10).

Nun ist die Anamnese nicht nur ein hinsichtlich der Diagnostik informatives Instrument, sie ist auch ein billiges Instrument - insbesondere vom Standpunkt des Patienten aus. Viele Patienten empfinden die anamnestische Exploration als angenehme Aussprache. Selbst wenn die emotionale Atmosphäre vom Arzt in andere Richtung gesteuert wird - was gelegentlich sinnvoll ist - ist die Aussprache noch weit weniger belastend als eine körperliche Untersuchung, eine Blutentnahme, Röntgenuntersuchung oder viele andere Untersuchungsmöglichkeiten und diagnostische Eingriffe.

Für den Arzt ist die Bilanz nicht ganz so positiv, denn die Erhebung einer Anamnese kostet Zeit. In der eingangs geschilderten Situation der Allgemeinmedizin wird diese Zeit über Jahre in kleinen Portionen von wenigen Minuten pro Kontakt aufgebracht. Als Ergebnis sammelt sich das an, was dem Arzt als Vorinformation zur Verfügung steht.

In vielen anderen Situationen besteht diese Vorinformation nicht und es muss Zeit aufgewandt werden, um die Information zu erfragen. Der tatsächlich erforderliche Zeitaufwand ist wesentlich abhängig von Erfahrung und Geschick des behandelnden Arztes. Insgesamt ist also aus der Sicht des Arztes die Anamnese ein aufwendiges Verfahren. Die erforderliche Zeit ist in manchen Situationen schwer aufzubringen, das Ergebnis ist nur bei ausreichend erfahrenen - bei hohen Ansprüchen auch nur bei ausreichend begabten - Ärzten verlässlich.

Der Mangel an Objektivität, Vollständigkeit und Auswertbarkeit der freien Anamnese hat in den vergangenen 3 Jahrzehnten dazu geführt, die anamnestische Technik zu verbessern und durch standardisierte Verfahren zu ergänzen. Unter diesen ist insbesonders der Einsatz von Fragebogen mit und ohne Computerunterstützung verbreitet angewendet worden (9). In einem Gesundheitssystem, das die Einflussnahme auf verbreitete und volkswirtschaftlich bedeutungsvolle Krankheiten in den Vordergrund stellt, sollten diese Techniken weiterhin verbessert werden. In der Beeinflussung der besonders wichtigen Krankheitsgruppen (Herz/Kreislauferkrankungen, bösartige Neubildungen, rheumatische Erkrankungen, Mutter- und Säuglingssterblichkeit (3)) kommt den Massnahmen der Prävention und der Langzeitbehandlung besondere Bedeutung zu. Dementsprechend ist in zahlreichen Empfehlungen zu Gesundheitsprogrammen auf die Notwendigkeit zur

- Verbesserung der Datenlage und Information im Gesundheitswesen (3, S.40),
- systematischen Überprüfung vorhandener Früherkennungsmassnahmen auf Wirksamkeit und Wirtschaftlichkeit (3, S.24),
- Entwicklung verbesserter Verfahren und neuer Techniken für die Früherkennung mit gutem Kosten-Nutzen-Verhältnis (3, S.24)
- Entwicklung von Methoden zur
  -- Vergleichbarkeit von Befunden und
  -- Validierung von Diagnoseinstrumenten

hingewiesen worden. Insbesondere sind auch von den im Rahmen der grossen Krebskonferenz gebildeten Fachbereichkommissionen Empfehlungen zur Verbesserung auf dem Gebiet der Dokumentation und der anamnestischen Diagnostik verabschiedet worden.

3. Wege zur Standardisierung der Anamnese

3.1 Bisherige Erfahrungen

Die ersten systematischen Untersuchungen über die Verwendbarkeit und den Nutzen von Anamnesefragebogen in der Medizin wurden von BRODMAN et al. Ende der vierziger Jahre publiziert (1). Sie lösten mit zunehmender Verfügbarkeit von Computern in den 50er und 60er Jahren eine vielfältige Aktivität aus (für Literaturübersichten vergleiche 9,12,13), die zu folgenden wichtigen Ergebnissen führten:

- Patienten sind willens und in der Lage, umfangreiche Fragenkataloge, auch unter Bewältigung technischer Schwierigkeiten - etwa der Handhabung von Datenendgeräten - zu bearbeiten.
- Der Wert der so erfassten Daten kann für den Arzt gross sein, ist es aber selten, weshalb die meisten Fragen nicht akzeptiert werden.
  --Viele Fragenkataloge enthalten Fragen, die für den Arzt irrelevant sind.
  --Die Fragen sind häufig so formuliert, dass sie vom Patienten nur schlecht zu beantworten sind.
- Der Aufwand für die Erstellung eines Fragebogens wird meist unterschätzt. Einfache Fragensammlungen lassen sich leicht erstellen, bringen aber kaum verwendbare Ergebnisse. Sorgfältige Entwicklung erfordert einen sehr erheblichen Aufwand.
- Ein Hauptproblem ist die Darstellung der erfassten Information für

den Arzt. Die Auflistung der gegebenen Antworten ist nicht ausreichend, da deren Interpretation schwieriger ist, als die Erhebung der benötigten Information im anamnestischen Gespräch.

3.2 Zu lösende Probleme

Der Versuch, die vom Patienten verfügbare Information für den Arzt sicherer und mit weniger Aufwand als bisher verfügbar zu machen, setzt daher die Lösung der folgenden Probleme voraus:

1. Spezifikation eines auf den Informationsbedarf des Arztes abgestimmten Frageninstrumentes.
2. Formulierung der Fragen in der Form, dass die vom Arzt benötigte Information vom Patienten erfasst wird.
3. Verarbeitung der Antworten in eine den Bedürfnissen des Arztes adäquate Form der Präsentation.

Diese drei Probleme müssen integrierend gelöst werden. Eine Konsequenz ist die Abkehr von einfachen Fragebogen, auf denen Fragen präsentiert und Antworten durch Ankreuzen vom Patienten ausgewählt werden. Die Lösung ist auf unterschiedliche Weise denkbar, hat aber jeweils in mehrfachem Zusammenhang den Einsatz von Datenverarbeitungsanlagen zur Voraussetzung. In der Folge sollen bisher durchgeführte Versuche zur Lösung der Probleme skizziert und die Ergebnisse diskutiert werden.

3.3 Lösungswege

3.3.1 Spezifikation des Fragenkataloges

Da prinzipiell fast jedes Ereignis im Leben eines Menschen im Rahmen einer Anamneseerhebung Bedeutung erlangen kann, tendieren die aufgestellten Fragenkataloge leicht dazu, sehr umfangreich zu werden. Wir hatten daher vor einigen Jahren vorgeschlagen, zunächst den Informationsbedarf des Arztes zu definieren (8,9) und dann von daher zur Formulierung der Fragen überzugehen. Die Definition des Informationsbedarfs kann als eine Anzahl von Entscheidungen spezifiziert werden, die vom Arzt zu treffen sind. Es sollte natürlich berücksichtigt werden, ob für diese Entscheidungen vom Patienten Information verfügbar gemacht werden kann.

Dieses Verfahren wurde von BUENTE konsequent für die Spezifikation einer Basisanamnese für allgemeinmedizinische Belange eingesetzt (2) und das Ergebnis von WEFER an ca.300 Patienten erprobt (15). Zur Definition des Informationsbedarfs diente eine Liste von etwa 60 Problemen

(Krankheiten, Diagnosen), die von Allgemeinärzten erarbeitet worden war. Hierzu wurden von 7 Ärzten über 1500 Fragen formuliert, die anschliessend kondensiert, ausgewählt, geordnet und aufeinander abgestimmt wurden, wodurch ein Fragenkatalog von 195 Fragen resultierte, der von Patienten in der Erprobungsphase durch Ankreuzen von Antworten bearbeitet wurde.

Die Bewertung der Ergebnisse war in mehrfacher Hinsicht verblüffend. Der Fragenumfang war identisch mit dem des Fragenkataloges von BRODMAN (1). Der Vergleich mit einem früher von uns an der Medizinischen Hochschule Hannover erprobten Fragebogen (MSHF-VIII)(9), der unter Bezug auf Fragensammlungen entstanden war, zeigte, dass die Fragenkomplexe nicht mehr enthalten waren, die bei Ärzten für wenig relevant gehalten wurden (9). Dieser Effekt war eingetreten, ohne dass auf andere Fragebogen und die damit erzielten Ergebnisse direkt Bezug genommen wurde.

Weiterhin konnte durch die Untersuchungen von WEFER (15) nachgewiesen werden, dass die Akzeptanz bei Patienten deutlich gegenüber unserem früher erprobten Fragebogen (MSHF-VIII) angestiegen war. Es fielen nicht nur die Antworten auf Fragen zur Verständlichkeit, zur Belastung etc., sehr positiv aus. Es sank auch der Anteil fehlender Antworten von ca. 10% im alten Fragebogen auf ca. 3% in dem von BUENTE.

Besonders überraschend empfanden wir das Ergebnis des Vergleichs mit dem Fragebogen von BRODMAN. Es zeigte sich, dass trotz praktisch gleichen Gesamtumfanges und als sehr ähnlich anzunehmender Zielsetzung nur 1/3 der Fragen als inhaltlich gleich angesehen werden konnten, während 2/3 der Fragen unterschiedliche Themen betrafen. Seinerzeit interpretierten wir diesen Befund als Indiz dafür, dass geringe Unterschiede in der Zielsetzung - etwa Unterschiede in der epidemiologischen Situation in den USA in den 40er Jahren bei BRODMAN einerseits und in Deutschland in den 70er Jahren bei BUENTE andererseits - dazu führen, dass deutliche Unterschiede im Fragenspektrum resultieren.

Insgesamt schien danach der eingeschlagene Weg erfolgversprechend. Allerdings musste die Frage zunächst offen bleiben, ob der von den Ärzten definierte Informationsbedarf abgedeckt wurde. Erkenntnisse hierüber ergaben sich erst in einer weiteren Untersuchung.

3.3.2 Erfassung des ärztlichen Informationsbedarfs

Eine Untersuchung, die von SEELOS durchgeführt wurde, ergab die Gelegenheit, die skizzierten Ergebnisse zu überprüfen und zu erweitern. Ziel war die Konstruktion einer Screening-Anamnese für den

Vertrauensärztlichen Dienst (VäD), den gemeinsamen Gutachterdienst der gesetzlichen Krankenversicherung. Er verfügt (Stand 1980) über 579 Dienststellen im Bereich von 17 Landesversicherungsanstalten (LVA) und der Allgemeinen Ortskrankenkasse (AOK), Berlin. In ihm sind 989 Vertrauensärzte für rund 90% der Gesamtbevölkerung der BRD (35 Mio. Versicherte, 22 Mio. mitversicherte Familienangehörige) zuständig, die Arbeitsunfähigkeit, Verordnung von Heil- und Hilfsmitteln, Rehabilitationsmassnahmen und dergleichen zu begutachten.
Für diesen Bereich wurde nach dem geschilderten Verfahren ein weiterer Fragenkatalog in drei Stufen (Version I, Version II, Version III) entwickelt und in einem Grossversuch mit über 7000 Probanden und 5650 auswertbaren Fragebogen erprobt. Dabei zeigten sich folgende interessante Resultate:

- Der resultierende Katalog hatte wiederum grössenordnungsmässig den gleichen Umfang wie der von BRODMAN und der von BUENTE (184 Fragen).
- Die Gütekriterien hinsichtlich der Akzeptanz durch Patienten waren mit denen von WEFER vergleichbar oder besser (Reliabilität der Fragen Version II durchschnittlich 0,89, Anteil fehlender Antworten Version II 1% mit n=214, Version III 1,9% mit n=5650).
- Nur 40% der Fragen von SEELOS waren in dem Katalog von BUENTE enthalten. In diesem Falle konnte auch das Problemspektrum verglichen werden. 87% der bei BUENTE verwendeten Probleme waren in dem bei SEELOS spezifizierten Katalog enthalten, umgekehrt lag die Relation bei 71%. Wiederum resultierte also aus vergleichsweise geringen Unterschieden in der Zielsetzung ein deutlich unterschiedliches Fragenspektrum.

Die wesentlichen Vorteile unserer neueren Untersuchung lagen aber darin, dass die hier vorliegenden institutionellen Voraussetzungen die Durchführung des Grossversuchs mit Anwendung des Anamneseschemas in 54 vertrauenärztliche Dienststellen gestatteten und insbesondere Gelegenheit gaben, zur Beantwortung der Frage Stellung zu nehmen, ob und inwieweit das spezifizierte Problemspektrum vom erarbeiteten Fragenkatalog abgedeckt wird. Dazu wurden aus den Antwortmustern Sensitivität und Spezifität sowie der U-Wert - ein informationstheoretisch begründetes Mass (9,12,14) - für jede Frage zu jeder Problemkategorie mit mehr als 10 Fällen im Material berechnet. Für 17 Problemkategorien von 94 spezifizierten waren weniger als 10 Fälle verfügbar. Das im Feldversuch erfasste Fallmaterial war dabei in seiner

Verteilung dem Fallmaterial des VäD von 1979 weitgehend ähnlich. Die Ergebnisse waren wiederum überraschend, allerdings eher im Sinne einer Enttäuschung hinsichtlich der gehegten Erwartungen.
Die Problemkategorien, für die die höchsten Validitätsmasse einzelner Fragen erreicht wurden, sind (in absteigender Reihenfolge) in Tabelle 1 angegeben. Wie hieraus ersichtlich ist, sind die gut erfassbaren Problemkategorien dadurch gekennzeichnet, dass sie abgrenzbar sind, dass die durch sie erzeugten Symptome eindrucksvoll und handfest greifbar sind, und dass die Probleme im allgemeinen Sprachgebrauch so verwurzelt sind, dass man den Patienten gegebenfalls direkt fragen kann, ob das Problem bei ihm besteht, bzw. ob die Diagnose bei ihm gestellt wurde. Die überwiegende Zahl der Probleme ist nicht so charakterisiert und ist daher schlecht erfassbar.

Problem Nr.	Problem-Kategorie	n	Max U-Wert	Frage Nr.	Frage
29	Asthma bronchiale	72	0,48	113	Haben Sie Asthma
51	Adnexitis (Eileiterentzündung)	29	0,33	179	Haben Sie Schmer zen im Unterleib
53	Erkrankung der Mamma	17	0,23	102	Haben Sie Verhaer tungen in der Brust beobachtet
20	Hypertonie	723	0,21	122	Wurden Sie wegen zu hohem Blut druck behandelt
28	Chronische Bronchitis	212	0,20	114	Leiden Sie unter Husten

Tabelle 1: Die am besten erfassten Problemkategorien in der Reihenfolge der maximal erreichten U-Werte.

Insgesamt zeigte sich, dass die Ergebnisse qualitativ nur wenig vom früher am Datenmaterial des relativ arbiträr spezifizierten Fragenkataloges MSHF-VIII erhobenen Befundes (9) abwichen. Wie

seinerzeit am begrenzten Untersuchungsmaterial von 524 Probanden ergab sich wiederum, dass nur wenige Problemkategorien hinlänglich sicher erfasst werden. Zudem waren es weitgehend dieselben Problemkategorien, sodass es von daher den Anschein hat, als ob der durch den aufwendigen Prozess der Fragenspezifikation erhoffte Gewinn an Validität nicht eingetreten ist.
Dabei ist noch zu berücksichtigen, dass die verwendeten Validitätsmasse (U-Wert, Sensitivität, Spezifität) selbst eine begrenzte Validität haben. Das wird deutlich, wenn man die mit den formulierten Fragen verbundene ärztliche Intention (Bedeutung der Frage für eine gegebene Problemkategorie, für die sie vom Ärzteteam spezifiziert war) vergleicht mit der Beziehung zwischen Frage und Problemen, die durch die Validitätsmasse ausgewiesen wird. Das kommt insbesondere dadurch zustande, dass im Fallmaterial Kombinationen von Krankheiten vorkommen. Wenn nun eine seltene Erkrankung immer mit einer anderen häufigeren assoziiert ist, weisen die verwendeten Schätzer eine hohe Validität aus. Insgesamt sind etwa 70% der als valide ausgewiesenen Assoziationen von Fragen mit Problemkategorien in Einklang mit der ärztlichen Erfahrung, während bei 30% Abweichungen vorkommen.

4. Diskussion

Der geschilderte Ansatz hat einerseits Erfolge, andererseits Enttäuschungen erbracht:

- Erfolgreich war eine Optimierung des Interface mit dem Patienten, die durch 2 unabhängige Versuche mit fast gleichen Resultaten nachgewiesen werden konnte,sowie
- die Tatsache, dass man Information darüber bekommen hat, ob der von den Ärzten definierte Informationsbedarf vom Anamneseschema abgedeckt wurde.
- Enttäuschend war das Ausbleiben einer umfassenden Verbesserung der Erfassung der für den Arzt wichtigen Informationen, sowie die Lösung der Probleme einer Datenrepräsentation.
- Da eine kompakte Präsentation wenig valider Informationen erfahrungsgemäss eher Verwirrung stiftet, als dass sie nützt, ist insbesondere auch die Frage einer verbesserten Dokumentation der erhobenen Daten für den Arzt weiterhin offen.

Gleichwohl ist das Ergebnis unserer Arbeiten ein Anamneseschema im Sinne eines diagnostischen Screeninginstrumentes verfügbar, welches sich hinsichtlich der geforderten Gütekriterien besser verhält, als die bisher beschriebenen. Insbesonders lässt sich mit der angewandten

Methodik angeben, was der Fragenkatalog in Bezug auf die unterschiedlichen Problemkategorien leistet.
Zwar ist es möglich, durch Anwendung differenzierter statistischer Techniken, die insbesondere die Beziehung zwischen Problemkombinationen und Antwortmustern berücksichtigen, eine graduelle Verbesserung zu erreichen. Es stellt sich jedoch die Frage, ob der dem Verfahren zugrunde liegende statistische Ansatz prinzipiell ausreicht. Von den Anwendungsfeldern, in denen dieser statistische Ansatz fruchtbar war, wie etwa der der automatischen Klassifikation von Zellbildern und Elektrokardiogrammen, unterscheidet sich das hier bearbeitete Problemgebiet in mehrfacher Hinsicht:

- Der Entscheidungsraum ist nicht einfach abzugrenzen und aufzuteilen.
- Insbesondere ist eine erschöpfende Aufteilung in diskrete Klassen schwierig.
- Die Einheiten des Entscheidungsraumes wie auch die zur Klassifikation herangezogenen sind unscharf definiert.
- Der Grad dieser Unschärfe variiert.

Es erscheint daher nötig, dass zur wirksamen Verbesserung der Situation grundsätzlich andere Wege untersucht werden. Diese könnten etwa darin bestehen, die gesuchte Information vom Patienten durch situationsgemäss ausgewählte und an das Verständnisniveau hochgradig angepasste Fragen umfassend abzuklären. Dabei könnte auch der Entscheidungsspielraum des Arztes differenziert berücksichtigt werden. Unter Umständen bieten die modernen Techniken der künstlichen Intelligenz hier eine Lösungsmöglichkeit. Allerdings wäre dazu die Frage sorgfältig zu untersuchen, ob gegenüber dem skizzierten erreichten Zustand ein Gewinn möglich ist, der die umfassende Überarbeitung aller bisherigen Konzepte vom Interface mit den Beteiligten bis zur Lösung der Datenschutzproblematik sinnvoll erscheinen lässt.

LITERATUR

(1) Brodman, K., Erdman, A.J., Wolff, H.G.: Cornell Medical Index. An Adjunct to Medical Interview. J.A.M.A. 140, (1949) 530-534

(2) Buente, W.: Zielorientierte Konstruktion eines Anamnese fragebogens. Dissertation, Med.Hochschule Hannover, 1976

(3) Bundesminister für Forschung und Technologie. Programm der Bundesregierung zur Förderung der Forschung und Entwicklung im Dienste der Gesundheit 1978-81. (BMFT: Bonn 1978)

(4) Hampton et al. : Relative Contribution of History Taking, Physical Examination and Laboratory Investigation to Diagnosis and Management of Medical Outpatients. Br.Med.J.Z. (1975) 486-489

(5) Hartmann, F.: Die Anamnese. Klinik der Gegenwart 10 (1965) 691-718

(6) Hegglin, R.: Differentialdiagnose Innerer Krankheiten. (Thieme: Stuttgart 1966)

(7) Lauda, E.: Die interne Diagnostik in ihrer geschichtlichen Entwicklung aus ihren Anfängen bis zur Gegenwart. Med.Klin. 53 (1958) 1157-1166

(8) Möhr, J.R.: Methoden zur Konstruktion und Bewertung von Frage bögen zur Erfassung einer Basisanamnese. Verh.Dtsch.Ges.Inn.Med. 80 (1974) 930-932

(9) Möhr, J.R.: Computer Assisted Medical History. In: Reichertz, p.l., Goos, G., (Hrsg.): Informatics and Medicine. An Advanced Course. (Springer: Berlin, Heidelberg, New York 1977) 460-578

(10) Möhr, J.R.. Haehn, K.D. (Hrsg.): Verdenstudie: Strukturanalyse allgemeinmedizinischer Praxen (Deutscher Ärzteverlag: Köln 1977)

(11) Nüssel, E.: Das ärztliche Gespräch und die Anamnese. Deutsch. med.Journ. 19 (1968) 45-51

(12) Raufmann, W.: Untersuchungen zur Entwicklung eines adaptiven lernfähigen Systems zur automatisierten Klassifikation medizinischer Daten. Diplomarbeit, Med.Hochschule Hannover (1976)

(13) Seelos, H.-J.: Computerunterstützte Symptomanamnese - Design und Realisierung für den Bereich des vertrauensärztlichen Dienstes. Dissertation, Heidelberg, in Vorbereitung

(14) Sterling, T., Glaser, M., Habermann, S., Pollak, S.: Robot Data Screening: A Solution to Multivariate Type Problems in Biological and Social Sciences. Domm.A.C.M. 9 (1966) 512-532

(15) Wefer, B.: Anamneseerhebung in einer Allgemeinpraxis, Ergebnisse der Erprobung einer zielorientierten Fragenbogenkonstruktion. Dissertation, Med.Hochschule, Hannover (1978)

MODELLUNTERSUCHUNGEN ZUM FLÜSSIGKEITSHAUSHALT DES MENSCHLICHEN KÖRPERS

A. Schmidt
Hautklinik, Klinikum Nürnberg

B. Schmidt
Informatik IV, Universität Erlangen-Nürnberg

Zusammenfassung:

Die Regelungsmechanismen, die den Flüssigkeitshaushalt des menschlichen Körpers steuern, sind von außerordentlicher Komplexität. Die Wirkungszusammenhänge und ihre wechselseitigen Abhängigkeiten sind für den Arzt oft nicht mehr überschaubar.
Das vorgestellte Simulationsmodell erlaubt es, die wesentlichen Einflußgrößen und Abhängigkeiten, die den Flüssigkeitshaushalt bestimmen, darzustellen und zu untersuchen. Es ist geplant, insbesondere den Einfluß von krankhaften Veränderungen zu analysieren, wie sie zum Beispiel bei Verbrennungen auftreten.

Das Modell berücksichtigt:

- Kreislaufsystem
- Nierenfunktion
- Hormonsteuerung
- Elektrolythaushalt

Es werden Ergebnisse von Untersuchungen mit Hilfe des Modells vorgestellt.

1. Das Einsatzfeld des Simulationsmodells

Die Hautklinik der Städtischen Krankenanstalten Nürnberg besitzt eine Station zur Behandlung von Verbrennungen. Bei der Behandlung von Verbrennungen spielt die Bekämpfung des Schockzustandes aufgrund von Flüssigkeitsmangel eine bedeutende Rolle. In diesem Zusammenhang entstand das Simulationsmodell für Modelluntersuchungen des Flüssigkeitshaushaltes des menschlichen Körpers.

1.1 Das Modell als Hilfe bei Diagnose und Therapie

Die Regelungsmechanismen, die den Flüssigkeitshaushalt des menschlichen Körpers steuern, sind von außerordentlicher Vielfalt. Die Wirkungszusammenhänge und ihre wechselseitigen Abhängigkeiten sind für den Arzt oft nicht mehr überschaubar.
Bild 1 gibt einen Eindruck von der Komplexität der Abläufe.

Das hier vorgestellte Simulationsmodell erlaubt es, die Regelvorgänge innerhalb des menschlichen Körpers nachzuspielen. Das heißt, daß das Simulationsmodell die wesentlichen Einflußgrößen und Abhängigkeiten, die den Flüssigkeitshaushalt bestimmen, darstellen und untersuchen kann. Damit hat der Arzt die Möglichkeit, die Konsequenzen einer vorgeschlagenen Therapie vor dem tatsächlichen Einsatz am Modell zu überprüfen.

Bild 2 zeigt ein Beispiel. In diesem Fall wird dem Patienten 2,4 l Flüssigkeit innerhalb von 4 Stunden verabreicht. Die Konsequenzen für

* extrazelluläres Volumen
* extrazelluläre NaCl-Konzentration
* arteriellen Blutdruck
* Aldosteron-Spiegel
* Antidiuretische Hormon-Konzentration
* Urinausscheidungsrate

in Abhängigkeit der Zeit lassen sich am Modell darstellen.
Es ist geplant, das Simulationsmodell auf dem Klinikrechner zu implementieren, so daß Modellergebnisse auf dem Terminal am Krankenbett zugänglich sind.

1.2 Das Modell als integrierter Teil des geschlossenen rechnergesteuerten Intensiv-Therapie-Systems GRITS

An der Hautklinik der Städtischen Krankenanstalten Nürnberg wurde das geschlossene, rechnergesteuerte Intensiv-Therapie-System GRITS entwickelt. Aufgabe des Systems ist es, Infusionsautomaten so zu steuern, daß die für den Flüssigkeitshaushalt des menschlichen Körpers charakteristischen Parameter den Normbereich nicht verlassen. Die Steuerung der Infusionspumpen erfolgt mit Hilfe eines Prozeßrechners aufgrund von on-line ermittelten Meßdaten. Das Systems läuft bereits seit längerem im Routinebetrieb (/1/).

Jeder Regelungsvorgang verlangt ein Modell des zu regelnden Systems. Das Modell ermöglicht es hierbei, aus der Differenz zwischen Ist- und Sollwert die Art und Größe der erforderlichen Korrektur zu ermitteln. Es ist geplant, das Simulationsmodell in das Intensiv-Therapie-System GRITS zu integrieren.

2. Flüssigkeitshaushalt des menschlichen Körpers und Modellbildung

Modellbildung bedeutet in jedem Falle einen Abstraktionsprozeß, der aus der Vielgestaltigkeit des zu untersuchenden Systems die relevanten Größen extrahiert und von zufälligen Nebensächlichkeiten absieht.
Das auf diese Weise ermittelte theoretische Modell muß in einem nachfolgenden Schritt über die Implementierung in ein reales, ablauffähiges Modell umgesetzt werden.

2.1 Theoretische Modelle

Die Literatur kennt bereits eine größere Zahl theoretischer Modelle für den Flüssigkeitshaushalt des menschlichen Körpers. Sie unterscheiden sich im wesentlichen durch ihre Genauigkeit, d.h., durch die Anzahl der berücksichtigten Zustandsvariablen. Als Beispiel sei auf die Modelle von /2/, /3/ und /4/ verwiesen.
In der Regel vermögen ausführlichere Modelle das Systemverhalten exakter darzustellen, da sie eine größere Zahl von Einflußgrößen berücksichtigen. Dem Modellumfang werden jedoch durch die folgenden drei Überlegungen Grenzen gesetzt:

* Der Aufwand, der erforderlich ist, um ein Modell zu implementieren und zu betreiben, wächst nicht proportional zur erzielten Genauigkeit. Das heißt, daß von einer gewissen Grenze an ein geringfügiger Zuwachs an Modellgenauigkeit durch einen hohen Aufwand erkauft werden muß.
  Aufwand heißt im vorliegenden Fall auch Speicherplatzbedarf und Rechenzeit für den Ablauf des Modells auf der Rechenanlage der Klinik.
* Die Modellgenauigkeit hat sich an den Anforderungen der Praxis zu orientieren. Es kann nicht das Ziel sein, ein Modell zu entwickeln, das eine Variable sehr genau zu bestimmen vermag, wenn dem behandelndem Arzt bereits eine Trendanalyse genügt.
* Die Genauigkeit der Modellergebnisse hängt nicht nur von der Genauigkeit des Modells, sondern auch von der Genauigkeit der Eingabedaten ab. Es ist wiederum nicht sinnvoll, ein Modell zu entwickeln, dessen Fehler unter 10% liegt, wenn die Eingabedaten für das Modell selbst mit einem Fehler von z.B. 50% behaftet sind.

Die vorgenannten Überlegungen haben dazu geführt, daß zunächst das im Vergleich zu anderen theoretischen Modellen relativ einfache Modell von Cameron implementiert wurde.

2.2 Modellimplementierung

Das Modell von Cameron liegt zunächst als System von Differentialgleichungen vor. Es handelt sich also um ein reines zeitkontinuierliches Modell.
Das Modell mußte jedoch erweitert werden, um zeitdiskrete Vorgänge wie z.B. Medikamentengabe, Infusionsbeginn und dgl. erfassen zu können. Damit wird das Modell ein typischer Vertreter für kombinierte diskret-kontinuierliche Systeme.

Die Simulationstechnik hat in den letzten Jahren auf dem Gebiet der kombinierten Modelle beachtliche Fortschritte erzielt. So sind z.B. zahlreiche Simulationssprachen zur Behandlung kombinierter Modelle entwickelt worden (siehe /5/).

Das vorliegende Modell wurde mit Hilfe von GPSS-FORTRAN Version 3 implementiert. GPSS-FORTRAN Version 3 ist hierbei die erweiterte und verbesserte Fassung von GPSS-FORTRAN Version II (siehe /6/).

3. Modellbeschreibung und Modellergebnisse

Um die nachfolgenden Ergebnisse korrekt interpretieren zu können, ist eine kurze Modellbeschreibung erforderlich.

3.1 Die qualitativen Wechselwirkungen

Bild 1 zeigt die wesentlichen Abhängigkeiten. Ein Pfeil bedeutet hierbei eine Wirkung. Das Vorzeichen gibt an, ob eine Änderung der bewirkten Größe die abhängige Größe gleichsinnig oder gegensinnig beeinflußt.

Beispiel:
Bild 1 zeigt, daß eine Änderung des Plasma-Volumens eine Änderung der Plasma-Proteinkonzentration und eine Änderung des arteriellen Druckes zur Folge hat. Die Vorzeichen geben an, daß eine Erhöhung des Plasma-Volumens eine Erniedrigung der Protein-Konzentration und eine Erhöhung des Blutdruckes (Druckes im re. Vorhof) nach sich zieht.
Aus Bild 1 ist weiterhin ersichtlich, daß das Plasma-Volumen seinerseits von der Urinfluß-Rate, der Trink-Rate, der Lymphrückfluß-Rate und der kapillaren Filtrationsrate beeinflußt wird.
Die in Bild 1 dargestellten qualitativen Wechselwirkungen werden im Modell durch das Gleichungssystem quantifiziert. Einzelheiten hierzu findet man in /2/.

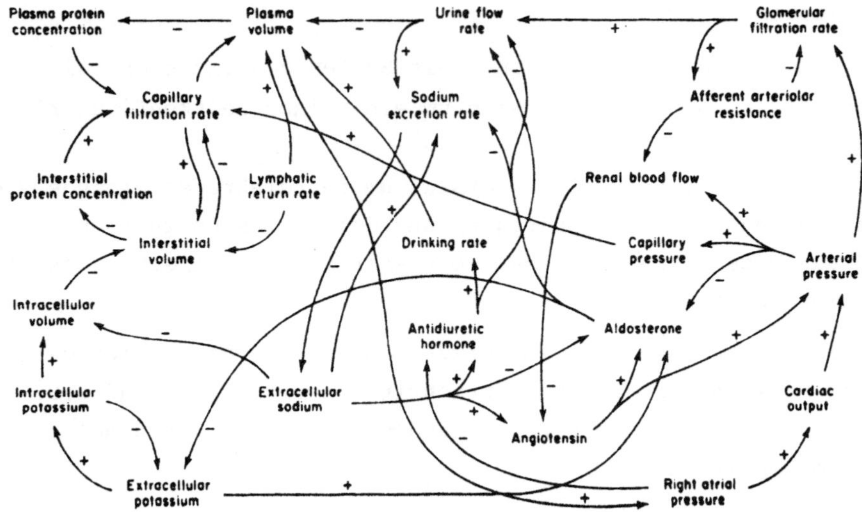

Bild 1: Qualitative Wechselwirkungen des Modells

3.2 Erhöhung der Flüssigkeitszufuhr

In der Regel wird es so sein, daß sich das Modell zu Anfang in einem stabilen Zustand befindet. Dieser Modellzustand entspricht dem Zustand des Patienten. Nun ist es möglich, durch Änderung einer oder mehrerer Variablen einen modifizierten Zustand im Modell herzustellen und den zeitlichen Ablauf zu verfolgen.

In Bild 2 wird z.B. von einer stabilen Situation ausgehend, die Flüssigkeitszufuhr einmalig für die Dauer von 4 Stunden um 2,4 l erhöht. Der Körper reagiert zunächst wie erwartet mit einer Erhöhung des extrazellulären Volumens (Plasma-Volumen + interstitielles Volumen) und der Urin-Ausscheidung, während die extrazelluläre NaCl-Konzentration und der antidiuretische Hormonspiegel abfallen. Der arterielle Blutdruck steigt während der Zeit der Flüssigkeitszufuhr geringfügig an. Bemerkenswert ist, daß sowohl das extrazelluläre Volumen als auch der arterielle Blutdruck nach Ende der Flüssigkeitszufuhr unter dem Normalwert liegen. Weiterhin fällt auf, daß der Körper erst nach 20 Stunden in den Ausgangszustand zurückgekehrt ist.

3.3 Erhöhung der NaCl-Zufuhr

Aufgrund der komplexen Rückkopplungsvorgänge ist der menschliche Körper in der Lage, Störungen auszuregeln und sich auf einen neuen stabilen Zustand einzustellen.
Bild 3 zeigt das Einschwingen auf den neuen Zustand nach der kontinuierlichen Erhöhung der NaCl-Zufuhr um den Faktor 4.

Alle gezeigten Ergebnisse sind in voller Übereinstimmung mit den Ergebnissen, die /2/ angibt.
Die Beispiele sollen stellvertretend zeigen, inwieweit ein Simulationsmodell den behandelnden Arzt unterstützen kann. Es ist wesentlich, daß das Modell dem behandelnden Arzt Informationen über das Verhalten des Patienten zur Verfügung stellt, die zur Diagnose und Therapie beitragen. Diese Informationen sind dem Arzt ohne Modell in der Regel auf Grund der verwickelten Rückkopplungsvorgänge innerhalb des menschlichen Körpers nicht zugänglich.

4. Modellakzeptanz

Die Probleme, die sich bei der Modellentwicklung und beim Modelleinsatz ergeben, sind beachtlich. Zunächst ist die Datenbeschaffung und Modellvalidierung schwierig. Da dieses Problem bekannt ist, soll an dieser Stelle nicht darauf eingegangen werden. Es sei angemerkt, daß auch unsere Arbeit in vollem Umfang hiervon betroffen wird.

Modellakzeptanz betrifft den Einsatz eines Modells in der Routine der Alltagspraxis. Die Frage, ob ein Modell tatsächlich auch in regelmäßigem Gebrauch zur Entscheidungsfindung eingesetzt wird, muß häufig negativ beantwortet werden. Man hat den Eindruck, daß viele, auch sehr aufwendige und anspruchsvolle Modelle ihr Dasein beenden, indem eine einmalige Modellbeschreibung publiziert wird, die niemand mehr liest.
Das Problem der Modellakzeptanz sollte in verstärktem Maße ins Bewußtsein gerückt werden.
Es ist das Ziel des vorliegenden Projektes, nicht nur ein Modell zu erstellen, sondern sich auch dafür einzusetzen, daß das Modell im Klinikbereich als Hilfsmittel der Diagnose und Therapie verwendet wird.

Die Probleme der Modellakzeptanz sind sehr vielfältig und können an dieser Stelle nicht erschöpfend behandelt werden. Es soll genügen, einige Punkte zur Diskussion zu stellen, deren Erfüllung die Modellakzeptanz verbessern könnte. (Es soll angemerkt werden, daß die Akzeptanz von Modellen viel mit der Akzeptanz von EDV-Systemen im allgemeinen zu tun hat. In einigen Aspekten ergeben sich Unterschiede).

* Einfachheit der Modelle
  Die Struktur des Modells muß überschaubar bleiben. Ein Modell, dessen Elemente und Funktionen dem Anwender nicht einsichtig sind, wird (mit Recht) auf Skepsis stoßen.

* Beschränkung bei den Eingabe-Daten
  Die Eingabedaten, die das Modell verlangt, müssen relativ einfach zu beschaffen sein. Außerdem muß sich der Datenumfang in Grenzen halten.

* Aufbereitung der Ausgabedaten
  Die Ergebnisse der Modelluntersuchung müssen so dargestellt werden, daß sie dem Anwender sowohl einen schnellen Überblick als auch gezielte Detailinformation ermöglichen. Übersichtlichkeit, leichte Lesbarkeit usw. sind hierbei selbstverständliche Anforderungen.

* Permanente Modellbetreuung
  Es sollte eine Fachkraft verfügbar sein, die das Modell kennt und die ständige Betreuung übernimmt.
  Häufig entstehen Modelle als wissenschaftliche Arbeiten an Hochschulen. Die Arbeit gilt mit der Fertigstellung des Modells als abgeschlossen. In der Regel verläßt der Autor die Hochschule, um sich auf einem anderen Arbeitsgebiet zu betätigen. Das Modell bleibt als Leiche zurück, um deren Wiederbelebung sich niemand kümmert.

* Praxisnahe Problemfelder für den Modelleinsatz
  Es ist anzustreben, daß Modelle für Bereiche erstellt werden, die für den Anwender von Bedeutung sind. Diese Forderung ist nicht selbstverständlich: Im allgemeinen kommt der Wunsch nach einem Modell noch nicht vom Anwender. Dem Anwender sind die modernen Verfahren der Simulationstechnik nicht so vertraut, als daß er von seiner Seite aus beurteilen könnte, ob ein Modell für seine Fragestellungen brauchbar ist.
  Bisher stammen Modelle zumeist aus dem wissenschaftlichen Bereich; sie sind entstanden, ohne daß praxisbezogene Notwendigkeit sie gefordert hätte.
  Die Simulationstechnik steht noch vor der Aufgabe, den Anwender von der Nützlichkeit und Brauchbarkeit dieses Verfahrens zu überzeugen. Das tut sie am eindrucksvollsten, indem sie auf den Gebieten Ergebnisse liefert, die für die Anwender von Bedeutung sind.

Literatur

/1/ A. Schmidt, G. Weber, A. Geiger: Geschlossenes rechnergesteuertes Intensiv-Therapie-System (GRITS), Biomed. Technik, Bd. 25, September 1980

/2/ W. H. Cameron: A Model Framework for Computer Simulation of Overall Renal Function, Journal Biol., Vol. 66, 1977

/3/ U. Ranft: Zur Mechanik und Regelung des Herzkreislaufsystems, Medizinische Informatik und Statistik Bd. 6, Springer Verlag 1978

/4/ N. Ikedo, F. Marumo, M. Shirataka, T. Sato: A Model of Overall Regulation of Body Fluids, Annals of Biomedical Engineering, Vol. 7, 1979

/5/ T. Ören: Software for Simulation of Combined Continuous and Discrete Systems: A state-of-the-art report. Simulation 28, 1977

/6/ B. Schmidt: GPSS-FORTRAN, Informatik Fachberichte Bd. 6, Springer Verlag 1978

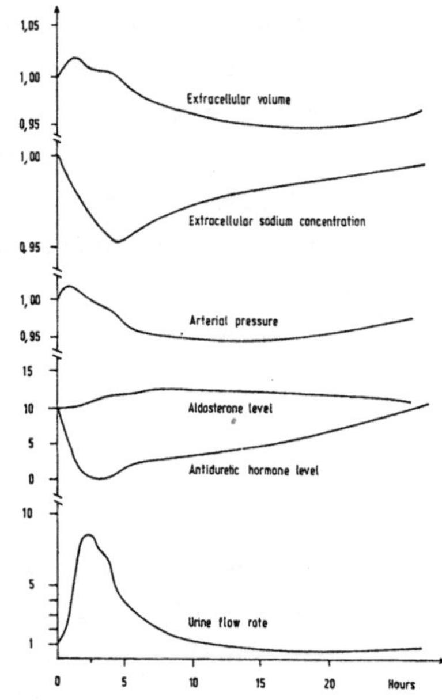

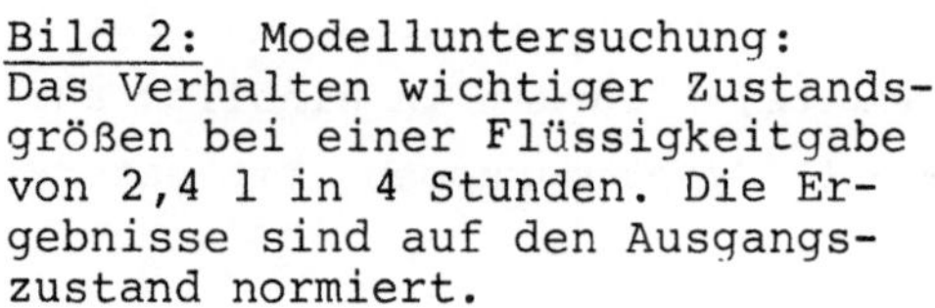
Bild 2: Modelluntersuchung: Das Verhalten wichtiger Zustandsgrößen bei einer Flüssigkeitgabe von 2,4 l in 4 Stunden. Die Ergebnisse sind auf den Ausgangszustand normiert.

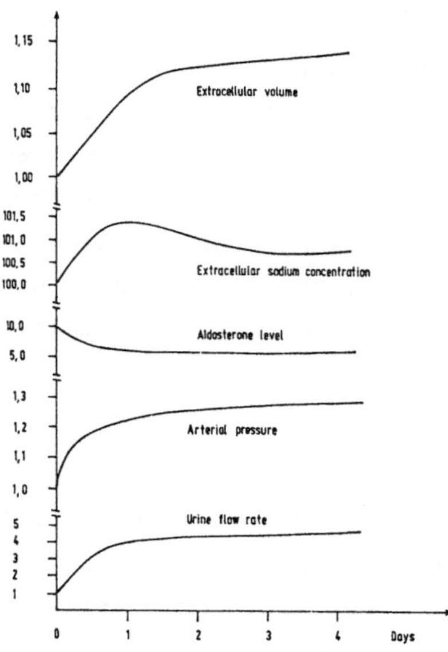

Bild 3: Das Verhalten bei Erhöhung der NaCl-Einnahme um das Vierfache. Die Ergebnisse sind auf den Ausgangszustand normiert.

EIN FUZZY ALGORITHMUS ZUR DIAGNOSTISCHEN KLASSIFIZIERUNG IN DER CRANIALEN COMPUTER-TOMOGRAPHIE (CCT)

Günter Tusch
Medizinische Hochschule Hannover
Institut für Medizinische Informatik
(Direktor Prof. Dr. P.L. Reichertz)

Zusammenfassung:

Dieser Beitrag behandelt eine Anwendung der Theorie der fuzzy Mengen in der cranialen Computer Tomographie (CCT)(8). Benutzt wird ein von ADLASSNIG publiziertes Modell der klinischen Entscheidungsfindung verbunden mit einem eigenen mathematischen Ansatz. Der daraus resultierende Algorithmus basiert 1. auf einem speziellen Begriff von "Mittelwert" und "Abstand" von fuzzy Mengen und 2. auf einer Tabelle mit Beziehungen von Symptomen und Diagnosen. Der Tabelle lag eine Beschreibung dieser Beziehungen zu Grunde, die durch fuzzy Mengen dargestellt werden. Nach Eingabe eines Symptommusters wird der Mittelwert der fuzzy Mengen, die die Beziehungen zwischen allen "vorhandenen" Symptomen und einer Diagnose beschreiben, berechnet. Er dient als Hinweis auf die Entscheidungsfindung.

1. EINLEITUNG

Die Theorie der fuzzy Mengen hat sich seit der Begründung durch L.A.Zadeh im Jahre 1965 rasch entwickelt (s.a. (5)). Es wurden Anwendungen auf verschiedenen Gebieten versucht, so seit einigen Jahren auch auf dem Gebiet der Medizin. Allerdings gibt es hier erst seit kurzem praktische Ansätze (vgl. auch (1),(3)). In diesem Beitrag werden erste Ergebnisse einer konkreten Erprobung des fuzzy Ansatzes an einem Modell dargestellt. Dabei wird als Verknüpfung von fuzzy Mengen nicht wie üblich Durchschnitt und Vereinigung, sondern ein speziell definiertes "gewichtetes Mittel" gewählt.

2. DAS MODELL

Das im folgenden beschriebene Entscheidungsmodell wurde auf ein Problem der cranialen Computer-Tomographie (CCT) angewandt. In der Abteilung Neuroradiologie der MHH (Prof.Dr. H. Vogelsang)(+) dokumentieren Ärzte seit 5 Jahren mit Hilfe eines dafür entwickelten Dokumentationsbogen Computertomogramme. Weil das Modell zunächst nur für 5 Tumordiagnosen(s.u.) getestet werden sollte, wurden in Hinblick auf diese Differentialdiagnosen 25 Symptome (7 Symptomgruppen mit unter-

---

(+) Prof. Vogelsang sei für die Unterstützung besonders gedankt.

schiedlichen Ausprägungen: Zahl der Herde, Herdstruktur(nativ), Ödeme, Lokalisation(Ödeme), Ventrikelform und -lage, Sulci und Cisternen, Pinealis) aus dem Dokumentationsbogen für die Klassifizierung ausgewählt. Es standen Daten von 802 Tumorfällen zur Verfügung, davon Malignome 297, Semimalignome 128, Metastasen 194, Fehlbildungstumore 63, Benignome 120.

In Bezug auf die Symptome wurde nur unterschieden zwischen "vorhanden" und "nicht vorhanden/ nicht erhoben". Es handelte sich also um dichotome Variablen und es wurde als Vergleich zum fuzzy Ansatz eine (lineare) Diskriminanzanalyse (SPSS-Prozedur mit Mahalanobis-Abstand(2)) durchgeführt. Bei der Reklassifikation ergab sich eine Trefferquote von nur 57,5% in bezug auf die Arztdiagnosen.

Das hier vorgeschlagene Modell verfolgt die Ziele, medizinisches Wissen in (fuzzy-)logischen Beziehungen zu speichern und dem Arzt eine oder mehrere Diagnosen vorzuschlagen, um seine Entscheidung zu erleichtern.

2.1 Das medizinische Modell

Der hier vorgestellte Algorithmus basiert auf einem ärztlichen Entscheidungsmodell, das ADLASSNIG (1) vorgeschlagen hat:

Vor jeder Diagnose prüft der Arzt den Zusammenhang zwischen einem bestimmten Symptom S_{i*} und einer bestimmten Diagnose D_{j*}.

Er betrachtet dabei die beiden folgenden Fragen:

1) Wie oft tritt das Symptom S_{i*} bei der Diagnose D_{j*} auf? (Vorhandensein)

2) Wie oft handelt es sich um die Diagnose D_{j*}, wenn das Symptom S_{i*} vorhanden ist? (Beweiskraft)

Auf Grund seiner Ausbildung und mit Hilfe seiner Erfahrung und von Fachbüchern gibt der Arzt auf diese beiden Fragen Antworten. Aus den Antworten leitet er einen Hinweis auf die Diagnose ab, je nachdem, ob das Symptom vorhanden ist oder nicht ($^{+}S_iD_j$-Hinweis bzw. $^{-}S_iD_j$-Hinweis). Für alle in Betracht kommenden Kombinationen der Symptome S_i, $i=1,\dots,n$, und Diagnosen D_j, $j=1,\dots,m$, wird nun ein $^{+}S_iD_j$- bzw. $^{-}S_iD_j$-(Einzel-)Hinweis abgeleitet. Entsprechend dem vorhandenen Symptommuster wird nun aus den entsprechenden Einzelhinweisen für jede Diagnose ein Gesamthinweis bestimmt und die Diagnose mit dem größten Gesamthinweis ausgewählt.

2.2 Das mathematische Modell

Das im folgenden verwendete zugehörige mathematische Modell weicht von ADLASSNIG's Vorschlag ab:

1) Ein Arzt füllt zu Anfang zwei Fragebögen (Tabellen) aus, in denen er auf die Fragen: "Wie oft tritt Ihrer Meinung nach das Symptom S_{i*} bei der Diagnose D_{j*} auf?" (Vorhandensein), bzw. "Wie häufig ist das Symptom S_{i*} in Bezug auf die Diagnose D_{j*} beweisend?" (Beweiskraft) antwortet.

2) Die Antworten des Arztes werden durch fuzzy Mengen beschrieben.

3) Für die Entscheidung werden nur die vorhandenen Symptome berücksichtigt.

4) Für Vorhandensein und Beweiskraft der vorhandenen Symptome werden nach den unten diskutierten Algorithmen Gesamthinweise auf alle Diagnosen D_j, $j=1,\ldots,m$, berechnet.

5) Die Diagnosen mit "sehr sehr niedrigen" Gesamthinweisen werden aus der Entscheidung ausgeschlossen ("unzutreffende Diagnosen").

6) Aus den restlichen Diagnosen werden diejenigen mit dem "höchsten" Gesamthinweis gewählt (Es können mehrere sein). Diese gelten als "zutreffend".

3. DARSTELLUNG DER FUZZY MENGEN

DEFINITION:

Sei X eine Menge (von Objekten, die hinsichtlich einer "fuzzy" Aussage zu bewerten sind), sie heiße Universum.
Dann heißt $A := \{(x,\mu_A(x)),\ x \in X\}$ eine fuzzy Menge von X.
Dabei ist $\mu_A : X \dashrightarrow [0,1]$ eine Funktion, welche als Zugehörigkeitsfunktion von A bezeichnet wird. Der Funktionswert $\mu_A(x)$ heißt auch Mitgliedschaftsgrad von x bzgl. A.
Man schreibt wie folgt: $A := \int_X x/\mu_A(x)$

Soll z.B. "hohe Häufigkeit" durch eine fuzzy Menge beschrieben werden, so sei etwa 0.8 der Mitgliedschaftsgrad von 60% für das Universum [0,100] (in %).
ZADEH hat die Zugehörigkeitsfunktion als Erweiterung des Wertebereichs der charakteristischen Funktion auf [0,1] eingeführt.
Er hat in (5) die S- und π-Funktion als (Standard-)Zugehörigkeitsfunktion wie folgt definiert ($x,\alpha,\beta,\gamma \in \mathbb{R}$):

$$S(x;\alpha,\gamma) := \begin{cases} 0 & \text{für } x<\alpha \\ 2\left(\frac{x-\alpha}{\gamma-\alpha}\right)^2 & \text{für } \alpha \leq x \leq \frac{\alpha+\gamma}{2} \\ 1-2\left(\frac{x-\gamma}{\gamma-\alpha}\right)^2 & \text{für } \frac{\alpha+\gamma}{2} < x \leq \gamma \\ 1 & \text{für } x > \gamma \end{cases}$$

$$\Pi(x;\beta,\gamma) := \begin{cases} S(x;\gamma-\beta,\gamma) & \text{für } x \leq \gamma \\ 1 - S(x;\gamma,\gamma+\beta) & \text{für } x > \gamma \end{cases}$$

Zur Darstellung der Häufigkeiten und Hinweise wurden die folgenden drei Ansätze verfolgt, das Universum der fuzzy Mengen war dabei immer [0,100] (Häufigkeiten von 0 bis 100% der Fälle). Die Antworten sind vorgegeben (vgl. Tafel 1 bzw. Tafel 2 und (7)).

immer	→	S(94,97)
fast immer	→	Π(6.25,93.75)
sehr oft	→	Π(12.5,87.5)
oft	→	Π(25,75)
mehr oder weniger oft	→	Π(37.5,62.5)
mittel	→	Π(50,50)
mehr oder weniger selten	→	Π(37.5,37.5)
selten	→	Π(25,25)
sehr selten	→	Π(12.5,12.5)
fast nie	→	Π(6.25,6.25)
nie	→	1-S(3,6)

Tafel 1

immer	→	S(75,87.5)
fast immer	→	Π(40,60)
sehr oft	→	Π(45,55)
oft	→	Π(30,30)
mehr oder weniger oft	→	Π(26,26)
mittel	→	Π(25,25)
mehr oder weniger selten	→	Π(21,21)
selten	→	Π(20,20)
sehr selten	→	Π(15,15)
fast nie	→	Π(10,10)
nie	→	1-S(3,6)

Tafel 2

Schreibweise: a → b bedeute: "Die Zugehörigkeitsfunktion der die Bedeutung von a beschreibenden fuzzy Menge sei b"

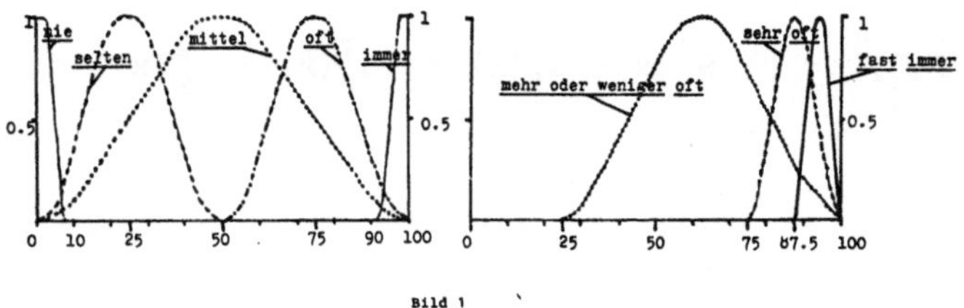

Bild 1

1) Ansatz (intuitiv)
Siehe Tafel 1 und Bild 1.

2) Ansatz (empirisch)
Die ersten der 5 dokumentierten Jahrgänge wurden statistisch ausgewertet und die ermittelten Häufigkeiten mit den entsprechenden Werten der "Vorhandensein"-Tabelle des Arztes in Beziehung gesetzt.Dies diente als Grundlage zur Neubestimmung der Π-Funktionen. Stark abweichende Werte wurden dabei nicht berücksichtigt. Die Wahl fiel auf die Werte in Tafel 2.

3) Ansatz (kombiniert)
Die Darstellung durch die Π-Funktion geschah wie bei Ansatz 1. Allerdings wurde die "Vorhandensein"-Tabelle des Arztes entsprechend den statistisch ermittelten Häufigkeiten mit der Π-Darstellung in Einklang gebracht. Dadurch wurden Diskrepanzen wie teilweise bei 2. vermieden, allerdings konnte natürlich die "Beweiskraft"-Tabelle nicht entsprechend modifiziert werden.

4. ABSTAND UND MITTELWERT

Der Gesamthinweis auf eine Diagnose wurde durch "linguistische Approximation" (vgl. (5)) ermittelt, d.h. er wird durch den Hinweis mit dem kleinsten Abstand dargestellt. Die Hinweise wurden wie folgt sprachlich beschrieben:
Total hoch, sehr sehr hoch, sehr hoch, hoch, mehr oder weniger hoch, mittel, mehr oder weniger niedrig, niedrig, sehr niedrig, sehr sehr niedrig, total niedrig.
Diese Worte wurden wie die Häufigkeiten beschrieben
(z.B. total hoch -> S(94,97), sehr hoch -> (62.5,93.75)). Hier wurde der folgende Abstand verwendet:

DEFINITION: (vgl. Bild 2)

Seien A und B fuzzy Mengen von $\mathbb{R}$ mit

$$\mu_A(x) := \Pi(x;\beta_1,\gamma_1) \quad \text{und} \quad \mu_B(x) := \Pi(x;\beta_2,\gamma_2)$$

Ferner sei

$$\left.\begin{array}{l} S_l^i(x) := S(x;\gamma_i-\beta_i,\gamma_i) \\ S_r^i(x) := 1-S(x;\gamma_i,\gamma_i+\beta_i) \end{array}\right\} \quad i=1,2$$

Der p-Abstand d_p sei dann definiert durch

$$d_p(A,B) := \left| \int_{\mathbb{R}} S_l^1(x) - S_l^2(x) + (S_r^1(x) - S_r^2(x))\, dx \right|$$

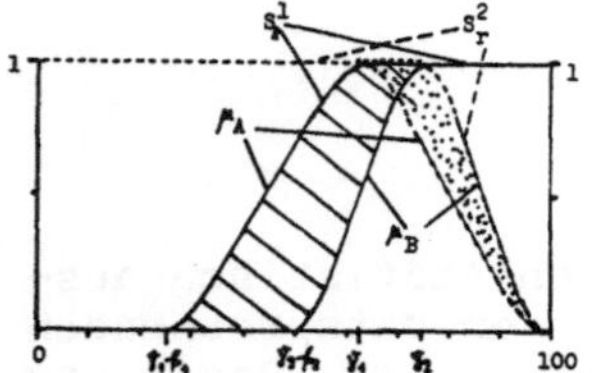

[gepunktet] ≙ $\int_{-\infty}^{+\infty} S_r^1(x)-S_r^2(x)\,dx$

[schraffiert] ≙ $\int_{-\infty}^{+\infty} S_l^1(x)-S_l^2(x)\,dx$

Bild 2

Der d_p-Abstand von zwei fuzzy Mengen A und B ist nur dann 0, wenn $A \subset B$ bzw. $B \subset A$ ist. Der Abstand ist umso größer, je weiter die Träger beider fuzzy Mengen "auseinander" liegen (Träger von A und B heißen die Teilmengen des Universums, auf denen die Mitgliedschaftsgrade positiv sind).

4.1 Algorithmen zur Berechnung des Gesamthinweises

Es wurden zwei Algorithmen getestet. Grundlage für beide ist das im folgenden definierte Mittel:

DEFINITION:

Seien $A_1, A_2, \ldots, A_n$ fuzzy Mengen von $\mathbb{R}$ mit

$$\left.\begin{array}{l} \mu_{A_i} := \Pi(\beta_i, \gamma_i) \\ \text{und } \sum \xi_i = 1, \ \xi_i \in \mathbb{R} \end{array}\right\} \quad i=1,\ldots,n$$

Dann sei das (gewichtete) Mittel definiert durch

$$M_{(\xi_1,\ldots,\xi_n)}(A_1,\ldots,A_n) = \int_{\mathbb{R}} \Pi(x; (\sum \xi_i \cdot \beta_i), (\sum \xi_i \cdot \gamma_i))/x$$

Das gewichtetet Mittel zweier fuzzy Mengen A und B mit $\xi_1 = \xi_2 = 0.5$ entspricht dem intuitiven Begriff des "Mittelwertes". Es ist symmetrisch in A und B und es gilt:

$$d_p(A, M_{(0.5,0.5)}(A,B)) = d_p(B, M_{(0.5,0.5)}(A,B)) = \frac{1}{2} d_p(A,B)$$

4.1.1 Algorithmus I

Aus allen fuzzy Mengen V_i und B_i, die "Vorhandensein" und "Beweiskraft" der vorhandenen Symptome beschreiben, wird der folgende Mittelwert gebildet:

$$M_{VB_i} := M_{(\lambda, (1-\lambda))}(V_i, B_i)$$

Daraus wird der Gesamthinweis durch

$$G := M_{(\frac{1}{n},\ldots,\frac{1}{n})}(M_{VB_1},\ldots,M_{VB_n})$$

gebildet, wobei n die Anzahl der vorhandenen Symptome ist.

4.1.2 Algorithmus II

Der Gesamthinweis G_{II} wird durch

$$G_{II} := M_{(\lambda_1,\ldots,\lambda_n)}(V_1,\ldots,V_n)$$

gebildet, wobei V_i die "Vorhandensein" beschreibenden fuzzy Mengen sind und λ_i der Mittelpunkt des Intervalls ist, das die α-Niveaumenge (vgl. (5)) von B_i darstellt (Beweiskraft). Eine α-Niveaumenge ist die Teilmenge des Universums, auf der der Mitgliedschaftgrad größer oder gleich α ist.

α wird in Hinblick auf ein vorgegebenes Datenmaterial optimiert.
(Die Niveaumengen der B_i sind abgeschlossene und reelle Intervalle, da das zugrundeliegende Universum [a,b] abgeschlossen und reell ist, da S und Π stetig und die B_i konvexe fuzzy Mengen sind.)
Für die mathematischen Tatbestände sei auch auf (4) verwiesen.

5. ERGEBNIS

Die Algorithmen I und II wurden auf die Darstellungen 1., 2. und 3. angewandt, nachdem ein Arzt der Abteilung Neuroradiologie der MHH die entsprechenden Vorhandensein- bzw. Beweiskraft-Fragebögen ausgefüllt hatte.

Als vorläufiges Ergebnis läßt sich feststellen: Der Prozentsatz der Ausgaben mit ein bis drei Diagnosevorschlägen (d.h. die Hälfte aller möglichen) lag zwischen 70 und 95% (Trefferquote zwischen 76 und 55%). Beispielsweise erzielte Algorithmus II Ansatz 3 einen Prozentsatz von 92% (Trefferquote 70% - allerdings wurden Malignome,Semimalignome und Metastasen eindeutig bevorzugt (92%, 61%, 65%)).

Algorithmus I mit Ansatz 1 fand 70% richtige Diagnosen, jedoch deutlich geringere Prozentsätze bei Metastasen und Fehlbildungstumoren. Algorithmus II mit Ansatz 1 fand 64% richtige Diagnosen mit 84% Ausgaben mit bis zu 3 Vorschlägen. Semimalignome und Fehlbildungstumore wurden dabei jedoch nur zu 35 bzw. 30% richtig bewertet.

Sensitivität und Spezifität wurden ähnlich wie in der Literatur (z.B. (9)) berechnet. Da der Algorithmus mehrere Diagnosen vorschlägt, wurden Effizienz und Spezifität relativ niedrig.

6. DISKUSSION

Der Arbeit liegen die Schätzungen eines einzelnen Arztes in Bezug auf Vorhandensein und Beweiskraft von Symptomen bei bestimmten Diagnosen zugrunde. ADLASSNIG hatte vorgeschlagen, Durchschnitt und Vereinigung von fuzzy Mengen zur Berechnung des Gesamthinweises zu verwenden. Hier wurde der gewichtete Mittelwert gewählt.

Es scheint, daß Algorithmus I zwar eine insgesamt niedrigere, dafür aber gleichmäßigere Trefferquote über alle Diagnosen ergibt, während Algorithmus II eine gewisse Abhängigkeit von der Anzahl der Tumorfälle zu haben scheint (allerdings auch die Diskriminanzanalyse).

Ein anderes Problem ist die Darstellung der fuzzy Mengen. Hier wurde zunächst vorwiegend ein Ansatz durch Π-Funktionen versucht. Es bieten sich noch Ansätze mit S-Funktionen und einer "erweiterten S- und Π-Funktion" an (vgl. (4)).

Teilweise unterlagen beim 2. Ansatz die empirisch ermittelten Häufigkeiten in Bezug auf einen Arztwert großen Schwankungen.

Insgesamt wurde die bessere Trefferquote gegenüber der Diskriminanzanalyse durch ein weniger an Eindeutigkeit erkauft.

Einen andereren Aspekt, der sich speziell auf die CCT-Anwendung bezieht, sieht man an der Schematisierung des Informationsflusses beim Arzt bzw. Computer (Bild 3):

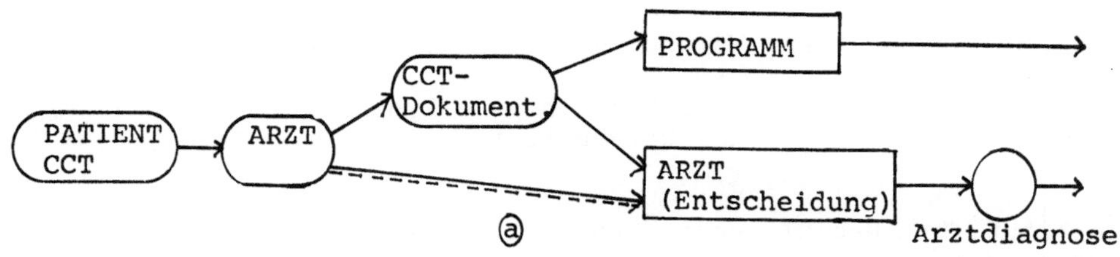

Bild 3

Einige Anzeichen sprechen dafür, daß der Arzt auf dem Weg @ Zusatzinformationen bekommt (z.B. Krankengeschichte, vgl. (6) bzgl. der Bestimmung der Metastasen), die der Algorithmus nicht erhält.
Vor allem der letzte Punkt wird in der weiteren Arbeit zu einer Erweiterung des Modells führen.

LITERATUR

1) Adlaßnig,K.P., A fuzzy Logical Model of Computer-Assisted Diagnosis. Meth.Inform.Med. 19(3) 141-148 (1980)

2) Nie,N.H., Hull,C.H., Jenkins,G.J., Steinbrenner,K., Bent,D.H., SPSS. Statistical Package for the Social Sciences (Second Edition). New York, McGraw Hill (1975)

3) Reichertz,P.L. in diesem Band

4) Tusch,G. Fuzzy Mengen und Anwendungen.
Diplomarbeit am Institut für Praktische Mathematik und Darstellende Geometrie (Prof. G. Bertram), Universität Hannover (1980)

5) Zadeh,L.A. The Concept of a Linguistic Variable and its Application to Approximate Reasoning. San Jose, California. IBM Research Laboratory, RJ 1355 (Nr. 21042). (1974)

6) Weiske,R. Die axiale CT in der Diagnostik von Hirnmetastasen. Z.Allg.Med. 57, 391-399 (1981)

7) Hersh,H.M., Caramazza,A., A Fuzzy Set Approach to Modifiers and Vagueness in Natural Language. Journal of Experimental Psychology: General 105(3), 254-276 (1976)

8) Kazner,E., Lanksch,W., Steinhoff,H., Wilske,J., Die axiale Computer-Tomographie des Gehirnschädels - Anwendungsmöglichkeiten und klinische Ergebnisse. Fortschritte der Neurologie-Psychiatrie und ihrer Grenzgebiete 10, 487-574 (1975)

9) Fordon,W.A., Bezdek,J.C., The Application of Fuzzy Set Theory to Medical Diagnosis in:Gupta,M.M., Ragade,R.K., Yager,R.R., (editors) Advances in Fuzzy Set Theory and Applications. Amsterdam, North-Holland Publishing Company (1979)

STRUKTUR DER WISSENSBASIS FÜR EIN AI-SYSTEM ZUR UNTERSTÜTZUNG ÄRZTLICHER DIAGNOSTISCHER UND THERAPEUTISCHER ENTSCHEIDUNGEN

Werner Horn, Walter Buchstaller, Robert Trappl

Institut für Medizinische Kybernetik
der Universität Wien

Am Institut für Medizinische Kybernetik der Universität Wien wird versucht, durch Anwendung von Methoden der Artificial Intelligence ein Konsultationssystem aufzubauen, das den Arzt sowohl bei diagnostischen als auch therapeutischen Entscheidungen unterstützen soll. Darüberhinaus soll das System den Verlauf einer (oder mehrerer) beim Patienten diagnostizierten Krankheit(en) verfolgen und den Therapieerfolg bewerten.

Die vorliegende Arbeit beschreibt die für die Lösung dieser Aufgabe entwickelte Struktur eines Semantischen Netzes, sowie das zur Erzeugung dieser Struktur entwickelte Definitionssystem KSDS (Knowledge Structure Definition System).

EINLEITUNG

Am Institut für Medizinische Kybernetik der Universität Wien wird versucht ein Konsultationssystem aufzubauen, dessen Einsatzbereich die primärärztliche Versorgung ist. Das Ziel des Projektes ist die Entwicklung eines Systems, das den Praktischen Arzt oder Arzt der Fachgrundversorgung bei seinen diagnostischen und therapeutischen Entscheidungen unterstützt.

Daraus ergibt sich unmittelbar folgende Konsequenz: Der angesprochene medizinische Bereich ist nicht ein eng begrenzter Spezialbereich, sondern ein weit gespannter. Zumal handelt es sich um ein stark "diffuses" Wissensgebiet, d.h. das Wissen läßt sich nur schwer explizit darstellen. Dies ist aber eine Voraussetzung, die gerade die Anwendung von Methoden der Artificial Intelligence notwendig und wirkungsvoll erscheinen läßt (Amarel, et al. /1/, Feigenbaum /2/). Wir versuchen ein Expertensystem aufzubauen, das Wissen von Experten in das System einzubringen, und für der Arzt in der Primärversorgung anwendbar zu machen.

Noch eine zweite Überlegung führte uns zum Aufbau eines AI-Systems: die Frage der Akzeptanz durch den Benutzer. Voraussetzung für die Akzeptanz scheint zu sein, daß das System seine eigenen

Schlußfolgerungen erklärt. Es muß nach außen hin begründen, warum es zu einer bestimmten Diagnose, bzw. Therapie kommt. Das von Shortliffe entwickelte System zur Entscheidungsunterstützung bei der Verordung von Antibiotika bei infektiösen Erkrankungen MYCIN /3/ weist hier einen Weg. Dabei ist wichtig, daß das System sehr gute Interaktionsmöglischkeiten besitzt, die eine Kommunikation zwischen Arzt und System in (eingeschränkter) natürlicher Sprache erlauben.

Betrachtet man die wenigen bisher bestehenden Systeme, so zeigen sich grundsätzlich zwei Ansätze:

1. Systeme, die ihr Wissen in Regeln speichern (z.B. MYCIN /3/). Diese Systeme versuchen durch Anwendung ihrer Regeln zu diagnostischen und therapeutischen Schlüssen zu kommen. Dabei ist es aber sehr schwer, Hierarchien zu defineren, um z.B. topographische Zuordungen zu erlauben. Reggia /4/ hat hier die Inadäquatheit beim Problem der neurologischen Lokalisation aufgezeigt. Da im Allgemeinen immer alle Regeln verwendet werden können, wird man bei System mit großem Umfang wahrscheinlich Methoden finden müssen, die die Anzahl der gleichzeitig aktiven und aktivierbaren Regeln einschränken, um den Suchraum zu beschränken und in vernünftigen Zeiten zu Schlüssen zu kommen. Aus diesen Gründen wurden Systeme, die ausschließlich auf Regeln basieren, bisher nur für sehr eng eingegrenzte Probleme angewandt (z.B. VM /5/).

2. Systeme mit medizinischem Wissen in Form eines Semantischen Netzes. Hier werden medizinische Konzepte definiert, welche durch Relationen miteinander verknüpft sind. Bei Vorliegen von Patientendaten werden Hypothesen (in Form bestimmter Konzepte) generiert und danach auf ihr Zutreffen getestet. Dabei können zur Entscheidungsfindung sowohl logische als auch auf numerischen Berechnungen basierende Schlüsse gezogen werden (Szolovits und Pauker /6/). Erste erfolgversprechende Resultate wurden damit auch auf einem, von den Daten gesehen, umfangreichen Gebiet erzielt: INTERNIST /7,8/ unterstützt die Diagnose von internen Erkrankungen und enthält über 400 Krankheiten und 3000 Manifestationen.

Aufgrund der bisherigen Erkenntnisse bei Konsultationssystemen haben wir unsere Wissensbasis als Semantisches Netz aufgebaut (Horn, et al. /9/). Wir haben bis jetzt die Struktur dieses Netzes definiert, und sind derzeit dabei, das Netz mit medizinischen Daten zu füllen, die für den Primärversorgungsbereich relevant erscheinen.

STRUKTUR DER WISSENSBASIS

Die Schlüsselstellung beim Aufbau eines Konsultationssystems nimmt die Wahl der Repräsentationsform ein. Wie schon in der Einleitung aufgezeigt, kann die Repräsentation des Problems den Anwendungsbereich so sehr einschränken, daß eine Erweiterung der Wissensbasis nicht möglich ist (vgl. MYCIN /3/, CASNET /10/). Dies veranlaßte uns, ein System zu entwicklen, das sowohl eine explizite Definition der Struktur der Wissensbasis, als auch eine spätere Modifikation erlaubt.

In dem von uns entwickelten Metasystem KSDS (Knowledge Structure Definition System) sind derzeit vier medizinische Konzepte definiert, die als Knotentypen im Semantischen Netz aufgenommen sind:

- Manifestationen,
- Krankheiten und Krankheitsgruppen,
- Diagnostische Prozeduren, und
- Therapeutische Prozeduren.

Mit Hilfe von derzeit 33 Relationstypen werden diese vier Knotentypen untereinander verbunden.

STRUKTURELLER AUFBAU DER KNOTEN UND RELATIONEN DES NETZES

Um eine möglichst einfache und leicht handhabbare Struktur aufzubauen, werden Knoten- und Relationstypen in der Strukturbeschreibung in der gleichen Weise spezifiziert (vgl. Bild 1 \`Beispiel eines Knotentyps\` und Bild 2 \`Beispiel eines Relationstyps\`).

Die Beschreibung der Struktur der Knoten und Relationen erfolgt in vier Teilen, welche am Beispiel des Knotentyps \`Krankheit(sgruppen)\` (Bild 1) und des Relationstyps \`durchzuführende therapeutische Prozeduren\` (Bild 2) erklärt wird.

1. Der <u>Definitionsteil</u> (ersten zwei Zeilen von Bild 1 und 2) enthält
   - die Definition, ob es sich um die Struktur eines Knotens oder einer Relation handelt;
   - eine eindeutige Identifikation des Knoten- (\`D\`) bzw. Relationstyps (\`BEH\`);
   - den Namen der definierten Struktur (Spalte 2);
   - einen Vermerk, ob Erklärungen bei der Definition der Wissensbasis

KNOTEN [1]	Name [2]	Erkl[3]
D	Krankheit(sgruppe)	Y

DESKRIPTOREN:

	Name[1]	Ab[2]	Wrt[3]	Len	Pos	Def[4]
01	Name der Krankheit(sgruppe)	NAME	C80	80	1	0
02	Klassifikationscode	CODE	C10	10	81	0
03	Typ der Krankheit(sgruppe)	ART	D.ART	4	91	2
04	Haeufigkeit	HAUF	INT4	4	95	0
05	Intensitaet, Bedrohlichkeit	INTS	INTENS	4	99	99
06	Interferenz mit Patientenbefinden	INTF	INTERF	4	103	99
07	mittlere Krankheitsdauer	DAU	ZEIT	4	107	99
08	Periodizitaet	PERI	PERIOD	4	111	1
09	Frequenz des Auftretens	FREQ	FREQ	4	115	99
10	Penetranz (Erkenn-/Verfuegbarkeit)	PENE	PENETR	4	119	1
11	Therapeutisierbarkeit	THER	THERAP	4	123	99
12	Prognose	PROG	PROGN	4	127	1
13	Intervall fuer Verlaufskontrolle	KONT	ZEIT	4	131	99

RELATIONEN:

	Typ	Name	Len	Endknoten
01	GRP	zuzuordnen den Gruppen	8	D
02	KRKH	Krankheiten dieser Gruppe	4	D
03	HIER	uebergeordnete Gruppe	8	D
04	SUB	untergeordnete Elemente	8	D
05	URS	ist moegliche Folge der Krankheiten	8	D
06	FOLG	moegliche Folgekrkh., Komplikationen	12	D
07	ASS	assoziierte Krankheiten	12	D
08	KOMB	ist eine Kombination von	4	D
09	ELEM	ist Teil der Krankheit	4	D
10	PHAS	zerfaellt in die Phasen	6	D
11	FPH	Folgephase	4	D
12	MANI	manifestiert sich in	8	M
13	EXKL	wird exkludiert (zweifelhaft) durch	8	M
14	DPR	fuehre die diagn.Prozeduren durch	10	P
15	BEH	durchzufuehrende ther.Prozeduren	22	T

ERKLAERUNGEN:
(Detaillierte Erlaeuterungen der definierten Deskriptoren und Relationen und ihrer Verwendung fuer den Experten, der die Wissensbasis aufbaut; entfaellt hier aus Platzgruenden).

<u>Bild 1</u>: Strukturbeschreibung des Knotens \`Krankheit(sgruppe)\`

verwendet werden können (Spalte 3); und

- falls eine Relation definiert wird: den Typ der Knoten, die durch diese Relation verbunden werden (Spalten 4,5). Daraus folgt, daß eine Relation genau zwei fix definierte Knotentypen verbindet, in unserem Beispiel den Knotentyp \`Krankheit(sgruppe) (D)\` mit dem Knotentyp \`Therapeutische Prozedur (T)\`.

2. Der <u>Deskriptoren-Teil</u> bescheibt die Attribute des Knotens bzw. der Relation (\`DESKRIPTOREN\` in Bild 1 und 2). Dies entspricht den \`Slots\` in der Terminologie der \`Frames\` (Minsky /11/).

```
RELATION[1] Name [2]                          Erkl[3]  von[4]  nach[5]
    BEH     durchzufuehrende ther.Prozeduren     Y        D       T

DESKRIPTOREN:
   Name[1]                                  Ab[2] Wrt[3] Len Pos Def[4]
Ø1 Praeferenz                               PRAE  INT      2   1     1
Ø2 Notwendigkeit der Therapie               NOTW  NOTW     4   3    99
Ø3 erwarteter Krkh.status nach Behandlung   STAT  STATUS   4   7     2
Ø4 Strategie, falls Beh. erfolgreich        ERFR  STRAT    4  11     1
Ø5 Strategie, falls Beh. erfolglos          ERFL  STRAT    4  15    99

ERKLAERUNGEN:
  ....
```

Bild 2: Strukturbeschreibung der Relation durchzufuehrende therapeutische Prozeduren

Die Attribute von Knoten und Relationen haben eine unterschiedliche Bedeutung, da in der Wissensbasis nur die Knoten gespeichert werden. Die Relationen werden bei den Knoten gespeichert (siehe Relationen-Teil). Daraus folgt, daß die Knoten Attribute haben müssen, die eine eindeutige Identifizierung erlauben (`Name`, `Klassifikationscode` in unserer Wissensbasis).

Die in Bild 1 aufgezeigten Deskriptoren des Knotentyps `Krankheit(sgruppe)` definieren Attribute, die das diagnostische Vorgehen steuern (Häufigkeit, Bedrohlichkeit, Bedeutung der Krankheit für den Patienten), das Zeitverhalten der Krankheit beschreiben (Dauer, Frequenz, Periodiziät, Prognose), sowie das sich daraus ableitende Intervall für eine Verlaufskontrolle und die Möglichkeit einer Therapie angeben. Die Knoten des Typs `D` bezeichnen nicht nur klinische Krankheitseinheiten, sondern auch Krankheitsgruppen (`Semantische Dimensionen`, Wingert /12/), welche durch klassifizierende und hierarchisierende Relationen miteinander verbunden sind (siehe Relationen-Teil). Das Attribut `Typ` definiert, ob es sich um eine klinische Krankheitseinheit oder um eine nosologische, topographische, ätiologische, morphologische oder dysfunktionelle Klassifikation (Krankheitsgruppe) handelt.

Die Attribute der Relationen bezeichnen Werte, die mit der Relation assoziiert werden, z.B. Grad des Zusammenhangs, Reihenfolge, Konsequenzen, Erwartungen. Diese Werte kommen zum Tragen, wenn versucht wird, beim Schlußfolgern entlang der Relation fortzuschreiten. In unserem Beispiel (Bild 2) wird, nachdem eine bestimmte Krankheitshypothese angenommen wurde, auf Grund der `BEH`-Relationen versucht werden, geeignete therapeutische Prozeduren zu finden. Die

Reihenfolge der Auswahl wird dabei von den Attributen \`Präferenz\` und \`Notwendigkeit\` gesteuert werden. Bei Zweitkonsultationen wird der Therapieerfolg durch Vergleich von (auf Grund von \`STAT\`) erwarteten und aktuellen Krankheitszustand überprüft, und das weitere Vorgehen abhängig von \`ERFR\` und \`ERFL\` gewählt werden.

Für jedes Attribut wird eine Zeile in der Beschreibung verwendet. Jede Zeile enthält

- den Namen des Deskriptors (Spalte 1);
- eine Abkürzung des Namens zur schnellen Referenzierung (Spalte 2);
- einen Verweis auf erlaubte Werte (Spalte 3). Dieser Verweis bezeichnet den Namen einer Gruppe von erlaubten \`Primitives\`, die in einer eigenen Datenbasis gespeichert sind. Die Werte, die in der Wissensbasis für den Deskriptor verwendet werden, müssen aus dieser Liste der erlaubten Primitives entnommen werden. Dies unterstützt die einheitliche und konsistente Verwendung der Deskriptoren, ermöglicht eine Konsistenzprüfung und erleichtert die natürlichsprachliche Interaktion;
- die sich aus dem Wert automatisch errechnenden Angaben über Länge und Position des Deskriptors in der internen Darstellung; und
- die Angabe eines Standardwertes (Default), der angenommen wird, wenn vom Experten beim Aufbau der Wissensbasis keine näheren Angaben gemacht werden (Spalte 4). Der Defaultwert bezeichnet einen Wert in der Liste der Primitives.

3. Der <u>Relationen-Teil</u> definiert die von dem Element ausgehenden Relationen (\`RELATIONEN\` in Bild 1). Da derzeit aus Gründen der Einfachheit und Durchschaubarkeit noch keine Sub-Relationen, d.h. Relationen die von anderen Relationen ausgehen, erlaubt sind, entfällt dieser Teil bei der Beschreibung von Relationstypen.

In der Strukturbeschreibung eines Knotens sind im Relationen-Teil alle Relationen aufgelistet, die von diesem Knoten ausgehen. Dies entspricht der Konzeption, alle Informationen über eine Relation im Anfangsknoten der Relation zu speichern. Jede Zeile im Relationen-Teil definiert einen Relationstyp, der von diesem Knoten ausgeht. Endknoten und erforderliche Länge zum Speichern der Relation in der Wissensbasis ergibt sich automatisch aus der Beschreibung des Relationstyps in KSDS.

Die ersten zwei in Bild 1 dargestellten Relationstypen, die von einer \`Krankheit(sgruppe)\` ausgehen, bezeichnen klassifizierende Relationen zwischen Krankheiten und Krankheitsgruppen (`GRP`, `KRKH`). Dies erlaubt ein Schlußfolgern auf Grund z.B. topographischer Informationen, da bestimmte Manifestationen bestimmten Topographien zugeordnet werden. Nach Aktivierung einer topographischen Gruppe können danach die, der topographischen Gruppe zugeordneten Krankheiten als Hypothesen aktiviert werden.

Hierarchische Beziehungen werden durch die Relationen `HIER` und `SUB` dargestellt, patho-/nosogenetische Beziehungen durch die Relationen `URS` und `FOLG`. Mittels `KOMB` und `ELEM` kann eine Krankheit als Kombination anderer dargestellt werden. Sollte eine Krankheit sich in verschiedene Phasen aufteilen lassen, wobei jede Phase sich durch eine spezielle Symptomatik auszeichnet, so wird dies durch die Relationen `PHAS` und `FPH` definiert.

Manifestationen, deren Vorhandensein die Diagnose der Krankheit unterstützen bzw. verwerfen, werden durch die Relationen `MANI` und `EXKL` angesprochen. Auf diagnostische Prozeduren, die zur Klärung des Krankheitsstatus durchgeführt werden sollten, wird durch die Relation `DPR` verwiesen.

Die Relation `BEH` verweist auf alle therapeutischen Prozeduren, welche bei Vorliegen der Krankheit angewendet werden können. Eine detaillierte Beschreibung der Relation ist in Bild 2 angeführt.

4. Der Erklärungen-Teil erhält detaillierte Erklärungen zum definierten Knoten- bwz. Relationstyp, sowie Informationen für den Experten, die ihn beim Aufbau der Wissensbasis unterstützen sollen. Die Erklärungen können vom Interaktionsmodul aufgerufen werden.

DISKUSSION

Das Strukturdefinitionssystems KSDS bietet folgende Vorteile:

- es existiert eine explizite und sichtbare Definition der Struktur der Wissensbasis;
- die Struktur kann interaktiv verändert werden;
- die interne Speicherstruktur wird von KSDS bestimmt;
- KSDS formatiert eine bereits existierende Wissensbasis neu, falls Modifikationen der Struktur vorgenommen werden;

- das Interaktionssystem zum Aufbau der Wissensbasis durch Experten aktiviert Substrukturen des Netzes, um spezifische Aufgaben durchzuführen (Aufnahme von Informationen über spezifische Relationen, Konsistenzprüfung);
- das Module des Verarbeitungssystems werden als Operationen über die Netzstruktur definiert werden. Ein Modul definiert dabei eine spezifische Aufgabe unter Verwendung einer oder weniger Relationen (z.B. aktiviere Krankheiten auf Grund topographischer Informationen, suche mögliche therapeutische Prozeduren, prüfe Kontraindikationen). Im Laufe einer Konsultation werden nur wenige Module gleichzeitig aktiv sein, entsprechend dem sequentiellen Vorgehen des Arztes;
- Erfahrungen mit AI-Systemen haben gezeigt, daß sich ein gut funktionierendes System langsam aus einem schlecht funktionierenden entwickelt. Dazu werden schrittweise Verbesserungen und Änderungen der Struktur notwendig sein. KSDS unterstützt die leichte Durchführbarkeit solcher Modifikationen.

LITERATUR

/1/ Amarel S., et al.: Panel on Applications of Artificial Intelligence, Proc. 5th IJCAI, MIT, Cambridge, USA; 1977.

/2/ Feigenbaum E.A.: The Art of Artificial Intelligence: Themes and Case Studies of Knowledge Engineering, in Michie D.(ed.), Expert Systems in the Micro Electronic Age, Edinburgh Univ.Press, Edinburgh; 1977.

/3/ Shortliffe E.H.: Computer-Based Medical Consultations: MYCIN, Elsevier, New York; 1976.

/4/ Reggia J.A.: Representing and Using Medical Knowledge for the Neurological Localization Problem, Univ.Maryland, College Park, CS-TR-693; 1978.

/5/ Fagan L.M., Shortliffe E.H., Buchanan B.G.: Computer-Based Medical Decision Making: from MYCIN to VM, Automedica, 3,97-106; 1980.

/6/ Szolovits P., Pauker S.G.: Categorical and Probabilistic Reasoning in Medical Diagnosis, Artif. Intell., 11,115-144; 1978.

/7/ Pople H.E., Myers J.D., Miller R.A.: DIALOG: a Model of Diagnostic Logic in Internal Medicine, Proc. 4th IJCAI, Tbilisi, USSR; 1975.

/8/ Pople H.E.: The Formation of Composite Hypotheses in Diagnostic Problem Solving: an Exercise in Synthetic Reasoning, Proc. 5th IJCAI, MIT, Cambridge, USA; 1977.

/9/ Horn W., Buchstaller W., Trappl R.: Knowledge Structure Definition for an Expert System in Primary Medical Care, Proc. 7th IJCAI, Vancouver, Canada; 1981.

/10/ Weiss S.M., Kulikowski C.A., Safir A.: Glaucoma Consultation by Computer, Comput. Biol. Med., 8,25-40; 1978.

/11/ Minsky M.: A Framework for Representing Knowledge, in Winston P.H.(ed.), The Psychology of Computer Vision, McGraw-Hill, New York; 1975.

/12/ Wingert F.: Medizinische Informatik, Teubner, Stuttgart; 1979.

Mustererkennung und -wiedererkennung am Beispiel der biochemischen Schilddrüsendiagnostik.

Sator,H., Vogt,W., Nagel,D., Knedel,M.

Institut für Klinische Chemie am Klinikum Großhadern
der Ludwig-Maximilians-Universität
Postfach 701260, 8000 München 70

Zusammenfassung

Über die Verwendung des Referenzbereiches zur Interpretation klinisch-chemischer Meßwerte hinaus werden in der klinischen Chemie zur Zeit zwei aussagefähigere Modelle verwendet, das Modell des "predictive value" und die Diskriminanzanalyse. Beide Modelle haben jedoch den Nachteil, daß sie meist auf der Mithilfe der zu untersuchenden klinisch-chemischen Parameter gestellten Enddiagnosen eines Patientenkollektivs basieren. Wir entwickelten daher ein Modell, das ohne diese Basis arbeitet.
Von einem Patientenkollektiv mit Verdacht auf Schilddrüsenerkrankungen wurden sieben Parameter gemessen und einem Clusteralgorithmus (KMEANS und Ward) unterworfen (Mustererkennung). Die auf diese Weise gewonnenen Cluster waren unabhängig von der klinischen Diagnose, konnten aber größtenteils interpretiert werden. Die Reklassifizierung (Musterwiedererkennung) erfolgt durch den gleichen Algorithmus wie die Klassifizierung und ist mit diesem somit verträglich.

Einleitung

Eine der Aufgaben der klinischen Chemie ist die Unterstützung des am Krankenbett tätigen Arztes bei der Suche nach der richtigen Diagnose. Diese Entscheidungsfindung basiert noch heute, trotz überzeugender Gegenargumente, weitgehend auf der Interpretation vieler Einzelergebnisse an Hand sogenannter "Normal- oder Referenzbereiche".
Die seit wenigen Jahren vorgeschlagene Verwendung des Modells des "predictive value" oder der Diskriminanzanalyse an Stelle der Referenzbereiche ist bereits ein deutlicher Schritt vorwärts. Auch gegenüber diesen Verfahren bestehen Vorbehalte, die uns veranlaßten, nach einem neuen Modell zu suchen.

Kritik am Modell des "predictive value"

Das Modell des "predictive value" ist geeignet, folgende Fragen zu beantworten:

1. Hat der Patient eine bestimmte Krankheit?
2. Kann man zwischen diesem und anderen Patienten unterscheiden, die diese Krankheit nicht haben, aber ähnliche Symptome zeigen?
3. Mit welcher Wahrscheinlichkeit kann diese Entscheidung getroffen werden?

Die quantitativ bestimmten Daten werden jedoch zu einem sehr frühen Zeitpunkt zu binären Qualitativdaten reduziert, die Entscheidungsgrenzen sind starr, wenn sie einmal aufgestellt sind und schließlich ist eine korrekte und komplette Enddiagnose für das ausgewählte Kollektiv eine absolute Voraussetzung für die Erstellung diagnostischer Kriterien. Diese Enddiagnose darf aber nur unter Ausschluß der klinisch-chemischen Meßwerte erstellt werden. Andernfalls würde sich die wie auch immer geartete Beurteilung der Meßwerte in der Enddiagnose wiederspiegeln, die anschließend herangezogen wird, um an Hand dieser Meßwerte diagnostische Entscheidungskriterien zu erstellen. Zudem stellt sich dann die Frage, wozu man überhaupt diese Werte braucht, wenn eine Enddiagnose auch ohne Laborwerte möglich ist.

Kritik an der Diskriminanzanalyse

Die Diskriminanzanalyse beantwortet zwei Fragen:

1. Wie gut können zwei oder mehr Gruppen mit Hilfe klinisch-chemischer Meßergebnisse getrennt werden und
2. mit welcher Wahrscheinlichkeit kann ein Patient mit einer bestimmten Wertekonstellation einer bestimmten diagnostischen Gruppe zugeordnet werden?

Bei diesem Verfahren bleibt die in den Daten enthaltene Information so lange wie möglich erhalten. Trotzdem wird auch hier zur Erstellung der Diskriminanzfunktionen die Enddiagnose benötigt. Darüberhinaus ist eine Normalverteilung der Daten Voraussetzung für die optimale Lösung.

Forderungen an das Modell

Die oben vorgebrachten Vorbehalte gegenüber den gebräuchlichen Verfahren veranlaßten uns, eine Alternative zu suchen. Dabei sollten folgende Punkte erfüllt werden:

1. Umwandlung der Informationen der Einzeldaten in eine "Gesamtinformation", in die die Kombination der Einzelinformationen eingeht. Diese soll den diagnostischen Entscheidungsprozeß der Kliniker erleichtern und verbessern.
2. Unabhängigkeit von Befunden und Diagnosen der Kliniker. Alleinige Beschränkung auf die Daten der klinischen Chemie.
3. Anwendbarkeit des Modells in der Praxis, d.h. geringer Rechenaufwand.

Methoden und Material

Das zur Entwicklung und zur Testung des neuen Modells benötigte Patientenmaterial setzte sich aus 592 Patienten mit Verdacht auf Schilddrüsenerkrankung zusammen [1]. Jeweils sieben klinisch-chemische Kenngrößen wurden gemessen. Die erhaltenen Daten wurden nach einer Datentransformation und Normierung einem nichthierarchischen Clusteralgorithmus (KMEANS [2]) unterworfen (Mustererkennung). Zur Reduzierung der für diesen Algorithmus benötigten Durchläufe mit verschiedenen Anfangskonstellationen und zur Ermittlung einer sinnvollen Clusteranzahl wurden die Daten zuvor mit einem hierarchischen Verfahren (Ward [3]) vorgruppiert. An Hand der Ergebnisse konnte eine sinnvolle Anzahl von Clustern und damit die Startkonfiguration für den KMEANS-Algorithmus gefunden werden. Da sich der KMEANS-Algorithmus auch zur Reklassifizierung (Musterwiedererkennung) verwenden läßt, wurde er von uns auch hierfür eingesetzt.

Ergebnisse und Diskussion

An die Algorithmen zur Klassifizierung und Reklassifizierung wurden von uns folgende Forderungen gestellt:

1. Verträglichkeit: Jeder Patient aus dem Ursprungskollektiv sollte durch das Reklassifizierungsverfahren dem Cluster wieder zugeordnet werden, in das er auf Grund des Klassifizierungsverfahrens gehörte.
2. Der Reklassifizierungsalgorithmus sollte geringen Rechenzeitaufwand und Speicherplatz erfordern.
3. Der Reklassifizierungsalgorithmus sollte auch mit weniger Parametern, als zur Klassifizierung herangezogen wurden, arbeiten.
4. Unabhängigkeit von der statistischen Verteilung der Grundgesamtheit.

Punkt 1 wird überraschenderweise selten gefordert, erscheint uns jedoch besonders wichtig. Er ist durch die Wahl des gleichen Verfahrens zur Klassifizierung sowie zur Reklassifizierung erfüllt. Die Punkte 2, 3 und 4 werden durch den KMEANS-Algorithmus ebenfalls erfüllt. Obwohl die Ergebnisse der Klassifizierung hinsichtlich der Enddiagnose uns zufriedenstellten, konnten sie biochemisch und klinisch nur teilweise interpretiert werden. Hier ist aber darauf hinzuweisen, daß es nicht unser Ziel sein konnte, durch die Klassifizierung klinische Diagnosen möglichst genau anzunähern, da an der Eignung von Diagnosen als Gruppierungsmerkmal berechtigte Zweifel angemeldet werden müssen. Möglicherweise sind Gruppierungen, die heute nicht relevant erscheinen, später doch bedeutsam, wenn genügend Erfahrungen mit diesem Modell gesammelt wurden.

Kritische Punkte und Ausblick

Folgende kritische Anmerkungen sind zu diesem Modell zu machen:

1. Die Wahl der klinisch-chemischen Kenngrößen, der Transformationsfunktionen, sowie der Anzahl der Cluster erfolgt subjektiv und beeinflußt in entscheidendem Maße die Ergebnisse des Modells.
2. Zur Zuordnung von Patienten zu den Clustern wurden alle Kenngrößen benötigt, die zur Klassifizierung herangezogen wurden. Damit würde das Modell in der routinemäßigen Anwendung zu teuer. Wir haben deshalb eine Strategie entwickelt, mit der Patienten mit einer gewissen Wahrscheinlichkeit auch mit weniger als der vollen Anzahl an Kenngrößen Clustern zugeordnet werden können. Dabei ist die Auswahl der benötigten Kenngrößen ein Teil der Strategie. Sie erfolgt für jeden Patienten individuell und wird nicht mehr vom Kliniker vorgegeben.
3. Die einmal erstellten Gruppierungen sind starr, und folgen nicht den sich wandelnden Gegebenheiten einer Klinik (veränderte Zusammensetzung des Kollektivs). Es ist daher notwendig, entweder von Zeit zu Zeit neue Gruppierungen zu erstellen, oder eine Methode zu entwickeln, die es zuläßt, daß sich die Gruppierungen gemäß dem aktuellen Patientengut dynamisch ändern.

Sicherlich kann das hier vorgestellte Modell nicht auf alle klinisch-chemischen Bereiche gleichermaßen angewendet werden. Es ist jedoch sicherlich auch noch für andere diagnostische Fragestellungen, wie die Differentialdiagnose des Herzinfarktes, geeignet.

Literatur

[1] Vogt,W., Sandel,P., Schwarzfischer,P., Braun,S.L., Langfelder,CH., Knedel,M.: Cluster-oriented discriminant analysis; taxonomic classification of the thyroid function. Clin.Chem.Acta, 112, 213 (1981).

[2] Späth,H.: Cluster Analyse-Algorithmen. München-Wien, R.Oldenbourg Verlag, (1977).

[3] Ward,J.H.: Hierarchical grouping to optimize an objective function. J.Am.Stat.Ass., 58, 236 (1963).

Lecture Notes in Computer Science

Vol. 53: Mathematical Foundations of Computer Science. Proceedings 1977. Edited by J. Gruska. XII, 608 pages. 1977.

Vol. 54: Design and Implementation of Programming Languages. Proceedings 1976. Edited by J. H. Williams and D. A. Fisher. X, 496 pages. 1977.

Vol. 55: A. Gerbier, Mes premières constructions de programmes. XII, 256 pages. 1977.

Vol. 56: Fundamentals of Computation Theory. Proceedings 1977. Edited by M. Karpiński. XII, 542 pages. 1977.

Vol. 57: Portability of Numerical Software. Proceedings 1976. Edited by W. Cowell. VIII, 539 pages. 1977.

Vol. 58: M. J. O'Donnel, Computing in Systems Described by Equations. XIV, 111 pages. 1977.

Vol. 59: E. Hill, Jr., A Comparative Study of Very Large Data Bases. X, 140 pages. 1978.

Vol. 60: Operating Systems, An Advanced Course. Edited by R. Bayer, R. M. Graham, and G. Seegmüller. X, 593 pages. 1978.

Vol. 61: The Vienna Development Method: The Meta-Language. Edited by D. Bjørner and C. B. Jones. XVIII, 382 pages. 1978.

Vol. 62: Automata, Languages and Programming. Proceedings 1978. Edited by G. Ausiello and C. Böhm. VIII, 508 pages. 1978.

Vol. 63: Natural Language Communication with Computers. Edited by Leonard Bolc. VI, 292 pages. 1978.

Vol. 64: Mathematical Foundations of Computer Science. Proceedings 1978. Edited by J. Winkowski. X, 551 pages. 1978.

Vol. 65: Information Systems Methodology. Proceedings 1978. Edited by G. Bracchi and P. C. Lockemann. XII, 696 pages. 1978.

Vol. 66: N. D. Jones and S. S. Muchnick, TEMPO: A Unified Treatment of Binding Time and Parameter Passing Concepts in Programming Languages. IX, 118 pages. 1978.

Vol. 67: Theoretical Computer Science, 4th GI Conference, Aachen. March 1979. Edited by K. Weihrauch. VII, 324 pages. 1979.

Vol. 68: D. Harel. First-Order Dynamic Logic. X, 133 pages. 1979.

Vol. 69: Program Construction. International Summer School. Edited by F. L. Bauer and M. Broy. VII, 651 pages. 1979.

Vol. 70: Semantics of Concurrent Computation. Proceedings 1979. Edited by G. Kahn. VI, 368 pages. 1979.

Vol. 71: Automata. Languages and Programming. Proceedings 1979. Edited by H. A. Maurer. IX, 684 pages. 1979.

Vol. 72: Symbolic and Algebraic Computation. Proceedings 1979. Edited by E. W. Ng. XV, 557 pages. 1979.

Vol. 73: Graph-Grammars and Their Application to Computer Science and Biology. Proceedings 1978. Edited by V. Claus, H. Ehring and G. Rozenberg. VII, 477 pages. 1979.

Vol. 74: Mathematical Foundations of Computer Science. Proceedings 1979. Edited by J. Bečvář. IX, 580 pages. 1979.

Vol. 75: Mathematical Studies of Information Processing. Proceedings 1978. Edited by E. K. Blum, M. Paul and S. Takasu. VIII, 629 pages. 1979.

Vol. 76: Codes for Boundary-Value Problems in Ordinary Differential Equations. Proceedings 1978. Edited by B. Childs et al. VIII, 388 pages. 1979.

Vol. 77: G. V. Bochmann, Architecture of Distributed Computer Systems. VIII, 238 pages. 1979.

Vol. 78: M. Gordon, R. Milner and C. Wadsworth, Edingburgh LCF. VIII, 159 pages. 1979.

Vol. 79: Language Design and Programming Methodology. Proceedings, 1979. Edited by J. Tobias. IX, 255 pages. 1980.

Vol. 80: Pictorial Information Systems. Edited by S. K. Chang and K. S. Fu. IX, 445 pages. 1980.

Vol. 81: Data Base Techniques for Pictorial Applications. Proceedings, 1979. Edited by A. Blaser. XI, 599 pages. 1980.

Vol. 82: J. G. Sanderson, A Relational Theory of Computing. VI, 147 pages. 1980.

Vol. 83: International Symposium Programming. Proceedings, 1980. Edited by B. Robinet. VII, 341 pages. 1980.

Vol. 84: Net Theory and Applications. Proceedings, 1979. Edited by W. Brauer. XIII, 537 Seiten. 1980.

Vol. 85: Automata, Languages and Programming. Proceedings, 1980. Edited by J. de Bakker and J. van Leeuwen. VIII, 671 pages. 1980.

Vol. 86: Abstract Software Specifications. Proceedings, 1979. Edited by D. Bjørner. XIII, 567 pages. 1980.

Vol. 87: 5th Conference on Automated Deduction. Proceedings, 1980. Edited by W. Bibel and R. Kowalski. VII, 385 pages. 1980.

Vol. 88: Mathematical Foundations of Computer Science 1980. Proceedings, 1980. Edited by P. Dembiński. VIII, 723 pages. 1980.

Vol. 89: Computer Aided Design – Modelling, Systems Engineering, CAD-Systems. Proceedings, 1980. Edited by J. Encarnacao. XIV, 461 pages. 1980.

Vol. 90: D. M. Sandford, Using Sophisticated Models in Resolution Theorem Proving. XI, 239 pages. 1980.

Vol. 91: D. Wood, Grammar and L Forms: An Introduction. IX, 314 pages. 1980.

Vol. 92: R. Milner, A Calculus of Communication Systems. VI, 171 pages. 1980.

Vol. 93: A. Nijholt, Contett-Free Grammars: Covers, Normal Forms, and Parsing. VII, 253 pages. 1980.

Vol. 94: Semantics-Directed Compiler Generation. Proceedings, 1980. Edited by N. D. Jones. V, 489 pages. 1980.

Vol. 95: Ch. D. Marlin, Coroutines. XII, 246 pages. 1980.

Vol. 96: J. L. Peterson, Computer Programs for Spelling Correctin. VI, 213 pages. 1980.

Vol. 97: S. Osaki and T. Nishio, Reliability Evaluation of Some Fault-Tolerant Computer Architectures. VI, 129 pages. 1980.

Vol. 98: Towards a Formal Description of Ada. Edited by D. Bjørner and O. N. Oest. XIV, 630 pages. 1980.

Vol. 99: I. Guessarian, Alebraic Semantics. XI, 158 pages. 1981.

Vol. 100: Graphtheoretic Concepts in Computer Science. Edited by H. Noltemeier. X, 403 pages. 1981.

Vol. 101: A. Thayse, Boolean Calculus of Differences. VII, 144 pages. 1981.

Vol. 102: J. H. Davenport, On the Integration of Algebraic Functions. 1-197 pages. 1981.

Vol. 103: H. Ledgard, A. Singer, J. Whiteside; Directions in Human Factors of Interactive Systems. VI. 190 pages. 1981.

Vol. 104: Theoretical Computer Science. Edited by P. Deussen. VII, 261 pages. 1981.

Vol. 105: Distributed Systems – Architecture and Implementation. Edited by B. Lampson, M. Paul and H. J. Siegert. XIII, 510 pages. 1981.

Vol. 106: The Programming Language Ada. X, 243 pages. 1981.

Vol. 107: International Colloquium on Formalization of Programming Concepts. Proceedings. Edited by J. Diaz and I. Ramos. VII, 478 pages. 1981.

Lecture Notes in Computer Science